World History

Ancient Civilizations

Douglas Carnine

Carlos Cortés

Kenneth Curtis

Anita Robinson

McDougal Littell

A DIVISION OF HOUGHTON MIFFLIN COMPANY

Nefertiti

The Buddha

African Mask

Athena

Olmec head

Caesar Augustus

World History

Ancient Civilizations

Douglas Carnine

Carlos Cortés

Kenneth Curtis

Anita Robinson

McDougal Littell

A DIVISION OF HOUGHTON MIFFLIN COMPANY

Senior Consultants

Douglas Carnine

Douglas Carnine is Professor of Education and Director of the National Center for Improving the Tools of Educators at the University of Oregon. He is the author of seven books and more than 100 other scholarly publications, primarily in the areas of instructional design and effective instructional strategies for diverse learners. Dr. Carnine is a member of the National Institute for Literacy Advisory Board.

Carlos E. Cortés

Carlos E. Cortés is Professor Emeritus of History at the University of California, Riverside. He has edited three major book series on Latinos in the United States. He has many other books, articles, documentaries, and educational materials to his credit. Fluent in Portuguese and Spanish, he often focuses on issues of multiculturalism, diversity, and media representation. Dr. Cortés has served on the summer faculty of the Harvard Institutes for Higher Education since 1990 and on the faculty of the Summer Institute for Intercultural Communication since 1995.

Kenneth R. Curtis

Kenneth R. Curtis is Professor of History and Liberal Studies at California State University, Long Beach, where he is Faculty Advisor to the California History/Social Science Project. He has been closely involved with the College Board's course and examination in Advanced Placement World History, serving as Chief Reader and as a member of the Test Development Committee. Dr. Curtis has co-authored a number of college-level world history texts.

Anita T. Robinson

Anita T. Robinson is Program Director for a Teaching American History/Department of Education grant. She served as a Master Lead Teacher and Social Studies Specialist in the Los Angeles Unified School District. Mrs. Robinson is an expert professional development presenter. Her topics include standards-based instruction, engaging English learners, literacy support, technology, visual literacy, and "big ideas."

Acknowledgments begin on page R110.
ISBN-13: 978-0-618-34791-9 ISBN-10: 0-618-34791-7

Printed in the United States of America.
6 7 8 9–DWO–10 09 08 07 06

Consultants and Reviewers

Reading Consultant

MaryEllen Vogt
Professor Emeritus,
California State University,
Long Beach, California
President of International Reading Assocation, 2004-2005

English Learner Consultants

Mary Lou McCloskey
Georgia State University,
Atlanta, Georgia
President of TESOL, 2002-2003

Lydia Stack
Administrator, San Francisco Unified School District
San Francisco, California

Content Consultants

The content consultants reviewed the text for historical depth and accuracy and for clarity of presentation.

David G. Atwill
Department of History and Religious Studies
Pennsylvania State University
University Park, Pennsylvania

Douglas C. Baxter
Department of History
Ohio University
Athens, Ohio

Roger Beck
Department of History
Eastern Illinois University
Charleston, Illinois

Beverly Bossler
Department of History
University of California, Davis
Davis, California

Philip Cunningham
Boston College
Chestnut Hill, Massachusetts

Susan L. Douglass
Council on Islamic Education
Fountain Valley, California

Joël DuBois
Humanities and Religious Studies Department
California State University, Sacramento
Sacramento, California

Vincent Farenga
Department of Comparative Literature
University of Southern California
Los Angeles, California

Claudio Fogu
Department of History
University of Southern California
Los Angeles, California

Charles L. Geshekter
Department of History
California State University, Chico
Chico, California

Erik Gilbert
Department of History
Arkansas State University
Jonesboro, Arkansas

Charles Hallisey
University of Wisconsin
Madison, Wisconsin

Dakota L. Hamilton
Department of History
Humboldt State University
Arcata, California

Charles C. Haynes
First Amendment Center
Arlington, Virginia

Lezlie Knox
Department of History
Marquette University
Milwaukee, Wisconsin

Geoffrey Koziol
Department of History
University of California, Berkeley
Berkeley, California

John Wolte Infong Lee
Department of History
University of California, Santa Barbara
Santa Barbara, California

Maritere Lopez
Department of History
California State University, Fresno
Fresno, California

Shabbir Mansuri
Council on Islamic Education
Fountain Valley, California

Jacob Meskin
Shoolman Graduate School of Jewish Education
Hebrew College
Newton, Massachusetts

Phillip Naylor
Department of History
Marquette University
Milwaukee, Wisconsin

Lawrence Okamura
Department of History
University of Missouri, Columbia
Columbia, Missouri

Robert Patch
Department of History
University of California, Riverside
Riverside, California

David D. Phillips
Department of History
University of California, Los Angeles
Los Angeles, California

Swami Tyagananda
Hindu Chaplain
Harvard University
Cambridge, Massachusetts

Kenneth Baxter Wolf
Department of History
Pomona College
Claremont, California

R. Bin Wong
Department of History
University of California, Los Angeles, California

Teacher Consultants

The following educators provided ongoing review during the development of the program.

John J. Brill
Bellevue School District
Bellevue, Washington

Merrell Frankel
Berendo Middle School
Los Angeles, California
2003 CCSS Middle Level Teacher of the Year
2004 NCSS Middle Level Teacher of the Year

Kathryn Friemann
West Middle School
Wayzata, Minnesota

Patricia Martins
John T. Nichols Middle School
Middleborough, Massachusetts

Ronnie Moppin
Sunny Vale Middle School
Blue Springs, Missouri

Susan Morris
West Deptford Middle School
West Deptford, New Jersey

Jose Rodriguez
Bellevue School District
Bellevue, Washington

Shanniska Smith
Ransome Middle School
Charlotte, North Carolina

Mark Stewart
Dublin School District
Dublin, Ohio

Unit 1

Introduction to World History

Technology
For more on early human societies . . .
ClassZone.com

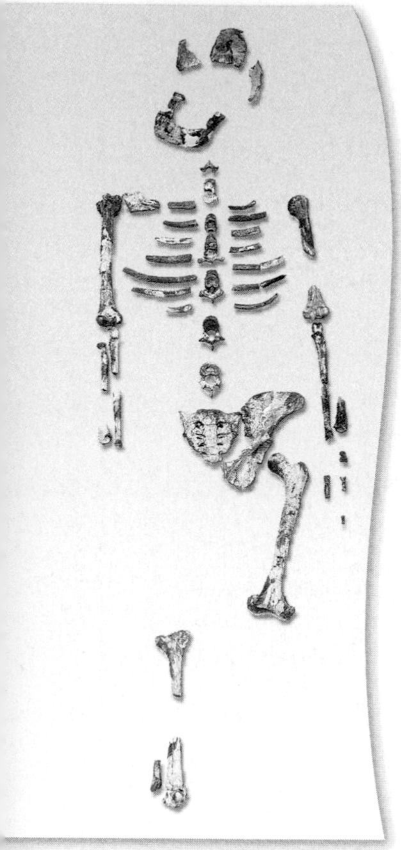

▲ **Lucy** (p. 31)

▲ **Spear Thrower** (p. 50)

Unit 2

Early Civilizations of Southwest Asia

Technology
For more on Southwest Asia . . .
ClassZone.com

▲ **Sumerian Pottery** (p. 98)

▲ **Detail from Ishtar Gate** (p. 123)

Iranian Valley (p. 129) ▼

Unit 3 Ancient Africa

Technology
For more on ancient Africa . . .
ClassZone.com

▲ **Double Crown of Egypt** (p. 166)

▲ **Kuba Mask** (p. 207)

▼ **Pyramids** (p. 165)

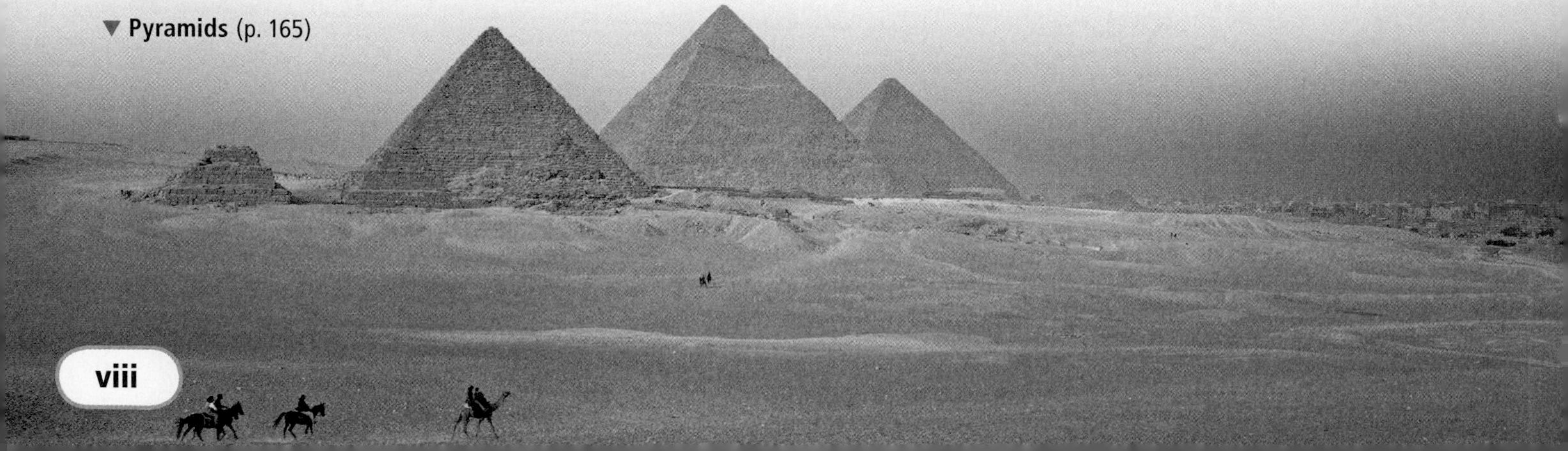

Unit 4

Ancient Asian and American Civilizations

Technology
For more on ancient Asian and American civilizations . . . ClassZone.com

▲ The Deity Shiva (p. 226)

▲ Terra Cotta Army (p. 267)

▲ Olmec Head (p. 302)

Unit 5

The Roots of Western Ideas

Technology
For more on the roots of western ideas . . . ClassZone.com

▲ Fortress of Masada (p. 344)

▲ Greek Vase (p. 360)

▲ Alexander the Great (p. 406)

Unit 6 The World of Ancient Rome

Technology
For more on the world of ancient Rome . . .
ClassZone.com

▲ **Brutus** (p. 436)

▲ **Byzantine Cross** (p. 466)

▲ **Aqueducts** (p. 517)

Reference

Reading & Writing Support

Before You Read Strategies

Reading Activities

Writing Activities

Writing About History

Reading & Writing Support

Visual Vocabulary

Visual Vocabulary

Minted coins is a term for coins that are issued by the government and are official money.

Vocabulary Strategies

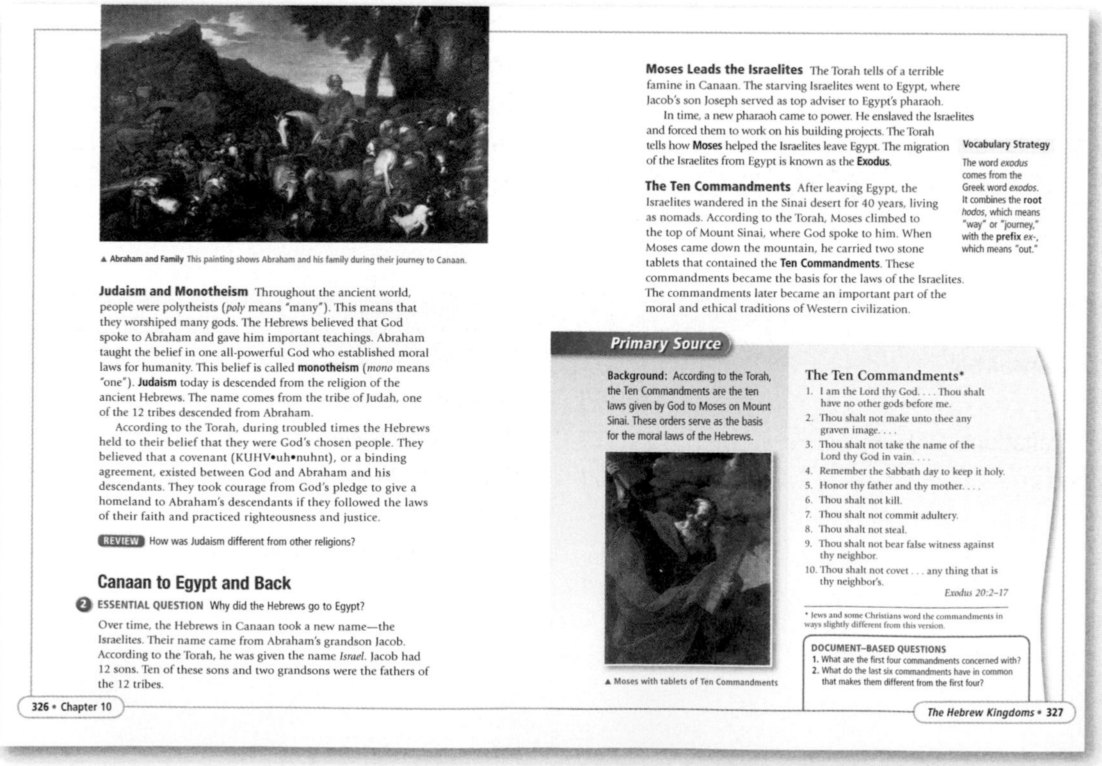

▲ **Abraham and Family** This painting shows Abraham and his family during their journey to Canaan.

Judaism and Monotheism Throughout the ancient world, people were polytheists (*poly* means "many"). This means that they worshiped many gods. The Hebrews believed that God spoke to Abraham and gave him important teachings. Abraham taught the belief in one all-powerful God who established moral laws for humanity. This belief is called **monotheism** (*mono* means "one"). **Judaism** today is descended from the religion of the ancient Hebrews. The name comes from the tribe of Judah, one of the 12 tribes descended from Abraham.

According to the Torah, during troubled times the Hebrews held to their belief that they were God's chosen people. They believed that a covenant (KUHV•uh•nuhnt), or a binding agreement, existed between God and Abraham and his descendants. They took courage from God's pledge to give a homeland to Abraham's descendants if they followed the laws of their faith and practiced righteousness and justice.

REVIEW How was Judaism different from other religions?

Canaan to Egypt and Back

2 ESSENTIAL QUESTION Why did the Hebrews go to Egypt?

Over time, the Hebrews in Canaan took a new name—the Israelites. Their name came from Abraham's grandson Jacob. According to the Torah, he was given the name *Israel*. Jacob had 12 sons. Ten of these sons and two grandsons were the fathers of the 12 tribes.

326 • Chapter 10

Moses Leads the Israelites The Torah tells of a terrible famine in Canaan. The starving Israelites went to Egypt, where Jacob's son Joseph served as top adviser to Egypt's pharaoh.

In time, a new pharaoh came to power. He enslaved the Israelites and forced them to work on his building projects. The Torah tells how **Moses** helped the Israelites leave Egypt. The migration of the Israelites from Egypt is known as the **Exodus**.

Vocabulary Strategy

The word *exodus* comes from the Greek word *exodos*. It combines the **root** *hodos*, which means "way" or "journey," with the **prefix** *ex-*, which means "out."

The Ten Commandments After leaving Egypt, the Israelites wandered in the Sinai desert for 40 years, living as nomads. According to the Torah, Moses climbed to the top of Mount Sinai, where God spoke to him. When Moses came down the mountain, he carried two stone tablets that contained the **Ten Commandments**. These commandments became the basis for the laws of the Israelites. The commandments later became an important part of the moral and ethical traditions of Western civilization.

Primary Source

Background: According to the Torah, the Ten Commandments are the ten laws given by God to Moses on Mount Sinai. These orders serve as the basis for the moral laws of the Hebrews.

▲ Moses with tablets of Ten Commandments

The Ten Commandments*

1. I am the Lord thy God. . . . Thou shalt have no other gods before me.
2. Thou shalt not make unto thee any graven image. . . .
3. Thou shalt not take the name of the Lord thy God in vain. . . .
4. Remember the Sabbath day to keep it holy.
5. Honor thy father and thy mother. . . .
6. Thou shalt not kill.
7. Thou shalt not commit adultery.
8. Thou shalt not steal.
9. Thou shalt not bear false witness against thy neighbor.
10. Thou shalt not covet . . . any thing that is thy neighbor's.

Exodus 20:2–17

* Jews and some Christians word the commandments in ways slightly different from this version.

DOCUMENT–BASED QUESTIONS
1. What are the first four commandments concerned with?
2. What do the last six commandments have in common that makes them different from the first four?

The Hebrew Kingdoms • 327

Features

Comparisons Across Cultures

Geography

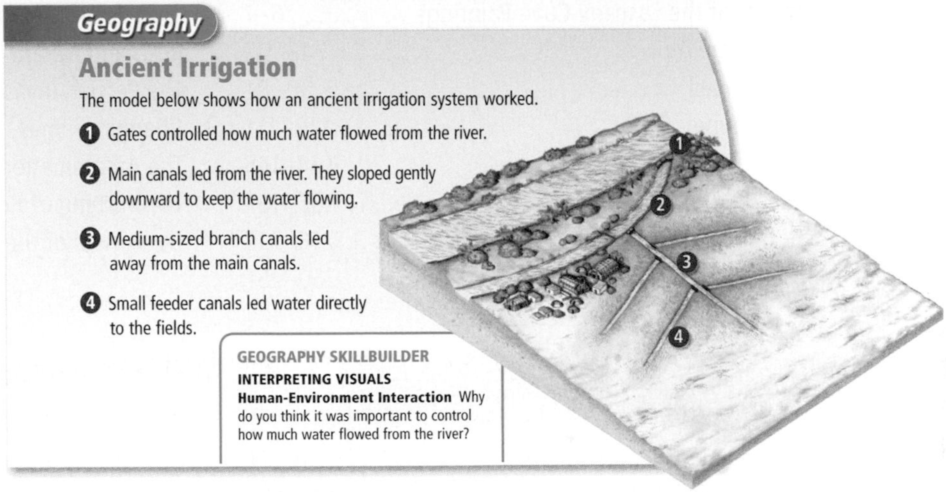

Geography
Ancient Irrigation
The model below shows how an ancient irrigation system worked.
1 Gates controlled how much water flowed from the river.
2 Main canals led from the river. They sloped gently downward to keep the water flowing.
3 Medium-sized branch canals led away from the main canals.
4 Small feeder canals led water directly to the fields.
GEOGRAPHY SKILLBUILDER
INTERPRETING VISUALS
Human-Environment Interaction Why do you think it was important to control how much water flowed from the river?
1
2
3
4

History Makers

Primary Sources

Features

Skillbuilders

Starting with a Story

Daily Life

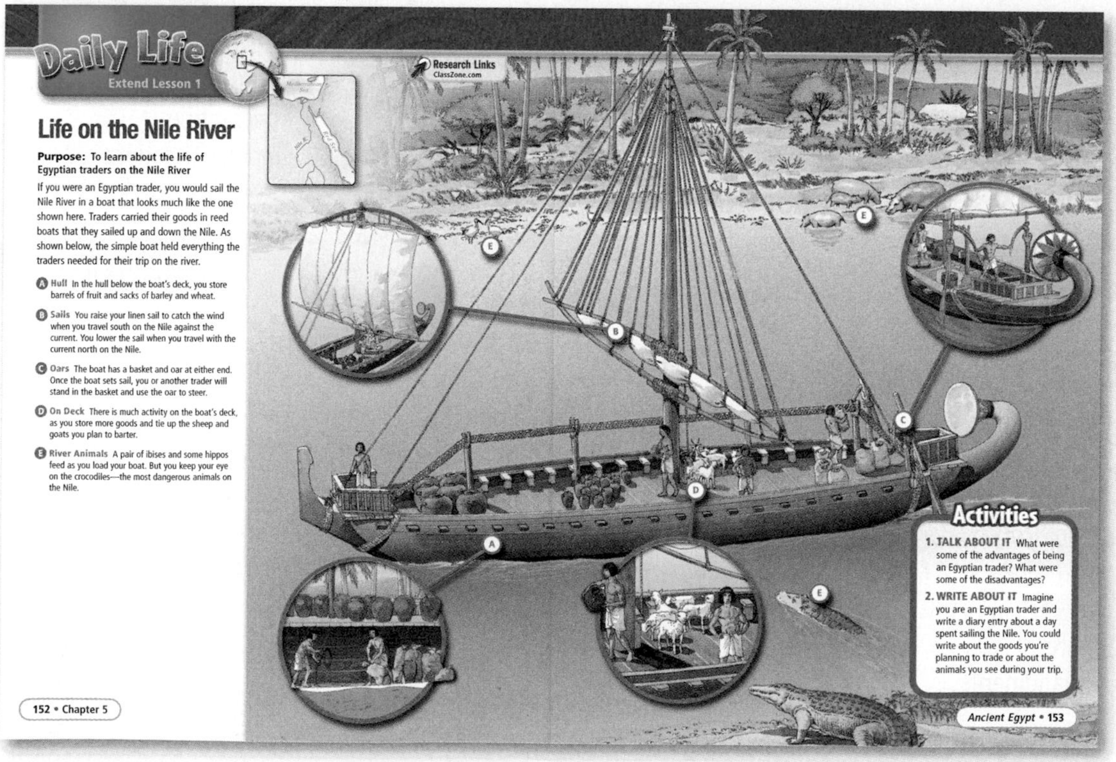

Connect to Today

Literature Connections

Reader's Theater

Activities

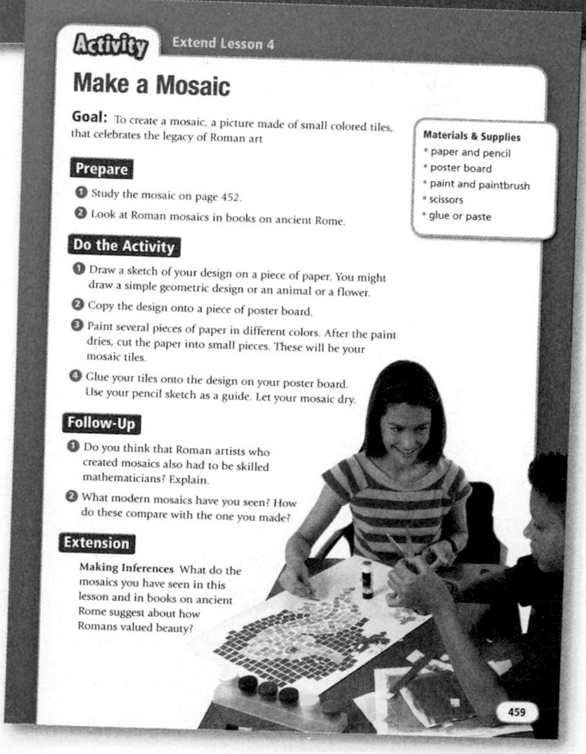
Activity Extend Lesson 4

Make a Mosaic

Goal: To create a mosaic, a picture made of small colored tiles, that celebrates the legacy of Roman art

Materials & Supplies
- paper and pencil
- poster board
- paint and paintbrush
- scissors
- glue or paste

Prepare
1. Study the mosaic on page 452.
2. Look at Roman mosaics in books on ancient Rome.

Do the Activity
1. Draw a sketch of your design on a piece of paper. You might draw a simple geometric design or an animal or a flower.
2. Copy the design onto a piece of poster board.
3. Paint several pieces of paper in different colors. After the paint dries, cut the paper into small pieces. These will be your mosaic tiles.
4. Glue your tiles onto the design on your poster board. Use your pencil sketch as a guide. Let your mosaic dry.

Follow-Up
1. Do you think that Roman artists who created mosaics also had to be skilled mathematicians? Explain.
2. What modern mosaics have you seen? How do these compare with the one you made?

Extension

Making Inferences What do the mosaics you have seen in this lesson and in books on ancient Rome suggest about how Romans valued beauty?

459

Infographics & Interactives

Infographics

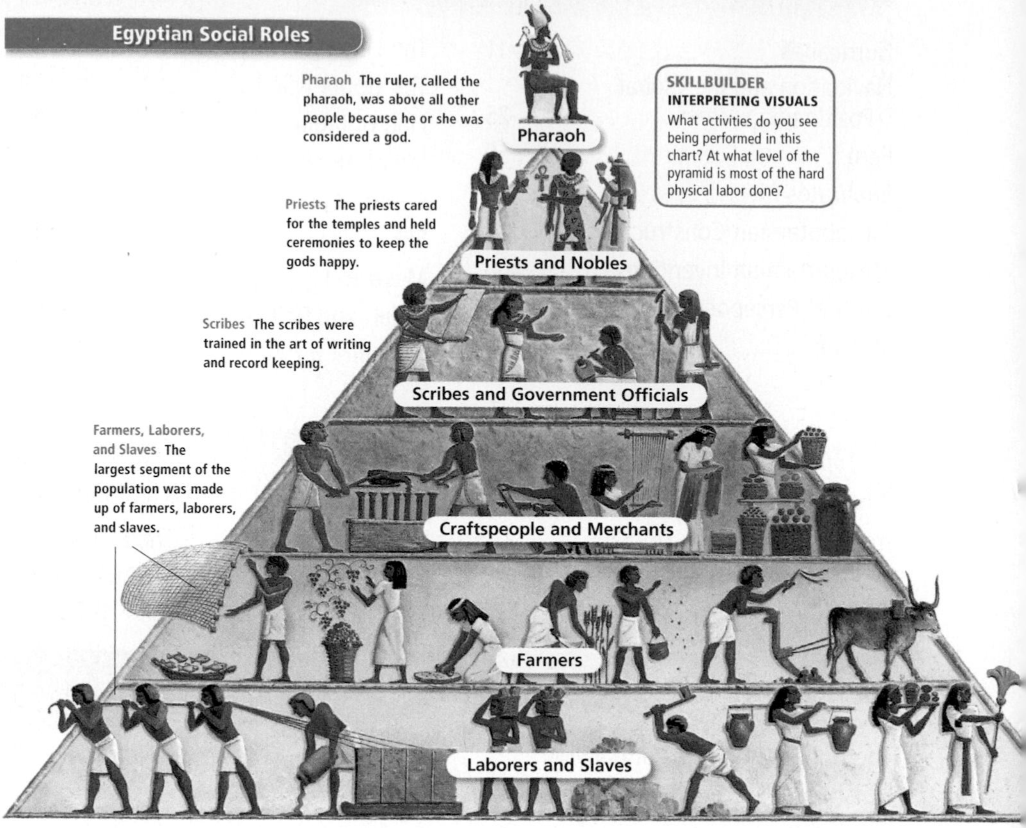

Egyptian Social Roles
Pharaoh The ruler, called the pharaoh, was above all other people because he or she was considered a god.
Pharaoh
SKILLBUILDER
INTERPRETING VISUALS
What activities do you see being performed in this chart? At what level of the pyramid is most of the hard physical labor done?
Priests The priests cared for the temples and held ceremonies to keep the gods happy.
Priests and Nobles
Scribes The scribes were trained in the art of writing and record keeping.
Scribes and Government Officials
Farmers, Laborers, and Slaves The largest segment of the population was made up of farmers, laborers, and slaves.
Craftspeople and Merchants
Farmers
Laborers and Slaves

INTERACTIVE Maps and Visuals

Maps

Visuals

Maps

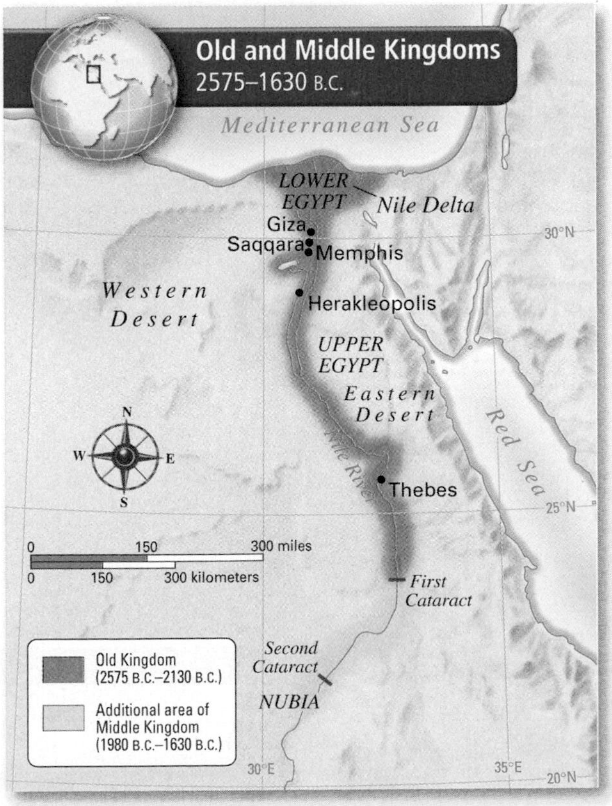

Old and Middle Kingdoms
2575–1630 B.C.
Mediterranean Sea
LOWER EGYPT
Nile Delta
Giza
Saqqara
Memphis
30°N
Western Desert
Herakleopolis
UPPER EGYPT
Eastern Desert
Red Sea
Nile River
Thebes
25°N
N
S
E
W
0 150 300 miles
0 150 300 kilometers
First Cataract
Second Cataract
NUBIA
Old Kingdom (2575 B.C.–2130 B.C.)
Additional area of Middle Kingdom (1980 B.C.–1630 B.C.)
30°E
35°E
20°N

Maps

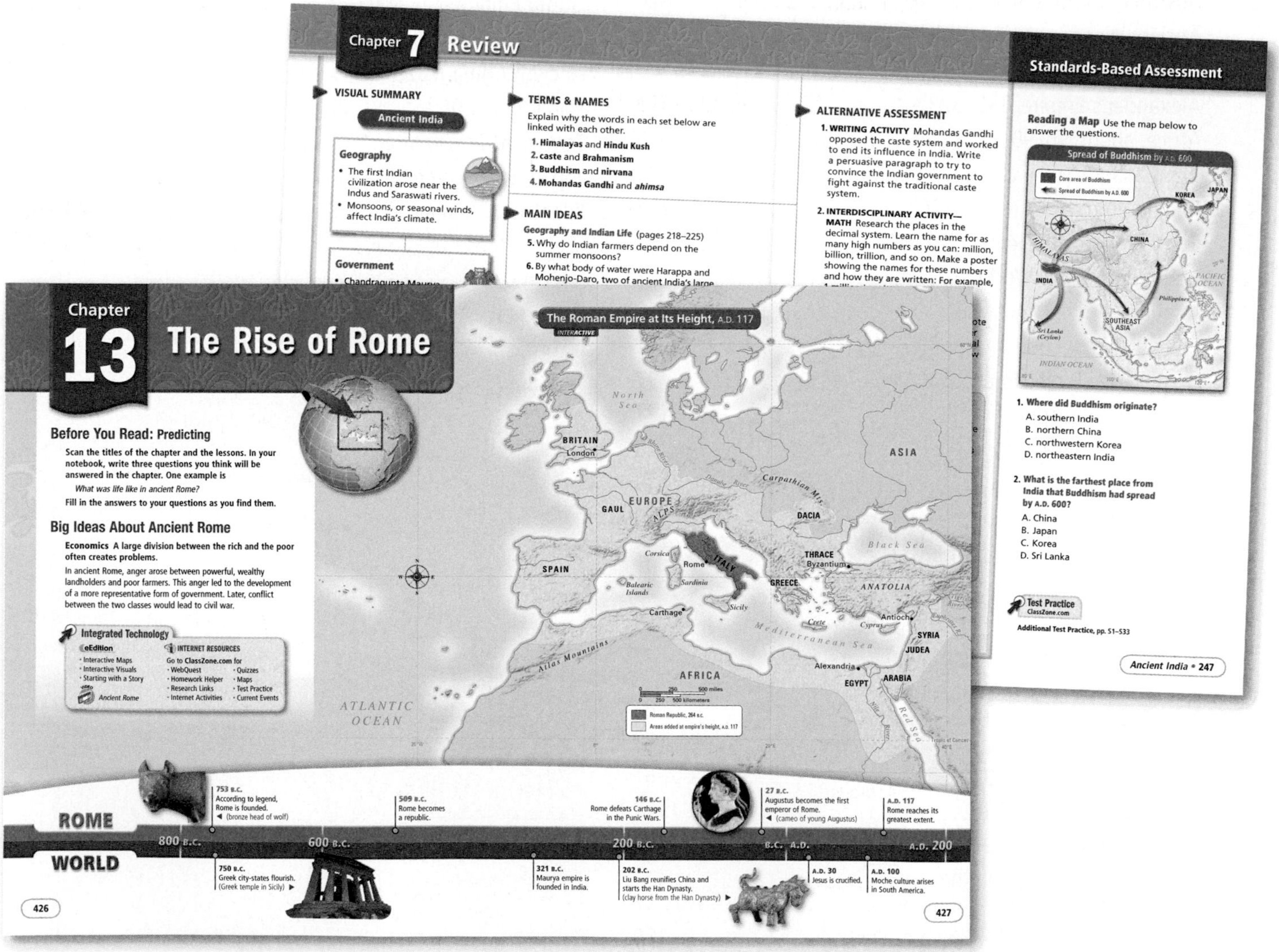

Chapter 7 Review
Standards-Based Assessment
Chapter 13 The Rise of Rome
The Roman Empire at Its Height, A.D. 117
Before You Read: Predicting
Big Ideas About Ancient Rome
ROME
WORLD
426
427
Ancient India • 247

Charts & Time Lines

Charts

Time Lines

Greek and Roman Gods

Description	Greek	Roman
Supreme god	Zeus	Jupiter
Supreme goddess	Hera (wife of Zeus)	Juno (wife of Jupiter)
God of the sea	Poseidon	Neptune
God of music and poetry	Apollo	Apollo
Goddess of love and beauty	Aphrodite	Venus
God of war	Ares	Mars

SKILLBUILDER
INTERPRETING VISUALS
Why do you think the Romans were so deeply influenced by Greek religion?

Jupiter This statue of Jupiter shows the god riding an eagle—his symbol—and throwing a lightning bolt. ▼

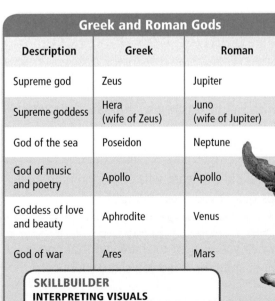

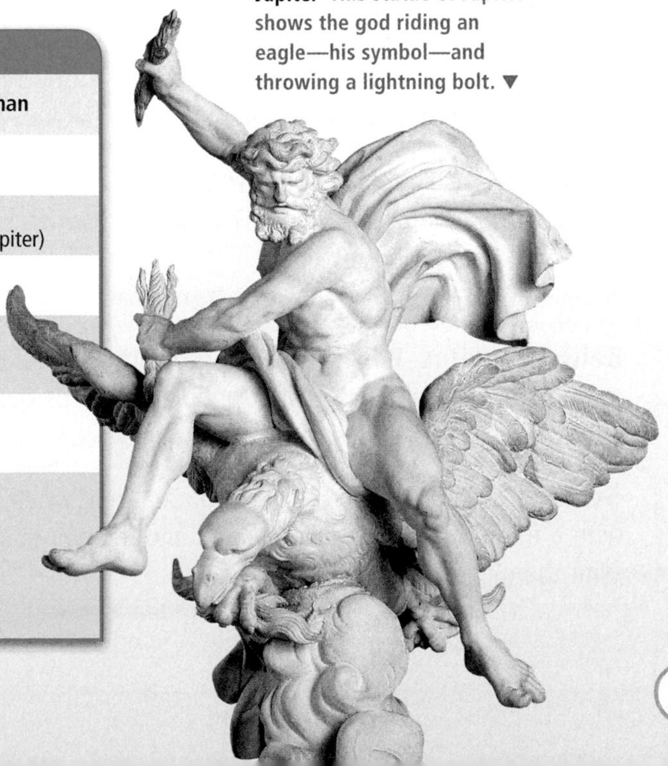

Historical Themes and Big Ideas

Beginning with Your Own Experience

Welcome to the study of world history. It is a big topic—the story of the most important things that ever happened to human beings. This book covers more than 5,000 years of that history.

You may be wondering how you will learn all the facts about such a long period of time. The best way is to sort the information into categories (similar groupings). The broad categories are called themes. This opening section of the book will introduce you to six major themes of history.

Let's begin with your life. Although you may not know it, you have already had many experiences that will help you to understand the themes. Consider the questions below and discuss your answers with your classmates.

Geography Is your town or city near a lake, an ocean, or mountains? What is the weather like? How do the landscape and the weather affect the way you live?

Culture Have you ever met someone from another place—another country, another state, or another city? In what ways did that person act differently from you? In what ways did he or she act like you?

Economics Are you always able to buy all the things you want? How do you decide what to buy when you don't have enough money for everything?

Government In your school, what would happen if every student could come to class at whatever time he or she wanted? Leave class whenever he or she wanted? Talk out loud anytime, even during tests?

Belief Systems When you were growing up, how did you learn what were the right and wrong ways of behaving? What people or groups taught you those things?

Science & Technology Think about a time when you wanted to share important news with a friend or relative who lived in another city or state. How did you share your news with them?

Understanding Historical Themes

As you and your classmates shared your answers, you probably discovered you had many different experiences. But you probably also found that you had things in common too.

For example, some people who live near the ocean like to surf, while others prefer fishing. Still others play beach volleyball. Some people who live directly on the coast build sea walls to protect their homes. Each of those activities is a different response to living by the ocean. Yet, what these people have in common is that the place where they live affects their lives.

Once you understand what a group of facts has in common, you are ready to talk about themes. The six themes of this history program are described below. As you read this book, you will notice that many statements and questions are labeled by one of these themes.

Geography

Geography refers to the characteristics of a physical place, the ways that environment affects human life, and the ways that humans change the environment. It also refers to the movement of people, goods, and ideas from place to place.

Culture

Culture is the way of life that a society or group shares. It includes the way people act, the way they express themselves, and the way they are organized.

Economics

Economics includes the ways that people use their limited resources to satisfy their needs and desires. It also refers to the ways that societies produce wealth and how they organize labor.

Government

Government refers to the system of laws and authority that a society uses to guide or control its members.

Belief Systems

Belief systems are often religions, which are beliefs in a god or gods. Belief systems may also be systems of ethics, or principles of right and wrong.

Science & Technology

The theme of science and technology includes discoveries, inventions, and improved methods of doing things.

Looking for Big Ideas

As you read this book, you will begin to notice that certain patterns occur over and over in history. Different societies go through similar stages, make similar choices, or organize themselves in similar ways. We call those patterns the **Big Ideas** of history.

For example, many of the ancient societies that you will study began in river valleys because such places were good for farming and transportation. Therefore, one of the Big Ideas in this book is:

THEME	BIG IDEA
Geography	**Civilizations developed in places that supported agriculture or trade or both.**

As you can see from that example, the Big Idea is a statement of the historical pattern. The first page of every chapter lists a Big Idea, which introduces a pattern that occurs in the chapter. Each Big Idea starts with a theme, as shown above. Think about the Big Idea before you start to read. It will help you know what to focus on as you study.

In this book, you will encounter 12 different Big Ideas, two for each theme:

Big Ideas are Patterns in History

Geography	Civilizations developed in places that supported agriculture or trade or both.	Migration, trade, warfare, and the action of missionaries spread ideas and beliefs.
Culture	Ways of living change as humans interact with each other.	Many societies rely on family roles and social classes to keep order.
Economics	Societies trade the surplus goods that they produce to obtain goods they lack.	Nomadic peoples often attacked settlements to gain the goods that civilizations produce.
Government	Governments create law codes and political bodies to organize a society.	New ideas and beliefs can challenge a government's authority, leading to change.
Belief Systems	Many religions and belief systems start with the ideas of a teacher or prophet.	Belief systems and religions may shape governments and societies.
Science & Technology	New scientific discoveries change human understanding of the world.	New inventions and techniques change the way humans live their daily lives.

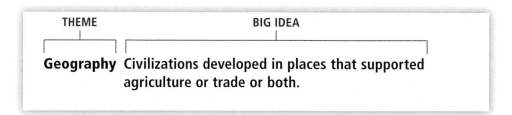

Asking Historical Questions

You can use themes and Big Ideas to ask questions about historic periods and people. As you read this book, ask yourself questions that you will try to answer as you read. This approach will help you understand the importance of various facts and will help you remember them.

Sample Historical Questions

Geography How has the place where people lived been important in influencing how they lived? What effect does landscape and weather have on human life?

Culture Throughout history, what have cultures learned about each other? How have they learned it, and how have they borrowed from other cultures to change themselves?

Economics Have societies always been able to acquire what they needed or wanted? When societies are limited in what they can acquire, how do they choose what to do without?

Government Throughout history, how have societies developed laws to guide the behavior of their members? How did those laws affect the way people lived together?

Belief Systems Throughout history, how have societies developed ideas of right and wrong? How do different belief systems compare?

Science & Technology In different time periods, how have people solved the problem of spreading information over long distances? What other problems of daily life have people solved by using inventions, discoveries, or new techniques?

To help guide your reading, we have included historical questions in every lesson of this book. They appear at the beginning of each section and are labeled **ESSENTIAL QUESTIONS**. By looking for the answers to these questions as you read, you will focus on the most important information in each lesson.

Be careful when you ask historical questions. Don't assume that life in the past was the same as life today. For example, consider this question: In the past, how did people get rid of a ruler they didn't like?

Because we have frequent elections in the United States, we can vote officials out of office. However, in the past, most societies were ruled by a monarch who controlled the army. It was difficult to replace such powerful rulers.

In conclusion, as you study world history, remember these three tips:

- Consider how facts and details relate to the six themes.
- Look for the patterns explained in the Big Ideas.
- Ask and answer historical questions.

STRATEGIES for TAKING TESTS

This section will help you develop and practice the skills you need to study history and to take tests. Part 1, **Strategies for Studying History,** shows you the features of this book. It also shows you how to improve your reading and study skills.

Part 2, **Test-Taking Strategies and Practice,** gives you strategies to help you answer the different kinds of questions that appear on tests. Each strategy is followed by a set of questions you can use for practice.

CONTENTS

Part 1: Strategies for Studying History

Reading is the central skill in the effective study of history or any other subject. You can improve your reading skills by using helpful techniques and by practicing. The better your reading skills, the more you will remember what you read. The next four pages show how some of the features of *World History: Ancient Civilizations* can help you learn and understand history.

Preview Chapters Before You Read

Each chapter begins with a two-page chapter opener. Study these pages to help you get ready to read.

1. Read the chapter title for clues to what will be covered in the chapter.
2. Study the **Before You Read** section. The activities in this section will help to guide your reading.
3. Preview the time line and note the years covered in the chapter. Consider the important events that took place during this time period. Study the map to get an idea of where these events took place.

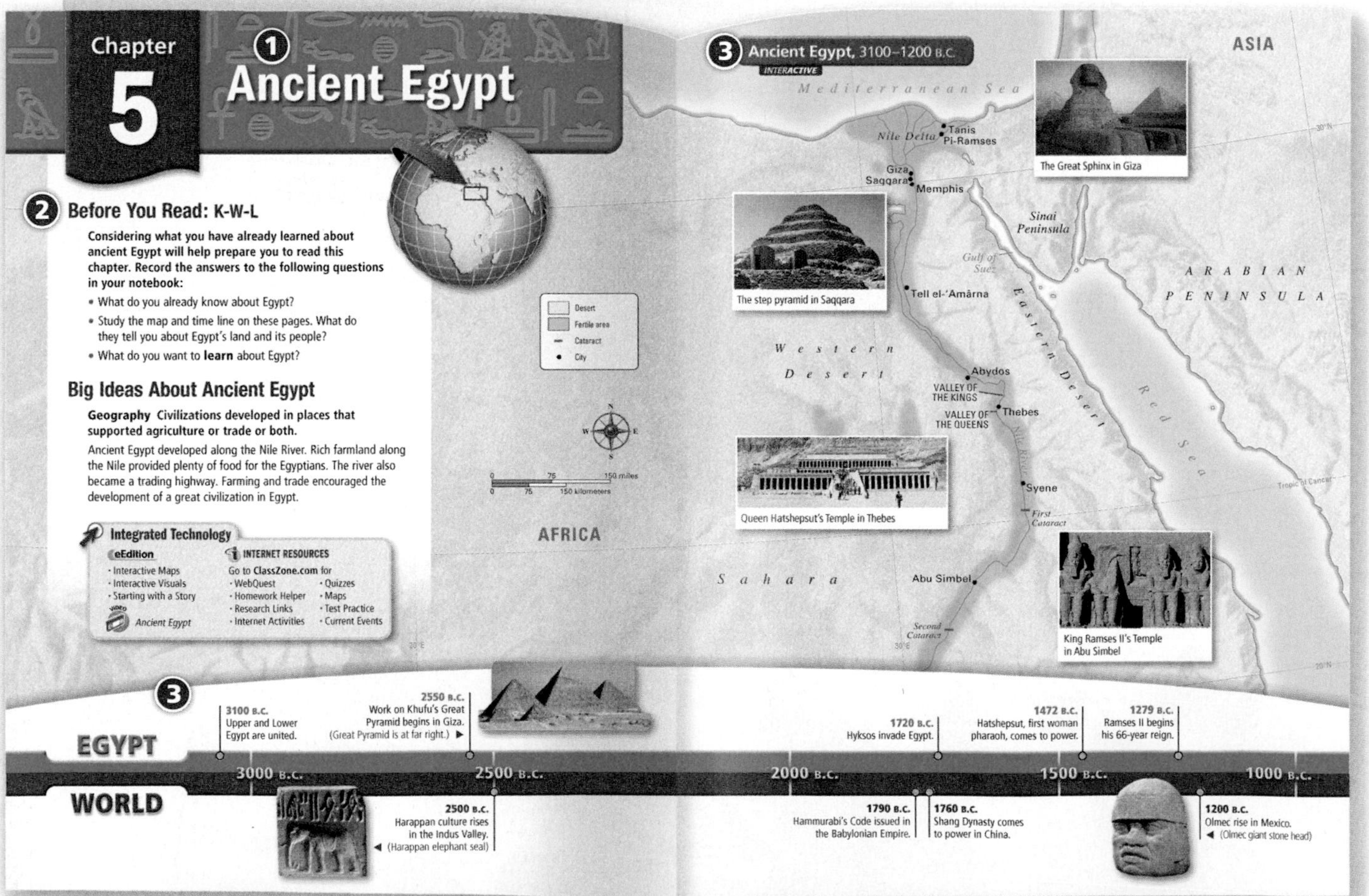

Preview Lessons Before You Read

Each chapter consists of either three or four lessons. These lessons focus on specific time periods or on particular historical themes.

1. Study the information under the heading **Main Ideas.** It tells you what is important in the lesson.
2. Preview the **Terms & Names** list. This list tells you the topics that will be covered in the lesson.
3. Read the paragraph under the head **Build on What You Know.** This relates the content of the lesson to your personal experience or to subjects you've already studied.
4. Notice the structure of the lesson. Red heads label the major topics; run-in heads signal smaller topics within those major topics. Together, these heads provide you with a quick outline of the lesson.
5. Check the **Words to Know** list. It defines common words that are used in the lesson.

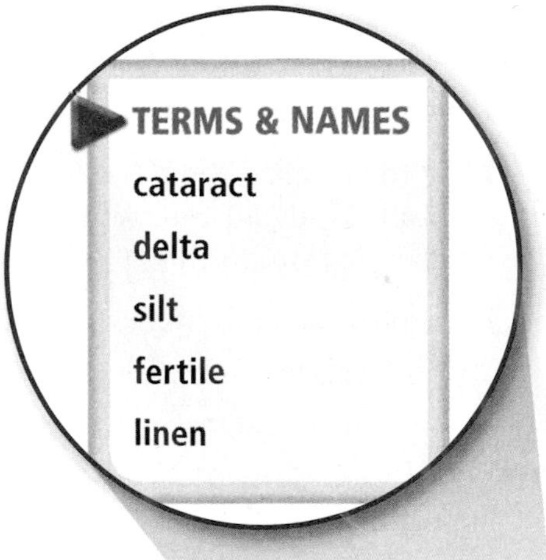

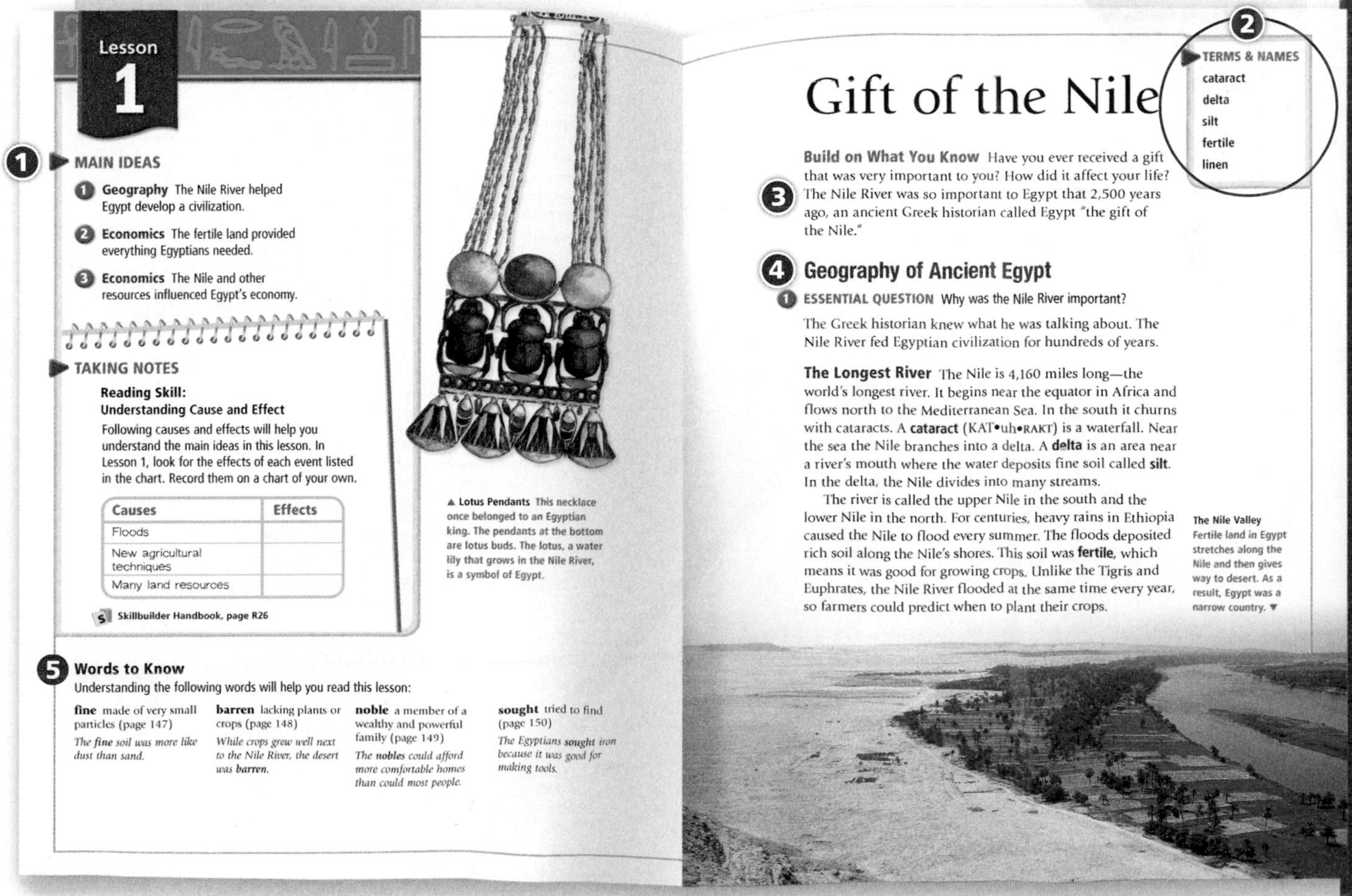

Lesson 1

1 **MAIN IDEAS**

1 **Geography** The Nile River helped Egypt develop a civilization.

2 **Economics** The fertile land provided everything Egyptians needed.

3 **Economics** The Nile and other resources influenced Egypt's economy.

TAKING NOTES

Reading Skill: Understanding Cause and Effect

Following causes and effects will help you understand the main ideas in this lesson. In Lesson 1, look for the effects of each event listed in the chart. Record them on a chart of your own.

Causes	Effects
Floods	
New agricultural techniques	
Many land resources	

Skillbuilder Handbook, page R26

5 **Words to Know**

Understanding the following words will help you read this lesson:

fine made of very small particles (page 147)
The fine soil was more like dust than sand.

barren lacking plants or crops (page 148)
While crops grew well next to the Nile River, the desert was barren.

noble a member of a wealthy and powerful family (page 149)
The nobles could afford more comfortable homes than could most people.

sought tried to find (page 150)
The Egyptians sought iron because it was good for making tools.

▲ **Lotus Pendants** This necklace once belonged to an Egyptian king. The pendants at the bottom are lotus buds. The lotus, a water lily that grows in the Nile River, is a symbol of Egypt.

Gift of the Nile

2 TERMS & NAMES: cataract, delta, silt, fertile, linen

3 **Build on What You Know** Have you ever received a gift that was very important to you? How did it affect your life? The Nile River was so important to Egypt that 2,500 years ago, an ancient Greek historian called Egypt "the gift of the Nile."

4 **Geography of Ancient Egypt**

1 **ESSENTIAL QUESTION** Why was the Nile River important?

The Greek historian knew what he was talking about. The Nile River fed Egyptian civilization for hundreds of years.

The Longest River The Nile is 4,160 miles long—the world's longest river. It begins near the equator in Africa and flows north to the Mediterranean Sea. In the south it churns with cataracts. A **cataract** (KAT•uh•RAKT) is a waterfall. Near the sea the Nile branches into a delta. A **delta** is an area near a river's mouth where the water deposits fine soil called **silt**. In the delta, the Nile divides into many streams.

The river is called the upper Nile in the south and the lower Nile in the north. For centuries, heavy rains in Ethiopia caused the Nile to flood every summer. The floods deposited rich soil along the Nile's shores. This soil was **fertile**, which means it was good for growing crops. Unlike the Tigris and Euphrates, the Nile River flooded at the same time every year, so farmers could predict when to plant their crops.

The Nile Valley Fertile land in Egypt stretches along the Nile and then gives way to desert. As a result, Egypt was a narrow country. ▼

Use Active Reading Strategies as You Read

Now you're ready to read the chapter. Read one lesson at a time, from beginning to end.

❶ Ask and answer questions as you read. Look for the **Essential Question** under each main heading. Finding the answer to this question will help guide your reading.

❷ Look for the story behind the events. Study the captions and any boxed features for additional information and interesting sidelights on the lesson content.

❸ Try to visualize the people, places, and events you read about. Studying the pictures, maps, and other illustrations will help you do this.

❹ Read to build your vocabulary. Use the **Vocabulary Strategy** in the margin to find the meaning of unfamiliar words.

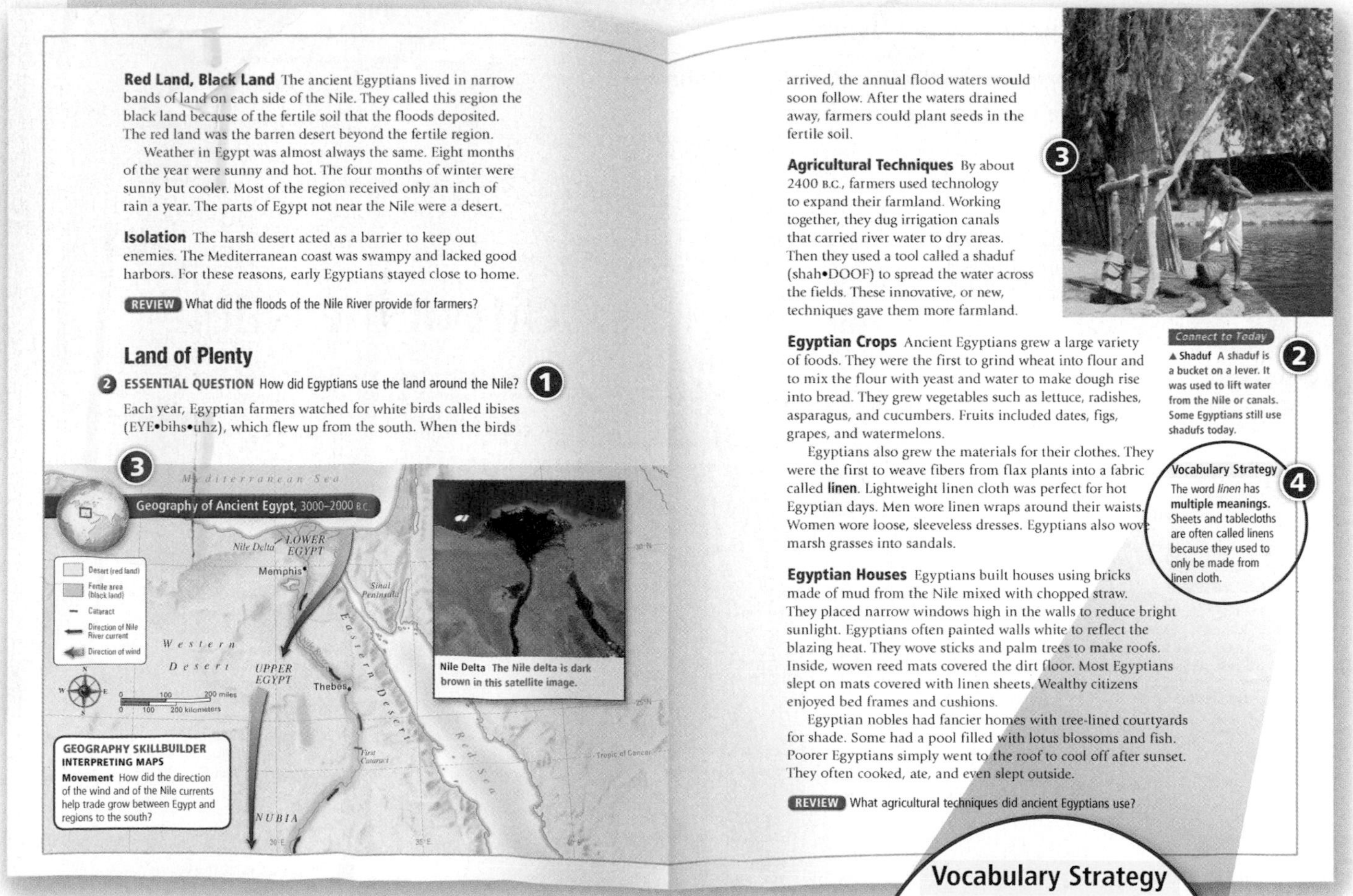

Red Land, Black Land The ancient Egyptians lived in narrow bands of land on each side of the Nile. They called this region the black land because of the fertile soil that the floods deposited. The red land was the barren desert beyond the fertile region.

Weather in Egypt was almost always the same. Eight months of the year were sunny and hot. The four months of winter were sunny but cooler. Most of the region received only an inch of rain a year. The parts of Egypt not near the Nile were a desert.

Isolation The harsh desert acted as a barrier to keep out enemies. The Mediterranean coast was swampy and lacked good harbors. For these reasons, early Egyptians stayed close to home.

REVIEW What did the floods of the Nile River provide for farmers?

Land of Plenty

❷ **ESSENTIAL QUESTION** How did Egyptians use the land around the Nile? ❶

Each year, Egyptian farmers watched for white birds called ibises (EYE•bihs•uhz), which flew up from the south. When the birds arrived, the annual flood waters would soon follow. After the waters drained away, farmers could plant seeds in the fertile soil.

❸

Geography of Ancient Egypt, 3000–2000 B.C.

GEOGRAPHY SKILLBUILDER
INTERPRETING MAPS
Movement How did the direction of the wind and of the Nile currents help trade grow between Egypt and regions to the south?

Nile Delta The Nile delta is dark brown in this satellite image.

Agricultural Techniques By about 2400 B.C., farmers used technology to expand their farmland. Working together, they dug irrigation canals that carried river water to dry areas. Then they used a tool called a shaduf (shah•DOOF) to spread the water across the fields. These innovative, or new, techniques gave them more farmland.

❸

Connect to Today

▲ **Shaduf** A shaduf is a bucket on a lever. It was used to lift water from the Nile or canals. Some Egyptians still use shadufs today. ❷

Egyptian Crops Ancient Egyptians grew a large variety of foods. They were the first to grind wheat into flour and to mix the flour with yeast and water to make dough rise into bread. They grew vegetables such as lettuce, radishes, asparagus, and cucumbers. Fruits included dates, figs, grapes, and watermelons.

Egyptians also grew the materials for their clothes. They were the first to weave fibers from flax plants into a fabric called **linen**. Lightweight linen cloth was perfect for hot Egyptian days. Men wore linen wraps around their waists. Women wore loose, sleeveless dresses. Egyptians also wove marsh grasses into sandals.

Vocabulary Strategy ❹
The word *linen* has **multiple meanings.** Sheets and tablecloths are often called linens because they used to only be made from linen cloth.

Egyptian Houses Egyptians built houses using bricks made of mud from the Nile mixed with chopped straw. They placed narrow windows high in the walls to reduce bright sunlight. Egyptians often painted walls white to reflect the blazing heat. They wove sticks and palm trees to make roofs. Inside, woven reed mats covered the dirt floor. Most Egyptians slept on mats covered with linen sheets. Wealthy citizens enjoyed bed frames and cushions.

Egyptian nobles had fancier homes with tree-lined courtyards for shade. Some had a pool filled with lotus blossoms and fish. Poorer Egyptians simply went to the roof to cool off after sunset. They often cooked, ate, and even slept outside.

REVIEW What agricultural techniques did ancient Egyptians use?

Vocabulary Strategy
The word *linen* has **multiple meanings.** Sheets and tablecloths are often called linens because they used to only be made from linen cloth.

Review and Summarize What You Have Read

When you finish reading a lesson, review and summarize what you have read. If necessary, go back and reread information that was not clear the first time through.

1. Answer the **Review** questions at the end of each section of the lesson.
2. Reread the main headings and the run-in headings for a quick summary of the major points covered in the lesson.
3. Study any charts, graphs, or maps in the lesson. These visual materials usually provide a condensed version of the information in the lesson.
4. Complete all of the questions in the **Lesson Review.** This will help you think critically about what you have just read.

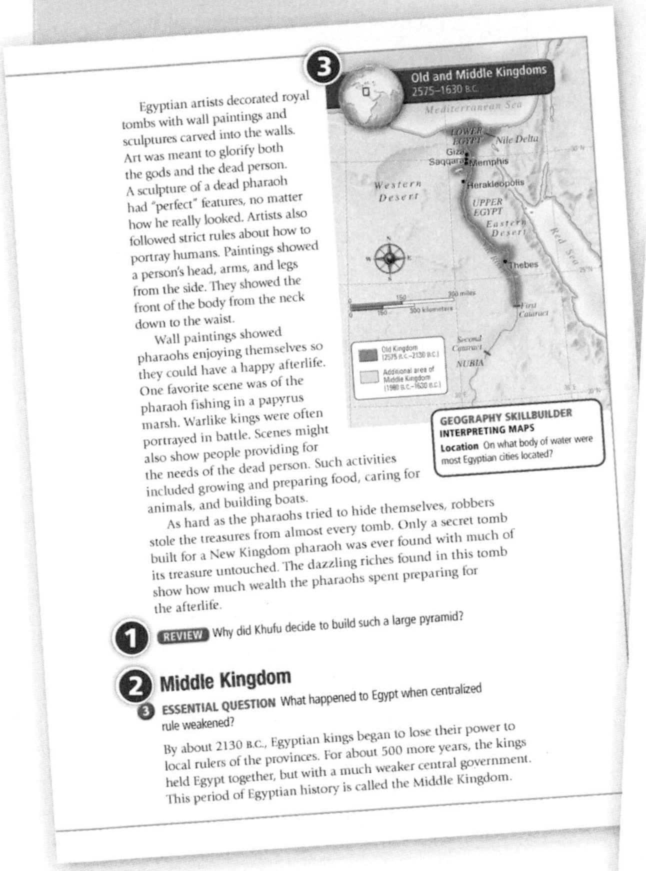

Egyptian artists decorated royal tombs with wall paintings and sculptures carved into the walls. Art was meant to glorify both the gods and the dead person. A sculpture of a dead pharaoh had "perfect" features, no matter how he really looked. Artists also followed strict rules about how to portray humans. Paintings showed a person's head, arms, and legs from the side. They showed the front of the body from the neck down to the waist.

Wall paintings showed pharaohs enjoying themselves so they could have a happy afterlife. One favorite scene was of the pharaoh fishing in a papyrus marsh. Warlike kings were often portrayed in battle. Scenes might also show people providing for the needs of the dead person. Such activities included growing and preparing food, caring for animals, and building boats.

As hard as the pharaohs tried to hide themselves, robbers stole the treasures from almost every tomb. Only a secret tomb built for a New Kingdom pharaoh was ever found with much of its treasure untouched. The dazzling riches found in this tomb show how much wealth the pharaohs spent preparing for the afterlife.

1 REVIEW Why did Khufu decide to build such a large pyramid?

2 **Middle Kingdom**

3 **ESSENTIAL QUESTION** What happened to Egypt when centralized rule weakened?

By about 2130 B.C., Egyptian kings began to lose their power to local rulers of the provinces. For about 500 more years, the kings held Egypt together, but with a much weaker central government. This period of Egyptian history is called the Middle Kingdom.

GEOGRAPHY SKILLBUILDER
INTERPRETING MAPS
Location On what body of water were most Egyptian cities located?

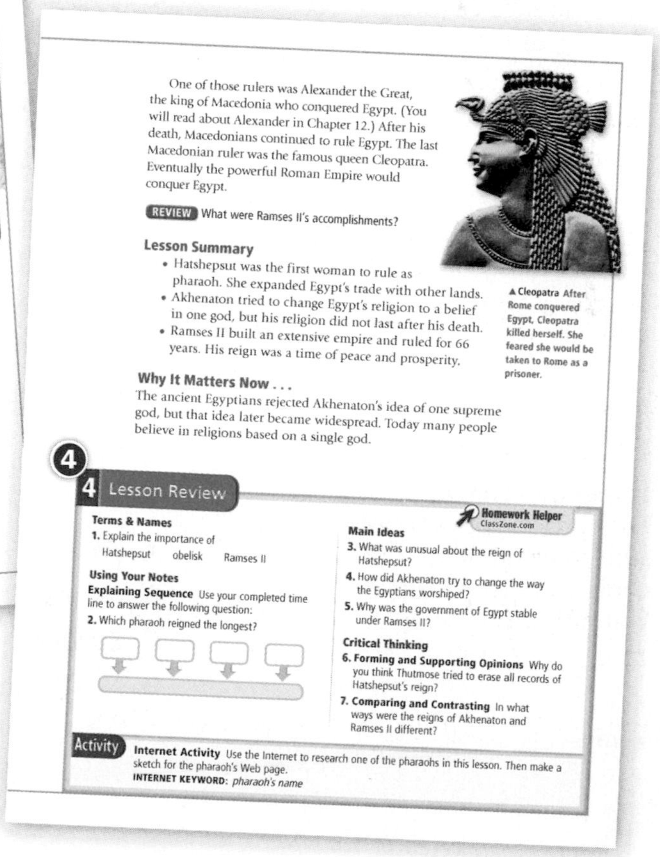

One of those rulers was Alexander the Great, the king of Macedonia who conquered Egypt. (You will read about Alexander in Chapter 12.) After his death, Macedonians continued to rule Egypt. The last Macedonian ruler was the famous queen Cleopatra. Eventually the powerful Roman Empire would conquer Egypt.

REVIEW What were Ramses II's accomplishments?

Lesson Summary

- Hatshepsut was the first woman to rule as pharaoh. She expanded Egypt's trade with other lands.
- Akhenaton tried to change Egypt's religion to a belief in one god, but his religion did not last after his death.
- Ramses II built an extensive empire and ruled for 66 years. His reign was a time of peace and prosperity.

▲ **Cleopatra** After Rome conquered Egypt, Cleopatra killed herself. She feared she would be taken to Rome as a prisoner.

Why It Matters Now . . .

The ancient Egyptians rejected Akhenaton's idea of one supreme god, but that idea later became widespread. Today many people believe in religions based on a single god.

4 **4 Lesson Review**

Homework Helper ClassZone.com

Terms & Names
1. Explain the importance of
Hatshepsut obelisk Ramses II

Using Your Notes
Explaining Sequence Use your completed time line to answer the following question:
2. Which pharaoh reigned the longest?

Main Ideas
3. What was unusual about the reign of Hatshepsut?
4. How did Akhenaton try to change the way the Egyptians worshiped?
5. Why was the government of Egypt stable under Ramses II?

Critical Thinking
6. **Forming and Supporting Opinions** Why do you think Thutmose tried to erase all records of Hatshepsut's reign?
7. **Comparing and Contrasting** In what ways were the reigns of Akhenaton and Ramses II different?

Activity
Internet Activity Use the Internet to research one of the pharaohs in this lesson. Then make a sketch for the pharaoh's Web page.
INTERNET KEYWORD: *pharaoh's name*

Part 2: Test-Taking Strategies and Practice

Use the strategies in this section to improve your test-taking skills. First read the tips on the left page. Then use them to help you with the practice items on the right page.

Multiple Choice

A multiple-choice question is a question or incomplete sentence and a set of choices. One of the choices correctly answers the question or completes the sentence.

❶ Read the question or incomplete sentence carefully. Try to answer the question or complete the sentence before looking at the choices.

❷ Look for key words in the question. They may help you figure out the correct answer.

❸ Read each choice with the question. Don't decide on your final answer until you have read all of the choices.

❹ Rule out any choices that you know are wrong.

❺ Sometimes the last choice is *all of the above.* Make sure that the other choices are all correct if you pick this answer.

answers: 1 (D); 2 (C); 3 (B); 4 (A)

❶ 1. The Andes mountains run through

❸ choices

A. Colombia.
B. Ecuador.
C. Peru.
D. all of the above

❺ Before selecting *all of the above,* make sure that all of the choices are, indeed, correct.

2. Paleontologists study

A. cultures.
B. modern societies.
C. fossils.
D. ancient art.

3. Which is an essential characteristic of a civilization?

❷ The word *essential* is key here. All of the choices are characteristics of some civilizations, but record keeping is essential to all.

A. warfare
B. record keeping
C. pyramids
D. machines

❹ You can eliminate *D* because you know many civilizations lacked machines.

4. Where did Buddhism originate?

A. Asia
B. Africa
C. Europe
D. North America

For more test practice online . . .
TEST PRACTICE
CLASSZONE.COM

Directions: Read the following questions and choose the *best* answer from the four choices.

1. Which of the following is *not* a form of government?

A. aristocracy
B. monarchy
C. oligarchy
D. philosophy

2. In 431 B.C., Sparta and Athens fought the

A. Trojan War.
B. Peloponnesian War.
C. Persian War.
D. Civil War.

3. Olmec civilization developed in

A. China.
B. western Africa.
C. Beringia.
D. Meso-America.

4. Which of the following was invented during China's Han Dynasty?

A. paper
B. bronze
C. steel
D. silk

Primary Sources

Sometimes you will need to look at a document to answer a question. Some documents are primary sources. Primary sources are written or made by people who either saw an event or were actually part of the event. A primary source can be a photograph, letter, diary, speech, or autobiography.

1. Look at the source line to learn about the document and its author. Consider how reliable the information might be.
2. Skim the article to get an idea of what it is about. As you read, look for the main idea. The main idea is the writer's most important point. Sometimes it is not directly stated.
3. Note any special punctuation. For example, ellipses (. . .) mean that words and sentences have been left out.
4. Ask yourself questions about the document as you read.
5. Review the questions. This will give your reading a purpose and also help you find the answers more easily. Then reread the document.

answers: 1 (C); 2 (A)

The Eruption of Mount Vesuvius, A.D. 79

(2, 4) My mother now began to beg, urge, and command me to escape as best I could. . . . I replied that I would not be saved without her. Taking her by the hand, I hurried her along. . . . And now came the ashes, but at first sparsely. I turned around. Behind us, an ominous thick smoke, spreading over the earth like a flood, followed us. . . . To be heard were only the shrill cries of women, the wailing of children, the shouting of men. Some were calling to their parents, others to their children, others to their wives—knowing one another only by voice. (3)

(1) —Pliny the Younger, from letters written to the historian Tacitus

This text is from a personal letter.

(5)

1. Pliny is describing a

A. flood.
B. tidal wave.
C. volcanic eruption.
D. war.

2. Which sentence *best* expresses the idea of this passage?

A. People were very frightened.
B. Pliny disagreed with his mother.
C. Thick smoke spread over the earth like a flood.
D. Pliny got separated from his mother.

For more test practice online . . .
TEST PRACTICE
CLASSZONE.COM

Directions: Use the passage to answer the following questions.

> He [the historian] must not be misled by the exaggerated fancies of the poets, or by the tales of chroniclers who seek to please the ear rather than speak the truth. . . . At such a distance of time he must make up his mind to be satisfied with conclusions resting upon the clearest evidence which can be had. . . . Of the events of the war I have not ventured to speak from any chance information, nor according to any notion of my own; I have described nothing but what I either saw myself, or learned from others of whom I made the most careful and particular enquiry. The task was a laborious one, because eye-witnesses of the same occurrences gave different accounts of them, as they remembered or were interested in the actions of one side or the other.
>
> —Thucydides, *The Peloponnesian War*

1. What does Thucydides think of poets?

A. They are reliable.
B. They are good storytellers.
C. They exaggerate.
D. They lie.

2. The task of writing the history of the war was difficult because

A. eyewitnesses gave different accounts of the same events.
B. the poets exaggerated.
C. Thucydides did not see any of the events himself.
D. the soldiers lied to Thucydides.

Secondary Sources

A secondary source is an account of events by a person who did not actually experience them. The author often uses information from several primary sources to write about a person or event. Biographies, many newspaper articles, and history books are examples of secondary sources.

1. Read the title to get an idea of what the passage is about. (The title here indicates that the passage is about what and how the Romans ate.)
2. Skim the paragraphs to find the main idea of the passage.
3. Look for words that help you understand the order in which events happen.
4. Ask yourself questions as you read. (You might ask yourself, Why were Roman dinner parties dignified or disgusting?)
5. Review the questions to see what information you will need to find. Then reread the passage.

answers: 1 (D); 2 (A)

❶ Roman Eating Habits

The ordinary Roman was not a great eater of meat. . . . At home, porridge and bread were the staple food of most Romans, many of whom in the city had to rely on [government distribution of] corn . . . for their needs. . . .

In the well-to-do homes the regimen was different. [Breakfast], for those who wanted it, might be bread dipped in wine, or with cheese, dried fruits, or honey. The equivalent of lunch was . . . again a light meal, often consisting of leftovers from the previous day. The main meal of the ❸ day . . . was eaten in the middle of the afternoon, after work and the bath, and could, and often did, go on for hours. ❷ Dinner-parties were elaborate, and could be dignified or ❹ disgusting affairs, depending on the . . . host and his choice of guests. Overindulgence was the rule rather than the exception. Cicero wrote to his friend Atticus that when Julius Caesar stopped overnight at his country villa . . . in 45 B.C. . . . Caesar "had a bath at about one . . . oiled his body, and came to dinner. He [ate and drank] to excess, with obvious enjoyment." . . . Dinner guests reclined on their left elbow at an angle of about 45 degrees from the table, on couches set against three sides of it, and ate with their fingers.

—Antony Kamm, *The Romans: An Introduction*

❺

1. Which was a food eaten by Romans for breakfast?
   - **A.** bread
   - **B.** honey
   - **C.** dried fruits
   - **D.** all of the above

Remember that an opinion is a statement that cannot be proved. A fact is a statement that can be proved.

2. Which of the following statements about Roman dinner parties is an opinion?
   - **A.** They were disgusting affairs.
   - **B.** They were eaten in the middle of the afternoon.
   - **C.** They were eaten after work.
   - **D.** Guests ate with their fingers.

For more test practice online . . .
TEST PRACTICE
CLASSZONE.COM

Directions: Use the passage to answer the following questions.

Polynesian Canoes

The Polynesian voyaging canoe, one of the great ocean-going craft of the ancient world, was the means by which generations of adventurous voyagers were able to extend the human frontier far out into the Pacific, discovering and colonizing a vast realm of Oceanic islands. By 1000 B.C., when Mediterranean sailors were sailing in their land-locked sea, the immediate ancestors of the Polynesians had reached the previously uninhabited archipelagoes of Fiji, Tonga, and Samoa, in the middle of the Pacific Ocean. Their descendants went on from there to settle all of the habitable islands in a huge triangular section of the ocean bounded by the Hawaiian archipelago, tiny Easter Island, and the massive islands of New Zealand—an area equivalent to most of Europe and Asia combined.

The canoes in which people spread into the Pacific were not only humankind's first truly ocean-going craft, but also embodied a unique way of gaining the stability needed to carry sail in rough, open ocean waters. . . [This involved] adding outrigger floats to one or both sides of a single canoe hull, or by joining two hulls together by means of crossbeams and coconut-fiber lashings to make the so-called double canoe.

—Ben Finney, "The Polynesian Voyaging Canoe." From *New World and Pacific Civilizations: Cultures of America, Asia, and the Pacific,* edited by Goran Burenhult.

1. The Polynesians used voyaging canoes to colonize
   A. a small area of the Pacific.
   B. a large area of the Pacific.
   C. most of Europe and Asia.
   D. Australia and New Guinea.

2. The Polynesians gave their canoes the stability needed to handle the rough ocean waters by adding
   A. outrigger floats.
   B. more sails.
   C. ballasted hulls.
   D. wooden keels.

Political Cartoons

Cartoonists who draw political cartoons use both words and art to express opinions about political issues.

1. Try to figure out what the cartoon is about. Titles and captions may give clues.
2. Use labels to help identify the people, places, and events represented in the cartoon.
3. Note when and where the cartoon was published.
4. Look for symbols—that is, people, places, or objects that stand for something else.
5. The cartoonist often exaggerates the physical features of people and objects. This technique will give you clues as to how the cartoonist feels about the subject.
6. Try to figure out the cartoonist's message and summarize it in a sentence.

answers: 1 (B); 2 (A)

❶ NEXT!

❹ The cartoonist uses the swastika, a symbol used during World War II.

❺ The swastika looks like a huge, frightening machine. It can easily crush Poland.

❷ The label "Poland" tells which country is the subject of the cartoon's title.

Daniel Fitzpatrick / *St. Louis Post-Dispatch*, August 24, 1939.

❸ The date is a clue that the cartoon refers to the beginning of World War II.

1. What does the swastika in the cartoon stand for?

A. the Soviet Union
B. Nazi Germany
C. the Polish army
D. Great Britain

❻ **2.** Which sentence *best* summarizes the cartoonist's message?

A. Germany will attack Poland next.
B. Poland should stop Germany.
C. Germany will lose this battle.
D. Poland will fight a civil war.

For more test practice online . . .
TEST PRACTICE
CLASSZONE.COM

Directions: Use the cartoon to answer the following questions.

The Granger Collection, New York

Benjamin Franklin (1754)

1. What do the sections of the snake in the cartoon represent?

A. army units
B. states
C. Native American groups
D. colonies

2. Which phrase *best* states the message of the cartoon?

A. "East is East, and West is West, and never the twain shall meet."
B. "Taxation without representation is tyranny."
C. "United we stand, divided we fall."
D. "Out of many, one."

Charts

Charts present facts in a visual form. History textbooks use several different types of charts. The chart that is most often found on tests is the table. A table organizes information in columns and rows.

1. Read the title of the chart to find out what information is represented.
2. Read the column and row headings. Sometimes further information on headings is provided in footnotes.
3. Notice how the information in the chart is organized.
4. Compare the information from column to column and row to row.
5. Try to draw conclusions from the information in the chart.
6. Read the questions and then study the chart again.

③ This chart compares two empires.

Two Great Empires: Han China and Rome

Han Dynasty—202 B.C. to A.D. 220	Roman Empire—27 B.C. to A.D. 476
• Empire replaced rival kingdoms	• Empire replaced republic
• Centralized, bureaucratic government	• Centralized, bureaucratic government
• Built roads and defensive walls	• Built roads and defensive walls
• Conquered many diverse peoples in regions bordering China	• Conquered many diverse peoples in regions of three continents
• At its height—area of 1,500,000 square miles and a population of 60,000,000	• At its height—area of 1,300,000 square miles and a population of 54,000,000
• Chinese became common written language throughout empire	• Latin did not replace other written languages in empire
• Ongoing conflict with nomads	• Ongoing conflict with nomads
• Empire fell apart; restored by Sui Dynasty after 581	• Empire fell apart; never restored

⑤ The two empires shared some of the same features.

1. Which was a characteristic shared by both Han China and Rome?
   - **A.** Both empires were restored after they fell apart.
   - **B.** Both empires replaced republics.
   - **C.** Both had a population of 60,000,000.
   - **D.** Both had an ongoing conflict with nomads.

   Use the information in the chart to find similarities between the two empires.

2. The Han Dynasty exceeded the Roman Empire in
   - **A.** population.
   - **B.** army.
   - **C.** completed building projects.
   - **D.** government agencies.

answers: 1 (D); 2 (A)

For more test practice online . . .
TEST PRACTICE
CLASSZONE.COM

Directions: Use the chart to answer the following questions.

Ancient Civilizations				
Feature	China	Egypt	Indus Valley	Mesopotamia
Location	River valley	River valley	River valley	River valley
Period	2000 B.C.–400 B.C.	3100 B.C.–600 B.C.	2500 B.C.–1500 B.C.	3500 B.C.–2000 B.C.
Specialized workers	Priests; government workers, soldiers; crafts people in bronze and silk; farmers	Priests; government workers, scribes, soldiers; workers in pottery, stone; farmers	Priests; government officials; workers in pottery, bricks; farmers	Priests; government officials, scribes, soldiers; workers in pottery, textiles; farmers
Institutions	Walled cities; oracle-bone reading	Ruling class of priests and nobles; education system	Strong central government	Ruling class of priests and nobles; education for scribes
Record keeping	Pictographic writing	Hieroglyphic writing	Pictographic writing	Cuneiform writing
Advanced technology and artifacts	Writing; making bronze and silk; irrigation systems	Papyrus; mathematics; astronomy, engineering; pyramids; mummification; medicine	Irrigation systems; indoor plumbing; seals	Wheel; plow; sailboat; bronze weapons

1. Which civilization appeared first?

A. China
B. Egypt
C. Indus Valley
D. Mesopotamia

2. The Indus Valley civilization did *not* have

A. irrigation systems.
B. walled cities.
C. government officials.
D. indoor plumbing.

Line and Bar Graphs

Graphs show numbers in visual form. Line graphs are useful for showing changes over time. Bar graphs make it easy to compare numbers.

1. Read the title of the graph to find out what information is represented.
2. Study the labels on the graph.
3. Look at the source line that tells where the graph is from. Decide whether you can depend on the source to provide reliable information.
4. See if you can make any generalizations about the information in the graph. For example, you might note that the Agricultural Revolution began when global temperatures rose.
5. Read the questions carefully and then study the graph again.

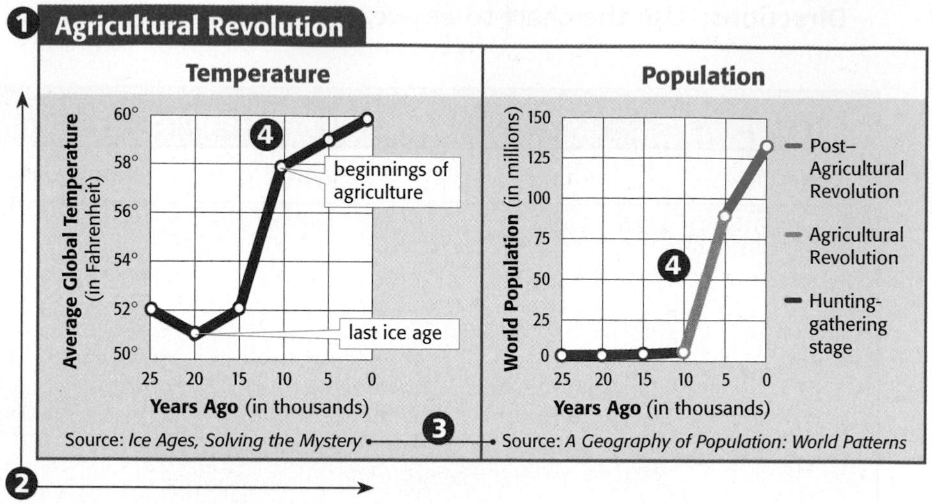

5

1. When was the world coldest?
   A. 1,000 years ago
   B. 5,000 years ago
   C. 25,000 years ago
   D. 20,000 years ago

2. During the Agricultural Revolution, world population
   A. rose rapidly.
   B. declined rapidly.
   C. rose slightly.
   D. declined slightly.

answers: 1 (D); 2 (A)

Directions: Use the graphs to answer the following questions.

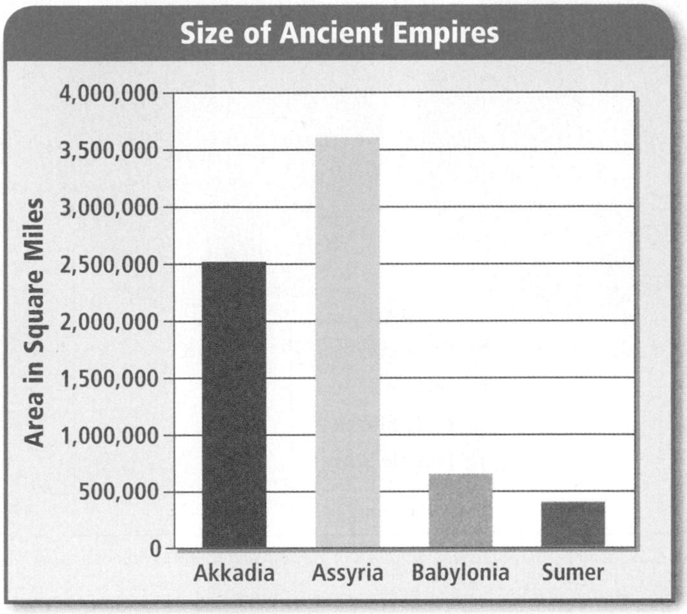

Source: *Institute for Research on World Systems*

1. Which empire was the largest?

A. Babylonia
B. Assyria
C. Sumer
D. Akkadia

Population of Four Ancient Cities

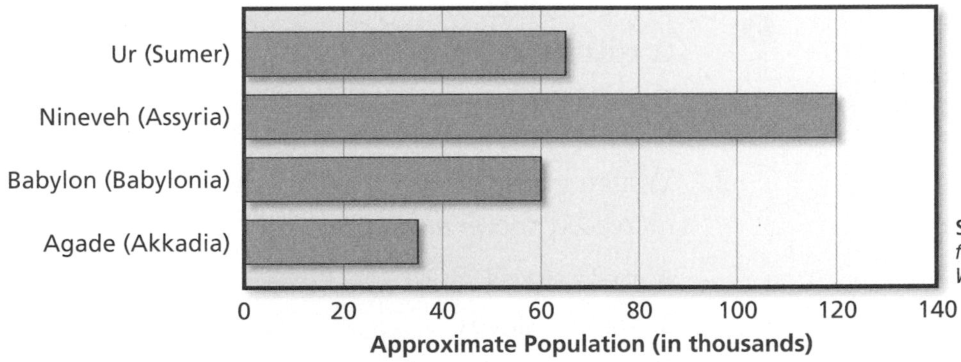

Source: *Institute for Research on World Systems*

2. Which city had a population of approximately 60,000 people?

A. Agade
B. Nineveh
C. Babylon
D. Ur

Pie Graphs

A pie, or circle, graph shows the relationship among parts of a whole. These parts look like slices of a pie. Each slice is shown as a percentage of the whole pie.

1. Read the title of the chart to find out what information is represented.
2. The graph may provide a legend, or key, that tells you what different slices represent.
3. The size of the slice is related to the percentage. The larger the percentage, the larger the slice.
4. Look at the source line that tells where the graph is from. Ask yourself if you can depend on this source to provide reliable information.
5. Read the questions carefully, and study the graph again.

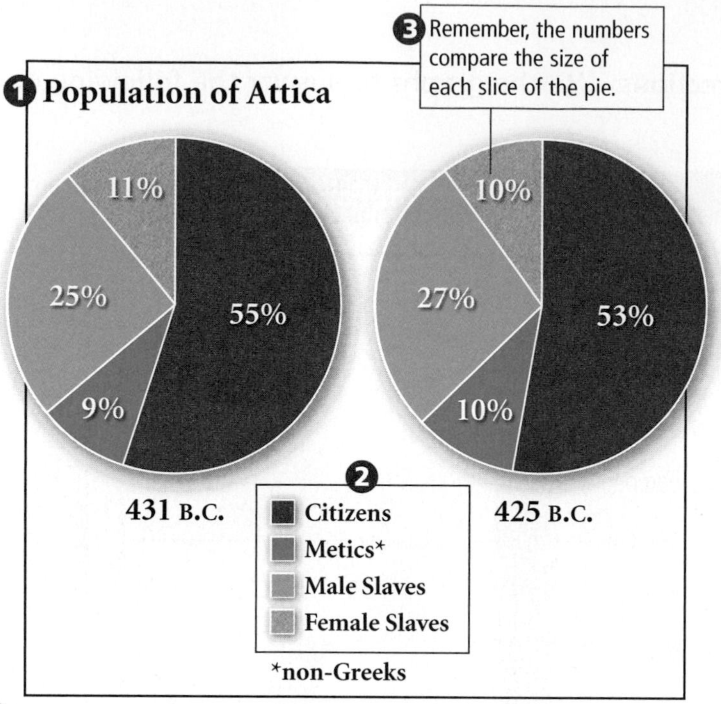

4 **Source:** *A. W. Gomme, The Population of Athens in the Fifth and Fourth Centuries* B.C.

5

1. Which group made up the majority of Attica's population in both years?
   A. female slaves
   B. male slaves
   C. citizens
   D. metics

2. Which group's percentage of the population increased the *most* between 431 B.C. and 425 B.C.?
   A. male slaves
   B. female slaves
   C. citizens
   D. metics

answers: 1 (C); 2 (A)

For more test practice online . . .
TEST PRACTICE
CLASSZONE.COM

Directions: Use the graph to answer the following questions.

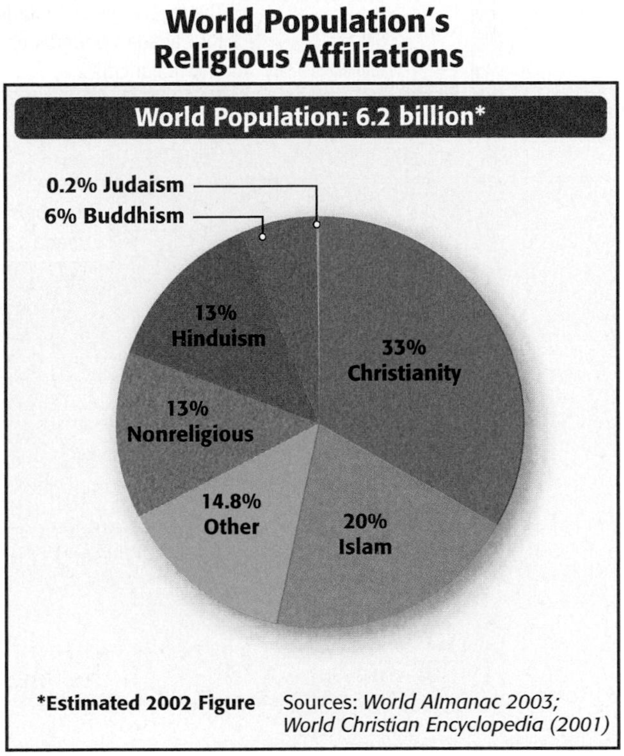

1. To which religion does the largest number of people belong?
   A. Islam
   B. Christianity
   C. Judaism
   D. Hinduism

2. The religion that has the smallest percentage of followers worldwide is
   A. Judaism
   B. Buddhism
   C. Other
   D. Christianity

Political Maps

Political maps show the divisions within countries. A country may be divided into states, provinces, and so on. The maps also show where major cities are. They may also show mountains, oceans, seas, lakes, and rivers.

1. Read the title of the map. This will give you the subject and purpose of the map.
2. Read the labels on the map. They also give information about the map's subject and purpose.
3. Study the key or legend to help you understand the symbols and colors on the map.
4. Use the scale to estimate distances between places shown on the map. Maps usually show the distance in both miles and kilometers.
5. Use the North arrow to figure out the direction of places on the map.
6. Read the questions. Carefully study the map to find the answers.

answers: 1 (B); 2 (B)

❶ Canada and Its Provinces

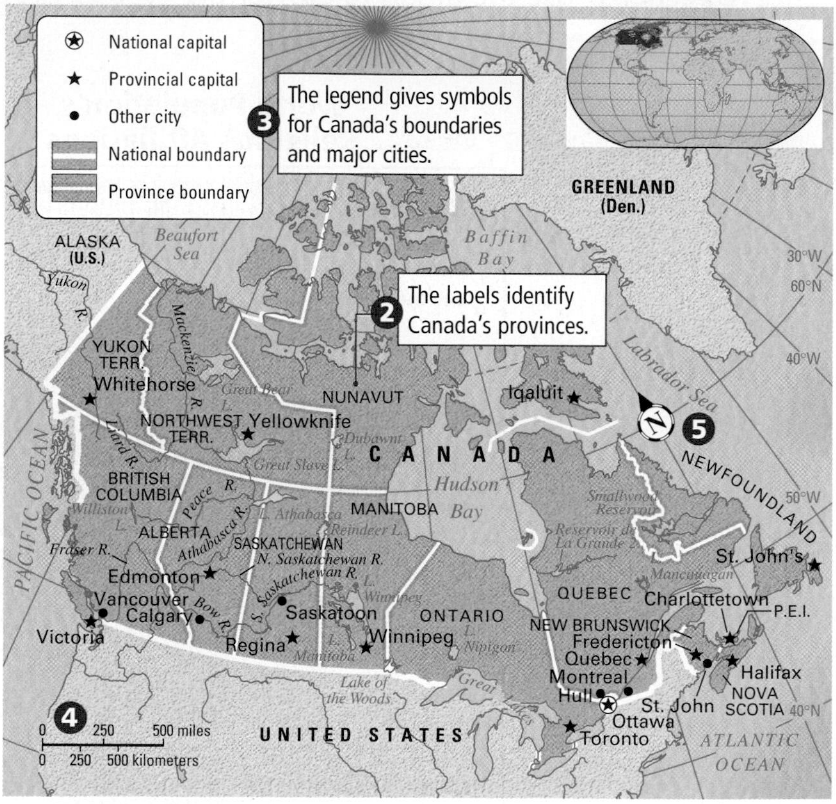

❻

1. Which province or territory is the farthest west?
   - **A.** Northwest Territories
   - **B.** Yukon Territory
   - **C.** British Columbia
   - **D.** Alberta

2. About how many miles is the United States-Canada border from the Great Lakes west to Vancouver on the Pacific Ocean?
   - **A.** 1,000
   - **B.** 1,500
   - **C.** 2,000
   - **D.** 2,500

Directions: Use the map to answer the following questions.

The Roman Empire, A.D. 400

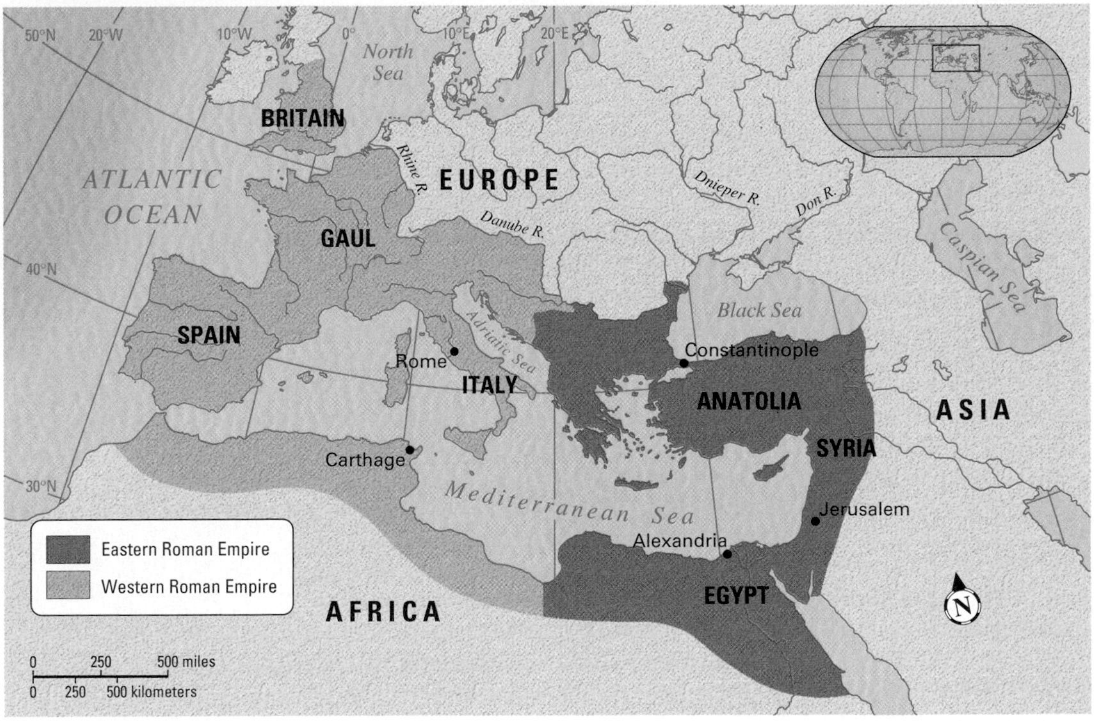

1. On which body of water was Syria located?
   - **A.** Atlantic Ocean
   - **B.** Mediterranean Sea
   - **C.** Caspian Sea
   - **D.** North Sea

2. The southernmost country in the Eastern Roman Empire was
   - **A.** Syria.
   - **B.** Gaul.
   - **C.** Spain.
   - **D.** Egypt.

Thematic Maps

Thematic maps focus on special topics. For example, a thematic map might show a country's natural resources or major battles in a war.

1. Read the title of the map. This will give you a general idea of the subject and purpose of the map.
2. Read the labels on the map. They also give information about the map's subject and purpose.
3. Study the key or legend to help you understand the symbols on the map. (The arrows show where Buddhism spread.)
4. Ask yourself whether the symbols show a pattern.
5. Read the questions. Carefully study the map to find the answers.

answers: 1 (D); 2 (D)

❶ **The Spread of Buddhism**

❷ The labels name the major areas of South Asia and East Asia. The dates show when Buddhism first came to each area.

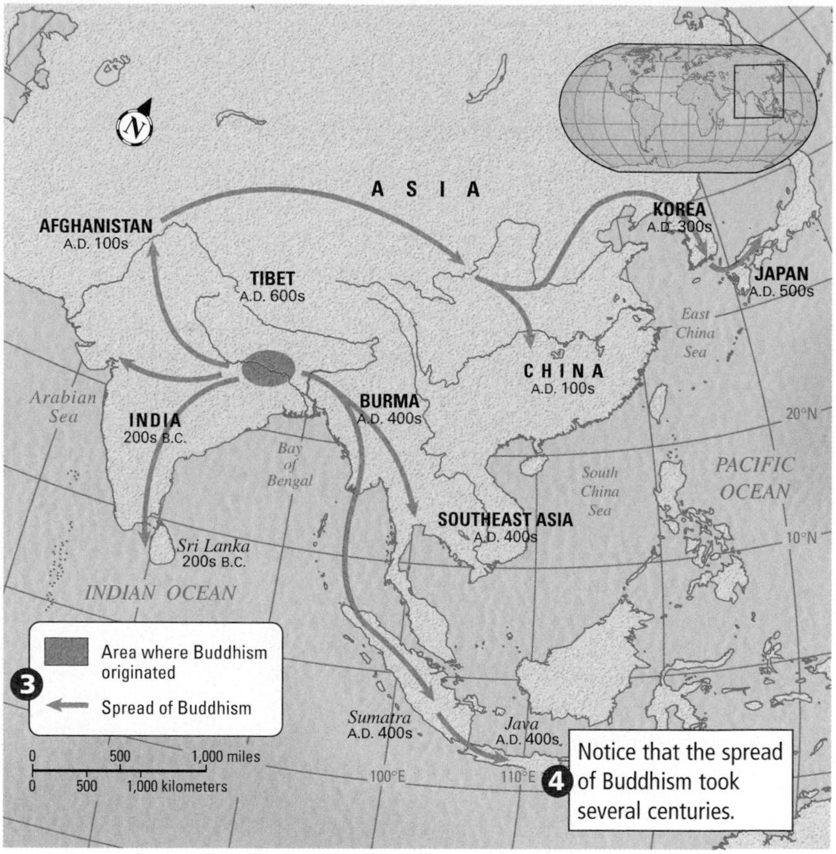

❸ (key)

❹ Notice that the spread of Buddhism took several centuries.

❺

1. To which area did Buddhism spread after A.D. 550?

A. Java
B. China
C. Japan
D. Tibet

2. When did Buddhism spread to the islands of Java and Sumatra?

A. A.D. 100s
B. A.D. 300s
C. 200s B.C.
D. A.D. 400s

For more test practice online . . .
TEST PRACTICE
CLASSZONE.COM

Directions: Use the map to answer the following questions.

The Christian Conquest of Muslim Spain

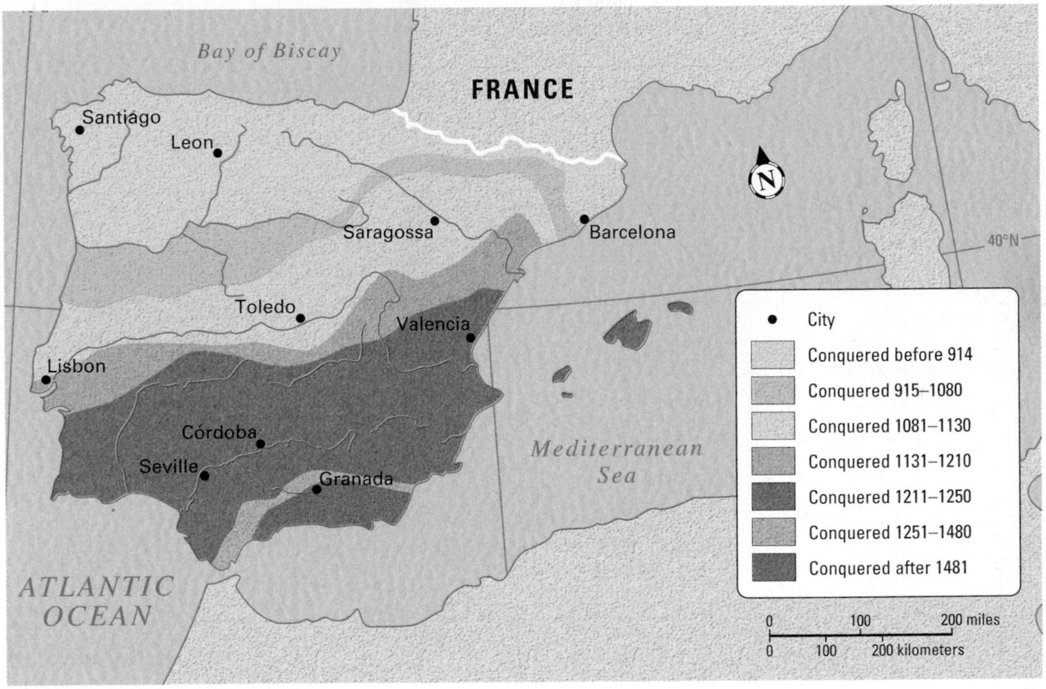

1. When did Christians conquer the easternmost city shown on the map?
   A. before 914
   B. between 1081 and 1130
   C. between 1211 and 1250
   D. after 1481

2. By 1480, how much of Spain did Christians control?
   A. only a small portion
   B. about one-third
   C. about one-half
   D. almost all of the land

Time Lines

A time line is a chart that lists events in the order in which they occurred. Time lines can be vertical or horizontal.

1. Read the title to learn what subject the time line covers.
2. Note the dates when the time line begins and ends.
3. Read the events in the order they occurred.
4. Think about what else was going on in the world on these dates. Try to make connections.
5. Read the questions. Then carefully study the time line to find the answers.

1 Domestication of Plants and Animals

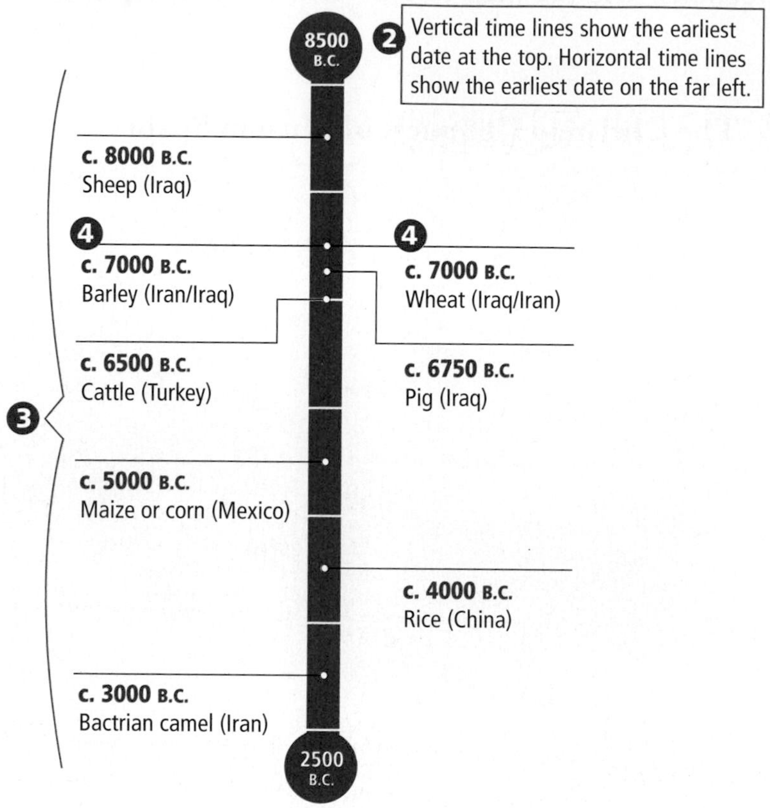

5

1. How many plants and animals were domesticated between 6000 B.C. and 2000 B.C.?

   A. 2
   B. 3
   C. 4
   D. 6

2. Which animal was the second to be domesticated?

   A. pig
   B. sheep
   C. Bactrian camel
   D. cattle

answers: 1 (B); 2 (A)

Directions: Use the time line to answer the following questions.

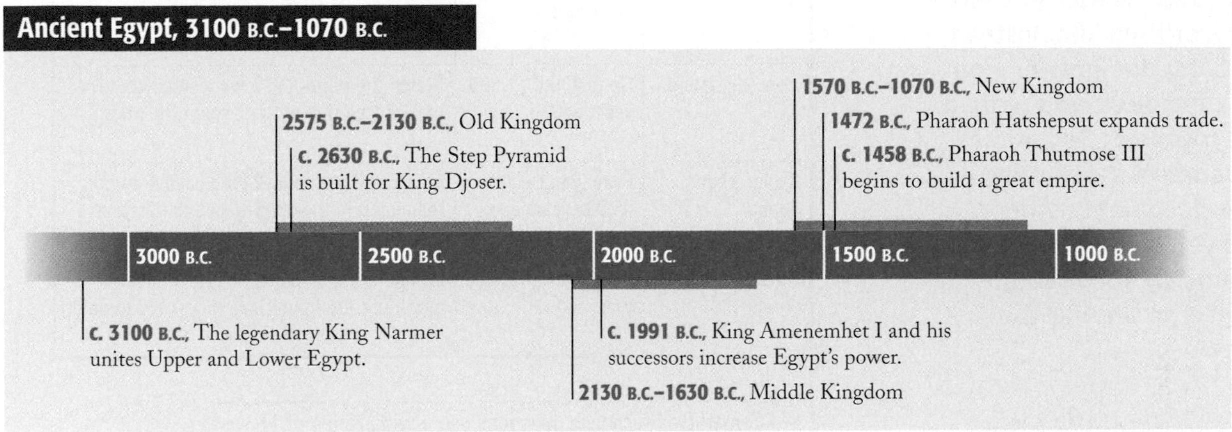
Ancient Egypt, 3100 B.C.–1070 B.C.
1570 B.C.–1070 B.C., New Kingdom
1472 B.C., Pharaoh Hatshepsut expands trade.
c. 1458 B.C., Pharaoh Thutmose III begins to build a great empire.
2575 B.C.–2130 B.C., Old Kingdom
c. 2630 B.C., The Step Pyramid is built for King Djoser.
3000 B.C.
2500 B.C.
2000 B.C.
1500 B.C.
1000 B.C.
c. 3100 B.C., The legendary King Narmer unites Upper and Lower Egypt.
c. 1991 B.C., King Amenemhet I and his successors increase Egypt's power.
2130 B.C.–1630 B.C., Middle Kingdom

1. When did Pharaoh Hatshepsut expand trade?

A. c. 1458
B. c. 1472
C. c. 2630
D. c. 3100

2. What happened after Pharaoh Hatshepsut expanded trade?

A. The Step Pyramid was built.
B. King Amenemhet I and his successors increased Egypt's power.
C. The Middle Kingdom began.
D. Pharaoh Thutmose III began to build a great empire.

Constructed Response

Constructed-response questions focus on a document, such as a photograph, cartoon, chart, graph, or time line. Instead of picking one answer from a set of choices, you write a short response. Sometimes you can find the answer in the document. Other times you will use what you already know about a subject to answer the question.

1. Read the title of the document to get an idea of what it is about.
2. Study the document.
3. Read the questions carefully. Study the document again to find the answers.
4. Write your answers. You don't need to use complete sentences unless the directions say so.

1 Determining the Age of Archaeological Finds

Method	Age Range	Process
Written records	Up to about 5,000 years ago	Use written records of known age to date artifacts found along with them.
Tree-ring dating	Up to about 11,000 years ago	Match the pattern in a wooden object to a master tree-ring pattern; count the rings.
Radiocarbon dating	From about 300 to 45,000 years ago	Measure the amount of radioactive carbon remaining in the object (used to date the remains of plants and animals).
Potassium-argon dating	More than 1,000,000 years ago	Compare the amounts of potassium and argon present in volcanic rock (used to date bones and tools found in the rock).

2 Constructed-response questions use a wide range of documents. These include short passages, cartoons, charts, graphs, maps, time lines, posters, and other visual materials. This document is a chart of archaeological procedures.

3

1. What are two methods of dating artifacts?

   4 *radiocarbon dating and potassium-argon dating*

2. Which dating method would be best to use on burned grain found at an archaeological site?

   radiocarbon dating, because it is used on plants

3. How could written records found in the remains of an ancient Roman city be used to date other artifacts from the same site?

   Written records can be used to date mateials up to 5,000 years old. If the records were dated, they could be used to find the age of artifacts buried with them.

For more test practice online . . .
TEST PRACTICE
CLASSZONE.COM

Directions: Read the following passage from an art history book. Then answer the questions that follow.

The Meaning of Cave Paintings

Because [the cave paintings] were hidden away in order to protect them from intruders, they must have been considered important. There can be little doubt that they were made as part of a ritual. But of what kind? The standard explanation, based on "preliterate" societies of modern times, is that they are a form of hunting magic. According to this theory, in "killing" the image of an animal, people of the Late Stone Age thought they had killed its vital spirit. . . .

There is growing agreement that cave paintings must embody a very early form of religion. If so, the creatures found in them have a spiritual meaning that makes them the distant ancestors of the animal divinities and their half-human, half-animal cousins [of Ancient Egypt and Minoan civilizations]. . . . Such an approach accords with animism—the belief that nature is filled with spirits—which was found the world over in the indigenous societies that survived intact until recently.

—H. W. and Anthony F. Janson, *History of Art: The Western Tradition* (2004)

1. Why were the cave paintings hidden away?
2. What is the standard explanation for cave paintings?
3. Many scientists believe that the cave paintings are evidence of an early form of religion. If this is true, what is also true about the animals in the paintings?

Extended Response

Extended-response questions, like constructed-response questions, focus on a document of some kind. However, they are more complicated and require more time to complete. Some extended-response questions ask you to present the information in the document in a different form. For example, you might be asked to present the information in a chart in graph form. Other questions ask you to complete a document such as a chart or graph. Still others require you to apply your knowledge to information in the document to write an essay.

1. Read the title of the document to get an idea of what it is about.
2. Carefully read directions and questions.
3. Study the document.
4. Sometimes the question may give you part of the answer.
5. The question may require you to write an essay. Write down some ideas to use in an outline. Then use your outline to write the essay. (A good essay will contain the ideas shown in the rubric to the right.)

❶ **Hammurabi's Code**

❸

If a son has struck his father, they shall cut off his hand.

If a [noble] has destroyed the eye of a [noble], they shall destroy his eye.

If he has broken another [noble's] bone, they shall break his bone.

If he has destroyed the eye of a commoner or broken the bone of a commoner, he shall pay one mina of silver.

If he has destroyed the eye of a [noble's] slave or broken the bone of a [noble's] slave, he shall pay one-half [the slave's] value.

If a [noble] has knocked out the tooth of a [noble], they shall knock out his tooth.

If he has knocked out a commoner's tooth, he shall pay one-third mina of silver.

❷ Hammurabi's Code is often described as "an eye for an eye." Is this an accurate description of the code? Is the code applied equally to all people? Explain your answer. ❹

The question gives you an idea of what people think about Hammurabi's Code.

❺ **Essay Rubric:** The best essays will point out that the strict "eye for an eye" rule only applies in some situations, such as when a noble destroys the eye of another noble. The description is accurate for nobles losing an eye, but not entirely accurate for other crimes that involve people who are not nobles. If someone wrongs a commoner by destroying his eye or breaking his bone, the commoner will receive a payment of one mina of silver. In this case, the wrongdoer would not lose an eye or have a bone broken. If a noble knocks a commoner's tooth out, he has to pay the commoner, but if a noble knocks another noble's tooth out, he gets his own tooth knocked out. The code does not seem to apply equally to all people. The code implies that a noble who harmed another noble was dealt with more harshly than a noble who harmed a commoner.

For more test practice online . . .
TEST PRACTICE
CLASSZONE.COM

Directions: Complete the chart. Then use the information in the chart to answer the following question.

The Development of Civilization	
Key Achievements	Impact
• Invention of Tools	•
• Mastery over fire	• People were able to keep warm and cook food.
• Development of language	•
• Breakthroughs in farming technology	•
• Domestication of animals	• Animals could be bred for certain traits. Animals became more dependable.
• Food surpluses	• More people could live in one place, and there were fewer food shortages.
• Specialized workers	•
• Record keeping	•
• Advanced technology	•

1. Which achievements do you think had the most influence on the development of civilization? Why?

Document-Based Questions

To answer a document-based question, you usually have to study more than one document. First you answer questions about each document. Then you use those answers and information from the documents as well as your own knowledge of history to write an essay.

1. Read the Historical Context section. It will give you an idea of the topic that will be covered in the question.
2. Read the Task section carefully. It tells you what you will need to write about in your essay.
3. Study each document. Think about the connection the documents have to the topic in the Task section.
4. Read and answer the questions about each document. Think about how your answers connect to the Task section.

Introduction

1 **Historical Context:** After the Persian War, Athens became the most powerful city-state in Greece. Many other city-states, including Sparta, felt threatened by Athens' rise to power. Eventually, Sparta declared war on Athens. In this Peloponnesian War, Athens was devastated.

2 **Task:** Discuss the effects of the Peloponnesian War on Athenians.

Part 1: Short Answer

Study each document carefully. Answer the questions that follow.

3 Document 1: The Peloponnesian War—A Summary

The Peloponnesian War, 431 B.C.–404 B.C.

Causes	Military Strategies	Outcomes
Anger at Athenian grab for power and prestige. Fear of Athens' status as a powerful naval empire. Anger at Athenian attempts to colonize lands of other city-states.	Athens and allies: Avoid land battles and rely on sea power. Sparta and allies: Focus on land battles; cut off Athenian food supply by laying waste to countryside.	Sparta victorious, becomes leading Greek city-state. Athens loses its empire, power, wealth, and prestige.

4 **How did Sparta intend to win the war?**

focus on land battles and cut off Athens' food supply by laying waste to the countryside

Document 2: Reaction to an Athenian Defeat

They were beaten at all points and altogether; all that they suffered was great; they were destroyed, as the saying is, with a total destruction, their fleet, their army, everything was destroyed, and few out of many returned home. Such were the events in Sicily. . . .

When the news was brought to Athens, for a long while they disbelieved even the most respectable of the soldiers who had themselves escaped from the scene of action and clearly reported the matter, a destruction so complete not being thought credible. . . . Already distressed at all points and in all quarters, after what had now happened, they were seized by a fear and consternation quite without example. . . . [T]hey began to despair of salvation.

—Thucydides, *The Peloponnesian War*

This passage deals with the Athenian defeat at Syracuse. How did Athenians react to this loss?

with utter disbelief and then with fear, dismay, and despair

Document 3: The Cost of the Peloponnesian War

The economic consequences of the war were grave. Commerce by land and sea was disrupted. . . . Agriculture suffered in most of Greece. . . . A good deal of territory was [ruined], and livestock and farming implements destroyed as well as growing vines and olive trees. . . .

In Athens, as many as fifty thousand people had probably died of the plague. . . .War casualties seem to have included at least five thousand . . . soldiers and twelve thousand sailors. . . . Probably the number of adult male citizens in 403 was half what it had been in 431.

—Sarah B. Pomeroy and others,
A Brief History of Ancient Greece

What was the human cost of the Peloponnesian War to Athens?

some 17,000 war casualties and as many as 50,000 from the plague, perhaps as much as half of the population of adult male citizens

5 Part 2: Essay

Write an essay describing the Peloponnesian War's effect on Athens. Use information from the documents, your short answers, and your knowledge of history. 6

5 Read the essay question carefully. Then write a brief outline for your essay.

6 Write your essay. The first paragraph should introduce your topic. The middle paragraphs should explain it. The closing paragraph should restate the topic and your conclusion. Support your ideas with quotations or details from the documents. Add other supporting facts or details from your knowledge of world history.

7 A good essay will contain the ideas in the rubric below.

7 **Essay Rubric:** The best essays will state that Athens was devastated. It lost its empire, power, wealth, and prestige (Document 1). Its economy was destroyed, and the human losses it suffered were immense (Document 3). Further, Athenians suffered a huge psychological blow because they could not believe that they could have been so thoroughly defeated (Document 2). This made them fear greatly for the future.

Introduction

Historical Context: By the time Rome was an empire, wealth and social status made a huge difference in the way people lived. Roman society was divided into three main social classes: the elite, the "more humble," and the slaves.

Task: Discuss how the life of an elite Roman would have been different from that of a "more humble" person or a slave.

Part 1: Short Answers

Study each document carefully. Answer the questions that follow.

Document 1: Roman Dinner Party

This painting found at Pompeii shows some elite Romans being entertained at a dinner party. What were elite dinner parties like?

Document 2: A Schoolboy's Life

> Before it is light I wake up, and, sitting on the edge of my bed, I put on my shoes and leg-wraps because it is cold. . . . Taking off my nightshirt I put on my tunic and belt; I put oil on my hair, comb it, wrap a scarf around my neck and put on my white cloak. Followed by my school attendant and my nurse I go to say good morning to daddy and mummy and I kiss them both. I find my writing things and exercise book and give them to a slave. I set off to school followed by my school attendant. . . .
>
> I go into the schoolroom and say "Good morning master." He kisses me and returns my greeting. The slave gives me my wax tablets, my writing things and ruler. . . . When I finish learning my lesson I ask the master to let me go home to lunch. . . . Reaching home I change, take some white bread, olives, cheese, dried figs, and nuts and drink some cold water. After lunch I go back to school where the master is beginning to read. He says, "Let's begin work."
>
> —A Roman schoolboy, quoted by F. R. Cowell, *Everyday Life in Ancient Rome*

How did the schoolboy's day differ from his slave's?

Document 3: Poorer Neighborhoods

> But here we inhabit a city supported for the most part by [planks]: for that is how the [landlord] holds up the tottering house, patches up gaping cracks in the old wall, bidding the [tenants] sleep at ease under a roof ready to tumble about their ears. No, no, I must live where there are no fires, no nightly alarms.
>
> —Juvenal, *Satires III*

What is housing like in the poorer neighborhoods?

Part 2: Essay

Write an essay describing the differences between the lives of elite Romans, poor Romans, and slaves. Use information from the documents, your short answers, and your knowledge of history to write your essay.

RAND McNALLY

World Atlas

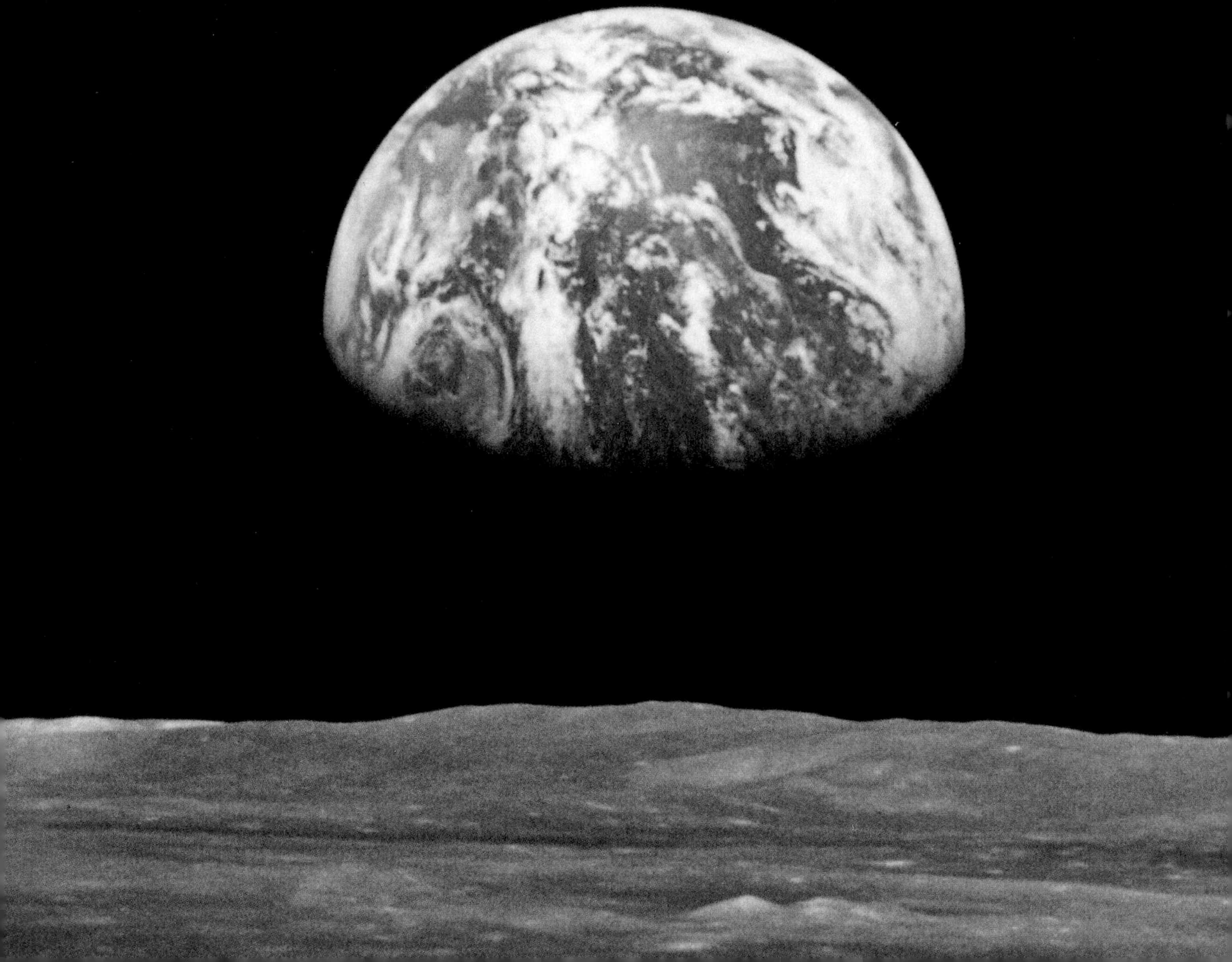

Contents

Complete Legend for Physical and Political Maps

Symbols

Lake

Seasonal Lake

River

Waterfall

Canal

▲ Mountain Peak

Cities

■ **Los Angeles** — City over 1,000,000 population

▣ **Calgary** — City under 1,000,000 population

✪ ***Paris*** — National Capital

Boundaries

International Boundary

Secondary Boundary

Type Styles Used to Name Features

CHINA	Country
O N T A R I O	State, Province, or Territory
PUERTO RICO (U.S.)	Possession
A T L A N T I C O C E A N	Ocean or Sea
A l p s	Physical Feature
Borneo	Island

Land Elevation and Water Depths

Land Elevation

Meters	Feet
3,000 and over	9,840 and over
2,000 - 3,000	6,560 - 9,840
500 - 2,000	1,640 - 6,560
200 - 500	656 - 1,640
0 - 200	0 - 656

Water Depth

Meters	Feet
Less than 200	Less than 656
200 - 2,000	656 - 6,560
Over 2,000	Over 6,560

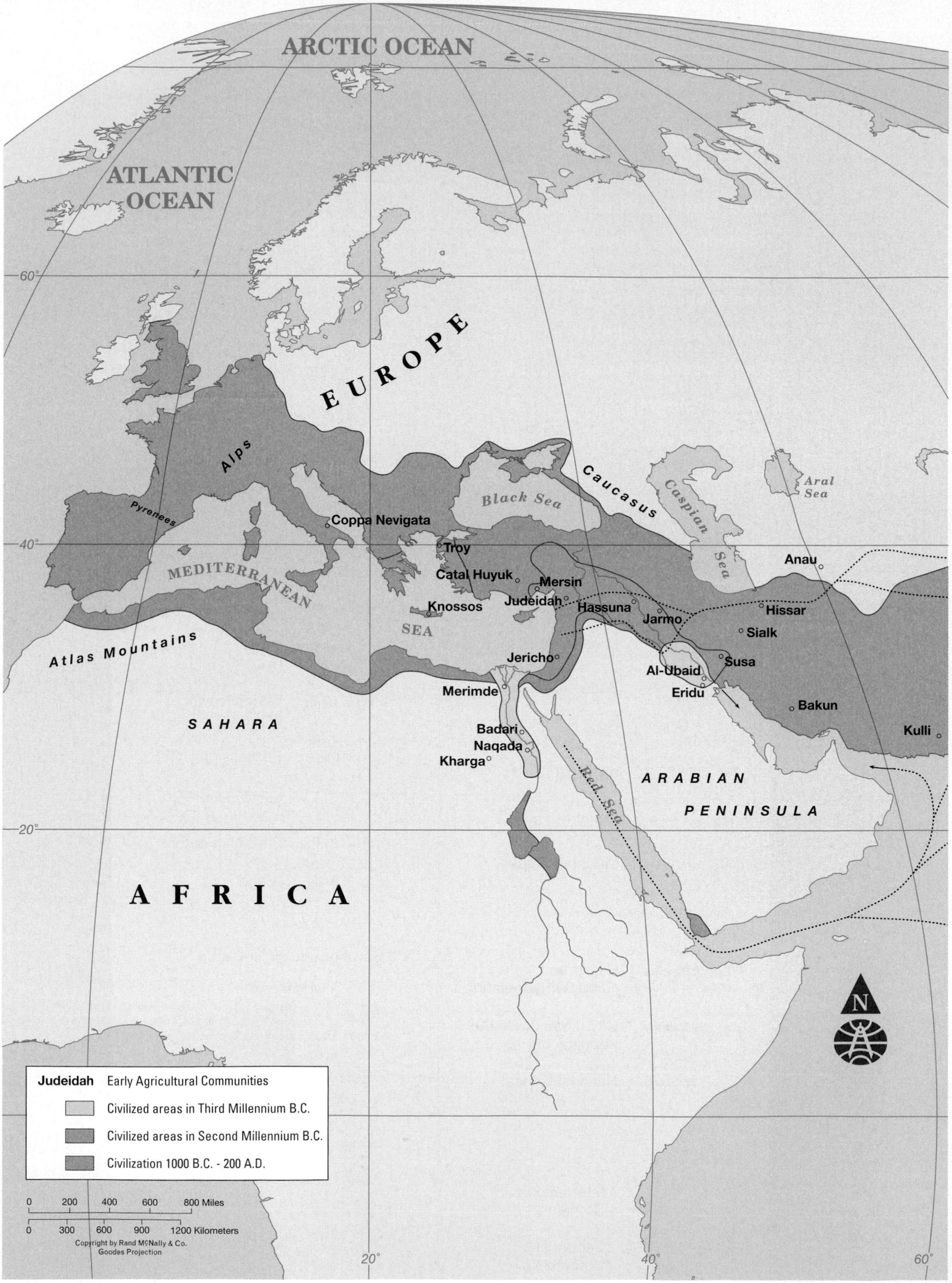
ARCTIC OCEAN
ATLANTIC OCEAN
EUROPE
Alps
Pyrenees
Caucasus
Black Sea
Caspian Sea
Aral Sea
MEDITERRANEAN SEA
Coppa Nevigata
Troy
Catal Huyuk
Mersin
Judeidah
Knossos
Hassuna
Jarmo
Anau
Hissar
Sialk
Jericho
Susa
Al-Ubaid
Eridu
Bakun
Kulli
Merimde
Badari
Naqada
Kharga
Atlas Mountains
SAHARA
ARABIAN PENINSULA
Red Sea
AFRICA
N
60°
40°
20°
20°
40°
60°
Judeidah Early Agricultural Communities
Civilized areas in Third Millennium B.C.
Civilized areas in Second Millennium B.C.
Civilization 1000 B.C. - 200 A.D.
0 200 400 600 800 Miles
0 300 600 900 1200 Kilometers
Copyright by Rand McNally & Co.
Goodes Projection

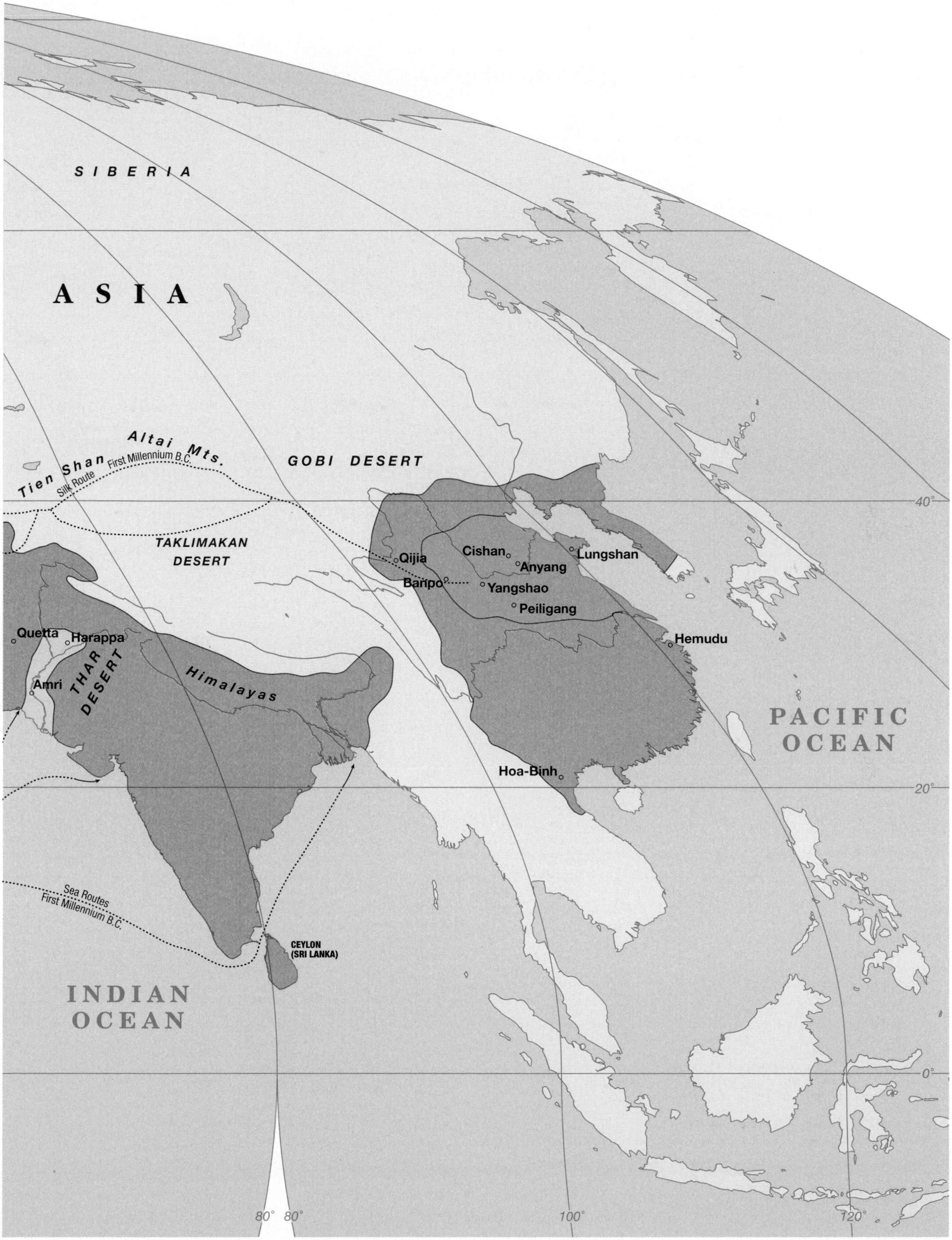
SIBERIA
ASIA
Altai Mts.
Tien Shan
Silk Route
First Millennium B.C.
GOBI DESERT
TAKLIMAKAN DESERT
Qijia
Cishan
Lungshan
Anyang
Banpo
Yangshao
Peiligang
Hemudu
Quetta
Harappa
Amri
THAR DESERT
Himalayas
PACIFIC OCEAN
Hoa-Binh
Sea Routes
First Millennium B.C.
CEYLON (SRI LANKA)
INDIAN OCEAN
40°
20°
0°
80°
80°
100°
120°

ARCTIC OCEAN
GREENLAND (Den.)
Baffin Bay
Arctic Circle
ICELAND
FAROE IS. (Den.)
UNITED KINGDOM
IRELAND
London
FRANCE
PORTUGAL
SPAIN
RUSSIA
ALASKA (U.S.)
Yukon
Hudson Bay
CANADA
Aleutian Islands
Newfoundland
Montréal
Ottawa
Missouri
Chicago
New York
Washington D.C.
UNITED STATES
Colorado
Mississippi
Los Angeles
Houston
Azores (Port.)
MOROCCO
Canary Islands (Sp.)
W. SAHARA
MIDWAY IS. (U.S.)
Tropic of Cancer
Gulf of Mexico
ATLANTIC
BAHAMAS
MEXICO
Hawaiian Islands (U.S)
CUBA
DOM. REP.
HAITI
PUERTO RICO (U.S.)
Mexico City
BELIZE
JAMAICA
Caribbean Sea
CAPE VERDE
MAURITANIA
MALI
SENEGAL
THE GAMBIA
GUINEA-BISSAU
GUINEA
Niger
BURK. FASO
SIERRA LEONE
COTE D'IVOIRE
GHANA
LIBERIA
GUAT.
HOND.
EL SAL.
NIC.
PACIFIC
COSTA RICA
PANAMA
Caracas
TRINIDAD AND TOBAGO
VENEZUELA
GUYANA
SURINAME
FRENCH GUIANA
COLOMBIA
Equator
KIRIBATI
Galapagos Islands (Ecuador)
ECUADOR
Amazon
PERU
BRAZIL
OCEAN
OCEAN
SAMOA
AMERICAN SAMOA
COOK ISLANDS (N.Z.)
TONGA
FRENCH POLYNESIA
BOLIVIA
ST. HELENA (U.K.)
Tropic of Capricorn
PARAGUAY
Rio de Janeiro
Easter Island (Chile)
ARGENTINA
CHILE
URUGUAY
Buenos Aires
N
0 1000 2000 Miles
0 1000 2000 3000 Kilometers
Copyright by Rand McNally & Co.
Robinson Projection
FALKLAND IS. (U.K.)
South Georgia (U.K.)
South Orkney Is. (U.K.)
South Shetland Is. (U.K.)
Antarctic Circle
Weddell Sea
180° 165° 150° 135° 120° 105° 90° 75° 60° 45° 30° 15°
75° 60° 45° 30° 15° 0° 15° 30° 45° 60° 75°

ARCTIC OCEAN
Franz Josef Land
Spitsbergen (Nor.)
Novaya Zemlya
Yenisey
Lena
Ob'
NORWAY
FINLAND
SWEDEN
EST.
LAT.
LITH.
North Sea
DEN.
R U S S I A
Volga
Moscow
Sea of Okhotsk
Bering Sea
NETH.
POLAND
BELARUS
GERMANY
BEL.
CZ.
SLVK.
UKRAINE
AUS.
HUNG.
MOLD.
SWITZ.
KAZAKHSTAN
MONGOLIA
ITALY
CRO.
BOS.
SERB.
ROM.
Black Sea
BUL.
Rome
ALB.
MA.
GEO.
Caspian Sea
UZBEKISTAN
KYRG.
ARM.
AZER.
NORTH KOREA
GREECE
TURKEY
TURKMENISTAN
TAJIK.
Beijing
Sea of Japan
JAPAN
SOUTH KOREA
Mediterranean Sea
Crete
CYPRUS
SYRIA
C H I N A
Tokyo
TUNISIA
LEB.
ISRAEL
IRAQ
IRAN
AFGHANISTAN
Cairo
JORDAN
Chang Jiang (Yangtze)
Shanghai
ALGERIA
KUWAIT
PAKISTAN
NEPAL
BHU.
Ganges
LIBYA
EGYPT
SAUDI ARABIA
QATAR
U.A.E.
PACIFIC
TAIWAN
Kolkata (Calcutta)
BNGL.
Tropic of Cancer
Red Sea
OMAN
MYANMAR
NORTHERN MARIANA ISLANDS (U.S.)
Mumbai (Bombay)
INDIA
LAOS
WAKE ISLAND (U.S.)
NIGER
Nile
ERITREA
YEMEN
Arabian Sea
Bay of Bengal
THAILAND
South China Sea
VIETNAM
GUAM (U.S.)
CHAD
SUDAN
Bangkok
CAMBODIA
PHILIPPINES
BENIN
NIGERIA
Addis Ababa
DJIBOUTI
OCEAN
Lagos
ETHIOPIA
SOMALIA
PALAU
CENTRAL AFRICAN REPUBLIC
SRI LANKA
BRUNEI
FED. STATES OF MICRONESIA
MARSHALL ISLANDS
CAMEROON
MALAYSIA
EQUAT. GUIN.
Congo
UGANDA
KENYA
MALDIVES
SINGAPORE
GABON
RWANDA
Borneo
New Guinea
Equator
REP. OF CONGO
DEM. REP. OF CONGO
BURUNDI
Sumatra
TANZANIA
SEYCHELLES
Jakarta
INDONESIA
PAPUA NEW GUINEA
SOLOMON ISLANDS
COMOROS
Java
EAST TIMOR
ANGOLA
INDIAN
ZAMBIA
MALAWI
MOZAMBIQUE
Coral Sea
VANUATU
MADAGASCAR
MAURITIUS
NEW CALEDONIA (Fr.)
FIJI
ZIMBABWE
NAMIBIA
BOTSWANA
REUNION (Fr.)
Tropic of Capricorn
AUSTRALIA
OCEAN
SWAZILAND
SOUTH AFRICA
LESOTHO
Darling
Sydney
Cape Town
NEW ZEALAND
Tasmania
Kerguelen Islands (Fr.)
SOUTHERN OCEAN
Antarctic Circle
ANTARCTICA
15°
30°
45°
60°
75°
90°
105°
120°
135°
150°
165°
180°

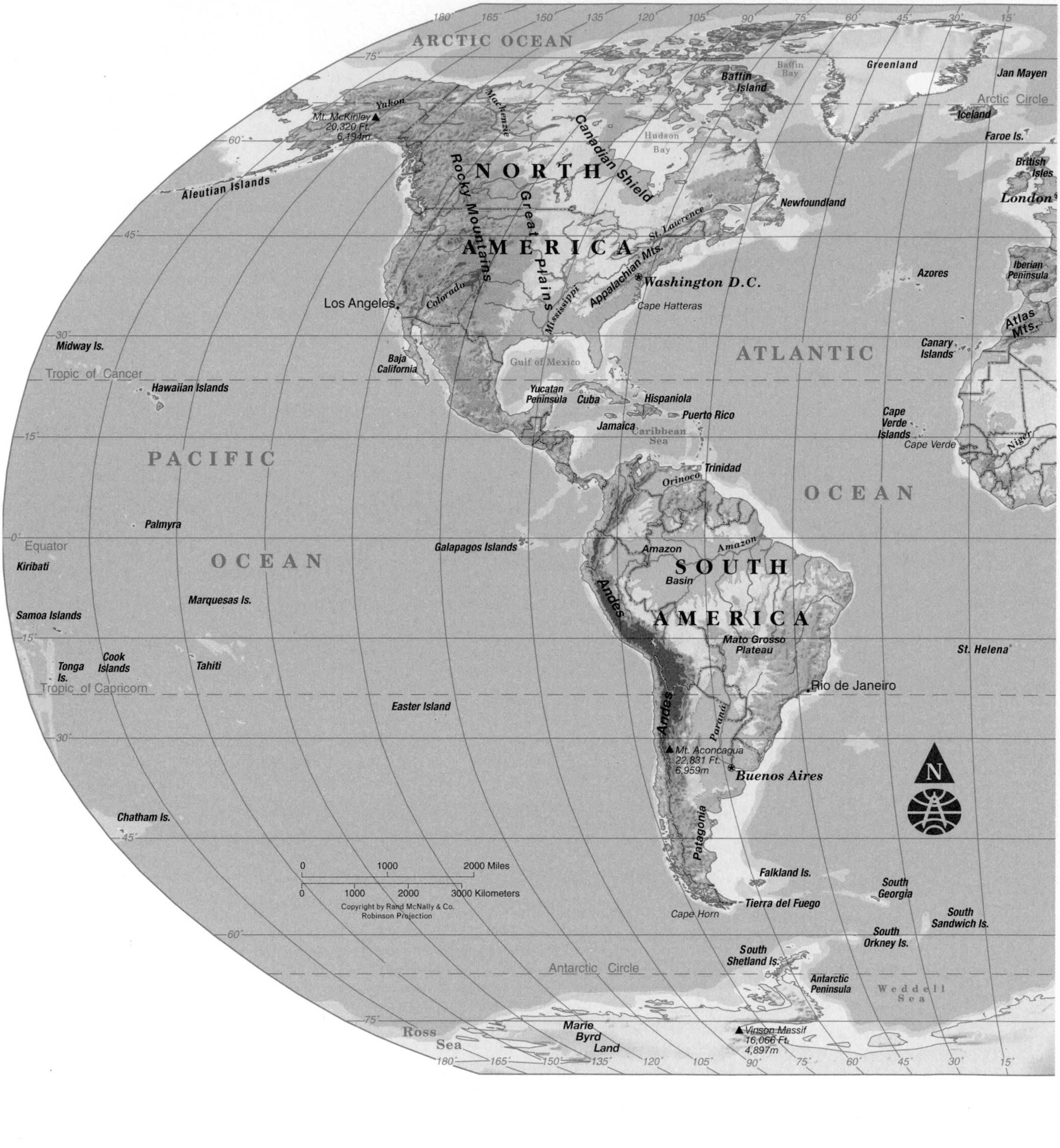
ARCTIC OCEAN
Greenland
Jan Mayen
Baffin Island
Baffin Bay
Arctic Circle
Iceland
Faroe Is.
Yukon
Mt. McKinley
20,320 Ft.
6,194m
Mackenzie
Canadian Shield
Hudson Bay
British Isles
London
Aleutian Islands
NORTH AMERICA
Rocky Mountains
Great Plains
Newfoundland
St. Lawrence
Appalachian Mts.
Washington D.C.
Azores
Iberian Peninsula
Los Angeles
Colorado
Mississippi
Cape Hatteras
Atlas Mts.
Midway Is.
Baja California
Gulf of Mexico
ATLANTIC
Canary Islands
Tropic of Cancer
Hawaiian Islands
Yucatan Peninsula
Cuba
Hispaniola
Puerto Rico
Jamaica
Caribbean Sea
Cape Verde Islands
Cape Verde
Niger
PACIFIC
Trinidad
Orinoco
OCEAN
Palmyra
Equator
Galapagos Islands
Amazon
Kiribati
OCEAN
SOUTH AMERICA
Basin
Andes
Samoa Islands
Marquesas Is.
Mato Grosso Plateau
St. Helena
Tonga Is.
Cook Islands
Tahiti
Tropic of Capricorn
Rio de Janeiro
Easter Island
Paraná
Mt. Aconcagua
22,831 Ft.
6,959m
Buenos Aires
N
Chatham Is.
Patagonia
0 1000 2000 Miles
0 1000 2000 3000 Kilometers
Copyright by Rand McNally & Co.
Robinson Projection
Falkland Is.
South Georgia
Tierra del Fuego
Cape Horn
South Sandwich Is.
South Orkney Is.
South Shetland Is.
Antarctic Circle
Antarctic Peninsula
Weddell Sea
Ross Sea
Marie Byrd Land
Vinson Massif
16,066 Ft.
4,897m

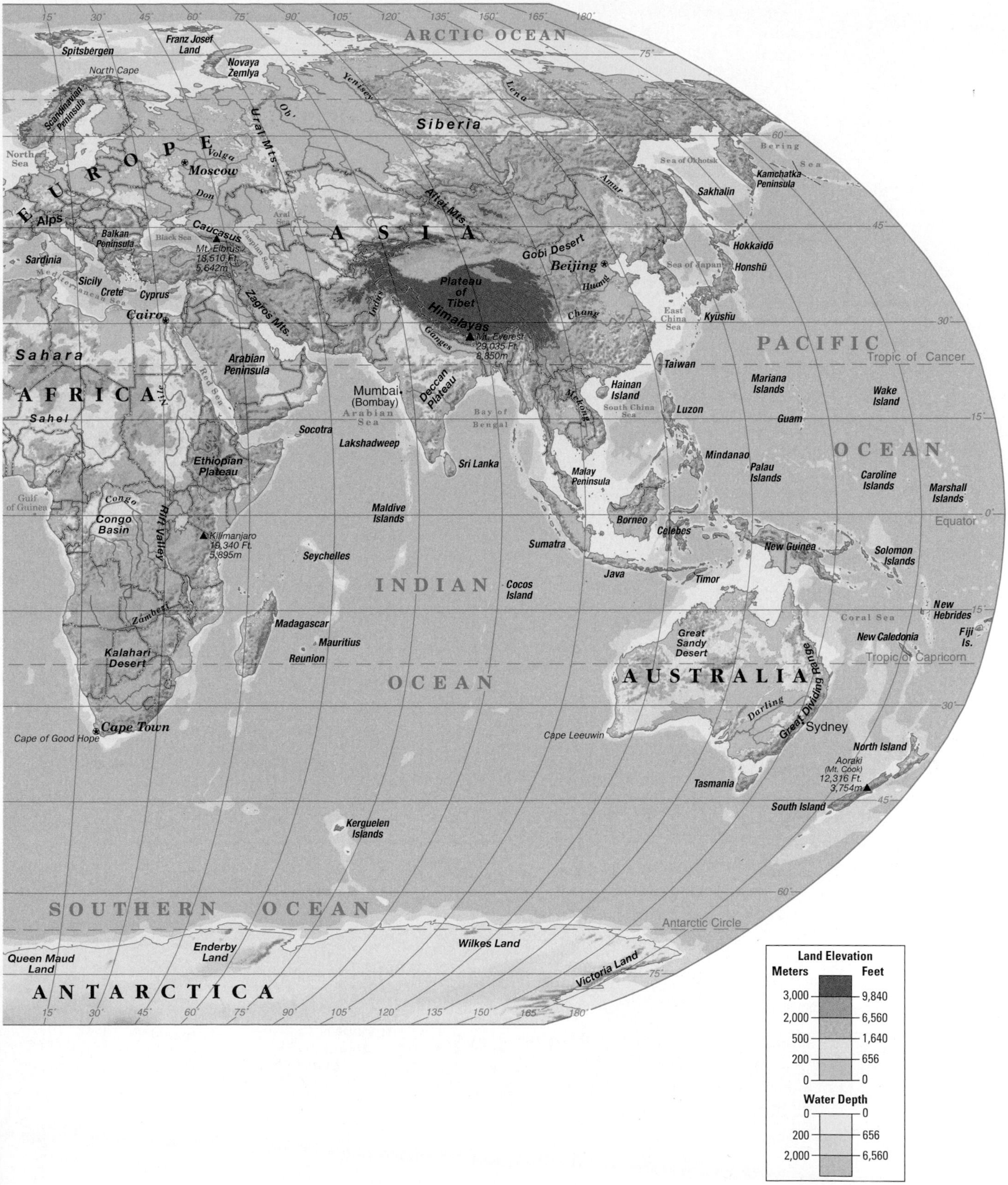
ARCTIC OCEAN
Spitsbergen
Franz Josef Land
Novaya Zemlya
North Cape
Scandinavian Peninsula
Yenisey
Lena
Ob'
Ural Mts.
Siberia
North Sea
E U R O P E
Volga
Moscow
Don
Bering Sea
Sea of Okhotsk
Kamchatka Peninsula
Sakhalin
Amur
Altai Mts.
Alps
Balkan Peninsula
Black Sea
Caucasus
Mt. Elbrus 18,510 Ft. 5,642m
Caspian Sea
Aral Sea
A S I A
Gobi Desert
Beijing
Hokkaidō
Sea of Japan
Honshū
Sardinia
Mediterranean Sea
Sicily
Crete
Cyprus
Cairo
Zagros Mts.
Plateau of Tibet
Himalayas
Indus
Ganges
Mt. Everest 29,035 Ft. 8,850m
Huang
Chang
East China Sea
Kyūshū
PACIFIC
Tropic of Cancer
Sahara
Arabian Peninsula
Red Sea
Nile
A F R I C A
Sahel
Mumbai (Bombay)
Deccan Plateau
Arabian Sea
Bay of Bengal
Mekong
Taiwan
Hainan Island
South China Sea
Luzon
Mariana Islands
Guam
Wake Island
Socotra
Lakshadweep
Ethiopian Plateau
Sri Lanka
Mindanao
Palau Islands
OCEAN
Caroline Islands
Marshall Islands
Gulf of Guinea
Congo
Congo Basin
Rift Valley
Malay Peninsula
Maldive Islands
Borneo
Celebes
Equator
Kilimanjaro 19,340 Ft. 5,895m
Seychelles
Sumatra
New Guinea
Solomon Islands
Java
Timor
INDIAN
Cocos Island
Zambezi
Madagascar
Mauritius
Reunion
Coral Sea
New Hebrides
New Caledonia
Fiji Is.
Great Sandy Desert
Kalahari Desert
Tropic of Capricorn
OCEAN
AUSTRALIA
Great Dividing Range
Darling
Cape Town
Cape of Good Hope
Cape Leeuwin
Sydney
North Island
Aoraki (Mt. Cook) 12,316 Ft. 3,754m
Tasmania
South Island
Kerguelen Islands
SOUTHERN OCEAN
Antarctic Circle
Queen Maud Land
Enderby Land
Wilkes Land
Victoria Land
ANTARCTICA
15° 30° 45° 60° 75° 90° 105° 120° 135° 150° 165° 180°
75° 60° 45° 30° 15° 0° 15° 30° 45° 60° 75°
Land Elevation
Meters Feet
3,000 9,840
2,000 6,560
500 1,640
200 656
0 0
Water Depth
0 0
200 656
2,000 6,560

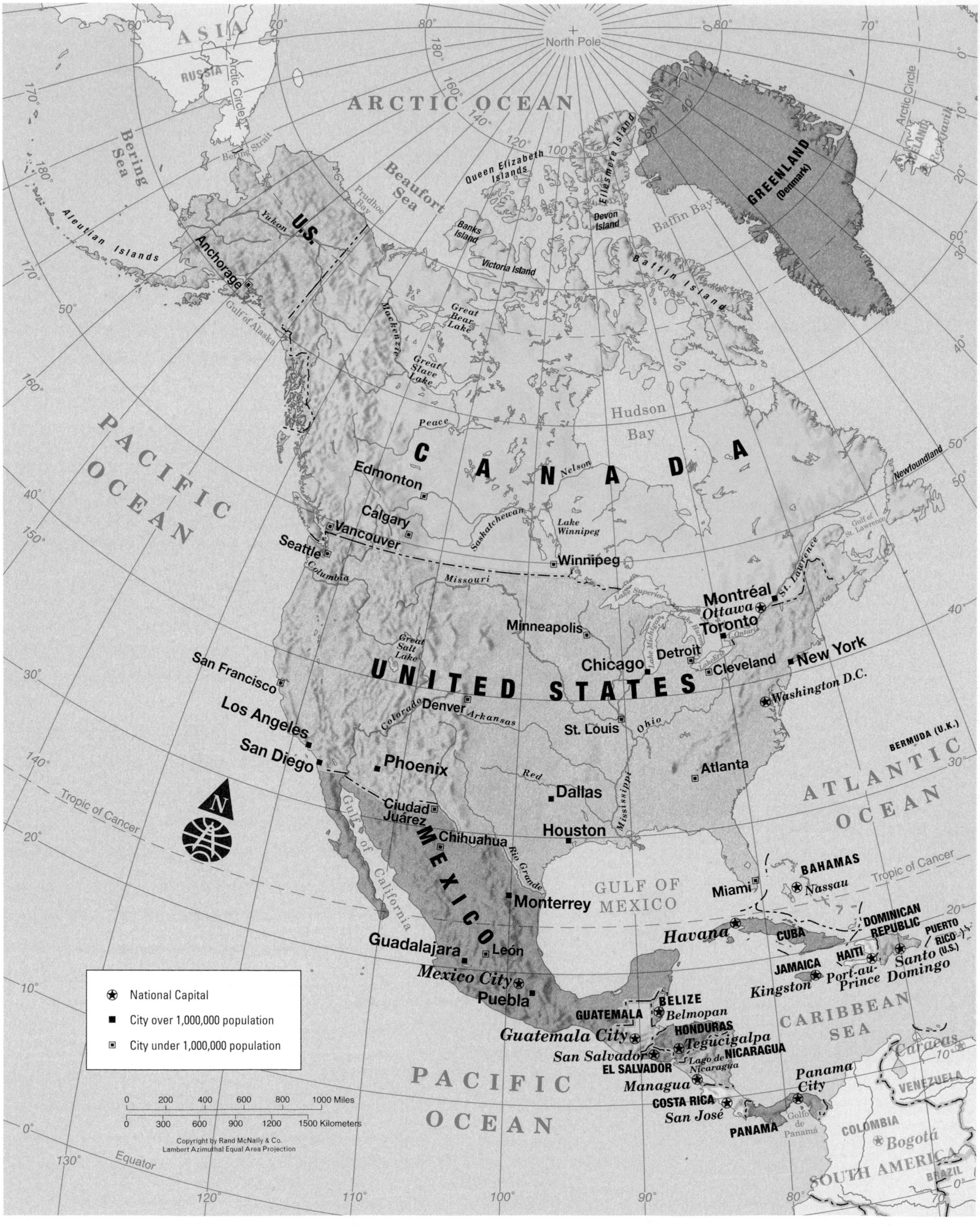
North Pole
ARCTIC OCEAN
ASIA
RUSSIA
Arctic Circle
Bering Strait
Bering Sea
Aleutian Islands
Beaufort Sea
Prudhoe Bay
Queen Elizabeth Islands
Ellesmere Island
Devon Island
Banks Island
Victoria Island
Baffin Bay
Baffin Island
GREENLAND (Denmark)
ICELAND
Reykjavík
U.S.
Yukon
Anchorage
Gulf of Alaska
Mackenzie
Great Bear Lake
Great Slave Lake
Peace
Hudson Bay
CANADA
Nelson
Edmonton
Calgary
Saskatchewan
Lake Winnipeg
Winnipeg
Vancouver
Seattle
Columbia
Missouri
Newfoundland
Gulf of St. Lawrence
St. Lawrence
Lake Superior
Montréal
Ottawa
Toronto
L. Ontario
Lake Huron
Lake Michigan
Lake Erie
Minneapolis
Great Salt Lake
Detroit
Chicago
Cleveland
New York
Washington D.C.
San Francisco
UNITED STATES
Denver
Colorado
Arkansas
Ohio
St. Louis
Los Angeles
San Diego
Phoenix
Red
Dallas
Mississippi
Atlanta
BERMUDA (U.K.)
PACIFIC OCEAN
ATLANTIC OCEAN
Tropic of Cancer
Ciudad Juárez
Chihuahua
Rio Grande
Houston
MEXICO
Gulf of California
Monterrey
GULF OF MEXICO
Miami
BAHAMAS
Nassau
Havana
CUBA
DOMINICAN REPUBLIC
PUERTO RICO (U.S.)
HAITI
Port-au-Prince
Santo Domingo
JAMAICA
Kingston
Guadalajara
León
Mexico City
Puebla
BELIZE
Belmopan
GUATEMALA
Guatemala City
HONDURAS
Tegucigalpa
San Salvador
EL SALVADOR
Lago de Nicaragua
NICARAGUA
Managua
COSTA RICA
San José
Panama City
PANAMA
Golfo de Panamá
CARIBBEAN SEA
Caracas
VENEZUELA
COLOMBIA
Bogotá
SOUTH AMERICA
BRAZIL
Equator
National Capital
City over 1,000,000 population
City under 1,000,000 population
0 200 400 600 800 1000 Miles
0 300 600 900 1200 1500 Kilometers
Copyright by Rand McNally & Co.
Lambert Azimuthal Equal Area Projection

RAND McNALLY

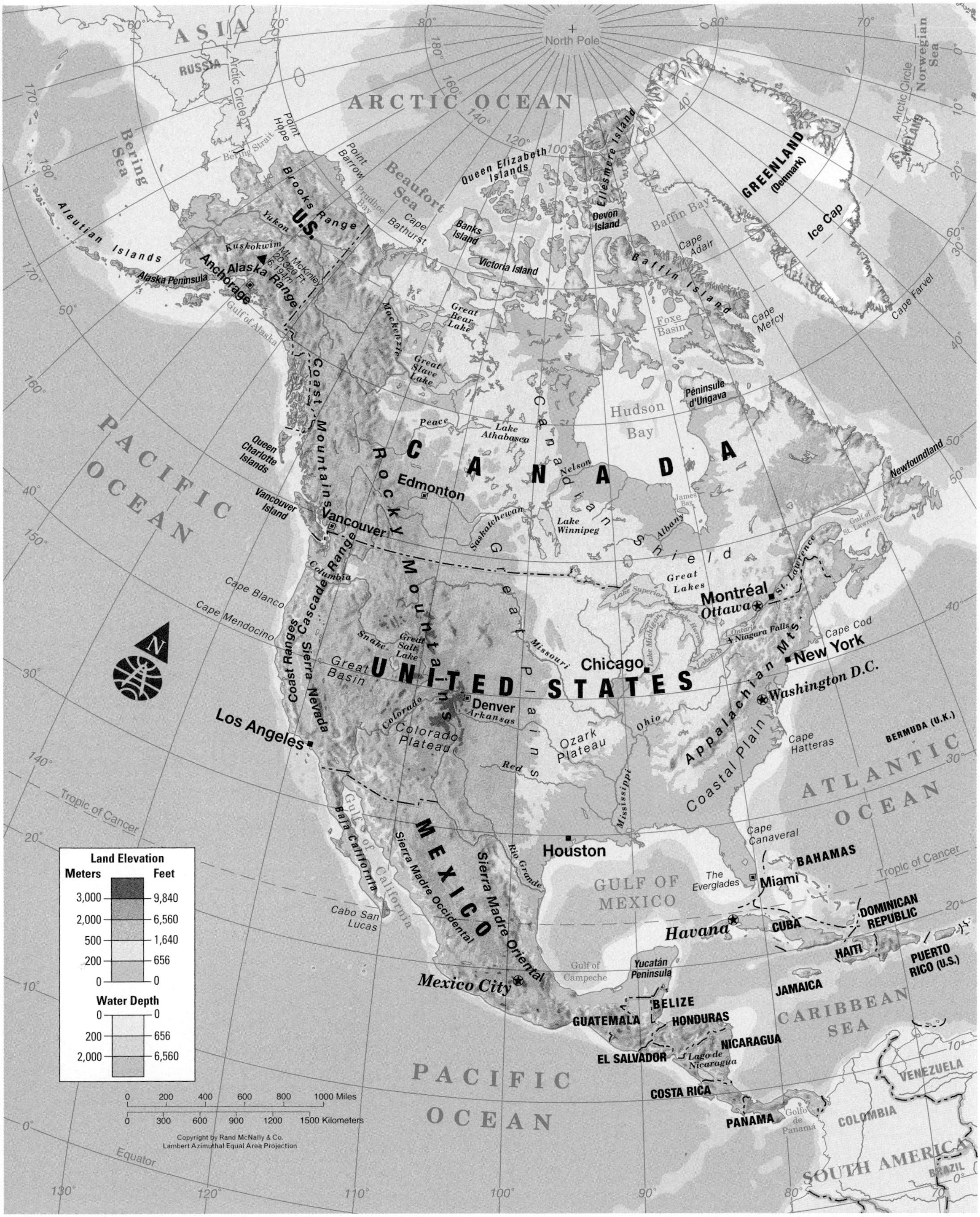
ASIA
RUSSIA
Arctic Circle
North Pole
ARCTIC OCEAN
Bering Sea
Bering Strait
Point Hope
Point Barrow
Prudhoe Bay
Beaufort Sea
Cape Bathurst
Queen Elizabeth Islands
Ellesmere Island
Devon Island
Banks Island
Victoria Island
GREENLAND (Denmark)
Ice Cap
Baffin Bay
Cape Adair
Baffin Island
Cape Mercy
Cape Farvel
Foxe Basin
ICELAND
Norwegian Sea
Aleutian Islands
Alaska Peninsula
Anchorage
Alaska Range
Mt. McKinley 20,320 ft. 6,194 m
Kuskokwim
Yukon
Brooks Range
U.S.
Gulf of Alaska
Mackenzie
Great Bear Lake
Great Slave Lake
Peace
Lake Athabasca
Coast Mountains
Queen Charlotte Islands
Vancouver Island
Vancouver
Edmonton
CANADA
Rocky Mountains
Canadian Shield
Saskatchewan
Nelson
Lake Winnipeg
Albany
James Bay
Hudson Bay
Péninsule d'Ungava
Newfoundland
Gulf of St. Lawrence
St. Lawrence
PACIFIC OCEAN
Columbia
Cascade Range
Cape Blanco
Cape Mendocino
Coast Ranges
Sierra Nevada
Snake
Great Salt Lake
Great Basin
Great Plains
Missouri
Lake Superior
Lake Michigan
Lake Huron
Lake Erie
Lake Ontario
Great Lakes
Niagara Falls
Montréal
Ottawa
Cape Cod
New York
Chicago
UNITED STATES
Denver
Arkansas
Colorado
Colorado Plateau
Los Angeles
Ozark Plateau
Ohio
Appalachian Mts.
Washington D.C.
Coastal Plain
Cape Hatteras
BERMUDA (U.K.)
ATLANTIC OCEAN
Red
Mississippi
Tropic of Cancer
Gulf of California
Baja California
MEXICO
Sierra Madre Occidental
Sierra Madre Oriental
Rio Grande
Houston
Cape Canaveral
BAHAMAS
The Everglades
Miami
GULF OF MEXICO
Cabo San Lucas
Havana
CUBA
DOMINICAN REPUBLIC
HAITI
PUERTO RICO (U.S.)
JAMAICA
Gulf of Campeche
Yucatán Peninsula
Mexico City
BELIZE
GUATEMALA
HONDURAS
CARIBBEAN SEA
NICARAGUA
EL SALVADOR
Lago de Nicaragua
COSTA RICA
PANAMA
Golfo de Panamá
VENEZUELA
COLOMBIA
SOUTH AMERICA
BRAZIL
Equator
Land Elevation
Meters
Feet
3,000 — 9,840
2,000 — 6,560
500 — 1,640
200 — 656
0 — 0
Water Depth
0 — 0
200 — 656
2,000 — 6,560
0 200 400 600 800 1000 Miles
0 300 600 900 1200 1500 Kilometers
Copyright by Rand McNally & Co.
Lambert Azimuthal Equal Area Projection
130° 120° 110° 100° 90° 80° 70°

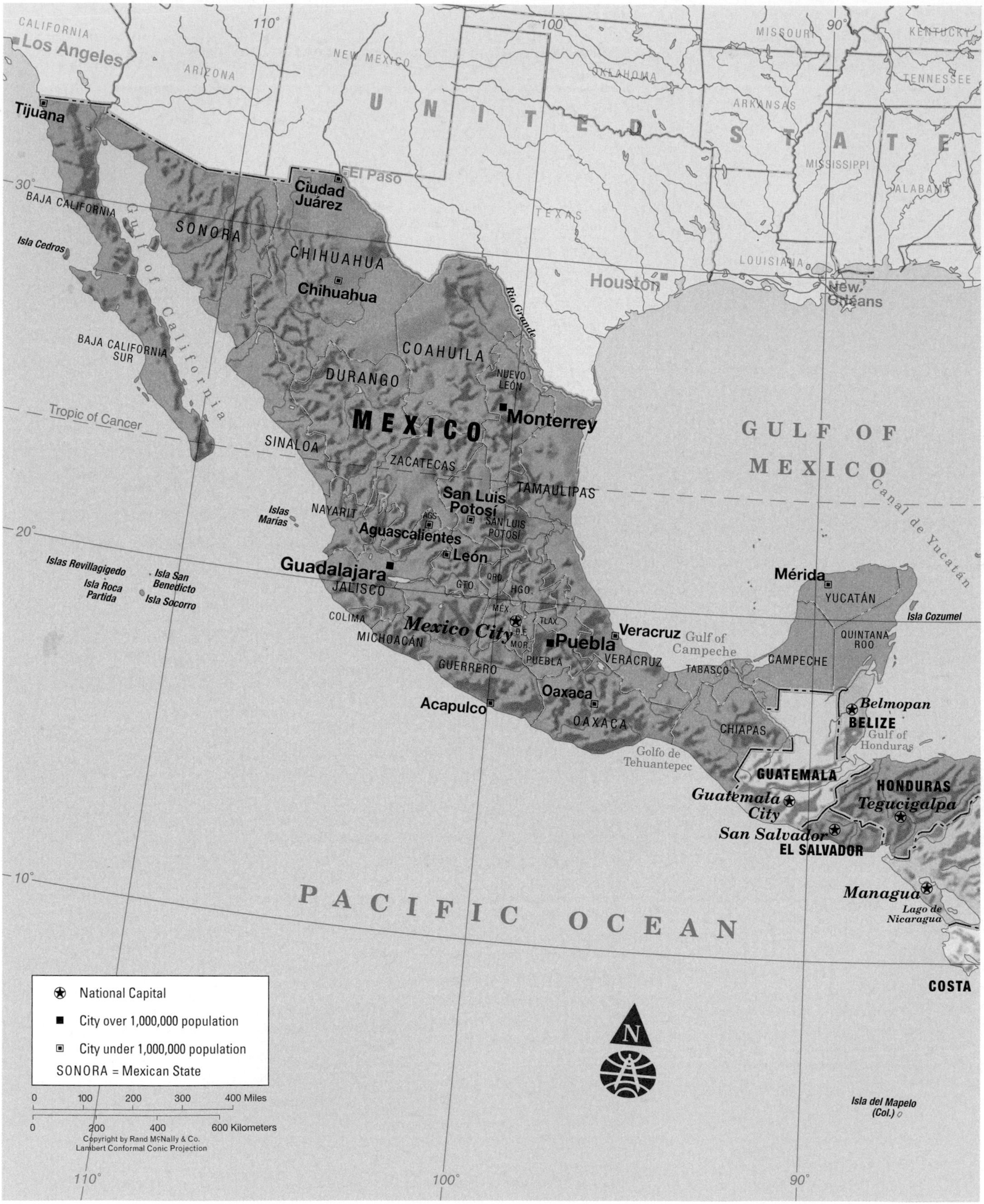

CALIFORNIA
Los Angeles
ARIZONA
NEW MEXICO
UNITED STATES
OKLAHOMA
MISSOURI
KENTUCKY
TENNESSEE
ARKANSAS
MISSISSIPPI
ALABAMA
TEXAS
LOUISIANA
Houston
New Orleans
El Paso
Tijuana
Ciudad Juárez
BAJA CALIFORNIA
SONORA
Gulf of California
Isla Cedros
CHIHUAHUA
Chihuahua
Rio Grande
BAJA CALIFORNIA SUR
COAHUILA
DURANGO
NUEVO LEÓN
Monterrey
Tropic of Cancer
MEXICO
SINALOA
ZACATECAS
TAMAULIPAS
San Luis Potosí
SAN LUIS POTOSÍ
GULF OF MEXICO
Canal de Yucatán
Islas Marías
NAYARIT
AGS.
Aguascalientes
León
Guadalajara
JALISCO
Islas Revillagigedo
Isla San Benedicto
Isla Roca Partida
Isla Socorro
GTO.
QRO.
HGO.
MÉX.
TLAX.
D.F.
MOR.
COLIMA
MICHOACÁN
Mexico City
Puebla
PUEBLA
Veracruz
VERACRUZ
Gulf of Campeche
Mérida
YUCATÁN
Isla Cozumel
QUINTANA ROO
CAMPECHE
TABASCO
GUERRERO
Acapulco
Oaxaca
OAXACA
CHIAPAS
Golfo de Tehuantepec
Belmopan
BELIZE
Gulf of Honduras
GUATEMALA
Guatemala City
HONDURAS
Tegucigalpa
San Salvador
EL SALVADOR
Managua
Lago de Nicaragua
COSTA
PACIFIC OCEAN
Isla del Mapelo (Col.)
30°
20°
10°
110°
100°
90°
N
National Capital
City over 1,000,000 population
City under 1,000,000 population
SONORA = Mexican State
0 100 200 300 400 Miles
0 200 400 600 Kilometers
Copyright by Rand McNally & Co.
Lambert Conformal Conic Projection

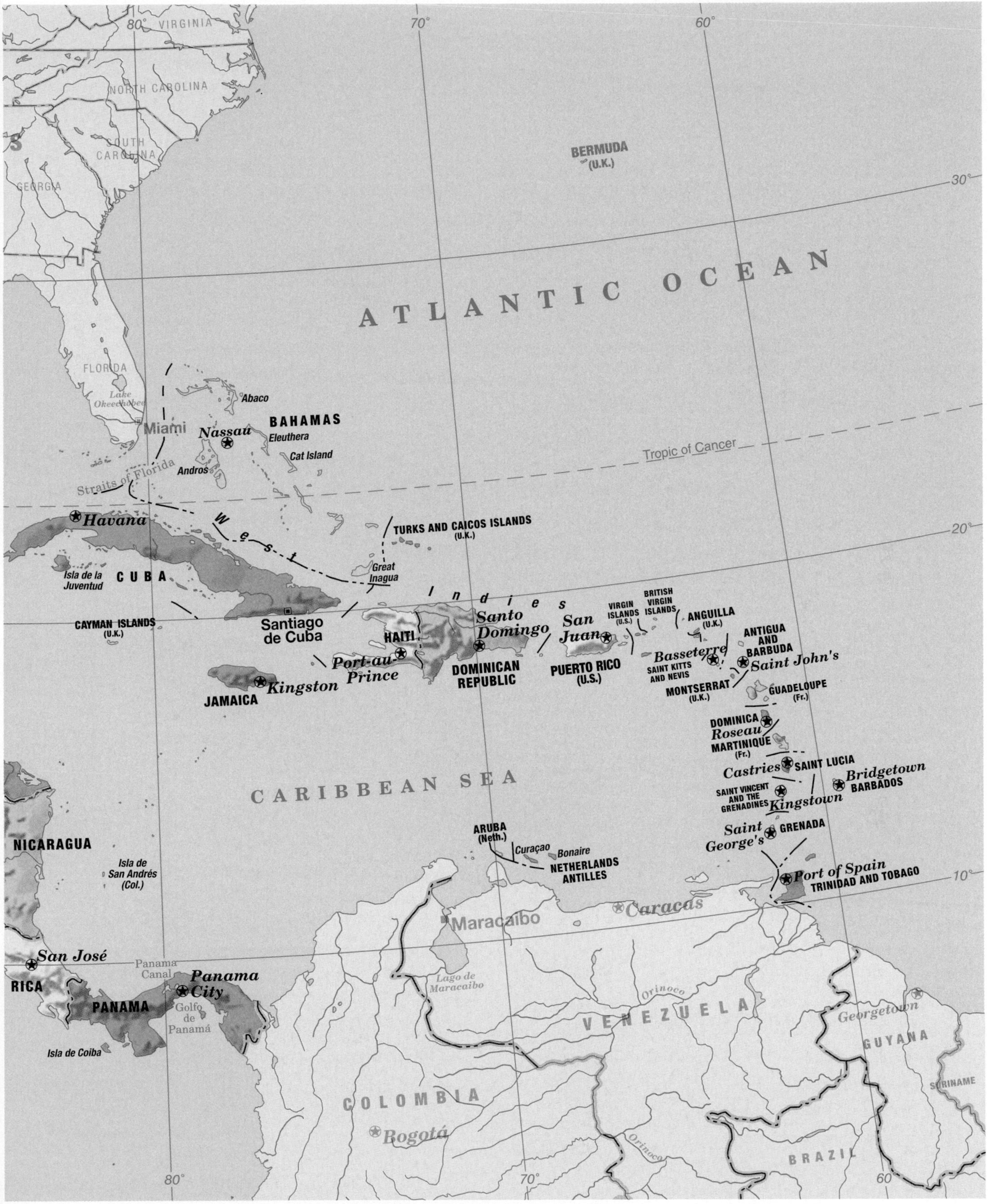
VIRGINIA
NORTH CAROLINA
SOUTH CAROLINA
GEORGIA
FLORIDA
Lake Okeechobee
Miami
BERMUDA (U.K.)
ATLANTIC OCEAN
Tropic of Cancer
Straits of Florida
Abaco
BAHAMAS
Nassau
Eleuthera
Cat Island
Andros
West Indies
Havana
TURKS AND CAICOS ISLANDS (U.K.)
Great Inagua
Isla de la Juventud
CUBA
CAYMAN ISLANDS (U.K.)
Santiago de Cuba
HAITI
Port-au-Prince
Santo Domingo
DOMINICAN REPUBLIC
San Juan
PUERTO RICO (U.S.)
VIRGIN ISLANDS (U.S.)
BRITISH VIRGIN ISLANDS
ANGUILLA (U.K.)
ANTIGUA AND BARBUDA
Basseterre
SAINT KITTS AND NEVIS
Saint John's
MONTSERRAT (U.K.)
GUADELOUPE (Fr.)
DOMINICA
Roseau
MARTINIQUE (Fr.)
Castries
SAINT LUCIA
Bridgetown
BARBADOS
SAINT VINCENT AND THE GRENADINES
Kingstown
Saint George's
GRENADA
Port of Spain
TRINIDAD AND TOBAGO
JAMAICA
Kingston
CARIBBEAN SEA
ARUBA (Neth.)
Curaçao
Bonaire
NETHERLANDS ANTILLES
NICARAGUA
Isla de San Andrés (Col.)
San José
RICA
Panama Canal
Panama City
PANAMA
Golfo de Panamá
Isla de Coiba
Maracaibo
Lago de Maracaibo
Caracas
Orinoco
VENEZUELA
Georgetown
GUYANA
SURINAME
COLOMBIA
Bogotá
BRAZIL
80°
70°
60°
30°
20°
10°

RAND McNALLY

GULF OF MEXICO
Havana
CUBA
DOMINICAN REPUBLIC
HAITI
JAMAICA
PUERTO RICO (U.S.)
Lesser Antilles
NORTH AMERICA
MEXICO
BELIZE
HONDURAS
GUATEMALA
EL SALVADOR
NICARAGUA
COSTA RICA
PANAMA
CARIBBEAN SEA
ATLANTIC OCEAN
Barranquilla
Maracaibo
Caracas
TRINIDAD AND TOBAGO
Orinoco
VENEZUELA
Georgetown
GUYANA
Paramaribo
SURINAM
Cayenne
FRENCH GUIANA
Medellín
Magdalena
Bogotá
Cali
COLOMBIA
Galapagos Islands (Ec.)
Quito
ECUADOR
Guayaquil
Putumayo
Japurá
Negro
Amazon
Manaus
Tapajós
Belém
Tocantins
Equator
Madeira
Juruá
BRAZIL
Fortaleza
Ucayali
PERU
Recife
Lima
Lake Titicaca
La Paz
BOLIVIA
Salvador
Brasília
Goiânia
Sucre
Belo Horizonte
Paraná
PARAGUAY
Rio de Janeiro
São Paulo
Asunción
Curitiba
Tropic of Capricorn
Isla San Ambrosio (Chile)
Isla San Felix (Chile)
Pôrto Alegre
Córdoba
Rosario
URUGUAY
Archipiélago Juan Fernández (Chile)
Santiago
Buenos Aires
Montevideo
Río de la Plata
PACIFIC OCEAN
Concepción
CHILE
ARGENTINA
N
Chiloé
Archipiélago de los Chonos
ATLANTIC OCEAN
National Capital
City over 1,000,000 population
City under 1,000,000 population
FALKLAND ISLANDS (U.K.)
West Falkland
East Falkland
Strait of Magellan
Tierra del Fuego
0 200 400 600 800 1000 Miles
0 300 600 900 1200 1500 Kilometers
Copyright by Rand McNally & Co.
Lambert Azimuthal Equal Area Projection
South Georgia (U.K.)
South Sandwich Islands (U.K.)
Drake Passage
South Shetland Islands (U.K.)
South Orkney Islands (U.K.)
110° 100° 90° 80° 70° 60° 50° 40° 30° 20° 10°
20° 10° 0° 10° 20° 30° 40° 50°

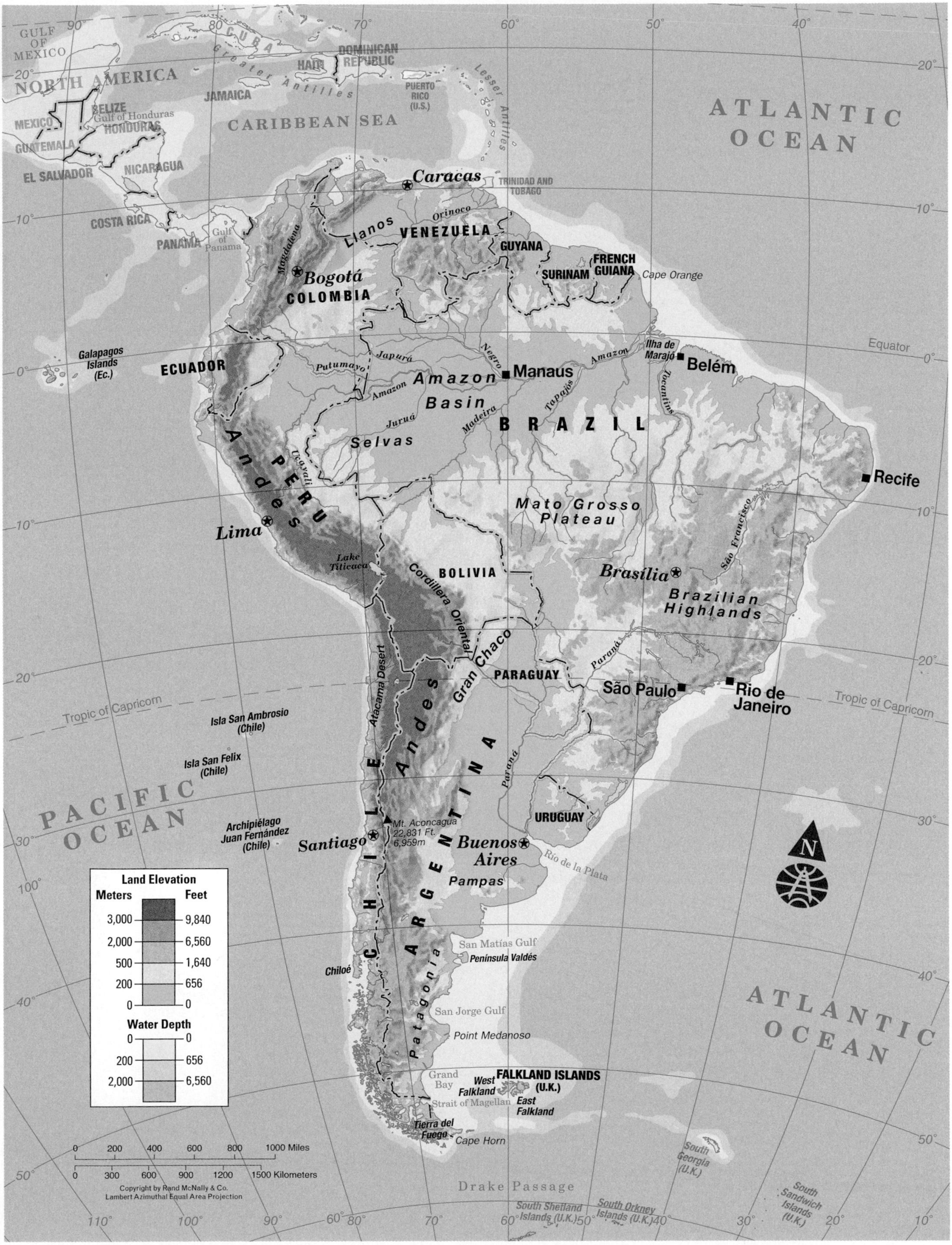

GULF OF MEXICO
NORTH AMERICA
CUBA
Greater Antilles
HAITI
DOMINICAN REPUBLIC
JAMAICA
PUERTO RICO (U.S.)
Lesser Antilles
MEXICO
BELIZE
Gulf of Honduras
HONDURAS
GUATEMALA
EL SALVADOR
NICARAGUA
CARIBBEAN SEA
ATLANTIC OCEAN
COSTA RICA
PANAMA
Gulf of Panama
Caracas
TRINIDAD AND TOBAGO
Orinoco
Llanos
VENEZUELA
GUYANA
SURINAM
FRENCH GUIANA
Cape Orange
Magdalena
Bogotá
COLOMBIA
Galapagos Islands (Ec.)
ECUADOR
Equator
Ilha de Marajó
Belém
Negro
Japurá
Putumayo
Amazon
Manaus
Amazon Basin
Tapajós
Tocantins
Juruá
Madeira
BRAZIL
Selvas
Ucayali
Andes
PERU
Recife
Mato Grosso Plateau
São Francisco
Lima
Lake Titicaca
Cordillera Oriental
BOLIVIA
Brasília
Brazilian Highlands
Gran Chaco
Paraná
Atacama Desert
PARAGUAY
São Paulo
Rio de Janeiro
Tropic of Capricorn
Isla San Ambrosio (Chile)
Isla San Felix (Chile)
PACIFIC OCEAN
CHILE
ARGENTINA
URUGUAY
Archipiélago Juan Fernández (Chile)
Mt. Aconcagua 22,831 Ft. 6,959m
Santiago
Buenos Aires
Río de la Plata
Pampas
N
Land Elevation
Meters
Feet
3,000
9,840
2,000
6,560
500
1,640
200
656
0
0
Water Depth
0
0
200
656
2,000
6,560
San Matías Gulf
Península Valdés
Chiloé
Patagonia
San Jorge Gulf
Point Medanoso
ATLANTIC OCEAN
Grand Bay
West Falkland
FALKLAND ISLANDS (U.K.)
East Falkland
Strait of Magellan
Tierra del Fuego
Cape Horn
South Georgia (U.K.)
0 200 400 600 800 1000 Miles
0 300 600 900 1200 1500 Kilometers
Copyright by Rand McNally & Co.
Lambert Azimuthal Equal Area Projection
Drake Passage
South Shetland Islands (U.K.)
South Orkney Islands (U.K.)
South Sandwich Islands (U.K.)
90° 80° 70° 60° 50° 40° 30° 20° 10° 100° 110°
20° 10° 0° 10° 20° 30° 40° 50°

RAND McNALLY

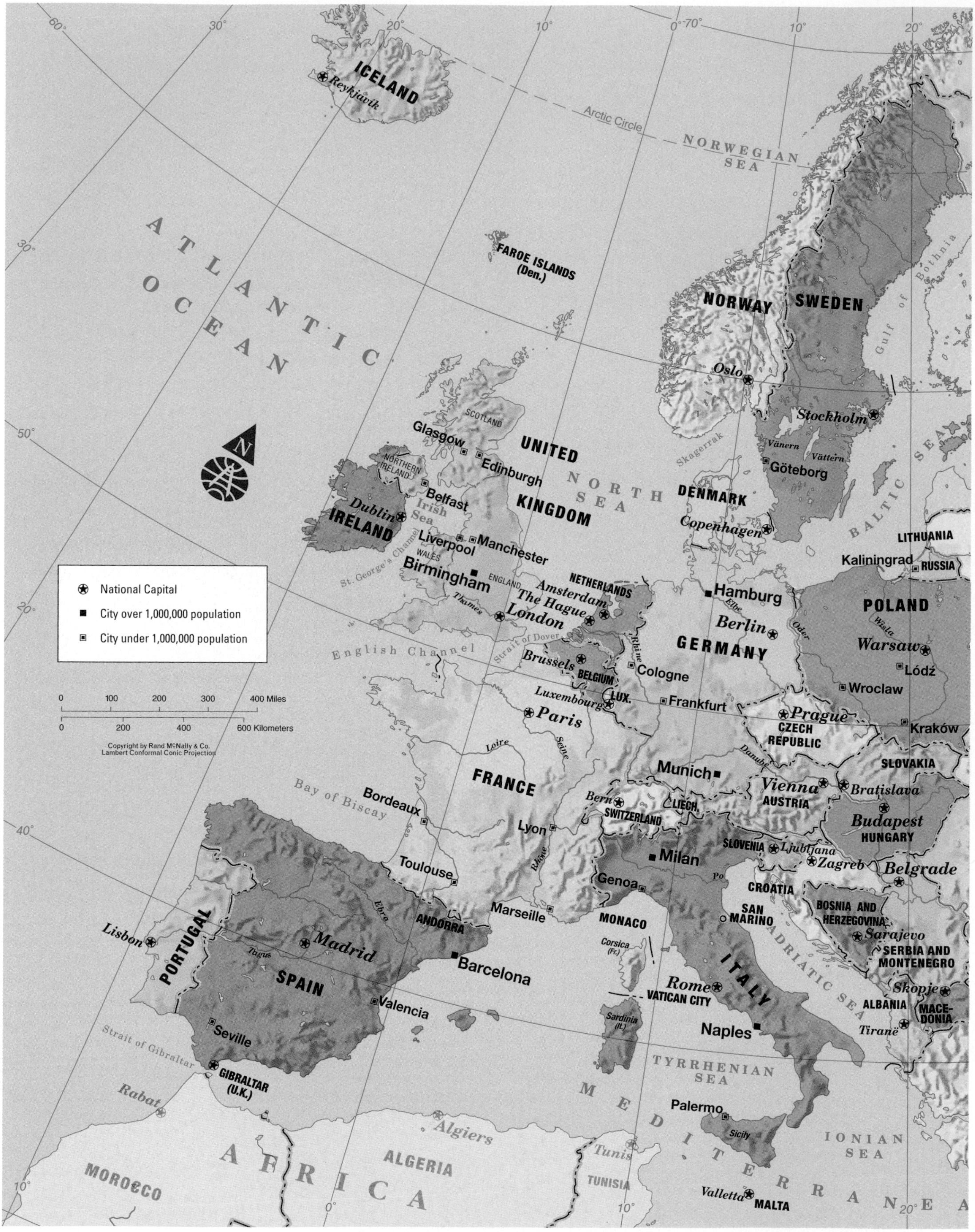
ICELAND
Reykjavík
Arctic Circle
NORWEGIAN SEA
ATLANTIC OCEAN
FAROE ISLANDS (Den.)
NORWAY
SWEDEN
Gulf of Bothnia
Oslo
Stockholm
Vänern
Vättern
Göteborg
Skagerrak
SCOTLAND
Glasgow
Edinburgh
UNITED KINGDOM
NORTH SEA
NORTHERN IRELAND
Belfast
Irish Sea
Dublin
IRELAND
DENMARK
Copenhagen
BALTIC SEA
LITHUANIA
Kaliningrad
RUSSIA
Liverpool
Manchester
WALES
St. George's Channel
Birmingham
ENGLAND
Thames
London
NETHERLANDS
Amsterdam
The Hague
Hamburg
Elbe
POLAND
Berlin
Oder
Wisla
Warsaw
Łódź
Wroclaw
Kraków
English Channel
Strait of Dover
Brussels
BELGIUM
Rhine
Cologne
GERMANY
Luxembourg
LUX.
Frankfurt
Prague
CZECH REPUBLIC
SLOVAKIA
Paris
Seine
Loire
FRANCE
Danube
Munich
Vienna
Bratislava
AUSTRIA
Budapest
HUNGARY
Bay of Biscay
Bordeaux
Bern
LIECH.
SWITZERLAND
Lyon
Rhône
SLOVENIA
Ljubljana
Zagreb
Belgrade
Milan
Po
Toulouse
Genoa
CROATIA
BOSNIA AND HERZEGOVINA
Sarajevo
SERBIA AND MONTENEGRO
SAN MARINO
Ebro
ANDORRA
Marseille
MONACO
ADRIATIC SEA
Lisbon
PORTUGAL
Madrid
Tagus
SPAIN
Barcelona
Corsica (Fr.)
ITALY
Rome
VATICAN CITY
Skopje
MACEDONIA
ALBANIA
Tiranë
Valencia
Sardinia (It.)
Naples
Seville
Strait of Gibraltar
GIBRALTAR (U.K.)
TYRRHENIAN SEA
Rabat
MEDITERRANEAN SEA
Palermo
Sicily
IONIAN SEA
Algiers
Tunis
AFRICA
ALGERIA
MOROCCO
TUNISIA
Valletta
MALTA
National Capital
City over 1,000,000 population
City under 1,000,000 population
0 100 200 300 400 Miles
0 200 400 600 Kilometers
Copyright by Rand McNally & Co.
Lambert Conformal Conic Projection
60° 30° 20° 10° 0° 70° 10° 20°
30° 50° 20° 40° 10° 0° 10° 20°

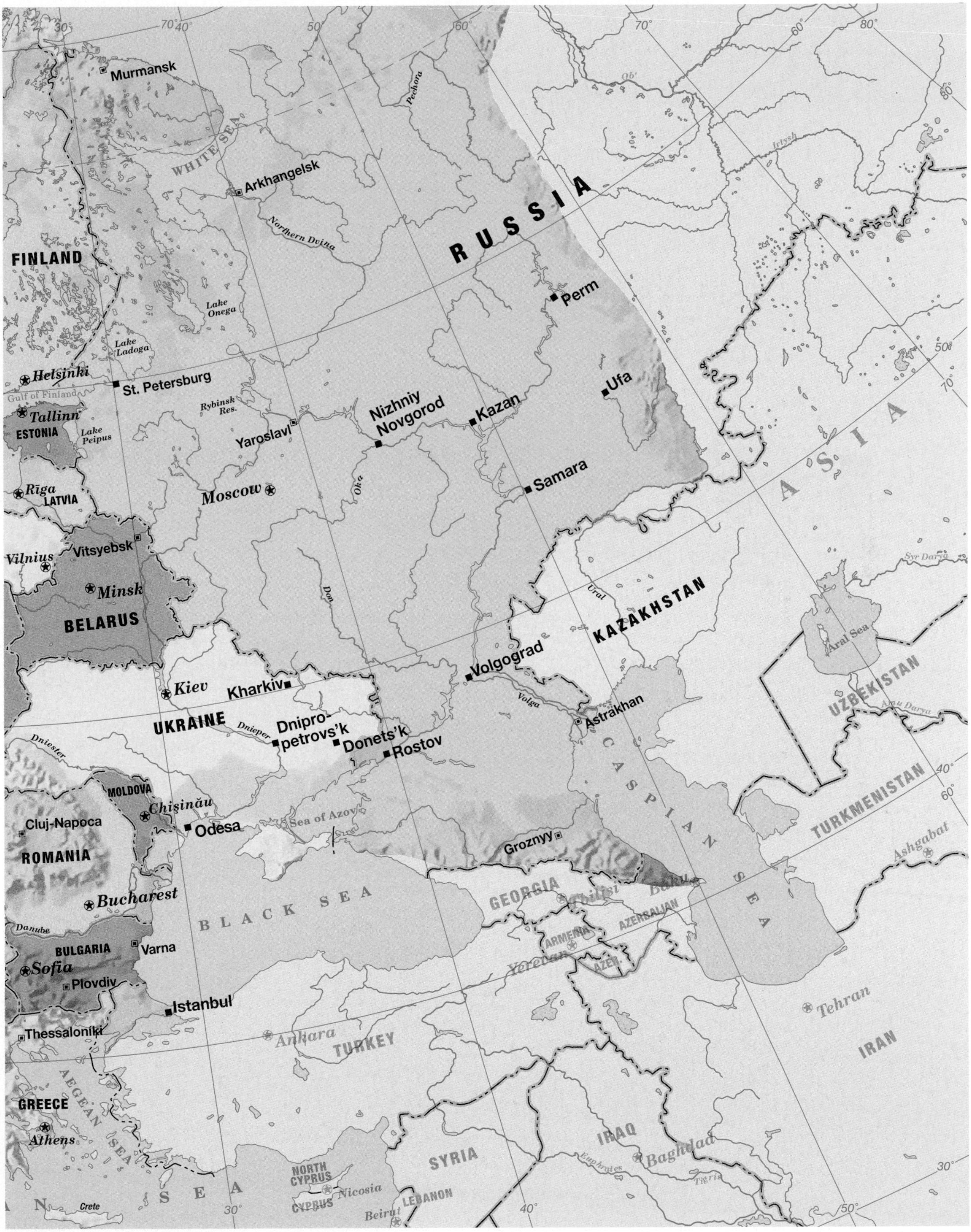
RUSSIA
FINLAND
ESTONIA
LATVIA
BELARUS
UKRAINE
MOLDOVA
ROMANIA
BULGARIA
GREECE
TURKEY
GEORGIA
ARMENIA
AZERBAIJAN
AZER.
KAZAKHSTAN
UZBEKISTAN
TURKMENISTAN
IRAN
IRAQ
SYRIA
LEBANON
NORTH CYPRUS
CYPRUS
ASIA
Murmansk
Arkhangelsk
Perm
Ufa
Kazan
Nizhniy Novgorod
Yaroslavl
St. Petersburg
Helsinki
Tallinn
Riga
Vilnius
Vitsyebsk
Minsk
Moscow
Samara
Volgograd
Astrakhan
Kiev
Kharkiv
Dnipropetrovs'k
Donets'k
Rostov
Odesa
Chişinău
Cluj-Napoca
Bucharest
Varna
Sofia
Plovdiv
Istanbul
Thessaloniki
Athens
Ankara
Groznyy
Tbilisi
Baku
Yerevan
Tehran
Ashgabat
Baghdad
Nicosia
Beirut
Crete
WHITE SEA
BLACK SEA
CASPIAN SEA
AEGEAN SEA
Sea of Azov
Aral Sea
Gulf of Finland
Lake Onega
Lake Ladoga
Lake Peipus
Rybinsk Res.
Pechora
Northern Dvina
Oka
Don
Volga
Ural
Dnieper
Dniester
Danube
Ob'
Irtysh
Syr Darya
Amu Darya
Euphrates
Tigris
30°
40°
50°
60°
70°
80°

ICELAND
Arctic Circle
NORWEGIAN SEA
Lofoten Islands
Torneälven
Lap
Luleälven
Umeälven
Scandinavian Peninsula
Gulf of Bothnia
ATLANTIC OCEAN
FAROE ISLANDS (Den.)
NORWAY
SWEDEN
Glåma
Klarälven
Dalälven
Hebrides
Orkney Islands
Stockholm
Skagerrak
Vänern
Vättern
Öland
BALTIC SEA
Land Elevation
Meters
Feet
3,000
9,840
2,000
6,560
500
1,640
200
656
0
0
Water Depth
0
0
200
656
2,000
6,560
UNITED KINGDOM
NORTH SEA
DENMARK
Irish Sea
IRELAND
St. George's Channel
Great Britain
Bornholm (Den.)
RUSSIA
Thames
London
NETHERLANDS
Elbe
Northern European
Berlin
Oder
POLAND
Strait of Dover
English Channel
GERMANY
BELGIUM
Rhine
Wisła
0
100
200
300
400 Miles
0
200
400
600 Kilometers
Copyright by Rand McNally & Co.
Lambert Conformal Conic Projection
LUX.
Paris
Paris Basin
Seine
Loire
Black Forest
Bohemian Forest
CZECH REPUBLIC
SLOVAKIA
Danube
FRANCE
Bay of Biscay
Saône
Jura
SWITZERLAND
LIECH.
AUSTRIA
HUNGARY
Great Hungarian Plain
Dordogne
Massif Central
Rhône
Alps
SLOVENIA
Drava
CROATIA
Po
Douro
Duero
Ebro
Pyrenees
ANDORRA
Apennines
SAN MARINO
BOSNIA AND HERZEGOVINA
Dinaric Alps
Balkan
SERBIA AND MONTENEGRO
Lisbon
PORTUGAL
Iberian Peninsula
Tagus
SPAIN
MONACO
Corsica (Fr.)
ADRIATIC SEA
Rome
ITALY
ALBANIA
MACEDONIA
Balearic Islands
Minorca
Majorca
Ibiza
Sardinia (It.)
Pindus Mts.
Strait of Gibraltar
GIBRALTAR (U.K.)
TYRRHENIAN SEA
MEDITERRANEAN
Algiers
Sicily
IONIAN SEA
AFRICA
ALGERIA
MOROCCO
TUNISIA
MALTA
60°
50°
40°
30°
20°
10°
0°

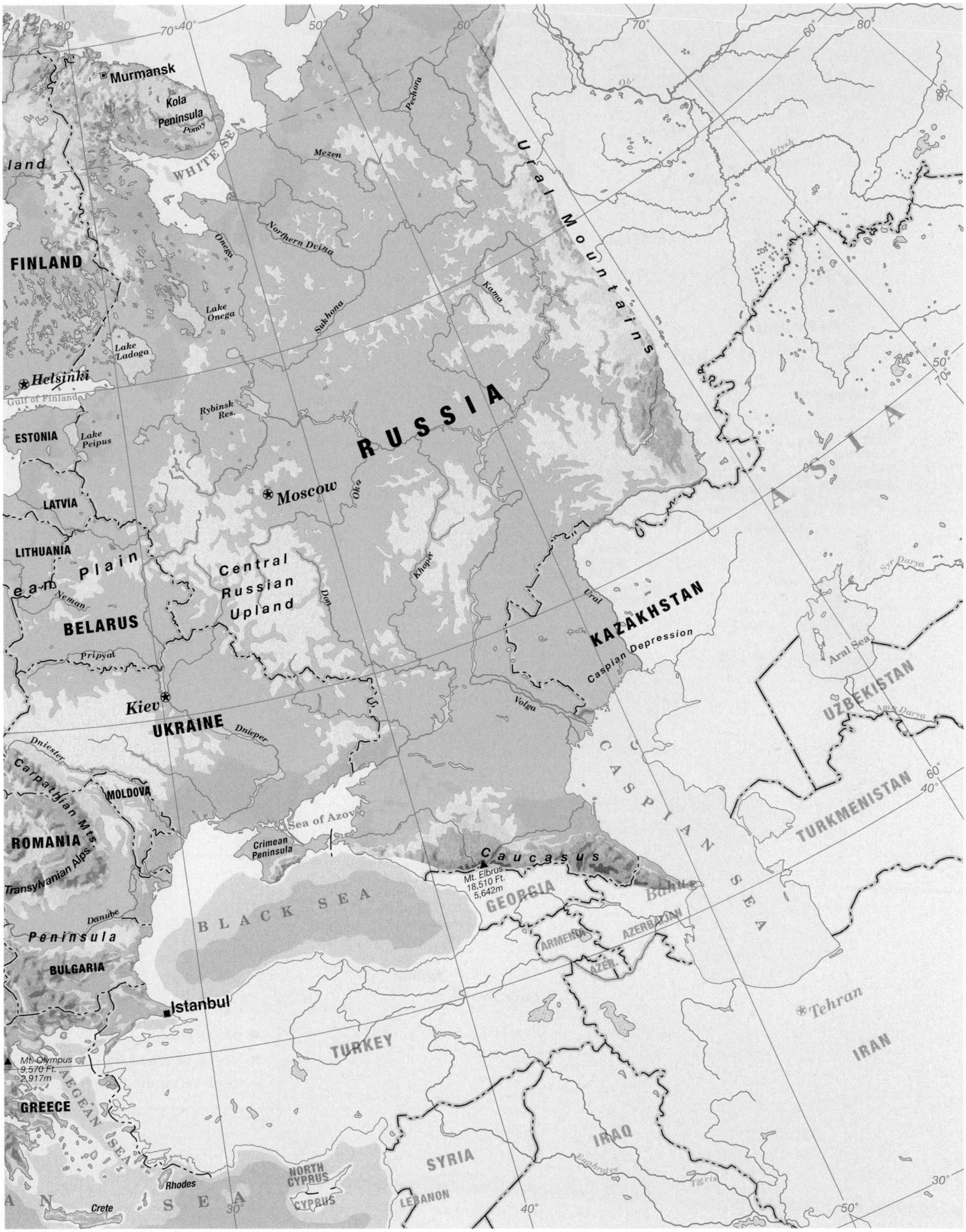

RAND McNALLY

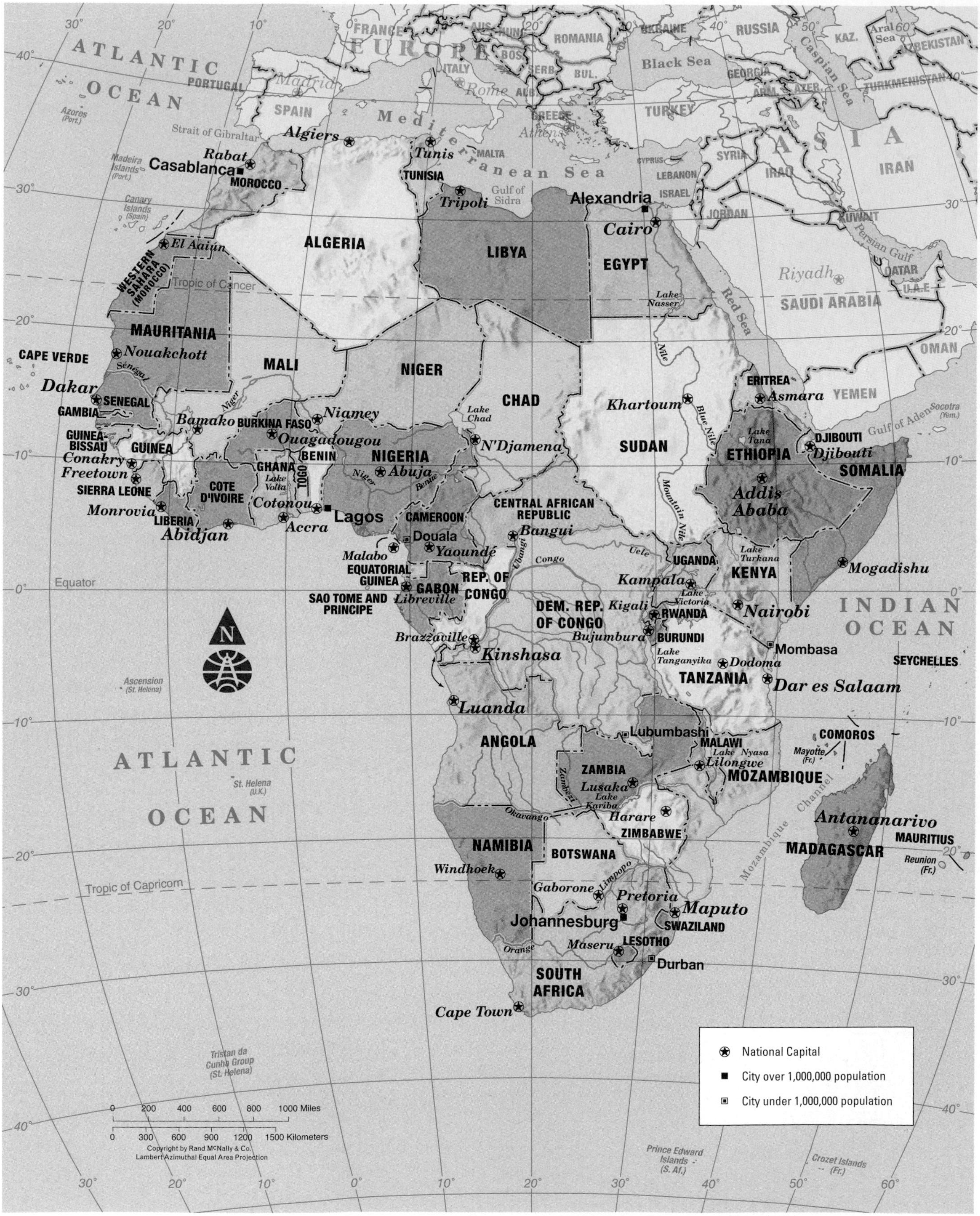
ATLANTIC OCEAN
PORTUGAL
SPAIN
FRANCE
EUROPE
ITALY
ROMANIA
BUL.
UKRAINE
RUSSIA
KAZ.
Aral Sea
UZBEKISTAN
Black Sea
GEORGIA
Caspian Sea
ARM.
AZER.
TURKMENISTAN
TURKEY
GREECE
ALB.
BOS.
SERB.
Madrid
Rome
Athens
Mediterranean Sea
Azores (Port.)
Strait of Gibraltar
Algiers
Tunis
MALTA
TUNISIA
CYPRUS
LEBANON
ISRAEL
SYRIA
IRAQ
IRAN
ASIA
JORDAN
KUWAIT
Persian Gulf
QATAR
U.A.E.
Riyadh
SAUDI ARABIA
OMAN
YEMEN
Socotra (Yem.)
Gulf of Aden
Madeira Islands (Port.)
Rabat
Casablanca
MOROCCO
Canary Islands (Spain)
Gulf of Sidra
Tripoli
Alexandria
Cairo
EGYPT
LIBYA
ALGERIA
El Aaiún
WESTERN SAHARA (MOROCCO)
Tropic of Cancer
Lake Nasser
Red Sea
Nile
MAURITANIA
Nouakchott
CAPE VERDE
MALI
NIGER
CHAD
SUDAN
Khartoum
Blue Nile
ERITREA
Asmara
Sénégal
Dakar
SENEGAL
GAMBIA
Niger
Bamako
BURKINA FASO
Niamey
Ouagadougou
Lake Chad
N'Djamena
Lake Tana
ETHIOPIA
DJIBOUTI
Djibouti
SOMALIA
GUINEA-BISSAU
GUINEA
Conakry
Freetown
SIERRA LEONE
Monrovia
LIBERIA
COTE D'IVOIRE
Abidjan
GHANA
Lake Volta
TOGO
BENIN
Accra
Cotonou
Lagos
NIGERIA
Abuja
Benue
CAMEROON
Douala
Yaoundé
Malabo
EQUATORIAL GUINEA
CENTRAL AFRICAN REPUBLIC
Bangui
Ubangi
Uele
Mountain Nile
Addis Ababa
Congo
UGANDA
Lake Turkana
KENYA
Mogadishu
Equator
SAO TOME AND PRINCIPE
Libreville
GABON
REP. OF CONGO
Kampala
Lake Victoria
DEM. REP. OF CONGO
Kigali
RWANDA
Nairobi
INDIAN OCEAN
Bujumbura
BURUNDI
Mombasa
Brazzaville
Kinshasa
Lake Tanganyika
Dodoma
SEYCHELLES
TANZANIA
Dar es Salaam
Ascension (St. Helena)
Luanda
Lubumbashi
MALAWI
COMOROS
ANGOLA
Lake Nyasa
Mayotte (Fr.)
Lilongwe
ZAMBIA
Lusaka
Zambezi
MOZAMBIQUE
Mozambique Channel
St. Helena (U.K.)
Lake Kariba
Okavango
Harare
ZIMBABWE
Antananarivo
MAURITIUS
MADAGASCAR
NAMIBIA
BOTSWANA
Reunion (Fr.)
Windhoek
Limpopo
Tropic of Capricorn
Gaborone
Pretoria
Maputo
Johannesburg
SWAZILAND
Orange
Maseru
LESOTHO
Durban
SOUTH AFRICA
Cape Town
National Capital
City over 1,000,000 population
City under 1,000,000 population
Tristan da Cunha Group (St. Helena)
0 200 400 600 800 1000 Miles
0 300 600 900 1200 1500 Kilometers
Copyright by Rand McNally & Co.
Lambert Azimuthal Equal Area Projection
Prince Edward Islands (S. Af.)
Crozet Islands (Fr.)
30° 20° 10° 0° 10° 20° 30° 40° 50° 60°
40° 30° 20° 10° 0° 10° 20° 30° 40°

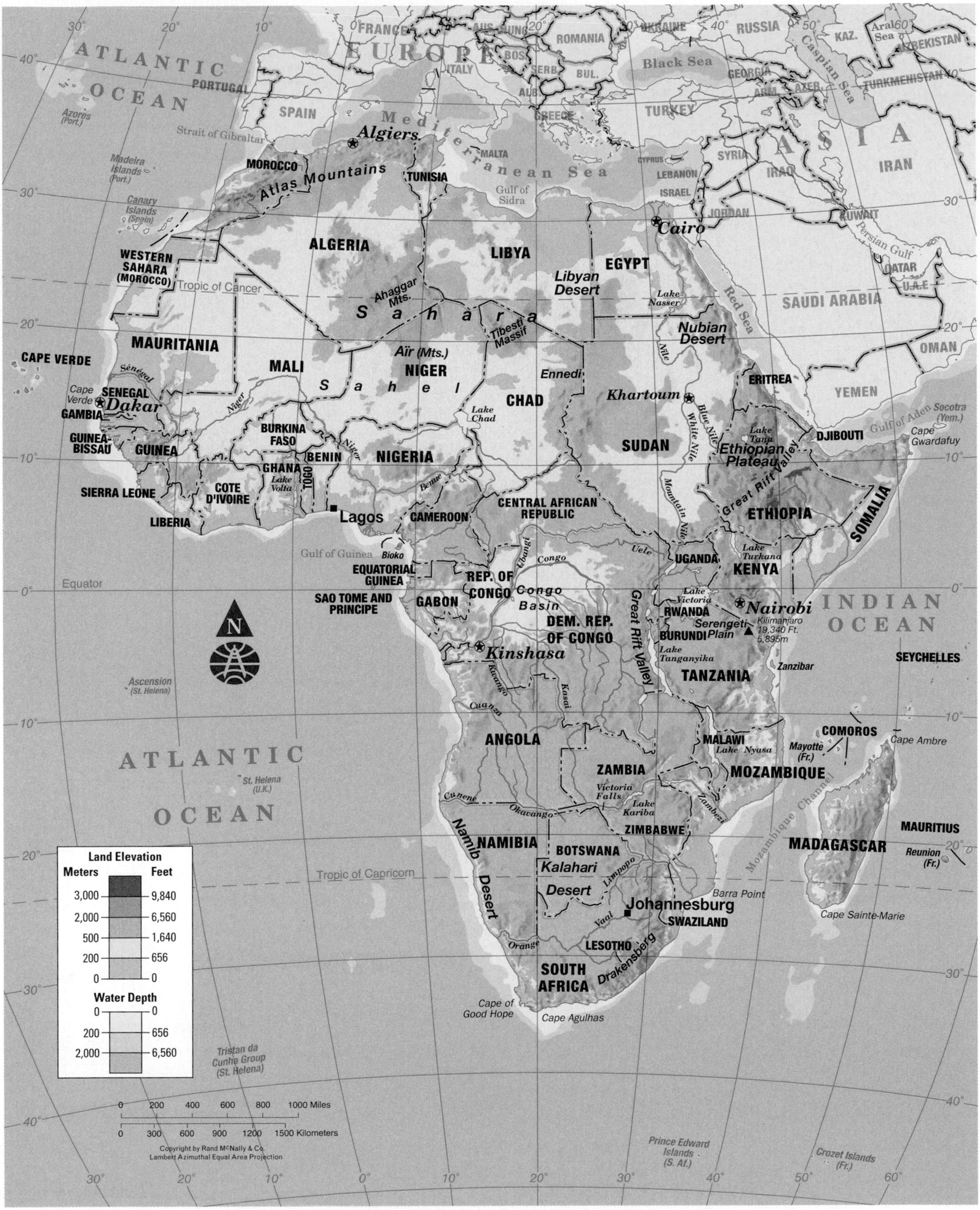
ATLANTIC OCEAN
Azores (Port.)
Madeira Islands (Port.)
Canary Islands (Spain)
PORTUGAL
SPAIN
FRANCE
EUROPE
ITALY
AUSTRIA
HUNG.
BOS.
SERB.
ALB.
GREECE
ROMANIA
BUL.
UKRAINE
RUSSIA
KAZ.
UZBEKISTAN
TURKMENISTAN
Aral Sea
Black Sea
Caspian Sea
GEORGIA
ARM.
AZER.
TURKEY
CYPRUS
SYRIA
LEBANON
ISRAEL
JORDAN
IRAQ
IRAN
KUWAIT
Persian Gulf
QATAR
U.A.E.
SAUDI ARABIA
OMAN
YEMEN
ASIA
Strait of Gibraltar
Mediterranean Sea
Algiers
MALTA
Gulf of Sidra
MOROCCO
Atlas Mountains
TUNISIA
ALGERIA
LIBYA
EGYPT
Cairo
Libyan Desert
Lake Nasser
Red Sea
Nubian Desert
Nile
WESTERN SAHARA (MOROCCO)
Tropic of Cancer
Ahaggar Mts.
Sahara
Tibesti Massif
MAURITANIA
CAPE VERDE
Sénégal
MALI
Aïr (Mts.)
NIGER
Sahel
Ennedi
CHAD
Lake Chad
Khartoum
Blue Nile
White Nile
SUDAN
ERITREA
Lake Tana
Ethiopian Plateau
DJIBOUTI
Gulf of Aden
Socotra (Yem.)
Cape Gwardafuy
Cape Verde
SENEGAL
Dakar
GAMBIA
GUINEA-BISSAU
GUINEA
BURKINA FASO
Niger
BENIN
NIGERIA
GHANA
Lake Volta
TOGO
SIERRA LEONE
COTE D'IVOIRE
LIBERIA
Lagos
Benue
CAMEROON
CENTRAL AFRICAN REPUBLIC
Mountain Nile
Great Rift Valley
ETHIOPIA
SOMALIA
Gulf of Guinea
Bioko
EQUATORIAL GUINEA
SAO TOME AND PRINCIPE
Ubangi
Congo
Uele
UGANDA
Lake Turkana
KENYA
Equator
REP. OF CONGO
GABON
Congo Basin
DEM. REP. OF CONGO
Lake Victoria
RWANDA
BURUNDI
Serengeti Plain
Nairobi
Kilimanjaro 19,340 Ft. 5,895m
INDIAN OCEAN
Kinshasa
Lake Tanganyika
Zanzibar
TANZANIA
SEYCHELLES
Ascension (St. Helena)
Kwango
Kasai
Cuanza
ANGOLA
MALAWI
Lake Nyasa
COMOROS
Mayotte (Fr.)
Cape Ambre
ZAMBIA
MOZAMBIQUE
St. Helena (U.K.)
Victoria Falls
Lake Kariba
Zambezi
Mozambique Channel
Cunene
Okavango
ZIMBABWE
MAURITIUS
Namib Desert
NAMIBIA
BOTSWANA
Kalahari Desert
Limpopo
MADAGASCAR
Reunion (Fr.)
Tropic of Capricorn
Barra Point
Johannesburg
Vaal
SWAZILAND
Cape Sainte-Marie
Orange
LESOTHO
Drakensberg
SOUTH AFRICA
Cape of Good Hope
Cape Agulhas
Tristan da Cunha Group (St. Helena)
Prince Edward Islands (S. Af.)
Crozet Islands (Fr.)
N
Land Elevation
Meters Feet
3,000 — 9,840
2,000 — 6,560
500 — 1,640
200 — 656
0 — 0
Water Depth
0 — 0
200 — 656
2,000 — 6,560
0 200 400 600 800 1000 Miles
0 300 600 900 1200 1500 Kilometers
Copyright by Rand McNally & Co.
Lambert Azimuthal Equal Area Projection
40° 30° 20° 10° 0° 10° 20° 30° 40° 50° 60°

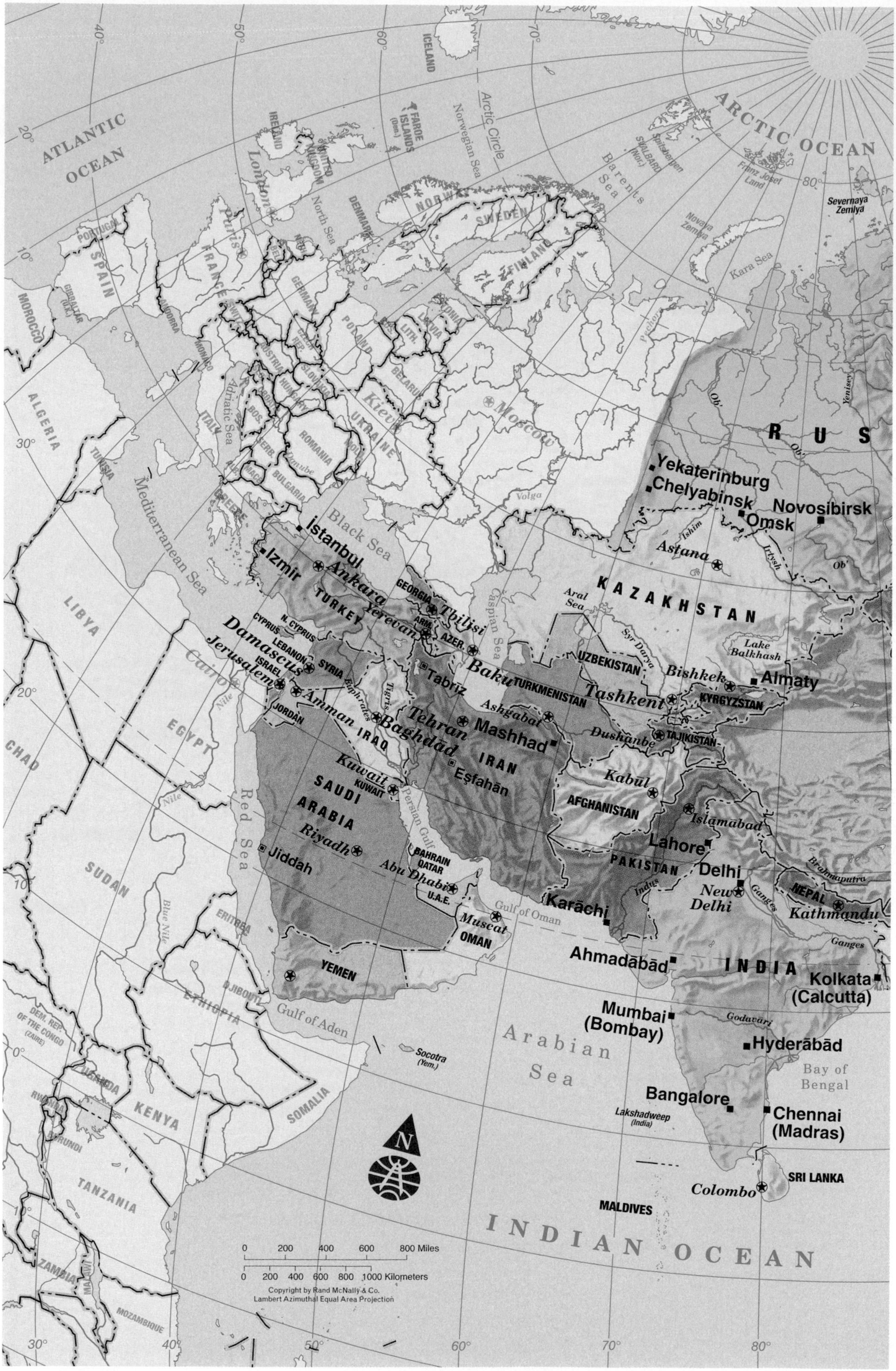

RAND McNALLY

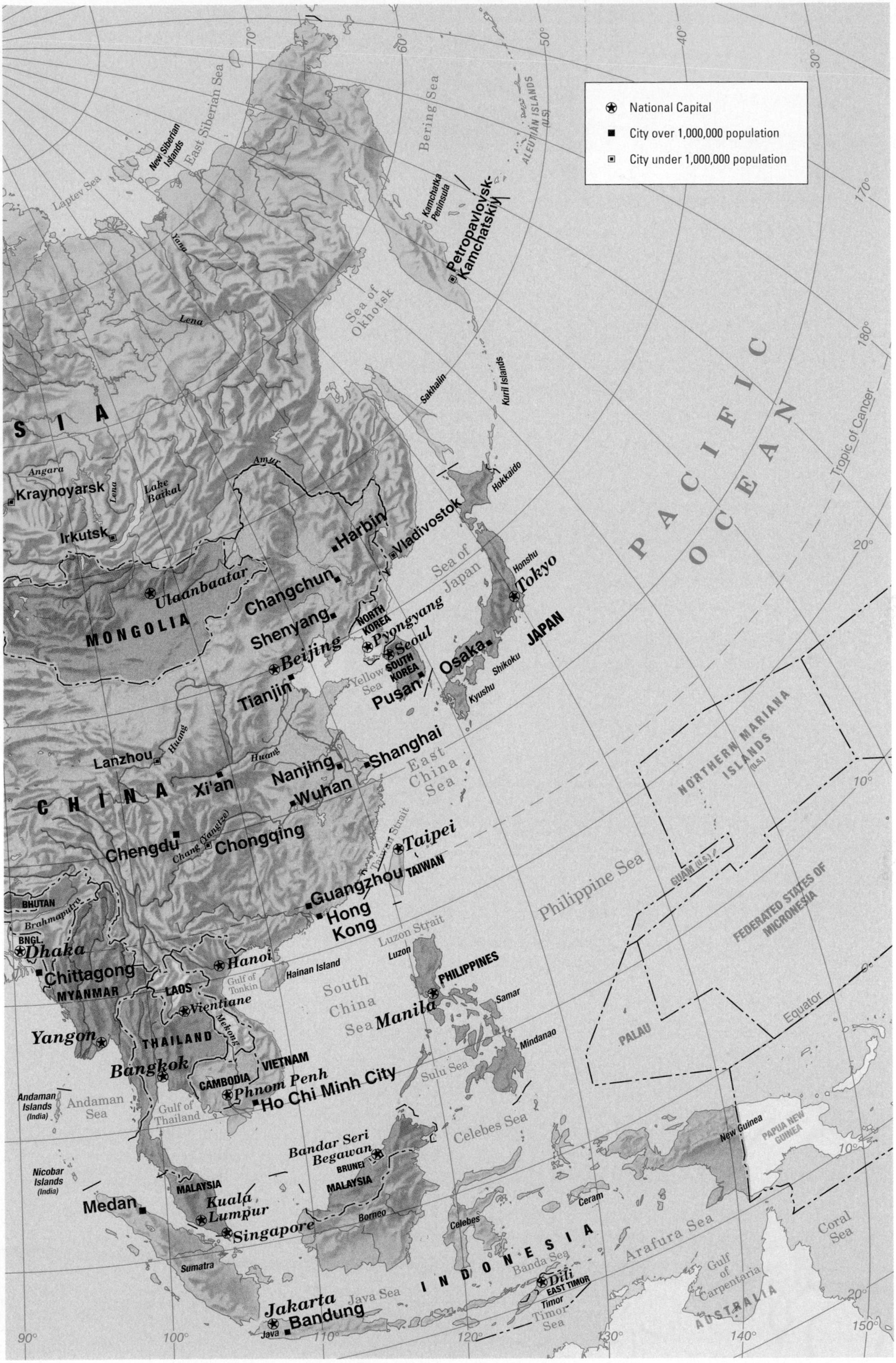
National Capital
City over 1,000,000 population
City under 1,000,000 population
New Siberian Islands
East Siberian Sea
Laptev Sea
Bering Sea
ALEUTIAN ISLANDS (U.S.)
Kamchatka Peninsula
Petropavlovsk-Kamchatskiy
Yana
Lena
Sea of Okhotsk
Sakhalin
Kuril Islands
P A C I F I C
O C E A N
Tropic of Cancer
S I A
Angara
Kraynoyarsk
Lena
Lake Baikal
Amur
Irkutsk
Hokkaido
Harbin
Vladivostok
Sea of Japan
Honshu
Tokyo
Ulaanbaatar
Changchun
MONGOLIA
Shenyang
NORTH KOREA
Pyongyang
Seoul
SOUTH KOREA
Beijing
Yellow Sea
Tianjin
Pusan
Osaka
Shikoku
Kyushu
JAPAN
NORTHERN MARIANA ISLANDS (U.S.)
Lanzhou
Huang
Xi'an
Nanjing
Shanghai
East China Sea
C H I N A
Wuhan
Chengdu
Chang (Yangtze)
Chongqing
Taiwan Strait
Taipei
TAIWAN
Philippine Sea
GUAM (U.S.)
FEDERATED STATES OF MICRONESIA
BHUTAN
Brahmaputra
Guangzhou
Hong Kong
BNGL.
Dhaka
Chittagong
Hanoi
Luzon Strait
Luzon
Hainan Island
Gulf of Tonkin
MYANMAR
LAOS
South China Sea
PHILIPPINES
Vientiane
Samar
Manila
Yangon
THAILAND
Mekong
PALAU
Equator
Bangkok
CAMBODIA
VIETNAM
Mindanao
Sulu Sea
Phnom Penh
Ho Chi Minh City
Andaman Islands (India)
Andaman Sea
Gulf of Thailand
Celebes Sea
Bandar Seri Begawan
BRUNEI
New Guinea
PAPUA NEW GUINEA
Nicobar Islands (India)
MALAYSIA
MALAYSIA
Medan
Kuala Lumpur
Singapore
Borneo
Celebes
Ceram
Coral Sea
Sumatra
I N D O N E S I A
Banda Sea
Dili
EAST TIMOR
Arafura Sea
Gulf of Carpentaria
Timor
Timor Sea
Jakarta
Bandung
Java Sea
Java
AUSTRALIA
90°
100°
110°
120°
130°
140°
150°
70°
60°
50°
40°
30°
20°
10°
0°
170°
180°

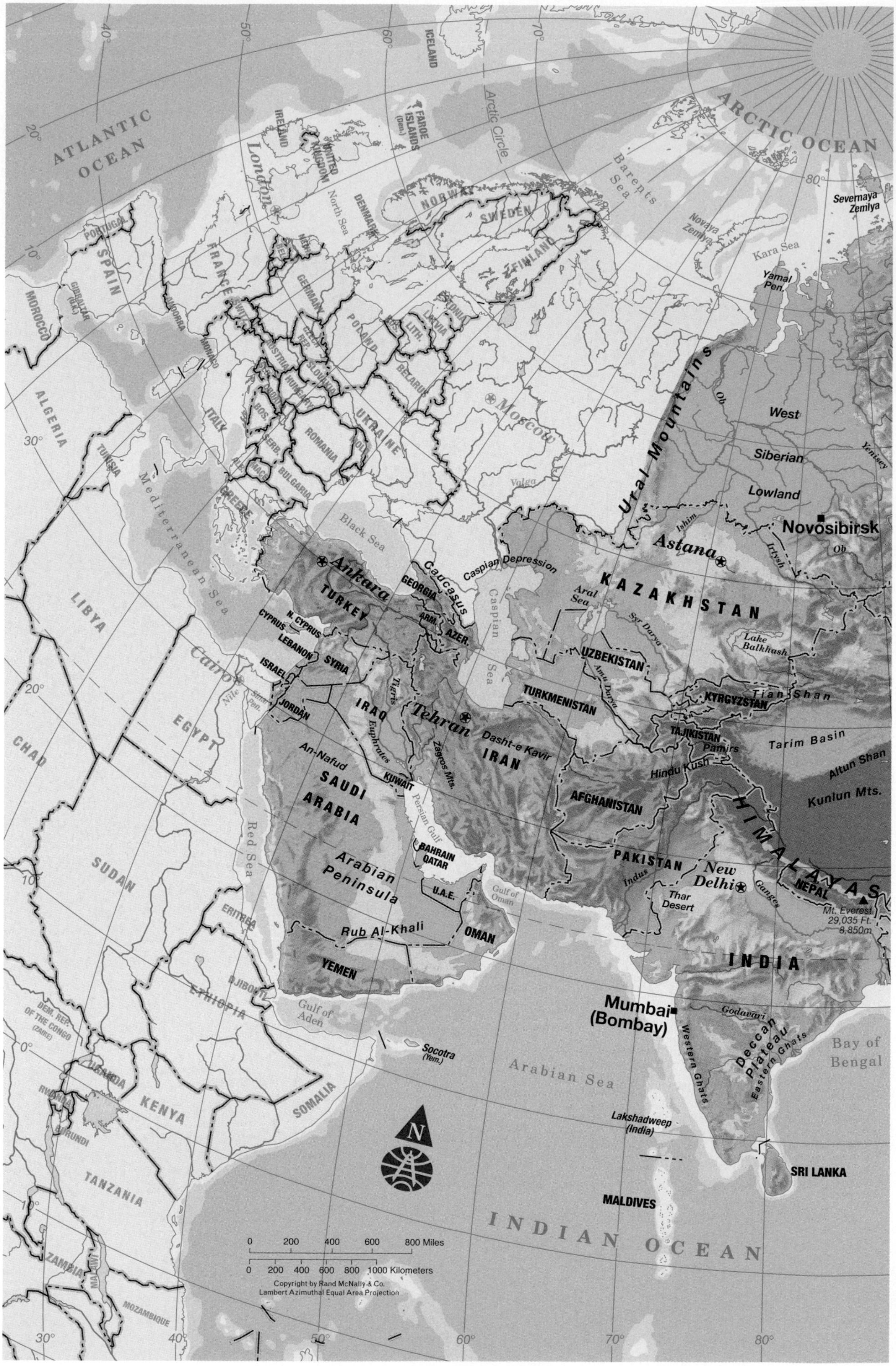
ATLANTIC OCEAN
ARCTIC OCEAN
Arctic Circle
ICELAND
FAROE ISLANDS (Den.)
IRELAND
UNITED KINGDOM
London
North Sea
DENMARK
NORWAY
SWEDEN
FINLAND
Barents Sea
Novaya Zemlya
Severnaya Zemlya
Kara Sea
Yamal Pen.
PORTUGAL
SPAIN
GIBRALTAR (U.K.)
MOROCCO
ANDORRA
MONACO
FRANCE
GERMANY
POLAND
LITH.
LATVIA
BELARUS
AUSTRIA
SLOVAKIA
HUNGARY
ROMANIA
UKRAINE
ITALY
BULGARIA
GREECE
ALGERIA
TUNISIA
Moscow
Volga
Ural Mountains
Ob
West
Siberian
Lowland
Yenisey
Ishim
Irtysh
Novosibirsk
Astana
Mediterranean Sea
Black Sea
Ankara
TURKEY
GEORGIA
Caucasus
ARM.
AZER.
Caspian Depression
Caspian Sea
Aral Sea
KAZAKHSTAN
Syr Darya
Lake Balkhash
UZBEKISTAN
Amu Darya
TURKMENISTAN
KYRGYZSTAN
Tian Shan
TAJIKISTAN
Pamirs
Tarim Basin
Altun Shan
Kunlun Mts.
Hindu Kush
LIBYA
N. CYPRUS
CYPRUS
LEBANON
SYRIA
ISRAEL
Cairo
Nile
Sinai Pen.
JORDAN
IRAQ
Tigris
Euphrates
Tehran
Dasht-e Kavir
IRAN
Zagros Mts.
EGYPT
CHAD
An-Nafud
KUWAIT
SAUDI ARABIA
Persian Gulf
AFGHANISTAN
HIMALAYAS
PAKISTAN
Indus
New Delhi
Ganges
NEPAL
Mt. Everest 29,035 Ft. 8,850m
Thar Desert
Red Sea
BAHRAIN
QATAR
Arabian Peninsula
U.A.E.
Gulf of Oman
SUDAN
ERITREA
Rub Al-Khali
OMAN
YEMEN
INDIA
DJIBOUTI
ETHIOPIA
Gulf of Aden
Mumbai (Bombay)
Godavari
DEM. REP. OF THE CONGO (ZAIRE)
Socotra (Yem.)
Western Ghats
Deccan Plateau
Eastern Ghats
Bay of Bengal
Arabian Sea
UGANDA
KENYA
RWANDA
BURUNDI
SOMALIA
Lakshadweep (India)
SRI LANKA
TANZANIA
MALDIVES
INDIAN OCEAN
ZAMBIA
MALAWI
MOZAMBIQUE
N
0 200 400 600 800 Miles
0 200 400 600 800 1000 Kilometers
Copyright by Rand McNally & Co.
Lambert Azimuthal Equal Area Projection
40°
50°
60°
70°
80°
20°
10°
30°
0°

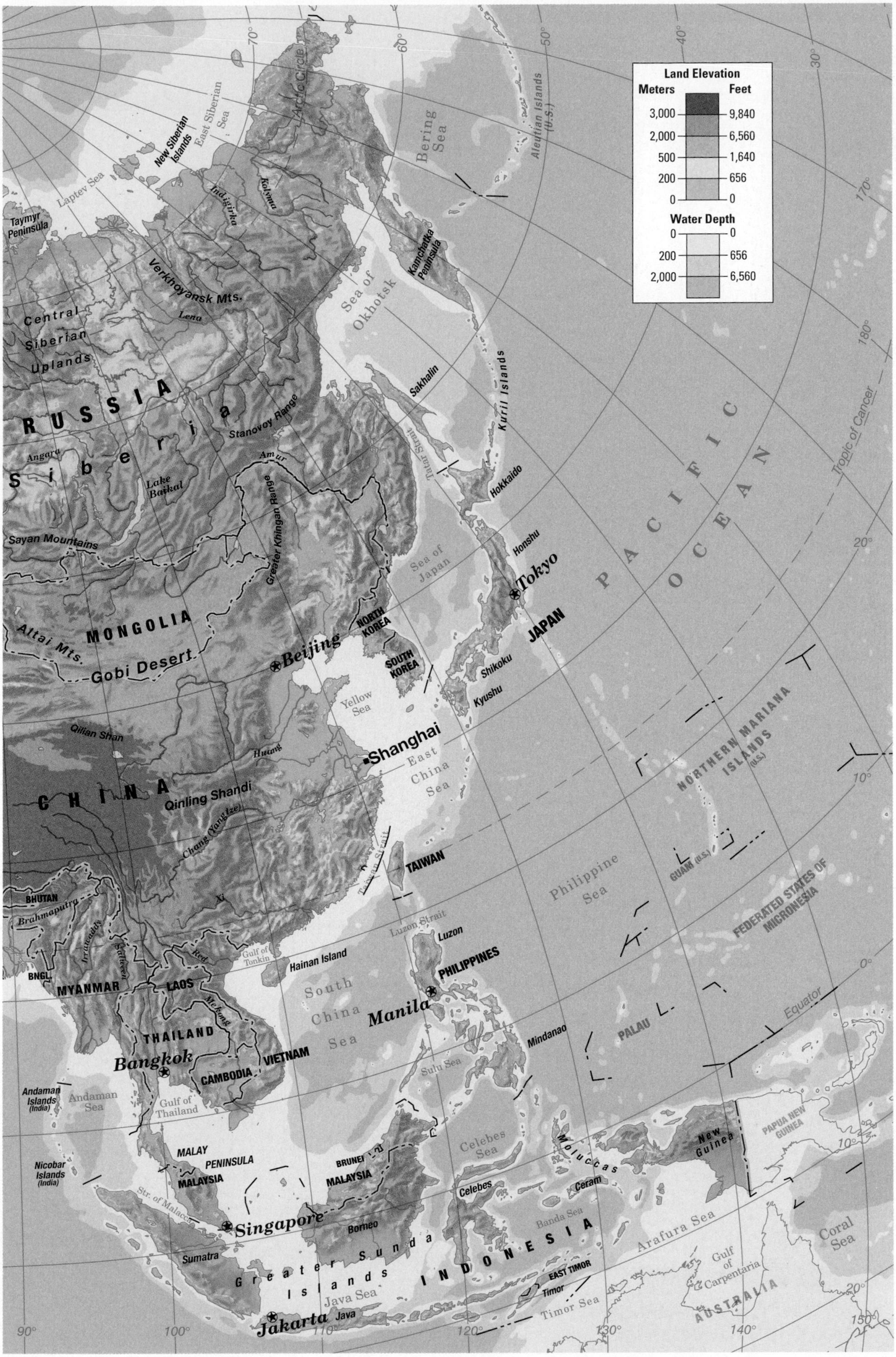

Land Elevation
Meters
Feet
3,000 — 9,840
2,000 — 6,560
500 — 1,640
200 — 656
0 — 0
Water Depth
0 — 0
200 — 656
2,000 — 6,560
Arctic Circle
East Siberian Sea
New Siberian Islands
Laptev Sea
Taymyr Peninsula
Indigirka
Kolyma
Bering Sea
Aleutian Islands (U.S.)
Verkhoyansk Mts.
Lena
Central Siberian Uplands
Sea of Okhotsk
Kamchatka Peninsula
Kuril Islands
Sakhalin
RUSSIA
Siberia
Stanovoy Range
Angara
Amur
Lake Baikal
Tatar Strait
Hokkaido
Sayan Mountains
Greater Khingan Range
Sea of Japan
Honshu
Tokyo
PACIFIC OCEAN
Tropic of Cancer
MONGOLIA
Altai Mts.
Gobi Desert
Beijing
NORTH KOREA
SOUTH KOREA
JAPAN
Shikoku
Kyushu
Yellow Sea
Qilian Shan
Huang
Shanghai
East China Sea
NORTHERN MARIANA ISLANDS (U.S.)
CHINA
Qinling Shandi
Chang (Yangtze)
Taiwan Strait
TAIWAN
GUAM (U.S.)
Philippine Sea
FEDERATED STATES OF MICRONESIA
BHUTAN
Brahmaputra
Irrawaddy
Salween
Xi
Red
Gulf of Tonkin
Hainan Island
Luzon Strait
Luzon
PHILIPPINES
BNGL.
MYANMAR
LAOS
Mekong
South China Sea
Manila
PALAU
Equator
THAILAND
Bangkok
CAMBODIA
VIETNAM
Sulu Sea
Mindanao
Andaman Islands (India)
Andaman Sea
Gulf of Thailand
Celebes Sea
Moluccas
New Guinea
PAPUA NEW GUINEA
MALAY PENINSULA
BRUNEI
MALAYSIA
Nicobar Islands (India)
Celebes
Ceram
Str. of Malacca
Singapore
Borneo
Banda Sea
Arafura Sea
Coral Sea
Sumatra
Greater Sunda Islands
INDONESIA
EAST TIMOR
Timor
Gulf of Carpentaria
Java Sea
Timor Sea
AUSTRALIA
Jakarta
Java
90°
100°
110°
120°
130°
140°
150°
70°
60°
50°
40°
30°
20°
10°
0°
170°
180°

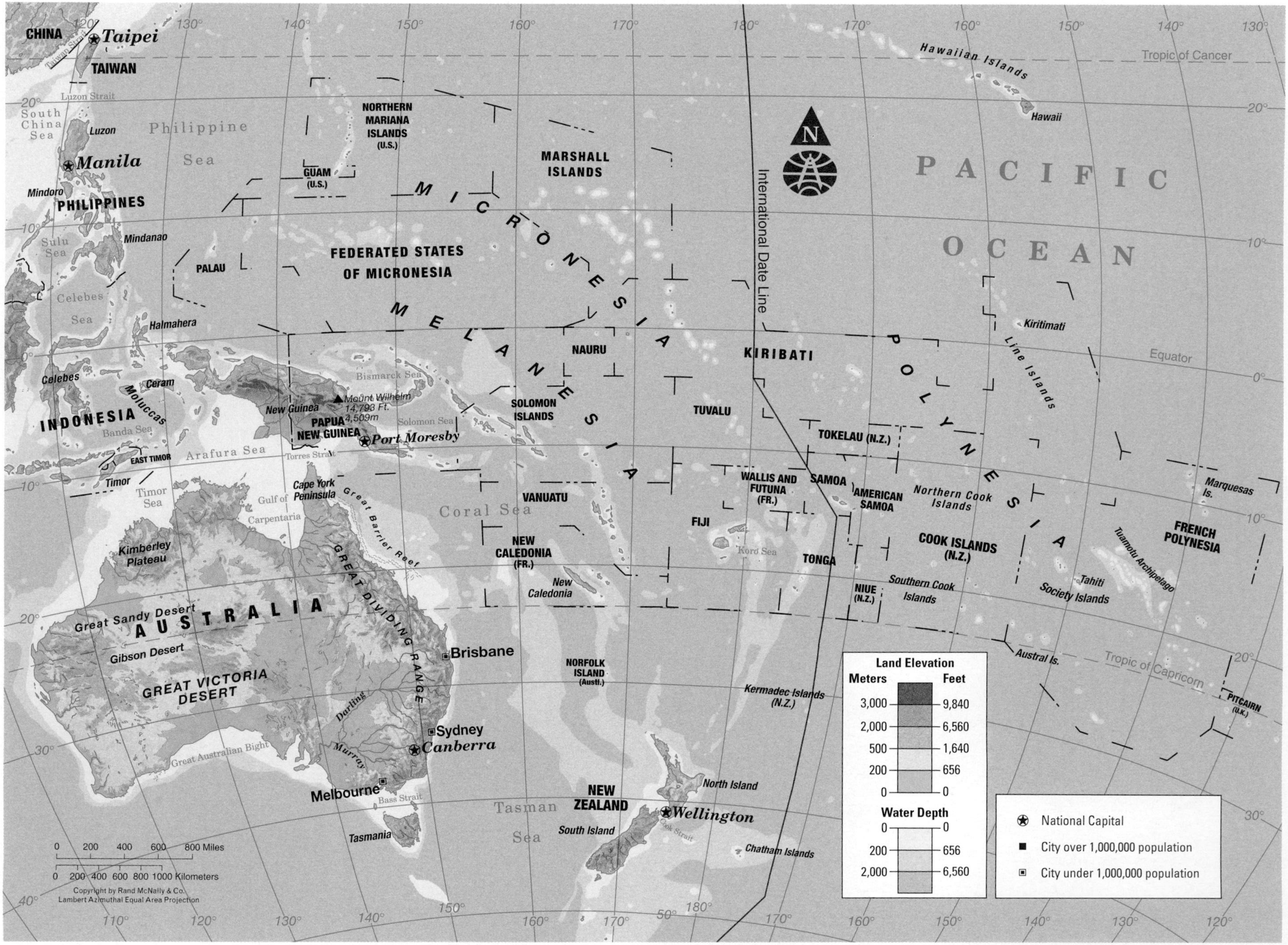
CHINA
Taipei
TAIWAN
Taiwan Strait
Luzon Strait
South China Sea
Luzon
Philippine Sea
Manila
Mindoro
PHILIPPINES
Mindanao
Sulu Sea
Celebes Sea
Halmahera
Celebes
Ceram
Moluccas
INDONESIA
Banda Sea
EAST TIMOR
Timor
Timor Sea
Arafura Sea
PALAU
NORTHERN MARIANA ISLANDS (U.S.)
GUAM (U.S.)
FEDERATED STATES OF MICRONESIA
MARSHALL ISLANDS
MICRONESIA
MELANESIA
POLYNESIA
NAURU
KIRIBATI
TUVALU
SOLOMON ISLANDS
Bismarck Sea
Solomon Sea
New Guinea
Mount Wilhelm 14,793 Ft. 4,509m
PAPUA NEW GUINEA
Port Moresby
Torres Strait
Cape York Peninsula
Gulf of Carpentaria
Great Barrier Reef
Coral Sea
VANUATU
NEW CALEDONIA (FR.)
New Caledonia
WALLIS AND FUTUNA (FR.)
FIJI
Koro Sea
SAMOA
AMERICAN SAMOA
TOKELAU (N.Z.)
TONGA
NIUE (N.Z.)
Northern Cook Islands
COOK ISLANDS (N.Z.)
Southern Cook Islands
International Date Line
Hawaiian Islands
Hawaii
Tropic of Cancer
PACIFIC OCEAN
Kiritimati
Line Islands
Equator
Marquesas Is.
FRENCH POLYNESIA
Tuamotu Archipelago
Tahiti
Society Islands
Austral Is.
Tropic of Capricorn
PITCAIRN (U.K.)
Kimberley Plateau
Great Sandy Desert
AUSTRALIA
Gibson Desert
GREAT VICTORIA DESERT
GREAT DIVIDING RANGE
Great Australian Bight
Darling
Murray
Brisbane
Sydney
Canberra
Melbourne
Bass Strait
Tasmania
NORFOLK ISLAND (Austl.)
Kermadec Islands (N.Z.)
Tasman Sea
NEW ZEALAND
North Island
South Island
Wellington
Cook Strait
Chatham Islands
Land Elevation
Meters
Feet
3,000 — 9,840
2,000 — 6,560
500 — 1,640
200 — 656
0 — 0
Water Depth
0 — 0
200 — 656
2,000 — 6,560
National Capital
City over 1,000,000 population
City under 1,000,000 population
0 200 400 600 800 Miles
0 200 400 600 800 1000 Kilometers
Copyright by Rand McNally & Co.
Lambert Azimuthal Equal Area Projection
N

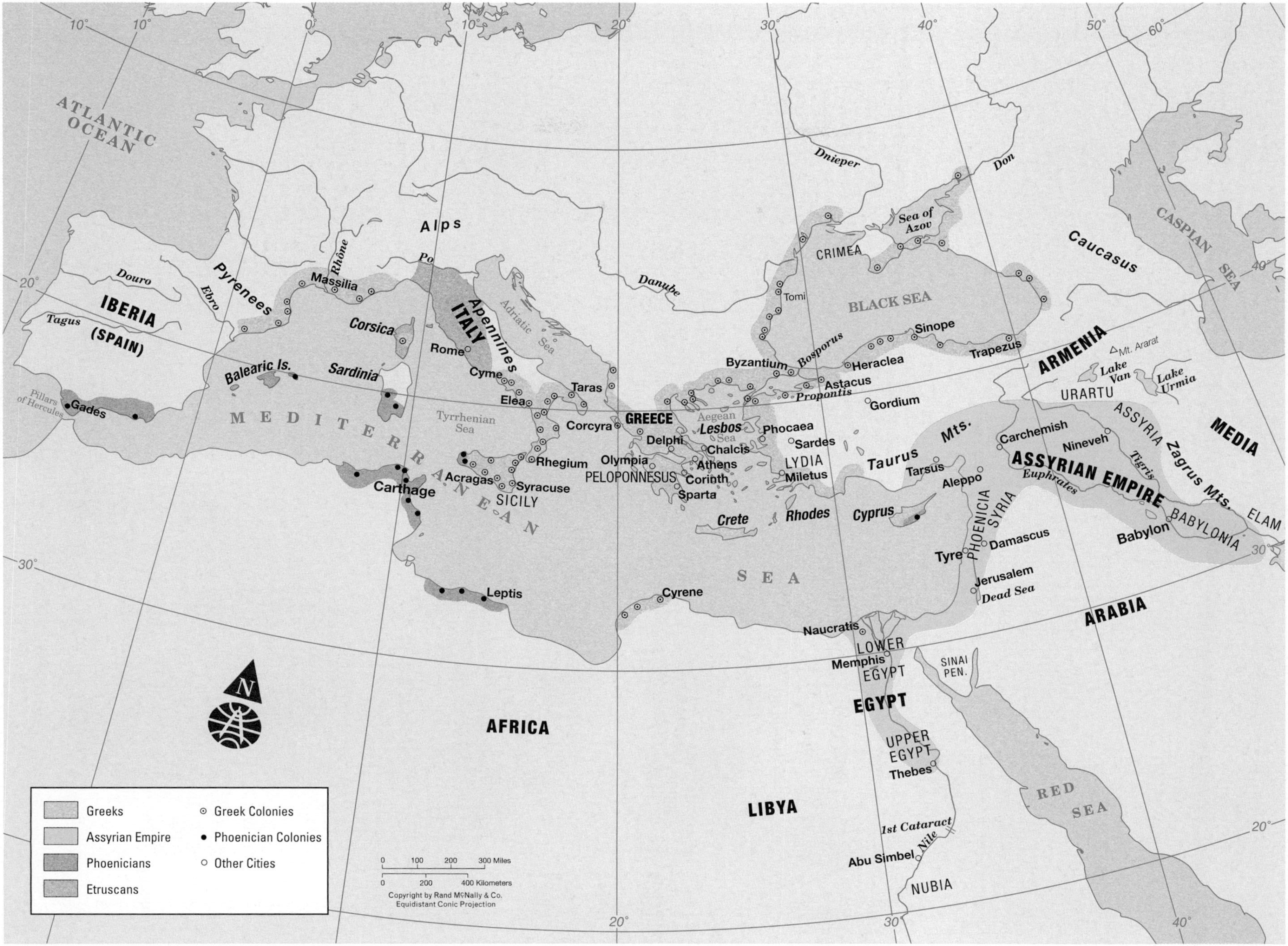
ATLANTIC OCEAN
IBERIA (SPAIN)
Douro
Tagus
Ebro
Pyrenees
Pillars of Hercules
Gades
Balearic Is.
Massilia
Rhône
Alps
Po
Corsica
Sardinia
ITALY
Apennines
Rome
Cyme
Elea
Taras
Adriatic Sea
Tyrrhenian Sea
MEDITERRANEAN SEA
Carthage
Acragas
Syracuse
SICILY
Rhegium
Corcyra
GREECE
Delphi
Olympia
PELOPONNESUS
Athens
Corinth
Sparta
Chalcis
Lesbos
Aegean Sea
Crete
Rhodes
Phocaea
Sardes
LYDIA
Miletus
Byzantium
Bosporus
Propontis
Astacus
Heraclea
Gordium
Danube
Tomi
BLACK SEA
CRIMEA
Dnieper
Don
Sea of Azov
Sinope
Trapezus
Caucasus
CASPIAN SEA
ARMENIA
Mt. Ararat
Lake Van
Lake Urmia
URARTU
ASSYRIA
MEDIA
Zagrus Mts.
ELAM
Nineveh
Carchemish
Tigris
Euphrates
ASSYRIAN EMPIRE
BABYLONIA
Babylon
Taurus Mts.
Tarsus
Aleppo
Cyprus
PHOENICIA
SYRIA
Tyre
Damascus
Jerusalem
Dead Sea
ARABIA
Cyrene
Leptis
AFRICA
LIBYA
Naucratis
LOWER EGYPT
Memphis
SINAI PEN.
EGYPT
UPPER EGYPT
Thebes
RED SEA
1st Cataract
Nile
Abu Simbel
NUBIA
N
Greeks
Assyrian Empire
Phoenicians
Etruscans
Greek Colonies
Phoenician Colonies
Other Cities
0 100 200 300 Miles
0 200 400 Kilometers
Copyright by Rand McNally & Co.
Equidistant Conic Projection

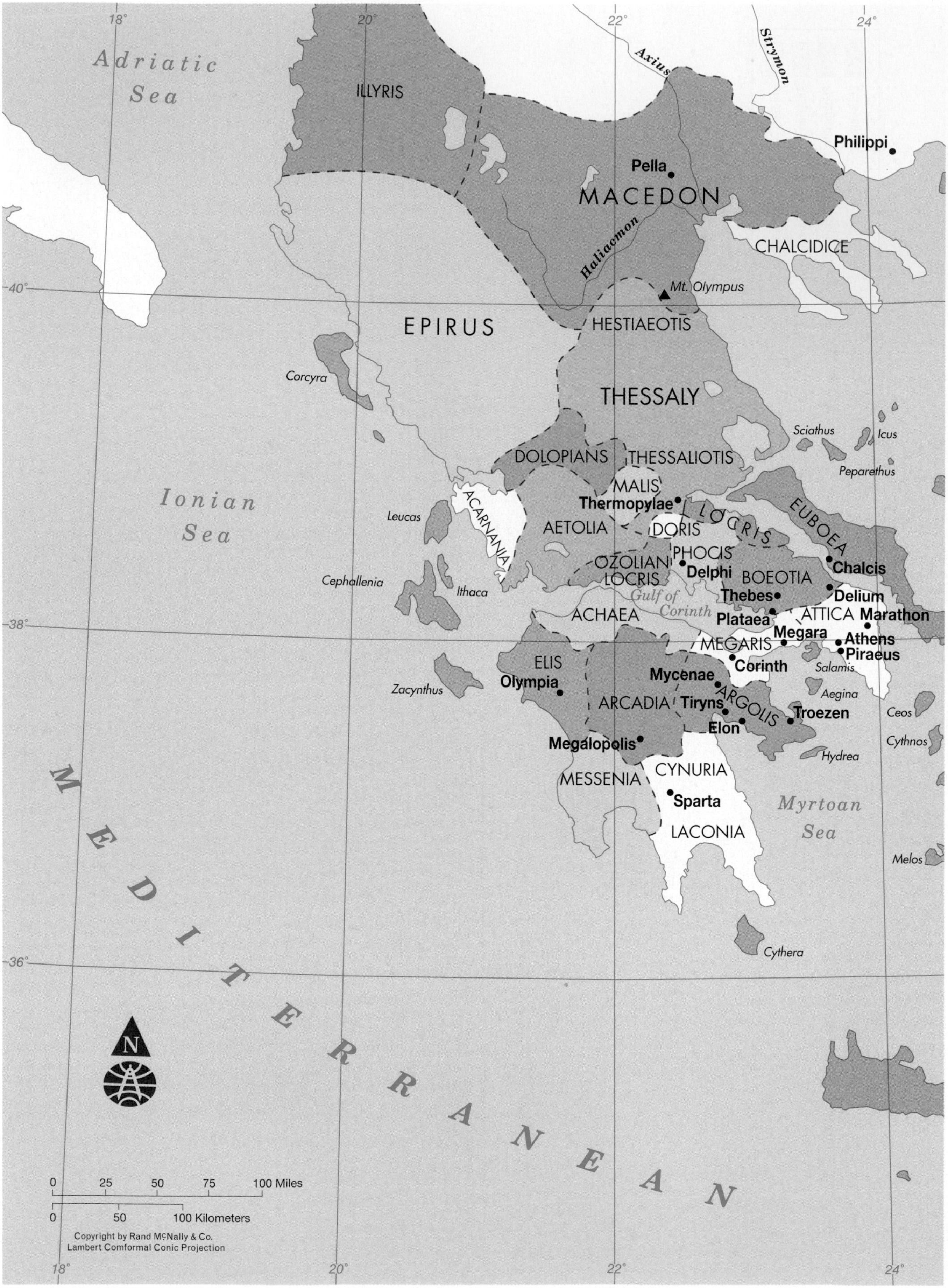

18°
20°
22°
24°
40°
38°
36°
Adriatic Sea
Axius
Strymon
ILLYRIS
Philippi
Pella
MACEDON
Haliacmon
CHALCIDICE
Mt. Olympus
EPIRUS
HESTIAEOTIS
Corcyra
THESSALY
Sciathus
Icus
Peparethus
DOLOPIANS
THESSALIOTIS
MALIS
Thermopylae
Ionian Sea
Leucas
ACARNANIA
AETOLIA
DORIS
LOCRIS
EUBOEA
PHOCIS
OZOLIAN LOCRIS
Delphi
BOEOTIA
Chalcis
Cephallenia
Ithaca
Gulf of Corinth
Thebes
Delium
ACHAEA
Plataea
ATTICA
Marathon
Megara
MEGARIS
Athens
Piraeus
ELIS
Corinth
Salamis
Zacynthus
Olympia
Mycenae
Aegina
ARCADIA
Tiryns
ARGOLIS
Troezen
Ceos
Elon
Cythnos
Megalopolis
Hydrea
MESSENIA
CYNURIA
Sparta
Myrtoan Sea
LACONIA
Melos
Cythera
MEDITERRANEAN
N
0 25 50 75 100 Miles
0 50 100 Kilometers
Copyright by Rand McNally & Co.
Lambert Comformal Conic Projection

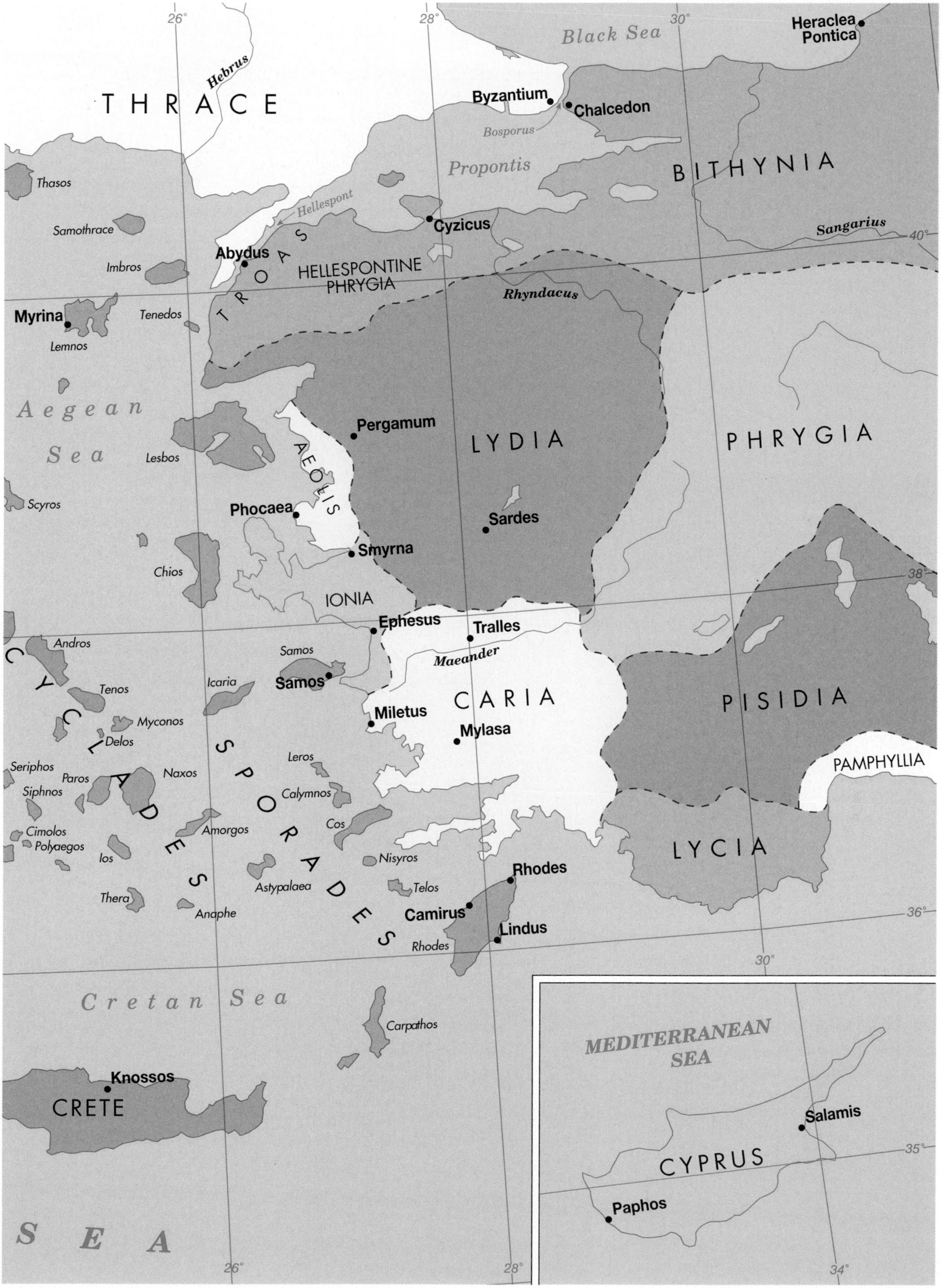
THRACE
Hebrus
Black Sea
Heraclea Pontica
Byzantium
Chalcedon
Bosporus
Propontis
BITHYNIA
Thasos
Samothrace
Hellespont
Cyzicus
Sangarius
Imbros
Abydus
TROAS
HELLESPONTINE PHRYGIA
Rhyndacus
Myrina
Tenedos
Lemnos
Aegean Sea
Pergamum
LYDIA
PHRYGIA
Lesbos
AEOLIS
Scyros
Phocaea
Sardes
Smyrna
Chios
IONIA
Ephesus
Tralles
Andros
Samos
Maeander
CYCLADES
Tenos
Icaria
Samos
CARIA
PISIDIA
Myconos
Miletus
Delos
Mylasa
SPORADES
Seriphos
Paros
Naxos
Leros
PAMPHYLLIA
Siphnos
Calymnos
Cimolos
Amorgos
Cos
LYCIA
Polyaegos
Ios
Nisyros
Rhodes
Astypalaea
Telos
Thera
Anaphe
Camirus
Lindus
Rhodes
Cretan Sea
Carpathos
Knossos
CRETE
SEA
MEDITERRANEAN SEA
Salamis
CYPRUS
Paphos
26°
28°
30°
34°
35°
36°
38°
40°

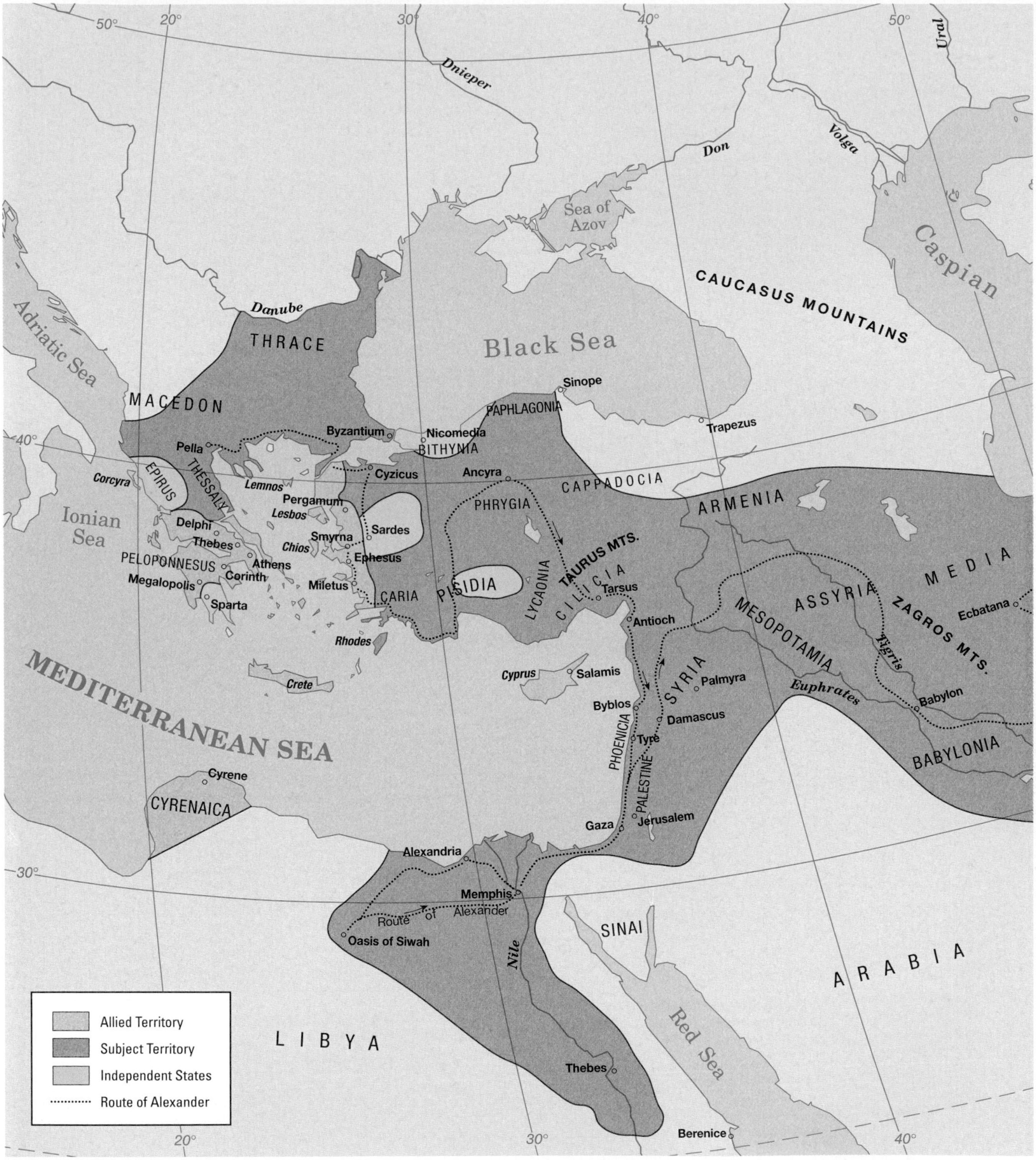

Dnieper
Don
Volga
Ural
Sea of Azov
Caspian
CAUCASUS MOUNTAINS
Danube
THRACE
Black Sea
Adriatic Sea
MACEDON
Sinope
PAPHLAGONIA
Trapezus
Byzantium
Nicomedia
BITHYNIA
Pella
EPIRUS
THESSALY
Corcyra
Lemnos
Cyzicus
Ancyra
CAPPADOCIA
ARMENIA
Pergamum
Lesbos
Sardes
PHRYGIA
Ionian Sea
Delphi
Thebes
Chios
Smyrna
Ephesus
TAURUS MTS.
MEDIA
PELOPONNESUS
Athens
Corinth
Megalopolis
Miletus
CARIA
PISIDIA
LYCAONIA
CILICIA
Tarsus
ASSYRIA
ZAGROS MTS.
Ecbatana
Sparta
Antioch
MESOPOTAMIA
Rhodes
Tigris
MEDITERRANEAN SEA
Cyprus
Salamis
SYRIA
Palmyra
Euphrates
Babylon
Crete
Byblos
Damascus
PHOENICIA
Tyre
BABYLONIA
Cyrene
PALESTINE
CYRENAICA
Gaza
Jerusalem
Alexandria
Memphis
Route of Alexander
SINAI
Oasis of Siwah
Nile
ARABIA
Allied Territory
Subject Territory
Independent States
Route of Alexander
LIBYA
Red Sea
Thebes
Berenice
50°
20°
30°
40°
50°
40°
30°
20°
30°
40°

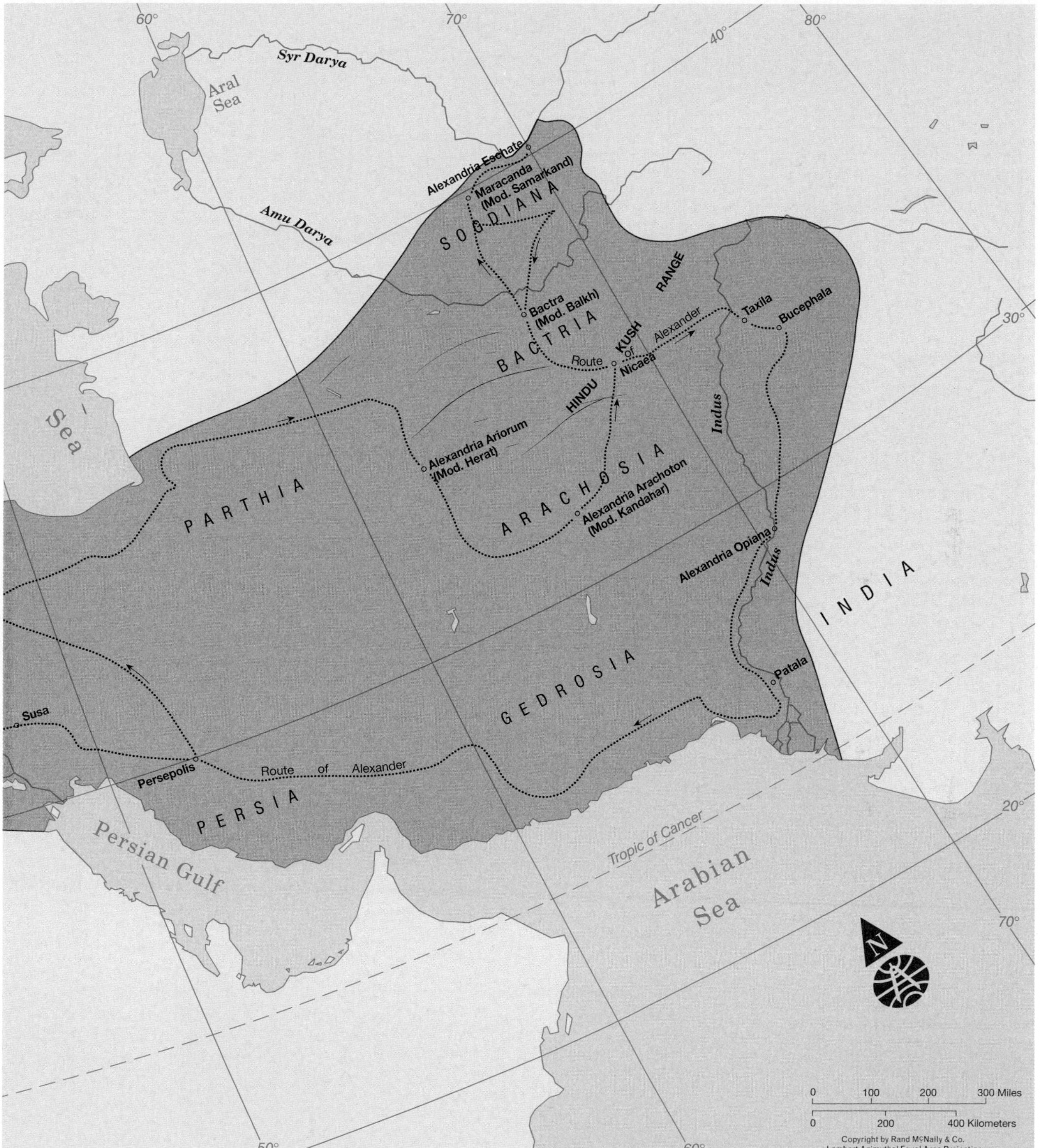
Syr Darya
Aral Sea
Amu Darya
Sea
Alexandria Eschate
Maracanda (Mod. Samarkand)
SOGDIANA
Bactra (Mod. Balkh)
BACTRIA
HINDU KUSH RANGE
Route of Alexander
Nicaea
Taxila
Bucephala
Indus
Alexandria Ariorum (Mod. Herat)
ARACHOSIA
Alexandria Arachoton (Mod. Kandahar)
PARTHIA
Alexandria Opiana
INDIA
Patala
GEDROSIA
Susa
Persepolis
PERSIA
Persian Gulf
Tropic of Cancer
Arabian Sea
60°
70°
80°
40°
30°
20°
50°
0 100 200 300 Miles
0 200 400 Kilometers
Copyright by Rand McNally & Co.
Lambert Azimuthal Equal Area Projection

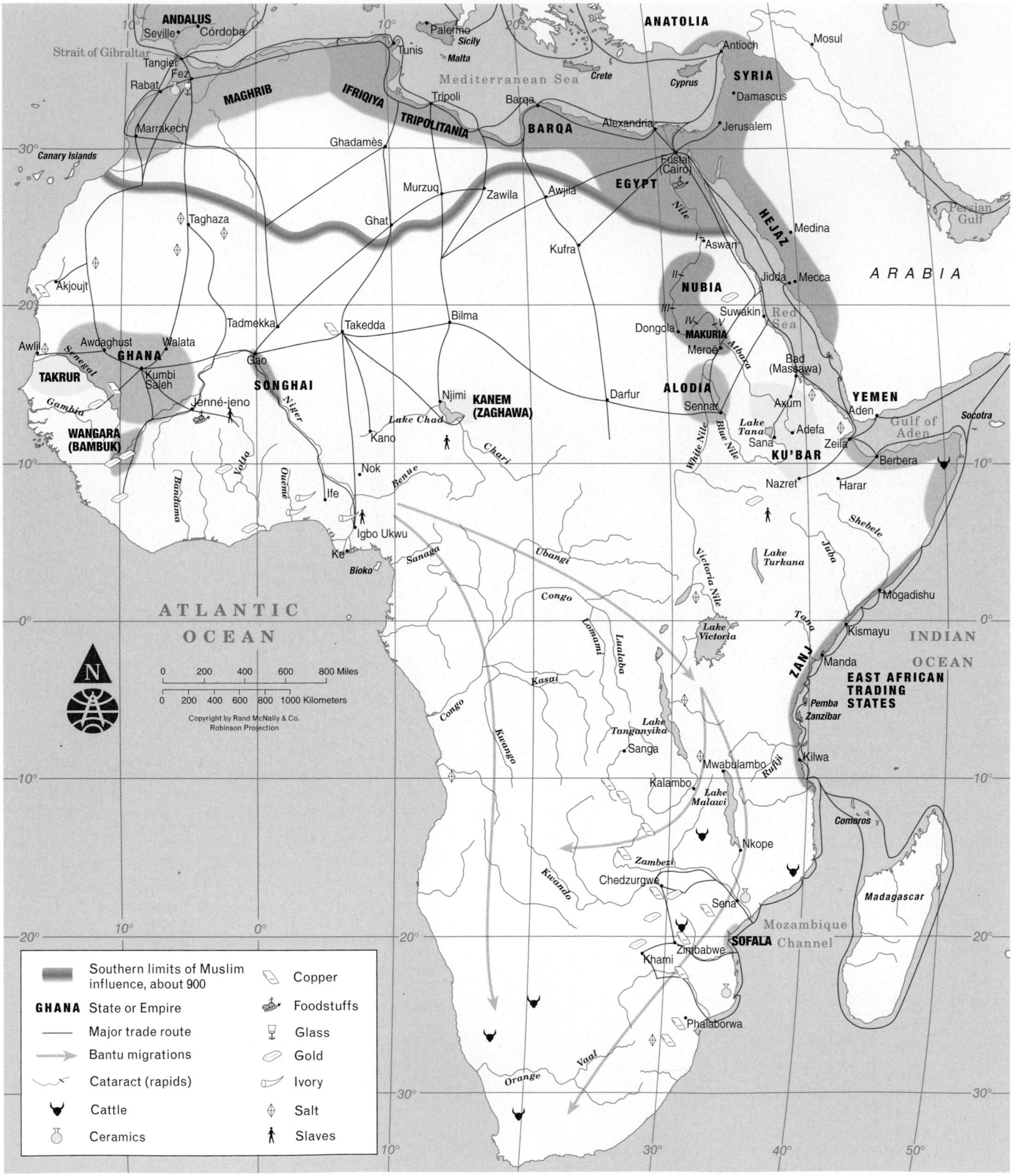

ANDALUS
Seville
Córdoba
Strait of Gibraltar
Tangier
Fez
Rabat
Marrakech
MAGHRIB
IFRIQIYA
TRIPOLITANIA
Tunis
Palermo
Sicily
Malta
Mediterranean Sea
Crete
Cyprus
ANATOLIA
Antioch
Mosul
SYRIA
Damascus
Jerusalem
Tripoli
Barqa
BARQA
Alexandria
Fustat (Cairo)
EGYPT
Canary Islands
Ghadamès
Murzuq
Zawila
Awjila
Ghat
Taghaza
Kufra
Nile
HEJAZ
Medina
Aswan
Jidda
Mecca
ARABIA
Persian Gulf
NUBIA
Akjoujt
Tadmekka
Takedda
Bilma
Dongola
MAKURIA
Suwakin
Red Sea
Meroë
Atbara
Awlil
Awdaghust
Walata
GHANA
Senegal
TAKRUR
Kumbi Saleh
Gao
SONGHAI
Niger
Gambia
Jenné-jeno
WANGARA (BAMBUK)
Njimi
KANEM (ZAGHAWA)
Lake Chad
Kano
Darfur
ALODIA
Sennar
Bad (Massawa)
Axum
YEMEN
Aden
Gulf of Aden
Socotra
Lake Tana
Sana
Adefa
Zeila
KU'BAR
Berbera
Harar
Nazret
White Nile
Blue Nile
Chari
Volta
Bandama
Ouémé
Nok
Benue
Ife
Igbo Ukwu
Ke
Bioko
Sanaga
Ubangi
Shebele
Juba
Lake Turkana
Victoria Nile
Mogadishu
Congo
Lomami
Lualaba
Lake Victoria
Tana
Kismayu
ATLANTIC OCEAN
INDIAN OCEAN
ZANJ
Manda
EAST AFRICAN TRADING STATES
Pemba
Zanzibar
N
0 200 400 600 800 Miles
0 200 400 600 800 1000 Kilometers
Copyright by Rand McNally & Co.
Robinson Projection
Kasai
Congo
Kwango
Lake Tanganyika
Sanga
Mwabulambo
Rufiji
Kilwa
Kalambo
Lake Malawi
Comoros
Nkope
Zambezi
Kwando
Chedzurgwe
Sena
Madagascar
Mozambique Channel
SOFALA
Zimbabwe
Khami
Phalaborwa
Vaal
Orange
10° 0° 10° 20° 30° 40° 50°
30° 20° 10° 0° 10° 20° 30°
Southern limits of Muslim influence, about 900
GHANA State or Empire
Major trade route
Bantu migrations
Cataract (rapids)
Cattle
Ceramics
Copper
Foodstuffs
Glass
Gold
Ivory
Salt
Slaves

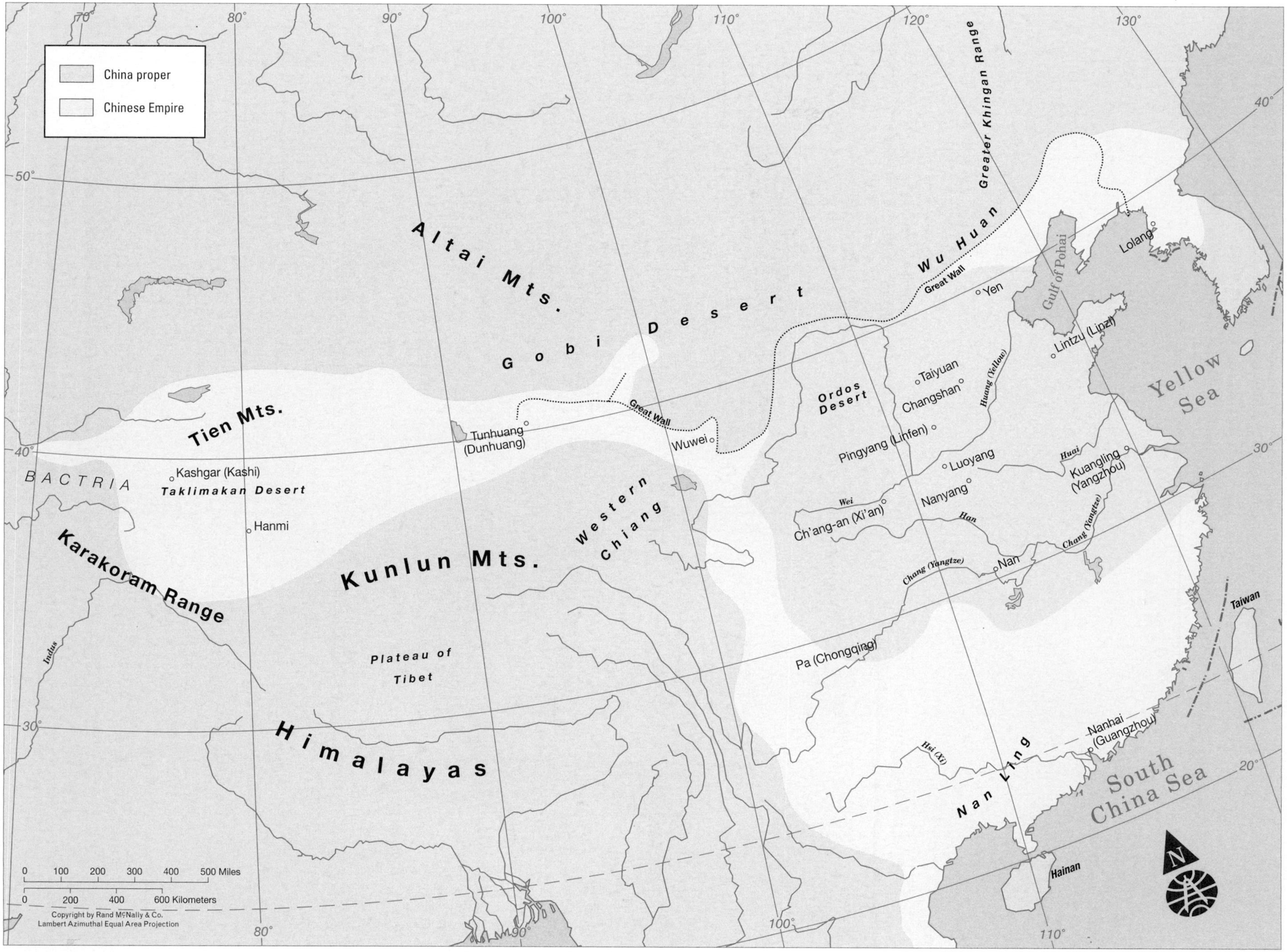
China proper
Chinese Empire
Altai Mts.
Gobi Desert
Tien Mts.
BACTRIA
Kashgar (Kashi)
Taklimakan Desert
Hanmi
Karakoram Range
Kunlun Mts.
Western Chiang
Plateau of Tibet
Himalayas
Indus
Tunhuang (Dunhuang)
Great Wall
Wuwei
Wu Huan
Greater Khingan Range
Yen
Gulf of Pohai
Lolang
Lintzu (Linzi)
Ordos Desert
Taiyuan
Changshan
Huang (Yellow)
Pingyang (Linfen)
Luoyang
Wei
Ch'ang-an (Xi'an)
Nanyang
Han
Huai
Kuangling (Yangzhou)
Chang (Yangtze)
Nan
Pa (Chongqing)
Yellow Sea
Taiwan
Hsi (Xi)
Nan Ling
Nanhai (Guangzhou)
South China Sea
Hainan
0 100 200 300 400 500 Miles
0 200 400 600 Kilometers
Copyright by Rand McNally & Co.
Lambert Azimuthal Equal Area Projection

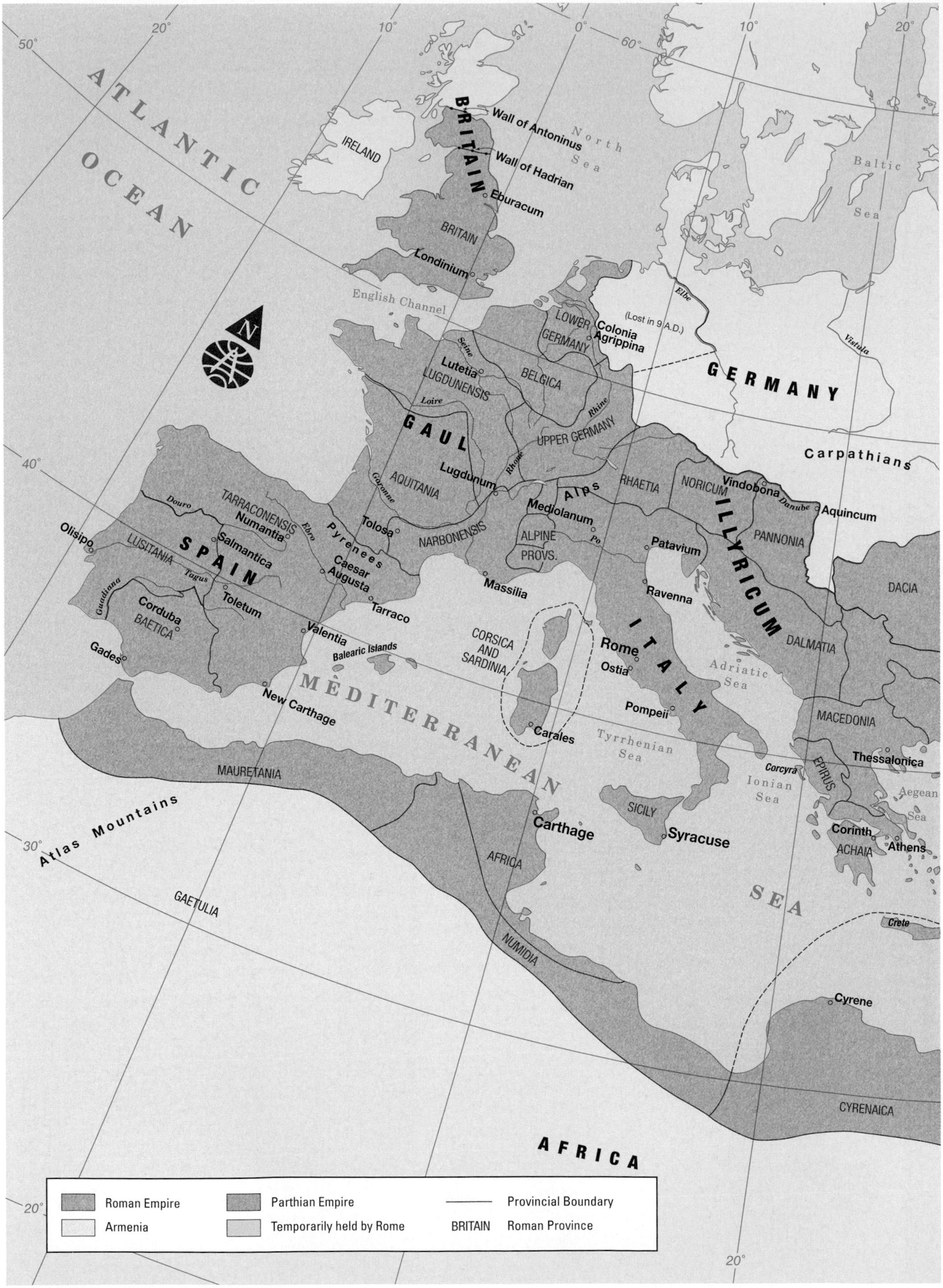
ATLANTIC OCEAN
IRELAND
BRITAIN
Wall of Antoninus
Wall of Hadrian
Eburacum
Londinium
North Sea
Baltic Sea
English Channel
LOWER GERMANY
Colonia Agrippina
(Lost in 9 A.D.)
Elbe
Vistula
GERMANY
Seine
Lutetia
LUGDUNENSIS
BELGICA
Loire
Rhine
GAUL
UPPER GERMANY
Carpathians
Lugdunum
Rhone
AQUITANIA
Garonne
Alps
RHAETIA
NORICUM
Vindobona
Danube
Aquincum
ILLYRICUM
PANNONIA
Douro
TARRACONENSIS
Numantia
Ebro
Pyrenees
Tolosa
NARBONENSIS
Mediolanum
Po
ALPINE PROVS.
Patavium
Olisipo
LUSITANIA
SPAIN
Salmantica
Caesar Augusta
Tagus
Toletum
Tarraco
Massilia
Ravenna
DACIA
Guadiana
Corduba
BAETICA
Gades
Valentia
Balearic Islands
CORSICA AND SARDINIA
Rome
Ostia
ITALY
DALMATIA
Adriatic Sea
MEDITERRANEAN
New Carthage
Pompeii
Carales
Tyrrhenian Sea
MACEDONIA
Thessalonica
Corcyra
EPIRUS
Ionian Sea
Aegean Sea
MAURETANIA
SICILY
Syracuse
Carthage
Corinth
ACHAIA
Athens
Atlas Mountains
AFRICA
GAETULIA
SEA
Crete
NUMIDIA
Cyrene
CYRENAICA
AFRICA
Roman Empire
Armenia
Parthian Empire
Temporarily held by Rome
Provincial Boundary
BRITAIN Roman Province
50°
40°
30°
20°
10°
0°
60°

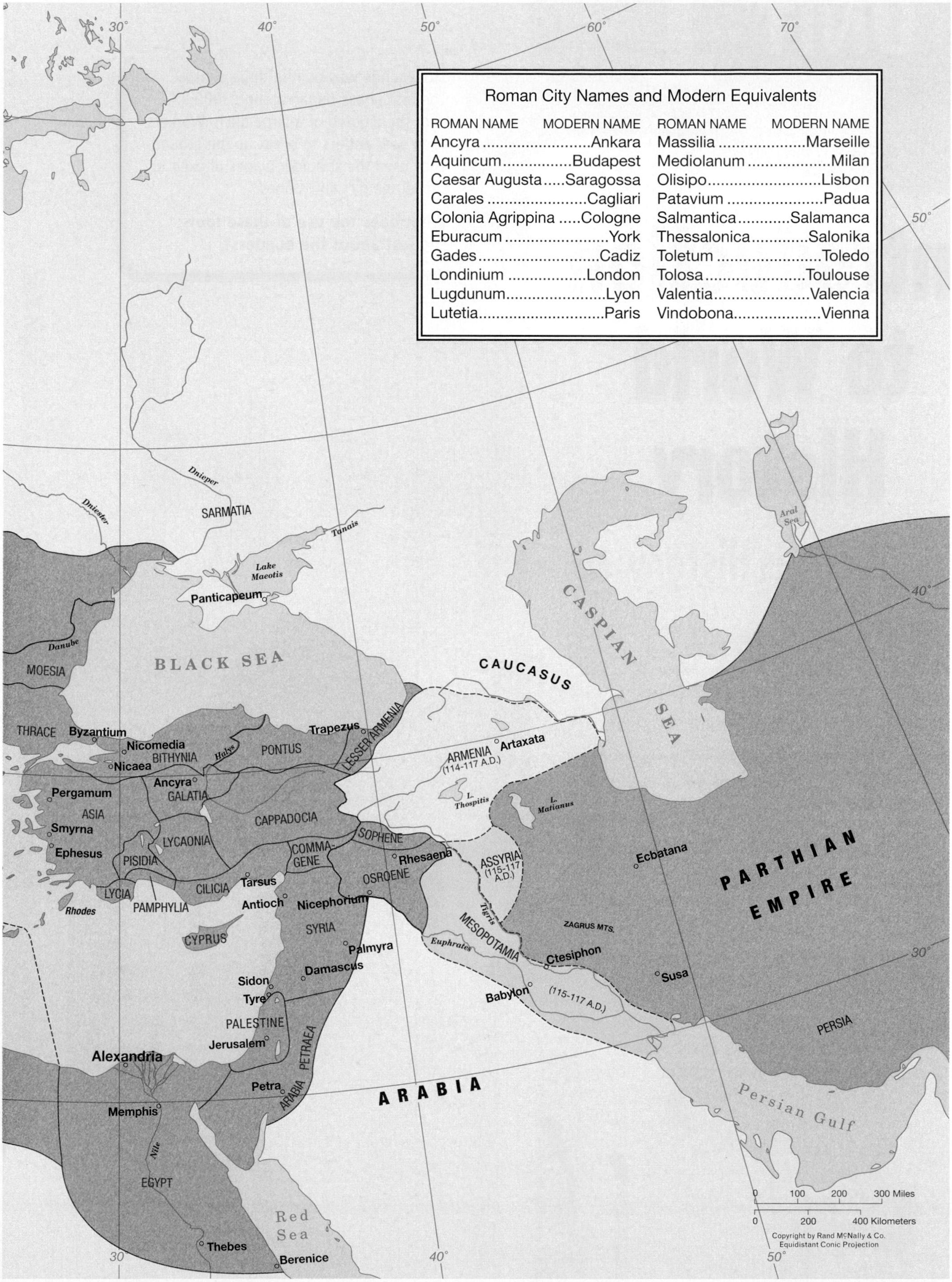

Roman City Names and Modern Equivalents

ROMAN NAME	MODERN NAME	ROMAN NAME	MODERN NAME
Ancyra	Ankara	Massilia	Marseille
Aquincum	Budapest	Mediolanum	Milan
Caesar Augusta	Saragossa	Olisipo	Lisbon
Carales	Cagliari	Patavium	Padua
Colonia Agrippina	Cologne	Salmantica	Salamanca
Eburacum	York	Thessalonica	Salonika
Gades	Cadiz	Toletum	Toledo
Londinium	London	Tolosa	Toulouse
Lugdunum	Lyon	Valentia	Valencia
Lutetia	Paris	Vindobona	Vienna

UNIT 1

Introduction to World History

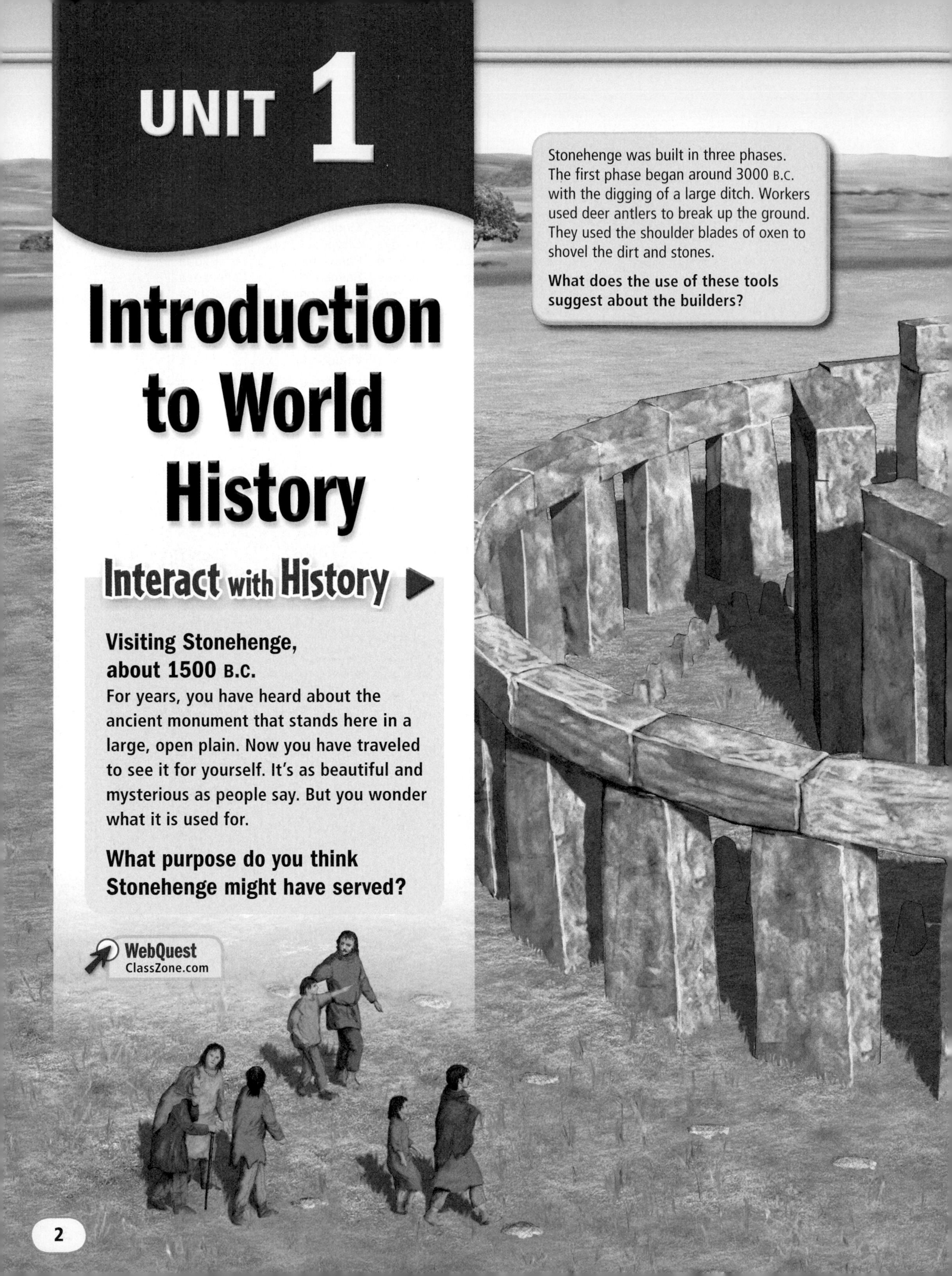

Interact with History

Visiting Stonehenge, about 1500 B.C.

For years, you have heard about the ancient monument that stands here in a large, open plain. Now you have traveled to see it for yourself. It's as beautiful and mysterious as people say. But you wonder what it is used for.

What purpose do you think Stonehenge might have served?

Stonehenge was built in three phases. The first phase began around 3000 B.C. with the digging of a large ditch. Workers used deer antlers to break up the ground. They used the shoulder blades of oxen to shovel the dirt and stones.

What does the use of these tools suggest about the builders?

WebQuest
ClassZone.com

Some of the stones line up with the rising and setting sun. Many people believe that Stonehenge was used to serve as a calendar or to predict eclipses of the moon.

Why would ancient societies want to use a calendar to divide time into days, months, and seasons?

The outer ring of stones was built during the third phase, around 2500 B.C. Some of the stones weighed as much as 50 tons. For years, people believed that only giants could have built Stonehenge.

What conclusions can you draw about what Stonehenge meant to the people who built it?

Chapter 1

The Tools of History

Before You Read: Knowledge Rating

Recognizing what you already know about each of these terms can help you understand the chapter.

hominid   artifact   fossil

In your notebook, rate how well you know each term.

3 = I know what this word means.
2 = I've seen this word before, but I don't know what it means.
1 = I've never seen this word before.

Define each term in your notebook as you read.

Big Ideas About the Tools of History

Science and Technology New scientific discoveries change human understanding of the world.

Geographers look for new ways to help us understand our place in the world. Archaeologists make discoveries that tell us about our earliest ancestors. Their findings answer questions about the past and provide insight into our lives today.

Integrated Technology

eEdition
- Interactive Maps
- Interactive Visuals
- Starting with a Story

INTERNET RESOURCES
Go to **ClassZone.com** for
- WebQuest
- Homework Helper
- Research Links
- Internet Activities
- Quizzes
- Maps
- Test Practice
- Current Events

German scientist Alfred Wegener proposed the continental drift theory in 1912. He claimed that more than 200 million years ago Earth was a single mass of land called Pangaea, meaning "all Earth." Eventually, the mass split apart, and its pieces have been moving ever since. You'll learn how this movement has affected Earth and its people in Chapter 1.

WORLD

5,000,000 B.C.

4.5 million B.C.
First hominids appear.
◀ (footprint of a hominid)

2.5 million B.C.
Paleolithic Age begins.
◀ (Paleolithic hand ax)

1,000,000 B.C.

1.6 million B.C.
Homo erectus appears.

Continental Drift Theory

INTERACTIVE

200 million years ago
Earth was a single mass of land surrounded by water.

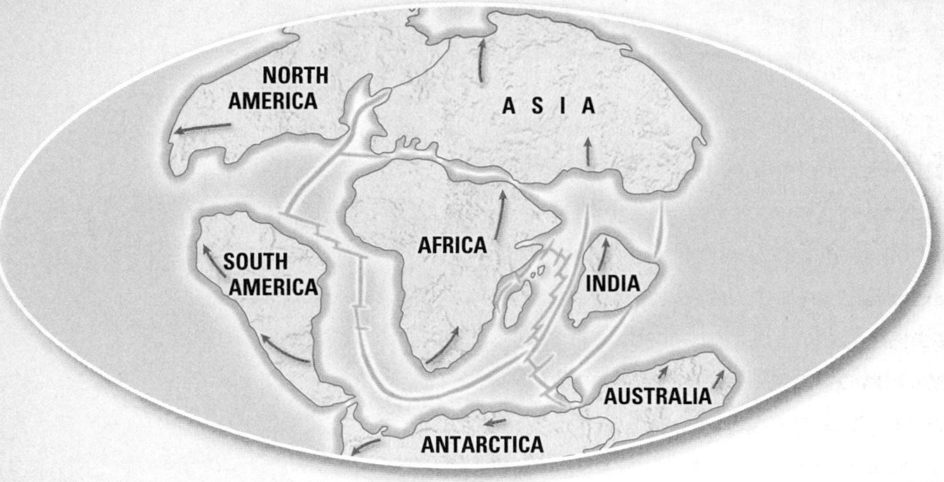

65 million years ago
The mass split apart, and the parts moved in different directions.

Today
The continents continue to drift apart.

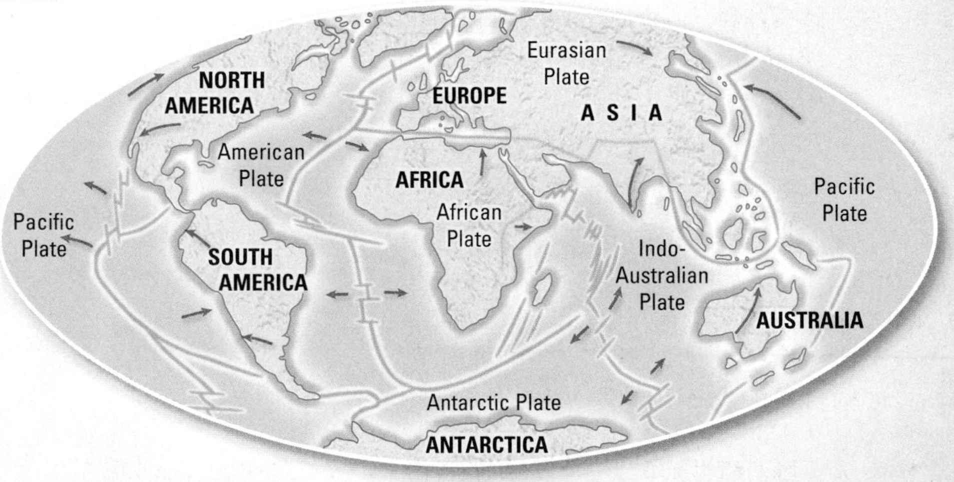

500,000 B.C. — 100,000 B.C. — 5000 B.C.

200,000 B.C.
Neanderthals appear.

8000 B.C.
Neolithic Age begins.
◀ (Neolithic clay mask)

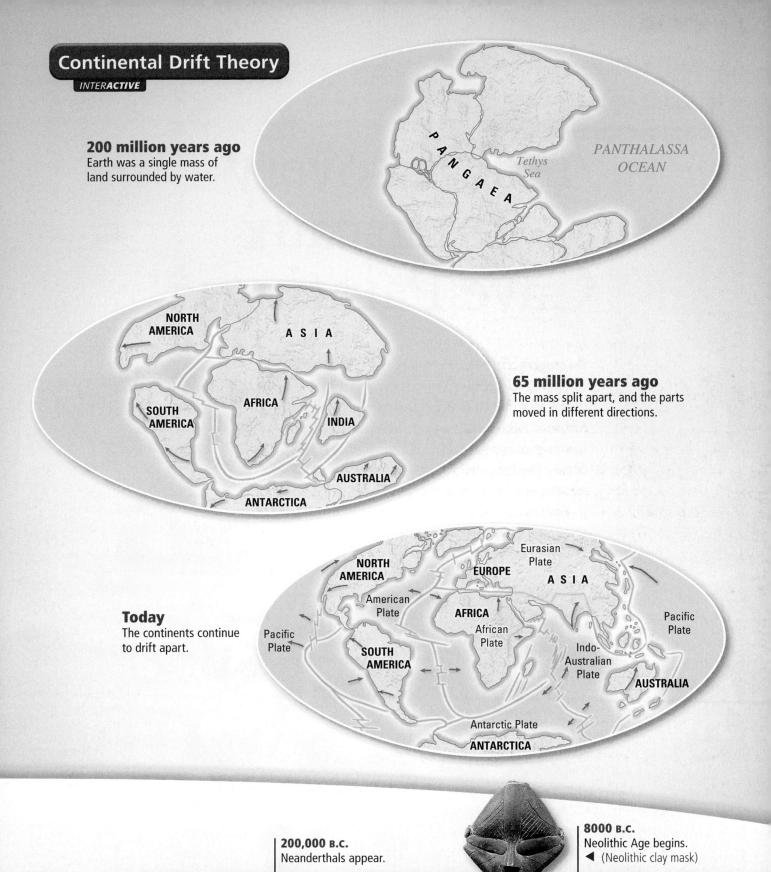

40,000 B.C.
Cro-Magnons appear.
◀ (Cro-Magnon skull)

Starting with a Story

The Discovery of the Lascaux Cave Paintings

Background: On September 12, 1940, four teenage boys explored a cave in the French countryside. It looked as if no one else had been there for years. But the walls were covered with strange paintings of animals in vivid colors of red, yellow, and brown. The boys had stumbled across a cave filled with masterpieces by prehistoric artists.

Now step inside the Lascaux (la•SKOH) Cave and discover the paintings with the teenage explorers.

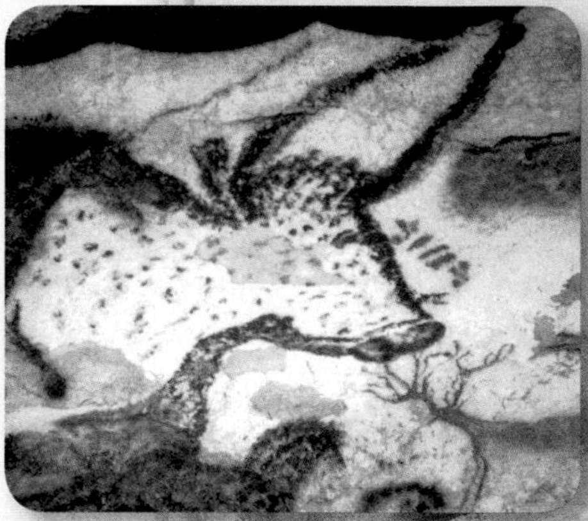

Painting in the Lascaux Cave ▶

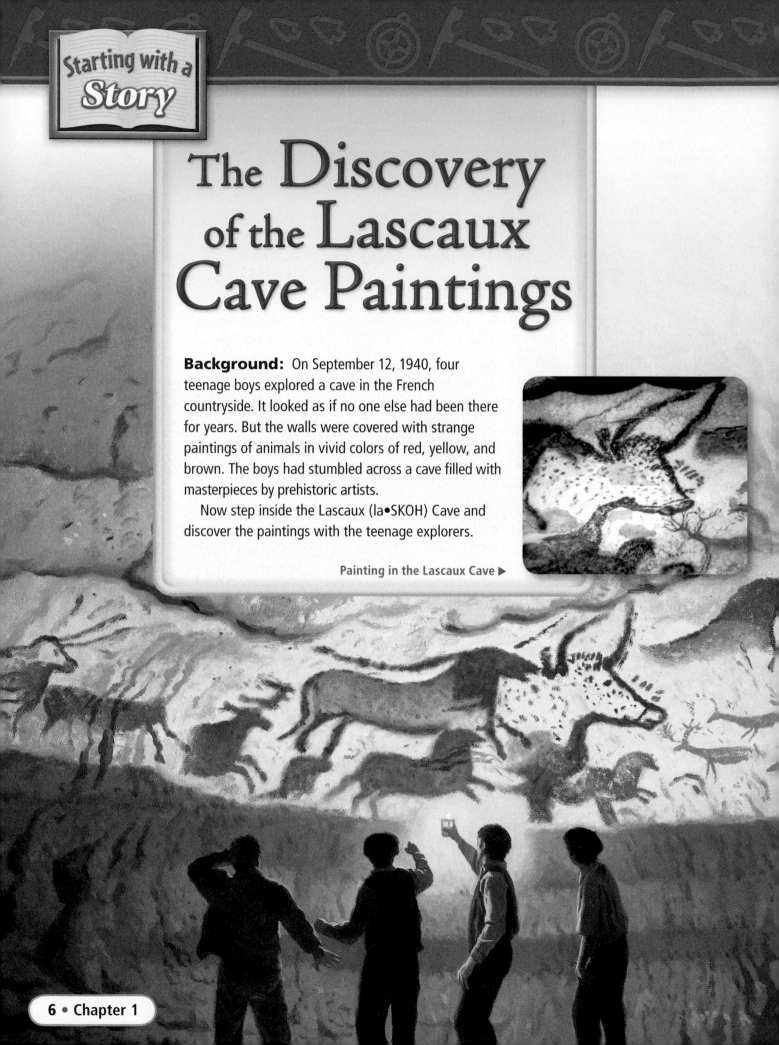

On September 8, Marcel went on a treasure hunt. For years, people had talked about a secret underground passage in the countryside around their French village. They said that the passage led to hidden treasure. The French teenager thought he had found it when he discovered the opening to a long vertical shaft. Four days later, on September 12, Marcel and three of his friends returned to explore it.

This time, Marcel brought an oil lamp to light the way. One after the other, the boys wriggled down the long passageway. Finally, they tumbled into a huge cavern, and Marcel held up the lamp. By its flickering light, they noticed a narrow, high passage. The friends entered the passage, and Marcel shone the light on its walls. What the French teenagers saw amazed them.

Herds of horses, oxen, and deer stampeded across the curving cave wall. The colorful animals seemed to leap off the walls. Excitedly, the teenagers ran through the cave and found room after room of paintings. They had found the real treasure of Lascaux.

At first the four teenagers promised to keep their great discovery a secret. But this secret was too hard to keep. They told their teacher, who contacted an expert. The expert said that the boys were probably the first modern people to lay eyes on this art. The paintings had been sealed in the Lascaux Cave for at least 17,000 years.

The cave walls are covered with more than 1,500 pictures of animals. Many of the animals include those that the early people of Lascaux hunted. Historians believe that the people told stories about the animals and sang as the artists painted them. But these oral stories are lost forever.

What do these cave paintings tell you about the people who painted them?

Reading & Writing

1. **READING: Speaker** This story is told by a third-person narrator. How would the story be different if Marcel or one of his friends told it?
2. **WRITING: Explanation** Research to find out what has happened to the Lascaux Cave, and write a paragraph explaining your findings.

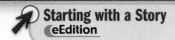

Lesson 1

MAIN IDEAS

1. **Geography** Continents, landforms, and bodies of water shape our planet.
2. **Geography** Geographers organize information into five themes.
3. **Geography** Where people live has an impact on how they live.

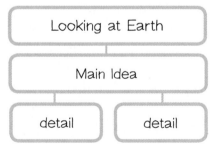

▲ **Earth** This "blue marble" image of Earth was put together using a collection of satellite pictures taken in 2001. It is the most detailed true-color image ever produced of Earth.

TAKING NOTES

Reading Skill: Summarizing

When you summarize, you supply only main ideas and important details. Identify the main ideas and important details in each section of Lesson 1. Then put them in your own words and record them in a diagram like the one below.

Looking at Earth

Main Idea

detail | detail

Skillbuilder Handbook, page R3

Words to Know

Understanding the following words will help you read this lesson:

theme topics of discussion (page 11)
*The **themes** students addressed in their first class were all related to geography.*

precise very definite or exact (page 11)
*She used a special map to identify the **precise** location of the valley.*

interaction when two or more things affect each other (page 11)
*Clothing styles sometimes reflect the **interaction** between humans and their environment.*

influence to have an effect or impact on something (page 12)
*The climate **influenced** the types of shelters people built.*

The World's Geography

TERMS & NAMES
geography
continent
landform
climate
vegetation

Build on What You Know How would you describe your town? Is the land flat or hilly? Does a river run nearby? Who lives in your town? When you answer these questions, you describe your town's geography. Your town is part of the world's geography.

Looking at Earth

1 ESSENTIAL QUESTION What do geographers study?

Scientists study the land and water that cover Earth. They also study how people live on Earth. The study of Earth and its people is called **geography**.

Continents Earth is divided into seven large landmasses called **continents**. You can see the continents on the map below. From largest to smallest, the continents are Asia, Africa, North America, South America, Antarctica, Europe, and Australia.

Continents of the World

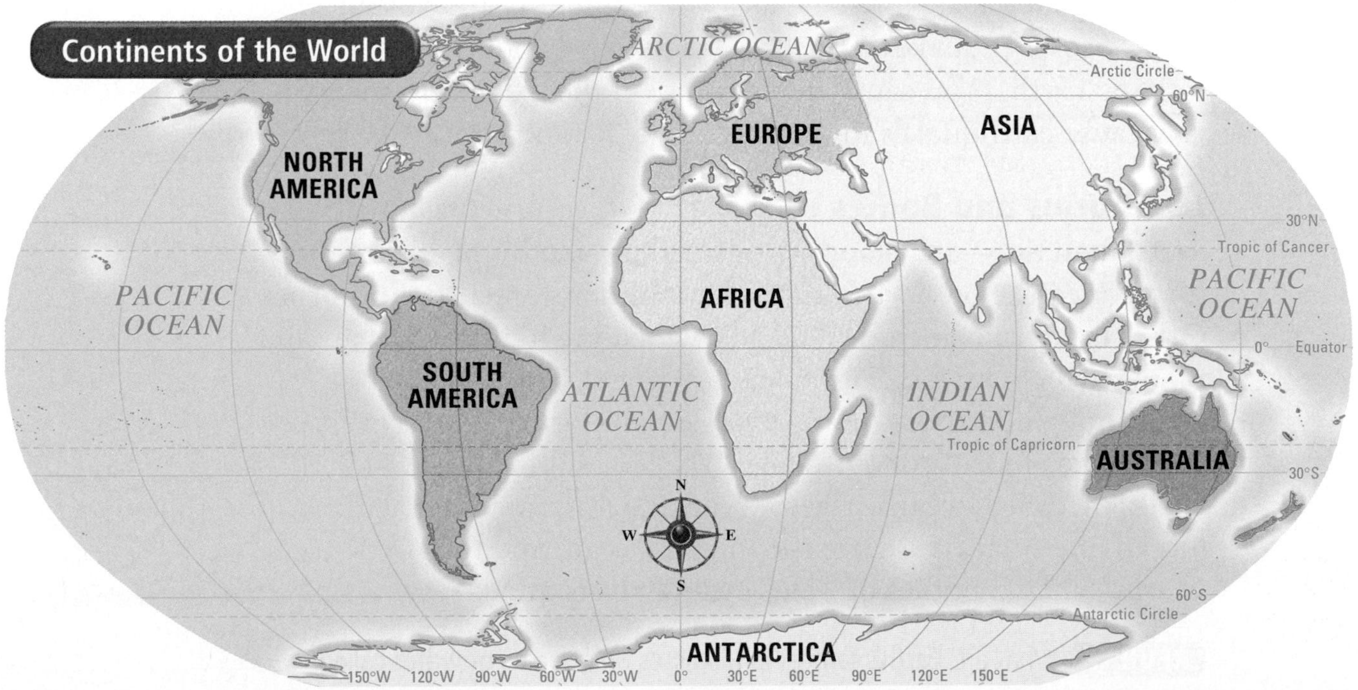

Geography Handbook

Geography

Earthquakes

At about 5:12 A.M. on April 18, 1906, the ground shook along the west coast of the United States. The earthquake was centered around San Francisco and destroyed much of the city, as shown in the photograph on the upper right.

The San Francisco earthquake was caused by plates sliding along a fault line, or break in Earth's crust. The diagram on the lower right shows their movement.

1. Plate A slides in one direction.
2. Plate B slides in the opposite direction.
3. The plates move past each other at the fault line, causing an earthquake.

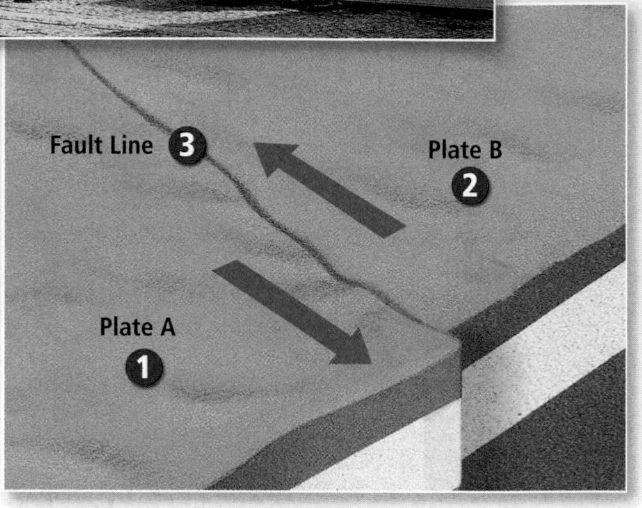

GEOGRAPHY SKILLBUILDER
INTERPRETING VISUALS Human-Environment Interaction Based on the photograph above, what are some of the effects of earthquakes?

Shifting Plates Scientists believe that the continents lie on large moving plates. Plate movements form mountains and volcanoes and cause earthquakes. The movements slowly but continually reshape Earth. (You can learn more about the plate movements that cause earthquakes in the Geography feature above.)

Landforms and Bodies of Water Two continents—Australia and Antarctica—are islands. An island is a **landform**, or naturally formed feature on Earth's surface. Mountains are also landforms. Other landforms include plateaus, which are high, flat areas, and plains, which are large, level areas of grassland.

Although Earth has many kinds of landforms, water covers about three-fourths of our planet. The largest bodies of water on Earth are called oceans. The four major oceans are the Pacific Ocean, the Atlantic Ocean, the Indian Ocean, and the Arctic Ocean. Smaller bodies of water include rivers and lakes.

REVIEW What are Earth's largest landmasses and bodies of water called?

Themes of Geography

2 ESSENTIAL QUESTION What are the five themes of geography?

Geographers use five themes of geography to describe Earth. The five themes help us understand our world and how we fit into it.

- **Location** The geographic question, Where is it? refers to location. Location can identify a precise spot or tell where one place is in relation to another.
- **Place** The question, What is it like? refers to place. Place includes physical characteristics as well as human ones, like language, religion, and politics.
- **Region** The question, How are places similar or different? refers to region. Region compares physical and human characteristics.
- **Movement** The question, How do people, goods, and ideas move from one location to another? refers to movement.
- **Human-Environment Interaction** The question, How do people relate to the physical world? refers to human-environment interaction. People learn to use and change what the environment offers them.

REVIEW Which two geographic themes are most concerned with people?

How Environment Affects People

3 ESSENTIAL QUESTION How does climate affect people's lives?

You probably wear a coat in cold weather and dress in light clothing in warmer weather. Of course, different people may develop different ways of adapting to the same area. But your environment—particularly its climate—has a big impact on the way you live.

Connect to Today

Hurricanes Natural disasters have a great impact on people and their homes. This photograph shows people fleeing during a 1998 hurricane in Florida. ▼

Climate Weather refers to the temperature and conditions in a particular place at a particular time. **Climate**, on the other hand, describes the weather conditions in a place over a long period of time. Climate can influence where people live. For example, the harsh conditions of a cold, wet climate may prevent people from settling in that region.

Climate also has a big impact on the type of **vegetation**, or plant life, that grows in a location. For instance, thick jungle vegetation grows well in a tropical climate with heavy rainfall, while crops may be difficult to grow in a hot, dry climate.

REVIEW How does environment affect people?

Lesson Summary

- Earth's largest landmasses, called continents, are surrounded by oceans.
- The five themes of geography help us explain our place in the world.
- Climate can affect how and where people live.

Why It Matters Now . . .

Geography helps us learn more about our neighbors and the ways we affect the world we share.

1 Lesson Review

Homework Helper
ClassZone.com

Terms & Names

1. Explain the importance of

geography landform vegetation
continent climate

Using Your Notes

Summarizing Use your completed diagram to answer the following question:

2. What are Earth's main geographic features?

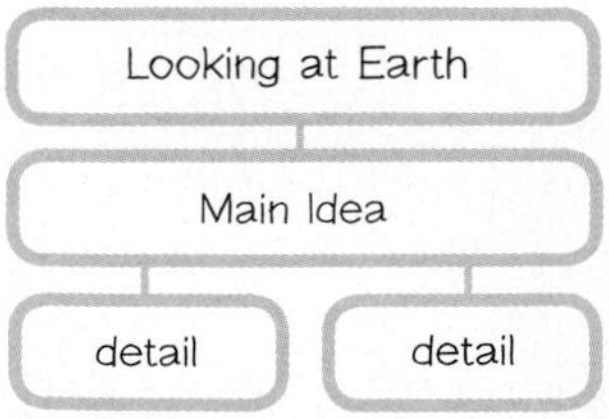

Main Ideas

3. Name three examples of landforms and three examples of bodies of water.

4. How do the five themes of geography help geographers?

5. How does the climate where you live affect your life?

Critical Thinking

6. Understanding Cause and Effect What might be the result if the climate of a region suddenly became much colder?

7. Making Inferences Since more people live on Asia than on any other continent, what can you infer about Asia's environment?

Activity

Planning a Mural Work with a group of classmates to plan a mural that represents the physical features, climate, and vegetation in your town.

Activity Extend Lesson 1

Make a Geography Themes Poster

Goal: To understand that the five themes of geography relate to people's everyday lives

Materials & Supplies
- poster board
- magazines
- scissors
- tape or glue
- pen or pencil

Prepare

1. Reread "The Five Themes of Geography" on page 11.
2. Think about pictures that would illustrate each theme's question.

Do the Activity

1. Get together with a group of four other classmates. Each member should choose a different geography theme.
2. Look through magazines and cut out a picture that illustrates your theme. Note that the group member who selects region will need to find and compare two pictures to illustrate the theme.
3. After all members of the group have found their pictures, arrange all five illustrations on a poster.
4. Label each picture with its theme. Write a caption explaining how the picture answers the theme's question.

Follow-Up

1. What does the picture illustrating movement show?
2. What similarities and differences do the pictures illustrating region show?

Extension

Making a Brochure Use the five themes of geography to make a brochure about your community. Find or draw pictures that illustrate the themes.

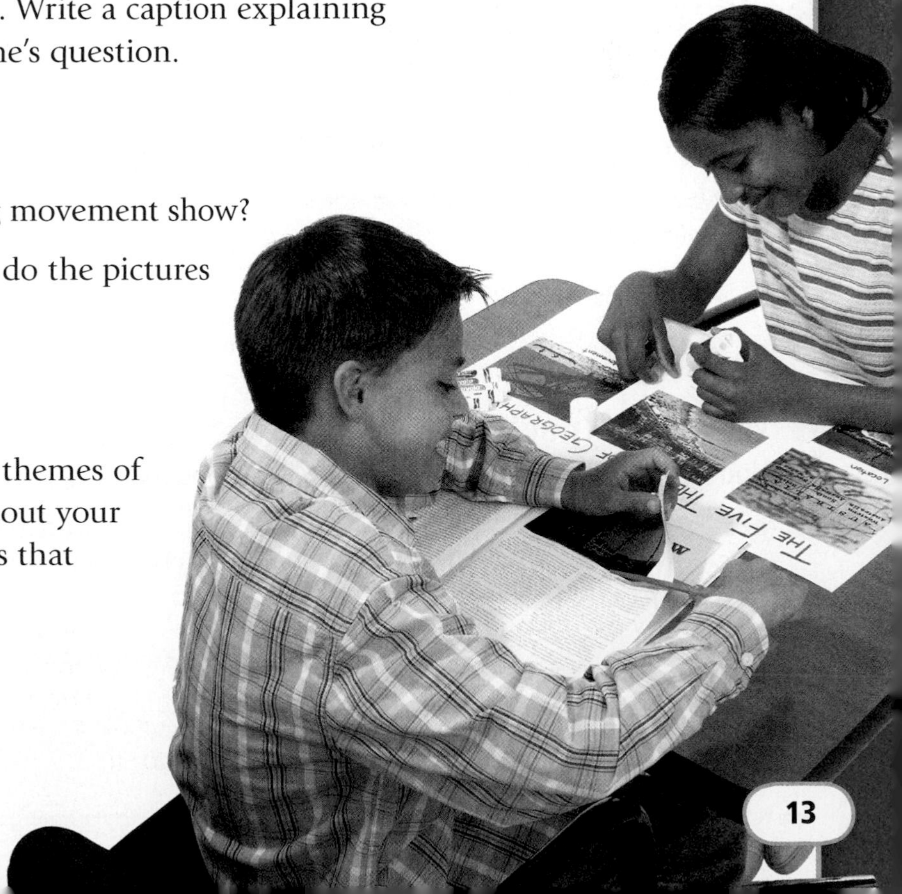

Lesson 2

MAIN IDEAS

1. **Geography** Geographers use maps and globes to measure and describe Earth.
2. **Geography** We use maps to see natural and human-made features and to understand patterns.
3. **Geography** Maps have changed over time to reflect people's increasing understanding of the world.

▲ **Compass** Early navigators used compasses, like this early Chinese one, to figure out where they were. Invented by the Chinese, the compass opened up the world to exploration and helped geographers make more accurate maps.

TAKING NOTES

Reading Skill: Comparing and Contrasting

When you compare and contrast two things, you look for ways in which they are similar and different. In Lesson 2, compare maps and globes, two types of maps, and two periods of mapmaking. Record their similarities and differences in a Venn diagram like the one below.

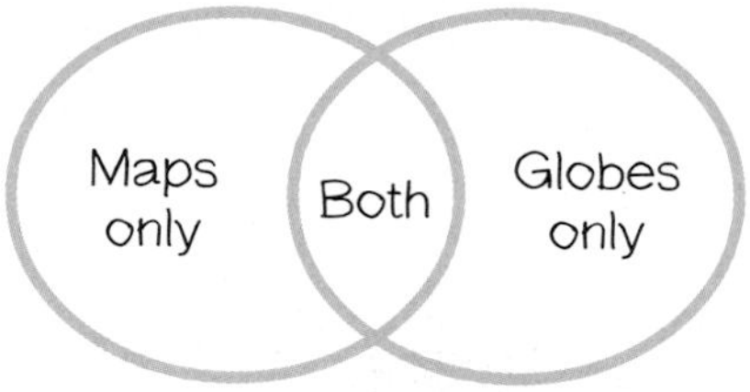

Skillbuilder Handbook, page R4

Words to Know

Understanding the following words will help you read this lesson:

prefer to like better (page 15)

*The geographer said she would **prefer** to see the site herself.*

symbol a thing that stands for something else (page 16)

*They were unable to identify the meaning or purpose of the **symbols**.*

indicate show or point out (page 16)

*On the map, arrows were used to **indicate** the direction in which the water currents flowed.*

How Maps Help Us Study History

TERMS & NAMES
longitude
latitude
hemisphere
political map
physical map
thematic map

Build on What You Know You probably use maps when you visit the mall, get on a bus, or take a trip with your family. The skills you use to read those maps can be applied to read any map.

The Geographer's Tools

1 ESSENTIAL QUESTION What are the geographer's tools?

Geographers use both globes and maps to represent Earth. Both tools have advantages and disadvantages.

Globes One advantage of a globe is that it looks more like Earth, since both are round. A globe shows the viewer exactly how continents and oceans appear on Earth's curved surface. A globe also shows the true shapes, locations, and relative sizes of Earth's landforms and bodies of water.

Maps A map, on the other hand, is a flat representation of Earth's surface. It can be drawn to any size. No flat map can ever be as accurate as a globe. That is because Earth's surface is distorted somewhat when it is flattened to create a map. In other words, a map can alter how Earth really looks. But most people prefer to use maps because they do have several advantages. For one thing, a map lets you measure distances much more easily. For another, a map lets you see the world at a glance. Most important, it's much easier to carry a map because you can fold it up!

Globes One disadvantage of using a globe is that you can view only half of Earth at a time. This globe shows parts of North and South America. ▼

Annual Rainfall in Australia

1 Title
2 Compass rose
3 Symbols
4 Legend
5 Lines of longitude
6 Lines of latitude
7 Scale
8 Labels
9 Colors

INDIAN OCEAN

Tropic of Capricorn

3
★ National capital
• Other city

4 Annual Rainfall in Inches

Over 40 (100 cm)
20–40 (50–100 cm)
10–20 (25–50 cm)
Under 10 (25 cm)

AUSTRALIA

Perth
Brisbane
Adelaide
Sydney
Canberra★
Melbourne

Coral Sea
Tasmania

0 500 1000 miles
0 500 1000 kilometers

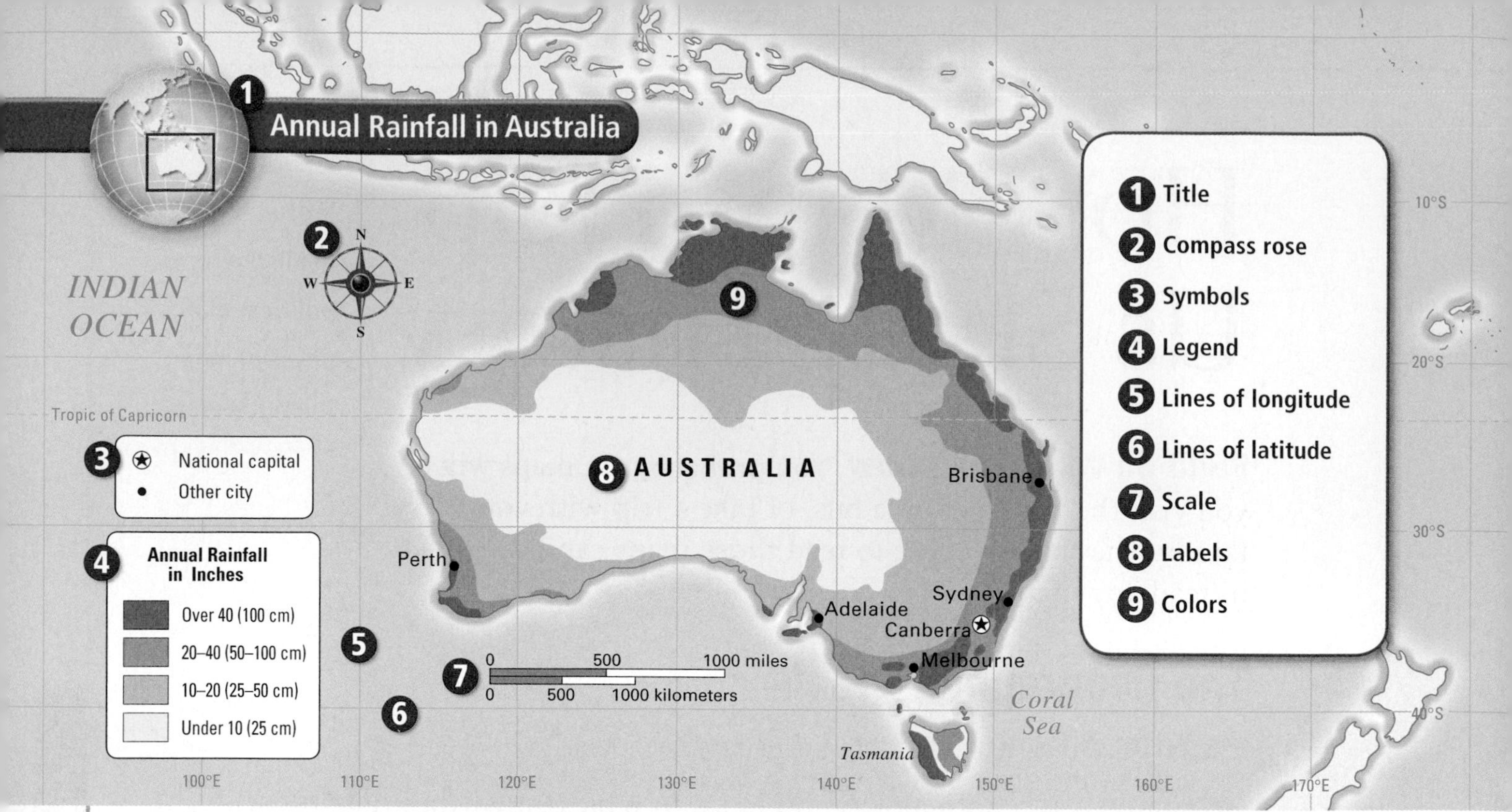

Reading a Map Most maps have nine features, as shown in the map above. These features, described below, help you read and understand maps.

- **Title** The title tells the subject of the map and gives you an idea of what information is shown.
- **Compass rose** The compass rose shows directions: north, south, east, and west.
- **Symbols** Symbols represent such items as capital cities and natural resources. The map legend explains what the symbols mean.
- **Legend** The legend, or key, lists and explains the symbols and colors used on the map.
- **Lines of longitude** These are imaginary lines that measure distances east and west of the prime meridian.
- **Lines of latitude** These are imaginary lines that measure distances north and south of the equator.
- **Scale** A scale can be used to figure out the distance between two locations on a map.
- **Labels** Labels indicate the names of cities, landforms, and bodies of water.
- **Colors** Colors represent a variety of information on a map. The map legend explains what the colors mean.

Map Projections As you have already learned, flat maps distort Earth's surface. Mapmakers try to control this distortion by using different projections. A projection is a way of showing the curved surface of Earth on a flat map. Compare the three common projections shown below.

Mercator Projection The Mercator (muhr•KAY•tuhr) projection shows most of the continents as they look on a globe. However, the projection stretches out the lands near the north and south poles. For example, the island of Greenland is actually one-eighth the size of South America.

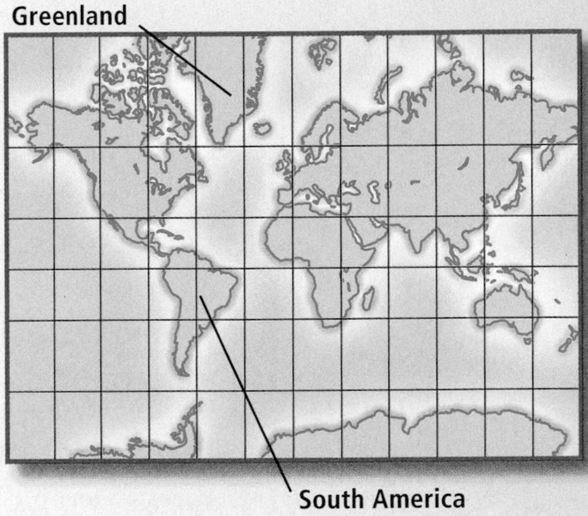

Homolosine Projection The homolosine (hoh•MAHL•uh•SYN) projection divides the oceans. This projection fairly accurately shows the sizes of landmasses. But distances on the map are not correct.

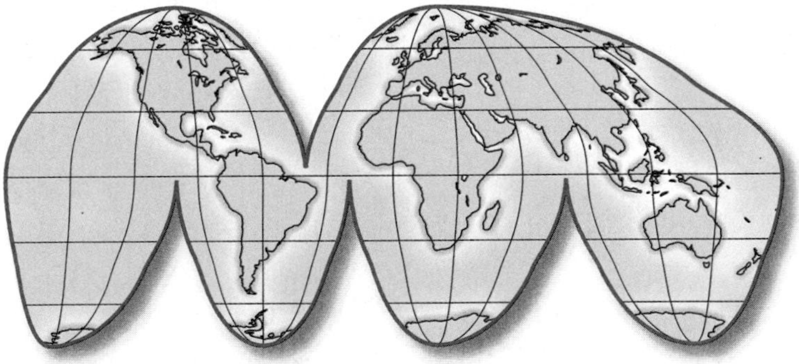

Robinson Projection The Robinson projection is often used in textbooks. It shows all of Earth with nearly the true sizes and shapes of the continents and oceans. However, the shapes of the landforms near the poles appear flat.

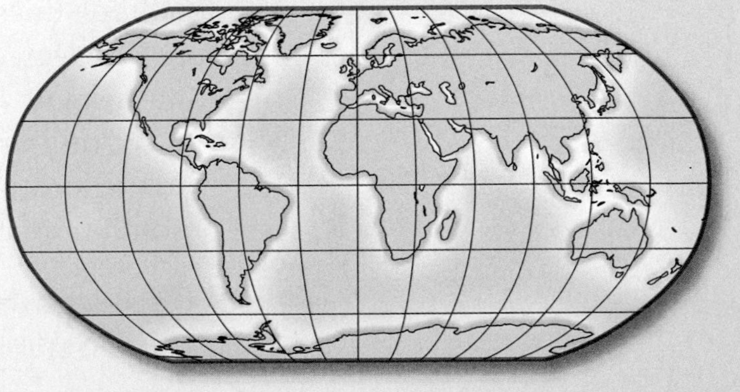

Geography Handbook

The Geographic Grid

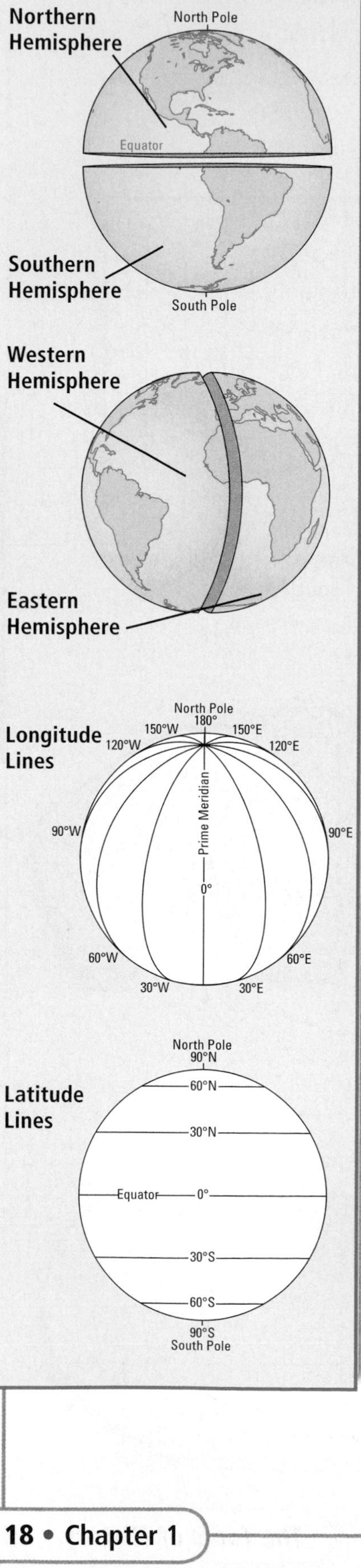

Hemispheres To study Earth, geographers divide the globe into equal halves. Each half is called a **hemisphere**. An imaginary line called the equator divides the globe into north and south halves. The half of Earth north of the equator is called the Northern Hemisphere. The half south of the equator is called the Southern Hemisphere.

Geographers use another imaginary line to divide Earth east from west. This line is called the prime meridian. The half of Earth west of the prime meridian is called the Western Hemisphere. The half east of the prime meridian is called the Eastern Hemisphere. As you can see in the diagram on the left, the United States is located in the northern and western hemispheres.

The Geographic Grid The diagram also shows two globes marked with lines of latitude and longitude. As you have already learned, latitude lines lie to the north and south of the equator. Longitude lines go around Earth over the poles. These lines run east and west of the prime meridian.

Geographers use a grid system to find the point where a latitude line and a longitude line cross. This point identifies an absolute location—the exact place on Earth where a city or other geographic feature can be found. Remember that location is one of the themes geographers use to describe Earth.

Absolute location is expressed using the coordinates, or set of numbers, of the latitude and longitude lines. These coordinates are measured in degrees. Every place on Earth has only one absolute location. For example, as you can see on the map on the following page, the absolute location of Rio de Janeiro, Brazil, is 23° south latitude, 43° west longitude.

REVIEW How do the latitude and longitude lines on a map help geographers?

Different Maps for Different Purposes

2 ESSENTIAL QUESTION What different maps do we use to see natural and human-made features and to understand patterns?

Different maps help us see different things. The three basic types of maps are political maps, physical maps, and thematic maps. You have probably used all of these different types of maps.

Political Maps **Political maps** show the features people have created, such as cities, states, provinces, territories, and countries. State and country boundaries can also be outlined on these types of maps. A political map of a smaller area, such as a state, often shows county boundaries.

Here are some of the questions the features of a political map, like the one below, might help you answer:

- Where on Earth's surface is this area located?
- What is the size and shape of the area? How might its size or shape affect its people?
- Who are the area's neighbors?
- How populated does the area seem to be?

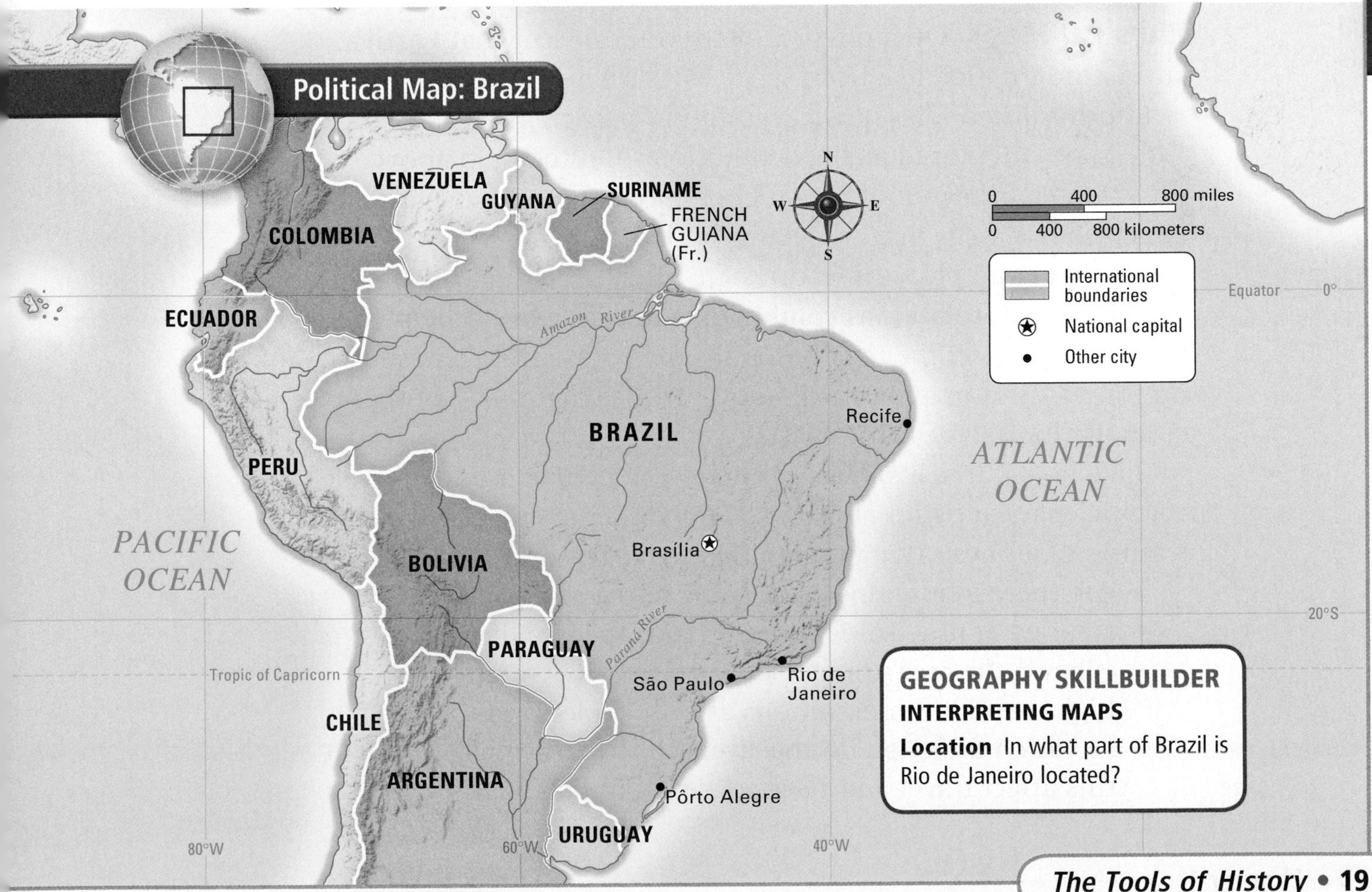

GEOGRAPHY SKILLBUILDER
INTERPRETING MAPS
Location In what part of Brazil is Rio de Janeiro located?

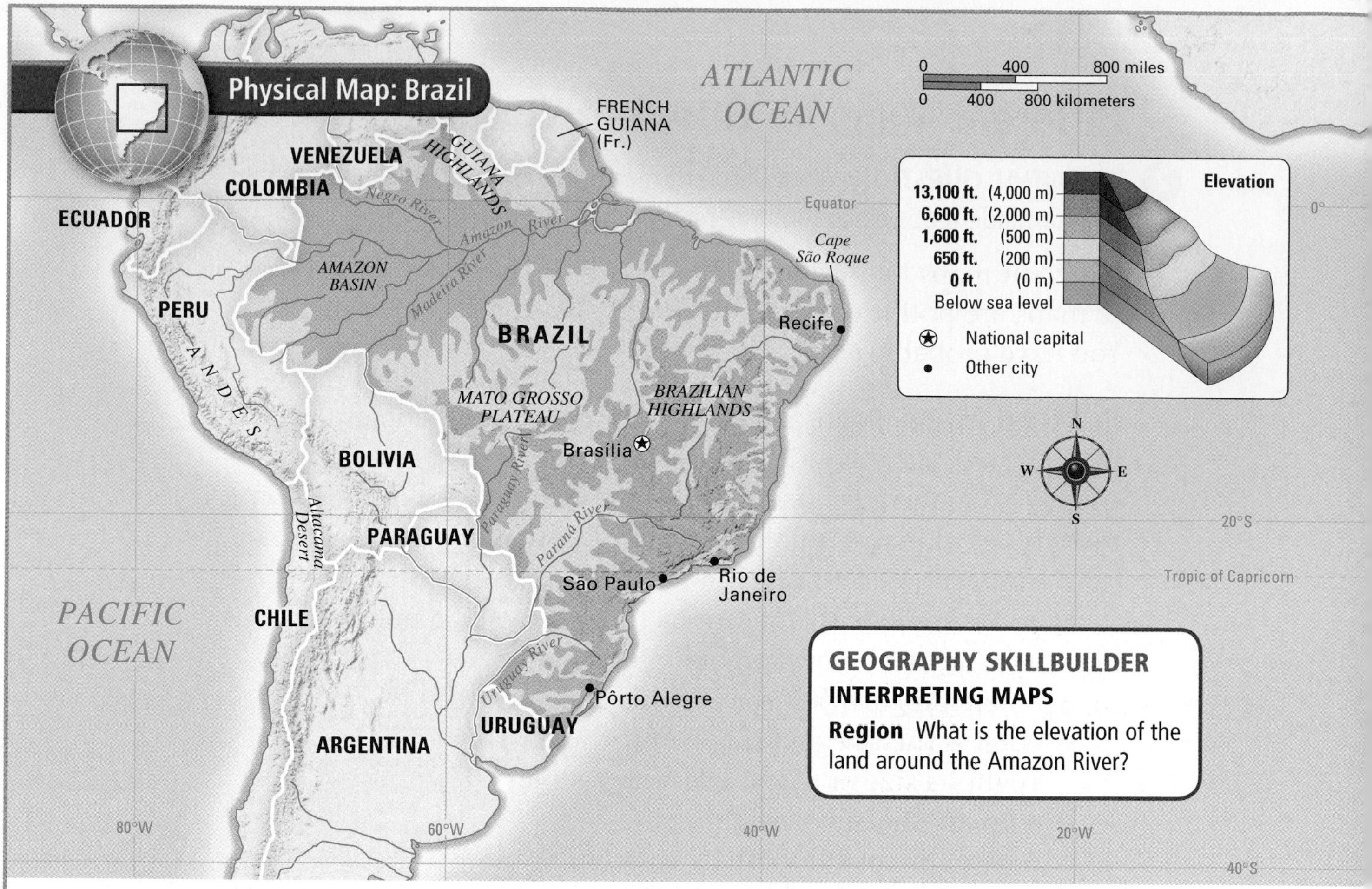

GEOGRAPHY SKILLBUILDER
INTERPRETING MAPS
Region What is the elevation of the land around the Amazon River?

Physical Maps On a physical map, you can see what Earth's surface might look like from space. **Physical maps** show the landforms and bodies of water found in particular areas. Colors are often used to show elevations. On the map above, for example, brown indicates higher, more mountainous areas. Green shows areas that are relatively flat.

Political and physical features are often shown on one map. When this information is combined, you can use it to help you better understand the region. For instance, find the cities shown on the physical map of Brazil above. Notice that many of these cities are located near the coast.

Like political maps, physical maps can help you understand specific characteristics of places. Here are some questions the features of a physical map might help you answer:

- Are there mountains or plateaus in the area?
- Near what physical features do most people live?
- What is the area's range of elevation? How might higher and lower elevations affect people's lives?
- In which direction do the rivers flow? How might this affect travel and transportation in the area?

Thematic Maps A **thematic map** includes certain information about a place or region. For example, the thematic map on this page shows the climates in Brazil.

Thematic maps can use colors, symbols, lines, or dots to help you see patterns. The map's title and legend will help you understand the theme and the information presented. In this textbook, you will find thematic maps on such topics as historical events, vegetation, and population density.

In fact, a thematic map can show just about any kind of information you can imagine. Here are just a few of the questions different thematic maps can help you answer:

- Where in the world do people speak Spanish?
- What are the natural resources of Africa?
- What is the best route for sailing across the Atlantic?
- Where and when did key battles take place during World War II?
- Where were the major trade routes in Asia in ancient times?

Vocabulary Strategy

Thematic and *theme* belong to the same **word family.** Both words refer to a topic.

REVIEW Which type of map might help you find the highest mountain in Brazil?

Geography Handbook

Thematic Map: Climates of Brazil

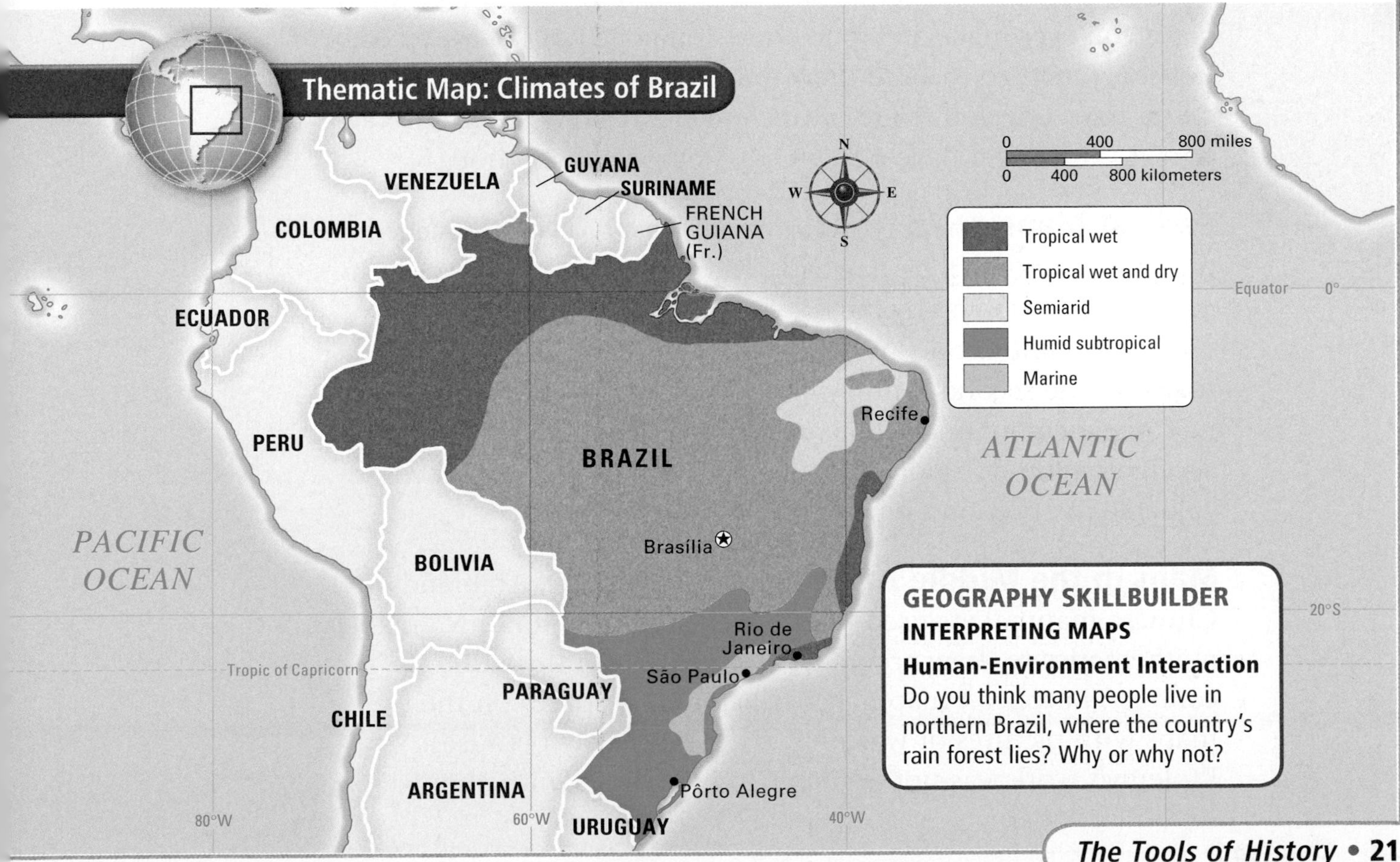

GEOGRAPHY SKILLBUILDER
INTERPRETING MAPS
Human-Environment Interaction
Do you think many people live in northern Brazil, where the country's rain forest lies? Why or why not?

▲ **Map from the Past** This map of North and South America was drawn by European mapmakers in 1570. As you can see, the mapmakers had only a rough idea of what the two continents looked like.

How Maps Change

3 **ESSENTIAL QUESTION** How have maps changed to reflect people's increasing understanding of the world?

Have you ever made a map to show someone how to get to your house? A map you would draw today would probably be much better than one you made in first grade. Maps showing different parts of the world have also greatly improved over time.

Earliest Maps The very earliest maps were probably scratched on the ground or drawn on tree bark. The oldest surviving maps were carved on clay tablets by the Babylonians around 2300 B.C.

The ancient Greeks made great advances in developing maps. In the second century A.D., a Greek astronomer and mathematician named Ptolemy (TAHL•uh•mee) produced an eight-volume work called *Geography.* This work contained valuable instruction on preparing maps.

Maps in the Middle Ages In the Middle Ages, Arab and Chinese mapmakers used their knowledge of astronomy and mathematics to draw accurate maps of parts of the world. By contrast, European mapmakers filled empty spaces on their maps with pictures or warnings. This was partly because Ptolemy's work was not available to Europeans until about 1405.

European maps greatly improved after 1569, when a Flemish mapmaker named Gerhardus Mercator showed the curved surface of Earth on a flat map. His Mercator projection, which you learned about on page 17, helped explorers plot straight routes on maps.

▲ **Ptolemy** Ptolemy's *Geography* remained one of the most important geographical works until 1496, when explorers began to prove some of his statements wrong.

Today's Maps Many modern maps are made with the help of the satellites of the Global Positioning System (GPS). You will learn more about this system in the Connect to Today feature on page 24.

REVIEW What were some of the results as maps improved?

Lesson Summary

- Maps and globes have different advantages as tools used to measure and describe Earth.
- Political, physical, and thematic maps show us different things about the world and our place in it.
- Over time, maps have become more accurate.

Why It Matters Now . . .

We still use maps to find our way around and to learn more about familiar and unfamiliar places.

2 Lesson Review

Homework Helper
ClassZone.com

Terms & Names

1. Explain the importance of

longitude	hemisphere	physical map
latitude	political map	thematic map

Using Your Notes

Comparing and Contrasting Use your completed Venn diagram to answer the following question:

2. How are maps and globes similar?

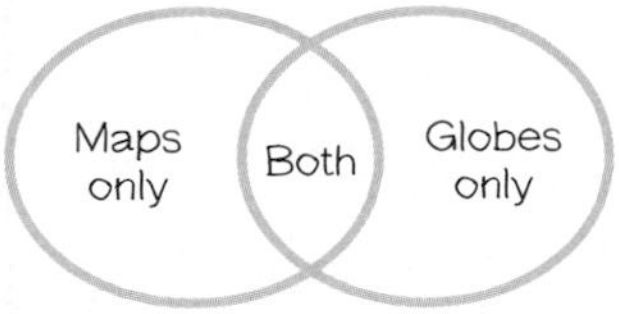

Main Ideas

3. Would you use a map or a globe to see a continent's exact shape? Explain why.

4. Describe the three types of maps.

5. Why were European maps in the Middle Ages so inaccurate?

Critical Thinking

6. Drawing Conclusions Why did European mapmakers in the Middle Ages sometimes leave empty spots on their maps?

7. Making Inferences What impact do you think improved mapmaking had on explorers?

Activity

Making a Map Create a thematic map of your neighborhood or school, showing, for example, populations, buildings, or numbers of people who own pets. Be sure to include a legend to explain any colors or symbols on your map.

Research Links
ClassZone.com

Navigation and the Global Positioning System

Purpose: To learn about Global Positioning System, which is used to determine locations on Earth

Throughout history, people have tried to figure out where they were and how they could find their way to another place. The earliest explorers and sailors navigated by the stars. However, this method wasn't much use on a cloudy night. Today, navigators still look to the sky to find their location. But now they are guided by the orbiting satellites of the Global Positioning System, or GPS. These satellites can pinpoint any spot on Earth in any weather.

Past

The Sextant For several hundred years, sailors used sextants, like the one shown below, to navigate. A sextant is a device that measures the angle between two objects. A navigator used the mirrors on a sextant to sight the horizon and the sun or a star. The angle between the two appeared on the sextant's scale. The navigator in the illustration at the right is using a sextant.

Present

GPS Satellites Twenty-four GPS satellites, such as the one shown here, orbit Earth. Receivers detect their signals and determine location within about 30 feet. GPS was originally developed for the military, but the system can also be used to create maps, track threatened wildlife, and help fire trucks and ambulances respond to an emergency.

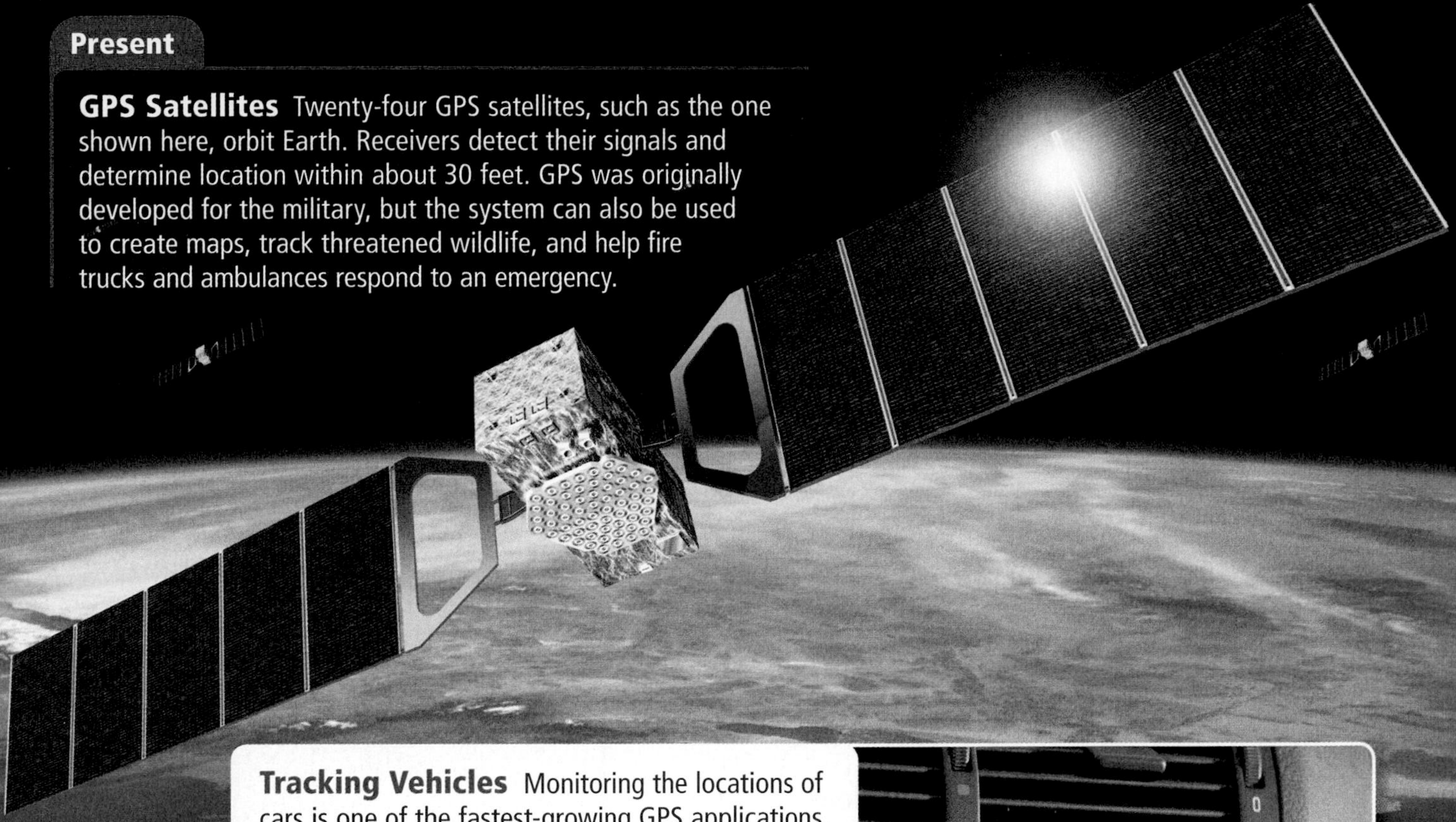

Tracking Vehicles Monitoring the locations of cars is one of the fastest-growing GPS applications. Drivers can also use GPS map displays to plan trips.

Tracking Children Receivers mounted on watches help parents keep track of wandering children. The system finds a child and shows his or her location on a detailed map.

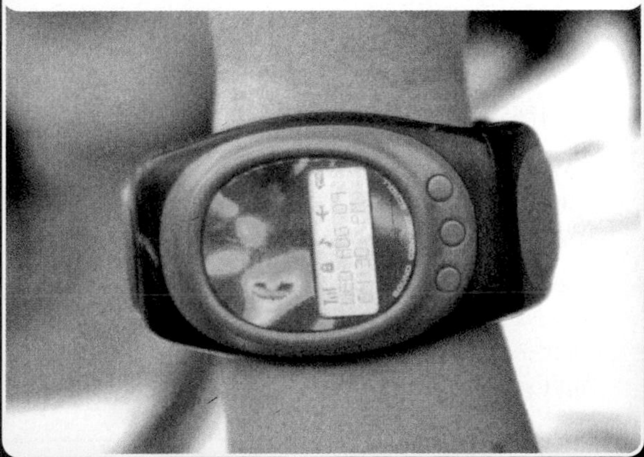

Activities

1. **TALK ABOUT IT** What uses for GPS can you think of?
2. **WRITE ABOUT IT** Write a dialogue in which a modern navigator explains the uses and benefits of GPS technology to an early explorer.

Lesson 3

MAIN IDEAS

1. **Science and Technology** Archaeologists are scientists who work to uncover the story of early people.
2. **Science and Technology** Archaeologists have found evidence that tells us a great deal about early humans.
3. **Culture** Human culture developed during the prehistoric period known as the Stone Age.

TAKING NOTES

Reading Skill: Finding Main Ideas

The main idea of a passage is a sentence that sums up its most important point. Details in the passage help support the main idea. As you read Lesson 3, use a diagram like the one below to identify the main idea of each section.

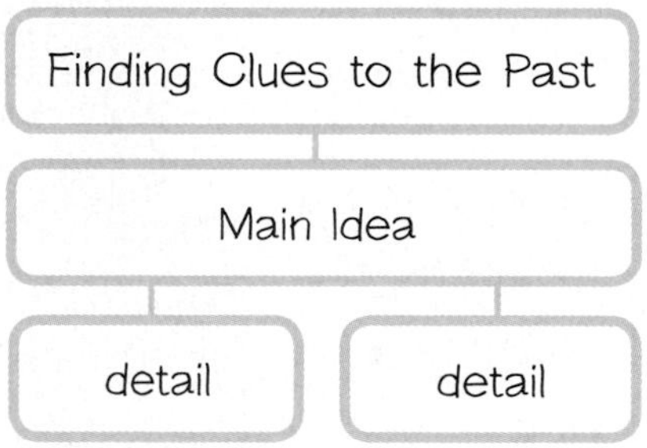

Skillbuilder Handbook, page R2

▲ **Footprint** This footprint was made by a humanlike being about 3.6 million years ago. Footprints and other remains are the kind of evidence archaeologists study to learn about the past.

Words to Know

Understanding the following words will help you read this lesson:

remains parts of a dead body (page 28)

*They were able to determine the age at which the man died from his **remains**.*

dawn to first appear or begin (page 32)

*After the Stone Age **dawned**, society slowly began to change.*

sophisticated complicated or complex (page 33)

*Their remarkable variety of tools suggests that their society was very **sophisticated**.*

How Archaeologists Study the Past

TERMS & NAMES
artifact
fossil
hominid
Paleolithic Age
Mesolithic Age
Neolithic Age

Build on What You Know When you read a detective story, you use clues in the story to try to solve the mystery. Now you will find out how people solve the mysteries of the past without any written clues.

Finding Clues to the Past

1 **ESSENTIAL QUESTION** How do archaeologists uncover the story of early peoples?

When you think about most researchers at work, you probably imagine them in libraries and book-lined studies. A day at the office for an archaeologist, on the other hand, often means sifting through the dirt in a small plot of land. Archaeologists are scientists who learn about early people by digging up and studying the traces of early settlements. On archaeological digs, these scientists search for bones and other evidence that might tell them about life long ago.

Archaeologists The archaeologists at this dig site use small shovels and brushes to carefully unearth and examine their findings. ▼

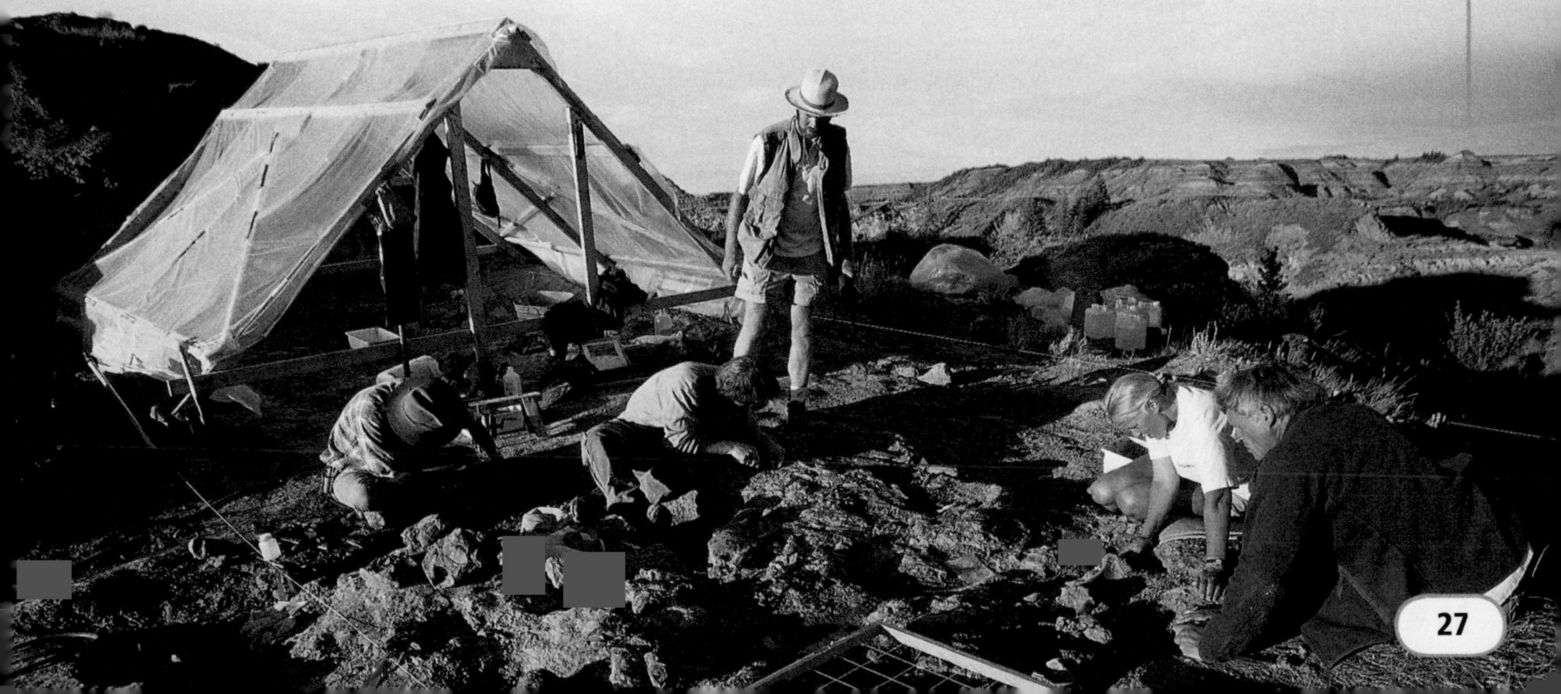

Working Together Archaeologists work with teams of other researchers and scientists to make new discoveries about how prehistoric people lived. Some of the other scientists help archaeologists figure out when **artifacts**, or human-made objects, were made and what they might mean. The artifacts can help archaeologists answer old questions and lead them to ask new ones.

Scientists called anthropologists often work with archaeologists too. Anthropologists study culture, which is the way of life of a group of people. Culture includes a people's beliefs, common language, and shared ways of doing things. The information collected by anthropologists helps archaeologists make connections between the past and present.

Studying Fossils Evidence of early people can be found in **fossils**, remains of early life preserved in the ground. Human fossils often consist of small pieces of teeth, skulls, and other bones. Figuring out the approximate age of fossils is one of the archaeologist's greatest challenges. Archaeologists use complicated techniques to calculate the ages of ancient fossil remains and artifacts.

REVIEW What do archaeologists do?

Hominid Development

This time line is based on the findings of archaeologists.

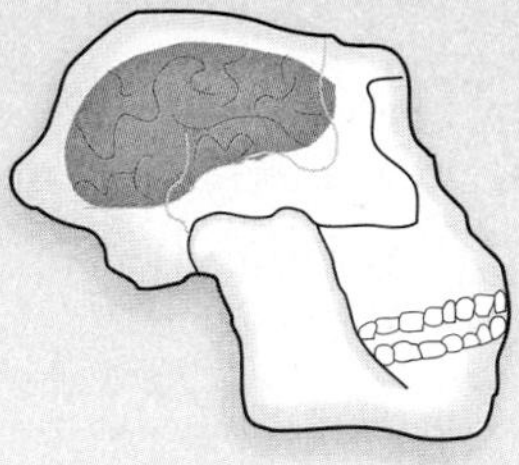

Australopithecine
- lived from about 4.5 million to 1 million B.C.
- found in southern and eastern Africa
- first humanlike creature to walk upright

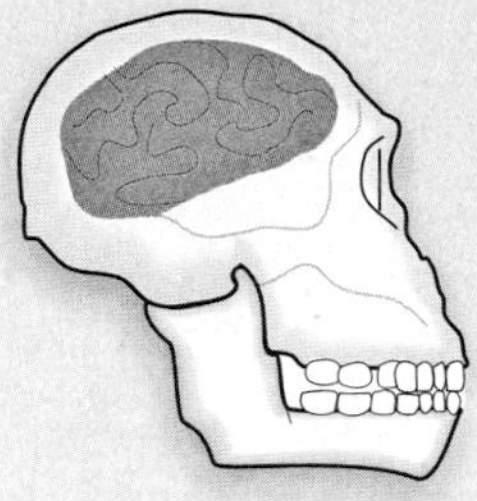

Homo habilis
- lived from about 2.5 million to 1.5 million B.C.
- found in East Africa
- first to make stone tools

4 million B.C.

3 million B.C.

Homo habilis

Australopithecine

The Search for Early Humans

2 ESSENTIAL QUESTION What have archaeologists learned about early humans from the evidence they have found?

The search for our earliest ancestors has taken archaeologists to Africa, where most scientists believe that humans began. There, they have answered many questions about the first humans.

Earliest Humans Some of the earliest humanlike beings that archaeologists have found are called australopithecines (aw•STRAY•loh•PIHTH•ih•SYNZ). These beings and other creatures that walk on two feet—including humans—are called **hominids**. Most scientists believe that australopithecines learned to walk on East African grasslands about 4.5 million years ago.

About 2.5 million years ago, a hominid called *Homo habilis* (HOH•moh HAB•uh•luhs), which means "man of skill," also appeared in East Africa. Archaeologists believe that these hominids used stone tools to cut meat and crack open bones.

Most scientists believe that *Homo erectus* (HOH•moh ih•REHK•tuhs), or "upright man," first appeared about 1.6 million years ago. Scientists think this hominid may have gradually developed into our own large-brained species, *Homo sapiens* (HOH•moh SAY•pee•uhnz), or "wise man."

Vocabulary Strategy

Hominid comes from the Latin **root word** *homo*, meaning "man." The names of human species, such as *Homo sapiens*, all derive from this root word.

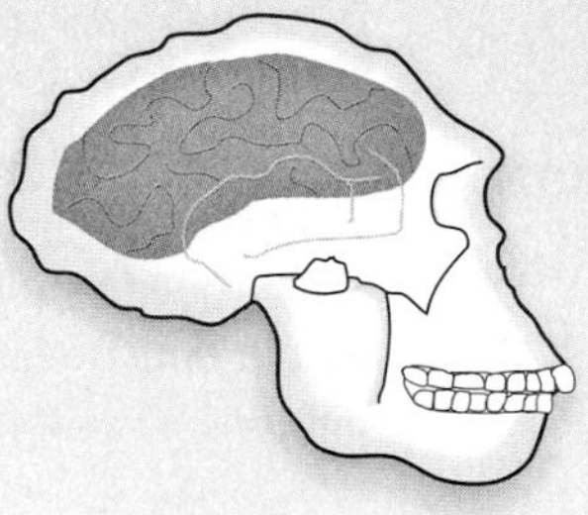

Homo erectus
- lived from about 1.6 million to 250,000 B.C.
- found in Africa, Asia, and Europe
- first to move out of Africa

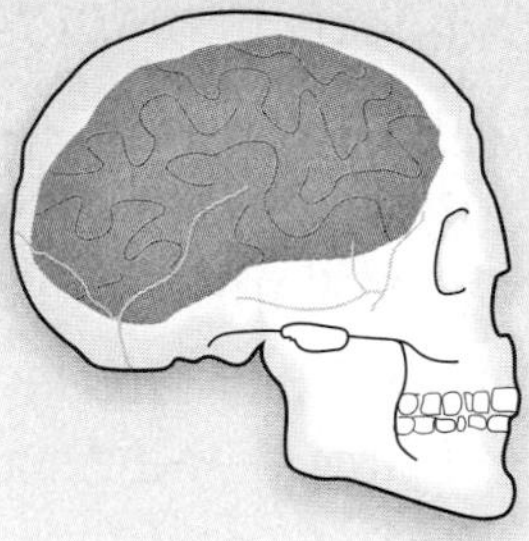

Homo sapiens
- has lived from about 400,000 B.C. to the present
- Early *Homo sapiens* found in Africa, Europe, and Asia
- physically modern humans

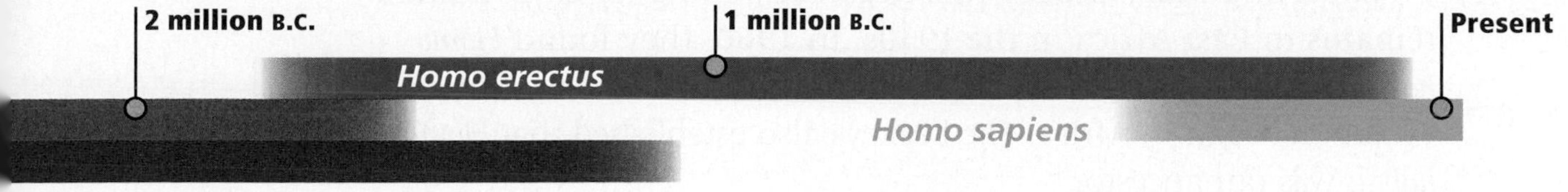

Archaeological Finds in East Africa, 1960–1993

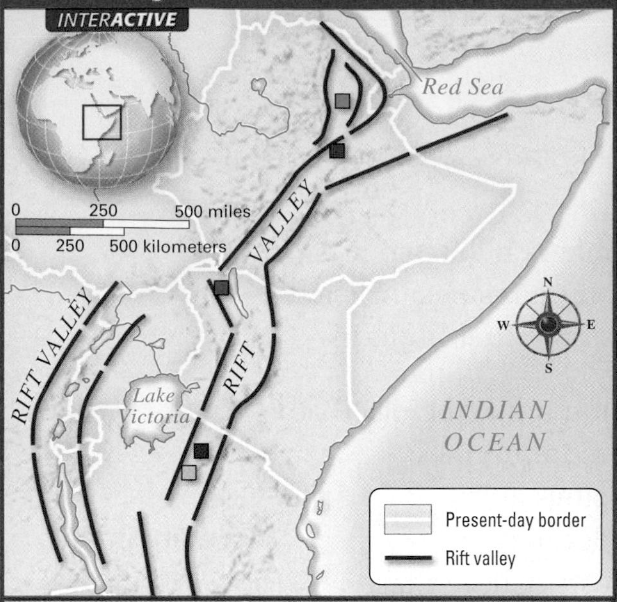

Archaeological Sites

- **1960** Louis and Mary Leakey find *Homo habilis* fossils. (Olduvai Gorge, Tanzania)
- **1974** Donald Johanson finds Lucy. (Hadar, Ethiopia)
- **1978** Mary Leakey finds hominid footprints. (Laetoli, Tanzania)
- **1984** Richard Leakey finds an almost complete *Homo erectus* skeleton. (West Turkana, Kenya)
- **1992–1993** Tim White finds fossils of a new species. (Aramis, Ethiopia)

▲ **Rift Valleys** Many archaeological digs have been carried out in East Africa's rift valleys. These valleys average 30 to 40 miles wide. They were formed as continental plates pulled apart over millions of years.

Modern Humans Human culture developed significantly with the appearance of *Homo sapiens*. Early *Homo sapiens* buried their dead, created cave paintings, and made sharper tools. In time, these humans began to farm, developed writing systems, and built complex villages. Some physically modern *Homo sapiens*, called Cro-Magnons (kroh•MAG•nuhnz), first appeared about 35,000 years ago. Cro-Magnons migrated from North Africa to Europe and Asia.

Important Finds Our understanding of early people is based on the findings of many archaeologists and anthropologists. Some of the most significant contributions have been made by the Leakeys, a family of British archaeologists.

Louis and Mary Leakey first began searching for early human remains in East Africa in the 1930s. In 1960, they found *Homo habilis* fossils in East Africa. Their discoveries showed that human evolution began in Africa. The Leakeys also established that *Homo habilis* was our ancestor.

In 1974, American archaeologist Donald Johanson discovered an unusually complete skeleton of an australopithecine. He and his team named the hominid Lucy. You will learn more about Lucy in the History Makers feature below. In 1978, Mary Leakey uncovered more information about australopithecines. She also became the first to discover a set of footprints made by these hominids. You can see a photograph of one of these footprints on page 26.

Primary Source Handbook
See the excerpt from *Disclosing the Past,* page R35.

The Leakeys' son, Richard, also became an important archaeologist. He and his team found a 1.6-million-year-old skeleton of a *Homo erectus* in 1984. It is one of the most complete skeletons ever found.

More recent findings have added to our understanding of early humans. In the early 1990s, American anthropologist Tim White found apelike fossils that led to the naming of a new hominid species. In 2002, a team of archaeologists found a hominid skull in Chad. The 6- to 7-million-year-old skull belongs to our earliest human ancestor so far discovered. (You can read an excerpt from a novel about archaeologists and their discoveries in the Literature Connection on page 34.)

REVIEW What are the names of some early hominids?

History Makers

Lucy (lived around 3.5 million B.C.)

On November 30, 1974, Professor Donald Johanson and his student Tom Gray were searching the hot, dry ground of Hadar, Ethiopia. There they discovered a tiny piece of an arm bone. Several other bones lay nearby. They belonged to a type of australopithecine Johanson had never seen before.

Excited by the find, members of the expedition went back and retrieved 40 percent of the creature's skeleton, which is shown here. The pelvis indicated that she was female, and the archaeologists named her Lucy, after the Beatles' song "Lucy in the Sky with Diamonds."

At about 3.5 million years old, Lucy was older than any hominid discovered up to that time. She had a smallish brain, like a chimp's, and very long arms. But she walked upright. Lucy challenged the theory that a bigger brain had led to walking.

The Stone Age

3 ESSENTIAL QUESTION Who lived and what happened during the prehistoric period known as the Stone Age?

The invention of tools, the mastery of fire, and the development of language and farming are some of humankind's most important achievements. Scientists believe that these advances took place during the prehistoric period known as the Stone Age. This period dawned when hominids made and used the first stone tools.

The Stone Age is often divided into three phases: the Old Stone Age, the Middle Stone Age, and the New Stone Age. The Old Stone Age, also called the **Paleolithic** (PAY•lee•uh•LIHTH•ihk) **Age**, lasted from about 2.5 million to 8000 B.C. The Middle Stone Age, also called the **Mesolithic** (MEHZ•uh•LIHTH•ihk) **Age**, occurred roughly between 10,000 and 6000 B.C. This period served as a sort of bridge between the Old and New Stone Age. The New Stone Age, or **Neolithic** (NEE•uh•LIHTH•ihk) **Age**, began about 8000 B.C. and ended as early as 3000 B.C. You can compare the characteristics of the three periods in the chart below.

The Stone Age

Period	Dates	Characteristics
Paleolithic Age	2.5 million–8000 B.C.	• *Homo habilis, Homo erectus,* and *Homo sapiens* lived during this period. • Early humans lived as hunters and gatherers. • People used simple stone tools with single sharp edges to cut and chop.
Mesolithic Age	10,000–6000 B.C.	• Mesolithic peoples developed needles and thread, harpoons, and spear throwers. • They began to control fire and develop language. • In some places, people specialized in hunting particular animals. • Gatherers developed grindstones to prepare the vegetables they collected.
Neolithic Age	8000–3000 B.C.	• Only *Homo sapiens* lived during this period. • People learned to polish stone tools and make pottery. • They began to grow crops, raise animals, and settle in villages.

Paleolithic Age figure ▶

Neolithic Age figure ▶

The development of farming in the Neolithic Age greatly changed people's lives. Instead of wandering from place to place, people began to settle down and build communities. As time passed, these early humans' skills and tools for surviving and adapting to the environment became more sophisticated. You will learn more about these early people and their communities in Chapter 2.

REVIEW What achievements occurred during the Stone Age?

Australopithecine Skull
These hominids had small brains, but their thumbs could cross their palms. This meant that they could pick up small objects and use tools. ▼

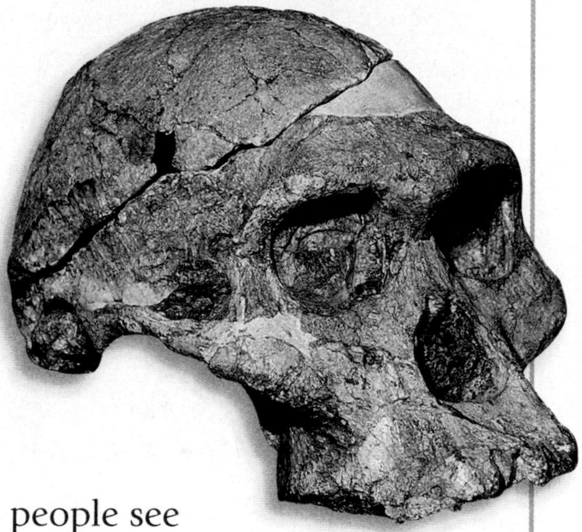

Lesson Summary

- Studying ancient artifacts and fossils helps reveal early human history.
- The first humanlike creatures developed in Africa.
- During the Stone Age, people began to use tools, control fire, speak, grow crops, and raise animals.

Why It Matters Now . . .

Learning about our common beginnings can help people see that our similarities outweigh our differences.

3 Lesson Review

Homework Helper
ClassZone.com

Terms & Names

1. Explain the importance of

artifact	hominid	Mesolithic Age
fossil	Paleolithic Age	Neolithic Age

Using Your Notes

Finding Main Ideas Use your completed diagram to answer the following question:

2. What is the main idea of the section "The Search for Early Humans"?

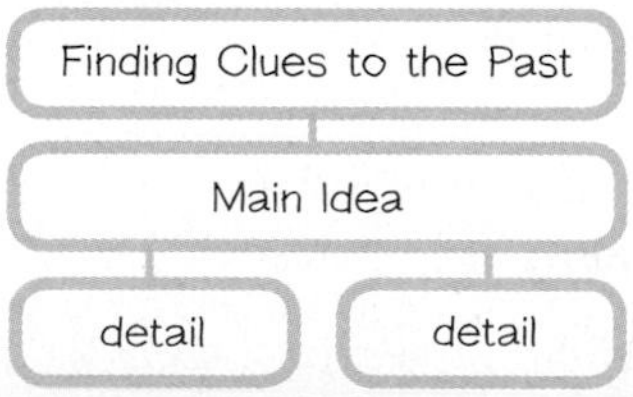

Main Ideas

3. What can archaeologists learn by studying artifacts and fossils?
4. What have archaeologists learned about early hominids?
5. How did people live during the Paleolithic and Mesolithic ages?

Critical Thinking

6. **Understanding Continuity and Change** What kinds of changes probably encouraged the development of early hominid societies?
7. **Identifying Issues and Problems** Why is studying early people so hard?

Activity

Internet Activity Use the Internet to research one of the archaeologists named in this lesson. Present your findings, including pictures and maps, on a poster you can share with the class.
INTERNET KEYWORD: *archaeologist's name*

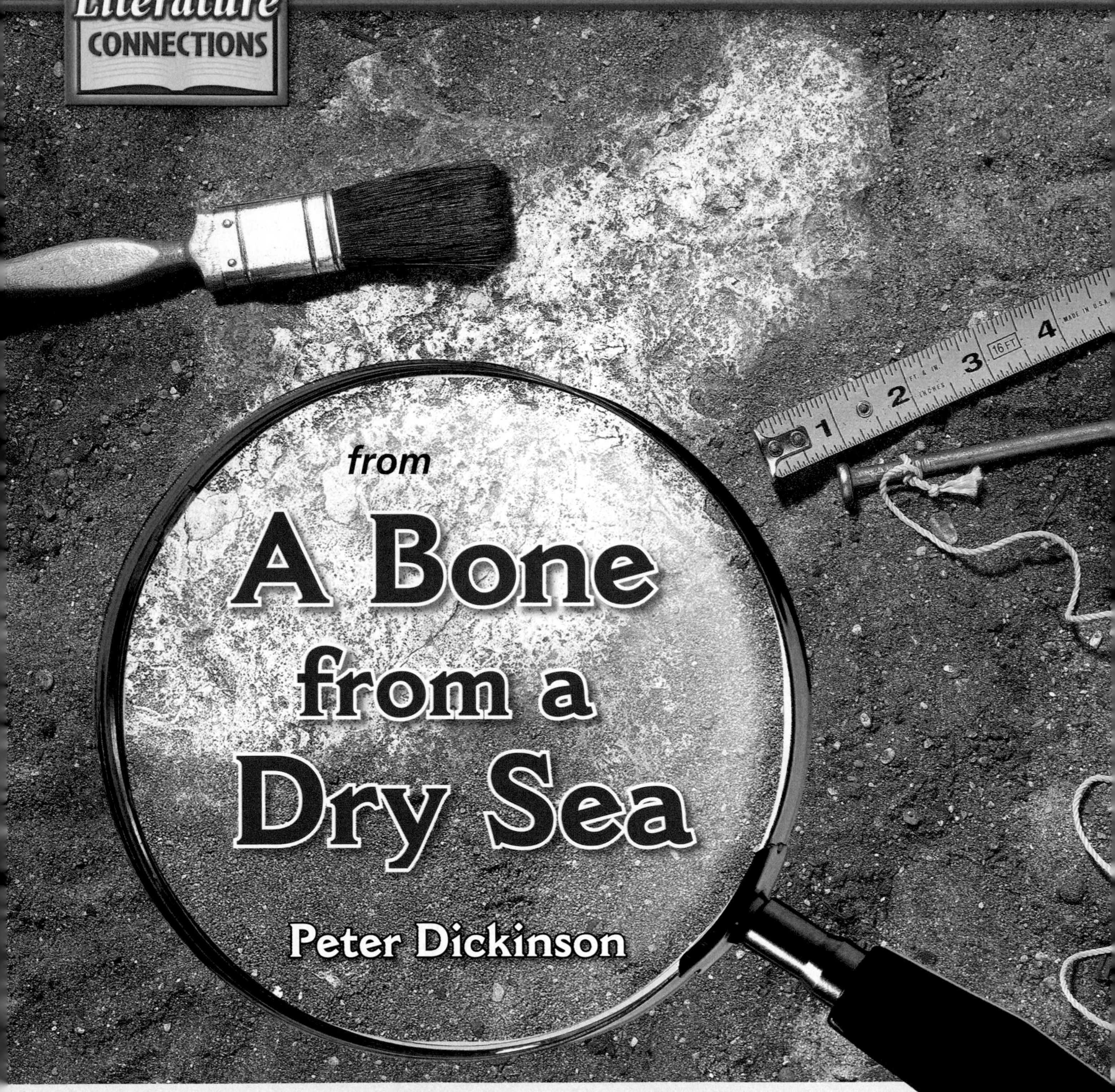

from

A Bone from a Dry Sea

Peter Dickinson

Background: In the novel *A Bone from a Dry Sea* by Peter Dickinson, 12-year-old Lavinia (Vinny for short) is happy living with her mother, her stepfather Colin, and her half-brothers in England. But she misses her father, Sam, an archaeologist. So Vinny asks to join her father in Africa, where he is part of a team searching for hominid fossils.

One day, Vinny goes to explore a site with the team leader, Dr. Joe Hamiska. And then Vinny makes her own discovery.

It seemed to be thin and flat and to lie almost level in the hill so that its left edge actually broke through the sloping line of tuff.[1] The outer edge had been snapped off where it reached the surface, and the right corner, about half a square inch, was cracked and loose from the main bit. [Vinny] was working not down but sideways into the hill, digging out a hollow like a miniature quarry[2] with the bone as its floor. Dr. Hamiska's boots crunched on the rock above her. She rose to let him see what she'd been doing.

"That's great," he said. "We'll have to employ you full-time."

"What is it? Do you know?"

"A fragment of scapula, I think. Shoulder blade to you, Vinny. Some fair-sized beast. Don't try and lever it out or you'll break it—you'll have to undercut it first. Look how the sequence[3] runs at the back there—that's beautiful."

"Do you think it was killed in the eruption?"

"Could be, could be. Your father's here to answer questions like that. The ash would have been soft, mind you, so the creature could have died after the eruption and then the bones partly embedded themselves. Lend me your trowel, will you? I could get a column of the sequence out there—something to show them on Thursday. Blind them with science, eh?"

Still chuckling, he forced the blade vertically down at the back of Vinny's quarry, as if he were cutting the first slice out of a birthday cake. The slice broke in two when he eased it out but he fitted the pieces together and laid them carefully out on the slope.

"Now if you'll ask Jane for a bag and a label," he said, "and then we'll—Hold it! Hold everything!"

▲ **Trowel** Archaeologists use trowels, or small shovels, to carefully dig for bones and artifacts.

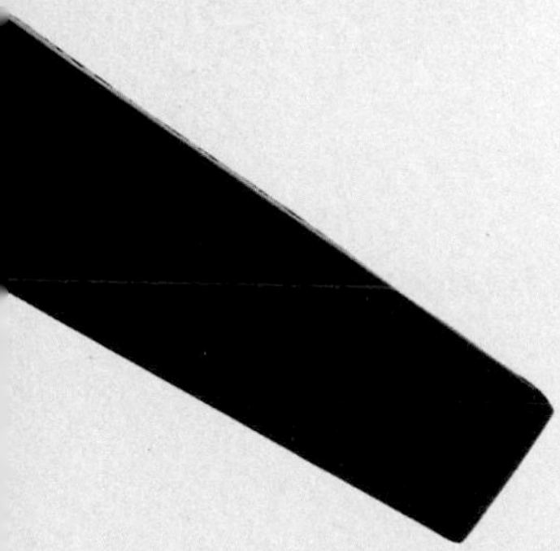

---

1. **tuff:** a layer of fossilized ash from a volcanic eruption.
2. **quarry:** hole in the ground.
3. **sequence:** layers of earth.

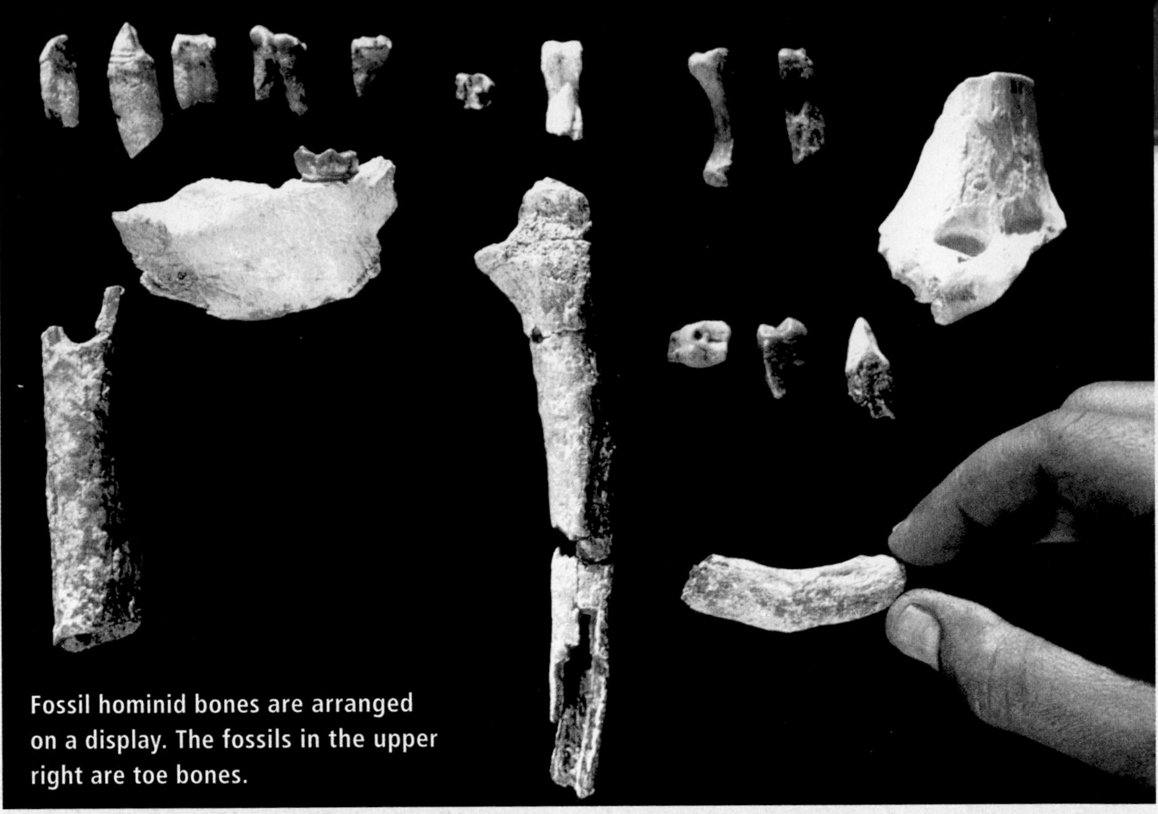
Fossil hominid bones are arranged on a display. The fossils in the upper right are toe bones.

He pushed his sunglasses onto his forehead and stared into the slice-shaped cut he had made. His breath hissed between closed teeth. With Vinny's brush he swept the loose bits from a pale lump which had been exposed on one side of the cut, just above the tuff. He took a magnifying glass from his shirt pocket and gazed intently through it.

"Jane," he called. "Come here a moment."

He'd changed. A moment before he'd been the friendly old professor showing off to the visitor. Now he'd forgotten she was there. Mrs. Hamiska came and crouched beside him. Every line of their bodies expressed enthralled[4] excitement. Two terriers at the same rabbit hole.

"Oh, yes," said Mrs. Hamiska. "I think so. I really do think so."

"Whoopee!" bellowed Dr. Hamiska, standing and flinging his cap into the air. It landed halfway down the hillside.

"Let me have a go," said Mrs. Hamiska. "You're a bit too excited."

REVIEW Why do you think Dr. Hamiska is so excited?

Without waiting for an answer she started to chip the clay away from the other side of the cut. Vinny fetched Dr. Hamiska's cap, and then helped him measure and peg out an area around the find. Standing on the rock he began to draw a sketch map. By now Mrs. Hamiska had opened the cut enough for Vinny to see that the fossil was a stubby cylindrical[5] bone with a bulge at each end.

"Is it part of someone's hand?" she said.

---

4. **enthralled:** absorbed with interest.
5. **cylindrical:** circular, in the shape of a cylinder.

"Their foot, Vinny, their foot!" crowed Dr. Hamiska. "It's a distal phalanx—a toe bone to you, Vinny. You are looking at the left big toe of a creature that walked on its hind legs five million years ago! It's going to be datable by the tuff! And either my name's not Joseph Seton Hamiska or the rest of the skeleton is all there, right under our feet! The oldest fossil hominid yet found! I knew it! I knew it! I knew the moment I woke up that this was my day, and this was going to be the place! Whoopee!"

You could have heard his shouts a mile across the plain. Mrs. Hamiska straightened and watched him, like Mom watching Colin and the boys let the sea run into the moat[6] of their sandcastle, yelling with triumph as it swirled around their ramparts.[7]

"I think you'd better get Sam out here, darling," she said.

"Yes, yes, of course. And Fred and the others—as many witnesses as we can. . . . I'll call them up."

He charged down the hill toward the jeep, where he'd left the two-way radio, but halfway down he stopped and turned.

"Vinny!" he shouted. "Didn't I tell you, the moment I set eyes on you, you were going to bring us luck!"

REVIEW What does Vinny's discovery lead Dr. Hamiska to find?

---

6. **moat:** water-filled ditch around a castle.
7. **ramparts:** defense barriers around a castle.

Reading & Writing

1. **READING: Character** What impact does Dr. Hamiska's personality have on the story?
2. **WRITING: Narration** What do you think will happen next? Write a scene in which Dr. Hamiska and Vinny present their find to the rest of the team.

Lesson 4

MAIN IDEAS

1. **Culture** Historians often ask questions about the past in order to understand the present.
2. **Culture** Historians use a variety of methods to help them answer questions about what happened in the past.
3. **Culture** Historians examine evidence and draw conclusions as they answer historical questions.

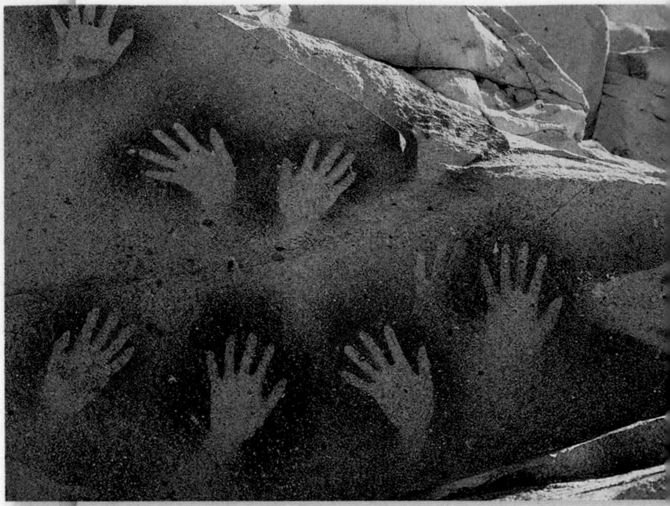

▲ Cave Paintings Caves throughout the world have ancient paintings of human hands. These hand paintings were found in a cave in Argentina. Historians believe that the hands marked territorial ownership or served as the artists' signature.

TAKING NOTES

Reading Skill: Categorizing

When you categorize information, you organize similar kinds of information into groups. In Lesson 4, you will read about the three main jobs of a historian. Record what you learn in a web diagram like the one below.

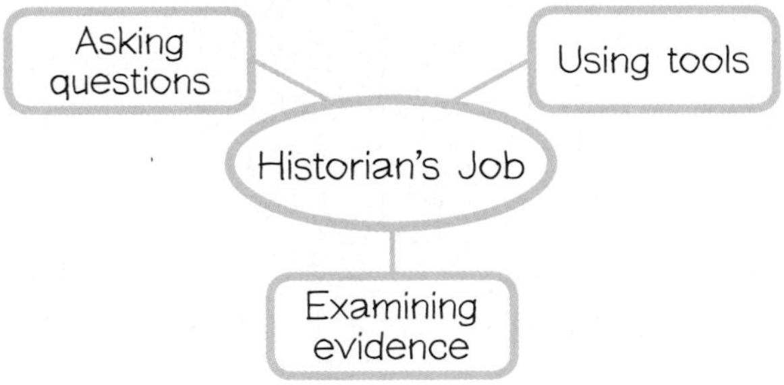

Skillbuilder Handbook, page R6

Words to Know

Understanding the following words will help you read this lesson:

recounting telling in detail (page 39)

*Her **recounting** of the tribe's origins was filled with dramatic descriptions and memorable details.*

system group of things that work together as a whole (page 40)

*Their belief **systems** mostly came from the society in which they lived.*

quarry open pit from which stones are taken (page 43)

*Historians don't know how workers moved the enormous stones from the **quarries** to the building sites.*

How Historians Study the Past

TERMS & NAMES
primary source
secondary source
oral history

Build on What You Know You may know where your parents or ancestors came from and some of the stories about them. Relatives and their stories help people understand their family history. Now learn what historians use to help them understand the past.

Understanding the Past

1 **ESSENTIAL QUESTION** What questions do historians ask to help them understand the past?

People investigate their family history to find out about their ancestors. In the process, however, they also find out about themselves. We study world history for the same reasons.

Why Study History? What has already happened to a person, a family, or a society affects what will occur today and in the future. But history is much more than simply recounting and studying past events. Examining a historical event also involves studying a society's culture, religion, politics, and economics.

When historians examine past events, they try to find patterns. They look for causes and effects that explain how and why events happened. They also try to understand why some ideas and traditions last and why others die out. Just as important, historians attempt to see the past through the eyes of the people who lived it. By doing so, historians gain greater insight into human nature and answer important historical questions.

Storyteller This West African griot, or storyteller, memorizes and tells the stories that make up his village's history. ▼

Asking Historical Questions As historians study the past, they ask themselves questions like those below. These questions help historians compare different societies and draw conclusions about the past.

- How have groups or societies interacted, and what have been the results?
- How have leaders governed societies?
- How have belief systems developed and changed?
- How have societies dealt with differences among their people?
- How have societies tried to protect people's security?
- How are societies similar and different?

REVIEW Why do we study history?

The Historian's Tools

2 ESSENTIAL QUESTION What methods do historians use to help them answer questions about what happened in the past?

When you hang up a picture, you use a hammer to pound in the nail. Historians also use tools to do their job. These tools include primary sources, secondary sources, and oral history.

Primary Sources A **primary source** is something written or created by a person who witnessed a historical event. You will learn about an ancient primary source on the next page. Primary sources include letters, diaries, eyewitness articles, videotapes, speeches, and photographs. Artifacts, such as the human-made tools below, are also primary sources.

Artifacts

These ax heads from different prehistoric periods show historians how early peoples' toolmaking ability advanced over time.

▲ 200,000 B.C. In the Paleolithic Age, humans made tools by chipping stone.

▲ 3000 B.C. In the Neolithic Age, humans learned to polish tools.

▲ 600 B.C. By the Bronze Age, humans had learned to shape a thin ax head.

Primary Source

The Rosetta Stone

The Rosetta Stone is a primary source from ancient Egypt that dates back to 196 B.C. Historians found the stone in 1799. They know now that the three different kinds of writing on the stone record the deeds of a young Egyptian ruler. The first writing is shown in the top inset. The other two writings are shown in the bottom inset. But no one could read much of the first two writings until 1822, when a French scholar cracked their code. The Rosetta Stone provided important information about the writing system of the ancient Egyptians.

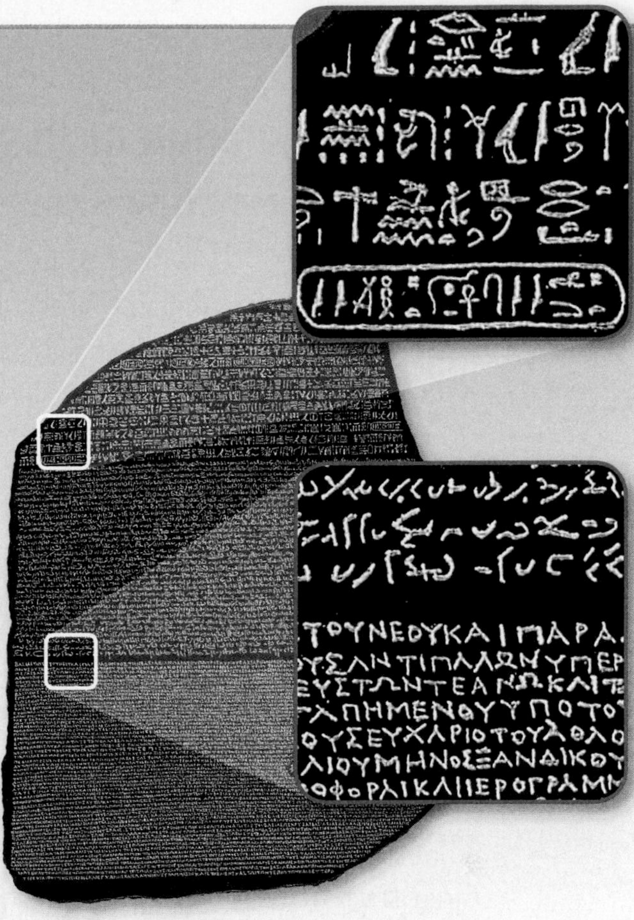

DOCUMENT–BASED QUESTION
What questions did the Rosetta Stone help historians answer?

Secondary Sources Historians also use secondary sources to learn about past events. **Secondary sources** are written after a historical event by people who did not witness the event. Books, paintings, and media reports that are based on primary sources and appear after an event are all secondary sources. Sometimes secondary sources are the only ones that are available. They can sometimes provide more balanced views of an event than primary sources.

Oral History When cultures have no written records, historians rely on oral history as a resource. **Oral history** is made up of all the unwritten verbal accounts of events. It includes the stories, customs, and songs that a culture has told and passed from generation to generation. For example, West African storytellers, like the one shown on page 39, have memorized and told family histories and the traditions and stories of their villages for hundreds of years.

REVIEW What tools do historians use to learn about the past?

How Knowledge of the Past Changes

3 ESSENTIAL QUESTION What steps do historians take as they answer historical questions?

Detectives use fingerprints and other evidence to solve crimes. Historians act as detectives too. They use evidence from primary, secondary, and oral sources.

Fact or Fiction? Historical evidence isn't always as simple as a bloodstain at a crime scene. Historians sometimes have more information than they can use when they try to answer a question. They must sort through all of the information and choose what's most important and most trustworthy as evidence.

In addition, sometimes what historians thought was true turns out to be false. For instance, one historian proved that the so-called mummy's curse was false. According to legend, the curse would kill anyone who entered the tomb of an ancient Egyptian ruler.

▲ **King Tut's Tomb** This photograph shows the interior of King Tut's tomb. Some people believed that exposure to the tomb killed Lord Carnarvon.

Many people believed the curse had caused the death of English archaeologist Lord Carnarvon. He died suddenly in 1923, shortly after entering the tomb of ancient Egyptian ruler "King Tut." People believed that the other archaeologists who had entered the tomb between 1923 and 1926 would also die as a result of the curse. However, a historian later examined the archaeologists' death records. Their average age at death was 70 years. The evidence did not support the existence of the mummy's curse.

Drawing Conclusions The mummy's curse was easy to disprove. But not all historical questions are so easily answered. Sometimes different historians arrive at different conclusions based on the same facts.

On pages 2–3, you learned that Stonehenge was built out of stones dragged from faraway quarries. Most historians agree that the monument was begun around 3000 B.C. as a place of worship. Earlier theories held that it was built as a temple for a group of priests who practiced magic. However, later experts realized that the monument was finished long before these priests lived in the area. Today some historians suggest that the builders of Stonehenge were sun worshipers. But other experts maintain that Stonehenge will never reveal all its secrets.

REVIEW How are historians like detectives?

Lesson Summary

- Asking historical questions can help solve mysteries about the past.
- A historian's most important tools are primary sources, secondary sources, and oral histories.
- Examining evidence can lead to a new answer to a question or deepen a mystery.

Why It Matters Now . . .

The answers to historical questions can help people as they respond to today's events and challenges.

4 Lesson Review

Homework Helper
ClassZone.com

Terms & Names

1. Explain the importance of
   primary source   secondary source   oral history

Using Your Notes

Categorizing Use your completed web diagram to answer the following question:

2. What is the difference between primary and secondary sources?

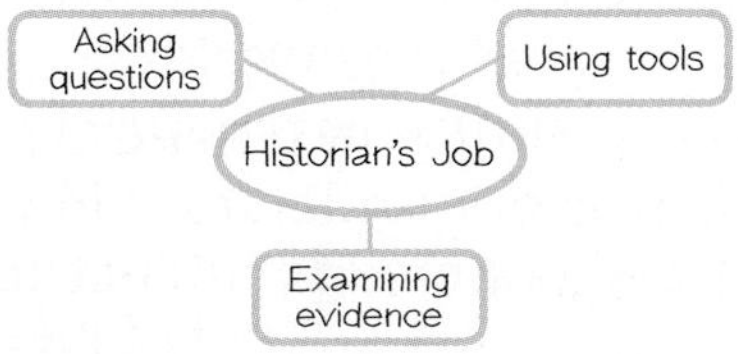

Main Ideas

3. Name two of the questions historians ask themselves when they study the past.
4. What resources do historians particularly rely on when a society does not have a written history?
5. What do historians do when they sort through evidence, such as that involving the "curse" of King Tut's tomb?

Critical Thinking

6. **Distinguishing Fact from Opinion** List two facts and two opinions about Stonehenge.
7. **Comparing and Contrasting** Compare a historian's job with that of an archaeologist.

Activity

Recording an Oral History Interview an older relative about a historical event that occurred in his or her lifetime. Use the interview to write down what you learned about the event.

Chapter 1 Review

VISUAL SUMMARY

The Tools of History

Geography

- Earth is shaped by continents, landforms, and bodies of water.
- Physical features, climate, and vegetation affect where people live.
- People use political, physical, and thematic maps to learn about the world.

Culture

- Primary and secondary sources and oral histories answer questions about the past.
- Our earliest human ancestors first lived in Africa.
- Tools, use of fire, language, and farming developed during the Stone Age.

Science & Technology

- Fossils and artifacts reveal much about human development.
- Dating methods help determine a fossil's age.

TERMS & NAMES

Explain why the words in each set below are linked with each other.

1. **climate** and **vegetation**
2. **longitude** and **latitude**
3. **Paleolithic Age** and **Neolithic Age**
4. **primary source** and **secondary source**

MAIN IDEAS

The World's Geography (pages 8–13)

5. What do geographers study?
6. How might the climate where you live affect your life?

How Maps Help Us Study History (pages 14–25)

7. What do political maps show?
8. Why have maps changed throughout history?

How Archaeologists Study the Past (pages 26–37)

9. What do archaeologists study to learn about early humans?
10. According to scientists, which hominid developed into *Homo sapiens?*

How Historians Study the Past (pages 38–43)

11. What kinds of questions do historians ask when they study the past?
12. What are three examples of primary sources?

CRITICAL THINKING

Big Ideas: Science and Technology

13. **EXPLAINING HISTORICAL PATTERNS** What does the continuing effort to develop and improve maps throughout history tell us about people and their place in the world?
14. **RECOGNIZING CHANGING INTERPRETATIONS OF HISTORY** Why is our understanding of the lives of early hominids subject to change?
15. **EVALUATING INFORMATION** What does the steady development of tools in the hunter-gatherer societies suggest about early humans' intelligence?

ALTERNATIVE ASSESSMENT

1. **WRITING ACTIVITY** Apply one of the historical questions listed on page 40 to your city or state. Write a paragraph in which you answer the question.

2. **INTERDISCIPLINARY ACTIVITY—SCIENCE** Learn more about the movements of continental plates. Draw a series of diagrams demonstrating the different types of plate movement.

3. **STARTING WITH A STORY**
Starting with a Story
Use the composition you wrote about the Lascaux Cave to create a dialogue between the four teenage explorers. Express their reactions to the cave's fate.

Technology Activity

4. **CREATING A VIRTUAL MUSEUM**
Use the Internet or library to learn more about one of the early hominids discussed in this chapter. Then work with a group of classmates to create a virtual museum exhibit on how early humans lived.
   - Provide information about where these early hominids lived, what they ate, what tools and skills they used, and how they survived.
   - Use maps, visuals, and sounds to engage your viewers' interest.
   - Include documentation of your sources.

Research Links
ClassZone.com

Reading Maps Use the map below to answer the questions.

Population Distribution in Africa, 2000

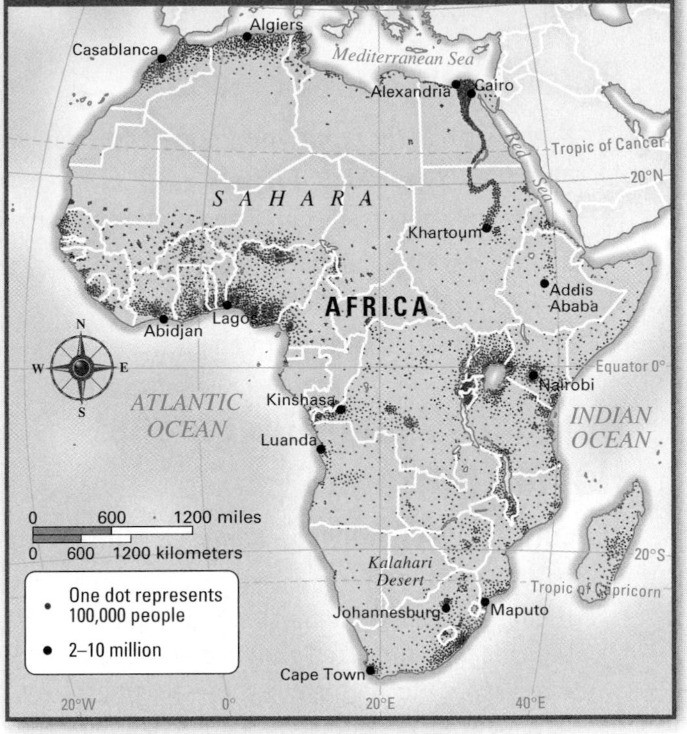

1. **Where do most people live in Africa?**
   A. along the continent's coasts, rivers, and lakes
   B. in the southwestern part of the continent
   C. in the deserts
   D. along the equator

2. **Why do you think most Africans live in these areas?**
   A. to be near the deserts
   B. to live in Africa's interior
   C. to be near water sources
   D. to live in a warm climate

Test Practice
ClassZone.com

Additional Test Practice, pp. S1–S33

Chapter 2 The Earliest Human Societies

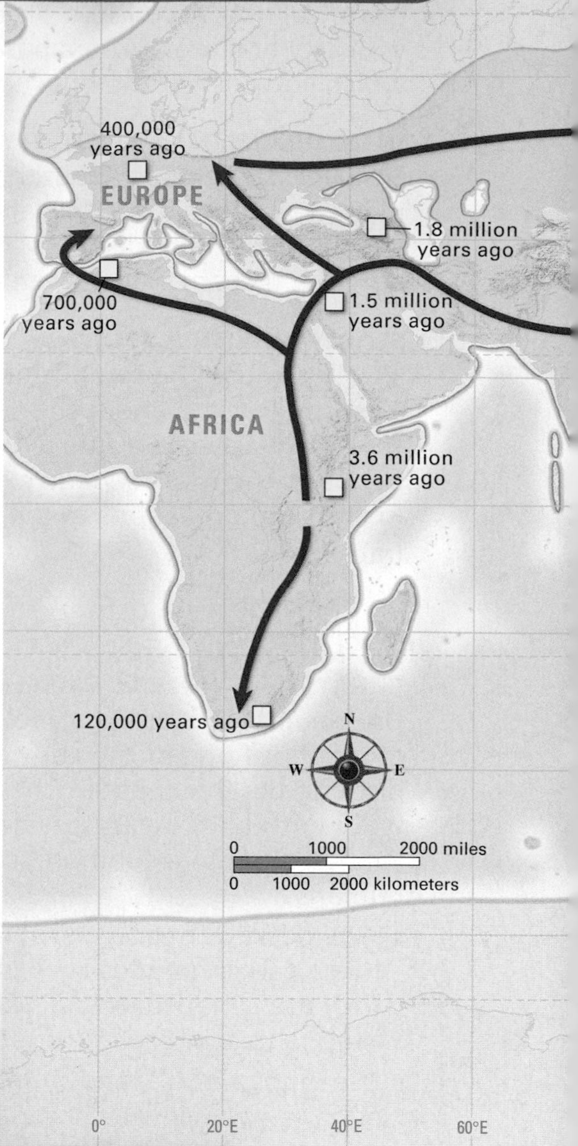

Before You Read: K-W-L

K-W-L stands for what you know, what you want to know, and what you have learned.

- What do you already know about early human societies?
- Study the map and the time line. What do they tell you about where early humans lived?
- What do you want to learn about the earliest human societies?

Big Ideas About the Earliest Human Societies

Culture **Ways of living change as humans interact with one another.**

The first humans hunted animals and gathered plants for food. Then, as they interacted with one another, they developed tools and weapons to aid them in these activities. New, more settled ways of living developed as people shared ideas.

Integrated Technology

eEdition
- Interactive Maps
- Interactive Visuals
- Starting with a Story

INTERNET RESOURCES
Go to **ClassZone.com** for
- WebQuest
- Homework Helper
- Research Links
- Internet Activities
- Quizzes
- Maps
- Test Practice
- Current Events

WORLD

500,000 B.C.

500,000 B.C.
Early humans learn how to control fire.
(19th-century lithograph) ▶

40,000 B.C.
Cro-Magnons appear.

Early Human Migration to 10,000 years ago

INTERACTIVE

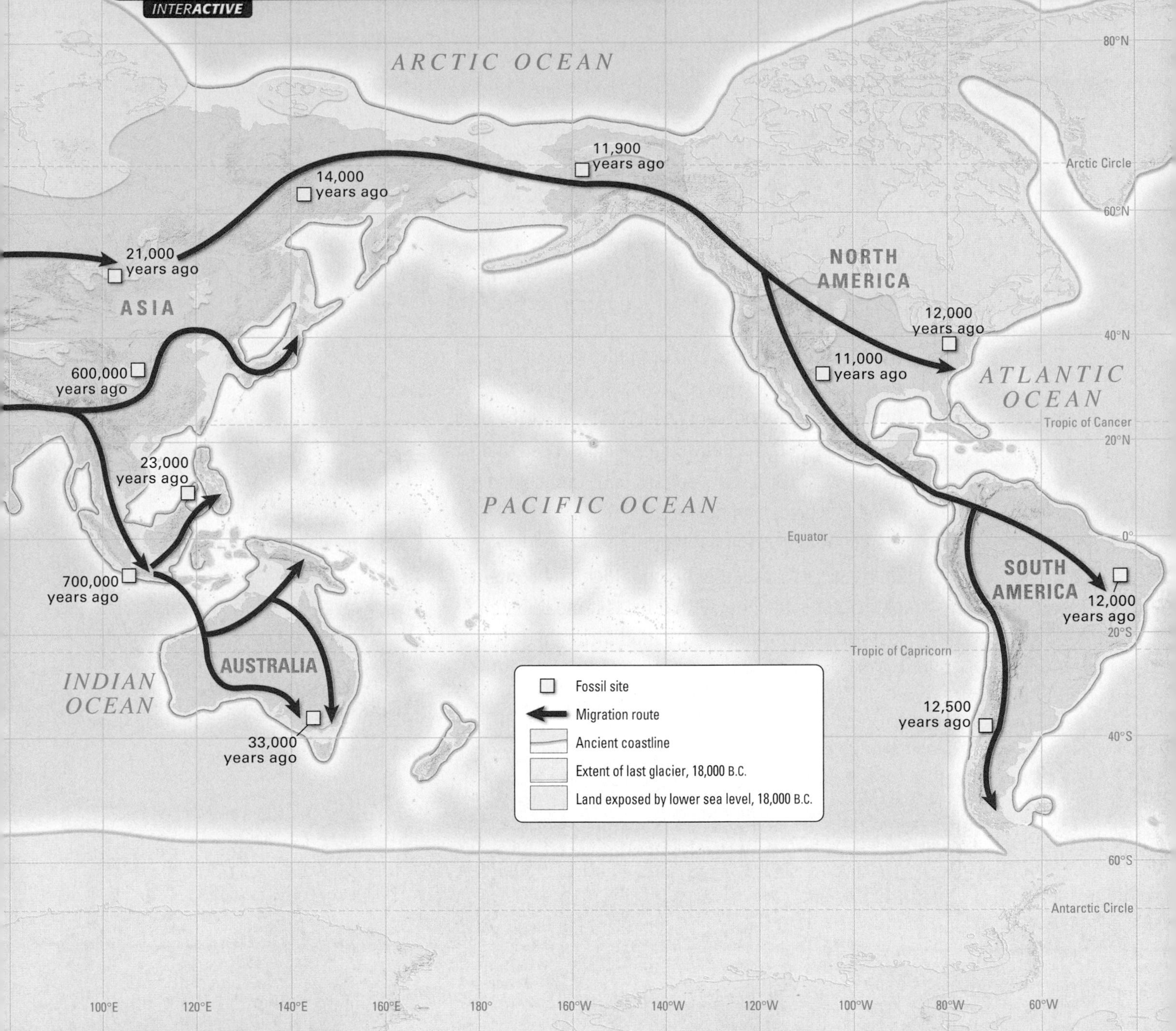

8000 B.C.
First agriculture takes place with tools such as this wooden plow. ▶

5000 B.C.
First cities begin to develop.

10,000 B.C. — **5000 B.C.**

10,000 B.C.
Last ice age ends.
▲ (glacier dividing, Alaska)

9000 B.C.
Domestication of animals begins.

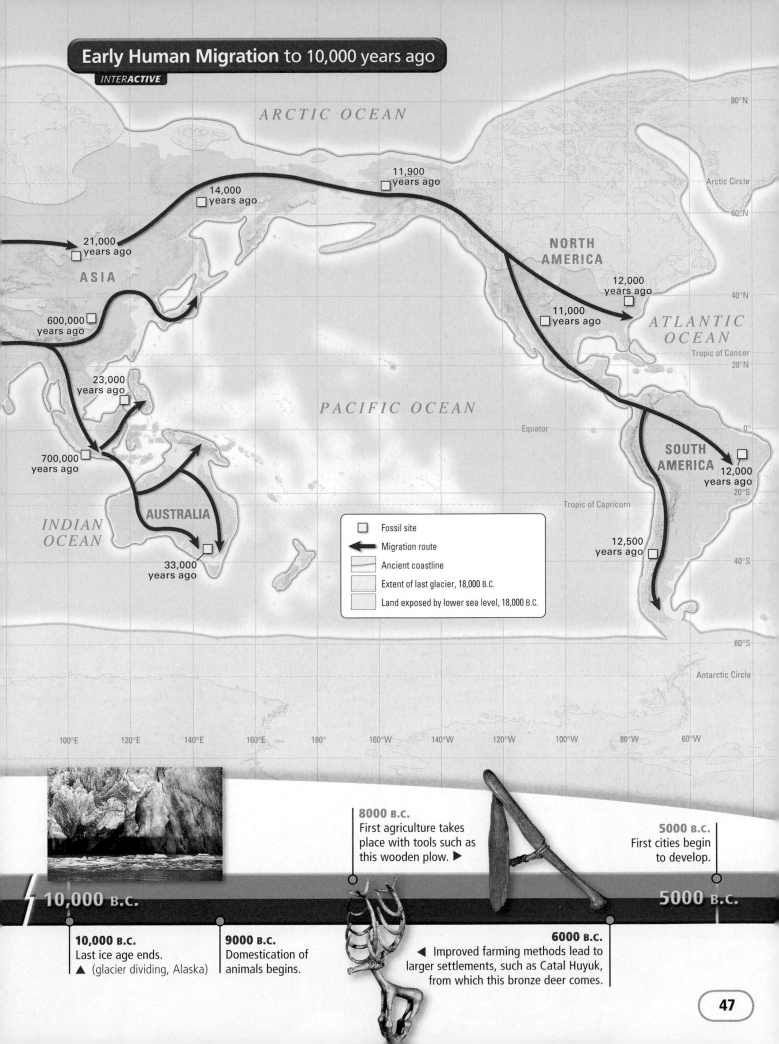

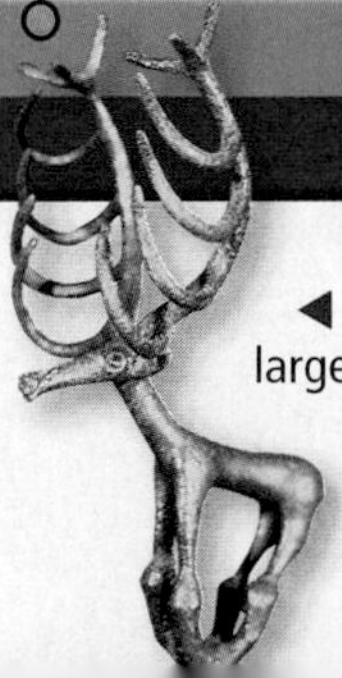

6000 B.C.
◀ Improved farming methods lead to larger settlements, such as Catal Huyuk, from which this bronze deer comes.

Starting with a Story

The Hunter OF THE Alps

Background: In 1991, a couple hiking in the Alps in Europe discovered the frozen body of a man. Ancient-looking tools and weapons lay near the body. A scientist studying early humans announced that this hunter was 5,300 years old. His body and belongings were well preserved by the cold.

Scientists nicknamed him the Iceman. They found an arrowhead in his shoulder. The contents of his stomach showed that his last meal, eaten just hours before his death, had included deer, barley, and wheat.

The hunter's body found in the Alps ▶

Starting with a Story
eEdition

Primary Source Handbook

See the excerpt from *The Man in the Ice*, page R36.

The hunter had been walking since dawn. The air in the Alps was cold, but the morning fog had cleared up during the course of the day. He was glad of his warm fur hat, goatskin clothes, and grass cloak.

He had spent most of his life walking in these mountains. He had worn out many pairs of deerskin shoes. The ones he was wearing had soles of bearskin.

On this day, the mountain seemed steeper than usual. It might have been his age. The hunter was over 40, one of the oldest people in his community. But he could still easily carry everything he needed. His leather quiver contained a bow, arrow shafts, and arrows with flint heads. He was also carrying a flint dagger and an ax made of wood from a yew tree, with a copper blade. His belt pouch held three flint tools, a bone awl, and a piece of tinder. He also carried a medicine kit in case he became sick or injured.

Suddenly a man lunged toward him. The hunter struggled with him in an attempt to escape. He managed to free himself from the man's grasp and knock the ax out of his hand. He bounded away across the icy landscape. As he looked back, he saw that others had joined the pursuit.

As the hunter turned to run, he felt a searing pain in his shoulder. He'd been shot from behind with an arrow. With his last bit of strength, he struggled farther up the mountain. He found a narrow cave in the ice and managed to hide from his enemies. As night approached, it turned very cold, and snow began to fall. Snow covered the dying hunter, and his body remained undisturbed for more than 5,000 years. He was discovered by hikers in 1991, when an unusually warm year caused the ice to thaw. His body then was studied by scientists, revealing much about how prehistoric people lived.

What do you think life was like for early humans?

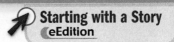

Reading & Writing

1. **READING: Reading Aloud** One way to read text fluently and accurately is to rehearse it. With a partner, read the text aloud. Practice those parts that give you trouble to gain the full dramatic effect.
2. **WRITING: Description** Imagine that you are going to make a documentary film about the hunter. Write a brief description of the film.

Lesson 1

MAIN IDEAS

1. **Geography** Early humans adapted to the natural environment.
2. **Culture** Humans created tools to ensure survival and to improve life.
3. **Culture** Early humans developed language, religion, and art.

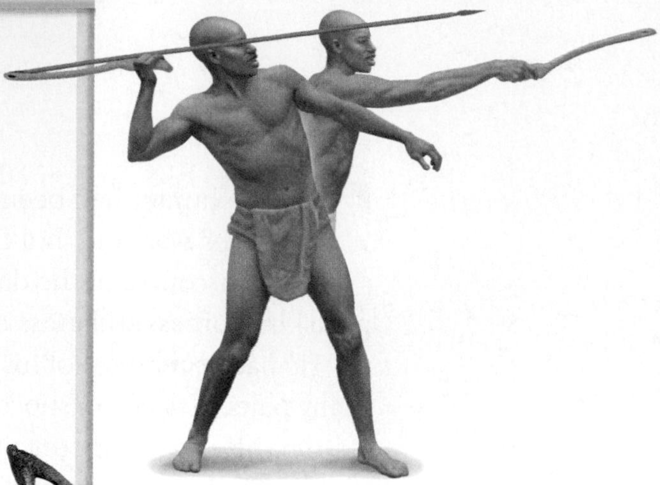

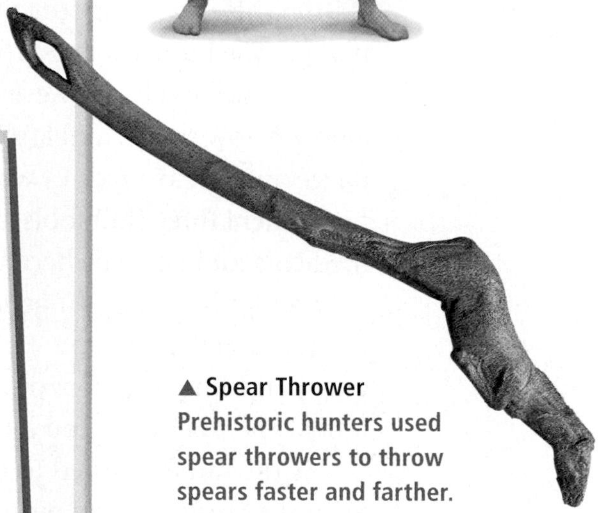

▲ **Spear Thrower**
Prehistoric hunters used spear throwers to throw spears faster and farther. These devices greatly improved their ability to hunt animals.

TAKING NOTES

Reading Skill: Summarizing

To summarize is to condense information into fewer words. Identify the main ideas and important details in this lesson. Then put them into your own words and record them in a graphic organizer like the one below.

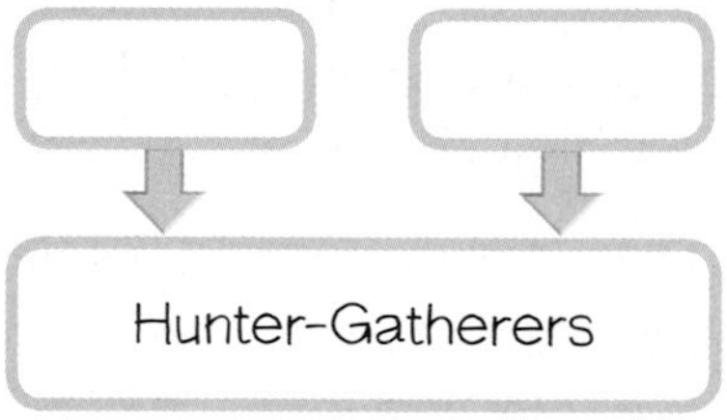

Skillbuilder Handbook, page R3

Words to Know

Understanding the following words will help you read this lesson:

band a group of people or animals acting together (page 52)
*Small **bands** of hunters searched for animals to kill for their meat and skins.*

community a group of people with close ties living in one area (page 52)
*Hunters provided meat for the new **communities**, which had grown large.*

apply to put into action or use (page 53)
*They were able to **apply** their knowledge of stone carving to make tools and weapons.*

spirit the part of a being believed to control thinking and feeling; the soul (page 54)
*He asked the tree's **spirit** to forgive him before he took its bark to use for his shelter.*

Hunters and Gatherers

TERMS & NAMES
hunter-gatherer
nomad
migration
technology
religion

Build on What You Know Have you ever gone camping? How would you survive if you got lost in the woods? Where would you find food and water? In this chapter, you will learn how early humans got food to eat, how they lived, and what tools they used.

Early Humans' Way of Life

1 ESSENTIAL QUESTION How did early humans interact with the environment?

Like early humans, you interact with the natural environment every day, often without thinking about it. You interact with the weather by wearing boots in the snow or sunglasses in the sunshine. Even your food is a product of the environment.

Hunter-Gatherers Adapt to Environments Early humans were **hunter-gatherers**. They hunted animals and gathered plants for food. When hunter-gatherers no longer had enough to eat, they moved to another location.

Early humans also depended on the natural environment for shelter. Some groups lived in caves and rock shelters. People who lived on plains or in desert areas may have made shelters out of branches, plant fibers, or animal skins.

African Savannah This photograph shows the kind of landscape over which the first hunter-gatherers roamed. Savannahs cover 40 percent of the African continent. ▼

Small Bands Hunter-gatherers lived together in small bands, each made up of several families. The size of a group—probably around 30 people—reflected the number of people who could live off the plants and animals in a given region. Men hunted and fished. Women gathered foods, such as berries and nuts from plants that grew wild. They cared for the children, who also worked.

Early Humans on the Move Hunter-gatherers were **nomads**, people who move from place to place. Movement often was limited. Groups returned to the same places with the changes of seasons. At certain times of the year, these early bands joined together, forming larger communities. There was probably time for storytelling, meeting friends, and finding marriage partners.

Early humans also moved to new and distant lands. The act of moving from one place to settle in another is called **migration**. Migrations may have been the result of people's following animals to hunt. By around 15,000 B.C., hunter-gatherers had migrated throughout much of the world. They even traveled across a land bridge connecting Siberia and Alaska. In this way, they entered the Americas.

Distribution of Hunter–Gatherers, 15,000 B.C.–A.D. 2000

INTERACTIVE

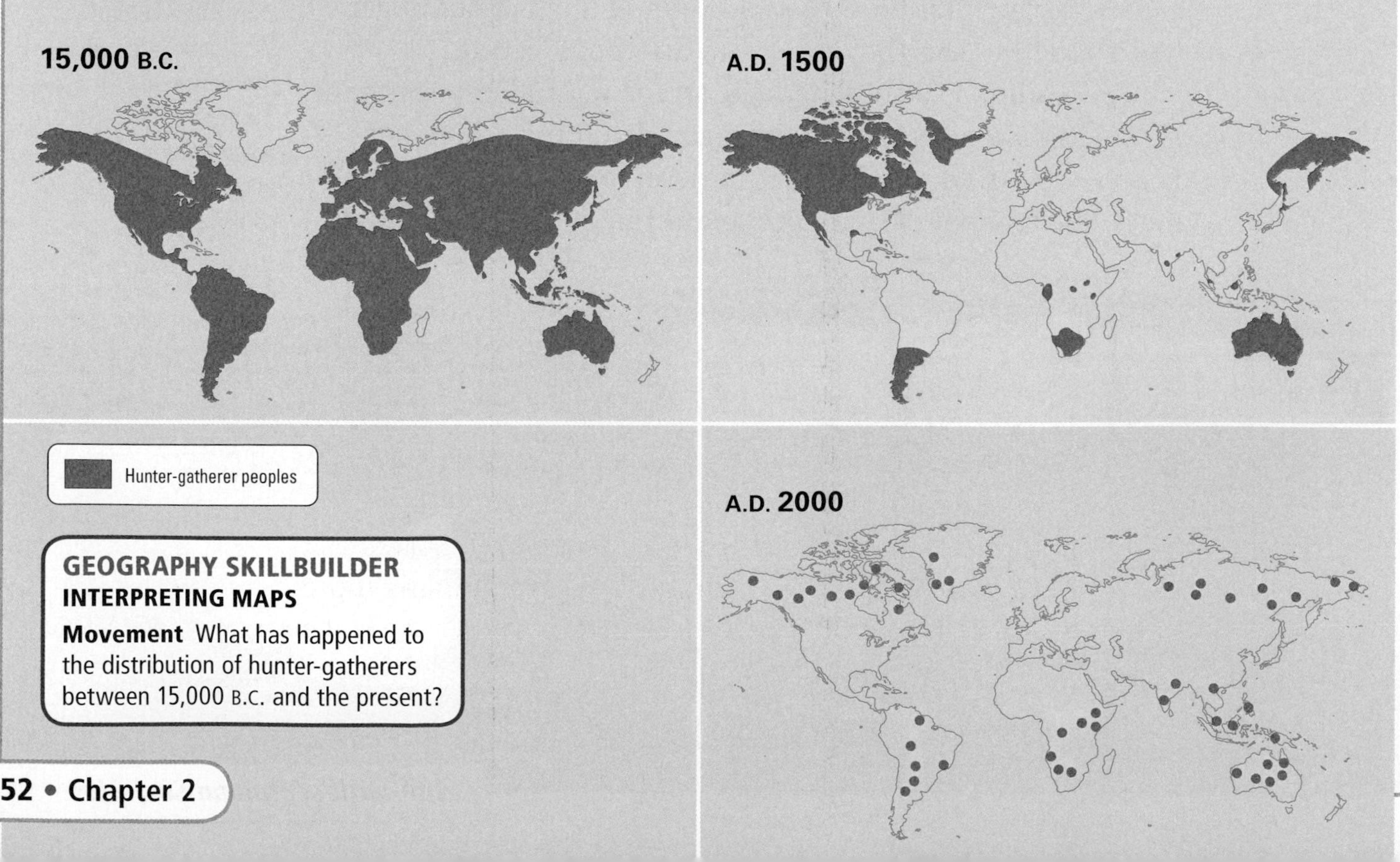

GEOGRAPHY SKILLBUILDER
INTERPRETING MAPS
Movement What has happened to the distribution of hunter-gatherers between 15,000 B.C. and the present?

The arrival of a migrating group in the territory of another people could lead to both good and bad outcomes. Everyone benefited when knowledge and tools were shared. However, people sometimes turned violent when they felt threatened by newcomers. They feared that the newcomers might try to take their territory. Sometimes they may have feared them just because they were different.

REVIEW Why did hunter-gatherers move often?

▲ **Early Tools** Among the tools used by early humans were the mattock (a digging tool), the harpoon, and the ax.

The Development of Tools

2 ESSENTIAL QUESTION What were some tools created by early humans?

Imagine that you are planning a camping trip. Think about what tools you will take to make sure your trip is safe and enjoyable. Like you, early humans relied on tools.

The Use of Fire Around 500,000 years ago, early humans learned to make and control fire. Fire provided heat and light, and it enabled people to cook food. A good fire offered protection from animals. Early humans also used fire to temper, or harden, tools made of metal.

The Development of Technology **Technology** consists of all of the ways in which people apply knowledge, tools, and inventions to meet their needs. Technology dates back to early humans. At least 2 million years ago, people made stone tools for cutting. Early humans also made carrying bags, stone hand axes, awls (tools for piercing holes in leather or wood), and drills.

In time, humans developed more complex tools, such as hunting bows made of wood. They learned to make flint spearheads and metal tools. Early humans used tools to hunt and butcher animals and to construct simple forms of shelter. Technology—these new tools—gave humans more control over their environment. These tools also set the stage for a more settled way of life.

REVIEW How did early humans use fire?

Vocabulary Strategy

You can figure out what *technology* means from its **root** and **suffix.** The Greek root *techn* means "craft" or "skill." The suffix *-logy* means "study of." *Technology* means "the study and application of crafts or skills."

Early Human Culture

3 ESSENTIAL QUESTION What kind of culture did early humans create?

What sets humans apart from other creatures? Art, language, and religion are special to humans and help create their culture.

Language Human language probably developed as a result of the need for people to work together. One theory suggests that the need for cooperation during the hunt spurred language development. Hunters needed to be able to talk to one another in order to outsmart, trap, and kill animals for food. Another theory suggests that the cooperation needed to gather and share food led to the development of language.

Religion **Religion** is the worship of God, gods, or spirits. Early humans probably believed that everything in nature, including rocks, trees, and animals, had a spirit. Some archaeologists believe that early cave paintings of animals were made to honor the spirits of animals killed for food.

Comparisons Across Cultures

Prehistoric Cave Art

Prehistoric people in different parts of the world painted scenes on cave walls. Such rock paintings are among the oldest art in the world.

The cave art on the top was done by a Native American artist in Utah. The painting shows a holy man holding a snake. Snakes were seen as links between the human and underground worlds.

The painting at the bottom was done by an Australian Aboriginal artist. It shows a dreamtime spirit. Dreamtime is a supernatural past in which ancestor spirits shaped the natural world.

SKILLBUILDER
INTERPRETING VISUALS
Making Inferences What do these examples tell you about early human art? On the basis of their art, how important does religion seem to have been in the lives of prehistoric peoples?

Art Prehistoric art gives us insights into humans' daily life and shared beliefs. Early humans created art in caves and rock shelters. They also created art they could carry with them.

More than 200 sites of early cave art have been discovered in France and Spain. Cave paintings thousands of years old show lively images of bulls, stallions, and bison. Prehistoric art exists in Africa, Asia, Europe, Australia, and the Americas.

Jewelry and figurines are examples of portable art. Early humans may have worn these items. Other items may have had religious meaning. Art also included music, dance, and stories—art that could be performed anywhere.

REVIEW What were the main elements of prehistoric culture?

Antler Headdress This red-deer antler headdress, which is about 9,500 years old, may have been used as a disguise in hunting or worn in hunting ceremonies. ▼

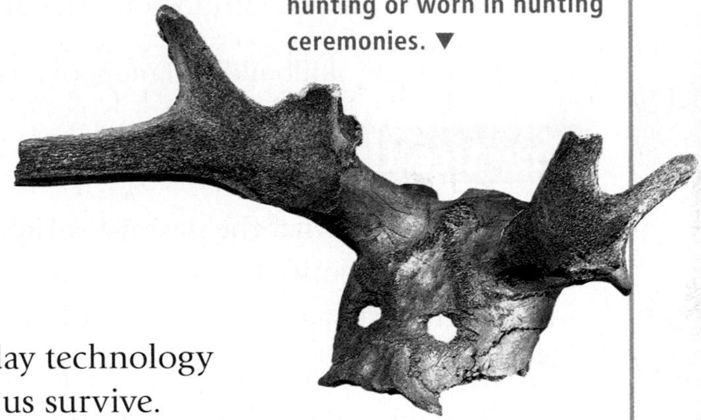

Lesson Summary

- Hunter-gatherers were nomads.
- Fire and tools improved lives.
- Early humans created language, religion, and art.

Why It Matters Now . . .

Early humans created the first tools. Today technology continues to improve our lives and help us survive.

1 Lesson Review

Homework Helper ClassZone.com

Terms & Names

1. Explain the importance of

hunter-gatherer	migration	religion
nomad	technology	

Using Your Notes

Summarizing Use your completed graphic organizer to answer the following question:

2. How did hunter-gatherers live?

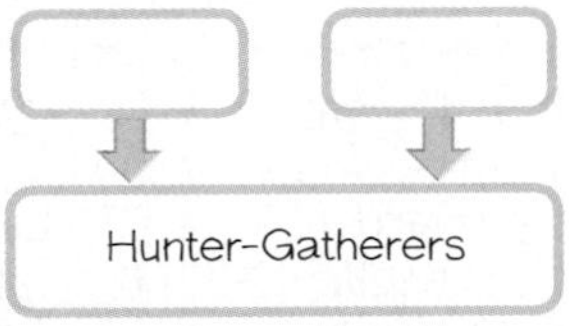

Main Ideas

3. How did prehistoric people use available natural resources for food, housing, and clothing?
4. How did the development of tools change the life of early humans?
5. Where are some of the places that prehistoric art has been found?

Critical Thinking

6. **Comparing and Contrasting** How was cave art different from other kinds of art created by early humans?
7. **Drawing Conclusions** What does their art tell us about early humans?

Activity

Making a Map Use the map on pages A6-A7 of the Atlas to sketch a world outline map. You will add to this map in later units. Use the map on page 52 to mark the location of the hunter-gatherer group closest to where you live.

Skillbuilder Extend Lesson 1

Finding Main Ideas

Goal: To identify the main idea of a passage in order to better understand hunter-gatherer societies

Learn the Skill

A main idea is the most important point in a paragraph or a passage. A main idea may or may not be stated in so many words. In the example to the right, the main idea is not stated. To find the main idea of a passage, identify the topic. Then, as you read, ask yourself this question: What main idea do the details and examples support?

See the Skillbuilder Handbook, page R2.

Practice the Skill

1. Ask yourself what the passage at right, titled "Hunter-Gatherer Societies," is about. Identify the topic by first looking at the title. The title tells you this passage is about what hunter-gatherer societies were like.
2. Look at the first and last sentences of each paragraph. These sentences often give clues to the main idea. See if any one sentence sums up the point of the whole passage. In this passage the main idea comes from combining the ideas in these sentences.
3. Read the entire passage. Look for details about the topic. What main idea do they explain or support? This passage contains details about both the good and the bad parts of hunter-gatherers' lives.
4. Use a chart like the one below to state the topic and list the supporting details. Use the information you record to help you state the main idea. This chart is based on the passage you just read.

Example:

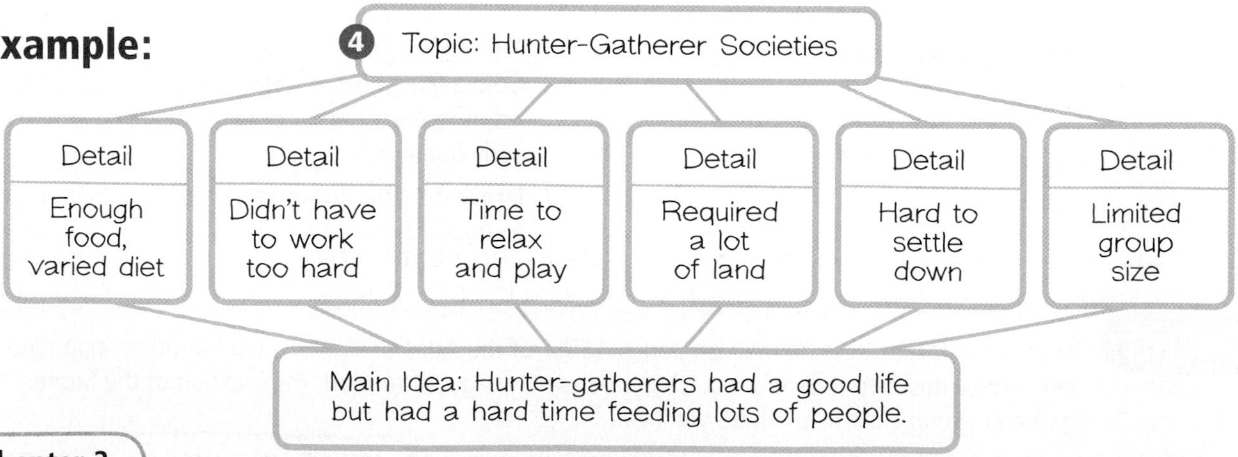

Secondary Source

Ideas about life in hunter-gatherer societies have changed since the 1960s. Until then, most scholars thought that ancient peoples' lives were very hard. Now many scholars have changed their minds. They have based their ideas on studies of hunter-gatherers in the modern world—groups who still live by hunting animals and gathering plants for food.

❶ *Hunter-Gatherer Societies*

▲ **Game Animals** This rock painting in Tanzania shows the possible favorite game animals of hunters.

❸

❷ Many scholars now believe that the lives of most hunter-gatherers were quite good. Their environment gave them all the kinds of food they needed. They had a varied diet of meat, fish, fruit, and wild plants. This diet was healthy and balanced. Usually, hunting and gathering did not require too much time and energy. People had time to relax, visit with friends, and play games. ❷

❷ Yet there were limits to the hunter-gatherer way of life. A lot of land was required to support a group of people. The group needed to roam across 7 to 500 square miles per person to get enough food. It was hard to settle in villages because people needed to move often to find food. They owned only what they could carry, and their houses had to be very simple. The groups had to be small, probably no more than about 30 people. As groups consumed the food in various areas, it became harder for societies to feed their people just by hunting and gathering. ❷

Apply the Skill

Turn to Chapter 1, Lesson 2, pages 17–19. Read "Different Maps for Different Purposes." Make a chart like the one at left to help you find the main ideas. Identify the topic, the most important details, and the main idea of the passage.

Lesson 2

MAIN IDEAS

1. **Science and Technology** New technologies supported an agricultural revolution.
2. **Culture** Agriculture made a big change in how people lived.
3. **Geography** Farming developed independently in many areas of the world.

TAKING NOTES

Reading Skill: Understanding Cause and Effect

Identifying causes and effects will help you understand the relationships among events in this lesson. In Lesson 2, look for the effects of the cause listed in the chart below. Record them in a chart of your own.

Cause	Effects
Agricultural revolution	1.
	2.
	3.

Skillbuilder Handbook, page R26

▲ **Pottery** This pottery figure from Hungary is holding a sickle, a farming tool. The figure represents a deity, or god, and dates back to about 4500 B.C.

Words to Know

Understanding the following words will help you read this lesson:

grazing animal an animal that feeds on growing grass (page 59)
*Humans could keep herds of **grazing animals** after they learned to grow grasses.*

develop to grow or cause to grow (page 60)
*As the number of villages in the region increased, a more complex economy **developed.***

fertile good for plants to grow in (page 60)
*Few people lived in the desert because it lacked water and **fertile** soil.*

Learning to Farm and Raise Animals

TERMS & NAMES
domesticate
agriculture
slash-and-burn
irrigation

Build on What You Know In the United States today, few people are farmers. However, in early human societies, almost everyone was a farmer. Today, because of technology, one farmer can raise enough food to feed many people.

The Beginnings of Agriculture

1 ESSENTIAL QUESTION What new farming tools and methods did early farmers invent?

Early humans were nomadic. They moved around in search of food. By around 8000 B.C., though, they had learned to modify the environment by growing plants and raising animals.

Climate Changes Global warming resulted in the retreat of the Ice Age glaciers. This retreat meant that early humans could move into new areas. As temperatures rose, the growing season became longer. Wild grasses spread and were **domesticated** by humans—that is, humans learned to grow and tend the grasses. This skill provided humans and grazing animals with more grain to eat.

Connect to Today

Peru A shepherd tends her sheep in the Andes Mountains of Peru. Sheep were among the first animals that humans learned to domesticate. ▼

The Domestication of Animals Early humans learned to domesticate animals such as sheep and goats around 9000 B.C. People raised them for food and clothing.

Domesticated animals offered a reliable source of meat and milk products. After people killed an animal, they used its skin to make clothing and shelters. They made harpoons, needles, and other tools from the bones.

The Agricultural Revolution Food gatherers noticed that grain sprouted from spilled seed. Around 8000 B.C., people got the idea of **agriculture**—planting seeds to raise crops.

Agricultural revolution is the name given to the shift from food gathering to food raising. The agricultural revolution brought about changes in tools and technology. People made hoes to loosen the soil, sticks to dig holes, and sickles to harvest grain.

Early farmers practiced **slash-and-burn** agriculture. They cut and then burned trees and brush to clear land for crops. After a number of growing seasons, soil often became poor. People then moved on to a new location.

REVIEW What was the impact of new tools on early humans?

Settlements Begin

2 ESSENTIAL QUESTION Why did villages develop?

People learned to be better farmers as their tools improved. Groups often remained in the same areas instead of moving around every few years. They began to develop permanent settlements.

Farming Villages Develop Fertile soil produced bigger and better crops. This attracted farmers. River valleys had soil that was especially rich. Their soil was better than that in fields that had been cleared by slashing and burning. Farmers settled in villages and went out to the fields to work. Villages grew to hold several thousand people. People lived in shelters made of mud, bricks, logs, and hides.

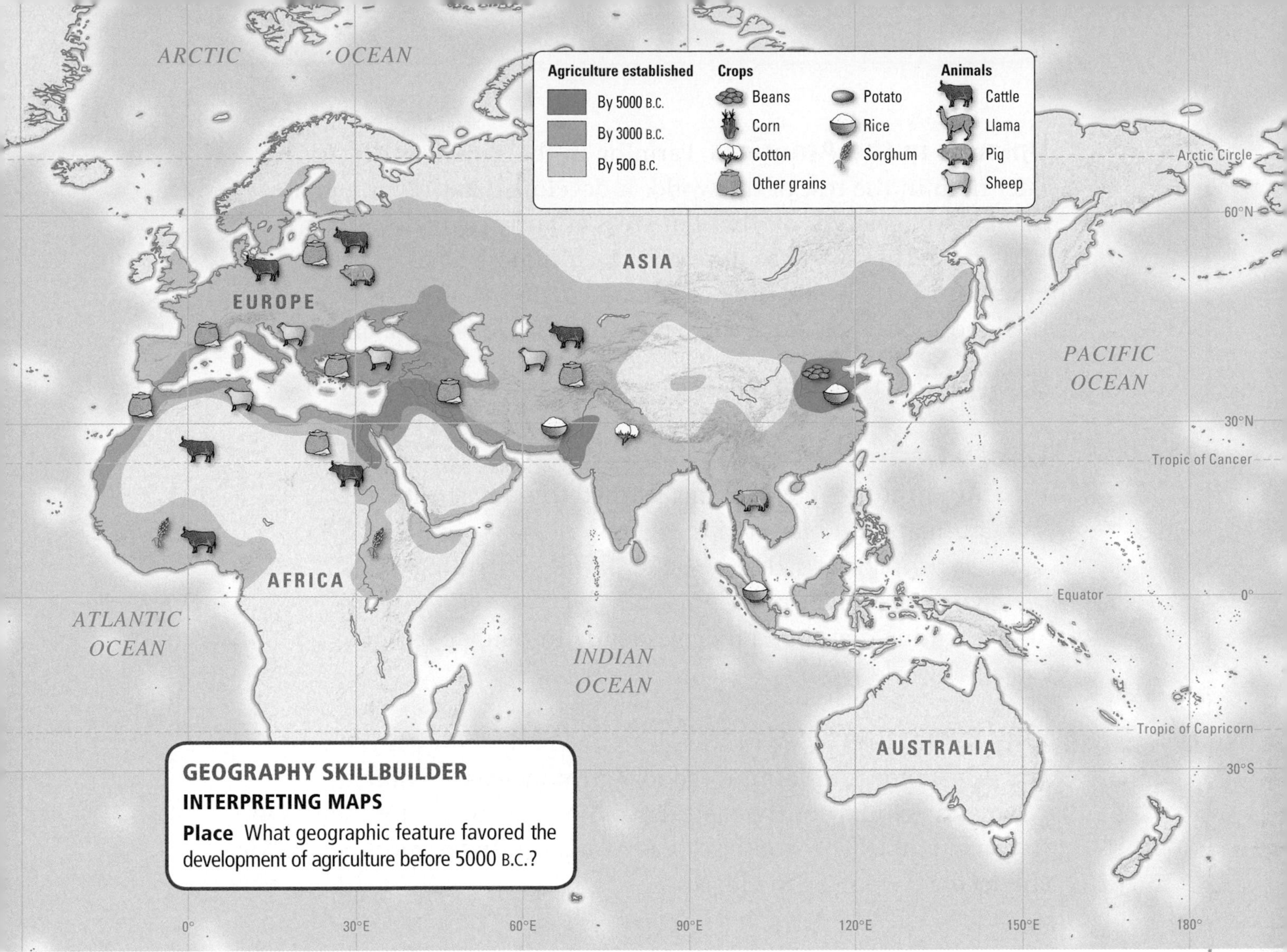

GEOGRAPHY SKILLBUILDER
INTERPRETING MAPS
Place What geographic feature favored the development of agriculture before 5000 B.C.?

Village life provided many advantages. Food was more plentiful. People living in larger groups could more easily withstand attacks by nomadic bands. Village life also had disadvantages, including the risks of fire, disease, and flood.

REVIEW How did farming change the way people lived?

Farming Develops in Many Places

3 ESSENTIAL QUESTION Where did farming develop?

About 8000 B.C., people in different parts of the world began to develop farming. Early farmers invented new methods of farming.

River Valleys in Africa and Asia Early farming developed in areas where water was available, such as in river valleys. These included the Huang He in China and the Nile in Africa. African farmers along the Nile were among the first to use **irrigation**—the watering of crops. They built irrigation systems of dikes and canals.

Uplands in the Americas Farming in the Americas developed later than in the rest of the world. It developed mainly in upland regions—plateaus and other flat areas at fairly high elevations. Farmers in the Americas developed techniques suited to the environment. The terracing of land to create flat areas helped adapt the land for raising crops such as corn, beans, potatoes, and squash.

REVIEW What crops did early farmers raise in the Americas?

Lesson Summary

- After the Ice Age, humans learned to domesticate animals and plant crops.
- As people learned to be better farmers, farming villages developed.
- Farming developed independently in many parts of the world.

Why It Matters Now . . .

The development of farming led to a great increase in human population. Today most people depend on agriculture for their food. In some parts of the world, such as Africa and India, most people are still farmers who live in villages.

2 Lesson Review

Homework Helper
ClassZone.com

Terms & Names

1. Explain the importance of

domesticate
agriculture
slash-and-burn
irrigation

Using Your Notes

Understanding Cause and Effect Use your completed chart to answer the following question:

2. What new technologies developed for growing and harvesting grain?

Cause	Effects
Agricultural revolution	1.
	2.
	3.

Main Ideas

3. What farming techniques were part of the agricultural revolution?
4. How did agriculture change the way people lived together?
5. In what geographical regions did farming develop in Asia, Africa, and the Americas?

Critical Thinking

6. **Cause and Effect** How did the end of the Ice Age affect the way people lived?
7. **Comparing and Contrasting** Compare the areas in which farming developed in Asia and Africa with those in which farming developed in the Americas. How were they different and similar?

Activity

Internet Activity Use the Internet to research farming techniques used by early farmers. Design one scene or panel of a mural on a blank sheet of paper.
INTERNET KEYWORD: *prehistoric farming tools*

Activity Extend Lesson 2

Grow a Plant

Goal: To understand the development of agriculture

Prepare

Your teacher will assign you to work in a group. He or she will recommend some fast-growing seeds. For each type of seed, you will learn about the effects of soil, light, and water.

Soil	potting soil	sand	subsoil
Sunlight	full sunlight	partial sunlight	minimal or no sunlight
Water	daily	every 3 days	every 5 days

Materials & Supplies

- plant pots, paper cups, or milk cartons
- potting soil
- sand
- subsoil (found 50–60 cm beneath topsoil)
- water
- three types of fast-growing seeds
- plastic wrap
- rubber bands

Do the Activity

1. Attach a label to each of the pots being used. Fill each pot with soil and moisten the soil. Plant two seeds in each pot. Cover each pot with plastic wrap, secured by a rubber band.
2. Once shoots appear, remove the plastic wrap. Pots being used to test for sunlight should be placed in locations that get different amounts of light. The amount of sunlight for all other pots should remain constant.
3. Record your observations over 4–6 weeks. Observations should include plant height, number of leaves, and greenness.

Follow-Up

1. At the end of the period, which plant was healthiest? What challenges do your observations suggest early farmers faced?
2. How have technological advances helped farmers?

Extension

Making a Presentation Each group should display its plants. As a class, discuss the ideal conditions for growing seeds.

Lesson 3

MAIN IDEAS

1. **Culture** Some simple farming villages expanded and developed into more complex villages.
2. **Culture** A cultural pattern involving early forms of government, specialized workers, and social classes began to develop in complex villages.
3. **Culture** The way of life in a complex village was different from that in a simple farming village.

TAKING NOTES

Reading Skill: Categorizing

Sorting information into groups helps you understand differences among the groups. In Lesson 3, look for the following three categories of information about the first communities. Record examples or details for each category in a web diagram.

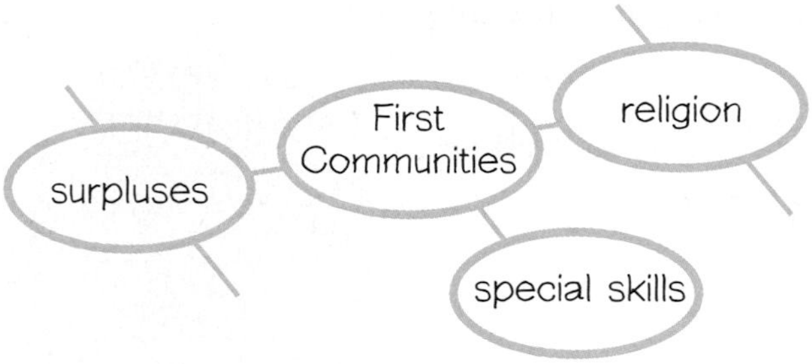

S Skillbuilder Handbook, page R6

▲ **Brooch** This prehistoric brooch was used for fastening a cloak at the neck. It was found on the bank of the Thames River in England.

Words to Know

Understanding the following words will help you read this lesson:

potter a person who makes objects, such as pots, from moist clay hardened by heat (page 66)
*The **potter** gave plates and bowls to the farmer.*

encourage to help to bring about; to foster (page 66)
*Great increases in food production **encouraged** population growth.*

inhabitant a resident of a place (page 67)
*Artifacts found in the ancient city give clues about the religious life of its **inhabitants.***

suggest to show indirectly (page 68)
*The presence of certain kinds of rocks would **suggest** that a volcano was located nearby.*

The First Communities

TERMS & NAMES
surplus
specialization
artisan
social class
government

Build on What You Know Do you live in the country, a small town, a city, or a suburb? In the distant past, simple farming villages developed, over hundreds of years, into more complex villages and eventually into cities.

Villages Around the World

1 ESSENTIAL QUESTION How did farming villages develop?

When villages prospered, they were able to support more people. Their populations grew. People's skills became more specialized. Village economies became more varied.

Surpluses Boost Development As agricultural techniques improved, farmers sometimes produced **surpluses**—more than what they needed to survive. For example, farmers might grow more grain than their families or village could use. The extra was an economic surplus.

Surpluses in early farming villages were not limited to food. Surpluses also included materials for making cloth and other products. Sheep raisers, for example, may have had surplus wool. Surpluses of food and other materials in good seasons helped villages survive bad seasons.

Moroccan Village
This modern village in the Atlas Mountains of Morocco in North Africa continues a way of life that has lasted for thousands of years. ▼

People Develop Different Skills As farmers began producing surpluses, not everyone had to raise food. People began specializing in other kinds of work. A **specialization** is a skill in one kind of work.

Potters and weavers probably were among the first to specialize. They made products that everyone could use. Potters made vessels for carrying and storing water and food. Weavers created cloth from spun cotton, wool, and flax—the plant from which linen is made. Potters and weavers traded their products for food.

Certain people in a community were regarded as holy. These holy people, or shamans, interpreted natural events such as rain or fire. They explained the meaning of a good or bad harvest. They were also healers. They were thought to be in contact with the spiritual world. Such people evolved into the priests of the first cities.

▲ **Necklace and Pottery** People with special skills made different objects. The pottery jar was made about 1800 B.C. The necklace is roughly the same age. Both were produced by early civilizations in Southwest Asia.

The way of life in a village was new and very different. Hunter-gatherers led a nomadic life, moving from place to place. Villagers settled in one place and no longer depended on hunting and gathering for food. Instead, farmers worked to raise enough food for everyone in the village. Work became more specialized, with nonfarmers trading their goods and services for food.

REVIEW How did surpluses affect village life?

Simple Villages Grow More Complex

2 ESSENTIAL QUESTION How did life in villages become more complex?

Surpluses and specialization led to the growth of villages. Life became more complex in certain villages as they developed.

A Changing Way of Life Extra food and other supplies meant that more people could live together. In this way, surpluses encouraged the growth of villages and populations. Surpluses also led to increased trade. People in one village might trade their surplus food for the surplus tools in another village.

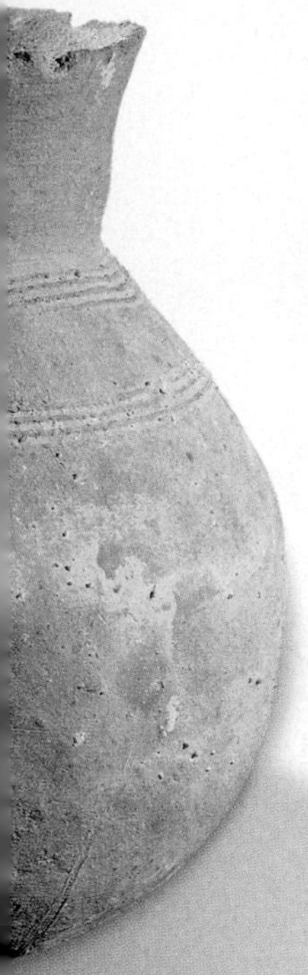

Workers became more specialized. Potters, weavers, and other craftspeople often spent years learning their skills. People trained in skills or crafts are called **artisans**. Carpenters, toolmakers, cloth makers, and potters are all artisans. People with similar skills developed into occupational classes. In this way, specialization led to the development of social classes. A **social class** is a group of people with similar customs, background, training, and income, such as farmers, craftspeople, priests, or rulers.

Vocabulary Strategy

Artisan means "a skilled worker or craftsperson." Its **antonym,** or opposite, is *unskilled worker.* The movement from unskilled to skilled workers represented an important change.

As ancient communities grew into larger villages, people felt the need for laws and leadership to keep order and settle disputes. People developed early forms of **government**—that is, ways of creating order and providing leadership. Early humans made laws to make their communities both safer and more stable.

From Simple to Complex Villages A complex village had a larger population than a simple village, with people living closer together. The larger population had a greater supply of skills, ideas, and needs. As a result, life in a complex village was more varied and complicated than that in a simple village.

REVIEW What are some examples of specialized labor?

Life in a Complex Village

3 ESSENTIAL QUESTION How did life in a complex village compare with that in a simple village?

Complex villages were not like the cities of today. Although one of these villages may have had as many as 5,000 people, it would be quite small by today's standards. However, thousands of years ago, a village with a population of 5,000 would have been very large.

Technology was still in its early stages. Electricity, rapid transit, sewer systems, and concrete buildings support today's huge city populations. In ancient times, these tools and technologies had not yet been invented. Most farming villages had only a few hundred inhabitants.

Characteristics of Complex Villages

Larger populations	thousands of people
Beginnings of government	leaders; laws or other means of settling disputes
Public buildings	shrines and other accommodations for gatherings of people
Specialized workers	artisans and other skilled workers
Social classes	groups with similar trainings and incomes
Trade	exchange of surplus goods

Primary Source

Artifacts

Primary sources include artifacts, or objects, from the past. Artifacts include tools, weapons, sculptures, and jewelry made by human beings. These objects can tell us much about ancient peoples and cultures.

- The seal at the top was found in a burial site in Catal Huyuk. (chah•TAHL hoo•YOOK) It was used as a stamp to show ownership. None of the designs is repeated on the many seals that have been found.
- The dagger at the bottom was also found in Catal Huyuk. It has a snake handle. The blade is made of flint imported from Syria. It was probably used in religious ceremonies or rituals.

DOCUMENT–BASED QUESTION
What conclusions can you draw about the life of the people in Catal Huyuk by looking at these artifacts?

Catal Huyuk Catal Huyuk is an example of a complex village. Its ruins are at least 8,000 years old, and it had a population of about 5,000. Archaeologists began unearthing and studying Catal Huyuk in 1961.

Catal Huyuk is located in Turkey, where agriculture developed fairly early. (See map on page 61.) The bones of many water birds found at Catal Huyuk suggest that the village was built in a marshy area. Farming probably took place in outlying areas.

A Village Develops Although Catal Huyuk had a small population, its site has yielded evidence of the complex life of its dwellers. The layout of the village shows that people lived in clusters of permanent buildings. Houses had similar floor plans, although the bricks used to build them varied in size.

Other buildings served as shrines, where religious ceremonies took place. Wall paintings in the shrines have religious meaning. Small amounts of charred grain and other offerings to the gods show that these buildings were sacred sites.

The people of Catal Huyuk developed special skills, such as making tools. Artisans also created luxury items, such as mirrors and metal beads. They produced cloth, wooden vessels, and simple pottery. Artists created murals on the clay walls of many buildings. Specialization established Catal Huyuk as a center of trade, culture, and influence.

▲ **Wall Painting**
This painting shows a red bull surrounded by humans. It was painted on the inside wall of a shrine in the village of Catal Huyuk.

REVIEW What characteristics of Catal Huyuk identify it as a complex village?

Lesson Summary

- Improved farming techniques enabled village farmers to grow surplus food.
- Simple villages sometimes grew into complex villages.
- Catal Huyuk is the site of an early complex village.

Why It Matters Now . . .

The development of complex villages was an important step in the change from simple villages to cities.

3 Lesson Review

Homework Helper
ClassZone.com

Terms & Names

1. Explain the importance of

surplus	artisan	government
specialization	social class	

Using Your Notes

Categorizing Use your completed web diagram to answer the following question:

2. Why were pottery and weaving among the first skills to be developed?

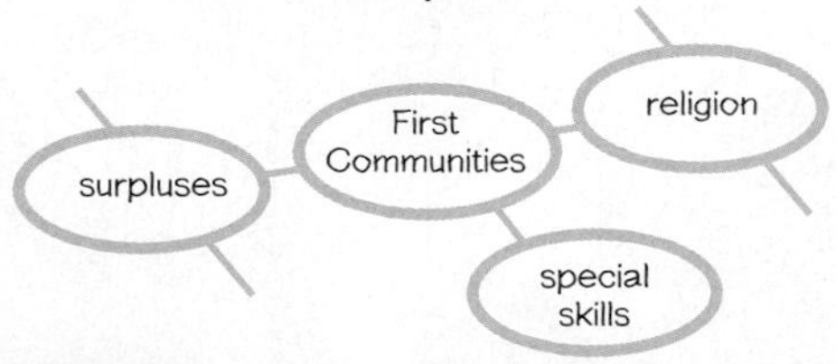

Main Ideas

3. Why did surpluses lead to the growth of trade?

4. What are the basic characteristics of a complex village?

5. How does its inhabitants' way of life indicate that Catal Huyuk was a complex village?

Critical Thinking

6. Comparing and Contrasting What would be the pros and cons of living as a nomad? in a simple village? in a complex village?

7. Making Inferences How did specialization help to establish social classes?

Activity

Planning a Museum Display Plan a museum display showing specializations that people practiced in early villages. On a poster, make a two-column chart. List the display items on the left. Opposite each item, write a brief description.

Daily Life

Extend Lesson 3

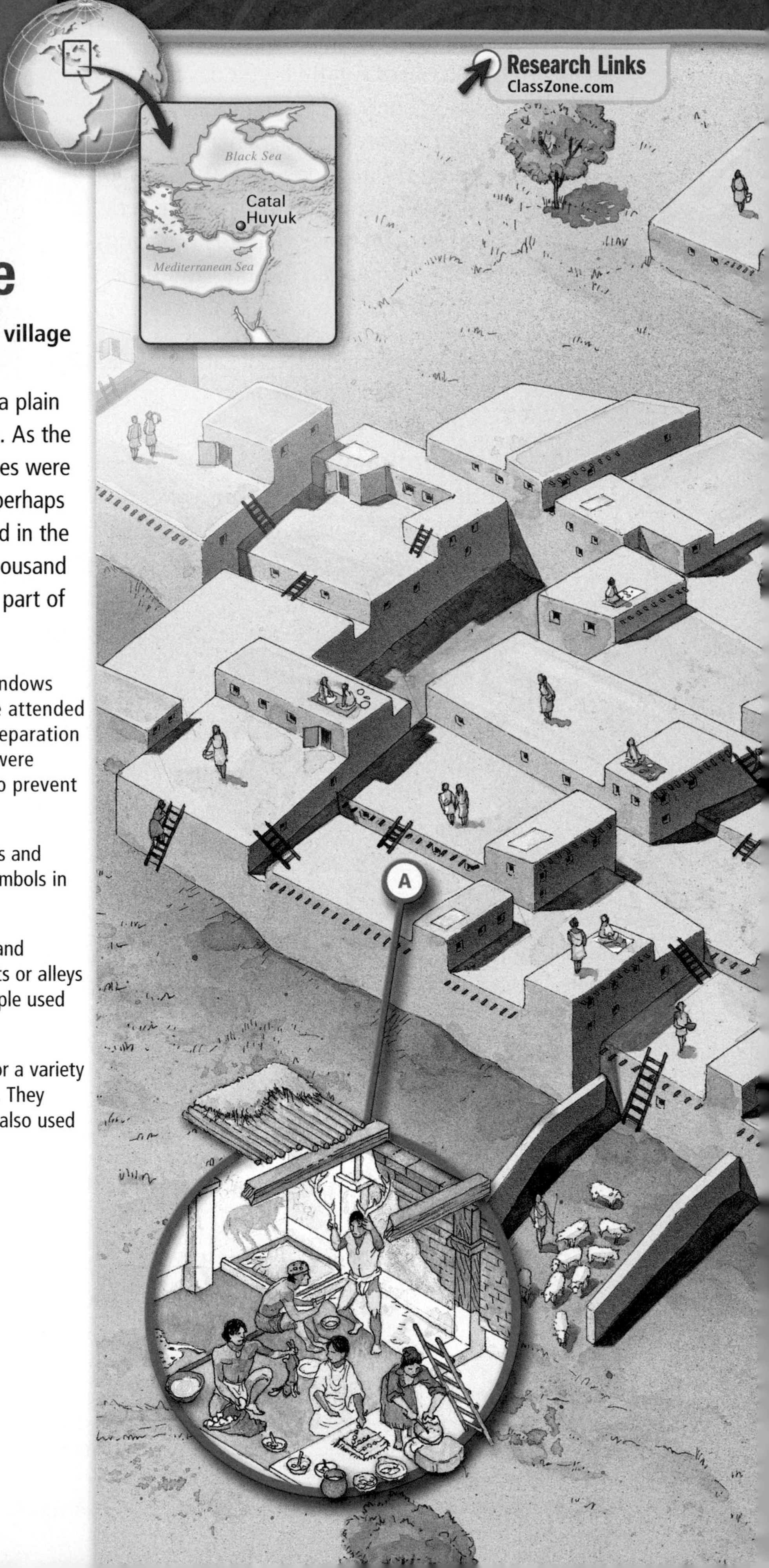

Research Links
ClassZone.com

Living in a Complex Village

Purpose: To learn about life in a village around 7000 B.C.

Catal Huyuk was located on a river in a plain that was well suited for growing crops. As the settlement prospered, permanent homes were built of mud brick. Around 7000 B.C., perhaps as many as 5,000 or 6,000 people lived in the town, which contained more than a thousand houses. Many different activities were part of daily life in the town.

A House Interiors The houses had windows and doors. Within the houses, people attended to their daily chores, including the preparation of food. The clay hearths and ovens were built in and had curbs around them to prevent embers from spreading.

B Shrines Shrines contained bulls' heads and horns. These were common religious symbols in the village.

C Houses with Ladders Over a thousand houses were packed together. No streets or alleys separated the houses. For security, people used ladders to enter the village.

D Rooftops People used the rooftops for a variety of purposes. They traveled across roofs. They slept on the roofs in hot weather. They also used the roofs to dry their crops in the sun.

Activities

1. **TALK ABOUT IT** What were some of the advantages of living in a village like Catal Huyuk?
2. **WRITE ABOUT IT** This illustration shows a variety of scenes in an early village. Choose one of the scenes and write a brief story about it.

Chapter 2 Review

VISUAL SUMMARY

The Earliest Human Societies

Geography

- Early humans adapted to their environment.
- Hunter-gatherers lived a nomadic life in pursuit of animals.
- Farming developed in many parts of the world.

Science & Technology

- Humans desire to explore the world and solve problems.
- Weapons and tools helped hunter-gatherers to survive.
- New technologies developed to support the agricultural revolution.

Culture

- Early humans developed language, religion, and art.
- Agriculture caused a change in how people lived.
- Simple farming villages developed into complex villages.

TERMS & NAMES

Explain why the words in each pair below are linked with each other.

1. **hunter-gatherer** and **nomad**
2. **irrigation** and **slash-and-burn**
3. **specialization** and **artisan**

MAIN IDEAS

Hunters and Gatherers (pages 50–57)

4. How did hunter-gatherers interact with the environment?
5. Why was the development of technology important to early humans?

Learning to Farm and Raise Animals (pages 58–63)

6. How did the domestication of animals affect people's lives?
7. How did environmental conditions influence the locations of early farms?

The First Communities (pages 64–71)

8. What factors caused simple villages to develop into complex villages?
9. In what ways was life in Catal Huyuk more complex than life in a simple farming village?

CRITICAL THINKING

Big Ideas: Culture

10. **FINDING MAIN IDEAS** As early communities grew larger, how did village life change?
11. **UNDERSTANDING CAUSE AND EFFECT** How did the development of tools affect agriculture?
12. **UNDERSTANDING CONTINUITY AND CHANGE** What were some of the changes that occurred in the way people lived as they changed from a nomadic to a settled way of life?

ALTERNATIVE ASSESSMENT

1. **WRITING ACTIVITY** Choose one of the examples of early art shown in this chapter. Write one or two paragraphs about an event that might have inspired the work of art or about a story that the art is attempting to tell.

2. **INTERDISCIPLINARY ACTIVITY—SCIENCE** Make a chart comparing early farming in the Americas with that in African and Asian river valleys. Include the following factors: type of terrain, crops grown, and farming techniques. Use books and the Internet to find information.

3. **STARTING WITH A STORY** Review the description you wrote of your documentary. Create a storyboard with simple sketches of the scenes you will include. Write a brief caption for each.

Technology Activity

4. **CREATING A MULTIMEDIA PRESENTATION** Use the Internet or library resources to research an early complex village, such as Catal Huyuk. Jericho is another example of a complex village. Create a multimedia presentation that includes
   - information and visuals of the layout of the village and its buildings and structures
   - images of artifacts and other evidence of culture
   - a map showing the village's location
   - text for each slide
   - documentation of your sources

Research Links
ClassZone.com

Reading Charts Use the chart below to answer the questions.

The Domestication of Animals

Animal	Location	Use
llama	South America	transport, meat
turkey	North America	meat
guinea pig	South America	meat
horse	Asia (southwestern steppes)	transport
dog	Asia (possibly China)	guarding, herding, hunting
camel	Asia (central and Near East)	transport
cat	Africa	killing mice and rats
sheep	Europe, Asia, Africa	meat, wool
goat	Asia	milk, meat
pig	Europe, Asia	meat
cattle	Europe, Asia, Africa	milk, meat
chicken	Asia (southeastern)	meat, eggs

1. How were turkeys, guinea pigs, and pigs used?

A. protection
B. meat
C. transport
D. clothes

2. Which animals were domesticated in South America?

A. turkey, pig
B. horse, goat
C. llama, guinea pig
D. camel, cattle

Test Practice
ClassZone.com

Additional Test Practice, pp. S1–S33

Writing About History

Writing Model
ClassZone.com

Narratives:
A Story About Early Humans

Purpose: To write a narrative for a class magazine about early humans
Audience: Your class

In this unit, you read stories about teenagers who discovered cave paintings, anthropologists who found Lucy's skeleton, and the ice man's fate. Another name for a story is a **narrative.**

Some narratives are based mostly on imagination. Historians, though, write narratives about events that really happened. Their stories are based on facts. But without the ability to interpret information, a historian could not turn the factual evidence from artifacts into a story of the past.

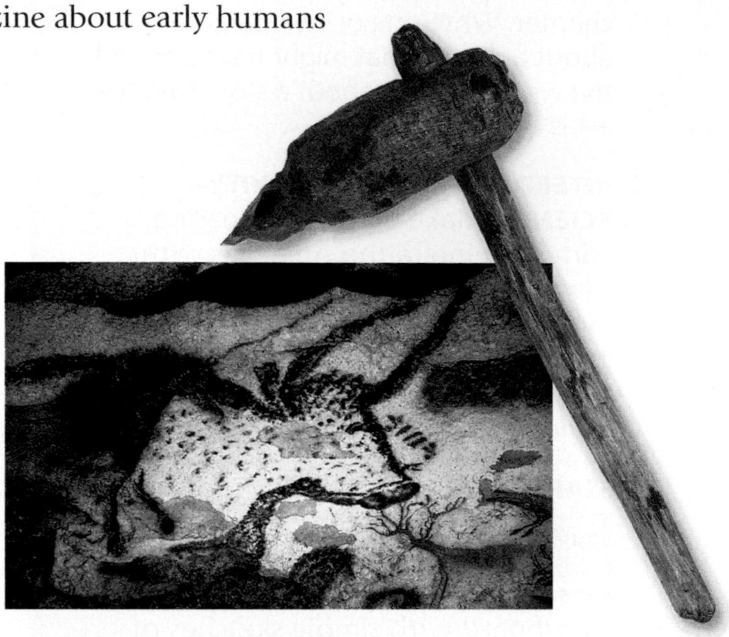

▲ Lascaux Cave painting and prehistoric tool

Organization & Focus

Your assignment is to write a narrative about early humans. A narrative has three basic parts. The **beginning** sets the scene and starts the action. The **body** presents a conflict. The **resolution** settles the conflict and ends the story. The first step in writing a narrative is to focus on a topic.

Choosing a Topic Here are some ways to help you think of topics about early humans to write about.

- Note facts or ideas from Chapters 1 and 2 that might make a good narrative.
- Review the images in these chapters. What story might exist behind each one?
- Talk to a classmate. Share ideas that might work as good stories.

Identifying Purpose and Audience For this writing assignment, your purpose and audience are provided above. In general, to plan a narrative, consider the following two questions:

- Why are you writing this story? Thinking about what interests you about this topic will help you decide on your purpose.
- Who will read this story? Your writing will change based on the ages, education levels, and interests of your audience.

Finding Details Organize information about your topic in a chart like the one below. List words and phrases that will make the narrative vivid and engaging.

Narrative Elements	Main Point	Vivid Details
What is the setting?		
Who are the characters?		
What is the point of view of the person telling the story?		
What is the main conflict?		
How is the conflict resolved?		

Outlining and Drafting Create an outline for your story using the details from your chart. Then write the first draft. Transition words and phrases, such as *later, next,* and *the following day,* can tell the order of events. Include dialogue if you wish.

Research & Technology

You can find information to use in your narrative in a library or on the Internet. Use notecards to record facts and ideas that will help you decide what to write. Try to make your story as real as possible.

Technology Tip Before you go online, have a search strategy. Identify specific questions and keywords. Ask a librarian to recommend search engines and directories.

Evaluation & Revision

Work on your narrative until you are ready to share it. Here are some ways to check your draft and improve it.

- Read it aloud and ask for feedback.
- Write a title.
- Check all details.

When you are done, create a neat, clean copy.

Self-Check

Does my narrative have

- ☐ historical information?
- ☐ a conflict?
- ☐ a beginning, middle, and end?
- ☐ interesting characters?

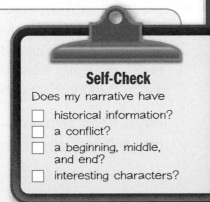

Publish & Present

To create the magazine, divide up these tasks.

- Design front and back covers and create illustrations.
- Organize the stories and create a table of contents.
- Think of a title for the magazine.
- Share the magazine with other social studies classes.

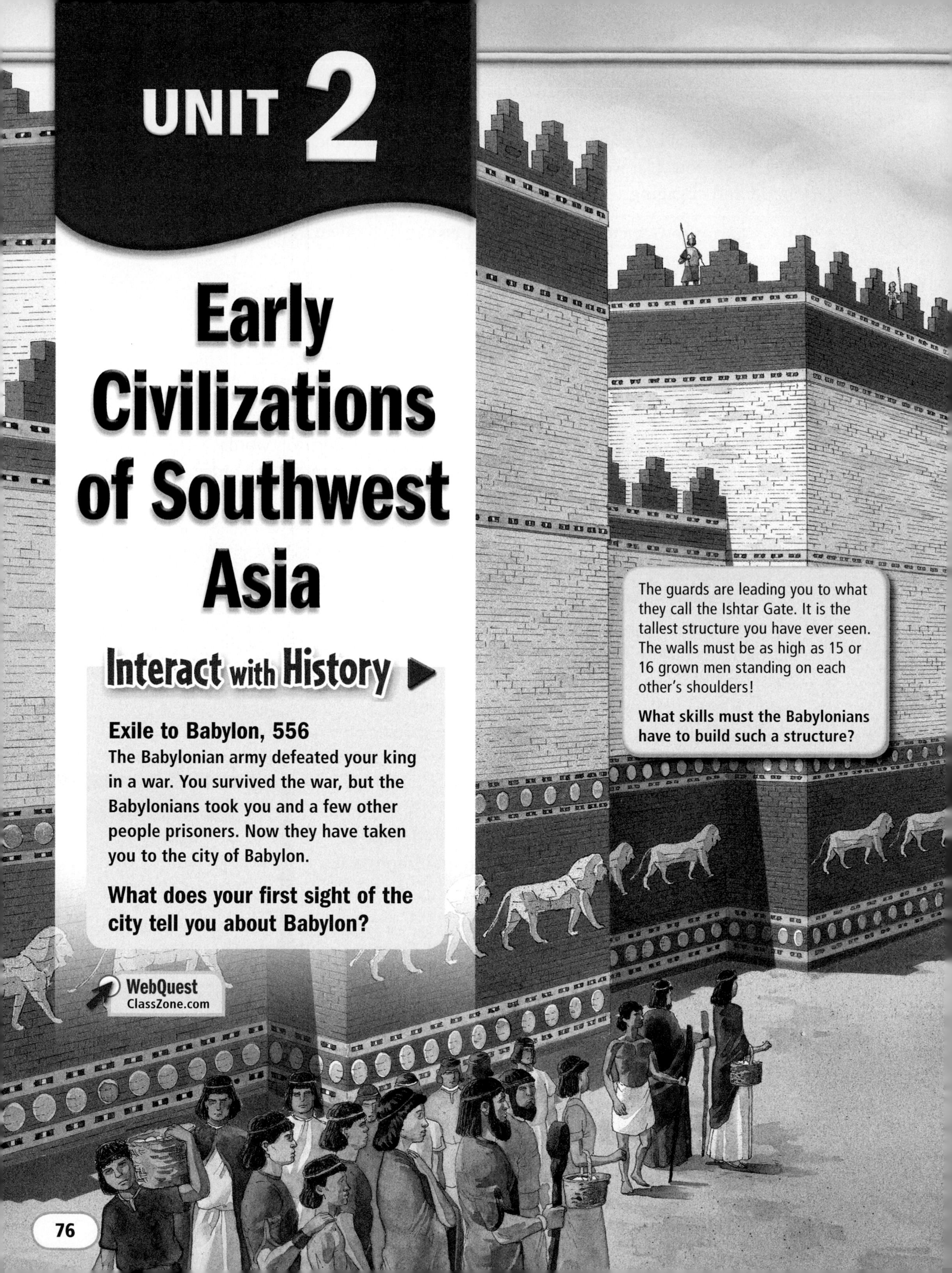

UNIT 2

Early Civilizations of Southwest Asia

Interact with History

Exile to Babylon, 556

The Babylonian army defeated your king in a war. You survived the war, but the Babylonians took you and a few other people prisoners. Now they have taken you to the city of Babylon.

What does your first sight of the city tell you about Babylon?

The guards are leading you to what they call the Ishtar Gate. It is the tallest structure you have ever seen. The walls must be as high as 15 or 16 grown men standing on each other's shoulders!

What skills must the Babylonians have to build such a structure?

WebQuest
ClassZone.com

Chapter 3
Ancient Mesopotamia
Chapter 4
Early Empires
On top of the gate and the surrounding walls stand armed men. They hold spears and bows and arrows. You didn't realize that the army that defeated your king was only a part of the full strength of Babylon.
What purpose do the soldiers on the wall serve?
The bricks of the gate are the most amazing color—a blue that is as dark as the evening sky. Pictures of dragons and bulls decorate the walls.
What qualities do bulls and dragons have in common? Why might the Babylonians admire them?

Chapter 3 Ancient Mesopotamia

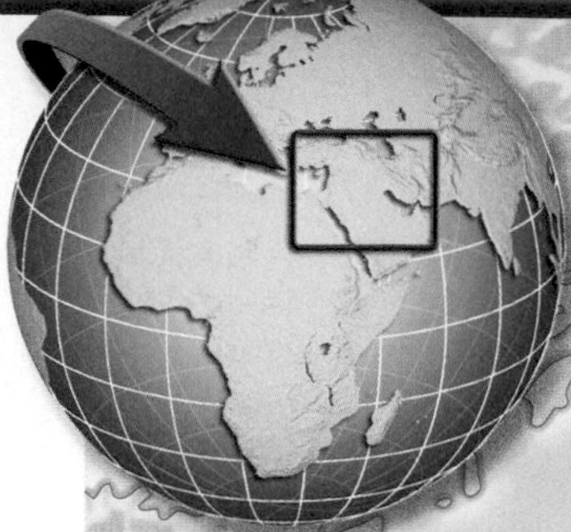

Before You Read: Previewing Key Concepts

The Big Idea below is a general historical idea. Rewrite this idea as three questions that can be answered as you read this chapter. One example is:

How did the geography of ancient Mesopotamia help agriculture develop?

Look for the answers to your questions as you read.

Big Ideas About Ancient Mesopotamia

Geography Civilizations arise in geographic locations that help the development of agriculture or trade or both.

Mesopotamia is a region that has two great rivers. They provided ancient people with water for drinking and for crops. When the rivers flooded, they deposited fresh soil on the land, making it good for farming. In addition, it was easy to move trade goods by boat down the rivers.

Integrated Technology

eEdition
- Interactive Maps
- Interactive Visuals
- Starting with a Story

VIDEO *Ancient Mesopotamia*

INTERNET RESOURCES

Go to **ClassZone.com** for
- WebQuest
- Homework Helper
- Research Links
- Internet Activities
- Quizzes
- Maps
- Test Practice
- Current Events

AFRICA

20°E

30°E

MESOPOTAMIA

5000 B.C.
People by the Euphrates River begin to irrigate crops.
(jug, about 3000 B.C.) ▶

5000 B.C. | 4600 B.C. | 4200 B.C.

WORLD

4000 B.C.
A dry period begins in Africa, causing the Sahara to spread.
◀ (the Sahara today)

Mesopotamia, 2400 B.C.

INTERACTIVE

3500 B.C.
Farming villages grow into cities.

3000 B.C.
The first system of writing is in use.
◄ (tablet, about 2100 B.C.)

2400 B.C.
King Urukagina of Lagash reforms government.

3400 B.C. | 3000 B.C. | 2600 B.C. | 2200 B.C.

3100 B.C.
King Narmer unifies Egypt.

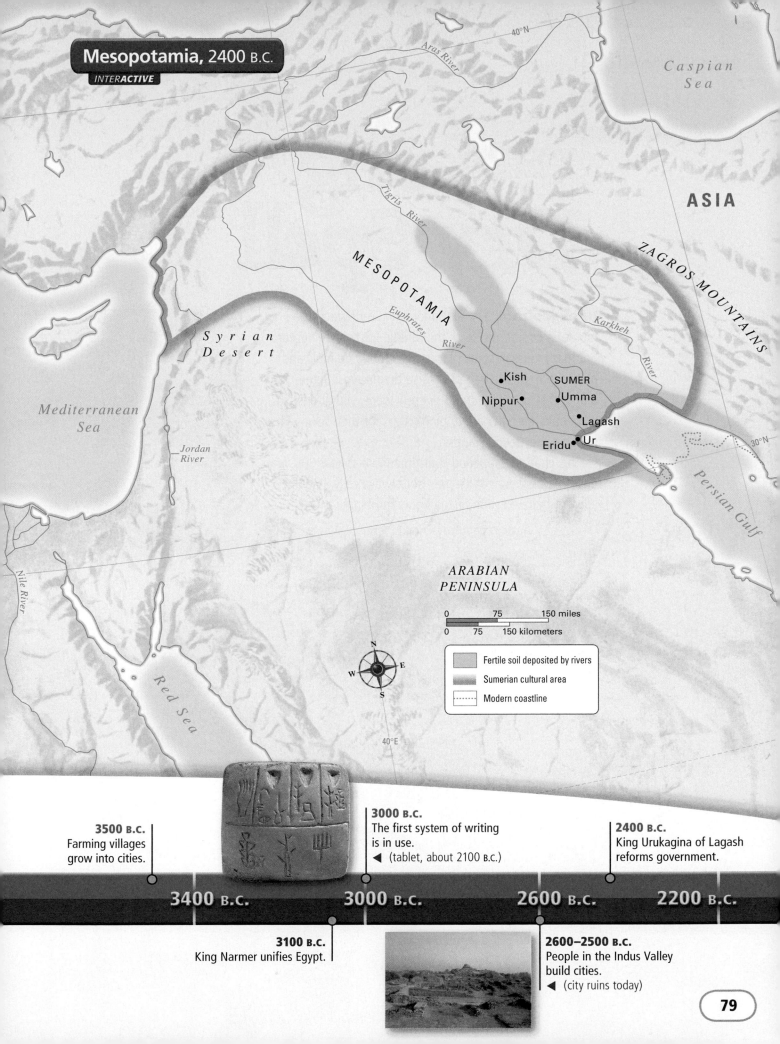

2600–2500 B.C.
People in the Indus Valley build cities.
◄ (city ruins today)

Starting with a Story

THE Long Dry Spell

Background: The first people in Southwest Asia (sometimes referred to as the Middle East) were hunters and gatherers. In some places, they found animals and plants that people began to raise themselves. Some plants that people learned to grow were wild grains. So as people learned how to plant crops for themselves, they began to settle in villages.

This change happened over time more than 8,000 years ago. The new way of life was not always easy. Imagine you are there as your village fights for its life.

Ancient people learned to grow wheat for food. ▶

You are a farmer in Southwest Asia. The oldest members of your family decided several years ago to settle in a new village near a river. They knew the river had something special about it that would make this place suitable for farming.

Every year the river floods and puts a fresh layer of rich, dark mud on the fields. This mud provides moisture to the soil and somehow seems to help plants grow. You depend on the flood to be able to farm.

This year the flood never happened because there wasn't enough rain. With no moisture, the soil was hard when you were ready to plant. Your sharpened digging stick barely penetrated the soil enough for you to put the seeds in the ground.

Now the weather is hot and dry, and the tiny plants are struggling to survive. Every day the scorching sun beats down on them. Their leaves wilt. Large cracks are appearing in the ground, and crops are dying.

The brutal heat makes it difficult to work. Yet every day you must walk to the river with animal-skin bags to get water for the plants. You repeat the trip hour after hour, until your legs feel like they won't support you any longer. Your back aches from carrying water and from bending over your crops. The plants need every drop of moisture they can get. But the heat of the sun seems to evaporate the water as soon as it hits the ground.

At times like this, farming seems like fighting a losing battle. If your crops die, your family won't have enough food. Trudging back and forth to the river, you pray to the gods for help. Sick with worry, you wonder how to avoid this situation in the future.

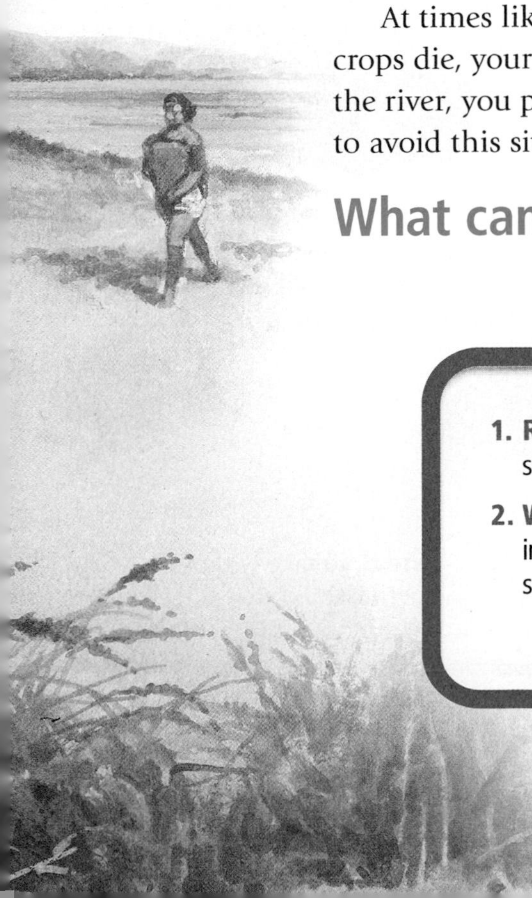

What can you invent to make farming easier?

Reading & Writing

1. **READING: Setting** Setting is the place and time of a story. How did setting influence the problem in this story?
2. **WRITING: Explanation** Write a description of your invention. Explain how it works step by step. Conclude by summarizing how the invention will change farming.

Lesson 1

MAIN IDEAS

1. **Geography** The land between the Tigris and Euphrates rivers was a good region for agriculture.
2. **Geography** The environment of Mesopotamia presented several challenges to the people who lived there.
3. **Geography** Mesopotamians changed their environment to improve life.

TAKING NOTES

Reading Skill: Summarizing

To summarize is to restate a passage in fewer words. After you read Lesson 1, write a sentence or two summarizing each of the three main sections. Use a chart like this one to record your summaries.

Geography of Mesopotamia
The rivers of Mesopotamia were important because . . .
Mesopotamians watered their crops by . . .
Because of a lack of resources, . . .

Skillbuilder Handbook, page R3

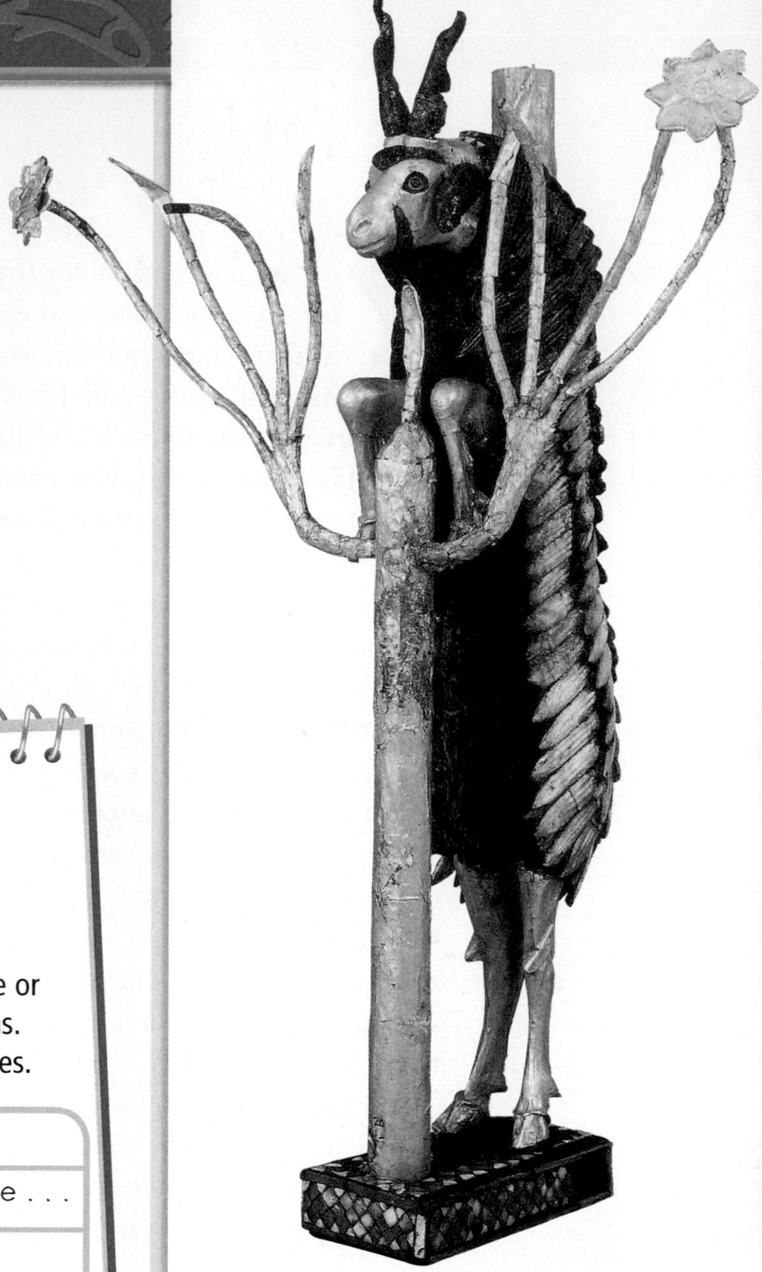

▲ **Ram** This figurine shows a ram caught in a thicket. It is made of gold, shell, and a blue stone called lapis.

Words to Know

Understanding the following words will help you read this lesson:

current a flowing part of a river or stream (page 83)

*Experienced travelers knew how **currents** affected boats on the river.*

swell to increase in size or volume (page 84)

*The farmers knew that the river would **swell**, pour over its low banks, and flood their fields.*

clog to block up (page 85)

*The water slowed to a trickle because the canal through which it flowed was **clogged** with dirt.*

steal to take without permission (page 85)

*The thieves planned to sneak into the village at night to **steal** food and valuables.*

Geography of Mesopotamia

TERMS & NAMES
- Mesopotamia
- floodplain
- silt
- semiarid
- drought
- surplus

Build on What You Know Think of a time when you have seen pictures of a flood on television or in newspapers. Floods cause destruction by washing away objects in their path. Do you think a flood can also have good consequences?

The Land Between Two Rivers

1 ESSENTIAL QUESTION How did the land between the Tigris and Euphrates rivers support agriculture?

The Tigris (TY•grihs) and Euphrates (yoo•FRAY•teez) rivers are in Southwest Asia. They start in the mountains of what are now Turkey and Kurdistan. From there they flow through what is now Iraq southeast to the Persian Gulf. (See the map on pages 78–79.)

Mesopotamia The region where these two rivers flow is called **Mesopotamia** (MEHS•uh•puh•TAY•mee•uh). The name means "land between the rivers." This land was mostly flat with small, scrubby plants.

The rivers provided water and means of travel. In ancient times, it was easier to travel by boat than over land. Boats can carry heavy loads. River currents helped move boats that were traveling down river. Also, few roads existed.

Connect to Today

Euphrates River Even today, people of Mesopotamia farm the land next to the Euphrates River. The flat land by a river is a floodplain. ▼

Fertile Soil Almost every year, rain and melting snow in the mountains caused the rivers to swell. As the water flowed down the mountains, it picked up soil. When the rivers reached the plains, water overflowed onto the **floodplain**, the flat land bordering the banks. As the water spread over the floodplain, the soil it carried settled on the land. The fine soil deposited by rivers is called **silt**. The silt was fertile, which means it was good for growing crops.

A Semiarid Climate Usually, less than 10 inches of rain fell in southern Mesopotamia a year. Summers were hot. This type of climate is called **semiarid**. Although the region was dry, ancient people could still grow crops because of the rivers and the fertile soil. Farming villages were widespread across southern Mesopotamia by 4000 B.C.

Vocabulary Strategy

The **prefix** *semi-* means "half." The word *arid* means "dry." A *semiarid* region has some rain, but remains fairly dry.

REVIEW What made Mesopotamia a good region for farming?

Controlling Water by Irrigation

2 ESSENTIAL QUESTION How did the climate affect farmers?

Being a farmer is difficult. Crops need the right amount of water to thrive. The floods and the semiarid climate in Mesopotamia meant that farmers often had either too much water or too little.

Geography

Ancient Irrigation

The model below shows how an ancient irrigation system worked.

1. Gates controlled how much water flowed from the river.
2. Main canals led from the river. They sloped gently downward to keep the water flowing.
3. Medium-sized branch canals led away from the main canals.
4. Small feeder canals led water directly to the fields.

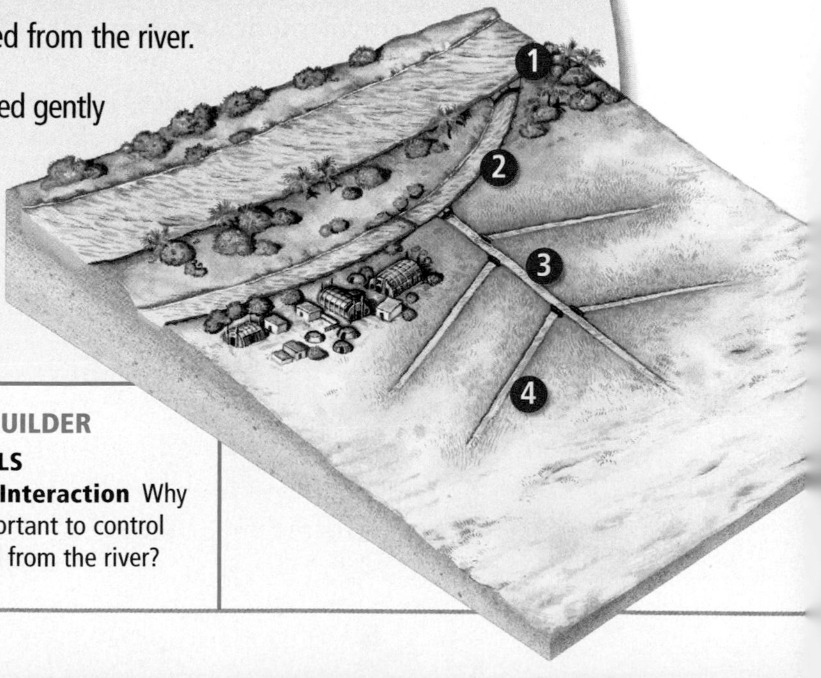

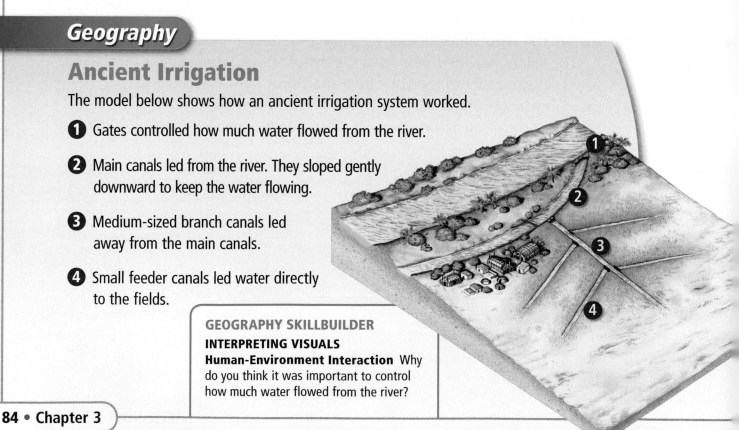

GEOGRAPHY SKILLBUILDER

INTERPRETING VISUALS

Human-Environment Interaction Why do you think it was important to control how much water flowed from the river?

Floods and Droughts The yearly flood was unpredictable. No one knew when the flood would occur. It might come in April or as late as June. Farmers could not predict when to plant. Also, the flood's size depended on how much snow melted in the mountains in spring and how much rain fell. If there was too much, the flood might be violent and wash everything away. If there was too little rain and melting snow, the flood would not come.

A **drought** is a period when not enough rain and snow fall. In a semiarid region, drought is a constant danger. During a drought, the river level would drop, making it hard to water crops. If crops failed, people starved.

Irrigation By about 6000 B.C., farmers built canals to carry water from the rivers to their fields. Such a system is called irrigation. Often, the silt in the water clogged the canals. Workers had to clean out the silt to keep the water flowing. They also built dams to hold back excess water during floods.

REVIEW How did Mesopotamians water their crops during droughts?

Finding Resources

3 **ESSENTIAL QUESTION** How did Mesopotamians cope with a lack of resources?

Since the beginning of time, humans have had to solve problems in the environment. For example, Mesopotamia had no forests to provide wood. The region also lacked stone and minerals, such as metals.

Mud Houses and Walls Because of that lack of resources, Mesopotamians had few building materials. Since they could not build with wood or stone, they used mud for bricks and plaster. However, mud buildings crumbled easily and had to be repaired often.

Also, Mesopotamia was easy to invade because it had few mountains or other natural barriers. As a result, people from other regions often came to steal from the Mesopotamians or conquer them. The ancient Mesopotamians wanted to protect themselves, but they had no trees or stone to build barriers. So people built mud walls around their villages.

Connect to Today

▲ **Building of Mud and Reeds** This style of building has been used in the region for at least 5,000 years and is still used today.

Finding Resources Mesopotamians obtained some stone, wood, and metal outside their own land. They were able to trade for these things because they grew a surplus of grain. **Surplus** means more than they needed for themselves.

Jobs such as digging canals, building walls, and trading had to be done over and over. Community leaders began to organize groups of people to do the work at the right time. Lesson 2 explains more about the organization of society.

REVIEW Why was trade important in Mesopotamia?

Lesson Summary

- The Tigris and Euphrates rivers made the soil of Mesopotamia good for growing crops.
- The people of Mesopotamia developed an irrigation system to bring water to crops.
- Mesopotamia had few resources. People traded surplus crops to get what they needed.

Why It Matters Now . . .

The Mesopotamians had to overcome a lack of resources. Today people still work to solve shortages of water, food, and resources.

1 Lesson Review

Homework Helper
ClassZone.com

Terms & Names

1. Explain the importance of

Mesopotamia	silt	drought
floodplain	semiarid	surplus

Using Your Notes

Summarizing Use your completed chart to answer the following question:

2. How did the Mesopotamians change the environment to deal with geographic challenges?

Geography of Mesopotamia
The rivers of Mesopotamia were important because . . .
Mesopotamians watered their crops by . . .
Because of a lack of resources, . . .

Main Ideas

3. What did the Tigris and Euphrates rivers provide for ancient Mesopotamians?
4. How did the lack of natural resources affect Mesopotamians?
5. How did Mesopotamian farmers obtain the right amount of water for their crops?

Critical Thinking

6. **Understanding Causes** How was irrigation connected to trade?
7. **Drawing Conclusions** How did Mesopotamians create a successful society?

Activity

Writing Job Descriptions Create a job description for a worker in Mesopotamia. Some possible jobs include irrigation system planner, canal digger, wall builder, trader, and project scheduler. Form a small group, and share your job descriptions.

Activity Extend Lesson 1

Make a Diagram

Goal: To explore the geographic relationship between resources and settlement in river valley civilizations

Materials & Supplies
- posterboard
- colored markers or pencils
- ruler
- books on earth science or encyclopedias

Prepare

1. Reread the paragraph "Fertile Soil" on page 84. Also, research the processes by which rivers pick up soil, carry it to other places, and deposit it on floodplains.
2. Learn the terms *erosion* and *deposition.*

Do the Activity

1. Create a diagram showing a river flowing from mountains through a floodplain to a gulf. (Use the diagram at right as a model.) Draw an arrow to show which way the river is flowing.
2. Label the following areas: mountains, river, floodplain, gulf.
3. Color the fertile region green. (Use the map on page 79 as a model.)
4. Add captions to explain how rivers pick up soil and how they deposit it on the floodplain.

Follow-Up

Where do you think ancient farmers built villages? Explain.

Extension

Writing a Comparison Research in books or ask a science teacher which U.S. river systems deposit soil on floodplains. Write a paragraph comparing those river systems to the ones in Mesopotamia.

Lesson 2

MAIN IDEAS

1. **Culture** Food surpluses, new technology, and advanced social organization led to a complex way of life. It is called civilization.
2. **Government** A new type of government developed in Sumer that included a city and its surrounding lands.
3. **Government** Religion dominated life in Sumer, but in time, powerful men who were not priests became the political rulers.

TAKING NOTES

Reading Skill: Making Generalizations
As you read Lesson 2, use your own words to record information about Sumer on a chart like this. You will be asked to make a generalization, or broad judgment, later.

Civilization in Sumer	
Advanced cities	
Specialized workers	
Complex institutions	
Record keeping	
Advanced technology	

Skillbuilder Handbook, page R8

▲ **Votive Statues** Sumerian artists made these statues to worship the gods when people were busy doing other things. Notice how big their eyes are from gazing at the gods.

Words to Know

Understanding the following words will help you read this lesson:

advanced beyond others in development or progress (page 89)
*Historians have studied the **advanced** societies that lived in Mesopotamia.*

mouth the part of a river that empties into a larger body of water (page 92)
*The **mouths** of the Tigris and Euphrates rivers are in the Persian Gulf.*

hometown the town in which one is born or raised (page 92)
*The **hometown** of the religious leader Abraham was Ur.*

foothill a low hill at the start of a mountain range (page 93)
*The travelers approached the **foothills** of the Zagros Mountains.*

The First Civilization

TERMS & NAMES
- civilization
- Sumer
- city-state
- ziggurat
- polytheism
- king

Build on What You Know Cities today have a wide range of cultural options. These include sports, entertainment, museums, and restaurants. They also offer people the chance to gain a good education or a promising job. As you are about to read, even the earliest cities were places of opportunity and culture.

The Rise of Civilization

1 ESSENTIAL QUESTION How did civilization develop in the region of Sumer?

The rise of agriculture enabled people to settle in villages. They didn't have to search for food. As more people decided to live in communities, villages grew larger. In time, they became cities. City leaders had to start organizing workers to solve problems, such as building and cleaning irrigation canals. Over time, society and culture grew more complex. These changes led to an advanced form of culture called **civilization**. Most historians think the first civilization rose about 3300 B.C. in **Sumer**, which was a region in southern Mesopotamia.

Ruins of Ur The ancient Sumerian city of Ur once stood on the banks of the Euphrates. The river has shifted over time. Now it is ten miles away. ▼

Traits of Civilization Five traits characterize civilization: advanced cities, specialized workers, complex institutions, record keeping, and advanced technology.

1. **Advanced Cities** Civilization is closely linked to life in cities. At first, cities became important because farmers needed a place to store and trade their surplus grain. As cities grew, they began to offer other advantages. For example, the cities of Sumer had large temples where people prayed. Cities also offered many different types of work.

2. **Specialized Workers** In general, a society needs food surpluses before civilization can develop. Having a food surplus allows people to do other types of work besides farming. Workers can specialize, which means to do a job that requires special skills. For example, Sumerian workers built houses, made jewelry, sewed clothes, or created pottery. When people specialize, the quality of their work improves because they can develop their skill.

    Because cities are crowded, people must learn to live together. They also have to cooperate on projects, such as building irrigation canals. As a result, some people took on

Civilization in Sumer

Basic Traits of Civilization	Examples from Sumer
Advanced cities	Kish, Nippur, Ur 
Specialized workers	priest, king, artisan 
Complex institutions	the temple, the army, schools 
Record keeping	writing 
Advanced technology	irrigation, bronze tools 

Kings City-states in ancient Sumer were ruled by kings. King Gudea ruled the city-state Lagash. ▶

the job of organizing society. In early Sumerian cities, priests did that job. They ran society and acted as judges.

3. **Complex Institutions** In time, religion and government became institutions. An institution is a group of people who have a specific purpose. Often it exists to help society meet its needs. For example, schools are institutions that exist to educate children. An army is an institution that exists to protect a society. Sometimes society uses an army to conquer others.

4. **Record Keeping** Societies must keep track of many things. For example, the rulers may want to measure the food supplies stored in the city. Keeping records usually involves writing, but not always. In Mesopotamia, people started by using wooden counting sticks. Later, they invented the world's first system of writing. (You will learn about this in Lesson 3.)

5. **Advanced Technology** Societies advance as people learn better ways to do things. For example, the people of Sumer learned to use canals to irrigate crops. They also created new tools and used new materials. For instance, the Sumerians began to make tools of bronze (a mixture of copper and tin). Bronze tools replaced tools made of copper, which is a softer metal.

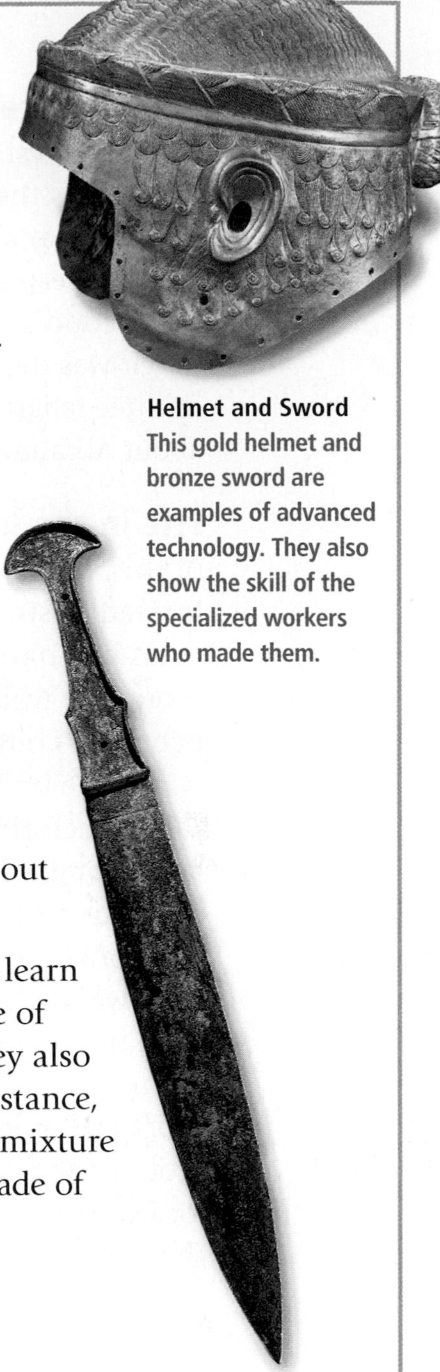

Helmet and Sword
This gold helmet and bronze sword are examples of advanced technology. They also show the skill of the specialized workers who made them.

REVIEW Why was Sumer a good example of civilization?

Sumerian City-States

2 ESSENTIAL QUESTION What new type of community developed in Sumer?

Sumerian cities offered many advantages to people who lived in the surrounding lands. Cities were centers of trade, learning, and religion. Most people still lived in the countryside. Even so, over time the cities began to rule the surrounding lands and villages.

A community that included a city and its nearby farmlands was called a **city-state**. The nearby land might include several villages. Between 10,000 and 100,000 people might have lived in a city. Each city-state ruled itself.

The City-States of Sumer By 3000 B.C., Sumer had at least 12 city-states. Some of the more famous ones were Kish, Nippur, and Ur. As the map on page 94 shows, most city-states were located near the mouths of the Tigris and Euphrates rivers. The land was especially fertile there. As a result, farmers grew more food. Food surpluses supported a larger population.

Ur was the hometown of Abraham, who is an important person in three religions: Judaism, Christianity, and Islam. You will read about Abraham in Chapter 10.

Life in the City The cities of Sumer grew gradually. Because of this, they did not look the way many U.S. cities look today. Instead of straight streets that cross at right angles, Sumerian cities had narrow, winding streets. As you learned in Lesson 1, protective walls surrounded the city. Gates in the wall allowed people to come and go.

People built their houses of mud walls that were several feet thick. Such thick walls helped to keep out heat. Narrow tunnels ran through the walls, carrying fresh air from the outside into the house. People first made the doorways by placing a horizontal beam over two vertical posts. Then they built the mud walls around the doorways.

A house consisted of a series of rooms arranged around a courtyard. The builders covered the courtyard with a loose roof of palm leaves over wooden planks. This roof helped protect people from the hot sun. The cooking area was usually located out in the courtyard so the smoke could escape through gaps in the roof.

The Ziggurat: City Center If you were to visit a Sumerian city, one building would stand out from all the rest. The largest and most important structure in a Sumerian city was the temple. It was called a **ziggurat** (ZIHG•uh•RAT). Ziggurats were first built about 2200 B.C.

The ziggurat was not just a temple; it was the center of city life. The ziggurat functioned as a sort of city hall. This was because the priests ran the irrigation systems. People came to the ziggurat to pay the priests for their services with grain and other items. As a result, the priests controlled the storage of surplus grain. The priests ended up controlling much of the wealth of the city-state.

REVIEW What was life like in Sumerian cities?

Changes in Leadership

3 ESSENTIAL QUESTION How did the leadership of Sumer change?

As you just read, priests played an important political role in Sumer. People also went to them to ask the gods for help. The priests advised the people on how to act to please the gods.

Sumerian Religion The Sumerians believed in many gods and goddesses. A belief in many gods and goddesses is called **polytheism**. Sumerians believed that four main gods created the world and ruled over it. These were the gods of sky, wind, foothills (hills that are near mountains), and fresh water. Each city-state worshiped its own god. In addition, Sumerians had thousands of lesser gods. The Sumerians believed their gods looked and acted like people.

Vocabulary Strategy

The **prefix** *poly-* means "many," and the **root word** *theism* means "belief in a god."

Ziggurat

INTERACTIVE

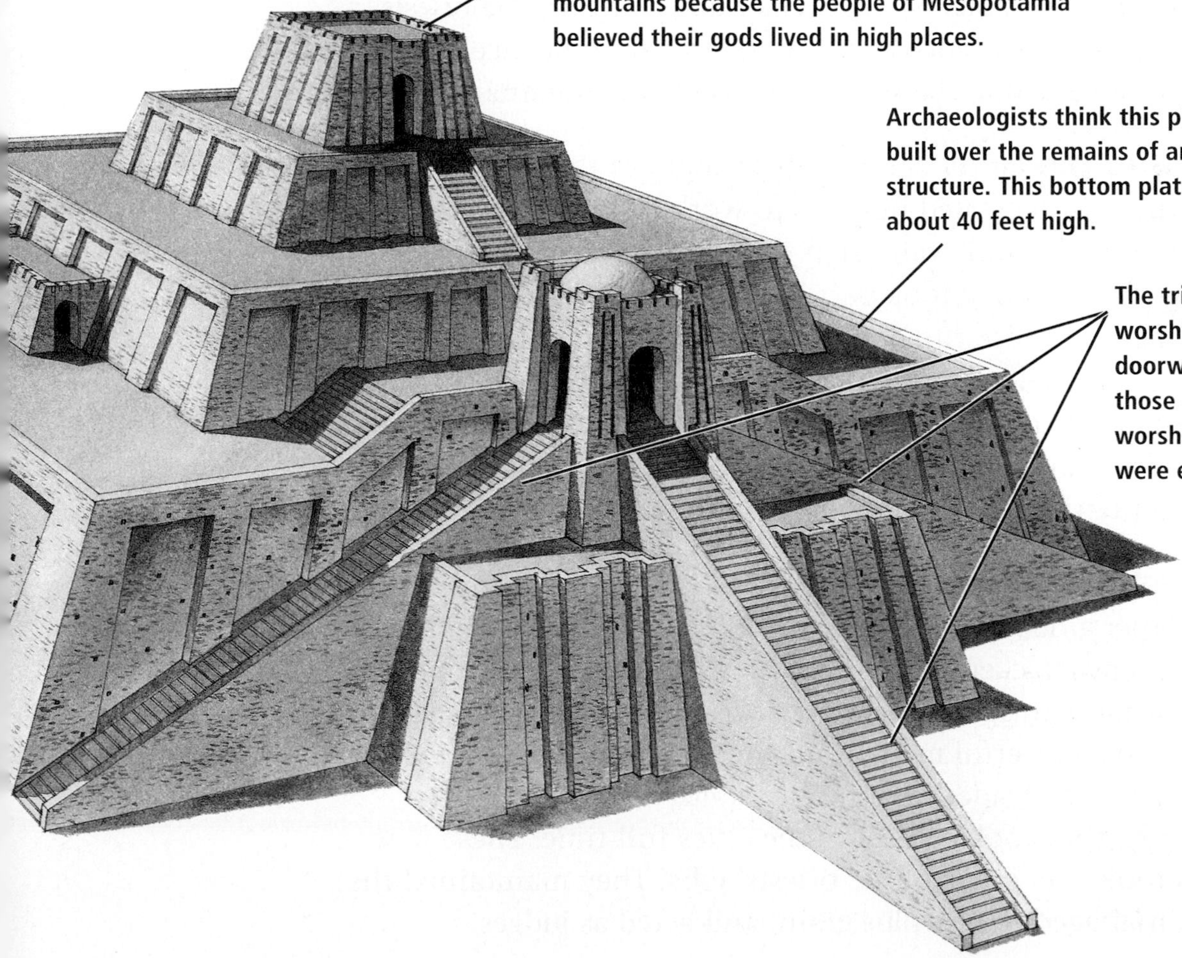

The shrine, or holy place, was in this small structure at the top. Ziggurats were built to look like mountains because the people of Mesopotamia believed their gods lived in high places.
Archaeologists think this platform was built over the remains of an earlier structure. This bottom platform was about 40 feet high.
The triple stairway led worshipers up to three arched doorways. Passing through those doorways helped worshipers to realize they were entering a holy place.

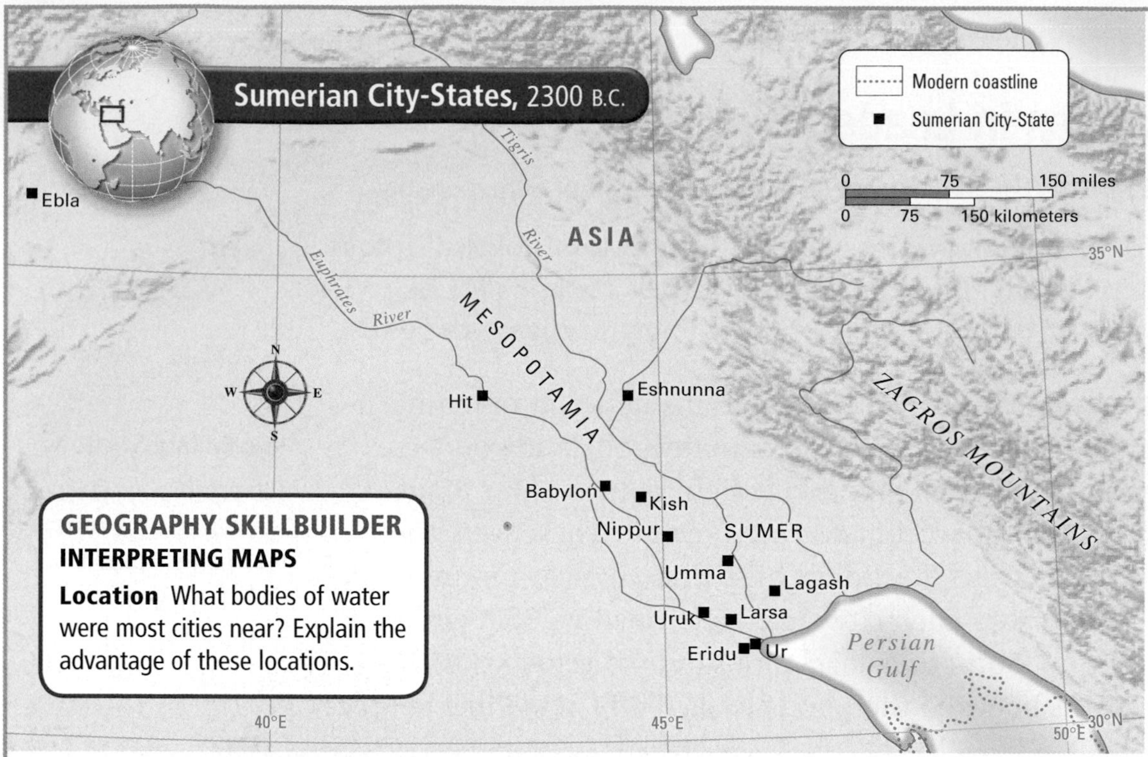

GEOGRAPHY SKILLBUILDER
INTERPRETING MAPS
Location What bodies of water were most cities near? Explain the advantage of these locations.

Priests Become Leaders Life in Sumer had many dangers, such as floods, droughts, and invasions. The Sumerians believed the gods could prevent these troubles. To protect their cities, people tried to please the gods. Each god had many priests. The priests worked to satisfy the gods and claimed to have influence with them. Because of that claim, people accepted the priests as leaders.

Service to the Gods Sumerians thought of the gods as rich landowners who created humans to work for them. Priests, ordinary people, and even rulers said prayers and made offerings to the gods. Everyone took part in rituals and followed religious rules. Many of those rituals took place at the ziggurat.

Sumerians believed that the souls of dead people went to the land of no return. It was a gloomy place that was also called the underworld. Some scholars think the hardships of Sumerian life caused Sumerians to expect continued unhappiness after death.

New Leaders in Sumer Around 3000 B.C., as city-states became richer, other groups of people began to attack them to take their wealth. Some attackers came from other regions. Others came from rival city-states. In such dangerous times, the people of the city-state often asked a powerful man to rule them and protect the city.

At first, such leaders led the city-states only during wars. Eventually, they took control of the cities full-time. These new leaders took over some of the priests' jobs. They maintained the canals, managed the surplus grain, and acted as judges.

In time, this new type of ruler became a **king**, who is the highest-ranked leader of a group of people. The area a king ruled was called a kingdom. Sumer became a kingdom under one king by 2375 B.C.

The priests still remained important because their job was to keep the gods happy and keep evil away. The people believed that the gods let the kings rule.

REVIEW How did kings take over as rulers of Sumer?

▲ **Ring** A Sumerian artisan created this ring about 3000 B.C.

Lesson Summary

- Sumer had a complex society and culture. Historians consider it the first civilization.
- Sumerian city-states were a form of government that included cities and the land around them.
- Priests were the first leaders in Sumer, but kings became leaders when the need for defense grew.

Why It Matters Now . . .

Cities first became important in Sumer. People today still move to cities to find jobs, education, and culture.

2 Lesson Review

Homework Helper
ClassZone.com

Terms & Names

1. Explain the importance of

civilization	city-state	polytheism
Sumer	ziggurat	king

Using Your Notes

Making Generalizations Use your completed chart to answer the following question:

2. What is the relationship between specialized workers and complex institutions? State your answer as a generalization.

Civilization in Sumer	
Advanced cities	
Specialized workers	
Complex institutions	
Record keeping	
Advanced technology	

Main Ideas

3. Why are food surpluses necessary for civilization to develop?
4. In what way did the ziggurat function like a city hall?
5. What did people in Sumer think their gods were like?

Critical Thinking

6. **Making Inferences** Why was a priest's job so important in Sumer?
7. **Understanding Cause and Effect** How did warfare change the government in Sumer?

Activity

Making a Poster Create a poster listing the five traits of civilization and giving examples from a modern society, such as the United States.

Reading a Map

Goal: To use a map to draw conclusions about the evolution of written language

Learn the Skill

Maps are representations of features on Earth's surface. Some maps show political features such as borders. Other maps show physical features such as mountains. A third type of map is the thematic map, which shows specific types of information such as where certain languages are spoken.

See the Skillbuilder Handbook, page R9.

Practice the Skill

1. Read the title of the map at the right. It will tell you what information the map shows. This thematic map shows where the first writing systems developed.
2. Read the map key. It is usually in a box. It will tell you what the various symbols and colors on the map mean. Notice that on this map, color is used to show the time period a written language developed. A photograph of one of the writing systems accompanies the map.
3. Notice the relationship among the various regions shown on the map. See what conclusions you can draw. For example, this map shows that Sumer and Egypt were the first regions where people used writing systems. The next regions to have writing systems were located next to Sumer and Egypt. From this, you can draw the conclusion that writing spread from Sumer and Egypt to their neighbors.
4. Sometimes, you can use maps as a source of information for written documents or visual presentations. The time line below presents the information on the map in a different way.

Example:

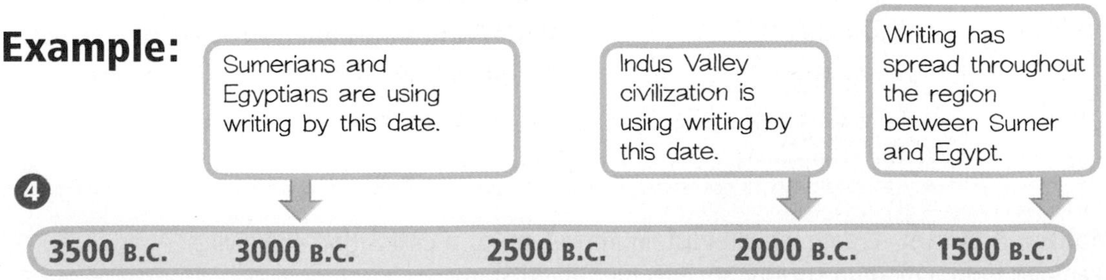
Sumerians and Egyptians are using writing by this date.
Indus Valley civilization is using writing by this date.
Writing has spread throughout the region between Sumer and Egypt.
4
3500 B.C.
3000 B.C.
2500 B.C.
2000 B.C.
1500 B.C.

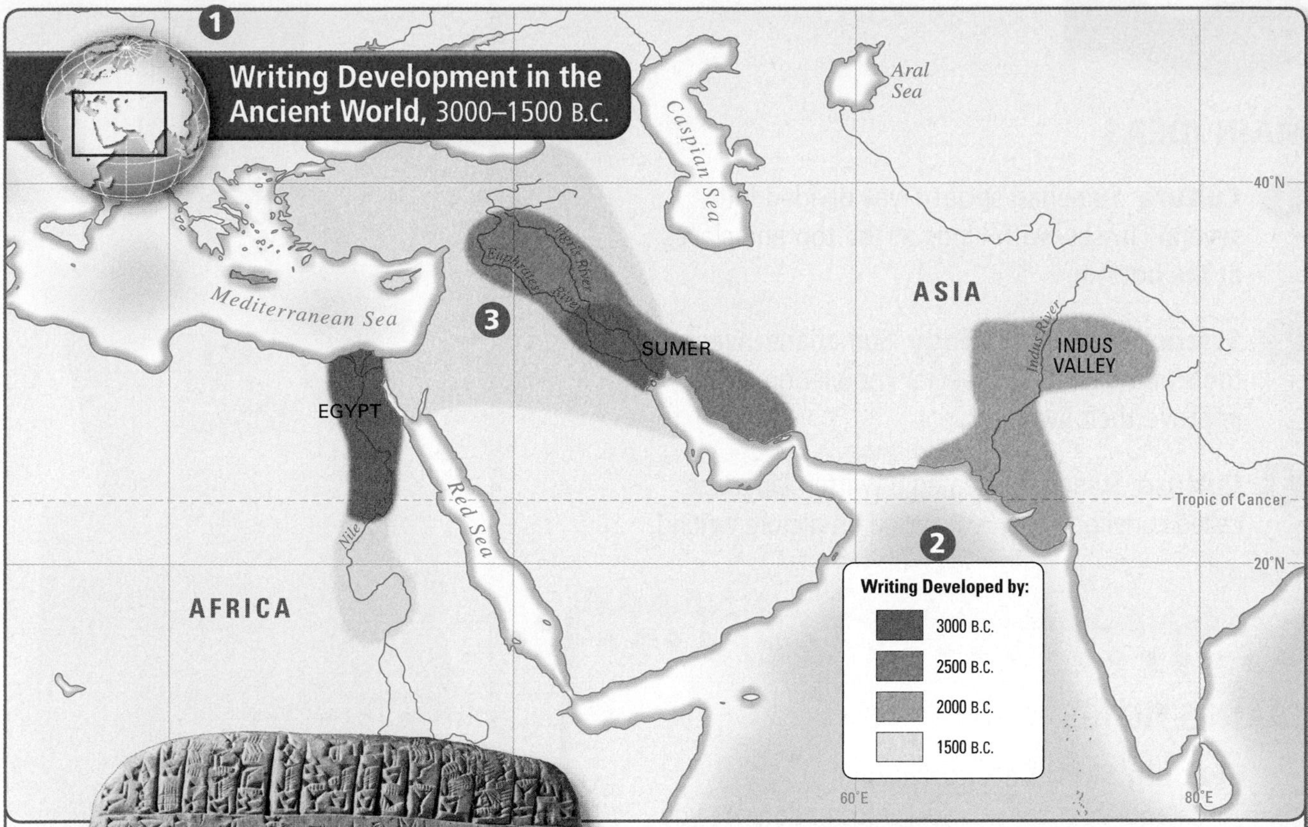

◀ **Cuneiform was the type of writing that developed in Sumer.**

Apply the Skill

Look at the map on pages 78–79. It is a thematic map showing the region where the Tigris and Euphrates rivers deposited fertile soil and the region where Sumerian culture was found. Write a brief description of the relationship between these two regions.

Lesson

3

MAIN IDEAS

1. **Culture** Sumerian society was divided into several classes, with kings at the top and slaves at the bottom.
2. **Science and Technology** Sumerians invented tools and developed special knowledge to improve their lives.
3. **Culture** Sumerians created a written language called cuneiform that was based on picture writing.

TAKING NOTES

Reading Skill: Categorizing
To categorize means to sort information. As you read Lesson 3, take notes about life in Sumer. Use a chart like this one to categorize the information you gather.

Life in Sumer		
Society	Technology	Writing

Skillbuilder Handbook, page R6

▲ **Woman with Pottery**
The woman shown in this figurine holds a pot that was probably made on a potter's wheel—a Sumerian invention.

Words to Know

Understanding the following words will help you read this lesson:

desirable having pleasing qualities (page 99)
He had little power, so he was always assigned the least ***desirable*** *jobs.*

daily taking place every day (page 100)
The Sumerians may have invented the wheel, which most people now use ***daily.***

label to mark an object with a name or symbol that identifies it (page 101)
The merchant wanted to ***label*** *the food items that were for sale.*

reed the hollow stem of a tall grass (page 102)
The writing tool was made from a ***reed*** *like those growing in the swamp.*

Life in Sumer

TERMS & NAMES
bronze
pictograph
stylus
cuneiform
scribe

Build on What You Know Think about society today. Consider the differences between the people who have money and power and the people who don't have much of either one. Similar differences existed in ancient Sumer.

Sumerian Society

1 ESSENTIAL QUESTION What were the social classes that made up Sumerian society?

As Sumerian society grew more complex, it divided into several social groups, or classes. Many societies are divided into unequal classes. Class systems often define who usually has power and who usually does the less desirable jobs.

Social Classes The king and the priests were at the top of the upper classes of Sumer. The Sumerians believed their kings and priests had a link to the gods, so they had great influence over people. The upper class also included landowners, government officials, and rich merchants.

The in-between classes included all free people. Most people in Sumer were in this group, including many farmers and artisans. Slaves made up the lowest class.

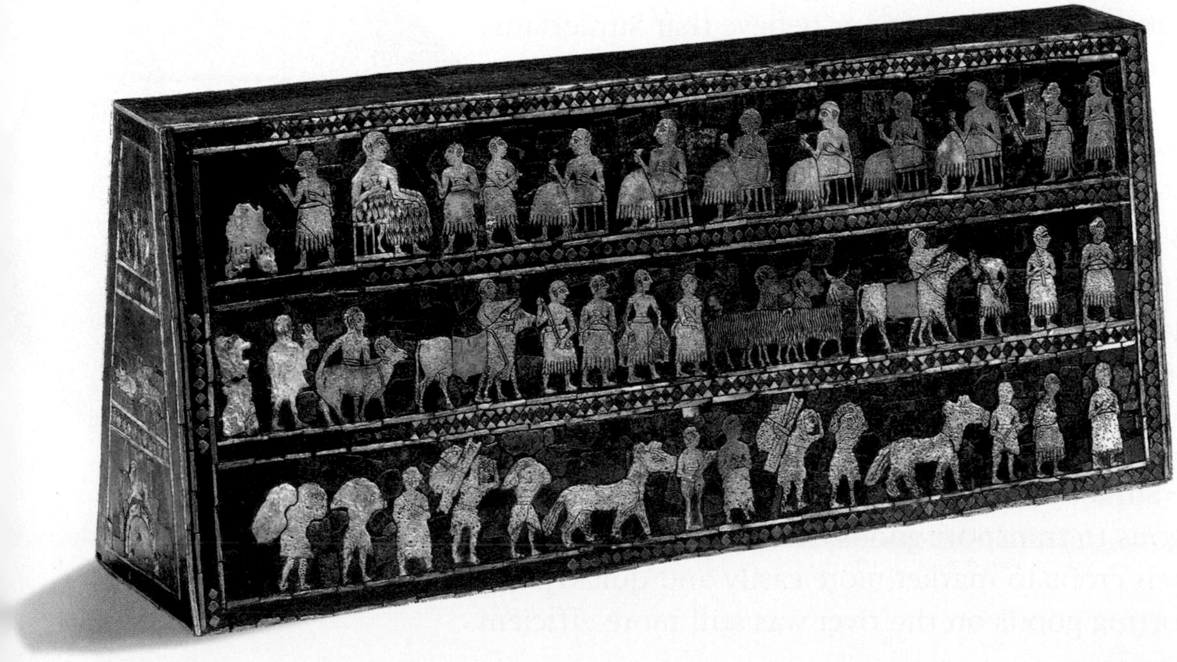

◀ **The Standard of Ur** A standard is a flag or symbol carried on a pole. This decorated panel shows many people in Sumerian society, including farmers. The panel is about 8.5 inches by 19.5 inches.

Slaves Some past societies have used slaves as a source of cheap labor. Most slaves in Sumer were taken as prisoners during war. In other cases, if Sumerian parents died or were very poor, their children might become slaves who worked in the temple. At times, a free person might borrow more money than he or she could repay. Such persons became slaves until they worked off the debt.

Slaves had some rights. They could conduct business and borrow money. Slaves could also buy their freedom.

Role of Women All of the social classes included women, so their social positions varied widely. In general, women in early Sumer had more rights than they did in later Mesopotamia.

Some upper-class women became priestesses, which was a role of honor. Free women could own land, and they could work as merchants and artisans, such as weavers. Still, the main role for most women was raising their children.

REVIEW Why were kings and priests in the highest class?

Sumerian Science and Technology

2 ESSENTIAL QUESTION What tools did the Sumerians invent?

Sumerians were good at solving problems. They invented tools and developed special knowledge to improve their lives. They were first to invent some of the things we use daily.

Wheel Early wheels were usually made from wood with tires made of leather. ▼

Early Inventions Historians believe that Sumerians may have invented the plow (about 6000 B.C.) and the wheel (about 3500 B.C.). These inventions helped Sumerians a great deal in their daily lives.

The plow was the first important tool invented to help farmers. The first plows were often simple digging sticks with handles. They could be pulled or pushed, first by people, then by animals. Plows broke up hard soil, which made planting easier. Also, water could sink more deeply into plowed soil. As a result, the roots of plants received more water.

The Sumerians used the wheel in many ways, such as on wagons to transport goods. Wheeled wagons helped farmers take their crops to market more easily and quickly. However, transporting goods on the river was still more efficient.

One special kind of wheel was the potter's wheel. Before the invention of the potter's wheel, people made pottery by shaping coils of clay by hand. With the potter's wheel, Sumerians could make more pottery faster. Pots were important storage containers for surplus food.

Sumerians were among the first people to use **bronze**, a mixture of copper and tin. Bronze was stronger than copper so tools lasted longer and stayed sharper. Bronze tools became another item that Sumerians could trade.

▲ **Nail Head** This bronze figurine of a god decorates a nail. It shows both the technical and artistic skills of the ancient Sumerians.

Mathematics The Sumerians developed arithmetic to keep records of crops and trade goods. Their number system was based on the number 60. So today, we have 60 seconds in a minute and 60 minutes in an hour. Circles contain 360 degrees. Eventually, the measurement of time helped with the creation of calendars.

Sumerians used a triangle and a measuring rope to set land boundaries. They understood geometric shapes such as rectangles, triangles, and squares. They used those shapes to make bricks, build ramps, and dig canals.

REVIEW How did new tools make life better for the Sumerians?

Creation of Written Language

3 ESSENTIAL QUESTION How did the Sumerians invent writing?

Sumerians invented writing by 3000 B.C. to meet the needs of business. As trade expanded, merchants needed records of exchanges. They also wanted to label goods.

Picture Writing At first, Sumerians used clay tokens that had an image of a product, such as a cow, to keep track of goods. They sealed the tokens in clay containers to make sure that no one tampered with them. The Sumerians marked the outside of the containers so people would know what was inside them.

The marks outside the container would be a symbol of the product. Such symbols are known as **pictographs**, which means "picture writing." In time, Sumerians stopped using tokens. They just drew the pictographs on clay tablets.

Visual Vocabulary

pictograph

Primary Source

Background: Cuneiform was used to write many kinds of records. These were often written on small clay tablets like the one shown. Cuneiform was also used for literature, such as proverbs. A proverb is a short saying containing wisdom or advice. Proverbs are found in many cultures.

It is not always easy to understand the meaning of ancient proverbs because every culture is different. What do you think these proverbs mean?

from *Sumerian Proverbs*

Translated by Edmund I. Gordon

Whoever has walked with truth generates life.

Tell a lie and then tell the truth; it will be considered a lie!

He acquires many things; he must keep close watch over them.

Possessions are sparrows in flight which can find no place to alight.

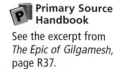

DOCUMENT–BASED QUESTION
Judging from these proverbs, how did the Sumerians feel about truth? How did they feel about possessions?

Cuneiform At first, pictographs showed actual objects. Later, they also stood for ideas. In time, the Sumerians began to use pictographs to stand for sounds too. By combining sounds, they could write more words.

The Sumerians used a sharpened reed called a **stylus** to press markings into a clay tablet. Because of its shape, the stylus made marks that were wedge shaped. Over time, the Sumerians stopped using pictures and began to use symbols made entirely of these wedge shapes. This wedge-shaped writing is called **cuneiform** (KYOO•nee•uh•FAWRM).

The writing system was very complex. The Sumerian language contained about 600 different symbols. Learning all those symbols took years. As a result, few people were able to read and write. The people who specialized in writing were called **scribes**. They were professional record keepers. Other people in Sumerian society respected them highly.

Written History At first, Sumerians used records mostly for business dealings. Later, people started writing about wars, floods, and the reigns of their kings. These records are Sumer's written history.

Primary Source Handbook
See the excerpt from *The Epic of Gilgamesh*, page R37.

Other cultures in Mesopotamia and elsewhere adopted the cuneiform writing system from the Sumerians. Archaeologists have found thousands of cuneiform tablets in Southwest Asia. One king owned a library of more than 24,000 clay tablet records and histories from all over the region of Mesopotamia.

REVIEW Why were scribes highly respected in Sumer?

▲ **Scribe** This sculpture of a scribe was made later in Mesopotamian history. Notice that he is holding a stylus.

Lesson Summary

- Sumerian society had several classes. Kings and priests were at the top of society. Slaves were at the bottom.
- Inventions, such as the wheel and the plow, and mathematical knowledge improved Sumerian life.
- The Sumerians created a system of writing to record business transactions and histories.

Why It Matters Now . . .

The Sumerians developed the first system of writing. Writing makes it easier for people to pass on knowledge from generation to generation.

3 Lesson Review

Homework Helper
ClassZone.com

Terms & Names

1. Explain the importance of

bronze, stylus, scribe, pictograph, cuneiform

Using Your Notes

Categorizing Use your completed chart to answer the following question:

2. Which invention or technology do you think was most important? Explain why.

Life in Sumer		
Society	Technology	Writing

Main Ideas

3. How did religion affect who was in the upper class?

4. Why was the plow such an important tool for farmers?

5. How did writing evolve in Sumer?

Critical Thinking

6. Making Inferences Why was the invention of cuneiform an important development?

7. Drawing Conclusions Why do historians identify the beginning of history with the beginning of writing?

Activity

Internet Activity Choose one of the Sumerian inventions and use the Internet to research it. Then give a presentation on its importance. Include visuals with captions in your presentation.
INTERNET KEYWORDS: *plow, wheel, cuneiform*

Connect to Today

Extend Lesson 3

Research Links
ClassZone.com

Mesopotamian Inventions

Purpose: To learn about the ancient Mesopotamian inventions of the plow, board games, and the potter's wheel

The ancient Mesopotamians are a good example of people who solved problems—and changed history by doing so. They invented technology that helped to grow crops and to create pottery more efficiently. Ever since, people all over the world have used those inventions. But don't think that ancient Mesopotamians were so serious that they worked all the time. They also invented some ways to have fun!

Plow

▶ **Past** The sun can bake the soil as hard as a brick. Seeds thrown on top of such hard ground usually don't sprout. Because of this, early farmers had to find a way to loosen the soil. They invented the plow, which has a blade that cuts into soil and turns it over. The plow helped farmers to grow surplus crops.

▼ **Present** Today's plows are bigger and use metal blades to turn over the soil. Now tractors instead of animals pull plows. Even there, we owe a debt to the ancient Mesopotamians. We wouldn't have tractors without the wheel—and they invented that too.

plow

Board Games

▼ **Past** This game comes from a tomb at Ur. Scholars think the goal was to move your pieces from one end to the other while an opponent blocked the narrow bridge.

▶ **Present** Checkers is a board game that many people still enjoy. The object is to capture all of your opponent's pieces.

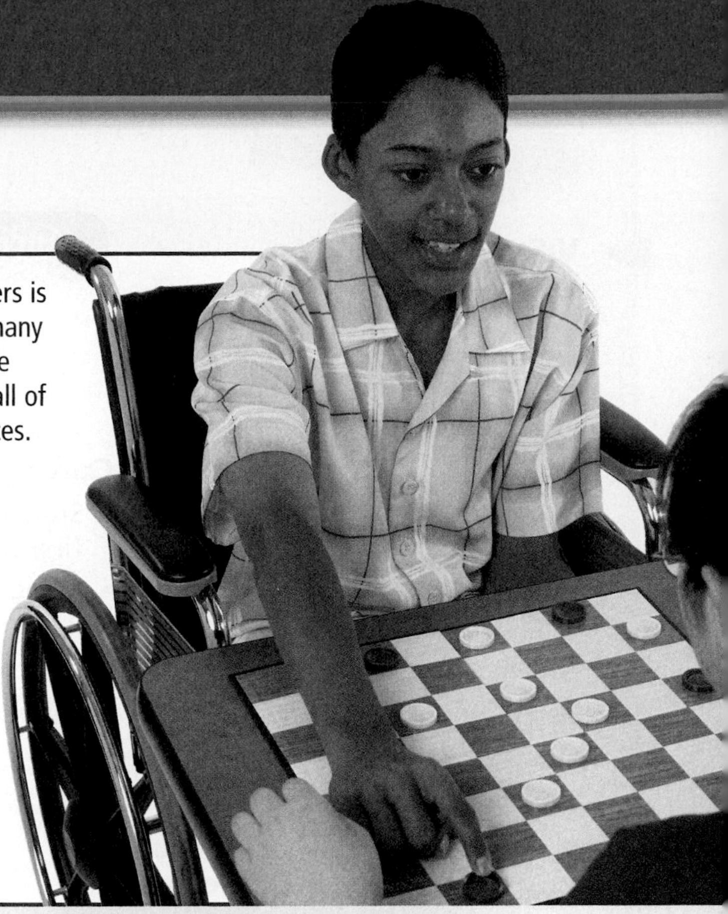

Pottery

▶ **Past** It is possible to create pottery entirely by hand, but the potter's wheel provides several advantages. Artisans can make pots with more even, streamlined shapes. And the process is much faster, so artisans could produce more pots than before.

▼ **Present** If you go to any craft fair, you can still find pottery that artisans make on a simple potter's wheel. Many people create pottery as a way to express their artistic side.

Activities

1. **TALK ABOUT IT** Which of these inventions has had the greatest effect on your life? Explain.
2. **WRITE ABOUT IT** Create instructions for the ancient board game shown here. Write them out, using a numbered, step-by-step format.

Chapter 3 Review

VISUAL SUMMARY

Ancient Mesopotamia

Geography
- Rivers made agriculture possible.
- Challenges included floods, drought, and lack of resources.

Culture
- Sumerians developed the first writing system.
- Sumerian society was divided into classes.

Belief Systems
- Sumerians worshiped many gods.
- The temple was called a ziggurat.

Government
- City-states were the form of government throughout Sumer.
- First, priests ruled in Sumer. Later, powerful men became kings.

Science & Technology
- Irrigation helped provide a steady source of water for crops.
- Sumerians invented the wheel and the plow.

TERMS & NAMES

Explain why the words in each set below are linked with each other.

1. **floodplain** and **silt**
2. **Sumer** and **civilization**
3. **ziggurat** and **polytheism**
4. **pictograph** and **cuneiform**

MAIN IDEAS

Geography of Mesopotamia (pages 82–87)

5. How did the flooding of the Tigris and Euphrates rivers both help and hurt farmers?
6. Why was irrigation so important to agriculture in Mesopotamia?

The First Civilization (pages 88–97)

7. How did advances in agriculture contribute to the rise of cities?
8. What role did the temple play in Sumerian society?

Life in Sumer (pages 98–105)

9. What roles did women and slaves have in Sumerian religion?
10. What are the characteristics of Sumerian cuneiform writing?

Standards-Based Assessment

CRITICAL THINKING Big Ideas: Geography

11. UNDERSTANDING CAUSES How did the geography of Mesopotamia help civilization develop there?

12. EXPLAINING HISTORICAL PATTERNS Judging from the history of Sumer, what geographic conditions would help other ancient civilizations to develop?

13. UNDERSTANDING EFFECTS How did inventions and special knowledge support agriculture in Sumer?

ALTERNATIVE ASSESSMENT

1. WRITING ACTIVITY Review the section "Changes in Leadership" on pages 93–95. Decide whether you think kings or priests made better leaders in ancient Sumer. Then write a persuasive paragraph trying to convince readers to adopt your position.

2. INTERDISCIPLINARY ACTIVITY—SCIENCE Use books or the Internet to research bronze. Make a poster that explains how bronze is made, what it was used for, and how it helped the economy of Sumer. Use photocopies or draw examples of bronze objects.

3. STARTING WITH A STORY

Starting with a Story

Review the invention that you thought of to help the farmer. How did your ideas compare with what you learned in the chapter? Draw pictures for a wall mural that would illustrate the development of agriculture techniques in Mesopotamia.

Technology Activity

4. PLANNING A MULTIMEDIA PRESENTATION
Use the Internet or the library to research scribes in Sumer. Work with a partner to plan a multimedia presentation.

- Who could become a scribe?
- How were scribes educated?
- What kinds of work did they do?

Research Links
ClassZone.com

Reading a Chart Use the chart below to answer the questions.

Early Development of Writing

word	pictograph	cuneiform
bird		
cow		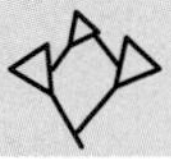
fish	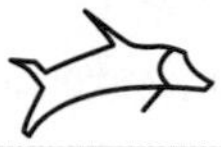	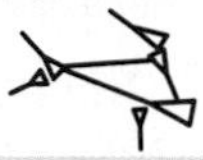
mountain		
water		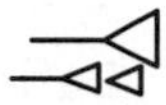

1. What do all of the words on the chart have in common?

A. They name a person's actions.
B. They name abstract ideas.
C. They name human emotions.
D. They name things from nature.

2. Which of the following statements is true of the way cuneiform looked?

A. It was made of realistic pictures of objects.
B. It was similar to our alphabet.
C. It was made of wedges and lines.
D. It used symbols that were larger than pictographs.

Test Practice
ClassZone.com

Additional Test Practice, pp. S1–S33

Chapter

4 Early Empires

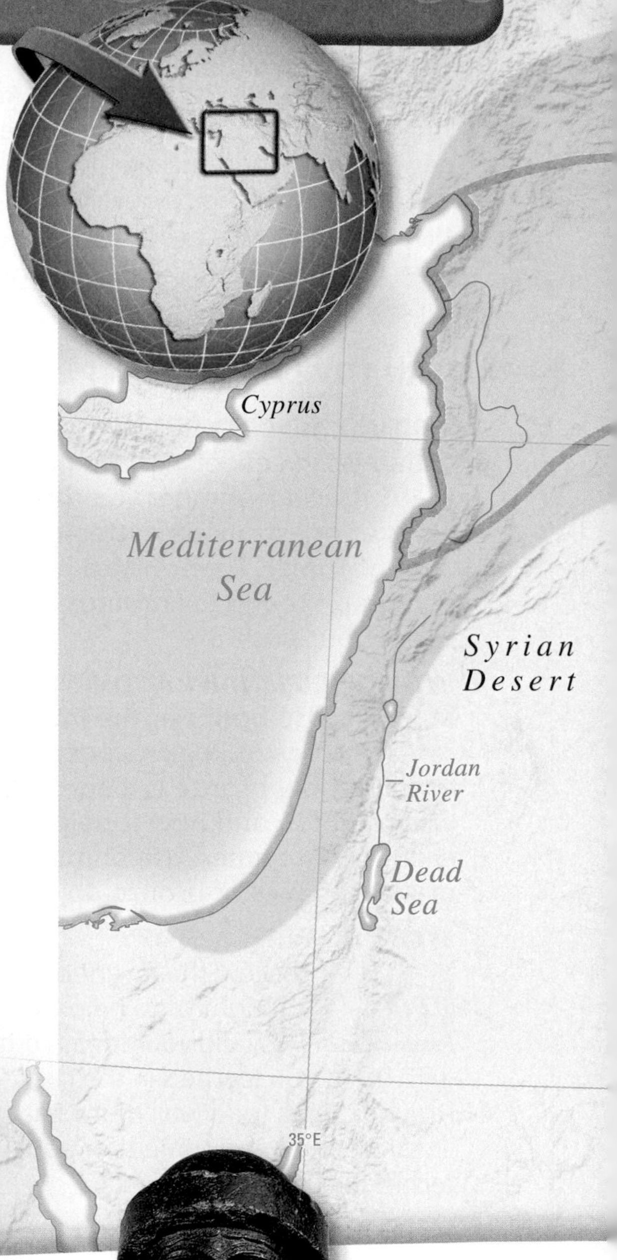

Before You Read: Knowledge Rating

Recognizing what you already know about each of these terms can help you understand the chapter:

Fertile Crescent   tribute   toleration

In your notebook, rate how well you know each term:

3 = I know what this word means.
2 = I've seen this word before, but I don't know what it means.
1 = I've never seen this word before.

Define each term in your notebook as you read.

Big Ideas About Early Empires

Government Governments create law codes and political bodies to organize a society.

As societies grew, new ways of governing developed to provide people with safety and security. During the early empires, leaders developed law codes to bring fair laws to societies. The leaders also set up new ways to organize and rule vast lands with many different groups of people.

Integrated Technology

eEdition
- Interactive Maps
- Interactive Visuals
- Starting with a Story

INTERNET RESOURCES
Go to **ClassZone.com** for
- WebQuest
- Homework Helper
- Research Links
- Internet Activities
- Quizzes
- Maps
- Test Practice
- Current Events

EARLY EMPIRES

2334 B.C. Sargon builds an empire.

1792 B.C. Hammurabi's Code developed in Babylonian Empire. (statue of Hammurabi) ▶

1850 B.C. — 1650 B.C. — 1450 B.C.

WORLD

1700 B.C. Indus River Valley civilization declines. ◀ (Harappan seal)

1570 B.C. The New Kingdom in Egypt begins.

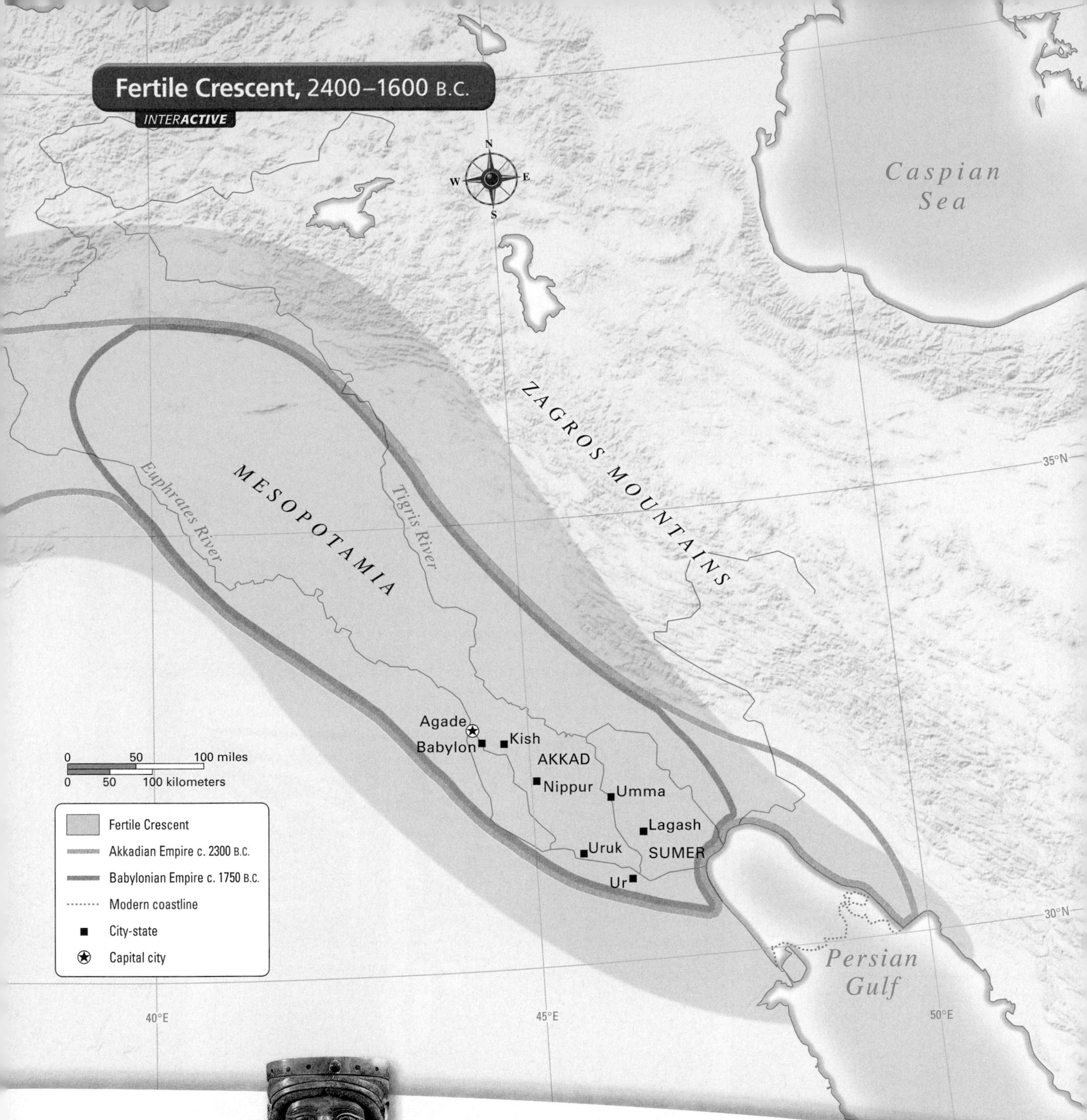

850 B.C. Assyrian Empire reaches its peak. ◄ (ivory head)

550 B.C. Persian Empire is largest in world.

1050 B.C. | **850 B.C.** | **650 B.C.**

1027 B.C. Zhou Dynasty is founded in China. ◄ (bronze vessel)

750 B.C. Greek city-states flourish.

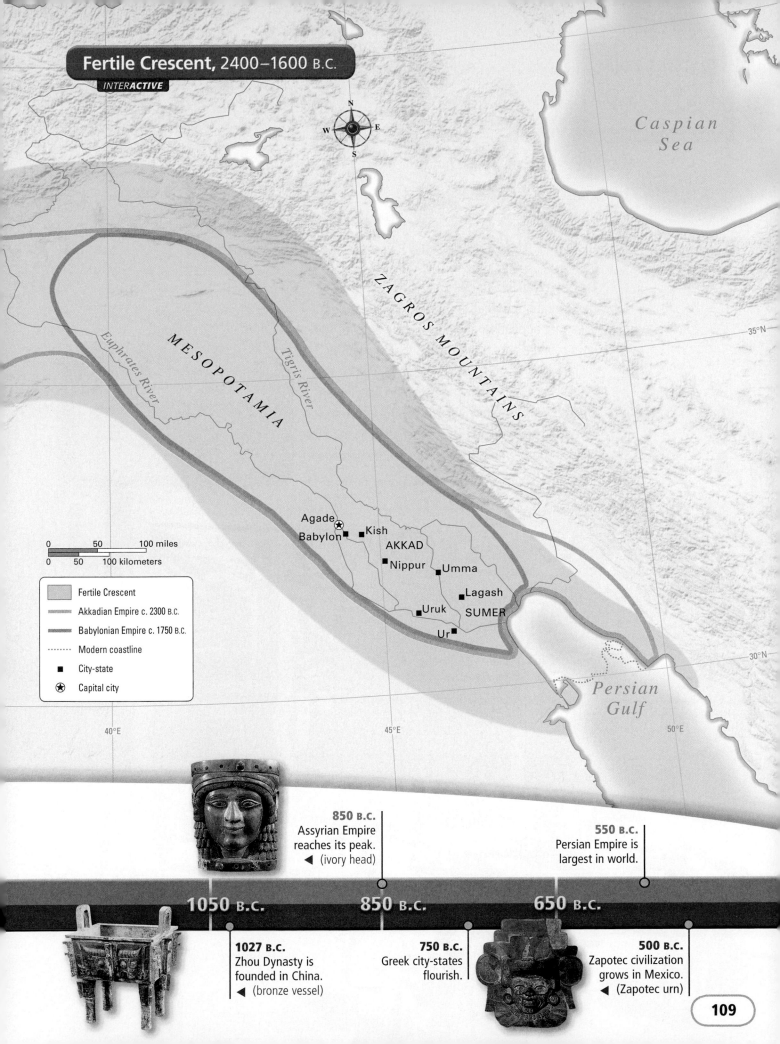

500 B.C. Zapotec civilization grows in Mexico. ◄ (Zapotec urn)

Starting with a Story

Day of Misfortune

Background: To build unity in his empire, Hammurabi, the ruler of Babylon, created a set of laws that applied to all people in the empire. The laws covered acts that affected the community, such as business conduct and crime. Imagine that you live in a brand-new house in the Babylonian Empire. Unfortunately, the roof of the house has caved in. Now, you and your father are talking to the builder about who is responsible for the damage.

Model of a typical Mesopotamian house ▶

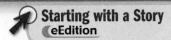

My father pointed to the house and said to the builder, "You can see the damage." I stood with them in front of our ruined house. The roof of our new house had a huge hole in it. The roof supports had fallen through the second floor and into the first floor.

My father turned to me. "Stay here, son," he said. He took the builder inside with him. They looked up at the sky from the first floor.

I could tell that my father was getting angry. The builder seemed not to care. "You made mistakes when you built my house," my father told him, his voice rising. "I paid you the right number of shekels, so you have to rebuild at your expense." "No," the builder snapped. His face looked mean. I watched his shifty eyes as he snarled, "There's nothing that says I have to do it."

"Oh, yes there is!" cried my father. "The code of laws by King Hammurabi says a builder has to make repairs at his own expense if a house falls down. Not only that, the law says you have to pay for everything that was damaged in the house."

My father kept talking to the builder. "You are lucky no one was home at the time. If the collapse had killed me, by law you would have been put to death." For the first time, the builder looked a bit worried.

"If my son, here, had been killed, your son would have had to die." My father seemed to be getting somewhere now. The builder looked more worried.

The builder started to back away from us. Then he started running. "Stop! Come back here!" my father shouted at him. I turned to my father. "Isn't he going to obey the code of law? What do we do next?"

Why are laws necessary?

Reading & Writing

1. **READING: Theme** A theme is the subject or idea that a story is about. Look at the illustration and think about the question at the end of the story. Talk with a partner to decide what the theme of this story is. As you read other stories in this book, watch to see if this theme recurs.
2. **WRITING: Persuasion** Imagine that you are the father in this story. Write a persuasive speech listing your complaints about the builder of your house. Then present your speech to your classmates.

Lesson

1

MAIN IDEAS

1. **Geography** Powerful city-states expanded to control much of Mesopotamia.
2. **Government** Babylon built a large empire in the Fertile Crescent.
3. **Government** Hammurabi created one of the first codes of law.

TAKING NOTES

Reading Skill: Summarizing

Summarizing means restating the main idea and important details about a subject. As you read Lesson 1, make a summary statement about each of the topics listed. Record them on a list of your own.

Topic	Statement
Geography	
A strong king	
A law code	

Skillbuilder Handbook, page R3

▲ **Bust of Sargon** Sargon of Akkad created the world's first empire 4,500 years ago.

Words to Know

Understanding the following words will help you read this lesson:

ambitious eager to gain success, fame, or power (page 113)

*Many Mesopotamian leaders were **ambitious**, but few were as successful as Sargon of Akkad.*

pattern a series of events that occur repeatedly (page 114)

*The decline, as well as the creation, of empires is an important historical **pattern**.*

governor a person chosen to rule over a colony or territory (page 114)

*Emperors selected **governors** who would carry out the emperors' policies.*

class a group of persons that are usually alike in some way (page 115)

*The upper **class** of a society usually has more wealth, resources, and power than do other classes.*

Mesopotamian Empires

TERMS & NAMES
empire
emperor
Fertile Crescent
Hammurabi
code of law
justice

Build on What You Know How big is the state where you live? What kinds of activities take place in the capital of your state? Most of the Mesopotamian city-states were smaller than the state you live in. The city-states were centers of culture and power.

The First Empire Builders

1 ESSENTIAL QUESTION Who controlled Mesopotamia?

From about 3000 to 2000 B.C., ambitious kings of the city-states of Sumer fought over land. The land was flat and easy to invade. More land would give more wealth and power to the king. However, no single king was able to control all of the city-states in Mesopotamia.

Sargon Builds an Empire About 2350 B.C., a powerful leader named Sargon took control of both northern and southern Mesopotamia. Sargon of Akkad is known as the creator of the first empire in world history. An **empire** brings together many different peoples and lands under the control of one ruler. The person who rules is called an **emperor**.

Sumerian Ruins Doorways are visible in these ruins of the once important Sumerian city of Uruk. ▼

The Akkadian Empire Sargon's empire was called the Akkadian Empire. Eventually, Sargon ruled over lands that stretched in a curve from the Mediterranean Sea through Mesopotamia to the Persian Gulf. This region is called the **Fertile Crescent** (see map on page 109). Unlike the dry region around it, the Fertile Crescent had rich soil and water that made the area good for farming.

Sargon's conquests helped to spread Akkadian ideas and ways of life. One of the most important ideas shared in the empire was the Akkadian system of writing.

The creation of an empire is a pattern that repeats in history. Empires are important because they change the way people live. They may bring peace to the peoples there. They encourage trade, which makes more goods available. Empires often include people from several cultures. The ideas, technology, and customs of the different peoples may be shared by all.

REVIEW How do empires change the lives of people who live in them?

▲ **Statue of Hammurabi**
This statue from about 1760 B.C. shows Hammurabi praying.

The Babylonian Empire

2 ESSENTIAL QUESTION Which empires ruled the Fertile Crescent?

The empire of Akkad lasted for about 200 years. It fell apart because of attacks by outside peoples. Fighting also took place among city-states within the empire.

Babylonians Expand About 2000 B.C., people known as the Amorites began to invade and take control of the city-states of Sumer. They chose the city of Babylon, which was located on the Euphrates River, for their capital.

From 1792 to 1750 B.C., a powerful Amorite king named **Hammurabi** (HAM•uh•RAH•bee) ruled the Babylonian Empire. Hammurabi expanded control over many city-states. Soon, his empire stretched across Mesopotamia and other parts of the Fertile Crescent.

Hammurabi used governors to help him control the lands. He sent out people to collect tax money and appointed judges to help keep order. Hammurabi also watched over agriculture, irrigation, trade, and the construction of buildings.

REVIEW How did Hammurabi control his huge empire?

Hammurabi's Law Code

3 ESSENTIAL QUESTION Why did Hammurabi create a law code?

Hammurabi ruled a vast empire of many peoples with different ideas, ways of life, and sets of laws. He needed a set of rules that all his people could obey.

A Code of Laws Hammurabi believed a **code of law** would help to control the empire. A code of law is a set of written rules for people to obey. He sent out people to collect the existing rules. After studying these rules, Hammurabi put together a single code of law. The code, written in cuneiform, was displayed on huge pillars near a temple.

Primary Source Handbook
See the excerpt from the Code of Hammurabi, page R38.

Justice for All The code's goal was to bring **justice**, fair treatment of people, to the people. In addition to identifying acts of wrongdoing, the code gave rights to people living in the land. Even women and children had rights, which was not the case in many ancient cultures. Punishments were different for each social class. (See Primary Source below.)

Primary Source

Background: Hammurabi's Code is sometimes called the "eye for an eye" code. It included 282 laws covering business, property, and conduct toward other people. The laws help us understand what was important to the people in Hammurabi's empire.

This scene is from the upper section of a pillar with the law code of Hammurabi. The laws were written on the lower section so that people could see them. ▶

from *Code of Hammurabi*
Translated by L. W. King

195. If a son strike his father, his hands shall be hewn [cut off].
196. If a man put out the eye of another man, his eye shall be put out.
197. If a man break another man's bone, his bone shall be broken.
202. If any one strike the body of a man higher in rank than he, he shall receive sixty blows with an ox-whip in public.
204. If a freed man strike the body of another freed man, he shall pay ten shekels in money.
205. If the slave of a freed man strike the body of a freed man, his ear shall be cut off.

DOCUMENT–BASED QUESTION
What do the laws tell you about justice at the time?

Hammurabi's Legacy The code established the idea that the government should provide protection and justice for the people. Hammurabi wanted to replace the belief in personal revenge as a way of solving problems. Hammurabi's Code set out the belief that society should be run by the rule of law. That means the law should be applied to all people, not just a few. By placing the laws on pillars where they could be seen, it also suggests everyone has a right to know the laws and the punishments for breaking them.

REVIEW What was the purpose of Hammurabi's Code?

Lesson Summary

- Sargon of Akkad built an empire of many different peoples under one ruler and one government.
- Hammurabi expanded the Babylonian Empire and brought its peoples together by wise government.
- Hammurabi created a single code of law that set up well-defined rules of treatment for all.

Why It Matters Now . . .

Hammurabi's Code established the idea that rule of law is an important part of society. Rule of law that guarantees fair treatment is practiced in most countries today.

1 Lesson Review

Homework Helper
ClassZone.com

Terms & Names

1. Explain the importance of

empire	Fertile Crescent	code of law
emperor	Hammurabi	justice

Using Your Notes

Summarizing Use your completed chart to answer the following question:

2. How does a strong king become an emperor?

Topic	Statement
Geography	
A strong king	
A law code	

Main Ideas

3. Which empires gained control of the Fertile Crescent?
4. Why did Hammurabi think his empire needed a single code of law?
5. What basic ideas about the law did Hammurabi's Code set up?

Critical Thinking

6. **Making Inferences** How did the geography of Mesopotamia affect the history of the region?
7. **Drawing Conclusions** Why is the development of Hammurabi's Code an important landmark in the growth of civilization?

Activity

Creating a Code of Law Develop a code of law for use in your classroom. Include penalties for failing to meet the rules. Have classmates compare your list with theirs.

Activity Extend Lesson 1

Build a Monument

Goal: To evaluate the reign of Hammurabi and to create a monument detailing his accomplishments

Materials & Supplies
- gray or tan construction paper
- markers
- scissors and tape
- ruler

Optional: books on Babylonia, Hammurabi, and U.S. presidential monuments

Prepare

1. Research the reign of Hammurabi. Make a list of his accomplishments.
2. Reread the information on Hammurabi on pages 114–116 in this chapter.
3. Research existing monuments to U.S. presidents or other world leaders.

Do the Activity

1. Look at your list of Hammurabi's achievements. Decide which are the most impressive and should be listed on the monument.
2. Brainstorm how you might show the achievements of Hammurabi visually.
3. Sketch a suitable monument for Hammurabi.
4. Transfer your drawing to construction paper. Cut it out and tape it together.

Follow-Up

1. Which of Hammurabi's accomplishments did you select? Why?
2. Why do people erect monuments to leaders?

Extension

Design Contest Have a design contest with others in your class to select the most appropriate design for Hammurabi's monument.

Lesson 2

MAIN IDEAS

1. **Science and Technology** Assyria built a military machine that was greatly feared by others in the region.
2. **Government** Assyria used several different methods to control its empire.
3. **Government** The Chaldeans replaced the Assyrians as the main power in Mesopotamia and other parts of the Fertile Crescent.

TAKING NOTES

Reading Skill: Understanding Cause and Effect

Finding causes and effects will help you understand the events in Lesson 2. Look for the effect of each cause listed in the chart. Fill in the effects on a chart of your own.

Causes	Effects
Assyrian military machine	
Cruelty to captured peoples	
Huge empires	

Skillbuilder Handbook, page R26

▲ **Jeweled Pendant** This ornament for a necklace is made from gold and precious stones. It shows a sacred palm tree.

Words to Know

Understanding the following words will help you read this lesson:

battering ram a large wooden beam used to knock down walls or gates (page 119)

*The **battering ram** bashed open the fortress gate.*

treasury the place in a country or empire where money is kept and managed (page 120)

*The emperor was pleased that so much money was flowing into the **treasury**.*

loom to stand high above (page 122)

*The walls of the city **loomed** above the plains below.*

wonder a very unusual or remarkable thing (page 122)

*Many of the **wonders** of the ancient world no longer exist.*

Assyria Rules the Fertile Crescent

TERMS & NAMES
exile
tribute
Hanging Gardens of Babylon

Build on What You Know In the last lesson, you learned that early empires in Mesopotamia conquered land that stretched into the Fertile Crescent. These empires needed strong armies and wise leaders to hold them together. When the Babylonian Empire fell, another took its place—Assyria.

A Mighty Military Machine

1 **ESSENTIAL QUESTION** How was Assyria able to build an empire?

Assyria was located in northern Mesopotamia, an area of rolling hills. To protect their lands, the rulers built a powerful army and set out to control the neighboring lands. The Assyrian army proved they were second to none.

A Powerful Army The Assyrians fought fiercely on foot, on horseback, and with chariots. Assyrian soldiers used the latest inventions for war. They carried iron swords and iron-tipped spears. Few of their enemies had iron weapons. The Assyrians attacked city walls with battering rams. They used ladders to scale the walls of cities. They even dug tunnels under city walls to get soldiers inside.

Once inside the city, they slaughtered the inhabitants. One Assyrian king boasted that he had destroyed 89 cities, 820 villages, and had burned the city of Babylon. As a result, the Assyrians were greatly feared by other peoples.

Stone Carving Assyrian warriors attack the walls and burn a neighboring city. ▼

Harsh Treatment of Captured People The Assyrians were cruel to the peoples they defeated. Enemies who surrendered were allowed to choose a leader. But those who refused to submit to Assyrian control were taken captive. The Assyrians killed or made slaves of captives. They speared enemy leaders and burned their cities. They sent captured peoples into **exile**. This means that they forced people to move from their homelands to other lands, often far away.

REVIEW Why were the Assyrians feared by their enemies?

Assyria Builds a Huge Empire

2 ESSENTIAL QUESTION How did Assyria control its empire?

Between 850 and 650 B.C., the Assyrians conquered many lands. They added Syria, Babylonia, Egypt, and Palestine to the empire. Assyria reached its peak of power under the rule of Ashurbanipal (AH•shur•BAH•nuh•PAHL) from 668 to 627 B.C. Under his leadership, the Assyrians controlled almost all of the Fertile Crescent.

A Huge Empire The Assyrian Empire grew so large that it needed to be very well organized. The Assyrians governed the conquered lands by choosing a governor or native king from that land to rule under their direction. The Assyrians provided the army that protected all of the lands.

Each ruler in a conquered land had to send **tribute** to the Assyrian emperor. This meant that the ruler had to pay for the protection given by the Assyrian army. Tribute brought money and goods into the empire's treasury. If any ruler failed to pay tribute, the army destroyed cities in that land. People of the land were forced into exile.

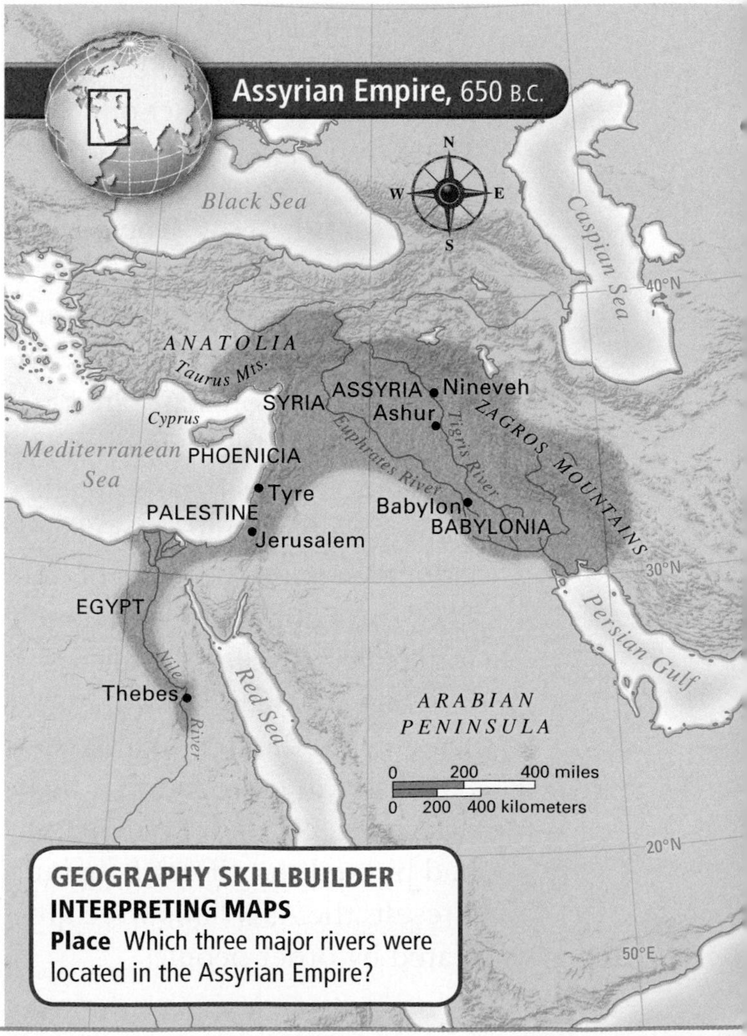

GEOGRAPHY SKILLBUILDER
INTERPRETING MAPS
Place Which three major rivers were located in the Assyrian Empire?

History Makers

Ashurbanipal (c. 668–627 B.C.)

Ashurbanipal, an Assyrian king, sent people to find and bring back copies of writings from throughout the empire. His collection contained over 20,000 cuneiform tablets. The collection included dictionaries, myths, and stories. He kept writings on special subjects such as science, geography, medicine, and religion. He even had some reports by spies.

Ashurbanipal set up a huge library in the capital at Nineveh (shown at the left). The library organized the collected texts by subject, like books in a modern library. However, Nineveh's enemies leveled the library. When archaeologists dug up the library's ruins, they found tablets. The tablets became the main source of information about ancient Mesopotamia.

◀ This is an artist's idea of what the library in Nineveh looked like.

The Assyrians made many enemies by their cruel actions. The leaders worried that exiled peoples might try to gather a force strong enough to defeat the Assyrians. They were right. The Assyrians had to put down many revolts.

Assyria Crumbles In 609 B.C., the Assyrian Empire fell. Two of its enemies, the Medes (meedz) and the Chaldeans (kal•DEE•uhnz), joined forces to defeat the Assyrians. These forces completely destroyed the city of Nineveh by burning it to the ground. For centuries afterward, only mounds of earth marked the location of the once great capital.

REVIEW Why did the Assyrians receive tribute?

A New Babylonian Empire

3 ESSENTIAL QUESTION Who replaced the Assyrian Empire?

In time, Assyria's neighbors, the Chaldeans, ruled much of the former Assyrian empire. The city of Babylon became the capital of the Chaldeans' new empire. Remember that Babylon was the capital of the first Babylonian empire. Sometimes the Chaldeans are called the New Babylonians.

Chaldeans Take Assyrian Lands The Chaldean Empire reached its peak between 605 and 562 B.C. The Chaldeans were led by Nebuchadnezzar II (NEHB•uh•kuhd•NEHZ•uhr) who drove the Egyptians out of Syria and captured trading cities on the Mediterranean coast.

Like the Assyrians, the Chaldeans faced revolts by captured people. The Hebrews, a group of people living in lands near the Mediterranean Sea coast, rebelled in 598 B.C. Nebuchadnezzar seized Jerusalem, which was the capital city of the Hebrews. The Hebrews' sacred temple there was destroyed. The Chaldeans held thousands of Hebrews captive in Babylon for about 50 years.

Height of Wealth and Power Nebuchadnezzar rebuilt the city of Babylon and constructed the huge, colorful Ishtar Gate. Processions into the city went through this gate. An enormous ziggurat loomed 300 feet above the city. Chaldean astronomers used the tower to study the skies. It is said that to please his wife, Nebuchadnezzar built an artificial mountain covered with trees and plants. It was called the **Hanging Gardens of Babylon**. The gardens were built in such a way that they appeared to float above the ground. They became one of the Seven Wonders of the World. (See the Reader's Theater, pages 124–127.)

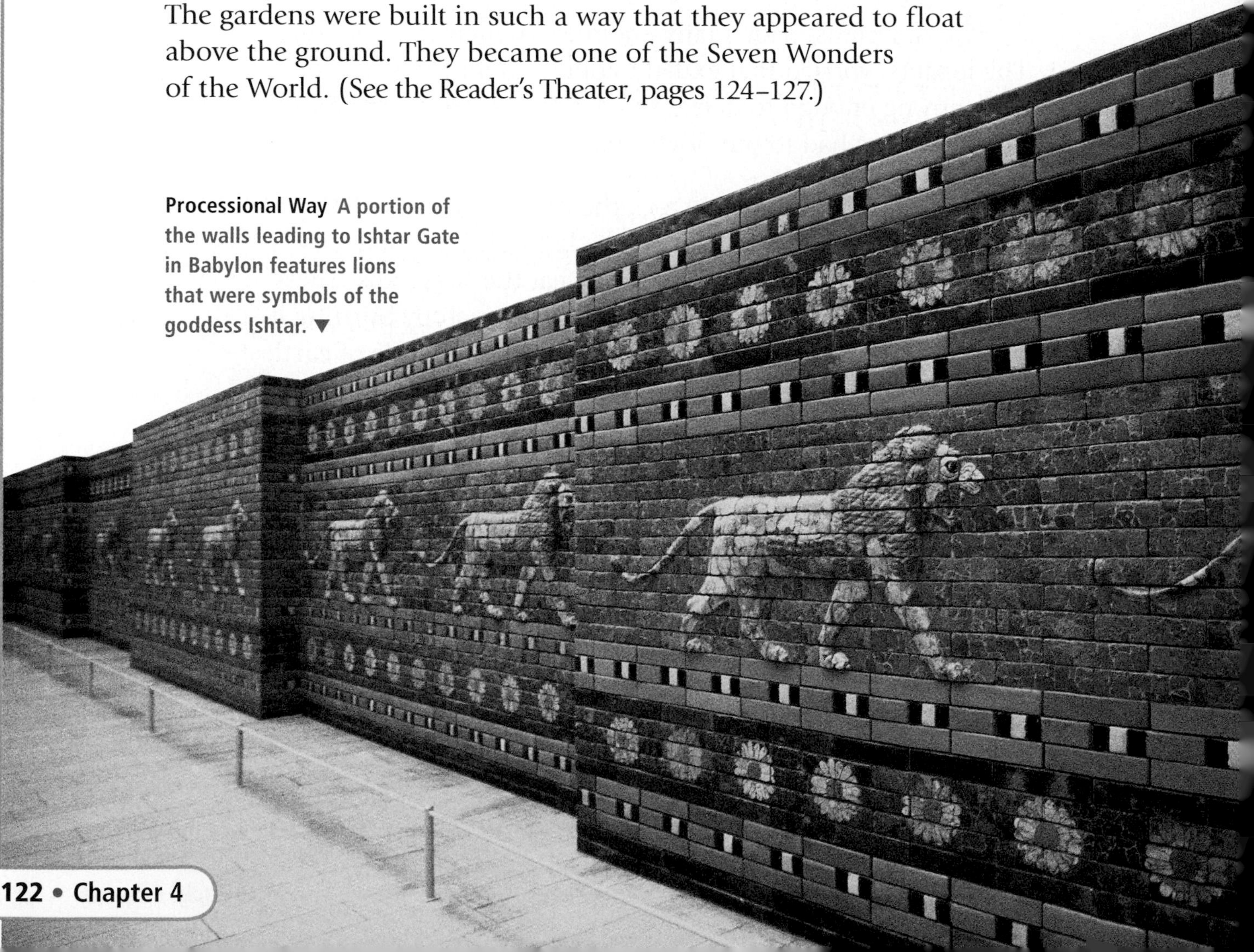

Processional Way A portion of the walls leading to Ishtar Gate in Babylon features lions that were symbols of the goddess Ishtar. ▼

The Empire Fades Weak rulers followed Nebuchadnezzar II. In addition to the weak rulers, internal conflicts about religion upset and divided the Chaldeans. This made it easy for Cyrus of Persia to conquer the land. You will learn more about Cyrus in the next lesson.

REVIEW What were some features of the Chaldean capital of Babylon?

▲ **Detail from the Ishtar Gate** This is one of the mythical dragons found on the Ishtar Gate. The dragons were believed to dwell in ancient Babylon.

Lesson Summary

- The Assyrian military used new kinds of weapons and ways of fighting. The military was very cruel to captured peoples.
- The Assyrians' highly organized government controlled the conquered lands.
- The Chaldeans conquered Assyrian lands. Their empire reached its peak under Nebuchadnezzar II.

Why It Matters Now . . .

The Assyrian Empire showed that to control large areas of land with many people, an empire must have a highly organized government and a strong military.

2 Lesson Review

Homework Helper
ClassZone.com

Terms & Names

1. Explain the importance of
exile   tribute   Hanging Gardens of Babylon

Using Your Notes

Understanding Cause and Effect Use your completed chart to answer the following question:

2. What caused Assyria to improve its methods of government?

Causes	Effects
Assyrian military machine	
Cruelty to captured peoples	
Huge empires	

Main Ideas

3. What tactics did the Assyrians use to defeat their enemies?

4. How did the Assyrians maintain control of their lands?

5. What happened to the Hebrews when they rebelled against the Chaldeans?

Critical Thinking

6. Making Inferences What can happen when a country follows a policy of cruelty toward captured peoples, as Assyria did?

7. Comparing In what ways were the Assyrians and the Chaldeans alike?

Activity

Internet Activity Use the Internet to research the wonders of Babylon under Nebuchadnezzar II. Create a guide for tourists.

INTERNET KEYWORDS: *Babylon, Nebuchadnezzar*

THE HANGING GARDENS OF BABYLON

Background: The year is 580 B.C. The place: Babylon, an ancient city in what is now Iraq. The ruler, Nebuchadnezzar II, is currently the most powerful king in the region. To strengthen his power, he has married Amytis, a princess from a land called Media, which was located in present-day Iran.

CAST OF CHARACTERS

Amytis: (uh•MIH•tuhs) queen and wife of Nebuchadnezzar II

Sammu: slave to the royal family

Nebuchadnezzar II: (NEHB•uh•kuhd•NEHZ•uhr) King of the Chaldeans

Merodach: (mih•ROH•DAK) the royal architect

Essam: the royal engineer

Narrator

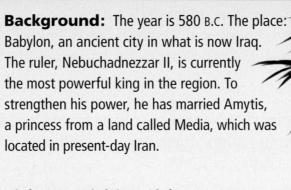

Amytis: Sammu, did you bring my palm oil? My face is as dry as the desert wind in this dreadful land!

Sammu: Right here, my queen.

Narrator: Amytis has been very unhappy since King Nebuchadnezzar brought her from Media. She is a Median princess, and the king married her to help keep peace between the two lands. But Amytis is so miserable. If she insists on returning to Media, her father will not be pleased. Look, here come the king and the queen.

Amytis: You said that I would live in a paradise as your wife. But I think I left paradise when I left Media.

Nebuchadnezzar: But my queen, Babylon is one of the largest and most beautiful cities in the world. Look at the great city walls, the Tower of Babel, the paved boulevards.

Amytis: In the Median mountains where I lived, the breezes were comfortable. The trees provided cool shade and sweet fruit. It's so hot and dusty here. It's nothing like my beautiful Media!

Narrator: Nebuchadnezzar knew that he must please Amytis to keep peace with her father in Media. He hurries to speak with her.

Nebuchadnezzar: My sweet, what if I give you what you desire? Cool gardens, green trees, flowers, and clear water right here in Babylon. Will you stay?

Amytis: Of course. But how can you do that?

Nebuchadnezzar: (*boasting*) I am the most powerful king the world has known. I will find a way. Sammu, fetch my royal architect and engineer.

Sammu: Yes, my king.

Nebuchadnezzar: Merodach, I charge you to create a spectacular mountain garden, right here on the palace grounds. It must have trees and flowers and clear running water. Essam, you will take the plans and figure out how to make this work. Do you both understand?

Merodach and Essam: Yes, my king. It will be done.

Narrator: Months later the king, the royal architect, and the royal engineer go over the architect's plans.

(continued)

Merodach: We can build a huge tower with terraces that will be filled with dirt. We will import trees that grow in our queen's Median homeland: date palms, cypress, fig, and pomegranate. Perfumed flowers too. And we can clear spaces for shaded canopies to protect our fair queen from the midday sun. Of course, we will need something to keep evil spirits away from her precious soul. I propose guarding the stairway with giant statues of winged lions that have copies of your majesty's head. The gods themselves could not offer better protection.

Nebuchadnezzar: Her own green mountain, in the midst of this desert! Amytis would love that. Remember just one thing: it rarely rains here. We can irrigate our flat farmlands from the rivers, but how will we move water uphill to keep an entire forest alive?

Essam: (*smiling*) I've designed what I call a chain pump. My system uses a large wheel at the bottom of the "mountain," and one at the top. They are connected by a chain, from which hang many buckets for water. As slaves turn the

◀ **Hanging Gardens** This is an artist's idea of what the Hanging Gardens looked like.

bottom wheel, the chain dips buckets into an irrigation pool and carries them upward. At the top, the buckets dump into an upper pool with channels to carry water to every plant in the monument.

Nebuchadnezzar: Well done, both of you! Let's get started immediately.

Merodach: Your worship, these hanging gardens will probably be the most expensive building project ever. And the chain pump will need to be operated by shifts of men all day and night. It will require much gold and many slaves.

Nebuchadnezzar: Not a problem. Since I captured Jerusalem, we have a fresh supply of both gold and slaves.

Narrator: Nebuchadnezzar built his Hanging Gardens of Babylon, and they were called one of the Seven Wonders of the World. Nebuchadnezzar presented the gardens to Amytis.

Nebuchadnezzar: Amytis, my sweet, here are your new gardens. Now, perhaps, you will not want to go home to Media.

Amytis: Oh, my king! They are the most wonderful gardens ever!

Narrator: Amytis loves her human-made mountain, and spends almost all of her time there. This has made life easier for the king. Nebuchadnezzar and Amytis enjoy relaxing in the gardens.

Amytis: Sammu, we need more pomegranates and dates in this basket. Go pick us some, then come back and fan me.

Sammu: Yes, my queen. Right away.

Amytis: My king, I think we should invite the Egyptian pharaoh for a royal visit. I want all the world to see and admire my beautiful gardens. They will be a vision of beauty for all eternity!

Narrator: Amytis was partially right. There was nothing like the Hanging Gardens of Babylon anywhere. But somewhere along the line they were destroyed, along with the Chaldean civilization. The only way you can see them now, my friends, is with your imagination.

Activities

1. **TALK ABOUT IT** What do you think might have happened to the Hanging Gardens?
2. **WRITE ABOUT IT** Write a new scene in which Amytis has a party for the Egyptian royal family to show off her Hanging Gardens of Babylon. What might guests see and do at such an elegant event?

Lesson 3

MAIN IDEAS

1. **Geography** Persia's location between Mesopotamia and India was a bridge between eastern and western Asia.
2. **Government** Cyrus used a policy of toleration to control the Persian Empire.
3. **Government** To better govern, Persia divided its lands into smaller units.

TAKING NOTES

Reading Skill: Identifying Issues and Problems
A study of problems faced by rulers in Lesson 3 can help you understand the growth of governments. Use a Venn diagram to identify the issues and problems faced by Cyrus and Darius.

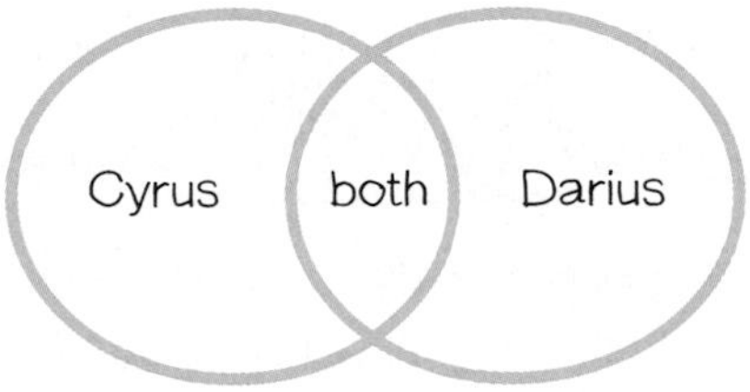

Skillbuilder Handbook, page R28

▲ **Drinking Vessel** A winged lion decorates a gold drinking vessel. Winged lions symbolizing speed and power were associated with Persia.

Words to Know

Understanding the following words will help you read this lesson:

isolate to keep apart from others (page 129)
*The mountains that **isolated** Persia from the rest of the Fertile Crescent slowed trade between the two regions.*

semiprecious not quite as valuable as the most expensive (page 129)
*Opals are **semiprecious** gems.*

policy a course of action chosen by a government (page 131)
*The new emperor's harsh **policy** toward conquered peoples resulted in a rebellion.*

wise showing intelligence and good judgment (page 131)
*The peace of his rule showed that he had made **wise** choices about how to govern.*

Persia Controls Southwest Asia

TERMS & NAMES
Anatolia
toleration
province
satrap
Royal Road

Build on What You Know In Lessons 1 and 2, you learned about empires that were built in the lands of the Fertile Crescent. To the east of these empires was the land of the Medes, which was called Media. These lands bridged east and west Asia.

A Land Between East and West

1 **ESSENTIAL QUESTION** What was the land of the Persians like?

The Medes controlled lands that included the Persians. Modern-day Iran lies on Persian land. It is marked by geographic differences.

Mountains, Deserts, and a Plateau The area Persia would control was isolated from the rest of the Fertile Crescent. Mountain ranges cut off the land from the sea and from the rest of the continent. These ranges are the Zagros, the Caucasus (KAW•kuh•sus), and the Hindu Kush. (See the map on page 130.) Most people lived at the edge of a high plateau in the middle of the region or in mountain valleys. Iron, copper, and semiprecious gems could be found in the land.

Iranian Valley Fertile valleys still exist between the mountain ranges in the lands once known as Persia. ▼

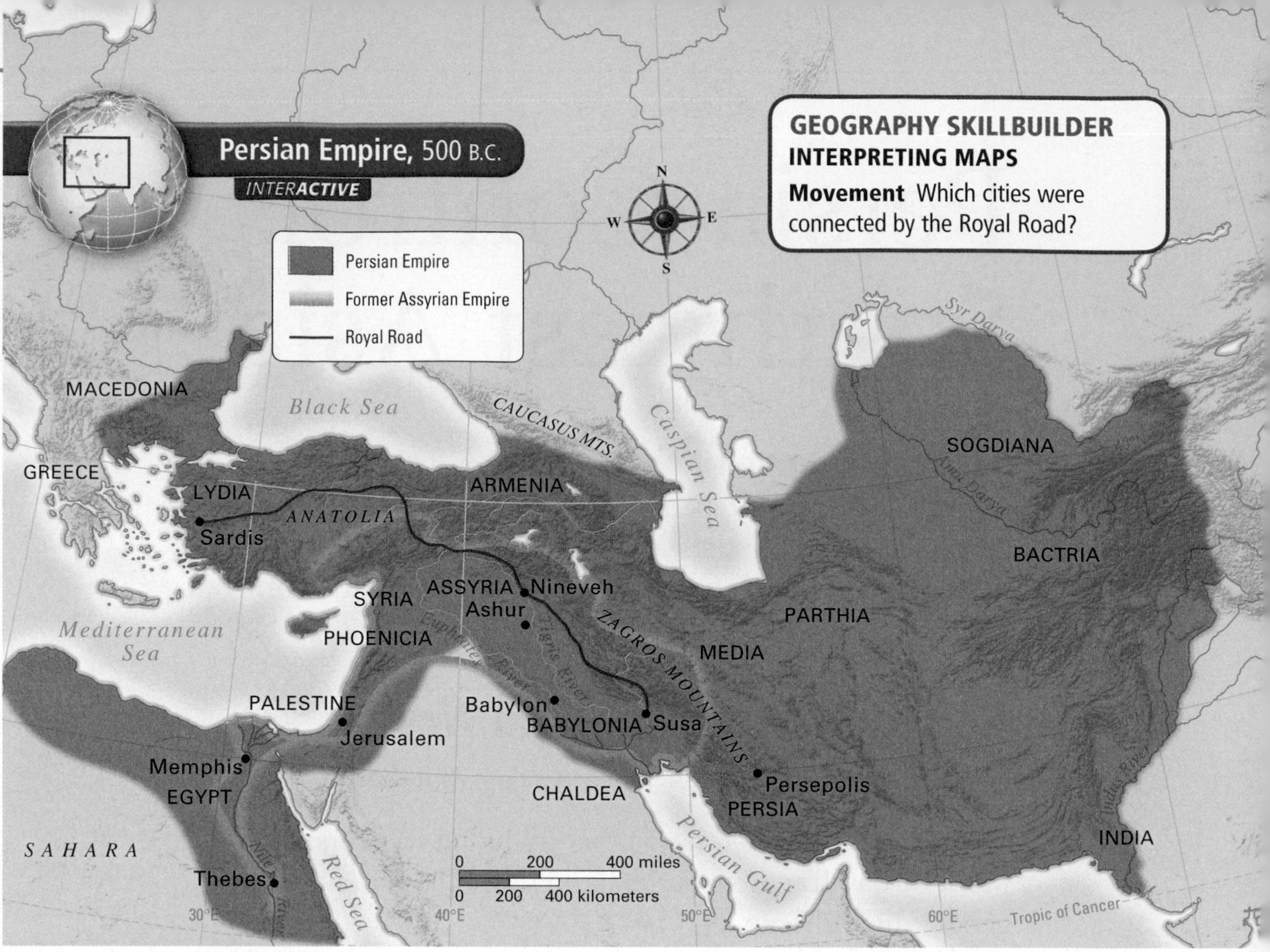

Persians Occupy the Land Nomadic invaders often swept in and occupied the lands of the Medes. The nomads came from the plains of Central Asia. They were related to other nomadic people who would later move into Europe and into India. The result of these invasions was much mixing of nomads' customs with other societies that lived there. About 1000 B.C., Persians entered the region. They created many tiny kingdoms that thrived through trade in horses and minerals with eastern and western Asia. These kingdoms grew in power and began to threaten the Medes' control of the land.

REVIEW How did the presence of nomadic tribes affect Persia?

Cyrus Founds the Persian Empire

2 ESSENTIAL QUESTION What was the rule of Cyrus like?

The Medes ruled Persia until a brilliant, powerful Persian king named Cyrus (SY•ruhs) took control. He was known as Cyrus the Great. Cyrus had a vision of conquering the lands around Persia and uniting these lands as one large empire. Then he set out to accomplish his goal.

Comparisons Across Cultures

Treatment of Captured Peoples

Ashurbanipal and the Assyrians	Cyrus, Darius, and the Persians
Used policies of cruelty	Used policies of toleration
Tortured leaders	Allowed leaders to remain in power
Burned cities	Did not destroy homes
Sent people into exile	Allowed people to keep their own gods and culture
Collected tribute	Collected tribute

▲ This is an artist's idea of the surrender of a conquered leader to Assyrian king Sennacherib.

Fearless Military Leader Cyrus led swift, deadly attacks in the region. First, Cyrus conquered **Anatolia**, also called Asia Minor. It lies within modern-day Turkey. Then, between 550 and 539 B.C., Cyrus conquered the Fertile Crescent lands that had once been controlled by the Assyrians and the Chaldeans. His empire was immense.

A Wise Emperor Cyrus needed ways to control lands filled with many different peoples. Unlike the Assyrians who ruled through cruelty, Cyrus set up a policy of **toleration**. This meant allowing people to keep their customs and beliefs. Cyrus allowed the conquered peoples to continue to worship their own gods, speak their own languages, and practice their own ways of life. However, they did have to pay tribute.

Cyrus's policies of respect and toleration made friends instead of enemies. For example, the Hebrew people (see Lesson 2) who had been captured by the Chaldeans greatly liked Cyrus because he freed them. He also allowed them to rebuild their temple and the city of Jerusalem. Cyrus's policy of toleration made governing the empire much easier. There were fewer revolts, and the people lived in peace.

REVIEW Why can Cyrus be considered a wise emperor?

Darius Expands the Empire

3 ESSENTIAL QUESTION How did Darius control his empire?

Cyrus built a stable empire of many peoples by his policy of toleration. After he died, a weak, less-tolerant ruler faced rebellions in the empire. Then a strong leader named Darius (duh•RY•uhs) came to power.

Darius Extends Persian Control The new emperor, Darius I, spent his first years as emperor dealing with rebellious peoples. After he put down the revolts, he moved to conquer lands as far east as India. The Persian Empire grew to 2,800 miles from east to west. (The distance from New York City to Los Angeles is about 2,500 miles.)

Political Organization The empire was so large that Darius added new policies to those set up by Cyrus. Darius divided the empire into 20 **provinces**. Each province, which was an area of land similar to a state, had a local government.

Darius set up governors called **satraps** (SAY•traps) to carry out his orders in the provinces and to collect taxes. He appointed a military commander for each satrap. He also sent out spies called "king's eyes and ears" to be sure his satraps followed orders. These policies allowed him to have greater control over all of the lands.

Connect to Today

Ruins at Persepolis
Winged and bearded bull-like figures guard the Gate of All Nations at the Persian royal palace. ▼

Uniting the Empire The policy of provinces ruled by satraps was only one way to unite the empire. Darius started the use of a **Royal Road**, or road for government purposes. The Royal Road was 1,775 miles long. The eastern end of the road was in Susa, and the western end was in Sardis on the Anatolian Peninsula. Royal messages were sent by a relay of messengers.

About every 15 miles there was a relay station where the messengers could get a fresh horse. Royal messages could move from one end of the road to the other in about seven days. Military troops and mail also moved along it from all parts of the empire to the capital. The road also promoted trade and business throughout the empire.

Darius set up a law code based on Hammurabi's model. From the Lydians, a conquered people, Darius took the idea of *minted coins*. The coins were good throughout the empire. They promoted business and made it easy to pay taxes.

Visual Vocabulary

Minted coins is a term for coins that are issued by the government and are official money.

Enemies of Persia Darius planned a march against Egyptian rebels in 486 B.C., but he died that year. His son Xerxes (ZURK•seez) had to deal with Egypt. You will read about Egypt in the next chapter. Xerxes would also have to deal with the Greeks. You will read about them in Chapter 11.

REVIEW Why did Darius divide the empire into provinces?

Lesson Summary

- Tiny Persian kingdoms thrived due to trade.
- Cyrus the Great ruled the Persian Empire with a policy of toleration.
- Darius formed provinces and appointed satraps to improve government.

Why It Matters Now . . .

The Persians showed that lands ruled with policies of toleration could be stable and peaceful.

3 Lesson Review

Homework Helper
ClassZone.com

Terms & Names

1. Explain the importance of

Anatolia	province	Royal Road
toleration	satrap	

Taking Notes

Identifying Issues and Problems Use your completed Venn diagram to answer the following question:

2. What common problems did Cyrus and Darius face during their reigns?

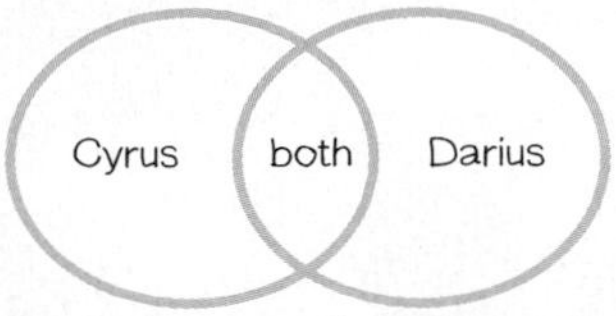

Main Ideas

3. How did people in early Persian kingdoms earn their living?
4. How did Cyrus treat the Hebrew people in the lands he captured?
5. In what ways did the Royal Road and minted coins help Darius unite the empire?

Critical Thinking

6. **Making Inferences** How did Cyrus's policy of toleration change the way empires were ruled?
7. **Comparing and Contrasting** How did the policies of Cyrus and Darius contrast with those of the Assyrians?

Activity

Making a Map Take out the world map you created in Chapter 2. Add to the map by outlining the expansion of the Persian Empire under Darius.

Daily Life

Extend Lesson 3

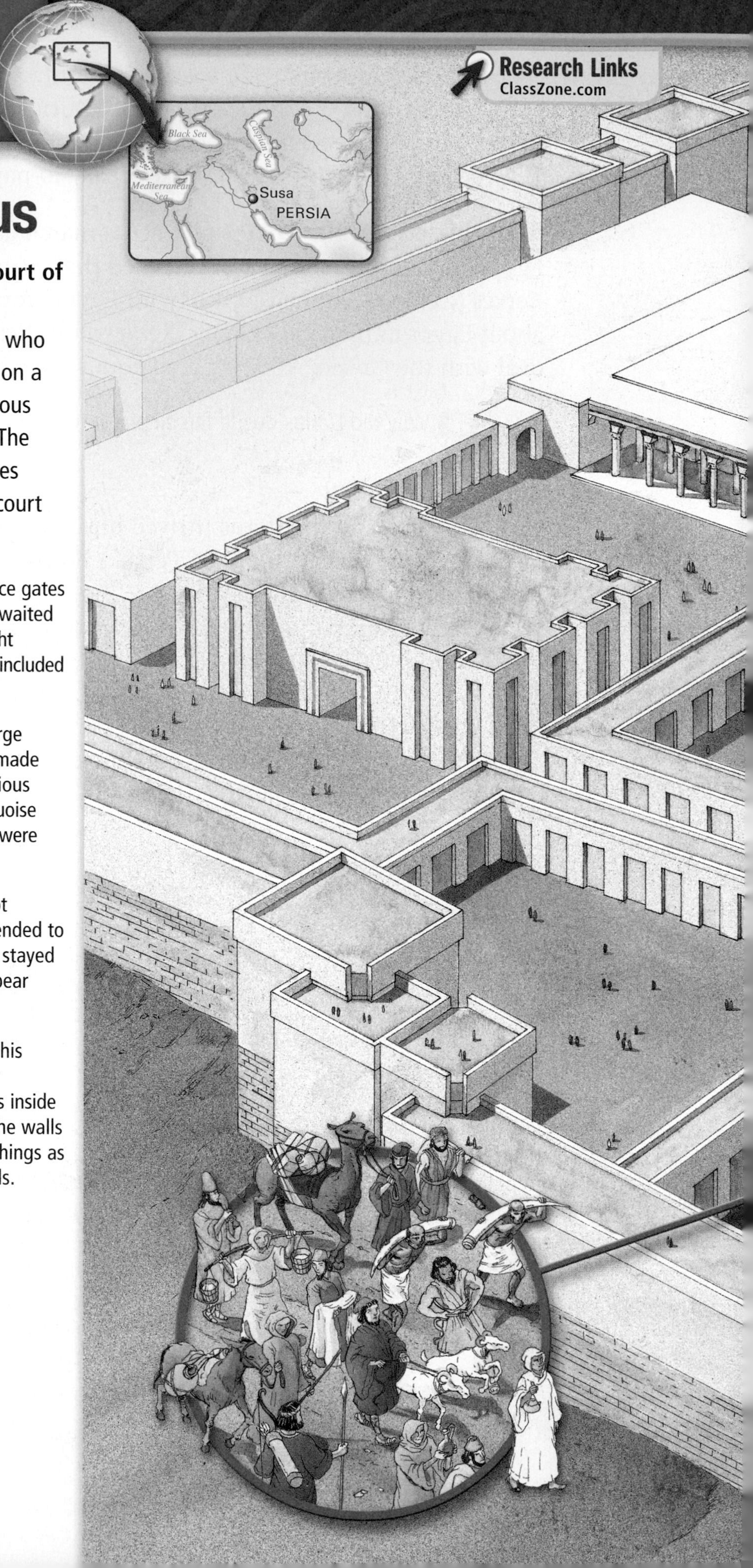

Research Links
ClassZone.com

The Court of Darius

Purpose: To learn about life at the court of the Persian emperor Darius

Darius's palace was designed to impress all who came there. It was set on the base of a hill on a platform 50 feet above the plain. Its enormous size proclaimed the power of the emperor. The palace at Persepolis was one of three palaces used by the Persian emperors. Darius held court here in the wintertime.

A Entrance Gate The palace had two entrance gates where representatives of conquered peoples waited to present tribute to the emperor. They brought animals such as bulls and horses. Other tribute included gold, ivory, cloth, grain, and precious gems.

B Treasure Room The treasure room held large quantities of gold and silver. Some of it was made into serving plates and drinking vessels. Precious stones such as lapis lazuli, carnelian, and turquoise decorated some of these pieces. Other stones were used in fine jewelry.

C Ladies' Court Upper-class women were not expected to do any work. Many servants attended to the ladies of the court. The women generally stayed in the ladies' court unless commanded to appear before the emperor.

D Audience Hall Darius met with officials of his empire and received ambassadors from other countries in this hall. The hall had 36 columns inside and 36 columns outside to support the roof. The walls featured brightly colored tiles showing such things as human-headed lions and ranks of royal guards.

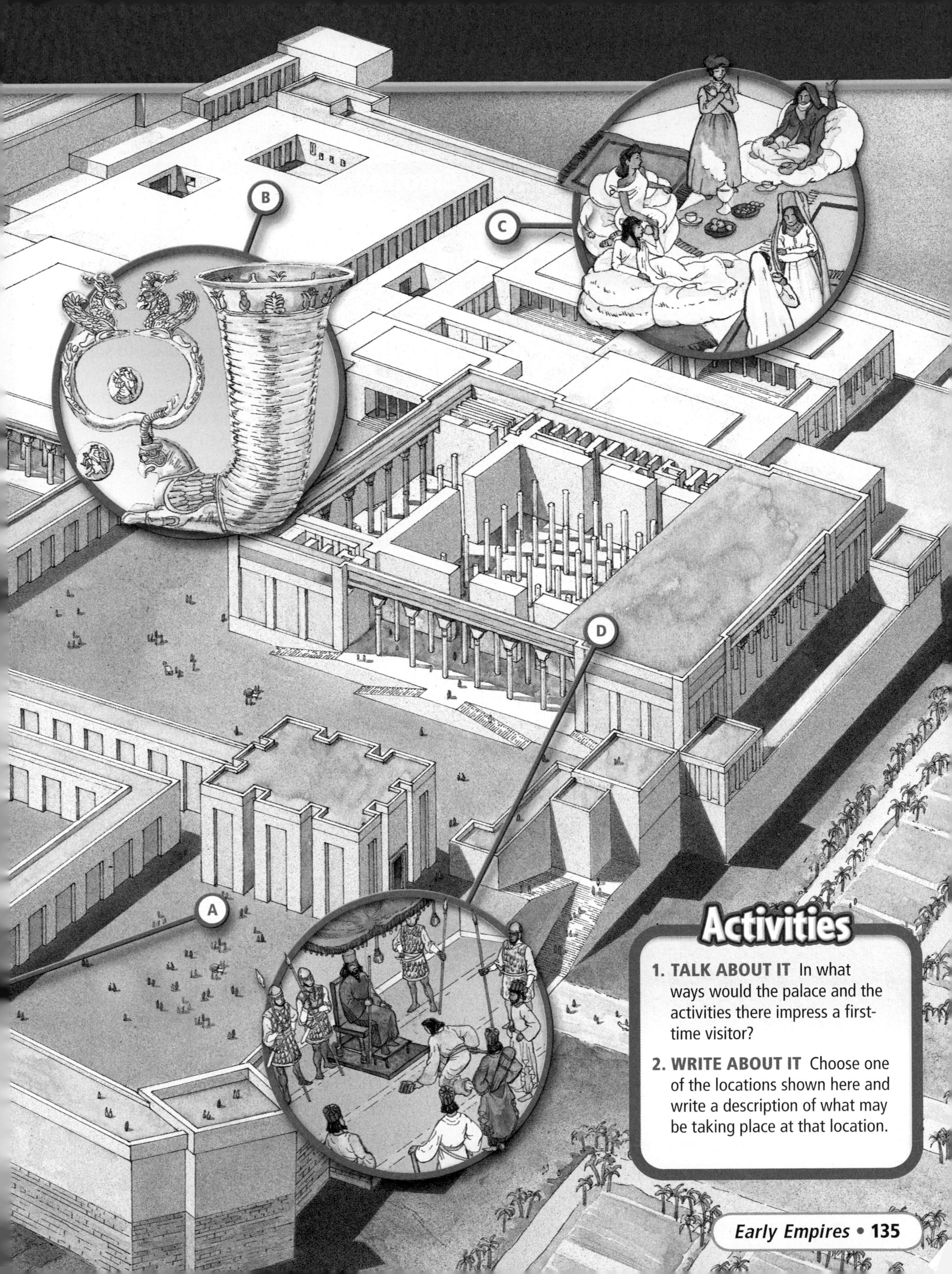

Activities

1. **TALK ABOUT IT** In what ways would the palace and the activities there impress a first-time visitor?
2. **WRITE ABOUT IT** Choose one of the locations shown here and write a description of what may be taking place at that location.

Chapter 4 Review

VISUAL SUMMARY

Early Empires

Government

- First empire is created.
- Code of law developed.
- Empire divided into smaller units for easier rule.
- Policies of toleration are used to control captured people.

Culture

- System of writing helps record keeping.
- Library is built by Ashurbanipal.
- Hanging Gardens are built by Nebuchadnezzar.
- Tower of Babel rises above the city of Babylon.

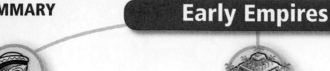

Economics

- Tribute used to support the empire.
- Minted coins help business and the government.
- Royal Road links the Persian Empire.

TERMS & NAMES

Explain why the words in each set below are linked with each other.

1. **empire, Fertile Crescent,** and **Anatolia**
2. **Hammurabi, code of law,** and **justice**
3. **province, satrap,** and **Royal Road**

MAIN IDEAS

Mesopotamian Empires (pages 112–117)

4. Which lands are a part of the region known as the Fertile Crescent?
5. How do empires change the lives of the people who live in them?
6. Why was Hammurabi's Code a step toward better government?

Assyria Rules the Fertile Crescent (pages 118–127)

7. Why were the Assyrians able to build such a large empire?
8. How did Assyrians treat peoples with different religious beliefs and ways of life?
9. Why did conquered people have to pay tribute?

Persia Controls Southwest Asia (pages 128–135)

10. What policies did Cyrus use to keep his empire under control?
11. Why did Darius expand his government?
12. Why was the Persian Royal Road important?

CRITICAL THINKING
Big Ideas: Government

13. **MAKING INFERENCES** How does a uniform code of law improve a leader's ability to rule effectively?
14. **EXPLAINING HISTORICAL PATTERNS** What pattern of governmental leadership can be seen in the reigns of Hammurabi, Cyrus, and Darius?
15. **COMPARING** How successful were the policies of Assyria compared with those of Persia?

ALTERNATIVE ASSESSMENT

1. **WRITING ACTIVITY** Select two rulers from this chapter to compare and contrast. Write an expository paragraph about them.
2. **INTERDISCIPLINARY ACTIVITY—SCIENCE AND TECHNOLOGY** Use printed sources or the Internet to research ancient warfare equipment such as that the Assyrians invented. Create a poster to illustrate your findings.
3. **STARTING WITH A STORY**
Starting with a Story
Review the story titled "Day of Misfortune." Work with a few classmates to rewrite the story as a scene in a play. Include an ending that tells what happened to the builder. Perform your scene.

Technology Activity

4. **MAKING A MULTIMEDIA PRESENTATION**
Use the Internet or printed sources to find illustrations of Mesopotamian or Persian objects found by archaeologists. Work with a small group to make a multimedia presentation.
- What objects were found?
- What activities do they represent?

Research Links
ClassZone.com

Reading Tables Use the table below to answer the questions.

Size and Population of Ancient Empires

Empire	Empire Size in Square Miles	Major City	City Size (Approximate Population)
Akkadia	2,509,664	Agade	35,000
Sumer	386,102	Ur	65,000
Babylonia	640,930	Babylon	60,000
Assyria	3,602,333	Nineveh	120,000

Source: *Institute for Research on World Systems*

1. **Which of the following statements about empire land size is correct?**
   A. Assyria's land size is much smaller than Babylonia's land size.
   B. Assyria's land size is much larger than Sumer's land size.
   C. Sumer's land size and Babylonia's land size are about the same.
   D. All of the empires are about the same size.

2. **Based on the population size of the major cities, which statement is correct?**
   A. Agade and Nineveh were the largest cities.
   B. Babylon and Nineveh were similar in size.
   C. Babylon and Ur were similar in size.
   D. Nineveh was ten times larger than any other city.

Test Practice
ClassZone.com

Additional Test Practice, pp. S1–S33

Writing About History

Writing Model
ClassZone.com

Expository Writing: Explanations

The Origins and Impacts of Empires

Purpose: To write an expository composition about empires

Audience: Your learning partner

In this unit, you read many explanations. For example, you read how the land in Mesopotamia became fertile because of flooding and how fertile land made crops grow. These explanations are examples of **expository writing,** or writing that informs. Historians use expository writing to explain past events and their impact on human life.

◀ Sargon

Organization & Focus

Your assignment is to write a 500- to 700-word expository composition about the origins or impacts of empires. An expository composition has three main parts. The **introduction** gets the reader interested and states a clear thesis, or main idea. The **body** provides supporting details in the form of facts and examples. The **conclusion** summarizes the information and restates the thesis.

Historical expositions often have chronological sequence or cause and effect as their organizational pattern. In this essay, cause-and-effect organization will best help you to explain the origins or impacts of empires.

Choosing a Topic Reread pages 113–114. With a learning partner, identify paragraphs that deal with the causes of the rise of empires and those that deal with empires' effects. Finally, you and your partner should divide the topic, so that one will write about the origins and the other about the impacts.

Identifying Purpose and Audience When your purpose is to explain, you need to use facts and examples to support your main idea. Through discussion, try to get an idea of what kinds of facts and examples will help your learning partner understand your thesis.

Research & Technology

> **Technology Tip** To do additional research on the Internet, you might visit an online database, or collection of well-organized information. Your librarian might be able to suggest a database with information on your topic.

Finding Details Review Chapters 3 and 4. Look for information to support your thesis, and record it in a chart like the one below. Review your notes and create categories for them. Possible categories include the themes of this program: Geography, Culture, Economics, Government, Belief Systems, and Science & Technology. Use your category names as key words to search for more information.

Thesis:	
Supporting Facts	Supporting Examples

Outlining and Drafting When you have the facts and examples you need, decide on the best order for them. One possibility is order of importance, with the most important information saved for last. Another is a category-by-category order with the categories arranged for logical flow. Outline your composition, and then compose the first draft.

Evaluation & Revision

When revising, pay attention to the order of your ideas and the flow of paragraphs. Use the Self-Check to see if your explanation accomplishes its purpose. When you are satisfied that it does, prepare a final copy. Use your word processor to check spelling.

Self-Check

Does my explanation have

- ☐ a clear introduction, with the main idea, or thesis, stated?
- ☐ supporting examples and facts logically arranged?
- ☐ a conclusion that restates the main idea?

Publish & Present

Exchange compositions with your partner, and read his or her work. Then discuss what you learned from reading your partner's composition and from writing your own.

UNIT 3

Ancient Africa

Interact with History ▶

Building the Great Pyramid, about 2550 B.C.

You are an overseer working to build the tomb of the pharaoh, or ruler. Many laborers and skilled craftspeople will be needed to complete the pyramid in time.

What problems might you face in building a pyramid?

Thousands of workers were needed to build the pyramid. Many were farmers who worked during the season when the Nile was flooded.

What different types of workers would you need to build the pyramid?

WebQuest
ClassZone.com

Chapter 5
Ancient Egypt

Chapter 6
Kush and Other African Kingdoms

Each stone block weighed about 2.5 tons—which is about as heavy as a small pickup truck. The ancient Egyptians had not started using the wheel yet. So they had to drag the blocks on sleds up wooden ramps.

What are some of the dangers involved in this process?

Artisans had to finish rough stone blocks to be the perfect size and shape. This created a huge pile of stone chips. Archaeologists are not sure if the finishing was done at the quarry or at the pyramid site.

What are the advantages of finishing the blocks at the quarry? at the pyramid?

Chapter 5

Ancient Egypt

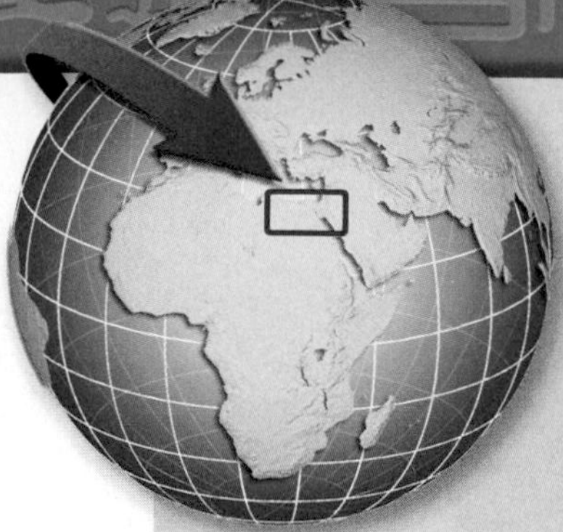

Before You Read: K-W-L

Considering what you have already learned about ancient Egypt will help prepare you to read this chapter. Record the answers to the following questions in your notebook:

- What do you already know about Egypt?
- Study the map and time line on these pages. What do they tell you about Egypt's land and its people?
- What do you want to **learn** about Egypt?

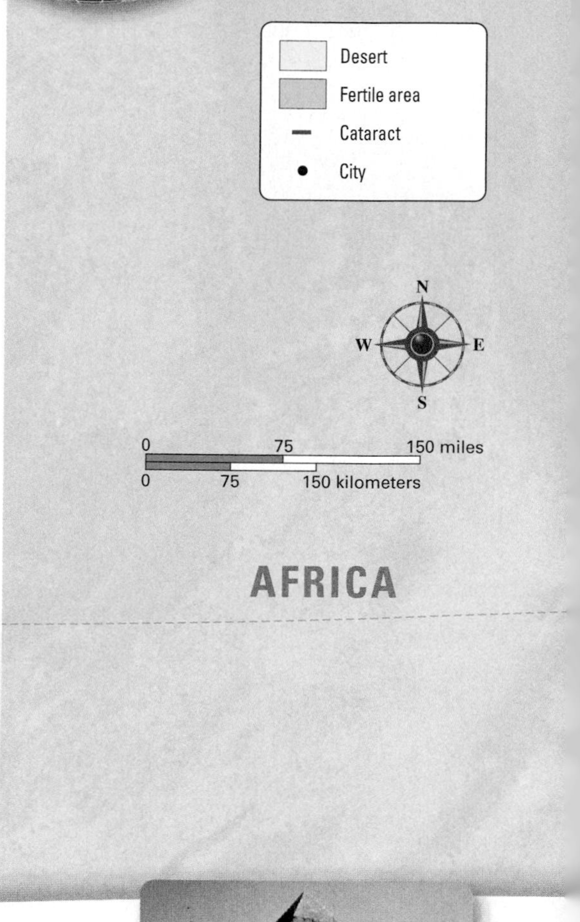

Big Ideas About Ancient Egypt

Geography **Civilizations developed in places that supported agriculture or trade or both.**

Ancient Egypt developed along the Nile River. Rich farmland along the Nile provided plenty of food for the Egyptians. The river also became a trading highway. Farming and trade encouraged the development of a great civilization in Egypt.

Integrated Technology

eEdition
- Interactive Maps
- Interactive Visuals
- Starting with a Story

VIDEO *Ancient Egypt*

INTERNET RESOURCES

Go to **ClassZone.com** for
- WebQuest
- Homework Helper
- Research Links
- Internet Activities
- Quizzes
- Maps
- Test Practice
- Current Events

EGYPT

3100 B.C. Upper and Lower Egypt are united.

2550 B.C. Work on Khufu's Great Pyramid begins in Giza. (Great Pyramid is at far right.) ▶

3000 B.C. — 2500 B.C.

WORLD

2500 B.C. Harappan culture rises in the Indus Valley. ◀ (Harappan elephant seal)

Ancient Egypt, 3100–1200 B.C.

INTERACTIVE

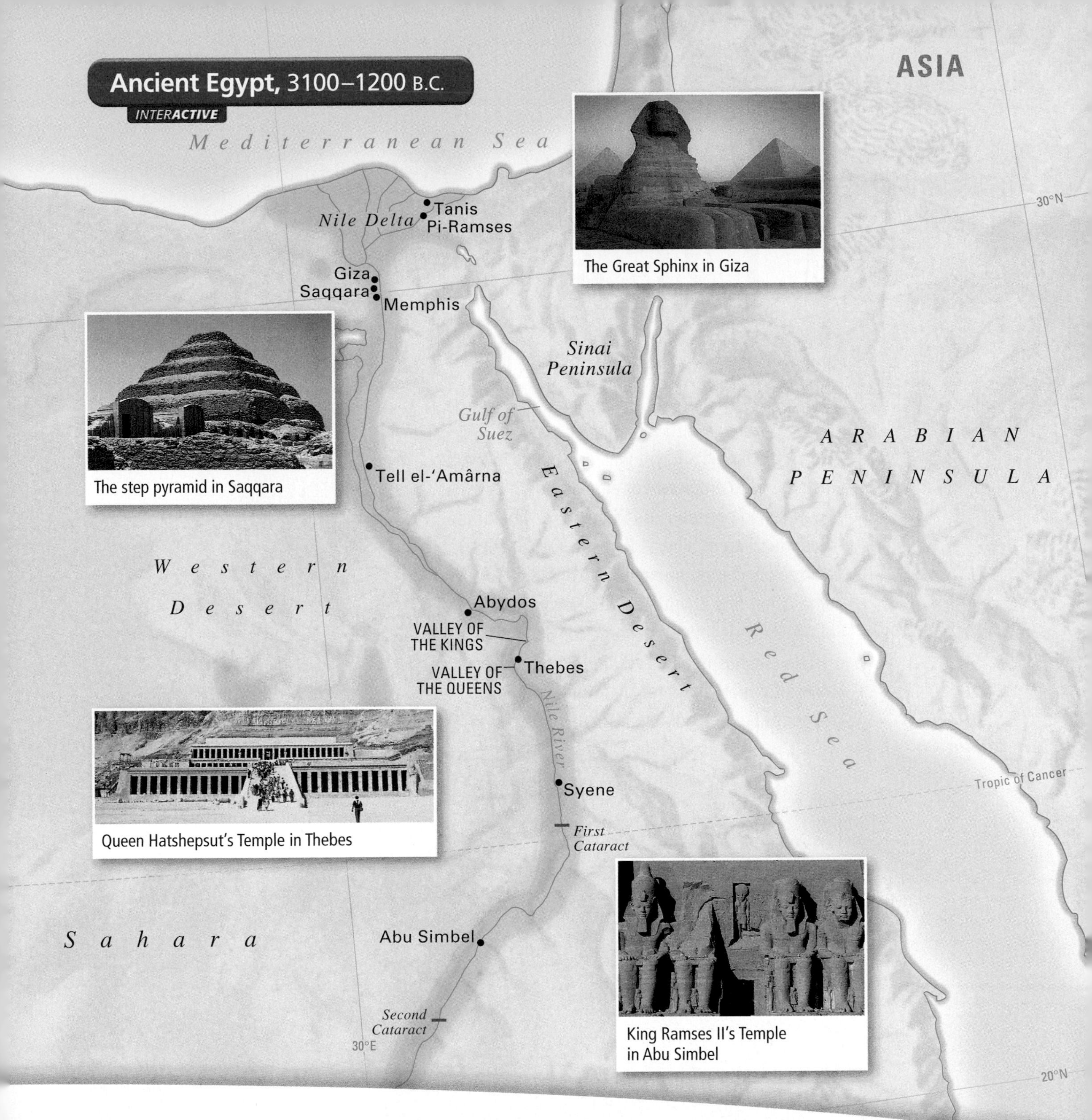

The Great Sphinx in Giza

The step pyramid in Saqqara

Queen Hatshepsut's Temple in Thebes

King Ramses II's Temple in Abu Simbel

1720 B.C.
Hyksos invade Egypt.

1472 B.C.
Hatshepsut, first woman pharaoh, comes to power.

1279 B.C.
Ramses II begins his 66-year reign.

2000 B.C. — 1500 B.C. — 1000 B.C.

1790 B.C.
Hammurabi's Code issued in the Babylonian Empire.

1760 B.C.
Shang Dynasty comes to power in China.

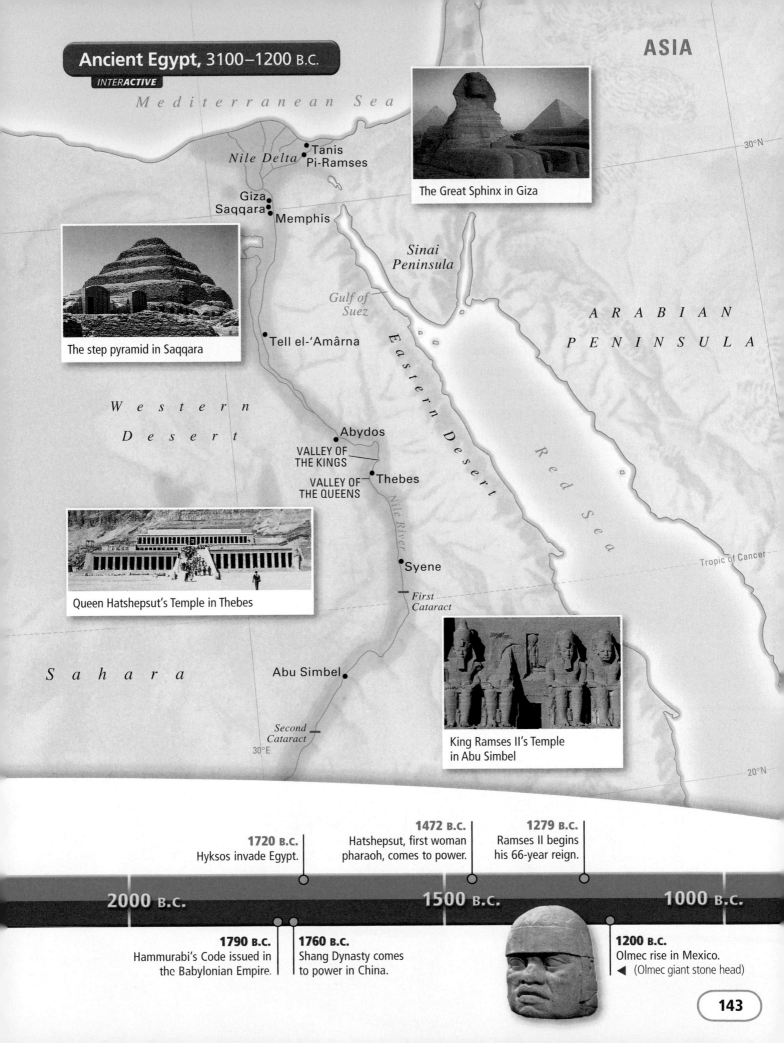

1200 B.C.
Olmec rise in Mexico.
◀ (Olmec giant stone head)

Starting with a Story

THE DEATH OF RAMSES II

Background: Egypt was one of the longest-lasting world empires. For almost 3,000 years, kings called pharaohs ruled the land. One of the most dazzling of all was Ramses II (RAM•SEEZ), who reigned from about 1279 to 1213 B.C. At a time when few Egyptians lived beyond the age of 40, Ramses II was in charge for 66 years!

Now he has finally died, and Egypt prepares for his funeral. Imagine you are there as the leader of Egypt's golden age is laid to rest.

Statue of Ramses II ▶

You are a professional mourner, a person whose job is to cry at funerals. In the past, you've helped to bury some important people—but never a pharaoh! Your white mourning robe is spotless. You spent hours preparing the wreath of flowers to crown your head.

No one remembers any other pharaoh. Ramses II ruled Egypt when your grandparents were children. Some people thought he would live forever. Now he's dead and headed for his tomb in the Valley of the Kings. The ceremony began at his temple at Abu Simbel. At that temple, four 66-foot statues of Ramses II guard the entrance. Inside the secret chambers, priests preserved the pharaoh's body for burial.

Next, a royal barge carried Ramses' casket on the Nile River. Inside is the pharaoh's mummy, wrapped in orange linen and wearing a gold mask. Hundreds of important Egyptians are waiting at the tomb.

It's time to begin the procession. You line up with other mourners behind a group of slaves carrying Ramses' most important possessions. There is his sword! Could it be the one he carried into battle when he fought Egypt's enemy, the Hittites? Who will stop the Hittites now?

Tearing your hair and beating your chest, you wail your song of sorrow: "Great lord of our empire! Provider of lasting peace! Builder of temples that reach for the sun! Don't leave us! Without you, we are fatherless children!"

Sometimes you fake your cries at funerals, but today you mean every word. Trembling with fear, you wonder what will happen now.

What do you hope the new pharaoh will be like?

Reading & Writing

1. **READING: Reading Aloud** What parts of this story benefit most from being read with appropriate intonation and expression?
2. **WRITING: Narration** Suppose you are waiting to hear Ramses' son, the new pharaoh, speak for the first time. Write a brief scene in which you discuss your hopes and fears for Egypt with others in the crowd.

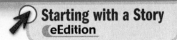

Lesson 1

MAIN IDEAS

1. **Geography** The Nile River helped Egypt develop a civilization.
2. **Economics** The fertile land provided everything Egyptians needed.
3. **Economics** The Nile and other resources influenced Egypt's economy.

TAKING NOTES

Reading Skill: Understanding Cause and Effect

Following causes and effects will help you understand the main ideas in this lesson. In Lesson 1, look for the effects of each event listed in the chart. Record them on a chart of your own.

Causes	Effects
Floods	
New agricultural techniques	
Many land resources	

Skillbuilder Handbook, page R26

▲ **Lotus Pendants** This necklace once belonged to an Egyptian king. The pendants at the bottom are lotus buds. The lotus, a water lily that grows in the Nile River, is a symbol of Egypt.

Words to Know

Understanding the following words will help you read this lesson:

fine made of very small particles (page 147)
*The **fine** soil was more like dust than sand.*

barren lacking plants or crops (page 148)
*While crops grew well next to the Nile River, the desert was **barren**.*

noble a member of a wealthy and powerful family (page 149)
*The **nobles** could afford more comfortable homes than could most people.*

sought tried to find (page 150)
*The Egyptians **sought** iron because it was good for making tools.*

Gift of the Nile

TERMS & NAMES
cataract
delta
silt
fertile
linen

Build on What You Know Have you ever received a gift that was very important to you? How did it affect your life? The Nile River was so important to Egypt that 2,500 years ago, an ancient Greek historian called Egypt "the gift of the Nile."

Geography of Ancient Egypt

1 **ESSENTIAL QUESTION** Why was the Nile River important?

The Greek historian knew what he was talking about. The Nile River fed Egyptian civilization for hundreds of years.

The Longest River The Nile is 4,160 miles long—the world's longest river. It begins near the equator in Africa and flows north to the Mediterranean Sea. In the south it churns with cataracts. A **cataract** (KAT•uh•RAKT) is a waterfall. Near the sea the Nile branches into a delta. A **delta** is an area near a river's mouth where the water deposits fine soil called **silt**. In the delta, the Nile divides into many streams.

The river is called the upper Nile in the south and the lower Nile in the north. For centuries, heavy rains in Ethiopia caused the Nile to flood every summer. The floods deposited rich soil along the Nile's shores. This soil was **fertile**, which means it was good for growing crops. Unlike the Tigris and Euphrates, the Nile River flooded at the same time every year, so farmers could predict when to plant their crops.

The Nile Valley
Fertile land in Egypt stretches along the Nile and then gives way to desert. As a result, Egypt was a narrow country. ▼

Red Land, Black Land The ancient Egyptians lived in narrow bands of land on each side of the Nile. They called this region the black land because of the fertile soil that the floods deposited. The red land was the barren desert beyond the fertile region.

Weather in Egypt was almost always the same. Eight months of the year were sunny and hot. The four months of winter were sunny but cooler. Most of the region received only an inch of rain a year. The parts of Egypt not near the Nile were a desert.

Isolation The harsh desert acted as a barrier to keep out enemies. The Mediterranean coast was swampy and lacked good harbors. For these reasons, early Egyptians stayed close to home.

REVIEW What did the floods of the Nile River provide for farmers?

Land of Plenty

2 ESSENTIAL QUESTION How did Egyptians use the land around the Nile?

Each year, Egyptian farmers watched for white birds called ibises (EYE•bihs•uhz), which flew up from the south. When the birds

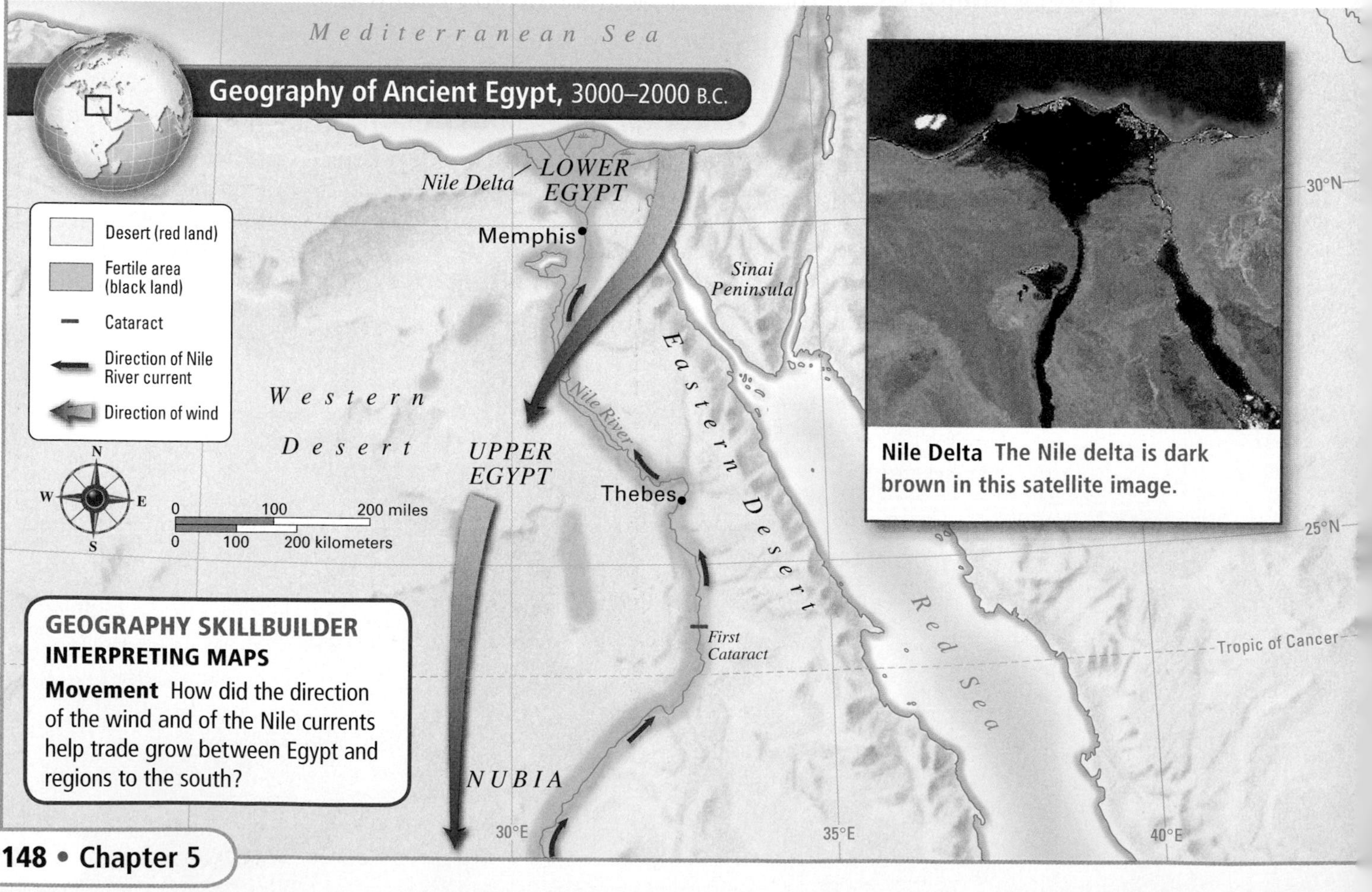

Nile Delta The Nile delta is dark brown in this satellite image.

GEOGRAPHY SKILLBUILDER
INTERPRETING MAPS
Movement How did the direction of the wind and of the Nile currents help trade grow between Egypt and regions to the south?

arrived, the annual flood waters would soon follow. After the waters drained away, farmers could plant seeds in the fertile soil.

Agricultural Techniques By about 2400 B.C., farmers used technology to expand their farmland. Working together, they dug irrigation canals that carried river water to dry areas. Then they used a tool called a shaduf (shah•DOOF) to spread the water across the fields. These innovative, or new, techniques gave them more farmland.

Connect to Today

▲ **Shaduf** A shaduf is a bucket on a lever. It was used to lift water from the Nile or canals. Some Egyptians still use shadufs today.

Egyptian Crops Ancient Egyptians grew a large variety of foods. They were the first to grind wheat into flour and to mix the flour with yeast and water to make dough rise into bread. They grew vegetables such as lettuce, radishes, asparagus, and cucumbers. Fruits included dates, figs, grapes, and watermelons.

Egyptians also grew the materials for their clothes. They were the first to weave fibers from flax plants into a fabric called **linen**. Lightweight linen cloth was perfect for hot Egyptian days. Men wore linen wraps around their waists. Women wore loose, sleeveless dresses. Egyptians also wove marsh grasses into sandals.

Vocabulary Strategy

The word *linen* has **multiple meanings.** Sheets and tablecloths are often called linens because they used to only be made from linen cloth.

Egyptian Houses Egyptians built houses using bricks made of mud from the Nile mixed with chopped straw. They placed narrow windows high in the walls to reduce bright sunlight. Egyptians often painted walls white to reflect the blazing heat. They wove sticks and palm trees to make roofs. Inside, woven reed mats covered the dirt floor. Most Egyptians slept on mats covered with linen sheets. Wealthy citizens enjoyed bed frames and cushions.

Egyptian nobles had fancier homes with tree-lined courtyards for shade. Some had a pool filled with lotus blossoms and fish. Poorer Egyptians simply went to the roof to cool off after sunset. They often cooked, ate, and even slept outside.

REVIEW What agricultural techniques did ancient Egyptians use?

Geography Shapes Egyptian Life

3 ESSENTIAL QUESTION What economic activities developed in Egypt?

▲ **Hunter** This wall painting from a tomb shows a man hunting marsh birds.

Egypt's economy depended on farming. However, the natural resources of the area allowed other economic activities to develop too.

Mining The Egyptians wanted valuable metals that were not found in the black land. For example, they wanted copper to make tools and weapons. Egyptians looked for copper as early as 6000 B.C. Later they learned that iron was stronger, and they sought it as well. Ancient Egyptians also desired gold for its bright beauty. The Egyptian word for gold was *nub. Nubia* was the Egyptian name for the area of the upper Nile that had the richest gold mines in Africa.

Mining minerals was difficult. Veins (long streaks) of copper, iron, and bronze were hidden inside desert mountains in the hot Sinai Peninsula, east of Egypt. Even during the cool season, chipping minerals out of the rock was miserable work.

Egyptians mined precious stones too. They were probably the first people in the world to mine turquoise (TUR•KWOYZ). The Egyptians also mined lapis lazuli (LAP•ihs LAZ•uh•lee). These beautiful blue stones were used in jewelry.

Fishing and Hunting The Nile had fish and other wildlife that Egyptians wanted. To go on the river, Egyptians made lightweight rafts by binding together reeds. They used everything from nets to harpoons to catch fish. One ancient painting even shows a man ready to hit a catfish with a wooden hammer.

More adventurous hunters speared hippopotamuses and crocodiles along the Nile. Egyptians also captured quail with nets. They used boomerangs to knock down flying ducks and geese. (A boomerang is a curved stick that returns to the person who threw it.)

Transportation and Trade Eventually, Egyptians equipped their reed boats with sails and oars. The Nile then became a highway. The river's current was slow, so boaters used paddles to go faster when they traveled north with the current. Going south, they raised a sail and let the winds that blew in that direction push them.

The Nile provided so well for Egyptians that sometimes they had surpluses, or more goods than they needed. They began to trade with each other. Ancient Egypt had no money, so people exchanged goods that they grew or made. This method of trade is called bartering.

REVIEW How did geography affect Egypt's economy?

Turquoise Jewelry This bracelet has turquoise and other precious stones. ▼

Lesson Summary

- The Nile River created a fertile land in a desert.
- The Egyptians used technology to expand their farms and grow many crops.
- Ancient Egyptians also mined, fished, hunted, and traded.

Why It Matters Now . . .

Ancient Egyptians invented many things we use today, such as yeast bread, turquoise jewelry, and linen clothes.

1 Lesson Review

Homework Helper ClassZone.com

Terms & Names

1. Explain the importance of

cataract   silt   linen
delta   fertile

Using Your Notes

Understanding Cause and Effect Use your completed chart to answer the following question:

2. How did new agricultural techniques make the Egyptians more prosperous?

Causes	Effects
Floods	
New agricultural techniques	
Many land resources	

Main Ideas

3. Why did Egypt develop along the Nile?
4. How did irrigation canals expand farmland in Egypt?
5. How did trade along the Nile come about?

Critical Thinking

6. **Making Inferences** How did climate affect the daily lives of Egyptians?
7. **Drawing Conclusions** Analyze the gifts of the Nile in terms of innovation and cultural endurance.

Activity

Making a Sketch Create a sketch showing the different types of economic activities that took place in ancient Egypt.

Daily Life

Extend Lesson 1

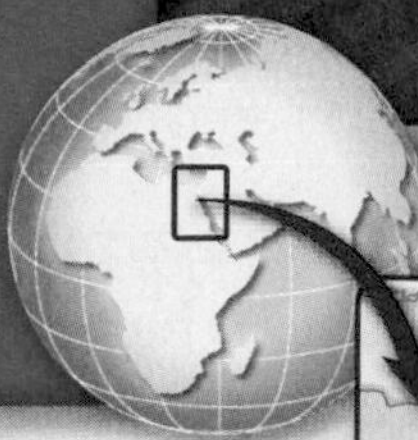

Life on the Nile River

Purpose: To learn about the life of Egyptian traders on the Nile River

If you were an Egyptian trader, you would sail the Nile River in a boat that looks much like the one shown here. Traders carried their goods in reed boats that they sailed up and down the Nile. As shown below, the simple boat held everything the traders needed for their trip on the river.

A Hull In the hull below the boat's deck, you store barrels of fruit and sacks of barley and wheat.

B Sails You raise your linen sail to catch the wind when you travel south on the Nile against the current. You lower the sail when you travel with the current north on the Nile.

C Oars The boat has a basket and oar at either end. Once the boat sets sail, you or another trader will stand in the basket and use the oar to steer.

D On Deck There is much activity on the boat's deck, as you store more goods and tie up the sheep and goats you plan to barter.

E River Animals A pair of ibises and some hippos feed as you load your boat. But you keep your eye on the crocodiles—the most dangerous animals on the Nile.

Activities

1. **TALK ABOUT IT** What were some of the advantages of being an Egyptian trader? What were some of the disadvantages?
2. **WRITE ABOUT IT** Imagine you are an Egyptian trader and write a diary entry about a day spent sailing the Nile. You could write about the goods you're planning to trade or about the animals you see during your trip.

Lesson 2

MAIN IDEAS

1. **Economics** Egyptians developed a complex society with many different jobs and social roles.
2. **Science and Technology** Egyptians made advances in calendars, geometry, medicine, and other areas.
3. **Belief Systems** Egyptians believed in many gods and a happy life after death.

TAKING NOTES

Reading Skill: Categorizing Sorting information into groups helps you understand patterns in history. In Lesson 2, look for three categories of Egyptian culture and details about them. Record the information on a web diagram.

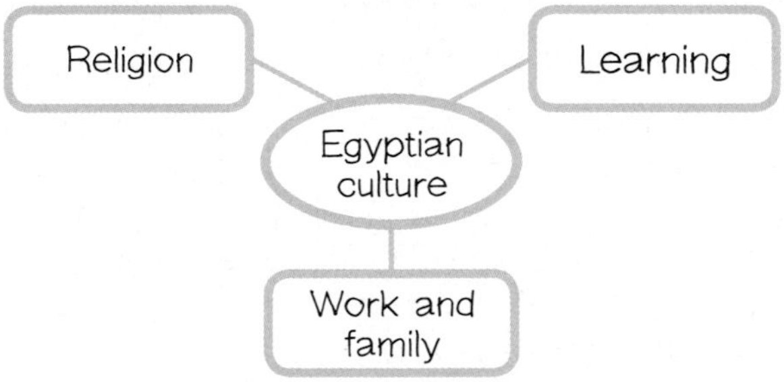

Skillbuilder Handbook, page R6

▲ **Cat Mummy** Some Egyptians made their dead pets into mummies and gave them a formal burial. Cats were especially honored in Egypt.

Words to Know

Understanding the following words will help you read this lesson:

formal carried out in a ceremonial manner (page 156)
*The priest obeyed the church's **formal** rituals as he performed the service.*

garment a piece of clothing (page 156)
*The **garments** that priests wore were made of linen.*

deed an action done by a person (page 160)
*People were judged more by their **deeds** than by their words.*

Life in Ancient Egypt

TERMS & NAMES
scribe
hieroglyph
papyrus
afterlife
embalm
mummy

Build on What You Know As you have seen, Egypt prospered along the Nile. This prosperity made life easier and provided greater opportunities for many Egyptians.

Work and Family Life

1 ESSENTIAL QUESTION How did work and social roles affect people in ancient Egypt?

When farmers produce food surpluses, the society's economy begins to expand. Cities emerge as centers of culture and power, and people learn to do jobs that do not involve agriculture. For example, some ancient Egyptians learned to be **scribes**, people whose job was to write and keep records.

Specialized Jobs As Egyptian civilization grew more complex, people took on jobs other than that of a farmer or scribe. Some skilled artisans erected stone or brick houses and temples. Other artisans made pottery, incense, mats, furniture, linen clothing, sandals, or jewelry.

A few Egyptians traveled to the upper Nile to trade with other Africans. These traders took Egyptian products such as scrolls, linen, gold, and jewelry. They brought back exotic woods, animal skins, and live beasts.

Luxor, Egypt Skilled artisans helped to build this temple and the shafts with pointed tops, which are called obelisks. ▼

Rulers and Priests As Egypt grew, so did its need to organize. Egyptians created a government that divided the empire into 42 provinces. Many officials worked to keep the provinces running smoothly. Egypt also created an army to defend itself.

One of the highest jobs in Egypt was to be a priest. Priests followed formal rituals and took care of the temples. Before entering a temple, a priest bathed and put on special linen garments and white sandals. Priests cleaned the sacred statues in temples, changed their clothes, and even fed them meals.

Egyptian Social Roles

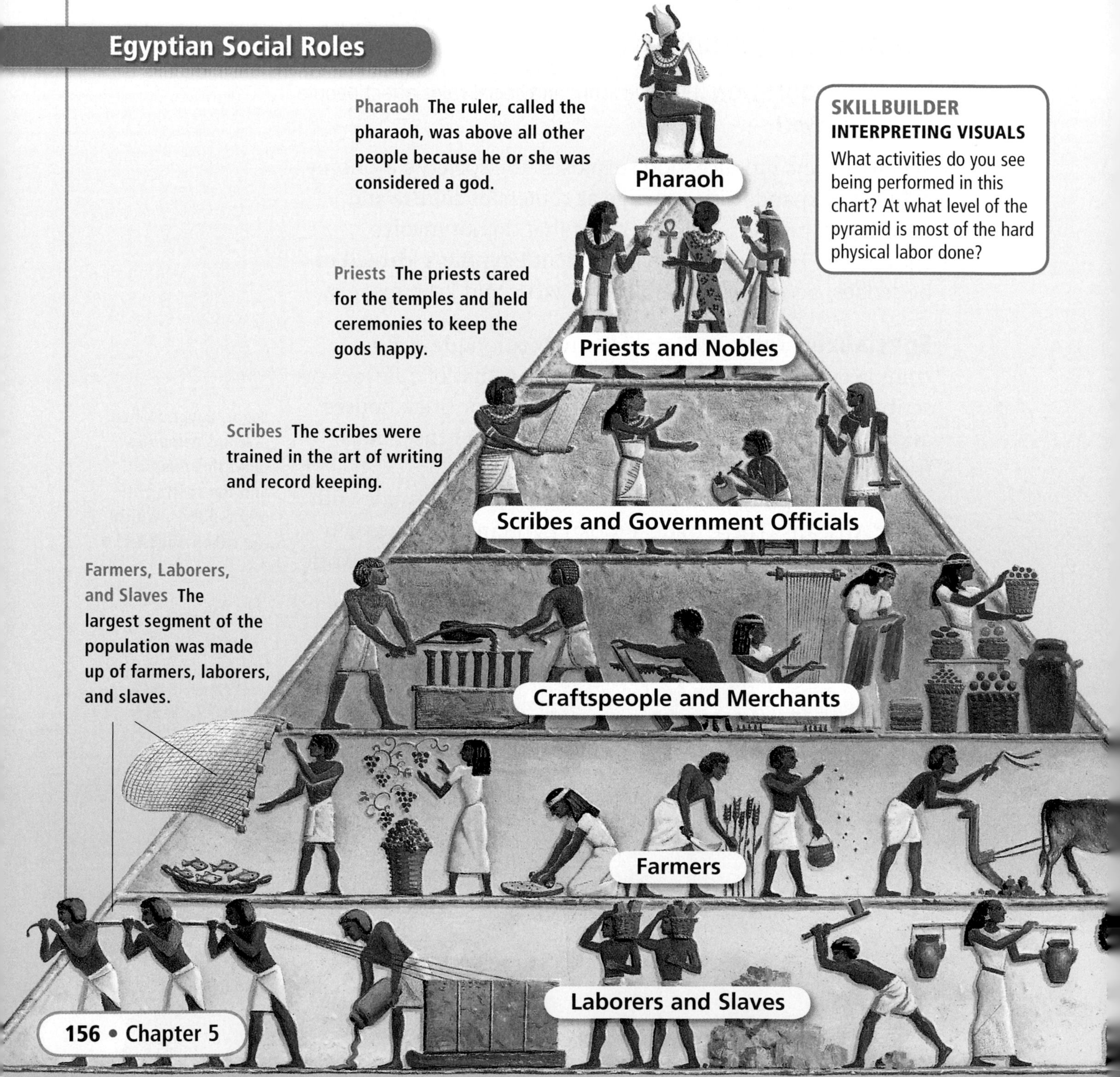

Pharaoh The ruler, called the pharaoh, was above all other people because he or she was considered a god.

Priests The priests cared for the temples and held ceremonies to keep the gods happy.

Scribes The scribes were trained in the art of writing and record keeping.

Farmers, Laborers, and Slaves The largest segment of the population was made up of farmers, laborers, and slaves.

SKILLBUILDER
INTERPRETING VISUALS
What activities do you see being performed in this chart? At what level of the pyramid is most of the hard physical labor done?

Together, the priests and the ruler held ceremonies to please the gods. Egyptians believed that if the gods were angry, the Nile would not flood. As a result, crops would not grow, and people would die. So the ruler and the priests tried hard to keep the gods happy. By doing so, they hoped to maintain the social and political order.

Slaves Slaves were at the bottom of society. In Egypt, people became slaves if they owed a debt, committed a crime, or were captured in war. Egyptian slaves were usually freed after a period of time. One exception was the slaves who had to work in the mines. Many died from the exhausting labor.

Life for Women Egypt was one of the best places in the ancient world to be a woman. Unlike other ancient African cultures, in Egyptian society men and women had fairly equal rights. For example, they could both own and manage their own property.

The main job of most women was to care for their children and home, but some did other jobs too. Some women wove cloth. Others worked with their husbands in fields or workshops. Some women, such as Queen Tiy, even rose to important positions in the government.

Childhood Children in Egypt played with toys such as dolls, animal figures, board games, and marbles. Their parents made the toys from wood or clay. Boys and girls also played rough physical games with balls made of leather or reeds.

Boys and some girls from wealthy families went to schools run by scribes or priests. Most other children learned their parents' jobs. Almost all Egyptians married when they were in their early teens.

REVIEW What were the levels of Egyptian society?

Expanding Knowledge

2 ESSENTIAL QUESTION How did learning advance in ancient Egypt?

As in many ancient societies, much of the knowledge of Egypt came about as priests studied the world to find ways to please the gods. Other advances came about because of practical discoveries.

Astronomy Egyptian priests studied the sky as part of their religion. About 5,000 years ago, they noticed that a star now called Sirius (SIHR•ee•uhs) appeared shortly before the Nile began to flood. The star returned to the same position in 365 days. Based on that, Egyptians developed the world's first practical calendar.

Geometry The Egyptians developed some of the first geometry. Each year the Nile's floods washed away land boundaries. To restore property lines, surveyors measured the land by using ropes that were knotted at regular intervals.

Geometric shapes such as squares and triangles were sacred to Egyptians. Architects used them in the design of royal temples and monuments.

Medicine Egyptian doctors often prepared dead bodies for burial, so they knew the parts of the body. That knowledge helped them perform some of the world's first surgery. Some doctors specialized in using medicines made of herbs.

Egyptian medicine was far from perfect. Doctors believed that the heart controlled thought and the brain circulated blood, which is the opposite of what is known now. Some Egyptian treatments would raise eyebrows today. One "cure" for an upset stomach was to eat a hog's tooth crushed inside sugar cakes!

Hieroglyphs Beginning about 3000 B.C., Egyptians developed a writing system using hieroglyphs. **Hieroglyphs** (HY•uhr•uh•GLIHFS) are pictures that stand for different words or sounds. Early Egyptians created a hieroglyphic system with about 700 characters. Over time the system grew to include more than 6,000 symbols.

The Egyptians also developed a paper-like material called **papyrus** (puh•PY•ruhs) from a reed of the same name. Egyptians cut the stems into strips, pressed them, and dried them into sheets that could be rolled into scrolls. Papyrus scrolls were light and easy to carry. With them, Egyptians created some of the first books.

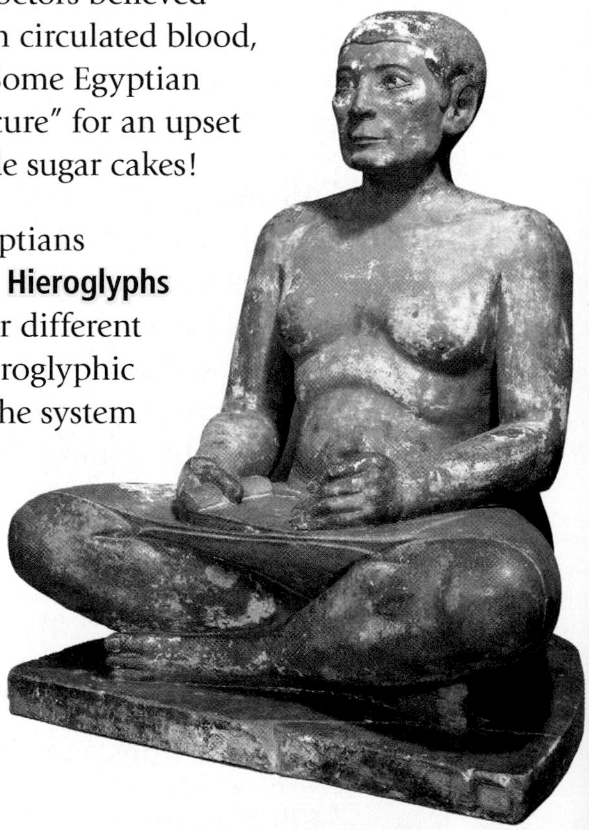

▲ **Scribe** A person who wanted to be a scribe had to study many years to learn all of the hieroglyphs.

REVIEW What advances in learning did the Egyptians make?

Primary Source

Hieroglyphs

The ancient Egyptians used hieroglyphs in many ways, as shown in this carving of Senusret I, a ruler from the 1900s B.C.

- They could be simple picture writing. For example, a wavy line might mean "water."
- Some pictures stood for ideas. A circle often meant Re, the sun god.
- Finally, some signs also came to represent sounds. For example, the signs below represent the name of Cleopatra, a foreign queen who would later rule Egypt.

KL E O P A T-R A-T

DOCUMENT–BASED QUESTION
What do you think is the purpose of the hieroglyphs on this carving?

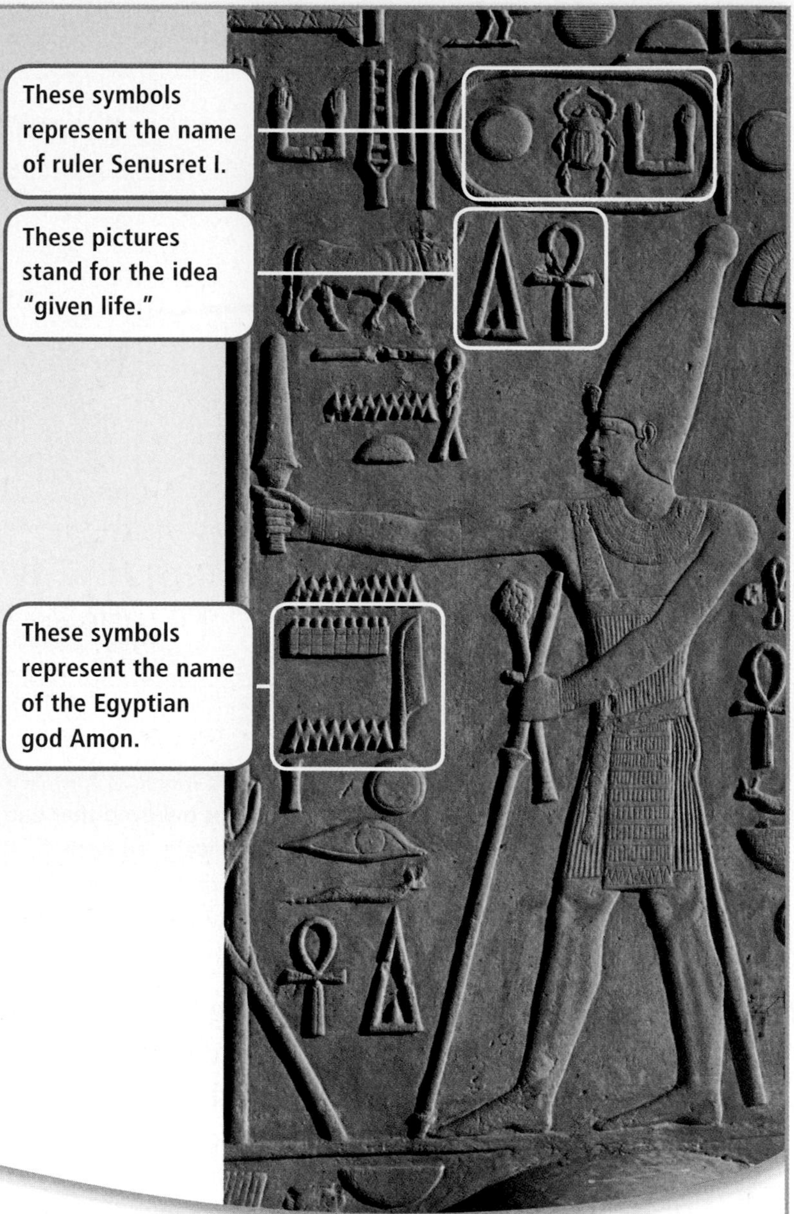
These symbols represent the name of ruler Senusret I.
These pictures stand for the idea "given life."
These symbols represent the name of the Egyptian god Amon.

Beliefs and Religion

3 ESSENTIAL QUESTION What religious beliefs did Egyptians hold?

We know from their writing and their art that, in general, the Egyptians had a positive view of life. The black land provided most of the Egyptians' needs. As a result, they did not have to struggle to make a living.

Life After Death Their positive outlook shaped their religion and led them to believe that the gods favored them. Egyptians believed that their prosperity could continue with a happy afterlife. An **afterlife** is a life believed to follow death. Not every ancient culture shared Egyptians' beliefs. For example, the Sumerians thought that the afterlife was miserable.

Vocabulary Strategy
Afterlife is a **compound word.** You can divide it into the words *after* and *life.* An afterlife is a life believed to follow death.

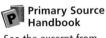

▲ **Judgment of the Dead** Egyptians believed that bad deeds made a heart heavy. They thought that the god Anubis weighed each dead person's heart, as shown in this Egyptian art. If it was lighter than a feather, the reward was a happy afterlife. If the heart was heavier than a feather, Anubis fed it to a monster.

Many Gods As you have learned in Chapter 3, polytheism is a belief in many gods. The Egyptians worshiped gods that were related to the afterlife and to parts of nature—such as the sun, the river, and plant life. Some of the most important Egyptian gods included

- Re (ray)—the sun god (later called Amon-Re)
- Osiris (oh•SY•rihs)—a god who judged Egyptians after death
- Isis (EYE•sihs)—a fertility goddess who was Osiris' wife
- Anubis (uh•NOO•bihs)—a god of the dead

Making Mummies Egyptians thought they would need their bodies in the afterlife, so they embalmed dead people. **Embalm** means to preserve a body after death. First, embalmers removed all organs except the heart. Next, they filled the body with a mixture of salt and herbs to create a mummy. A **mummy** is a body that has been dried so it won't decay. When dry, the mummy was wrapped in hundreds of yards of linen strips. The whole process of embalming and wrapping took about 70 days. Embalming was expensive, and not everyone could afford it.

Primary Source Handbook

See the excerpt from the *Book of the Dead*, page R39.

The mummy was placed in a coffin inside a tomb. The tomb also held everyday objects, furniture, and food. Scenes from the person's life were painted on the walls. The Egyptians expected these pictures to become real so that the dead person could use them in the afterlife.

REVIEW What did the Egyptians think happened after death?

Anubis Egyptians believed the jackal-headed god Anubis weighed their hearts after death. ▼

Lesson Summary

- The Egyptians developed a calendar, early geometry, medical knowledge, and hieroglyphic writing.
- Ancient Egypt had a complex society with specialized jobs. Women and slaves lived better there than in many other ancient lands.
- The Egyptians believed in many gods related to nature. They also believed in a happy afterlife.

Why It Matters Now . . .

The ancient Egyptians were the first people known to develop a formal religion based on a belief in the afterlife. Such a belief is part of most religions today.

2 Lesson Review

Homework Helper
ClassZone.com

Terms & Names

1. Explain the importance of

scribe	papyrus	embalm
hieroglyph	afterlife	mummy

Using Your Notes

Categorizing Use your completed web diagram to answer the following question:

2. What jobs did Egyptians hold?

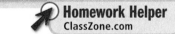

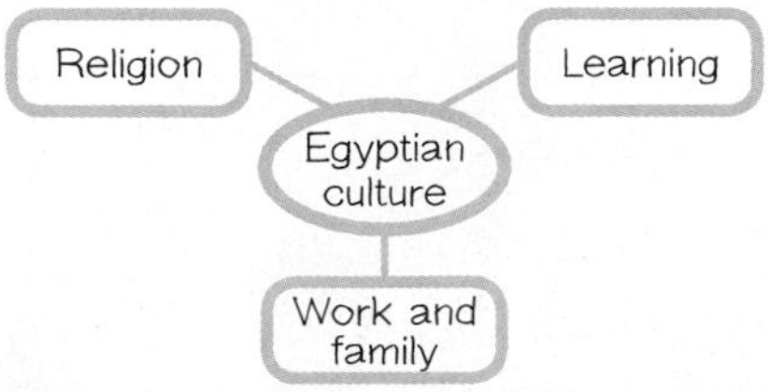

Main Ideas

3. Why were some Egyptians able to become artisans?

4. How were hieroglyphs used?

5. What duties did priests have?

Critical Thinking

6. Understanding Cause and Effect Why were Egyptian discoveries in astronomy and medicine important?

7. Making Generalizations How did the Nile affect the Egyptians' view of the afterlife?

Activity

Writing in Hieroglyphs Use the hieroglyphs shown on page 159 to write a few words.

Connect to Today

Extend Lesson 2

Research Links
ClassZone.com

The Legacy of Egypt

Purpose: To learn about the impact that Egyptian knowledge and learning have on people today

You may feel little connection with the ancient Egyptians as you learn about their civilization. Yet our civilization owes a great deal to the Egyptians. They left behind a rich heritage in science and mathematics that we continue to build on today.

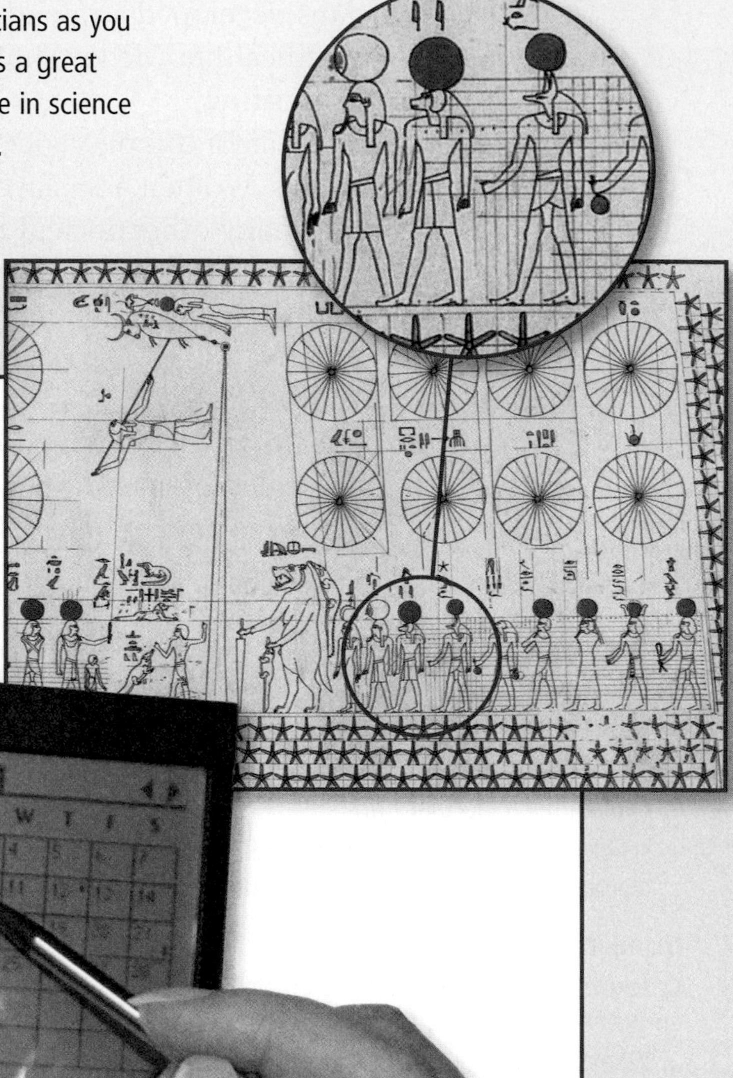

Calendars

▶ **Past** Around 4000 B.C., the Egyptians developed a 365-day calendar based on the star Sirius. This fragment from a tomb painting shows the Egyptian concept of time. The red circles represent the months of the year. The large circles, which are divided into 24 hours, symbolize religious holidays.

▶ **Present** The Egyptian calendar is the basis for the modern Western calendar. Still, the calendar in the handheld computer shown here can do things that ancient Egyptians never dreamed of—including measuring minutes and seconds. Egyptians did not have names for units of time smaller than an hour.

Medical Knowledge

▼ **Past** Egyptian doctors treated physical injuries, such as wounds and broken bones, much like doctors today. They examined the patient, conducted tests, and made their diagnosis. Egyptians were also the first to use surgical instruments, such as those shown here.

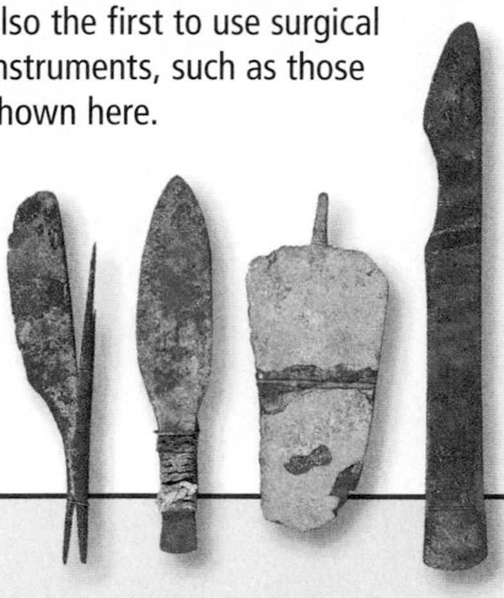

▶ **Present** Egyptian medicine provided the foundation for modern medicine. Our instruments have become more sophisticated, such as those used for laser surgery. But doctors today still use the three categories that Egyptians used to describe a patient's condition: favorable, uncertain, and unfavorable.

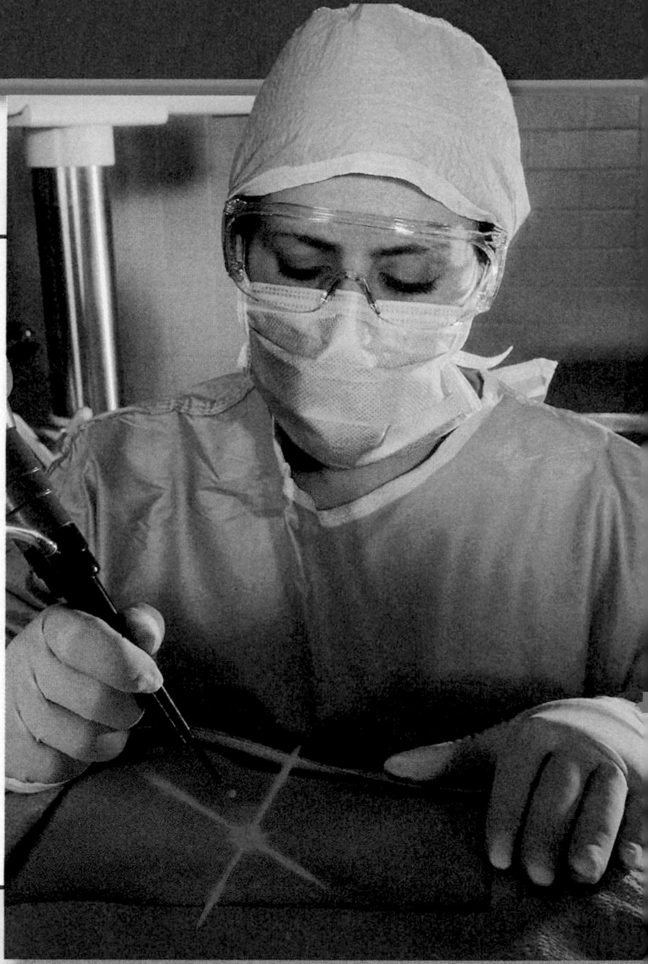

Architecture

▶ **Past** Egyptians measured fields using such geometric shapes as triangles. Architects also used this shape when they built their great stone pyramids. You will learn more about Egyptian pyramids in the next lesson.

▼ **Present** The magnificent pyramids of ancient Egypt have left their mark on Western architecture. The glass pyramid at the Louvre Museum in Paris is just one example of Egyptian influence.

Activities

1. **TALK ABOUT IT** What do these advances in knowledge and learning tell you about ancient Egyptian civilization?
2. **WRITE ABOUT IT** What will our civilization be remembered for? Write a paragraph telling what you think our legacy will be.

Lesson 3

MAIN IDEAS

1. **Government** Egypt united under a central government that ruled for centuries.
2. **Culture** Pharaoh Khufu built a huge monument to proclaim his glory.
3. **Government** Egypt entered a period of change as centralized rule weakened.

TAKING NOTES

Reading Skill: Summarizing To summarize means to condense information into fewer words. Jot down the main ideas and important details in Lesson 3 in a diagram like the one below. Then use them to help you write a summary of the lesson.

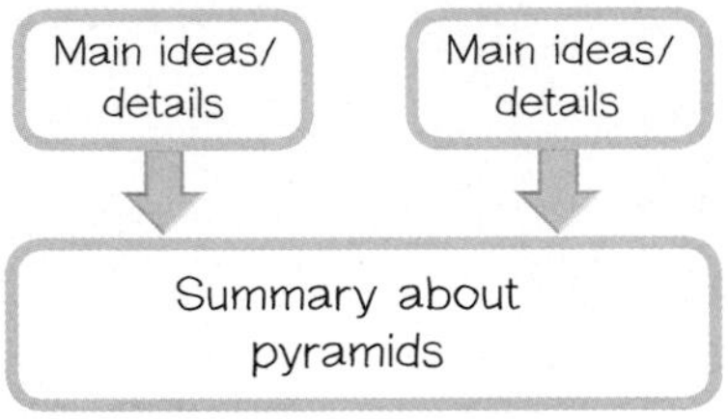

Skillbuilder Handbook, page R3

▲ Ankh The ankh (ahnk) was a symbol of life for ancient Egyptians. Tomb art often shows pharaohs and gods holding ankhs.

Words to Know

Understanding the following words will help you read this lesson:

inherit to receive something from a person who has died (page 165)
When the king died, his son would ***inherit*** *the throne.*

triangle a shape with three sides (page 166)
Each side of the pyramid was a ***triangle,*** *but the base had four sides.*

portray to show by means of a picture (page 169)
Artists had to follow rules about how to ***portray*** *humans in their paintings.*

The Pyramid Builders

TERMS & NAMES
dynasty
succession
pharaoh
pyramid
step pyramid
Khufu

Build on What You Know You have read about the upper and lower Nile. There were also two kingdoms called Upper Egypt and Lower Egypt. They united into a strong empire.

The Old Kingdom

1 ESSENTIAL QUESTION What kind of government ruled Egypt after it was united?

Legend says a king named Narmer united Upper and Lower Egypt. Some historians think Narmer actually represents several kings who gradually joined the two lands. After Egypt was united, its ruler wore the Double Crown. It combined the red Crown of Lower Egypt with the white Crown of Upper Egypt. (See page 166.)

The First Dynasty The first dynasty of the Egyptian empire began about 2925 B.C. A **dynasty** (DY•nuh•stee) is a line of rulers from the same family. When a king died, one of his children usually took his place as ruler. The order in which members of a royal family inherit a throne is called the **succession**. More than 30 dynasties ruled ancient Egypt.

Historians divide ancient Egyptian dynasties into the Old Kingdom, the Middle Kingdom, and the New Kingdom. The Old Kingdom started about 2575 B.C., when the Egyptian empire was gaining strength.

Pyramids These structures, called pyramids, were built as monuments over the tombs of rulers. ▼

Crown of Upper Egypt

Crown of Lower Egypt

Double Crown of Upper and Lower Egypt

Pharaohs Rule The king of Egypt became known as the **pharaoh** (FAIR•oh). The word *pharaoh* meant "great house," and it was originally used to describe the king's palace. Later it became the title of the king himself. The pharaoh ruled from the capital city of Memphis.

The ancient Egyptians thought the pharaoh was a child of the gods and a god himself. Egyptians believed that if the pharaoh and his subjects honored the gods, their lives would be happy. If Egypt suffered hard times for a long period, the people blamed the pharaoh for angering the gods. In such a case, a rival might drive him from power and start a new dynasty.

Because the pharaoh was thought to be a god, government and religion were not separate in ancient Egypt. Priests had much power in the government. Many high officials were priests.

REVIEW How were religion and government linked in ancient Egypt?

Khufu's Great Pyramid

2 ESSENTIAL QUESTION How did Pharaoh Khufu proclaim his glory?

The first rulers of Egypt were often buried in an underground tomb topped by mud brick. Soon, kings wanted more permanent monuments. They replaced the mud brick with a small pyramid of brick or stone. A **pyramid** (PIHR•uh•mihd) is a structure shaped like a triangle, with four sides that meet at a point.

About 2630 B.C., King Djoser (ZHOH•suhr) built a much larger pyramid over his tomb. It is called a **step pyramid** because its sides rise in a series of giant steps. It is the oldest-known large stone structure in the world.

Visual Vocabulary

pyramid

step pyramid

The Great Pyramid About 80 years later, a pharaoh named **Khufu** (KOO•FOO) decided he wanted a monument that would show the world how great he was. He ordered the construction of the largest pyramid ever built. Along its base, each side was about 760 feet long. The core was built from 2.3 million blocks of stone.

Building the Great Pyramid was hard work. Miners cut the huge blocks of stone using copper saws and chisels. These tools were much softer than the iron tools developed later. Other teams of workers pulled the stone slabs up long, sloping ramps to their place on the pyramid. Near the top of the pyramid, the ramps ended. Workers dragged each heavy block hundreds of feet and then set it in place.

Farmers did the heavy labor of hauling stone during the season when the Nile flooded their fields. Skilled stonecutters and overseers worked year-round. The Great Pyramid took nearly 20 years to build. An estimated 20,000 Egyptians worked on it. A city called Giza (GEE•zuh) was built for the pyramid workers and the people who fed, clothed, and housed them.

History Makers

Khufu (ruled during the 2500s B.C.)

Khufu was one child who followed his father's example. His father, Snefru (SNEHF•ROO), was a warrior king who brought prosperity to Egypt. Snefru celebrated his deeds by building the first true pyramid as his burial monument.

Khufu liked the pyramid's design, but he decided that bigger was even better. His Great Pyramid was the tallest structure on Earth for over 4,300 years. Can you imagine the spectacular riches a ruler like that must have included in his tomb? We can only imagine because grave robbers emptied the chambers inside the pyramid long ago. The only object left from Khufu's funeral is a ship discovered in 1954. This 125-foot ship was meant to transport Khufu's soul through the afterlife along the path of the sun god.

Grave Robbers Eventually, Egyptians stopped building pyramids. One reason is that the pyramids drew attention to the tombs inside them. Grave robbers broke into the tombs to steal the treasure buried with the pharaohs. Sometimes they also stole the mummies.

Egyptians believed that if a tomb was robbed, the person buried there could not have a happy afterlife. During the New Kingdom, pharaohs began building more secret tombs in an area called the Valley of the Kings. The burial chambers were hidden in mountains near the Nile. This way, the pharaohs hoped to protect their bodies and treasures from robbers.

Inside the Tombs Both the pyramids and later tombs had several passageways leading to different rooms. This was to confuse grave robbers about which passage to take. Sometimes relatives, such as the queen, were buried in the extra rooms.

Tombs were supposed to be the palaces of pharaohs in the afterlife. Mourners filled the tomb with objects ranging from food to furniture that the mummified pharaoh would need. Some tombs contained small statues that were supposed to be servants for the dead person.

The Great Pyramid of Khufu

INTERACTIVE

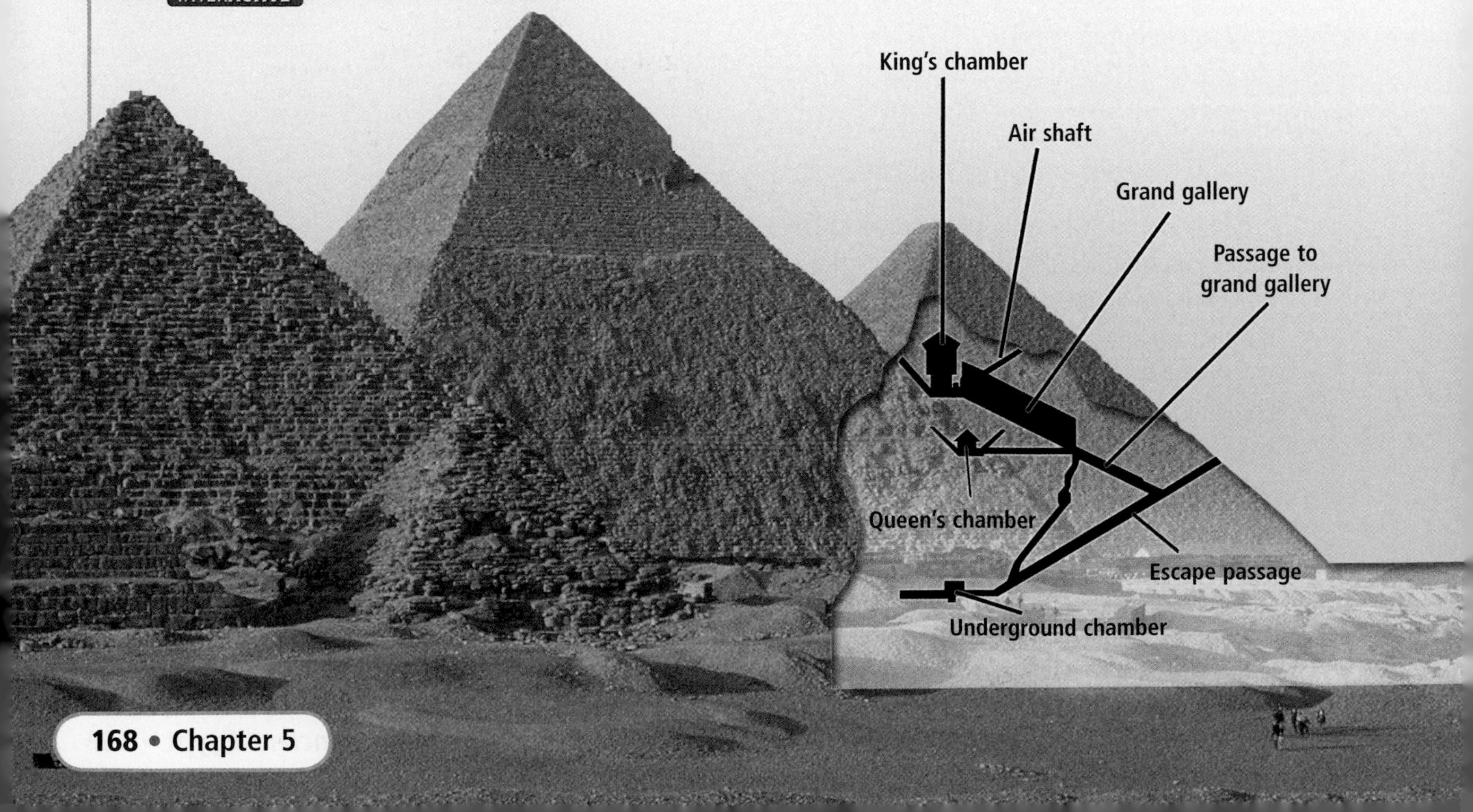

Egyptian artists decorated royal tombs with wall paintings and sculptures carved into the walls. Art was meant to glorify both the gods and the dead person. A sculpture of a dead pharaoh had "perfect" features, no matter how he really looked. Artists also followed strict rules about how to portray humans. Paintings showed a person's head, arms, and legs from the side. They showed the front of the body from the neck down to the waist.

Wall paintings showed pharaohs enjoying themselves so they could have a happy afterlife. One favorite scene was of the pharaoh fishing in a papyrus marsh. Warlike kings were often portrayed in battle. Scenes might also show people providing for the needs of the dead person. Such activities included growing and preparing food, caring for animals, and building boats.

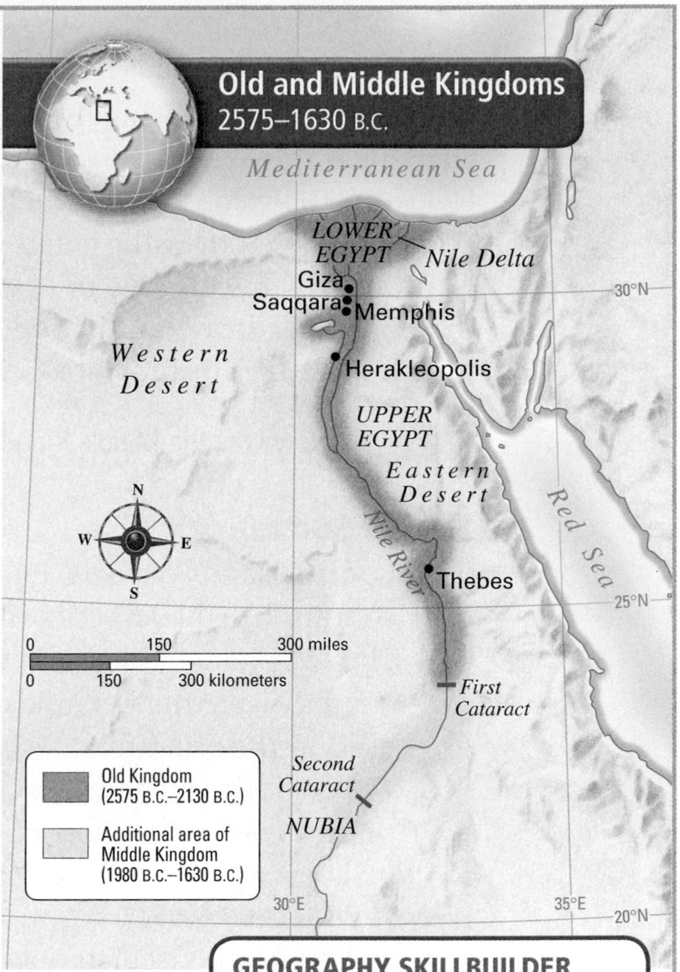

GEOGRAPHY SKILLBUILDER
INTERPRETING MAPS
Location On what body of water were most Egyptian cities located?

As hard as the pharaohs tried to hide themselves, robbers stole the treasures from almost every tomb. Only a secret tomb built for a New Kingdom pharaoh was ever found with much of its treasure untouched. The dazzling riches found in this tomb show how much wealth the pharaohs spent preparing for the afterlife.

REVIEW Why did Khufu decide to build such a large pyramid?

Middle Kingdom

3 **ESSENTIAL QUESTION** What happened to Egypt when centralized rule weakened?

By about 2130 B.C., Egyptian kings began to lose their power to local rulers of the provinces. For about 500 more years, the kings held Egypt together, but with a much weaker central government. This period of Egyptian history is called the Middle Kingdom.

Invasions Rulers during the Middle Kingdom also faced challenges from outside Egypt. A nomadic people called the Hyksos (HIHK•sohs) invaded Egypt from the northeast. Their army conquered by using better weapons and horse-drawn chariots, which were new to Egyptians. After about 100 years, the Egyptians drove out the Hyksos and began the New Kingdom. You will study this period in Lesson 4.

REVIEW How was the Middle Kingdom different from the Old Kingdom?

Lesson Summary

- For thousands of years, Egypt remained a unified country ruled by a series of dynasties.
- The Egyptians built pyramids to honor pharaohs. Tombs inside the pyramids held treasures to be used in the afterlife.
- The Middle Kingdom was a time when the central government lost power to the provinces.

Why It Matters Now . . .

Ancient Egypt still fascinates people. Books and movies portray the mystery of mummies and tombs. People wear jewelry and use household objects modeled on Egyptian artifacts.

3 Lesson Review

Homework Helper
ClassZone.com

Terms & Names

1. Explain the importance of

dynasty	pharaoh	step pyramid
succession	pyramid	Khufu

Using Your Notes

Summarizing Use your completed diagram to answer the following question:

2. What was the purpose of the pyramids?

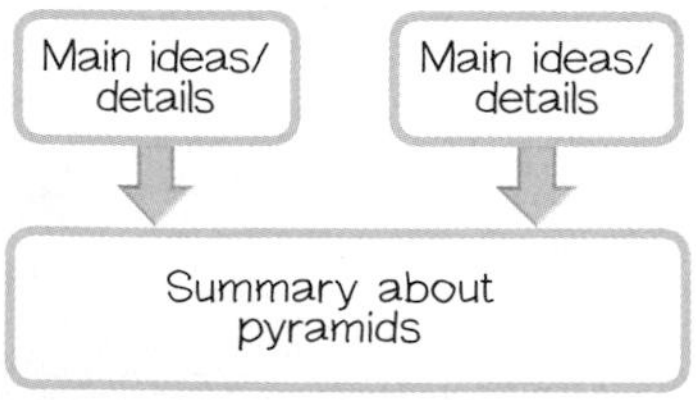

Main Ideas

3. Why were religion and government not separate in ancient Egypt?

4. What were some of the main features of Egyptian art?

5. What group was able to conquer Egypt during the Middle Kingdom?

Critical Thinking

6. Evaluating Information Why did Egypt experience a period of change during the Middle Kingdom?

7. Making Decisions Did pyramids accomplish their purpose? Consider what they did for a pharaoh while he lived and after he died.

Activity

Writing a Narrative Look at the illustration on pages 140–141 and reread "The Great Pyramid" on page 167. Write a narrative story about one of the workers.

Activity Extend Lesson 3

Make A Pyramid

Goal: To understand the art and architecture of ancient Egypt by creating a pyramid and decorating its walls

Materials & Supplies
- yellow or tan construction paper
- ruler and protractor
- scissors and tape
- markers

Optional: Book on Egyptian tombs

Prepare

1. Research Egyptian pyramids and art. Study the images in this chapter and in books about Egypt.
2. Reread the information on pyramids on pages 166–169.

Do the Activity

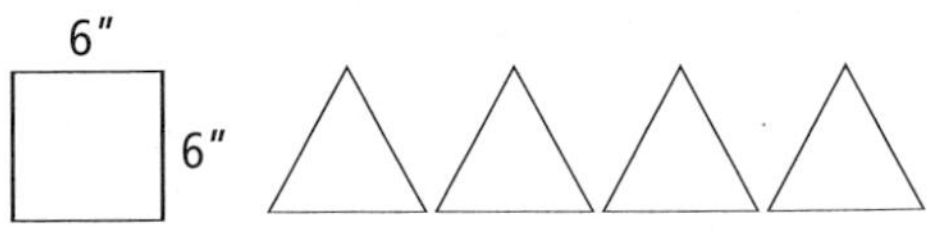

1. Draw and cut out a six-inch square. Then draw and cut out four six-inch equilateral triangles (triangles whose sides are of equal length).

2. Decorate one side of each triangle with the type of art you think would be found inside a tomb.

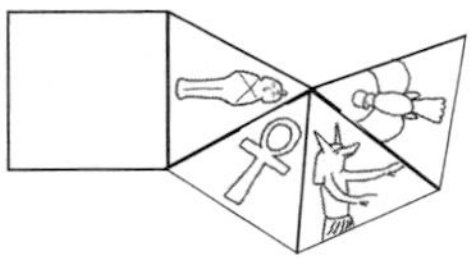

3. Tape the four triangles together so that their top points meet. Then tape the bottom sides of three of the triangles to three sides of the square base. Make sure the art goes on the inside.
4. Leave one of the triangles unattached to the square so you can see inside.

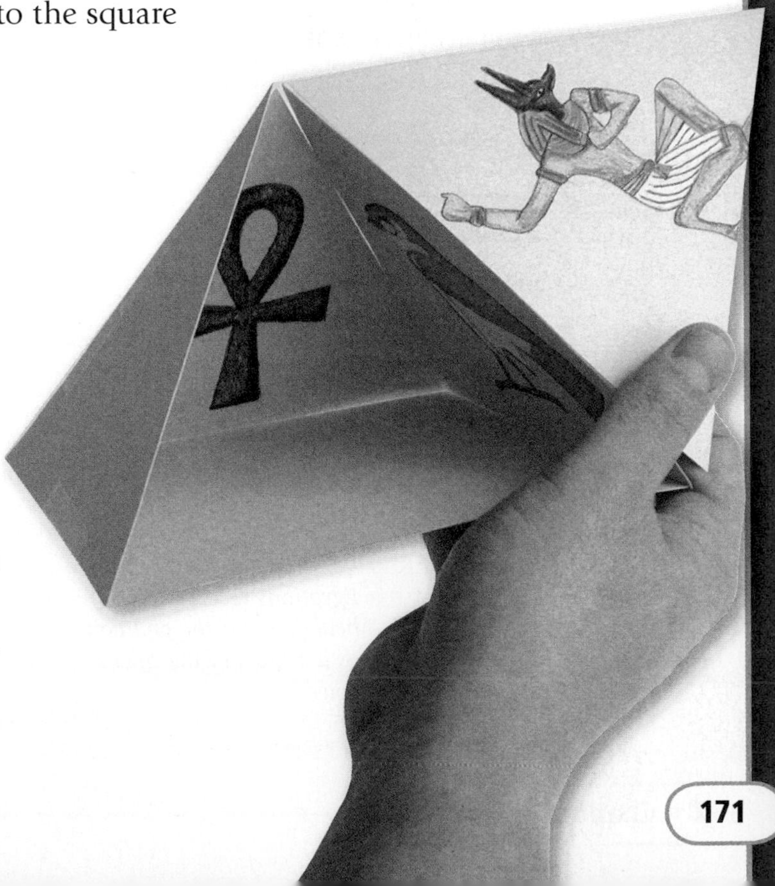

Follow-Up

1. How is an understanding of geometry related to building a pyramid?
2. How do the images that you put inside the pyramid relate to Egyptian beliefs?

Extension

Making a Presentation Show your pyramid to the class. Explain why you created your art and how it expresses Egyptian beliefs about life after death.

Lesson

4

MAIN IDEAS

1. **Economics** Queen Hatshepsut ruled as pharaoh and expanded trade during the New Kingdom.
2. **Belief Systems** Akhenaton tried to change Egyptian religion by replacing the old gods with one god called Aton.
3. **Government** Ramses II ruled Egypt for decades and created a stable empire.

TAKING NOTES

Reading Skill: Explaining Chronological Order and Sequence

Placing events in sequence means putting them in order based on the time they happened. As you read Lesson 4, note things that happened in the reigns of the pharaohs discussed. Create a time line like the one below to put events in order.

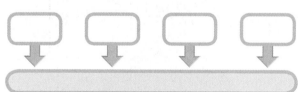

Skillbuilder Handbook, page R15

▲ **King Tut** British archaeologist Howard Carter found the tomb of New Kingdom pharaoh Tutankhamen in 1922. The mummy was protected by this gold mask.

Words to Know

Understanding the following words will help you read this lesson:

reign the time when a ruler is in power (page 173)

*Usually a ruler's **reign** lasted as long as he or she lived.*

reserve to keep for a special use (page 173)

*Egyptians **reserved** a headdress for the pharaoh as a symbol of the ruler's power.*

status a position, rank, or standing given to someone or something (page 175)

*As the **status** of the god increased, more people worshiped it.*

The New Kingdom

TERMS & NAMES
Hatshepsut
obelisk
Ramses II

Build on What You Know You read a little about the dazzling reign of Ramses II in Starting with a Story. He was a powerful pharaoh of the New Kingdom.

A Woman Pharaoh

1 **ESSENTIAL QUESTION** What was the significance of Queen Hatshepsut's rule?

The New Kingdom included some of Egypt's most powerful rulers. These pharaohs set up a new capital city of Thebes, 450 miles south of the old capital at Memphis. They strengthened Egypt by expanding the empire.

Taking Power Queen **Hatshepsut** (hat•SHEHP•SOOT) was the first woman to rule as pharaoh. She was the wife of a pharaoh who died soon after he took power. Hatshepsut then ruled with her stepson, Thutmose III (thoot•MOH•suh). In 1472 B.C., she declared herself the only ruler. She wore a false beard reserved for pharaohs alone.

Trade Grows Unlike other New Kingdom pharaohs, Hatshepsut did not only expand Egypt by waging war. She also wanted to make Egypt richer through trade. Her biggest trading expedition crossed the eastern desert to the Red Sea. Large ships sailed south to an African land called Punt (poont). Traders brought back rare herbs, spices, scented woods, live monkeys, and potted trees for making incense.

Hatshepsut's Temple Queen Hatshepsut had this temple constructed to honor herself. It was cut into a mountain. ▼

Hatshepsut's Monuments Like other pharaohs, Hatshepsut was eager to proclaim her glory. One type of monument she erected was the obelisk (AHB•uh•lihsk). An **obelisk** is a four-sided shaft with a pyramid-shaped top. (See page 155.) Hatshepsut had tall obelisks carved from blocks of red granite. On them, artisans used hieroglyphs to record her great deeds.

Mysterious End After ruling 15 years, Hatshepsut disappeared. She may have died peacefully, or Thutmose III may have killed her. After her death, Thutmose became pharaoh and tried to destroy all records of Hatshepsut's reign. We know about her because archaeologists restored her damaged temple and tomb.

REVIEW How did Hatshepsut try to make Egypt richer?

A Reforming Pharaoh

2 ESSENTIAL QUESTION How did Akhenaton try to change Egyptian religion?

As you read earlier, the Egyptians believed that angry gods caused suffering. In spite of this, one pharaoh dared to defy the gods.

New Kingdom Trade Routes, 1570–1070 B.C.

INTERACTIVE

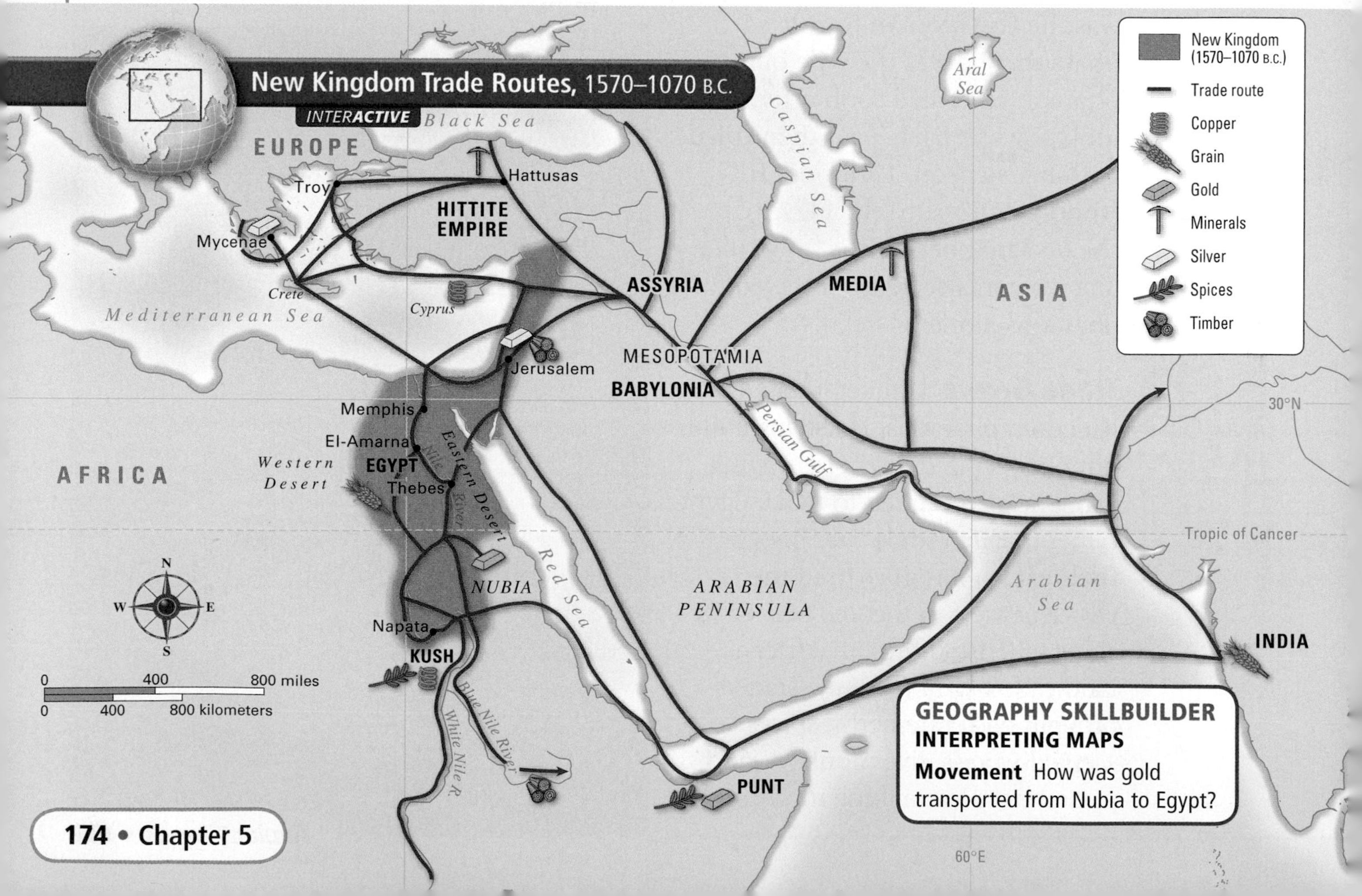

GEOGRAPHY SKILLBUILDER
INTERPRETING MAPS
Movement How was gold transported from Nubia to Egypt?

A New Belief When Akhenaton (AH•kuh•NAHT•n) became pharaoh in 1353 B.C., he lifted a sun god called Aton to the highest status. He then closed the temples of other gods. In this way, he promoted the worship of one god for the first time in Egyptian history.

Priests who served the other gods suddenly lost power. They became furious. They also feared that the pharaoh's actions had angered the old gods. To avoid conflict with those priests, Akhenaton moved about 200 miles away from them to a new capital city called Akhetaton (AH•kuh•TAHT•n).

▲ **Nefertiti** Historians consider this bust to be a realistic image of Akhenaton's wife, Nefertiti (NEHF•uhr•TEE•tee).

Realistic Art Akhenaton's new ways of thinking affected art. As Lesson 3 explained, Egyptian artwork usually tried to show perfect beauty. Under Akhenaton, that changed. For the first time, a pharaoh was shown realistically. For example, carvings of Akhenaton show his large stomach.

Reform Ends Akhenaton's new religion did not last long. Three years after his death, a young relative named Tutankhamen (TOOT•ahng•KAH•muhn) became pharaoh in 1333 B.C. This boy relied on advisers to help him rule Egypt. They convinced Tutankhamen to reject the new religion and worship the old gods.

REVIEW What reforms did Akhenaton make?

A Powerful Pharaoh

3 ESSENTIAL QUESTION How did Ramses II expand Egypt?

In 1279 B.C., 44 years after Tutankhamen died, **Ramses II** (RAM•SEEZ) took the throne. His 66-year reign was among the longest in history. He expanded the Egyptian empire.

Empire Builder Unlike Hatshepsut, Ramses II—also called Ramses the Great—wanted to make Egypt powerful through war. Under Ramses' rule, Egypt extended its territory south into the African kingdom of Nubia. The empire also stretched to the eastern rim of the Mediterranean Sea. There it bordered the empire of a people called the Hittites.

▲ **Abu Simbel** Four giant statues of Ramses guarded his temple at Abu Simbel, which was near the Nile. Each statue was as tall as a six-story building.

Military Leader The Egyptians and Hittites had long been enemies. Soon after he became pharaoh, Ramses led an army into battle against the Hittites. Nobody really won the battle, but Ramses claimed victory. His real success came after the battle. The treaty he negotiated with the Hittites was the first known peace treaty in world history.

Ramses' Reign Ramses was bold in honoring himself. He built a city called the House of Ramses. Four 66-foot statues of himself guarded his temple. The statues' ears were three feet long! Unlike Akhenaton, Ramses did not want his statues to show how he really looked. He wanted to appear godlike.

Ramses II reigned until 1213 B.C., when he was more than 90 years old. Having one ruler for 66 years made the Egyptian government *stable*. His reign was also a time of peace. After the treaty with the Hittites, no enemy threatened Egypt while Ramses ruled.

Vocabulary Strategy

Stable is a **multiple-meaning** word. Here it means "not likely to change."

Life was calm and happy in other ways too. The Nile flooding was even more reliable than usual during Ramses' reign. Egyptian crops were more plentiful than ever.

Egypt's Decline Egypt was never quite the same after Ramses died. Gradually, the central government weakened. After about 1070 B.C., a series of foreign powers ruled Egypt.

One of those rulers was Alexander the Great, the king of Macedonia who conquered Egypt. (You will read about Alexander in Chapter 12.) After his death, Macedonians continued to rule Egypt. The last Macedonian ruler was the famous queen Cleopatra. Eventually the powerful Roman Empire would conquer Egypt.

REVIEW What were Ramses II's accomplishments?

▲ **Cleopatra** After Rome conquered Egypt, Cleopatra killed herself. She feared she would be taken to Rome as a prisoner.

Lesson Summary

- Hatshepsut was the first woman to rule as pharaoh. She expanded Egypt's trade with other lands.
- Akhenaton tried to change Egypt's religion to a belief in one god, but his religion did not last after his death.
- Ramses II built an extensive empire and ruled for 66 years. His reign was a time of peace and prosperity.

Why It Matters Now . . .

The ancient Egyptians rejected Akhenaton's idea of one supreme god, but that idea later became widespread. Today many people believe in religions based on a single god.

4 Lesson Review

Homework Helper
ClassZone.com

Terms & Names

1. Explain the importance of

Hatshepsut   obelisk   Ramses II

Using Your Notes

Explaining Sequence Use your completed time line to answer the following question:

2. Which pharaoh reigned the longest?

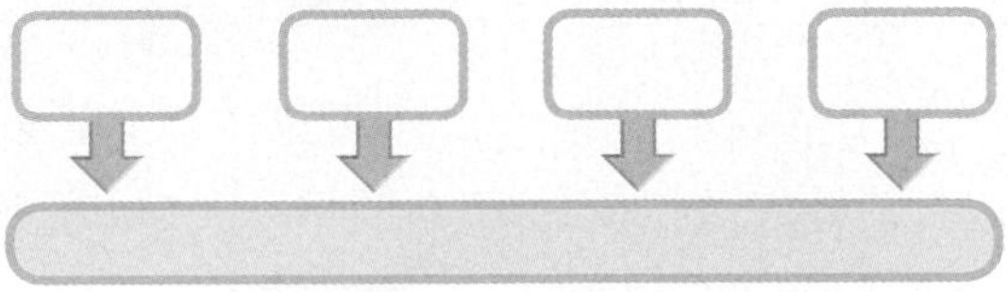

Main Ideas

3. What was unusual about the reign of Hatshepsut?

4. How did Akhenaton try to change the way the Egyptians worshiped?

5. Why was the government of Egypt stable under Ramses II?

Critical Thinking

6. Forming and Supporting Opinions Why do you think Thutmose tried to erase all records of Hatshepsut's reign?

7. Comparing and Contrasting In what ways were the reigns of Akhenaton and Ramses II different?

Activity

Internet Activity Use the Internet to research one of the pharaohs in this lesson. Then make a sketch for the pharaoh's Web page.

INTERNET KEYWORD: *pharaoh's name*

Hatshepsut's EXPEDITION to PUNT

Background: In about 1472 B.C., a queen named Hatshepsut (hat•SHEHP•SOOT) took the title of pharaoh of Egypt. She wanted to make her country powerful and rich. Hatshepsut decided that trade would bring wealth to Egypt.

CAST OF CHARACTERS

Narrator

Hatshepsut: woman pharaoh of Egypt

Senmut: (SEHN•muht) Hatshepsut's most trusted adviser

Thutmose III: (thoot•MOH•suh) Hatshepsut's nephew and co-ruler

Nehesy: (neh•HEH•see) commander of the expedition to Punt

Sailor

Chief: ruler of Punt

Chief's Wife

Court Official

First Treasure Bearer

Second Treasure Bearer

Third Treasure Bearer

Fourth Treasure Bearer

▲ **Sailors rowing** Although Hatshepsut's ships had sails, the sailors had to row if the wind died.

Narrator: When King Thutmose II died, his son Thutmose III became pharaoh. Because the boy was so young, his stepmother, Queen Hatshepsut, ruled in his place. Within a few years, the queen proclaimed herself to be pharaoh. Hatshepsut also had big plans for Egypt. She discussed her plans with Senmut.

Hatshepsut: I want to make Egypt great again. I want to repair the old temples and build new ones.

Senmut: Great Pharaoh, such a plan will please the gods. But where will Egypt gain the fine building materials to carry out such projects?

Hatshepsut: The god Amon-Re (AH•muhn•RAY) has told me to trade with the land of Punt, which is rich in valuable goods. We will send a trading expedition there.

Thutmose III: (*angry whisper*) This is terrible news. If Hatshepsut succeeds in her plan, she will earn great glory. I will never get rid of her and be able to rule by myself.

Narrator: After hearing of Hatshepsut's plan for the expedition to Punt, Senmut sent for Nehesy. He was a skilled sea captain.

Nehesy: You sent for me, your highness?

Hatshepsut: Our ancient writings tell of a rich land called Punt. To reach it, you must sail the length of the Red Sea and then down the coast of the lands to the south. Do you think you can find this place?

▲ **Hatshepsut** **The royalty of Egypt wore colorful jewelry, as shown on this figure of Hatshepsut.**

Nehesy: Oh, yes. I'm sure I can find this land.

Hatshepsut: Good. I want you to take a fleet and sail to Punt. Take my trusted adviser Senmut with you. He will trade with the people of Punt and bring back materials to make our temples great again.

Narrator: Nehesy did as the pharaoh commanded. He gathered together five great ships. Each was about 80 feet long and had a single giant sail.

Senmut: Are you sure you can make this voyage, Nehesy? Our people are used to sailing on the Nile, not on the wide seas.

(continued)

Nehesy: When the wind is behind the sail, it will push us forward. When the wind dies or blows the wrong way, my 30 oarsmen will row the ship.

Senmut: That sounds like a good plan, but are you sure we will be safe?

Nehesy: We are perfectly safe. I have given orders that we must always stay within sight of the coast, so we cannot get lost.

Senmut: All right, Nehesy. I believe the voyage is in good hands under your leadership.

Narrator: After many months, the fleet came to a land with huge trees. The Egyptians could see a village with round huts that had cone-shaped thatch roofs.

Sailor: Look over there! I think that's the land of Punt! We made it!

Narrator: The ruler of the country and his wife came to meet the ships and learned they were from Egypt.

Chief: How did you come here? We thought this land was unknown to Egypt.

Chief's Wife: Did you come down the roads of the heavens? You must have followed the sun's path.

Senmut: We sailed down the Red Sea and then along the coast of this land. O Great Chief, I bring you greetings from Pharaoh Hatshepsut. I have brought many gifts to honor you. I also have trade goods to exchange for the goods of your country.

Chief: Come to my house. My servants will prepare a meal for us, and you and I can bargain.

Narrator: Senmut showed the Chief of Punt the trade items he had brought.

Senmut: My people are good metal workers. I have brought you bronze daggers and axes, and also beautiful necklaces. We also brought wheat bread, dried fruits, and honeycakes.

Narrator: The chief and Senmut agreed to a trade. Then the Egyptians loaded their ships and returned home. When they reached the coast of Egypt, they traveled over land to the capital at Thebes.

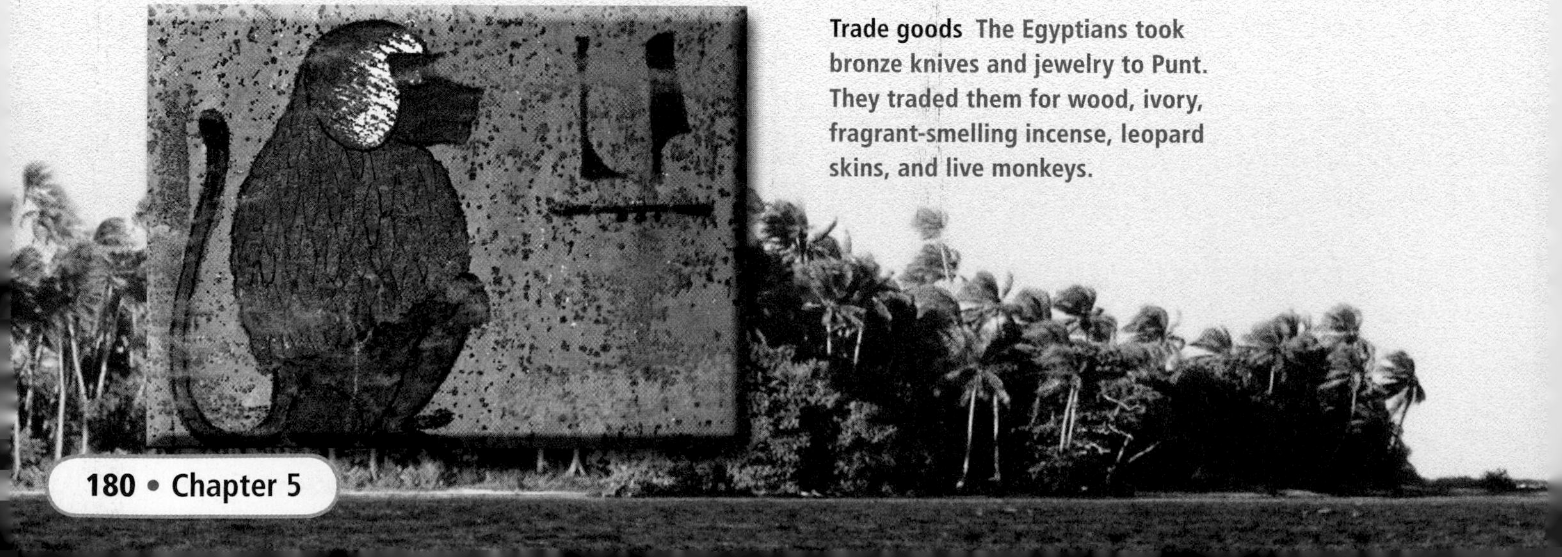

Trade goods The Egyptians took bronze knives and jewelry to Punt. They traded them for wood, ivory, fragrant-smelling incense, leopard skins, and live monkeys.

Court Official: O Great Hatshepsut, your expedition to Punt has returned. Senmut has arrived with a caravan of goods from the ships.

Hatshepsut: Show him in.

Senmut: Your highness, the chief of Punt greeted us with friendliness, and our trade mission was successful. We have gained many great treasures for Egypt. I will have them brought before you.

First Treasure Bearer: Great Pharaoh, I bring you chests of gold.

Hatshepsut: Good. I will use this to adorn my obelisks and other monuments.

Second Treasure Bearer: Highness, I bring logs of dark ebony wood and great tusks of ivory. Our artisans can use these materials to make beautiful things.

Third Treasure Bearer: Mighty Pharaoh, I bring baboons and monkeys for your amusement. And leopards for their exotic spotted skins.

Fourth Treasure Bearer: Your highness, I bring great quantities of incense.

Hatshepsut: This will please the priests, who burn incense in the temples.

Senmut: Great Pharaoh, we have saved the best treasure for last. The Chief of Punt sold us 31 myrrh trees, which his people carefully planted in tubs for the journey. I will plant the trees in the courtyard of your great temple. With the sap of these trees, our priests can make their own incense.

Hatshepsut: Senmut, you have done well. And Nehesy, I am pleased with you too.

Nehesy: Thank you, your highness.

Thutmose III: (*angry whisper*) I was certain this trade mission would fail. But it has succeeded more than Hatshepsut dared to hope. She is right that the priests will be happy. Now they will love Hatshepsut and support her rule. I must wait for a better time to seize the throne.

Narrator: Years later, Thutmose III did become the sole pharaoh of Egypt. No one knows what happened to Hatshepsut. Maybe Thutmose killed her or maybe she died of old age. We do know that Thutmose tried to erase her name from history. He failed, and the record of Hatshepsut's deeds still amazes the world.

Activities

1. **TALK ABOUT IT** What qualities of a good ruler did Hatshepsut have?
2. **WRITE ABOUT IT** Write a new scene in which Senmut and the chief bargain over the exchange of goods. Show how each person tried to get the most he could from the exchange.

Chapter 5 Review

VISUAL SUMMARY

Ancient Egypt

Geography
- Nile provided silt and water, transportation.
- Desert acted as a natural barrier.

Economy
- Traded with parts of Africa, Arabia, and Mediterranean countries
- A prosperous land with many specialized jobs

Belief Systems
- Many gods; pharaoh was one
- Believed in a happy afterlife

Science & Technology
- Developed calendar, astronomy, medicine
- Developed written language—hieroglyphs

Government
- Upper and Lower Egypt united as one country
- Pharaohs and dynasties kept control; priests served as officials

TERMS & NAMES

Explain why the words in each set below are linked with each other.

1. **delta** and **silt**
2. **scribe** and **hieroglyph**
3. **dynasty** and **pharaoh**
4. **Hatshepsut** and **Ramses II**

MAIN IDEAS

Gift of the Nile (pages 146–153)

5. Why was the Nile so valuable for trade and transportation?
6. How did Egyptian farmers use the Nile to expand their farmland?

Life in Ancient Egypt (pages 154–163)

7. What are the characteristics of the hieroglyphic system?
8. Why did the Egyptians embalm bodies?

The Pyramid Builders (pages 164–171)

9. Why did the Egyptians have such great respect for the pharaohs?
10. What items were found inside pyramids?

The New Kingdom (pages 172–181)

11. What were the important accomplishments of Queen Hatshepsut?
12. Why was the reign of Ramses II so successful?

CRITICAL THINKING Big Ideas: Geography

13. DRAWING CONCLUSIONS How did the geography of Egypt help civilization develop there?

14. UNDERSTANDING CAUSE AND EFFECT How did the geography of ancient Egypt affect the building of pyramids and other structures?

15. EXPLAINING HISTORICAL PATTERNS Why do you think successful agriculture encourages the development of civilizations?

ALTERNATIVE ASSESSMENT

1. WRITING ACTIVITY Write a descriptive paragraph about an artifact in the chapter. Identify the object and the page on which it is found.

2. INTERDISCIPLINARY ACTIVITY—SCIENCE Research to learn about the Egyptian calendar. Make a poster explaining the calendar.

3. STARTING WITH A STORY
Starting with a Story
Review the narrative you wrote about the new pharaoh. Draw a picture that illustrates the scene.

Technology Activity

4. CREATING A MULTIMEDIA PRESENTATION
Use the Internet or the library to research and compare Egyptian pyramids with those of Meso-America. Work with a partner to make a multimedia presentation.

- Include maps that show where pyramids are located in Egypt and Meso-America.
- Show slides of pyramids from Egypt and Meso-America.
- Supply text for each slide.
- Provide documentation of your sources.

Research Links
ClassZone.com

Reading Charts Use the chart below to answer the questions.

Pyramids Around the World

PYRAMID	LOCATION & APPROX. DATE	HEIGHT (meters)	NOTES
Djoser step pyramid	Saqqara, Egypt 2630 B.C.	60	First step pyramid
Bent pyramid	Dahshur, Egypt 2600 B.C.	105	First attempt at a true pyramid
Khufu's Great Pyramid	Giza, Egypt 2550 B.C.	147	True pyramid
Pyramid of the Sun	Teotihuacán, Mexico 100 B.C.	65	Step pyramid
Temple of the Giant Jaguar	Tikal, Guatemala A.D. 700	45	Step pyramid

Sources: *Encyclopedia Britannica; World Book*

1. Which of the following pyramids is not in Egypt?
A. Djoser step pyramid
B. Bent pyramid
C. Khufu's Great Pyramid
D. Temple of the Giant Jaguar

2. Which of the following is tallest?
A. Djoser step pyramid
B. Bent pyramid
C. Pyramid of the Sun
D. Temple of the Giant Jaguar

Test Practice
ClassZone.com

Additional Test Practice, pp. S1–S33

Chapter 6 Kush and Other African Kingdoms

Before You Read: Knowledge Rating

Recognizing what you already know about each of these terms can help you understand the chapter:

Kush	Meroë	Aksum
Ezana	griot	Bantu

In your notebook, rate how well you know each term:

3 = I know what this word means.
2 = I've seen this word, but I don't know what it means.
1 = I've never seen this word before.

Define each term in your notebook as you read.

Big Ideas About the Kush Civilization

Culture **Ways of living change as humans interact with each other.**

Kush civilization was influenced by Egyptian culture. Kush was under the rule of Egypt for hundreds of years. Kush adopted Egyptian customs, religion, hieroglyphs, and architecture. Later, Kush conquered Egypt. The two cultures influenced each other.

Integrated Technology

eEdition
- Interactive Maps
- Interactive Visuals
- Starting with a Story

INTERNET RESOURCES
Go to **ClassZone.com** for
- WebQuest
- Homework Helper
- Research Links
- Internet Activities
- Quizzes
- Maps
- Test Practice
- Current Events

AFRICA

751 B.C.
Piankhi, a Kushite king, conquers Memphis in Egypt.

500 B.C.
Nok people make iron tools.
(Nok head) ▶

800 B.C. — 650 B.C. — 500 B.C.

WORLD

461 B.C.
Age of Pericles begins in Greece.
◀ (marble bust of Pericles)

Vegetation Regions of Africa

INTERACTIVE

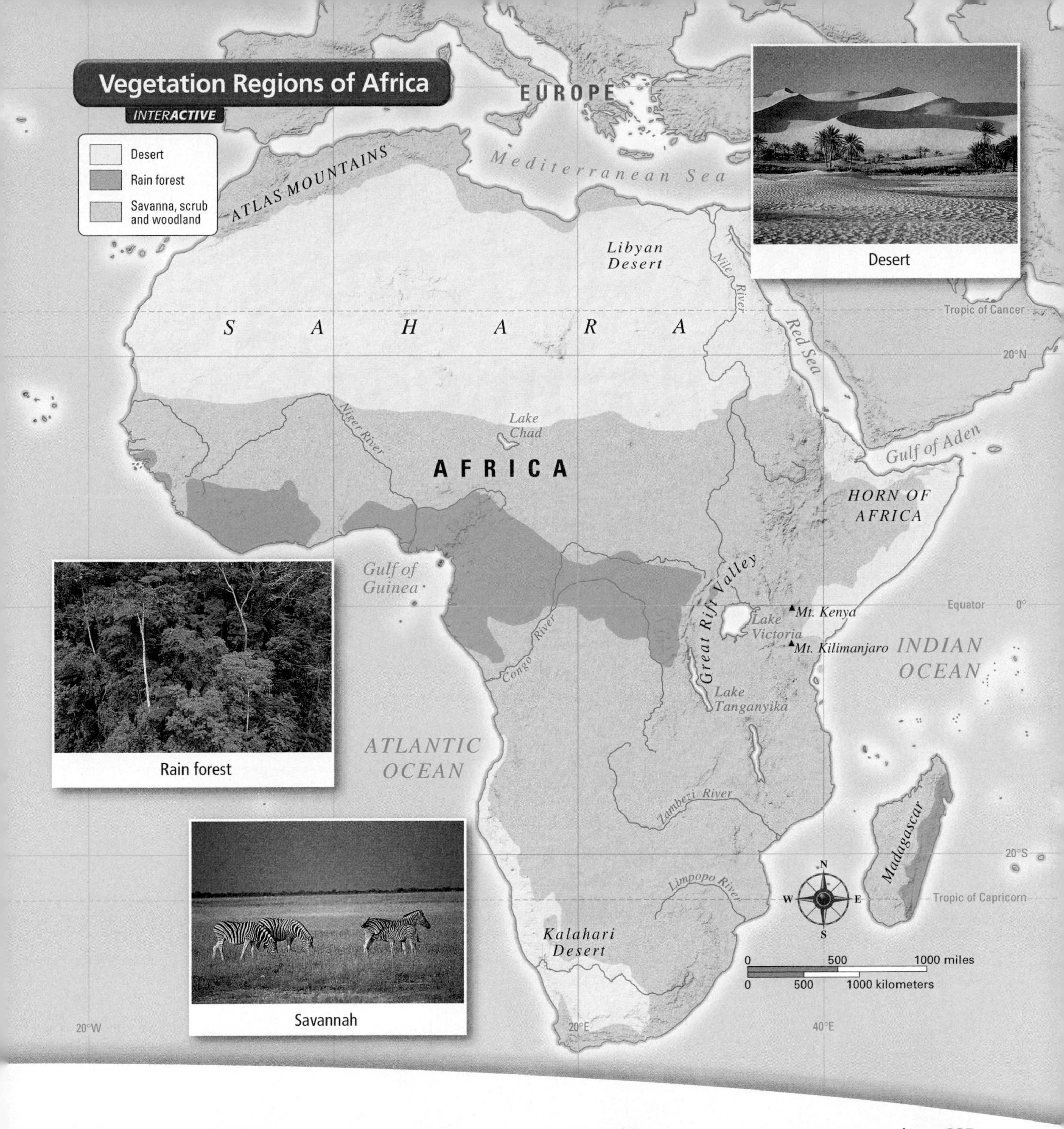

Desert

Rain forest

Savannah

146 B.C. African city of Carthage destroyed by Rome.

27 B.C. Pax Romana begins.

A.D. 100 Bantu migrations under way.

A.D. 105 Chinese invent paper. (illuminated manuscript, Tang Dynasty) ▶

A.D. 325 King Ezana rules Aksum.

200 B.C. | 50 B.C. | A.D. 100 | A.D. 250 | A.D. 400

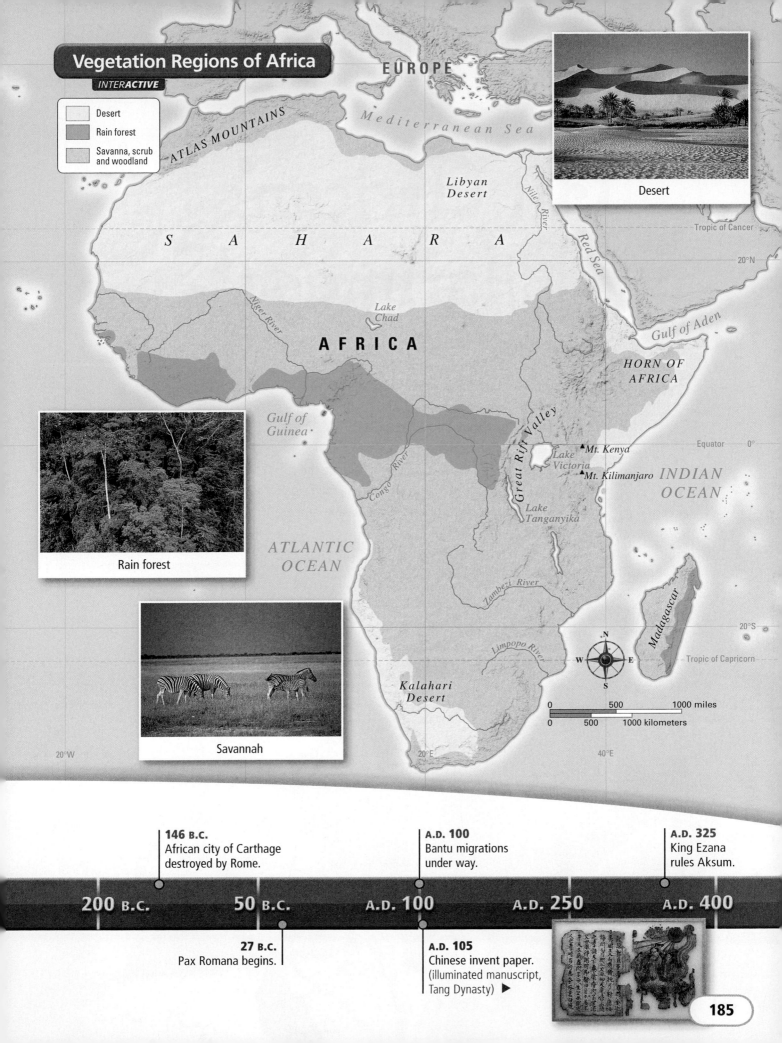

Starting with a Story

An African's Pilgrimage

Background: In the third century A.D., a Babylonian prophet wrote that there were four great kingdoms on Earth. These were the kingdoms of China, Persia, Rome, and the African kingdom of Aksum. Rome and Aksum made Christianity their official religion. In 324, Constantine became the Roman Empire's first Christian ruler. Around the same time, King Ezana became the first Christian ruler of Aksum. As you read the following story, think about what it would be like to live in Africa's Christian kingdom.

Church in Aksum, Ethiopia ▶

There was a young boy in Aksum. His father was an important official in the court of King Ezana. The father was a devoted servant of the king, and he adopted Christianity after the king made it Aksum's official religion. After his conversion, the father worked hard to raise his son as a Christian. He spent many hours helping him to read the Bible, and the boy grew to love the sacred book's stories and lessons. Even so, it was not until his father took him on a pilgrimage to the Christian holy places that he became truly dedicated to the new faith.

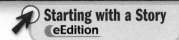

The boy still recalled with great pleasure the day they sailed from the port city of Adulis. King Ezana and Bishop Frumentius had provided resources and guides to take them to Jerusalem. With such preparation, they departed with few cares. On the way to the holy city, the guides ordered stops at many sites familiar from the Bible. One of the most meaningful was Sinai, the mountain where God gave Moses the Ten Commandments. The boy would never forget standing on Sinai's sacred summit and gazing over the surrounding scene. On the way to Jerusalem, they also stopped in Bethlehem, the birthplace of Jesus.

Jerusalem, however, was the spiritual peak of the journey. The boy walked with pilgrims from all over the Christian world as they visited the most important sites. The boy took careful notes because he was expected to report to the king about what he had seen. He met another boy his age and the boy's father, who had traveled to Jerusalem from Constantinople. The young Aksumite traveler was able to speak some Greek and make himself understood to the travelers from Constantinople. He acquired a rich supply of experiences and information to report to his king.

What experiences might the boy take back to Aksum from his pilgrimage?

Reading & Writing

1. **READING: Main Ideas** The main idea sums up the most important point of a paragraph or selection. With a partner, list one or two main ideas from the above passage.
2. **WRITING: Comparison and Contrast** Write a two-paragraph essay in which you compare what the boy's ideas about Jerusalem might have been before his trip with what he might have learned on the journey.

Lesson 1

MAIN IDEAS

1. **Geography** The region of Nubia had connections with Egypt.
2. **Government** A powerful king of Kush conquered Egypt and ruled as pharaoh.
3. **Economics** Meroë was an important economic center linking Egypt and the interior of Africa.

▲ **Nubian Pottery** This Nubian pottery vessel decorated with giraffes is an example of the goods traded in Kush.

TAKING NOTES

Reading Skill: Explaining Sequence

To sequence events means to put them in order based on the time they happened. As you read Lesson 1, make a note of things that happened in the Kushite kingdoms. Create a time line like the one below to put events in order.

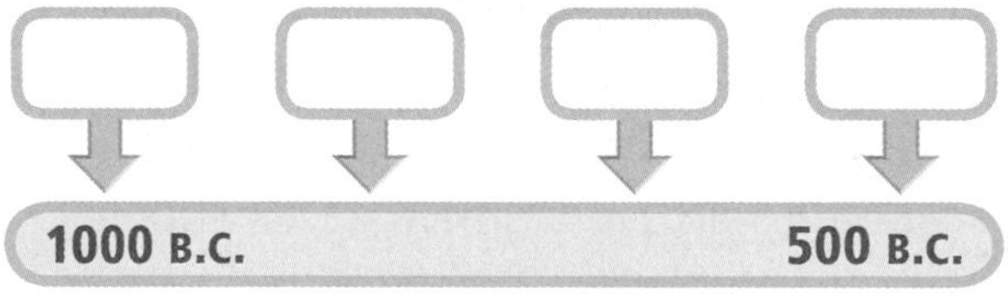

Skillbuilder Handbook, page R15

Words to Know

Understanding the following words will help you read this lesson:

boundary a border or line where something comes to an end (page 189)

*At midday, the caravan crossed the **boundary** of Nubia into Egypt.*

official a person who holds a position of authority (page 190)

*Even though he was Nubia's top **official**, he was still responsible to Egypt.*

navigate to guide the course of a ship or aircraft (page 191)

*To **navigate** the Nile River, traders had to know the locations of waterfalls.*

mine to gather rocks or minerals from an underground hole (page 192)

*They **mined** in order to find minerals they could use to make tools and weapons.*

Nubia and the Land of Kush

TERMS & NAMES
- Nubia
- Kush
- Piankhi
- Meroë
- smelting

Build on What You Know Have you ever traveled on a river or visited a river town? The Egyptians lived downstream on the lower, or northern, end of the Nile River. Now you will learn about another culture that developed to the south that interacted with Egypt and other parts of Africa.

The Region of Nubia

1 **ESSENTIAL QUESTION** In what ways were Nubia and Egypt connected?

Nubia (NOO•bee•uh) is the name for a geographic region of Africa. (See the map at the top of the next page.) Nubia extended from the southern boundary of Egypt southward to include present-day Sudan. Its southern boundary was south of the Nile River's sixth cataract.

Upper and Lower Nubia Like Egypt, Nubia was divided into upper (southern, upstream) and lower (northern, downstream) areas. Like the Egyptians, the people of Nubia lived along the Nile. However, in southern Nubia, unlike in Egypt, a climate that provided greater moisture meant farming was not limited to the Nile valley.

REVIEW What geographic feature connected Egypt and Nubia?

Connect to Today

▼ The Upper Nile The Nile River begins in Burundi and then travels north through Uganda, Sudan (shown below), and Egypt before it empties into the Mediterranean Sea.

The Kush Civilization

2 ESSENTIAL QUESTION What were some of the achievements of Piankhi?

Egypt controlled parts of Nubia between 2000 and 1000 B.C. During these centuries, Nubia was a source of goods for Egypt. But as Egypt declined, a Nubian kingdom called **Kush** became a power in the region.

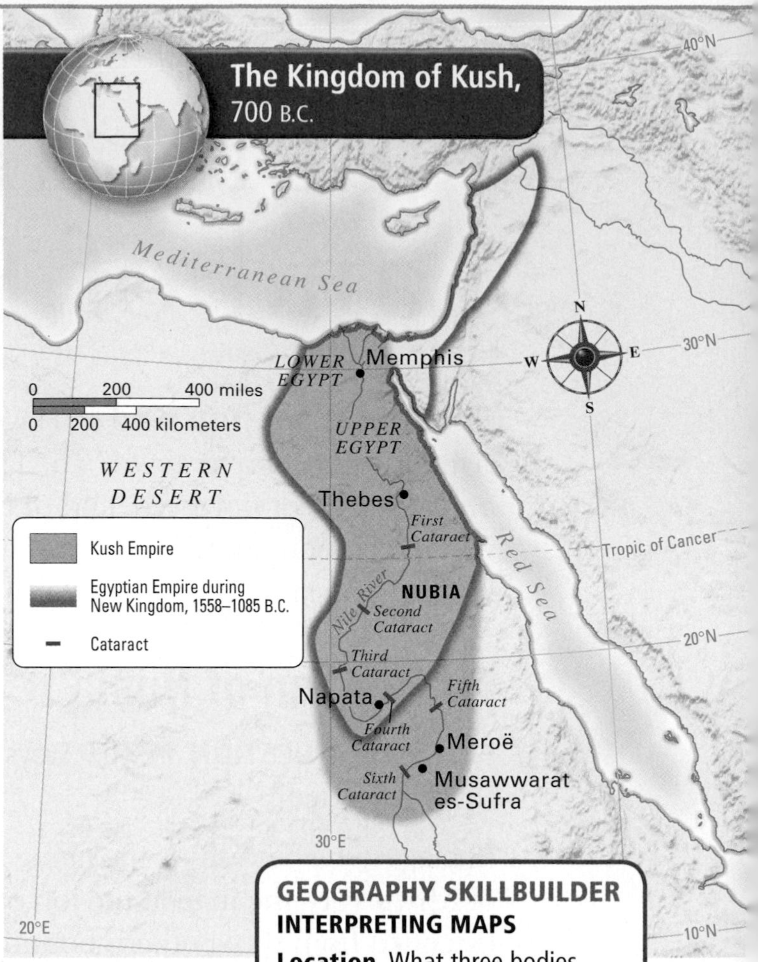

GEOGRAPHY SKILLBUILDER
INTERPRETING MAPS
Location What three bodies of water were important to the kingdom of Kush?

Cultural Relations Between Egypt and Kush

Cultural Relations Between Egypt and Kush In ancient times, Nubia had a strong influence on Egypt. For example, some scholars believe Nubia's monarchy was the earliest in human history. Later, this monarchy was developed in the person of the Egyptian pharaoh.

Then, when Egypt ruled Nubia, the Egyptian pharaoh appointed an official to govern the region. Contact with Egypt resulted in cultural exchanges. Egypt influenced the art and architecture of the Nubian region, including the emerging kingdom of Kush. Nubians also worshiped some of the gods sacred to Egyptians.

Young Kushite nobles went to Egypt where they learned the Egyptian language. They also adopted the customs and clothing styles of the Egyptians. They brought back royal rituals and a hieroglyphic writing system to Kush. Egyptian pyramids were also adapted by builders in Kush.

Vocabulary Strategy

Use context clues to figure out the meaning of *sacred.* The rest of the sentence tells you that the word sometimes means "worthy of religious respect or reverence."

Kush Rises to Power In the 700s B.C., the Nubian kingdom of Kush conquered all of upper and lower Egypt. In 751 B.C., **Piankhi** (PYANG•kee)—a Kushite king—attacked the Egyptian city of Memphis. By about 36 years later, Piankhi had gained control of Egypt.

From this point on, two periods make up the history of Kush. Each period is based on the location of the capital and king's tomb. The city of Napata was the capital during this first period. Meroë (MEHR•oh•EE) was the capital during the second.

Political and Commercial Relations with Egypt Piankhi united Egypt and Kush. Nubia established its own dynasty, or line of royal rulers, on the throne of Egypt. Piankhi was declared Egypt's pharaoh. His reign marked the beginning of Egypt's 25th Dynasty. Although he was the pharaoh, Piankhi did not live in Egypt. Instead, he chose to live in Napata, the capital of Kush.

Primary Source Handbook
See the excerpt from Piankhi's Monument, page R40.

Napata was located at the head of a road used to move goods around the Nile River's cataracts. Traders used the road when boats loaded with goods were unable to navigate the rough water on certain sections of the river. Nubia was rich in goods that were scarce in Egypt: ivory, animal skins, timber, and minerals. This led to a lively trade along the Nile. Napata was the center for the spread of Egyptian goods and culture to Kush's other trading partners in Africa and beyond.

The Decline of Kush Taharqa (tuh•HAHR•kuh) was a later Kushite ruler of Egypt. Taharqa spent much of his reign fighting the Assyrians, who had invaded and conquered Egypt in 671 B.C.

The Assyrians carried iron weapons that were more powerful than the bronze weapons of the Kushites. A large part of the Assyrian army was made up of foot soldiers, who were armed with bows and arrows.

History Makers

Piankhi (ruled during the 700s B.C.)

Piankhi was a Kushite king who knew when to fight and when to make peace. When a Libyan chief threatened Upper Egypt, Piankhi decided to fight. He defeated the Libyans' land army and their river fleet as well. At the time, Egypt had many weak princes who ruled small areas. They welcomed Piankhi's protection. The Egyptian priests also were eager to have Piankhi come to their defense.

Around 750 B.C., Piankhi united Egypt and became the pharaoh. This marked the beginning of the 25th Dynasty. Having accomplished what he set out to do, Piankhi went home to Napata. There he had a stone slab built that celebrated his deeds. The slab lasted longer than his dynasty, which ended after about 100 years.

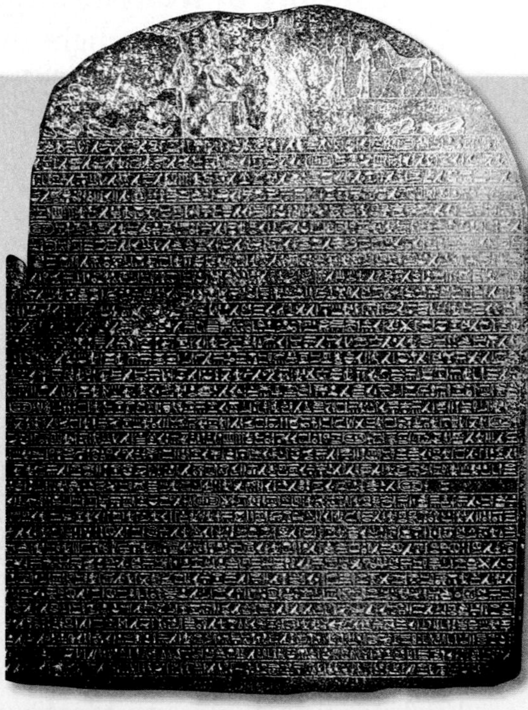

▲ **Monument** This black granite monument, which is six feet high, was discovered in Napata. The image of Piankhi is at the center, upper right.

Horses and Chariots Some Assyrians drove chariots. The Assyrian army also was the first army to have a cavalry—men on horseback.

The Kushite armies under Taharqa were no match for the Assyrians, who took control of Egypt and parts of Kush. After their defeat, the Kushite kings retreated south.

REVIEW How did Piankhi become the Egyptian pharaoh?

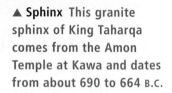

▲ **Sphinx** This granite sphinx of King Taharqa comes from the Amon Temple at Kawa and dates from about 690 to 664 B.C.

The Kushite Capital of Meroë

3 ESSENTIAL QUESTION Why was the Kushite city of Meroë an important economic center?

The Kushite kings eventually chose a new capital, **Meroë**, in about 590 B.C. Meroë was located on the Nile and on trade routes leading from the Red Sea to the interior of Africa. It had access to gold and iron.

An Economy of Ironworking and Trade The defeat of Kush by the Assyrians taught the Kushites that they needed iron weapons. The people of Kush learned to smelt iron. **Smelting** is the heating of material from Earth's crust to separate the elements it contains. The Kushites mined rock containing iron ore. Then they heated the rock in small earthen furnaces. The heat caused the iron to separate from other minerals.

Meroë was an ideal location for producing iron. The city was close to iron ore deposits. The Kushites set up smelting furnaces to process the deposits. Meroë traded its iron in central and east Africa, and in Arabia.

Ivory, gold, and products made from them were traded at Meroë. These items were in demand in many other parts of the world. Trade was especially active with Egypt, which was under Greek rule beginning in the fourth century B.C.

A Rich Culture Develops Some of the gods worshiped by the Kushites in Napata and Meroë were similar to those of Egypt. This similarity was especially true of the sun god Amon-Re and Isis, goddess of the moon. Other gods were Nubian in origin.

In Nubia, women played an important role. Amanirenas and Amanishakheto were important Nubian queens. Queen Amanitore and her husband ruled beginning around 12 B.C.

The people of Kush developed a written language. They appear to have at first used hieroglyphics similar to those used by the Egyptians. Later, their language changed to an alphabet of 23 symbols. The language has not yet been translated.

Royal tombs in Kush were built of stone. They were pyramid-shaped with steep sides. These tombs included a chapel attached to the side. Kushite kings were often mummified to preserve their bodies. These traditions continued in Nubia even after they had died out in Egypt.

REVIEW In what ways was Meroë economically important?

▲ **Armlet** This armlet dates from Meroë in the late first century B.C. It is made of gold with fused-glass inlays. On the hinge is the figure of a goddess.

Lesson Summary

- Nubia and Egypt interacted with each other.
- The Kushite king Piankhi conquered Egypt.
- The Kushite capital of Meroë was a trade center.

Why It Matters Now . . .

By studying the history of Nubia, we learn of the important role played by Africans in ancient history.

1 Lesson Review

Homework Helper
ClassZone.com

Terms & Names

1. Explain the importance of

Nubia Piankhi smelting
Kush Meroë

Using Your Notes

Explaining Sequence Use your completed time line to answer the following question:

2. What event marked the end of the Kushite kingdom based in Napata?

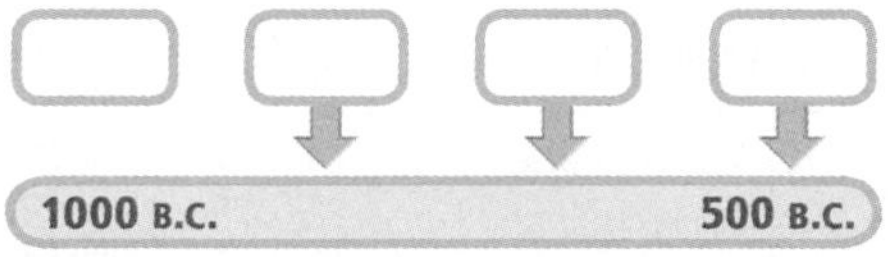

Main Ideas

3. How was the Nile important to the relationship between Nubia and Egypt?

4. What was the most significant achievement of Piankhi's rule?

5. Why did the people of Meroë learn to smelt iron?

Critical Thinking

6. Comparing How did Piankhi's reign differ from that of Taharqa in the control of Egypt?

7. Drawing Conclusions What factors made the Kushites move their capital to Meroë?

Activity

Making a Map Pull out the world outline map you began in the activity for Chapter 2, Lesson 1. Place the Nubian kingdom of Kush on the map, along with its two capitals of Napata and Meroë.

Explaining Geographic Patterns

Goal: To identify the importance of minerals and trade to the economic system of the Kush Empire

Learn the Skill

Recognizing geographic patterns involves seeing the overall shape, organization, or trend of specific geographic characteristics. Look at the chart at the bottom of this page for examples of geographic patterns. Trade routes make up one type of geographic pattern. You read about the Kush Empire and trade in Lesson 1. Trade routes went in and out of Kush in every direction, by land and by sea.

See the Skillbuilder Handbook, page R16.

Practice the Skill

1. Look at the title of the map at right to get an idea of the geographic pattern—trade routes and minerals—that it shows.
2. Identify significant mineral deposits, such as gold and iron, on this map by using the symbols in the legend.
3. Look at the map to see in what areas trade routes developed. Which part of the continent, if any, was largely untouched by Kush trade routes?
4. Check the map to see how the location of resources contributed to the development of trade routes.
5. There are many different examples of geographic patterns. Some of these are given below.

Examples:

5

GEOGRAPHIC PATTERNS

Weather Cycles	Economic Changes	Languages	Trade Routes
Monsoon winds in India follow a predictable pattern: winter—from northeast; summer—from southwest.	Oil has transformed the economies of some North African countries.	Bantu languages spread across Africa as a result of Bantu migrations.	Triangular trade developed between Africa, America, and Europe; Silk Roads crossed Asia.

Trade Map

The Kush Empire was a center of trade. As the mineral wealth of the Nile valley flowed out of Kush to Egypt (among other places), luxury goods from India and Arabia flowed in. Trade routes developed both over land and by sea to carry goods in and out of Kush.

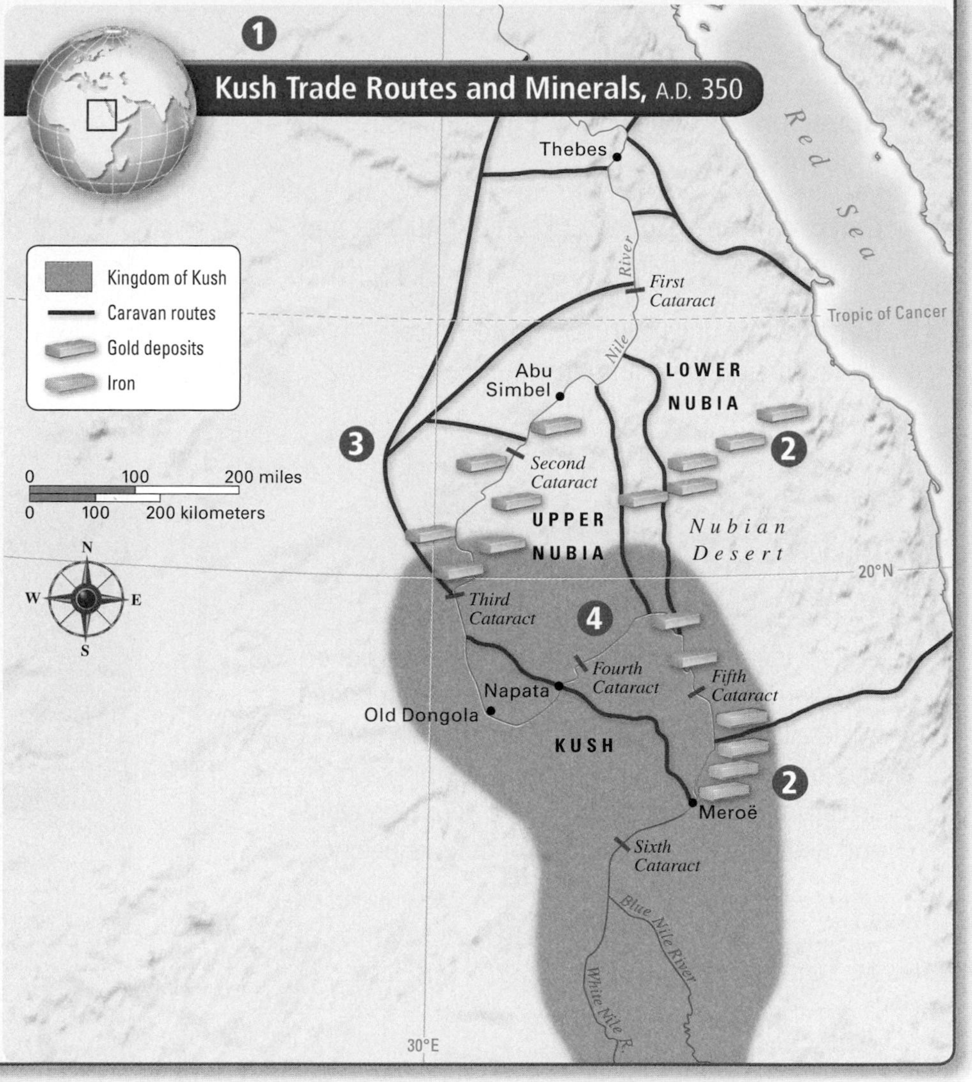

Apply the Skill

Look at the maps on the distribution of hunters and gatherers in Chapter 2, Lesson 1, page 52. Make notes on the geographic patterns that you see developing across the time span of the three maps on that page.

Lesson 2

MAIN IDEAS

1. **Government** A new power, Aksum, rises south of Egypt.
2. **Culture** Ezana expands Aksum's influence and converts to Christianity.
3. **Culture** Aksum's cultural and technical achievements were long lasting.

TAKING NOTES

Reading Skill: Finding Main Ideas

A main idea sums up the most important point of a paragraph or passage. Main ideas are supported by details and examples. Identify the main ideas and important details in Lesson 2 about Aksum's achievements. Then put them into your own words and write them in a diagram like the one below.

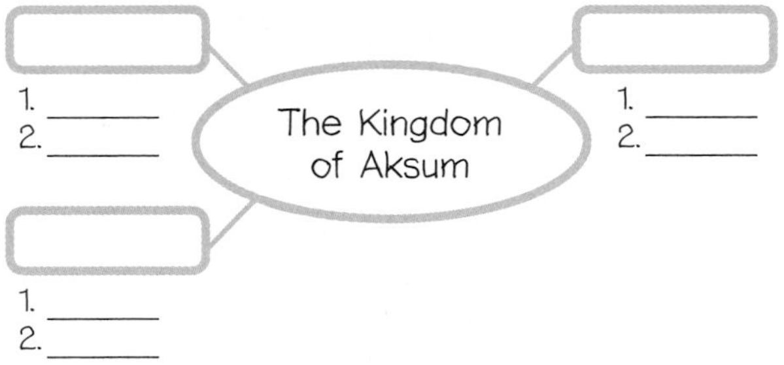

Skillbuilder Handbook, page R2

▲ **Pillar** This towering stone pillar was built around A.D. 400 to celebrate Aksum's achievements.

Words to Know

Understanding the following words will help you read this lesson:

legend a story handed down from earlier times (page 197)

*Many societies have a **legend** that explains their origins.*

network a pattern, such as that made by crisscrossing routes (page 198)

*An extensive trading **network** spanned the waters of the Red Sea.*

infant a child in the earliest period of life (page 198)

*If an **infant** inherits the throne, someone else must govern.*

unique one of a kind (page 199)

*The influence of two cultures on a region can produce a new and **unique** culture.*

The Kingdom of Aksum

TERMS & NAMES
- **Aksum**
- **Horn of Africa**
- **Adulis**
- **Ezana**
- **terrace**

Build on What You Know In Lesson 1 you learned about the kingdom of Kush. South of Kush, a new African kingdom arose as a leading center of political and economic power.

The Rise of Aksum

1 ESSENTIAL QUESTION Why did trade become important to Aksum?

The kingdom of Kush fell when Meroë was destroyed by a king of **Aksum** (AHK•SOOM). Kush was conquered by Aksum. Aksum was located in modern-day Ethiopia and Eritrea.

Perfect Trade Location Aksum arose in the **Horn of Africa**, an area shaped like a rhinoceros horn. (See map below.) This location gave Aksum access to trade to the Red Sea, Mediterranean Sea, Indian Ocean, and the Nile valley.

Arab traders built colonies and trading posts there. They found the location ideal for exchanging goods from the Indian Ocean trade, Persia, and Africa. Aksum was a meeting place for African, Arabian, and other peoples.

A legend traces the founding of the Ethiopian dynasty of Aksum to Menelik, son of King Solomon of Israel and the Queen of Sheba.

Ethiopia This photograph shows present-day Ethiopia (highlighted on map), where the ancient kingdom of Aksum was located. ▼

An International Trading Hub Like Kush, Aksum became a trading hub, or center, from which trade spread out in many directions. Traders came from Egypt, other parts of Africa, Arabia, the eastern Mediterranean, Persia, and India.

Adulis (ah•DOO•lihs), a city on the Red Sea, was the main trading port of Aksum. There traders exchanged salt, ivory, cloth, brass, iron, gold, glass, olive oil, and wine. Animal traders purchased animals such as giraffes and elephants.

REVIEW What made Aksum's location ideal for trade?

King Ezana Expands Aksum

2 ESSENTIAL QUESTION What was the effect of King Ezana on religion?

At the beginning, Aksum was small. Then, in the A.D. 300s, a bold king added territory and built a powerful nation.

A Trading Nation **Ezana** (AY•zah•nah) was a strong king who rose to power in Aksum in A.D. 325. First he took control of a trading colony on the coast of the Arabian peninsula. Then, in 350, he conquered Kush and burned Meroë to the ground.

Around this time, the empire of Aksum expanded inland and along the coast of the Red Sea. As a result, the kingdom controlled a large trading network.

Ezana had become king as an infant. While he was being educated, Ezana's mother ruled on his behalf. One of Ezana's teachers taught him about Christianity. When Ezana began to rule he converted to Christianity. He also made Christianity the official religion of Aksum. The Christian church in Aksum was linked to Alexandria, in Egypt, rather than to Rome.

REVIEW How did Ezana influence the culture of Aksum?

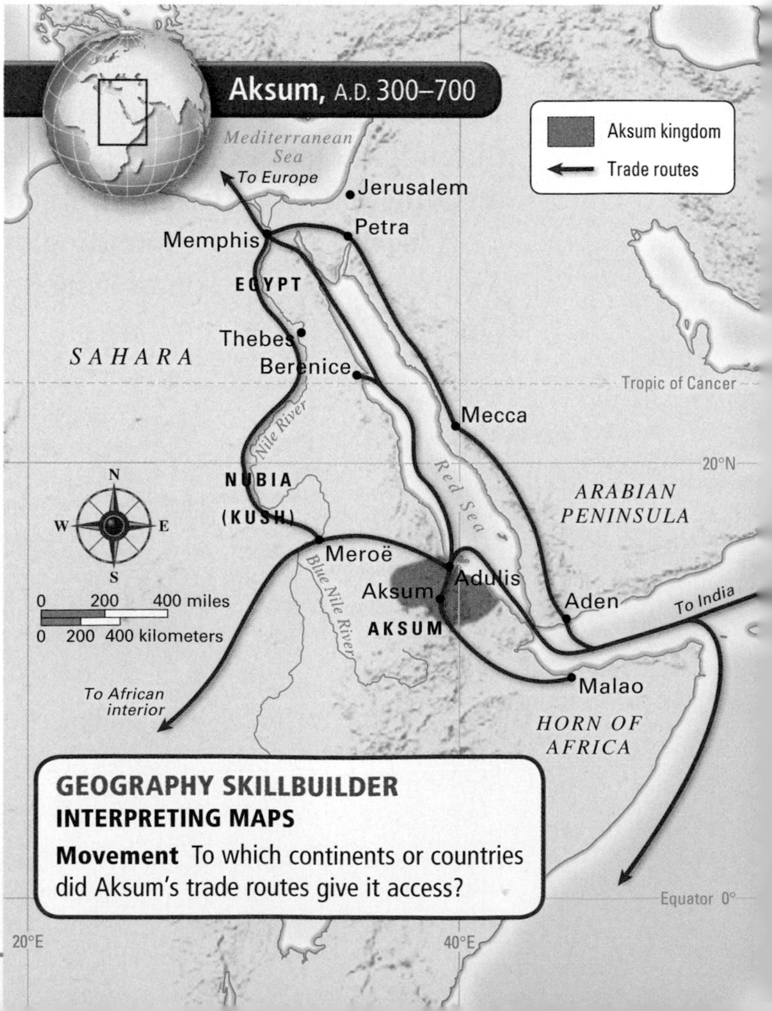

GEOGRAPHY SKILLBUILDER
INTERPRETING MAPS
Movement To which continents or countries did Aksum's trade routes give it access?

Primary Source

Background: African rulers in Egypt, Kush, and Aksum had accounts of their military campaigns carved onto stone pillars and thrones.

They followed a standard format. First they described the reasons for going to war. Then they described the war itself. Next they noted the campaign's results. Finally, they gave thanks to the gods or God for victory. The passage quoted on the right was carved onto a throne for King Ezana to celebrate his victory.

from *Aksum: An African Civilization of Late Antiquity*

By Stuart Munro-Hay

And I set up a throne here in Shado [in Aksum] by the might of the Lord of Heaven who has helped me and given me supremacy. May the Lord of Heaven reinforce my reign. And, as he has now defeated my enemies for me, may he continue to do so wherever I go. As he has now conquered for me, and has submitted my enemies to me, I wish to reign in justice and equity, without doing any injustice to my peoples.

◄ **Aksum Crown** This is an early crown from the Christian kingdom of Aksum.

DOCUMENT–BASED QUESTION
Whom is King Ezana thanking? What are his goals for ruling?

Aksum's Achievements

3 ESSENTIAL QUESTION What were some of Aksum's achievements?

A unique culture rose in Aksum. Just as the people of Kush blended Nubian and Egyptian influences, so Aksum saw a coming together of cultural influences from the Horn of Africa and southern Arabia.

Architecture Among the most impressive of these achievements were the pillars of Aksum, which builders placed around the country. Some were 60 to more than 100 feet tall. Writing carved on the pillars celebrated great victories or achievements. Builders in Egypt and Kush had used pillars in a similar fashion.

Builders constructed Aksum's tall pillars without mortar. They were carved from single stone slabs. Features included false doors and windows. Builders and architects also built large temples. Later, richly decorated Christian churches replaced the temples.

A Written Language Aksum had a written language called Ge'ez (gee•EHZ). Arabian migrants brought the language to Aksum. Ge'ez became the basis for three languages that are used in Ethiopia and Eritrea today—Amharic, Tigrinya, and Tigre. Ge'ez is still used in the Ethiopian Church.

Terraced Farming The landscape of Aksum was rugged and hilly. To adapt the land for farming, farmers built terraces. A **terrace** is a leveled-off area of land. Being flat, terraces hold moisture better than hilly land does. Terraced farming increased the amount of land that could be cultivated. Aksum's farmers also built canals, dams, and holding ponds to bring mountain water to the fields.

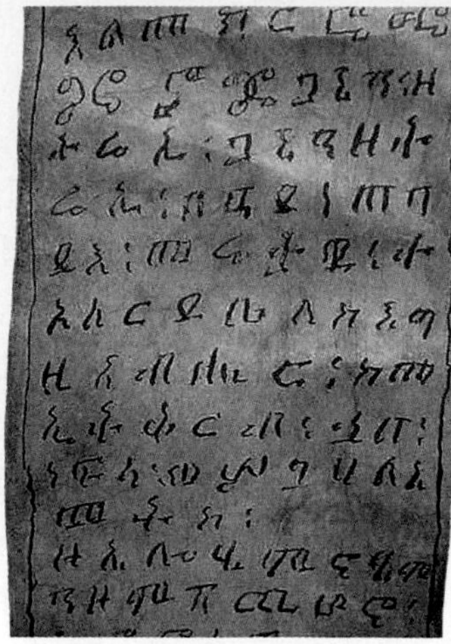
▲ **Scroll** Text written in the Ge'ez language

REVIEW How did Aksum farmers increase productivity?

Lesson Summary

- Aksum became a powerful trading center.
- King Ezana expanded Aksum's empire.
- Aksum's unique culture had long-lasting effects.

Why It Matters Now . . .

Many Ethiopians today are Christians, the religion of King Ezana.

2 Lesson Review

Homework Helper
ClassZone.com

Terms & Names

1. Explain the importance of

Aksum	Adulis	terrace
Horn of Africa	Ezana	

Using Your Notes

Finding Main Ideas Use your completed diagram to answer the following question:

2. What were some of Aksum's major achievements?

Main Ideas

3. What factors led to the rise of Aksum?

4. How did Ezana expand Aksum's power?

5. What kinds of structures were built in Aksum, and what purpose did they serve?

Critical Thinking

6. Drawing Conclusions What did the pillars of Aksum reveal about the culture?

7. Making Inferences In what ways did the adoption of Christianity as the official religion affect the culture of Aksum?

Activity

Designing a Coin Write a short motto for King Ezana. The motto should say something memorable about him or his reign. Draw a coin showing the motto and sketch Ezana.

Activity Extend Lesson 2

Design a Pillar

Goal: To understand the architecture of Kush and Aksum, and the purpose it served, by creating a pillar and decorating its sides

Materials & Supplies
- poster board
- pens, pencils, or markers
- scissors

Prepare

1. Look at the example of a pillar from Aksum on page 196 and read the caption.
2. Reread the information on the monument of Pianhki in Kush (page 191) and the pillars of Aksum (page 199) in this chapter.

Do the Activity

1. Draw a pillar to fill up a poster board.
2. Design drawings to celebrate the achievements of one of the following: your school, your neighborhood, your city, your state, or your country.
3. Color your drawings with crayons or magic markers.
4. Cut out the pillar from the poster board so that it is free-standing.
5. Give a title to the pillar you have designed.

Follow-Up

1. Why might a pillar be an effective way to celebrate achievement?
2. How do the images you used on your pillar celebrate achievement?

Extension

Making a Presentation Display your pillar in the classroom. Explain what your pillar is meant to celebrate and how it expresses the beliefs of your community.

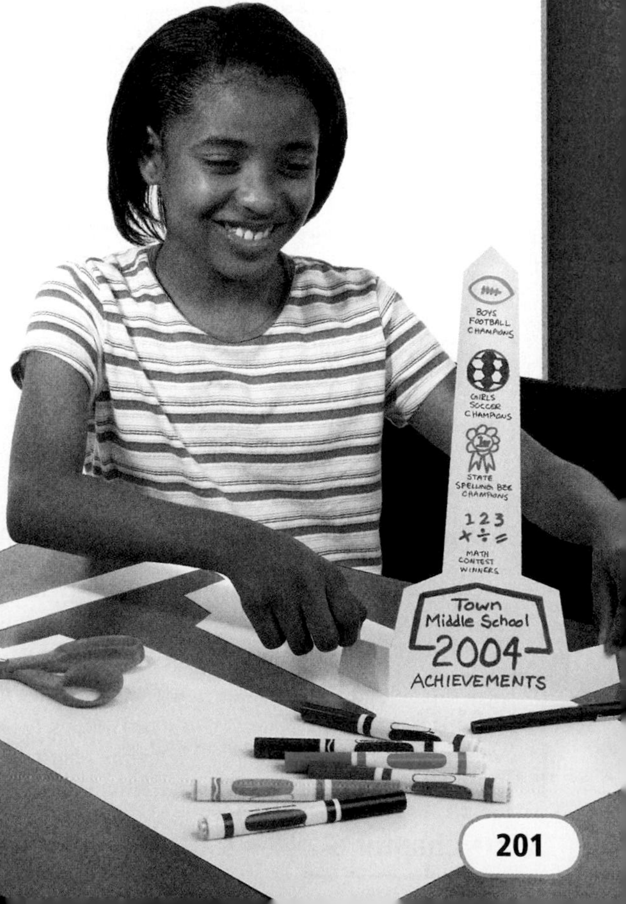

Lesson 3

MAIN IDEAS

1. **Geography** The people of west, central, and southern Africa adapted to life in a variety of environments.
2. **Economics** The Nok people were the first ironworkers of West Africa.
3. **Geography** Migration by the Bantu people from West Africa populated central and southern Africa.

TAKING NOTES

Reading Skill: Explaining Geographic Patterns

Recognizing geographic patterns means seeing the overall shape or trend of geographic characteristics. In Lesson 3, look for details about the nomadic migrations of the Bantu people of Africa. Record the information on a web diagram.

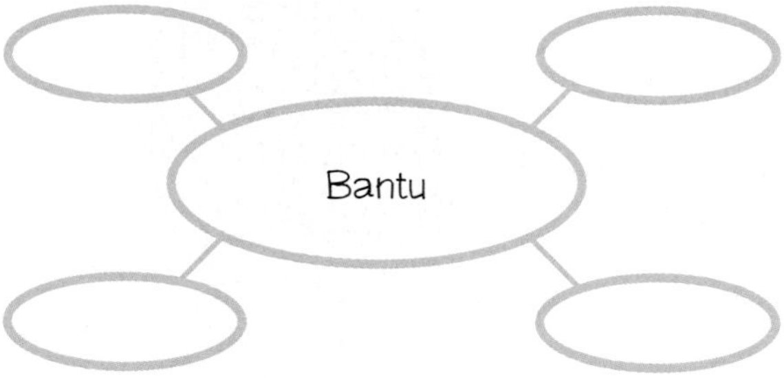

Skillbuilder Handbook, page R16

▲ **Sculpture** This Nok terra cotta (ceramic clay) sculpture depicts a seated dignitary, a person of high status.

Words to Know

Understanding the following words will help you read this lesson:

alternate to happen in turns, first one and then the other (page 203)

The rainy and dry seasons ***alternate,*** *giving the sense of an unending cycle.*

ironsmith a person who works with iron (page 205)

The farmer visited several ***ironsmiths*** *to see which one would repair his tools for the lowest cost.*

herd to tend to or watch over sheep, cattle, or other animals (page 206)

Some groups of Africa's Bantu people were renowned for their ***herding*** *skills.*

intermarry to marry a member of another group (page 207)

Individuals from the two cultures ***intermarried.***

West, Central, and Southern Africa

TERMS & NAMES
- animism
- griot
- Nok
- Bantu
- migration

Build on What You Know You have been learning about some of the people living in eastern Africa. You will now learn about the people of west, central, and southern Africa.

Early Life in Africa

1 ESSENTIAL QUESTION What were some of the environments that the people of west, central, and southern Africa had to adapt to?

As the Sahara dried up, about 4000 B.C., people moved south into West Africa around the Niger River, just as they had moved eastward into the Nile valley. West, central, and southern Africa included savannahs (flat, grassy, mostly treeless plains) and rain forests.

Regions of Africa: West, Central, and Southern Africa

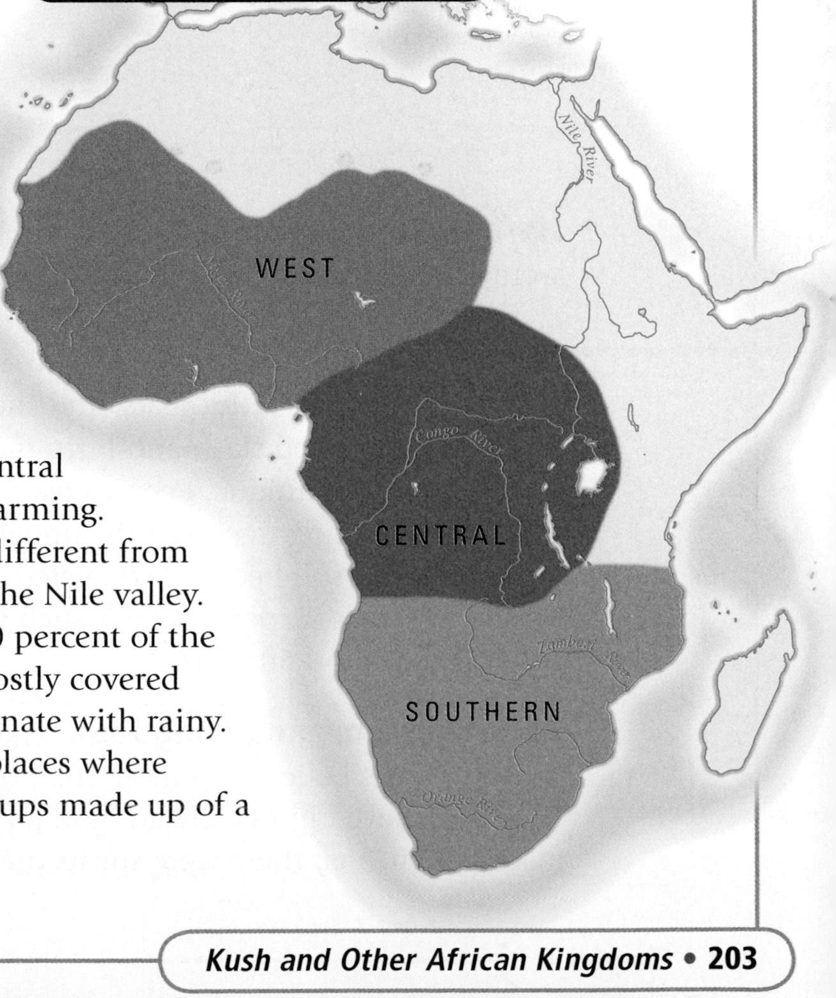

A Variety of Environments

The rain forests in west and central Africa did not support much farming. People's lives there were very different from the settled lives of farmers in the Nile valley. Savannahs cover more than 40 percent of the African continent. They are mostly covered with grasses. Dry seasons alternate with rainy. These savannahs became the places where most people lived in small groups made up of a number of families.

Geography

Desertification

The Sahara has been expanding for thousands of years. This expansion of dry, desertlike conditions into fertile areas is called desertification.

Normally, desertification results from nature's long-term climate cycles. However, as the illustrations show, human activity has sped up the process.

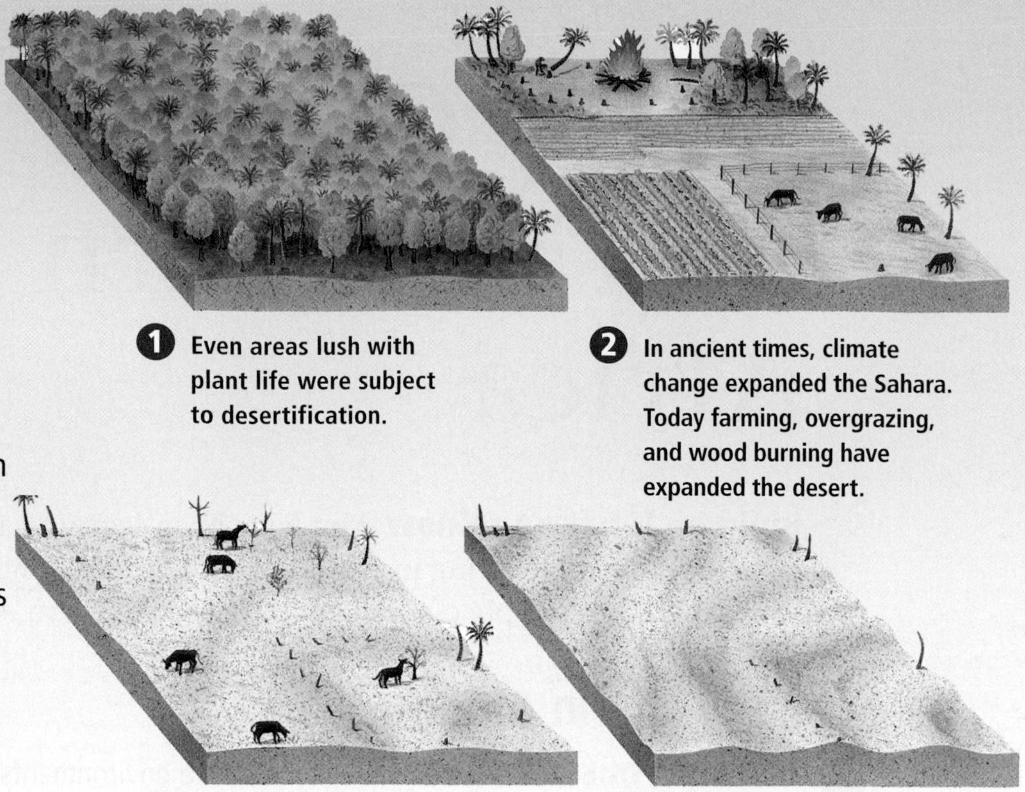

1. Even areas lush with plant life were subject to desertification.
2. In ancient times, climate change expanded the Sahara. Today farming, overgrazing, and wood burning have expanded the desert.
3. Due to overuse of the land for farming, grazing, and burning wood for fuel, dry grasses died and were replaced by shrubs.
4. Because there was less plant life covering the soil, rain evaporated quickly. The wind then carried away the fertile topsoil, leaving barren wasteland.

GEOGRAPHY SKILLBUILDER
INTERPRETING VISUALS
Human-Environment Interaction
What impact would desertification be likely to have on people in the areas affected?

Herding and Farming South of the Sahara, the savannahs were filled with herds of animals. Mainly because of climate change and also desertification, shown above, the soil was thin and not ideal for farming. As a result, many people were herders. These people kept cattle, goats, and sheep.

Others practiced slash-and-burn farming. This was a very early farming technique. People cleared the land by cutting down and burning trees and the undergrowth. After a few years, the thin soil became exhausted. Then the people moved on to new areas. Experts believe such farming began in Africa sometime around 6000 B.C.

Belief Systems and Language Like other ancient peoples, most Africans believed in more than one god, though they usually believed in one creator god greater than the others. They also thought that there were spirits present in animals, plants, or natural forces. This belief that everything possesses a soul is called **animism**.

These early societies did not have a written language. They preserved their history by telling stories. In some places, storytellers known as **griots** (gree•OHZ) kept the history alive. Their stories were lively retellings of past events.

REVIEW How did people live on the plains of Africa?

The Nok Culture

2 ESSENTIAL QUESTION What role did ironworking play in Nok culture?

Many early peoples in West Africa made objects out of materials that decayed, such as plant fiber. Few artifacts survived. However, archaeologists have found evidence of one culture that made objects that have survived.

Sculpture This Nok sculpture shows a half-human, half-bird creature. ▼

Ironworkers Between the Benue and Niger rivers—a distance of about 300 miles—scientists have found small clay statues. In addition, they discovered waste products from ironmaking, charcoal, and iron-smelting furnaces. Archaeologists were surprised to find that iron had been produced in this area before 500 B.C. They had thought, based on previous evidence, that ironmaking occurred only in the eastern part of Africa.

One early West African people who produced iron were called the **Nok**. They lived in an area that today is southeastern Nigeria. It appears that the Nok did not follow the pattern of some early ironmakers in other parts of the world, who first produced copper and then bronze. Instead, the Nok seem to have moved right into ironmaking. They were among the first western African people to make iron.

Using Iron To produce iron, the Nok mined iron ore. Then they smelted the iron. Ironsmiths worked the iron into tools and weapons.Some of the tools and weapons made their way into trade routes across West Africa.

REVIEW What was the pattern of some early ironworkers, and how did the Nok differ?

The Bantu Migrations

3 ESSENTIAL QUESTION Where did the Bantu peoples first live, and where did they move to?

The **Bantu** people lived in the same area as the Nok. The Bantu spread across Africa in what was one of the greatest movements in history. They slowly moved south and east along a frontier, opening up new lands to farming and herding. The Bantu brought farming and iron to Africa south of an imaginary line from Nigeria in the west to Kenya in the east.

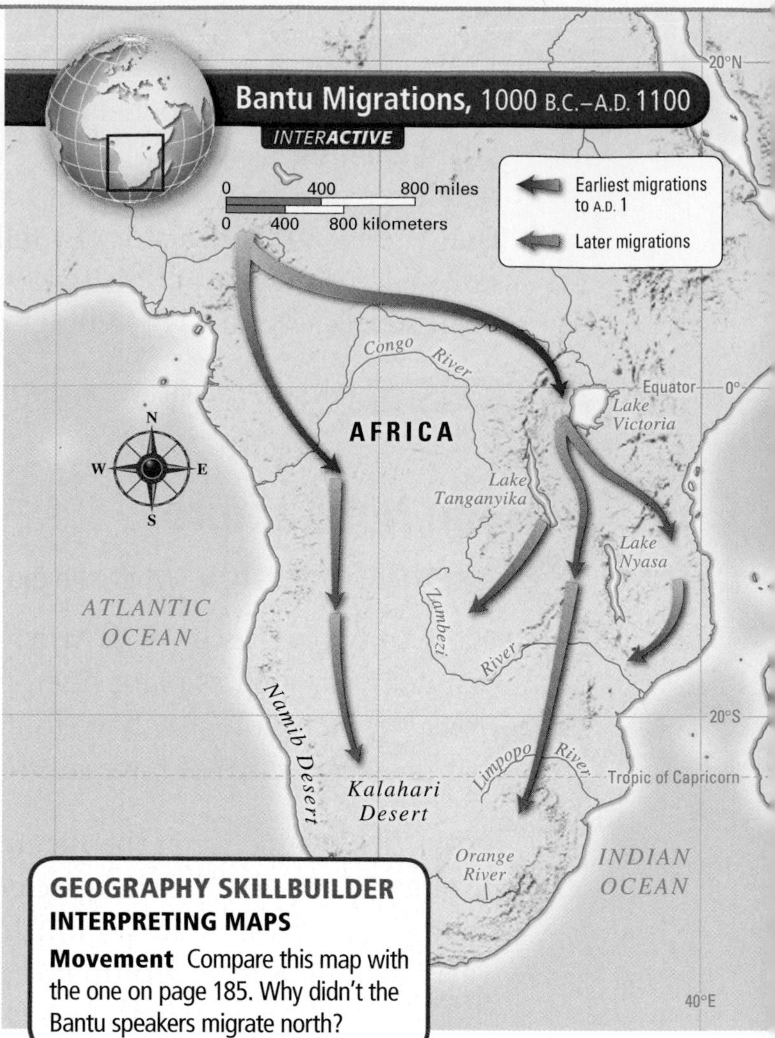

GEOGRAPHY SKILLBUILDER
INTERPRETING MAPS
Movement Compare this map with the one on page 185. Why didn't the Bantu speakers migrate north?

Bantu Speakers Some African peoples spoke similar languages based on a parent language that historians called Bantu. The word *Bantu* itself means "the people." The Bantu-speaking peoples were not one group. They were many groups who had similar cultures. They were farmers, herders, and eventually ironworkers.

Migration Begins About 3,000 years ago the Bantu speakers began moving out of their lands near the Benue and Niger rivers in West Africa. They migrated south and east. A **migration** is a move from one region to another.

The migration of the Bantu was a slow process that took thousands of years. Some groups eventually settled in the rain forest along the Congo River. Some Bantu lived in small villages and farmed along the riverbanks. Later, Bantu-speaking groups moved south beyond the forest to the grasslands of southern Africa. There they began raising animals such as cattle and growing grain crops. Bantu farmers adapted the way they farmed to their new environments.

Bantu speakers kept their ability to make iron. Ironmaking set them apart from others living in areas to which the Bantu migrated. Their iron tools helped them in their main task of farming.

Effects of Migration The Bantu speakers moved to areas where other people already lived. The Bantu adopted cattle herding from peoples near present-day Lake Victoria. They displaced hunting-gathering peoples. Bantu speakers exchanged ideas and customs with people in the areas they entered, and intermarried with them. They shared their knowledge of ironmaking and agriculture. As the Bantu speakers migrated, their languages spread.

REVIEW To which areas of Africa did the Bantu speakers migrate?

Mask This mask was created by a Kuba craftsperson. The Kuba were a Bantu-speaking people. ▼

Lesson Summary

- Early societies living on the savannah south of the Sahara practiced herding and farming.
- The Nok made iron tools for use and for trade.
- Migration of Bantu speakers spread the Bantu language and culture.

Why It Matters Now . . .

Despite the great variety of languages and cultures in Bantu-speaking Africa, there are also connections based on a common heritage.

3 Lesson Review

Homework Helper
ClassZone.com

Terms & Names

1. Explain the importance of

animism | Nok | migration
griot | Bantu

Using Your Notes

Explaining Geographic Patterns Use your completed web diagram to answer the following question:

2. In what two ways did most of the peoples of West Africa support themselves and their families?

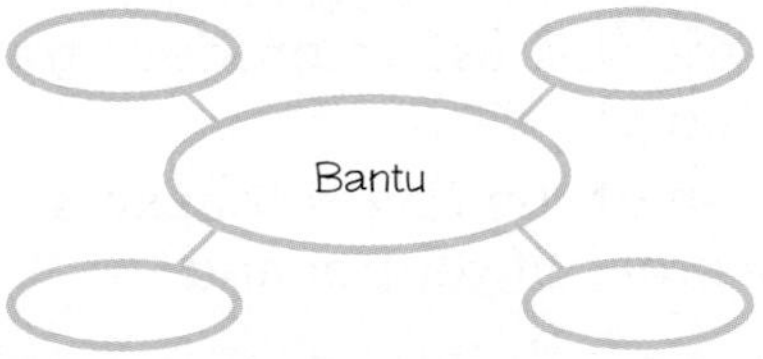

Main Ideas

3. Why did people living on the plains of central Africa practice herding?
4. Why were archaeologists surprised to discover that the Nok produced iron?
5. Why was the migration of Bantu speakers so slow?

Critical Thinking

6. **Understanding Causes** Why did the Bantus overwhelm the people into whose territory they migrated?
7. **Comparing** Compare the importance of ironmaking in the Nok and Bantu cultures.

Activity

Internet Activity Use the Internet to research the Bantu migrations. Then create a chart showing the causes and effects of the migrations.

INTERNET KEYWORD: *Bantu migrations*

Chapter 6 Review

VISUAL SUMMARY

Kush and Other African Kingdoms

Geography

- Nubia and Egypt interacted over the centuries.
- The people of Africa lived in different environments.
- Bantu speakers traveled from West Africa to central and southern Africa.

Government

- The Kush kingdoms conquered Egypt and ruled Egypt and Nubia.
- The kingdom of Aksum absorbed Kush in the region of Nubia.

Economics

- The Kushite kingdom of Meroë was an economic center linking Egypt and the interior of Africa.
- The Nok people were accomplished ironworkers.

Culture

- The kingdom of Aksum converted to Christianity.
- Aksum's achievements in architecture, language, and farming were long-lasting.

TERMS & NAMES

Explain why the words in each set below are linked with each other.

1. **Piankhi** and **Kush**
2. **Aksum** and **Adulis**
3. **Bantu** and **migration**

MAIN IDEAS

Nubia and the Land of Kush (pages 188–195)

4. How did geography help to increase trade between Nubia and Egypt?
5. In what way did iron contribute to the economic and commercial development of Meroë?

The Kingdom of Aksum (pages 196–201)

6. What official act of King Ezana led to lasting cultural change?
7. What is the cultural legacy of Ge′ez?

West, Central, and Southern Africa (pages 202–207)

8. What processes did the Nok use to produce trade goods? to produce tools?
9. How did the migration of the Bantu speakers affect culture in the areas of central and southern Africa?

CRITICAL THINKING Big Ideas: Culture

10. **UNDERSTANDING CAUSE AND EFFECT** How did contact with Egypt affect Nubian culture?
11. **DRAWING CONCLUSIONS** What impact might Meroë's importance as a trade center have had on the interaction of cultures?
12. **COMPARING AND CONTRASTING** What two cultural influences did Aksum blend?

ALTERNATIVE ASSESSMENT

1. **WRITING ACTIVITY** You have read about the Bantu migrations in Lesson 3. Write a report about what the migrations might have been like. Read your report to the class.
2. **INTERDISCIPLINARY ACTIVITY—GEOGRAPHY** Work with a partner or a small group. Brainstorm places on or near the Nile that you have learned about in Chapter 6. Draw a map showing each place on your list. Draw symbols or add labels to indicate why each place was important.
3. **STARTING WITH A STORY** Starting with a Story Review the essay you wrote in which you compared your ideas about Jerusalem before and after your trip. Write a 60-second TV news story about your journey.

Technology Activity

4. **CREATING A NEWSLETTER** Use the Internet and library to research desertification. Create a newsletter about the topic.
   - Present information on desertification's rate of growth.
   - Show how it has affected Africa.
   - Show what is being done about desertification.

Research Links
ClassZone.com

Reading Charts Use the chart below to answer the questions.

Interaction of Egypt and Kush	
Language	Kushites brought back hieroglyphic writing to Kush from Egypt.
Religion	Kushites worshiped many Egyptian gods, but had some distinct gods of their own.
Architecture	Kushites built pyramids similar to those of Egypt, but with steeper sides. They also sometimes built temples onto the sides of pyramids.
Art	Kushites produced wall paintings, pottery, jewelry, and sculpture.
Burial practices	Kings were buried in splendid stone-faced pyramids.
Government	The ruler was treated as a god.

1. **What objects were important in both architecture and burial practices?**
   A. sculptures
   B. pyramids
   C. jewelry
   D. hieroglyphics

2. **How would you describe the relationship between Egypt and Kush?**
   A. They influenced each other greatly.
   B. They did not have much influence on each other.
   C. They were enemies.
   D. They had no relationship at all.

Test Practice
ClassZone.com

Additional Test Practice, pp. S1–S33

Writing About History

Writing Model
ClassZone.com

Research Reports:
Daily Life in Ancient Times

Purpose: To write a research report on an aspect of daily life in ancient times

Audience: Someone involved in a similar aspect of your daily life

You read many details in this unit that showed what life in ancient Egypt was like: a hog's tooth crushed in a sweet cake, priests feeding meals to statues, children playing with animal toys. How do historians know these things? They do research. By studying primary and secondary sources, they piece together an understanding of daily life. You can learn more about daily life in ancient times by writing a research report yourself. A **research report** is a composition that pulls together information from several primary sources or secondary sources or both.

▲ Egyptian mural of a hunter

Organization & Focus

Your assignment is to write a 500- to 700-word research report about an aspect of daily life in ancient Egypt or Kush. Possible topics include education, meals, clothing, religion, or sports and games. In addition to an introduction, body, and conclusion, research reports also have a **bibliography**—a list of the sources used in preparing the report.

Choosing a Topic Review Chapters 5 and 6 looking for information on daily life. Think about which aspect of ancient daily life seems most connected to your daily life today. For example, if you are an athlete, you might be especially interested in sports in ancient times. Focus on your subject so that you can cover it thoroughly in your report.

Identifying Purpose and Audience Your purpose is to make ancient history seem meaningful and alive to a reader. Choose a reader who shares your interest in your topic. For example, if you are writing about sports, you might choose your soccer coach for your audience.

Finding Details Look for vivid details about your topic, such as the objects people used, the ways they behaved, and any laws, rules, or rituals they had. Take notes on a graphic organizer like the one below.

Aspect of Daily Life		
Objects	Behaviors	Laws, Rules, or Rituals

Research & Technology

Plan on using at least four different sources for your research report.

- a primary source
- an encyclopedia article
- a Web site
- a book

As you research, take notes on note cards. On each card, record the source—the title, author, publisher, date, page number, or Web address. You will need this information for your bibliography.

Technology Tip Fortunately for students of ancient civilization, translations of some documents, as well as photographs of some artifacts, are online. Start your Internet research by visiting ClassZone.com, which has links to sites about life in the ancient world.

Outlining and Drafting Group your note cards into categories and arrange the categories in a logical order. Use your categories and notes to outline your report. Follow the outline as you write your draft.

Evaluation & Revision

Share your first draft with test readers to see what still needs work. You may need to do any of the following:

- Add more information or stronger examples.
- Take something out that doesn't belong.
- Move something to a better, more logical location.

When you are satisfied with your report, prepare your bibliography. Use your language arts textbook or school handbook to find the correct format for each source.

Self-Check

Does my report have

- ☐ a clearly focused topic?
- ☐ supporting details drawn from the sources required?
- ☐ a strong conclusion?
- ☐ a bibliography in the proper format?

Publish & Present

Make a neat final copy of your report. Give it to your reader and explain why you chose him or her. Invite comments on your report.

UNIT 4

Ancient Asian and American Civilizations

Interact with History ▶

A Pilgrimage to Sanchi, about 50 B.C.
Stupas are Buddhist holy places. They were built to hold relics, or physical remains, of the Buddha—the teacher whose ideas are the basis of Buddhism. A Buddhist king began to build the Great Stupa at Sanchi, India, in the 200s B.C.

Why do people build holy places?

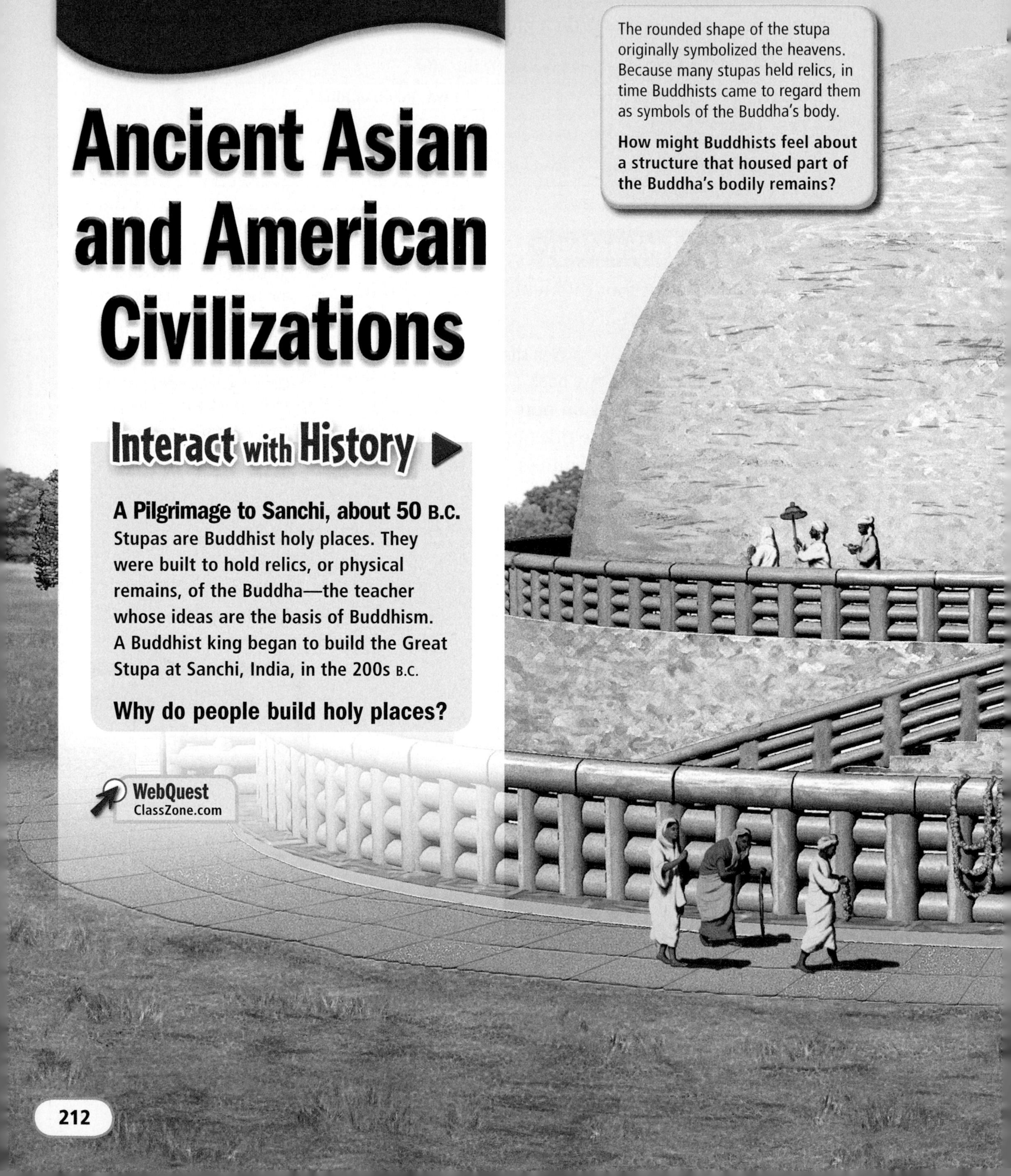

The rounded shape of the stupa originally symbolized the heavens. Because many stupas held relics, in time Buddhists came to regard them as symbols of the Buddha's body.

How might Buddhists feel about a structure that housed part of the Buddha's bodily remains?

WebQuest
ClassZone.com

Chapter 7
Ancient India

Chapter 8
Ancient China

Chapter 9
Ancient America

This is the Southern Gateway. Some of the carvings show scenes of the Buddha's birth. Others show events from the life of Asoka, the king who started building this monument. He ruled India according to Buddhist law.

What lessons might these carved scenes be designed to teach?

Worshipers brought offerings of flowers, lamps, and other gifts. Some lay flat on the ground in worship. Others walked around the stupa several times, thinking about the Buddha. To ancient Indians, the circular path stood for the daily path of the sun and the cycle of life and death.

Why would thinking about life and death help a person to worship?

Chapter 7 Ancient India

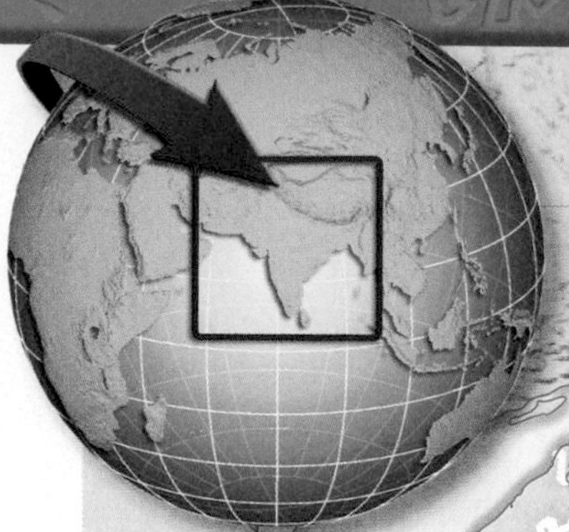

Before You Read: Knowledge Rating

Recognizing what you already know about each of these terms can help you understand the chapter.

In your notebook, rate how well you know each term.

3 = I know what this word means.

2 = I've seen this word, but I don't know what it means.

1 = I've never seen this word before.

Define each term as you read.

Big Ideas About Ancient India

Culture Many societies rely on family roles and social roles to keep order.

Indians saw themselves as belonging to one of four social classes called castes. These broad classes were divided into many smaller groups based on jobs. In time, a fifth group of people called the untouchables came to be considered the lowest group in society.

Integrated Technology

eEdition
- Interactive Maps
- Interactive Visuals
- Starting with a Story

INTERNET RESOURCES

Go to **ClassZone.com** for
- WebQuest
- Homework Helper
- Research Links
- Internet Activities
- Quizzes
- Maps
- Test Practice
- Current Events

INDIA

2500 B.C.
Well-planned cities are thriving by the Indus River.
◄ (necklace, 3000 to 2000 B.C.)

1500 B.C.
Aryans begin to migrate into India.

2500 B.C. 2000 B.C. 1500 B.C.

WORLD

1472 B.C.
Queen Hatshepsut begins to rule Egypt.
◄ (statue of Hatshepsut, late 1400s B.C.)

India: Physical Geography and Resources, 300s B.C.

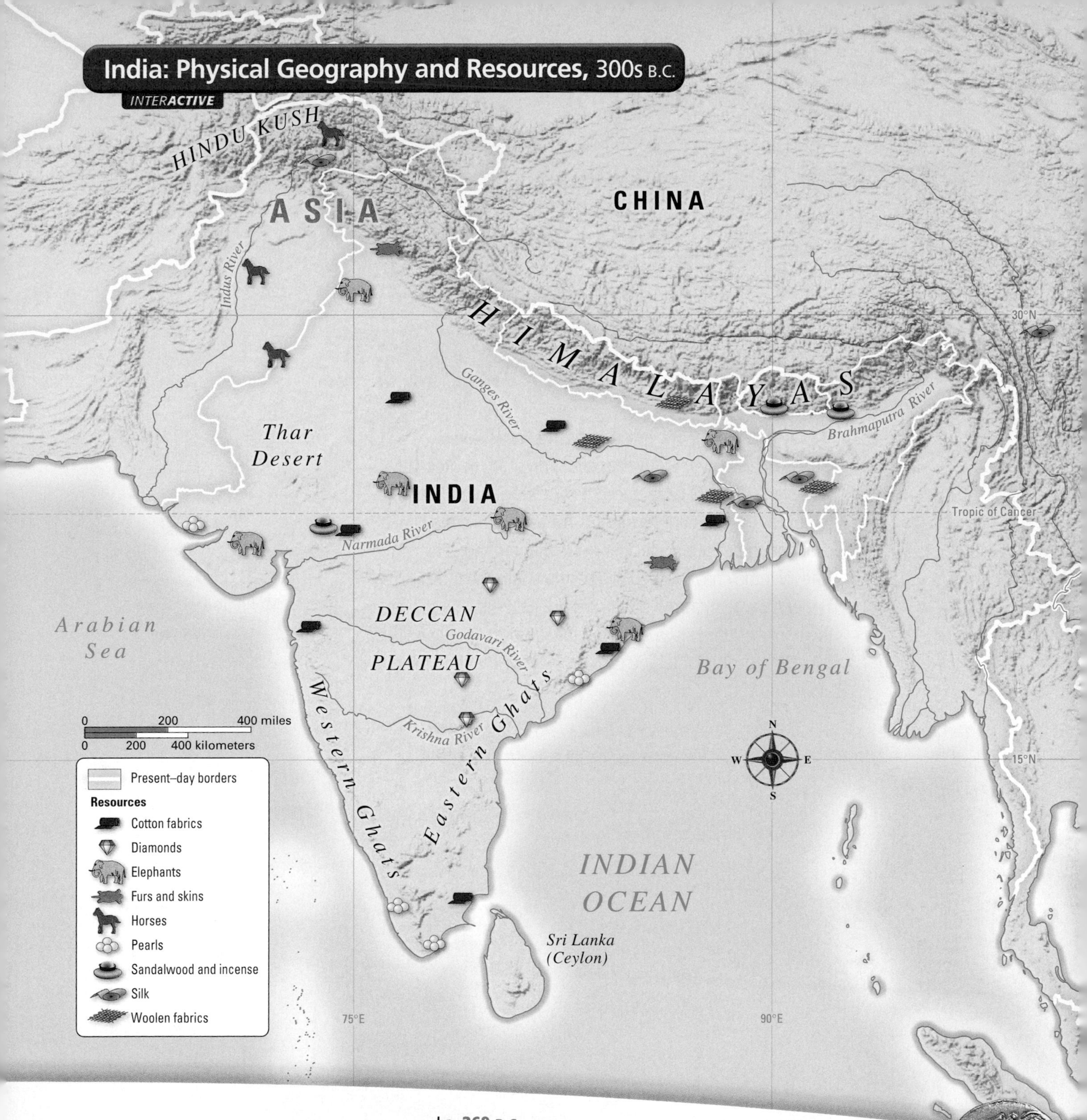

563 B.C.
Siddhartha Gautama, who will become the Buddha, is born.

c. 269 B.C.
King Asoka, who ruled by Buddhist principles, takes the throne.

c. A.D. 375
Chandra Gupta II begins to rule.
(coin, A.D. 300s) ▶

500 B.C. — 200 B.C. — A.D. 100 — A.D. 400

500 B.C.
The Nok people are using iron in West Africa.

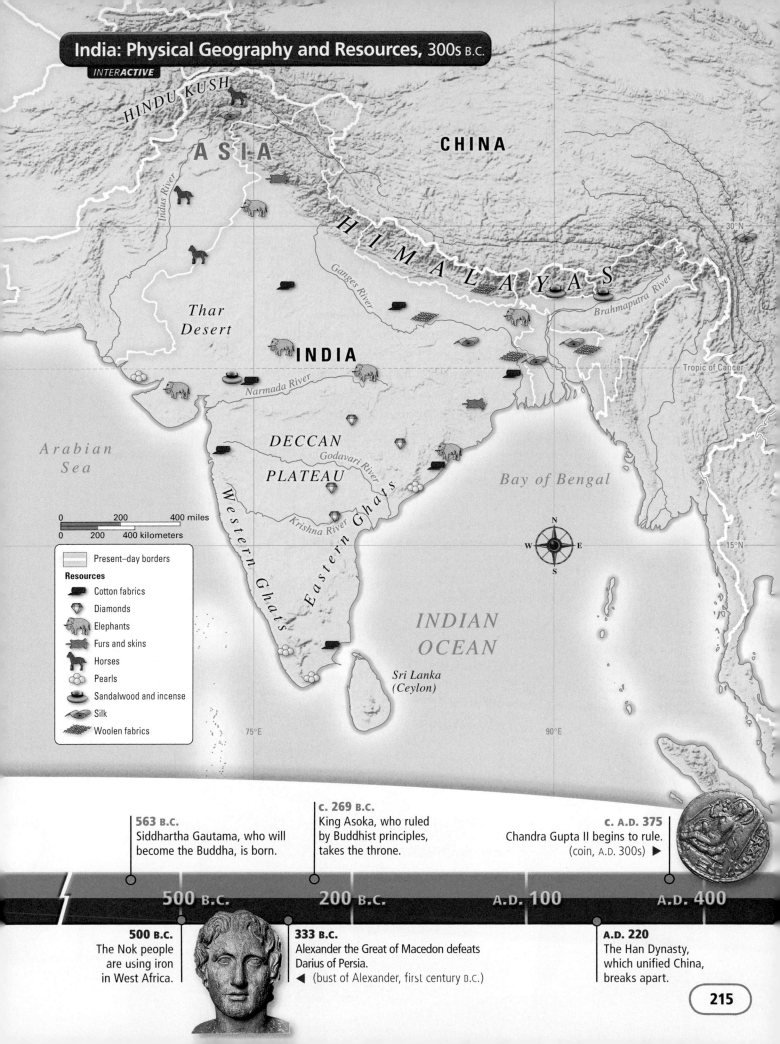

333 B.C.
Alexander the Great of Macedon defeats Darius of Persia.
◀ (bust of Alexander, first century B.C.)

A.D. 220
The Han Dynasty, which unified China, breaks apart.

Starting with a Story

Saraswati EARTHQUAKE

Background: For many years, the Saraswati (suh•RUHS•wuh•tee) River existed only in myth. Recently, however, scientists have traced its historic path and begun to unlock the secret of its decline. An earthquake may have changed the course of smaller rivers that fed the Saraswati. One river may have turned west to flow into the Indus River. The extra water caused disastrous floods. People who lived on the banks of the Saraswati faced the opposite problem. Their river disappeared. Imagine you live in a city that had been built along the Saraswati.

The Saraswati River ▶

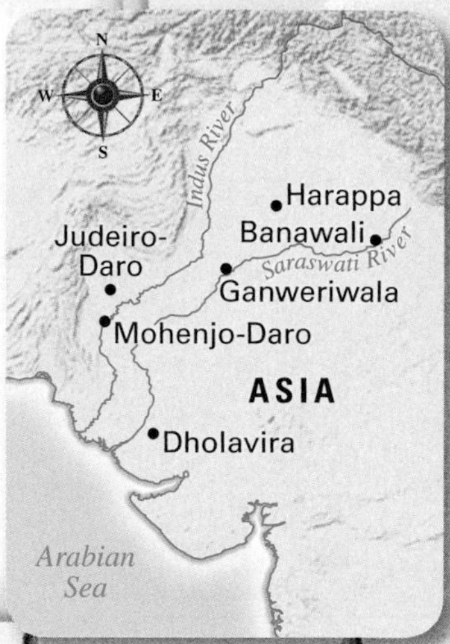

You are a trader. For years, you have made a good living sailing a boat down the Saraswati River to the Arabian Sea and then to Mesopotamia. There you sold Indian goods: precious woods, gold, deep red beads, milky white pearls, ivory combs, and fine-spun cotton. In exchange, you bought silver, tin, wool fabric, and grain.

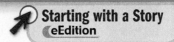

One day, everything suddenly changes. Returning from a trip, you dock your boat in the dockyard built next to the river and go home. Early the next morning, you awake from a sound sleep to feel the house shaking. Dishes clatter, and screams rise from the street. When the shaking finally stops, you cautiously step outside to find out what happened.

The scene outside is shocking. The top floor of the two-story house next door has toppled over, exposing the stairway. Littering the street are piles of mud bricks from the upper stories of other buildings.

Back inside the house, you pick up the broken pieces of painted plates. As you clean up the mess, you have no idea that an even worse disaster is about to strike.

Several hours later, you go outside to check on your neighbors. Walking past the river, you notice that the water level has dropped. All day, it falls until finally nothing is left but a few puddles in the low places of the riverbed. One by one, the boats in the dockyard settle in the mud.

Surely, you tell yourself, the river will return. But the days pass, and nothing changes. Finally, you face the awful fact that the Saraswati has probably dried up forever. You and your neighbors must decide what to do.

Should you rebuild your city or move?

Reading & Writing

1. **READING: Setting** The setting is the time and place of a story. How does the setting contribute to the problem the trader faces?
2. **WRITING: Persuasion** Imagine that you joined a group of your neighbors discussing whether to stay or leave. When they asked for your opinion, you said you wanted to think about it. Now write a letter explaining your opinion and reasons for it. Discuss the costs and benefits of staying versus the costs and benefits of leaving.

Lesson 1

MAIN IDEAS

1. **Geography** In India, mountains and seasonal winds shape the climate and affect agriculture.
2. **Government** The earliest Indian civilization built well-organized cities near the Indus River.
3. **Culture** Harappan civilization produced writing, a prosperous way of life, and a widely shared culture.

TAKING NOTES

Reading Skill: Making Generalizations

A generalization is a broad judgment based on information. As you read Lesson 1, record information on a chart like the one below. Later, you will be asked to make a generalization.

Geography and Indian Life	
Physical geography of India	
Cities in the Indus Valley	
Harappan culture	

Skillbuilder Handbook, page R8

▲ **Priest-King** Scholars believe this seven-inch-tall sculpture is of a priest or king from the ancient city of Mohenjo-Daro.

Words to Know

Understanding the following words will help you read this lesson:

range a group of things in a line or row, such as mountains (page 220)
*Of all of the mountain **ranges** on Earth, the Himalayas are the highest.*

deposit to put or lay down (page 220)
*The river **deposited** soil and debris that it had swept up a great distance upstream.*

mysterious difficult to understand (page 221)
*Experts have not figured out the meaning of the **mysterious** writing that appears on the objects.*

site a location or position (page 223)
*Though expecting to find the **site** of religious buildings at the ruined city, archaeologists found none.*

Geography and Indian Life

TERMS & NAMES
- subcontinent
- Hindu Kush
- Himalayas
- monsoon
- Harappan civilization
- planned city

Build on What You Know Have you ever visited a part of the United States with a different climate? Some regions of the country receive much more rainfall than other regions do. As you are about to learn, India has two distinct seasons: a rainy season and a dry season.

Physical Geography of India

1 **ESSENTIAL QUESTION** How do mountains and seasonal winds shape the climate of India?

India is a **subcontinent**, which is a large landmass that is like a continent, only smaller. The subcontinent includes present-day Bangladesh, Bhutan, India, Nepal, and most of Pakistan. It is often referred to as South Asia. Geographers think the kite-shaped Indian subcontinent used to be a separate land. It inched north until it hit Asia. The collision pushed up mountains where the two lands met.

Ganges River The Ganges is one of the major rivers of India. Most Indians consider it holy. As the photograph shows, the banks of the Ganges today are heavily populated. ▼

Mountains and Waterways Those high mountains tower over the northern borders of India. They form several mountain ranges, including the **Hindu Kush** (HIHN•doo kush) and the **Himalayas** (HIHM•uh•LAY•uhs).

In addition to tall mountains, the subcontinent has several great rivers. These include the Ganges (GAN•JEEZ) and the Indus. Like other rivers you have studied, these two rivers carry water for irrigation. The silt they deposit makes the land fertile. The Indus River valley was the home of the first Indian civilization. In ancient times, another river called the Saraswati (suh•RUHS•wuh•tee) ran parallel to the Indus. The Saraswati area was also home to great cities. However, it dried up, perhaps because of an earthquake. (See Starting with a Story on pages 216–217.)

The Arabian Sea, Indian Ocean, and Bay of Bengal surround India. Ancient Indians sailed these waters to other ancient lands, such as Mesopotamia. This travel helped encourage trade.

Climate The tall mountains help block cold north winds from reaching much of India. As a result, temperatures are generally warm there. In addition, seasonal winds called **monsoons** shape India's climate. Because of the monsoon, India has a dry season in the winter and a rainy season

Vocabulary Strategy

The word *monsoon* is also sometimes used as a **synonym** for the summer rainy season.

Geography

Monsoons

A monsoon is a seasonal wind. India and Pakistan have two main monsoons: a summer monsoon and a winter monsoon.

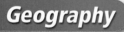

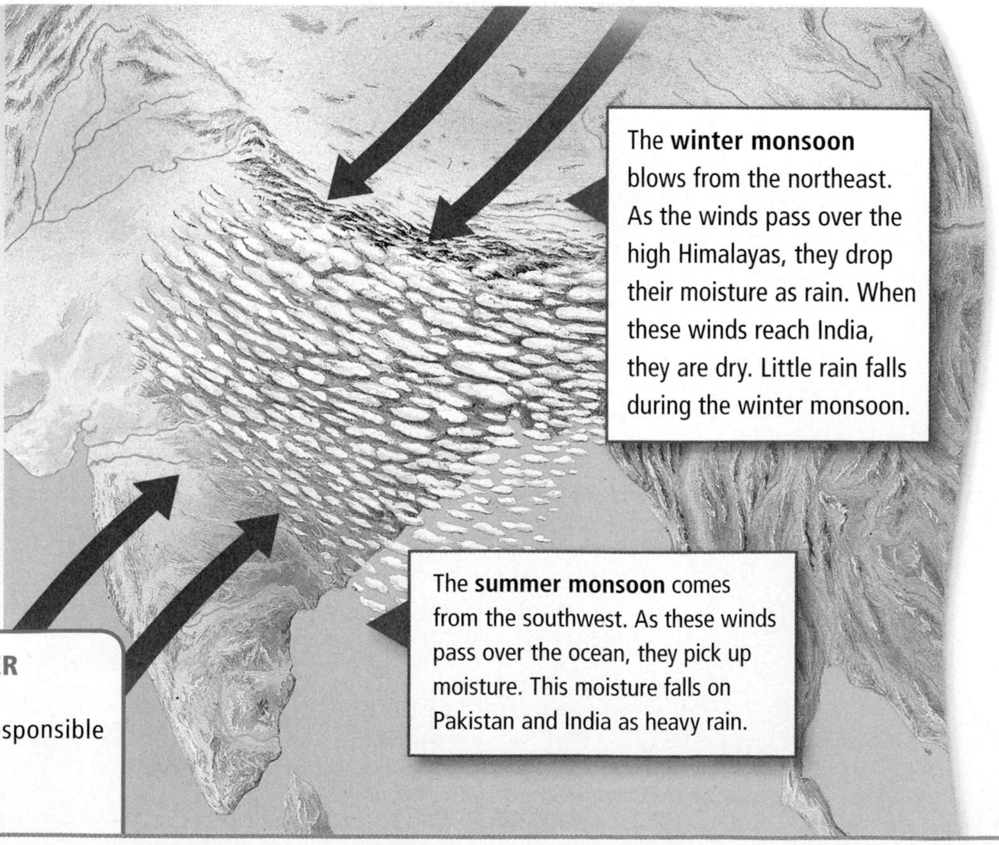

The **winter monsoon** blows from the northeast. As the winds pass over the high Himalayas, they drop their moisture as rain. When these winds reach India, they are dry. Little rain falls during the winter monsoon.

The **summer monsoon** comes from the southwest. As these winds pass over the ocean, they pick up moisture. This moisture falls on Pakistan and India as heavy rain.

GEOGRAPHY SKILLBUILDER
INTERPRETING VISUALS
Region Which monsoon is responsible for causing a rainy season?

in the summer. The summer monsoon provides rain for India's crops. But these rains can also cause severe floods.

REVIEW How do India's rivers and climate affect agriculture?

Cities in the Indus Valley

2 ESSENTIAL QUESTION Why was the earliest Indian civilization located near the Indus River?

Huge earth mounds dot the Indus Valley. Near them, people found burnt bricks and tiny stone seals covered with a mysterious writing. These finds caused further exploration of the mounds. Archaeologists uncovered the ruins of an ancient civilization.

▲ **Indus Valley Seal**
This seal clearly shows an elephant, but scholars don't know why. No one has figured out how to read the pictographs above the animal.

Early Inhabitants History in the Indus River valley followed the same pattern as in Sumer and Egypt. As in other regions, civilization along the Indus River began with agriculture. The earliest farmers raised wheat and barley. By 3000 B.C., they were growing cotton and making it into fabric—the first people in Asia to do so. They domesticated cattle, sheep, goats, and chickens. They also learned how to make copper and bronze tools, which were more effective than stone tools.

People in the villages traded with one another. Over time, the Indus Valley people began to trade with people from farther away. The wealth they gained from trade helped them to develop a more complex culture.

Great Cities By 2500 B.C., some villages had grown to be great cities. The Indus and Saraswati valleys contained hundreds of cities. At least 35,000 people may have lived in the largest and best-known cities, Mohenjo-Daro (moh•HEHN•joh•DAHR•oh) and Harappa (huh•RAP•uh). Harappa gave its name to the entire Indus River culture. Today that ancient culture is called **Harappan civilization**.

This civilization featured **planned cities**, which were cities that were built according to a design. Architects surrounded these cities with heavy brick protective walls. City streets crossed each other in a neat grid with square corners. Along the streets were homes, shops, and factories. The cities also had large public buildings that may have been used for religious or government functions.

Dealing with Problems People in large cities always have to deal with the problem of removing human waste. Harappan cities were very advanced in that area. Almost every house contained a bathroom and a toilet. Underground sewers carried away the waste.

People need to use much planning and organization to build such complex cities. Because of that, historians believe the ancient Harappans must have had powerful leaders. We do not know if priests or kings or a combination of both ruled the Harappans, but their government must have been strong.

REVIEW How was Harappan civilization similar to other ancient civilizations?

Harappan Culture

3 ESSENTIAL QUESTION What were the cultural features of Harappan civilization?

A mysterious form of writing covered the stone seals that people found in the ruined cities. Some of those seals may have indicated types of trade goods.

Some scholars think that the 500 pictographs, or picture signs, of Harappan writing may stand for words, sounds, or both. But they don't really know. No one has figured out how to read the writing of Harappan civilization. Until someone learns to read it, the only way we can learn about the civilization is by studying artifacts.

Harappan Religion Archaeologists have not identified the site of any temples for specific gods. But they have found evidence of religion. Mohenjo-Daro had a huge public bath that may have been used for religious rituals. (Many religions have rituals linked to cleansing. For example, Christian baptism stands for the act of washing away sin.) Archaeologists have found figures of animals, such as bulls, that Indians still regard as holy. They also found clay figurines that may be goddesses or simply dolls.

A Widespread and Prosperous Culture People across a wide region shared Harappan culture. Harappan cities spread across an area that was about 500,000 square miles in size. That region was nearly twice as big as Texas is today. Even so, these cities shared a common design. Those shared designs show how widely the culture had spread.

Harappan people used standard weights and measures. Across the region, they made similar bronze statues and clay toys. These artifacts show that the Harappans could afford to have more than just basic necessities. This was because they gained wealth from agriculture and trade. Archaeologists have found seals from the Indus Valley as far away as Mesopotamia. Indians traded timber, ivory, and beads. Mesopotamians sold the Indians silver, tin, and woolen cloth.

Mohenjo-Daro The ruins of the ancient city show how carefully planned it was. The streets were at right angles, and the walls were well built. The smaller photograph is the Great Bath, which was probably a public bathhouse. ▼

▲ **Pot** This pot was found in the cemetery in the city of Harappa.

Challenges to Harappan Life Around 2000 to 1500 B.C., earthquakes shook the region. These quakes probably caused the Saraswati River to dry up. The same natural disaster may have caused the Indus River to flood. The problems forced people to leave their cities. Harappan civilization went into decline. As you will read in Lesson 2, another group of people soon took the place of Harappan civilization.

REVIEW How is the Harappan writing similar to hieroglyphs?

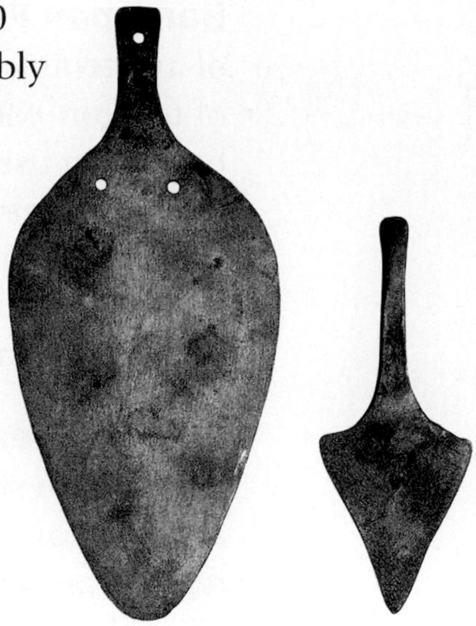

▲ **Copper Tools** Farmers used these tools for tasks such as weeding and leveling soil.

Lesson Summary

- The rivers of India and the seasonal monsoons helped make agriculture possible.
- Agricultural wealth led to the rise of a complex civilization in the Indus Valley.
- The prosperous Harappan culture lasted for about 800 years.

Why It Matters Now . . .

Ancient Indians developed products that are still important today. They were the first people to domesticate chickens and the first Asians to produce cotton cloth.

1 Lesson Review

Homework Helper ClassZone.com

Terms & Names

1. Explain the importance of

subcontinent	Himalayas	Harappan civilization
Hindu Kush	monsoon	planned city

Using Your Notes

Making Generalizations Use your completed chart to answer the following question:

2. What are advantages and disadvantages of having monsoons?

Geography and Indian Life	
Physical geography of India	
Cities in the Indus Valley	
Harappan culture	

Main Ideas

3. What evidence showed archaeologists that an ancient civilization had existed in the Indus Valley?
4. What economic activities allowed Harappan civilization to begin along the Indus and Saraswati rivers?
5. What evidence suggested that Harappan civilization was prosperous?

Critical Thinking

6. **Framing Historical Questions** What questions do you still have about Harappan culture?
7. **Understanding Cause and Effect** What are two positive and two negative effects of India's great rivers?

Activity

Doing a Dig Find a toy, tool, or object in your house or classroom. Study it and describe it as if you were an archaeologist. List five things that it tells you about its owner.

Activity Extend Lesson 1

Make a Climate Graph

Goal: To learn about the physical setting that supported the Harappan civilization by creating a bar graph showing average monthly rainfall

Materials & Supplies
- graph paper
- colored markers, pencils, or pens
- ruler

Prepare

1. Look at examples of bar graphs in your textbooks. Notice how such graphs are constructed. Learn the meaning of the terms *vertical axis* and *horizontal axis.*
2. Study the chart at right of average monthly rainfall in Islamabad, Pakistan—a city located near the site of ancient Harappa.

Average Monthly Rainfall in Islamabad, Pakistan

Month	Rainfall (inches)
Jan.	2.3
Feb.	2.1
Mar.	2.7
Apr.	2.1
May	1.6
June	1.2
July	10.1
Aug.	9.9
Sep.	3.8
Oct.	1.0
Nov.	0.7
Dec.	1.6

Source: www.worldclimate.com

Do the Activity

1. On a piece of graph paper, draw the horizontal axis and the vertical axis. On the vertical axis, mark 11 one-inch measurements up the side and label them.
2. Below the horizontal axis, write the names of all 12 months. You may abbreviate the names. Space them evenly.
3. For each month, draw a bar whose height indicates the average amount of rainfall.

Follow-Up

As you learned in Lesson 1, the summer monsoon blows over the Indian Ocean and the Arabian Sea and brings rain to the Indian subcontinent. Look at your graph. In what months does the summer monsoon occur? Would ancient farmers have wanted to plant before or after the summer monsoon? Explain.

Extension

Creating a Line Graph Use almanacs or the Internet to research the average monthly temperatures in Islamabad. Create a line graph to convey this information.

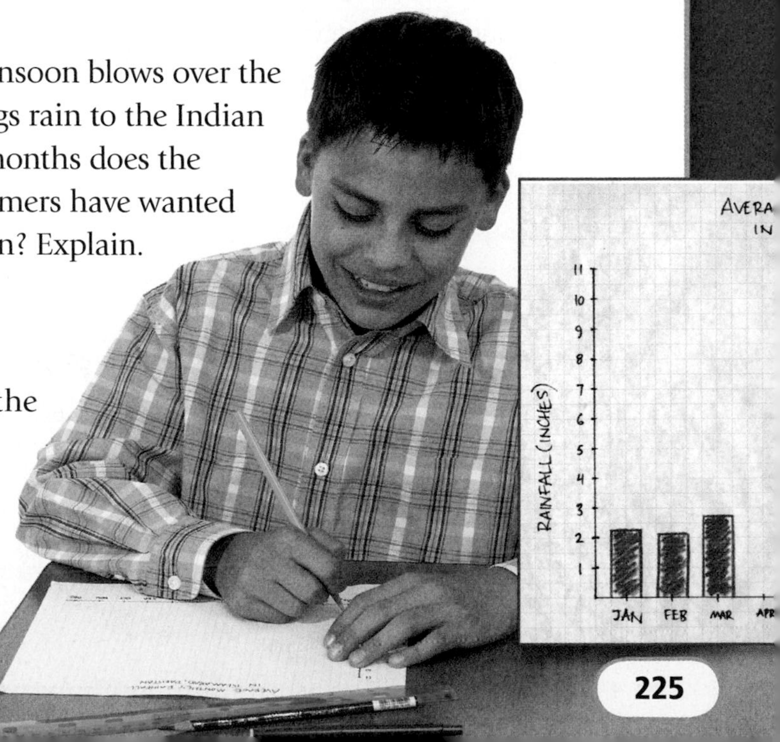

Lesson 2

MAIN IDEAS

1. **Culture** A group of nomadic people moved into India and took over what was left of Harappan civilization.
2. **Government** Under Aryan rule, Indian society developed a distinct system of social classes that still affects India today.
3. **Belief Systems** Over time, the belief of the Aryans developed into the religion of Hinduism.

TAKING NOTES

Reading Skill: Summarizing

To summarize is to restate a passage in fewer words. After you read Lesson 2, write a paragraph summarizing each of the three main sections. Use a chart like the one below to record your summaries.

The Origins of Hinduism
The Aryans migrated ...
Aryan culture changed India by ...
The main characteristics of Hinduism are ...

Skillbuilder Handbook, page R3

▲ **Shiva** One of the most important deities of Hinduism is Shiva, the destroyer. This statue shows him dancing on the demon of ignorance.

Words to Know

Understanding the following words will help you read this lesson:

dialect a variety of a language spoken in a region or by a group (page 227)

*The Aryans spoke a **dialect** of Indo-European.*

chariot a cart with two wheels that is pulled by horses (page 227)

*After the battle, they saw horses pulling **chariots** that no longer carried riders.*

doctrine a principle or belief that a religion considers to be true (page 230)

*A **doctrine** that is held by one religion may not be held by another.*

The Origins of Hinduism

TERMS & NAMES
- Aryan
- caste
- Brahmanism
- Hinduism
- reincarnation
- karma

Build on What You Know In Chapter 5, you learned how Egypt battled the Hittites. The Hittites belonged to a group of peoples who all spoke dialects of a language called Indo-European. Scholars believe that the Indo-Europeans may have originally come from Central Asia.

Aryans Move Into India

1 ESSENTIAL QUESTION Who were the Aryans?

Most Indo-Europeans were nomads. They lived in family groups or clans and herded cattle, sheep, and goats. They also were warriors who rode horse-driven chariots. They fought with long bows and arrows and with bronze axes.

The Indo-European Migrations Around 2000 B.C., something drove the Indo-Europeans from their homeland. Historians do not know if a drought, a plague, or an invasion made them leave. Different groups moved to different regions. The Hittites went to Southwest Asia. Many other Indo-Europeans settled in parts of Europe.

Hindu Kush This mountain range runs along the northwest border of the Indian subcontinent. The Aryan people crossed these mountains to enter India. ▼

The Aryan Migrations In about 1500 B.C., the **Aryans** (AIR•ee•uhnz) traveled east into India. According to some historians, the Aryans belonged to the larger Indo-European group. In contrast to the city-dwelling Harappans, the Aryans were herders. They lived in simple houses. They spoke an Indo-European language called Sanskrit.

Did Aryan warriors in chariots conquer the walled cities and force the Harappans to flee south? For years, history books told that story. But new research suggests a different tale. Two hundred years before the Aryans arrived, the largest Harappan cities lay in ruins. As Lesson 1 explained, this destruction may have been the result of earthquakes and floods.

REVIEW Who were the Aryans, and where did they come from?

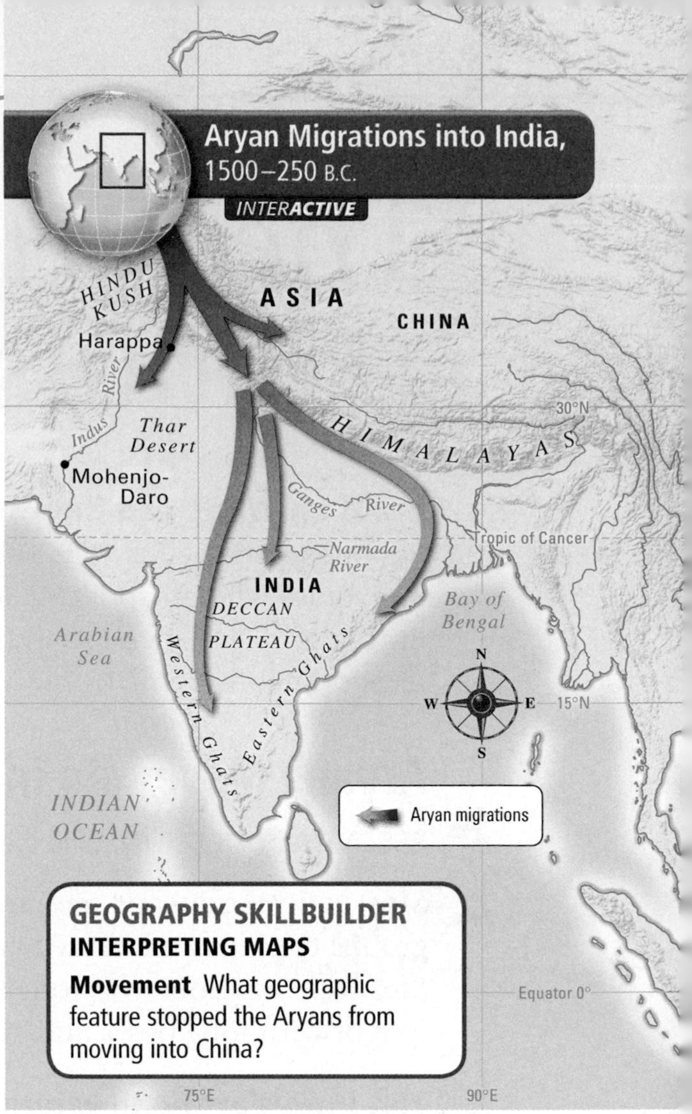

GEOGRAPHY SKILLBUILDER
INTERPRETING MAPS
Movement What geographic feature stopped the Aryans from moving into China?

Changes to Indian Life

2 ESSENTIAL QUESTION How was Aryan society organized?

The Aryans entered India gradually. They practiced a mysterious religion that appealed to many Dravidians—the people living in India when they arrived. As a result, Aryan religion and language spread. In turn, the Dravidians taught the Aryans about city life. Because of these interactions, India developed a complex, blended culture.

The Caste System Aryan society was organized into classes: warriors, priests, and commoners. As Indian society grew more complex, these classes developed into what was later called the caste system. A **caste** is a social class whose members are identified by their job. Because there are thousands of different jobs, thousands of groups exist. Broadly, those groups are organized into four categories. (See the chart on the next page.)

After many centuries, another group came into being that was considered below all other groups. This group was called the untouchables. They had to do the jobs no one else wanted.

The Caste System

Indian society divided itself into a complex structure of social classes based partially on jobs. This class structure is called the caste system.

▲ Sweeper This sweeper did not choose his job. In traditional India, jobs were passed down from father to son.

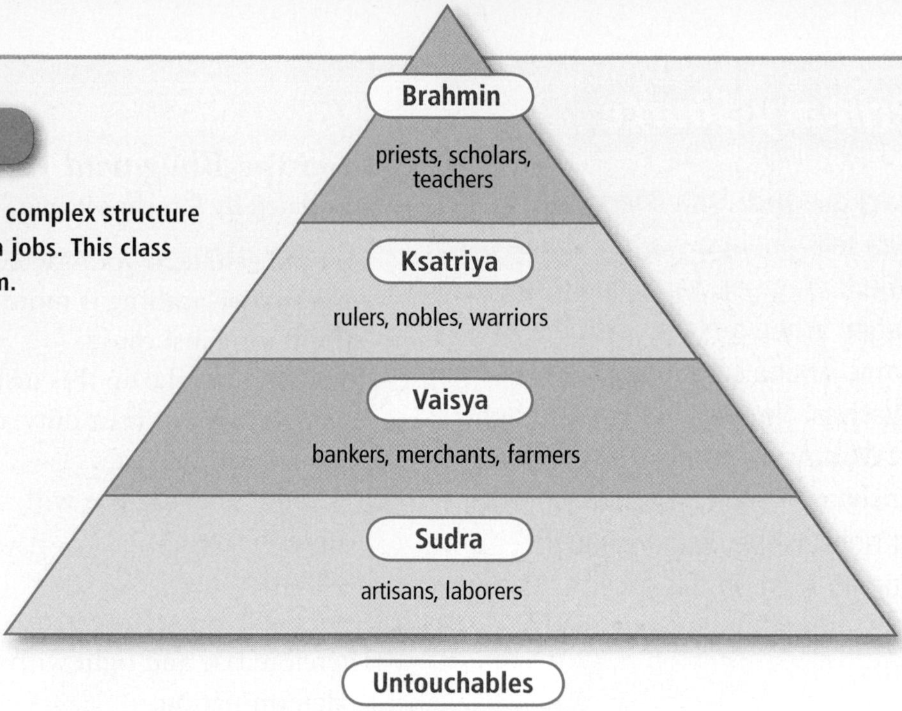

Untouchables were considered outside the system and below it. They did jobs no one else wanted, such as being sweepers and disposers of dead bodies.

Aryan Beliefs and Brahmanism The early religion of the Aryans is now called **Brahmanism**, after the name of the Aryan priests, or Brahmins. The Aryans worshiped many nature deities. The Brahmins made sacrifices to those deities by offering animals to a sacred fire. Over time, the ceremonies became more and more complex. Some lasted for days—or even months. The rituals of the Aryan religion and many hymns to their deities are found in ancient Sanskrit sacred texts called the Vedas.

As time passed, Indians began to question how the world came into being. These questions led to changes in contemporary religious ideas. One change was a belief that one spirit governed the universe.

Later, Indians wrote about their ancient history in such works as the *Mahabharata* (MAH•huh•BAH•ruh•tuh)—an epic poem that retells many legends. The *Bhagavad Gita* (BAH•guh•vahd GEE•tuh) is part of the *Mahabharata*. (See the Primary Source on page 230.)

Primary Source Handbook
See the excerpt from the *Bhagavad Gita*, page R41.

REVIEW What is the caste system?

Hinduism: The Religion of India

3 ESSENTIAL QUESTION How did the religion of Hinduism develop?

The *Bhagavad Gita* is an important sacred text of Hinduism. **Hinduism** is the modern name for the major religion of India, which grew out of early Brahmanism.

Primary Source

Background: The *Bhagavad Gita* tells about a warrior, Prince Arjuna. A great war is about to begin. When he looks at the enemy army, Arjuna sees many friends and relatives. He does not want to fight.

With Arjuna is his chariot driver, Krishna. In reality, Krishna (shown at right) is the deity Vishnu in human form. In this excerpt, Krishna tells Arjuna that he must do his duty.

from the *Bhagavad Gita*

Translated by Ranchor Prime

Do not hesitate in your sacred duty as a warrior.
For a soldier nothing is more sacred than the
fight for a just cause. . . .
If you do not take up this just fight,
you will fail in your duty and your
honor will be lost. . . .
If you die in battle you will
enter heaven.
If you win
you will enjoy the earth.
Therefore rise and fight with
determination.
Fight for the sake of fighting.
Look equally on happiness
and distress, gain and
loss, victory and defeat.
In this way you will not incur sin.

DOCUMENT–BASED QUESTION
What arguments does Krishna use to convince Arjuna that the outcome of the battle is not important?

Many Deities Hindus worship many deities. Although they believe in many deities, Hindus also recognize one supreme God or life force. Hindus consider the other deities to be parts of the one universal God. The three most important of the other deities are Brahma, the creator; Vishnu, the protector; and Shiva, the destroyer. (Shiva destroys the world so that it can be created anew.) Shiva's wife, Kali, also has many worshipers.

Many Lives Hindus believe in **reincarnation**, which means that each person has many lives. What a person does in each life determines what he or she will be in the next life, according to a doctrine called **karma**. Deeds (good or evil) cause a person to be reborn in a higher or lower life form. (Hindus believe that animals, like humans, have the supreme life force in them. For that reason, many Hindus are vegetarians. They will not eat animals.)

Reincarnation creates a repeating cycle of birth, life, death, and rebirth. The cycle ends only when a person achieves a mystical union with God. To achieve that, a person must come to realize that his or her soul and God's soul are one.

Vocabulary Strategy

The word *reincarnation* uses the **prefix** *re-*, which means "again," and the **root** *carn*, which means "flesh." Therefore, reincarnation means that the soul takes on another body.

Many Paths to God Hindus believe they connect with God by following their own individual path. Part of that path concerns one's job, which is linked to the caste system. Devout Hindus must faithfully carry out their assigned duties in life.

Hindus have a choice of spiritual practices to grow closer to God. Two of these are also popular in Western countries. Meditation is the practice of making the mind calm. Yoga is a complex practice that includes exercise, breathing techniques, and diet.

REVIEW How can Hindus believe in one God and many different deities at the same time?

Lesson Summary

- After Harappan civilization declined, Aryan people brought their culture to India.
- Aryan society developed a class structure that was based on jobs and is called the caste system.
- Hindus worship many deities. They believe in reincarnation and karma.

Why It Matters Now . . .

Hindusim ranks third among world religions in the number of followers (after Christianity and Islam).

2 Lesson Review

Homework Helper
ClassZone.com

Terms & Names

1. Explain the importance of

Aryan	Brahmanism	reincarnation
caste	Hinduism	karma

Using Your Notes

Summarizing Use your completed chart to answer the following question:

2. How did Hinduism grow out of the beliefs of Brahmanism?

The Origins of Hinduism
The Aryans migrated . . .
Aryan culture changed India by . . .
The main characteristics of Hinduism are . . .

Main Ideas

3. How did the Aryan culture differ from Harappan culture?
4. What was the social structure of the Aryan caste system?
5. How does karma relate to reincarnation?

Critical Thinking

6. **Recognizing Changing Interpretations** What changed the long-held theory that Aryans drove out the Harappan people?
7. **Drawing Conclusions from Sources** What values of a warrior culture does the passage from the *Bhagavad Gita* express?

Activity

Internet Activity Use the Internet to learn about Hindu customs concerning one of these topics: the Ganges River, cows, funerals, diet. Present your findings to the class in an oral presentation.

INTERNET KEYWORDS: *Hinduism, Ganges*

Lesson 3

MAIN IDEAS

1. **Belief Systems** A teacher called the Buddha developed a new religion that focused on helping people to escape suffering.
2. **Government** The Maurya rulers united northern India into the first great Indian empire.
3. **Culture** About 500 years after Asoka's death, a new ruler united northern India and began a golden age of culture.

TAKING NOTES

Reading Skill: Comparing and Contrasting

To compare and contrast is to look for similarities and differences. As you read Lesson 3, compare and contrast the Maurya and Gupta empires. Record your notes on a Venn diagram like the one below.

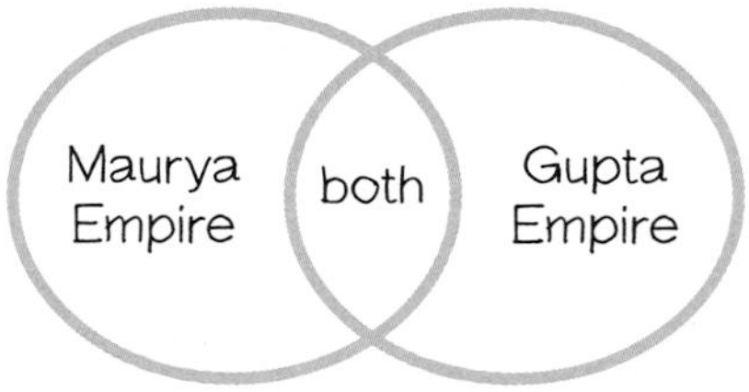

Skillbuilder Handbook, page R4

▲ Lion **The king Asoka adopted many Buddhist principles. He had his laws and policies carved on pillars in public places. The capitals, or tops, of the pillars were decorated with sculpture.**

Words to Know

Understanding the following words will help you read this lesson:

enlightened having spiritual knowledge or understanding (page 233)
*The religious leader's most devoted followers said he was **enlightened** and pure.*

spy a secret agent who obtains information about an enemy (page 235)
*The king used information he received from his **spies** to punish or eliminate his foes.*

flourish to do well; to prosper (page 238)
*The arts of India **flourished** during the rule of Chandra Gupta II.*

estimate to guess; to calculate roughly (page 238)
*She **estimated** the size of the circle by using a mathematical formula.*

Buddhism and India's Golden Age

TERMS & NAMES
ahimsa
Buddhism
Siddhartha Gautama
nirvana
dharma
Asoka

Build on What You Know As you know, Hinduism is the modern name for the major religion that is practiced in India. Other religions also had their beginnings in India. One of these is the religion of Jainism. Jains teach ***ahimsa*** (uh•HIHM•SAH), which means "nonviolence." Jains practice *ahimsa* very strictly. They believe that every living thing has a soul and should not be hurt. Some Jains even wear masks to avoid accidentally breathing in small insects.

The Rise of Buddhism

1 **ESSENTIAL QUESTION** What are the main teachings of the religion of Buddhism?

Another religion called Buddhism also began in India. **Buddhism** is based on the teachings of **Siddhartha Gautama** (sihd•DAHR•tuh GAW•tuh•muh). He was a prince who gave up his wealth and position to try to understand the meaning of life. Later, when he began to teach what he had learned, he was called the Buddha, or enlightened one.

◀ **Resting Buddha** This carving of a sleeping Buddha is in the Ajanta Caves in India.

History Makers

Siddhartha Gautama (c. 563 to 483 B.C.)

According to Buddhist teaching, as Siddhartha Gautama sat meditating, an evil spirit tempted him to stop seeking truth. First the spirit sent beautiful women, but Siddhartha ignored them. Then flaming rocks began to rain down on him. But as they drew close to Siddhartha, they became flower petals. Finally, the evil spirit asked what right Siddhartha had to look for truth. Siddhartha touched the ground, and a voice thundered, "I bear you witness"—which means to testify in one's favor.

That night Siddhartha's meditation grew even deeper, and he received his great insights. He had become the Buddha. The evil spirit decided to tempt him one last time. "No one will understand your deep truths," the spirit taunted.

The Buddha simply answered, "Some will understand."

The Buddha's Life and Teachings Siddhartha was born a Hindu prince. A priest had predicted that he would become a wandering holy man. To prevent this, Siddhartha's father gave his son every luxury and sheltered him. Siddhartha did not see old age, illness, death, or poverty until he was 29. When he finally did see such troubles, they upset him. He fled his home to search for peace in a world of suffering.

For six years, Siddhartha starved himself, but this sacrifice did not help him find the answers he sought. Then he sat under a fig tree and meditated until he found understanding. This gave him insights into reality, which he called the Four Noble Truths.

1. People suffer because their minds are not at ease.
2. That condition comes from wanting what one doesn't have or from wanting life to be different.
3. People can stop suffering by not wanting.
4. People can stop wanting by following the Eightfold Path.

The Eightfold Path involved having the right opinions, desires, speech, actions, job, effort, concentration, and meditation. This path, the Buddha taught, could lead to **nirvana** (neer•VAH•nuh), or the end of suffering. Reaching nirvana broke the cycle of reincarnation that Buddhists, as well as Hindus, believed in.

The Buddha believed in the practice of *ahimsa*. But he didn't worship Hindu deities. He also rejected the idea that people in the upper castes were holier than others.

Connect to Today

▲ **Indian Flag** In the center of the flag of modern India is a Buddhist symbol—the wheel of dharma.

Buddhism Changes After the Buddha died, his followers gathered his teachings to pass on to others. These collected teachings are called the **dharma** (DAHR•muh), which means the true nature of things. Dharma is often shown symbolically as a wheel.

Monks and nuns—men and women who live in religious communities—helped develop the formal religion of Buddhism. Other Buddhists became wandering holy men and tried to live as the Buddha had.

Over time, Buddhism split into many branches. Some branches stressed the importance of being a monk and studying the Buddha's life. Others stressed meditation. Some Buddhists taught that ordinary people could become Buddhas. Such holy people could work to save others through acts of mercy and love. Most Buddhists worshiped the Buddha as a divine being.

REVIEW How could a Buddhist achieve an end to suffering?

The Maurya Empire

2 **ESSENTIAL QUESTION** How did the Maurya rulers unite northern India into the first great Indian empire?

One reason Buddhism became so influential is that a famous Indian king ruled by its teachings. As you will read, he was the third king of the Maurya dynasty, which united India.

A United India For centuries, separate Aryan kingdoms battled each other. Around 550 B.C., Magadha (MAH•guh•duh), a northeastern kingdom, began to gain strength. About 321 B.C., Chandragupta Maurya (CHUHN•druh•GUP•tuh MOWR•yuh) became king of Magadha. He conquered much territory. His Maurya Empire soon covered much of the subcontinent.

Chandragupta controlled his empire by using spies to learn what people did and an army of soldiers to keep order. Many officials ran the government. To pay these people, Chandragupta taxed land and crops heavily. Surprisingly, legend says that he became a nonviolent Jainist monk at the end of his life.

Asoka, the Buddhist King The greatest Maurya king was Chandragupta's grandson **Asoka** (uh•SOH•kuh), who began to rule in 269 B.C. Early in Asoka's reign, he fought a bloody war and conquered a neighboring kingdom. Afterwards, Asoka decided to rule by Buddhist teachings. He gave up constant warfare. He tried to rule peacefully by law instead.

Asoka had his policies carved on rocks and pillars. Rocks that survive from his reign advise people to be truthful and kind. Others urge people not to kill living things.

As a result of Asoka's patronage, Buddhism attracted people to its monastic order. Asoka and the Buddhist rulers that followed him sent missionaries to bring new converts to Buddhism. At the same time, he let people of other religions worship freely. Asoka's officials planted trees, dug wells, set up hospitals, and built rest houses along main roads. These improvements allowed people to travel in more comfort than before. Better travel conditions helped traders and officials.

Changes to Hinduism The popularity of Buddhism meant that fewer people were worshiping Hindu deities. Early Hinduism had a set of complex sacrifices that only priests could perform. They conducted the rites in Sanskrit, which few people spoke anymore. This caused people to feel distant from the deities. Many people turned to Buddhism instead. Rulers who had come under the influence of Buddhism encouraged this shift.

Hindu thought began to change. Poets began to write hymns of praise to the deities Vishnu and Shiva. These poems were written in languages that common people spoke, instead of in Sanskrit.

The poems became popular across India. As a result, many Indians felt a renewed love for their Hindu deities. This renewal of interest in Hinduism occurred at the same time as a decline in Buddhism. Eventually, Buddhism lost most of its followers in India. By that time, however, it had spread to many other countries in Asia.

REVIEW What were some of Asoka's accomplishments?

Vishnu The deity Vishnu remains one of the most popular deities in India. This Indian miniature dates from the 1700s. ▼

The Golden Age of the Guptas

3 ESSENTIAL QUESTION Who were the Guptas, and when did they rule India?

The Maurya Empire collapsed shortly after Asoka died because of poor rule and invasions. Five centuries of conflict followed until the Gupta (GUP•tuh) family took control.

The Gupta Empire Like the Mauryas, the Guptas began as leaders in Magadha. Chandra Gupta I became king in A.D. 320. (He was not related to Chandragupta Maurya.) Right away, he married a king's daughter and gained new lands. Later, his son enlarged the empire by fighting wars. But Chandra Gupta's grandson, Chandra Gupta II, was the greatest ruler of the family. During his reign (A.D. 375 to 415), India had a golden age—a time of great accomplishment.

GEOGRAPHY SKILLBUILDER
INTERPRETING MAPS
Region Which empire was larger? Describe the differences in the regions the two empires controlled.

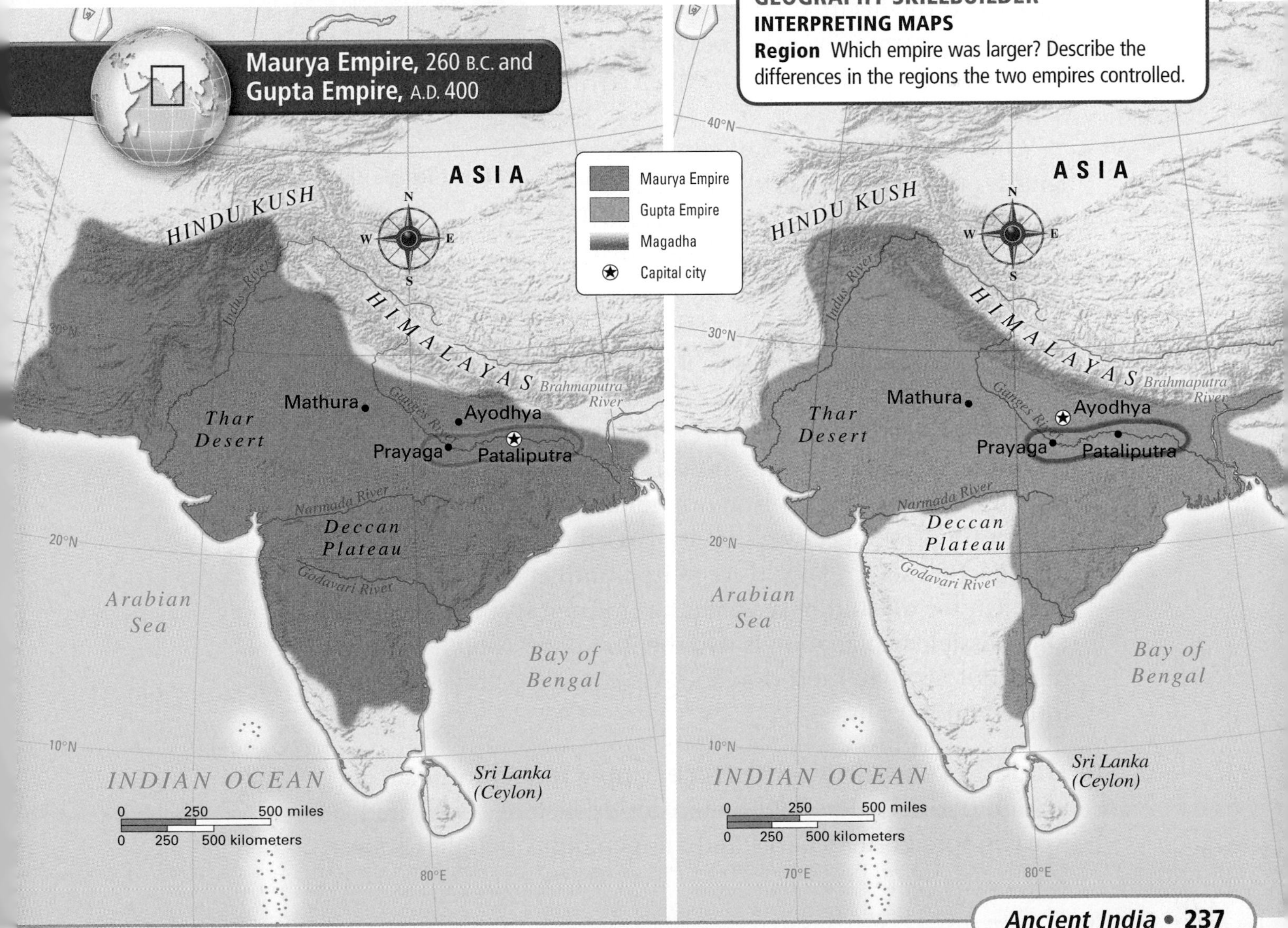

Art and Literature Under Chandra Gupta II, Indian arts flourished. Architects erected gracefully designed temples. Artists painted murals and sculpted statues, many of which had religious subjects.

Kalidasa (KAH•lee•DAH•suh) wrote brilliant Sanskrit plays and poems. His most famous play is about a young woman named Sakuntala (SAH•koon•TAH•lah). The king falls in love with her and promises to marry her. Later he forgets her because of a curse laid on him. The couple are reunited in heaven. Today Kalidasa is considered one of the greatest writers India ever had.

▲ **Vishnu Temple** During the Gupta period, Hindu temples began to be built with pyramid-shaped roofs. This architectural style remained very influential. (See the photograph of Angkor Wat on page 241.)

Mathematics, Science, and Metallurgy Indian scholars invented the numeral system we use today. They developed the decimal system and the symbol for zero. (The Maya of Central America also came up with the idea of zero independently.)

One mathematician figured out the length of a year. He also estimated the value of pi. Pi is the number that is used to calculate the length of a circle's boundary.

Doctors added new techniques to the ancient practice of Ayurvedic (EYE•yuhr•VAY•dihk) medicine. It is one of the oldest systems of medicine in the world. It promotes health by using diet, exercise, and other methods to maintain energy in the body.

Indian artisans developed advanced methods of metallurgy (metal working). In Delhi, an iron pillar erected about A.D. 400 towers almost 23 feet over the city. No other people were able to manufacture such a large piece of iron until at least 1,000 years later. Unlike most iron, the pillar has resisted rust for 16 centuries. One possible explanation is that the iron pillar contains more phosphorous than most iron does. As a result, a protective coating formed on the surface.

Trade Spreads Indian Culture Gupta India profited from foreign trade. Traders sold Indian goods such as cotton and ivory to foreign merchants. Indian merchants bought Chinese goods such as silk. They resold these goods to traders who were traveling west.

Both traders and missionaries spread Indian culture and beliefs. Hinduism spread to parts of Southeast Asia. Buddhism gradually spread to Central Asia, Sri Lanka (formerly called Ceylon), China, and Southeast Asia.

REVIEW Why was the period of Gupta rule a golden age for India?

Lesson Summary

- A new religion called Buddhism taught people to escape suffering by following a path of right living.
- Influenced by Buddhism, King Asoka tried to rule with peace, law, and good works.
- Under Gupta rule, India had a golden age. The arts, science, metallurgy, and trade prospered.

Why It Matters Now . . .

The spread of Hinduism and Buddhism shaped Asian cultures. Many Asian people still practice those religions today.

▲ **Iron Pillar** This pillar from the Gupta period stands more than 20 feet high and weighs about 1,300 pounds.

3 Lesson Review

Homework Helper
ClassZone.com

Terms & Names

1. Explain the importance of

ahimsa	Siddhartha Gautama	dharma
Buddhism	nirvana	Asoka

Using Your Notes

Comparing and Contrasting Use your completed Venn diagram to answer the following question:

2. How were the Maurya and Gupta empires of India alike?

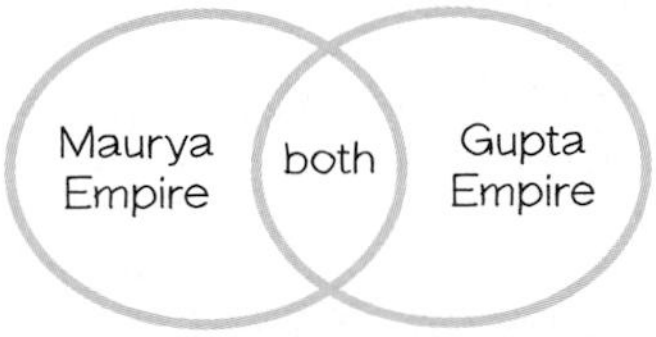

Main Ideas

3. The Buddha's Eightfold Path stressed right behavior in eight areas. What were they?

4. How did Buddhism influence Asoka as a ruler?

5. What were the important achievements in Indian literature?

Critical Thinking

6. Comparing Was Hinduism or Buddhism more similar to ancient Egyptian religion? Why?

7. Assessing Credibility of Primary Sources If historians found an engraved rock pillar from Asoka's time, would that be a primary source or a secondary source? Explain.

Activity

Writing Rules With a group of your friends, agree on three or four basic rules for social conduct. Print your rules on a poster and display it in the classroom.

Lesson 4

MAIN IDEAS

1. **Belief Systems** Hinduism and Buddhism are practiced in countries besides India and have also influenced people of other faiths.
2. **Culture** The artistic styles of ancient India influenced other cultures and continue to be used today.
3. **Culture** The decimal system, numerals, and the concept of the zero transformed the ability to do mathematical calculations.

TAKING NOTES

Reading Skill: Categorizing To categorize means to sort information. As you read Lesson 4, take notes about the legacy of India. Use a chart like this one to categorize your information.

Legacy of India		
Religion	Arts	Mathematics

Skillbuilder Handbook, page R6

▲ **Mohandas Gandhi** In the early 20th century, Britain ruled India as a colony. Gandhi was one of the men who led the fight against foreign rule, but he practiced *ahimsa* while doing so. He took part only in nonviolent protests.

Words to Know

Understanding the following words will help you read this lesson:

practice to follow the teachings of a religion (page 241)

About 1 million Americans ***practice*** *Hinduism.*

translate to express in a different language (page 242)

More than one writer has ***translated*** *the* Bhagavad Gita *into English.*

place the position of a numeral (page 243)

In the number 761, a 6 is in the tens ***place.***

The Legacy of India

TERMS & NAMES
Mohandas Gandhi
Hindu-Arabic numerals

Build on What You Know In ancient times, trade spread Indian religion and art to other parts of Asia. Indian culture continues to influence our modern world today.

India's Religious Legacy

1 **ESSENTIAL QUESTION** How did the religions of India affect other cultures?

Yoga is as old as the *Bhagavad Gita* and as new as the yoga classes taught in health clubs. Its popularity shows that the ancient religious traditions of India are still very much alive.

Hinduism and Buddhism Today Four out of five people living in India today are Hindus. Hindus also live in Nepal, Sri Lanka, Malaysia, and many other countries. Also, about 1 million people in the United States practice Hinduism.

Buddhism did not remain strong in India. Not even 1 percent of Indians today are Buddhists. But the religion is popular in Asia, Western Europe, and the United States.

Angkor Wat The Hindu temples at Angkor Wat in Cambodia show how Hinduism and Indian artistic styles spread to Southeast Asia. ▼

Hindu and Buddhist Influences In the mid-1900s, Indian leader **Mohandas Gandhi** (MOH•huhn•DAHS GAHN•dee) used *ahimsa* (nonviolence) in his fight against British rule. His life inspired U.S. civil rights leader Martin Luther King Jr. In the 1950s and 1960s, King led nonviolent protests to gain rights for African Americans.

Today Hindu and Buddhist influences continue. For example, millions of people from other religions meditate and practice yoga.

REVIEW Which of India's original religions remains most popular in India?

▲ **Dance of the *Ramayana*** **Indian culture has strongly influenced Southeast Asia. This dancer in Thailand is performing a piece from an Indian epic called the *Ramayana*.**

India's Artistic Legacy

2 ESSENTIAL QUESTION How have the Indian arts influenced other cultures?

The arts of India have strongly influenced the world. For example, in many Southeast Asian nations, people perform plays based on the ancient Sanskrit epic the *Mahabharata*. The *Bhagavad Gita* has been translated into many languages and is read around the world.

Indian art and architecture have shaped other cultures. For example, ancient Indian artists developed visual symbols to show the Buddha's holiness. These symbols include features such as a topknot of hair. Artists have used such symbols to portray the Buddha ever since. In northwestern Cambodia, ancient builders erected a large Hindu temple called Angkor Wat. Indian influences are seen in the design of those temples.

REVIEW What types of Indian art have influenced other societies?

The Legacy of Indian Mathematics

3 ESSENTIAL QUESTION How does the mathematical knowledge of ancient India affect our lives today?

The numerals we use originated in India. People in India have been using the numerals for 1 to 9 for more than 2,000 years. Arab traders brought these numerals to the West. As a result, we call them Arabic numerals, or **Hindu-Arabic numerals**.

The number system first developed in India and used today is called the decimal system. The name comes from the Latin word *decem,* which means "ten." In a number such as 5,555, each numeral is worth ten times as much as the numeral to its right. The place of a numeral—the ones place, the tens place, the hundreds place, and so on—tells how much that numeral is worth.

The decimal system would not work without a symbol for zero. It would be impossible to write a number like 504 without some way to show that the tens place was empty. In India, the use of the zero goes back about 1,400 years.

REVIEW How does the zero make the decimal system possible?

Lesson Summary

- Hinduism and Buddhism are major world religions.
- Indian literature and art shaped other cultures.
- Without the zero, the way we do mathematical calculations would be impossible.

Why It Matters Now . . .

Every day you use at least ten things that were invented in India. You can count on it!

4 Lesson Review

Homework Helper
ClassZone.com

Terms & Names

1. Explain the importance of

Mohandas Gandhi   Hindu-Arabic numerals

Using Your Notes

Categorizing Use your completed chart to answer the following question:

2. Which of India's legacies has made the biggest impact on your life? Explain.

Legacy of India		
Religion	Arts	Mathematics

Main Ideas

3. What ancient Hindu and Buddhist practice inspired both Mohandas Gandhi and Martin Luther King Jr.?

4. Which ancient Indian arts influenced Southeast Asian culture?

5. What number system did Indian mathematicians invent?

Critical Thinking

6. Making Generalizations What are three main ways Indian religion, art, music, literature, and dance reached the rest of the world?

7. Explaining Sequence How did Indian numerals come to be called Arabic numerals?

Activity

Making a Travel Poster Research one of the Indian legacies you learned about. Advertise it on a travel poster about "Old and New India."

Connect to Today
Extend Lesson 4

Research Links
ClassZone.com

Indian Health Practices

Purpose: To learn about ancient Indian medicine

Magazines often feature articles that give health tips. It's a popular subject. In recent years, such articles have focused on diet and exercise. Today a person who eats vegetarian food, practices yoga, and uses scented oils to produce a calm atmosphere is considered modern. But these are not new ideas about how to live a healthy life. Each of them dates back to ancient India.

Yoga

▶ **Past** This 3,500-year-old seal from Mohenjo-Daro shows a man meditating in a yoga pose. The word *yoga* means "joining" or "union." The purpose of yoga is to help humans unite with the supreme force of the universe. Yoga includes many practices, including exercise, breathing techniques, meditation, and service to others.

▶ **Present** The form of yoga that most Americans know is an exercise routine that consists of practicing certain poses. Each pose is designed to promote balance and to help energy flow through the body in certain ways. In recent decades, this form of yoga has become one of the most popular types of exercise in the United States.

Ayurvedic Medicine

▼ **Past** This ancient system of medicine teaches that each person is made of five elements—space, air, fire, water, and earth—but the combinations differ. As a result, everyone is unique and must have unique remedies. An Ayurvedic physician tries to bring the five elements into a better balance. Remedies include cleansing treatments, special diets, herbs and spices like those below, and oils with healing fragrances.

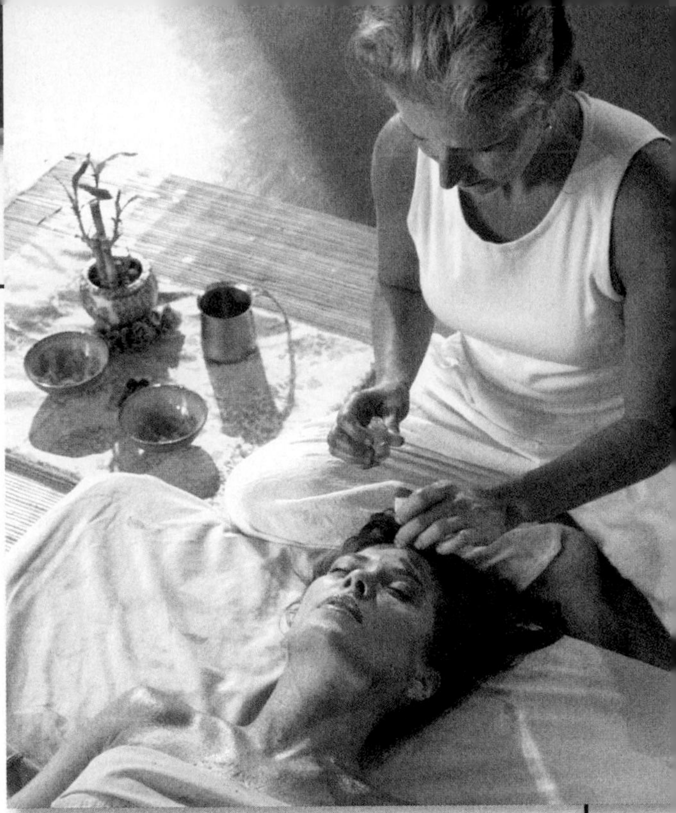

▲ **Present** Today some people use Ayurvedic treatments in addition to Western medicine. For example, this woman is having her forehead massaged with healing oil.

Vegetarianism

▼ **Past** Since ancient times, Hindus have believed that some animals—such as the cow—are sacred. More generally, they believe that animals also share in the universal life force. Because they respect this life force, devout Hindus do not eat meat.

▶ **Present** Indian cooking features a wide variety of vegetarian dishes. Common foods are rice and *dals* (a type of lentils). Some foods are highly spiced. This meal is being served on banana leaves.

Activities

1. **TALK ABOUT IT** Why do you think yoga has become so popular in the United States?
2. **WRITE ABOUT IT** Use books or the Internet to find out how to eat enough protein on a vegetarian diet. Write a brief explanation of how to do this.

Chapter 7 Review

VISUAL SUMMARY

Ancient India

Geography

- The first Indian civilization arose near the Indus and Saraswati rivers.
- Monsoons, or seasonal winds, affect India's climate.

Government

- Chandragupta Maurya ruled harshly. He used spies, his army, and many officials.
- Asoka tried to rule peacefully, influenced by Buddhism.

Belief Systems

- Hinduism is a religion that worships God in many forms and believes in reincarnation.
- Buddhism teaches people to follow a middle way according to the Eightfold Path.

Culture

- Indian artistic styles spread to other regions of Asia.
- Indians invented the zero, Hindu-Arabic numerals, and the decimal system. They were skilled metal workers.

TERMS & NAMES

Explain why the words in each set below are linked with each other.

1. **Himalayas** and **Hindu Kush**
2. **caste** and **Brahmanism**
3. **Buddhism** and **nirvana**
4. **Mohandas Gandhi** and ***ahimsa***

MAIN IDEAS

Geography and Indian Life (pages 218–225)

5. Why do Indian farmers depend on the summer monsoons?
6. By what body of water were Harappa and Mohenjo-Daro, two of ancient India's large cities, located?

The Origins of Hinduism (pages 226–231)

7. What cultural impact did the Aryan migrations have on India?
8. How does Hinduism differ from many religions that worship many deities?

Buddhism and India's Golden Age (pages 232–239)

9. What are the Four Noble Truths?
10. Why was the reign of Chandra Gupta II considered India's golden age?

The Legacy of India (pages 240–245)

11. How did a Hindu belief influence the U.S. civil rights movement?
12. What makes the Indian idea of the zero so important?

CRITICAL THINKING Big Ideas: Culture

13. **UNDERSTANDING EFFECT** How did the caste system maintain social order?
14. **ANALYZING ECONOMIC AND POLITICAL ISSUES** In what way was the caste system related to economic status?
15. **MAKING INFERENCES** How do you think the Buddha felt about the caste system? Why?

ALTERNATIVE ASSESSMENT

1. **WRITING ACTIVITY** Mohandas Gandhi opposed the caste system and worked to end its influence in India. Write a persuasive paragraph to try to convince the Indian government to fight against the traditional caste system.

2. **INTERDISCIPLINARY ACTIVITY—MATH** Research the places in the decimal system. Learn the name for as many high numbers as you can: million, billion, trillion, and so on. Make a poster showing the names for these numbers and how they are written: For example, 1 million is written 1,000,000.

3. **STARTING WITH A STORY** Starting with a Story Review the essay you wrote about the Saraswati River disaster. Draw an editorial cartoon to persuade others to follow your suggestion.

Technology Activity

4. **DESIGNING A WEB PAGE** Use the Internet and the library to find out more about Buddhism in the United States. Then design a Web page using pictures, maps, or graphs to convey the information.
   - Which immigrant groups in the United States practice Buddhism?
   - In what states or regions are the most Buddhists to be found?
   - What is Zen Buddhism?
   - What other forms of Buddhism are practiced in the United States?

Research Links
ClassZone.com

Reading a Map Use the map below to answer the questions.

Spread of Buddhism by A.D. 600

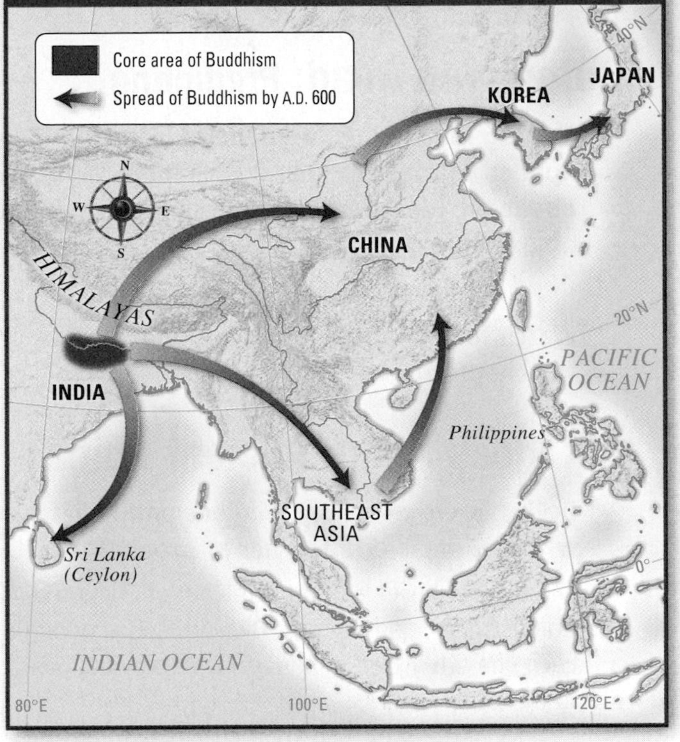

1. Where did Buddhism originate?

A. southern India
B. northern China
C. northwestern Korea
D. northeastern India

2. What is the farthest place from India that Buddhism had spread by A.D. 600?

A. China
B. Japan
C. Korea
D. Sri Lanka

Test Practice
ClassZone.com

Additional Test Practice, pp. S1–S33

Chapter

8 Ancient China

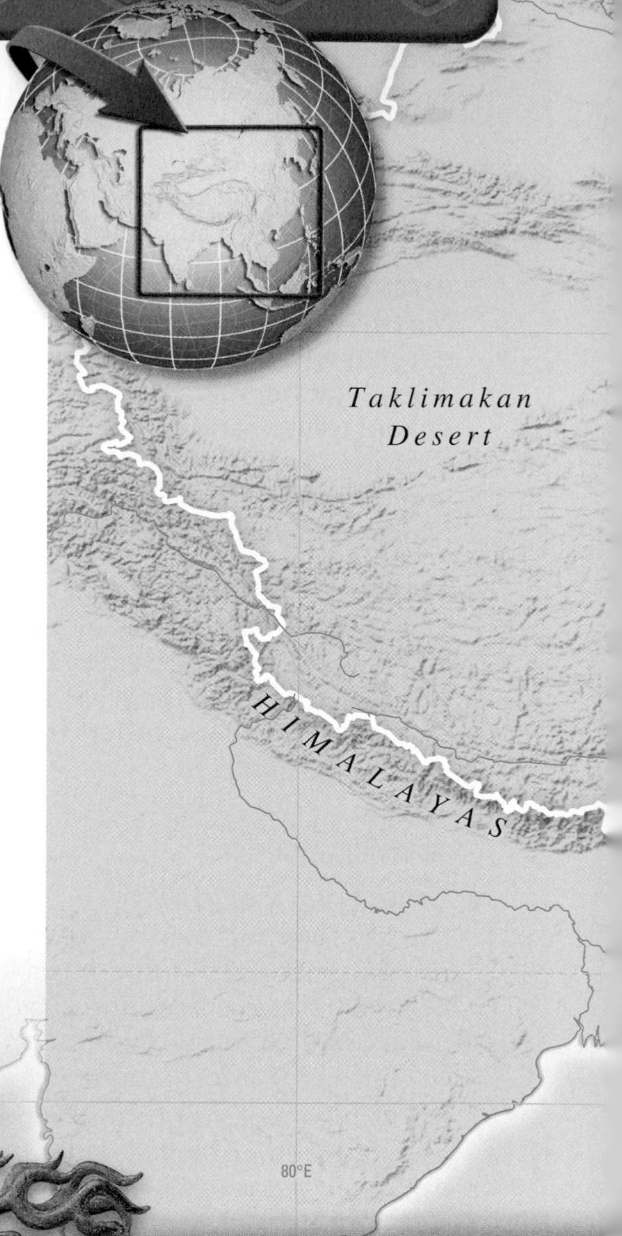

Before You Read: Predicting

The Big Idea below is a general historical idea that will be applied to the region in this chapter. Write three questions about the idea that can be answered as you read. Here is an example:

What religions are practiced in China?

Watch for the answers to your questions as you read the chapter.

Big Ideas About Ancient China

Belief Systems Many religions and belief systems start with the ideas of a teacher or prophet.

Three major belief systems came out of China. They are Legalism, Confucianism, and Daoism. They developed during a time of unrest. Each one attempted to find a way of bringing peace and harmony to the land.

Integrated Technology

eEdition
- Interactive Maps
- Interactive Visuals
- Starting with a Story

VIDEO *Ancient China*

INTERNET RESOURCES

Go to **ClassZone.com** for
- WebQuest
- Homework Helper
- Research Links
- Internet Activities
- Quizzes
- Maps
- Test Practice
- Current Events

CHINA

1766 B.C.
Shang Dynasty established.
(jade stag pendant) ▶

1027 B.C.
Zhou Dynasty founded.

1800 B.C. — **1500 B.C.** — **1200 B.C.**

WORLD

1792 B.C.
Hammurabi begins his reign.

1200 B.C.
Olmec culture in Mexico begins.
(Olmec man with jaguar cub) ▶

551 B.C.
Confucius born.
◀ (portrait of Confucius)

403 B.C.
Period of Warring States begins.

202 B.C.
Liu Bang becomes the first emperor of the Han Dynasty.

600 B.C. | 300 B.C. | B.C. A.D. | A.D. 300

751 B.C.
Piankhi of Kush conquers Egypt.

509 B.C.
Roman Republic established.
(ruins of the Roman Colosseum) ▶

Starting with a Story

The Minister of Justice Comes to Town

Background: Around 500 B.C., the Duke of Lu appointed Confucius the minister of justice. Tradition has it that crime almost disappeared from the area in response to the teachings and actions of Confucius. In this story, Confucius is visiting a village in his district. The people wonder about the new minister of justice and the stories told about what he teaches and how he acts. You have joined others in the village gathering to meet Confucius.

Wooden sculpture of Confucius ▶

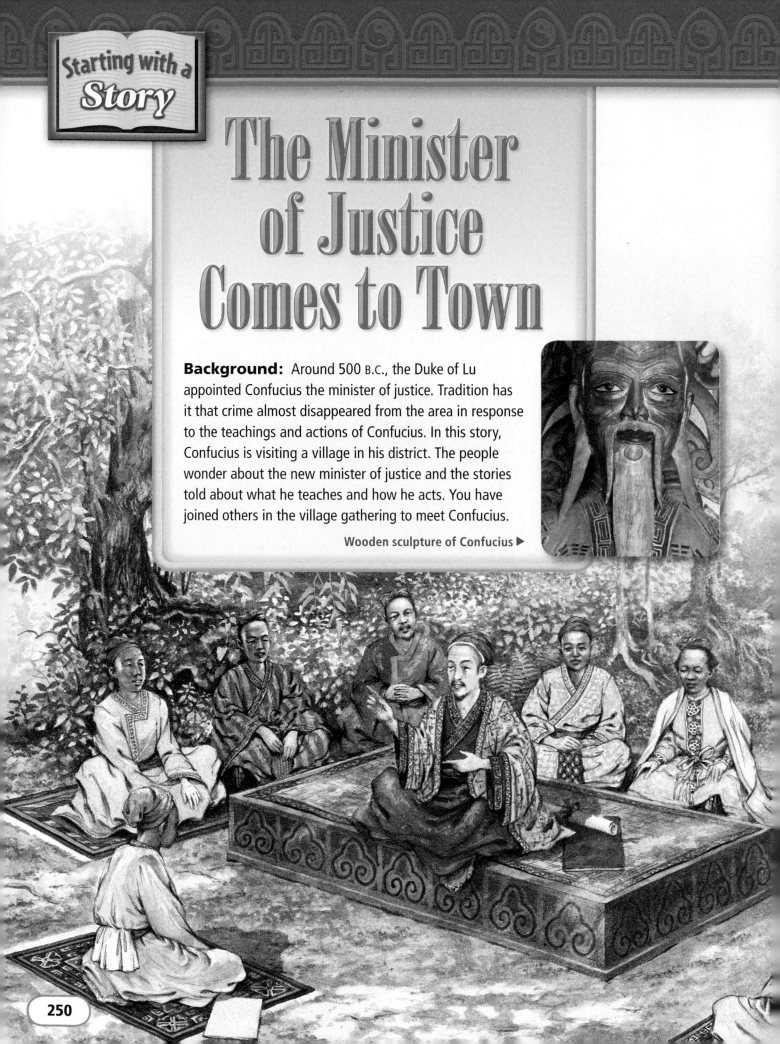

Starting with a Story
eEdition

We saw his oxcart coming in the distance. It was Confucius, the great teacher. We waited, excited at his presence. He was our minister of justice. We had heard stories about how crime and violence had disappeared from villages where he was the main official. We thought this sounded too good to be true.

"I am happy that you came," he said, to greet us all. Then he began to speak. "We need to change our ways of living so that we can all live in peace with each other. I have studied how to make this happen." Then he said that peace required us to learn how to treat each other kindly.

He said that we must behave properly with our family members, our neighbors, and the rulers. He went on, "In our families we must show respect for our parents and our ancestors. We must be righteous, or do what is right rather than what brings us profit. Each of us must know our place. Each has a duty to another."

I asked if that meant the government officials, too. They were always cheating the people and acting as if they were gods. Confucius quickly responded. "That includes the highest rulers," he said. "They must set examples of goodness for us. In turn, we must obey them as their subjects."

"Teacher," I asked, "is that all? Will that make crime and violence go away?" He replied, "It may seem too simple, but it will work. However," he cautioned, "all must agree to respect and honor each other."

He rose to leave. I, for one, was willing to try out his ideas. Did anyone else feel the way I did?

What impact do you think Confucius' ideas will have on the village?

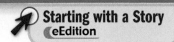

Reading & Writing

1. **READING: Character and Plot** What character trait does Confucius suggest is important in creating a peaceful society? How do you think Confucius' ideas will be accepted in the village?
2. **WRITING: Persuasion** Write a letter to the village members explaining why Confucius' ideas will lead to a more peaceful village.

Lesson 1

MAIN IDEAS

1. **Geography** Natural barriers isolate China's fertile river valleys from other parts of Asia.
2. **Government** The Shang Dynasty ruled China's earliest civilization, which arose near the Huang He.
3. **Government** Claiming approval from the gods, the Zhou conquered the Shang and took over China.

TAKING NOTES

Reading Skill: Explaining Geographic Patterns

Facts about geography can help you understand settlement patterns in history. As you read, take notes on the natural barriers and the farming area of China. Record the information on a Web diagram placing the North China Plain in the center circle.

Skillbuilder Handbook, page R16

▲ **Shang Bronze Drinking Vessel** The Shang were famous for their excellent bronzework.

Words to Know

Understanding the following words will help you read this lesson:

millet a plant that people grow for its grain (page 254)

*Farmers in the northern part of China grow **millet**.*

nomad a member of a group that has no fixed home and moves from place to place with the seasons (page 254)

*The Chinese fought against invading **nomads**.*

favor support or approval (page 256)

*His recent failures led the leader to believe that he had lost the **favor** of the gods.*

mandate an official order or command (page 256)

*The approval of the Chinese gods was considered a **mandate** for a ruler.*

Geography Shapes Life in Ancient China

TERMS & NAMES
- oracle bone
- pictograph
- dynastic cycle
- Mandate of Heaven

Build on What You Know What makes the area you live in a good place for people to live? Think about how the geographic features of your area have affected life there.

Geographic Features of China

1 ESSENTIAL QUESTION What effect did the physical features of China have on its early development?

The river valley pattern you studied in Mesopotamia, Egypt, and the Indus Valley was repeated in China. Its civilization developed because two rivers brought water and silt that made farming possible. Cities grew along the banks of the river.

Isolated by Barriers Located on the eastern side of Asia, China lies about the same distance north of the equator as the United States. China's lands are bordered on the east by the Yellow Sea, East China Sea, and the Pacific Ocean. Deserts edge the northern and western lands. To the north is the Gobi Desert and to the west lies the Taklimakan Desert. The Pamir, Tian Shan, and Himalaya mountain ranges form a tight curve on the western border.

Unlike the regions of the Nile and Fertile Crescent, where civilizations interacted with each other, China was geographically isolated. The huge mountain chains, vast deserts, and large expanses of water made the spread of ideas and goods to China difficult. As a result, Chinese civilization developed along very distinct lines.

Gobi Desert One of the largest deserts in the world, the Gobi covers more land than Texas and California combined. ▼

Two River Systems Two major rivers flow toward the Pacific Ocean. The Chang Jiang (chahng jyahng), or the Yangtze, is found in central China. The Huang He (hwahng huh) to the north is also known as the Yellow River. Their floodwaters deposit yellowish silt that makes fertile soil. In ancient times, most Chinese farming was done in the very rich land between these rivers. This land, called the North China Plain, has always been the center of Chinese civilization.

▲ **Chang Jiang (Yangtze River)** This river is the longest river in Asia. It has been and still is a major trade route throughout China. Like the Huang He, it, too, carries yellow silt.

A Varied Climate China has a varied climate like the United States. Western China is dry like the western United States. The north has seasons like New England. The southeast is like the U.S. south. These different climates allow a variety of crops to be produced. Rice is grown in the moist south, while wheat and millet are grown in the drier north lands. (See map on page 283.)

REVIEW Why was the North China Plain the center of Chinese civilization?

The Shang Dynasty

2 ESSENTIAL QUESTION How did the Chinese language develop?

Around 2000 B.C., farming settlements along the Huang He began to grow into cities. An early civilization began there, and Chinese culture today evolved from that ancient beginning. Therefore, we can say that China is the oldest continuous civilization in the world.

Shang Kings About 1766 B.C., Shang family kings began to control some cities. They set up a dynasty, or rule by generations of one family. The kings were responsible for religious activities. They claimed to rule with the gods' permission. Shang kings controlled the central portion of the North China Plain; their relatives ruled distant areas. The Shang used chariots to defend themselves against the nomads who lived to the north and west. They made war with nomadic people like the Zhou (joh).

Shang Families In Shang culture, respect for one's parents and ancestors was very important. Family was closely tied to religion. The Chinese believed that the spirits of their ancestors could bring good fortune to the family. Families paid respect to the father's ancestors by making animal sacrifices in their honor. Men ruled within the family.

Developing Language The Shang kings claimed to be able to influence the gods to help people. Shang kings received messages from the gods through **oracle bones**. These were animal bones or turtle shells on which Shang royal priests scratched questions to the gods. Next, they touched the bones with heated rods to make them crack. The royal priests interpreted the cracks and scratched the answers on the bones. These scratch marks were an early form of a writing system.

Like other ancient peoples, the Shang developed their system of writing with **pictographs**. This system of writing used simple drawings, or characters, for words or ideas. As you can see in the chart to the right, the pictographs are very similar to the modern Chinese characters. Compared to the English alphabet of 26 letters, the Chinese system of writing used a huge number of symbols. To be barely able to read and write, a person had to know at least 1,500 characters. An educated person had to know at least 10,000 characters.

One unique thing about the Chinese system of writing is that you can read Chinese without being able to speak it. (A person who speaks a language other than English can still understand 2 + 2 = 4.) The writing system helped unify a large and varied land.

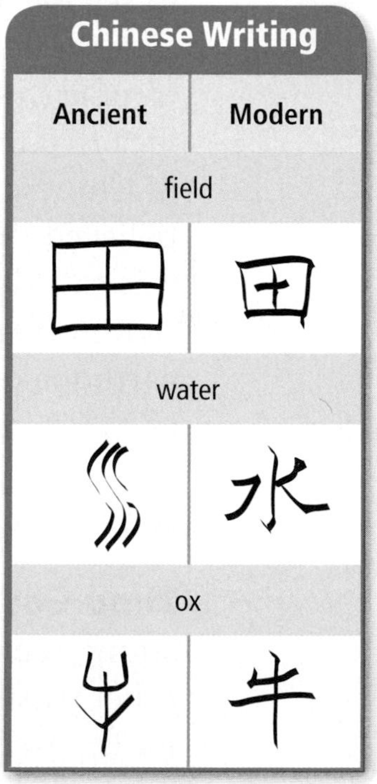

REVIEW How did the Shang develop writing?

The Zhou Dynasty

3 ESSENTIAL QUESTION How were the Zhou able to conquer Shang lands?

The Zhou people moved down from the northwest. They clashed with the Shang on many occasions. Around 1027 B.C., the Zhou ruler Wu Wang led a force that defeated the Shang.

This oracle bone made of a shoulder blade has inscriptions scratched on it.

Chinese Writing

Ancient	Modern
field	
田	田
water	
巛	水
ox	
屮	牛

Dynastic Cycle

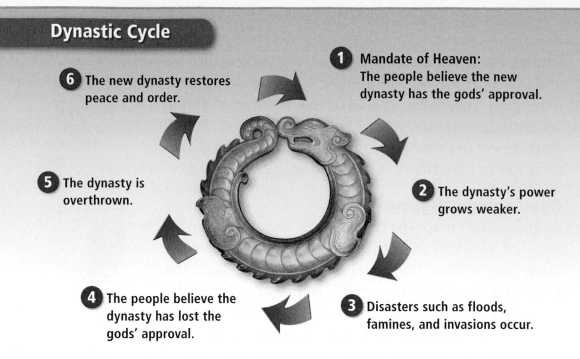

1 Mandate of Heaven: The people believe the new dynasty has the gods' approval.
2 The dynasty's power grows weaker.
3 Disasters such as floods, famines, and invasions occur.
4 The people believe the dynasty has lost the gods' approval.
5 The dynasty is overthrown.
6 The new dynasty restores peace and order.

The Zhou and the Dynastic Cycle The Zhou kings established a new dynasty in China. Chinese dynasties rose and fell in a pattern. Historians call the pattern of the rise and fall of dynasties in China the **dynastic cycle**. Look at the diagram above to see the pattern.

Like the ancient Egyptians, the Zhou kings thought that trouble would come if rulers lost heaven's favor. Eventually, the idea that a good ruler had approval from the gods became a part of Chinese culture. When a ruler was bad or foolish, the people believed the approval of the gods would be taken away. This idea was called the **Mandate of Heaven**. The Chinese people believed that troubles such as peasant uprisings, invasions, floods, or earthquakes meant that the Mandate of Heaven had been taken away. Then it was time for new leaders.

The Zhou adopted many Shang ways. This started a pattern of Chinese culture that developed until the present day.

Zhou Government Like the Shang, the Zhou did not have a strong central government. Kings put people with family ties or other trusted people in charge of regions. Those local rulers, or lords, owed loyalty and military service to the king. In return, the king promised to help protect their lands. As their towns became cities, the lords grew stronger. More groups came under their rule. The lords became less dependent on the king. They began to fight among themselves and with other peoples. The lands they added to their control expanded Chinese territory.

The Time of the Warring States Invasion of Chinese lands was a constant theme in Chinese history. After 800 B.C., nomads from the north and west invaded China. In 771 B.C., invaders destroyed the capital city of Hao and killed the king. The king's family escaped to Luoyang and set up a new capital. Because the kings were weak, the lords fought constantly. This led to a period called the Time of the Warring States, which began around 403 B.C.

REVIEW How did the idea of the Mandate of Heaven help the Zhou take over the Shang?

Lesson Summary

- River valleys supported the rise of Chinese civilization, while some geographic features helped to isolate China from outside contact.
- The Shang developed a dynasty and a culture that included a system of writing.
- The Zhou claimed to rule using the idea of the Mandate of Heaven.

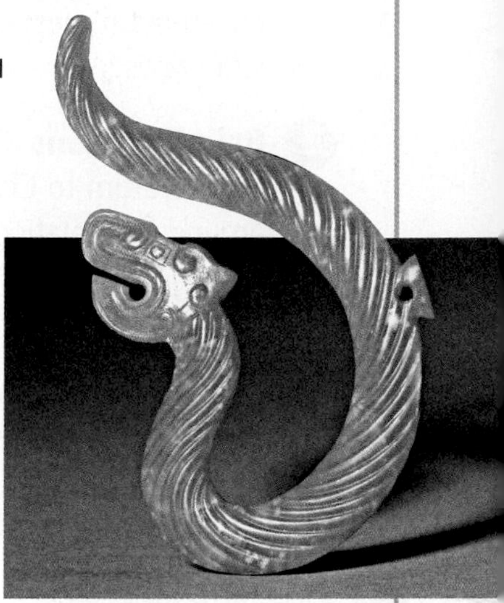

▲ **Jade Dragon Pendant** The dragon is a symbol of power and excellence.

Why It Matters Now . . .

The culture developed by the Shang and the Zhou still influences Chinese ways of life today.

1 Lesson Review

Homework Helper
ClassZone.com

Terms & Names

1. Explain the importance of
   oracle bone — dynastic cycle
   pictograph — Mandate of Heaven

Using Your Notes

Explaining Geographic Patterns Use your completed graphic to answer the following question:

2. How did geographic barriers affect Shang and Zhou relations with outside peoples?

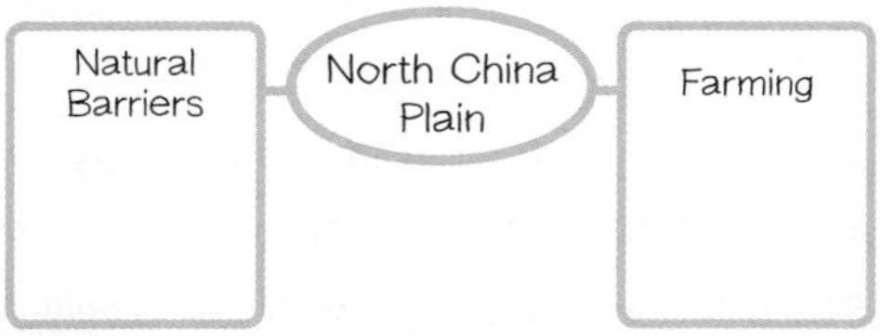

Main Ideas

3. Why did Shang settlements begin along the Huang He?
4. How did the Shang develop a Chinese language?
5. How would the Chinese people know that a ruler had lost the Mandate of Heaven?

Critical Thinking

6. **Understanding Cause and Effect** How did the belief in the Mandate of Heaven help the change in government from the Shang to the Zhou?
7. **Comparing** In what ways was the settling of the Huang He Valley similar to settlements in other world regions?

Activity

Creating Elements of Language Develop pictographs and use them in a sentence about your classroom. Have classmates try to determine what you wrote.

Lesson 2

MAIN IDEAS

1. **Belief Systems** Legalists believed that the government must control people through strict laws.
2. **Belief Systems** Confucius taught that order would return to China if society was organized around five relationships.
3. **Belief Systems** The followers of Daoism taught that people could find virtue by living in harmony with nature.

TAKING NOTES

Reading Skill: Comparing

Comparing can help you see the similarities and differences among sets of things. In this lesson, look for details about the three Chinese philosophies. Identify points that all three philosophies consider important in a chart similar to the one below.

Legalism	Confucianism	Daoism

Skillbuilder Handbook, page R4

▲ Symbol: The Way This Chinese symbol is called Dao. It means "the Way" or "the path." It is made up of two characters. The red one means "go forward," and the green one means "head." Taken together, they mean "the way to understanding."

Words to Know

Understanding the following words will help you read this lesson:

wicked mean, bad, or evil (page 259)
*Some people believe that humans are naturally **wicked**.*

relationship a connection or tie between people (page 260)
*Social customs can have a significant effect on the kinds of **relationships** people have with one another.*

conduct the way someone acts; behavior (page 260)
*Their **conduct** violated rules laid down by the philosopher Confucius.*

complement to work well with (page 263)
*When two people or things **complement** each other, they are said to exist in harmony.*

China's Ancient Philosophies

TERMS & NAMES
- philosophy
- Legalism
- Confucianism
- filial piety
- Daoism

Build on What You Know In the last lesson, you learned about the Time of the Warring States in China. During this time, Chinese society experienced much disorder. Warlords and kings fought with each other to gain control of lands. Scholars wondered what it would take to bring peace to the land. They developed three ways of thinking: Legalism, Confucianism, and Daoism. Each was a **philosophy**, or a study of basic truths and ideas about the universe.

Legalism

1 **ESSENTIAL QUESTION** How did Legalism suggest that society be controlled?

One philosophy was **Legalism**, or a belief that rulers should use the legal system to force people to obey laws. Those who followed this belief system saw disorder in society. These people decided that a strong government was the answer to China's problems.

Strict Laws and Harsh Punishments Legalists believed that human nature is wicked and that people do good only if they are forced to do it. Legalists believed that the government must pass strict laws to control the way people behaved. They believed that harsh punishments were needed to make people afraid to do wrong.

School of Confucius Confucius, second figure from the left, meets with his students. ▼

An Increase in Government Control Shang Yang, a supporter of Legalism, wanted to force people to report lawbreakers. In fact, he thought people who did not report lawbreakers should be cut in two. Legalists taught that rulers should reward people who do their duty.

Legalists did not want people to complain about the government or question what it did. They favored arresting people who questioned the government or taught different ideas. They also taught that rulers should burn books that contained different philosophies or ideas.

REVIEW Why did Legalists want a strong government?

Confucianism

2 ESSENTIAL QUESTION What actions did Confucius believe would bring order to China?

Confucius lived from 551 to 479 B.C., in a time of much conflict and unrest in China. He developed ideas to end conflict and have peace in all relationships. According to Confucius, respect for others was absolutely necessary for peace and harmony. Government leaders should set a good example so that people would see what was correct. Confucius' students collected his ideas and recorded them in a book called the *Analects*. The book tells of Confucius' teachings, which together form a belief system known as **Confucianism**.

Connect to Today

Ceremony Children in Taiwan take part in a ceremony honoring Confucius.▼

The Five Relationships Confucius taught a code of proper conduct for people. In Confucianism there were five basic relationships. Each type of relationship had its own duties and its own code of proper conduct. Here are the five relationships.

- father and son
- elder brother and junior brother
- husband and wife
- friend and friend
- ruler and subject

Notice that the relationships fall into two basic categories: proper conduct in the family and proper conduct in society.

Primary Source

Background: Confucius taught filial piety, or respect for one's parents and ancestors. In this selection, he discusses filial piety with his students. He focuses on propriety, or concern about what is proper or correct in society.

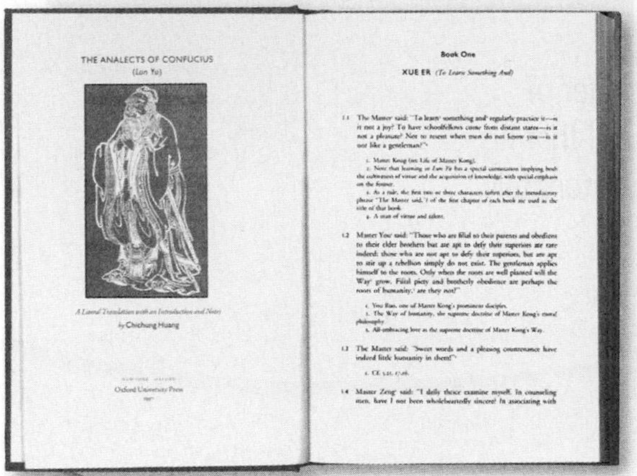
THE ANALECTS OF CONFUCIUS

(Lun Yu)

Book One

XUE ER

from the *Analects*

By Confucius

Translated by James Legge

"The filial piety of now-a-days means the support of one's parents. But dogs and horses likewise are able to do something in the way of support; — without reverence, what is there to distinguish the one support given from the other?" . . .

Mang I asked what filial piety was. The Master said, "It is not being disobedient." . . .

Fan Chih said, "What did you mean?" The Master replied, "That parents, when alive, should be served according to propriety; that, when dead, they should be buried according to propriety; and that they should be sacrificed to according to propriety."

DOCUMENT–BASED QUESTION
What can you infer from Confucius' teachings about the place of the family in society?

Proper Conduct Confucius believed good conduct and respect began at home. Husbands had to be good to their wives. Wives had to obey every decision of their husbands. Brothers had to be kind to brothers, but a younger brother always had to follow the wishes of his older brother. One of Confucius' most important teachings was about **filial piety**, or treating parents with respect. The Primary Source above is about filial piety.

Confucius was also concerned with people's behavior in society. Authority should be respected. The ruler's responsibility was to live correctly and treat his subjects with respect. If a ruler led in a right, moral way, a subject's duty was to obey. If these behaviors were followed, there would be peace in the society.

Primary Source Handbook
See the excerpt from the *Analects* of Confucius, page R42.

The Impact of Confucianism Confucianism set out clear family and social roles. By following these roles, the Chinese people found ways to avoid conflict and live peacefully. Many rulers tried to live up to Confucius' model for a good ruler. By encouraging education, Confucius laid the groundwork for fair and skilled government officials.

REVIEW How did Confucius think rulers should behave?

History Makers

Confucius (551–479 B.C.)

The name Confucius is a translation of the Chinese title *Kongfuzi.* It means "Master Kong."

Confucius began his career at the age of 19 as supervisor of a noble family's herds. He then spent years in study and acting as a tutor to children of rich families. He wanted to be a government official so that he could try out his ideas of ways to change society. One of the ideas he taught may sound familiar to you. He said, "What you do not want done to yourself, do not do to others."

Finally, at the age of 51, Confucius was appointed the minister of justice in his home state of Lu. Legend says he was so successful that his town was free of crime and a model of correct behavior. Unfortunately, Confucius had to leave his post and felt he was a failure.

Daoism

3 ESSENTIAL QUESTION What did the Daoists believe about society?

The third philosophy is said to have begun with Laozi (low•dzuh). No one knows if he really existed, but some say he lived in the 500s B.C. The name Laozi means "Old Master." The book of his teachings is the *Dao De Jing* (*The Book of the Way of Virtue*). The teachings of Laozi are called **Daoism** (DOW•IHZ•uhm). They contrast sharply with Legalism and Confucianism.

Primary Source Handbook
See the excerpt from the *Dao De Jing,* page R43.

The Way Daoists believed that a universal force called the Dao, or the Way, guides all things. All creatures, except humans, live in harmony with this force. To relate to nature and each other, each human being had to find an individual way, or Dao. The individual had to learn to live in harmony with nature and with inner feelings.

Following the Way Daoists did not argue about good and bad, and they did not try to change things. They accepted things as they were. They did not want to be involved with the government.

Daoists tried to understand nature and live in harmony with its rhythms. This included the idea of yin and yang, or two things that interact with each other. The yin (black) stands for all that is cold, dark, and mysterious. The yang (white) represents all that is warm, bright, and light. The forces complement each other. The forces are always changing and evolving. Understanding yin and yang helped a person understand how he or she fits into the world.

In the next lesson you will learn how the three philosophies influenced the way in which the rulers of China controlled their lands.

▲ **Yin and Yang Symbol** The outer circle represents "everything". The inner shapes represent the interaction of the forces—Yin and Yang.

REVIEW Why did Daoism teach that each human had to find an individual way to follow in life?

Lesson Summary

- Legalists believed humans are wicked and need strict laws with harsh punishments.
- Confucius taught a code of proper conduct, including respect, that humans could learn.
- Daoists held the view that each human must find an individual moral path to follow.

Why It Matters Now . . .

The teachings of Confucianism and Daoism remain influential in China and the world today.

2 Lesson Review

Homework Helper ClassZone.com

Terms & Names

1. Explain the importance of

philosophy Confucianism Daoism
Legalism filial piety

Using Your Notes

Comparing Use your completed graphic to answer the following question:

2. Which of the Chinese philosophies stressed the importance of family?

Legalism	Confucianism	Daoism

Main Ideas

3. How did Legalists believe governments should keep peace among people?

4. What was the purpose of Confucius' five relationships?

5. What did Daoists believe about nature?

Critical Thinking

6. Comparing and Contrasting How did the Legalists' views of human nature contrast with those of the Confucians?

7. Making Inferences How might a Daoist respond to Confucius' teachings?

Activity

Creating Classroom Rules Choose one of the three Chinese philosophies and create a set of classroom rules that reflect the basic ideas of that philosophy. Share your rules with others, and decide which rules you would like for your classroom.

Comparing and Contrasting

Goal: To analyze a passage to compare and contrast two Chinese philosophies

Learn the Skill

Comparing means looking at the similarities and differences between two or more things. **Contrasting** means examining only the differences between them. Historians compare and contrast events, personalities, beliefs, and situations in order to understand them.

See the Skillbuilder Handbook, page R4.

Practice the Skill

1. Look for two views about a subject that may be compared and contrasted. The sample passage at the right compares two ways of achieving a perfect society.
2. To find similarities in the views, look for clue words suggesting that two things are alike. Clue words include *both, like, as,* and *similarly.*
3. To find differences, look for clue words that show how two things are different. Clue words include *by contrast, however, except, yet,* and *unlike.*
4. Make a Venn diagram like the one below to help you identify similarities and differences between two things. In the overlapping area, list characteristics shared by both subjects. In the separate ovals, list characteristics not shared by the other. The chart below compares and contrasts two Chinese philosophers, Confucius and Laozi.

Example:

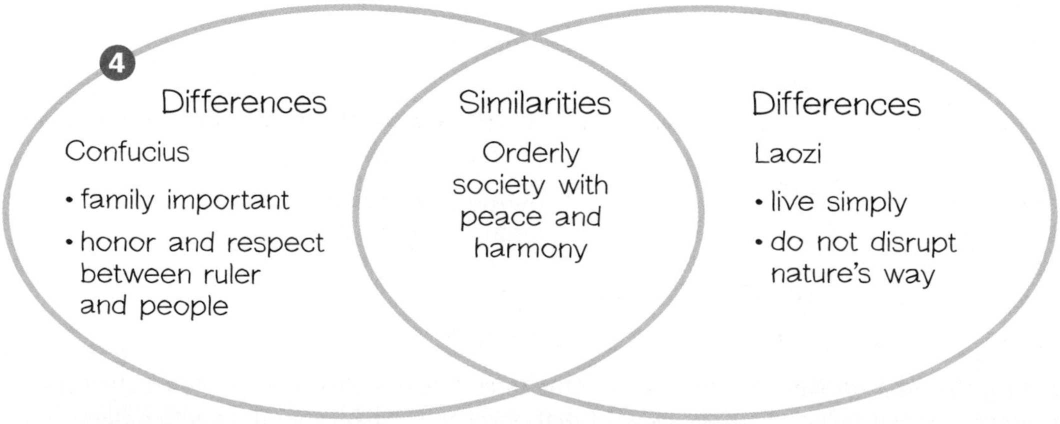

Secondary Source

In this selection, the ideas of two Chinese philosophers, Confucius and Laozi, are discussed. The paragraphs focus on how Confucius and Laozi thought people should live to achieve a perfect society.

▲ **Confucius** Confucius wanted to restore order and harmony to China by having all people show respect for one another.

Two Chinese Philosophies

In China, two philosophers, Confucius and Laozi, looked for ❶ a way to create a perfect society. ❷ Both philosophers wanted people to live in peace and to have an orderly society.

❸ However, the ideas of Confucius are quite different from those of Laozi. Confucius believed family was very important. He said that family members should respect each other. In the community and country, rulers should have respect for the people and the people should respect the ruler. If they do these things, the society will be stable and happy.

Laozi did not agree with the teachings of Confucius. ❸ Unlike Confucius, he believed organizations and human-made systems were not the way to live in harmony. ❸ Instead, Laozi taught that nature provides the best examples of living in harmony. He told his followers to observe the ways of nature and they would know how to live. He stressed living simply and not disrupting the ways of nature. If people did this, he said, there would be peace and harmony in the world.

▲ **Laozi** Laozi believed that the natural order of things was important. If people followed nature, they would have a good life.

Apply the Skill

Go back to Chapter 7, Lessons 2 and 3. (See pages 226–239.) Read the information on Hinduism and Buddhism. Make a Venn diagram like the one at the left to help you take notes on the two religions.

Lesson 3

MAIN IDEAS

1. **Government** Shi Huangdi conquered the warring states, unified China, and built a strong government.
2. **Government** The Han Dynasty took over China and established a strong empire that lasted 400 years.
3. **Culture** Life in Han China set a pattern that is still seen today.

TAKING NOTES

Reading Skill: Comparing and Contrasting

Comparing and contrasting means looking for similarities and differences that can help you understand developments in history. As you read, look for clue words such as *like* or *similarly* that indicate two things are alike in some ways. Compare and contrast the rule of the Qin and Han dynasties. Record your information on a Venn diagram.

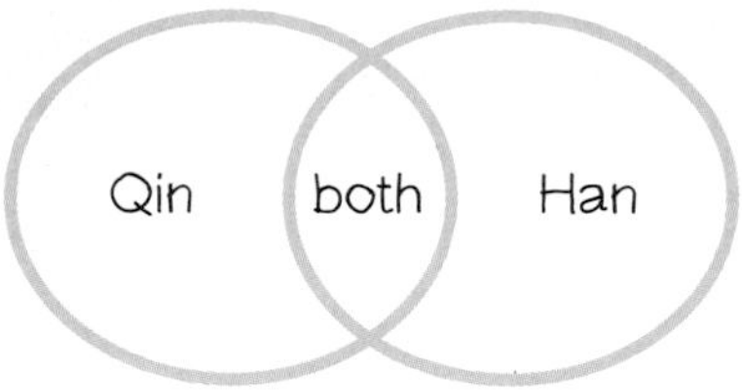

Skillbuilder Handbook, page R4

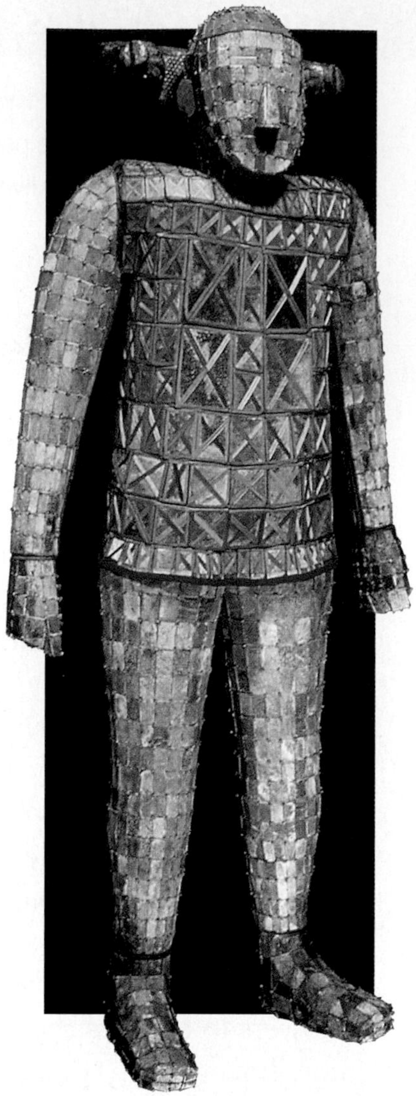

▲ **Jade Funeral Suit** This jade funeral suit is made up of 2,498 jade pieces sewn together with gold thread. The Chinese believed jade would preserve dead bodies for the afterlife.

Words to Know

Understanding the following words will help you read this lesson:

rival a competitor (page 267)
*Shi Huangdi viewed any government not under his control as a **rival** state.*

rebel to defy an authority (page 269)
*Tired of high taxes, the Chinese peasants **rebelled** against the emperor.*

martial having to do with military forces (page 270)
*Because Wudi used military force to gain land, he was known as a **martial** emperor.*

identify to see oneself as part of a group (page 270)
*People usually **identify** with groups that they admire or respect.*

The Qin and the Han

TERMS & NAMES
Qin
Shi Huangdi
Han Dynasty
bureaucracy

Build on What You Know At the end of the Zhou period, several states were still at war. As you recall, the Chinese believed in the Mandate of Heaven. According to that belief, wars and other troubles were signs that the ruling dynasty had lost heaven's favor. A new ruler was needed.

The Qin Unified China

1 ESSENTIAL QUESTION How did the Qin Dynasty unify China?

The new ruler of China came from the state of **Qin** (chihn). (Some scholars think the name of China may come from this word.) The new emperor took the name **Shi Huangdi** (shee•hwahng•dee). He would unify and expand China.

A Legalistic Ruler In 221 B.C., Qin ruler Shi Huangdi began ending internal battles between warring states. He then conquered rival states and drove out nomadic invaders. China grew larger than it had been under the Zhou.

Shi Huangdi believed in the Legalist way of running the country. He tried to wipe out Confucian teachings. He had 460 critics and Confucianists killed. He also ordered the burning of books that contained ideas he disliked.

Terra Cotta Army Thousands of clay soldiers were buried at the tomb of Shi Huangdi. ▼

Uniting China Shi Huangdi wanted a strong central government. To gain personal control of the government, he set out to weaken the noble families. He took land away from defeated nobles. Shi Huangdi also forced the nobles to live at the capital so he could watch them. These actions weakened the power of noble families and strengthened the emperor's power.

Shi Huangdi set out to unite the lands under his control. To link the lands together, he built highways and irrigation projects. He forced peasants to work on these projects and set high taxes to pay for them. He also set government standards for weights, measures, coins, and writing. These steps made it easier to trade and do business everywhere in China.

The Great Wall Shi Huangdi planned to build a long wall along China's northern borders to keep out invaders. He forced hundreds of thousands of peasants and criminals to build it. Many workers died from hard labor. The deaths caused great resentment among the people.

The first Great Wall linked smaller walls that had been built during the Time of the Warring States. The earliest walls were built of earth. Later stone and brick were used. The Great Wall has been rebuilt and extended many times.

The Qin Dynasty Ends Shi Huangdi died in 210 B.C. He was buried in an elaborate tomb. Near his tomb, an army of terra cotta (baked clay) soldiers was buried. Archaeologists discovered the soldiers in 1974. (See Literature Connections, pages 272–276.)

REVIEW Why did Shi Huangdi kill so many Confucianists?

The Great Wall Thousands of people visit a portion of the Great Wall during a holiday. ▼

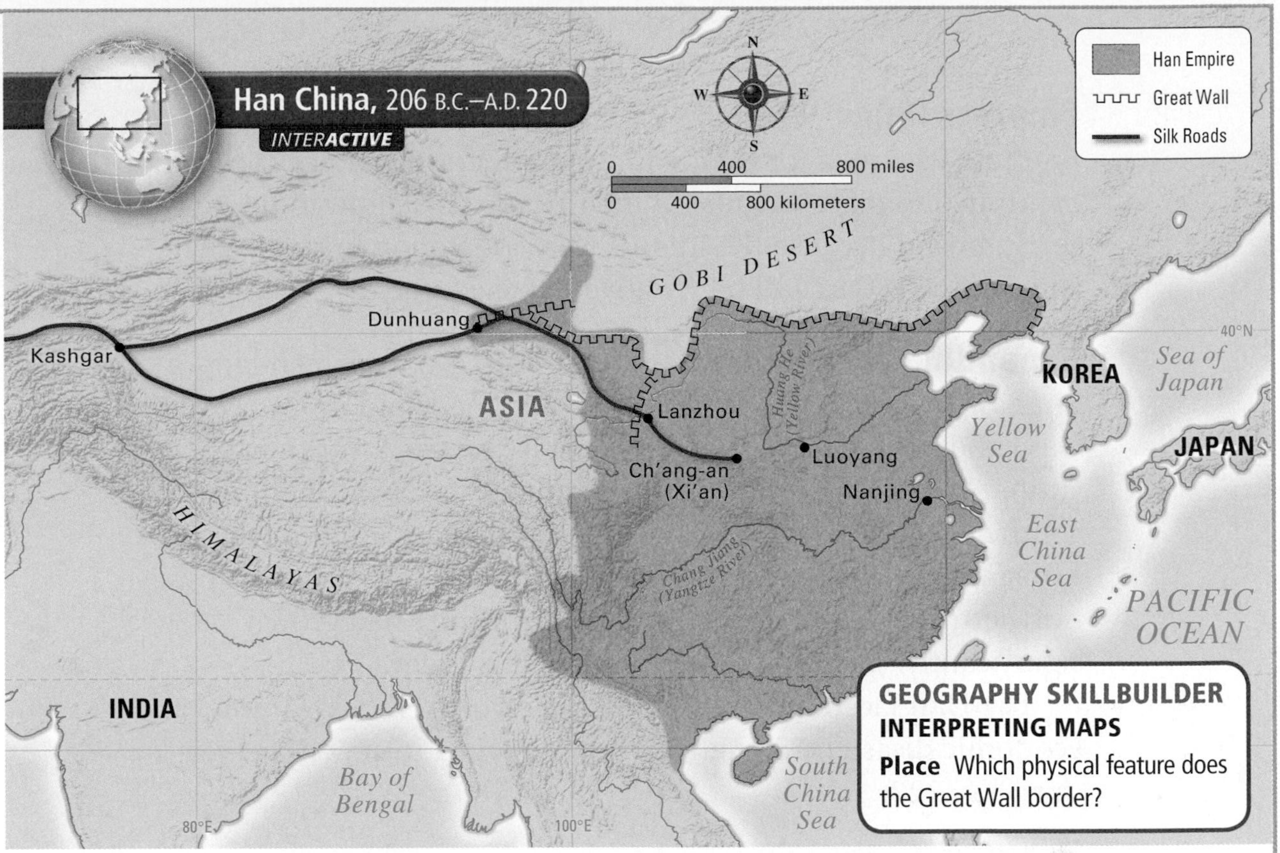

GEOGRAPHY SKILLBUILDER
INTERPRETING MAPS
Place Which physical feature does the Great Wall border?

The Han Dynasty

2 ESSENTIAL QUESTION How did the Han rule China?

Shi Huangdi's son was a less effective ruler than his father. People rebelled during his rule. A civil war broke out during the last years of his reign. Eventually, a military general named Liu Bang (lee•oo bahng) defeated the Qin forces. He ended the civil war and reunified China. In 202 B.C., he started the **Han Dynasty**. The Han Dynasty lasted until about 220 A.D., during the same time period as the Roman Empire.

Han Government Liu Bang kept the Qin policies of strong central government, but he lowered taxes. He made punishments less harsh. In Han China, peasant men owed the government a month of labor per year on the emperor's public projects. He put peasants to work building roads, canals, and irrigation projects.

The Han rulers set up a **bureaucracy**. In this way of governing, officials chosen by the ruler ran offices, or bureaus. The officials helped enforce the emperor's rule. The Han rulers put family members and trusted people in local government positions. They set up a system of tests to find the most educated and ethical people for the imperial bureaucratic state. To do this they tested individuals on their knowledge of Confucianism.

Empress Rules When Liu Bang died in 195 B.C., his widow, the Empress Lü, ruled for their young son. Lü outlived her son and continued to place infants on the throne. This allowed her to retain power because the infants were too young to rule. When she died in 180 B.C. all her relatives were executed.

Expanding the Empire From 141 to 87 B.C., a descendant of Liu Bang named Wudi (woo•dee) ruled the Han Empire. He was called the Martial Emperor because he used war to expand China. Wudi made many military conquests. He brought southern Chinese provinces, northern Vietnam, and northern Korea under his control. He chased nomadic invaders out of northern China. By the end of his rule, China had grown significantly, in fact nearly as large as it is today.

The Han faced rebellions, peasant revolts, floods, famine, and economic disasters. Somehow they managed to stay in power until A.D. 220.

REVIEW How did the Han rulers find people for government jobs?

Life in Han China

3 ESSENTIAL QUESTION What was life in Han China like?

Many Chinese today call themselves the people of the Han. They identify strongly with their ancient past. The Han were industrious people whose civilization prospered.

Daily Life in Han China A large part of the Han society lived and worked on farms. Farmers lived in villages near the lands they worked. Most lived in one- or two-story mud houses. Barns, pigsties, and storage buildings were also located there. Rich farmers probably had an ox or two to pull a plow. Poor farmers had to pull the plows themselves. Both rich and poor had a few simple tools to make farming a bit easier.

Chinese farmers wore simple clothing and sandals, much like clothing today. For the cooler months, their clothing was stuffed like a quilt. Farmers in the north raised wheat or millet. Those in the south raised rice. Families kept vegetable gardens for additional food. Fish and meat were available, but expensive. As a result, most people ate small portions of meat and fish.

Women of Han
These ladies of the Chinese court have elaborate dresses and hair styles. ▼

City Living Not everyone lived in the country. Han China had cities as well. The cities were centers of trade, education, and government. Merchants, craftspeople, and government officials lived there. In some ways, the cities were not too different from today's cities. They were crowded and had lots of entertainment, including musicians, jugglers, and acrobats. According to some writers, the cities also had street gangs.

REVIEW How were the lives of farmers different from those of city dwellers?

Flying Horse This bronze statue of a horse is considered one of the finest pieces of Han art. ▼

Lesson Summary

- In 221 B.C., the Qin ruler Shi Huangdi unified China and ruled by harsh Legalist principles.
- The Han Dynasty ruled over a large and successful land.
- The Han Chinese way of life is reflected in Chinese life today.

Why It Matters Now . . .

Strong government remains important in Chinese life today.

3 Lesson Review

Homework Helper
ClassZone.com

Terms & Names

1. Explain the importance of

Qin	Han Dynasty
Shi Huangdi	bureaucracy

Using Your Notes

Comparing and Contrasting Use your completed graphic to answer the following question:

2. In what ways were the Qin and Han dynasties similar?

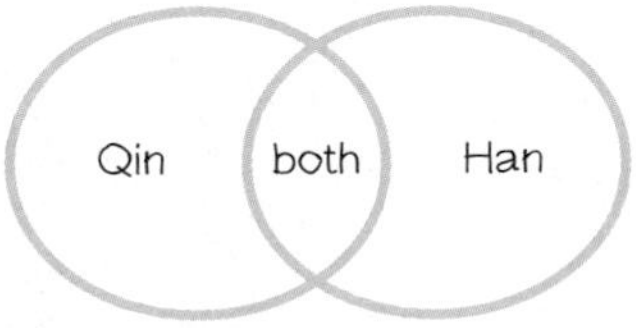

Main Ideas

3. What ruling style did Shi Huangdi choose, and how did it affect his rule?

4. Why was the ruler Wudi important in the achievements of the Han Dynasty?

5. How is the Chinese way of life today similar to that of Han China?

Critical Thinking

6. Making Inferences Why were Shi Huangdi's efforts to unify China important?

7. Comparing How were Shi Huangdi's methods of uniting his lands similar to those of Persian rulers?

Activity

Making a Map Take out the world map that you started in Chapter 2. Add the borders of Han China to the map and then draw the Great Wall of China. Choose an appropriate symbol for the wall.

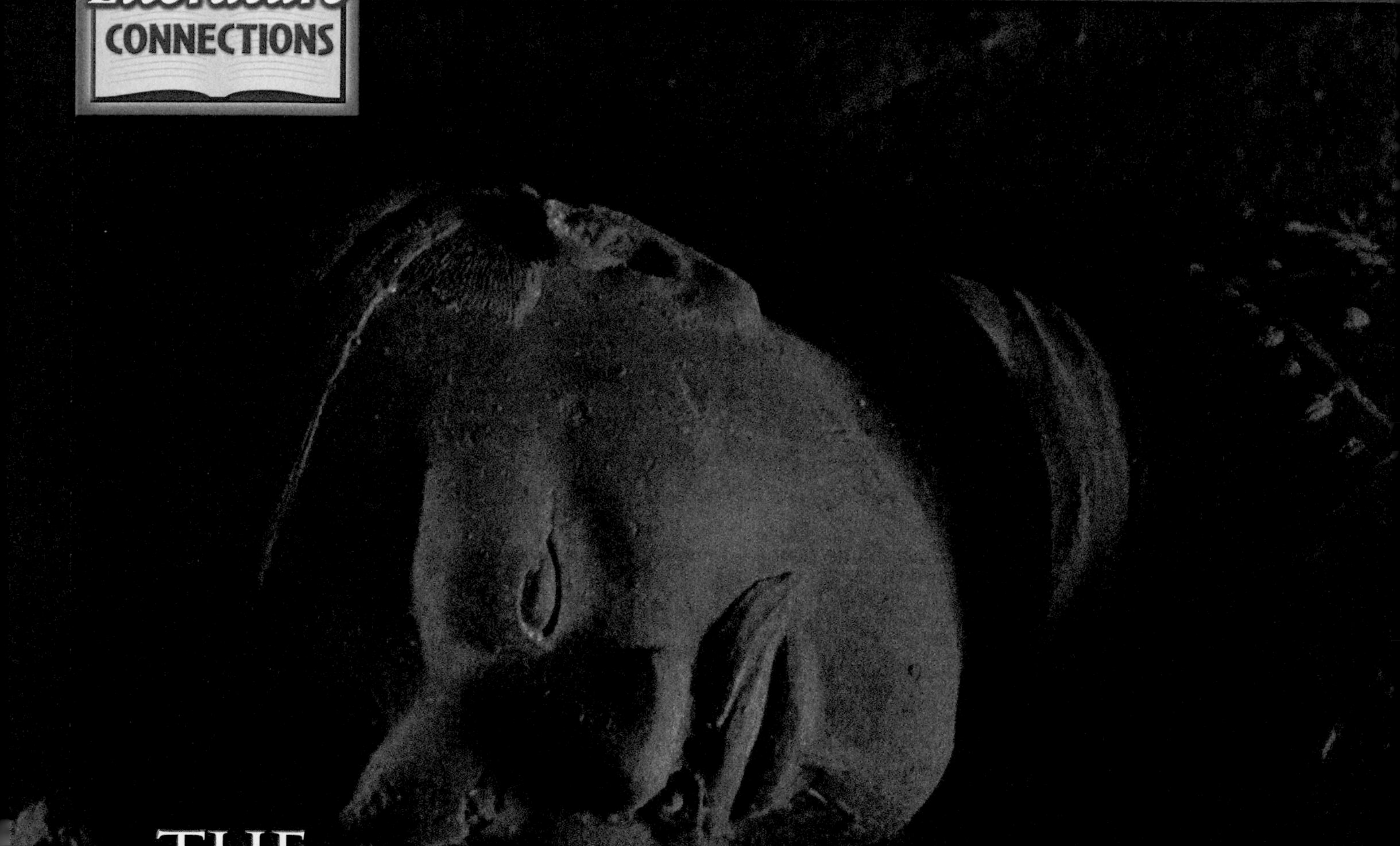

from THE EMPEROR'S SILENT ARMY

BY JANE O'CONNOR

Background: In 1974, three Chinese farmers digging a well hit a hard object. As they continued to dig, the clay head of a man dressed like an ancient soldier emerged from the ground. The farmers had stumbled across a clay army of about 7,500 soldiers complete with weapons and horse-drawn chariots. The army was buried at the site of the tomb of one of China's greatest emperors, Qin Shinhuang . [He is also known as Shi Huangdi (shee• hwahng•dee).]

BURIED SOLDIERS

Qin Shinhuang became emperor because of his stunning victories on the battlefield. His army was said to be a million strong. In every respect except for number, the terracotta army is a faithful replica of the real one.

So far terracotta troops have been found in three separate pits, all close to one another. A fourth pit was discovered, but it was empty. The entire army faces east. The Qin kingdom, the emperor's homeland, was in the northwest. The other kingdoms that had been conquered and had become part of his empire lay to the east. So Qin Shihuang feared that any enemy uprising would come from that direction.

The first pit is by far the biggest, more than two football fields long, with approximately six thousand soldiers and horses. About one thousand have already been excavated and restored. None of the soldiers in the army wears a helmet or carries a shield, proof of the Qin soldiers' fearlessness. But the archers stationed in the front lines don't wear any armor either. They needed to be able to move freely in order to fire their arrows with accuracy. And so these frontline sharpshooters, who were the first targets of an approaching enemy, also had the least protection.

Following the vanguard[1] are eleven long columns of foot soldiers and lower-ranking officers, the main body of the army, who once carried spears, battle-axes, and halberds[2]. The soldiers are prepared for an attack from any direction; those in the extreme right and extreme left columns face out, not forward, so that they can block enemy charges from either side. Last of all comes the rear guard, three rows of soldiers with their backs to the rest of the army, ready to stop an attack from behind.

Stationed at various points among the foot soldiers are about fifty charioteers who drove wooden chariots. Each charioteer has a team of four horses and is dressed in full-length armor. In some carts, a general rides beside the charioteer, ready to beat a drum to signal a charge or ring a bell to call for a retreat. . . .

1. **vanguard:** troops moving at the head of an army.
2. **halberd:** a long-handled weapon used as both spear and a battle-ax.

Pit 2 is far smaller than Pit 1. With an estimated 900 warriors of all different ranks, Pit 2 serves as a powerful back-up force to help the larger army in Pit 1. There are also almost 500 chariot horses and more than 100 cavalry horses.

The terracotta horses are Mongolian[3] ponies, not very big, but muscular and full of power. With their flaring nostrils, bared teeth, and bulging eyes, the chariot horses all look as if they are straining to gallop across a battlefield. The mane of each chariot horse is trimmed short and its tail is braided. That is so it won't get caught in the harness. . . .

Pit 3, by far the smallest, contains fewer than seventy warriors and only one team of horses. Archeologists think that Pit 3 represents army headquarters. That's because the soldiers are not arranged in an attack formation. . . .

Altogether, the three pits of warriors and horses make up an unstoppable army. . . .

REVIEW Which army groups are represented in each pit?

---

3. **Mongolian:** coming from the area of Mongolia.

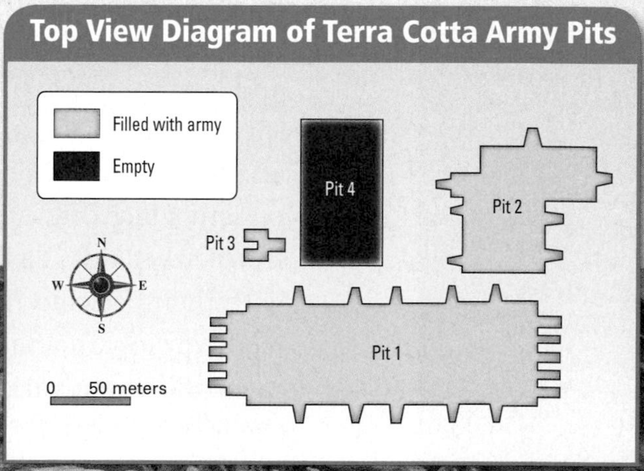

▼ **Pit 2 Soldiers** These are a backup force for the soldiers in Pit 1.

About two thousand soldiers have been unearthed, yet, amazingly, so far no two are the same. The army includes men of all different ages, from different parts of China, with different temperaments. A young soldier looks both excited and nervous; an older officer, perhaps a veteran of many wars, appears tired, resigned.[4] Some soldiers seem lost in thought, possibly dreaming of their return home; others look proud and confident. Although from a distance the figures appear almost identical, like giant-size toy soldiers, each is a distinct work of art. . . .

The uniforms of the terracotta figures are exact copies in clay of what real soldiers of the day wore. The soldier's uniform tells his rank in the army. The lowest-ranking soldiers are bareheaded and wear heavy knee-length tunics[5] but no armor. Often their legs are wrapped in cloth shin guards for protection.

The generals' uniforms are the most elegant. Their caps sometimes sport a pheasant feather; their fancy shoes curl up at the toes; and their fine armor is made from small iron fish scales. Tassels on their armor are also a mark of their high rank.

▲ Mongolian Ponies More than 600 horses were found in the tombs. Some were cavalry horses, and others pulled war chariots.

REVIEW How would you describe the uniforms of the soldiers?

---

4. **resigned:** giving in passively to sorrow or misfortune.
5. **tunic:** a loose-fitting knee-length garment.

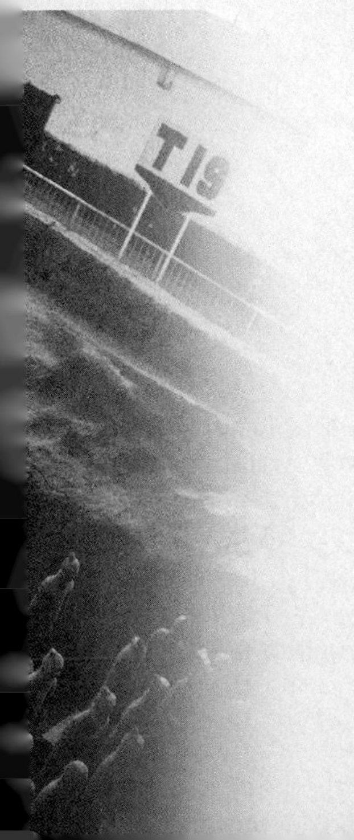

Reading & Writing

1. **READING: Finding Main Ideas** What information about the emperor's army can you gain from the text, pictures, and diagrams in the story?
2. **WRITING: Response to Literature** Write a speech asking for donations to continue the archaeological work at the site of the tomb. Deliver the speech to your classmates.

Lesson 4

MAIN IDEAS

1. **Geography** The Silk Roads brought cultural and economic changes to China.
2. **Belief Systems** Chinese philosophies such as Confucianism and Daoism had a lasting influence on East Asia.
3. **Science and Technology** During Han times, China made many advances in technology, agriculture, and trade.

▲ **Embroidered Silk Tapestry**
This Chinese tapestry shows the Buddha preaching at a site called Vulture Peak.

TAKING NOTES

Reading Skill: Categorizing

Sorting information into groups helps you understand important developments in history. Look for categories of ancient China's legacy and details about them. Record the information on a web diagram.

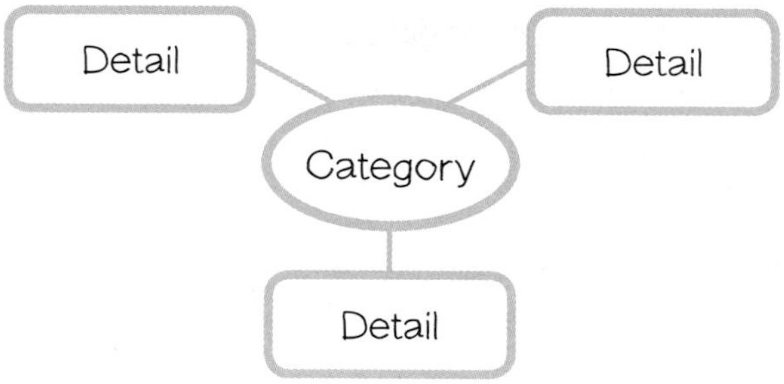

Skillbuilder Handbook, page R6

Words to Know

Understanding the following words will help you read this lesson:

luxury not really needed, but giving pleasure, enjoyment, or comfort (page 277)
*Some Chinese merchants made large sums of money selling **luxury** goods.*

sesame a plant that produces small seeds that can be used for oil and flavoring (page 277)
*She could smell the delightful aroma of **sesame** oil in the meal prepared by her host.*

standard a rule or practice that is accepted as a model (page 278)
***Standards** for behavior can originate in religions as well as philosophies, such as Confucianism.*

harness a set of straps used to attach an animal to a plow or vehicle (page 279)
*The new, improved **harness** that he bought for his horse nearly cut his workday in half.*

The Legacy of Ancient China

TERMS & NAMES
Silk Roads
trans-Eurasian
cultural diffusion

Build on What You Know Trade formed a part of Chinese life. Despite the geographic barriers that separated China from the lands to the west, trade caused Chinese contacts with other lands to increase.

The Silk Roads

1 **ESSENTIAL QUESTION** What kinds of goods moved along the Silk Roads?

During the time of the Han Dynasty, only the Chinese knew how to make silk. It was much desired as a luxury fabric by both the Chinese and people outside of China. Chinese silk was important in opening trading routes to the west.

A Trans-Eurasian Link Overland trade routes were called **Silk Roads** because traders carried silk and other goods on caravan trails. The trails stretched westward from China through central Asia to Mesopotamia and Europe. (See map on pages 278–279.) Because these trails stretched across two continents, Europe and Asia, they were called **trans-Eurasian**. China was part of a huge global trade network.

By 100 B.C., the Silk Roads were well established. Goods leaving China included silk, paper, and pottery. Exchange goods coming from the west included sesame seeds and oil, metals, and precious stones. One trade item the Chinese especially valued was Central Asian horses.

Cultural Diffusion Trade goods were not the only things that moved on the Silk Roads. Ideas and cultural customs moved on the Silk Roads, too. This spread of ideas and customs is called **cultural diffusion**. For example, such things as Central Asian military methods, Buddhism, and western cultural styles reached China. In turn, Chinese art, silks, and pottery influenced the cultures to the west.

Connect to Today

Silk A modern-day seller of silk sells his goods at the ancient Silk Road market at Kashgar in China. ▼

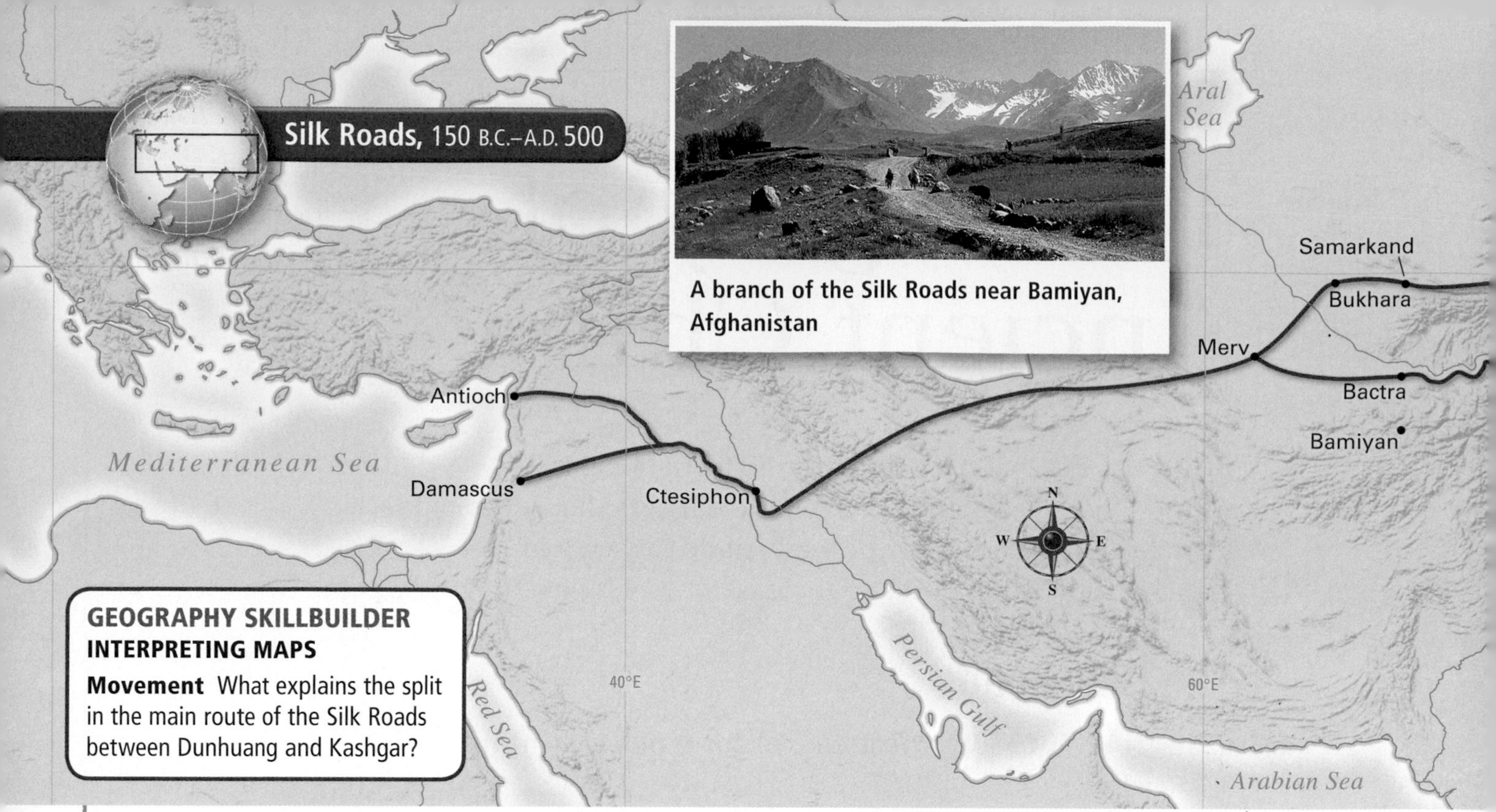

A branch of the Silk Roads near Bamiyan, Afghanistan

GEOGRAPHY SKILLBUILDER
INTERPRETING MAPS
Movement What explains the split in the main route of the Silk Roads between Dunhuang and Kashgar?

The Spread of Buddhism In Chapter 7, you learned about the beginnings of Buddhism in India. During the Han Dynasty, Buddhist missionaries entered China along the Silk Roads. Buddhism spread to Japan and Korea from China. Chinese Buddhists modified Buddhism to make it fit better with their own traditions.

REVIEW Why were the Silk Roads important to Chinese civilization?

Influential Ideas and Beliefs

2 ESSENTIAL QUESTION How important were Confucianism and Daoism?

Confucianism The standards set by Confucianism remained significant in Chinese government and education. Today, the legacy of Confucius' ideas about social duty are still important in Chinese villages. Confucianism also became a very influential philosophy in Japan, Korea, and Vietnam.

Daoism Daoism had a lasting influence in China. By the sixth century it was a religion with priests, rituals, and volumes of collected writings. Unlike Confucianism, however, Daoism remained primarily a Chinese belief system.

REVIEW Where is Confucianism practiced today?

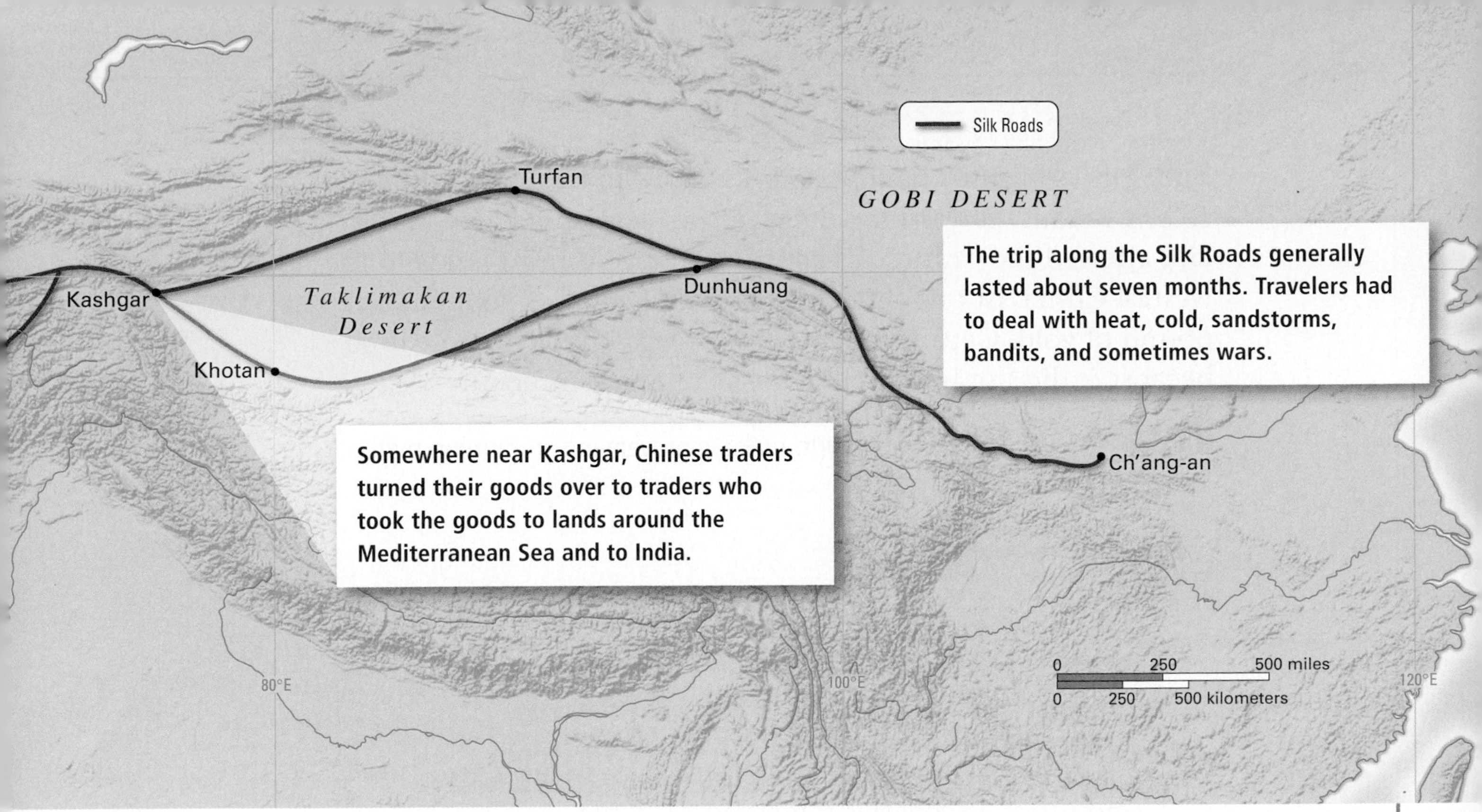
Silk Roads
GOBI DESERT
Turfan
Kashgar
Taklimakan Desert
Dunhuang
Khotan
Ch'ang-an
The trip along the Silk Roads generally lasted about seven months. Travelers had to deal with heat, cold, sandstorms, bandits, and sometimes wars.
Somewhere near Kashgar, Chinese traders turned their goods over to traders who took the goods to lands around the Mediterranean Sea and to India.
80°E
100°E
120°E
0 250 500 miles
0 250 500 kilometers

Chinese Inventions and Discoveries

3 ESSENTIAL QUESTION In which aspects of Chinese life did the Han make great advances?

China had a large and growing population to feed. Because agriculture was so important in China, most of the really important inventions during this period came about in agriculture.

Agricultural Improvements Chinese inventions made life easier for farmers and made more grain available for trade. For example, a better plow and farm tools helped increase crop production. The invention of a collar harness allowed horses to pull heavy loads. The wheelbarrow made it easier for farmers to move heavy loads by hand. Watermills used river power to grind grain. In a land of mostly farmers, these inventions were valuable.

Paper In A.D. 105, paper was invented in China. Before that time, books were made of costly silk. The inexpensive paper was made from a mixture of old rags, mulberry tree bark, and fibers from the hemp plant. Inexpensive paper made books available in a country that valued learning. Paper was important for a bureaucratic government that kept many records.

Silk Silk is beautiful and long lasting. It can be dyed brilliant colors. Because it was rare, it became an excellent trade product. Silk allowed the Chinese to get silver and gold from lands to the west of China. At one time, one pound of silk was equal to one pound of gold. Getting gold and silver was important to China because it did not have rich deposits of either mineral.

REVIEW Why was it necessary to make improvements in farming methods in ancient China?

Lesson Summary

- Trading routes called the Silk Roads brought goods and ideas to and from China.
- Confucianism and Daoism had a lasting influence in China.
- Chinese inventions in agriculture, paper making, and other discoveries improved daily life.

Why It Matters Now . . .

Ancient cultural patterns continue to influence life in China and elsewhere.

4 Lesson Review

Homework Helper
ClassZone.com

Terms & Names

1. Explain the importance of

Silk Roads   trans-Eurasian   cultural diffusion

Using Your Notes

Categorizing Use your completed graphic to answer the following question:

2. What ideas or goods did China give the ancient world?

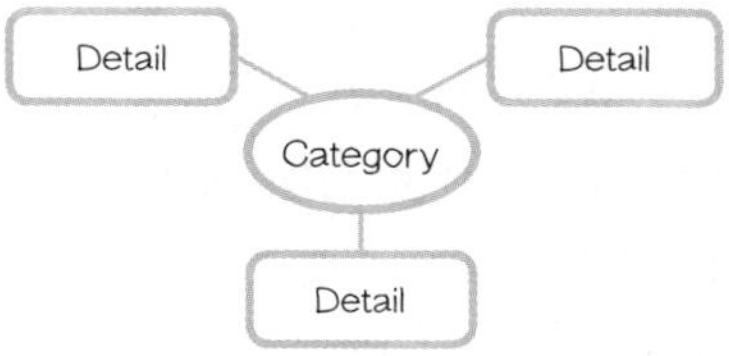

Main Ideas

3. What economic changes did the Silk Roads bring to China?

4. How did the Silk Roads aid in the spread of Buddhism?

5. Why were most of the early Chinese inventions related to agriculture?

Critical Thinking

6. Understanding Cause and Effect Why were the Silk Roads important to ancient China?

7. Making Inferences Why might Confucianism continue to influence life in Chinese villages?

Activity

Internet Activity Use the Internet to research how silk is made. Create a diagram showing the process. Be sure to clearly label all the steps.

INTERNET KEYWORD: *Silk making*

Activity Extend Lesson 4

Keep a Silk Roads Journal

Goal: To analyze the nature of goods, landscape, and means of transportation on the Silk Roads by writing journal entries about a trader's experience on the road

Materials & Supplies
- books on the Silk Roads
- writing paper and pen

Prepare

1. Research the products, landscape, and means of transportation found on the Silk Roads.
2. Reread the information and look at the map of the Silk Roads on pages 278–279 in this chapter.

Do the Activity

1. Imagine you are a Chinese trader about to start a trip on the Silk Roads. Decide what items you will trade.
2. Determine a route you would take starting at Chang'an and ending at Kashgar.
3. Decide what type of animals you will use.
4. Write three diary entries about your experience on the Silk Roads. Be sure to include information about the land you are traveling through and other traders you meet.

Follow-Up

1. How did climate and physical geography help you plan your trip?
2. What things must you think about when planning a long trip on the Silk Roads?

Extension

Making a Wall Map Work with a group to create a large map of the Silk Roads. Tape your map to the wall and have other students add products traded on the Silk Roads.

Chapter 8 Review

VISUAL SUMMARY

Ancient China

Science & Technology

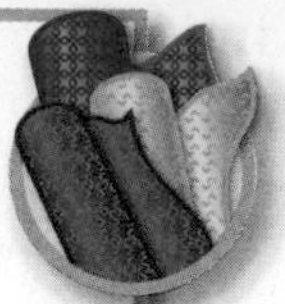

- Chinese master the art of bronzeworking.
- A language system develops.
- Advances in agricultural technology produce more food.
- Paper is invented.
- Silk is produced.

Geography

- Early farmers settle in the river valleys of the Huang He and Chang Jiang.
- Physical landforms make contact with other parts of the world difficult.
- Goods, ideas, Buddhism, and cultural practices moved along the Silk Roads.

Government

- Shang establish first dynasty.
- Mandate of Heaven establishes authority.
- Shi Huangdi and Qin unify China.
- Builders begin the Great Wall.
- Han Dynasty rules for 400 years.

Belief Systems

- Legalism calls for strict control of the people.
- Confucius teaches that the five relationships will bring harmony.
- Daoism promotes learning the way of nature to find harmony.

TERMS & NAMES

Explain why the words in each set below are linked with each other.

1. **Qin** and **Legalism**
2. **Han Dynasty** and **bureaucracy**
3. **filial piety** and **Confucianism**
4. **Silk Roads** and **cultural diffusion**

MAIN IDEAS

Geography Shapes Life in Ancient China (pages 252–257)

5. What made the Huang He so valuable to ancient Chinese civilization?
6. How did Chinese writing develop?

China's Ancient Philosophies (pages 258–265)

7. How did the Legalists and Daoists differ in their views of society?
8. What five basic human relationships did Confucius teach?

The Qin and the Han (pages 266–275)

9. Which policies of Qin ruler Shi Huangdi caused the greatest resentment among the people?
10. What advances in government did the Han make?

The Legacy of Ancient China (pages 276–281)

11. What are some ideas that reached ancient China because of the Silk Roads?
12. Why were agricultural improvements important in ancient China?

CRITICAL THINKING

Big Ideas: Belief Systems

13. **DRAWING CONCLUSIONS** How did the teachings of Confucius support the ancient Chinese family structure?
14. **UNDERSTANDING CAUSE AND EFFECT** How did Confucianism contribute to the development of the Chinese bureaucracy?
15. **FORMING AND SUPPORTING OPINIONS** Which of the three belief systems discussed in this chapter do you think would be the most effective in ruling a land? Explain.

ALTERNATIVE ASSESSMENT

1. **WRITING ACTIVITY** Write a diary entry as a person working on the Great Wall. Include a description of your work and also your views about having to do the work.
2. **INTERDISCIPLINARY ACTIVITY—SCIENCE** Research the paper-making process. Make a poster illustrating the process and tell how it changed Chinese lives.
3. **STARTING WITH A STORY** Review your letter on the impact of Confucian teachings on society. Write a paragraph supporting the view that strict laws, not simply respect, are needed to control society.

Technology Activity

4. **CREATING A MULTIMEDIA PRESENTATION** Use the library or the Internet to research the Qin tomb of Shi Huangdi and a tomb of an Egyptian ruler. Create a multimedia presentation on the tombs. Include
   - location of tombs
   - similarities and differences

Research Links ClassZone.com

Reading a Map The map below shows climates that are found in China and compares them to locations in North America. Answer the questions about the map.

Climate Comparisons, China and North America

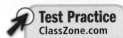

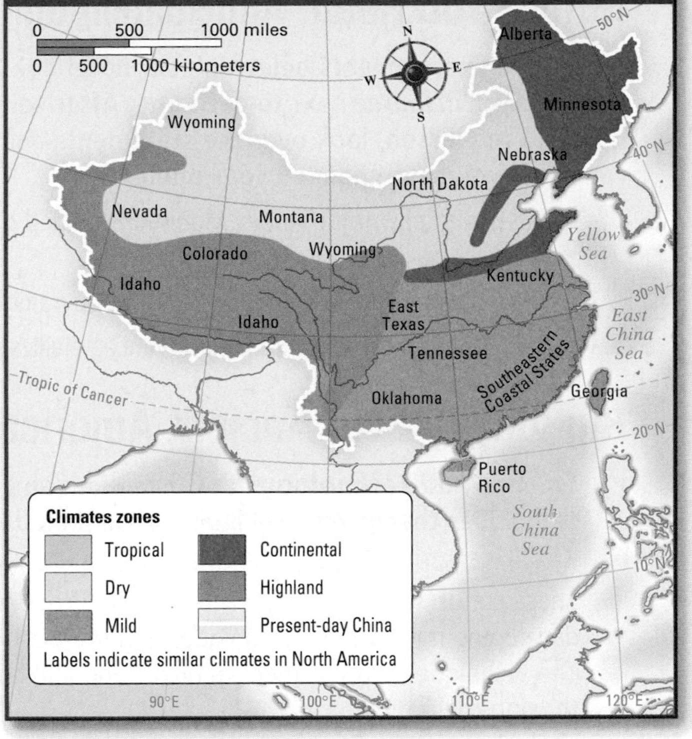

1. **The western lands of China are similar to which state of the United States?**
   A. Minnesota
   B. Idaho
   C. Kentucky
   D. Oklahoma

2. **Which area of China has a climate similar to Nebraska?**
   A. West Central
   B. East Central
   C. Northeast
   D. Far North

Test Practice ClassZone.com

Additional Test Practice, pp. S1–S33

Chapter 9 Ancient America

Before You Read: Anticipation Guide

Copy the statements below in your notebook. Write *agree* or *disagree* next to each one. After you have read the lesson, look over the statements again and see if you have changed your opinion.

- The geography of the Andes Mountains helped civilizations develop there.
- Some ancient American civilizations built pyramids.
- The Maya did not create a very advanced civilization.

Big Ideas About Ancient America

Science and Technology New inventions and techniques change the way humans live their daily lives.

Ancient American cultures arose in difficult environments. These cultures adapted to their challenging conditions by developing new farming techniques and irrigation systems. The techniques allowed them to grow food and build thriving civilizations.

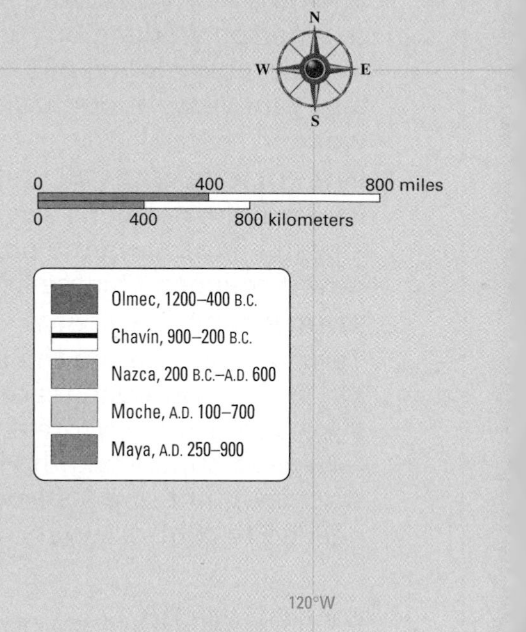

Integrated Technology

eEdition
- Interactive Maps
- Interactive Visuals
- Starting with a Story

VIDEO *Ancient Maya*

INTERNET RESOURCES
Go to **ClassZone.com** for
- WebQuest
- Homework Helper
- Research Links
- Internet Activities
- Quizzes
- Maps
- Test Practice
- Current Events

AMERICAS

1200 B.C.
Olmec build the Americas' first known civilization in southeastern Mexico.
(sculpture of Olmec wrestler) ▶

900 B.C.
Chavín culture arises in Peru and influences other cultures in South America.

1200 B.C. **900 B.C.**

WORLD

1200 B.C.
Attacked by invaders, Egyptian Empire begins to decline.
(Egyptian sphinx and pyramid) ▶

American Civilizations, 1200 B.C.–A.D. 900

INTERACTIVE

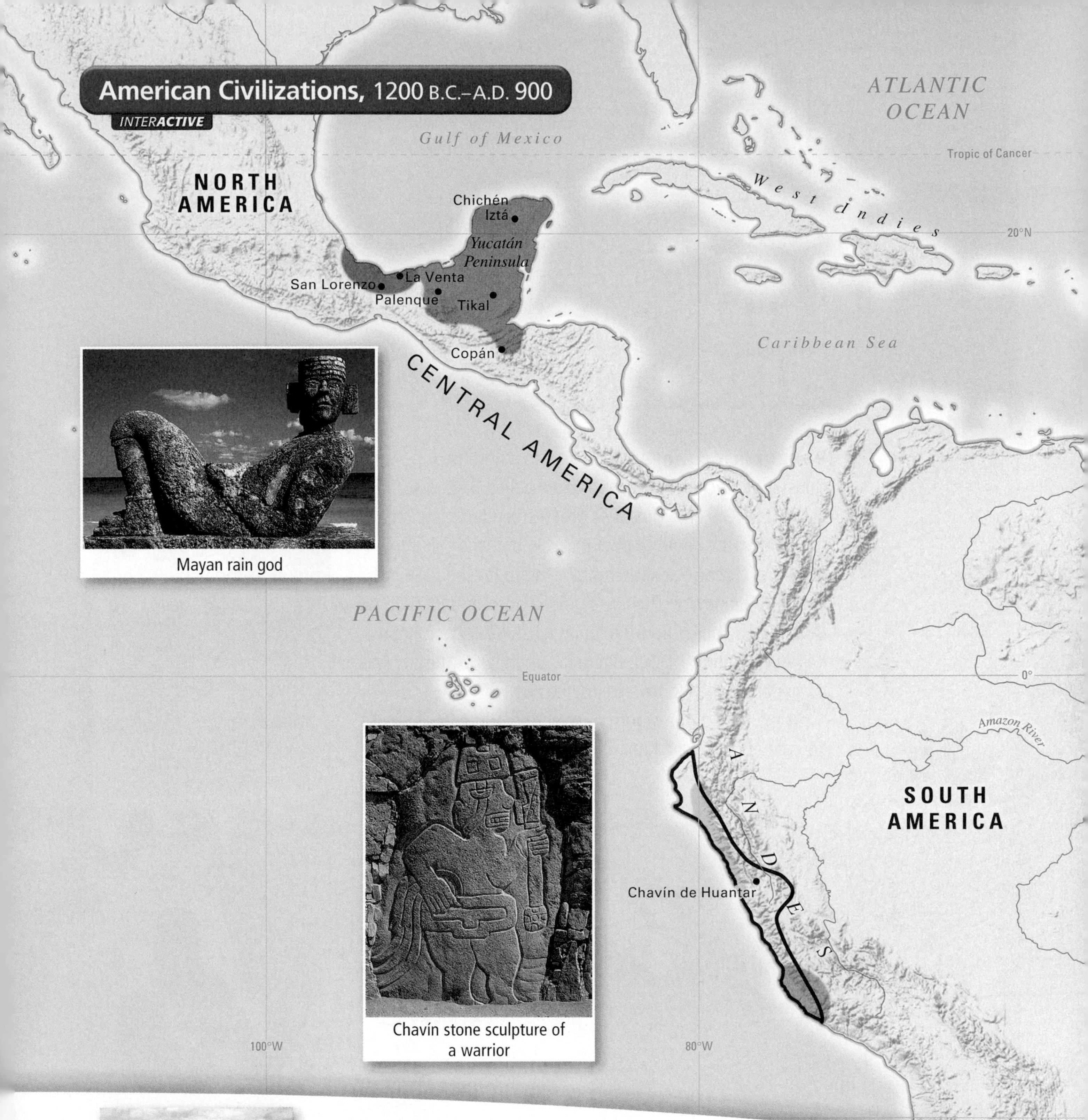

Mayan rain god

Chavín stone sculpture of a warrior

200 B.C.
Nazca culture arises in southern Peru.
◀ (Nazca Lines)

A.D. 100
Moche culture emerges and produces beautiful art.

A.D. 250
Classic Period of Mayan civilization begins.

300 B.C. — **B.C. A.D.** — **A.D. 300**

480 B.C.
Culture and science flourish during the Golden Age of Greece.

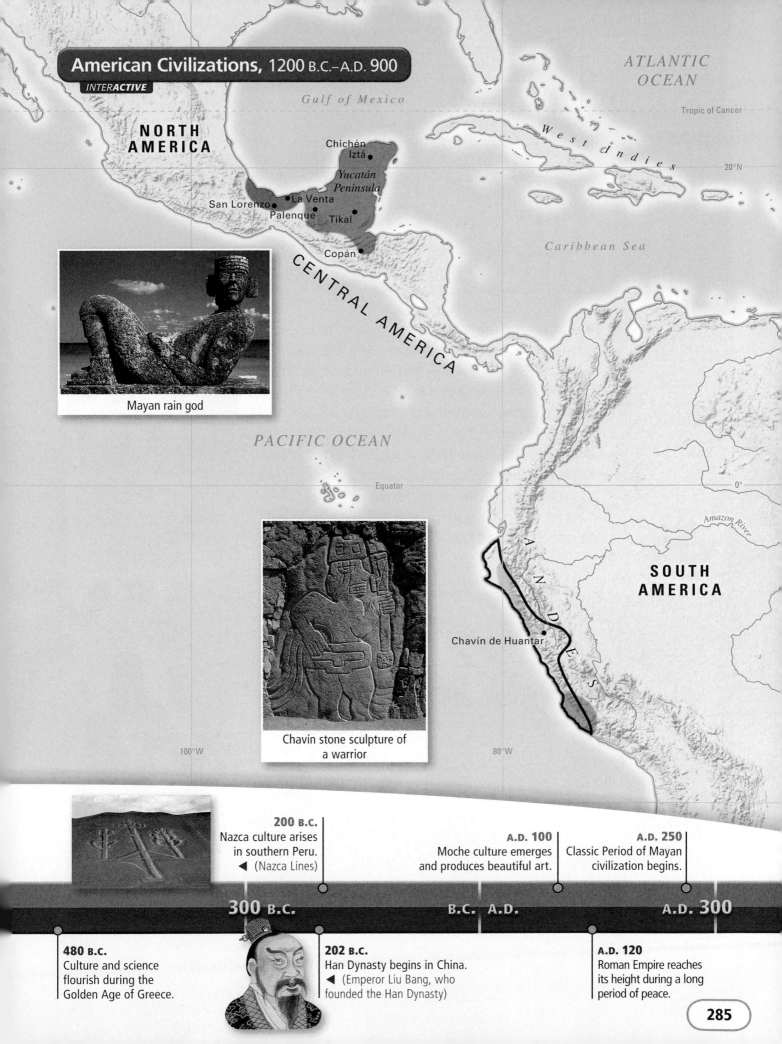

202 B.C.
Han Dynasty begins in China.
◀ (Emperor Liu Bang, who founded the Han Dynasty)

A.D. 120
Roman Empire reaches its height during a long period of peace.

Starting with a Story

King Pacal II and His Sons

Background: In southern Mexico stand the ruins of an ancient Mayan city-state called Palenque (pah•LEHNG•keh). The city's greatest leader, King Pacal II (pah•KAHL), came to power in A.D. 615 and ruled for 68 years. During Pacal's reign, Palenque reached the height of its power. The city's golden age continued under Pacal's two sons, Chan-Bahlum II (chan•BAH•loom) and Kan-Xul II (kahn•SHOOL). But then, around 800, the city was mysteriously abandoned. No one knows why.

At the time of the story, however, the future looks bright. You are about to see Kan-Xul become king of Palenque.

Pacal's jade death mask ▶

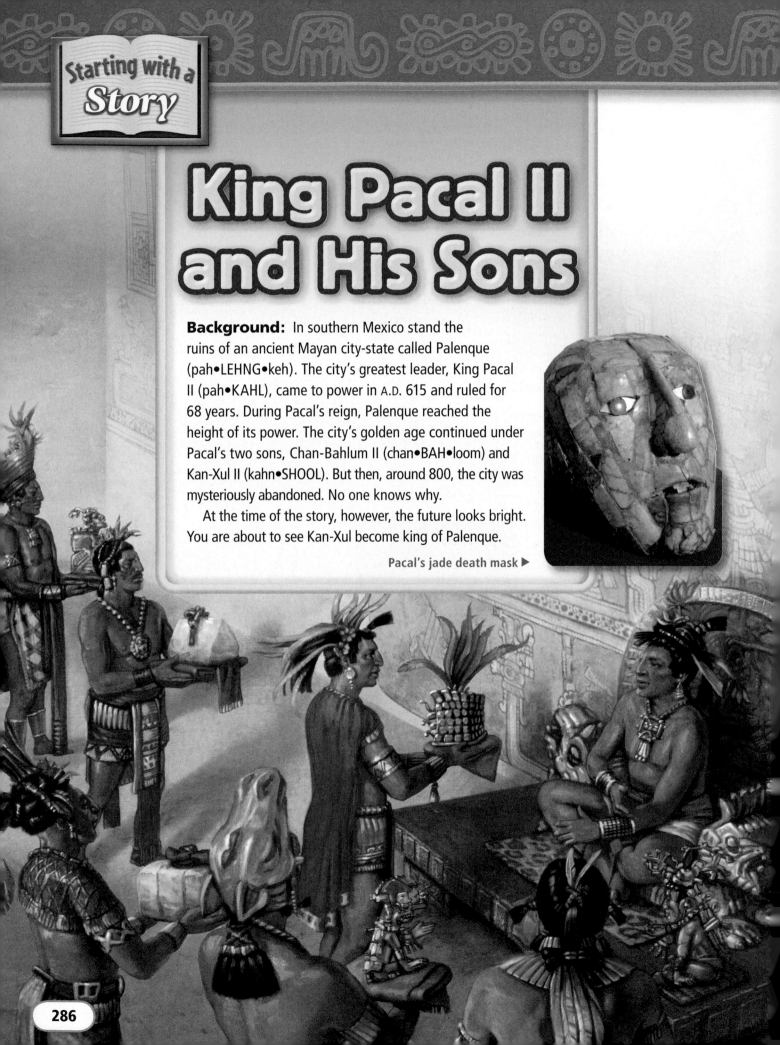

Starting with a Story
eEdition

As an attendant in the palace, you have much to do before the ceremony begins. But as you work, placing the gifts and offerings around the throne, you think about Kan-Xul's father.

Pacal the Great made Palenque one of the most powerful Mayan cities in the land. He had beautiful temples built and decorated them with wonderful jade ornaments and stone sculptures. After Pacal died, the city's artists carved statues of the king. They also made necklaces and rings for him to wear on his journey to the underworld. You were one of the few servants to catch a peek of the life-sized jade mask that was placed over the dead king's face. Now you're almost sorry you looked. Whenever you recall the unblinking gaze of its eyes, you shiver.

After Pacal's funeral, slaves carefully lowered a stone block to seal his tomb. The enormous block weighed as much as 70 men. A long speaking tube extended from the tomb. The tube let Pacal's sons talk and pray to their dead father.

Pacal's oldest son, Chan-Bahlum, ruled for 18 years. He continued his father's work. Now that he has died, his brother Kan-Xul will be the king. After you finish the preparations, you stand at the back of the room and watch the ceremony.

Kan-Xul sits on the jaguar throne. He receives the magnificent jade headdress that his father and brother wore before him. His mother stands at his side and watches as Kan-Xul accepts gifts from the noblemen of the city. You happily imagine the many kings who will certainly follow Kan-Xul. Then suddenly, you feel a strange chill. You remember the cold, staring eyes of Pacal's death mask. The eyes seem to behold a darker future. What do they see?

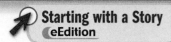

What can happen when a new leader takes power?

Reading & Writing

1. **READING: Supporting Citations** How was Pacal important to his sons and to the people of Palenque? Use citations from the story to support your answer.
2. **WRITING: Description** Imagine that you are a reporter covering the ceremony as Kan-Xul becomes king. Write a short news feature in which you describe what you see.

Lesson 1

MAIN IDEAS

1. **Geography** The physical geographies of North and South America are very different.
2. **Geography** The Andes provide a harsh environment for the people who live there.
3. **Geography** Mesoamerica has a variety of landforms and climates.

TAKING NOTES

Reading Skill: Comparing and Contrasting

When you compare and contrast two subjects, you discover how they are alike and how they are different. As you read Lesson 1, compare and contrast the geography of the Andes with the geography of Mesoamerica. Use a Venn diagram like the one below to record their similarities and differences.

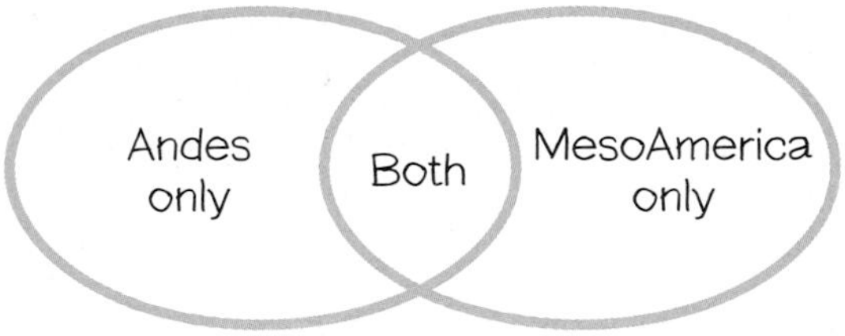

Skillbuilder Handbook, page R4

▲ **Quetzal Bird** The colorful quetzal (keht•SAHL) bird of Central America was greatly respected by the Maya. They used the bird's feathers to decorate the ceremonial robes of kings and priests.

Words to Know

Understanding the following words will help you read this lesson:

impact an effect (page 290)

*A region's climate has a major **impact** on the types of foods that it can produce.*

severe very harsh or extreme (page 291)

*The **severe** conditions in the Andes Mountains offer many challenges to people living there.*

subject likely to have or to get (page 292)

*Buildings can be in danger of collapse in a region that is **subject** to earthquakes.*

The Geography of the Americas

TERMS & NAMES
isthmus
tropical
Mesoamerica
Yucatán Peninsula
slash-and-burn agriculture

Build on What You Know Which do you like best—the mountains, the shore, the desert, the plains? You can find all of these regions in North America. In this lesson, you will compare the geography of North America with that of South America.

Physical Geography of the Americas

1 **ESSENTIAL QUESTION** What is the physical geography of the Americas like?

Look at the map of North and South America on the following page. You can see that the continents are connected. A narrow land bridge called an **isthmus** links them. However, the geographies and climates of the two continents are very different.

Major Landforms and Rivers Mountains run along the western parts of both continents. North America has a north-south mountain range called the Rocky Mountains. South America has a mountain range called the Andes.

Water flows down these ranges to the continents' great rivers. The major river system of North America is the Mississippi. The Amazon and Paraná (PAR•uh•NAH) rivers are the major systems of South America.

Amazon River Villagers of the Amazon rain forest paddle a canoe on the river. The Amazon carries more water to the sea than any other river in the world. ▼

A Variety of Climates The locations of the two continents has an impact on their seasons. As you can see on the map on this page, North America lies north of the equator. Most of South America lies south of it. As a result, the seasons are reversed. When it is summer in North America, it is winter in South America—and vice versa.

The locations of the continents also affect their climates. Much of North America has a mild or dry climate, with four distinct seasons. Most people live in these climates. Few people live in the northern regions of Canada, where the climate is very cold.

South America also has a wide range of climates. In addition, much of the continent receives a great deal of rainfall. In fact, about half of South America is warm and rainy. These warm and rainy areas are called **tropical** zones. Some areas of North America are also tropical. These areas lie mostly in Central America. The people who built ancient civilizations in this Central American area learned to live and thrive in its tropical climate.

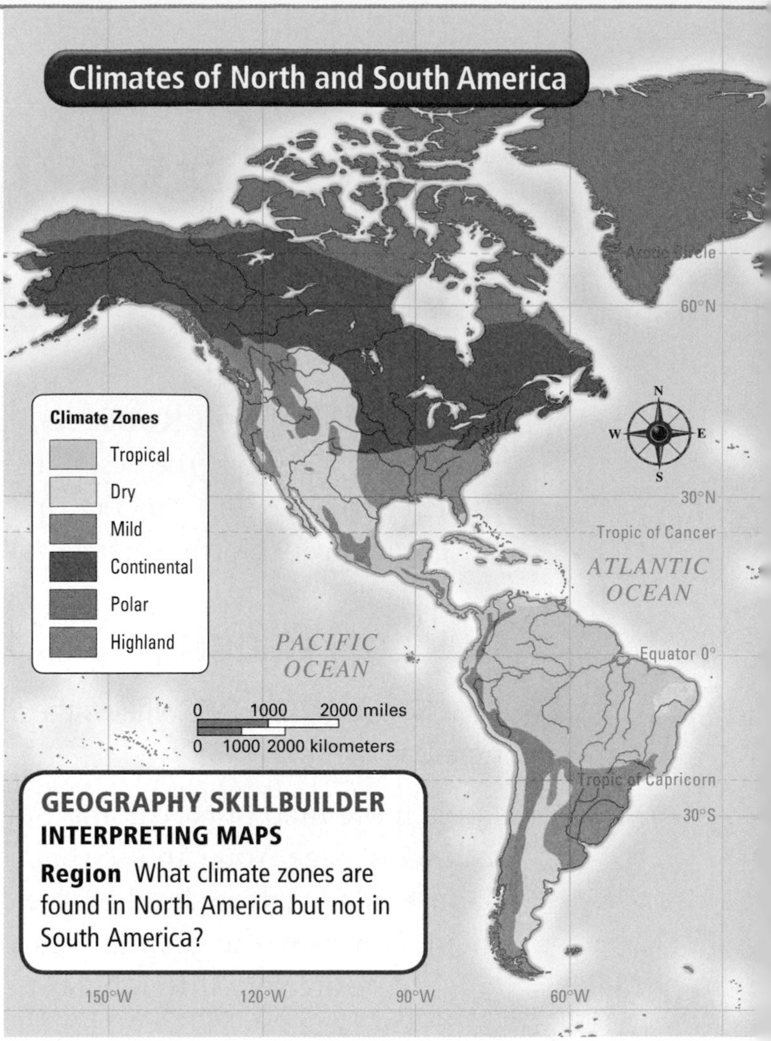

GEOGRAPHY SKILLBUILDER
INTERPRETING MAPS
Region What climate zones are found in North America but not in South America?

REVIEW What are some major differences between the geographies and climates of North America and South America?

Geography of the Andes

2 ESSENTIAL QUESTION What geographic features are characteristic of the Andes?

Ancient civilizations developed on both continents. Some arose high in South America's Andes Mountains. The Andes extend about 5,500 miles from Venezuela in the north to Chile at the southern tip of South America. They consist of very high plateaus surrounded by even higher peaks.

Tall Peaks The peaks of the Andes are the highest in the Americas. Many are over 20,000 feet, or almost four miles high. The highest elevations are covered only by a thin, stony soil. Lower down, the soil is a little richer.

The Andes' location along two colliding plates also makes life there hard. The plate movement causes volcanic activity and earthquakes in the Andes. The climate is severe too. At high altitudes it freezes, and in many places rainfall is unpredictable.

High Plateaus Over a long stretch of the Andes, the mountains split into two ranges. A large group of high plateaus lies between them. This area is filled with hills, valleys, plains, and deserts. A few large rivers water the area. But in the high desert regions, rain almost never falls.

As you might imagine, farming presents a challenge in the Andes. To grow their food, farmers in ancient Andean civilizations developed irrigation canals. These carried water to crops the farmers developed, such as potatoes.

REVIEW What makes the Andes a harsh environment?

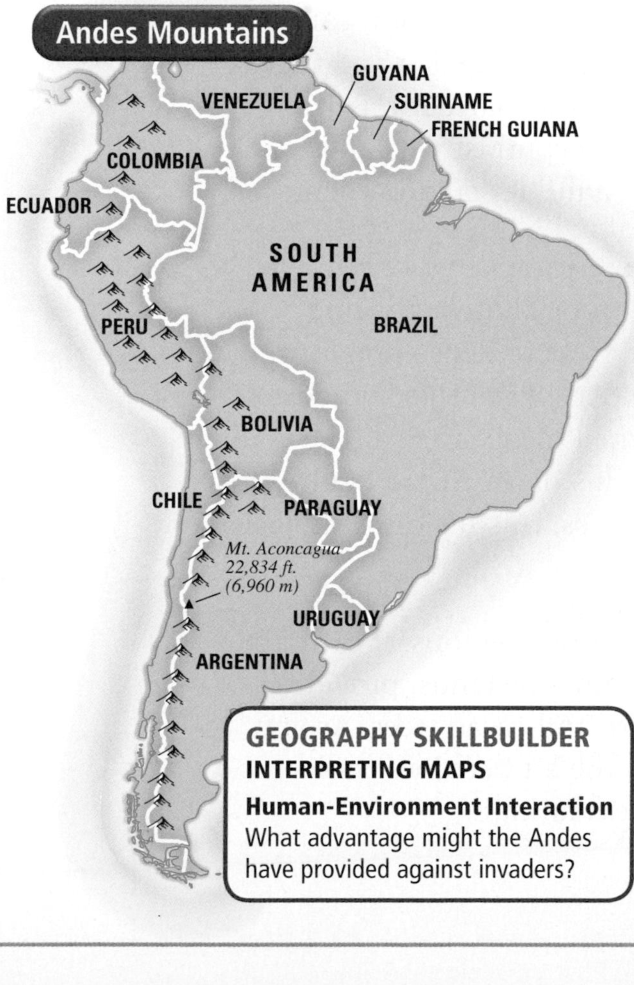

GEOGRAPHY SKILLBUILDER
INTERPRETING MAPS
Human-Environment Interaction
What advantage might the Andes have provided against invaders?

Andes The Andes are the longest mountain range in the world. The top photograph shows a high plateau region. The bottom one shows the more fertile valley region.

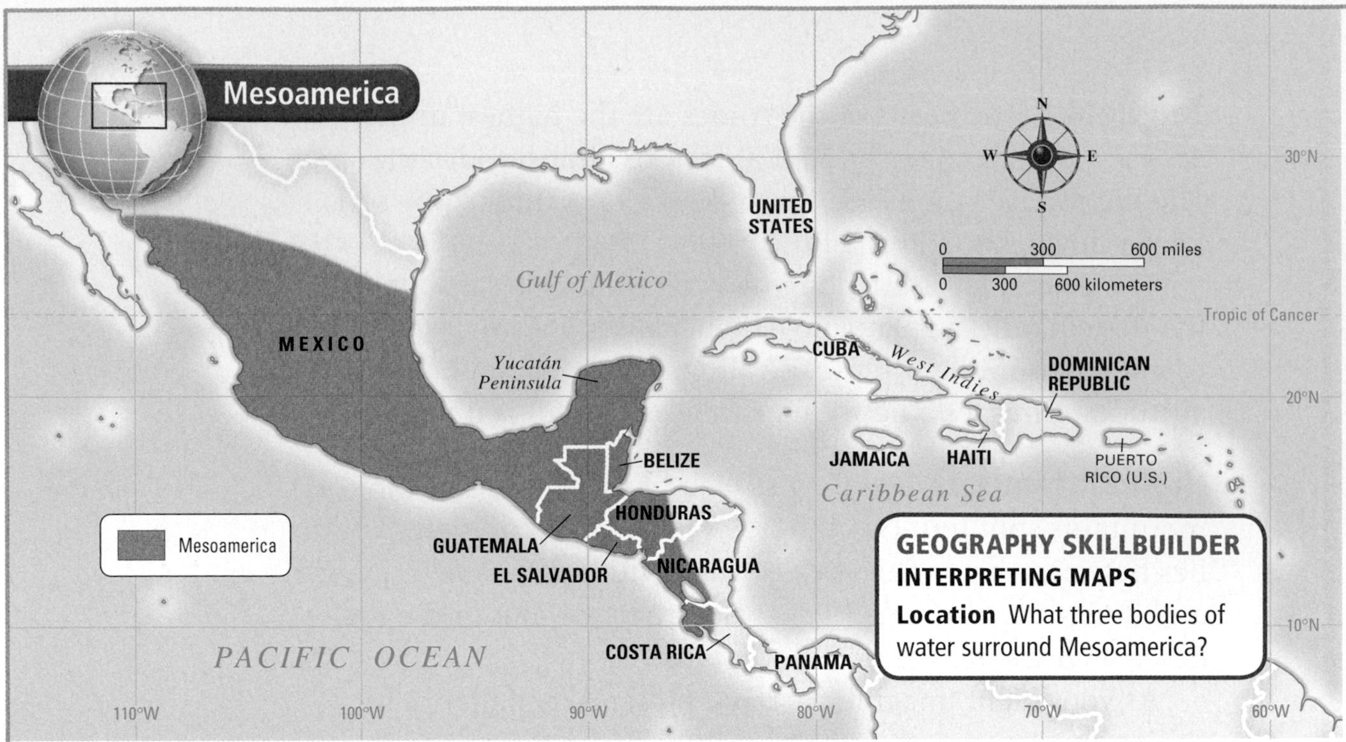

Geography of Mesoamerica

3 ESSENTIAL QUESTION How do the geography and climate of Mesoamerica contrast with those of the Andes?

Ancient civilizations arose in North America in a region called **Mesoamerica**. Mesoamerica includes southern Mexico and the Central American countries of Guatemala, El Salvador, Belize, and parts of Honduras and Nicaragua. In contrast with the Andes Mountains, Mesoamerica offers a milder environment.

The Land of Mesoamerica Mesoamerica has two main regions: highlands and lowlands. The tropical lowlands hug the coast of the Gulf of Mexico. These areas of dense jungle are also found on the **Yucatán** (YOO•kuh•TAN) **Peninsula**, which lies between the Gulf of Mexico and the Caribbean Sea. The highlands stretch between the mountains of the Sierra Madre mountain system. Like much of the Andes, this region is subject to earthquakes and volcanoes.

Climate Rainfall varies greatly in these two regions. It can rain more than 100 inches a year in the steamy lowlands, providing a good environment for palm, avocado, and cacao trees. As you climb toward the highlands, however, the air becomes cooler and drier. This region receives much less rainfall.

Early Mesoamerican farmers had to develop advanced agricultural practices to deal with both climates. In the dry highlands, farmers irrigated their fields, which produced corn, beans, and squash. In the lowlands, they practiced **slash-and-burn agriculture**. They cleared a patch of jungle by cutting back and burning it. When the field became less productive, farmers began again with a new piece of land.

REVIEW How does climate affect the two main regions in Mesoamerica?

Corn These ears of maize, or corn, are being sold in a Yucatán market. Corn was first developed in Mesoamerica. ▼

Lesson Summary

- North America and South America have contrasting climates and geographies.
- The Andes Mountains provided a challenging environment for ancient civilizations.
- The climates of Mesoamerica resulted in the development of different agricultural practices.

Why It Matters Now . . .

Today the potatoes developed in the Andes and the corn developed in Mesoamerica have become important crops in countries all over the world.

1 Lesson Review

Homework Helper
ClassZone.com

Terms & Names

1. Explain the importance of
   isthmus
   tropical
   Mesoamerica
   Yucatán Peninsula
   slash-and-burn agriculture

Using Your Notes

Comparing and Contrasting Use your completed Venn diagram to answer the following question:

2. How is the geography of the Andes and Mesoamerica similar?

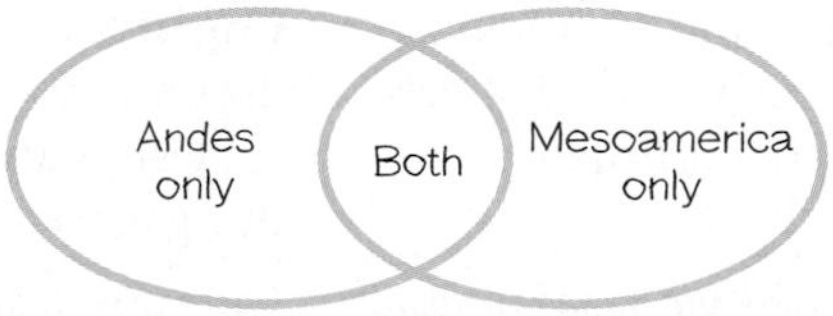

Main Ideas

3. Why are the seasons reversed in North and South America?
4. Why is farming a challenge in the Andes?
5. How did farmers grow crops in the rainy lowlands of Mesoamerica?

Critical Thinking

6. **Explaining Geographic Patterns** Why did farmers in the Andes and in Mesoamerica develop advanced agricultural techniques?
7. **Making Inferences** What might have happened if ancient peoples in the Americas had not adapted to their environments?

Activity **Making a Physical Map** Trace a map showing Mesoamerica and the western coast of South America. Label the major landforms, bodies of water, and regions in both places. Use a legend to identify any symbols or colors on the map.

Lesson 2

MAIN IDEAS

1. **Culture** The art of the Chavín, which featured religious images, influenced other cultures.
2. **Culture** The Nazca civilization left behind beautiful art and mysterious images.
3. **Science and Technology** The Moche created a complex system of agriculture that supported important city structures.

TAKING NOTES

Reading Skill: Drawing Conclusions

When you draw conclusions, you form opinions about what you have read. Draw conclusions about the three ancient Andean civilizations as you read Lesson 2. Use a diagram like the one below to record your conclusions.

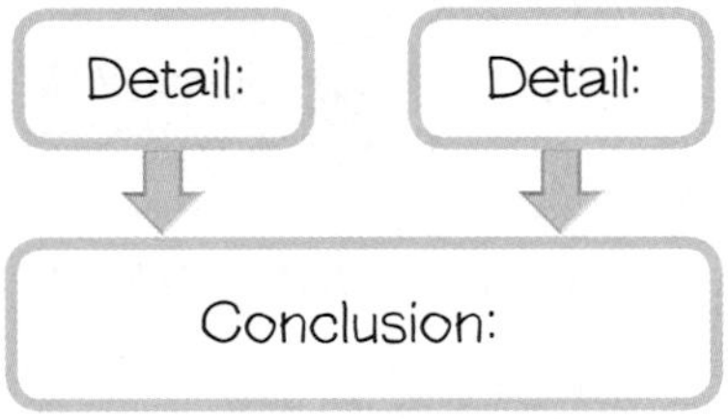

Skillbuilder Handbook, page R25

▲ **Chavín Art** This golden ornament of a snarling cat is typical of Chavín religious art. Some archaeologists believe that artwork featuring snarling cats was used in religious rituals of the Chavín.

Words to Know

Understanding the following words will help you read this lesson:

ruin the remains of something that has been destroyed or has decayed (page 295)
*Archaeologists study the **ruins** of ancient buildings.*

extensive large in quantity or area (page 296)
*Farming in the dry region required an **extensive** system of canals.*

wool the soft, thick, often curly hair of sheep and other animals (page 297)
*They used the **wool** of local animals to make clothing.*

engineer a person who uses scientific knowledge to design and build things (page 298)
*Only a skilled **engineer** could have built the irrigation system.*

Ancient Andean Civilizations

TERMS & NAMES
- Chavín
- textile
- Nazca
- aquifer
- Moche

Build on What You Know You have learned about the rugged landscape and harsh climate of the Andes Mountains. Now find out about the people who created civilizations in this tough environment.

The Chavín Civilization

1 ESSENTIAL QUESTION What was the Chavín civilization?

The ruins of a huge U-shaped temple stand high in the Andes of Peru in a place called Chavín de Huantar (chah•VEEN deh WAHN•tahr). The temple was built by a culture known as the **Chavín**. This culture flourished between about 900 and 200 B.C. Our understanding of the Chavín may increase as more discoveries are made. But for right now, the little we know is based on the ruins of the structures they built.

The Chavín Ruins Archaeologists believe that the Chavín civilization was united mainly by religion. Little is known about their political or economic organization. However, the religious images found at Chavín de Huantar tell us about their culture.

Chavín de Huantar Heads like this one decorated the outer walls of the temple of Chavín de Huantar. The heads may have been designed to frighten away evil spirits. ▼

Religion and Art Some archaeologists believe that Chavín de Huantar was a holy city. The culture's ruler-priests may have called on farmers, who made up most of the society, to build the religious center. The farmers probably worked at Chavín de Huantar to fulfill their religious duty. Followers of the Chavín religion probably traveled to the center for special festivals.

The Chavín culture spread across much of northern and central Peru. Archaeologists know this because they have found the Chavín art style in religious images throughout the northern coast of Peru. This style is seen in stone carvings and in beautiful black and red pottery. The Chavín also embroidered images into woven cloth called **textiles**.

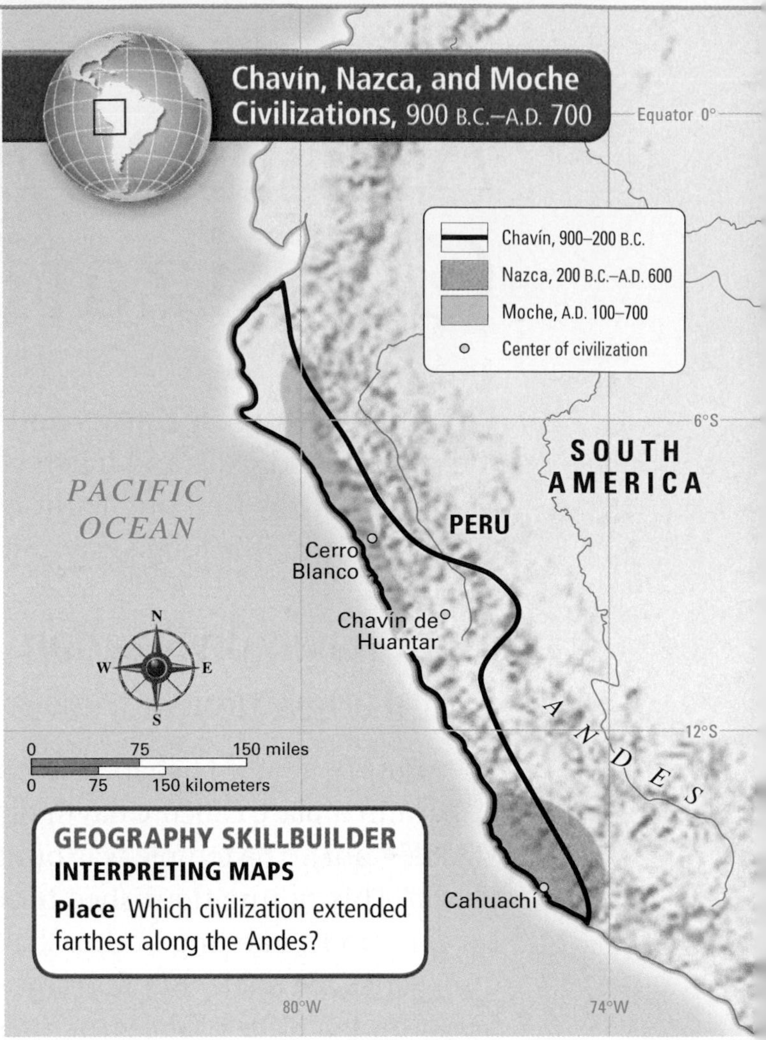

GEOGRAPHY SKILLBUILDER
INTERPRETING MAPS
Place Which civilization extended farthest along the Andes?

REVIEW How did the Chavín influence other cultures?

The Nazca Civilization

2 ESSENTIAL QUESTION How did the Nazca adapt to their harsh environment?

After the decline of the Chavín, other cultures arose in Peru. One of these was the **Nazca** (NAHZ•kuh) culture, which arose along the southern coast of present-day Peru. The Nazca prospered from around 200 B.C. to A.D. 600.

Irrigation and Agriculture Much about the Nazca remains a mystery. Like the Chavín, little is known about the political and economic structures of the Nazca. One of the things we do know about the Nazca is that they developed an extensive irrigation system. Their economy was based on farming, but the Nazca lived in an area that received less than an inch of rainfall a year. So to water their crops, the Nazca built a network of underground canals.

Art The Nazca civilization is also known for its beautiful pottery and textiles. Potters crafted bowls and double-spouted pitchers and decorated them with vividly painted people, birds, fish, fruits, and mythical creatures. Textile artists wove the wool of the alpaca, a camel-like animal, into ponchos, shirts, and headbands. They decorated these fine textiles with religious images and animals.

The Nazca Lines Probably the most striking legacy left behind by the Nazca are the Nazca Lines, which are shown below. To this day, no one knows the purpose of the Nazca Lines. Some people believe that the Nazca worshiped mountain or sky gods and created the drawings to please them. Other people believe the lines showed where surface water entered the plain. Still others say that the lines form a giant astronomical calendar and map. The latest theory is that some of them show the routes of **aquifers**, or underground water sources.

REVIEW What is the Nazca culture known for?

Geography

The Nazca Lines

Between 200 B.C. and A.D. 600, the Nazca made more than 1,000 pictures of birds, plants, animals, humans, and geometric shapes on the plains of southeastern Peru. The dry climate and winds in the region preserved the designs.

Most of the drawings are so big that you can't recognize them from the ground. The hummingbird (top) and parrot shown here, for example, are over 100 feet long. Some designs are more than 2,500 feet long. It's no wonder the Nazca Lines remained undiscovered until people saw them from airplanes in the 1920s.

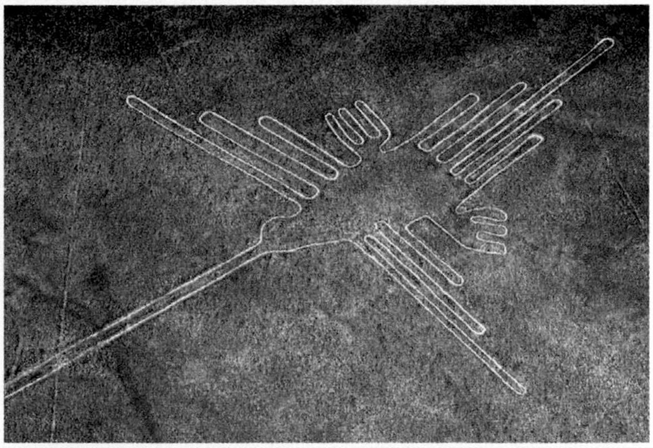

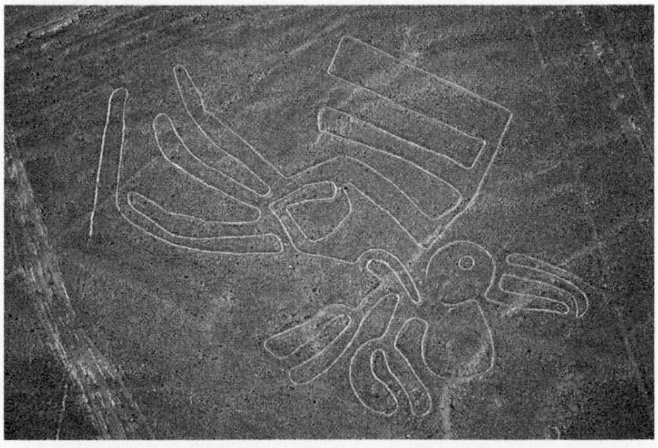

GEOGRAPHY SKILLBUILDER
INTERPRETING VISUALS
Human-Environment Interaction What do the lines suggest about the Nazca?

The Moche Civilization

3 ESSENTIAL QUESTION What does Moche art tell us about their civilization?

While the Nazca rose on the southern coast of Peru, the **Moche** (MOH•chay) culture dominated Peru's hot, dry northern coast between about A.D. 100 and 700. The culture is named for the city of Moche, which may have been the capital of the Moche civilization.

▲ **Moche Pottery** Archaeologists believe that this jug pictures an actual person. Some experts consider the Moche the most skilled artists of ancient America.

Agriculture Like the Nazca, the Moche used advanced farming techniques to make the most of their environment. The Moche channeled the rivers that flowed from the Andes Mountains into impressive irrigation systems. They used this water to grow corn, beans, squash, avocados, chile peppers, and peanuts. In fact, the Moche enjoyed a wide variety of foods. They hunted and fished, gathered snails and wild plants, and ate domesticated ducks and llamas.

City Structures In addition to being good engineers, the Moche were also skilled architects. Two large structures still stand in the city of Moche. The Temple of the Sun is a gigantic step pyramid, which you learned about in Chapter 5. The Temple of the Moon is a raised platform topped with big rooms and courtyards.

Some archaeologists believe that the temples may have served as centers of political power for the Moche. They think that nobles ruled over the people. The lower classes, made up of farmers and laborers, probably paid taxes for the repair of the temples and other city structures.

Art Recent discoveries of Moche tombs have increased our understanding of the Moche civilization. Archaeologists have found beautiful jewelry made of gold, silver, and turquoise. Leaders and the wealthy wore this jewelry. They also wore textiles covered with pictures of people, plants, and animals.

In addition, archaeologists have found pottery that tells us about Moche daily life. The pots show doctors with their patients, women weaving cloth, and musicians playing instruments. But we still don't know very much about Moche religious beliefs or why the civilization fell. One day, further archaeological discoveries may answer these questions.

REVIEW How have archaeologists learned about the Moche civilization?

▲ **Nazca Textile** This colorful poncho was made around A.D. 600. Nazca textiles were sometimes used to show the owner's standing in the society.

Lesson Summary

- Chavín religion spread to a large area along Peru's coast.
- The Nazca developed irrigation systems and etched mysterious lines on the ground.
- The Moche civilization built large cities where artists crafted beautiful jewelry and pottery.

Why It Matters Now . . .

The farming methods used by the ancient Andean civilizations can help people today bring water to their dry fields and develop crops that grow well there.

2 Lesson Review

Homework Helper
ClassZone.com

Terms & Names

1. Explain the importance of

Chavín	Nazca	Moche
textile	aquifer	

Using Your Notes

Drawing Conclusions Use your diagram to answer the following question:

2. What conclusions can you draw about the Chavín culture?

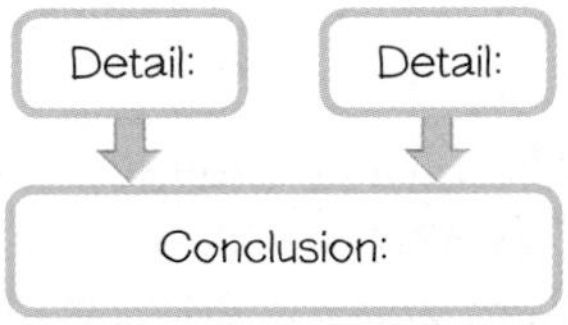

Main Ideas

3. How do archaeologists know that the Chavín influenced other cultures?

4. What are the Nazca Lines?

5. How have recent discoveries increased understanding of the Moche?

Critical Thinking

6. Comparing and Contrasting Compare and contrast characteristics of the Chavín, Nazca, and Moche civilizations.

7. Identifying Issues and Problems Why is it difficult to know more about the Chavín, Nazca, and Moche cultures?

Activity

Making a Nazca Line Drawing Sketch a plan for a Nazca Line drawing that would be 100 feet long. Be sure to indicate the scale you use in your drawing.

Lesson 3

MAIN IDEAS

1. **Geography** The Olmec lived in a fertile land and developed the first civilization in the Americas.
2. **Culture** The Olmec had a complex civilization with many great accomplishments in art and learning.
3. **Culture** Olmec culture spread to other groups of people in Mesoamerica through trade.

TAKING NOTES

Reading Skill: Categorizing

Sorting similar kinds of information into groups helps you understand patterns in history. As you read Lesson 3, look for three categories about Olmec civilization. Record the information you learn about them in a web diagram like the one below.

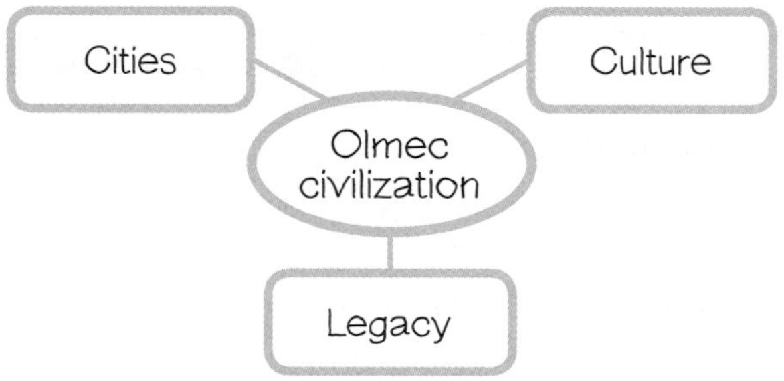

Skillbuilder Handbook, page R6

▲ **Olmec Figure** This Olmec jade figure shows an adult holding a baby. Jade was sacred to the Olmec. They traded throughout much of Mesoamerica to obtain it.

Words to Know

Understanding the following words will help you read this lesson:

scholar a person who knows a great deal about a topic (page 301)

*The discovery of new evidence can cause **scholars** to give up long-held beliefs.*

tomb a grave, chamber, or structure for holding a dead body (page 302)

*Important rulers often had large and elaborate **tombs** built for themselves.*

ton unit of weight equal to 2,000 pounds (page 302)

*Some of the sculptures weigh as much as 20 **tons**, which is roughly equal to the weight of ten automobiles.*

legacy something passed down from an ancestor or predecessor (page 303)

*The **legacy** of the Olmecs can be seen in many elements of Mayan culture.*

The Olmec of Mesoamerica

TERMS & NAMES
Olmec
mother culture

Build on What You Know You have learned about the ancient Andean civilizations in South America. Now you will read about the Olmec civilization, which arose even earlier in Mesoamerica. This North American region had better geographical conditions than the Andes.

The Earliest American Civilization

1 ESSENTIAL QUESTION What helped the Olmec develop the first civilization in the Americas?

Scholars of Mesoamerica used to think that in 1200 B.C., people lived only in villages. Then they discovered the remains of a city-based culture in Mexico's lowlands. Archaeologists named Mesoamerica's first known civilization the **Olmec** (AHL•mehk).

Geography Olmec civilization took root in the jungles along southern Mexico's Gulf coast. Rich soil along the rivers in the region produced generous corn crops for Mesoamerican farmers, just as the fertile soil around the Nile supported Egyptian farmers. As you have already learned, successful agriculture usually comes before the rise of cities.

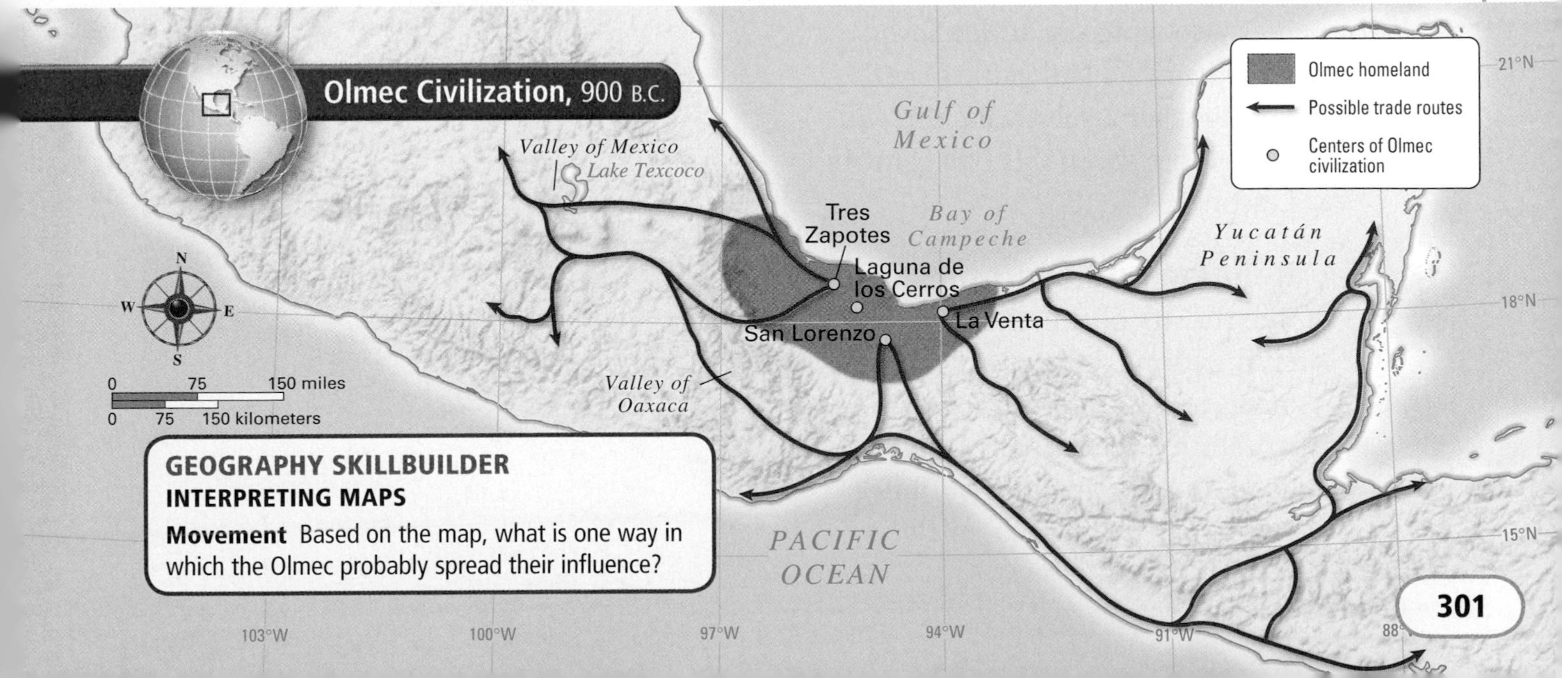

GEOGRAPHY SKILLBUILDER
INTERPRETING MAPS
Movement Based on the map, what is one way in which the Olmec probably spread their influence?

Cities The Olmec built several cities, which served as political centers. One of the cities, now called San Lorenzo, dates back to around 1150 B.C. Archaeologists have found earthen mounds, courtyards, and pyramids in the city. Another Olmec city, now called La Venta, rose around 900 B.C. A 100-foot pyramid discovered there probably once contained the tomb of a great Olmec ruler.

Archaeologists believe that Olmec cities were ruled by powerful dynasties. Administrators, engineers and builders, and artists came below the rulers in the rigid Olmec social structure. Farmers formed the society's largest and lowest class.

REVIEW Why were the Olmec able to build cities?

Olmec Culture

2 ESSENTIAL QUESTION What did the Olmec accomplish in art and learning?

San Lorenzo and La Venta have given archaeologists greater insight into Olmec culture. These cities give us a glimpse into Olmec accomplishments in art and learning.

Olmec Art Some of the most amazing finds were huge stone heads. Crafted with simple tools, some heads stand as tall as 9 feet and weigh as much as 20 tons.

Archaeologists do not know who or what the heads represent. They may represent Olmec rulers or gods. Since all of the faces stare out from underneath helmets, they may also represent athletes who played a ritual ball game played during religious festivals. You will learn more about this ball game in Lesson 4.

Religion and Learning Much like the art of the ancient Andean civilizations, Olmec art was often tied to religion. The Olmec worshiped a number of nature gods. But above all, the Olmec worshiped the jaguar spirit.

Olmec Head The stone used for the heads was carried up to 80 miles over mountain ranges, rivers, and swamps. ▼

Primary Source

Jaguar Sculpture

Background: Scholars have not yet been able to decipher Olmec writing. But images of a jaguar, a big cat that still prowls the jungles of Mesoamerica, appear on many Olmec carvings and other artifacts. The jaguar is an important symbol of Olmec culture. Some historians have even called the Olmec "the people of the jaguar."

The carvings often show an imaginary animal that is part human and part jaguar. Like the three-inch-high sculpture shown here, the creature usually has a snarling mouth and long, curved fangs. The Olmec worshiped the jaguar for its power. They believed that the jaguar could control nature and society.

DOCUMENT–BASED QUESTION
Why do you think the Olmec pictured the jaguar as part human?

Many Olmec sculptures represent this spirit as a half-human, half-jaguar creature. You can learn about these sculptures in the Primary Source feature above.

Advances in learning also reflect religious influence. Some archaeologists believe that the Olmec developed a calendar to keep track of religious ceremonies. They may also have used picture symbols to illustrate the calendar.

REVIEW How was Olmec art tied to religion?

Olmec Legacy

3 ESSENTIAL QUESTION How did the Olmec influence other cultures?

For reasons that are not fully understood, Olmec civilization ended some time after 400 B.C. Invaders, or the Olmec themselves, destroyed most of the monuments in cities such as San Lorenzo and La Venta.

Nevertheless, the Olmec legacy lived on in later Mesoamerican cultures. A large trading network throughout Mesoamerica helped spread Olmec influence. As a result, the Olmec are often called Mesoamerica's **mother culture**.

Vocabulary Strategy

You can use **context clues** to understand the meaning of the term *mother culture*. Words like *legacy*, *spread influence*, and *mother* suggest a culture that supported and inspired others.

Influences Other cultures were particularly influenced by Olmec art styles. These styles—especially the use of the jaguar—can be seen in the pottery and sculpture of later peoples. In addition, the Olmec left behind their ideas for cities, ceremonial centers, and ritual ball games. Their use of picture symbols may also have influenced later writing systems. The Olmec greatly influenced the Mayan civilization, which you will learn about in Lesson 4.

REVIEW Why is Olmec civilization called Mesoamerica's mother culture?

Lesson Summary

- Successful farming gave rise to a great civilization in Mexico's lowlands.
- The Olmec made great advances in art and learning.
- Trade spread Olmec influence throughout Mesoamerica.

Why It Matters Now . . .

The Olmec mother culture continues to influence the cultures of Mexico and Central America today.

3 Lesson Review

Homework Helper
ClassZone.com

Terms & Names

1. Explain the importance of

Olmec mother culture

Using Your Notes

Categorizing Use your completed web diagram to answer the following question:

2. What were important parts of Olmec culture?

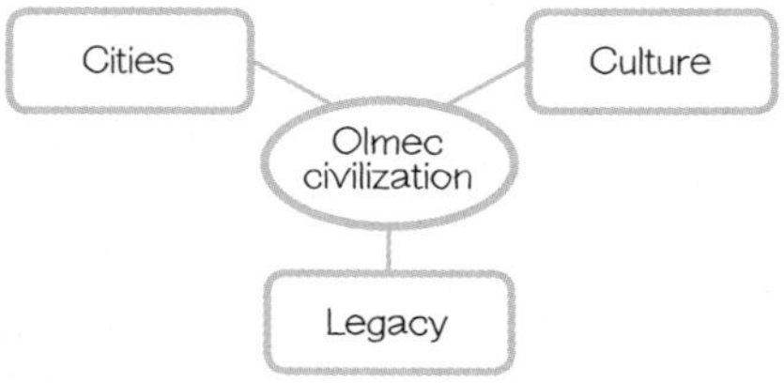

Main Ideas

3. How were classes in the Olmec social structure ordered?
4. What does Olmec art tell us about their religious beliefs?
5. What was the effect of Olmec trade in Mesoamerica?

Critical Thinking

6. **Recognizing Changing Interpretations of History** Why did historians change their minds about how people lived in ancient Mesoamerica?
7. **Comparing and Contrasting** How was the rise of Olmec civilization similar to that of ancient Egypt?

Activity

Writing a Letter Imagine that you are an Olmec artist. Write a letter in which you explain why the jaguar is important to you.

Activity Extend Lesson 3

Make a Shoebox Time Capsule

Goal: To understand that much of what we know about the Olmec and other ancient American civilizations is based on the artifacts archaeologists have found

Materials & Supplies
- paper
- colored pencils
- scissors
- shoebox

Prepare

1. Get together with a small group of classmates.
2. Discuss items that represent today's culture in the United States.

Do the Activity

1. Use the paper and colored pencils to draw two pictures of items that represent U.S. culture.
2. Cut out each drawing with the scissors.
3. Label your drawings.
4. Place all of your group's drawings in a shoebox. Label the box with your group name or number.

Follow-Up

1. Exchange shoeboxes with another group. What items did this group place in its shoebox?
2. Pretend you are archaeologists who have discovered the box 1,000 years from now. What insight does each artifact provide about U.S. culture in the 21st century?

Extension

Making Historical Interpretations With your group, take the drawings out of your shoebox. Erase the labels and tear small pieces off the drawings. Then put the drawings back and exchange shoeboxes once again with another group. Try to identify the "ruins" in the shoebox.

Lesson 4

MAIN IDEAS

1. **Geography** Mayan civilization rose in Central America as the Maya adapted to both highlands and lowlands.
2. **Culture** Mayan society was divided into classes and shaped by religion.
3. **Culture** The Maya produced beautiful art and made important advances in learning.

TAKING NOTES

Reading Skill: Summarizing

When you summarize, you supply only main ideas and important details. Identify the main ideas and important details in each section of Lesson 4. Then put them in your own words and record them in a diagram like the one below.

The Rise of the Maya

Main idea

Detail | Detail

Skillbuilder Handbook, page R3

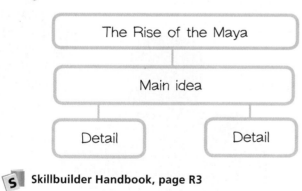

▲ **Mayan Mask** This jade mask, found in a tomb in Tikal, covered the face of a dead Mayan nobleman. The Maya believed that the nobleman would wear the mask during his voyage to the afterlife to protect him from evil spirits.

Words to Know

Understanding the following words will help you read this lesson:

plaza a public square in a town or city (page 308)

__Plazas__ have been a feature of Central American towns and cities since ancient times.

bed the ground under a body of water (page 309)

Soil found in the __beds__ of streams and rivers can be extremely fertile.

rotted decayed (page 309)

Many things __rotted__ quickly in the region's warm and humid climate.

bark the protective outer covering on trees (page 309)

The Mayan people used tree __bark__ to make paper.

The Mayan Civilization

TERMS & NAMES
Maya
maize
stele
glyph
codex

Build on What You Know You have learned that the Olmec influenced other cultures. Now you'll read about one of them, the Maya, who built a powerful civilization in Mesoamerica.

The Rise of the Maya

1 ESSENTIAL QUESTION Where did Mayan civilization rise?

As the Olmec declined, the **Maya** began to develop a civilization from present-day southern Mexico into northern Central America. This area included the lowlands in the north, the dry forests of the Yucatán Peninsula, and the dense jungles of present-day Mexico and Guatemala. The area also included the highlands in the south. This is a range of cool mountains stretching from southern Mexico to El Salvador.

Early Settlements By about 1500 B.C., people speaking Mayan languages first began settling lowland villages, where they farmed and traded. The first ceremonial centers, where the Maya practiced their religion, appeared in wealthier villages by 500 B.C. Eventually, these villages developed into cities.

Tikal The pyramid shown here is the Temple of the Jaguar. It stands in Tikal, one of the great Mayan cities. ▼

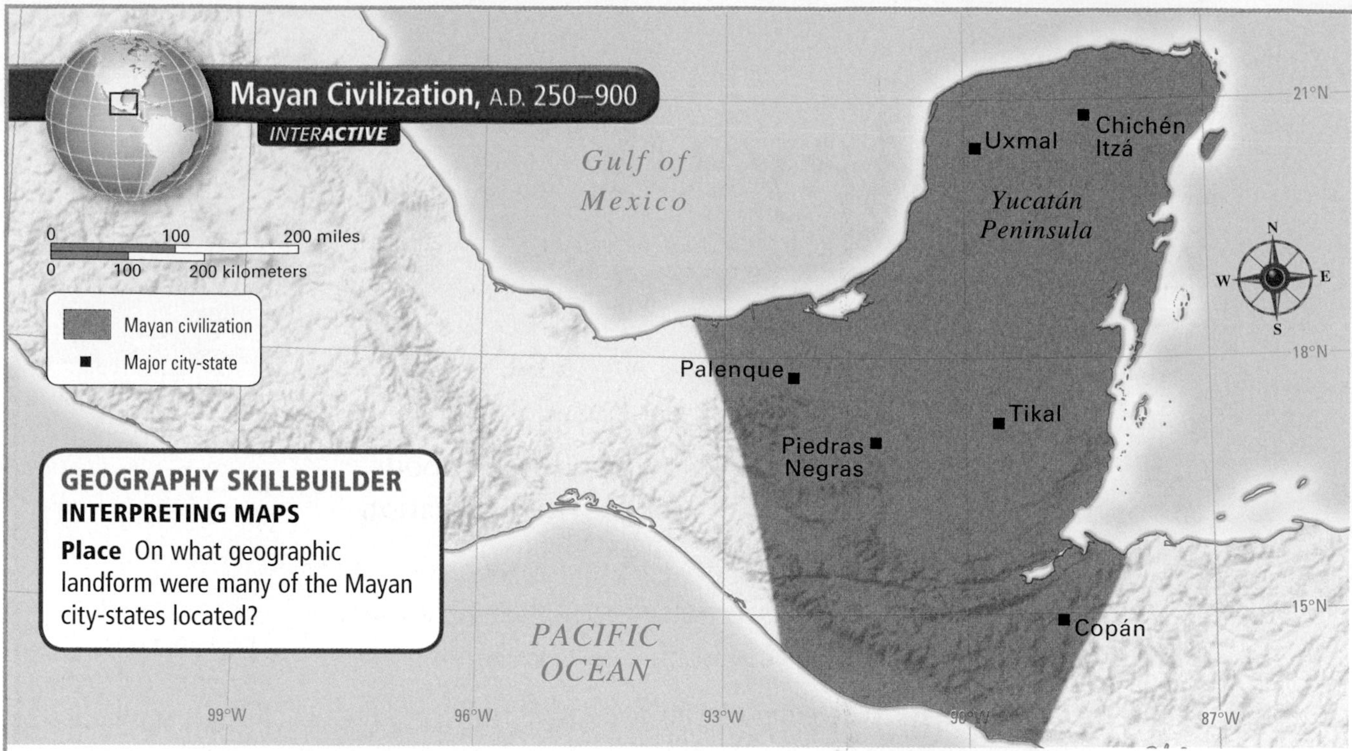

GEOGRAPHY SKILLBUILDER
INTERPRETING MAPS
Place On what geographic landform were many of the Mayan city-states located?

Classic Period Recent findings may cause the dates to change, but the period from A.D. 250 to 900 is traditionally known as the Classic Period of Mayan civilization. During this period, the Maya built magnificent city-states with temples, pyramids, and plazas.

Some of the largest city-states included Tikal (tee•KAHL), Copán (koh•PAHN), and Palenque. (You read about Palenque and some of its kings in Starting with a Story on page 286.) Each city-state was independent and was ruled by a king. However, the cities were linked through trade. Cities traded local products, such as salt, textiles, and jade.

REVIEW How did the Maya develop into a great civilization?

Mayan Life

2 ESSENTIAL QUESTION How was Mayan society structured?

Thousands of people lived in the city-states. Over time, a clear social structure developed. The Mayan king was at the top of this structure, followed by the noble class, made up of priests and leading warriors. Merchants and artisans came next, followed by farmers and then slaves. Slaves were mostly prisoners captured during wars.

Daily Life Most of the Mayan people lived and worked as farmers. They grew beans, squash, and **maize** (mayz), a type of corn. This corn crop was important to the Maya. In fact, according to Mayan legends, people had been created out of maize.

Mayan farmers used a variety of agricultural techniques, including irrigation. To irrigate dry areas, they dug canals that carried water to their fields. They also added rich soil from the canal beds to their fields to lift them above river level. To keep their families dry when the rivers flooded, the farmers built their houses on poles that raised the houses above the ground.

In contrast with the farmers, members of the noble class lived in decorated stone palaces. The Mayan nobles and their children wore beautiful clothes and jade beads.

Primary Source Handbook
See the excerpt from the *Popol Vuh*, page R44.

Religious Beliefs Mayan life was shaped by religion. The Maya prayed to many gods. Their supreme god was the lord of fire. Other gods included the god of the sun, goddess of the moon, and the gods of death, war, corn, and rain.

To gain favor with their gods, the Maya made offerings of animals, plants, and jade. Sometimes they even made human sacrifices. In most large cities, the Maya also played a ritual ball game on a huge court. One of the reasons the Maya played this game is because they believed it would bring life-giving rains. You will learn more about the Mayan ball game in the Daily Life feature on pages 312–313.

REVIEW How was Mayan life shaped by religion?

Stele This carved stone slab of a Mayan ruler stands in a ceremonial center at Copán. Artistic expression in Copán reached its height during the reign of this ruler. ▼

Mayan Culture

3 ESSENTIAL QUESTION What were Mayan achievements in art and learning?

Mayan art and learning were also linked to religion. Art was produced for religious ceremonies. Religious beliefs led to the development of the calendar and to advances in mathematics and astronomy.

Art Mesoamerica's tropical climate long ago rotted Mayan art made of wood, bark, feather, and gourds. Only pottery, sculpture, jade work, and **steles** (STEE•leez)—carved stone slabs—have survived. Steles were used to mark special religious dates and celebrate a ruler's reign.

Comparisons Across Cultures

Mayan and Egyptian Civilizations

The Mayan and the Egyptian civilizations built pyramids and developed writing systems that had striking similarities and differences. Both civilizations used their pyramids as tombs and filled them with treasure. But Mayan pyramids were also used for religious rituals.

Both the Egyptians and the Maya developed writing systems based on picture symbols. However, Mayan symbols—called glyphs—stood for whole words, syllables, or sounds. Egyptian symbols, called hieroglyphs, stood for sounds, ideas, or letters.

Mayan pyramid

Mayan glyphs

Egyptian pyramid

Egyptian hieroglyphs

SKILLBUILDER
INTERPRETING VISUALS
As you study the Mayan and Egyptian pyramids above, what other similarities and differences do you see?

Achievements in Math and Science In Chapter 7, you learned that ancient Indian mathematicians used a symbol for the zero and positions to show place. The Maya also developed these two important mathematical ideas.

Mayan astronomers and mathematicians applied these ideas to develop a calendar system. The 365-day calendar they created is nearly as accurate as a modern calendar. The calendar helped identify the best times to plant crops and attack enemies. It was also used to keep track of religious holidays.

Writing Only a few writing systems developed in the ancient world. The Maya developed the most advanced writing system in the ancient Americas. Mayan writing on steles and books contains symbolic pictures called **glyphs** (glihfs). Some of these glyphs stood for whole words, syllables, or sounds. The Maya used the glyphs to record important historical events in a bark-paper book called a **codex** (KOH•DEKS). Only four of these books have survived.

Abandoned Cities

Abandoned Cities By 900, the Maya had abandoned their great cities. To this day, no one knows why. Warfare, which broke out in the 700s, may have caused a decline. Overcrowding and overfarming may have led to food shortages. When Spanish conquerors arrived in the 1500s, only small, weak city-states remained. However, Mayan peoples still live in Mesoamerica. Many of them still speak the Mayan languages, as well as Spanish.

REVIEW How were art and learning linked to religion?

Connect to Today

▲ **Maya Today** The modern-day descendants of the ancient Maya follow many traditional practices. For example, these women carry corn much like their ancestors did.

Lesson Summary

- The Maya built magnificent cities.
- A clear class structure developed in the Mayan civilization.
- The Maya created lasting artworks, invented a writing system, and made great advances in astronomy and mathematics.

Why It Matters Now . . .

The influence of Mayan culture is found in the United States as a result of immigration from Mesoamerica.

4 Lesson Review

Homework Helper ClassZone.com

Terms & Names

1. Explain the importance of

Maya	stele	codex
maize	glyph	

Using Your Notes

Summarizing Use your completed diagram to answer the following question:

2. What is the main idea of the section "Mayan Life"?

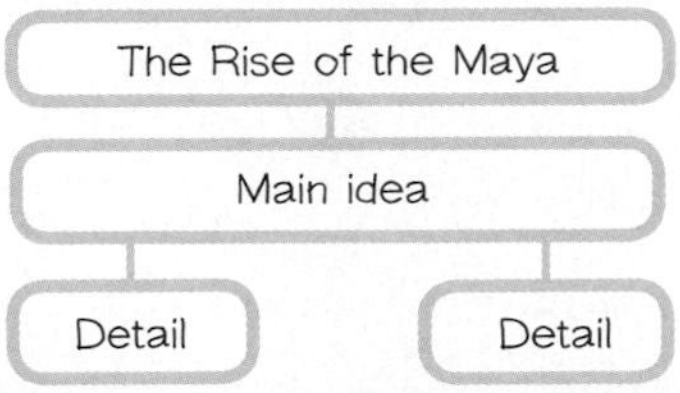

Main Ideas

3. What happened during the Classic Period in Mayan civilization?

4. Who belonged to the main classes in Mayan society?

5. Why did the Maya develop a calendar?

Critical Thinking

6. Understanding Cause and Effect Why do you think archaeologists were able to find many Mayan steles?

7. Comparing and Contrasting How did the Olmec influence Mayan culture and religion?

Activity

Internet Activity Use the Internet to learn more about the Mayan calendar. Create a poster with pictures and captions that shows how the Mayan system worked.

INTERNET KEYWORD *Mayan calendar*

Daily Life

Extend Lesson 4

Playing the Mayan Ball Game

Purpose: To learn about the rules and risks of the Mayan ball game

Ball courts, like this one in Copán, were found in every major Mayan city-state. Most players belonged to the noble class and considered it a great honor to play the Mayan ball game. But the stakes were high. The Maya believed that the gods rewarded the winning team's city with fertile soil and plentiful crops. However, the captain of the losing team was often sacrificed to the gods. Here are some typical features of the Mayan ball game.

A Spectators People crowded along the walls above the court to cheer on their team and favorite players.

B Temple At the end of the game, the captain of the losing team followed the priest up the staircase to the temple and accepted his fate.

C Steles The glyphs on the steles were meant to inspire the home team. They celebrated the city's king and the team's great victories.

D Goal It is thought that to win the game, players had to bounce the ball off of carved parrot heads set about 20 to 30 feet off the ground along the court. But this could take hours or even days.

E Players Players could not touch the ball with their hands or feet. They could only hit the solid, eight-pound rubber ball with their hips, knees, and elbows. Even though players wore heavy padding, they often got hurt.

Activities

1. **TALK ABOUT IT** What does this game tell you about Mayan culture?
2. **WRITE ABOUT IT** Imagine the action as the teams move down the court and put the ball in play. Then write descriptive copy of the action that a television sports announcer might read.

Chapter 9 Review

VISUAL SUMMARY

Ancient America

Geography
- The Andes provided a harsh environment for the Chavín, Nazca, and Moche civilizations.
- The Olmec and Maya lived in fertile land in Mesoamerica.

Culture
- Trade helped spread Olmec culture throughout Mesoamerica.
- Ancient Americans left behind beautiful carvings, pottery, and textiles.
- The Maya built pyramids and temples in their great city-states.

Science and Technology
- The Moche created irrigation systems.
- The Maya developed a calendar and the concept of zero.

TERMS & NAMES

Explain why the words in each set below are linked with each other.

1. **tropical** and **slash-and-burn agriculture**
2. **Nazca** and **aquifer**
3. **Olmec** and **mother culture**
4. **glyph** and **codex**

MAIN IDEAS

The Geography of the Americas (pages 288–293)

5. How did civilizations in the Americas arise in difficult environments?
6. Name some geographical differences between the Andes and Mesoamerica.

Ancient Andean Civilizations (pages 294–299)

7. How were art and religion linked in the Chavín and Nazca cultures?
8. How have archaeologists learned about the Chavín, Nazca, and Moche?

The Olmec of Mesoamerica (pages 300–305)

9. What was the importance of discovering ruins in San Lorenzo and La Venta?
10. What aspects of the Olmec civilization influenced other cultures?

The Mayan Civilization (pages 306–313)

11. Describe the geography of the area where Mayan civilization rose.
12. What artistic and architectural traditions did the Maya develop?

CRITICAL THINKING

BIG IDEAS: Science and Technology

13. **MAKING INFERENCES** What innovations of the early Andean cultures probably helped later civilizations survive?
14. **UNDERSTANDING CAUSE AND EFFECT** How did religious practices in ancient America lead to developments in science?
15. **EVALUATING INFORMATION** How did the development of the concept of zero help the Maya calculate numbers?

ALTERNATIVE ASSESSMENT

1. **WRITING ACTIVITY** Imagine that you have just flown over and discovered the Nazca Lines. Write a letter to a friend describing them and telling what you think they were used for.

2. **INTERDISCIPLINARY ACTIVITY—MATHEMATICS** Learn about the symbols the Maya used in their number system. Then use the symbols to write a few simple addition problems.

3. **STARTING WITH A STORY**
Starting with a Story
Review the news feature you wrote about the ceremony in Palenque. Use the feature to write a brief scene about what happened after the ceremony. Create dialogue and interesting characters to make the scene come alive.

Technology Activity

4. **WRITING A VIDEO SCRIPT**
Use the Internet or the library to find out about the hardships archaeologists and explorers suffered to uncover information about the Maya. Then work with a group of classmates to write a video script for a documentary about the explorers.
   - Include interviews with the archaeologists and explorers.
   - Write a dramatic scene describing their struggles.
   - Use maps and pictures to help illustrate the geography of Mesoamerica.

Research Links
ClassZone.com

Interpreting Visuals Use this Mayan clay figure of a warrior to answer these questions.

1. **What class in Mayan society did warriors belong to?**
   A. nobles
   B. merchants
   C. farmers
   D. slaves

2. **Which of the following indicates this warrior's class?**
   A. his modest appearance
   B. his frightened expression
   C. his humble pose
   D. his clothing and jewelry

Test Practice
ClassZone.com

Additional Test Practice, pp. S1–S33

Writing About History

Expository Writing: Comparison and Contrast

Two Ancient Civilizations

Purpose: To write a composition comparing and contrasting life in ancient India or China to life in the Americas

Audience: Your classmates

You just read about three ancient civilizations that developed over 3,000 years. How can you get a good understanding of the main ideas from such a long span of history? One way is to organize the information by similarities and differences. When you write an essay about similarities and differences, you are writing a type of expository composition called **comparison and contrast**.

▲ Hindu temple and pyramid in Tikal

Organization & Focus

Your assignment is to write a 500- to 700-word expository essay that compares and contrasts ancient Asian and American civilizations. Focus on just one aspect of life so that you can cover it thoroughly.

Choosing a Topic Study the Visual Summaries on pages 246, 282, and 314, and look for topics to compare and contrast. For example, the visual summaries of the three chapters group information by the themes of this book: Geography, Culture, Economics, Government, Belief Systems, and Science & Technology. By using one of the themes, you can compare and contrast an aspect of life in two cultures.

Identifying Purpose and Audience Your communication purpose in this assignment is to compare and contrast, and your audience is your classmates. However, there is another useful purpose for writing this essay. It will help you to review and draw meaning from the unit.

Finding Details Reread all the information in this unit about your topic. Take notes about important details. After you finish your notes, look for details that are similar and those that are different across the two cultures.

Outlining and Drafting You might organize and present your ideas in one of three possible ways, as the chart above right shows.

Ways to Organize Comparison and Contrast Details		
Point by Point	**Whole by Whole**	**Similarities & Differences**
Presents one aspect at a time, showing both comparisons (similarities) and contrasts (differences)	Presents each subject as a whole, pointing out comparisons and contrasts during the presentation of the second subject	Presents the similarities together and the differences together
Example:	**Example:**	**Example:**
1) Goods traded in China; goods traded in the Americas (how they were alike and different)	1) Trade in China (the goods traded and the effect of trade on the rest of the culture)	1) Trade in China and the Americas were alike in these ways.
2) Effect of trade on Chinese culture; effect of trade on ancient American cultures (how they were alike and different)	2) Trade in ancient America (the goods traded and the effect of trade on the rest of the culture, with references back to the first section using phrases such as "Unlike Chinese trade" or "As in China")	2) Trade in China and the Americas were different in these ways.

Decide which order works best for your topic and create an outline for your essay. Follow your outline as you draft your essay. Be sure to use transitions that highlight the comparisons, such as *like, also, as well,* and the contrasts, such as *in contrast, on the other hand, unlike.*

Research & Technology

As you draft your essay, you may need additional information. One good source would be an encyclopedia, either online or in print. Articles in the same encyclopedia often cover the same general topics for each civilization. That will help you to compare and contrast.

Technology Tip Make the settings in your word processor for margins, tabs, and spacing match the form your school requires. These settings are usually found in the Format menu.

Evaluation & Revision

When you have finished your first draft, put it aside for a day. Then read it as if you had never read it before, to see what might still need work. In particular, check the organization of ideas within and between paragraphs. Make revisions until you are satisfied.

Self-Check

Does my essay have

- ☐ a clear focus?
- ☐ a formal introduction?
- ☐ supporting evidence of similarities and differences?
- ☐ transitions that show comparisons and contrasts?
- ☐ a strong conclusion?

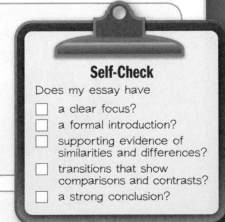

Publish & Present

Make a neat final copy of your essay that conforms to your school's guidelines. Share it with your classmates and take turns reading and commenting on each other's work.

UNIT 5

The Roots of Western Ideas

Interact with History

Visiting the Temple of Solomon, about 950 B.C.

You are a visitor from a small village in the countryside to the Temple built by King Solomon in the capital city of Jerusalem. The Temple is the center of religious life. Each year, there are a number of festivals that you attend in Jerusalem.

How might religion influence the laws of a society?

WebQuest
ClassZone.com

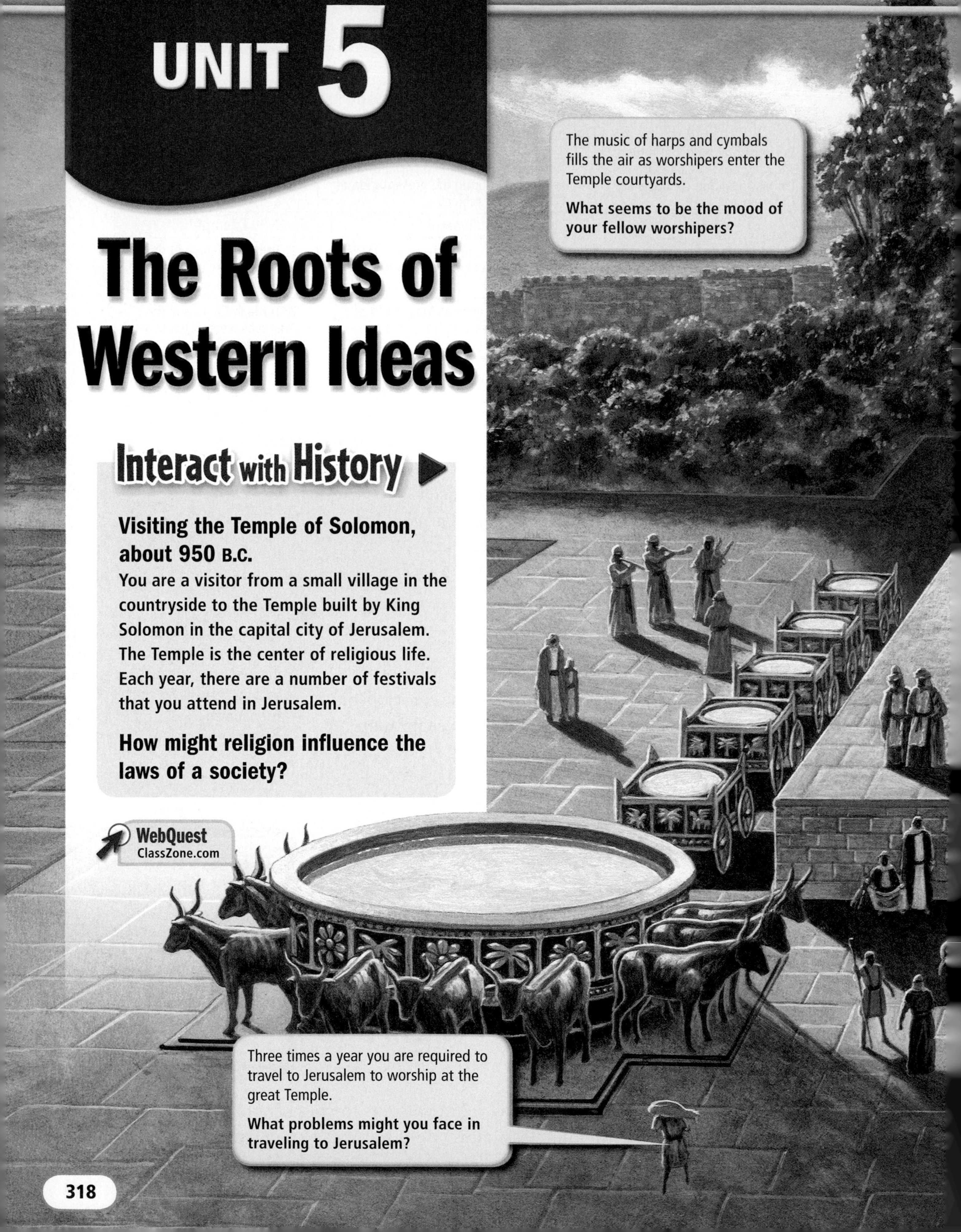

The music of harps and cymbals fills the air as worshipers enter the Temple courtyards.

What seems to be the mood of your fellow worshipers?

Three times a year you are required to travel to Jerusalem to worship at the great Temple.

What problems might you face in traveling to Jerusalem?

The smoke of gifts burned on a sacrificial fire floats through the air.

What gifts might you bring to the Temple?

Chapter 10 The Hebrew Kingdoms

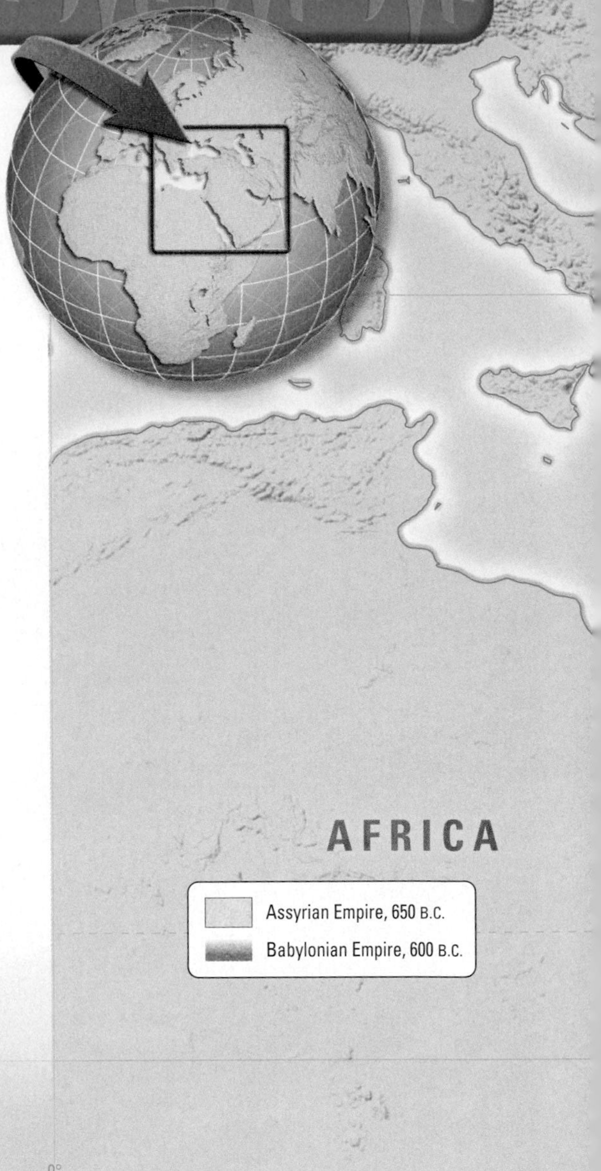

Before You Read: Predicting

Scan the title of the chapter and the lesson titles. Write three questions you think might be answered in the chapter. One example is

What were the origins of the Hebrew people?

As you find the answers to your questions as you read, write them in your notebook.

Big Ideas About the Hebrew Kingdoms

Belief Systems **Belief systems and religions may shape government and societies.**

Although the ancient Hebrews were a small group of people, their impact on world history has been great. The Hebrews have contributed to civilizations across Europe, Asia, and the Americas. The beliefs of the Hebrew people have been important in the development of religion and law in Western civilization.

Integrated Technology

eEdition

- Interactive Maps
- Interactive Visuals
- Starting with a Story

INTERNET RESOURCES

Go to **ClassZone.com** for

- WebQuest
- Homework Helper
- Research Links
- Internet Activities
- Quizzes
- Maps
- Test Practice
- Current Events

SOUTHWEST ASIA

1800 B.C.
Abraham and his family leave Ur on their way to Canaan. (Russian icon showing Abraham and Sara) ▶

c. 1250 B.C.
Moses leads Hebrews out of Egypt.

1800 B.C. — 1500 B.C. — 1200 B.C.

WORLD

1200 B.C.
Olmec civilization emerges in southeast Mexico. (Olmec jade head) ▶

Southwest Asia, 700–600 B.C.

INTER*ACTIVE*

586 B.C.
Babylonians capture Jerusalem and destroy Solomon's Temple.

A.D. 70
Romans under Titus destroy Herod's temple in Jerusalem. (bust of Titus) ▶

600 B.C. | 300 B.C. | B.C. A.D. | A.D. 300

771 B.C.
Nomads in China sack the Zhou capital and murder the monarch.

500 B.C.
Zapotecs found Monte Albán. (Zapotec urn from Monte Albán in Mexico) ▶

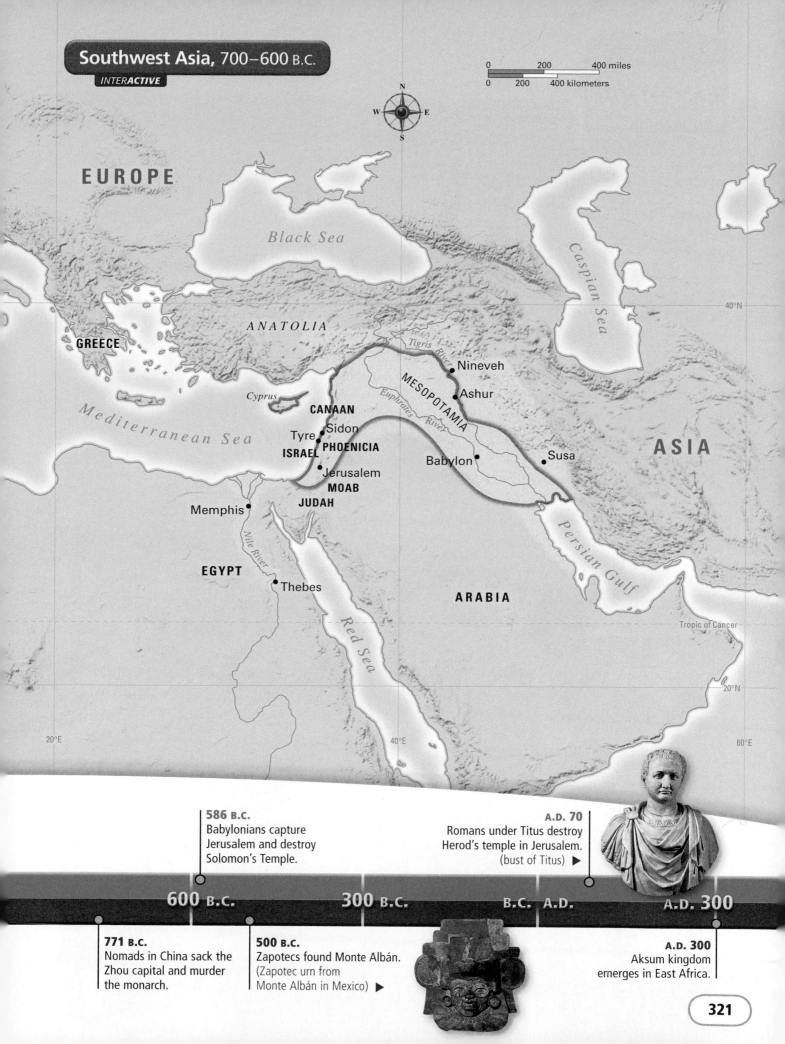

A.D. 300
Aksum kingdom emerges in East Africa.

Starting with a Story

Ruth and Naomi

Background: The Hebrews settled throughout parts of what are now Israel and Lebanon. Their laws, religious customs, and beliefs were different from those of other peoples in that region. However, Hebrews and other groups sometimes learned to understand each other.

One example of this understanding is the Hebrew Bible story of Ruth and Naomi. Naomi, with her husband and sons, had left Israel and moved to Moab, a land east of the Dead Sea in present-day Jordan. Naomi's sons married women from Moab, including Ruth. Ruth, who was not a Hebrew, was an ancestor of King David of Israel.

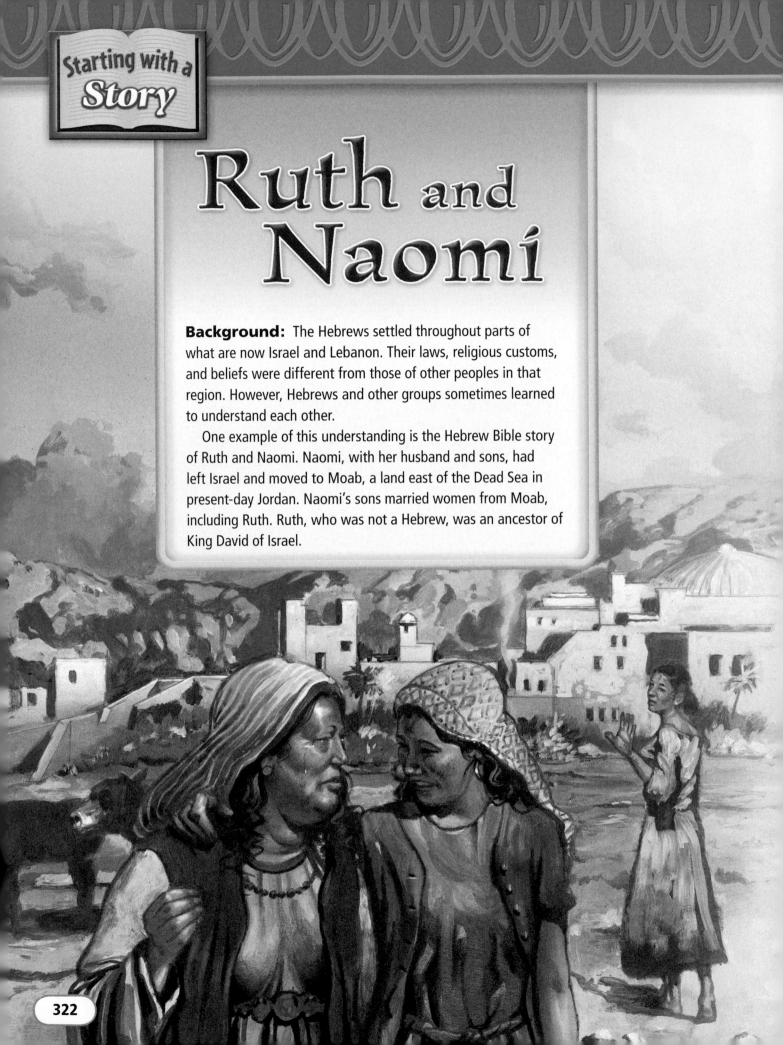

Starting with a Story
eEdition

Naomi, her husband, and their sons had come to live in Moab many years ago. They fled a famine in their native land. Once settled in Moab, one of the sons married Ruth, a woman of Moab. In this way, they all became one family.

Now Ruth's husband, father-in-law, and brother-in-law have all died. Ruth's mother-in-law, Naomi, tells her that she is going back to Israel. Ruth tells Naomi that she will go with her. Naomi is touched by Ruth's loyalty but thinks she should reconsider.

Naomi urges Ruth to stay in Moab, where Ruth will find a new husband among her own people. Ruth knows that the Hebrews have a different faith. They do not make statues of gods. They worship only one God.

Ruth thinks about the love and friendship she has for Naomi. She thinks about her dead husband, Naomi's son. Ruth thinks about which group of people, both of whom she loves, she will choose to live with. Then Ruth says to Naomi, "Wherever you go, I will go. Wherever you lodge, I will lodge. Your people shall be my people and your God my God."

When Naomi returns to Israel, Ruth goes with her out of loyalty to Naomi and her family. Later, Ruth marries a Hebrew and declares that she will worship his God. One of their descendants is David, the second king of Israel. David, one of the greatest figures in the history of the Hebrews, represents the coming together of different peoples and traditions.

How might Ruth's decision affect her understanding of other people and cultures?

Reading & Writing

1. **READING: Setting** The setting of the story is the time and place of the action. The time may be past, present, or future. The place may be real or imaginary. With a partner, discuss the time and place of the story of Ruth and Naomi.
2. **WRITING: Exposition** Imagine that you are Ruth. Write a letter to your great-grandson, King David of Israel. Explain to him what your homeland in Moab was like, why you chose to leave, and how your life changed when you moved to a new land.

Lesson 1

MAIN IDEAS

1. **Belief Systems** The Hebrews believed in one God and tried to follow his commandments.
2. **Geography** Enslaved Hebrews returned from Egypt to Canaan to reclaim land.
3. **Government** Hebrew leaders called judges attempted to rule according to their understanding of God's laws.

TAKING NOTES

Reading Skill: Understanding Cause and Effect

A cause makes something happen. An effect is a result of a cause. Following causes and effects will help you understand the main ideas in this lesson. In Lesson 1, look for the effects of each event or cause listed in the chart. Record them on a chart like the one below.

Causes	Effects
Abraham leaves Ur.	
Moses leads people out of Egypt.	
Moses climbs Mount Sinai.	

Skillbuilder Handbook, page R26

▲ **Torah Case** The Tik, or Torah case, shown above was made in Iraq in the early 20th century.

Words to Know

Understanding the following words will help you read this lesson:

shepherd a person who takes care of a group of sheep (page 325)

*A group of sheep that a **shepherd** watches over is usually called a flock.*

promise to pledge to do something (page 325)

*Some people believe that God **promised** to give the land of Israel to the Jews.*

fame great reputation; public esteem; renown (page 329)

*Some people gained **fame** for military feats and some for intellectual feats.*

The Origins of the Hebrews

TERMS & NAMES
- Abraham
- monotheism
- Judaism
- Moses
- Exodus
- Ten Commandments

Build on What You Know You have probably noticed that plants grow better in green, well-watered places. And you have learned how early cities developed in the Fertile Crescent. Within this region is an area that, partly because of its fertility, became the home of the Hebrews.

The Hebrew People in Canaan

1 ESSENTIAL QUESTION What is the central belief of the Hebrews?

The first five books of the Hebrew Bible are called the Torah (TAWR•uh). The Hebrews believed that these holy books, or scriptures, were given to them by God. The Torah gives the early history, laws, and beliefs of the Hebrews. It consists of Genesis, Exodus, Leviticus, Numbers, and Deuteronomy. Later, there were Commentaries, or interpretations, written about the Torah.

Primary Source Handbook
See the excerpt from the Hebrew Bible: The Creation, page R45.

From Ur to Canaan A shepherd named **Abraham** was the father of the Hebrews. Abraham lived in Ur, a city in Mesopotamia, about 1800 B.C. According to the Torah, God told Abraham to leave Ur and go to Canaan (KAY•nuhn). Abraham believed that if he went to Canaan, the land would belong to his descendants because it was promised to them by God. Because of this, the Hebrews thought of Canaan as the Promised Land. With his family, Abraham settled in Canaan. (See map below.)

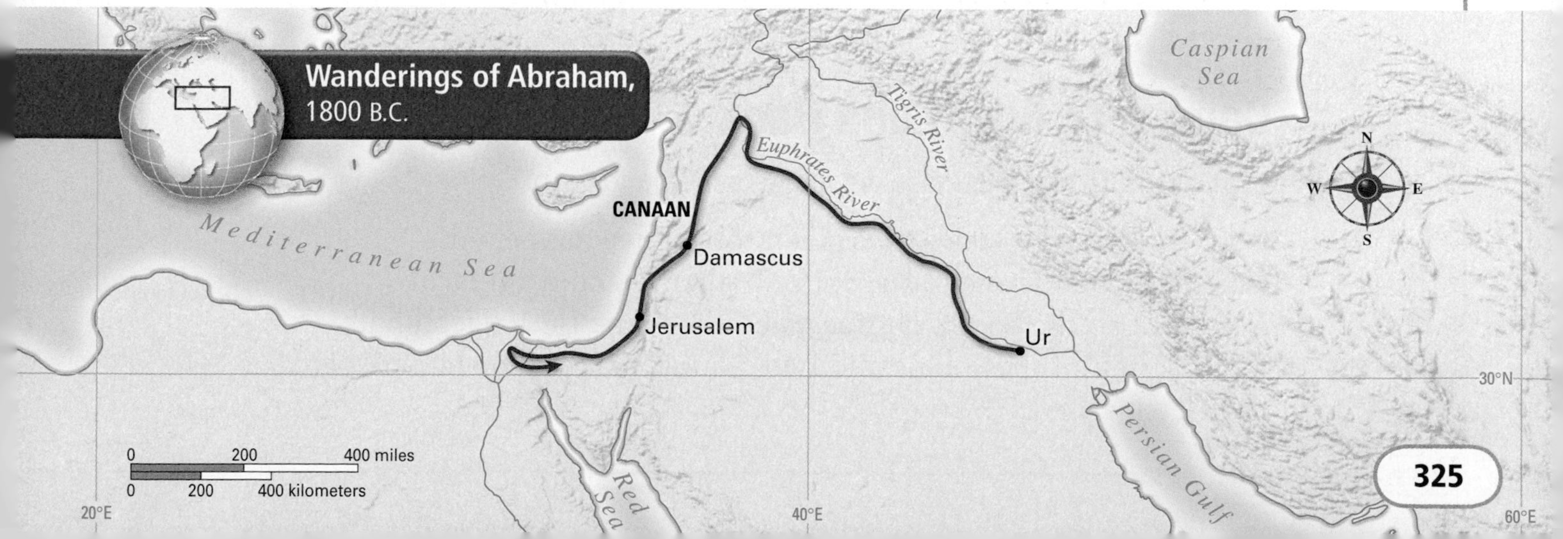

▲ **Abraham and Family** This painting shows Abraham and his family during their journey to Canaan.

Judaism and Monotheism Throughout the ancient world, people were polytheists (*poly* means "many" and *theos* means "god"). This means that they worshiped many gods. The Hebrews believed that God spoke to Abraham and gave him important teachings. Abraham taught the belief in one all-powerful God who established moral laws for humanity. This belief is called **monotheism** (*mono* means "one"). **Judaism** today is descended from the religion of the ancient Hebrews. The name comes from the tribe of Judah, one of the 12 tribes descended from Abraham.

According to the Torah, during troubled times the Hebrews held to their belief in God. They believed that a covenant (KUHV•uh•nuhnt), or a binding agreement, existed between God and Abraham and his descendants. They took courage from God's pledge to give a homeland to Abraham's descendants if they followed the laws of their faith and practiced righteousness and justice.

Primary Source Handbook

See the excerpt from the Hebrew Bible: Noah and the Flood, page R46.

REVIEW How was Judaism different from other religions?

Canaan to Egypt and Back

2 ESSENTIAL QUESTION Why did the Hebrews go to Egypt?

Over time, the Hebrews in Canaan took a new name—the Israelites. Their name came from Abraham's grandson Jacob. According to the Torah, he was given the name *Israel*. Jacob had 12 sons. Ten of these sons and two grandsons were the fathers of the 12 tribes.

Moses Leads the Israelites The Torah tells of a terrible famine in Canaan. The starving Israelites went to Egypt, where Jacob's son Joseph served as top adviser to Egypt's pharaoh.

In time, a new pharaoh came to power. He enslaved the Israelites and forced them to work on his building projects. The Torah tells how **Moses** helped the Israelites leave Egypt. The migration of the Israelites from Egypt is known as the **Exodus**.

Vocabulary Strategy

The word *exodus* comes from the Greek word *exodos*. It combines the **root** *hodos*, which means "way" or "journey," with the **prefix** *ex-*, which means "out."

The Ten Commandments After leaving Egypt, the Israelites wandered in the Sinai desert for 40 years, living as nomads. According to the Torah, Moses climbed to the top of Mount Sinai, where God spoke to him. When Moses came down the mountain, he carried two stone tablets that contained the **Ten Commandments**. These commandments became the basis for the laws of the Israelites. The commandments later became an important part of the moral and ethical traditions of Western civilization.

Primary Source

Background: According to the Torah, the Ten Commandments are the ten laws given by God to Moses on Mount Sinai. These orders serve as the basis for the moral laws of the Hebrews.

▲ Moses with tablets of Ten Commandments

The Ten Commandments*

1. I am the Lord your God who brought you out of the land of Eygpt, the house of bondage: You shall have no other gods besides Me.
2. You shall not make for yourself a sculptured image. . . .
3. You shall not swear falsely by the name of the Lord your God. . . .
4. Remember the Sabbath day and keep it holy. . . .
5. Honor your father and your mother. . . .
6. You shall not murder.
7. You shall not commit adultery.
8. You shall not steal.
9. You shall not bear false witness against your neighbor.
10. You shall not covet [desire]. . . anything that is your neighbor's.

Exodus 20:2–14

* Christians word the commandments in ways slightly different from this Jewish version.

DOCUMENT–BASED QUESTIONS

1. What are the first four commandments concerned with?
2. What do the last six commandments have in common that makes them different from the first four?

An Agreement Confirmed The Israelites believed that the giving of the commandments reaffirmed their covenant with God. They thought that God would protect them. The people, in turn, would obey his laws. They believed that God through his commandments had set down moral laws for all humanity.

REVIEW Who led the Israelites in their escape from slavery in Egypt?

Return to the Promised Land

3 ESSENTIAL QUESTION What role did the judges play in the life of the ancient Israelites?

By the time the Israelites returned to Canaan, many years had passed. The other groups who lived there were subject to powerful rulers who lived in walled cities. Moses picked Joshua to lead the people into Canaan.

The 12 Tribes of Israel The Israelites entering Canaan were organized into 12 tribes. Each tribe was named after one of Jacob's sons or grandsons. The men of these tribes became Joshua's troops. They formed a fighting force united by their goal of reclaiming the land from the city states. The first city to fall to the Israelites was Jericho. The movement to reclaim Canaan continued for 200 years.

Once the fighting ended, the Israelite soldiers became farmers and herders. The 12 tribes divided the land among themselves. Some received land in the mountains. Others settled on the plains. Tribes that lived near each other formed close ties, because they shared beliefs, problems, and enemies.

Judges This engraving portrays the judge Deborah. ▼

Judges Lead the Israelites During the 200 years of war, no single powerful leader led the Israelites. Instead, they sought advice from many different leaders called judges. These were highly respected men and women of the community.

The first judges acted as military leaders. Later judges gave advice on legal matters and helped settle conflicts. Judges such as Gideon, Samson, and Samuel gained fame throughout Canaan for their strength and wisdom. Deborah was one of the most famous judges. She inspired a small force of fighters to victory against a large Canaanite force near Mount Tabor.

The judges played a key role in keeping the 12 tribes united. When the Israelites lacked a strong judge as a leader, some tribes turned away from traditional religion. They made offerings to other gods. The judges spoke out against these practices.

REVIEW Who were some of the important judges of Israel?

Lesson Summary

- Abraham led the Hebrews to Canaan.
- Moses received the Ten Commandments from God.
- The judges led the Israelites in Canaan.

Why It Matters Now . . .

Judaism was the first monotheistic religion and influenced other world religions, particularly Christianity and Islam.

1 Lesson Review

Homework Helper
ClassZone.com

Terms & Names

1. Explain the importance of

Abraham	Judaism	Exodus
monotheism	Moses	Ten Commandments

Using Your Notes

Understanding Cause and Effect Use your completed chart to answer the following question:

2. What was one effect of each of the following causes shown in the chart?

Causes	Effects
Abraham leaves Ur.	
Moses leads people out of Egypt.	
Moses climbs Mount Sinai.	

Main Ideas

3. What religious beliefs made the Hebrews different from other ancient peoples?

4. What part did Moses play in the Exodus from Egypt?

5. Why did the return of the Hebrews to Canaan cause conflicts with other peoples living there?

Critical Thinking

6. Summarizing What covenant between God and the Hebrews did the Hebrews believe the Ten Commandments reaffirmed?

7. Drawing Conclusions How did the Hebrew belief in a Promised Land affect their actions in Egypt and Canaan?

Activity

Making a Map Trace the map that shows the route of Abraham and his family out of Ur on page 325. Add to the map the geographic challenges they faced.

THE EXODUS

Background: According to the Torah, God commanded Moses to lead the Hebrews out of slavery in Egypt. Moses went to the pharaoh and pleaded with him to let the Hebrew people go. After God sent a series of plagues, the pharaoh agreed. Then he changed his mind and led his troops to stop the Hebrews. The Exodus became an inspirational story to other people attempting to flee slavery, such as African Americans in the South before the Civil War. This version of the Exodus is taken from *The Children's Bible: The Old and New Testaments*.

▲ **Moses** This painting, titled ***The Parting of the Red Sea***, shows Moses leading the Hebrews in their flight from Egypt.

Continuing their journey from Succoth, the Israelites camped at Etham, at the edge of the wilderness. And the Lord went before them by day in a pillar of cloud to show them the way, and by night in a pillar of fire to give them light, so that they could travel by day and night. He did not take away from the people the pillar of cloud by day nor the pillar of fire by night.

It was told to the king of Egypt that the people had fled, and the hearts of Pharaoh and his servants were moved against the people, and they said: "Why have we done this, and let Israel free from serving us?"

Then Pharaoh made ready his chariots and took his people with him. He took six hundred chosen chariots, of all the chariots of Egypt, and put captains over all of them.

The Lord hardened the heart of Pharaoh, king of Egypt, and Pharaoh pursued the children of Israel, for the children of Israel had gone out proudly.

The Egyptians came after them, all the horses and chariots of Pharaoh, his horsemen and his army, and overtook them camping beside the sea, near Pihahiroth, before Baalzephon.

When Pharaoh came near, the children of Israel looked up, and, seeing the Egyptians marching after them, they were very frightened. Then the children of Israel cried out to the Lord, and they said to Moses:

"Were there no graves in Egypt? Have you brought us away to die in the wilderness? Why have you treated us in this way, in bringing us out of Egypt? Did we not tell you in Egypt, 'Let us alone, so that we may serve the Egyptians?' For it would have been better for us to serve the Egyptians than to die in the wilderness."

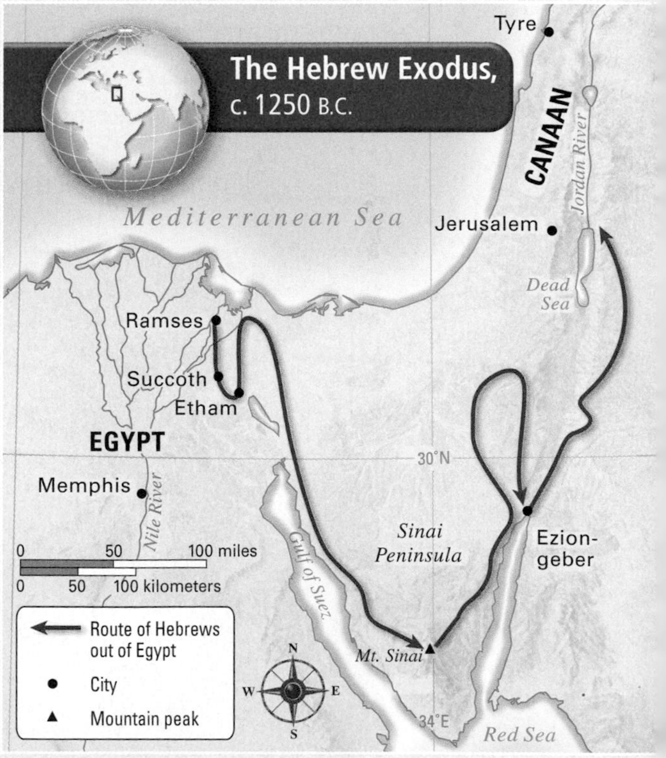

REVIEW Why were the Israelites upset?

"Do not be afraid," said Moses to the people. "Stand still and watch the power of the Lord to save you, as he will show you today, for the Egyptians whom you have seen today you shall never see again. The Lord will fight for you if you will be calm."

And God said to Moses: "Why do you cry to me? Tell the children of Israel to go forward. But you must lift up your rod and stretch out your hand over the sea, and divide it. And the children of Israel shall go on dry land through the middle of the sea.

"And you shall see that I will harden the hearts of the Egyptians, and they shall follow you. Then I will show my power over Pharaoh and over all his armies, his chariots and his horsemen. And the Egyptians shall know that I am the Lord, when I have shown my power."

Then the angel of God which went before the camp of Israel moved and went behind them. The pillar of cloud moved from in front of them and rose up behind them. It came between the camp of Israel and the camp of the Egyptians, but it gave light by night to Israel, so that the Egyptians did not come near Israel all that night.

Then Moses stretched out his hand over the sea, and the Lord caused the sea to go back by making a strong east wind blow all that night. It made the sea dry land, and the waters were divided.

The children of Israel walked into the middle of the sea upon the dry ground, and the waters were a wall on their right hand and on their left.

REVIEW What happened when Moses stretched his hand over the sea?

Exodus This depiction of Moses and the passage of the Red Sea is from a French illuminated manuscript, about 1250 A.D. ▶

The Egyptians pursued them and went into the middle of the sea after them, all Pharaoh's horses, his chariots and his horsemen.

▲ **Chariot** A pharaoh in his chariot hunts desert animals.

When morning came, the Lord looked down on the army of the Egyptians through the pillar of fire and the cloud, and troubled the forces of the Egyptians. He made the wheels fall off their chariots and made them drive heavily, so that the Egyptians said, "Let us flee from the children of Israel, for the Lord fights for them against the Egyptians."

Then God said to Moses: "Stretch out your hand over the sea, so that the waters may come together again and cover the Egyptians, their chariots and their horsemen."

Moses stretched out his hand over the sea, and the sea returned to its bed when the morning appeared. The Egyptians fled before it, but the Lord overthrew the Egyptians in the middle of the sea. The waters returned and covered the chariots and the horsemen, and all the forces of Pharaoh that had followed him into the sea. Not one of them survived.

But the children of Israel had walked on dry land in the middle of the sea, and the waters had formed a wall for them on their right hand and on their left. Thus the Lord saved Israel that day from the hands of the Egyptians, and the Israelites saw the Egyptians dead upon the sea shore.

When Israel saw the great work the Lord did against the Egyptians, the people stood in awe of the Lord, and believed in him and his servant Moses.

REVIEW Whom did the Israelites credit for the destruction of their enemies?

Reading & Writing

1. **READING: Character** With a partner, discuss the character of Moses as it is revealed in his actions. Then make a list of words that describe his character.
2. **WRITING: Narration** Write a dialogue between two soldiers in Pharaoh's army. Have them discuss their mission in pursuing the Hebrews.

Lesson 2

MAIN IDEAS

1. **Government** The Israelites built a small nation.
2. **Government** Conflict divided the Israelites and made them vulnerable to outside invaders.
3. **Belief Systems** The exiled Israelites returned to their homeland with beliefs that carried them through difficult times.

▲ **Mezuzah** Traditionally, Jews keep a scroll of an important scripture passage in a mezuzah (a container often attached to a doorpost) like the one shown here. This practice is in keeping with the teachings of Deuteronomy 6:9 and 11:20.

TAKING NOTES

Reading Skill:
Explaining Chronological Order and Sequence

To put events in sequence means to put them in order based on the time they happened. As you read Lesson 2, make a note of things that happened in the kingdoms of Israel and Judah. Use a time line like this one to put events in order.

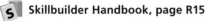

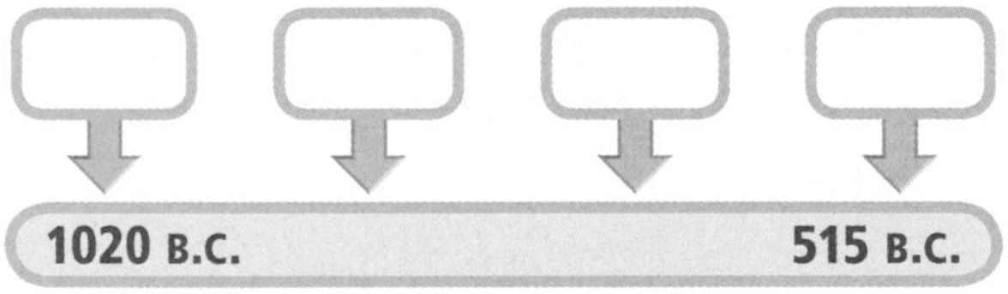

Skillbuilder Handbook, page R15

Words to Know

Understanding the following words will help you read this lesson:

dispute an argument or quarrel (page 336)

Often, kings act as judges, settling important legal ***disputes.***

outcome something that happens as a result or consequence (page 337)

The division of Israel was an ***outcome*** *of disagreements among the kingdom's different tribes.*

threat a warning of possible danger (page 337)

Faced with an external ***threat,*** *the tribes united to defend themselves.*

sustain to support the spirits of (page 338)

Sustained *by their religious faith, the Jews were able to overcome tremendous hardships.*

Kingdoms and Captivity

TERMS & NAMES
- David
- Solomon
- Babylonian Captivity
- Messiah
- prophets

Build on What You Know You have learned that the Israelites came back to Canaan from Egypt. When they returned, they fought to regain control of the land and clashed with their neighbors.

The Kingdom of Israel

1 ESSENTIAL QUESTION Who were some of the early kings of Israel?

The Israelites' belief in one God and their religious practices set them apart from others in the region. They traded with other groups in Canaan but did not adopt their culture or beliefs. However, sometimes individuals from different groups did mix. One such example is the story of Ruth and Naomi, which you read at the beginning of the chapter.

Saul and David About 1029 B.C., the Israelites faced the Philistines, another people in the area. The Philistines invaded and conquered Israelite territory.

The Israelites agreed to unite under one king in order to fight the Philistines, although many feared a king with too much power. A judge named Samuel shared these concerns, but helped select the first kings of the 12 tribes.

Connect to Today

Judah and Philistia A flock of sheep grazes in hills once part of the kingdom of Judah. ▼

History Makers

David (ruled during the 900s B.C.)

David organized a central government and made Jerusalem the capital of Israel. He expanded the borders of Israel and helped its economy grow by encouraging trade with Phoenicia, a neighbor on the Mediterranean coast.

According to the Hebrew Bible, David slew the Philistine giant Goliath. David, who was Israel's second king, was also a fine poet and musician. He is said to have written many of the beautiful prayers and songs found in the Hebrew Bible's Book of Psalms. By the time David died, Israel had become an independent and united kingdom mostly at peace with its neighbors.

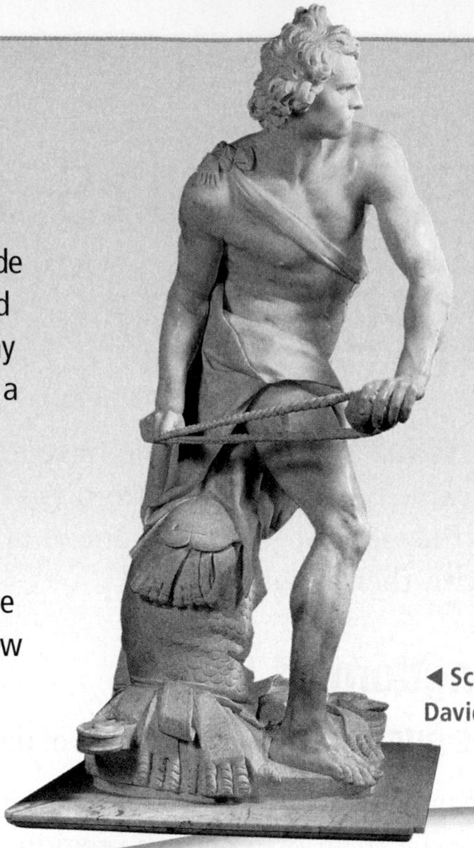

◀ Sculpture of David by Bernini

A New Leader The Israelites chose Saul, a respected military leader, as their first king in 1020 B.C. Under Saul, the Israelites fought the Philistines. These battles forced the Philistines to loosen their control over the Israelites. After Saul's death, the Israelites looked for a new leader.

According to the Hebrew Bible, Samuel chose a young man named **David** as the next king. The choice was a wise one. In about 1000 B.C., David and the Israelites drove out the Philistines. David won control of Jerusalem.

Primary Source Handbook
See the excerpt from the Hebrew Bible: Psalm 100, page R50.

Solomon David established a line of kings. He chose his son **Solomon** to succeed him. Solomon became the third king of Israel in about 962 B.C. Solomon, too, was a strong leader.

Primary Source Handbook
See the excerpt from the Hebrew Bible: Proverbs, page R49.

During Solomon's rule, Israel became a powerful nation. Solomon built on the trade ties between Phoenicia and Israel established by David. Solomon also formed new trade alliances.

Solomon oversaw many building projects. His most famous was the Temple in Jerusalem. (See pages 318–319.) The Temple became the center of religious life for the Israelites. People came there from all parts of the kingdom to say prayers and leave offerings. Many also came to ask the wise king to settle their disputes.

REVIEW Why did the Israelites decide to choose a king?

The Kingdom Divides

2 ESSENTIAL QUESTION What was the outcome of the conflict among the Israelites?

Faced by a threat of attack, Israelite tribes formed the kingdom of Israel. When the threat ended, the kingdom divided.

Israel and Judah King Solomon died in 922 B.C. When Solomon's son became king, the northern tribes refused to pledge their loyalty until he agreed to lighten their taxes and end their labor on building projects. When he refused, the tribes rebelled. Only the tribes of Judah and Benjamin remained loyal.

Israel split into two separate kingdoms. The northern part continued to be called Israel. The two tribes in the southern area, which included Jerusalem, called their new nation Judah. The words *Judaism* and *Jews* come from the name Judah.

Two separate kingdoms existed for about two centuries. Throughout this period, Jerusalem remained an important center of worship.

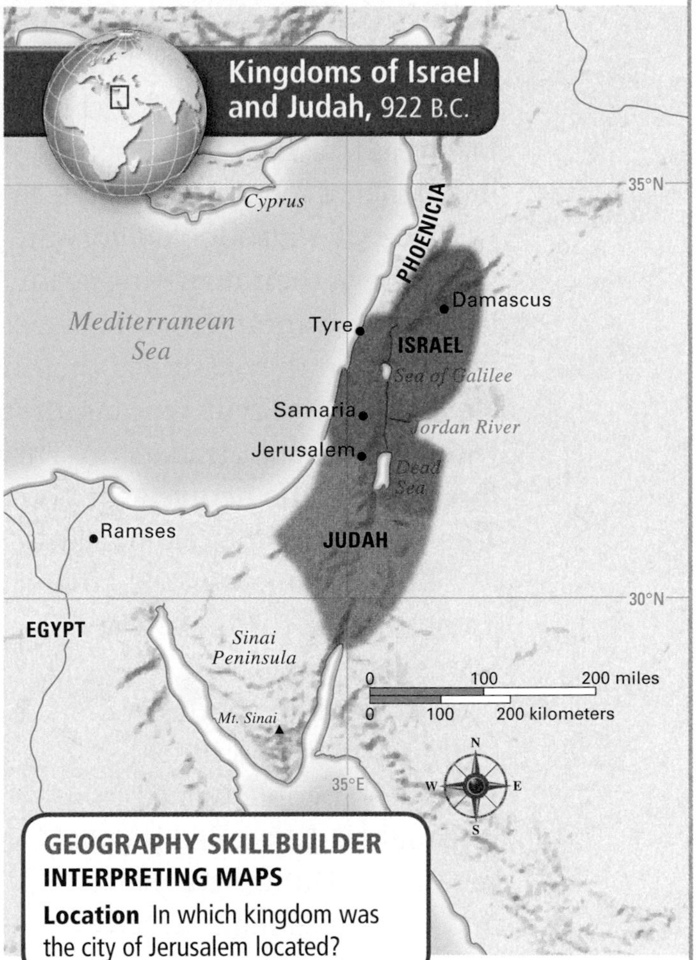

GEOGRAPHY SKILLBUILDER
INTERPRETING MAPS
Location In which kingdom was the city of Jerusalem located?

Assyrians and Babylonians Take the Land By 738 B.C., both kingdoms faced new threats to their independence from the Assyrians. The Assyrians forced Israel and Judah to pay tribute. In 722 B.C., Assyria invaded Israel, whose army was weak, and conquered it. The kingdom of Israel ended. Around 612 B.C., the Assyrian Empire fell to the Babylonians. (You read about this in Chapter 4.)

For many years, King Nebuchadnezzar ruled Babylonia. In 586 B.C., Nebuchadnezzar captured Jerusalem. When Judah's leaders resisted his rule, the Babylonians destroyed the Temple in Jerusalem. They took thousands of Jews to Babylon as slaves.

REVIEW What conflicts caused Israel to split into two kingdoms?

Jewish Exiles Return to Judah

3 ESSENTIAL QUESTION What hope sustained the Jews in exile?

The exiles from Judah spent about 50 years in Babylon. This time is known as the **Babylonian Captivity**. During this period, the Israelites became known as the Jews.

Beliefs During the Babylonian Captivity During their years in Babylon, the Jews struggled to keep their identity. They continued to observe religious laws, celebrate holy days, and worship as they had in Judah. They hoped someday to return to their homeland in Judah and rebuild the Temple in Jerusalem.

Primary Source Handbook
See the excerpt from the Hebrew Bible: Daniel in the Lions' Den, pages R47–48.

The exiles also looked forward to a time when they would have their own king again. Before the exile, Hebrew leaders were anointed, or had special oils poured on their heads, when they assumed their offices. The Hebrew word **Messiah** (mih•SY•uh) means an "anointed one" charged with some task or leadership. Throughout the centuries of foreign rule, the people kept hoping for their own king. This was sometimes expressed as a hope for an anointed king, an heir to the throne of David, a Messiah.

During times of trouble, both in Judah and in exile, the Jewish people turned to spiritual leaders called **prophets** for advice. These were men and women thought to have a special ability to interpret God's word. They warned the people when they strayed from the Jewish code of conduct. They criticized rulers who were not living according to God's laws. The prophets also comforted the people in times of trouble.

The Temple Is Rebuilt In 539 B.C., the Persians conquered Babylonia. As you learned in Chapter 4, Lesson 3, the Persian

Cyrus the Great This engraving shows Cyrus giving objects from the destroyed Temple to the Jews. ▼

king Cyrus set up a policy of religious toleration in his empire. In 538 B.C., Cyrus freed the Jewish exiles from captivity and allowed them to return to their homeland in Judah.

Soon after most of the exiles returned to Judah, they began rebuilding the Temple in Jerusalem. The beautiful Temple Solomon had built lay in ruins. Grass grew between the crumbling walls. Workers completed the new Temple sometime around 515 B.C.

REVIEW How did the exiles maintain their identity in Babylon?

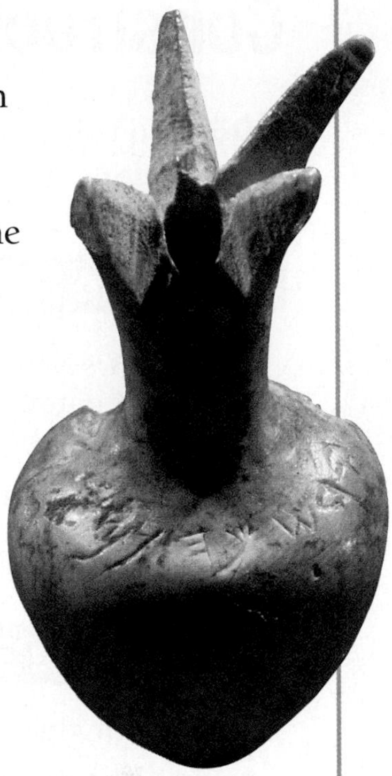

▲ **Ivory Pomegranate** This ivory fruit is believed to be the only remaining relic from Solomon's Temple. Almost two inches high, the object may have decorated an altar.

Lesson Summary

- Saul, David, and Solomon were the first kings of Israel.
- After the death of Solomon, the kingdom of Israel split into two smaller kingdoms—Israel and Judah.
- The Babylonian conquest destroyed the Temple and forced the people of Judah into exile in Babylon.

Why It Matters Now . . .

During the years in captivity, the exiles maintained the religious beliefs and practices that are part of Jewish life today.

2 Lesson Review

Homework Helper
ClassZone.com

Terms & Names

1. Explain the importance of

David	Babylonian Captivity	prophets
Solomon	Messiah	

Using Your Notes

Explaining Chronological Order and Sequence
Use your completed time line to answer the following question:

2. Which empire destroyed the kingdom of Israel, and which empire took the Jews into captivity?

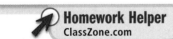

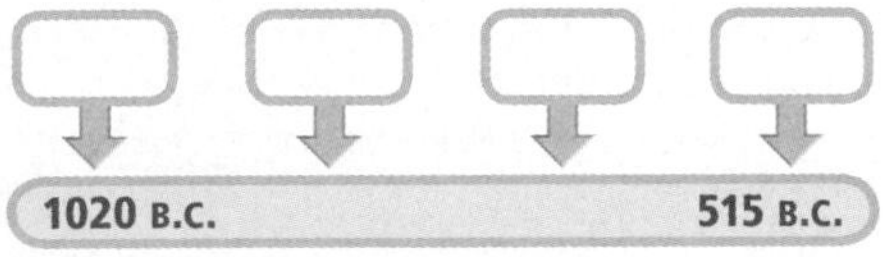

Main Ideas

3. What were Solomon's achievements as king of Israel?

4. What was the role of prophets in Jewish life in the ancient world?

5. What event ended the Babylonian Captivity?

Critical Thinking

6. Drawing Conclusions How did fighting among the tribes of Israel make it easier for their enemies to conquer them?

7. Making Inferences Why do you think Jewish exiles wanted to rebuild the Temple as soon as they returned to their homeland?

Activity

Writing a Narrative Look at the illustration on pages 318–319 and reread "Solomon" on page 336. Write a narrative story about one of the visitors or travelers to the Temple.

Skillbuilder

Extend Lesson 2

Constructing Time Lines

Goal: To construct a time line in order to understand events in the history of the Hebrews

Learn the Skill

Making a time line is a good way to understand material that includes a lot of dates. Events are placed on a time line in the order that they happened. When events are in the proper order, you can see the relationships among them.

See the Skillbuilder Handbook, page R14.

Practice the Skill

1. Look for clue words about time as you read the passage at right. These are words such as *first, next, then, before, after, finally,* and *by that time.* Some of these are identified for you in the passage.
2. Use specific dates provided in the text.
3. Look for phrases that link two events together to help you find an exact date. For example, to figure out the date of Solomon's death, subtract 40 (the number of years he ruled) from 962, the year his reign began. Remember that B.C. dates decrease as they move forward in time.
4. Use a time line like the one below to help you put the events in a passage in the right order. Look for the earliest date to know how to mark the beginning of the time line and latest to mark the end of the time line. This time line is based on the passage you just read.

Example:

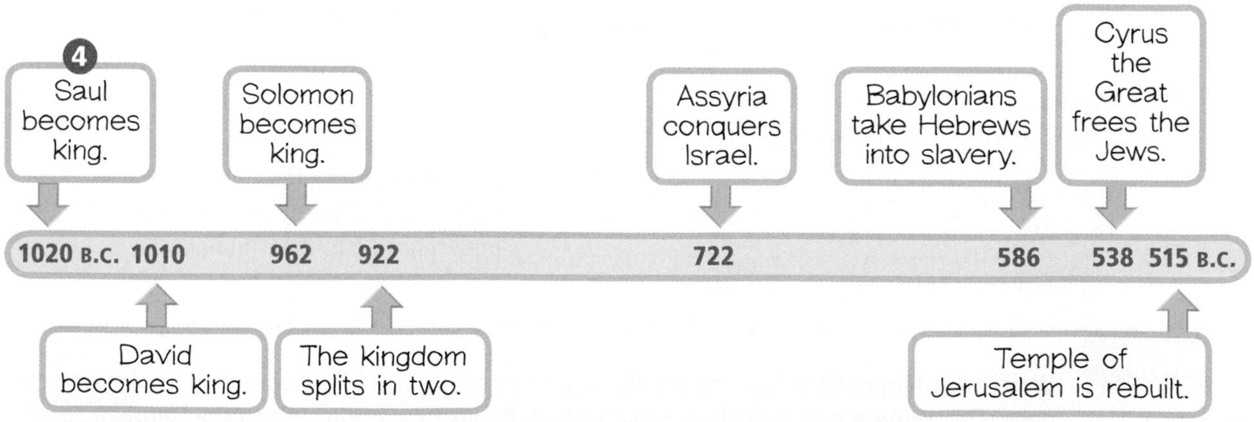

Secondary Source

In the following passage, the author describes the history of the Hebrew kingdoms. Notice that the passage covers a long period of time. Use the numbered strategies listed under Practice the Skill to help you follow the order of events.

▲ **Mosaic** King David and King Solomon are shown in this detail from a Byzantine mosaic of the 11th century.

The Rise and Fall of the Hebrew Kingdoms

The ❶ first king of Israel was Saul. He became king in ❷ 1020 B.C. His successor, King David, reigned from ❷ 1010 B.C. to 970 B.C. David expanded the kingdom and established a dynasty that lasted for about 400 years.

The kingdom of Israel reached its peak during the reign of David's son Solomon. He took the throne in ❷ 962 B.C. and reigned for ❸ 40 years. His greatest achievement was the construction of a great Temple in Jerusalem. ❶ After Solomon's death, the kingdom split in two. The northern kingdom was called Israel, and the southern kingdom was called Judah.

The kingdom was not as strong ❶ after the split. In ❷ 722 B.C., Assyria took over Israel but not Judah. ❶ Then in ❷ 586 B.C., the Babylonians conquered Judah. Thousands of Jews were taken to Babylon as slaves.

The Jews remained slaves in Babylon until ❷ 538 B.C. ❶ At that time, Cyrus the Great of Persia conquered the Babylonians. He freed the Jews and allowed them to return to Judah. ❶ After their return, the Jews rebuilt the Temple of Jerusalem. It was completed in ❷ 515 B.C.

Apply the Skill

Turn to Chapter 13, Lesson 3. Read the sections "Julius Caesar" and "Emperors Rule Rome." Make a time line like the one at left to show the order of events.

Lesson 3

MAIN IDEAS

1. **Government** Jews fought against foreign control and regained self-rule.
2. **Government** Jewish resistance to Roman control resulted in Jews being driven out of their homeland.
3. **Belief Systems** Living outside their homeland, many Jews remained loyal to their beliefs.

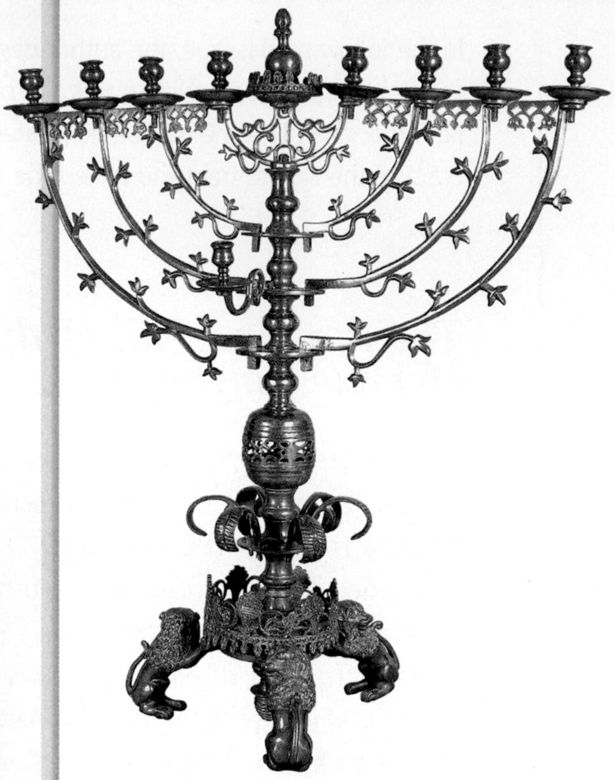

▲ **Menorah** This 18th-century brass menorah comes from eastern Europe. Most menorahs have seven branches. The nine-branched version is used in celebration of Hanukkah.

TAKING NOTES

Reading Skill: Comparing and Contrasting

Comparing and contrasting means finding ways in which two things are alike and different. In Lesson 3, look for ways in which the Syrians and Romans were alike and different in their treatment of Jewish rebellions and insert them in a Venn diagram like the one below.

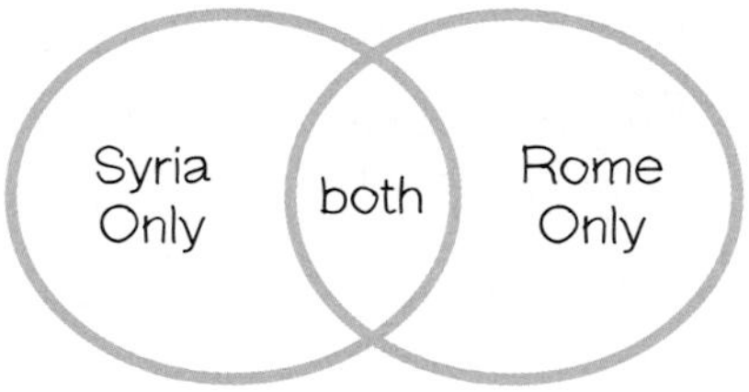

Skillbuilder Handbook, page R4

Words to Know

Understanding the following words will help you read this lesson:

observe to practice or celebrate in a customary way (page 343)

*People were no longer free to **observe** their own religion.*

appoint to choose or pick for an office, position, or duty (page 344)

*Leaders of the Roman Empire **appointed** officials to lead and govern their overseas territories.*

faithful loyal; devoted (page 345)

*The Jews remained **faithful** to their beliefs and established their religion in the new regions in which they settled.*

Rome and Judea

TERMS & NAMES
Diaspora
rabbi
synagogue

Build on What You Know The Jews returned to Judah from their long exile in Babylon. As they prepared for self-rule, they recalled how freedom had often been followed by foreign invasion.

Ruled by Foreigners

1 ESSENTIAL QUESTION What was the relationship of Judah to Syria?

The land of Judah lay in the path of conquering armies that marched across the eastern shores of the Mediterranean. Over the years, many different groups, including the Syrians, Greeks, and Romans, controlled the country.

Syria Controls Judah In 198 B.C., the Hellenistic kingdom of Syria seized control of Judah. Syrian rulers admired Greek culture. They introduced Greek ideas and beliefs to the Jewish people. Some Jews adopted aspects of Greek culture, and some began to worship Greek gods. Others did not begin to worship Greek gods. They continued to observe, or follow, Jewish religious beliefs and practices. Judah's first Syrian rulers allowed the Jews to practice their religion.

In 175 B.C., a new Syrian ruler ordered Jewish priests to make offerings to Greek gods. When the Jews refused, he outlawed their religion and placed statues of Greek gods in the Temple in Jerusalem. The Syrian ruler made it a crime to observe Jewish laws or study the Torah. Some Jews fled to the hills, where they prepared to fight back.

Ancient Ruins The ruins of this ancient Jewish house of worship are located in Capernaum in Israel. ▼

Rebels Fight Syria A Jewish priest along with his five sons led the fight to drive out the Syrians. One of his sons, Judah Maccabee, led the revolt.

Judah Maccabee had a difficult task. His tiny fighting force, called the Maccabees, faced the much larger, better-equipped Syrian army. But the Maccabees' knowledge of the countryside gave them an advantage. In battle after battle, the rebels defeated the Syrian forces. By 164 B.C., the Maccabees had regained control of Jerusalem.

REVIEW Why did the Jews rebel against their Syrian rulers?

Roman Control

2 ESSENTIAL QUESTION What was the result of Jewish resistance to Roman rule?

The independence of the Jews did not last. After less than a century of self-rule, another foreign power took control.

Rome Conquers Judea In 63 B.C., the Romans conquered Judah, which the Romans called Judea. Roman rulers kept strict control over Judea. The Jews were allowed to have Jewish kings and religious leaders, but these kings and leaders were appointed by Rome.

Resistance to Roman Rule The people of Judea disagreed about how to deal with the Romans. Some wanted to cooperate. Others favored fighting to free Judea.

In A.D. 66, a group of Jews known as the Zealots led a rebellion in Judea against Roman authority in the province. Roman leaders responded by sending General Vespasian to crush the uprising.

Some Jews feared the Romans would destroy the Temple. A teacher named Yohanan ben Zaccai hurried to Vespasian's camp. He asked the general to set aside a place for Jewish scholars to study. The school that ben Zaccai set up kept alive the traditions of the Jews.

Masada Zealots held out against the Romans in the fortress of Masada, which overlooks the Dead Sea in Israel. ▼

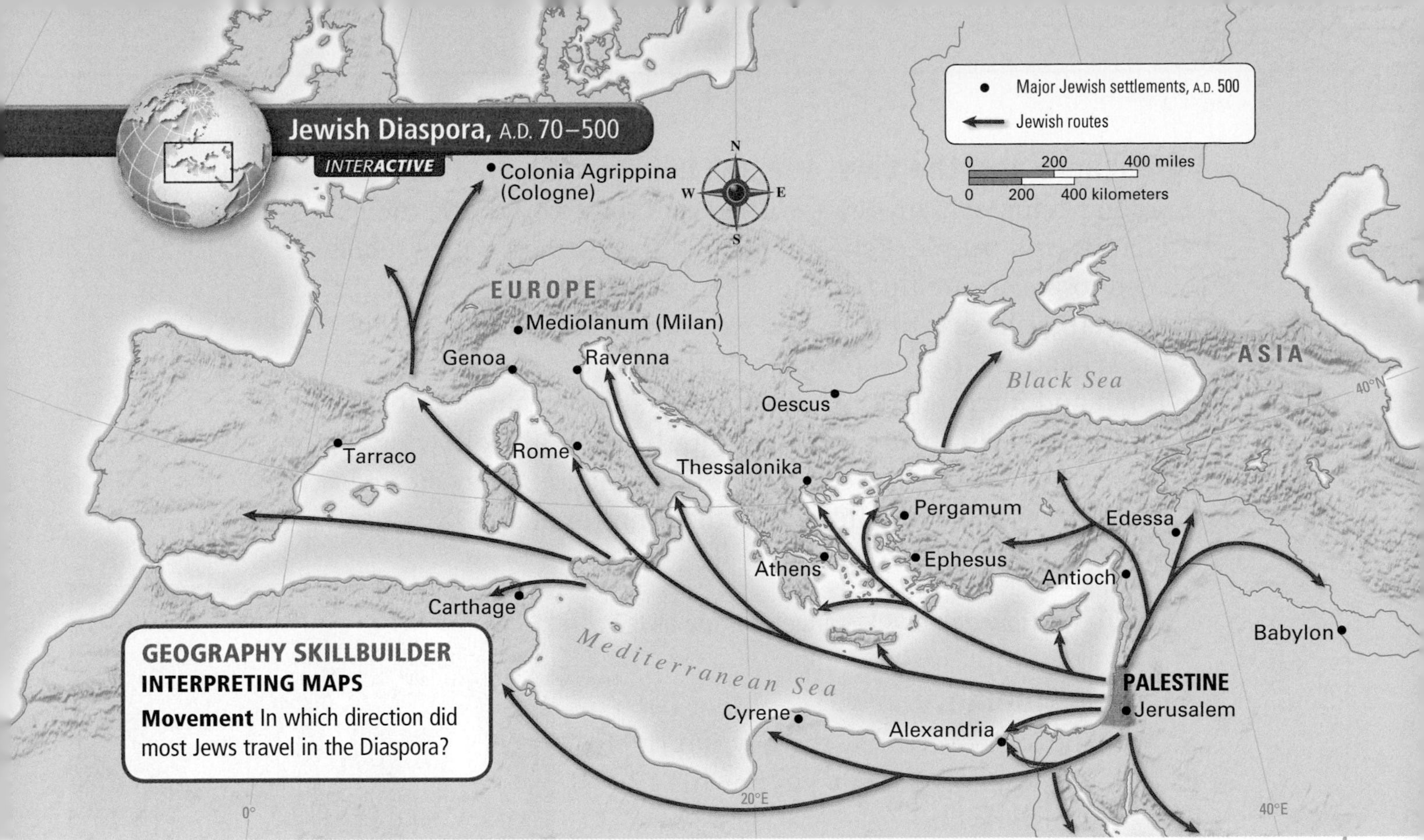

GEOGRAPHY SKILLBUILDER
INTERPRETING MAPS
Movement In which direction did most Jews travel in the Diaspora?

Vespasian put his son Titus in charge of the Roman troops in Judea. In A.D. 70, Titus put down the rebellion, burning the second Temple and taking Jerusalem. Some Zealots fought on at Masada, a fortress overlooking the Dead Sea, but it was taken.

The Diaspora The destruction by the Romans of the second Temple and of Jerusalem in A.D. 70 hastened the movement of the Jews out of Judea. This movement of the Jews to other parts of the world, which had begun peacefully centuries earlier, is known as the **Diaspora** (dy•AS•puhr•uh), a Greek word meaning "scattered." The Romans sent many Jews to Rome as slaves. Some Jews remained in Jerusalem.

REVIEW What was the lasting effect of Jewish resistance to Roman rule?

Judaism—An Ongoing Faith

3 ESSENTIAL QUESTION What happened to Jewish beliefs when the Jews were in exile?

Although the Jews were scattered throughout the Roman Empire, many stayed faithful to their religious beliefs. Despite their scattering, they continued to try to practice the biblical concepts of righteousness and justice.

Teachers and the Law After the Romans destroyed the second Temple, many Jews worried that they would lose their identity as a people. Religious leaders and teachers called **rabbis** tried to make sure this did not happen. Wherever Jews settled, they built places for prayer and worship called **synagogues**. At the synagogue, the people gathered to hear the rabbis read the Torah and interpretations, or Commentaries, on the Torah.

The Jews also held onto their faith by carefully following the laws and observing the customs of their religion. They created schools where Jewish children studied the Torah and learned the prayers of their faith.

REVIEW How did Jews keep their culture alive?

Lesson Summary

- The Jews overthrew their Syrian rulers.
- The Romans harshly put down a Jewish revolt.
- The Jews held onto their faith.

▲ **Torah** A rabbi and teenager read from the Torah.

Why It Matters Now . . .

The laws, rituals, and writings from this period are an important part of how Jews practice their religion today.

3 Lesson Review

Homework Helper ClassZone.com

Terms & Names

1. Explain the importance of

   Diaspora rabbi synagogue

Using Your Notes

Comparing and Contrasting Use your completed Venn diagram to answer the following question:

2. How were the Syrians and Romans alike and different in the way they dealt with Jewish rebellion?

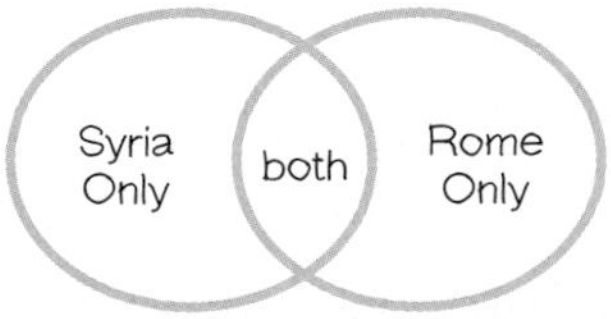

Main Ideas

3. What was the goal of the revolt led by Judah Maccabeus and his brothers against the Syrians?
4. How did the Romans punish the Jews of Judea for resisting Roman rule?
5. What are three ways Jews kept their faith strong after the Diaspora?

Critical Thinking

6. **Making Inferences** How did study keep the faith of the Jews alive?
7. **Drawing Conclusions** Why did the Diaspora change the way that the Jews practiced their religion?

Activity

Internet Activity Use the Internet to research one of the people in this lesson, such as Judah Maccabee or Yohanan ben Zaccai. Then make a sketch for the leader's Web page.
INTERNET KEYWORDS *Judah Maccabee, Yohanan ben Zaccai*

Activity Extend Lesson 3

Design a Fortress

Goal: To understand the history of the Hebrew kingdoms by designing a fortress such as the one at Masada

Materials & Supplies
- blank drawing paper
- pen, marker or colored pencils

Optional: book on forts and castles

Prepare

1. Research fortresses, including Masada.
2. You will need blank paper and a marker, a pen, or colored pencils.

Do the Activity

1. Draw a blueprint for a fortress from overhead, showing the location of all of the important features of the fort.
2. Draw the fortress from a different angle. For example, you might draw it as it would appear to those outside of it.
3. Call out various elements of your drawing and illustrate them in greater detail. For example, you might draw a close-up of watchtowers or a drawbridge.
4. Label the elements in your drawing, such as moats, drawbridges, walls, and so forth.

Follow-Up

1. How does a fortress represent self-defense rather than aggression?
2. What supplies might you need inside a fortress to withstand a long siege?

Extension

Making a Presentation Each person should show his or her drawing to the rest of the class and explain why a fortress might be important for survival. Drawings might be displayed on a wall in the classroom.

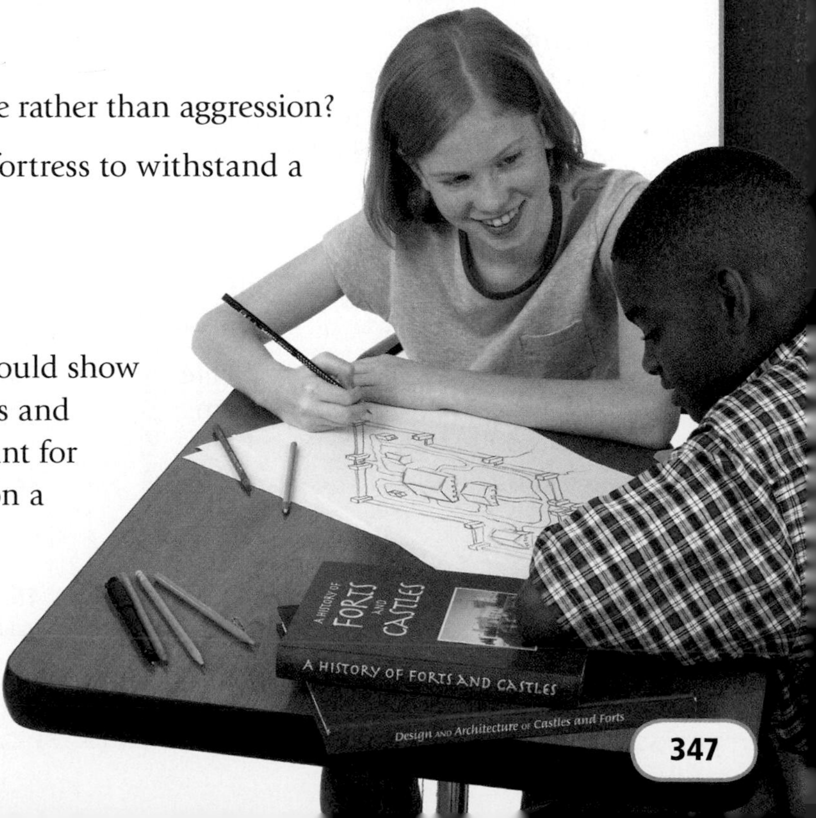

Chapter 10 Review

VISUAL SUMMARY

The Hebrew Kingdoms

Belief Systems

- The Hebrews worshiped one God.
- The beliefs of the Hebrews helped them survive difficult times.
- After being expelled from their homeland, most Jews remained loyal to their beliefs.

Geography

- Abraham left Mesopotamia to settle in Canaan.
- Hebrew slaves left Egypt and returned to Canaan.
- Hebrew captives left Babylon and returned to the kingdom of Judah.

Government

- The Hebrews built a small but influential nation, Israel, that later divided into the kingdoms of Israel and Judah.
- The Jews fought against foreign control by the Assyrians, Babylonians, and Romans.
- Jewish resistance to Roman rule hastened their departure from their homeland.

TERMS & NAMES

Explain why the words in each set below are linked with each other.

1. **Abraham** and **monotheism**
2. **Moses** and **Exodus**
3. **David** and **Solomon**
4. **rabbi** and **synagogue**

MAIN IDEAS

The Origins of the Hebrews (pages 324–333)

5. What made the religion of the Hebrews different from the religions of other groups in the ancient world?
6. Why might the Hebrew leader Moses be known as "The Lawgiver"?
7. What are three ways the judges helped the Hebrews?

Kingdoms and Captivity (pages 334–341)

8. How did Solomon's building projects help and hurt Israel?
9. What happened to the Israelites after Israel was conquered by the Assyrians?
10. How did the Babylonian conquest change the way the people of Judah lived?

Rome and Judea (pages 342–347)

11. How did the Maccabee victory affect the government of Judah?
12. Which group of Jews led the fight to resist Roman rule?
13. How did the Romans punish the people of Judea for rebelling?

CRITICAL THINKING

Big Ideas: Belief Systems

14. **MAKING INFERENCES** How did the Ten Commandments reflect Jewish beliefs?
15. **DRAWING CONCLUSIONS** What important Jewish belief was passed on to other religions?
16. **UNDERSTANDING CONTINUITY AND CHANGE** What beliefs and practices helped Jews pass on their religion?

ALTERNATIVE ASSESSMENT

1. **WRITING ACTIVITY** Choose one of the kings discussed in this chapter. Write a persuasive paragraph telling whether you think the person was a good king. Be sure to use information from the chapter to support your opinion.

2. **INTERDISCIPLINARY ACTIVITY—SCIENCE** According to tradition, the Hebrews wandered 40 years in the Sinai desert before entering Canaan. Use books or the Internet to research the climate, plants and animals, and the soil of the desert. Choose a plant or animal that lives in the desert. Make a poster showing how that animal or plant has adapted to life in the desert.

3. **STARTING WITH A STORY** Starting with a Story. Review the letter you wrote to your great-grandson. Draw a picture of some aspect of life in Moab or Israel to include with your letter.

Technology Activity

4. **MAKING A MULTIMEDIA PRESENTATION** Use the Internet or the library to find out more about Judah and the Maccabees. Working in a group, create a multimedia presentation.
   - Who were the Maccabees?
   - How were the Maccabees able to defeat a larger, better-equipped enemy?
   - How do Jews today commemorate the Maccabee victory?

Research Links
ClassZone.com

Interpreting Primary Sources The Ark of the Covenant was important to the Hebrews. It was said to contain the original tablets with the Ten Commandments given by God to Moses on Mount Sinai. Use the following description of the Ark from the Torah to answer the questions.

Primary Source

> Bezalel [a craftsman] made the ark of acacia wood—two and a half cubits long [about 50 inches], a cubit and a half wide, and a cubit and a half high. He overlaid it with pure gold, both inside and out, and made a gold molding around it. He cast four gold rings for it and fastened them to its four feet, with two rings on one side and two rings on the other. Then he made poles of acacia wood and overlaid them with gold. And he inserted the poles into the rings on the sides of the ark to carry it. He made the . . . cover of pure gold—two and a half cubits long and a cubit and a half wide. Then he made two cherubim [angels] out of hammered gold at the ends of the cover.
>
> Exodus *37:1–7*

1. **What precious metal is used in building the Ark?**

   A. silver
   B. gold
   C. platinum
   D. copper

2. **Why might the Hebrews have used precious metal?**

   A. long lasting
   B. tarnish resistant
   C. rust proof
   D. worthy of God

Test Practice
ClassZone.com

Additional Test Practice, pp. S1–S33

Chapter 11 Ancient Greece

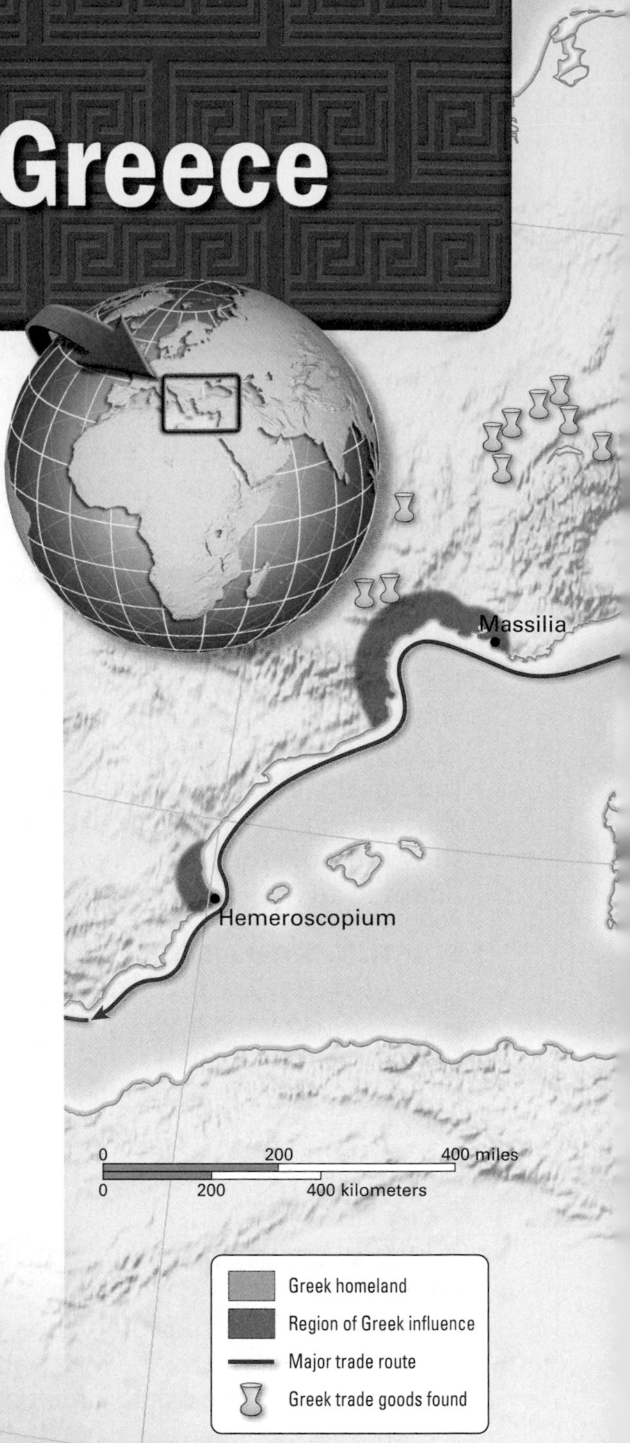

Before You Read: Predicting

Scan the title of the chapter and the lesson titles. Write three questions that you think will be answered in the chapter. One example might be

What were the main geographic features of Greece?

If you find the answer to any of your questions as you read, write it down in your notebook.

Big Ideas About Ancient Greece

Government **Governments create law codes and political bodies to organize a society.**

Mountains separated ancient Greece into regions, which were organized as separate city-states. Originally, kings ruled those city-states, but over time other forms of government evolved. The city-state of Athens developed direct democracy, in which all male citizens met in an assembly to make their own laws.

Integrated Technology

eEdition
- Interactive Maps
- Interactive Visuals
- Starting with a Story

VIDEO *Ancient Greece*

INTERNET RESOURCES

Go to **ClassZone.com** for
- WebQuest
- Homework Helper
- Research Links
- Internet Activities
- Quizzes
- Maps
- Test Practice
- Current Events

GREECE

1500 B.C.
Mycenaean civilization thrives in Greece.
(Mycenaean headpiece, 1500s B.C.) ▲

1050 B.C.
Dorians move into Greece.

1500 B.C. — **1000 B.C.**

WORLD

c. 1200 B.C.
Olmec culture rises in Mexico.
(Olmec sculpture of man with infant) ▶

1027 B.C.
Zhou Dynasty begins in China.

Greek Trade, 500 B.C.

INTERACTIVE

800 B.C.
Greeks use an alphabet.
(ring showing Greek letters, 400s B.C.) ▶

490 B.C.
Athenians win the Battle of Marathon.

700 B.C. — 400 B.C.

751 B.C.
Kush conquers Upper Egypt.

c. 563 B.C.
The Buddha is born.
(head of the Buddha, southeast Asia, A.D. 1100s) ▶

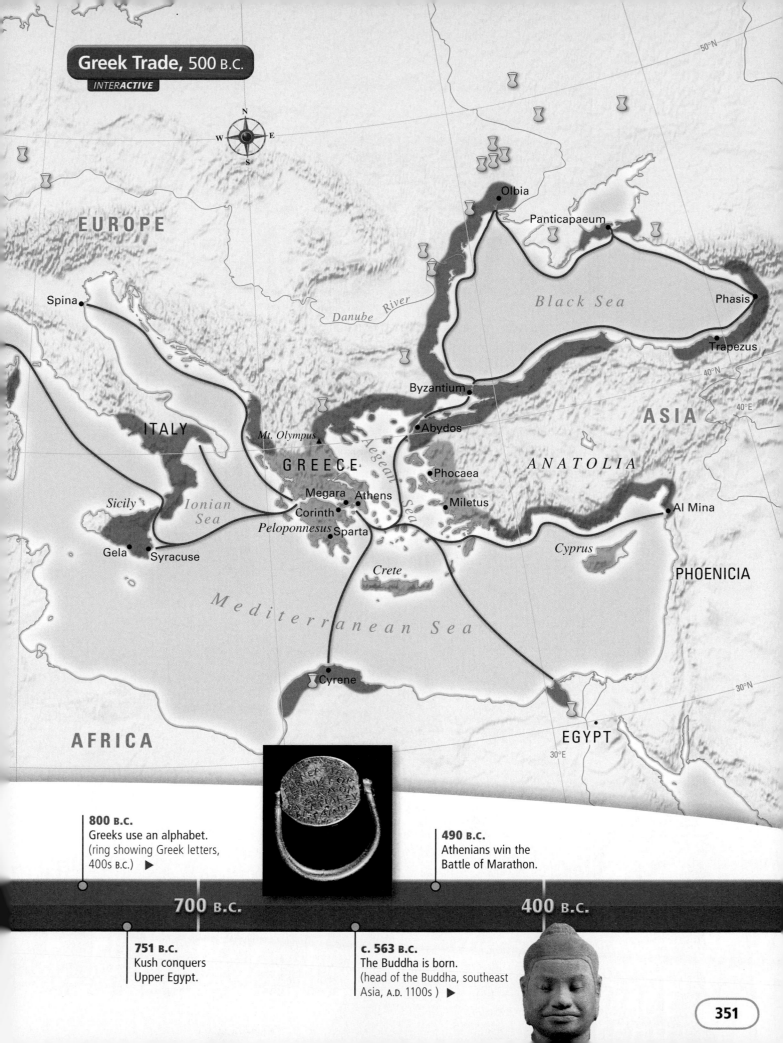

Starting with a Story

THE PERSIAN INVASION

Background: Ancient Greece was not a unified country. It was made up of independent city-states (states made of a city and its surrounding lands). Two of the leading city-states were Athens and Sparta. In 490 B.C., the mighty Persian Empire dominated Southwest Asia. The Persian king Darius decided to conquer Greece.

Darius and his army have just landed near Athens. Imagine that you are hearing the news in your home state of Sparta. Athens is 150 miles away. You wonder whether this fight has anything to do with you.

Sculpture of a Spartan warrior, possibly a king ▶

Starting with a Story
eEdition

You are a soldier in Sparta. All of the free men in Sparta are soldiers. Your father and grandfather were soldiers. All of the men in your family for more than 150 years have been soldiers.

Sparta's army is its great strength and the source of its pride. From the time you were a boy, you trained to be a soldier. You learned to be tough. You and your friends played at war, preparing for the real thing.

Athens is Sparta's main rival. Its way of life is different. Men there spend most of their time talking about politics. Boys in Athens study debate, music, and poetry. You wonder what kind of people would waste their time on such things.

An Athenian messenger has just arrived to tell the Spartan rulers that the Persian army has landed near Athens. He ran for two days to bring the news. He pleads with the rulers, "The enemy's force is enormous. There are 600 ships and more than 15,000 soldiers, many of them with horses. We have only about 10,000 soldiers. Athens desperately needs the help of your powerful army. Will you not join us in this fight?"

You've heard about the Persian Empire. Their rulers have been conquering their neighbors for more than 100 years. Their lands stretch from the Mediterranean Sea to the border of India. Persians now rule over Egypt.

Such a powerful empire might eliminate your rival for you. Then Sparta would be the greatest city-state in Greece. Why should Spartans die for men who would rather be politicians than warriors? Then a horrible thought occurs to you. What if the Persians don't stop with Athens? What if they decide to come after Sparta next?

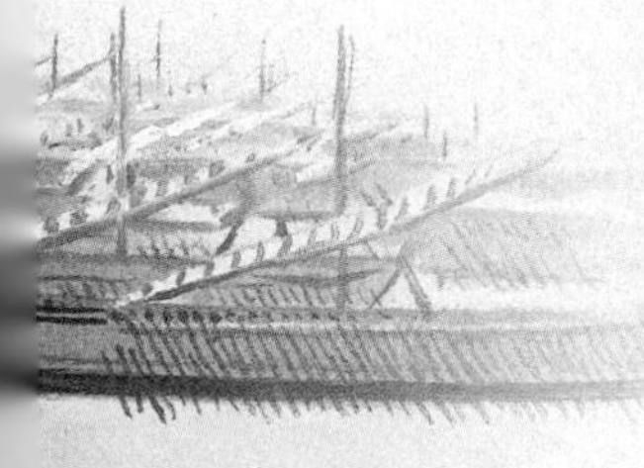

Do you help your rival against a greater enemy?

Reading & Writing

1. **READING: Compare and Contrast** How were Athens and Sparta similar and different? Compare and contrast them.
2. **WRITING: Persuasion** Suppose that the rulers of Sparta have asked your advice. Think about the reasons for and against helping Athens. Then write a letter to the ruler explaining what you think Sparta should do.

Lesson 1

MAIN IDEAS

1. **Geography** Rugged mountains divided Greece into many regions.
2. **Geography** The sea linked the regions of Greece to each other and to foreign regions. Sea trade became common.
3. **Culture** Trade helped the early Greeks develop a sophisticated culture.

▲ **Pottery Plate** The sea was very important to the ancient Greeks. For one thing, it provided them with a variety of seafood, as shown on this plate.

TAKING NOTES

Reading Skill: Understanding Effects

An effect is an event or action that is the result of a cause. Copy a chart like the one below on your own paper. As you read Lesson 1, look for the effects of the causes that are listed.

Causes	Effects
Mountains cover most of Greece.	
Several seas surround Greece.	
Greece traded with other regions.	

Skillbuilder Handbook, page R26

Words to Know

Understanding the following words will help you read this lesson:

mainland the main part of a country or territory (page 355)
*Surrounding the **mainland** are thousands of islands, which are part of Greece.*

rugged having a rough, jagged, or uneven surface (page 355)
*The country's **rugged** landscape made it difficult for people to travel.*

found to establish; to bring into being (page 356)
*Greek traders helped to **found** colonies where they could exchange their goods.*

collapse to break down or end suddenly (page 358)
*Greek culture took some time to recover after its early civilization **collapsed** about 1200 B.C.*

The Geography of Greece

TERMS & NAMES
peninsula
Peloponnesus
isthmus
Phoenician
alphabet

Build on What You Know Has construction or an accident ever blocked the road your family wanted to take? How did you get around the problem? Mountains prevented the ancient Greeks from traveling over land. This lesson will explain their other methods of travel.

Geography Shapes Ancient Greek Life

1 ESSENTIAL QUESTION What were the main features of the geography of Greece?

The mainland of Greece sticks out into the Mediterranean Sea. It is a **peninsula**, a body of land that has water on three sides. Greece also includes thousands of islands.

A gulf of water almost divides the Greek peninsula in two. The southern tip forms a second peninsula called the **Peloponnesus** (PEHL•uh•puh•NEE•suhs). A narrow strip of land called an **isthmus** (IHS•muhs) links the Peloponnesus to the rest of Greece. (See the map on page 351.)

Landscape and Climate

Mountains cover 70 to 80 percent of Greece. The mountains divided it into many regions. The uneven landscape made transportation over land difficult. Greece had no large rivers on which people could travel. The rugged landscape made it hard to unite Greece under a single government.

Greece has mild, rainy winters and hot, dry summers. In much of Greece, temperatures range from about 50°F in winter to 80°F in summer. The warm climate encouraged outdoor life. For example, outdoor athletic competitions such as races were an important part of Greek culture.

Coastline of Greece Because of its long coastline, Greece has many ports. This port, Piraeus, is near the capital and ancient city of Athens. ▼

Geography

Land Use in Greece

Mountains cover 70 to 80 percent of Greece. As a result, only about 20 to 30 percent of Greek land was good for farming. Even so, the ancient Greeks found ways to make the best use of the land that they had.

- They grew grain on the few open plains. Olive trees grew on the edges of those plains.
- The Greeks planted grapevines on the lower slopes of hills.
- Sheep and goats grazed on land that was too rocky or too infertile to grow crops.

Greece: Land Use

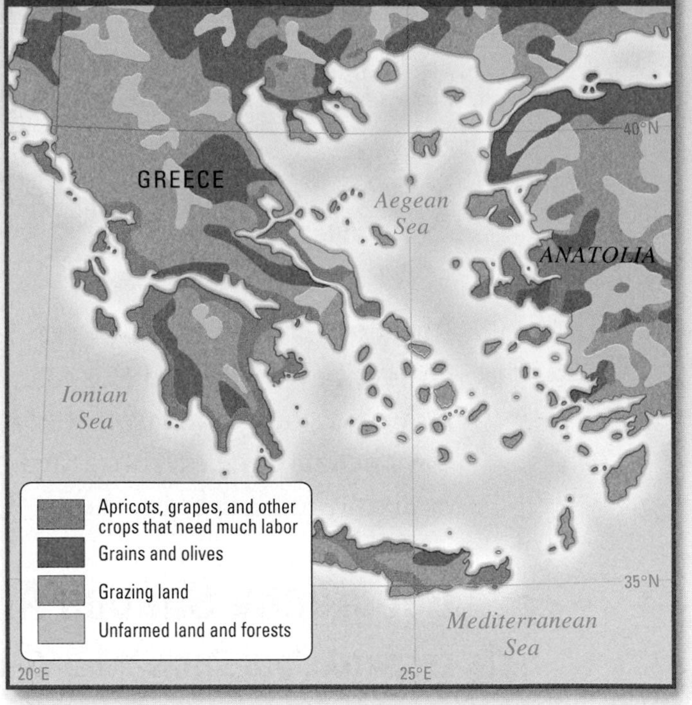

GEOGRAPHY SKILLBUILDER
INTERPRETING MAPS
Region Was more land used for growing grains and olives or for grazing animals?

Agriculture Greek land was rocky, so only about 20 to 30 percent of it was good for farming. Even so, more than half of all Greeks were farmers or herders. Most farmland was located in the valleys between mountains.

In Greek society, landowners were part of the upper class. In general, only men owned property. A person who owned land could support himself. He had enough wealth to pay for equipment such as helmets, shields, and swords. This allowed him to serve in the army and defend his homeland. As a result, people respected landowners, who had a higher place in society than merchants or poor people.

In order to get more farmland, the Greeks founded colonies in other regions. The western end of Anatolia had broad plains and rivers. The Greeks founded many colonies there.

Resources The lack of farmland was not the only problem. Greece also lacked natural resources such as precious metals. The Greeks had to find those resources somewhere else.

One resource that Greece did have was stone for building. Greece also had plenty of good sites for harbors.

REVIEW How did the mountains affect life in Greece?

Trade Helps Greece Prosper

2 ESSENTIAL QUESTION How did the sea affect Greek life?

Just as rivers influenced other ancient cultures, the sea influenced Greece. Greece has a long coastline, and most places in Greece are less than 100 miles from the coast. In fact, many cities were built directly on harbors.

Highways of Water Several seas played a major role in the life of ancient Greece. The largest was the Mediterranean Sea to the south. The Ionian and Aegean seas were branches of the Mediterranean. The Ionian Sea is west of Greece. The Aegean Sea is east of Greece.

These "highways of water" linked most parts of Greece to each other. The Greeks used the seas as transportation routes.

▲ **Greek Ship** In recent times, people built this ship to show how ancient Greek fishing ships looked.

A Seafaring People The Greeks became skilled sailors and shipbuilders. They built rowing ships for fighting and sailing ships for trading. Some warships had two or three levels of oars on each side. Most sailing ships had a single mast and square sail.

The Ionian and Aegean seas are not very large. Small ships could sail around them by staying near the coast or by sailing from island to island. Once the Greeks learned these routes, they could sail to other regions.

The sea was a source of fish, an important part of the Greek diet. The Greeks traded fresh fish from the sea to local ports along the coast. The Greeks also dried some kinds of fish so that they could be transported over great distances.

Trade and Commerce Greece did not produce much grain, but some regions produced surplus olive oil, wine, wool, and fine pottery. Greek city-states bought and sold surplus goods from each other. In addition, Greeks traded these items to other regions around the Black Sea and the Mediterranean Sea, including Egypt and Italy.

The main products that the Greeks bought were grain, timber for building, animal hides, and slaves. The Greeks also traded for nuts, figs, cheese, and flax, which was used to make linen.

REVIEW How did the sea help the Greek economy?

The Earliest Greeks

3 ESSENTIAL QUESTION How did trade influence Greek culture?

The Greek culture of sailing and trading developed over thousands of years. The earliest Greeks had moved onto the Greek peninsula about 2000 B.C.

Mycenaean Civilization The first Greek civilization was built on the Peloponnesus. It was named after its most important city, Mycenae (my•SEE•nee). A king ruled each city of Mycenaean Greece. The Mycenaeans were traders. Their culture featured writing, gold jewelry, bronze weapons, and fine pottery. Their civilization collapsed about 1200 B.C., perhaps because of invaders.

After the fall of the Mycenaeans, Greek culture declined. People no longer kept written records. Without such records, historians know little about the period from 1200 to 750 B.C.

New Advances in Greek Culture In time, Greek culture made advances again. One reason for this is that the Greeks learned from other people, such as the **Phoenicians** (fih•NISHSH•uhnz). They were another important trading people, who lived on the coast of the eastern Mediterranean. By trading with other people, the Phoenicians spread their system of writing. It used 22 symbols to stand for sounds. Such a system of symbols is called an **alphabet**.

Comparisons Across Cultures

Alphabets

Writing systems change over time. The Greeks borrowed the Phoenician alphabet of 22 letters but wrote the symbols differently. Also, the Greeks added two letters. Since the time of ancient Greece, their alphabet has evolved into the one used in the United States today.

▲ American Sign Language is a language for the deaf that uses gestures to convey meaning. It includes an alphabet.

Culture	Characters from Alphabet																												
Phoenician	𐤀	𐤁		𐤃	𐤄	𐤅	𐤂	𐤇	𐤈	𐤆		𐤊	𐤋	𐤌	𐤍	𐤏	𐤐	𐤑	𐤒	𐤓	𐤔	𐤕					𐤎		𐤆	
Greek	Α	Β		Δ	Ε	ꟻ	Γ	Η	Θ	Ι		Κ	Λ	Μ	Ν	Ο	Π			Ρ	Σ	Τ	Υ	Φ		Υ	Ξ		Ζ	∩
Modern English	A	B	C	D	E	F	G	H		I	J	K	L	M	N	O	P		Q	R	S	T	U		V	W	X	Y	Z	

The Greeks picked up the Phoenician alphabet between 900 and 800 B.C. They changed some letters to suit their language. The Greek alphabet later evolved into our own alphabet of 26 letters.

The Greeks also learned about coins from trading with other peoples. Coins were invented about 650 B.C. in Anatolia. Most parts of Greece were making their own coins by 500 B.C.

Eventually, the Greeks also developed new forms of literature and government. You will learn more about these developments in Lessons 2 and 3.

REVIEW What did the Greeks learn from trading with other peoples?

Greek Coins This coin is from the city of Athens, Greece. One side shows the goddess Athena, for whom Athens was named. The other side shows an owl, which was a symbol of Athena's wisdom. ▼

Lesson Summary

- The mountainous geography of Greece limited agriculture and political unity.
- The Greeks depended on the sea to connect with each other and with the wider world.
- Trade brought an alphabet and coins to Greece.

Why It Matters Now . . .

The Greek alphabet influenced the development of all Western alphabets, including the English alphabet.

1 Lesson Review

Homework Helper
ClassZone.com

Terms & Names

1. Explain the importance of

peninsula, Peloponnesus, isthmus, Phoenician, alphabet

Using Your Notes

Understanding Effects Use your completed chart to answer the following question:

2. What effects did the geography of Greece have on settlement patterns?

Causes	Effects
Mountains cover most of Greece.	
Several seas surround Greece.	
Greece traded with other regions.	

Main Ideas

3. How did the geography of the Greek peninsula affect the political organization of the region?

4. How did the seas affect Greek trade patterns?

5. How did trade with other peoples contribute to Greek civilization?

Critical Thinking

6. Analyzing Causes Why did the Greeks develop trade with other regions?

7. Contrasting What were two major differences between the civilizations of Greece and Mesopotamia?

Activity

Making a Map Take out the world map you started in Chapter 2. Using the map on page 351 as a model, add the Greek homeland to your map. You should also add the cities of Athens and Sparta.

Lesson 2

MAIN IDEAS

1. **Belief Systems** Like other ancient peoples, the Greeks believed their gods controlled the human and natural worlds.
2. **Belief Systems** The Greeks honored their gods by worshiping them and by holding festivals and games in their honor.
3. **Culture** Early Greek literature included stories that taught lessons, and long poems that told of adventures.

TAKING NOTES

Reading Skill: Making Generalizations

As you read Lesson 2, look for information that will help you make a generalization, or broad judgment, about the relationship between Greek beliefs and literature. Record the information on a chart like the one below.

Greek Religious Beliefs	Greek Literature

Skillbuilder Handbook, page R8

▲ **Greek Vase** This vase shows a scene from a Greek myth. The hero Heracles (also called Hercules) rescued Alcestis from the underworld after she offered to die in place of her husband, the king of Thessaly.

Words to Know

Understanding the following words will help you read this lesson:

hero a person who is admired for great courage or special achievements (page 360)
*Odysseus was a famous **hero** of ancient Greece.*

vivid producing clear mental images (page 361)
*People still enjoy reading the **vivid** stories that the Greeks told about their gods.*

public open to all people; not private (page 362)
*The Greeks built special places for **public** rituals and celebrations.*

javelin a light spear thrown by hand (page 363)
*The **javelin** throw is an Olympic event.*

Beliefs and Customs

TERMS & NAMES
- Zeus
- Mount Olympus
- myth
- Olympics
- epic poem
- fable

Build on What You Know Like other ancient peoples, the Greeks were polytheistic—they worshiped many gods. But you won't find gods with animal heads in Greece as you did in Egypt. Greek gods looked like humans, yet were more powerful and more beautiful than any human could be.

Greek Gods and Myths

1 ESSENTIAL QUESTION What was Greek religion like?

To the Greeks, the gods were not distant beings. They became involved in people's lives, and the Greeks loved to tell stories about them. These vivid tales showed that the gods were sometimes cruel and selfish.

The Gods of Greece The Greek gods had both divine and human qualities. For example, they were very powerful and could shape human events. Yet they had a wide range of human emotions, including love, anger, and jealousy. The gods and goddesses of Greece constantly competed with one another.

Zeus (ZOOS) was the ruler of the gods. The Greeks believed that he and 11 other major gods and goddesses lived on **Mount Olympus** (uh•LIHM•puhs), the highest mountain in Greece. (See the box on pages 362–363.) The Greeks also worshiped many less-important gods.

Each city had a special god or goddess to protect it. For example, Athena (one of the 12 who lived on Olympus) was the protector of Athens. She was the goddess of wisdom, a warrior, and the patron of crafts such as weaving.

Mount Olympus The ancient Greeks believed that their most important gods lived on this mountain. As a result, this group is frequently called the Olympian gods. ▼

Greek Mythology **Myths** are stories that people tell to explain beliefs about their world. Myths often begin as oral stories. Later they might be written down.

The Greeks created myths to explain the creation of the world and of human beings. Many myths described the gods and goddesses and how they related to one another and to humans. For example, the myth of Prometheus (pruh•MEE•thee•uhs) tells how he stole fire from the gods and gave it to humans. Zeus punished him for this by chaining him to a rock. Every day, an eagle ate his liver—which grew back every night. Today, Prometheus is seen as a hero who defied unjust authority.

Primary Source Handbook
See the Greek myth: "The Boy Who Flew," pages R54–55.

Other myths portrayed Greek heroes and heroines. The Reader's Theater on pages 366–369 is based on the myth of a young woman named Atalanta, who was a skilled hunter and runner.

REVIEW How were Greek myths and religion connected?

Honoring the Gods

2 ESSENTIAL QUESTION How did the Greeks honor their gods?

Like other ancient peoples, the Greeks believed it was important to honor the gods. An angry god could cause trouble. The Greeks created statues of the gods and built temples as places for the gods to live. They also held special events to honor the gods.

Holy Festivals Certain days of each month were holy to different gods and goddesses or to aspects of nature. For example, each month began with the new moon, and the festival of Noumenia was held. People celebrated holy days with sacrifices and public ceremonies.

The most important festivals honored the 12 Olympian gods. For example, there was a great festival to honor Athena. A new robe was woven for her statue in the main temple. The festival also included a procession, races and other athletic games, and poetry recitals.

Greek Gods and Goddesses

Zeus was the father of many other gods. Some of his children were Aphrodite, Apollo, Athena, and Hermes. ▼

The Olympics In Greece, games were always part of religious festivals. The largest and most elaborate of these were the Olympics. The **Olympics** were games held every four years as part of a major festival that honored Zeus. They took place in a stadium built in the city of Olympia. Only men competed in these contests.

The oldest records of winners at the Olympics date to 776 B.C. But the games might have been going on for centuries before that. The first Olympics included only a foot race. Over time, longer races and other events were added. Events included wrestling, the long jump, the javelin throw, and the discus throw. These games tested skills that were valuable to soldiers.

Unmarried girls competed in a festival to honor the goddess Hera. Hera was Zeus' wife, and her festival was held at the same time as the Olympics. This festival featured a foot race in three different age categories.

Connect to Today

▲ **Olympics for All** In modern times, a wider variety of athletes has the chance to compete in the Olympic games than ever before.

REVIEW Why did the Greeks hold the Olympics?

◀ Demeter was a fertility goddess who was especially linked with growing grain.

▲ Athena was the goddess of wisdom and also a warrior. Athena had no mother. She sprang from the forehead of Zeus.

Apollo was the god of archery, healing, music, poetry, and prophecy. Later, he was honored as the god of the sun. Zeus and Apollo were the most widely worshiped gods. ▶

Other Greek Gods and Goddesses

Ares	god of war
Aphrodite	goddess of love
Artemis	goddess of the hunt
Hephaestus	god of fire
Hera	wife of Zeus; protector of marriage
Hermes	messenger of the gods
Hestia	goddess of home life
Poseidon	god of the seas and earthquakes

Early Greek Literature

2 ESSENTIAL QUESTION What literature did the early Greeks produce?

In addition to stories about gods, the Greeks told stories about their ancient heroes. Much of what we know about the early Greeks comes from stories passed down through generations and from long poems that told stories. These long poems are called **epic poems**. According to tradition, a blind man, Homer, composed the most famous epics.

Primary Source Handbook
See the excerpt from the *Iliad*, pages R51–52.

Epics of Homer Homer's epic the *Iliad* is about the Trojan War, which started because a Trojan stole a Greek king's wife. In the *Iliad,* the Greeks surrounded the city of Troy for more than nine years, trying to capture it. The *Iliad* is famous for its portrayal of heroes. For example, no one could defeat the Greek warrior Achilles (uh•KIHL•eez). When he was a baby, his mother dipped him in a river that would make him live forever. But an arrow wounded Achilles in his one weak spot—the heel his mother held as she lowered him in the water—so he died.

Primary Source Handbook
See the excerpt from Aesop's Fables: The Wolf in Sheep's Clothing, page R53.

For centuries, people thought Homer's story was fiction. Around 1870, archaeologists discovered the ruins of ancient Troy. A real war did take place there, but it did not happen exactly as the *Iliad* portrays it.

Homer's other major epic was the *Odyssey.* It describes the adventures of the Greek hero Odysseus (oh•DIHS•YOOS) after the Trojan War. The Greek gods decided that Odysseus' trip home should take ten years. During that time, he and his men encountered many dangers. The gods sometimes helped Odysseus and sometimes worked against him.

These ancient stories still influence speech and art today. For instance, we use the phrase *Achilles' heel* to refer to a person's weakest area.

Aesop's Fables A **fable** is a short story, usually involving animals, that teaches a moral lesson. A storyteller named Aesop (EE•suhp) is credited with writing down many ancient Greek fables.

Achilles The ancient Greek epics still influence our culture. For example, in 2004, the movie *Troy* retold the story of the Trojan War. Here the warrior Achilles does battle. ▼

One of Aesop's best-known fables is "The Hare and the Tortoise." In it, a hare (rabbit) makes fun of a tortoise (turtle) for being slow. The tortoise challenges the hare to a race. The hare is so sure he will win that he lies down for a nap. The tortoise never stops but goes at a slow, steady pace to the finish line. The hare wakes up too late for his speed to save him. We still use this story today to encourage people to work steadily at a task that seems impossible to accomplish.

REVIEW Why are Homer's epics important?

Cyclops On Odysseus' long voyage, a one-eyed monster called a Cyclops made him and his men prisoners. The Cyclops ate several of the men before Odysseus defeated him. ▼

Lesson Summary

- The ancient Greeks created stories about their gods, who were important to their daily lives.
- The ancient Greeks honored their gods through festivals that included rituals and athletic games.
- Early Greeks wrote fables and epic poems.

Why It Matters Now . . .

Greek mythology, epics, and fables continue to influence our literature, language, and movies.

2 Lesson Review

Homework Helper
ClassZone.com

Terms & Names

1. Explain the importance of

Zeus	myth	epic poem
Mount Olympus	Olympics	fable

Using Your Notes

Making Generalizations Use your completed chart to answer the following question:

2. How were Greek religious beliefs and Greek literature linked? Write your answer as a generalization.

Greek Religious Beliefs	Greek Literature

Main Ideas

3. Why was mythology important to the lives of ancient Greeks?

4. What role did religious festivals play in Greek life?

5. How are the *Iliad* and the *Odyssey* connected?

Critical Thinking

6. Drawing Conclusions from Sources What lesson might the Greeks have learned from the myth of Prometheus?

7. Comparing and Contrasting In what key ways were the religions of Egypt and Greece similar and different?

Activity

Writing a Fable Consider a moral lesson that is important to you. Working with a group, create a story that uses animals to teach that lesson.

Atalanta's Last Race

Background: According to Greek myth, the father of Atalanta (AT•uh•LAN•tuh) wanted a son, not a daughter. So he left Atalanta to die in the wilderness as an infant. She was raised first by a mother bear and then by caring hunters. As a result, the beautiful young woman was skilled in running, hunting, and wrestling.

Cast of Characters

Narrator

Oeneus: (EEN•yoost) king of Calydon

Atalanta: a young Greek woman

Hunter: Atalanta's foster father

Meleager: (mehl•ee•AY•guhr) son of Oeneus

Iasus: (EYE•ah•suhs) father of Atalanta

Aphrodite: (AF•ruh•DY•tee) Greek goddess of love

Milanion: (my•LAN•ee•uhn) suitor of Atalanta

Spectator

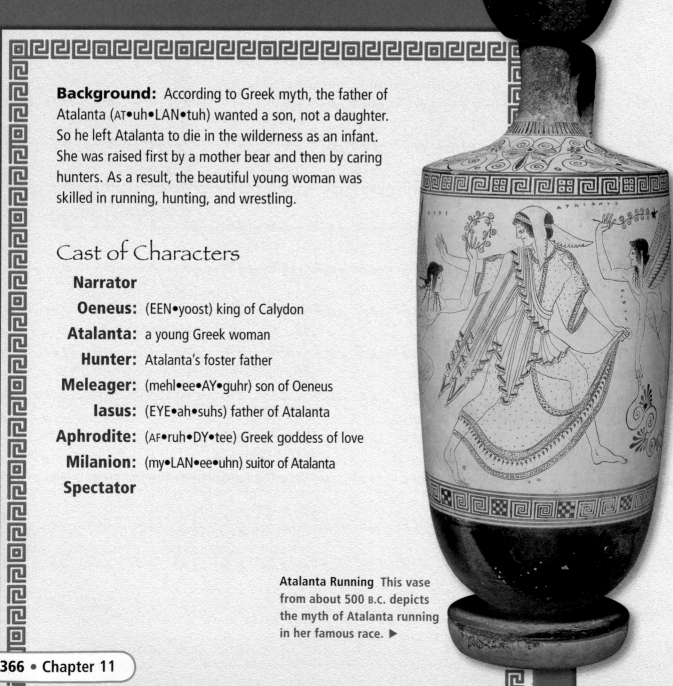

Atalanta Running This vase from about 500 B.C. depicts the myth of Atalanta running in her famous race. ▶

Narrator: The goddess Artemis (AHR•tuh•mihs) is angry at King Oeneus because he forgot to make sacrifices to her. So she has sent a wild boar to destroy his country of Calydon (KAL•ih•DAHN). The king has asked the best hunters in Greece for help. When they arrive, Atalanta is with them. She stands before the king, looking lovely in her simple woolen robe. A quiver of arrows hangs over her left shoulder. Her right hand clasps her bow.

Oeneus: Who are you, young woman? I have need of skilled hunters, not foolish girls.

Atalanta: Your majesty, I think you will find that I am as skilled as any man here. I have spent my life in the woods.

Hunter: I can speak for her, my lord. Atalanta has lived among us since she was a small girl. She once killed two centaurs[1] single-handedly. In our land, she is known as "the pride of the woods."

Oeneus: Very well, let us see what she can do. We need all the help we can get.

Narrator: The king's son Meleager falls in love with Atalanta instantly. Although some of the men dislike the idea of hunting with a woman, Meleager insists that she go with them.

Meleager: Come, Atalanta, you can hunt by my side. If you are as skilled as the hunters say, I will be glad of your presence. In fact, I should like you always near me.

Atalanta: I am happy to be your friend, Meleager, and I look forward to the hunt. But I only care for men as fellow hunters. I don't plan to ever get married.

Narrator: When the hunters surround the boar, it attacks and kills two men. Atalanta stays calm, and it is her arrow that first strikes the animal. Meleager then moves in for the kill.

(continued)

Artemis The goddess Artemis, sister of Apollo, was another female in Greek mythology who was a skilled hunter. ▶

1. **centaur (SEHN•TAWRZ):** a creature with the head, arms, and chest of a man, and the body and legs of a horse.

Meleager: Although it is my knife that has killed this beast, I insist that the honor go to Atalanta. She shall have the boar skin as a trophy.

Narrator: Meleager's uncles quarrel with him because he honored Atalanta. This quarrel leads to his death. But Atalanta's fame is just beginning. After defeating a great hero in a wrestling match, she meets her father, Iasus.

Iasus: Congratulations, daughter. I am very proud of you and would like to welcome you back to my home. I see that you will be almost like a son to me. But I understand that many young men want to marry you.

Atalanta: Don't worry, Father, I will never marry a man unless he can beat me in a foot race. (*Aside*) And I know there is no man alive who can do that.

Narrator: Atalanta enjoys defeating all the young men who come to race with her. No matter how fast they are, she is faster. She cares nothing for their promises of love. Her actions do not go unnoticed by Aphrodite, the goddess of love on Mount Olympus.

Aphrodite: It has come to my attention that there is a wild, young maiden who thinks she is too good for love. I may need to teach her a lesson.

Narrator: As it happens, a young man named Milanion wants very much to marry Atalanta. He is smart enough to know he cannot rely on his speed to beat her. He calls upon Aphrodite.

Milanion: Aphrodite, will you help me to marry Atalanta?

◀ **Running Girl** In Sparta, girls were trained in athletics because it taught them to be strong. Also, every four years at a festival in Hera's honor, unmarried girls competed in races.

Aphrodite: I will gladly help tame this young woman who refuses to honor me. Here are three magical golden apples. Their beauty is so dazzling that anyone who sees them will feel she must have them. Use them wisely and you will succeed.

Milanion: Thank you, goddess, for your wise and generous assistance.

Narrator: The day arrives when Milanion and Atalanta are to race. Atalanta looks so confident of her skill that Milanion almost despairs of being able to succeed in his plan.

Milanion: I must not lose courage. Aphrodite is on my side.

Narrator: The race begins. Milanion is swift, but Atalanta is pulling ahead. He rolls his first golden apple right in front of her.

Atalanta: Oh my! What is this? I've never seen anything so lovely. I'll just reach down and scoop it up.

Milanion: She barely lost her stride! I've caught up with her, but now she is racing ahead again. I've got to slow her down even more.

Narrator: This time, Milanion throws his apple to Atalanta's side. She has to move to the right to pick it up.

Spectator: Look, he's pulled ahead of her! But here she comes again, and the finish line is just ahead. Will she win this time?

Milanion: This is my last chance. I must distract her long enough for me to reach the goal ahead of her. Here goes.

Narrator: The third golden apple rolls right in front of Atalanta and onto the side of the racecourse. She sees it glinting in the green grass and follows it.

Atalanta: I must have that gorgeous glowing ball. But wait, what's this? Milanion is sprinting past me. He has won!

Milanion: (*panting for breath*) Atalanta, do not be angry with me. I only acted out of my great love for you. I will be extremely honored to be your husband.

Atalanta: I admire your skill and your wit. And I see that Aphrodite is your friend. I will honor my promise and be your wife.

Activities

1. **TALK ABOUT IT** Why might Atalanta prefer not to marry?
2. **WRITE ABOUT IT** Imagine that you are a spectator watching the race between Atalanta and Milanion. Write a paragraph describing the details of the race—the sights, the sounds, and other important impressions.

Lesson 3

MAIN IDEAS

1. **Government** Instead of being a unified country, Greece was organized into separate city-states.
2. **Government** Different political systems evolved in the various city-states. Some governments changed because of conflicts between rich and poor.
3. **Government** The city-state of Athens developed democracy, which is rule by the people.

TAKING NOTES

Reading Skill: Categorizing

To categorize means to sort information. As you read Lesson 3, use your own words to take notes about types of government on a chart like this one.

Types of Government		
Monarchy	Oligarchy	Democracy

Skillbuilder Handbook, page R6

▲ **Water Clock** A water clock was a device that used the flow of water to measure time. The Greeks used this clock to make sure that people in court kept their speeches short. (This clock runs out in about six minutes.)

Words to Know

Understanding the following words will help you read this lesson:

layout the plan or arrangement of something (page 372)

*The city's **layout** included space for a large public marketplace.*

supreme greatest in power or authority (page 373)

*The upper class began to question the **supreme** authority of the king.*

entitle to have rights and privileges (page 374)

*Greek women and slaves were not **entitled** to many of the benefits enjoyed by free male citizens.*

gradual happening little by little (page 374)

*Political change sometimes occurs suddenly, but often it is **gradual**.*

The City-State and Democracy

TERMS & NAMES
polis
aristocracy
oligarchy
tyrant
citizen
democracy

Build on What You Know As you read in Lesson 1, the Mycenaean civilization fell about 1200 B.C. After a decline, Greek culture gradually started to advance again. This led to the rise of Greek civilization. Like ancient Sumer, Greece was a region of people who shared a common language and common beliefs. In spite of that cultural unity, Greece was divided politically.

The Rise of City-States

1 **ESSENTIAL QUESTION** How was Greece organized politically?

In Lesson 1, you learned how geography divided Greece into small regions. Because of this, the basic form of government was the city-state. A city-state is a state made of a city and its surrounding lands. The colonies founded by Greeks around the Mediterranean were also city-states.

Greek City-States City-states became common in Greece about 700 B.C. In Greek, the word for city-state was **polis**. Most city-states were small. Geographic features, such as mountains, limited their size. Athens and Sparta were the largest Greek city-states. Their lands included the plains that surrounded the center city.

Most Greek cities had fewer than 20,000 residents. Because a city-state was fairly small, the people who lived there formed a close community.

Agora Most Greek cities, such as Athens shown here, had an agora—an open marketplace that also had temples and other public buildings. Men often met there to talk politics. ▶

▲ **Athens from the Air**
A modern artist painted this watercolor showing Athens and its surrounding lands. Notice how the Acropolis is much higher than everything else.

Layout of the City The center of city life was the agora. The agora was an open space where people came for business and public gatherings. Male citizens met there to discuss politics. Festivals and athletic contests were held there. Statues, temples, and other public buildings were found in and around the agora. (See Daily Life on pages 384–385.)

Many cities had a fortified hilltop called an acropolis. The word means "highest city." At first, people used the acropolis mainly for military purposes; high places are easier to defend. Later the Greeks built temples and palaces on the flat tops of these hills. Ordinary houses were built along the hill's base.

REVIEW What was the role of the agora in a Greek city?

Forms of Government

2 ESSENTIAL QUESTION What different political systems evolved in the city-states of Greece?

Each city-state of Greece was independent. The people of each one figured out what kind of government worked best for them. As a result, different city-states used different political systems. Some city-states kept the same system of government for centuries. Others slowly changed from one system to another.

Monarchs and Aristocrats The earliest form of government in Greece was monarchy (MAHN•uhr•kee). A monarch is a king or queen who has supreme power. Therefore, a monarchy is a government that a king or queen rules. Most Greek city-states started out as monarchies but changed over time.

Aristocracy (AR•ih•STAHK•ruh•see) is another name for the upper class or nobility. In Greece, the aristocracy were people who were descended from high-born ancestors. Some aristocrats believed that their ancestors were mythical heroes.

The Greek city-state of Corinth began as a monarchy. Later, an aristocracy ruled it. In fact, by the 700s B.C., most of the Greek city-states had moved from monarchy to rule by an aristocracy.

Vocabulary Strategy

The term *aristocracy* is from the Greek **root words** *aristos,* which means "best," and *kratos*, which means "power." The term *oligarchy* is from the **root words** *oligos,* which means "few," and *arkhe,* which means "rule."

Oligarchy Some city-states developed a political system called **oligarchy** (AHL•ih•GAHR•kee). Oligarchy means "rule by the few." It is similar to aristocracy because in both cases, a minority group controls the government.

The main difference between the two is the basis for the ruling class's power. When aristocrats rule, they do so because of their inherited social class. In an oligarchy, people rule because of wealth or land ownership. In some Greek city-states, an oligarchy replaced aristocratic rule. In others, the aristocracy and the oligarchy shared power.

Tyrants Poor people were not part of government in either monarchy, aristocracy, or oligarchy. Often, the poor came to resent being shut out of power. At times, they rebelled.

Sometimes a wealthy person who wanted to seize power made use of that anger. He would ask poor people to support him in becoming a leader. Such leaders were called tyrants. In Greece, a **tyrant** was someone who took power in an illegal way. Today the term *tyrant* means a cruel leader. To the Greeks, a tyrant was simply someone who acted like a king without being of royal birth. Some Greek tyrants worked to help the poor. Some created building programs to provide jobs. Others enacted laws canceling the debts that poor people owed to the wealthy.

Tyrants played an important role in the development of rule by the people. They helped overthrow the oligarchy. They also showed that if common people united behind a leader, they could gain the power to make changes.

REVIEW How were oligarchy and aristocracy similar?

Athens Builds a Limited Democracy

3 ESSENTIAL QUESTION How did limited democracy develop in Athens?

By helping tyrants rise to power, people in the lower classes realized they could influence government. As a result, they began to demand even more political power.

Citizenship One of the major legacies of ancient Greece is the idea of citizenship, which the Greeks invented. In today's world, a **citizen** is a person who is loyal to a government and who is entitled to protection by that government. To the Greeks, a citizen was a person with the right to take part in ruling the city-state. A citizen had to be born to parents who were free citizens. In much of ancient Greece, people of both upper and lower classes were citizens, but only upper-class citizens had power.

By demanding political power, the lower-class citizens were asking for a major change to their society. Such a change does not happen quickly. During the 500s B.C., two leaders in Athens made gradual reforms that gave people more power. Those leaders were Solon and Cleisthenes (KLIHS•thuh•NEEZ).

Solon and Cleisthenes In the 500s B.C., trouble stirred in Athens. Many poor farmers owed so much money that they were forced to work their land for someone else or to become slaves. The lower classes were growing angry with the rulers.

History Makers

Solon (c. 630 to 560 B.C.)

Solon was called one of the Seven Wise Men of Greece. Although he was the son of a noble family, he reduced the nobles' power. He is known for his political reforms and his poetry. Poetry was the way he communicated with the citizens.

About 600 B.C., Solon recited a poem to encourage the Athenians in a war. He persuaded them to resume the war and save the honor of Athens.

Solon's reforms did not make all Athenians happy. The nobles wished he had made fewer changes. Poor farmers wished that he had given them more land. Tired of having to justify his reforms, Solon left on a trip for ten years. He traveled to Egypt and Cyprus, among other places. He wrote poems about his journey.

About 594 B.C., the nobles elected Solon to lead Athens. He made reforms that helped prevent a revolt by the poor. First he freed people who had become slaves because of debts. He made a law that no citizen could be enslaved.

Solon also organized citizens into four classes based on wealth, not birth. Rich men had more power—yet this was still a fairer system than the old one that limited power to nobles. Solon allowed all citizens to serve in the assembly and help elect leaders. He also reformed the laws to make them less harsh.

Around 500 B.C., Cleisthenes increased the citizens' power even more. He took power away from the nobles. He organized citizens into groups based on place of residence, not wealth. Any citizen could now vote on laws.

Jury box and tokens Juries in Athens voted by putting tokens in this box. The token with the hollow center spoke meant "guilty," and the other meant "not guilty." ▼

Direct Democracy Athens moved toward an early form of democracy. **Democracy** is a government in which the citizens make political decisions. The Athenian style of democracy is called a direct democracy. In such a system, all the citizens meet to decide on the laws. (Indirect democracy, in which people elect representatives to make laws, is more common today. The United States is an example.)

PATTERNS in HISTORY Forms of Government

	Monarchy	Oligarchy	Direct Democracy
Who ruled	A king or queen ruled the government.	A small group of citizens ruled the government.	All citizens took part in the government (but not all people were citizens).
Basis for rule	Many kings or queens claimed that the gods gave them the right to rule. The monarch's son usually was the next ruler.	Aristocratic birth, wealth, or land ownership gave this group the right to rule.	Neither wealth nor social status affected the right to make decisions.
Type of rule	The king or queen often had supreme power over everyone else.	The ruling group ran the government for their own purposes.	Decisions were made by voting. The majority won.

Limited Democracy Athens had a limited democracy. It did not include all of the people who lived in the city-state. Only free adult males were citizens who could take part in the government. Women, slaves, and foreigners could not take part. Noncitizens were not allowed to become citizens.

REVIEW How did reformers change the government of Athens?

▲ **Ostracism** If Athenians thought someone was a danger to the city-state, they would ostracize, or send that person away for ten years. People voted to ostracize someone by scratching his or her name on a piece of pottery called an ostracon.

- The people of Greece lived in independent city-states.
- Greek city-states had various types of government: monarchy, oligarchy, and direct democracy.
- Over time, the male citizens of Athens gained the power to make political decisions.

Why It Matters Now . . .

Athens is often called the birthplace of democracy. Many people in today's world are seeking to replace other forms of government with democracy.

3 Lesson Review

Homework Helper
ClassZone.com

Terms & Names

1. Explain the importance of

polis	oligarchy	citizen
aristocracy	tyrant	democracy

Using Your Notes

Categorizing Use your completed chart to answer the following question:

2. In which form of government do the fewest people share power?

Types of Government		
Monarchy	Oligarchy	Democracy

Main Ideas

3. How did the geography of Greece lead to the rise of city-states?

4. What was the role of tyrants in the development of democracy in Greece?

5. What made democracy in Athens a limited democracy?

Critical Thinking

6. Understanding Causes What were the key factors leading to the rise of tyrants? Explain.

7. Drawing Conclusions Why was the invention of the idea of citizenship important to the development of democracy?

Activity

Making a Poster Find out how a person qualifies as a citizen in the United States. How can a noncitizen become a citizen? Make a poster comparing citizenship in Athens with citizenship in the United States.

Activity Extend Lesson 3

Make Vocabulary Cards

Goal: To learn English words that are based on Greek roots

Materials & Supplies

- a dictionary that gives word origins
- pens or pencils
- notecards
- a map of the United States

Prepare

1. The Greek word *polis*, which you learned in this chapter, is the root of many English words, including *politics*.
2. Other terms from the chapter use Greek words as prefixes and roots. For example, democracy comes from word *demos*, which means "the people," and *kratos*, which means "power."

Do the Activity

1. Working with a partner, find other words in the dictionary that are based on the Greek word *polis*. Look up words beginning with the letters *pol* and check their origin. Word origins are given at the beginning or the end of the definition.
2. Look up the following types of government in the dictionary: monarchy, aristocracy, oligarchy. Note the meaning of each term and the Greek roots of the words.
3. Make a vocabulary card for each word that comes from *polis* and for each of the government terms. Write the English word on the front of the card. On the back, write the word's meaning and origin.

Follow-Up

Take turns quizzing each other until you know the meaning of the words.

Extension

Locating Cities on a Map Use a map of the United States to find cities that end in *polis*, such as Indianapolis. Make a list.

Lesson 4

MAIN IDEAS

1. **Government** Sparta built a state in which every part of life was organized around the need to have a strong army.
2. **Government** Athenian citizens were expected to participate actively in government.
3. **Government** A Persian invasion endangered Greece, so some city-states united to fight their enemy.

▲ **Athena** The goddess Athena was associated closely with the city of Athens. She was wise and was supposed to give good advice in war. Because she is a warrior goddess, she is often shown wearing a helmet.

TAKING NOTES

Reading Skill: Comparing and Contrasting

Use a Venn diagram to take notes comparing and contrasting life in Sparta and Athens. Think about where you would rather have lived. Underline the details in your notes that influenced your decision.

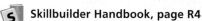

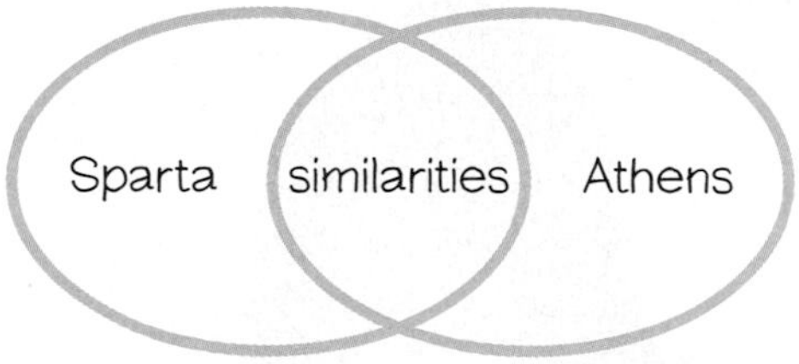

Skillbuilder Handbook, page R4

Words to Know

Understanding the following words will help you read this lesson:

supervisor a person who is in charge of a department (page 379)

*In Sparta, five **supervisors** ran the government.*

propose to suggest; or put forward for consideration (page 379)

*The group **proposed** a new law that it hoped would be approved by the Assembly.*

industry an enterprise in which goods are manufactured from raw materials (page 381)

*Some Greek slaves worked in the shield-making **industry**.*

clever smart; showing quick thinking and resourcefulness (page 382)

*A small army with a **clever** strategy can sometimes defeat a much larger force.*

Sparta and Athens

TERMS & NAMES
Athens
Sparta
helot
barracks
Marathon

Build on What You Know You've read about **Athens**. Its main rival was **Sparta**, a large city-state in the Peloponnesus. Life there was quite different from life in Athens.

Sparta's Military State

1 **ESSENTIAL QUESTION** What did Spartan society emphasize the most?

About 715 B.C., Sparta conquered a neighboring area to gain land. This conquest changed Sparta. The Spartans forced the defeated people to become slaves called **helots** (HEHL•uhtz). They worked mostly on farms and had to give the Spartans half their crops. The helots rebelled many times. Although they greatly outnumbered the Spartans and fought hard, the Spartans put down the revolts. Fear of these revolts led Sparta to become a state that focused everything on building a strong army.

Government and Society Sparta had a government that was part monarchy, part oligarchy, and part democracy. Two kings ruled Sparta, and five elected supervisors ran the government. The Council of Elders, made up of 30 older citizens, proposed laws. All Spartan citizens were part of the Assembly. It elected officials and voted on the laws proposed by the Council.

Three social groups made up Spartan society. Citizens lived in the city and spent all their time training to be soldiers. Free noncitizens lived in nearby villages. They had no political rights. The lowest group was the helots. Their labor fed Sparta, making it possible for free Spartans to be full-time soldiers.

Spartan Warrior As this statue shows, Spartans valued military strength. Probably only an officer of a high rank could wear the crested helmet shown here. ▶

Education The goal of Spartan society was to have a strong army. At age seven, boys moved into military houses called **barracks**. Their education stressed discipline, duty, strength, and military skill. (See Primary Source below.) The boys learned to read just enough to get by.

All male citizens entered the army at the age of 20 and served until they were 60. Even after men got married, they had to eat with their fellow soldiers.

Visual Vocabulary

Barracks

Women Spartan society expected its women to be tough, emotionally and physically. Mothers told their sons, "Bring back this shield yourself or be brought back on it." (Spartans carried dead warriors home on their shields.) Education for girls in Sparta focused on making them strong. They had athletic training and learned to defend themselves.

The emphasis on the army made family life less important in Sparta than in other Greek city-states. In Sparta husbands and wives spent much time apart. Women had more freedom. They were allowed to own property. A wife was expected to watch over her husband's property if he was at war.

REVIEW How did Spartan education support the military?

Primary Source

Background: Plutarch (PLOO•TAHRK) was a Greek historian who lived between A.D. 46 and about 120. One of the people he wrote about was Lycurgus (ly•KUR•guhs), the leader of Sparta who created its strong military institutions. This passage describes how boys were trained in Sparta by being placed in companies, or military units.

◀ Lycurgus discusses the meaning of education in this 17th-century painting.

from *Parallel Lives*

By Plutarch

(based on the translation by Aubrey Stewart and George Long)

As soon as the boys were seven years old Lycurgus took them from their parents and enrolled them in companies. Here they lived and ate in common and shared their play and work. One of the noblest and bravest men of the state was appointed superintendent of the boys, and they themselves in each company chose the wisest and bravest as captain. They looked to him for orders, obeyed his commands, and endured his punishments, so that even in childhood they learned to obey.

DOCUMENT–BASED QUESTION
What did Spartan boys learn that made them good soldiers?

Athens' Democratic Way of Life

2 ESSENTIAL QUESTION What was the government of Athens like?

As you learned in Lesson 3, over time Athens developed a direct democracy. All of its citizens met to vote on laws. Only free men were citizens.

Government and Society Athens had two governing bodies. The Council of Four Hundred took care of day-to-day problems. The Assembly voted on policies proposed by the council.

Citizens had to serve in the army whenever they were needed. They also had to serve on juries. Juries usually had several hundred people to hear charges against a person. In Athens, all citizens were equal in the courts. There were no professional lawyers or judges. Citizens argued their case directly before the jury.

▲ **Knucklebones Players** These two women are playing knucklebones, an ancient game similar to the child's game of jacks. It is called that because it was originally played with the knucklebones (anklebones) of a sheep.

Solon's reforms had organized citizens into four classes based on income. Foreigners, women, children, and slaves were not citizens.

Slaves made up one-third of the population. They worked in homes, agriculture, industry, and mines. Some slaves worked alongside their masters. Some even earned wages and were able to buy their freedom.

Education Boys of wealthy families started school at age six or seven. Education prepared them to be good citizens. They studied logic and public speaking to help them debate as adults in the Assembly. They also studied reading, writing, poetry, arithmetic, and music. Athletic activities helped them develop strong bodies.

Women Athenians expected women to be good wives and mothers. These roles were respected because they helped to keep the family and society strong. In addition, some women fulfilled important religious roles as priestesses in temples. In spite of their importance to society, Athenian women had much less freedom than Spartan women.

Women could inherit property only if their fathers had no sons. Girls did not attend school. They learned household duties from their mothers. A few learned to read and write.

REVIEW What were the duties of an Athenian citizen?

The Persian Wars

3 ESSENTIAL QUESTION What happened when Persia invaded Greece?

As you know, Persia conquered much of Southwest Asia. A king and a highly organized government ruled the resulting empire.

In the 500s B.C., Persia conquered Anatolia, a region with many Greek colonies. In 499 B.C., some Greeks in Anatolia revolted against Persian rule. Athens, which had a strong navy, sent ships and soldiers to help them. The revolt failed, but Persia decided to punish Athens for interfering. In 490 B.C., the Persians arrived near Athens on the plain of **Marathon**. The Athenians sent a runner to ask Sparta for help, but the Spartans came too late.

The Athenians were greatly outnumbered, so they had to use a clever plan. First they drew the Persians toward the center of the Greek line. Then the Greeks surrounded them and attacked. In close fighting, Greek spears were more effective than Persian arrows. The Persians lost 6,400 men. The Greeks lost only 192.

Legend says that a soldier ran from Marathon about 25 miles to Athens to tell of the victory. When he reached Athens, he collapsed and died. Modern marathons are based on his long run.

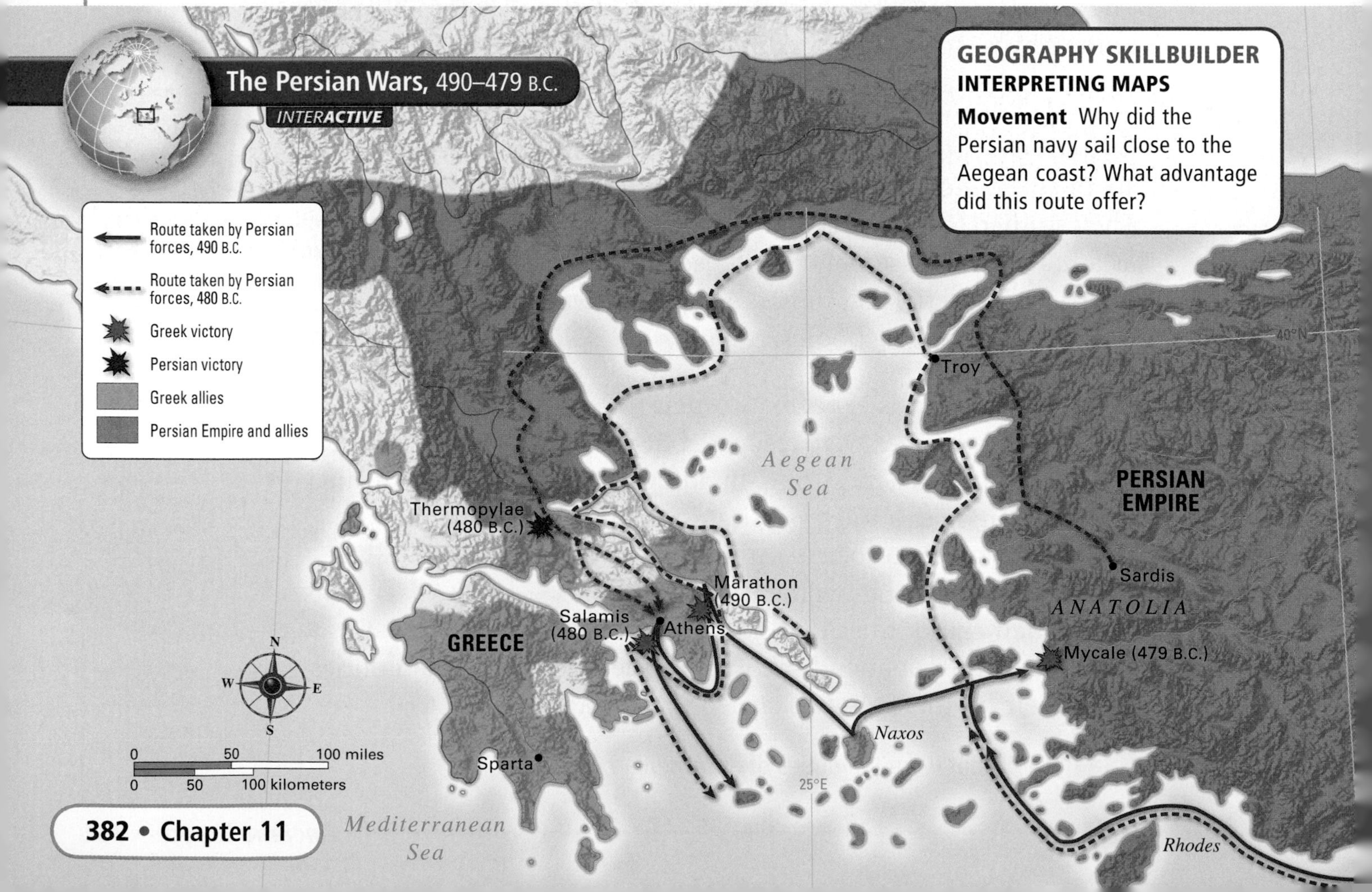

GEOGRAPHY SKILLBUILDER
INTERPRETING MAPS
Movement Why did the Persian navy sail close to the Aegean coast? What advantage did this route offer?

Greek Victory In 480 B.C., Persia again invaded Greece. In spite of past quarrels with each other, several Greek city-states united against Persia. An army of 300 Spartans guarded the narrow pass at Thermopylae (thuhr•MAHP•uh•lee) to stop a Persian army from reaching Athens. The Spartans held the pass for two days before the Persians killed them all. Their sacrifice gave the Athenians time to prepare for battle.

The Athenians left their city to fight a naval battle against the Persians. The battle took place in a narrow body of water where the large Persian fleet could barely move. Smaller, more mobile Greek ships sunk about 300 Persian ships, and the war ended. You will read more about Greece after the war in Chapter 12.

REVIEW How did the Persian Wars bring the Greek city-states together?

Lesson Summary

- Sparta organized its state around its strong army.
- Athens valued democratic government and culture.
- Some Greek city-states united to defeat the Persians.

Why It Matters Now . . .

Defeating the Persians allowed Greek democracy and culture to continue. This culture greatly influenced later world civilization.

4 Lesson Review

Homework Helper
ClassZone.com

Terms & Names

1. Explain the importance of

Athens	helot	Marathon
Sparta	barracks	

Using Your Notes

Comparing and Contrasting Use your completed Venn diagram to answer the following question:

2. What were some ways that Athens and Sparta were alike?

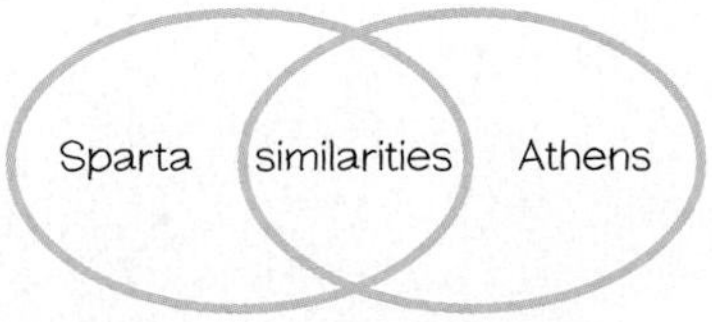

Main Ideas

3. What form of government existed in ancient Sparta?

4. How were direct democracy and education related in Athens?

5. What roles did Athens and Sparta play in defeating the Persians?

Critical Thinking

6. Understanding Causes How did the conquest of the helots make it necessary for Sparta to be a military state, and how did the conquest make such a state possible?

7. Contrasting How was the role of women different in Athens and Sparta?

Activity

Internet Activity Use the Internet to learn more about the Persian Wars. Then create one panel for a mural about the wars. Illustrate one battle or another event.

INTERNET KEYWORDS: *Battle of Marathon, Battle of Salamis, Thermopylae*

Daily Life

Extend Lesson 4

Research Links
ClassZone.com

Life in the Agora

Purpose: To learn about daily life in Athens

Imagine a place that is a shopping mall, city hall, sports arena, and place of worship all in one. The agora of an ancient Greek city was just such a place. An agora was an open space with buildings around it and roads leading into it. People went there to buy and sell goods, to worship at the nearby temples, and to take part in government. This illustration shows the agora of ancient Athens in about 500 B.C.

A Fish Seller Merchants set up stalls in the open space to sell goods. Because the Greeks lived near the sea, they ate much fish. Fresh fish was sold locally; it would spoil if it was transported very far. (Dried fish could be stored and traded to distant regions.)

B Cloth Seller Sheep could graze on land that was too poor to farm, so most Greeks wore clothes made from wool. They also wore some linen, made from flax bought in Egypt.

C Political Discussions Direct democracy required citizens to be very involved in government, so political discussions were popular in Athens. Because the weather was so mild, men often held such discussions outdoors.

D Shoemaker Craftspeople, such as this shoemaker, often set up shop in the stoa. A stoa was a building made of a roof held up by long rows of columns. Stoas were also used for political meetings and as places for teachers to meet with their students.

E Farmers Farmers sold their own vegetables, fruit, milk, and eggs at the market. First they had to transport the food to the city. Using an animal to carry the heavy load was the easiest method. Some poor farmers carried goods on their backs.

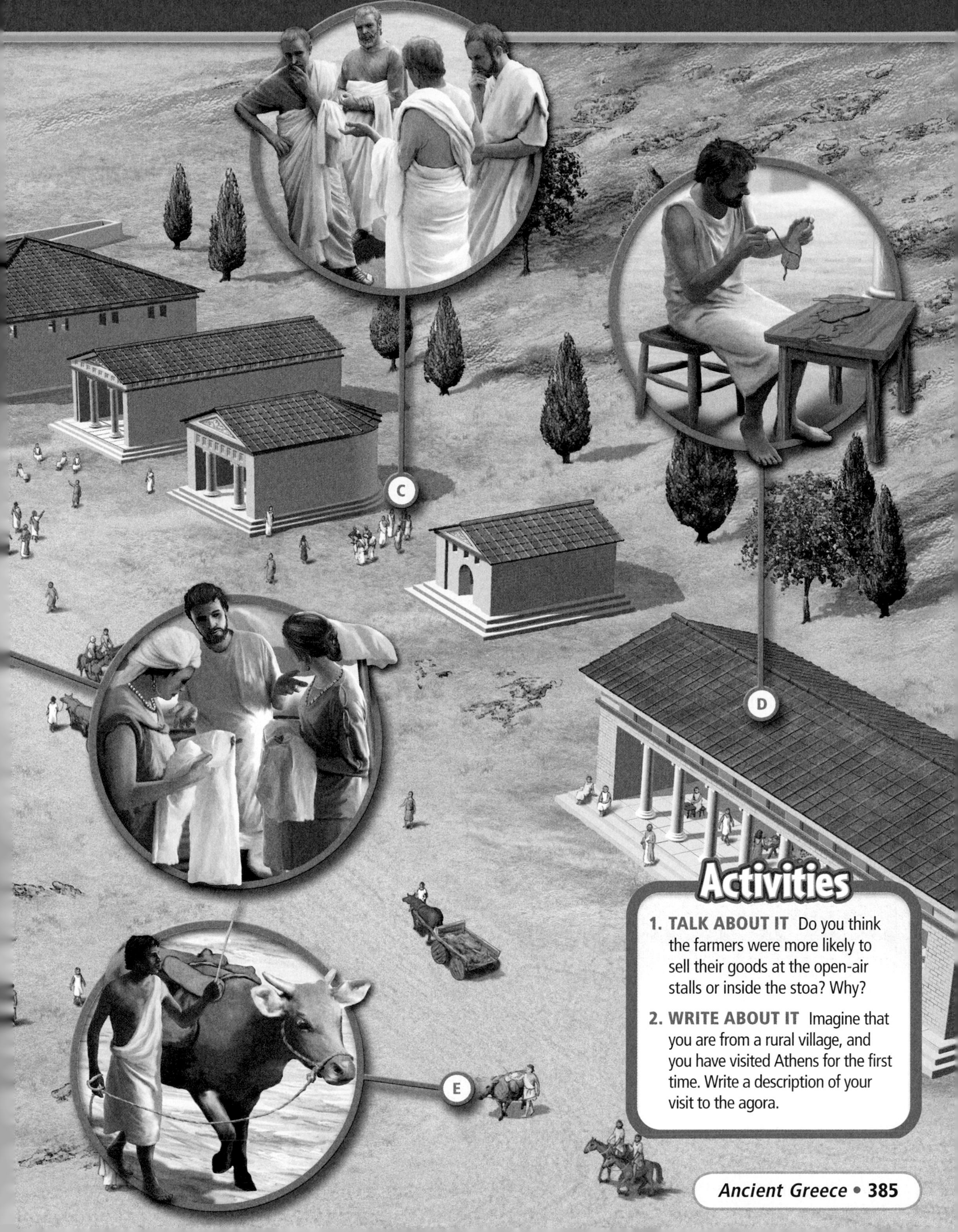

Activities

1. **TALK ABOUT IT** Do you think the farmers were more likely to sell their goods at the open-air stalls or inside the stoa? Why?
2. **WRITE ABOUT IT** Imagine that you are from a rural village, and you have visited Athens for the first time. Write a description of your visit to the agora.

Chapter 11 Review

VISUAL SUMMARY

Ancient Greece

Geography
- Greece did not have much good farmland.
- Most places in Greece were close to the sea. The Greeks used the seas as highways.

Economics
- The Greeks built their economy on farming and sea trade.
- They learned to use coins from other trading people.

Culture
- Early Greek literature included Aesop's fables and the epic poems the *Iliad* and the *Odyssey.*
- The Greeks learned the alphabet from the Phoenicians and adapted it to their language.

Government
- Different city-states had different forms of government, including monarchy, rule by aristocrats, and oligarchy.
- Athens developed limited, direct democracy.

TERMS & NAMES

Sort the words in the list below into three categories: geography, government, culture. Be prepared to explain your decisions.

1. **alphabet**
2. **aristocracy**
3. **democracy**
4. **fable**
5. **isthmus**
6. **myth**
7. **oligarchy**
8. **peninsula**
9. **polis**
10. **tyrant**

MAIN IDEAS

The Geography of Greece (pages 354–359)

11. How did the geography of Greece affect the location of cities?
12. What skills did the Greeks need to master to become successful traders?

Beliefs and Customs (pages 360–369)

13. In what ways did Homer use mythology?
14. How were epic poems and fables the same? How were they different?

The City-State and Democracy (pages 370–377)

15. How did government in Athens evolve into early forms of democracy?
16. How was Athenian democracy different from democracy in the world today?

Sparta and Athens (pages 378–385)

17. What roles did slaves play in Sparta and Athens?
18. How were Athens and Sparta different?

CRITICAL THINKING

Big Ideas: Government

19. ANALYZING POLITICAL ISSUES Why would the rugged geography make it difficult to unify Greece? Explain the potential problems.

20. EXPLAINING HISTORICAL PATTERNS Considering their cultures, why do you think democracy developed in Athens and not in Sparta?

21. UNDERSTANDING EFFECTS How did Solon's reforms change Athenian society?

ALTERNATIVE ASSESSMENT

1. **WRITING ACTIVITY** Review your notes about Sparta and Athens. Write an essay persuading your readers which city-state was better to live in and why.
2. **INTERDISCIPLINARY ACTIVITY—LITERATURE** Read several of Aesop's fables. Choose one besides *"The Hare and the Tortoise."* Make a poster illustrating the fable and its lesson.
3. **STARTING WITH A STORY** Review the letter you wrote about helping Athens. Write a report to the Spartan assembly. Describe the results of the Battle of Marathon, and recommend how Sparta and Athens should deal with Persia in the future.

Technology Activity

4. **DESIGNING A VIDEO GAME** Use the Internet or library to research the *Odyssey*. Work with a partner to design a video game about Odysseus' adventures as he journeyed home.
   - How did he escape from the Cyclops?
   - What were Scylla and Charybdis?
   - How did he escape from Calypso?

Research Links
ClassZone.com

Reading a Map Use the map and graph below to answer the questions.

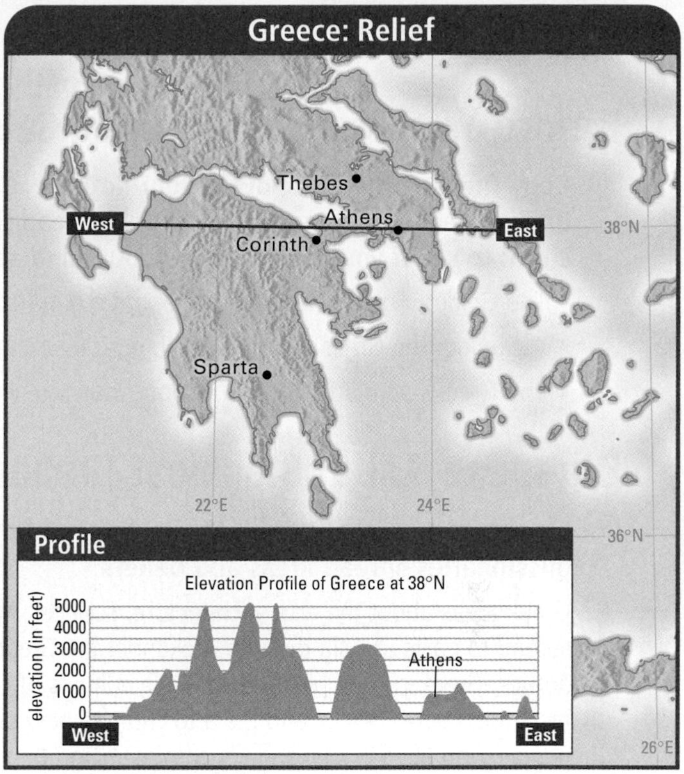

1. At what elevation is Athens located?

A. about 400 feet
B. about 650 feet
C. about 950 feet
D. about 1,200 feet

2. Which of the following general statements is supported by the elevation profile?

A. Greece is a country of many lakes.
B. Greece is a country of many plains.
C. Greece is a country of many harbors.
D. Greece is a country of many mountains.

Test Practice
ClassZone.com

Additional Test Practice, pp. S1–S33

Chapter 12 Classical Greece

Before You Read: Anticipation Guide

Copy the statements below in your notebook. Write *agree* or *disagree* next to each one. After you read the lesson, check to see if you have changed your mind about each.

- The Golden Age of Greece lasted about a hundred years.
- Alexander the Great's empire was bigger than the Persian empire.
- The Greeks studied philosophy more than science.

Big Ideas About Classical Greece

Geography Migration, trade, warfare, and the action of missionaries spread ideas and beliefs.

Greek ideas about the arts, architecture, sciences, and philosophy spread to parts of Asia through Alexander the Great and his armies. Greek culture blended with the cultures of conquered lands including Egypt, Persia, and India to create a new one. Millions of people who lived in Alexander's empire shared that new culture. The culture continued long after Alexander died.

Tholos Temple, Delphi

Integrated Technology

eEdition
- Interactive Maps
- Interactive Visuals
- Starting with a Story

INTERNET RESOURCES
Go to **ClassZone.com** for
- WebQuest
- Homework Helper
- Research Links
- Internet Activities
- Quizzes
- Maps
- Test Practice
- Current Events

GREECE

477 B.C. The Golden Age of Athens begins. (Parthenon) ▶

431 B.C. The Peloponnesian War begins.

500 B.C. **475 B.C.** **450 B.C.**

WORLD

500 B.C. Nok people of Africa make iron tools.

483 B.C. Siddhartha Gautama, the Buddha, dies.

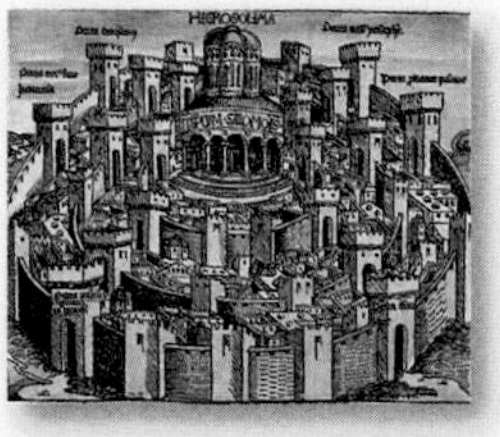

445 B.C. Jews rebuild the walls of Jerusalem. ◀ (illustration of Jerusalem)

The Greek City-States, 500 B.C.

INTERACTIVE

Lion Terrace, Delos

399 B.C.
Socrates is condemned to death.
(Socrates' bust) ▶

326 B.C.
The empire of Alexander the Great is at its peak.

400 B.C. | 375 B.C. | 350 B.C. | 325 B.C.

400 B.C.
Olmec civilization of Mexico begins to decline.
(Olmec man with infant) ▶

350 B.C.
African urban centers develop.

Starting with a Story

CHANGING TIMES

Background: Pericles (PEHR•ih•KLEEZ) was the leader in Athens from 460 to 429 B.C. One of his goals was to strengthen Athenian democracy. He proposed a plan that increased the number of paid political positions. When political positions were unpaid, only wealthy people could afford to serve. With the new plan even poor citizens could serve in the government.

This suggested change has caused a lot of people to talk about how times are changing. Some people say it is good, but others don't agree. You have been asked by Pericles to go to the marketplace and listen to what citizens are saying about his plan.

Bust of Pericles ▶

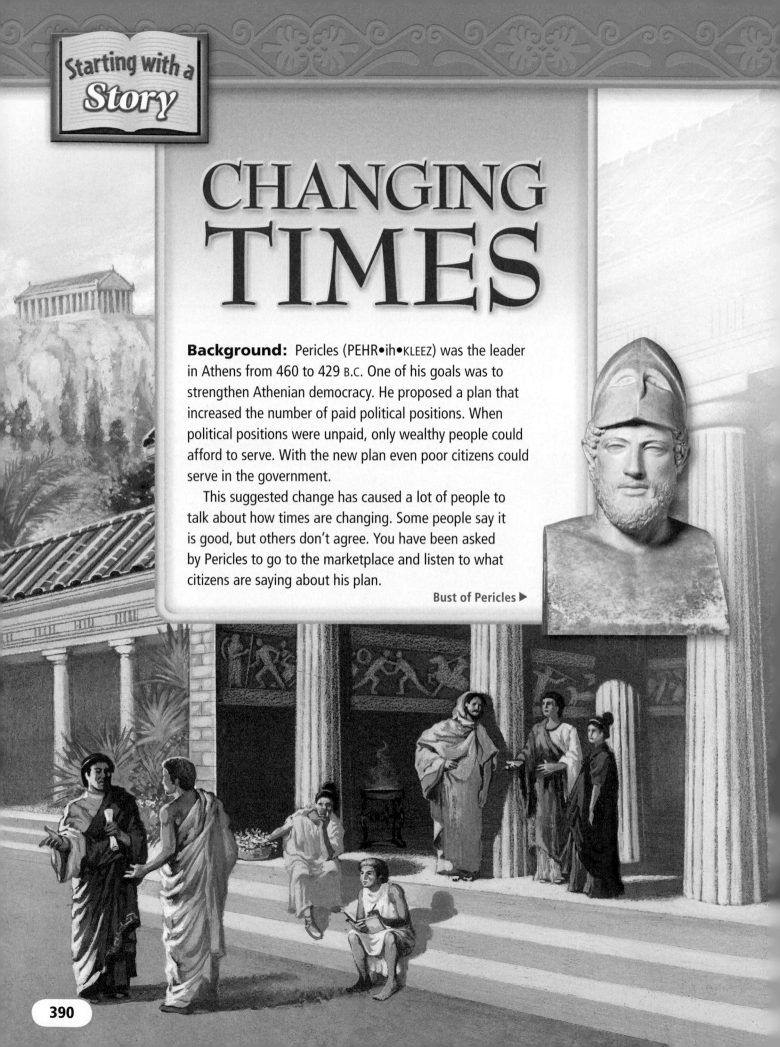

They were shouting. "Pericles wants more public officials to get paid," one of them hollered above the rest. "Poor citizens will be able to serve the government of Athens. I don't like that!"

The wealthy citizens were talking about the proposed policy change. Pericles was due to arrive at any moment. I was acting as his "eyes and ears" in the market place. Later, I would tell Pericles what I heard being said by the citizens of Athens.

"But I think Pericles is right," another man said. "Any citizen who wants to serve in the government should be able to do so. Pericles says being poor shouldn't prevent a man from serving our city."

"Yes," another man agreed. Several others nodded. "A poor man can serve Athens. A poor man is just as intelligent as a rich man. How can we ask the poor to obey our government if they cannot be public officials?"

"You're right. If a man is poor, it's not his fault!" piped up a fourth citizen. "Blame it on the gods!"

"Rich men are much better educated," a fifth man argued. "That's why only the rich should serve Athens."

Another man answered him. "But Pericles said that no one needs to be ashamed of poverty. The real shame is not trying to escape it."

Just then I heard footsteps. Pericles was coming! I needed to move away from the crowd. Later, he asked me if I had some advice for him based on what I heard. I knew what I would say and hoped he would agree with my advice.

What advice would you give Pericles?

Reading & Writing

1. **READING: Character and Plot** What character trait does Pericles show when supporting the rights of a poor citizen to serve in the government? What other character traits will he need to actually get the plan passed?
2. **WRITING: Persuasion** Think about what you heard. Think about the qualities needed to be a good public official. Then write a position paper outlining points that will help Pericles persuade people that his plan is the correct one.

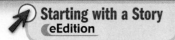

Lesson 1

MAIN IDEAS

1. **Government** Democracy expanded under the leadership of Pericles.
2. **Economics** Pericles expanded the wealth and power of Athens through the Delian League.
3. **Culture** Pericles launched a program to make Athens beautiful.

TAKING NOTES

Reading Skill: Finding Main Ideas

Identifying the main ideas and finding details about those ideas will help you understand the material in the lesson. In Lesson 1, look for three goals set by Pericles, and find details about them. Record the information in a web diagram.

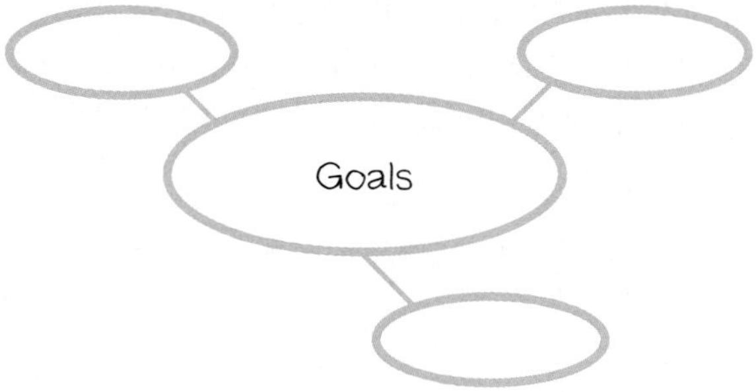

Skillbuilder Handbook, page R2

▲ **Porch of the Caryatids** The porch is part of the Erectheum, a temple that honors several gods and goddesses. The columns are sculptures of maidens (caryatids).

Words to Know

Understanding the following words will help you read this lesson:

ability a skill or talent (page 393)

*The **ability** that an individual possesses can be natural or the result of practice.*

league a group of people, organizations, or countries working together for a common goal (page 395)

*The city-states who joined the **league** promised to protect one another in the case of attack.*

glorify to bring honor, praise, and admiration to someone or something (page 396)

*The leader of Athens hired architects and artists to help **glorify** the city.*

ivory the substance that forms the tusks of animals such as elephants or walruses (page 396)

*Sculptors wanted **ivory** because it was an especially good material for carving.*

The Golden Age of Greece

TERMS & NAMES
- Pericles
- direct democracy
- Delian League
- Acropolis
- Parthenon

Build on What You Know Have you ever had a time when you were really successful in the things you were doing? A period of great achievement is sometimes called a golden age. Ancient civilizations, such as the Han Dynasty in China and the Gupta in India, had golden ages. Greece too had a golden age, during the time of Pericles.

Pericles Leads Athens

1 ESSENTIAL QUESTION What democratic changes did Pericles bring?

After the Persian Wars that you read about in Chapter 11, one of Athens' greatest leaders, **Pericles**, emerged. By 460 B.C., Pericles was the strongest leader in Athens. He remained the leader until his death 31 years later. He was so important that this time in Athens is often called the Age of Pericles.

Pericles had three goals for Athens. The first was to strengthen democracy. The second was to expand the empire. The third was to beautify Athens.

Pericles Strengthens Democracy

Remember that, before Pericles, leaders in Athens had begun to expand democracy. Pericles supported those reforms. He wanted, however, to change the balance of power between the rich and the poor.

About 430 B.C., Pericles gave his view of democracy in a speech honoring Athenian soldiers killed in war. "Everyone is equal before the law," he said. What counts in public service "is not membership of a particular class, but the actual ability which the man possesses."

Connect to Today

Ruins of Ancient Athens Parts of ancient Athens sit above the modern city. ▼

Paid Public Officials To spread power more evenly, Pericles changed the rule for holding public office. Most public officials were unpaid before he came to power. This meant that only wealthy people could afford to serve in government in Athens. Pericles increased the number of public officials who were paid. Now even poor citizens could hold a public office if elected or chosen randomly. However, to be a citizen an individual had to be a free male, over 18, and the son of Athenian-born parents.

Direct Democracy The form of democracy practiced in Athens was not the kind practiced in the United States today. The form used in Athens was called **direct democracy**. In a direct democracy all citizens participate in running the government. For example, all citizens in Athens could propose and vote directly on laws. By comparison, the United States has representative democracy, or a republic. U.S. citizens—male and female—elect representatives to take care of government business. These representatives propose and vote on laws. Study the chart on page 395 to find other differences.

REVIEW How is direct democracy different from representative democracy?

History Makers

Pericles (495–429 B.C.)

Pericles' speaking skills set him apart from other Athenians. He was so skilled that most regarded him as the best speaker of the time. Some people said that when he spoke, his words were like thunder and lightning.

Once, Pericles and another Athenian were involved in a wrestling match. Pericles lost. But his powers of speech were so great that he actually convinced the spectators that he won the match, even though they saw him lose!

His ability to speak so well made it possible for him to persuade Athenian citizens to back his reforms. These reforms brought about major changes in Athenian life. Unfortunately, toward the end of his life, Pericles was involved in several political scandals. As a result, he briefly stepped down from his position of leadership but later was reinstated. He is still thought of as one of the greatest leaders of Greece.

Comparisons Across Cultures

Athenian and U.S. Democracy

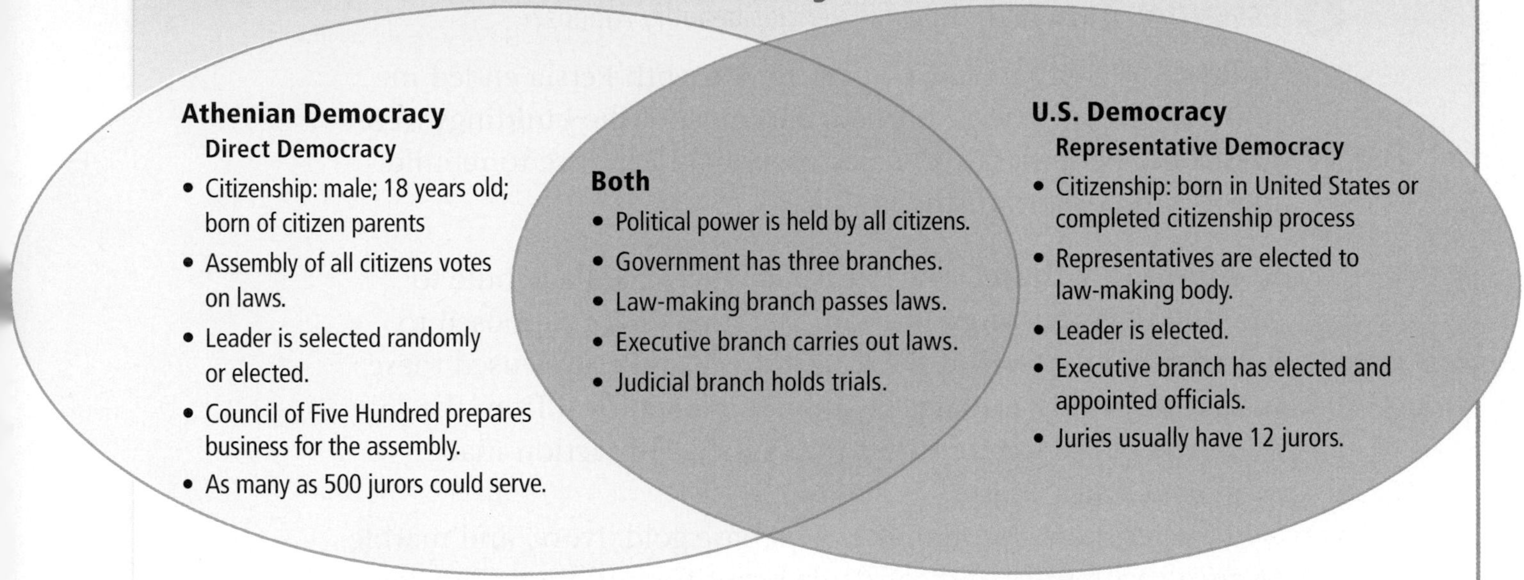

Athenian Democracy
Direct Democracy
• Citizenship: male; 18 years old; born of citizen parents
• Assembly of all citizens votes on laws.
• Leader is selected randomly or elected.
• Council of Five Hundred prepares business for the assembly.
• As many as 500 jurors could serve.
Both
• Political power is held by all citizens.
• Government has three branches.
• Law-making branch passes laws.
• Executive branch carries out laws.
• Judicial branch holds trials.
U.S. Democracy
Representative Democracy
• Citizenship: born in United States or completed citizenship process
• Representatives are elected to law-making body.
• Leader is elected.
• Executive branch has elected and appointed officials.
• Juries usually have 12 jurors.

Expanding the Empire

2 ESSENTIAL QUESTION How did Athens become more powerful?

Greek wealth depended on overseas trade. Athens was determined to protect its overseas trade and its homeland. At the end of the Persian War, the Greek city-states formed a league for mutual protection. It was called the **Delian League**.

Delian League Athens helped to organize this league. It was called the Delian League because its headquarters and treasury were located at first on the island of Delos. Pericles used money from the league's treasury to build a strong navy. The naval fleet was made up of at least 300 warships.

Athens Dominates the Delian League The fleet of Athens was the strongest in the Mediterranean region. Because Athens now had a superior navy, it took over leadership of the Delian League. In 454 B.C., the Delian League's treasury was moved to Athens. The transfer of the Delian League's treasury helped to strengthen Athens' power. Athens started treating the other members of the league as if they were conquered people, not allies. Eventually, Athens dominated all of the city-states to such an extent that they became part of an Athenian empire.

REVIEW How did the power of Athens expand?

Beautifying Athens

3 ESSENTIAL QUESTION How did Pericles beautify Athens?

Athens was a city in ruins when the war with Persia ended in 480 B.C. Parts of it were burned, and most of the buildings were destroyed. Pericles saw this destruction as a chance to rebuild, glorify, and beautify Athens.

Rebuilding Athens The Greek city-states paid a tribute to the Delian League organization. The funds were supposed to help build the power of the league. Instead, Pericles used these funds to beautify Athens. He did not ask approval from the members of the league to use the money. This action made other city-states angry.

Pericles spent the money to purchase gold, ivory, and marble to create sculptures and construct beautiful buildings. Pericles also used the money to pay artists, architects, and sculptors for these projects.

The Acropolis One of the areas rebuilt was the **Acropolis** (uh•KRAHP•uh•lihs), or the "high city" part of Athens. An acropolis is an area in a Greek city where important temples, monuments, and buildings are located. The Persians had destroyed the temples and smashed the statues in Athens during the war.

One of the buildings constructed was the **Parthenon** (PAHR•thuh•NAHN). Its purpose was to house a statue of Athena, a goddess. Athenians thought of her as a warrior who protected Athens. Athena was also the goddess of wisdom, arts, and handicrafts.

Acropolis The Parthenon, seen at right, is a temple dedicated to Athena. ▶

The Parthenon is considered the most magnificent building on the Acropolis. It is a masterpiece of architectural design, especially known for its graceful proportions and sense of harmony and order. Another temple on the Acropolis was one dedicated to Athena Nike, the goddess of victory. The most sacred site on the hill is the Erechtheum (ehr•ihic•THEE•uhm). It is considered the most beautiful example of Greek architecture. You can see its porch at the beginning of this lesson. Legend says it marks the site where the god Poseidon and the goddess Athena had a contest to see who would be the patron god of the city. Athena won.

REVIEW How did Pericles finance his program to make Athens beautiful?

Lesson Summary

- Pericles strengthened democracy in Athens by paying public officials.
- Pericles expanded the empire by building a strong naval fleet.
- Pericles rebuilt and beautified Athens.

Why It Matters Now . . .

Athenian democracy, art, and architecture set standards that remain influential in the world today.

1 Lesson Review

Homework Helper
ClassZone.com

Terms & Names

1. Explain the importance of

Pericles	Delian League	Parthenon
direct democracy	Acropolis	

Using Your Notes

Finding Main Ideas Use your completed graphic to answer the following question:

2. How did Pericles advance democracy?

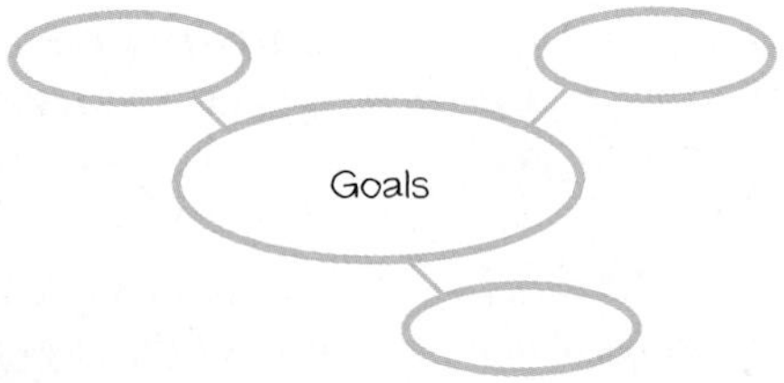

Main Ideas

3. What trait did Pericles believe was important to qualify for public service?

4. How did gaining control of the Delian League increase Athens' power?

5. Why was it important to rebuild and beautify the Acropolis in Athens?

Critical Thinking

6. Comparing and Contrasting How does the way Athenian citizens voted on laws compare with how U.S. citizens vote?

7. Determining Historical Context How was the Athenian view of a citizen different from the U.S. view of a citizen?

Activity

Making a Map Do some research on what buildings besides the Parthenon and the Erectheum were located on the Acropolis. Then draw a map showing their locations.

Lesson 2

MAIN IDEAS

1. **Government** Athens and Sparta and their allies fought a war over Athens' growing power.
2. **Government** Athens lost the Peloponnesian War.
3. **Government** More than 25 years of war weakened all of the Greek city-states.

TAKING NOTES

Reading Skill: Comparing and Contrasting

Comparing and contrasting the war strategies of Athens and Sparta will help you understand the outcome of the war. In Lesson 2, look for the differences between the war strategies of the two city-states. Record the differences on a chart like the one below.

War Strategy	
Athens	Sparta

Skillbuilder Handbook, page R4

▲ **Spartan Soldier** Sparta had the most powerful army of all the Greek city-states.

Words to Know

Understanding the following words will help you read this lesson:

ally a country that has joined with another for a special purpose (page 399)
*Sparta was joined by **allies**, who helped it fight the war.*

prestige importance in a group (page 399)
*Having **prestige** in the Delian League was important to Athens.*

strategy a plan for a series of actions designed to reach a specific goal (page 400)
*Each city-state based its **strategy** on its particular military strengths.*

countryside a rural or agricultural region, as opposed to an urban area (page 401)
*The **countryside** beyond the walls of the city-state was easy to attack.*

Peloponnesian War

TERMS & NAMES
Peloponnesian War
plague
truce

Build on What You Know In Chapter 11, you learned that important differences existed between Athens and Sparta. Tensions had been building between Athens and Sparta for years. Sparta did not like Athens growing more powerful.

The Outbreak of War

1 ESSENTIAL QUESTION What led Athens and Sparta to fight a war?

There were many differences between the city-states of Athens and Sparta. For example, Athens had a democratic form of government. Sparta had a culture that glorified military ideals. Both wanted to be the most powerful city-state in the region. This competition led to clashes between the two city-states and their allies.

Causes of the War There were three main reasons war broke out. First, some city-states feared Athens because of its grab for power and prestige. Second, under the leadership of Pericles, Athens grew from a city-state to a naval empire. Third, some Athenian settlers began to move into the lands of other city-states.

Trireme A trireme was a ship propelled by three tiers of oarsmen. Athens' fleet of triremes was the largest and best in the Mediterranean. ▼

Athens Disliked The other city-states also resented how Athens spent money from the Delian League, intended for the mutual protection of all the city-states. Athens used some of the money to beautify its city. Because of this practice several city-states tried to break free of Athenian power. Pericles' policy was to punish any city-state that resisted Athens.

Sparta headed a league of city-states to stand up to the power of the Delian League. It is called the Peloponnesian League because many of the city-states were located on the Peloponnesus. Finally, in 431 B.C., Sparta declared war on Athens. This conflict was called the **Peloponnesian War**.

Primary Source Handbook
See the excerpt from *History of the Peloponnesian War*, page R56.

REVIEW What were the causes of the war between Athens and Sparta?

The War Rages

2 ESSENTIAL QUESTION What happened during the Peloponnesian War?

Each side in the war had advantages and disadvantages. Sparta had the better land-based military force, and its location could not be attacked by sea. Athens had the better navy and could strike Sparta's allies by sea. These differences shaped the war strategy of each side.

Primary Source

Pericles' Funeral Oration

Background: Pericles spoke to honor Athenians killed in action during the first year of the Peloponnesian War, which began in 431 B.C. Parts of his speech paid tribute to democracy in Athens as well.

from ***The History of the Peloponnesian War***

By Thucydides (Translated by Rex Warner)

It is true that we are called a democracy, for the administration is in the hands of the many and not of the few. But while the law secures equal justice to all alike in their private disputes, the claim of excellence is also recognized; and when a citizen is in any way distinguished, he is preferred to the public service, not as a matter of privilege, but as the reward of merit. Neither is poverty a bar, but a man may benefit his country whatever be the obscurity [insignificance] of his condition.

DOCUMENT–BASED QUESTION
Why do you think Pericles praises Athenian life in a tribute to the war dead?

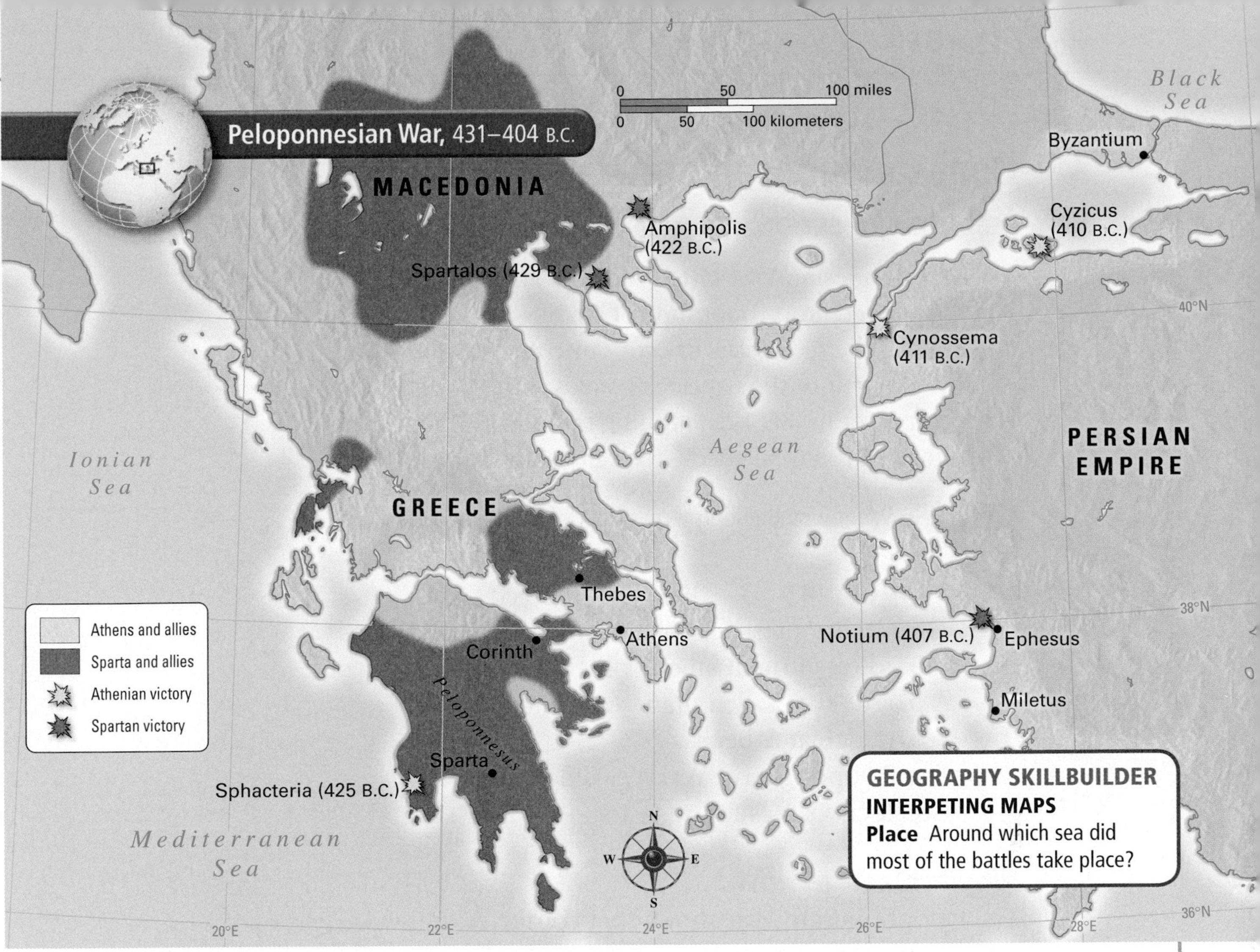

GEOGRAPHY SKILLBUILDER
INTERPETING MAPS
Place Around which sea did most of the battles take place?

Strategies of War Sparta's strategy was to cut off the Athenian food supply by destroying crops. The Spartans did this by taking control of the countryside around Athens.

Athens' strategy was to avoid battles on land and to rely on sea power. Pericles persuaded the Athenians to allow the Spartans to destroy the countryside. He brought people from the areas surrounding Athens inside the city walls. The people would be safe there and Athens would be supplied with food by sea.

Disaster Strikes Athens Because of Pericles' plan to bring people into Athens, the city became badly overcrowded. In the second year of the war, an outbreak of a **plague** took many lives in Athens. The plague was a disease that spread easily and usually caused death. Athens lost as many as one-third of its people and armed forces. Pericles, too, died from the plague.

In 421 B.C., Athens signed a **truce**, or an agreement to stop fighting. Athens finally surrendered to Sparta in 404 B.C.

REVIEW What caused Pericles' strategy to fail?

Consequences of the War

3 ESSENTIAL QUESTION What was the result of the Peloponnesian War?

The Peloponnesian War lasted for over 27 years. Cities and crops were destroyed, and thousands of Greeks died. All of the Greek city-states suffered losses of economic and military power.

To the north of the Greek city-states, King Philip II of Macedon came to power in 359 B.C. Planning to build an empire, he looked south toward the weakened Greek city-states.

REVIEW What was the long-term effect of the Peloponnesian War?

Lesson Summary

- The wealth, prestige, policies, and power of Athens caused resentment among other city-states.
- A plague that killed many Athenians helped Sparta defeat Athens.
- The Peloponnesian War weakened all of the Greek city-states for 50 years.

Why It Matters Now . . .

The Peloponnesian War shows that countries that wage war may lose power and prestige instead of gaining it.

2 Lesson Review

Homework Helper
ClassZone.com

Terms & Names

1. Explain the importance of

   Peloponnesian War   plague   truce

Using Your Notes

Comparing and Contrasting Use your completed graphic to answer the following question:

2. How was the war strategy of Athens different from that of Sparta?

War Strategy	
Athens	Sparta

Main Ideas

3. Why did smaller city-states resent Athenian control?
4. What was the Peloponnesian League and who led it?
5. Why did the Greek city-states lose power after the Peloponnesian War?

Critical Thinking

6. **Making Generalizations** What can happen to both sides in a war when the fighting goes on for many years?
7. **Making Inferences** What might have helped the Greek city-states to be more cooperative at the end of the Peloponnesian War?

Activity

Writing a Persuasive Composition Write a persuasive composition in which Pericles tries to convince people to leave their land and move into Athens to be safe from Spartan attacks.

Activity Extend Lesson 2

Create a Storyboard

Goal: To analyze the roles of Athens and Sparta in the Peloponnesian War and to create a storyboard portraying the events of that war

Materials & Supplies
- books on the Peloponnesian War
- poster board
- markers

Prepare

1. Research the roles Athens and Sparta played in the Peloponnesian War. Look for important events that occurred during this war.
2. Reread the information in Lesson 2 of this chapter.

Do the Activity

1. Make a list of six to eight events that occurred during the Peloponnesian War. Include events that were not battles.
2. Decide on a visual way to show the events you selected.
3. Divide the poster board into sections based on the number of events you selected.
4. Draw one event scene in each of the sections on the board.

Follow-Up

1. What event that was not a battle had a major influence on the course of the war?
2. Did Sparta actually win the war? Explain.

Extension

Making a Display Create a class storyboard by taking one section from each board made by the members of the class and taping them together. Then, using the storyboard display, explain the events of the war and their impact on Greece.

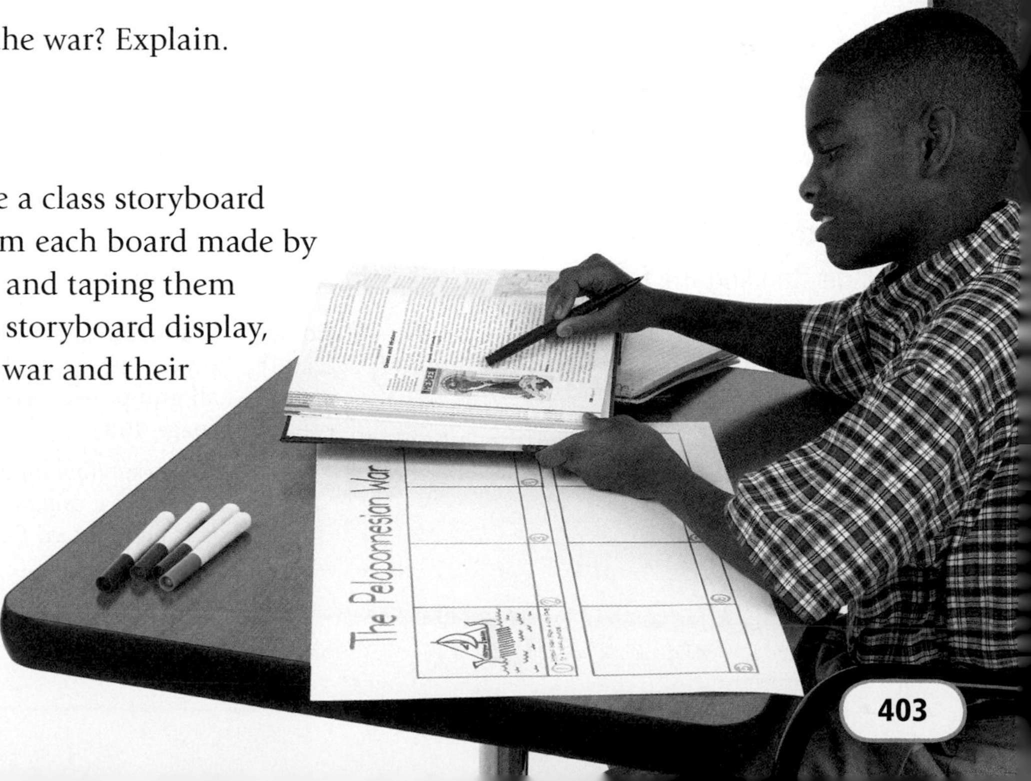

Lesson 3

MAIN IDEAS

1. **Government** Philip II of Macedonia conquered Greece.
2. **Government** Alexander built a huge empire that spread across parts of Europe and Asia.
3. **Geography** Alexander spread Greek culture and influence throughout his empire.

TAKING NOTES

Reading Skill: Understanding Cause and Effect

Following causes and effects can help you understand patterns in history. In this lesson, look for the effects of conditions listed in the chart. Record them on a chart of your own.

Causes	Effects
Weak governments	
New weapons of warfare	
Foreign conquests	

Skillbuilder Handbook, page R26

▲ **Philip II, King of Macedonia** Philip had dreams of defeating both the Greeks and the Persians.

Words to Know

Understanding the following words will help you read this lesson:

hostage a person taken by force to make sure the taker's demands are met (page 405)

*The city-state of Thebes held Philip **hostage**, but it did not treat him badly.*

tutor to give individual instruction to (page 406)

*The Greek philosopher Aristotle **tutored** the future king.*

common shared by two or more people or all group members (page 408)

*They were from different states, but a **common** language allowed them to communicate.*

style a way of dressing or behaving (page 408)

*By adopting the **styles** of conquered peoples, the invaders may have lessened the chance of rebellion.*

Alexander the Great

TERMS & NAMES
catapult
Alexander the Great
Hellenistic
Alexandria

Build on What You Know While the Greek city-states were busy fighting each other, a new power was rising in the north. The king there was strong. You have learned that a strong ruler can often unite a divided people.

The Kingdom of Macedonia

1 ESSENTIAL QUESTION Who conquered the Greek city-states?

The new power to the north of Greece was the country of Macedonia (MAS•ih•DOH•nee•uh). Its king, Philip II, was 23 years old, strong and fearless. He had plans to build an empire that included the lands of Greece and of Persia.

A Military Genius As a teenager, Philip had been a hostage in the Greek city of Thebes. There he observed its army and its military tactics. Philip learned of the advantages of a professional army, or an army of full-time soldiers, rather than one made up of citizen-soldiers.

Philip organized a well-trained professional army. He devised new battle formations and tactics. He experimented with the combined use of cavalry and infantry. He supplied his soldiers with new weapons, like the catapult. A **catapult** is a military machine that was used to hurl stones at enemy forces and city walls. His soldiers also used battering rams to smash through closed gates.

Alexander the Great The detail is from this mosaic. It shows Philip's son, Alexander, in battle. ▼

Philip Conquers Greece After conquering the lands around Macedonia, Philip focused on the Greek city-states. After the Peloponnesian War, the Greeks were too weak and disorganized to unite against Philip. In 338 B.C., Philip completed the conquest of the Greeks. Philip became the ruler of the Greek city-states. His dictatorial rule ended Greek democratic practices. He brought Greek troops into his army and prepared to attack Persia.

Alexander Takes Over However, in 336 B.C., Philip was assassinated at his daughter's wedding. His 20-year-old son Alexander took the throne. Many wondered if such a young man was ready to take control of Macedonia.

REVIEW Why were the Greek city-states open to an attack by Philip?

Alexander Tries to Conquer the World

2 ESSENTIAL QUESTION How did Alexander build an empire?

Alexander was well-prepared for the job of king. He had been tutored by the finest Greek scholars and trained in the Macedonian army. He continued his father's plan of creating an empire.

Alexander Defeats Persia Before Alexander could attack Persia, the Greek city-state of Thebes rebelled. Alexander destroyed the city. His cruel tactics made other Greek city-states too fearful to rebel. Next, Alexander moved his troops to Anatolia, where he attacked and defeated Persian forces. He used bold tactics, such as using thousands of troops to charge straight at the enemy. In the beginning, Alexander met sharp resistance from the Persians, but he was successful.

Next, instead of going directly to Persia, he turned south and entered Egypt, which the Persians controlled. The Egyptians welcomed Alexander because they hated the Persians. They even chose him to be their pharaoh. Alexander then moved his forces from Egypt across Mesopotamia toward Persia. Finally, he struck Persepolis, the royal capital of the Persians. By 331 B.C., Alexander controlled the Persian Empire.

Alexander Alexander rides his favorite horse Bucephalus. ▼

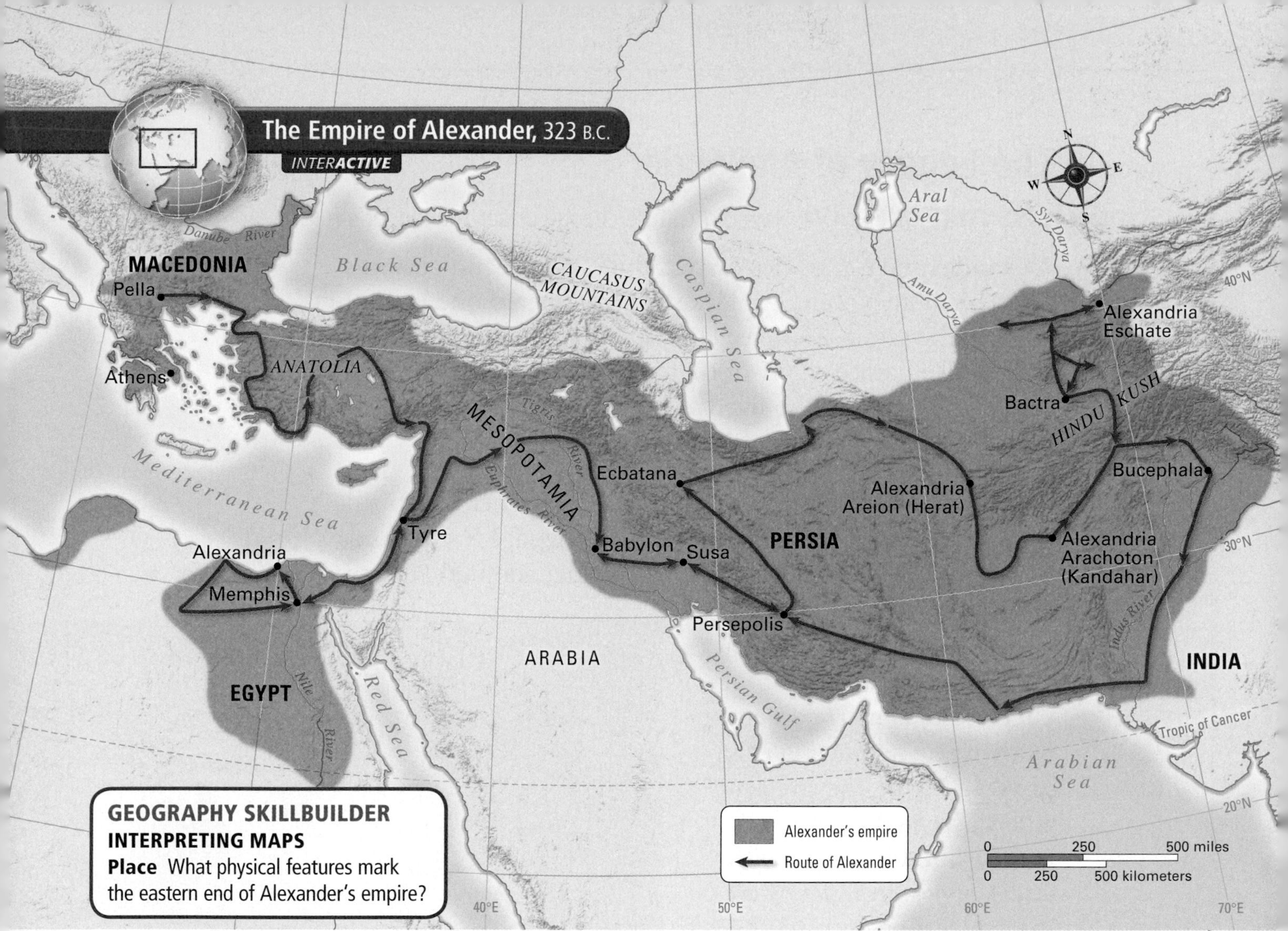

GEOGRAPHY SKILLBUILDER
INTERPRETING MAPS
Place What physical features mark the eastern end of Alexander's empire?

Alexander's Other Conquests In the next three years, Alexander pushed his armies eastward to conquer parts of Central Asia. In 326 B.C., they reached the Indus River Valley and India. Alexander urged his armies to continue eastward, but they refused to go any further. They had been fighting for 11 years and had marched thousands of miles from home. Alexander was forced to turn back.

In 323 B.C., Alexander and his armies returned to Babylon. While they paused there, Alexander fell ill with a fever and died within days. He was 32 years old. Although he did not live to an old age, he managed to create a great empire. Because of his achievements, he is remembered as **Alexander the Great**.

Alexander did not have time to unify his empire. After he died, military leaders fought among themselves to gain control of the empire. Not one of Alexander's generals was strong enough to take control of the entire empire. Eventually, three key generals divided the empire.

REVIEW How far eastward in Asia did Alexander build his empire?

The Legacy of Alexander

3 ESSENTIAL QUESTION How did culture change under Alexander's rule?

Alexander and his armies carried their culture and customs everywhere they went. As Alexander conquered one land after another, he set up colonies. He also built cities based on Greek culture. He named many of them Alexandria, after himself. The historian Plutarch, who lived a few centuries later, wrote that Alexander actually named 70 cities Alexandria.

A Blend of Cultures Alexander left Greeks behind to rule his lands. Greek became the common language in the lands he controlled. At the same time, Alexander adopted Persian clothing styles and Persian customs. He urged his armies to do the same. Some of the Greek settlers married Persian women and adopted Persian ways. In Egypt, the Greek rulers accepted Egyptian culture and blended it with Greek styles. In India, the same blending occurred.

This blend of Greek, Persian, Egyptian, and Indian styles and customs became known as **Hellenistic** culture. *Hellas* was the Greek name for Greece. This culture influenced the lands of the empire for hundreds of years. Learning was especially affected by the mingling of cultures. The combined knowledge of the Greeks, Egyptians, Arabs, and Indians made new discoveries possible in science and medicine. You will learn more about this in Lesson 4.

▲ Iranian Manuscript This manuscript depicts Hellenistic art. Aristotle, a Greek thinker, teaches astronomy to Persians. He is dressed in Persian-style clothing.

Alexandria The most famous of the Hellenistic cities was **Alexandria**, Egypt, which Alexander founded in 332 B.C. The city was an important center of learning until the second century A.D. A library there contained major collections of Greek, Persian, Egyptian, Hebrew, and other texts. Scholars from the Mediterranean area and from Asia came to Alexandria to study.

Also located in Alexandria was the Temple of the Muses. Muses are goddesses who rule the arts and sciences. Many examples of the arts and sciences were stored there. Today we call such a location a museum. Alexandria also had an enormous lighthouse whose light could be seen 35 miles away. It is considered one of the Seven Wonders of the World.

REVIEW How did Hellenistic culture develop?

▲ **Lighthouse at Alexandria**
The image above is an artist's idea of what the lighthouse may have looked like.

Lesson Summary

- Philip II, king of Macedonia, conquered Greece.
- Alexander the Great conquered the Persian Empire and parts of Central Asia.
- Hellenistic culture—a blend of Greek, Persian, Egyptian, and Indian cultures—was created.

Why It Matters Now . . .

The blended culture created by Alexander's empire forms a basis for culture in the countries that exist in those lands today.

3 Lesson Review

Homework Helper
ClassZone.com

Terms & Names

1. Explain the importance of

catapult
Alexander the Great
Hellenistic
Alexandria

Using Your Notes

Understanding Cause and Effect Use your completed graphic to answer the following question:

2. What were the effects of Alexander's conquest of a vast area?

Causes	Effects
Weak governments	
New weapons of warfare	
Foreign conquests	

Main Ideas

3. What happened to Greek democratic practices when Philip of Macedonia conquered Greece?

4. Why did Alexander's empire include Central Asia but not India?

5. How did Alexander spread Greek influence in new cities he founded?

Critical Thinking

6. Understanding Cause and Effect How did the Peloponnesian War lead to Alexander's success as a conqueror?

7. Making Inferences What made Hellenistic culture unique?

Activity

Calculating the Size of the Empire Go to the map on page 407. Use the scale to calculate the distance from east to west of Alexander's empire. How does it compare to the distance of the continental United States from east to west?

Lesson 4

MAIN IDEAS

1. **Culture** Greek art and architecture introduced new styles and concepts that set standards for generations of artists around the world.
2. **Culture** The Greek love of reason and logic influenced the development of Western knowledge.
3. **Science and Technology** Hellenistic science provided much of the scientific knowledge of the world until the modern age.

TAKING NOTES

Reading Skill: Finding Main Ideas

Looking for the main ideas as you read can help you understand the value of a period in history. As you read this lesson, look for the cultural and scientific contributions made by people of the Greek and Hellenistic cultures. Record these contributions on a list for each of the three headings in Lesson 4.

The Arts & Architecture	History & Philosophy	Science & Technology

Skillbuilder Handbook, page R2

▲ **Hellenistic Sculpture** This sculpture is titled *Winged Victory of Samothrace.* The sculpture features Nike, the goddess of victory.

Words to Know

Understanding the following words will help you read this lesson:

sponsor to support another person or thing (page 411)

*The city leader found the money to **sponsor** a play festival.*

troupe a group, especially of actors, singers, or dancers (page 411)

*The acting **troupe** spent months trying to memorize their lines from the play.*

proportion a pleasing balance of various parts of a whole (page 413)

*Greek buildings are famous for their graceful **proportions**.*

compound consisting of or using more than one (page 416)

*Archimedes used **compound** pulleys to move extremely heavy objects easily.*

The Legacy of Greece

TERMS & NAMES
drama
tragedy
comedy
ideal
philosophy

Build on What You Know You have learned about the great art, literature, and thought of Chinese and Indian civilizations. Greek civilization spread through the actions of Alexander the Great. Later, the Hellenistic culture spread to Mediterranean countries and into Asia.

The Arts and Architecture

1 ESSENTIAL QUESTION What new elements did Greek art and architecture introduce?

The Greeks invented drama as an art form. **Drama** was a written work designed for actors to perform. The Greeks built the first theaters in the western world.

Drama Greek drama was a part of every city's religious festival. Wealthy citizens spent money to sponsor the production of the dramas. Writers submitted plays to the city leader, who chose the ones he thought were the best. Then a play was assigned to a troupe of actors for production. When the plays were performed, contests were held to award prizes to the best writers.

Ancient Theater The theater at Epidaurus is built into a hillside. ▼

Actors The actors in plays were men, who also played the parts of women. The actors wore colorful costumes and masks to portray their characters. The stage sets were colorful as well. Dancing was important in Greek festivals and plays. Often the plays included a large chorus that danced, sang, and recited poetry. Drama had two forms: tragedy and comedy.

▲ **Dramatic Masks** The mask at the top represented comedy. The lower mask was used in tragedy.

Tragedy and Comedy The first form, **tragedy**, was a serious drama that presented the downfall of an important character, such as a king. Common themes for tragedy included love, war, and hate. One example is the hero in the play *Oedipus Rex* (EHD•uh•puhs rehks) by Sophocles (SAHF•uh•KLEEZ). In the play, a good, intelligent ruler named Oedipus kills a man. Later, Oedipus finds out that the man he killed was really his own father.

The second form of drama, called **comedy**, was a less serious dramatic work. Comedies often made fun of politics, important people, and ideas of the time. Comedies usually ended happily. Aristophanes (AR•ih•STAHF•uh•neez), who was born in the time of Pericles, was a great writer of comedy. One of his plays, *The Birds*, makes fun of those who would gain power. In the play, a king becomes a bird and founds a city in the sky. The city is called Cloudcuckooland. The hero blocks the gods from interfering with his rule and declares himself the king of the universe.

Sculpture Greek artists aimed to capture the **ideal** in their work. In other words, they tried to portray objects, including humans, in as perfect a form as possible. The artists tried to create a sense of order, beauty, and harmony in every work. Since the Greeks spent much of their time out-of-doors, works of art were located outside and were of a large scale. Many Greek sculptures portrayed the gods. The sculptures were placed in temples. These temples were built to honor the gods.

One of the most famous statues was created to honor the goddess Athena. In 447 B.C., Pericles appointed the sculptor Phidias (FIHD•ee•uhs) to direct the building of the Parthenon as a house for Athena. Phidias created a statue of Athena that was placed inside. He used gold and ivory to make the statue. It stood more than 30 feet tall when it was finished.

Architecture Greek architects designed temples, theaters, meeting places, and wealthy citizens' homes. Like the sculptors, the architects worked to create beautiful buildings with graceful proportions. Several distinct elements appeared in architectural works. One element was a column.

Often a series of columns, called a colonnade, was placed around the outside of a building. The space between the top of a column and the roof is called a *pediment*. Sculptures or paintings usually were placed in the pediments. The Parthenon displayed the temple form that was most often used (see page 396). It had a four-sided colonnade around a room built to house the statue of the goddess Athena. Sculptured designs that portrayed scenes in Athena's life were put in the pediments of the Parthenon.

Visual Vocabulary

pediment

REVIEW What was the goal of Greek artists?

Greek Columns

Ionic

This style has a thin column with a scroll-like design for its top.

Corinthian

The Greeks did not use this style much. The Romans copied it in the design of their temples.

Doric

This simple style has a plain top. It was used throughout Greece and its colonies.

History, Philosophy, and Democracy

2 ESSENTIAL QUESTION How did the Greek love of reason and logic influence the development of Western thought?

Perhaps the greatest legacy the Greeks left for the world was the idea of democracy and ways to run a government.

Democracy Becomes Reality The citizens of some Greek city-states practiced direct democracy. Unfortunately, citizenship was limited to a few people. But, for the first time, citizens had a voice in their government. The government was more open and more fair than any government had been. The Greeks' ideas have been copied in many places over time. Democracy continues to be a goal for many nations where it does not yet exist.

Herodotus and Thucydides The Greeks were among the first civilizations to write down their history. They did not just tell stories about their past. They examined the past to try to determine the facts and significance of a historical event.

Herodotus (hih•RAHD•uh•tuhs) has been called the Father of History. He was interested in learning and recording the stories about events. Herodotus was born in 484 B.C. and traveled widely as a young man. He wrote an account of the Persian Wars called *History.*

Another Greek historian, Thucydides (thoo•SIHD•ih•DEEZ), wrote a history of the Peloponnesian War. To make sure he was accurate, he used documents and eyewitness accounts to create his work. This approach set a standard for the writing of history.

The Search for Truth After the Peloponnesian War, Greek thinkers began to question their values. In this questioning they were like the Chinese thinkers before and during the Time of the Warring States. In the search to find answers, the Greeks developed **philosophy**, or the study of basic truths and ideas about the universe.

Greek Philosophers The three most famous Greek philosophers are Plato, Socrates, and Aristotle. ▼

Greek philosophers had two basic ideas about the universe. First, they assumed that the universe is put together in an orderly way. They believed that laws of nature control the universe. Second, the philosophers assumed that people could understand these laws. The philosophers used these two ideas when they sought the truth.

▲ **Death of Socrates** Socrates' supporters gather with him as he drinks poison.

Socrates Over a period of time, Greece had many famous philosophers. One of them was Socrates (SAHK•ruh•TEEZ), who lived from 470 to 399 B.C. He encouraged his young students to examine their beliefs by asking them a series of questions. This question-and-answer style of teaching is called the Socratic method.

Young people liked the teaching of Socrates. But his enemies accused him of causing young people to rebel. They brought him to trial. Socrates told the court that he was teaching young people to think about their values and actions. The jury did not agree with his actions and sentenced him to death. Socrates died by drinking a poison called hemlock.

Plato and Aristotle One of Socrates' best students was Plato. He was born about 427 B.C. Plato wrote about an ideal government in a book titled *The Republic*. He did not describe a democracy. Instead, he believed that a philosopher-king should rule. This king would be wise, calm, and reasonable—like a philosopher. Plato started an important school of higher learning called the Academy. It stayed open for about 900 years.

Aristotle

Aristotle (AR•ih•STAHT•uhl) was Plato's brightest student. Aristotle lived from 384 to 322 B.C. He invented a method of debating that followed rules of logic. Later, the rules of logic were applied to studies in science. Aristotle opened his own school in Athens called the Lyceum. In addition to his great philosophical work, Aristotle also spent three years tutoring Alexander the Great.

REVIEW How did Herodotus and Thucydides influence the writing of history today?

Science and Technology

3 ESSENTIAL QUESTION Why is Hellenistic science so important?

Hellenistic scholars preserved and expanded the scientific and mathematical knowledge of the thinkers of Greece, Egypt, and India.

Astronomy Some important discoveries about the planets and the stars came from scientists studying at Alexandria. For instance, Eratosthenes (EHR•uh•TAHS•thuh•NEEZ) found a way to estimate the circumference, or distance around Earth.

Another scientist at Alexandria, Aristarchus (AR•ih•STAHR•kus), studied the relationship of the sun, moon, and Earth to each other. He also estimated the size of the sun. The scientist Ptolemy (TAHL•uh•mee) studied the universe. Unfortunately for the world of science, Ptolemy placed Earth at the center of the universe. This incorrect view persisted for 1,400 years!

Mathematics and Physics Knowledge of very complicated mathematics is needed to do work in astronomy. Hellenistic mathematicians developed several kinds of math. The mathematician Euclid (YOO•klihd) created a geometry text complete with proofs for his work. The work of Euclid is still the basis for geometry.

Archimedes (AHR•kuh•MEE•deez) explained the law of the lever. As an inventor, he developed the compound pulley. He is also believed to have created a device to lift water. He intended his water-lifting device to be used for the irrigation of fields.

Greek Astronomy

Earth

Eratosthenes' estimate of the Earth's circumference was between 28,000 and 29,000 miles.

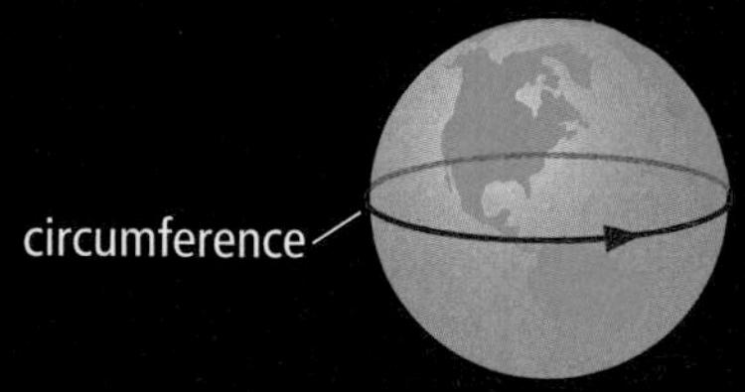

The actual circumference of Earth is 24,901.5 miles.

Sun

Aristarchus' estimate of the sun's size was 300 times the size of Earth.

The sun is actually 1.3 million times the size of Earth.

The Universe

Ptolemy's view of the universe placed Earth in the center.

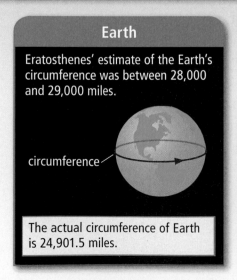

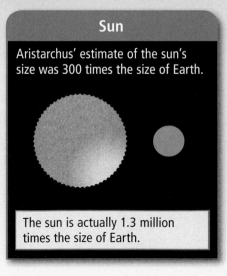

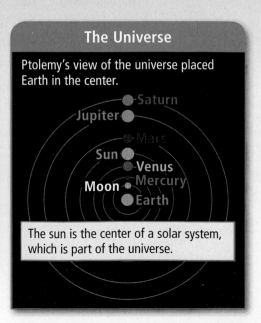

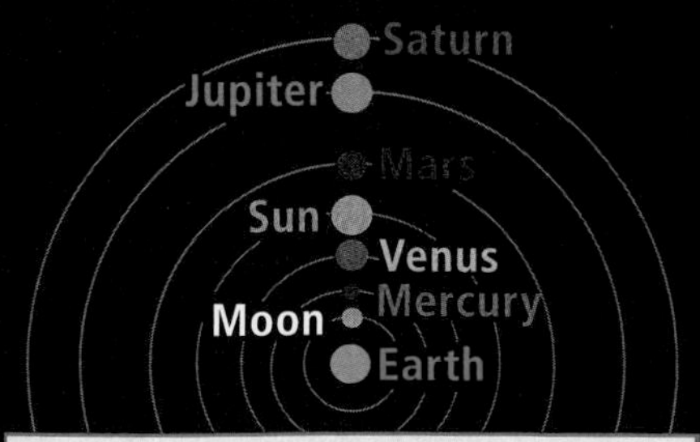

The sun is the center of a solar system, which is part of the universe.

The ideas of Archimedes were used to build pumps and eventually to create a steam engine.

The first noted female mathematician, Hypatia (hy•PAY•shuh), taught at Alexandria. Hypatia was also an astronomer. She wrote about the works of Ptolemy and about Euclid and geometry as well. She was also the leader of a philosophical movement based on the works of Plato.

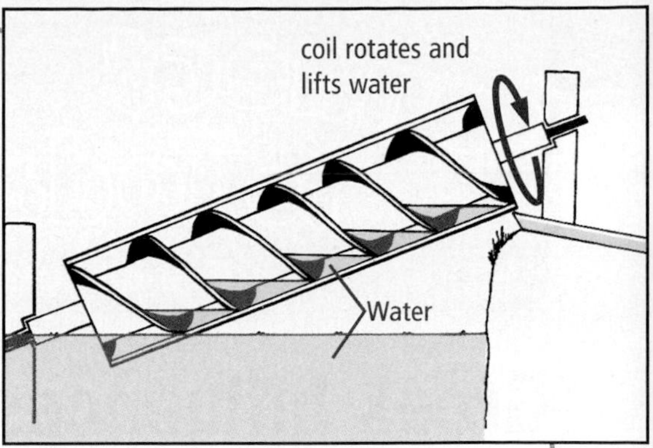

▲ **Archimedes' Water-Lifting Device** The device is a large coil open at both ends. It is placed inside a water tight tube. As the coil turns it brings up water from a lower level.

REVIEW In what areas of math and science did Greek thinkers work?

Lesson Summary

- Greek and Hellenistic writers, artists, and architects invented new and beautiful styles.
- Greek philosophy and history set standards of logic, reason, and record keeping.
- Hellenistic scientists made important discoveries about the world.

Why It Matters Now . . .

The Greek and Hellenistic cultures set enduring standards in art, philosophy, and science.

4 Lesson Review

Homework Helper
ClassZone.com

Terms & Names

1. Explain the importance of

drama, comedy, philosophy, tragedy, ideal

Using Your Notes

Finding Main Ideas Use your completed graphic to answer the following question:

2. What two ideas about the universe did Greek philosophers accept?

The Arts & Architecture	History & Philosophy	Science & Technology

Main Ideas

3. What qualities did Greek architects strive for in their work?

4. What teaching style is identified with Socrates, and what was it like?

5. What important discoveries about Earth, the planets, and the sun came from the scientists of Alexandria?

Critical Thinking

6. Determining Historical Context What was wrong with Ptolemy's theory?

7. Explaining Historical Patterns Why did both Chinese and Greek thinkers develop ideas about philosophy during times of war and disorder?

Activity

Internet Activity Use the Internet to research inventions of ancient Greeks. Design a Web page that illustrates and explains those inventions.
INTERNET KEYWORD: *Greek inventions*

Connect to Today

Extend Lesson 4

Research Links
ClassZone.com

Greek Influences Today

Purpose: To explore places where Greek influence can be found in today's world

The Greeks have influenced our ideas in many different areas. They strived to achieve the ideal in all areas of life. They paid especially close attention to those aspects of life that were a part of the polis. Today, we can clearly see the Greek influence in sports, architecture, and jury selection.

Olympics

▶ **Past** The Olympics were held in Olympia every four years. Only men could compete. Sports included boxing, wrestling, running, jumping, javelin and discus throwing, and events using horses. The image at the right shows an athlete arriving at the Olympics.

▼ **Present** The modern Olympics are held every four years. There are so many events that the games were split into the Summer Games and the Winter Games. Cathy Freeman (center), gold medal winner in the 400 meter dash in 2000, represented Australia.

Architecture

▼ **Past** Greek architects looked to nature to find the ideal form for building. They found a ratio in nature that they believed created perfect proportions. They used it in their buildings and especially with their columns. The result was a graceful structure like the Temple of Hephaestus.

▼ **Present** Many buildings copy the Greek style. The columns lend a sense of importance and authority to the building. The building below is the Lincoln Memorial in Washington, D.C.

Jury Selection

▶ **Past** Athens had a pool of about 6,000 qualified jurors. Trials required as many as 500 jurors. Jurors were paid. At right is a jury selection device from ancient Greece. Each juror had a metal plate with his name on it. The plates were randomly placed in the slots. Then rows of the plates were selected for a specific trial.

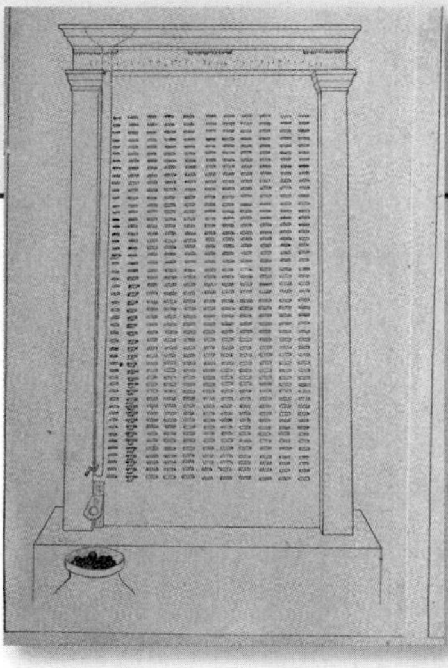

▼ **Present** The adult population of citizens of a district make up the jury pool. Jurors are randomly called to serve and are paid a small amount. Juries are made up of 12 persons, although there can be as few as 6. Potential jurors are sent a legal order to serve. The order must be obeyed.

Activities

1. **TALK ABOUT IT** Why do you think jurors are paid?
2. **WRITE ABOUT IT** Use the library or the Internet to research the development of the modern Olympic games. Write a research report describing your findings.

Chapter 12 Review

VISUAL SUMMARY

Classical Greece

Culture
- Developed the basis of western philosophy
- Established rules for the writing of history
- Set out rules of logic

Arts
- Created drama
- Used the ideal as the basis for the arts
- Set artistic standards for art and architecture

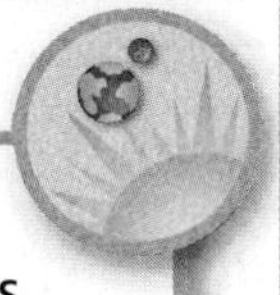

Science & Technology
- Made important discoveries about Earth and the planets
- Devised new mathematics
- Developed inventions such as compound pulley and water lifting devices

Government
- Created and used direct democracy
- Expanded citizen participation in government
- Alexander built an enormous empire including land in Asia, Africa, and Europe

TERMS & NAMES

Explain why the words in each set below are linked with each other.

1. **Pericles** and **direct democracy**
2. **Delian League** and **Peloponnesian War**
3. **Alexander the Great** and **Hellenistic**
4. **tragedy** and **comedy**

MAIN IDEAS

The Golden Age of Greece (pages 392–397)

5. How did the three goals of Pericles bring a Golden Age to Greece?
6. What aspects of Athenian direct democracy are similar to democracy as practiced by the United States?

Peloponnesian War (pages 398–403)

7. Why did other city-states in the Delian League resent Athens?
8. How did Athens and Sparta shape their war strategies?

Alexander the Great (pages 404–409)

9. How did the Peloponnesian War help Philip II of Macedonia conquer Greece?
10. How did Alexander the Great introduce Greek ideas to Egypt and Central Asia?

The Legacy of Greece (pages 410–419)

11. What qualities did Greek sculptors and architects seek to portray?
12. What are the basic ideas in Greek philosophy?

CRITICAL THINKING Big Ideas: Geography

13. **UNDERSTANDING CAUSE AND EFFECT** Why didn't the democratic ideas of Greek city-states spread throughout the empire of Alexander the Great?
14. **MAKING INFERENCES** How did the conquests of Alexander the Great change the cultures of the conquered lands?
15. **UNDERSTANDING CONTINUITY AND CHANGE** How did the Greek scientists expand knowledge about the world?

Standards-Based Assessment

ALTERNATIVE ASSESSMENT

1. **WRITING ACTIVITY** Review the section about Socrates in Lesson 4. Use books or the Internet to learn more about Socrates' trial. Working with a partner, write a short scene for a play about the trial of Socrates. Be sure to include parts for Socrates, his students, and his enemies.

2. **INTERDISCIPLINARY ACTIVITY—SCIENCE** Use books or the Internet to research the ideas of Archimedes about levers. Duplicate some of Archimedes' experiments. Prepare a lab report on your activities.

3. **STARTING WITH A STORY** Review your letter of advice to Pericles about paid public officials. Use the Internet to find what paid public positions exist in your hometown or state. Also find out what qualifications are required for those positions and how the positions are filled. Prepare a report with your findings.

Technology Activity

4. **CREATING A VIDEO SCRIPT** Use the Internet or the library to research modern buildings that show the influence of Greek architecture. Create a video script for a presentation on the influence of Greek architecture on modern buildings.
   Include
   - the location of the modern buildings
   - images of the modern and Greek buildings
   - comparisons of modern buildings and Greek buildings

Research Links
ClassZone.com

Using a Time Line The time line below shows changes in Greece from 479 B.C. to 323 B.C. Use it to answer the questions below.

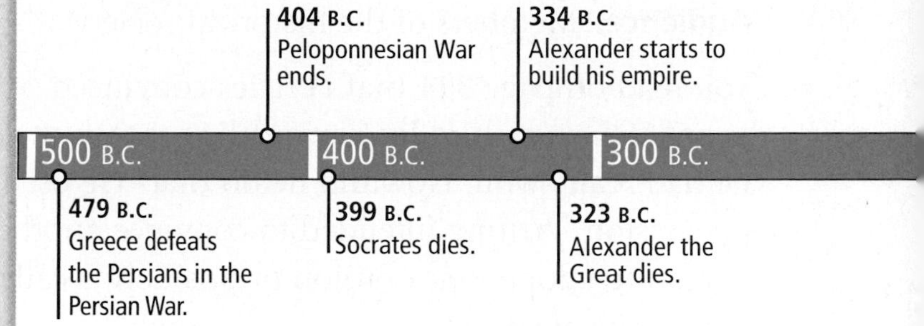
500 B.C.
400 B.C.
300 B.C.
479 B.C. Greece defeats the Persians in the Persian War.
404 B.C. Peloponnesian War ends.
399 B.C. Socrates dies.
334 B.C. Alexander starts to build his empire.
323 B.C. Alexander the Great dies.

1. **Which of the events listed above occurred first?**
   A. death of Socrates
   B. death of Alexander
   C. Peloponnesian War
   D. Persian War

2. **Which of the following statements is correct?**
   A. Socrates and Alexander lived at the same time.
   B. The Peloponnesian War ended before Alexander built an empire
   C. The Persian War occurred after the Peloponnesian War.
   D. It took Alexander 10 years to build his empire.

Test Practice
ClassZone.com

Additional Test Practice, pp. S1–S33

Writing About History

Writing Model
ClassZone.com

Persuasive Writing:
Honoring an Ancient Leader

Purpose: To persuade a historical society to honor the leader of your choice with a statue

Audience: Members of the historical society

You read on page 394 that Pericles convinced people who saw him lose a wrestling match that he had really won. How did he do that? He used persuasion. Writing intended to convince another person to adopt your opinion or position is called **persuasive writing**.

Pericles ▶

Organization & Focus

A historical society has raised money to erect a statue. Its goal is to honor the ancient Hebrew or ancient Greek who had the most-lasting influence on history. Your assignment is to write a 500- to 700-word letter to persuade the society to honor the leader of your choice.

Choosing a Topic Skim Chapters 10, 11, and 12. In your notebook, write the name of each leader you find. Take notes about his or her accomplishments and lasting influence. Even if you find a leader you want to recommend, keep reviewing the chapters. To write a good persuasive letter, you will need to show why your leader is a better choice than other leaders. So you will need details about them too. When you've finished, review your notes and make your choice.

Identifying Purpose and Audience Your purpose is to use facts, examples, and reasons to convince others to adopt your opinion. Your audience is the members of a historical society. Because they are familiar with history, you won't have to provide much background information. You can focus on giving solid and convincing reasons.

Finding Supporting Evidence Gather facts, examples, and reasons to prove that your leader is the best choice. Also, anticipate the leaders others might suggest, and gather evidence against those choices.

Outlining and Drafting Make an outline of the three main parts of your persuasive letter. The **introduction** should grab the readers' interest and state your recommendation. The **body** of your letter should offer facts and examples as supporting evidence for your recommendation. The body of your letter should also show why other recommendations—counterarguments—are not as good as yours. The **conclusion** should tie everything together and make a strong appeal.

Research & Technology

Give your readers a strong sense of your leader's personality. One way to do this is to describe actions that demonstrate the leader's best characteristics. You can find additional information about the life of your leader in the library or online. Record helpful information on a chart like the one below.

Technology Tip Not all information on the Internet is accurate. Learn to evaluate online sources. For example, museums and encyclopedias are reliable. If you have questions about a source, ask your teacher or librarian.

Characteristics	Actions that Demonstrate Them

Evaluation & Revision

Exchange first drafts with a classmate. Use the following guide to evaluate your partner's letter:

- Is the thesis statement clear?
- How strong are the main arguments and evidence?
- Were counterarguments addressed well?
- Were you convinced by the letter? Why or why not?

Listen carefully to your partner's comments. Rework your letter until you are satisfied that you have addressed your partner's major concerns.

Self-Check

Does my letter have

- ☐ an awareness of my audience and purpose?
- ☐ an introduction that states my recommendation?
- ☐ well-organized and convincing evidence?
- ☐ a strong conclusion with a final appeal?

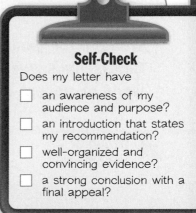

Publish & Present

Make a neat final copy of your letter. Make a sketch to go along with it to show what the statue might look like. Post your letter and drawing on the bulletin board and read what others have posted there.

UNIT 6

The World of Ancient Rome

Interact with History ▶

Watching the Games at the Colosseum, A.D. 80

Emperor Titus has invited all of Rome to celebrate the opening of the new Colosseum with 100 days of festivities and entertainment. Along with about 50,000 others, you have crowded into the arena to see the games. As the action gets underway, the crowd roars with excitement.

What do the games at the Colosseum suggest about the world of ancient Rome?

WebQuest
ClassZone.com

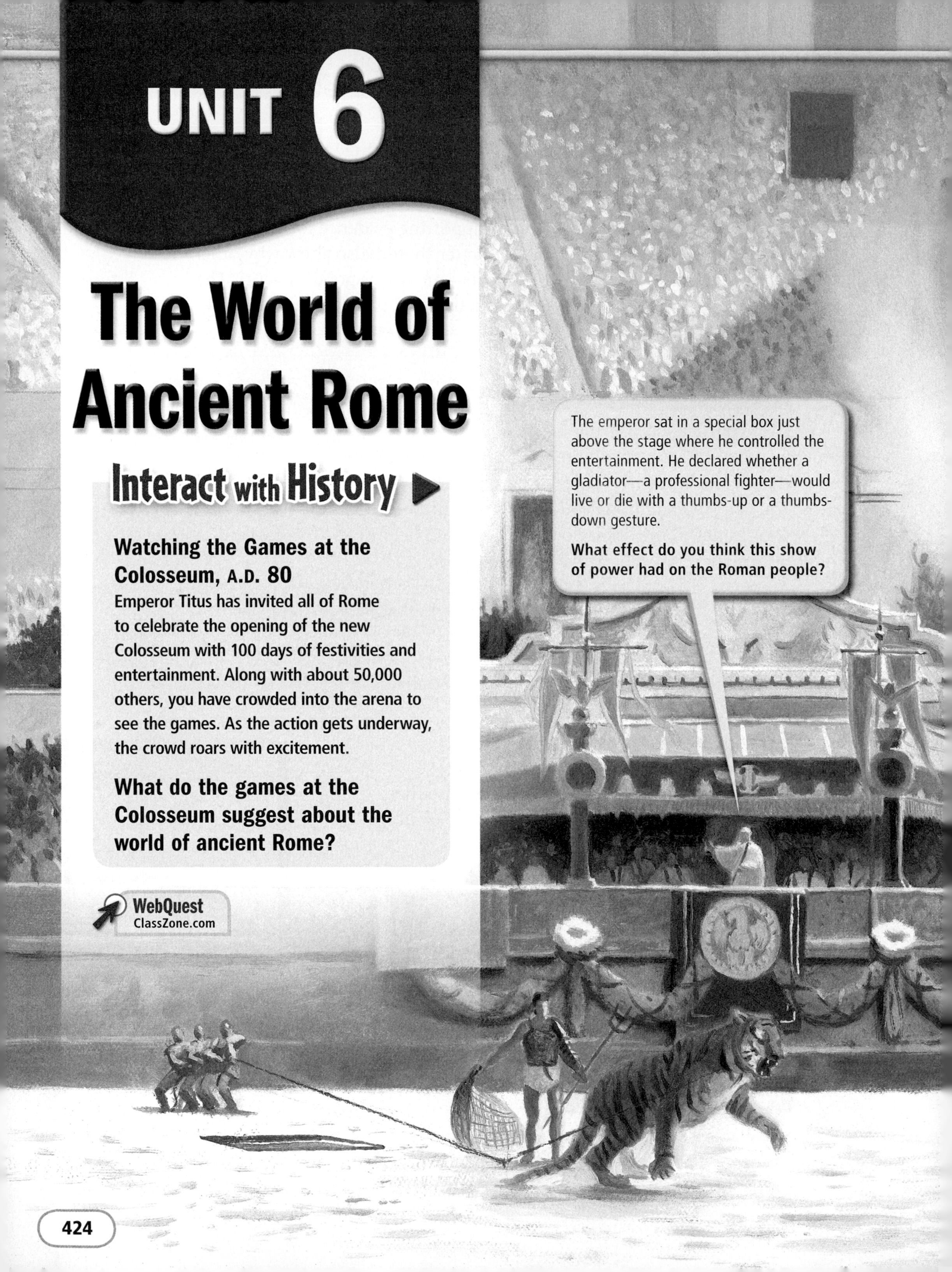

The emperor sat in a special box just above the stage where he controlled the entertainment. He declared whether a gladiator—a professional fighter—would live or die with a thumbs-up or a thumbs-down gesture.
What effect do you think this show of power had on the Roman people?

Spectators could quickly enter and exit the Colosseum through 80 arched entrances. Overhead stretched a cloth awning to protect the public from the sun. Beneath the arena, rope-operated elevators could bring thousands of animals to the surface at once.

How would you describe the architecture of the Colosseum?

The crowd might see lions attacking bulls or hunters killing unusual animals. But most eagerly anticipated were the games that pitted a gladiator against another person or a wild animal. Before they began to fight, the gladiators greeted the emperor: "We who are about to die salute you."

What traits do you think were necessary to be a gladiator?

Chapter

13 The Rise of Rome

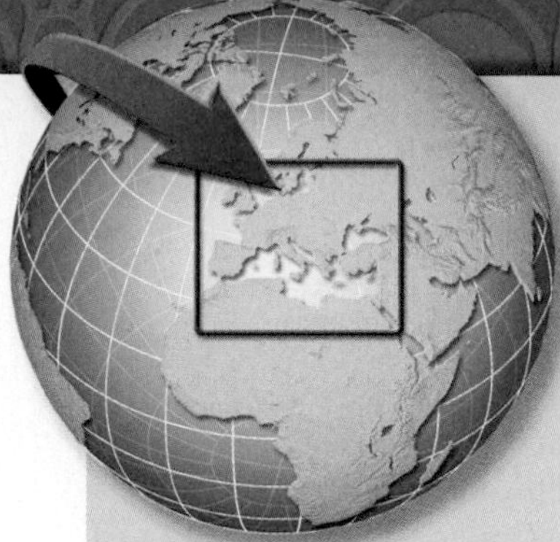

Before You Read: Predicting

Scan the titles of the chapter and the lessons. In your notebook, write three questions you think will be answered in the chapter. One example is

What was life like in ancient Rome?

Fill in the answers to your questions as you find them.

Big Ideas About Ancient Rome

Economics **A large division between the rich and the poor often creates problems.**

In ancient Rome, anger arose between powerful, wealthy landholders and poor farmers. This anger led to the development of a more representative form of government. Later, conflict between the two classes would lead to civil war.

Integrated Technology

eEdition
- Interactive Maps
- Interactive Visuals
- Starting with a Story

VIDEO *Ancient Rome*

INTERNET RESOURCES

Go to **ClassZone.com** for
- WebQuest
- Homework Helper
- Research Links
- Internet Activities
- Quizzes
- Maps
- Test Practice
- Current Events

ATLANTIC OCEAN

20°W

ROME

753 B.C.
According to legend, Rome is founded.
◄ (bronze head of wolf)

509 B.C.
Rome becomes a republic.

800 B.C. — 600 B.C.

WORLD

750 B.C.
Greek city-states flourish.
(Greek temple in Sicily) ►

The Roman Empire at Its Height, A.D. 117

INTERACTIVE

146 B.C.
Rome defeats Carthage in the Punic Wars.

27 B.C.
Augustus becomes the first emperor of Rome.
◀ (cameo of young Augustus)

A.D. 117
Rome reaches its greatest extent.

200 B.C. — B.C. | A.D. — A.D. 200

321 B.C.
Maurya empire is founded in India.

202 B.C.
Liu Bang reunifies China and starts the Han Dynasty.
(clay horse from the Han Dynasty) ▶

A.D. 30
Jesus is crucified.

A.D. 100
Moche culture arises in South America.

Starting with a Story

THE Assassination OF Julius Caesar

Background: In 49 B.C., Julius Caesar became the sole ruler of Rome. At first, Caesar was a popular and effective leader. But in time, the Senate, Rome's governing body, resented his power. On March 15, 44 B.C., some of the senators took action.

The Senate held a meeting on that fateful day. The senators entered one by one and, finally, Caesar came into the chamber. And then an incredible scene unfolded.

Bust of Julius Caesar ▶

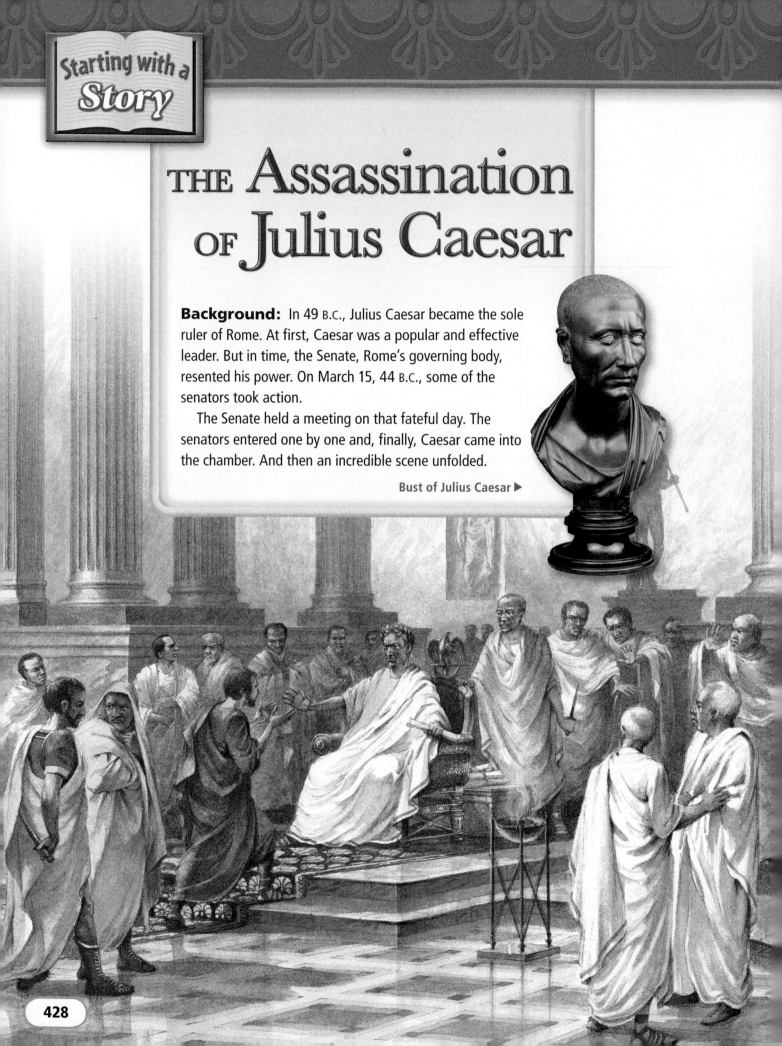

Caesar took his seat in the center of the chamber. According to custom, he was the only one allowed to sit. Before Caesar called the meeting to order, the senators talked in small groups. Then one of the men stepped forward to ask Caesar a question. He even grabbed Caesar's shoulder. Angrily, the ruler waved him away, but the senator seemed determined to gain his attention.

While Caesar argued with his questioner, another senator moved forward. Silently, he drew out a knife and wounded the ruler with his weapon. Caesar cried out in surprise and rose from his chair. He pulled out a knife from the folds of his toga and defended himself. The senator stumbled backward, but the others moved forward. They all drew out their knives. It was a plot!

Caesar made no sound as the senators attacked him. He pulled the hood of his toga over his head and adjusted the garment over his feet. As he fell to the ground, the toga covered his body. When the senators finally stepped back, Caesar was dead.

One of the senators ordered a pair of servants to remove the body. The people of Rome would soon learn that their ruler had been killed. No one—not even the senators—knew what would happen to Rome next.

What might drive people to overthrow their leader?

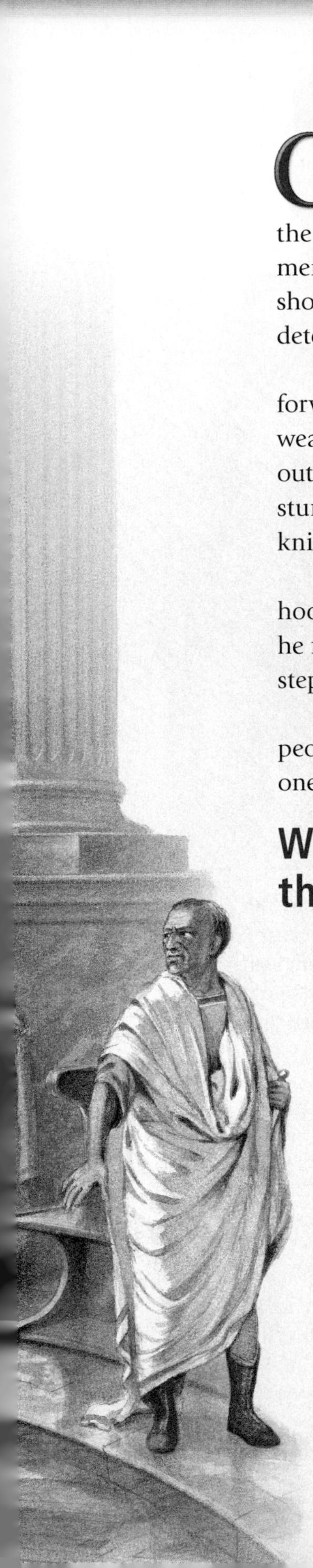

Reading & Writing

1. **READING: Setting** Setting is when and where a story takes place. How does this story's setting help the senators carry out their plot?
2. **WRITING: Persuasion** The date is March 14, 44 B.C. You are a Roman senator who opposes the plot against Caesar. Write a speech in which you explain and support your position for letting Caesar continue his rule.

Lesson 1

MAIN IDEAS

1. **Culture** Stories about the beginnings of Rome are a mix of legend and historical fact.
2. **Geography** The people who settled Rome chose a geographic location that was good for defense, travel, and trade.
3. **Economics** To survive, Roman farmers relied on discipline and hard work.

TAKING NOTES

Reading Skill: Categorizing

Sorting similar kinds of information into groups helps you understand patterns in history. As you read Lesson 1, look for details about the three categories given for ancient Rome. Record the information you learn about them in a web diagram like the one below.

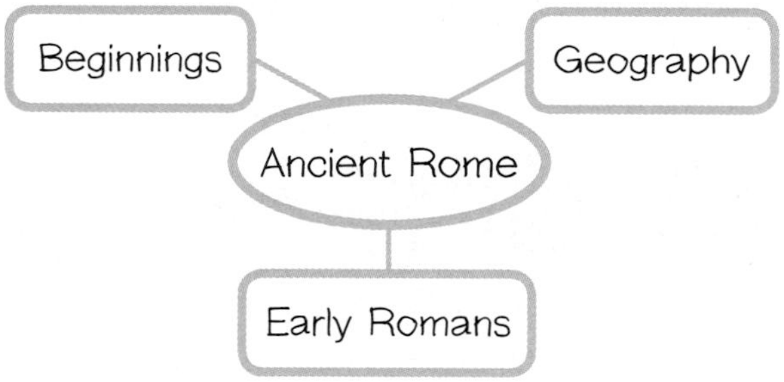

Skillbuilder Handbook, page R6

▲ **Symbol of Rome** This statue of the goddess Roma represents ancient Rome. Romans believed that the goddess protected them and their city.

Words to Know

Understanding the following words will help you read this lesson:

descendant a person related to a particular parent, grandparent, or other ancestor (page 432)

__Descendants__ of a Trojan warrior may have founded Rome.

abandon to leave behind, to desert (page 432)

At an early age, the twins were __abandoned__ by their mother.

vast very great in area or size (page 432)

The __vast__ Roman Empire would stretch from Britain to Egypt.

fetch to go after and return with; to get (page 435)

The farmer asked his daughter to __fetch__ a bucket of water from a nearby stream.

The Geography of Ancient Rome

TERMS & NAMES
- **Romulus**
- **legend**
- **Aeneas**
- **Remus**
- **republic**
- **peninsula**

Build on What You Know You have probably seen movies about ancient Rome, with its Colosseum and gladiators. These films show Rome at its height, but they only tell part of the story. The founding of the civilization owes much to its geography.

The Beginnings of Rome

1 ESSENTIAL QUESTION What is the early history of Rome?

The history of ancient Rome begins with the overthrow of foreign kings in 509 B.C. But Romans like to date the history of their city to 753 B.C. That is when a legendary hero called **Romulus** (RAHM•yuh•luhs) is said to have founded Rome.

A **legend** is a popular story from earlier times that cannot be proved. The legend about Rome's founding begins with **Aeneas** (ih•NEE•uhs), a hero of the Trojan War. You learned about the Trojan War in Chapter 11. According to the legend, Aeneas settled in Italy after Troy was destroyed.

Palatine Hill Traces of settlements dating from around 1000 B.C. have been found on the Palatine Hill. ▼

The Founding of Rome The legend continues with the twins Romulus and **Remus** (REE•muhs), the descendants of Aeneas according to some versions. They were abandoned by their mother but rescued by a wolf. When the twins grew up, they decided to found a city but fought over its location. Romulus killed his brother and traced Rome's boundaries around the Palatine Hill.

After Romulus, a series of Roman kings ruled the city. Sometime in the 600s B.C., however, the Etruscans conquered Rome. The Etruscans were a people from northern Italy. But the Romans wanted self-rule. In 509 B.C., they overthrew the Etruscan king and formed a republic. A **republic** is a government in which people elect their leaders. You will learn about the Roman Republic in Lesson 2.

REVIEW Why are the dates 753 B.C. and 509 B.C. important?

Rome's Geographic Location

2 ESSENTIAL QUESTION Why was Rome's location so favorable?

After the overthrow of the Etruscans, Rome grew from a city into a country and then into a vast empire. Its location helped make this growth possible.

Hills and River In reality, people founded Rome, not figures from legend. The first settlers of Rome were the Latins. They came from a region surrounding Rome. They chose the spot for its mild climate, good farmland, and strategic location.

The Latins and later settlers built Rome on seven steep hills. (See map at right.) During the day, settlers farmed the fertile plain at the base of the hills. At night, they returned to their hilltop homes, from which they could defend themselves against an enemy attack.

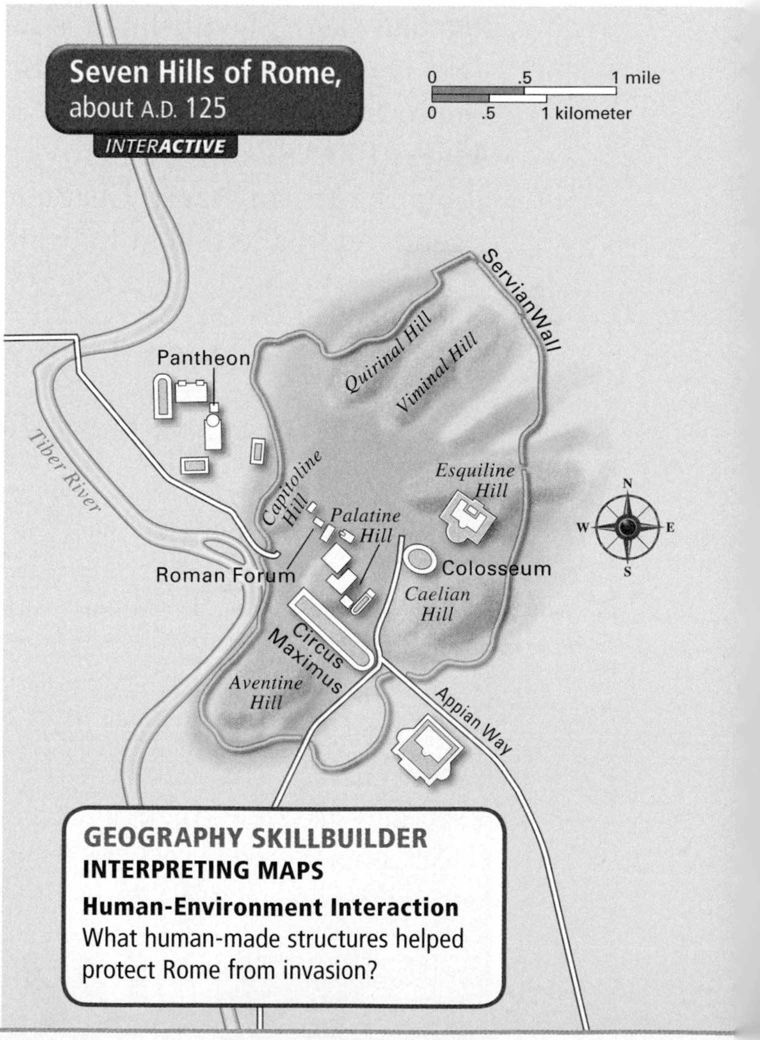

GEOGRAPHY SKILLBUILDER
INTERPRETING MAPS
Human-Environment Interaction
What human-made structures helped protect Rome from invasion?

Geography

The Tiber River

During Rome's earliest times, the Tiber provided a source of water for farming and drinking. Later, the river provided a route for travel and trade. Small ships could sail up the Tiber to Rome and down the Tiber to the Mediterranean. But the river also offered protection from invaders, since Rome was located away from the mouth of the sea.

GEOGRAPHY SKILLBUILDER
INTERPRETING VISUALS
Human-Environment Interaction
What does the photograph suggest about the importance of the Tiber to Romans today?

Rome had other advantages. It was located a short distance from the Mediterranean Sea on several ancient trade routes. It also lay next to the Tiber River. As you learned in the Geography feature above, this river played an important role in Rome's development.

Italian Peninsula Rome's location on the Italian Peninsula also played an important role in its development. The peninsula stretches south from Europe into the Mediterranean Sea. A **peninsula** is a piece of land surrounded on three sides by water. As you can see on the map on page 427, the Italian Peninsula is shaped like a boot. Its heel points toward Greece, while its toe points across the sea to Africa.

Italy's location on the Mediterranean made it relatively easy for Roman ships to reach the other lands around the sea. This position made it easier for Rome to eventually conquer and gain new territories. It also helped the development of trade routes.

The two main mountain ranges of Italy helped protect Rome. The Alps border Italy on the north, and the Apennines (AP•uh•NYNZ) form Italy's spine. But Italy's mountains didn't separate early settlements the way the mountains of Greece did. Italy also had more large plains than Greece. This made farming easier.

REVIEW How did its geography help Rome grow?

Lives of Early Romans

3 ESSENTIAL QUESTION What was life like for the early Romans?

Like many ancient peoples, the early Romans lived by farming. But even though the land was fertile, life on a Roman farm was not easy.

Working the Land Most early Romans worked small plots of land. They planted grains such as wheat and barley. They also grew beans, vegetables, and fruit. Later they learned to grow olives and grapes. They also raised pigs, sheep, goats, and chickens. They used oxen to pull their plows.

Farmers who owned land also served in the army. In fact, for a time only landowners were allowed to join the army. Roman leaders believed that property owners would fight harder to defend the city. Landowners were also able to pay for their own military equipment.

Over time, some farmers grew richer than others. They bought more land and built larger farms, or estates. A gap developed between small farmers and the owners of the estates. This gap would later produce divisions in Roman politics and government.

Farm Life At first, most Roman farmers lived in simple homes made of mud or timber. They did not have much furniture. In addition, the farmers lived in extended families. This large family group might have included grandparents, aunts and uncles, nieces and nephews, and cousins.

Connect to Today

Italian Farm Grapes, like these shown here, are still a popular crop in Italy. In ancient Rome, only wealthy farmers, who could afford to wait a few years to harvest the first crop, grew grapes. ▼

The members of a Roman farm family had to work very hard. They farmed the land with simple tools and fetched water from a well or nearby spring. The small amount of land on most farms had to produce enough food to feed the family. This meant that everyone had to be disciplined about his or her responsibilities.

The qualities of discipline, loyalty, and hard work that these early farmers developed would help Rome succeed. They were the qualities that made Roman armies so successful. When soldiers went to war, they had to obey orders and do their jobs. This attitude would help Rome conquer all of Italy.

REVIEW Why was discipline important to early Romans?

Lesson Summary

- Legend and fact shaped Rome's early history.
- Rome's geography encouraged the growth of Roman civilization.
- Roman society benefited from the hard work and discipline of Roman farmers.

Why It Matters Now . . .

There are still many cultural connections among Mediterranean areas of Europe, Asia, and Africa as a result of Rome's influence.

1 Lesson Review

Homework Helper
ClassZone.com

Terms & Names

1. Explain the importance of

Romulus	Aeneas	republic
legend	Remus	peninsula

Using Your Notes

Categorizing Use your web diagram to answer the following question:

2. Which category of information would you use to describe why Rome developed into a powerful civilization?

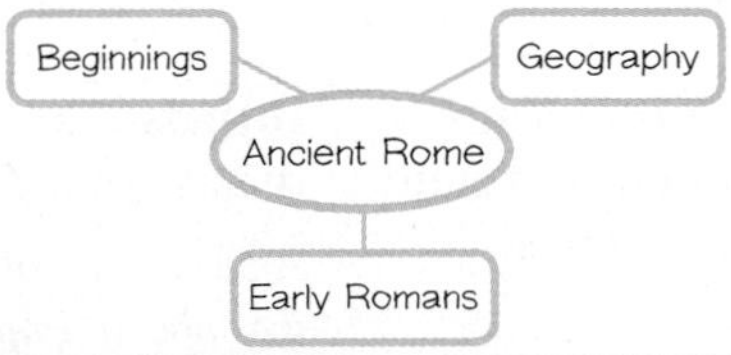

Main Ideas

3. What is the legend of Rome's founding?

4. How was Rome's location good for defense?

5. Why did early Romans have to work hard?

Critical Thinking

6. Making Inferences What does the legend about Rome's founding tell you about what was important to Romans?

7. Comparing and Contrasting Compare the role of the Tiber in the development of ancient Rome with that of the Nile in ancient Egypt.

Activity

Illustrating a Legend Draw a picture that illustrates a scene from the legendary founding of Rome.

Lesson 2

MAIN IDEAS

1. **Economics** Early Roman society was divided into two unequal classes.
2. **Government** The Roman Republic had a government divided into three parts, similar to the U.S. government today.
3. **Government** To gain more land and wealth, Rome began to expand by conquering neighboring peoples.

▲ **Founder** Lucius Junius Brutus helped found the Roman Republic. He led a citizen army that drove the last Etruscan king from Rome.

TAKING NOTES

Reading Skill: Understanding Cause and Effect

Causes explain why an event happens. Effects are the results of the event. As you read Lesson 2, look for the effects of each event listed in the chart below.

Causes	Effects
Romans no longer wanted a monarchy.	
Plebeians were not equal to the patricians.	
Rome expanded its territories.	

Skillbuilder Handbook, page R26

Words to Know

Understanding the following words will help you read this lesson:

resentment anger (page 437)
*The lower class felt deep **resentment** because the upper class held all the power.*

branch a part of something larger (page 438)
*Each of the Roman government's **branches** had a different duty to perform.*

province a political division similar to a state of the United States (page 438)
*To maintain order, Rome stationed troops in each of its **provinces**.*

impose to force or dictate (page 440)
*After a series of wars, Rome was able to **impose** its rule on the trading city of Carthage.*

The Roman Republic

TERMS & NAMES
patrician
plebeian
Senate
consul
Cincinnatus

Build on What You Know You have already learned that Rome overthrew its kings and formed a republic. This change to self-rule would not only affect Rome's government. It would also affect Roman society.

Early Strengths of Roman Society

1 **ESSENTIAL QUESTION** How was Roman society structured?

As Rome developed into a complex civilization, two classes arose. Inequalities between them would lead to conflict. This conflict, however, would eventually define Roman citizenship and the rights of citizens under Roman law.

Patricians and Plebeians The upper-class **patricians** (puh•TRIHSH•uhnz) were wealthy landowners who held all of the highest positions in government. The **plebeians** (plih•BEE•uhnz) were mostly common farmers. Like all male Roman citizens, they could vote, but they couldn't hold important government positions.

Resentment over the patricians' power caused tension. Finally, the patricians passed a written constitution, called the Twelve Tables, around 450 B.C. The Twelve Tables established basic rights and duties for Roman citizens.

REVIEW Why did the division of Roman society cause tension?

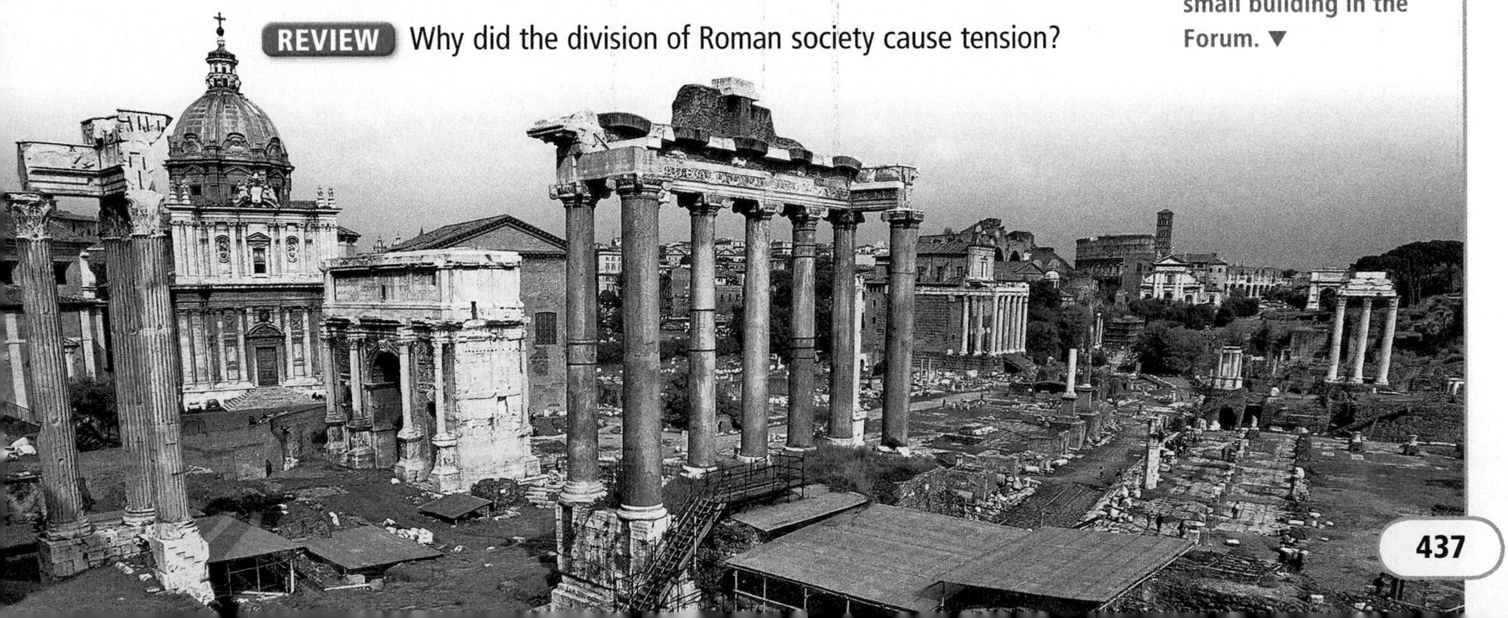

Roman Forum Ruins of the Roman Forum, the religious, cultural, and political heart of Rome, still stand today. In the early days of the republic, the Senate met in a small building in the Forum. ▼

Republican Government

2 ESSENTIAL QUESTION How was the republican government organized?

The leaders of the Roman Republic established a tripartite (try•PAHR•tyt) government. This type of government has three branches: executive, legislative, and judicial. The executive branch enforces a country's laws. The legislative branch makes the laws. And the judicial branch interprets the laws in court.

Legislative and Judicial The legislative branch of Roman government included the Senate and the assemblies. The **Senate** was a powerful body of 300 members that advised Roman leaders. Most senators were patricians. The assemblies were mainly made up of plebeians. Their representatives protected the rights of plebeians.

The judicial branch consisted of eight judges who served for one year. They oversaw the courts and governed the provinces.

Executive Two **consuls** led Rome's executive branch. They commanded the army and directed the government for one year. Each consul had the power to veto, or overrule, the other.

In times of crisis, the consuls could choose a dictator—a leader with absolute power—to rule in their place for a limited time. Around 460 B.C., a man named **Cincinnatus** (SIHN•suh•NAT•uhs) was made dictator to defend Rome from attack. According to legend, he defeated the enemy and returned power to the consuls in sixteen days.

Senators In this 19th-century painting, a speaker addresses his fellow members of the Roman Senate. ▼

Comparing Republican Governments

Executive

Rome

Two consuls, elected for one year: led government and commanded army

United States

A president, elected for four years: heads government and military

Legislative

Rome

Senate of 300 members: advised consuls and set policies

Assemblies: made laws and selected officials

United States

Senate of 100 members: makes laws and advises president

House of Representatives of 435 members: makes laws

Legal Code

Rome

Twelve Tables: basis of Roman law, which established citizens' legal, economic, property, and social rights

United States

U.S. Constitution: basis of U.S. law, which sets forth both individual rights and governmental powers

Judicial

Rome

Eight judges: oversaw courts and governed provinces

United States

Supreme Court of nine justices: interprets the Constitution and federal law

SKILLBUILDER
INTERPRETING VISUALS
What similarities do you see in the governments of the Roman Republic and the United States?

Legacy of Roman Law The U.S. government adopted several features of the Roman Republic. You can compare the two systems in the chart above. Like the Roman government, the United States has a tripartite system. The U.S. system of checks and balances makes sure that one branch of the government doesn't have too much power. This system is like the veto, which limited the power of Roman consuls. In addition, like Rome, the United States has a written constitution on which its government is based.

Citizenship is also an important part of a republican government. In the Roman Republic, only free adult males were citizens and could vote. Only these citizens enjoyed the protection of Roman law. They also were expected to perform civic duties. That means that they were expected to serve their nation. Cincinnatus showed civic duty by defeating the enemy and stepping down from power. American citizens show civic duty by voting, taking part in jury duty, and paying taxes.

REVIEW What made up the three branches of the Roman Republic?

The Republic Expands

3 ESSENTIAL QUESTION How did Rome expand?

For hundreds of years after the founding of the republic, Rome expanded its territories. By the 300s B.C., the Romans dominated central Italy. Eventually, they conquered the Etruscans to the north and the Greek city-states to the southeast. By 275 B.C., all of the Italian Peninsula was under Roman control.

In general, Rome did not impose harsh rule on conquered peoples. The republic offered Roman citizenship to most of the conquered peoples and allowed them to govern themselves. In return, they had to pay taxes and provide soldiers for the Roman army.

Vocabulary Strategy

The **specialized vocabulary** term *Punic Wars* refers to the series of wars between Rome and Carthage. Carthage was once a colony of Phoenicia, a group of sea-trading city-states on the Mediterranean. *Punic* comes from the Latin word *Phoenician*.

The Punic Wars Rome needed these soldiers to fight in the *Punic Wars,* which began in 264 B.C. The Punic Wars were a series of three long wars against Carthage, a rich trading city in North Africa.

Rome won each of the Punic Wars but almost lost the second. Hannibal, a general from Carthage, crossed the Alps with a herd of elephants and nearly captured Rome. The Roman general Scipio (SIHP•ee•OH) defeated him in 202 B.C. In 146 B.C., Rome finally captured and destroyed Carthage. By the end of the wars, Roman territory extended from Spain to Greece. (See the map below.)

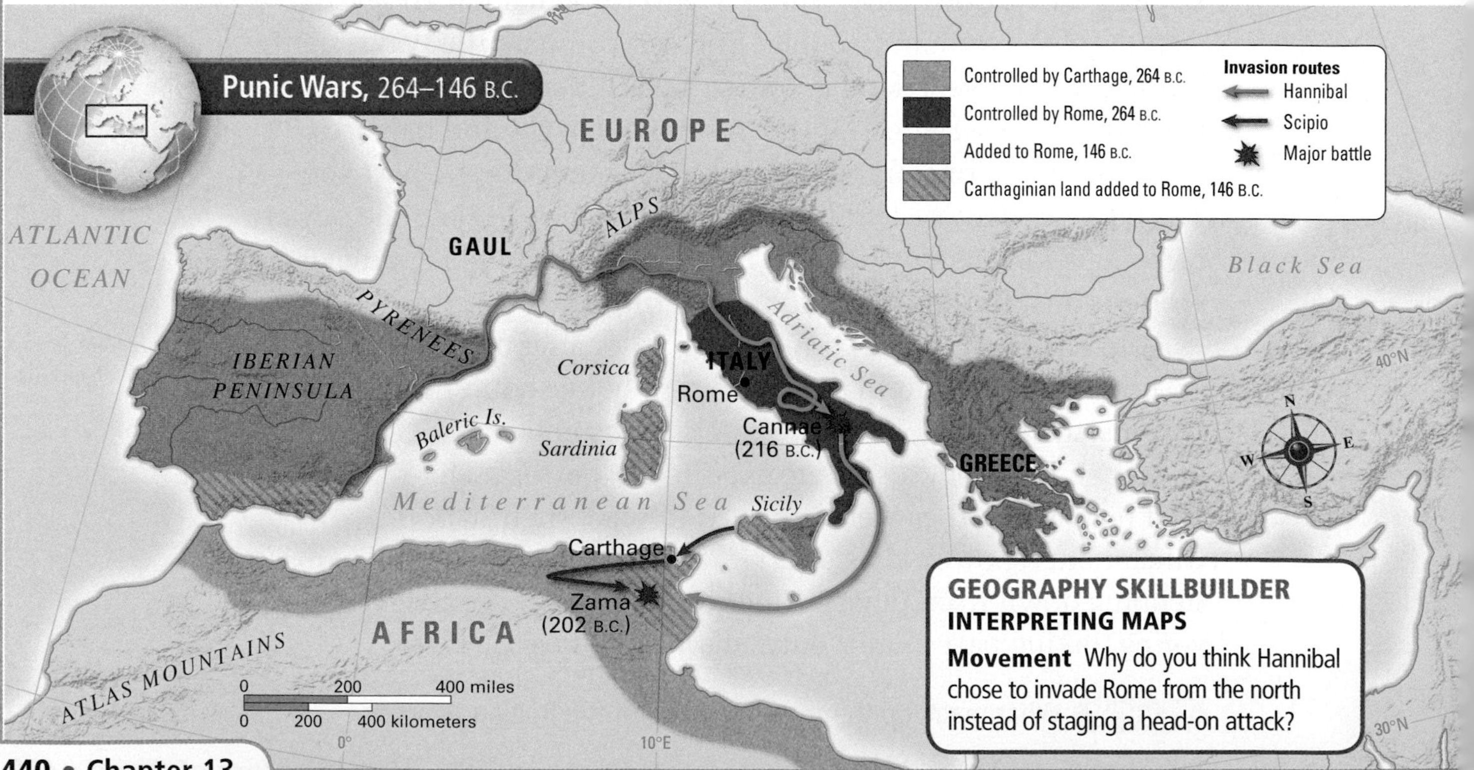

GEOGRAPHY SKILLBUILDER
INTERPRETING MAPS
Movement Why do you think Hannibal chose to invade Rome from the north instead of staging a head-on attack?

Effects of Expansion The Roman conquerors brought back great wealth and many slaves. They bought large estates and farmed them with slave labor. But because many small farmers couldn't compete, they lost their farms. As a result, unemployment and poverty increased. The gap between rich and poor grew wider. This, in turn, produced more anger and tension between the classes.

REVIEW What was the result of Roman expansion?

Lesson Summary

- Early Rome was divided into two classes—patricians and plebeians.
- The Roman Republic was a tripartite system that provided a model for the U.S. government.
- Roman expansion brought new lands and great wealth for Rome.

Why It Matters Now . . .

Some of the most basic values and institutions of the United States, such as civic duty and a separate judicial branch, began in the Roman Republic.

▲ **Laurel Wreath** Roman generals wore a wreath made of laurel leaves after winning a major battle. The Romans adopted this symbol of victory from ancient Greece.

2 Lesson Review

Homework Helper
ClassZone.com

Terms & Names

1. Explain the importance of

patrician, Senate, Cincinnatus, plebeian, consul

Using Your Notes

Understanding Cause and Effect Use your completed chart to answer the following question:

2. What happened when Romans no longer wanted a monarchy?

Causes	Effects
Romans no longer wanted a monarchy.	
Plebeians were not equal to the patricians.	
Rome expanded its territories.	

Main Ideas

3. In what ways were the Roman social classes unequal?

4. What is the legacy of Roman law?

5. What lands did Rome conquer?

Critical Thinking

6. Explaining Historical Patterns Why do you think the Roman Republican government has influenced the governments of other countries?

7. Making Inferences What benefits do you think the Romans gained from their treatment of conquered peoples?

Activity

Writing a Dialogue Write a brief dialogue between Cincinnatus and the consuls who appointed him dictator. Remember that he served for only one day.

Lesson 3

▶ MAIN IDEAS

1. **Government** Angry poor people, power-hungry generals, and ambitious politicians threatened the Roman Republic.

2. **Government** Julius Caesar gained absolute control of the republic but did not rule long.

3. **Government** After Caesar was assassinated, Augustus founded an empire that enjoyed peace and prosperity for about 200 years.

▶ TAKING NOTES

Reading Skill: Constructing Time Lines

When you place events in order on a time line, you get a sense of the relationships among events. Create a time line like the one shown below to keep track of the dates and events in Lesson 3.

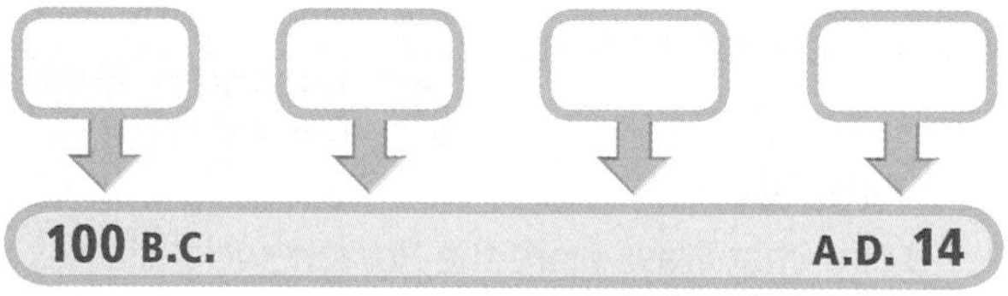

Skillbuilder Handbook, page R14

▲ **Imperial Eagle** A Roman soldier carried a bronze or silver image of an eagle raised on a pole, like the one shown in this small figurine, into battle. The eagle represented the strength of the Roman Empire.

Words to Know

Understanding the following words will help you read this lesson:

civic relating to citizenship and its rights and duties (page 443)

*They believed it was their **civic** duty to help solve their society's problems.*

campaign a series of military operations that form a part of a war (page 444)

*Julius Caesar's **campaign** against the Gauls lasted from 58 to 50 B.C.*

great-nephew the grandson of one's sister or brother (page 446)

*Augustus was related to Caesar as a **great-nephew**.*

marble a type of stone that can be highly polished (page 447)

*Roman artists and architects used **marble** to create beautiful sculptures.*

Rome Becomes an Empire

TERMS & NAMES
- civil war
- Julius Caesar
- Cicero
- Augustus
- Pax Romana

Build on What You Know In Lesson 2, you learned about the changes expansion brought to Roman society. Expansion would also change the balance of power in Rome's republican government. These changes would lead to the overthrow of the republic.

Conflicts at Home

1 ESSENTIAL QUESTION What led to conflict in Rome?

As Rome expanded, many wealthy Romans neglected their civic duties. They thought only about gaining even more power and wealth. This increased the differences between rich and poor. As a result, the threat of uprisings grew.

Reform Fails Reformers tried to relieve these problems. They wanted to break up the huge estates and give land to the poor. But the wealthy landowners in the Senate felt threatened. They opposed the reforms and had the reformers killed.

Connect to Today

Colosseum The Colosseum is a lasting symbol of the power of the Roman Empire. Many stadiums built since have been modeled on the Colosseum. ▼

Civil War At the same time, generals who had conquered other lands became ambitious for power at home. They hired poor farmers to serve under them as soldiers. Increasingly, these soldiers shifted their loyalty from the republic to their general. The generals' desire for power led to conflict.

Eventually, civil war broke out. A **civil war** is an armed conflict between groups within the same country. On one side were the generals who supported the cause of the plebeians. On the other were generals who were backed by patricians and senators.

A general named Marius fought for the plebeians, while a general named Sulla fought for the patricians. The struggle went on for years. Finally, in 82 B.C., the patricians won. Sulla took power and became a dictator.

Vocabulary Strategy

The word *civil* is part of a **word family** that includes the words *civic*, *civilian*, and *civilization*. They all come from the Latin root *civis*, meaning "citizen."

REVIEW Who fought in the civil war?

Julius Caesar

2 ESSENTIAL QUESTION Who was Julius Caesar?

After Sulla died, other generals rose to power. One of them was **Julius Caesar**. Caesar was born around 100 B.C. into an old noble family. He was a man of many talents and great ambition. But to achieve real power, he knew he had to win on the battlefield.

Military Leader Caesar first saw military action in Asia Minor—part of present-day Turkey—and Spain. But he proved himself to be a great general in Gaul, the area now known as France.

The Gauls were fierce fighters. But in a brilliant military campaign, Caesar defeated the Gauls and captured the entire region. His conquests won new lands and great wealth for Rome. The victories also won fame and fortune for Caesar.

▲ **Caesar** In this 19th-century wood engraving, soldiers bow down to Caesar after he won an important battle in 47 B.C. After the battle, Caesar had the following message sent back to Rome: "I came, I saw, I conquered."

Dictator for Life In addition to his military skills, Caesar was also a good politician. He gained a reputation as a reformer who supported the common people. This, plus his military fame, made him popular with the plebeians.

Primary Source Handbook
See the excerpt from *The Life of Caesar,* page R57.

But Caesar also had enemies. Many powerful Romans, including patrician senators, opposed Caesar. One of his opponents was **Cicero** (SIHS•uh•ROH), a key Roman consul and perhaps the greatest speaker in Roman history. Cicero was a strong supporter of the republic. He distrusted Caesar and the ruler's great desire for power. (You can learn more about the relationship between Cicero and Caesar by reading Cicero's letter in the Primary Source feature below.)

When Caesar returned from Gaul, the Senate ordered him to break up his army. Instead, he led his soldiers into Italy and began fighting for control of Rome. After several years, Caesar emerged victorious. In 46 B.C., he returned to Rome, where he had the support of the people and the army. That same year, the Senate appointed him the sole Roman ruler. In 44 B.C., Caesar was named dictator for life as opposed to the usual six months.

Primary Source

Background: Although Cicero opposed Caesar, he could still be polite to Rome's sole ruler. In 45 B.C., Cicero invited Caesar to be a guest in his home. The ruler arrived with 2,000 men. Cicero described the visit in a letter to a friend. In this excerpt from the letter, you can sense that Cicero is not comfortable with Caesar.

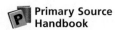

from *Cicero's Selected Works*

A Letter by Cicero
Translated by Michael Grant

In other words, we were human beings together. Still, he was not the sort of guest to whom you would say "do please come again on your way back." Once is enough! We talked no serious politics, but a good deal about literary matters. In short, he liked it and enjoyed himself. . . . There you have the story of how I entertained him—or had him billeted [camped] on me; I found it a bother, as I have said, but not disagreeable.

DOCUMENT–BASED QUESTION
Why do you think Cicero and Caesar avoided talking about politics?

Caesar's Reforms Caesar governed as an absolute ruler, but he started a number of reforms. He expanded the Senate by including supporters from Italy and other regions. He also enforced laws against crime and created jobs for the poor. Despite these reforms, some Romans feared that Caesar would make himself king. Not only would he rule for a lifetime, but his family members would also rule after him. Roman hatred of kings went back to the days of Etruscan rule.

▲ **Silver Coin** This coin was issued after Caesar's assassination. One side of the coin (*top*) shows a profile of one of the assassins. The other side shows a cap of liberty between two daggers. ▼

Assassination and Legacy Concern over Caesar's growing power led to his downfall. As you read in Starting with a Story, Caesar was assassinated in 44 B.C. by a group of senators. The leaders of the conspiracy were eventually killed or committed suicide.

Historians still disagree about Caesar's rule, just as Romans did at the time. Some say he was a reformer who worked to help the people. Others say he was a power-hungry tyrant. In either case, Caesar's rule and his death would bring an end to the republic.

REVIEW Why was Caesar killed?

Emperors Rule Rome

3 ESSENTIAL QUESTION What happened to Rome after Caesar's death?

After Caesar's death, several Roman leaders struggled to gain power. One of these men was Caesar's great-nephew and adopted son, Octavian (ahk•TAY•vee•uhn).

This struggle led to civil war, which lasted for years. The war destroyed what was left of the Roman Republic. Eventually, Octavian defeated his enemies. In 27 B.C., he became the unchallenged ruler of Rome. In time, he took the name **Augustus** (aw•GUHS•tuhs), which means "exalted one," or person of great rank and authority.

Augustus Rebuilds Rome Augustus was the first emperor of Rome, but he didn't use that title. He preferred to be called "first citizen." He restored some aspects of the republican government. Senators, consuls, and tribunes once again held office. But Augustus had power over all of them.

History Makers

Augustus (63 B.C.–A.D. 14)

As a child, Augustus was weak and sickly. He continued to suffer from illnesses throughout his life. Yet he lived a long life and became the powerful ruler of a great empire.

Despite his enormous power, Augustus liked to present himself as an average citizen with simple tastes. He lived in a small house and slept in a bedroom no larger than a cell. He wore plain robes woven by his wife. His favorite foods were those of the common people—bread, cheese, and olives. Augustus also believed in a strict moral code. He sent his own daughter into exile for not living up to this code.

Augustus once said that his highest honor was to be called the father of his country by the Roman people. But after his death, the Romans worshiped Augustus as a god.

Augustus governed well. He brought the provinces under control and strengthened the empire's defenses. He also began a civil service. A civil service is a group of officials employed by the government. The Roman civil service collected taxes, oversaw the postal system, and managed the grain supply.

Augustus also rebuilt and beautified Rome. He built grand temples, theaters, and monuments. He replaced many old brick buildings with structures in marble. Under Augustus, Rome became a magnificent imperial capital.

The Roman Peace The reign of Augustus began a long period of peace and stability in the Roman Empire. This period is called the **Pax Romana**, or "Roman Peace." The Pax Romana lasted for about 200 years. During this time, the empire grew to its greatest size, about 2 million square miles.

Under Augustus, the Roman army became the greatest fighting force in the world. Around 300,000 men served in the army. They guarded the empire's frontiers. They also built roads, bridges, and tunnels that helped tie the empire together. In addition, Augustus created a strong Roman navy that patrolled the Mediterranean Sea.

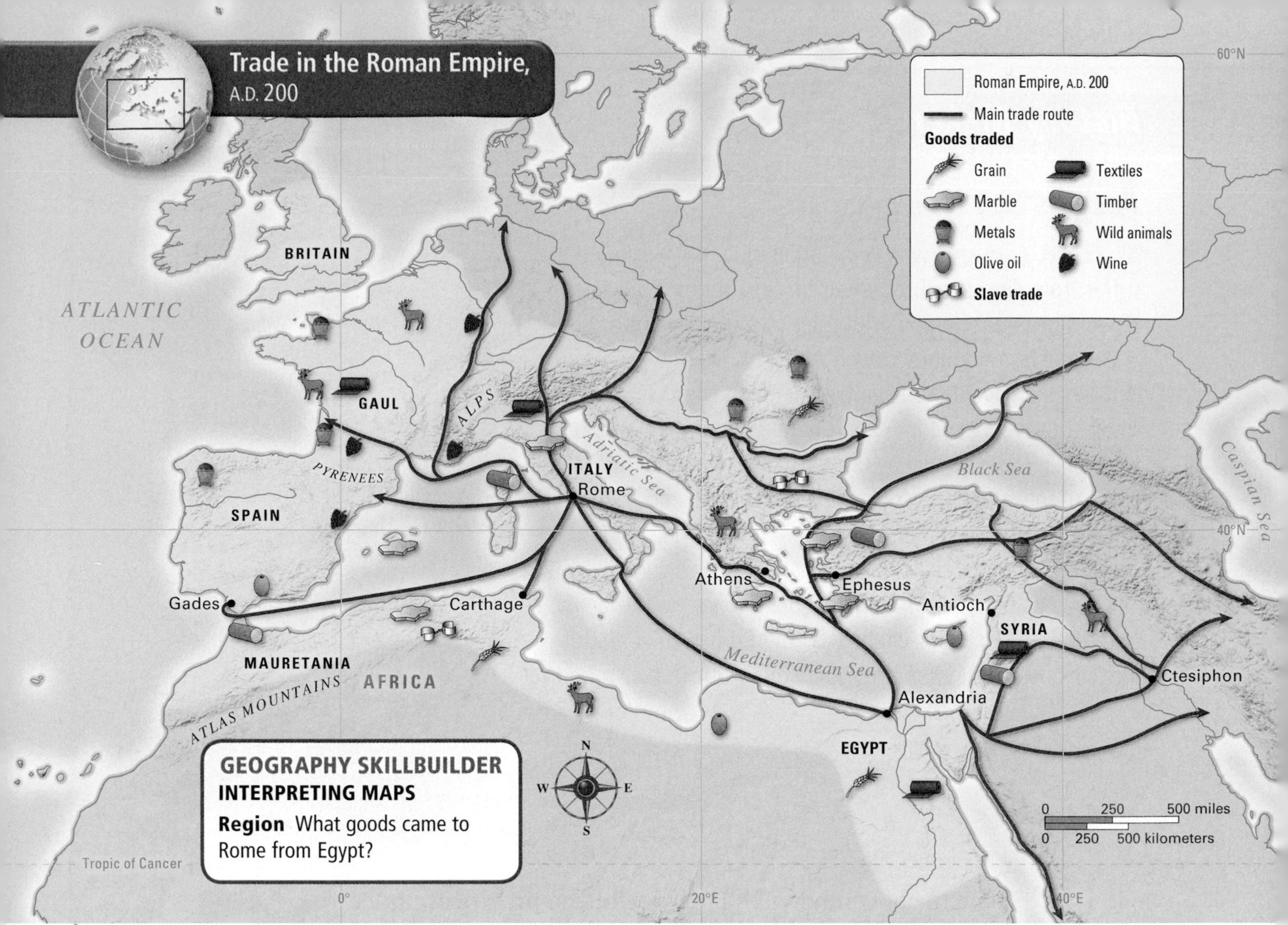

A Strong Economy The Pax Romana continued long after Augustus died in A.D. 14. Many other emperors ruled after Augustus. Some were good rulers, while others were not. But the government begun under Augustus was so effective that the empire continued to do well.

Agriculture and Trade Agriculture and trade helped the empire prosper. Farming remained the basis of the Roman economy, but industry also grew. The manufacture of pottery, metal goods, and glass increased. So did the production of wine, olive oil, and other food products.

The empire fostered economic growth through the use of trade routes. Traders sailed across the Mediterranean Sea to Spain, Africa, and western Asia. They also traveled by land to Gaul and other parts of Europe. Through trade, Rome acquired valuable goods not available at home. Traders brought back grain, ivory, silk, spices, gold and silver, and even wild animals. Much of this trade relied on the quality of Roman roads. It also relied on the security provided by the Roman military.

Currency The Roman economy was also united by a common currency, or money. In Augustus' time, a silver coin called a denarius (dih•NAHR•ee•uhs) was used throughout the empire. A common form of money made trade between different parts of the empire much easier. Traders could buy and sell without having to change their money into another currency.

Rome's expanding economy largely benefited those who were already wealthy. As a result, the division between rich and poor became deeper. You will learn about this division in Lesson 4.

REVIEW What were the contributions of the first Roman emperor?

Lesson Summary

- The results of Roman expansion produced social conflict and civil war.
- Julius Caesar gained power and became a dictator but was then assassinated.
- The reign of Augustus began a long period of imperial rule and peace in the Roman Empire.

▲ Motto SPQR stands for "the Senate and the people of Rome." This was the motto of the Roman Empire.

Why It Matters Now . . .

Rome faced the problems of how to maintain peace, law, and order. Modern governments face similar problems.

3 Lesson Review

Homework Helper
ClassZone.com

Terms & Names

1. Explain the importance of
   civil war — Cicero — Pax Romana
   Julius Caesar — Augustus

Using Your Notes

Constructing Time Lines Use your completed time line to answer the following question:

2. How long did Julius Caesar serve as dictator for life?

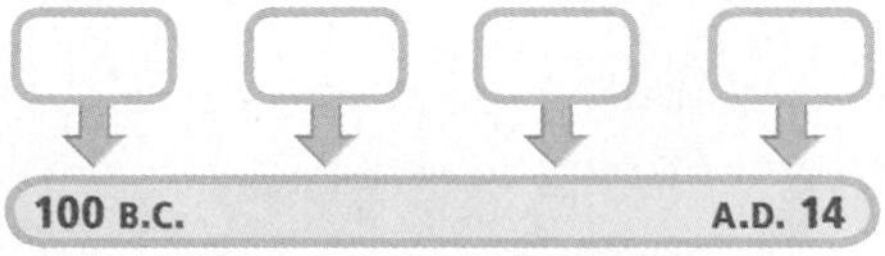

Main Ideas

3. How did expansion threaten the Roman Republic?
4. How did Caesar gain power?
5. How did Roman government change under Augustus?

Critical Thinking

6. **Summarizing** What events and circumstances brought the Roman Republic to an end?
7. **Understanding Cause and Effect** What factors encouraged economic growth during the Pax Romana?

Activity

Making a Map Add Rome to the world map that you have been working on throughout this book. Outline and label the Roman Empire at its height in A.D. 117.

Daily Life
Extend Lesson 3

Research Links
ClassZone.com

Life in a Roman Fort

Purpose: To learn about the daily life of a soldier in a Roman fort

The Romans built permanent forts on the frontiers of the empire. These forts helped Rome both defend and expand its empire. Some of the forts, like the one shown here, were located in Britain. Officers called centurions commanded the forts and the ordinary soldiers. Many Roman citizens joined the army but had to sign on for 25 years of service. Conquered peoples were also invited to join. They became Roman citizens when their service ended.

Each fort housed officers and about 500 soldiers. When they weren't on patrol, the soldiers spent much of their time in and around their barracks. Eighty men and one centurion lived in each barracks.

A Uniform and Equipment A soldier guarding the fort wore a wool tunic, protective chain mail, an iron helmet, and leather sandals. He carried a spear, a sword, and a shield with his unit's emblem.

B Centurion's Rooms A commander had several rooms to himself. Like all centurions, he wore a helmet with a crest that helped his soldiers identify him during a battle.

C Mess Rooms Eight men shared a pair of mess rooms. This is where they slept, cooked, and ate.

D Free Time The soldiers didn't have much free time, but when they did, they sometimes played games. Board games were popular pastimes.

E Weapons Soldiers defended the fort by throwing spears or shooting arrows at the enemy. Sometimes they also used this machine, called a ballista. It could throw steel-tipped arrows about 300 to 400 yards.

Activities

1. **TALK ABOUT IT** What words would you use to describe the life of a Roman soldier?
2. **WRITE ABOUT IT** Imagine you are a Roman soldier and write a diary entry describing a typical day.

Lesson
4

MAIN IDEAS

1. **Culture** Roles in Roman family life and society were clearly defined.
2. **Belief Systems** Roman religious beliefs were influenced by other cultures and linked with government.
3. **Culture** Although they were overcrowded and dirty, Roman cities were also places of interesting innovations and entertainments.

▲ **Household Mosaic** This mosaic was set in front of a house in Pompeii, an ancient Roman city. The words at the bottom of the mosaic tell visitors to "beware of dog."

TAKING NOTES

Reading Skill: Summarizing

When you summarize, you supply only main ideas and the most important details. Record the main ideas and important details in each section of Lesson 4 in a diagram like the one below.

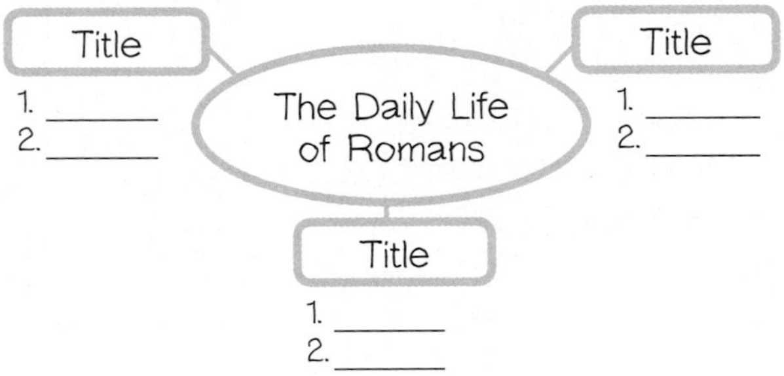

Skillbuilder Handbook, page R3

Words to Know

Understanding the following words will help you read this lesson:

cause a motive or reason for acting (page 453)
*Roman fathers only punished members of their families when they had good **cause**.*

private school a school that charges students for admission (page 454)
*The students' parents did not have enough money to send them to **private school**.*

shrine a place where sacred religious objects are kept (page 454)
*Before leaving, she paused at her household **shrine** and said a prayer.*

unrest disturbances or turmoil (page 456)
*The city's leaders tried to keep the population contented in order to avoid **unrest**.*

TERMS & NAMES
aqueduct
Colosseum
gladiator

The Daily Life of Romans

Build on What You Know Remember that, in the earliest days of Rome, extended families lived and worked on small farms. Family members knew what was expected of them. During the Roman Empire, family roles became more structured—and so did roles in society.

Family and Society

1 **ESSENTIAL QUESTION** How were the family and society organized?

The head of the Roman family was the father. He owned all the property and had control over other members of the household. The father's power was limited, however, by public opinion and custom. Roman society disapproved of a father punishing his family without good cause.

Women Women in a Roman family enjoyed more freedom than women in Greece. Like women in most parts of the world, Roman women were expected to run the household and take care of the children. But they also could inherit property, and they ran the family business when their husbands were away. Still, Roman women had little power outside the home and could not vote.

Emperor's Villa While most Romans lived in poor conditions, the emperors lived in luxury. A large number of slaves took care of this emperor's villa. ▼

Children Most parents gave their children some education at home. Boys from wealthy families were often sent to private schools, while daughters stayed at home and learned household skills. Girls usually married by age 14, while boys married later.

▲ **Upper-Class Woman** The young woman in this wall painting wears the clothes and hairstyle of a wealthy Roman citizen. The book and pen she holds are also signs of her class and education.

Social Classes Over time, Roman social classes changed. The old division between patricians and plebeians evolved into upper and lower classes. Patricians and some wealthy plebeians became part of the upper class. A new middle class also developed. Prosperous business leaders and officials belonged to this middle class. Farmers formed one of the lower classes.

Slaves made up the lowest—and largest—class in society. Up to one-third of the population were slaves. Some were prisoners of war. Others became slaves because their parents were slaves. Slaves were found throughout Roman society. They worked in low-level clerical positions. However, slaves also performed all jobs requiring physical labor. They worked in mines, on large estates, and as servants. Many suffered cruel treatment. Slave revolts were common, but none of them succeeded. Thousands of slaves died in these revolts.

REVIEW What were the roles in a typical Roman family?

Roman Beliefs

2 ESSENTIAL QUESTION What religious beliefs did the Romans hold?

Religious beliefs bound Roman society together. From the earliest times, the Romans worshiped hundreds of spirits. They believed that these spirits lived in everything around them, including rivers, woods, and fields. Roman families also believed that household gods protected them. They set up shrines in their homes to honor these spirits.

Religious Influences Later, Roman beliefs were influenced by other cultures. The Etruscans and Greeks particularly affected Roman religion. The Romans adopted the Etruscan idea of gods in human form. They also adopted Etruscan rituals designed to predict the future. The Romans believed these rituals could reveal whether a specific action, such as a battle, would have a good result.

The Romans borrowed many of their gods from the Greeks. For instance, the Roman god Jupiter, father of the gods, had many of the characteristics of the Greek god Zeus. Apollo, the Greek god of music and poetry, became a key Roman god of the same name. The chart below lists some of the gods that Rome borrowed from Greece.

Religion and Public Life As in ancient Egypt, religion and government were linked in Rome. Priests were government officials, and the emperor was the head of the church. Roman gods were also symbols of the state. Romans were expected to honor these gods in public ceremonies.

Over time, even the emperor himself became a god. At first, the Romans only worshiped emperors after death. But eventually they honored living rulers as gods. Loyalty to the emperor became the same as loyalty to the gods.

REVIEW What influences helped form Roman religion?

Greek and Roman Gods

Description	Greek	Roman
Supreme god	Zeus	Jupiter
Supreme goddess	Hera (wife of Zeus)	Juno (wife of Jupiter)
God of the sea	Poseidon	Neptune
God of music and poetry	Apollo	Apollo
Goddess of love and beauty	Aphrodite	Venus
God of war	Ares	Mars

SKILLBUILDER
INTERPRETING VISUALS
Why do you think the Romans were so deeply influenced by Greek religion?

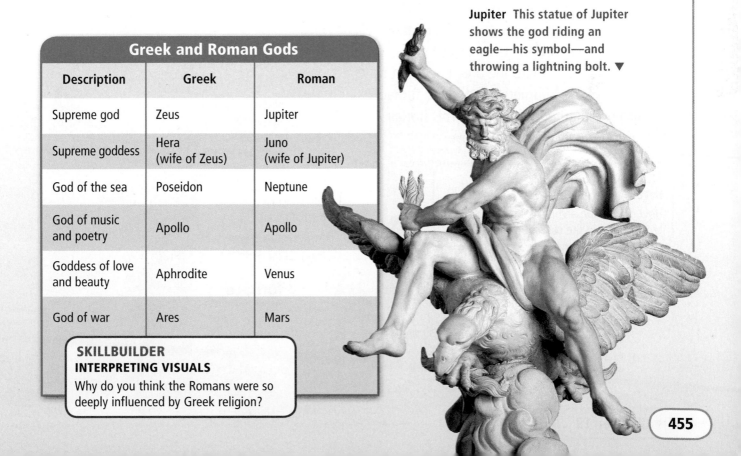

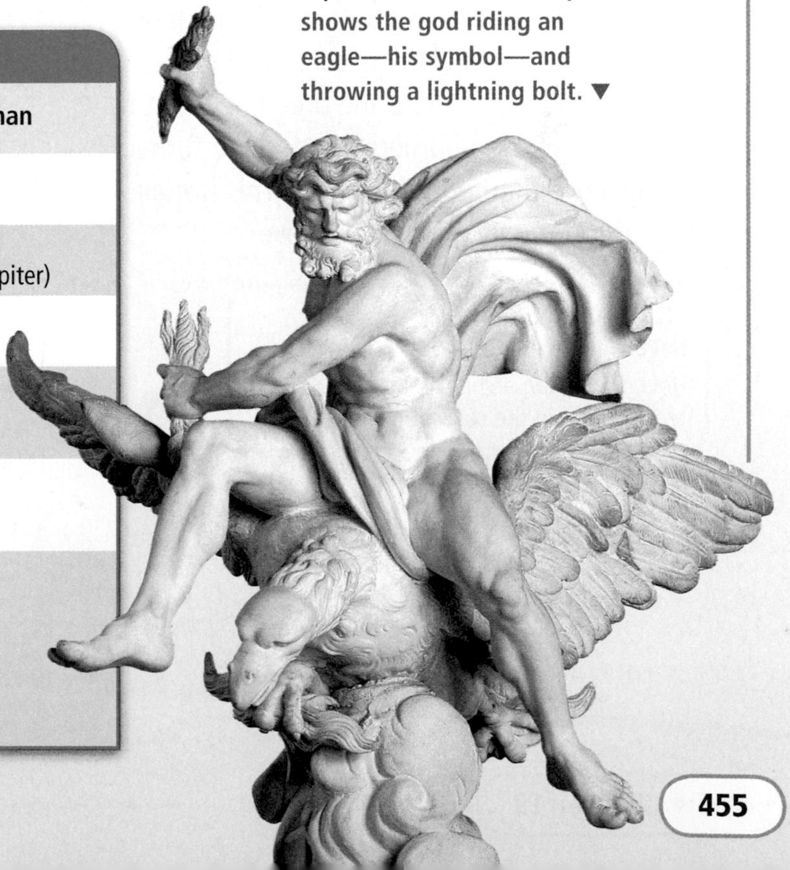

Jupiter This statue of Jupiter shows the god riding an eagle—his symbol—and throwing a lightning bolt. ▼

Life in Roman Cities

3 ESSENTIAL QUESTION What was life like in Roman cities?

At the height of the Roman Empire, the city of Rome had nearly 1 million people. Other Roman cities, such as Alexandria in Egypt, were also large. However, Rome was the center of the empire. People from all over the empire moved to Rome. This mix of people produced a lively blend of ideas and customs.

The Crowded City The number of people also created some problems. Rome's city center was crowded, dirty, and noisy. Much of the city's population was unemployed and poor. These people lived in large, rundown apartment buildings. They had small rooms with no running water or toilets. They often dropped their trash out the windows, sometimes injuring people walking in the streets below. Fire was also a constant danger. These problems were common in other Roman cities as well.

Poor Romans also had little to eat. Typical foods were bread, olives, and fruit. But the government provided free grain to keep people happy and avoid public unrest.

Architecture of the Roman Public Bath

Archaeologists have discovered that the typical Roman public bath was built on a foundation of pillars. Roman architects constructed a furnace that opened into the area beneath the bath. When slaves burned wood in the furnace, hot air flowed around the pillars. This hot air heated the rooms and water above.

SKILLBUILDER
INTERPRETING VISUALS
How did Roman architects make sure the temperature in the cold room stayed low?

Heat from the furnace was channeled beneath the bath house.
furnace

By contrast, wealthy Romans enjoyed a life of luxury. They lived in large, comfortable homes in the countryside. They spent their time going to the theater and enjoying themselves. They also held fancy dinner parties. These meals featured fine foods like dates, oysters, and ham. They also included unusual dishes like salted jellyfish, roast parrot, and boiled flamingo tongue.

Structures of City Life The Romans came up with a number of practical solutions to some of their urban problems. They built sewer and plumbing systems to improve sanitation. They also built **aqueducts** (AK•wih•DUHKTS) to carry fresh water from springs, streams, and lakes into towns. The water traveled through a system of channels and pipes. Most of these were underground. However, some were supported on high arched bridges. Many of these aqueduct bridges survive and are still used today.

Public baths were another important part of city life. Most towns and even most Roman forts had public bathhouses. Romans of all classes visited the baths to bathe and socialize. You can learn more about the architecture and technology of a typical Roman public bathhouse in the feature below.

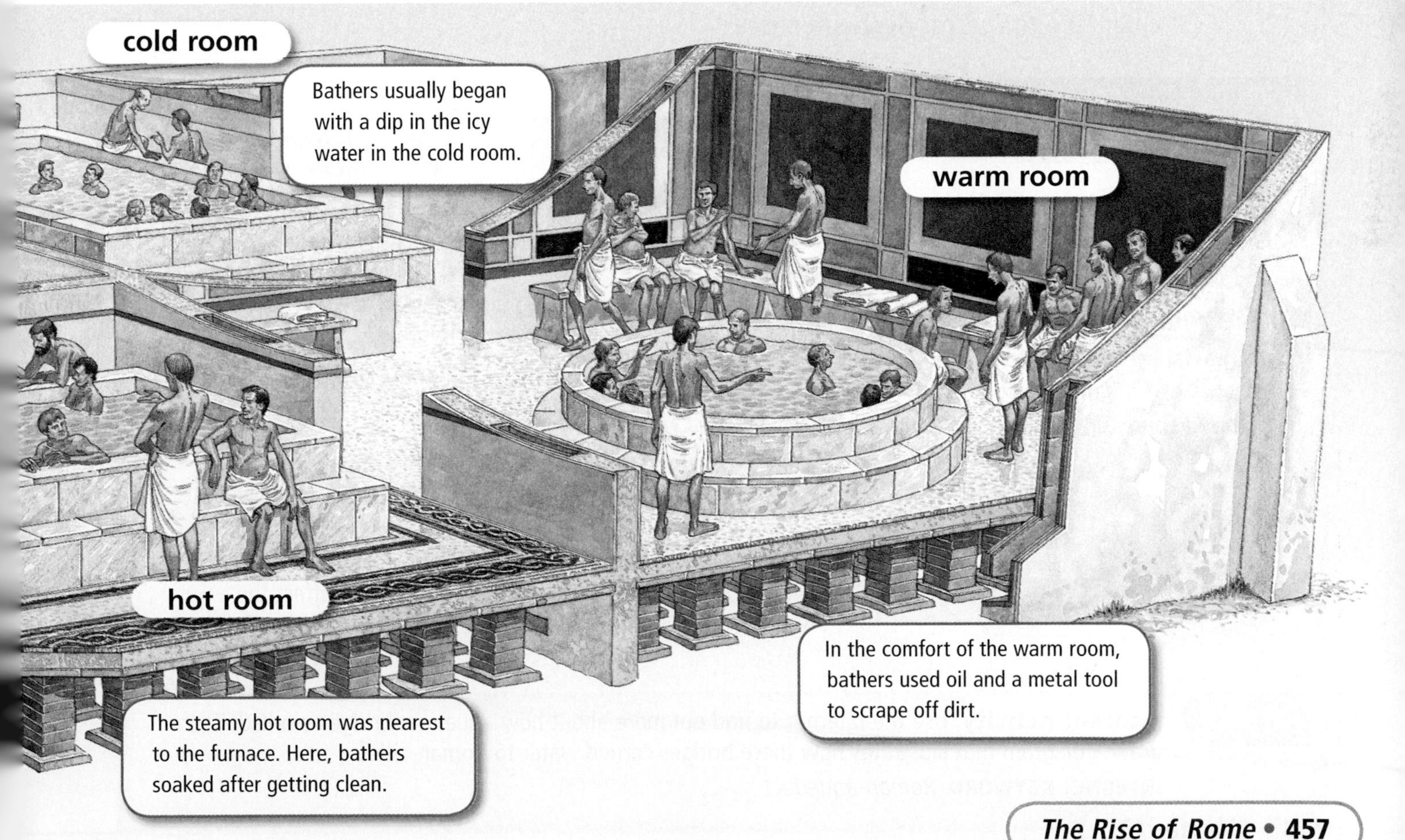

cold room
Bathers usually began with a dip in the icy water in the cold room.
warm room
hot room
In the comfort of the warm room, bathers used oil and a metal tool to scrape off dirt.
The steamy hot room was nearest to the furnace. Here, bathers soaked after getting clean.

Roman Sports To distract Romans from the problems of city life, the government provided entertainment at large public arenas. One of these was the Circus Maximus (MAK•suh•muhs), a large oval stadium used for chariot races. As you learned on pages 424–425, another famous arena was the **Colosseum**. There, Romans could watch **gladiators**, or trained warriors, fight to the death. The spectacles they watched combined bravery and violence, honor and cruelty.

Vocabulary Strategy

Colosseum comes from the Latin **root word** *colossus*, meaning "huge statue." The Colosseum was, in fact, named for a huge statue of an emperor that once stood beside the arena.

REVIEW How did the Roman government try to solve some of the problems of city life?

Lesson Summary

- Family life and social classes were important in ancient Rome.
- Romans worshiped many gods both privately at home and in public ceremonies.
- Roman city life was challenging, but the government tried to ease some of its problems.

Why It Matters Now . . .

Ancient Rome was a mixture of different cultures and beliefs, just like many modern societies.

4 Lesson Review

Homework Helper
ClassZone.com

Terms & Names

1. Explain the importance of

aqueduct Colosseum gladiator

Using Your Notes

Summarizing Use your completed diagram to answer the following question:

2. What architectural innovations improved Roman city life?

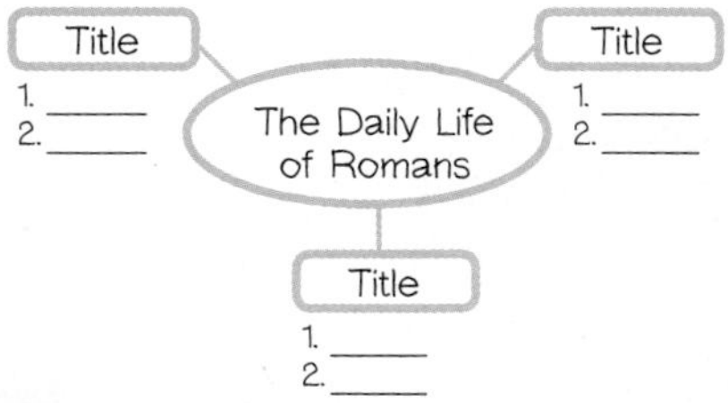

Main Ideas

3. Who belonged to the main social classes during the time of the Roman Empire?

4. What was the relationship of religion to government in ancient Rome?

5. What was the city of Rome like?

Critical Thinking

6. Forming and Supporting Opinions How would worshiping the emperor while he lived affect the Romans' view of their ruler?

7. Understanding Continuity and Change How did Rome's urban problems affect the development of cities in later civilizations?

Activity

Internet Activity Use the Internet to find out more about how aqueduct bridges worked. Then draw a diagram that illustrates how these bridges carried water to Roman cities.

INTERNET KEYWORD *Roman aqueduct*

Activity Extend Lesson 4

Make a Mosaic

Goal: To create a mosaic, a picture made of small colored tiles, that celebrates the legacy of Roman art

Materials & Supplies
- paper and pencil
- poster board
- paint and paintbrush
- scissors
- glue or paste

Prepare

1. Study the mosaic on page 452.
2. Look at Roman mosaics in books on ancient Rome.

Do the Activity

1. Draw a sketch of your design on a piece of paper. You might draw a simple geometric design or an animal or a flower.
2. Copy the design onto a piece of poster board.
3. Paint several pieces of paper in different colors. After the paint dries, cut the paper into small pieces. These will be your mosaic tiles.
4. Glue your tiles onto the design on your poster board. Use your pencil sketch as a guide. Let your mosaic dry.

Follow-Up

1. Do you think that Roman artists who created mosaics also had to be skilled mathematicians? Explain.
2. What modern mosaics have you seen? How do these compare with the one you made?

Extension

Making Inferences What do the mosaics you have seen in this lesson and in books on ancient Rome suggest about how Romans valued beauty?

Chapter 13 Review

VISUAL SUMMARY

The Rise of Rome

Geography
- Hills and the Tiber River helped protect Rome from enemies.
- Rome's location in Italy made it easier to reach and conquer other lands.

Culture
- Roman family life and society were highly structured.
- Romans built aqueducts and sanitation systems to ease the problems of city life.

Government
- The Roman Republic had a government divided into three parts.
- Roman government influenced modern republics.

Economics
- A vigorous trade developed in the Roman Empire.
- A common currency united the empire.

Belief Systems
- Romans worshiped many gods.
- Roman religion was linked with government.

TERMS & NAMES

Explain why the words in each set below are linked with each other.

1. **patrician** and **plebeian**
2. **Senate** and **consul**
3. **Julius Caesar** and **Augustus**
4. **gladiator** and **Colosseum**

MAIN IDEAS

The Geography of Ancient Rome (pages 430–435)

5. Describe the geography of Rome.
6. How did hard work and discipline help Roman civilization grow?

The Roman Republic (pages 436–441)

7. What powers did the executive branch have in the Roman Republic?
8. Why did the gap between patricians and plebeians widen with Rome's expansion?

Rome Becomes an Empire (pages 442–451)

9. What did Julius Caesar accomplish as ruler of the Roman Republic?
10. How did Augustus encourage the expansion of the Roman Empire?

The Daily Life of Romans (pages 452–459)

11. How did life differ for the rich and poor in Roman cities?
12. What structures in Roman cities have influenced modern structures?

CRITICAL THINKING Big Ideas: Economics

13. **EXPLAINING HISTORICAL PATTERNS** How did the advantages gained by some early farmers affect Rome's development?
14. **ANALYZING ECONOMIC AND POLITICAL ISSUES** How did class divisions bring about the end of the Roman Republic?
15. **IDENTIFYING ISSUES AND PROBLEMS** What steps did the empire take to avoid another civil war between rich and poor?

ALTERNATIVE ASSESSMENT

1. **WRITING ACTIVITY** Imagine that you are a plebeian in the Roman Empire. Write a journal entry about a day in your life. Describe where and how you live. Tell what you see and do on an ordinary day.

2. **INTERDISCIPLINARY ACTIVITY—CIVICS** Create a poster in which you use photographs and drawings to compare the Roman Republic with the U.S. republic.

3. **STARTING WITH A STORY** Starting with a Story. Review the speech you wrote trying to persuade other senators to let Julius Caesar live. Now that you have read the chapter, decide whether you think Caesar's death was good for Rome. Write a paragraph explaining and supporting your opinion.

Technology Activity

4. **RECORDING A NEWS REPORT** Work with a group of classmates to prepare a radio news report on the opening of the Colosseum. Use information from the chapter as the basis for your report. Do further research on the Internet, if necessary. Tape the news report and play it for your class.
   - Provide background information on the construction and opening of the Colosseum.
   - Interview gladiators and ordinary citizens to get their opinions of the arena and its entertainment.
   - Discuss what impact you think the Colosseum will have on public entertainment in the future.

Research Links
ClassZone.com

Interpreting Visuals Use the sculpture below, which shows Roman soldiers fighting from on top of their fort, to answer the questions.

1. What advantages do the Roman soldiers appear to have in this battle?

A. They are fighting on the ground.
B. They are fighting with bows and arrows.
C. They are fighting more fiercely.
D. They are fighting from inside their fort.

2. Which sentence best describes the Roman soldiers?

A. They all look frightened.
B. They all are on horseback.
C. They all carry shields and wear helmets.
D. They are not ready for battle.

Test Practice
ClassZone.com

Additional Test Practice, pp. S1–S33

Chapter 14 The Birth of Christianity

Before You Read: Previewing Key Concepts

The Big Idea below is a general historical idea that will be applied to the Mediterranean region in this chapter. Rewrite this idea as a question that can be answered as you read. Here is an example of a question:

How did Christian beliefs challenge Rome?

Watch for the answer(s) to your question as you read the chapter.

Big Ideas About the Birth of Christianity

Government New ideas and beliefs can challenge a government's authority, leading to change.

The Romans were in general tolerant of the religious beliefs of people they ruled. However, they did expect the people to worship the emperor and to allow temples to be built to Roman gods. Jews and Christians were unwilling to do either. This unwillingness caused conflict with Rome.

Integrated Technology

eEdition
- Interactive Maps
- Interactive Visuals
- Starting with a Story

INTERNET RESOURCES

Go to **ClassZone.com** for
- WebQuest
- Homework Helper
- Research Links
- Internet Activities
- Quizzes
- Maps
- Test Practice
- Current Events

MEDITERRANEAN REGION

26–29 Jesus conducts his public ministry.

70 Romans storm Jerusalem and destroy the Temple complex.

120 Roman Empire reaches its height under Hadrian.

A.D. 25 — 75 — 125

WORLD

65 Buddhism takes root in China.

100 Moche culture arises in South America.

(deer-head figure, Peru) ▶

Spread of Christianity in the Roman Empire, to A.D. 600

INTERACTIVE

180
Reign of Emperor Marcus Aurelius ends.

220
China's Han Dynasty falls.
(bronze horse, Han Dynasty) ▶

300
Aksum kingdom emerges in Africa.

313
Emperor Constantine ends persecution of Christians.
◀ (bust of Constantine)

175 | 225 | 275 | A.D. 325

Starting with a **Story**

The Burning of Rome

Background: Fire! In A.D. 64, wind swept flames across the Circus Maximus, Rome's huge racing arena. Afterward, much of the city lay in ruins. A nasty rumor about Rome's emperor, Nero, began to spread almost as fast as the fire had. People whispered that the unpopular emperor had set the fire so that he could rebuild Rome, including a grand new palace. The emperor said that the unpopular Christians had started the fire. But not all Romans blamed the Christians, as you will read.

Roman coin depicting Nero ▶

Starting with a Story
eEdition

The baker is opening his shop near Rome's Christian neighborhood. Every morning, Christians come to buy bread at his bakery. Some Romans hate the Christians because they keep to themselves and refuse to worship the Roman gods. It's true that they don't go to the theater and the races and their men don't join the army. They're also poor, and they wear old clothes. But they're good neighbors and good customers. The Christians the baker knows would never start a fire.

The baker was lucky. His shop still smells smoky, but at least it didn't burn in the fire. As he sets things back in order, he feels sad that his Christian customers suffered so terribly. Because they were unpopular, they were easy for the emperor to blame. To stop people from saying that he set the fire, Nero told everyone it was the fault of the Christians.

The baker has heard that hundreds of Christians who survived the fire died terrible deaths afterward. At Nero's order, many were burned, while others were hanged on crosses or ripped apart by dogs. Nero conducted these executions right in his gardens. The public was invited, but the baker was too disgusted to go.

It's difficult for the baker to understand the Christians' religion. Even so, he doesn't believe any group should suffer such an awful punishment. He wonders whether the Christians who survived will be too afraid to come back to buy his bread.

What do you think will happen to the Christians in Rome?

Reading & Writing

1. **READING: Character** An important person in a story is a main character. Think about the character of Nero in this story. With a partner, discuss the character of the emperor Nero as revealed in his actions. Then make a list of words to describe the emperor.

2. **WRITING: Persuasion** Imagine that you have observed Nero's executions of Christians. You know that they didn't set the fire. You want to persuade others to join a revolt against the cruel emperor. Think about the consequences of a revolt. Then make a poster to persuade others to support your cause.

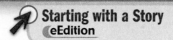

Lesson 1

MAIN IDEAS

1. **Belief Systems** Christianity built upon the Jewish belief in one God and the concept of a Messiah.
2. **Belief Systems** The disciples of Jesus came to believe that he was the Messiah.
3. **Belief Systems** According to the Gospels, Jesus was executed but rose from the dead. Christians believe that this makes freedom from sin and death possible for everyone.

TAKING NOTES

Reading Skill: Explaining Sequence

To sequence events is to put them in an order based on when they happened. As you read Lesson 1, make notes of things that happened in the life of Jesus. Create a time line like this one to sequence the events.

c. 4 B.C. — c. A.D. 29

Skillbuilder Handbook, page R15

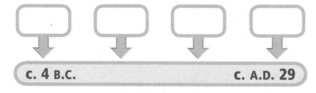

▲ **Cross** The cross is a symbol of Christianity. Some crosses are simple objects made of wood. Some are made of gold and adorned with jewels, like the one shown above.

Words to Know

Understanding the following words will help you read this lesson:

moral the lesson taught by a story (page 468)

*The **moral** of Jesus' story about the Good Samaritan is the importance of love.*

divine of, from, or like God (page 470)

*Some Jews began to believe that Jesus was more than human, possibly even **divine**.*

afterlife an existence or life thought to follow death (page 470)

*Christians believe that beyond death there is an **afterlife**.*

The Origins of Christianity

TERMS & NAMES
Jesus
Gospel
disciple
parable
crucifixion
resurrection

Build on What You Know Religion plays an important role in many people's lives, perhaps your own as well as others'. A new religion called Christianity grew out of Jewish beliefs and the ideas of a Jewish teacher named **Jesus**.

Christianity's Jewish Roots

1 ESSENTIAL QUESTION How did Christianity build on Jewish beliefs about the future?

In 63 B.C., the Romans conquered the Jewish kingdom of Judah, also called Judea. Although the Jews had their own kings, these Jewish rulers had to be approved by Rome.

During their history, the Jews had frequently been treated badly. Many wanted to be delivered from oppression and from foreign rulers. Some Jewish sacred writings promised a Messiah. Some people believed that this would be an earthly ruler sent by God. However, there were many different Jewish opinions about what to expect from a Messiah. Some believed that this ruler would be descended from King David, the ruler of Israel in the 900s B.C. Some Jews believed the Messiah would free them.

REVIEW What did some Jews believe the Messiah would do?

Connect to Today

Bethlehem This photograph shows the Church of the Nativity *(below left)* in Bethlehem, supposedly built upon the site of Jesus' birth. The building to the right is a monastery. ▼

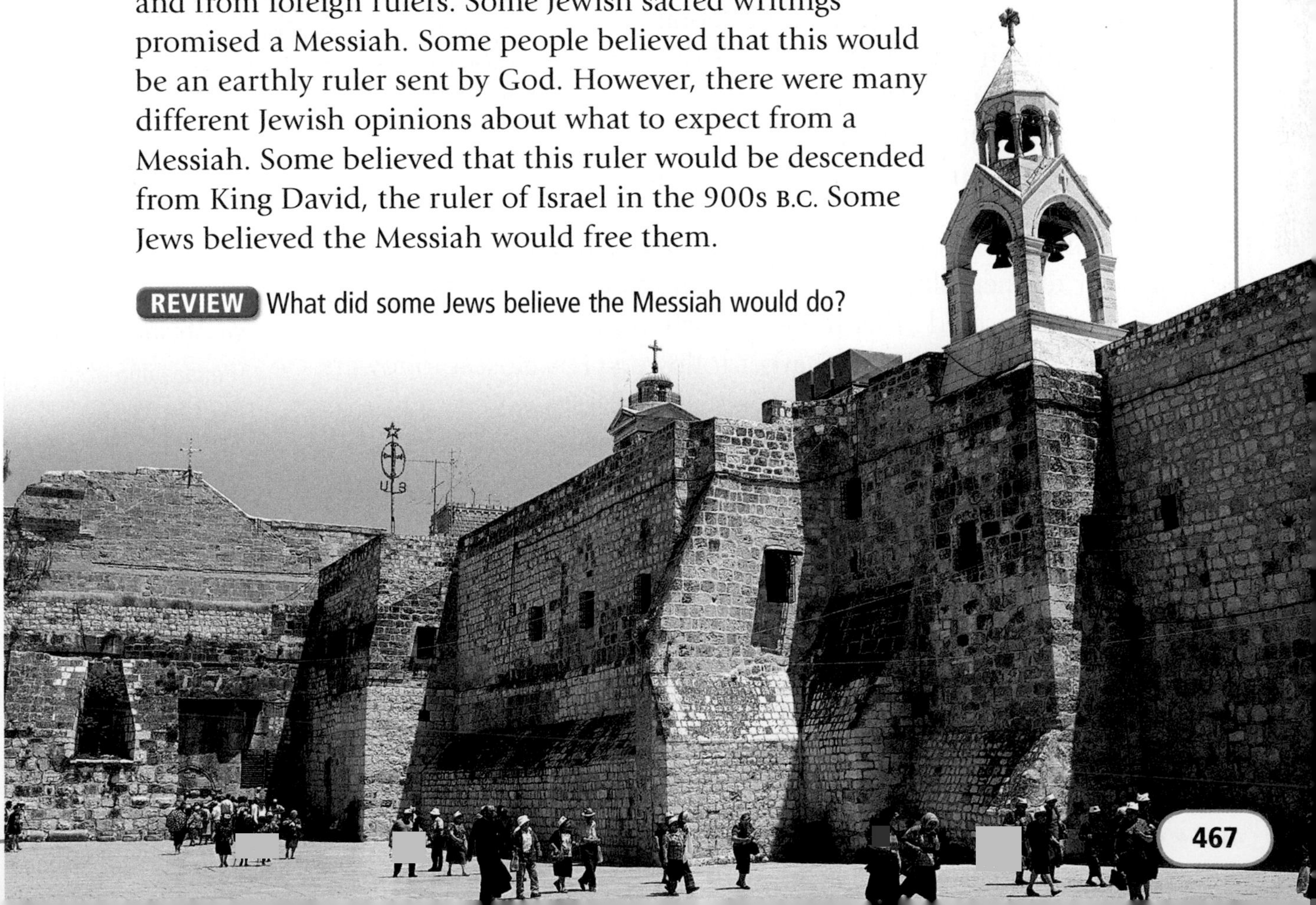

The Life of Jesus

2 ESSENTIAL QUESTION Who did the disciples of Jesus believe he was?

As a Jew born in the Roman province of Judea, Jesus followed many of the teachings of Judaism. However, he also taught certain ideas and practices that differed from what others were teaching.

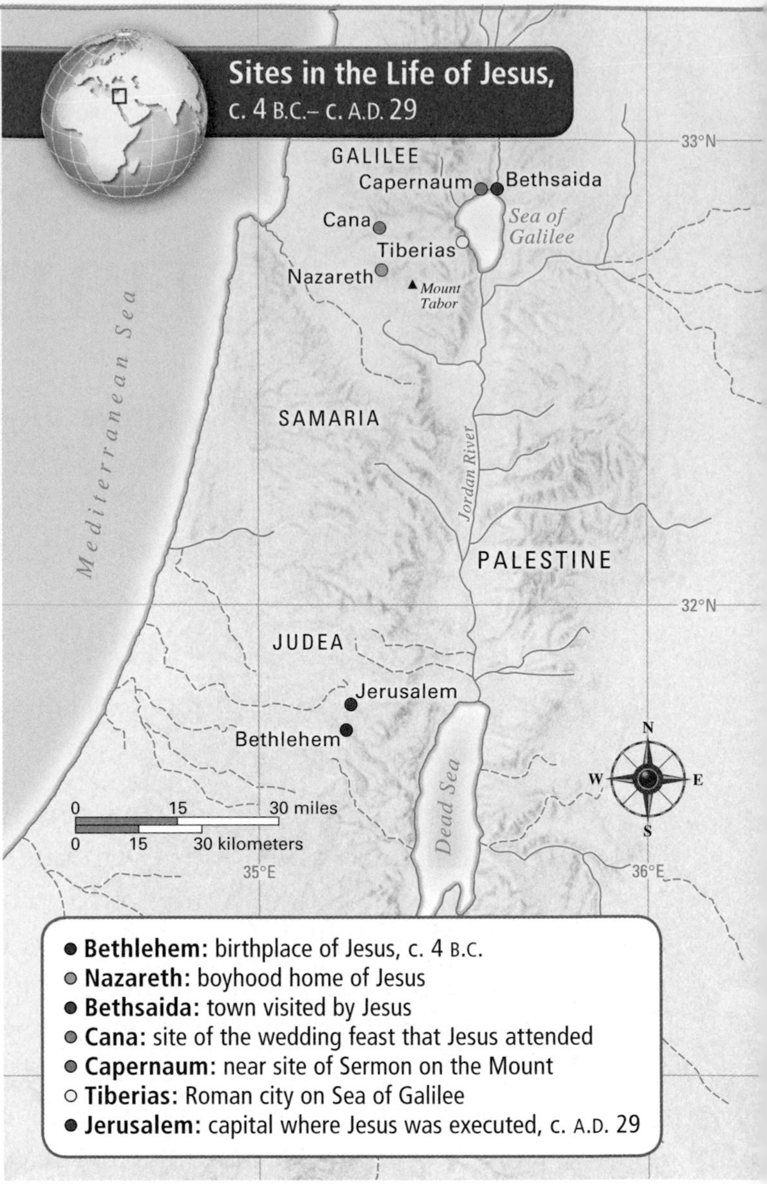

Birth and Early Life We know about Jesus from four accounts called the **Gospels**, written after his death by Matthew, Mark, Luke, and John. The Gospels and other writings make up the New Testament.

According to the Gospels, Jesus was born in Bethlehem and grew up in Nazareth. Christians would later celebrate his birth on the holiday of Christmas. In the Gospel account, Jesus was raised by Mary and by Joseph, a carpenter.

Jesus' Followers As a young adult, Jesus became a traveling teacher. Biblical accounts say he cured the sick and lame and performed other miracles, such as turning water to wine.

Jesus began to gather followers. His closest followers were called **disciples**. Jesus' 12 disciples were Peter, Andrew, James, John, Philip, Bartholomew, Thomas, Matthew, James (son of Alphaeus), Simon, Thaddaeus, and Judas Iscariot.

Vocabulary Strategy

The meaning of the word *disciple* can be figured out by using **context clues.** The rest of the sentence tells you that disciples are close followers. *Disciple* comes from a Latin word meaning "student" or "pupil."

The Teachings of Jesus Jesus preached justice, compassion, and the coming of God's kingdom. He often delivered these messages in the form of **parables**, or stories with morals. Three of Jesus' best-known parables are those of the Good Samaritan, the Prodigal Son, and the Lost Sheep. (See Literature Connection, pages 472–475.)

Jesus' most famous teachings were given in the Sermon on the Mount. The sermon opens with the Beatitudes (bee•AT•ih•TOODZ), or blessings. In this sermon, Jesus encouraged people not only to obey the law but also to change their hearts. People shouldn't simply refrain from killing; they should also love and pray for their enemies. Jesus encouraged his followers to live simply and humbly.

Despite his teachings, Jesus angered some people who heard him preach. For example, Jesus forgave people who had broken religious laws, but many Jewish leaders thought only God could grant this kind of forgiveness. Jesus also associated with sinners, whom religious leaders treated as outcasts. Most shocking was the claim of some of Jesus' followers that he was the Messiah they had long been waiting for.

REVIEW What form did Jesus' teachings often take?

Primary Source

Background: One of Jesus' most famous sermons is called the Sermon on the Mount. In this speech, he made a number of memorable statements that have become known as the Beatitudes. Some of them are at right. Below is the Sermon on the Mount as pictured in a French manuscript of the 1200s.

from *the Beatitudes*

- Blessed are the poor in spirit, for theirs is the kingdom of heaven.
- Blessed are those who mourn, for they shall be comforted.
- Blessed are the meek, for they shall inherit the earth.
- Blessed are those who hunger and thirst for righteousness, for they shall be satisfied.
- Blessed are the merciful, for they shall obtain mercy.
- Blessed are the pure in heart, for they shall see God.
- Blessed are the peacemakers, for they shall be called sons of God.

Matthew 5:3–9

DOCUMENT–BASED QUESTION
What do these sayings of Jesus suggest about his view of the oppressed? Does he seem to identify with the rich and powerful or the poor and weak?

The Death of Jesus

3 **ESSENTIAL QUESTION** What belief about Jesus did Christians think made an afterlife possible?

The claim that Jesus was the Messiah, or Jewish liberator and ruler, threatened the Romans because it questioned their political power and authority. The claim also shocked many Jewish leaders.

Arrest and Trial According to three of the Gospels, Jesus' followers hailed him as king when he journeyed to Jerusalem to celebrate the Jewish holy day of Passover. In that city's holy Temple, Jesus publicly criticized how the Temple was being run. Jesus was arrested and turned over to the Romans for punishment.

▲ **Tomb** This burial chamber dating from the time of Jesus was sealed with a round stone.

The Story of the Resurrection The Roman governor, Pontius Pilate, ordered Jesus to be executed by **crucifixion**, or hanging on a cross until he suffocated. After Jesus died, a huge stone was placed in front of the tomb where he was buried.

On the third day after his execution, according to the Gospels, some of his followers reported that the stone had moved and the tomb lay empty. Others said they had seen Jesus and had even walked and talked with him.

These accounts of Jesus' **resurrection**, or return to life, proved to many of his followers that he was divine. They came to believe that Jesus had been willing to give up his own life for the sake of God's kingdom. Through his death and resurrection, God was bringing new life into the world. This was a world in which sin would no longer prevail and even death would be defeated. Jesus' followers said anyone who believed this would share in the life of God.

According to Christians, Jesus' crucifixion took place on a Friday, and his resurrection on a Sunday. The Christian holidays Good Friday and Easter Sunday, which recall these two events, have been celebrated ever since.

REVIEW What event made Jesus' followers believe their leader was divine?

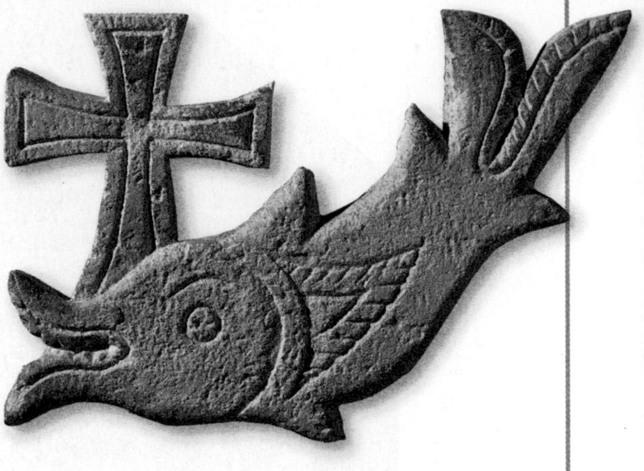

▲ **Relief Sculpture** The fish is a Christian symbol dating from ancient times. This fourth-century fish with a cross is from a Christian cemetery in Egypt.

Lesson Summary

- Some Jews believed a Messiah would give them political power and religious freedom.
- Jesus' teachings stressed compassion, justice, and the coming of God's kingdom.
- Accounts of Jesus' resurrection made some people believe Jesus was divine.

Why It Matters Now . . .

Jesus and his earliest followers were Jewish. Eventually, however, more and more non-Jews converted to Christianity. Today about a third of the people in the world are Christians.

1 Lesson Review

Homework Helper
ClassZone.com

Terms & Names

1. Explain the importance of

Jesus	disciple	crucifixion
Gospel	parable	resurrection

Using Your Notes

Explaining Sequence Use your completed graphic to answer the following question:

2. What actions of Jesus in Jerusalem preceded his arrest?

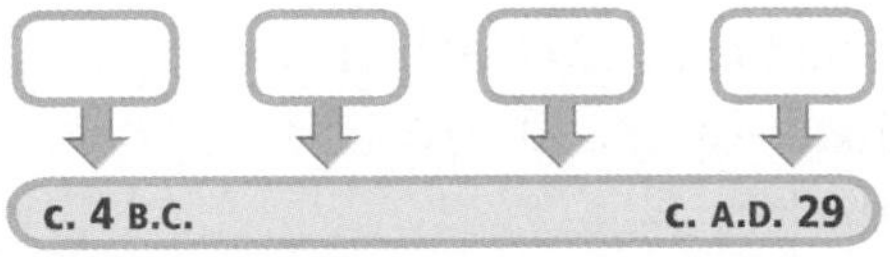

Main Ideas

3. What great power ruled over Judea in the time of Jesus? (See map on page 463.)

4. How do we know about Jesus' life and about his teachings?

5. What did accounts of Jesus' resurrection prove to his followers?

Critical Thinking

6. Determining Historical Context What historical conditions made some Jews in Judea likely to accept Jesus as their Messiah?

7. Drawing Conclusions Why might Jesus have used parables to deliver his message?

Activity

Writing a Parable Think of an important lesson you would like to teach. Then write a brief story to teach your lesson. Read your parable aloud to your class.

Two Parables of Jesus

Background: Jesus was a teacher. He often taught by telling parables, or stories that teach lessons. His teachings were based upon ideas from the Jewish tradition. Two of his most famous parables are those of the Good Samaritan and the Prodigal Son. The latter deals with God's call for the lost soul to repent. The version of the Prodigal Son is taken from *Everlasting Stories* by Lois Rock. (See page R58 in the Primary Source Handbook for the Parable of the Lost Sheep.)

The Good Samaritan

The scene Jesus uses for his parable is the rocky road from Jerusalem to Jericho. This trade route was dangerous and narrow, with sudden sharp curves that made it a favorite place for thieves. Also, the road dropped more than 3,400 feet in elevation in 17 miles. Jerusalem is 2,300 feet above sea level. Jericho is near the Dead Sea, which is 1,300 feet below sea level and the lowest place on Earth.

One day, as Jesus was talking with his disciples, a man stood up and approached him respectfully. "Teacher, I have a burning question to ask," he said. "What must I do to have everlasting life?

"What do the scriptures say?" Jesus asked him in return. "What do you think they mean?"

The man was quick to reply: "'Love the Lord your God with all your heart, and with all your soul, and with all your strength, and with all your mind' and, 'Love your neighbor as you love yourself.'"

"That's right," said Jesus. "Do this and you will live."

The man wanted to know more, so he asked Jesus, "And who is my neighbor?"

Jesus began a parable, one of the stories he was famous for when sharing his teachings. "Once there was a man on his way from Jerusalem to Jericho. Bandits attacked him. They beat him up, took his valuables, and left him there half dead."

Those listening to the parable thought what a fool the man must have been to travel alone on that dangerous road. Beaten, robbed of all he had. The poor man.

Jesus went on, "And by chance a man was going down that road. He saw the injured fellow, but walked by on the other side of the road."

"Next," said Jesus, "came another traveler. This person went over to look, then hurried away."

His listeners knew what was coming. There would be at least one more traveler—good parables needed someone who was different from the rest.

"A Samaritan who was traveling passed that way, . . ." A few in the crowd caught their breath. A stranger all the way from Samaria wouldn't be expected to help.

"He saw the man and had pity on him. He cleaned and bandaged his wounds, and then lifted him onto his own donkey. They went

The Good Samaritan The Samaritan helps the wounded traveler in this detail of a stained glass window. ▼

together down the steep road until they came to an inn. That night, the Samaritan cared for him, and when he left the next morning, he paid the innkeeper two days' wages. 'Take care of him,' he said to the innkeeper, 'and whatever more I owe you, I will pay on my way back.'"

Jesus asked, "What do you think? Which of the three was a neighbor to the man attacked by robbers?"

"The one who treated him kindly," replied the questioner.

Jesus said, "Go and do the same."

REVIEW Who treated the crime victim best?

The Prodigal Son

Jesus told this story:

"There was once a man who had two sons. They worked together on the land and made a good living. As he grew up, the younger son began to dream of what he would do if he had his father's riches, and then he made a plan.

"'Father,' he announced one day, 'when you die, I will inherit some of your wealth. I want to have it now, while I am young.'

"'My dear son, I fear you are making a mistake,' pleaded the father. But it was no use. Sorrowfully, his father divided his property between his two sons.

"Within days, the son sold it and set off for a country far away. There he found much on which to spend his money, with extravagant lodgings and stylish clothes and rich food. Friends gathered around him, eager to come to his parties. He was delighted. But his money soon dwindled away.

"Then, out of nowhere, famine struck the land and the price of everything soared. With nothing left to sell, the young man became desperate.

"He found himself a job . . . but it was of the very worst kind, looking after pigs. He carried a basketful of bean pods to the field they had

The Prodigal Son The father welcomes his returning son in this detail of a stained glass window. ▼

rooted into dust and tipped the food on the ground in front of them. I wish I could eat bean pods, he thought, as he watched them munching. No one gives me anything.

"He began to think of the family farm and the servants who had looked after the flocks. 'They always had more than enough to eat,' he remembered. Then he lifted his head. 'I shall go back to my father,' he said, 'and admit that I have done wrong.'

"So he made the long journey home. But while he was still a long way off, his father saw him. He ran to greet him and kissed him. The son hung his head. 'Father, I have sinned against God and against you. I am no longer fit to be called your son. Treat me as one of your hired workers.'

"His father simply waved his hand. 'Hurry!' he called to the servants. 'Bring a robe for my son, a ring for his finger, and shoes for his feet. Then let us prepare a feast.'

"So it was done. The party began, and the elder son returned from the fields to hear music and dancing. 'What's going on?' he asked a servant.

"'Your brother has come back,' he was told. 'Your father has prepared a feast to celebrate.'

"At that, the elder brother grew so angry he would not even go into the house. His father came out to welcome him in.

"'I have worked for you all these years and yet you have done nothing for me!' the son complained.

"The father replied, 'You are always here with me, and everything I have is yours. But we had to celebrate and be happy—your brother was dead, but now he is alive; he was lost, but now he has been found.'"

Primary Source Handbook

See the excerpt from the New Testament: Parable of the Lost Sheep, page R58.

REVIEW Why was the older brother angry?

Reading & Writing

1. **READING: Theme** In which of these parables does the theme of forgiveness seem important?
2. **WRITING: Narration** Imagine that you are the elder son in the Parable of the Prodigal Son. Write a narrative of your brother's return, in which you explain your point of view.

Lesson 2

MAIN IDEAS

1. **Belief Systems** The disciples of Jesus spread his teachings and tried to convince others to believe in him.
2. **Belief Systems** According to the Christian scriptures, after having a vision of Jesus, Paul became a leader of the Christian movement.
3. **Geography** Paul traveled to many of the great cities of the Roman Empire, seeking to convert people to Christianity.

TAKING NOTES

Reading Skill: Finding Main Ideas

Finding the main idea–the most important point–of a passage will increase your understanding of the material. This lesson discusses the changes in the early Christian Church. Record details about this main idea in a web diagram.

Skillbuilder Handbook, page R2

▲ **Communion Cup** This Russian chalice of gold and precious stones was made in 1598.

Words to Know

Understanding the following words will help you read this lesson:

charity the giving of money or help to people who are poor (page 477)

Many Jews and Christians feel that their religions call on them to practice ***charity.***

debate a discussion of opposing opinions; argument (page 478)

Early Christians had many ***debates*** *about the principles of their new religion.*

astonishment sudden great surprise or wonder (page 478)

The ***astonishment*** *he experienced led him to make important changes in his life.*

The Early Christians

TERMS & NAMES
Gentile
persecute
Paul
missionary
Epistle

Build on What You Know In Chapter 13 you learned that the Romans worshiped many gods. In contrast, the Jews worshiped one God and tried to obey God's law. The first Christians also obeyed the law of Moses.

Jesus' Disciples

1 **ESSENTIAL QUESTION** What did Jesus' disciples do after his death?

Jesus' first disciples were Jews. Eventually, they developed beliefs and practices that would cause a break from Judaism and became known as Christians.

The Early Church The disciples thought that Jesus had fulfilled Jewish prophecies about the Messiah. The disciples tried to convince other Jews to accept Jesus as the Messiah.

The early church stressed sharing property as well as practicing charity, helping prisoners, and taking common meals. Women and slaves were eager to join, perhaps because the new church taught that all its members were equal. These beliefs helped to set the early church apart from other religions of the time. The disciples hoped to spread Jesus' message and convert others to their beliefs.

Ephesus This view shows the ruins of a street and temple in the Roman city of Ephesus in Anatolia, where early Christians preached. ▼

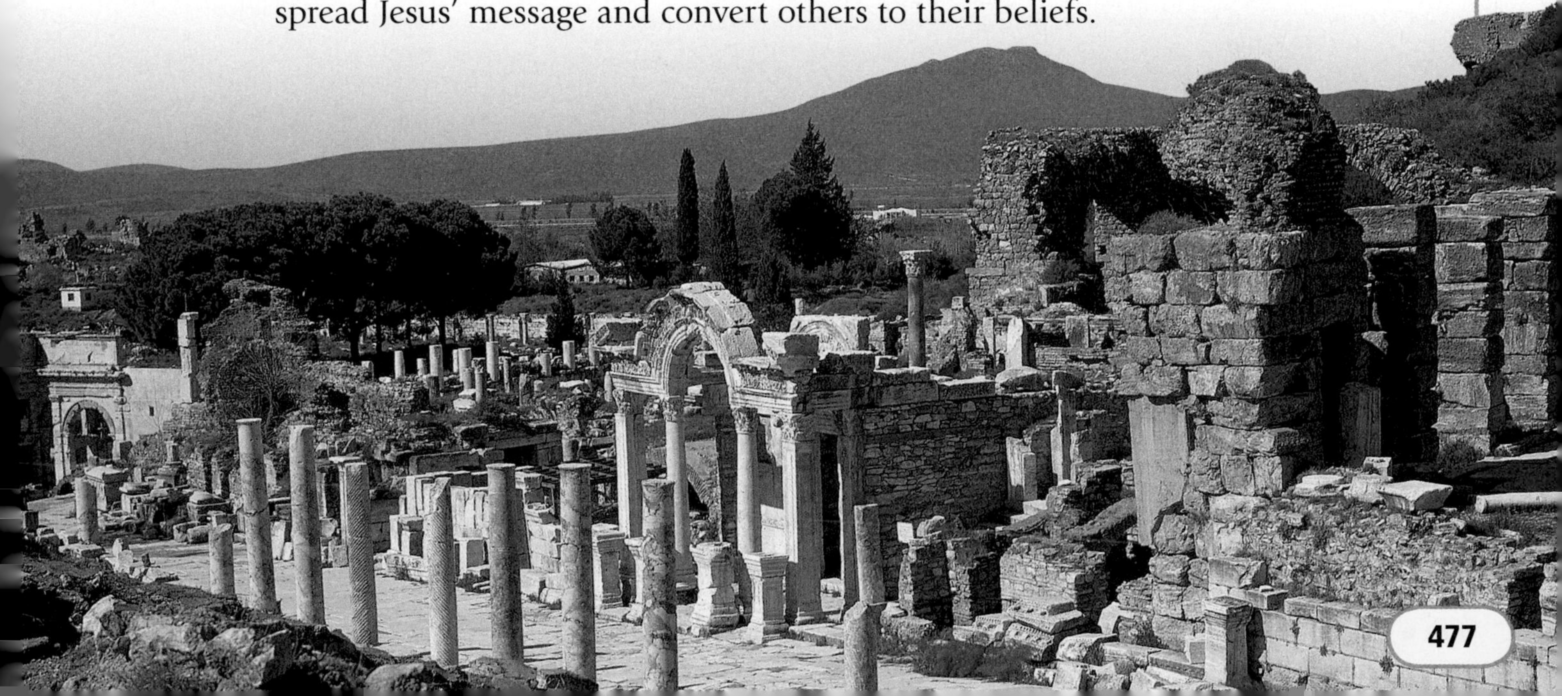

Conflict Arises The first members of Christian churches were Jewish converts to Christianity. The conversion of **Gentiles** (JEHN•TYLZ), or non-Jews, to Christianity sparked a debate. Some thought Gentiles should observe the Torah, while others thought that this was unnecessary.

At first, Roman leaders ignored the early Christians. Like the Christians themselves, the Romans viewed Christianity as a sect, or division, of Judaism. Jewish leaders disagreed with this view.

REVIEW On what beliefs was the early Christian church based?

The Conversion of Saul

2 ESSENTIAL QUESTION What change did Saul undergo?

One of the men who became an early leader of the Christian church was Saul, who had been born a Jew. Later he wrote about how his faith changed and how, as a young man, he had actively opposed the Christian church.

The Road to Damascus While on the road to Damascus, Saul experienced a sudden conversion. According to his own account, Saul felt that God had revealed Jesus as His son to him, and appointed him to proclaim Jesus among the Gentiles. Saul came to believe that Jesus was the Jewish Messiah.

Christianity's Early Years, c. 4 B.C.–A.D. 380

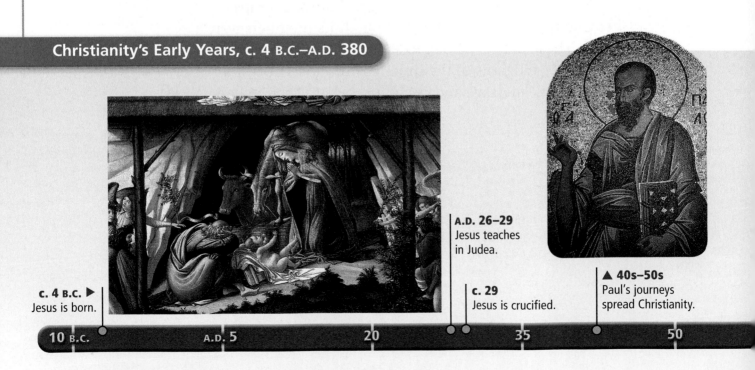

c. 4 B.C. ▶ Jesus is born.

A.D. 26–29 Jesus teaches in Judea.

c. 29 Jesus is crucified.

▲ **40s–50s** Paul's journeys spread Christianity.

10 B.C. | A.D. 5 | 20 | 35 | 50

Saul Becomes a Christian When Saul reached Damascus, he sought out members of the church and joined them. There he studied his new faith and began to convert Gentiles.

Saul's cultural and political background helped him convert a variety of nonbelievers. As a Pharisee, Saul knew Jewish law. He had been born in Tarsus, a city in Asia Minor heavily influenced by Greek culture. Saul held Roman citizenship. This allowed him to travel freely through the empire.

When he traveled, Saul used his Roman name, **Paul**. After three years, according to Christian scriptures, Paul was ready to travel as a **missionary**, or person who spreads his faith by converting others to his religion.

REVIEW What happened to Saul on the road to Damascus?

Paul's Journeys Spread Christianity

3 ESSENTIAL QUESTION Where did Paul travel, and why?

During Paul's lifetime, the Roman Empire was experiencing the Pax Romana, or "Roman peace." That made the empire's excellent roads safer for Paul's widespread travels.

The Journeys Nonetheless, Paul's travels weren't easy. He made four missionary journeys. Each one took several years. Paul wrote that he faced "dangers from rivers, dangers from bandits, . . . dangers in the wilderness, dangers at sea."

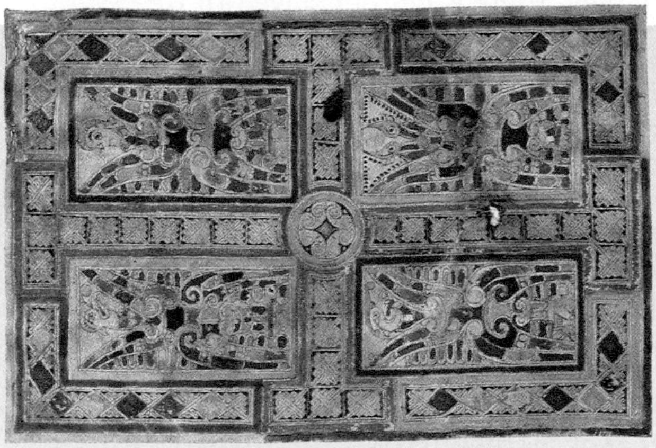

64
Roman persecution of Christians begins under Nero.

▲ 70s–90s
Gospels of Matthew, Mark, Luke, and John are written.

313 ▶
Roman emperor Constantine grants Christians freedom of worship.

380
Emperor Theodosius makes Christianity Rome's official religion.

65 80 95 400

Changes to Christianity

Paul and other Christian missionaries brought about changes that made it possible for Christianity to spread throughout the Roman Empire. For years, Paul and other early Christian leaders struggled over whether Gentiles had to become Jews before becoming Christians. Paul argued that conversion to Judaism was unnecessary. Paul's idea helped separate Christianity from Judaism. It also made the new religion more appealing to Gentiles. As a result, Christianity began to spread throughout the empire.

▲ **Paul** The apostle Paul was the most important early Christian missionary.

The Letters Almost everywhere Paul went, he started new churches. He kept in touch with these churches by writing letters, delivered by other missionaries. Paul's letters explained Christian beliefs and urged converts to live according to God's laws. He preached that salvation was available to all people if they accepted Jesus.

Paul's letters became an important part of the New Testament. They are among the **Epistles** ("letters"). In one famous Epistle, Paul wrote that believing in Jesus broke down all barriers between people: "There is neither Jew nor Greek, there is neither slave nor free, there is neither male nor female; for you are all one in Christ Jesus."

Paul's Death Paul had wanted to travel to Rome to speak before the emperor and spread his Christian faith. He did reach Rome, but not in the way he had hoped.

Near the end of his career, Paul returned to Jerusalem. He was taken into custody by the Romans when it was rumored that he had brought Gentiles into the Temple. After staying in prison for two years, Paul demanded to be tried before Caesar in Rome.

According to some who endeavor to reconstruct the history of early Christianity, Paul left on his final journey in late autumn A.D. 59. After arriving in Rome in early A.D. 60, Paul remained under house arrest for two years. He wrote several letters from captivity. Then, he suddenly stopped. Paul probably died in Rome, possibly after being **persecuted**—that is, opposed or harassed—by the Emperor Nero.

The Legacy of Paul Paul was the most influential of the early apostles, or messengers of Jesus, because of his many journeys and letters. He helped spread the church from Jesus' homeland out to the nations of the world.

REVIEW How did Paul change Christianity?

Lesson Summary

- Jesus' disciples tried to persuade other Jews and debated whether to seek Gentile converts.
- Saul became the most important early Christian missionary.
- Paul's conversion of Gentiles established Christianity as a new faith.

▲ **Relief Sculpture** This Roman sailing ship of the first century A.D. was the kind of ship in which Paul would have made many of his journeys.

Why It Matters Now . . .

More than any other person, Paul contributed to the growth of Christianity as a worldwide religion. All over the world, many churches and cities are named in his honor.

2 Lesson Review

Homework Helper ClassZone.com

Terms & Names

1. Explain the importance of

Gentile	Paul	Epistle
persecute	missionary	

Using Your Notes

Finding Main Ideas Use your completed diagram to answer the following question:

2. How did the Christian church change during Paul's lifetime?

Main Ideas

3. Why were women and slaves particularly eager to become Christians?

4. What qualifications did Paul possess that made him an effective missionary?

5. What decision made Christianity appealing to Gentile converts?

Critical Thinking

6. Understanding Cause and Effect How did the Pax Romana contribute to the spread of Christianity?

7. Assessing Credibility of Sources Why are the Epistles useful sources for learning about Paul's experiences?

Activity

Internet Activity Use the Internet to research Paul's journeys and make a thematic map of them. Use illustrations or symbols to show some things that happened to him.
INTERNET KEYWORD: *Paul's missionary journeys*

Lesson 3

MAIN IDEAS

1. **Government** Rome became hostile to Jews and Christians because both groups challenged Roman authority.
2. **Government** The Roman emperor Constantine accepted Christianity and ended persecutions.
3. **Government** The church developed into a complex institution with many levels of authority.

TAKING NOTES

Reading Skill: Finding Main Ideas

Finding the main idea—the most important point—of a passage will increase your understanding. This lesson discusses ways in which Rome's attitude toward Christianity changed. Record details about this main idea in a web diagram.

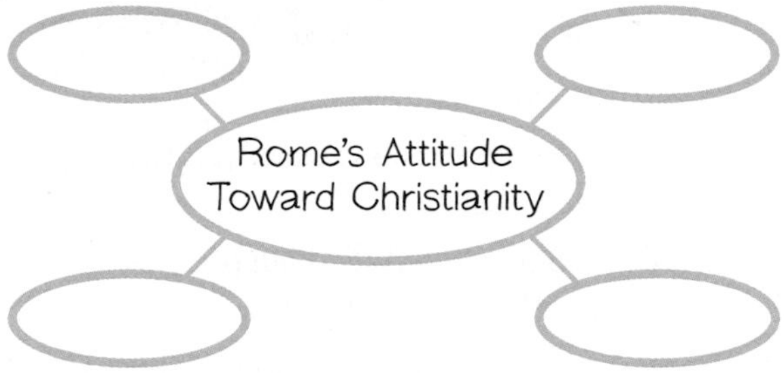

Skillbuilder Handbook, page R2

▲ **Bronze Statue The Roman emperor Valentinian holds aloft a Christian cross, showing the conversion of the Roman Empire to Christianity.**

Words to Know

Understanding the following words will help you read this lesson:

alien of or coming from another country; foreign (page 483)

*Some Roman leaders believed that **alien** religious beliefs might weaken their authority.*

waging conducting or carrying on (page 484)

*Constantine was **waging** a war for control of the Roman Empire.*

edict a statement by a ruler that has the force of law (page 484)

*The Roman emperor issued an **edict** that legalized Christianity.*

communion a ritual in which Christians remember Jesus by eating bread and drinking wine (page 486)

*Christians have different beliefs about the meaning and significance of **communion**.*

Rome and Christianity

TERMS & NAMES
bishop
pope
catholic
creed
Trinity

Build on What You Know In Chapter 13, you learned that the Roman religion included elements drawn from the religions of other peoples. An important issue facing the ancient world was how Rome would react to the new religion of Christianity.

Rome's Policy Toward Other Religions

1 ESSENTIAL QUESTION Why was Rome hostile to Christians and Jews?

Rome tolerated the alien religious practices of the people it conquered. It exempted Jews from the requirement to worship Roman gods, including the emperor. However, Rome would not let the religions of subject peoples inspire rebellion. When a Jewish revolt began in Jerusalem, the Romans destroyed the Temple.

A Christian Threat As more Gentiles joined the Christian movement, the Romans became alarmed. Some Gentiles claimed that they should not have to worship the emperor. The appeal of Christianity to slaves and women also caused alarm. Finally, Christian talk about a Lord who would establish a kingdom seemed to imply an end to the Roman Empire.

Connect to Today

Rome This view shows the Sant'Angelo Bridge over the Tiber River at dusk, with St. Peter's Basilica in the background. ▼

INTERACTIVE

The Roman Persecutions Roman doubts about Christianity soon led to active hostility. Nero blamed the Christians for a fire that leveled much of Rome in A.D. 64. Many Christians were tortured and killed because of their religion. Yet the conversions continued. During the Roman persecutions, catacombs—underground cemeteries with secret passages—provided a hiding place for Christians. However, a key event would bring the persecutions to an end.

REVIEW Why did the Romans feel threatened by Christianity?

▲ **Catacomb** This picture of a catacomb in Rome shows burial niches and a painting of Jesus.

The Conversion of Constantine

2 ESSENTIAL QUESTION What was Constantine's policy toward Christianity?

In A.D. 306, Constantine (KAHN•stuhn•TEEN) became the Roman emperor. Like those before him, he had allowed the persecution of Christians. In 312, however, he was waging a battle for leadership of Rome.

The Cross as Sign In the midst of the fighting, Constantine prayed for help. Later he reported seeing a Christian cross in the sky along with these words: "In this sign you will conquer." He ordered his soldiers to put the symbol of the cross on their shields and battle flags. Constantine and his troops were victorious.

The Legalization of Christianity The victorious Constantine immediately ended the persecution of Christians. Then, in the Edict of Milan, he made Christianity one of the empire's legal religions and returned property that had been seized during the persecutions. Constantine also built churches, used Christian symbols on coins, and made Sunday a holy day of rest and worship. But Rome's first Christian emperor delayed his own baptism, or formal conversion, until the end of his life.

History Makers

Constantine

Constantine was a fierce and successful warrior. He was also a serious student of his new religion. The emperor wrote a special prayer for his troops, and he even traveled with a movable chapel in a tent. Constantine decreed the building of many Christian churches in the Roman Empire.

Constantine established Constantinople (now Istanbul, Turkey) as a new capital. It was a center of Christianity for the next thousand years. He was buried in Constantinople's Church of the Apostles in A.D. 337. Memorials to the 12 apostles surrounded Constantine's tomb. The first Christian emperor considered himself to be Jesus' 13th apostle.

Christianity Changes Rome In 380, Emperor Theodosius decreed Christianity Rome's official religion. Eleven years later, Theodosius closed down all the pagan temples. "All the peoples we rule," he said, "shall practice that religion that Peter the Apostle transmitted to the Romans."

REVIEW What did the Edict of Milan decree?

Beginnings of the Roman Catholic Church

3 ESSENTIAL QUESTION What were some of the beliefs of the early church?

The practice of Christianity in Roman cities took on a common structure. Priests and deacons obeyed **bishops**, or local church leaders. Roman Catholic tradition says that Rome's first bishop was the apostle Peter. Much later, Rome's bishop gradually became the most important bishop, or **pope**. This was the beginning of the Roman Catholic Church. ***Catholic*** means "universal."

Beliefs and Practices Some early Christian writers, called church fathers, developed a **creed**, or statement of beliefs. This creed featured a belief in the **Trinity**, or union of three divine persons—Father, Son (Jesus), and Holy Spirit—in one God. A church father from North Africa, Augustine, wrote about a God who was present everywhere. The church also developed sacraments—religious rites—such as baptism and communion, based on events in the life of Jesus.

To live the ideal Christian life and to celebrate these sacraments together, Christian men and women formed communities called monasteries. As the church grew, men entered the higher orders of the church, becoming bishops, priests, and deacons. Christianity changed from a small sect to a powerful, wealthy religion.

REVIEW What is Rome's bishop called?

Lesson Summary

- Rome saw the new religion of Christianity as a threat.
- Constantine embraced Christianity in A.D. 312.
- The Roman Catholic Church traces its roots to the apostle Peter.

Why It Matters Now . . .

One-third of the people in the world today are Christian.

3 Lesson Review

Homework Helper
ClassZone.com

Terms & Names

1. Explain the importance of

bishop	catholic	Trinity
pope	creed	

Using Your Notes

Finding Main Ideas Use your completed diagram to answer the following question:

2. What decision made by Theodosius had a big impact on Roman religion?

Main Ideas

3. How did the Romans view Christianity at first?
4. What effect did the Edict of Milan have?
5. What three persons are said to make up the Trinity?

Critical Thinking

6. **Understanding Cause and Effect** What effect did Emperor Constantine have on the spread of Christianity?
7. **Making Inferences** Why do you think the bishop of Rome became the most important of all the bishops?

Activity

Making a Time Line Chart the important events in the early history of the church on a time line. Be sure to include the sources for your dates.

Make a World-Religions Pie Graph

Goal: To understand the sizes of the major religions of the world

Materials & Supplies
- blank sheet of paper
- markers or crayons of different colors
- a ruler to draw lines for sections of the pie graph
- research sources, such as world almanacs or encyclopedias

Prepare

1. Gather resources, such as world almanacs, encyclopedias, and books from the library.
2. Make a list of religions you find in these resources.

Do the Activity

1. Use the resources you've identified to find out the numbers of members of the major religions of the world. Major religions you might research include the following: Christianity, Islam, Judaism, Hinduism, and Buddhism. You might also have categories "Other" (for members of all the many other religions in the world) and "Nonreligious" (for residents of officially atheistic countries, such as China).
2. Construct a pie graph showing the size of each religion. The bigger the percentage of believers, the bigger the slice of the graph.
3. Choose a color for each religion or category, and color in each slice of the graph.

Follow-Up

1. Which religion has the most members?
2. Which religion has the second greatest number?
3. What other generalizations can you make on the basis of the graph?

Extension

Making a Presentation Display your completed pie graph in the classroom.

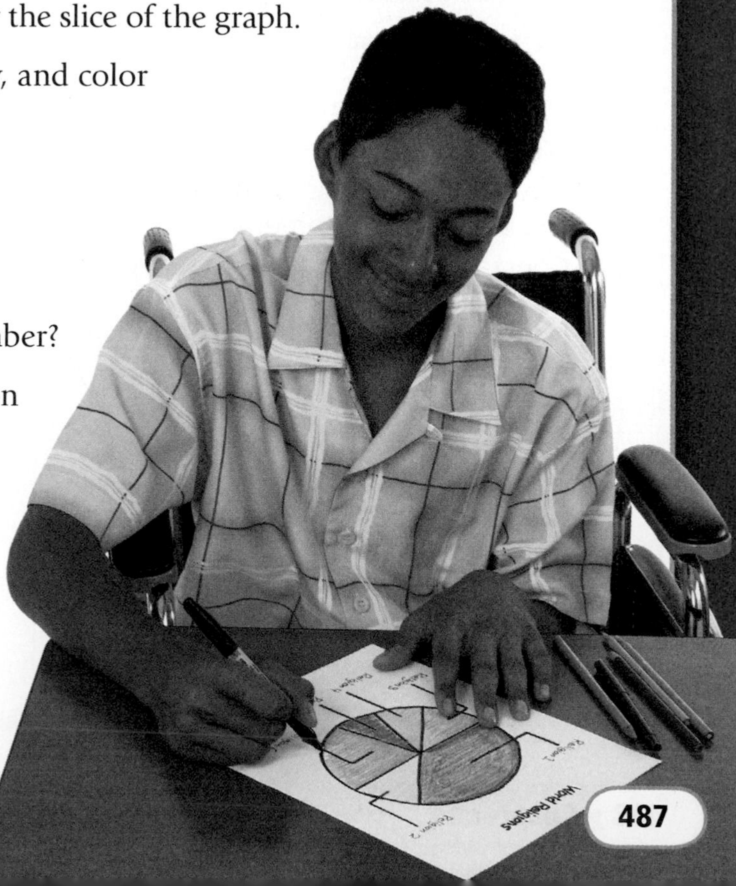

Chapter 14 Review

VISUAL SUMMARY

The Birth of Christianity

Belief Systems

- Christianity built upon Jewish beliefs.
- The disciples of Jesus believed that he was the Messiah.
- Christians believe that Jesus rose from the dead and that this made an afterlife possible.
- Jesus' disciples and, later, other apostles like Paul spread the teachings of Jesus.

Geography

- Paul traveled around the eastern Roman Empire trying to convince Gentiles to believe in Jesus.

Government

- Jews and Christians challenged the authority of Rome.
- Constantine converted to Christianity and made it one of the official religions of the empire.
- The Christian church developed into a complex institution.

TERMS & NAMES

Explain why the words in each pair below are linked with each other.

1. **Gospel** and **disciple**
2. **Paul** and **missionary**
3. **bishop** and **pope**

MAIN IDEAS

The Origins of Christianity (pages 466–475)

4. What is one important message from the Sermon on the Mount?
5. What events do the Christian holidays of Christmas, Good Friday, and Easter Sunday commemorate?

The Early Christians (pages 476–481)

6. What religion did Jesus and his earliest disciples follow?
7. What early decision helped attract Gentile converts to Christianity and separate it from Judaism?

Rome and Christianity (pages 482–487)

8. What happened to the Temple in Jerusalem in A.D. 70?
9. What are two examples of Christian sacraments?

CRITICAL THINKING

Big Ideas: Government

10. **MAKING INFERENCES** What beliefs did Jesus preach that might have brought him into conflict with Rome?
11. **DRAWING CONCLUSIONS** Why might Christians have been blamed by the Roman authorities for the fire that destroyed Rome in A.D. 64?
12. **SUMMARIZING** How did the emperor Constantine help spread Christianity?

Standards-Based Assessment

ALTERNATIVE ASSESSMENT

1. **WRITING ACTIVITY** Imagine that you were a reporter present at the Sermon on the Mount or one of the other events described in this chapter. Explain to your readers what you have seen. Describe the people present, the words spoken, and the meaning of the event. Remember the questions of the newspaper reporter as you write up your account:
   - Who?
   - What?
   - Where?
   - When?
   - How?
   - Why?

2. **INTERDISCIPLINARY ACTIVITY—GEOGRAPHY** Research how many miles Paul traveled on his various journeys. Describe the dangers he faced in various places. What dangers might a modern traveler face on the same routes? Using maps, make a brief oral report about your findings.

3. **STARTING WITH A STORY**
   Starting with a Story
   Review the poster you made about replacing Nero. Research what happened to Nero, and write the headline and first paragraph of a news story explaining his overthrow.

Technology Activity

4. **CREATING A MULTIMEDIA PRESENTATION**
   Use the Internet or library to research the sayings of Jesus and other religious leaders. Create a multimedia presentation in which you compare and contrast these sayings. Include
   - sayings of Buddha and Confucius
   - images of the religious leaders
   - a comparison chart
   - text for each slide
   - documentation of your sources

Research Links
ClassZone.com

Reading Charts Latin was the language of the western Roman Empire and the Roman Catholic Church. Use the chart below to answer the questions.

The Influence of Latin

Latin Word	Meaning	Related Words in English
pontifex	high priest	pontiff
dominus	lord	domain, dominion
senatus	supreme council of state	senate, senator
provincia	governed territory	province
legio	body of soldiers	legion, legionnaire
Caesar	emperor, prince	kaiser, czar
episcopus	overseer	episcopal, bishop
cardinalis	principal, pivotal	cardinal
sedes	seat	Holy See
catholicus	universal	catholic

1. **What two elements in the Roman world do the Latin words in the chart apply to?**
   A. Temple in Jerusalem and Roman Forum
   B. Roman army and roads
   C. Roman government and the Roman Catholic Church
   D. capitals of Rome and Constantinople

2. **What sorts of activities do the Latin words in the chart relate to?**
   A. sports and athletic competition
   B. music and entertainment
   C. government and authority
   D. business and commerce

Test Practice
ClassZone.com

Additional Test Practice, pp. S1–S33

Chapter 15

Rome's Decline and Legacy

Before You Read: K-W-L

Considering what you have already learned about Rome will help prepare you to read this chapter. Record the answers to the following questions in your notebook:

- What do you already know about Rome?
- Study the map on these pages. What does it tell you about what has happened in the Roman Empire?
- What do you want to learn about the legacy of Rome?

Big Ideas About Rome's Decline and Legacy

Economics Nomadic peoples often attack settlements to gain the goods that civilizations produce.

Roman armies spent a lot of time fighting people who wanted to enter the empire. Some nomads wanted the protection of the Roman Empire. Others wanted to take over Roman lands. They disrupted trade and took valuable goods.

Integrated Technology

eEdition
- Interactive Maps
- Interactive Visuals
- Starting with a Story

INTERNET RESOURCES

Go to **ClassZone.com** for
- WebQuest
- Homework Helper
- Research Links
- Internet Activities
- Quizzes
- Maps
- Test Practice
- Current Events

ROME

161
Marcus Aurelius begins his reign.
(relief of Marcus Aurelius) ▲

285
Diocletian reorganizes the empire.

324
Constantine reunifies the Roman Empire.

476
Western Roman Empire falls.

200 — 300 — 400

WORLD

220
Han Dynasty collapses.

325
King Ezana rules African kingdom of Aksum.
(pillar from Aksum) ▶

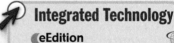

The Division of the Roman Empire, A.D. 395

INTERACTIVE

527
Justinian comes to power in the Byzantine Empire.
◀ (mosaic of Justinian)

1054
Christian church splits into two branches.

1453
Byzantine Empire falls to the Turks.

600 | 900 | 1200 | 1500

630
Muhammad unifies the people of the Arabian peninsula.

900s
Mayan civilization declines.
◀ (Mayan pyramid)

1279
Kublai Khan conquers China.
◀ (painting of Kublai Khan)

Starting with a Story

THE ARRIVAL OF THE GOTHS

Background: The Goths were Germanic peoples who lived north and east of the Western Roman Empire. In A.D. 375, a fierce Asian people called the Huns began to invade the Goths' territory. The Huns killed hundreds of people and burned villages and fields. Fearing for their lives, some Goths fled to the Western Roman Empire. There, they asked the Romans for protection. Imagine that you are an observer as the Goths arrive at the border of the Roman Empire.

Sculpture of a Roman soldier triumphing over a barbarian ▶

Fear of the Huns caused the western Goths to ask the Romans for protection. The Romans agreed to let the Goths cross the river into their empire. First, however, the Romans said the Goths must give up their weapons. But Goth warriors believed they had no honor without weapons. So they paid the Romans money or did favors for them in order to keep their weapons.

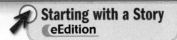

The river crossing was hard. The water was high and flowed swiftly. The floodwaters swept many people to their deaths.

Then the Goths entered a camp guarded by Roman soldiers. The governors of the region were supposed to feed the people. Instead, the Roman soldiers sold the people food—disgusting stuff that no Roman would eat. For example, some meat came from animals that died of disease. In exchange, the Romans took everything of value the Goths had.

Now the Romans are also buying Goth children and making them their slaves. Many Goth parents believe slavery is better than starvation. But they are bitter about making such a cruel choice.

Anger is growing. One Goth says, "We told the Romans that if they helped us, we would accept their religion and fight their enemies. As soon as we have nothing left to offer, they will starve us."

Some people propose going to the governors and explaining the Goths' suffering. "Maybe they will make the soldiers treat us better," one argues.

Others mutter about getting revenge. "We are men of honor. We still have weapons, and we can fight the Romans."

Should the Goths fight back or seek a peaceful solution?

Reading & Writing

1. **READING: Main Ideas** What is the main idea of this story? How do you think it might be related to the main idea of this chapter?
2. **WRITING: Persuasion** Write the outline for a speech in which you try to persuade the Goths whether to fight back or to seek peace. Be sure to give reasons supporting your decision. If possible, deliver your speech to the class.

Lesson 1

MAIN IDEAS

1. **Culture** A series of problems—including food shortages, wars, and political conflicts—weakened the Roman Empire.
2. **Government** Because the empire was so huge, Diocletian divided it into eastern and western regions to make governing more efficient.
3. **Government** Emperor Constantine reunited the eastern and western empires and tried to restore the Roman Empire to greatness.

TAKING NOTES

Reading Skill: Understanding Cause and Effect

Finding causes and effects will help you understand patterns in history. Look for the effect of each event listed in the chart below. Record them on a chart of your own.

Causes	Effects
Food shortages, wars, and political conflicts occur.	
Diocletian splits the empire.	
Constantine unites the empire.	

Skillbuilder Handbook, page R26

▲ Emperor Trajan's Column The surface of this 130-foot column is carved with scenes of Trajan's wars against outsiders.

Words to Know

Understanding the following words will help you read this lesson:

loyalty faithful support (page 496)
*Soldiers' **loyalty** to their military leaders might weaken if they are treated poorly or not paid.*

orderly free from violence (page 496)
*A good emperor will maintain an **orderly** society by providing for his subjects and protecting them.*

consult to go to for advice (page 497)
*Some leaders find they can govern more effectively if they **consult** with advisers.*

portion a part of a whole (page 498)
*The **portion** of the empire he received from his father did not satisfy his desire for more wealth and power.*

An Empire in Decline

TERMS & NAMES
mercenary
Diocletian
absolute ruler

Build on What You Know Did you ever have a problem you thought you could solve, then realized you could not find the right solution for it? In this lesson you will learn that the Roman Empire began to develop difficult problems for which there seemed to be no obvious solutions.

Weakness in the Empire

1 ESSENTIAL QUESTION What problems weakened Rome?

Primary Source Handbook
See the excerpt from the *Annals*, page R59.

After the death of Emperor Marcus Aurelius in A.D. 180, a series of problems began to weaken the empire. These economic and political problems were difficult to solve.

Economic Problems The empire could no longer feed its many people. Some farmland had been destroyed by warfare. But the biggest problem was improving farm production. With many slaves to do the work, plantation owners chose not to develop more-productive farming technology. As a result, the land wore out and harvests did not increase. Food shortages caused unrest.

The empire was running low on money. Taxes were high, so many people did not pay them. Without tax money, the government could not pay the army or buy needed services.

Hadrian's Wall
Hadrian's Wall marked the geographic border of the Roman Empire on the island of Britain. Like the Great Wall of China, this wall was supposed to help keep out invaders. ▼

Military Problems Rome was constantly at war with nomadic peoples in the north and northeast, as well as with the people who lived along its eastern borders. The empire needed larger armies to respond to so many threats, so it hired foreign mercenaries. A **mercenary** is a soldier for hire.

Mercenaries often had no loyalty to the empire. They pledged their allegiance to an individual military leader. Having armies that were loyal to only one man created independent military powers within the empire. In addition, mercenaries were not as disciplined as Roman soldiers. This lack of discipline made the army less effective. The result was a weakened defense along the empire's borders.

Vocabulary Strategy

The word *mercenary* can have **multiple meanings.** It has come to refer to anyone who, like the Roman mercenaries, does something only to get money.

Political and Social Problems The sheer physical size of the Roman Empire made it hard to govern. Government officials found it was not easy to obtain news about affairs in some regions of the empire. This made it more difficult to know where problems were developing. Also, many government officials were corrupt, seeking only to enrich themselves. These political problems destroyed a sense of citizenship. Many Romans no longer felt a sense of duty to the empire. Many chose to get rich in business rather than serve in the government.

Other aspects of Roman society also suffered. The cost of education increased, so poor Romans found it harder to become educated. In addition, distributing news across the large empire became more difficult. People grew less informed about civic matters.

REVIEW What problems weakened the Roman Empire?

Diocletian Divides the Empire

2 ESSENTIAL QUESTION What steps did Diocletian take to solve the empire's problems?

A rapidly changing series of emperors also weakened the government. During a 49-year period (from A.D. 235 to 284), Rome had 20 emperors. Some of them were military leaders who used their armies to seize control. With emperors changing so often, the Roman people had little sense of orderly rule.

The Tetrarchs This statue recognizes four emperors who ruled at the same time. ▼

Diocletian Restores Order In A.D. 284, the emperor **Diocletian** (DY•uh•KLEE•shunn) took power. He changed the way the army operated by permanently placing troops at the empire's borders. He also introduced economic reforms, including keeping prices low on goods such as bread, to help feed the poor.

During his reign, Diocletian no longer bothered to consult with the Senate. He issued laws on his own. Diocletian was an **absolute ruler**, one who has total power.

Splitting the Empire Diocletian soon realized that he could not effectively govern the huge empire. In A.D. 285, he reorganized it in two, taking the eastern portion for himself. He chose this area for its greater wealth and trade, and its magnificent cities. He appointed Maximian to rule the Western Empire. The two men ruled for 20 years.

In A.D. 306 a civil war broke out over control of the empire. Four military commanders—including Constantine—fought for control of the two halves of the empire.

REVIEW Why did civil war break out in the Roman Empire?

Constantine Continues Reform

3 ESSENTIAL QUESTION How did Constantine change the empire?

In Chapter 14, you learned that Constantine made it lawful to be a Christian. Now you will learn how he became emperor and reunited the Roman Empire.

A Single Emperor Constantine was a western Roman military commander who fought to gain control of Italy during the civil war. In A.D. 312, he entered Rome as the new emperor of the empire's western half. By A.D. 324, he had taken control of the Eastern Empire as well. The empire was reunited and Constantine became the sole emperor.

A New Capital In a bold move, Constantine shifted the empire's capital from Rome to Byzantium. Byzantium was an ancient Greek city located in what is now Turkey. At a crossroads between east and west, the city was well placed for defense and trade. Constantine enlarged and beautified his new capital, which he renamed Constantinople. Today the city is called Istanbul.

▲ **Bust of Constantine** Constantine was an important emperor who reunited the Roman Empire.

Final Division Constantine planned to have each of his three sons rule a portion of the empire after his death. His plan was unwise, for Constantius II, Constantine II, and Constans I created unrest by competing with one another. A period of conflict followed. In 395, the empire was permanently divided into east and west again.

REVIEW How did Constantine strengthen the Roman Empire?

Lesson Summary

- The Roman Empire declined because of a combination of economic, military, and political reasons.
- Diocletian reorganized the empire to increase efficiency in government.
- Constantine unified the empire and moved its capital to Byzantium, which he renamed Constantinople.

Why It Matters Now . . .

The mistakes made by the Roman emperors remind us that to retain power and control, rulers must successfully deal with many different problems.

1 Lesson Review

Homework Helper
ClassZone.com

Terms & Names

1. Explain the importance of

mercenary   Diocletian   absolute ruler

Using Your Notes

Understanding Cause and Effect Use your completed chart to answer the following question:

2. How do the causes and effects illustrate the decline of the empire?

Causes	Effects
Food shortages, wars, and political conflicts occur.	
Diocletian splits the empire.	
Constantine unites the empire.	

Main Ideas

3. Why was the empire in trouble economically?
4. What reforms did Diocletian introduce to solve the empire's problems?
5. What did Constantine do to try to restore the empire to greatness?

Critical Thinking

6. **Understanding Causes** How did constantly changing emperors affect the strength of the Roman Empire?
7. **Making Inferences** Of the problems listed in this lesson, which one was most difficult for the ordinary Roman?

Activity

Making a Collage Study the problems faced by the Roman Empire that were explained in this lesson. Then create a collage showing those problems.

Activity Extend Lesson 1

Hold a Debate

Goal: To debate the historical issue "What was the most serious problem in the late Roman Empire?"

Materials & Supplies
- note cards
- pens or pencils
- books on Roman history

Prepare

1. Form a small group with three or four other students. Assign roles such as reader, note taker, and presenter.
2. Reread pages 495–496. Take notes about the problems that the empire faced.
3. Read the quotations on this page. They offer different opinions about the problems faced by the empire.

Do the Activity

1. As a team, discuss the problems the quotations describe. Also, discuss other problems explained in this lesson.
2. Decide which problem was the most serious. Which was hardest for the empire to solve? List your reasons for your choice.
3. Hold a class debate. One student from each team should give a short speech explaining why the problem the team chose was the most serious. Finally, the class should discuss the various problems and reach a group decision.

from *The Book of the Ancient Romans* by **Dorothy Mills**

Perhaps the greatest danger of all to Rome . . . was the change in . . . the old Roman ideal of discipline and duty, of self-control and self-restraint. . . . By the second century A.D. there was practically none of it left.

from *The Ancient World: Rome* by **Sean Sheehan and Pat Levy**

So much time was spent [by soldiers and governors] fighting over who would be emperor that little attention was paid to the far reaches of the empire.

from *Ancient Rome* by **Judith Simpson**

By the third century A.D., the army was stretched too far and taxes were raised to cover the Empire's costs. Farmers who could not afford the taxes abandoned their farms, and cities suffered as the economy slumped and their markets declined.

from *History of the World: The Roman Empire* by **Don Nardo**

[After 192] Rome needed several good, strong emperors. . . . Instead, a long series of ambitious, weak, brutal, or inept [lacking skill] rulers occupied the throne.

Follow-Up

How would you respond to a person who said Rome fell because of barbarian invasions? Explain.

Extension

Doing Additional Research Use books or the Internet to research other problems of the empire. Write a paragraph summarizing what you have learned.

Lesson 2

MAIN IDEAS

1. **Economics** The Western Roman Empire was much weaker than the more prosperous Eastern Roman Empire.
2. **Geography** Invading groups of Germanic peoples overran the already weakened Western Empire.
3. **Government** Invading Germanic peoples raided Rome and overthrew the last Roman emperor, ending the Western Empire.

TAKING NOTES

Reading Skill: Explaining Sequence

Knowing the order in which events happen can help you understand the time period you are studying. In this lesson, look for events that bring about the fall of the Roman Empire. Use a time line like the one below to help you identify the sequence of events.

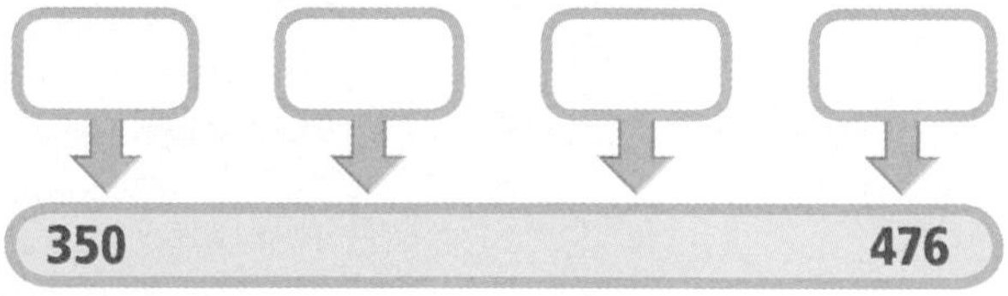

Skillbuilder Handbook, page R15

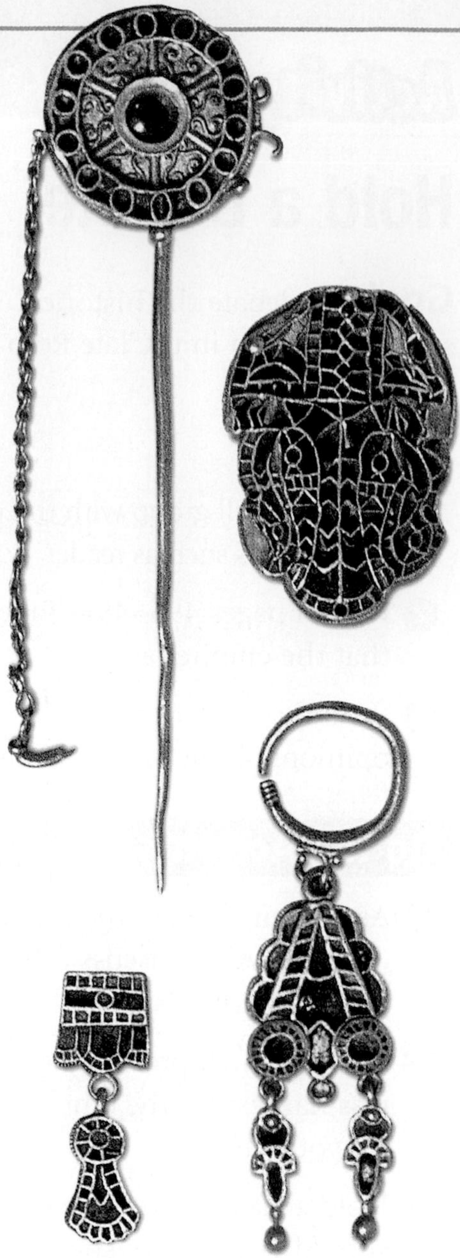

▲ **Gothic Jewelry** The Goths produced finely crafted jewelry from gold and semi-precious gems.

Words to Know

Understanding the following words will help you read this lesson:

bustle to move busily or excitedly (page 501)

*The market **bustled** with commerce as traders came from all over to sell goods.*

fortified strengthened against attack (page 501)

*They believed that invaders could never conquer such a heavily **fortified** city.*

chieftain a clan or tribal leader (page 502)

*A council of **chieftains** discussed the need to move their people to a new location.*

aftermath results of disaster or misfortune (page 505)

*The **aftermath** of the Goth invasion was the destruction of several villages.*

The Fall of the Roman Empire

TERMS & NAMES
barbarian
nomad
plunder

Build on What You Know You have learned how the Roman Empire was permanently split in A.D. 395. Now read about the fall of the Western Roman Empire.

The Two Roman Empires

1 ESSENTIAL QUESTION Why did the Western Roman Empire weaken?

When people talk about the fall of the Roman Empire, they mean the Western Roman Empire. You will learn about the growth of the Eastern Roman Empire in Lesson 3.

Wealthy East The Eastern Roman Empire was much stronger than the Western Roman Empire. The Eastern Empire's capital, Constantinople, bustled with traders from Asia, Africa, and Europe. As a result, the Eastern Empire had more wealth. Also, the eastern cities were larger and better fortified. And the Black Sea was a natural barrier that discouraged invasions. (See the map on page 503.)

Connect to Today

▼ Istanbul Today Constantinople is called Istanbul. The Blue Mosque is visible in the foreground of this aerial view of the city.

Weaker West In contrast, cities in the Western Empire were smaller and less prosperous. They were located farther away from the trade routes that provided both goods and wealth.

The cities of the west were more exposed to attack from groups of invaders along the northern border of the Roman Empire. Defense forces were widely scattered. They were often poorly paid, so they had little reason to risk their lives.

Invaders Raid Cities The invaders were often looking for goods to take or people to kidnap and sell as slaves. As attacks on cities increased, the inhabitants chose to leave. They were looking for safer surroundings. The less populated the cities became, the more vulnerable they were to attack.

REVIEW In what ways was the Western Empire weaker than the Eastern Empire?

Invading Peoples

2 ESSENTIAL QUESTION What groups moved into the Roman Empire?

Defense forces on the north and northeast borders of the Roman Empire grew weaker. **Nomads**—people who move from place to place—took advantage of this weakness and frequently attacked Roman towns and cities. These groups were known as Germanic peoples. The Romans had clashes with Germanic peoples along their northern borders for hundreds of years.

The Germanic Peoples A variety of groups made up the Germanic peoples. They all spoke languages that were part of a language family also called Germanic. The Goths mentioned in the opening story were a Germanic people.

Romans looked down on these groups but also feared them. To the Romans, the Germanic peoples were barbarians. The term **barbarian** originally meant someone who spoke a language the Greeks could not understand. Barbarian came to mean someone who was primitive and uncivilized. The Romans referred to the people who lived along the borders of the empire as barbarians. Later, the Romans applied the term to anyone living outside the empire.

Although the Romans thought the Germanic peoples were barbaric, they had a very complex culture. They were skilled metalworkers and fond of jewelry. Some groups had elected assemblies. War chiefs headed their military organizations. The Germanic peoples were loyal, especially to their chieftains.

Germanic Skull This skull still has its hair. The knot in the hair is a characteristic style of Germanic people. ▼

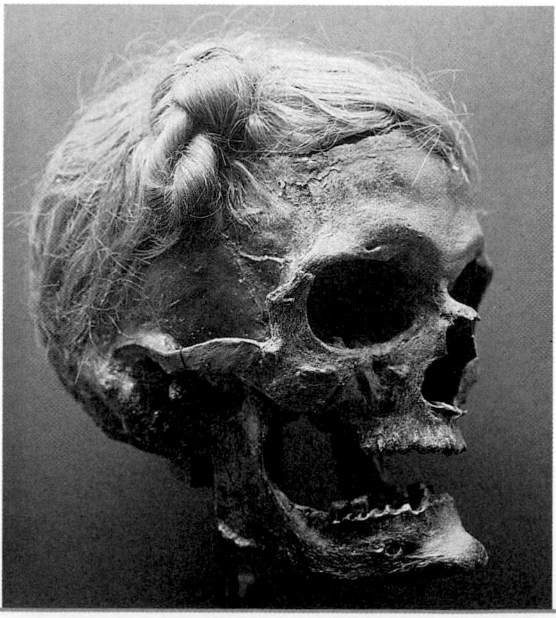

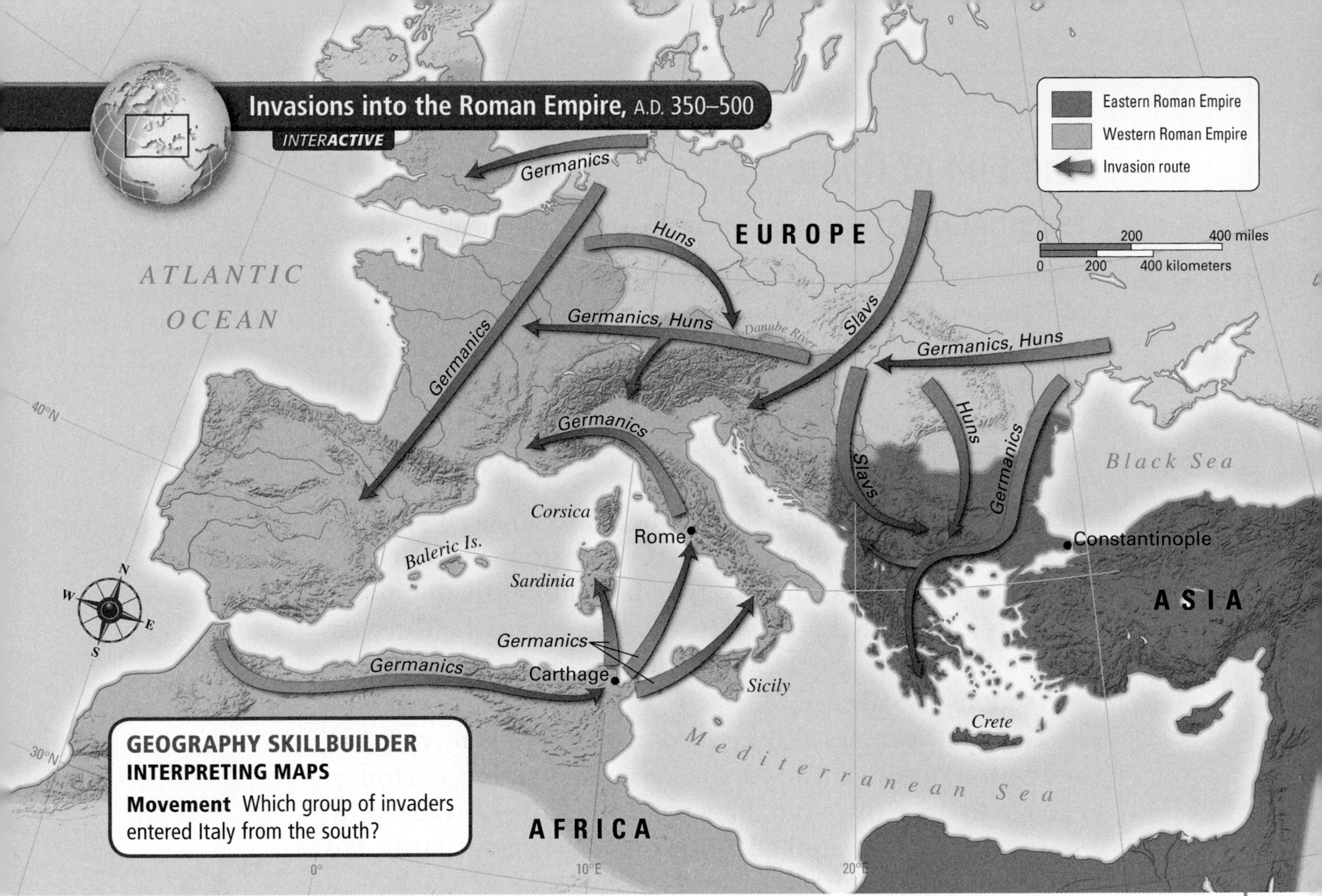

Invasions into the Roman Empire, A.D. 350–500

GEOGRAPHY SKILLBUILDER
INTERPRETING MAPS
Movement Which group of invaders entered Italy from the south?

The German Migrations In Chapters 2 and 6, you read about nomads. Nomads moved to a new location as their food ran out, or when they were driven out of an area by a stronger force. Nomads often fought for the right to remain in a new place. As Rome began to decline, groups of well-armed nomads posed a huge threat to other nomadic people living along the borders of the empire. The people on those borders would be driven into the Roman Empire by a stronger group of nomads.

Between 370 and 500 A.D., Central Asian nomads were pushing people out of their lands into both the Roman and the Chinese empires. The most important of these nomadic groups was the Huns.

The Huns moved across the grasslands of Asia into Germanic lands. They drove the Germanic peoples west and south into Roman territory. The Germanic peoples were looking for new places to settle and for the protection of the Roman armies. As you learned in the opening story, many Romans did not like the Germanic peoples and took advantage of them.

REVIEW Why did the Germanic peoples move into Roman territory?

The Fall of Rome

3 ESSENTIAL QUESTION How did the Western Roman Empire end?

Some people believe the barbarian invasions were the cause of Rome's fall. In reality, Rome gradually declined for many reasons. Corruption of government officials, indifferent citizens, and a breakdown of society contributed to the fall. Historians say a barbarian invasion of the city of Rome marked the beginning of the end for the Western Roman Empire.

Invaders Gain Ground In 410, the Goths attacked and plundered the city of Rome. **Plunder** means to loot, or to take things by force. It was the first time in centuries that nomadic invaders had entered Rome. After looting the city for three days, the Goths left. The city of Rome tried to recover and go on, but it was seriously weakened.

Germanic peoples also invaded what is now France, Spain, and northern Africa. The empire's army was no longer strong enough to drive them out. Italy was raided almost constantly.

In 445, the Huns united under the leadership of Attila. First his armies swept into the Eastern Empire. They attacked 70 cities and then moved into the Western Empire. These attacks placed great pressure on the Roman military.

Comparisons Across Cultures

The Decline of Empires: Roman and Han

Causes for Failure	Roman Empire 27 B.C.–A.D. 476	Han Empire 202 B.C.–A.D. 220
Political	A series of inexperienced and often corrupt emperors	A series of inexperienced emperors
	Division of the empire	No division of the empire
	Ongoing conflict with Germanic tribes	Ongoing conflict with nomads
Economic	Crushing tax burden	Crushing tax burden
	Gap between the rich and the poor	Gap between the rich and the poor
Social	Decline of patriotism and loyalty	Peasant revolts
	Food shortages	Floods that caused starvation and displacement of people

The Aftermath of Rome's Fall In A.D. 476, the last Roman emperor was removed from power. This date marks the fall of the Western Roman Empire. After Rome's fall, life changed in Western Europe in a number of ways.

- Roads and other public structures fell into disrepair.
- Trade and commerce declined.
- Germanic kingdoms claimed former Roman lands.
- The Roman Catholic Church became a unifying and powerful force.

The Eastern Empire continued for almost another thousand years. You will read about the Eastern Empire in Lesson 3.

REVIEW What caused the continued weakening of the Western Empire?

Lesson Summary

- The Western Roman Empire was less wealthy and harder to protect from invaders than the East.
- Germanic invaders further weakened the empire.
- In A.D. 476, the Western Roman Empire ceased to exist.

Why It Matters Now . . .

The decline and fall of empires is a repeating pattern of world history. Even large empires eventually break into smaller pieces.

2 Lesson Review

Homework Helper
ClassZone.com

Terms & Names

1. Explain the importance of
   barbarian   nomad   plunder

Using Your Notes

Explaining Sequence Use your completed time line to answer the following question:

2. What was the most significant event of the empire's downfall?

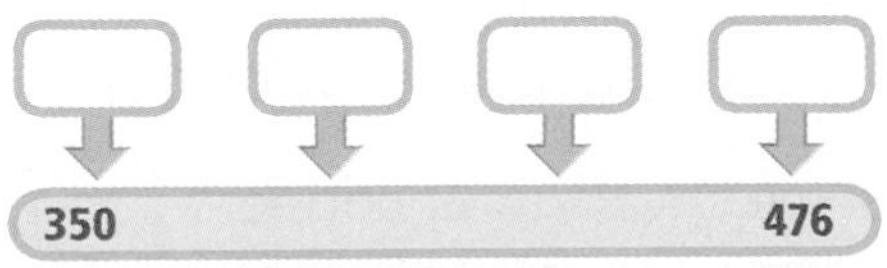

Main Ideas

3. Why was the Western Empire more likely to be invaded than the Eastern Empire?
4. What pushed the Germanic peoples south and west into Roman territory?
5. Why is A.D. 476 considered an important date in Roman history?

Critical Thinking

6. **Recognizing Changing Interpretations of History** How was the movement of the Huns into Europe related to the fall of Rome? Give reasons for your answer.
7. **Making Inferences** Why didn't the Romans make the Germanic peoples their allies?

Activity

Writing Newspaper Headlines Write a series of headlines that describe the fall of Rome. Base each headline on a major event or news story. Arrange the headlines in chronological order on a poster. When possible, provide a date for each.

Skillbuilder Extend Lesson 2

Drawing Conclusions from Sources

Goal: To draw conclusions about one of the reasons for the fall of Rome by reading and analyzing a secondary source

Learn the Skill

Drawing conclusions means reading carefully, analyzing what you read, and then forming an opinion based on facts about the subject. Often you must use your own common sense and your experiences to draw a conclusion.

See the Skillbuilder Handbook, page R25.

Practice the Skill

1. Read the passage at right carefully. Pay attention to the facts, statements that can be proved to be true. A few are labeled for you.
2. List the facts in a graphic organizer like the one below. It gives two examples of facts and conclusions you can draw from them for the passage you just read. Use your own experiences and common sense to understand how the facts relate to each other.
3. After reviewing the facts, write down the conclusion you have drawn.

Example:

Facts	Conclusion
Example 1 2 People failed to participate in government. 2 Government officials were not as qualified as they used to be.	3 People had less interest in good government.
Example 2 2 Fewer Romans served in the military. 2 Foreigners were hired to serve in the Roman military. 2 Foreigners had little loyalty to Rome.	3 Rome's army was not as powerful or as dedicated as it once was. These factors may have been some of the causes of the fall of Rome.

Secondary Source

Historians wonder about the reasons for the decline and fall of the Roman Empire. Most of them agree that there wasn't just one main reason the Roman Empire began to weaken. There were probably many reasons why the empire fell apart. The selection below discusses one of those possible reasons.

The Fall of the Roman Empire

Explaining the decline and fall of Rome is a difficult task for historians. Some historians look at the changes in the social and political attitudes of the Romans to find at least one cause for the weakening of the empire. For example, they believe that the nobles and people in the cities cared more about pleasing themselves than about the well-being of other people.

❶ Historians also know people failed to participate in the government. ❶ Some public officials were not as qualified to perform their jobs as others in the past had been.

▲ **Engraving** A Gothic leader forces the Roman emperor to surrender.

The backbone of the Roman Empire was its army. ❶ However, in the later years of the empire fewer men were willing to serve in the military. ❶ This made it necessary to hire foreigners to serve in the Roman army. ❶ Foreigners had little loyalty to Rome. They served because they were being paid to do so, not because they wanted to serve Rome. This lack of dedication weakened the army that was supposed to protect the empire.

Apply the Skill

Turn to page 380 in Chapter 11. Read the information on Spartan education. Make a chart like the one at left to help you draw conclusions about Spartan culture.

Lesson 3

MAIN IDEAS

1. **Culture** Roman culture continued in the Byzantine Empire for a thousand years after the fall of Rome.

2. **Belief Systems** Christianity developed different forms in the western and eastern parts of the former Roman Empire.

3. **Belief Systems** The Eastern Orthodox Church and the Roman Catholic Church had different relationships with governments.

TAKING NOTES

Reading Skill: Summarizing

Summarizing means restating the main idea and important details about a subject. As you read Lesson 3, make a summary statement about each of the topics listed. Record them on a chart like the one below.

Byzantine Empire	
Justinian	
Split in Christian church	
Role of church in government	

Skillbuilder Handbook, page R3

▲ **Mosaic of Justinian**
Justinian regained lost lands and briefly reunited the Eastern and Western Roman empires. He is considered one of the Byzantine Empire's most important emperors.

Words to Know

Understanding the following words will help you read this lesson:

preserve to maintain, protect from becoming worse (page 510)
*Scholars in the Byzantine Empire helped to **preserve** the culture of Rome.*

limit restricted; not occurring often (page 511)
***Limited** contact between the two cultures led their religions to develop differently.*

delegate a person chosen to speak and act for another (page 511)
*The head of the church employs **delegates** who help him carry out church business.*

Muslim a follower of the religion of Islam (page 512)
***Muslim** armies attacked Constantinople.*

The Byzantine Empire

TERMS & NAMES

- Byzantine Empire
- Justinian
- Justinian Code
- Roman Catholic Church
- Eastern Orthodox Church

Build on What You Know You read in Lesson 1 that Constantine renamed the city of Byzantium Constantinople. That city became the capital of the Eastern Roman Empire. Because of the city's original name, historians call the Eastern Roman Empire the **Byzantine Empire**.

A Continuing Empire

1 **ESSENTIAL QUESTION** How did Justinian restore the Eastern Roman Empire?

The Byzantine Empire continued for about 1,000 years after the fall of the Western Roman Empire. Like the emperors of the Western Roman Empire, the emperor of the Byzantine Empire was its absolute ruler. Also like the Western Roman Empire, the Byzantine emperors struggled to keep Germanic peoples, Huns, and others out of their lands. Despite their efforts, much Byzantine land was lost to invaders.

Justinian One emperor was able to restore control over the former lands of the Eastern Roman Empire. **Justinian** was emperor from A.D. 527 to 565. His armies reconquered lost territories, including Italy, northern Africa, and the southern coast of Spain. (See the map on page 511.)

Hagia Sophia Built by Justinian, Hagia Sophia was the greatest of all churches in Constantinople. Today it is a museum. ▼

Rebuilding Constantinople Justinian also began to rebuild Constantinople, which had suffered much damage from a revolt. He rebuilt the city walls. He also built schools, hospitals, law courts, and churches. The most famous church was Hagia Sophia (HAY•ee•uh soh•FEE•uh). Constantinople was again a glorious city.

Preserving Roman Culture Justinian appointed a committee to create a uniform code of law based on Roman law. These experts dropped outdated laws and rewrote others to make them clearer. The new code was called the **Justinian Code**. The code included laws on marriage, slavery, property ownership, women's rights, and criminal justice.

Although they spoke Greek, Byzantines thought of themselves as part of the Roman cultural tradition. Byzantine students studied Latin and Greek, and Roman literature and history. In this way, the east preserved Greek and Roman culture. In the former Western Empire, the Germanic peoples blended Roman culture with their own. However, they lost much of the scientific and philosophical knowledge of the Greeks and Romans.

REVIEW How did the Byzantine Empire preserve Roman culture?

History Makers

Empress Theodora (c. 500–548)

Theodora was an empress of Byzantium—which was unusual, considering her background. Theodora was an actress, and Byzantine society looked down on actresses. Yet Justinian, the heir to the throne, married Theodora in A.D. 525. His choice was a good one.

Justinian and Theodora became emperor and empress in 527. In 532, rioters threatened to overturn the government. Theodora urged Justinian not to flee. She herself refused to leave. Her courage inspired Justinian, and his generals put down the rebellion.

Later, Theodora had laws passed that helped women. Divorced women gained more rights. She founded a home to care for poor girls. She also offered protection to religious minorities.

▲ Theodora's mosaic portrait may still be seen in the Church of San Vitale in Ravenna, Italy.

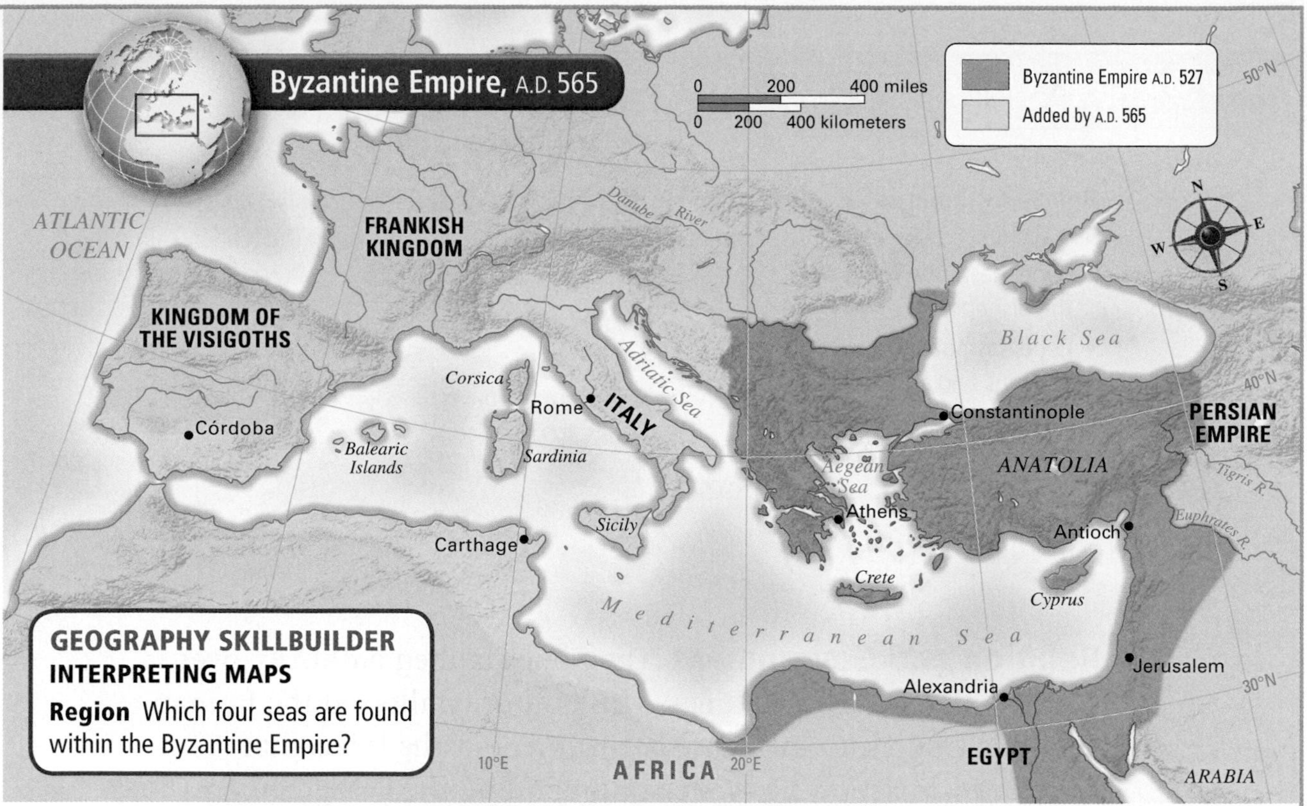

GEOGRAPHY SKILLBUILDER
INTERPRETING MAPS
Region Which four seas are found within the Byzantine Empire?

The Church Divides

2 ESSENTIAL QUESTION Why did the Christian church divide?

The division of the empire also affected the Christian church. Religious practices developed differently in the Christian churches of the east and of the west. Cultural practices and limited contact between the two areas caused these differences.

The Church Divides Another difference had to do with the authority of the emperor over church matters. In the east, the emperor had authority over the head of the church. In the west, there was no emperor and the pope began assuming more responsibilities in governing the former Western Empire.

Problems between the two churches began to grow. The pope claimed authority over the churches in both eastern and western empires. In A.D. 1054, delegates of the pope attempted to remove the eastern head of the church. The eastern church responded by refusing to recognize the authority of the pope.

Finally, the Christian church split in two. The church in the west became known as the **Roman Catholic Church**. *Catholic* means "universal." The church in the east became the **Eastern Orthodox Church**. *Orthodox* means "holding established beliefs." Over time, the split led to the development of two separate European civilizations. Each had its own view on the relationship between church and state.

Two Branches of Christianity in the 11th Century

Roman Catholic
- The leader, called the pope, has authority over the bishops.
- Pope has authority over all kings and emperors.
- Priests may not be married.
- Latin is used in services.

Similarities
- Faith is based on Jesus and the Bible.
- Leaders are priests and bishops.
- Both want to convert people to Christianity.

Eastern Orthodox
- The leader, called the patriarch, and the bishops run the church as a group.
- Emperor has authority over officials of the church.
- Priests may be married.
- Local languages such as Greek and Russian are used in services.

Religion and Government The pope claimed authority over Christian emperors and kings. This authority allowed the Roman Catholic Church to influence government in the lands that were once a part of the Western Roman Empire. Disagreements between the church and some kings and emperors of Western Europe would later cause major conflicts in European history.

In the Byzantine Empire, the emperor was the absolute ruler. He had power over the church as well as the government. This meant that the emperor had power over the spiritual head of the Eastern Orthodox Church. Overall, the Byzantine emperor had greater power than the emperors or kings in the west.

REVIEW How did governments and the Christian churches interact?

The Byzantine Empire Collapses

3 ESSENTIAL QUESTION What happened to the Byzantine Empire?

For many years after the division of the Roman Empire, the Byzantine Empire continued to carry on Roman traditions. But it was not easy. The Byzantine Empire faced constant threats from both the east and the west.

Constantinople Falls In the 600s, a new religion called Islam began in Arabia. Muslim armies arose and attacked nearby territories and Constantinople. Later, civil wars, as well as attacks by Ottoman Turks and Serbs, further weakened the empire. By 1350, all that remained of the Byzantine Empire was a tiny section of the Anatolian peninsula and a strip of land along the Black and Aegean seas.

Finally in 1453, an army of Ottoman Turks captured Constantinople. The city's conquest marked the end of the Byzantine Empire—a thousand years after the fall of the Western Roman Empire.

REVIEW What was a cause of the fall of the Byzantine Empire?

Lion of St. Mark The winged lion stands guard near the Byzantine-style Cathedral of St. Mark located in Venice, Italy. ▼

Lesson Summary

- Emperor Justinian regained much of the Roman Empire's land and helped preserve Roman law and culture.
- In 1054, the Christian church divided into the Roman Catholic and Eastern Orthodox churches.
- The pope of the Roman Catholic Church played a greater role in government in the west than the leader of the Eastern Orthodox Church played in the east.

Why It Matters Now . . .

Today millions of people practice their faith as members of the Roman Catholic Church or the Eastern Orthodox Church.

3 Lesson Review

Homework Helper ClassZone.com

Terms & Names

1. Explain the importance of

Byzantine Empire
Justinian
Justinian Code
Roman Catholic Church
Eastern Orthodox Church

Using Your Notes

Summarizing Use your completed chart to answer the following question:

2. In what ways did Justinian restore the Eastern Roman Empire?

Byzantine Empire	
Justinian	
Split in Christian church	
Role of church in government	

Main Ideas

3. How did Justinian preserve Roman law?

4. On what issue did the church in the east and in the west not agree?

5. In what way did the pope have a greater role in government in the west than the head of the church in the east?

Critical Thinking

6. Contrasting In what ways was the Eastern Roman Empire different from the Western Roman Empire?

7. Making Inferences Why did Christian practices develop differently in the eastern and western empires?

Activity

Internet Activity Use the Internet to research the Hagia Sophia. Plan a virtual field trip of the structure. Include information on its location, construction, and items that are inside the building.
Internet Keyword: *Hagia Sophia*

Lesson 4

MAIN IDEAS

1. **Culture** Roman culture was a unique blend of Roman and Greek ideas.
2. **Science and Technology** Roman advances in architecture and engineering have influenced builders throughout history.
3. **Culture** The spread of Christianity and the Roman system of law left a lasting legacy for the world today.

▲ **Bas-Relief** **The Roman soldiers seen here are examples of bas-relief sculpture, in which the figures stand out from the background.**

TAKING NOTES

Reading Skill: Finding Main Ideas

Identifying the main ideas and finding details about those ideas will help you understand the material in Lesson 4. Look for details about Roman legacies, and record the information on a web diagram like the one below.

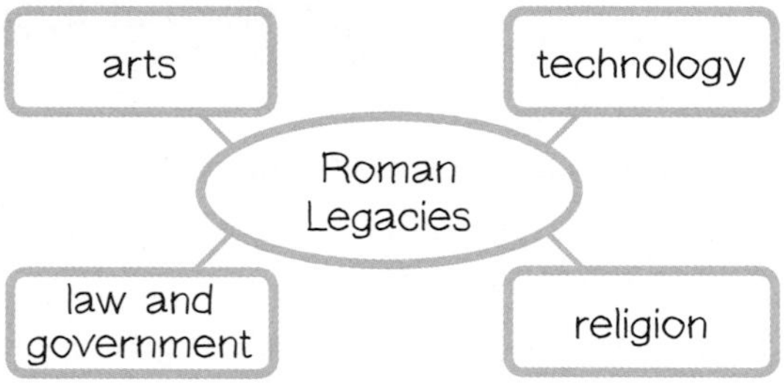

Skillbuilder Handbook, page R2

Words to Know

Understanding the following words will help you read this lesson:

tradition a belief or practice that is passed from one generation to the next (page 516)
*One culture will often adopt a **tradition** from another.*

model to create based on an example (page 516)
*The scholar could tell that the poem was **modeled** on the work of another poet.*

dome a rounded top or roof (page 517)
*The architect designed several enormous **domes** for the top of the building.*

rubble rough broken pieces of stone (page 518)
*The lowest layer of a Roman road is **rubble.***

The Legacy of Rome

TERMS & NAMES
- mosaic
- bas-relief
- epic
- oratory
- vault
- aqueduct

Build on What You Know You have already read that Greek and Hellenistic culture came before the Romans. Early in its history, Rome conquered Greece. Some of the Greek culture influenced Roman culture.

Roman Culture

1 ESSENTIAL QUESTION How did Roman culture differ from Greek culture?

Roman culture was based on values of strength, loyalty, and practicality. The Romans picked up Greek ideas about the artistic ideal and Greek styles of writing. The result was a culture that blended Roman practicality with elements of Greek idealism and style.

Art Roman artists were especially skillful at creating **mosaics**. A mosaic is a picture made from tiny pieces of colored stone or other material. One famous example shows Alexander the Great in battle (see page 405). This mosaic was found at Pompeii and measures 10 by 19 feet. Many mosaics show scenes of daily life.

◀ **Mosaic** This Roman mosaic was discovered in 2000 by archaeologists working in southeastern Turkey.

Sculpture Romans learned about sculpture from the Greeks but did not follow the Greek tradition of showing the ideal. Instead, the Romans created sculptures that were realistic portraits of **bas-relief**. In a bas-relief, slightly raised figures stand out against a flat background. See an example of this style on page 514.

Literature The Greeks also influenced Roman literature. Roman writers adopted the form of the **epic**, a long poem about a hero's adventures. The *Aeneid* by Virgil is a well-known Roman epic. Virgil modeled his poem on two Greek epics, the *Odyssey* and the *Iliad*. The *Aeneid* tells the adventures of the hero Aeneas, who survived the Trojan War, sailed to Italy, and founded Rome.

The works of the statesman Cicero provide a picture of Roman life and add to our knowledge of Roman history. Cicero's written works include his speeches. Cicero was a master of **oratory**, the art of public speaking. Oratory was an important means of persuasion for Roman politicians.

Romans also wrote about philosophy. For example, Emperor Marcus Aurelius wrote the *Meditations,* a work expressing the ideas of Stoicism. Stoicism teaches that the world was created by a divine plan. Duty and virtue help people to live by that plan.

Language Latin, the language of Rome, was spoken across the Western Empire. Over time, Latin evolved into a group of languages called the Romance languages. (The word *romance* comes from the word *Roman*.) Today, Romance languages are spoken in countries whose lands were once ruled by Rome. The chart below shows similarities among Romance languages.

REVIEW How did Roman culture influence the languages of Europe?

Latin Origins of Romance Words

Language	Word				
Latin	pater ("father")	nox ("night")	bonus ("good")	vita ("life")	mater ("mother")
Spanish	padre	noche	bueno	vida	madre
French	père	nuit	bon	vie	mere
Portuguese	pai	noite	bom	vida	mãe
Italian	padre	notte	buono	vita	madre
Romanian	tatã	noapte	bun	viatâ	mamâ

Technology, Engineering, and Architecture

2 ESSENTIAL QUESTION How did Roman ideas about architecture and engineering influence builders throughout history?

Greek architecture influenced Roman builders. You've already learned about the Greek building style, with its use of columns, pediments, and graceful proportions. The Romans used these elements but added their own ideas too.

New Styles of Architecture Roman builders were excellent engineers. They found new ways to improve the structure of buildings. These ideas included the use of arches, **vaults**, and domes. A vault is an arch that forms a ceiling or a roof.

Roman developments in building construction made it possible to build larger, taller buildings. Many modern buildings borrow Roman elements of design and structure. The dome of the U.S. Capitol building is a well-known example.

New Building Materials The Romans developed a form of concrete that was both light and strong. They poured the mixture into hollow walls or over curved forms to create strong vaults. Concrete is a common building material today.

Aqueducts The Romans built **aqueducts** to bring water to cities. An aqueduct is a waterway made by people. Aqueducts brought water to public fountains, where people collected water for their homes. Aqueducts also supplied water to public toilets and bathhouses. Eleven major aqueducts brought water to the city of Rome. The longest stretched for 57 miles. Aqueducts can still be found in France and Spain, lands that were once part of the Roman Empire.

Remains of a Roman Aqueduct This aqueduct is near Nîmes, France. It was constructed more than 2,000 years ago. ▼

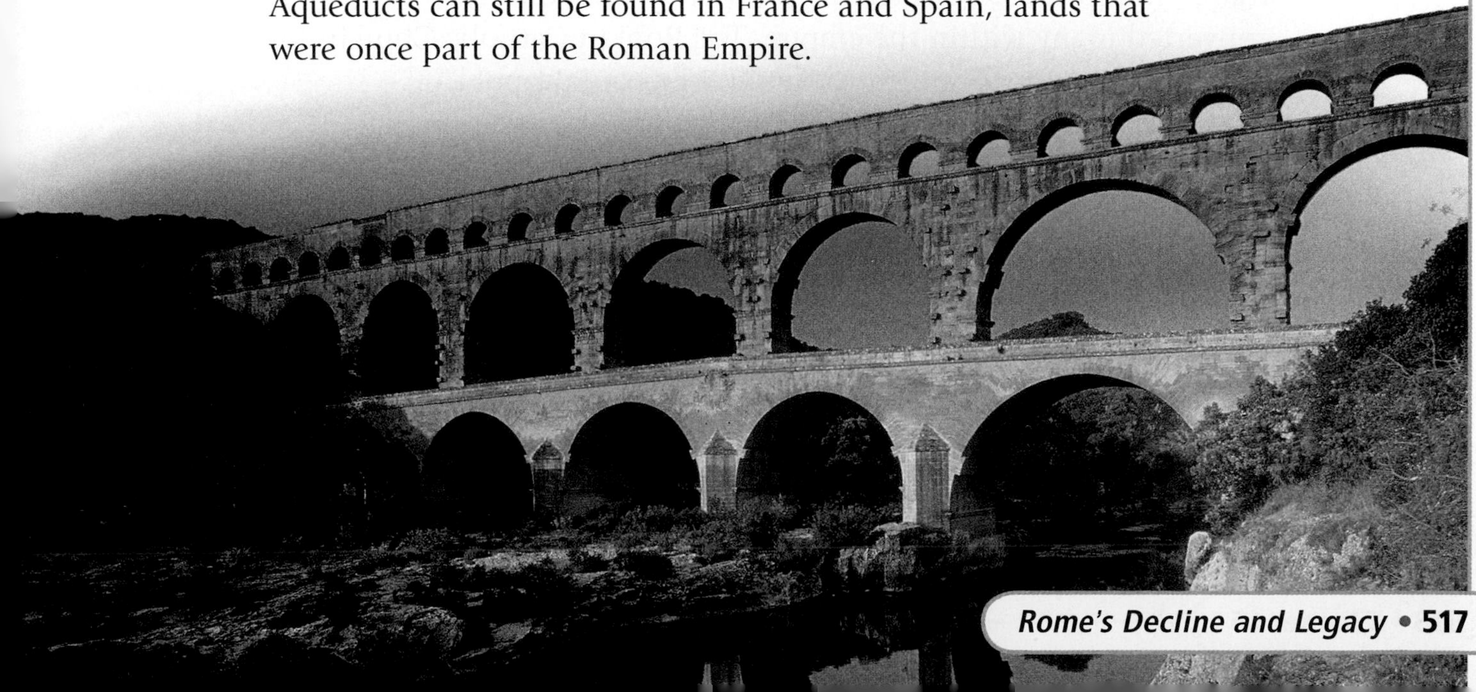

Roads The Romans are especially famous for the quality of their roads. In 312 B.C., Romans built the first of many roads. It was called the Appian Way, and it ran southeast from Rome. In time, a system of roads extended across much of the empire. Rome was the center of this network.

Many Roman roads were built so that soldiers could move quickly to places in the empire where they were needed. The road system also increased trade because merchants and traders could move their goods more easily. Although the road system helped hold the Roman Empire together, it also made it easier for its enemies to invade.

REVIEW What elements of Roman construction are still in use?

▲ **Roman Road Construction**
Roman roads were constructed in layers. The average width of a road was 15 to 18 feet.

Religion and Law

3 ESSENTIAL QUESTION What religious and legal legacies did Rome leave?

Past civilizations leave their mark through ideas as well as through objects. The western and eastern parts of the Roman Empire had great influence in the areas of religion and law.

Spreading Christianity The Roman Empire played a major role in the spread of Christianity. Christian missionaries converted many within the empire. The Roman Catholic Church became the powerful organization in Western Europe.

The Eastern Orthodox Church, which was the official religion of the Byzantine Empire, also spread Christianity. Many Russians and members of societies on the border of the Byzantine Empire became Eastern Orthodox Christians.

With both the Roman Catholic and Eastern Orthodox churches spreading Christianity, most of Europe and some parts of western Asia became Christian.

Roman Government and Law The structure of the Roman Republic influenced the writers of the U.S. Constitution. Roman senators made up the main political body of the republic. Early

U.S. citizens followed this example by providing for their own Senate in Article I of the Constitution.

Laws in today's democracies evolved from those of ancient Rome and Byzantine. These laws include the right to own property and to make contracts and write wills.

In the Roman Republic citizens had the right to equal treatment under the law. This principle of equality inspired the creators of democracies in the United States and France.

REVIEW Which elements of Roman law are found in U.S. law?

Lesson Summary

- Roman writers and artists were inspired by Greek culture, which they combined with their own ideas.
- Roman builders and engineers developed styles and construction methods that continue to be used.
- Roman laws and government continue to serve as models for modern countries.

Why It Matters Now . . .

Many areas of modern life—from government to architecture to language—still carry the mark of the Roman Empire.

4 Lesson Review

Homework Helper
ClassZone.com

Terms & Names

1. Explain the importance of

mosaic	epic	vault
bas-relief	oratory	aqueduct

Using Your Notes

Finding Main Ideas Use your completed web diagram to answer the following question:

2. What are some examples of Roman technology?

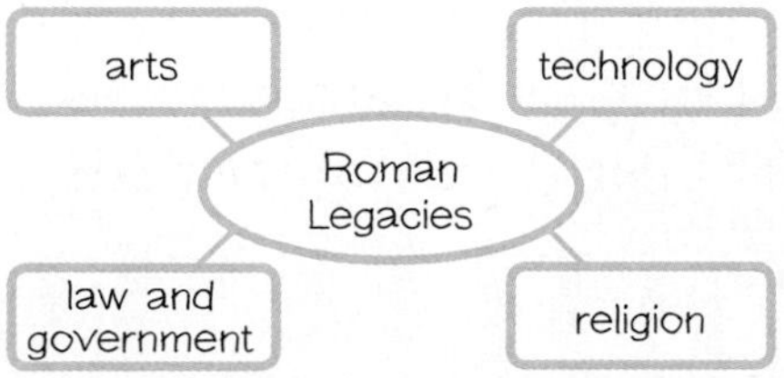

Main Ideas

3. How did Roman writers blend Greek literary styles with their own ideas?

4. How did the Romans influence language in modern-day Europe?

5. What role did the Byzantine Empire play in the spread of Christianity?

Critical Thinking

6. Framing Historical Questions Create a set of three questions about the Roman Empire that could be answered by historical study and research.

7. Forming and Supporting Opinions Which of Rome's legacies has had the greatest influence on life in the United States? Explain.

Activity

Designing a Bas-Relief Research examples of Roman bas-reliefs in books or on the Internet. Then create a sketch of your own bas-relief showing an aspect of life in ancient Rome.

Connect to Today

Extend Lesson 4

Research Links
ClassZone.com

Roman Influences Today

Purpose: To study the legacies of the Roman Empire that are present in today's life

The United States borrowed some Roman ideas about the structure of government. But the Romans also influenced culture in the United States in other ways. Their ideas about architecture and road-building can be seen in our buildings and our highway systems. The Christian church grew during Roman times. Today, millions of people practice the Christian faith that began in Roman times.

Domes

▶ **Past** Roman architects experimented with using a series of arches in a circle to create a dome. The dome of the Pantheon *(right)* is 142 feet high. The Pantheon was constructed to honor the gods. Later it became a Christian church and, finally, a national shrine in Italy.

▼ **Present** Architects for the U.S. Capitol building *(below right)* used the idea of the Roman dome. The dome of the Capitol is 287 feet high. It is topped by an almost 20-foot-tall statue called the Statue of Freedom.

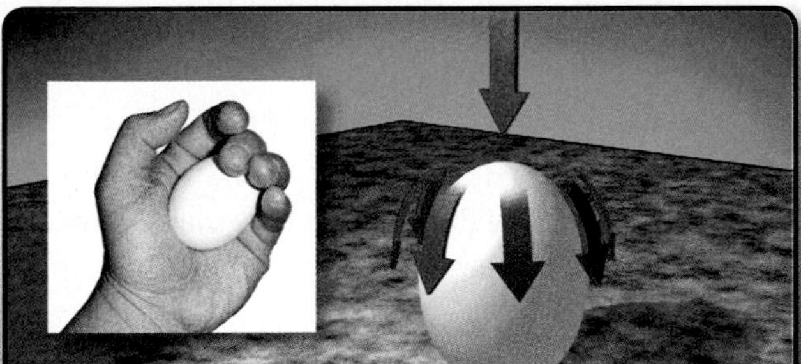

Dome Strength A dome is strong because pressure at the top of the structure is distributed evenly and travels down the curved sides. This gives the structure strength. A dome and an egg are similar. Although we often think of an egg as fragile, an egg can be very strong because it is shaped like a dome. If you try to crush an egg by pressing down on the top, it will not break.

Roads

▼ **Past** The Roman roads were constructed so that military forces could easily move throughout the empire. Under Diocletian, the Roman Empire had 372 main roads covering about 53,000 miles.

▶ **Present** The United States is a nation on the move. There are almost 4 million miles of roads. The interstate system covers 46,467 miles.

Religious Practice

▶ **Past** St. Peter *(right)* was one of Jesus' leading disciples. He became the first bishop of Rome. According to Roman Catholic tradition, the bishop of Rome became the head of the Christian church. Today the bishop of Rome is called the pope and heads the Roman Catholic Church. Rome is the spiritual center of the Church.

▼ **Present** Today the pope lives in a city-state called Vatican City. It is located within Rome. One of the largest Christian churches, St. Peter's Basilica, is located there. Tradition says St. Peter was buried beneath the basilica. In the photograph here the pope greets thousands of believers in St. Peter's Square.

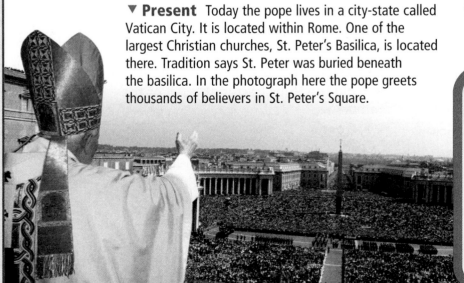

Activities

1. **TALK ABOUT IT** Are there any domed buildings where you live? If so, what activities take place there?
2. **WRITE ABOUT IT** Research information about Roman roads, including how the roads were built and their location in the empire. Write a research report on your findings.

Chapter 15 Review

VISUAL SUMMARY

Roman Empire

Government
- Absolute ruler, law codes

Belief Systems
- Spread Christianity

Science & Technology
- Roads, aqueducts, concrete, arches, domes

Culture
- Realism, bas-reliefs, mosaics, epics, oratory

Empire Splits

Western Roman Empire
- Roman Catholic
- Germanic migrations/invasions
- Ended A.D. 476

Eastern Roman Empire
- Eastern Orthodox
- Germanic/Muslim invasions
- Ended A.D. 1453

TERMS & NAMES

Explain why the words in each set below are linked with each other.

1. **Diocletian** and **absolute ruler**
2. **barbarian** and **nomad**
3. **Eastern Orthodox Church** and **Roman Catholic Church**
4. **vault** and **aqueduct**

MAIN IDEAS

An Empire in Decline (pages 494–499)

5. What economic and political problems weakened the Roman Empire?
6. Why did Diocletian believe reorganizing the empire would strengthen Rome?

The Fall of the Roman Empire (pages 500–507)

7. Why was the Western Roman Empire more likely to fall than the Eastern Roman Empire?
8. How did the Huns hasten the fall of the empire?

The Byzantine Empire (pages 508–513)

9. In what ways did the Byzantine Empire preserve the Roman culture?
10. What caused the Christian church to split in A.D. 1054?

The Legacy of Rome (pages 514–521)

11. What artistic styles did the Romans borrow from Greek culture?
12. How has Roman law shaped modern law?

Standards-Based Assessment

CRITICAL THINKING Big Ideas: Economics

13. **UNDERSTANDING CAUSES AND EFFECTS** How was economics a cause of Rome's downfall?
14. **ANALYZING ECONOMIC AND POLITICAL ISSUES** How are the nomadic attacks on Rome related to Rome's economic problems?
15. **MAKING INFERENCES** How did economics play a part in the survival of the Byzantine Empire?

ALTERNATIVE ASSESSMENT

1. **WRITING ACTIVITY** Imagine you lived in the city of Rome when the Goths attacked the city in A.D. 410. Write a description of the attack.
2. **INTERDISCIPLINARY ACTIVITY—LANGUAGE ARTS** Use books and the Internet to research Latin-based words in the English language. Make a list of five to ten terms used in everyday life. Create an illustrated chart listing the Latin word and an image of the concept the word represents.
3. **STARTING WITH A STORY** Review your speech explaining why the Goths should either seek peace or stand up to the Romans. Now outline a speech that takes the opposite view.

Technology Activity

4. **MAKING AN ILLUSTRATED MAP** Use the Internet to research the locations of Roman aqueducts. Make an illustrated map of the Roman Empire that shows their locations.
   - Display an image of the aqueduct located at each location.
   - Identify the location by city and modern-day country.
   - Document your sources.

Research Links
ClassZone.com

Reading a Map Use the map below to answer the questions.

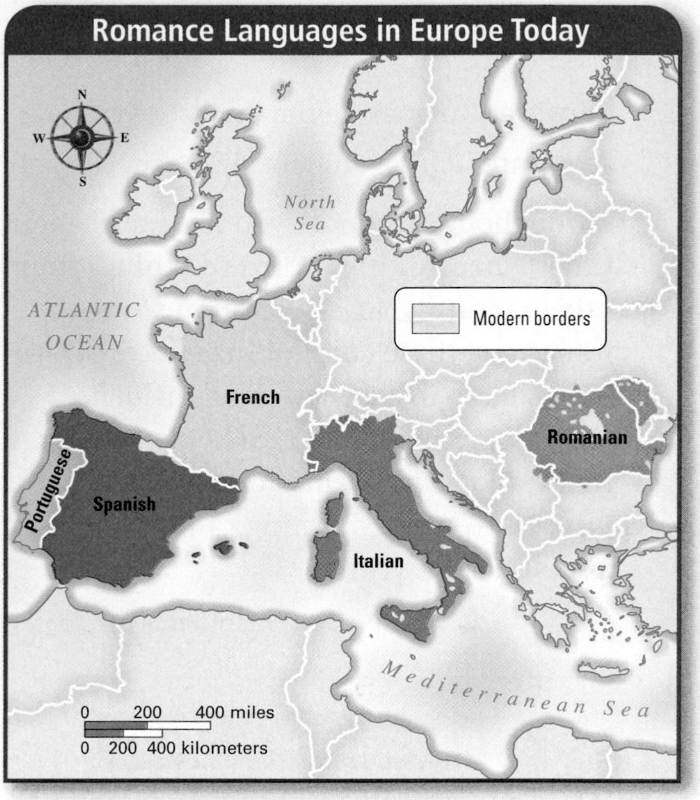

1. **The Romance languages are concentrated in which part of Europe?**
   A. north
   B. east
   C. southwest
   D. southeast

2. **Which statement best describes the pattern of Romance languages?**
   A. The pattern of languages is random.
   B. The Romance languages are found in the former Roman Empire.
   C. The Romance languages are dying out.
   D. The Romance languages spread throughout Europe.

Test Practice
ClassZone.com

Additional Test Practice, pp. S1–S33

Writing About History

Writing Model
ClassZone.com

Expository Writing: Problem and Solution

The Interaction of Cultures

Purpose: To analyze the impact of cultural borrowing

Audience: Other students in your class and school

Throughout this book, you have read about times when cultures borrowed things from other cultures. How can you measure the impacts of these cultural influences? One way is to analyze whether an influence created a problem or solved one. Writing that explores problems and solutions is a type of expository writing called **problem-and-solution** writing.

Alphabet on Greek ostracon (see page 376) ▶

Culture	Characters from Alphabet						
Phoenician	𐤀	𐤁	𐤂	𐤃	𐤄	𐤅	
Greek	Α	Β	Γ	Δ	Ε		
Modern	A	B	C	D	E	F	G

Organization & Focus

Your assignment is to (1) identify a time when one culture borrowed something important from another and (2) decide whether that borrowing solved a problem or created one. Then you will write a two- to three-page composition for a magazine that your class will publish.

Choosing a Topic Review the visual summaries in all the chapters. Take notes about cultural interactions—what caused them and how they affected the cultures that did the borrowing. If you need to, review the chapters for more information. When you have finished, choose one cultural interaction as the topic of your composition.

Identifying Purpose and Audience Your purpose is to analyze the problem or solution represented by an instance of cultural borrowing. Your readers are other students in your school. Keep their interests in mind as you write.

Analyzing Review your notes about the effects of cultural borrowing. Decide whether the borrowing you chose solved a problem or created a problem. For example, the Greeks' borrowing of the Phoenician alphabet solved their problem of not having a writing system.

Research & Technology

To decide whether the cultural borrowing was a problem or a solution, consider both short-term and long-term effects. Consider whether what was borrowed changed society or influenced even later cultures. Use a library and the Internet to research long-term effects.

Outlining and Drafting Consider how to organize your composition. Your outline might be in this form:

I. Introduction
II. Reasons for cultural borrowing
III. Effects of cultural borrowing
  A. On the receiver
  B. On the giver
IV. Identification as problem or solution
  A. Immediate outcomes
  B. Long-term outcomes
V. Conclusion

Use your completed outline as you draft your composition.

Technology Tip Many word-processing programs offer help with making outlines. Check the instruction manual or the help menu to see if your program will format an outline with the proper indents.

Evaluation & Revision

Many writers read their work several times, each time looking at a different aspect of their writing. The list below shows some aspects to review.

- **Ideas** In good compositions, the ideas are interesting, clearly presented, supported with details, and organized logically.
- **Sentence Variety** Using a variety of sentences makes a composition interesting to read. Good writers vary both the structure and the length of their sentences.
- **Word Choice** Precise words give the reader clear visuals. For example, instead of the word *trouble,* a writer might use the more specific word *riot.*

Self-Check

Does my composition have

- ☐ an introduction that grabs attention and states a thesis?
- ☐ an explanation of the effects of an instance of cultural borrowing?
- ☐ a thorough analysis of how the borrowing solved or created a problem?
- ☐ evidence to support that analysis?
- ☐ a strong conclusion?

Publish & Present

Make a neat final copy of your composition. With your classmates, discuss how to arrange the compositions, create a table of contents, and design a magazine cover. Share your magazine with other classes.

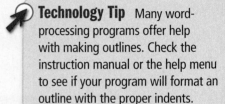

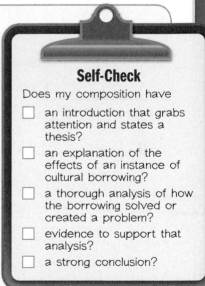

Reference Section

CONTENTS

1.1 Finding Main Ideas

Learn the Skill

The **main idea** is a statement that summarizes the subject of a speech, an article, a section of a book, or a paragraph. Main ideas can be stated or unstated. The main idea of a paragraph is often stated in the first or last sentence. If it is in the first sentence, it is followed by sentences that support that main idea. If it is in the last sentence, the details build up to the main idea. To find an unstated idea, you must use the details of the paragraph as clues.

Practice the Skill

The following paragraph deals with Indian mathematics, science, and technology during the reign of the Guptas. Use the strategies listed below to help you identify the main idea.

How to Find the Main Idea

Strategy ❶ Identify what you think may be the stated main idea. Check the first and last sentences of the paragraph to see if either could be the stated main idea.

Strategy ❷ Identify details that support the main idea. Some details explain that idea. Others give examples of what is stated in the main idea.

ADVANCES UNDER THE GUPTAS

❶ During the reign of the Guptas, Indians made significant advances in mathematics, science, and technology. ❷ Indian scholars developed the decimal system and the symbol for zero. ❷ They also invented the numeral system we use today. ❷ Meanwhile, Indian doctors made key contributions to Ayurvedic medicine. It is one of the oldest systems of medicine. It promotes health by using diet, exercise, and other methods to maintain energy in the body. ❷ Indian artisans developed advanced methods of working with metal. In Delhi, an iron pillar erected about A.D. 400 towers almost 23 feet over the city.

Make a Chart

Making a chart can help you identify the main idea and details in a passage or paragraph. The chart below identifies the main idea and details in the paragraph you just read.

MAIN IDEA: During the reign of the Guptas, Indians made significant advances in mathematics, science, and technology.			
DETAIL: Indian scholars developed the decimal system and the symbol for zero.	DETAIL: Indian scholars invented the numeral system we use today.	DETAIL: Indian doctors advanced Ayurvedic medicine.	DETAIL: Indian artisans developed advanced methods of working with metal.

Apply the Skill

Turn to Chapter 2, Lesson 3, "The First Communities." Read "Villages Grow More Complex" and create a chart that identifies the main idea and the supporting details.

1.2 Summarizing

Learn the Skill

When you **summarize,** you restate a paragraph, a passage, or a chapter in fewer words. You include only the main ideas and most important details. It is important to use your own words when summarizing.

Practice the Skill

The passage below describes early inventions that aided a group in ancient Mesopotamia known as the Sumerians. Use the strategies listed below to help you summarize the passage.

How to Summarize

Strategy ❶ Look for topic sentences that state the main idea or ideas. These are often at the beginning of a section or paragraph. Briefly restate each main idea in your own words.

Strategy ❷ Include key facts and any names, dates, numbers, amounts, or percentages from the text.

Strategy ❸ Write your summary and review it to see that you have included only the most important details.

EARLY INVENTIONS

❶ The plow and the wheel helped the Sumerians a great deal in their daily life. ❷ Plows helped to improve agriculture. They broke up hard soil, which made planting easier. In addition, rainfall often flowed deeper into plowed soil. As a result, the roots of plants received more water.

Meanwhile, Sumerians used the wheel in many ways. ❷ They built wheeled wagons, which helped farmers take their crops to market more easily and quickly. ❷ They also built potter's wheels, which enabled them to make pottery more quickly and efficiently.

Write a Summary

You should be able to write your summary in a short paragraph. The paragraph below summarizes the passage you just read.

❸ The plow and the wheel helped Sumerians in their daily life. Sumerians used plows to improve farming. They used wheels to construct transport wagons and to build potter's wheels, which helped them make pottery more quickly.

Apply the Skill

Turn to Chapter 1, Lesson 4, "How Historians Study the Past." Read "The Historian's Tools" and write a paragraph summarizing the passage.

Skillbuilder Handbook

1.3 Comparing and Contrasting

Learn the Skill

Comparing means looking at the similarities and differences among two or more things. **Contrasting** means examining only the differences among them. Historians compare and contrast events, personalities, behaviors, beliefs, and situations in order to understand them better.

Practice the Skill

The following passage describes the ancient Assyrian and Persian empires. Use the strategies below to help you compare and contrast these two empires.

How to Compare and Contrast

Strategy ❶ Look for two subjects that can be compared and contrasted. This passage compares the Assyrian and Persian empires.

Strategy ❷ To find similarities, look for clue words indicating that two things are alike. Clue words include *both, together, also,* and *similarly.*

Strategy ❸ To find contrasts, look for clue words that show how two things differ. Clue words include *by contrast, but, on the other hand,* and *yet.*

ASSYRIAN EMPIRE AND PERSIAN EMPIRE

❶ During ancient times, Assyria and Persia ❷ *both* developed into mighty empires. The Assyrians had a fierce army that conquered many lands. ❷ The Persians *also* had a powerful army. The Assyrians governed their empire by choosing the person to rule each region. ❷ *Similarly,* the Persians set up governors to carry out orders in the various regions of their empire. There were differences between the two empires, including the way in which they treated conquered peoples. The Assyrians were cruel to the groups they defeated. ❸ *By contrast,* the Persians largely respected the people they captured.

Make a Venn Diagram

Making a Venn diagram will help you identify similarities and differences between two things. In the overlapping area, list characteristics shared by both subjects. Then, in the separate ovals, list the characteristics that the two subjects do not share. This Venn diagram compares and contrasts the Assyrian and Persian empires.

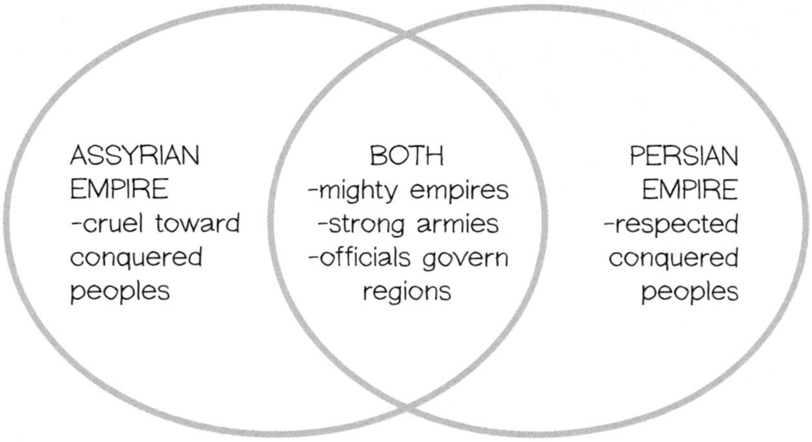

Apply the Skill

Turn to Chapter 1, Lesson 2, "How Maps Help Us Study History." Read "Different Maps for Different Purposes." Then make a Venn diagram showing similarities and differences between political and physical maps.

1.4 Making Inferences

Learn the Skill

Inferences are ideas that the author has not directly stated. **Making inferences** involves reading between the lines to interpret the information you read. You can make inferences by studying what is stated and using your common sense and previous knowledge.

Practice the Skill

The passage below examines the Kushite civilization in northern Africa. Use the strategies below to help you make inferences from the passage.

How to Make Inferences

Strategy ❶ Read to find statements of facts and ideas. Knowing the facts will give you a good basis for making inferences.

Strategy ❷ Use your knowledge, logic, and common sense to make inferences that are based on facts. Ask yourself, "What does the author want me to understand?" For example, from the facts about Kushite civilization, you can make the inference that trade was important to the Kushites.

KUSHITE CIVILIZATION

The Kushite kings chose a new capital, Meroë, in about 500 B.C. Meroë was located on the Nile River south of the Egyptian Empire. The city boasted abundant supplies of iron ore. ❶ As a result, the Kushite people manufactured iron weapons and tools. ❶ Merchants in Meroë traded iron goods for jewelry, fine cotton cloth, and glass bottles. ❶ In Kush, royal women held a significant degree of power. In the absence of the king, a queen ruled the country.

Make a Chart

Making a chart will help you organize information and make logical inferences. The chart below organizes information from the passage you just read.

❶ STATED FACTS AND IDEAS	❷ INFERENCES
The people of Kush manufactured iron weapons and tools.	The Kushite people possessed strong technological skills.
Merchants from Meroë exchanged iron goods for products from faraway lands.	Trade was an important part of the Kushite empire.
In Kush, royal women sometimes ruled.	In Kush, some women were influential and well respected.

Apply the Skill

Turn to Chapter 6, Lesson 2, "The Kingdom of Aksum." Read "Aksum's Achievements" and use a chart like the one above to make inferences about Aksum's civilization.

1.5 Categorizing

Learn the Skill

To **categorize** is to sort people, objects, ideas, or other information into groups, called categories. Historians categorize information to help them identify and understand patterns in historical events.

Practice the Skill

The following passage discusses the development of villages during ancient times. Use the strategies listed below to help you categorize information in a passage.

How to Categorize

Strategy ❶ First, decide what the passage is about.

Strategy ❷ Then find out what the categories will be. Look for different ways that villages became more complex. These will be your category headings.

Strategy ❸ Once you have chosen the categories, sort information into them. For example, how did the economy grow more complex? How did society grow more complex?

VILLAGES GROW MORE COMPLEX

Advances in agriculture and technology resulted in extra food and supplies. This meant that larger groups of people could live together in one place. ❶ As a result, villages soon grew larger and more complex. With fewer farmers needed, people learned new skills and crafts. ❷ They became carpenters, tool makers, and potters. As a result, a new and more diverse economic system emerged. Social systems also grew more diverse. ❷ As villages grew, social classes with varying wealth, power, and influence emerged. ❷ The growing populations of early villages also led to the creation of more organized political systems. Villagers established a government, or a system of ruling, to provide greater order and leadership.

Make a Chart

Making a chart can help you categorize information. The chart below shows how the information from the passage you just read can be categorized.

VILLAGES GROW MORE COMPLEX		
ECONOMIC	SOCIAL	POLITICAL
specialized workers; new professions	defined classes	creation of government

Apply the Skill

Turn to Chapter 7, Lesson 1, "Geography and Indian Life." Read "Physical Geography of India" and make a chart in which you categorize the physical geography of India.

1.6 Making Decisions

Learn the Skill

Making decisions involves choosing between two or more options, or courses of action. In most cases, decisions have consequences, or results. By understanding how historical figures made decisions, you can learn how to improve your own decision-making skills.

Practice the Skill

The passage below explains a decision Emperor Shi Huangdi faced about governing China. Use the strategies below to analyze his decision.

How to Make Decisions

Strategy ① Identify a decision that needs to be made. Think about what factors make the decision difficult.

Strategy ❷ Identify possible consequences of the decision. Remember that there can be more than one consequence to a decision.

Strategy ❸ Identify the decision.

Strategy ❹ Identify actual consequences that resulted from the decision.

HOW TO GOVERN

When Shi Huangdi became emperor in 221 B.C., China suffered from many internal battles between warring states. ① Shi Huangdi had to decide how to govern. ❷ If he imposed a strong and harsh rule, he could end the internal battles and restore order. However, the Chinese people might react angrily to such a strong government. ❷ If Shi Huangdi ruled with tolerance, the internal battles might continue. ❸ Shi Huangdi decided to rule harshly. ❹ Shi Huangdi's strong rule did bring order. ❹ However, his harsh rule caused great resentment among the people. After Shi Huangdi's death, the Chinese people rebelled.

Make a Flow Chart

A flow chart can help you identify the steps involved in making a decision. The flow chart below shows the decision-making process in the passage you just read.

① DECISION TO BE MADE: How should Shi Huangdi govern? Should he rule harshly or direct a more tolerant government?

→ ❷ POSSIBLE CONSEQUENCE: Harsh rule might lessen internal battles but anger the people.

→ ❷ POSSIBLE CONSEQUENCE: Tolerant rule might do little to halt the internal battles.

→ ❸ DECISION MADE: Rule harshly.

→ ❹ ACTUAL CONSEQUENCE: Shi Huangdi restored order. His rule caused resentment among the people, which eventually led to rebellion.

Apply the Skill

Turn to Chapter 4, Lesson 3, "Persia Controls Southwest Asia." Read "Cyrus Founds an Empire" and make a flow chart to identify Cyrus' decision about how to rule his empire.

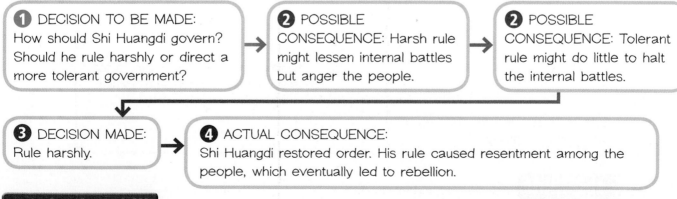

1.7 Making Generalizations

Learn the Skill

To **make generalizations** means to make broad judgments based on information. When you make generalizations, you should gather information from several sources.

Practice the Skill

The following three passages contain descriptions of Sparta. Use the strategies listed below to make a generalization about Sparta based on these descriptions.

How to Make Generalizations

Strategy ❶ Look for information that the sources have in common. For example, all three sources describe the military might of Sparta.

Strategy ❷ Form a generalization about these descriptions in a way that agrees with all three sources. State your generalization in a sentence.

LIFE IN SPARTA

❶ From the 5th century, the ruling class of Sparta devoted itself to war and diplomacy, deliberately neglecting the arts, philosophy, and literature. . . .
–*Encyclopaedia Britannica*

❶ From the age of seven a Spartan boy was educated and trained by the state to become a soldier.
–*Encyclopedia Americana*

❶ The Spartan people paid a high price for their military supremacy. All forms of individual expression were discouraged. ❶ As a result, Spartans did not value . . . artistic or intellectual pursuits.
–*World History: Patterns of Interaction*

Make a Diagram

Using a diagram can help you make generalizations. The diagram below shows how the information you just read can be used to generalize about Sparta.

<table>
<tr><td>❶ Spartan boys were trained from early on to be soldiers.</td><td rowspan="3">❷ GENERALIZATION
Sparta became a powerful military state by stressing military service and training over all other pursuits in society.</td></tr>
<tr><td>❶ Sparta discouraged artistic, intellectual, and other nonmilitary pursuits.</td></tr>
<tr><td>❶ The Spartans devoted themselves to war and military training.</td></tr>
</table>

Apply the Skill

Turn to Chapter 8, Lesson 2, "China's Ancient Philosophies." Read "Confucianism," and the primary source on page 261. Also read the History Maker feature about "Confucius" on page 262. Use a chart like the one above to make a generalization about Confucius.

2.1 Reading a Map

Learn the Skill

Maps are representations of features on Earth's surface. Some maps show political features, such as national borders. Other maps show physical features, such as mountains and bodies of water. By learning to use map elements, you can better understand how to read maps.

Practice the Skill

The following map shows the Sumerian city-states. Use the strategies listed below to help you identify the elements common to most maps.

How to Read a Map

Strategy 1 Read the title. This identifies the main idea of the map.

Strategy 2 Look for the grid of lines that forms a pattern of squares over the map. These numbered lines are the lines of latitude (horizontal) and longitude (vertical). They indicate the location of the area on Earth.

Strategy 3 Read the map key. It is usually in a box. The key will help you interpret the symbols or colors on the map.

Strategy 4 Use the scale and the pointer, or compass rose, to determine distance and direction.

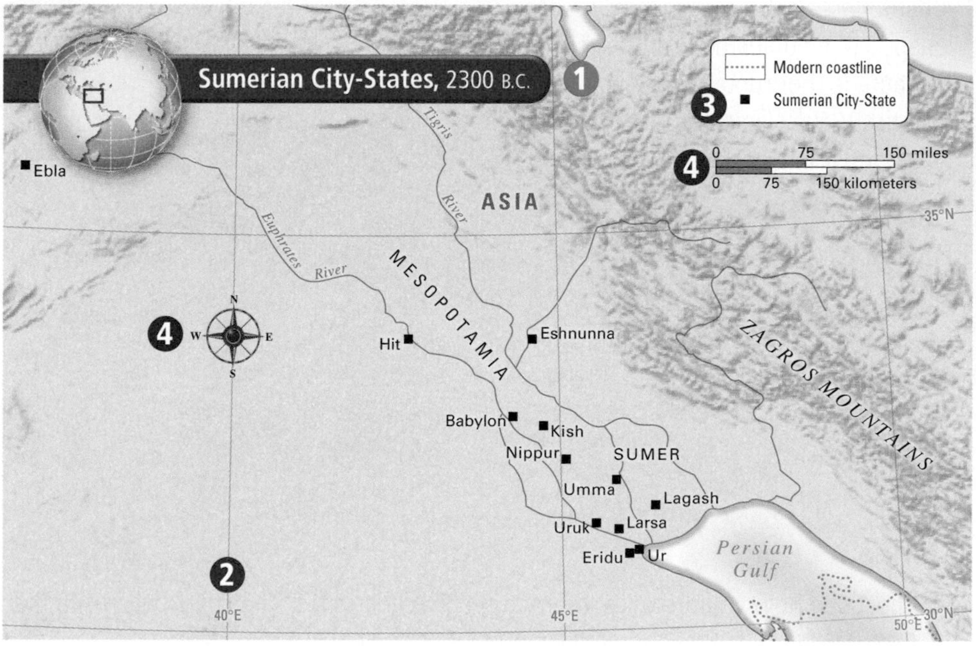

Make a Chart

A chart can help you organize information given on maps. The chart below summarizes information about the map you just studied.

TITLE	Sumerian City-States, 2300 B.C.
LOCATION	"between longitudes 50°E and 40°E and latitudes 30°N and 35°N, except for Ebla which is located between longitude 35°E and 40°E, just north of 35°N"
KEY INFORMATION	square = Sumerian city-state
SUMMARY	Sumerian city-states developed mostly along the southern regions of the Tigris and Euphrates rivers.

2.1 Reading a Map *(continued)*

Practice the Skill

The following map shows the Aryan invasions into India. Use the strategies listed below to help you identify the elements common to most maps.

How to Read a Map

Strategy 1 Read the title. This identifies the main idea of the map.

Strategy 2 Look for the grid of lines that forms a pattern of squares over the map. These numbered lines are the lines of latitude (horizontal) and longitude (vertical). They indicate the location of the area on Earth.

Strategy 3 Read the map key. It is usually in a box. The key will help you interpret the symbols or colors on the map.

Strategy 4 Use the pointer, or compass rose, to determine direction.

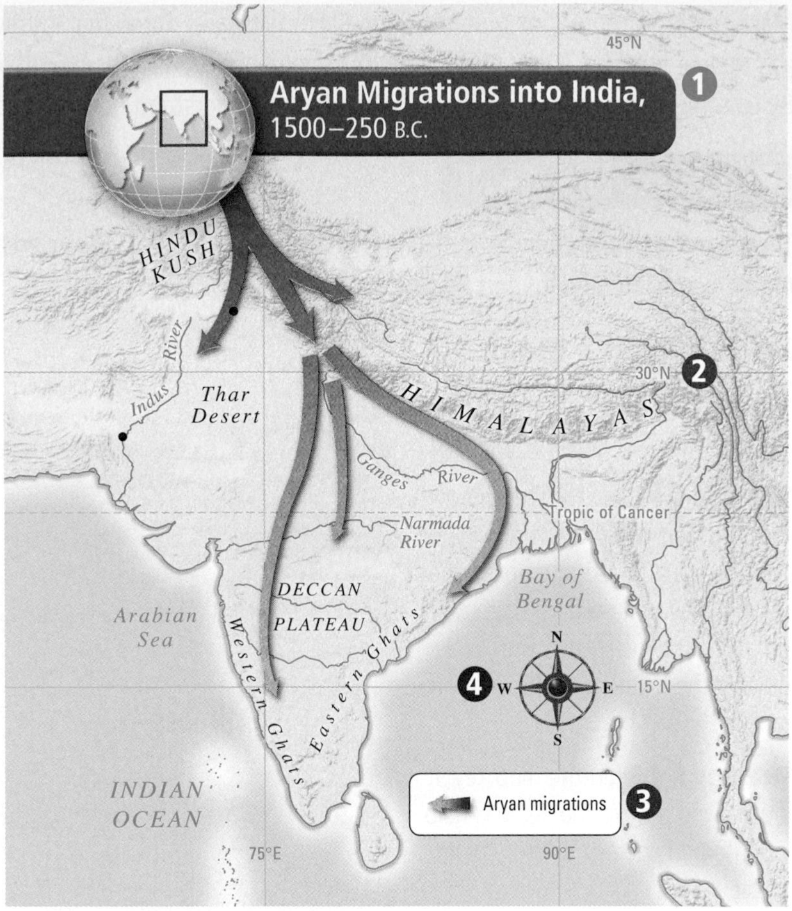

Make a Chart

A chart can help you organize information given on maps. The chart below summarizes information about the map you just studied.

TITLE	Aryan Migrations into India, 1500–250 B.C.
LOCATION	"between longitudes 75°E and 90°E and latitudes 30°N and the equator."
KEY INFORMATION	arrows = paths of Aryan migrations
SUMMARY	Over a roughly 1200-year period, the Aryans migrated south and settled throughout much of India.

Apply the Skill

Turn to Chapter 4, Lesson 2, "Assyria Rules the Fertile Crescent." Read the map entitled "Assyrian Empire, 650 B.C." and make a chart to identify information on the map.

2.2 Creating a Map

Learn the Skill

Creating a map involves representing geographical information. When you draw a map, it is easiest to use an existing map as a guide. On the map you draw, you can show geographical information. You can also show political information such as the area covered by empires, civilizations, and countries. In addition, maps can show data on climates, population, and resources.

Practice the Skill

Below is a map that a student created that shows the furthest extent of the Gupta Empire. Read the strategies listed below to see how the map was created.

How to Create a Map

Strategy 1 Select a title that identifies the geographical area and the map's purpose. Include a date in your title.

Strategy 2 Draw lines of latitude and longitude using short dashes.

Strategy 3 Create a key that shows the colors and symbols.

Strategy 4 Draw the colors and symbols on the map to show information.

Strategy 5 Draw a compass rose and scale.

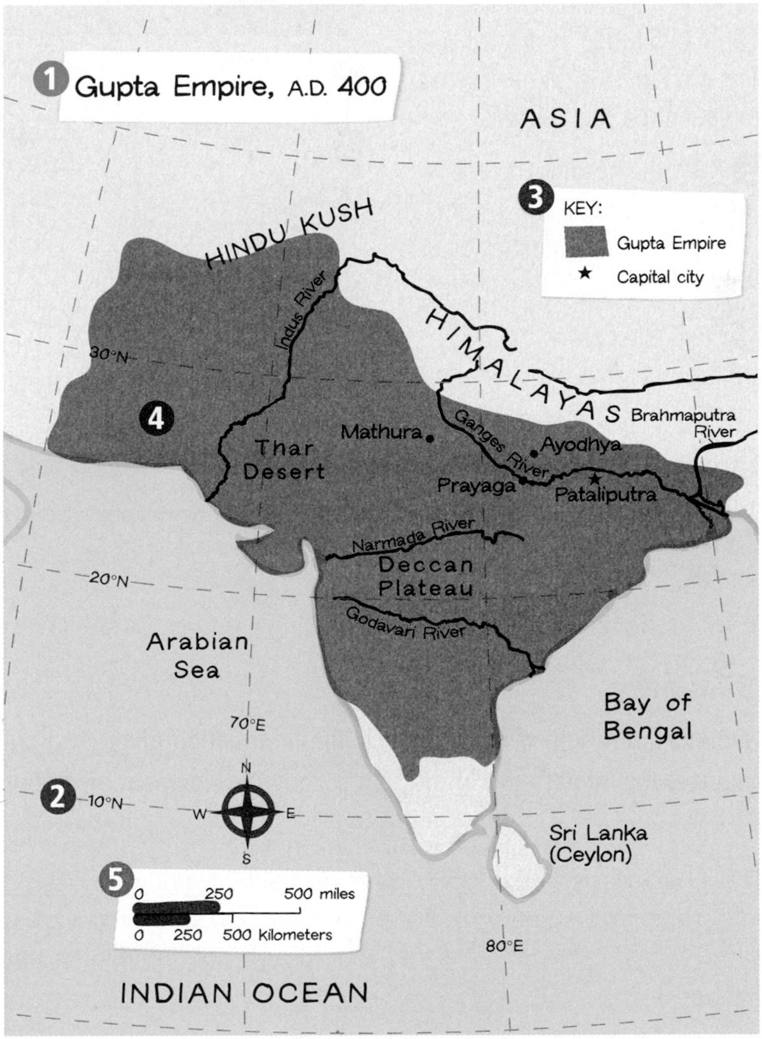

Apply the Skill

Turn to Chapter 8, Lesson 1, "Geography Shapes Life in Ancient China." Read "Isolated by Barriers" under "Geographic Features of China." Use the information in this passage and the strategies mentioned above to create a map of China that shows the approximate areas covered by the Gobi Desert and the Taklimakan Desert. Use the map on pages A6–A7 as a model for your map.

2.3 Interpreting Charts

Learn the Skill

Charts present information in a visual form. Charts are created by simplifying, summarizing, and organizing information. This information is then presented in a format that is easy to understand. Tables and diagrams are examples of commonly used charts.

Practice the Skill

The chart below focuses on the early development of writing. Use the strategies listed below to help interpret the information in the chart.

How to Interpret a Chart

Strategy ❶ Read the title. It will tell you what the chart is about. Ask yourself what kinds of information the chart shows.

Strategy ❷ Read the headings to see how the chart is organized. In this chart, information is organized by examples of pictograph and cuneiform.

Strategy ❸ Study the data in the chart to understand the facts that the chart was designed to show.

Strategy ❹ Summarize the information shown in each part of the chart. Use the title to help you focus on what information the chart is presenting.

❶ **Early Development of Writing**

❷ word	pictograph	cuneiform
❸ bird		
cow	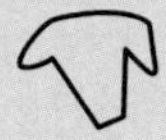	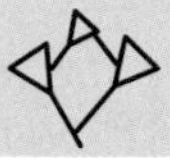
fish	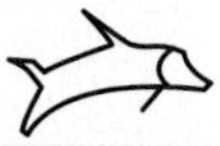	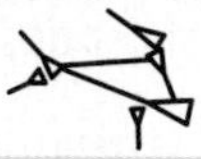
mountain		
water		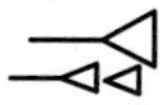

Write a Summary

Writing a summary can help you understand the information given in a chart. The paragraph below summarizes the information in the chart "Early Development of Writing."

❹ The chart depicts the early development of writing by showing examples of pictograph and cuneiform. By examining how each form of writing expressed the same word, one can see that pictograph and cuneiform had similarities and differences.

Apply the Skill

Turn to Chapter 12, Lesson 1, "The Golden Age of Greece." Study the political information presented in the chart entitled "Athenian and U.S. Democracy." Then write a paragraph in which you summarize what you learned from the chart.

2.4 Interpreting Graphs

Learn the Skill

Graphs use pictures and symbols, instead of words, to show information. There are many different kinds of graphs. Bar graphs, line graphs, and pie graphs are the most common. Line graphs show trends or changes over time.

Practice the Skill

The line graph below shows the relationship between the growth of farming (Agricultural Revolution) and the increase in the world population during the past 25,000 years. Use the strategies listed below to help you interpret the graph.

How to Interpret a Graph

Strategy ❶ Read the title to identify the main idea of the graph.

Strategy ❷ Read the vertical axis (the one that goes up and down) on the left side of the graph. In this graph, the vertical axis indicates the world population.

Strategy ❸ Read the horizontal axis (the one that runs across the bottom of the graph). In this graph, the horizontal axis shows the progression of time.

Strategy ❹ Look at any legends that accompany the graph in order to understand what colors and certain marks stand for.

Strategy ❺ Summarize the information shown in each part of the graph.

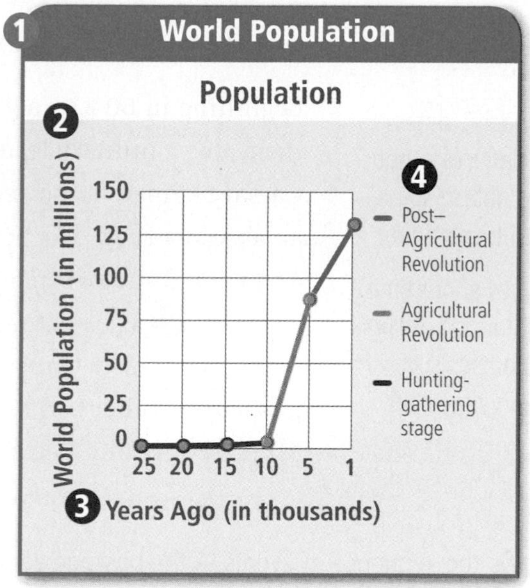

Source: *A Geography of Population: World Patterns*

Write a Summary

Writing a summary will help you understand the information in the graph. The paragraph below summarizes the information from the line graphs.

❺ As a result of the agricultural revolution, world population grew steadily over a period of 10,000 years.

Apply the Skill

Examine a current news magazine and look for any graphs that might be used to convey information. Write a summary of the information in the graph using the strategies you learned on this page. Share your graph and information with the class.

2.5 Constructing Time Lines

Learn the Skill

A **time line** is a visual list of events and dates shown in the order in which they occurred. Time lines show **sequence,** or the order in which events follow one another. The ability to sequence historical events by constructing a time line enables you to get an accurate sense of the relationship among those events.

Practice the Skill

The following passage shows the sequence of events in Rome's transition from a republic to an empire. Use the strategies listed below to help you construct a time line of the events.

How to Construct a Time Line

Strategy ❶ Look for specific dates provided in the text. The dates may not always read from earliest to latest, so be sure to match an event with the date

Strategy ❷ Look for clues about time that allow you to order events according to sequence. Words and phrases such as *day, week, year,* or *century* may help to sequence the events.

FROM REPUBLIC TO EMPIRE

Beginning in 60 B.C., a group of three leaders ruled Rome. Among them was a military leader named Julius Caesar. ❶ In 46 B.C., Caesar claimed all power for himself. Caesar governed Rome as an absolute ruler. His power made many officials jealous. ❶ In 44 B.C., a group of senators ambushed Caesar and stabbed him to death. ❷ The next *year,* Caesar's adopted son Octavian and two other leaders gained control of Rome. Octavian eventually pushed the other two aside. He took the title of Augustus, or "exalted one" and began his rule as emperor ❶ in 27 B.C.

Make a Time Line

The time line below shows the sequence of events in the passage you just read.

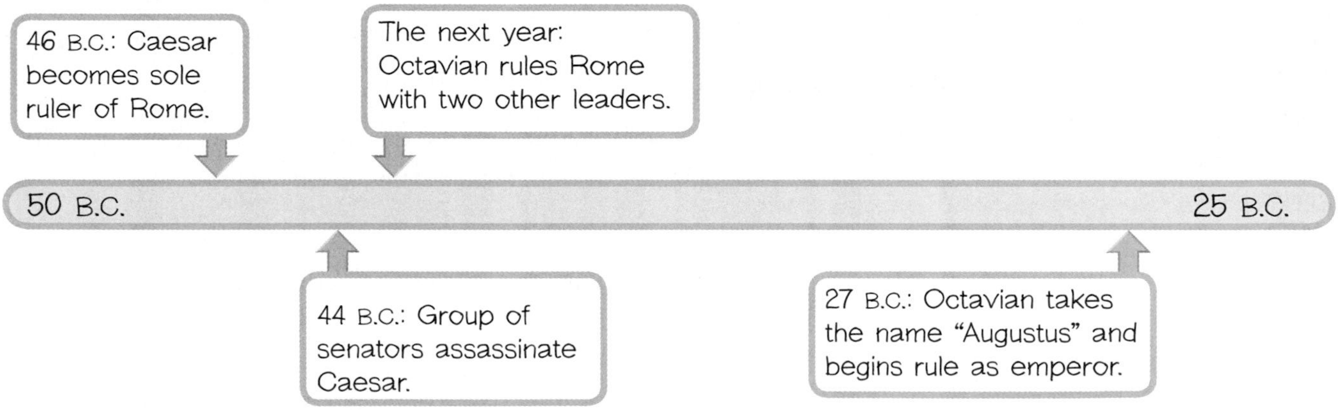
46 B.C.: Caesar becomes sole ruler of Rome.
The next year: Octavian rules Rome with two other leaders.
50 B.C.
25 B.C.
44 B.C.: Group of senators assassinate Caesar.
27 B.C.: Octavian takes the name "Augustus" and begins rule as emperor.

Apply the Skill

Turn to Chapter 4, Lesson 2, "Assyria Rules the Fertile Crescent." Read "Assyria Builds a Huge Empire" and "A New Babylonian Empire." Then make a time line showing the sequence of events in those two passages.

2.6 Explaining Chronological Order and Sequence

Learn the Skill

Explaining chronological order and sequence means identifying the order in which major historical events occur. Major events that follow each other in time are often linked by a series of occurrences.

Practice the Skill

The following passage deals with the captivity of ancient Israel. Use the strategies listed below to help you identify the major events and the series of occurrences that connect them.

How to Explain Chronological Order and Sequence

Strategy ❶ Look for specific dates provided in the text. The dates may not always read from earliest to latest, so be sure to match an event with the date.

Strategy ❷ Look for clues about time that allow you to order events according to sequence. Words and phrases such as *day, week, year,* or *century* may help to sequence the events.

THE BABYLONIAN CAPTIVITY

Solomon became the third king of Israel ❶ in 962 B.C. Soon after Solomon's death in ❷ in 922 B.C. Israel split into two separate kingdoms—Israel and Judah. Around 586 B.C., the Babylonians conquered both Israel and Judah. They took thousands of Jews to Babylon as slaves. These Jews spent roughly the ❷ next 50 years in Babylon. This time is known as the Babylonian Captivity. ❶ In 539 B.C., Persia conquered Babylonia. ❷ The next *year,* the Persian king Cyrus freed the Jewish slaves and allowed them to return to their homeland.

Make a Time Line

Making a time line can help you visualize chronological order. The time line below shows the order of events in the passage you just read.

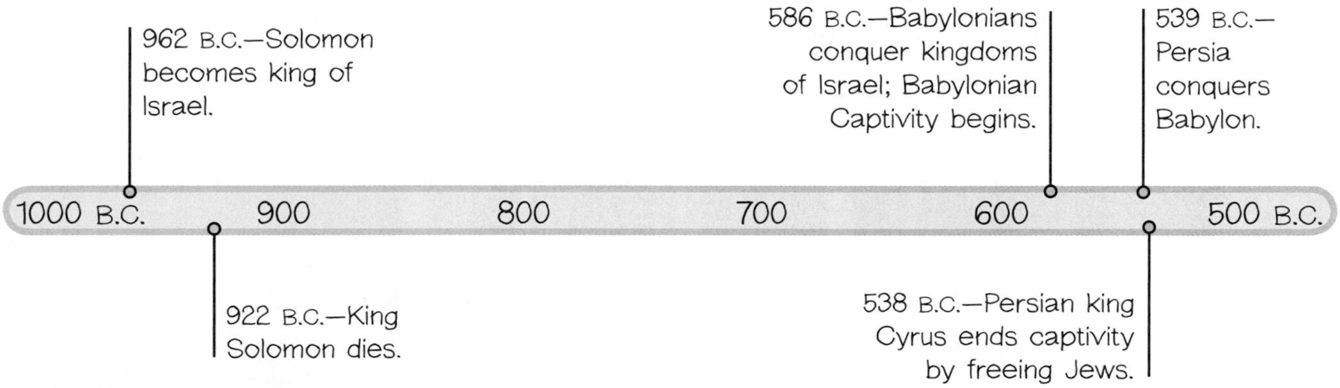
962 B.C.—Solomon becomes king of Israel.
586 B.C.—Babylonians conquer kingdoms of Israel; Babylonian Captivity begins.
539 B.C.—Persia conquers Babylon.
1000 B.C.
900
800
700
600
500 B.C.
922 B.C.—King Solomon dies.
538 B.C.—Persian king Cyrus ends captivity by freeing Jews.

Apply the Skill

Turn to Chapter 15, Lesson 2, "The Fall of the Roman Empire." Read "Invading People" and "The Fall of Rome." Then make a chart that shows the major events and connecting events and summarizes how the major events relate to each other.

2.7 Explaining Geographic Patterns

Learn the Skill

Explaining geographic patterns involves understanding the movement of such things as people, cultures, or ideas across the earth. Geographic patterns include the migration of people, the expansion or decline of empires, the growth of economic systems, and the spread of religion. Some maps show geographic patterns. By studying these maps, you can better understand the development of cultures, ideas, and political systems.

Practice the Skill

The following map deals with the spread of Buddhism. Use the strategies listed below to help you study this map and others that show geographic patterns.

How to Explain Geographic Patterns

Strategy 1 Locate the title of the map. The title usually identifies the geographic pattern shown on the map.

Strategy 2 Locate any shaded areas on the map. The shaded areas show important regions of the geographic pattern. On this map, the shaded area shows the region where the Buddhism originated.

Strategy 3 Identify any graphics on the map, such as arrows. Arrows are often used to show the movement of ideas, goods, or people. Use the compass rose to determine the directions that the arrows point.

Strategy 4 Using the above strategies, write a summary about the geographic pattern shown on the map.

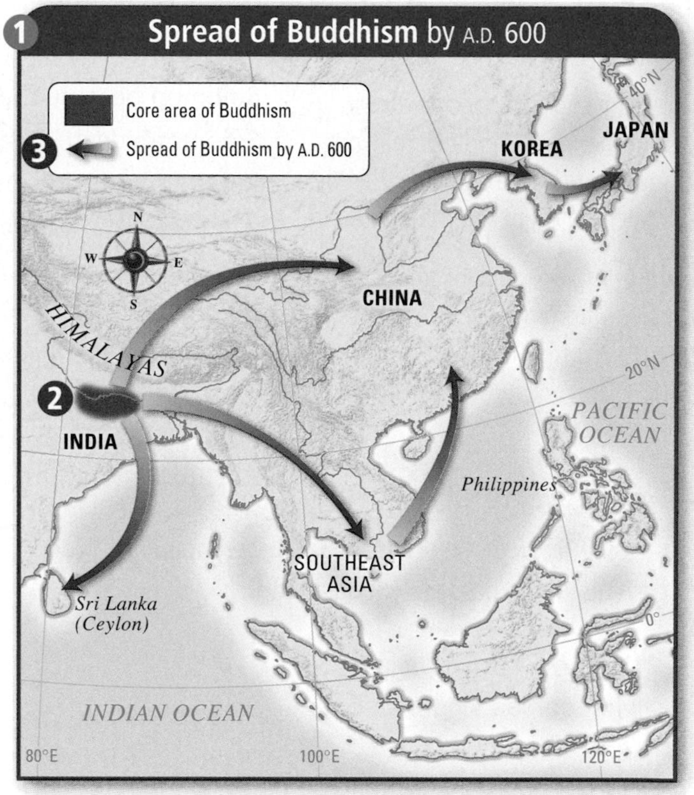

4 Buddhism began in India and spread southward and eastward. Its influence eventually reached China, Southeast Asia, Korea, Japan, and Sri Lanka.

Apply the Skill

Turn to Chapter 6, Lesson 3, "Western, Central, and Southern Africa." Study the map "Aryan Migrations into India, 1500–250 B.C." on page 228. Using the strategies mentioned above, write a summary of the geographic pattern shown on this map.

2.8 Creating a Model

Learn the Skill

When you **create a model,** you use information and ideas to show an event or a situation in a visual way. A model might be a poster or a diagram that explains how something happened. Or, it might be a three-dimensional model, such as a diorama, that depicts an important scene or situation.

Practice the Skill

The following sketch shows the early stages of a model of the Great Pyramid of Khufu's interior. Use the strategies listed below to help you create your own model.

How to Create a Model

Strategy 1 Gather the information you need to understand the situation or event. In this case, you need to be able to show parts of the inside of the Great Pyramid of Khufu.

Strategy 2 Visualize and sketch an idea for your model. Once you have created a picture in your mind, make an actual sketch to plan how the model might look.

Strategy 3 Think of symbols you may want to use. Since the model should give information in a visual way, think about ways you can use color, pictures, or other visuals to tell the story.

Strategy 4 Gather the supplies you will need. For example, for this model, you will need pictures of the Great Pyramid of Khufu and diagrams of the inside of this pyramid. You will also need art supplies. Then create the model.

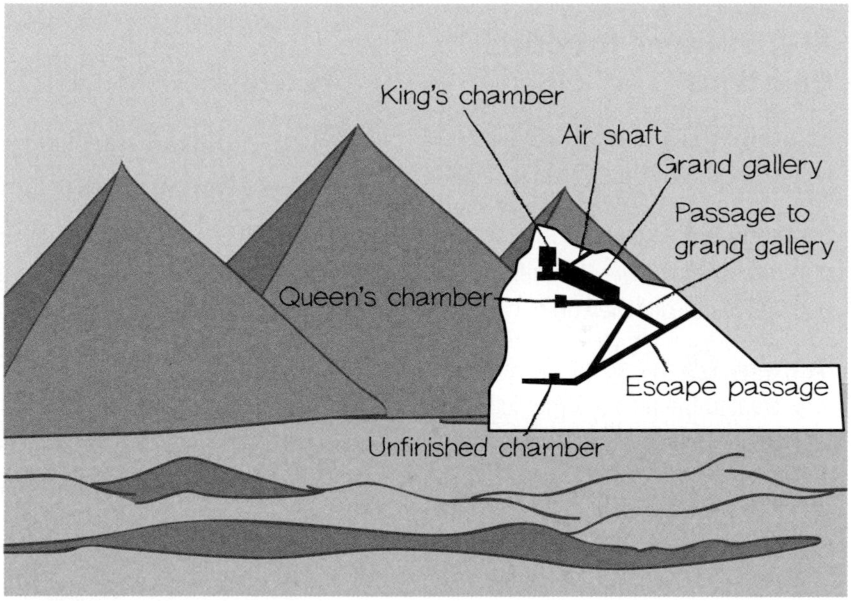

Apply the Skill

Turn to Chapter 12, Lesson 1, "The Golden Age of Greece" and read "Beautifying Athens." Also read descriptions and study images of the inside of the Parthenon. Then draw a diagram of the inside of the Parthenon. Include labels that identify parts of the Parthenon's interior.

3.1 Framing Historical Questions

Learn the Skill

Framing historical questions is important as you study primary sources—firsthand accounts, documents, letters, and other records of the past. As you analyze a source, ask questions about what it means and why it is significant. This will help you to better understand the information you read.

Practice the Skill

The following passage is an excerpt from a biography of Julius Caesar written by Roman scholar Caius Suetonius Tranquillus. This excerpt describes the assassination of Caesar. It mentions Spurinna, a prophet who had warned that harm would come to Caesar on the ides (15th) of March. Use the strategies listed below to help you frame historical questions.

How to Frame Historical Questions

Strategy ❶ Ask about the historical record itself. Who produced it? When?

Strategy ❷ Ask about the facts presented. Who were the main people? What did they do?

Strategy ❸ Ask about the person who created the record. What judgments or opinions does the author express?

Strategy ❹ Ask about the importance of the record. Does the record convey important historical information?

❶ CAIUS TRANQUILLUS, 1ST CENTURY B.C.

❷ He [Julius Caesar] entered the House [Senate] in defiance of portents [prophecies], laughing at ❷ Spurinna and calling him a false prophet, because the ides of March were come without bringing him harm. . . . As he took his seat, the ❷ conspirators gathered about him [Caesar] as if to pay their respects. . . . He [Caesar] saw that he was beset on every side by drawn daggers. . . . He was stabbed with three and twenty wounds, ❸ uttering not a word, but merely a groan at the first stroke, though some have written that when Marcus Brutus rushed at him, he said in Greek, "You too, my child?" . . . ❹

Make a Chart

Making a chart can help you list and answer questions about a historical source. The chart below lists historical questions and answers based on the passage you just read.

	QUESTIONS	ANSWERS
HISTORICAL RECORD	Who produced it? When?	Caius Suetonius Tranquillus; first century B.C.
FACTS PRESENTED	Who were the main people? What did they do?	Julius Caesar, Spurinna, Marcus Brutus, Conspirators The conspirators killed Caesar.
CREATOR	What were his opinions?	Caesar died without uttering a word.
IMPORTANCE	What is its importance?	Provides insight into the death of a famous historical figure

Apply the Skill

Turn to Chapter 6, Lesson 2, "The Kingdom of Aksum." Read the Primary Source on King Ezana of Aksum. Use a chart like the one shown here to ask and answer historical questions about this primary source.

3.2 Distinguishing Facts from Opinions

Learn the Skill

Facts are events, dates, statistics, or statements that can be proved to be true. **Opinions** are judgments, beliefs, and feelings. By understanding the difference between facts and opinions, you will be able to think critically when a person is trying to influence your own opinion.

Practice the Skill

The following passage describes the Greek philosopher Aristotle and some of his views on government. Use the strategies listed below to distinguish facts from opinions

How to Distinguish Facts from Opinions

Strategy ① Look for specific information that can be proved or checked for accuracy.

Strategy ② Look for assertions, claims, and judgments that express opinions. In this case, one speaker's opinion is addressed in quotation marks.

Strategy ③ Think about whether statements can be checked for accuracy. Then identify the facts and opinions in a chart.

ARISTOTLE'S VIEWS

① Artistotle was born in 384 B.C. in Stagira, a small town in northern Greece. At the age of 17, Aristotle entered a school directed by the noted philosopher Plato. ① Aristotle quickly became a standout student. Plato referred to him as the "intelligence of the school." Aristotle is considered one of the greatest thinkers in Western culture. He expressed views on a number of significant subjects, including politics and government. ② Aristotle believed the middle class was the most suited to rule, calling this group "the steadiest element" of society.

Make a Chart

The chart below analyzes the facts and opinions from the passage above.

③ STATEMENT	CAN IT BE PROVED	FACT OR OPINION
Aristotle was born in 384 B.C. in the town of Stagira.	Yes, check historical documents.	Fact
Aristotle became a standout philosophy student.	Yes, check Plato's comments; other historical records.	Fact
The middle class is the group most suited to rule.	No, this cannot be proved. It is what one speaker believes.	Opinion

Apply the Skill

Turn to Chapter 9, Lesson 2, "Ancient Andean Civilizations," and read the section entitled "The Nazca Civilization." Make a chart in which you analyze key statements to determine whether they are facts or opinions.

3.3 Detecting Historical Points of View

Learn the Skill

A **historical point of view** is an attitude that a person has about an event in the past. Detecting and analyzing different points of view can help you to better understand a historical figure's thoughts and actions.

Practice the Skill

The following passage describes the political rise of the Roman leader Julius Caesar. Use the strategies below to help you detect and analyze what historical points of view are expressed.

How to Detect Points of View

Strategy ❶ Look for clue words that indicate a person's view on an issue. These include words such as *believe, insist, support,* and *oppose.*

Strategy ❷ Look for reasons why someone has taken a particular point of view.

THE RISE OF CAESAR

Julius Caesar was a brilliant military leader who eventually became dictator of Rome. Although Rome had been a republic in which no single person held all the power, ❶ many people *supported* Caesar's rise to dictator. ❷ In addition to his military skills, Caesar was a good politician with a reputation as a reformer. All of this made him popular with the common people of Rome.

But some people opposed Caesar. One of his opponents was Cicero, a Roman politician. ❶ Cicero *believed* it was wrong for Caesar to have complete control over Rome. ❷ Cicero was a strong supporter of a republic. He opposed the idea of giving all political power to one person.

Make a Chart

Using a chart can help you detect and analyze historical points of view. The chart below analyzes the views in the passage you just read.

PERSON(S)	VIEW	REASONS
Common People	supported Caesar as dictator	military hero; reputation as a reformer
Cicero	opposed Caesar as dictator	favored a republic; distrusted rule by one person

Apply the Skill

Turn to Chapter 8, Lesson 3, "The Qin and the Han." Read "The Qin Unified China" and "The Han Dynasty." Then make a chart like the one above to analyze the different points of view taken by the two dynasties.

Skillbuilder Handbook

3.4 Determining Historical Context

Learn the Skill

Determining historical context means finding out how events and people were influenced by the context of their time. It means judging the past not by current values, but by taking into account the beliefs of the time.

Practice the Skill

The following passage is from the writings of the fourth-century Roman historian Ammianus Marcellinus. In this passage, Marcellinus describes the Huns, one of the groups that eventually invaded Rome and helped bring down the empire.

How to Determine Historical Context

Strategy ❶ Identify the historical figure, the occasion, and the date.

Strategy ❷ Look for clues to the attitudes, customs, and values of people living at the time. In this case, Marcellinus is expressing a view, most likely held by many Romans, that the outside invaders threatening their empire were uncivilized "barbarians."

Strategy ❸ Explain how people's actions and words reflected the attitudes, values, and passions of the era. Here, Marcellinus is issuing a warning of sorts to his fellow Romans that the Huns are wild and fierce fighters that need to be taken seriously.

Strategy ❹ Using the strategies mentioned above, write a conclusion about the historical context of the passage.

❶ from *The Chronicle of Events* (fourth century)
Ammianus Marcellinus

The nation of the Huns . . . ❷ surpasses all other barbarians in wildness of life. . . . And though [the Huns] do just bear the likeness of men (of a very ugly pattern), ❷ they are so little advanced in civilization that they . . . feed upon the . . . half-raw flesh of any sort of animal. . . . ❸ When attacked . . . they fill the air with varied and discordant cries. . . . They fight in no regular order of battle, but by being extremely swift and sudden in their movements, they disperse . . . spread havoc over vast plains, and . . . pillage the camp of their enemy almost before he has become aware of their approach.

❹ CONCLUSION
Like perhaps many Romans, Marcellinus considered the Huns far less civilized than the Romans themselves. As barbaric as the Romans thought they were, however, many probably agreed with Marcellinus that their fierce and chaotic fighting style made them a serious threat to the empire.

Apply the Skill

Turn to Chapter 12, Lesson 2, "Peloponnesian War." Read the Primary Source feature "Pericles' Funeral Oration." Using the above strategies, write a conclusion about the historical context of this passage.

3.5 Forming and Supporting Opinions

Learn the Skill

When you **form opinions,** you interpret and judge the importance of events and people in history. You should always **support your opinions** with facts, examples, and quotations.

Practice the Skill

The following passage describes characteristics of the Egyptian kings, known as pharaohs. Use the strategies listed below to form and support an opinion about these rulers.

How to Form and Support Opinions

Strategy ❶ Look for important information about the subject. Information can include facts, quotations, and examples.

Strategy ❷ Form an opinion about the subject by asking yourself questions about the information. For example, how important was the subject? How does it relate to similar subjects in your own experience?

Strategy ❸ Support your opinions with facts, quotations, and examples.

EGYPTIAN PHARAOHS

❶ The pharaoh stood at the center of Egypt's religion as well as its government and army. Egyptians believed that the pharaoh bore full responsibility for the kingdom's well being. ❶ Many Egyptians believed it was the pharaoh who caused the sun to rise, the Nile to flood, and the crops to grow. It was the pharaoh's duty to promote truth and justice. Egyptians believed that the pharaoh ruled even in death. ❶ As a result, they built giant pyramids to serve as elaborate resting places for pharaohs who passed away. These pyramids were remarkable engineering achievements that took the work of thousands of people.

Make a Chart

Making a chart can help you organize your opinions and supporting facts. The following chart summarizes one possible opinion about Egyptian pharaohs.

❷ OPINION	Egyptians viewed pharaohs as god-like and worshiped these rulers intensely.
❸ FACTS	Pharaohs served as the center of political and cultural life in Egypt. Many Egyptians looked to pharaohs to control nature. Thousands of Egyptian citizens worked to build elaborate pyramids to serve as tombs for deceased pharaohs.

Apply the Skill

Turn to Chapter 4, Lesson 2, "Assyria Rules the Fertile Crescent." Read "Assyria Builds a Huge Empire," and form your own opinion about the Assyrian Empire. Make a chart like the one above to summarize your opinion and the supporting facts and examples.

3.6 Evaluating Information

Learn the Skill

To **evaluate** is to make a judgment about something. Historians evaluate information about peoples, cultures, and events by determining what material is essential to the main point and whether or not the information is verifiable.

Practice the Skill

The following passage examines the rule of the Greek leader Solon. Use the strategies listed below to evaluate his rule.

How to Evaluate

Strategy ❶ Determine the major point of a passage. In this case, think about what Solon set out to achieve.

Strategy ❷ Look for statements that convey information relevant and essential to the main point. Think about how Solon achieved his goal.

Strategy ❸ Consider what text does not support the main point.

Strategy ❹ Ask whether most or all of the essential information can be verified in historical texts or other documents.

SOLON RULES ATHENS

Solon was the son of a noble family. ❶ After being elected leader of Athens, he made reforms that helped prevent a revolt by the poor. ❷ First, he freed people who had become slaves because they owed too much money. ❷ He also made a law that no citizen could be enslaved. ❷ In addition, Solon allowed all citizens to serve in the assembly and help elect leaders. Some powerful officials opposed the reform and criticized Solon. ❸ Tired of defending his actions, Solon left on a trip for ten years. He traveled to Egypt and Cyprus among other places.❹

Make a Diagram

The diagram below shows how to evaluate information and organize the essential material from the passage you just read.

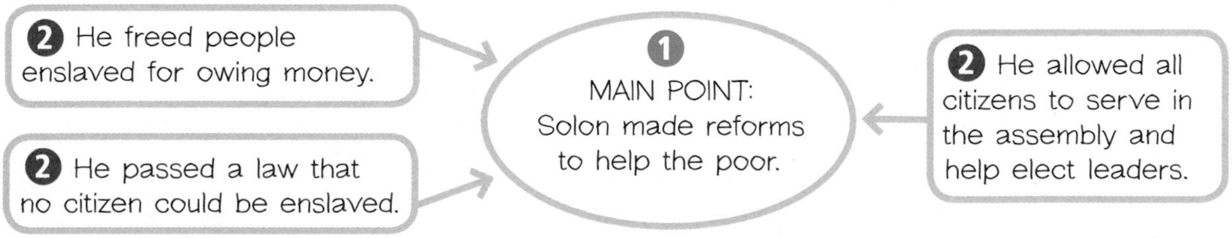

❷ He freed people enslaved for owing money.
❷ He passed a law that no citizen could be enslaved.
❶ MAIN POINT: Solon made reforms to help the poor.
❷ He allowed all citizens to serve in the assembly and help elect leaders.

Apply the Skill

Turn to Chapter 7, Lesson 3, "Buddhism and India's Golden Age." Read "Asoka, the Buddhist King" under "The Maurya Empire," and make a chart in which you decide what information is the most essential about the rule of Asoka.

3.7 Assessing Credibility of Sources

Learn the Skill

Assessing the credibility of sources means determining if the source material accurately portrays events, facts, and people. Primary sources are materials written or made by people who lived during a historical event. They include letters, diaries, articles, and photographs. Secondary sources are written after a historical event by people who were not present at the event. Books that appear long after an event are examples of secondary sources.

Practice the Skill

The following passage describes the Roman ruler Augustus. It includes both primary source and secondary source observations. Use the strategies listed below to help you assess the credibility of the sources.

How to Assess Credibility of Sources

Strategy 1 Determine the thesis, or main point, of the source.

Strategy 2 Check for details that support the thesis.

Strategy 3 Determine the credibility of primary sources. Is the speaker objective or not. Here, Augustus is speaking for himself.

THE EMPEROR AUGUSTUS

1 Despite his enormous power, Augustus liked to present himself as an average citizen with simple tastes. 2 He lived in a small house and wore plain clothes. His favorite foods were those of common people—bread, cheese, and olives. 2 In addition, he tried to present himself as a servant of the Roman people. In taking power, 3 Augustus is reported to have said, "What more have I to ask of the immortal gods than that I may retain this same unanimous approval of yours to the very end of my life?"

Make a Chart

Making a chart can help you assess the credibility of sources. The chart below organizes questions to ask about the credibility of sources.

Questions	Answers
What is the main idea?	Augustus portrayed himself as a humble ruler.
What are the supporting details?	He lived in a small house. He dressed and ate simply. He called himself a servant of the people.
Are the sources credible?	Secondary sources—can be verified in historical texts. Primary sources—views may vary; people may or may not trust what historical figures say about themselves.

Apply the Skill

Turn to Chapter 8, Lesson 2, "China's Ancient Philosophies." Read the "History Maker" feature on Confucius and use a chart like the one above to assess the credibility of the sources you encounter.

3.8 Drawing Conclusions from Sources

Learn the Skill

Drawing conclusions from sources means analyzing what you have read and forming an opinion about its meaning. To draw conclusions, look at the facts and then use your own common sense and experience to decide what the facts mean.

Practice the Skill

The following passage presents information about the Persian Empire. Use the strategies listed below to help you draw conclusions about the Persians.

How to Draw Conclusions from Sources

Strategy 1 Read carefully to understand all the facts or statements.

Strategy 2 List the facts and review them. Use your own experiences and common sense to understand how the facts relate to each other.

Strategy 3 After reviewing the facts, write down the conclusions you have drawn about them.

> THE PERSIAN EMPIRE
>
> The Persian Empire stretched some 2,800 miles from east to west. (1) The Persian king Darius divided the empire into 20 provinces. Each province, had a local government. Darius set up governors called satraps to rule the provinces. (1) Darius also built the Royal Road, a road for government purposes. The Royal Road was 1,775 miles long. The road greatly improved travel and communication across the empire. In addition, (1) Darius created standard coins throughout the empire. This made it easier for residents of the far-flung and diverse kingdom to conduct trade and other commercial activities.

Make a Diagram

Making a diagram can help you draw conclusions from sources. The diagram below shows how to organize facts to draw a conclusion about the passages you just read.

(2) FACTS

- Darius divided the empire into 20 provinces and installed governors to rule over each province.
- Darius created the Royal Road, which stretched for 1,775 miles and improved travel and communication throughout the empire.
- Darius created standard coins for use throughout the empire, which helped people conduct trade and commerce more easily.

(3) CONCLUSION

The Persians were a highly organized people who succeeded in bringing order and stability to their far-reaching empire.

Apply the Skill

Turn to Chapter 6, Lesson 3, "West, Central, and Southern Africa." Read the section titled "Nok Culture" and use the strategies on this page to draw conclusion about the Nok people.

4.1 Understanding Cause and Effect

Learn the Skill

A **cause** is an action in history that makes something happen. An **effect** is the historical event that is the result of the cause. A single event may have several causes. It is also possible for one cause to result in several effects. Historians identify cause-and-effect relationships to help them understand why historical events took place.

Practice the Skill

The following paragraph describes the growth of Christianity in the Roman Empire. Use the strategies below to help you identify the cause-and-effect relationships.

How to Analyze Causes and Recognize Effects

Strategy ❶ Ask why an action took place. Ask yourself a question about the title or topic sentence, such as, "How did Christianity spread?"

Strategy ❷ Look for the results (the effect). Ask yourself, What happened?

Strategy ❸ Look for the reasons why something happened (the cause). Search for clue words that signal causes, such as *cause* and *led to*.

❶ THE SPREAD OF CHRISTIANITY

In the decades after it developed, Christianity came under attack in the Roman Empire. Roman officials jailed and killed Christians mainly because they refused to worship Roman gods. ❷ Nonetheless, Christianity grew and spread throughout the Roman Empire. ❸ A major *cause* of its spread was the contribution of St. Paul the Apostle. St. Paul was a Jewish leader who converted to Christianity. He traveled throughout the Roman world preaching Christian beliefs and attracting followers. ❸ Another factor that *led to* the spread of Christianity was the decision by the Roman emperor Constantine to legalize Christianity and allow Christians to worship freely.

Make a Diagram

Using a diagram can help you understand causes and effects. The diagram below shows causes and an effect for the passage you just read.

CAUSE: Paul promoted Christianity across the empire. →

CAUSE: The emperor Constantine legalized Christianity. →

EFFECT: Christianity grew and spread throughout the empire.

Apply the Skill

Turn to Chapter 6, Lesson 3, "West, Central, and Southern Africa." Read "The Bantu Migrations." Then make a diagram about the causes and effects of the Bantu migrations.

4.2 Explaining Historical Patterns

Learn the Skill

When humans develop new ways of thinking and acting that are repeated by other people over time or in other places, these ways become historical patterns. **Explaining historical patterns** will help you better understand how and why certain ideas influence events and movements at different times in history.

Practice the Skill

The following passage discusses the recurring development of farming throughout the ancient world. Use the strategies listed below to help you explain the historical pattern.

How to Explain Historical Patterns

Strategy 1 Identify the historical movement or idea being examined.

Strategy 2 Identify previous or subsequent periods in history during which a similar movement or idea occurred.

THE DEVELOPMENT OF FARMING

About 10,000 years ago, humans began experimenting with planting seeds and growing plants. 1 This led to the development of farming. The foothills of the Zagros Mountains in northeastern Iraq appear to be a birthplace of agriculture. There, residents established a farming settlement as early as 9,000 years ago. Within a few thousand years, many other regions worldwide turned to farming. 2 About 7,000 years ago, residents along the Huang River in China cultivated a grain called millet. About 1,000 years later, people began growing rice in the Chang Jiang River delta. 2 Meanwhile, farmers in Mexico and Central America started growing corn, beans, and squash.

Make a Flow Chart

Making a flow chart can help you visualize historical patterns. The flow chart below helps to explain the historical pattern in the passage you just read.

The residents along the Zagros Mountains in Iraq developed farming 9,000 years ago.

→ Residents along China's rivers cultivated millet and rice in the centuries that followed.

→ Farmers in Mexico and Central America began to grow corn, beans and squash.

Apply the Skill

Turn to Chapter 12, Lesson 1, "The Golden Age of Greece." Read "Pericles Leads Athens." Use the information in the text as well as your own knowledge to create a flow chart about the development of democracy.

Skillbuilder Handbook

4.3 Identifying Issues and Problems

Learn the Skill

Identifying issues and problems means finding and understanding the difficulties faced by a particular group of people and the historical factors that contributed to these difficulties. By identifying historical issues and problems, you can learn to identify and understand problems in today's world.

Practice the Skill

The following paragraph describes the problems of floods and droughts in early Mesopotamia. Use the strategies listed below to find and understand these problems.

How to Identify Issues and Problems

Strategy 1 Look for the difficulties or problems faced by a group of people.

Strategy 2 Look for situations that existed at that time and place, which contributed to these problems.

Strategy 3 Look for the solutions that people or groups employed to deal with the problems.

FLOOD AND DROUGHT IN MESOPOTAMIA

1 In ancient Mesopotamia, farmers had to deal with both floods and droughts. 2 If too much rain fell, the rivers might overflow and wash everything away. Too little rain also created difficulties. 2 During a drought, the river levels dropped, making it hard to water crops.
3 To combat the lack of rain, farmers in Mesopotamia eventually built canals to carry water from the river to the fields. Such a system is called irrigation. 3 Farmers also built dams to hold back excess water during floods.

Make a Chart

Making a chart will help you identify and organize information about problems. The chart below shows the problem, the factors that contributed to the problem, and solutions to the problem in the passage you just read.

1 PROBLEM	2 CONTRIBUTING FACTORS	3 SOLUTIONS
Floods and droughts made farming difficult in ancient Mesopotamia.	Too much rain caused floods that washed everything away.	built canals to carry water from the river to the fields
	Drought caused the river level to drop, making it hard to water crops.	built dams to hold back excess water during floods

Apply the Skill

Turn to Chapter 13, Lesson 4, "The Daily Life of Romans." Read "Life in Roman Cities." Using the above chart as a model, identify the urban problems faced by ancient Romans.

4.4 Understanding Continuity and Change

Learn the Skill

Understanding continuity and change means understanding why certain political and social systems continue without major change for many years and why sometimes they undergo significant change. Continuity and change is a process that happens repeatedly throughout history.

Practice the Skill

The following passage describes the Han Dynasty of China. Use the strategies listed below to help you understand the continuity and change of this empire.

How to Understand Continuity and Change

Strategy ❶ Identify the system that is undergoing continuity and change. In this case, it is the Han Dynasty.

Strategy ❷ Identify the elements that contributed to the continuity of this system.

Strategy ❸ Identify the elements that contributed to the change of this system.

THE HAN DYNASTY

❶ The Han Dynasty began in China in 202 B.C. ❷ The Han rulers put family members and trusted people in local government positions. They set up a system of tests to find the most educated and ethical people for the imperial bureaucratic state. ❷ Under the Han, China witnessed improvements in education and numerous advances in technology and culture. ❷ Throughout its long reign, the Han Dynasty withstood rebellions, peasant revolts, floods, famine, and economic disasters. ❸ Eventually, however, these episodes of economic and political unrest made the empire weak. By 220, the Han Dynasty had disintegrated into three rival kingdoms.

Make a Chart

A chart can help you understand the main contributors to continuity and change. The chart below shows the possible reasons for the Han's long reign and eventual fall.

HAN DYNASTY FLOURISHES FOR 400 YEARS.	HAN DYNASTY COLLAPSES.
REASONS: • placed educated, ethical people in charge • promoted cultural and technological advances • withstood numerous challenges and disasters	REASONS: • could not remain strong amid continuous social and economic unrest

Apply the Skill

Turn to Chapter 4, Lesson 2, "Assyria Rules the Fertile Crescent." Read "Assyria Rules a Huge Empire." Using the above strategies, create a chart highlighting why the Assyrian Empire continued for many years and the changes that led to its decline.

4.5 Analyzing Economic and Political Issues

Learn the Skill

An **issue** is a matter of public concern. Issues in history are often economic or political. **Analyzing economic and political issues** means studying the various components of the issue in order to reach a better understanding of the issue and its impact on a particular event.

Practice the Skill

The following passage describes the growing difficulties that the Roman Empire faced in the centuries before it eventually fell. Use the strategies listed below to help you analyze the economic and political issues involved in Rome's decline.

How to Analyze Economic and Political Issues

Strategy 1 Identify the discussion of economic and political issues. Look for clue words and phrases such as *pay,* and *sources of wealth.* Then look for clue words and phrases such as *government, politician, ruler,* and *public affairs.*

Strategy 2 Determine what are the different components of each issue.

Strategy 3 Write an analysis that summarizes the issues.

INTERNAL WEAKNESSES OF ROME

During the second century, the empire stopped expanding. The end of new conquests meant an end to new 1 *sources of wealth.* 2 As a result, it grew harder for the government to *pay* for needed services, especially the army.

Meanwhile, the empire had to deal with other difficulties. 1 Over time, Roman *politics* grew increasingly corrupt. As a result, 2 citizens lost their sense of pride in 1 *government* and their interest in 1 *public affairs.*

Make a Diagram

Use this diagram to help you pull out the components of various economic and political issues in order to better analyze them.

3 ECONOMIC ISSUE	3 POLITICAL ISSUE
Components • The empire stops expanding, which ends new sources of wealth. • Government has fewer funds for needed services.	Components • Politics grows corrupt. • Residents lose civic pride and duty to empire.
Analysis With no new income, the Roman government became unable to pay for key services.	Analysis As the government became more corrupt, Romans lost their sense of civic duty.

Apply the Skill

Turn to Chapter 9, Lesson 4, "The Mayan Civilization." Read "Mayan Life" and "Mayan Culture." Using the above graphic as a model, analyze the economic and political issues in these passages.

4.6 Recognizing Changing Interpretations of History

Learn the Skill

Recognizing changing interpretations of history means identifying historical viewpoints that have changed over time. Historical interpretations often change when new evidence is found that causes historians to rethink an interpretation. When studying history, you should be able to identify both old and new interpretations of history—and any reasons for the change.

Practice the Skill

The following passage discusses hunter-gatherer societies. Use the strategies listed below to help you identify changing interpretations of history.

How to Recognize Changing Interpretations of History

Strategy ❶ Identify old interpretations of history.

Strategy ❷ Identify new interpretations of history.

Strategy ❸ Determine what factors led to the new interpretation.

Strategy ❹ Recognize any details that attempt to support the new interpretation.

HUNTER–GATHERER SOCIETIES

❶ For many years, scholars thought that life for hunter-gatherers was very hard. ❷ Now, many scholars believe that life for these ancient people was quite good. ❸ They have based their new beliefs on studies of hunter-gatherers in the modern world. ❹ Scholars now think that the surrounding environment gave hunter-gatherers all the kinds of food they needed. They had a varied diet of meat, fish, fruit, and wild plants. In addition, hunting and gathering did not require too much time and energy. People had time to relax, visit with friends, and play games.

Make a Chart

The chart below addresses changing historical interpretations about hunter-gatherer societies.

OLD INTERPRETATION	NEW INTERPRETATION	REASON	DETAILS
life difficult for hunter-gatherers	life good for hunter-gatherers	closer study of modern hunter-gatherers	healthy and well-balanced diet; didn't have to work too hard for food; had plenty of relaxation time

Apply the Skill

Turn to Chapter 1, Lesson 4, "How Historians Study the Past." Read "How Knowledge of the Past Changes." Using the above chart as a model, identify an old and new historical interpretation about the "mummy's curse."

4.7 Conducting Cost-Benefit Analyses

Learn the Skill

A **cost-benefit analysis** involves determining the economic costs and benefits of an action. Imagine, for example, that you own a lawn-mowing business. Your business would be economically beneficial if, at the end of the summer, the total amount of money you earned was greater than the costs of buying the mower, paying for gas, cleaning and repairing the tools, and so on. The ability to recognize the costs and benefits of an action in history will help you to better understand why people made the decisions they did.

Practice the Skill

The following passage examines the decision to travel the ancient Silk Roads that connected China and Europe. Use the strategies below to analyze the costs and benefits related to this issue.

How to Conduct a Cost-Benefit Analysis

Strategy ❶ Identify the historical topic or event that is under consideration.

Strategy ❷ Locate the potential costs of the action.

Strategy ❸ Identify the potential benefits associated with the action.

Strategy ❹ Determine what decision was made based on the cost-benefit analysis.

❶ THE SILK ROADS

The Silk Roads were a series of trade routes that connected Europe and China. The Silk Roads flourished primarily from the second century B.C. to the 1400s. ❷ The routes were not easy to travel. They stretched about 4,000 miles across harsh terrain of mountains and deserts. ❷ The journey was long and slow, as traders back then had to rely on horses or other animals to take them to their destination. ❷ The trip also could be dangerous. Travelers along the roads had to watch for bandits, who might rob or even kill them.

❸ However, the roads offered a way for people from different cultures to spread their ideas. ❸ The roads also presented traders with a way to introduce their goods to a new population of buyers. Merchants from China wanted to sell silk, paper, pottery, and other items to Westerners. Meanwhile, Westerners wanted to sell such items as sesame, metals, and precious stones to the people of the East. ❹ As a result, many people from both Europe and Asia made the long and difficult journey along the route.

(continued)

Make a Diagram

Making a diagram can help you organize the components of a cost-benefit analysis. The diagram below shows you how to create a cost-benefit analysis from the passage you just read.

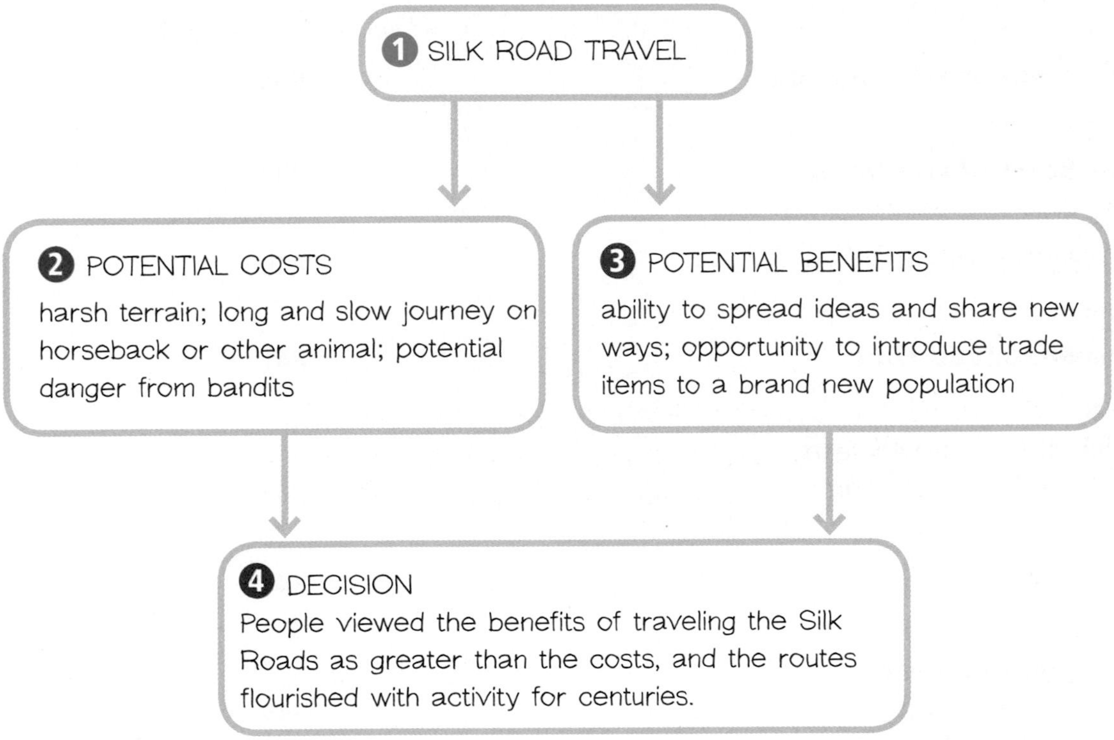

1 SILK ROAD TRAVEL
2 POTENTIAL COSTS
harsh terrain; long and slow journey on horseback or other animal; potential danger from bandits
3 POTENTIAL BENEFITS
ability to spread ideas and share new ways; opportunity to introduce trade items to a brand new population
4 DECISION
People viewed the benefits of traveling the Silk Roads as greater than the costs, and the routes flourished with activity for centuries.

Apply the Skill

Turn to Chapter 5, Lesson 3, "The Pyramid Builders." Read "Khufu's Great Pyramid." Then use the strategies you have learned to conduct a cost-benefit analysis of pyramid building in ancient Egypt.

Skillbuilder Handbook

CONTENTS

from *Disclosing the Past*

By Mary Leakey

Background: Mary Leakey and her husband, Louis, formed an archaeological partnership that lasted more than 30 years. They made many important discoveries in East Africa. In the following excerpt, Mary Leakey summarizes the importance of a set of prints.

▲ **Mary Leakey** Mary Leakey on site during excavations at Laetoli, Tanzania, in 1978

Primary Source

The discovery of the trails was immensely exciting—something so extraordinary that I could hardly take it in or comprehend its implications for some while. It was a quite different feeling from the discovery of a major hominid[1] fossil . . . because that happens to you all at once, and within a short time you know exactly what you have found. The Laetoli hominid trails were something that grew in extent, in detail and in importance over two seasons. But then again, there was an immediate impact in the vastness of our discovery because from a very early stage it was clear that we had before us unique evidence, of an unimpeachable[2] nature, to establish that our hominid ancestors were fully bipedal[3] a little before 3.5 million years ago—the kind of thing anthropologists had argued over for many decades, with no real hope of proving or disproving their views. The Laetolil Beds might not have included any foot bones among the hominid remains they had yielded to our search, but they had given us instead one of the most graphic alternative kinds of evidence for bipedalism one could dream of discovering. The essentially human nature and the modern appearance of the footprints were quite extraordinary.

1. **hominid:** a human or humanlike creature that walks on two feet.
2. **unimpeachable:** beyond doubt; unquestionable.
3. **bipedal:** walking on two feet.

DOCUMENT–BASED QUESTIONS

1. What sorts of prints did Leakey discover and investigate?
2. What did the prints prove beyond doubt?

Chapter Connection For more about the discoveries made by the Leakeys, see Chapter 1, Lesson 3.

from ***The Man in the Ice***

By Dr. Konrad Spindler

Background: Konrad Spindler led an international team of scientists who investigated the 5,300-year-old body of a man trapped in a glacier in the Alps. *The Man in the Ice* tells a fascinating detective story of how they discovered the identity of the figure they called the Iceman—who he was and where he came from.

Primary Source

Evidently overtaken by a blizzard or sudden fog, or both, the Iceman was in a state of total exhaustion. In a gully in the rock, perhaps familiar to him from previous crossings of the pass, he sought what shelter he could from the bad weather. With his failing strength he settled down for the night. He deposited his axe, bow and backpack on the ledge of the rock. It is possible that he consumed here the last of his food store: a piece of tough dried ibex[1] meat. Two bone splinters had inadvertently been left in the strip of meat as he cut it off: these he chewed off and spat out. Meanwhile it had grown dark. To press on might prove fatal. It was snowing ceaselessly, and in the gale the icy cold penetrated his clothes. A terrible fatigue engulfed his limbs. Between his will to survive and increasing indifference towards his physical danger he once more pulled himself together. He knew that to fall asleep meant death. He reeled forward a few more steps. He dropped his quiver. Below him there was only loose scree.[2] He tripped and fell heavily against a boulder. The container with the hot embers slipped from his hand; his cap fell off. Again pain pierced the right side of his chest. He only wanted a short rest, but his need for sleep was stronger than his willpower. . . . He turned on to his left side to dull the pain. He laid his head on the rock. His senses numbed, he no longer noticed the awkward position of his folded ear. His left arm, its muscles relaxed and probably slightly bent at the elbow, lay in front of him. His right arm was almost extended and was hanging down forward. His feet rested one on the other; the left shoe under the right. Soon his clothes froze to the rough ground. He was no longer aware that he was freezing to death. Overnight the body froze stiff.

▲ **The Iceman** The frozen mummy of a 5,300-year-old hunter called the Iceman is moved by scientists from its resting place in the Alps.

1. **ibex:** wild goat.
2. **scree:** loose rock.

DOCUMENT–BASED QUESTIONS

1. Why might falling asleep have been dangerous for the Iceman?
2. Why might the body of the Iceman have been so well preserved after 5,300 years?

Chapter Connection For more about the Iceman, see Chapter 2, Starting with a Story.

from *The Epic of Gilgamesh*

Translated by N. K. Sandars

Background: *The Epic of Gilgamesh* is one of the oldest surviving works of literature. Like most epics, it is based to some degree on fact. Most scholars think that Gilgamesh was a Sumerian king who ruled over the city of Uruk around 2700 B.C. In the centuries following his death, stories about him grew. Through the oral tradition of storytelling, Gilgamesh developed over time into a legendary figure. In the following excerpt, Enkidu (Gilgamesh's friend) has died, and Gilgamesh experiences for the first time the human emotions of grief and fear.

Primary Source

Bitterly Gilgamesh wept for his friend Enkidu; he wandered over the wilderness as a hunter, he roamed over the plains; in his bitterness he cried, "How can I rest, how can I be at peace? Despair is in my heart. What my brother is now, that shall I be when I am dead. Because I am afraid of death I will go as best I can to find Utnapishtim[1] whom they call the Faraway, for he has entered the assembly of the gods." So Gilgamesh traveled over the wilderness, he wandered over the grasslands, a long journey, in search of Utnapishtim, whom the gods took after the deluge;[2] and they set him to live in the land of Dilmun,[3] in the garden of the sun; and to him alone of men they gave everlasting life.

At night when he came to the mountain passes Gilgamesh prayed: "In these mountain passes long ago I saw lions, I was afraid and I lifted my eyes to the moon; I prayed and my prayers went up to the gods, so now, O moon god Sin, protect me." When he had prayed he lay down to sleep, until he was woken from out of a dream. He saw the lions round him glorying in life; then he took his axe in his hand, he drew his sword from his belt, and he fell upon them like an arrow from the string, and struck and destroyed and scattered them.

▲ **Gilgamesh** Assyrian stone relief of Gilgamesh

1. **Utnapishtim (OOT•nuh•PEESH•tuhm):** Friend of the Sumerian god Ea, he and his wife survive a flood and are the only mortals to be granted the gift of eternal life.
2. **deluge:** an unusually heavy flood.
3. **Dilmun:** a paradise in the world of the gods.

DOCUMENT–BASED QUESTIONS

1. Why is Gilgamesh grieving at the beginning of this excerpt?

2. What danger does Gilgamesh encounter as he begins his journey to find Utnapishtim, and how does he deal with the danger?

Chapter Connection For more about Sumerian civilization, see Chapter 3, Lessons 2 and 3.

from the **Code of Hammurabi**

Translated by L. W. King

Background: Hammurabi was a king of the Babylonian Empire who reigned between 1792 and 1750 B.C. Hammurabi's law code listed punishments ranging from fines to death. Often a punishment was based on the social class of the victim. Following are some examples of the laws.

Primary Source

8. If a man has stolen an ox, a sheep, a pig, or a boat that belonged to a temple or palace, he shall repay thirty times its cost. If it belonged to a private citizen, he shall repay ten times. If the thief cannot pay, he shall be put to death.

142. If a woman hates her husband and says to him "You cannot be with me," the authorities in her district will investigate the case. If she has been chaste and without fault, even though her husband has neglected or belittled her, she will be held innocent and may return to her father's house.

143. If the woman is at fault, she shall be thrown into the river.

196. If a man put out the eye of another man, his eye shall be put out.

198. If he put out the eye of a free man or break the bone of a free man, he shall pay one gold mina.[1]

199. If he put out the eye of a man's slave, or break the bone of a man's slave, he shall pay one-half of its value.

▲ **Pillar of Hammurabi**
Hammurabi receiving the laws from the god Shamash

1. **mina:** a unit of money in ancient Asia.

DOCUMENT–BASED QUESTIONS

1. Did the code apply equally to all people? Why or why not?

2. What was the point of making the punishments for crimes known to all?

Chapter Connection For more about Hammurabi's Code, see Chapter 4, Lesson 1, Primary Source.

from the ***Book of the Dead***

Translated by E. A. Wallis Budge

Background: The Egyptian *Book of the Dead* is a series of texts that assists the soul in the search for happiness in the afterlife. Egyptians believed that after death an individual faced 42 gods and testified about his or her behavior on Earth. That testimony was called the negative confession. Below you will see some of that confession.

Primary Source

Hail, Hept-khet, who comest forth from Kher-aha,
I have not committed robbery with violence.

Hail, Fenti, who comest forth from Khemenu,
I have not stolen.

Hail, Am-khaibit, who comest forth from Qernet,
I have not slain men and women.

Hail, Neha-her, who comest forth from Rasta,
I have not stolen grain.

Hail, Unem-besek, who comest forth from Mabit,
I have not stolen cultivated land.

Hail, Ari-em-ab-f, who comest forth from Tebu,
I have never stopped [the flow of] water.

Illustration This illustration comes from the *Book of the Dead.* ▼

DOCUMENT–BASED QUESTIONS

1. Why might stopping the flow of water have been a serious sin or crime in ancient Egypt?
2. What did Egyptians hope to do by making this confession?

Chapter Connection For more on beliefs about the afterlife in ancient Egypt, see Chapter 5, Lesson 2.

from **Piankhi's Monument**

Background: Piankhi was a Kushite king who overthrew a dynasty that had ruled Egypt for about 100 years. He gathered a large fleet and army and sailed northward to lay siege to the Egyptian city of Hermopolis. He was victorious and united the Nile valley from the delta in the north to his capital of Napata in the south. After his victory, Piankhi erected a monument in his homeland of Kush. On the monument were inscribed writings that celebrated his victory. The inscriptions contained a catalog of the riches of Egypt. An excerpt from the monument follows.

Primary Source

Hermopolis threw herself upon her belly and pleaded before the king. Messengers came forth and descended bearing everything beautiful to behold; gold, every splendid costly stone, clothing in a chest, and the diadem [crown] which was upon his head; the uraeus[1] which inspireth fear of him, without ceasing during many days. . . .

Then the ships were laden with silver, gold, copper, clothing, and everything of the Northland, every product of Syria and all sweet woods of God's-Land. His Majesty sailed upstream [south], with glad heart, the shores on his either side were jubilating. West and east were jubilating in the presence of his Majesty.

1. **uraeus:** a sacred serpent shown as an emblem of sovereignty on the headdress of ancient Egyptian rulers.

▲ **Piankhi's Monument** This black granite slab was discovered in Piankhi's capital of Napata.

Primary Source Handbook

DOCUMENT–BASED QUESTIONS

1. What were some of the riches that Piankhi gained in Egypt?
2. In what direction does Piankhi sail with the treasure he has acquired in Egypt?

Chapter Connection For more about Piankhi's monument, see Chapter 6, Lesson 1.

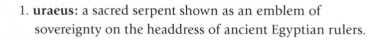

from the *Bhagavad Gita*

Translated by Barbara Stoler Miller

Background: The *Bhagavad Gita* is a beloved and widely translated religious work of India. It begins on the eve of battle, as the warrior-prince Arjuna sees his uncles, cousins, friends, and teachers lined up on the field against him. Overcome with grief at the thought of fighting against, and possibly killing, his relatives, Arjuna refuses to fight. The deity Krishna explains to Arjuna that as a warrior he has a sacred duty to fight.

Primary Source

Our bodies are known to end,
but the embodied self[1] is enduring,
indestructible, and immeasurable;
therefore, Arjuna, fight the battle!

He who thinks this self a killer
and he who thinks it killed,
both fail to understand;
it does not kill, nor is it killed.

It is not born,
it does not die;
having been,
it will never not be;
unborn, enduring,
constant, and primordial,[2]
it is not killed
when the body is killed.

Arjuna, when a man knows the self
to be indestructible, enduring, unborn,
unchanging, how does he kill
or cause anyone to kill?

1. **embodied self:** soul or spirit.
2. **primordial:** first; original.

War Chariot Arjuna is led into battle by his chariot driver, Krishna. ▶

DOCUMENT–BASED QUESTIONS

1. Why does Arjuna not want to fight?

2. What argument does Krishna use to urge Arjuna to fight?

Chapter Connection For more about the *Bhagavad Gita,* see Chapter 7, Lesson 2, Primary Source.

Primary Source Handbook

from the *Analects* of Confucius

Translated by Simon Leys

Background: The *Analects* is a collection of about 500 sayings, dialogues, and brief stories. It was put together over many years following the death of Confucius. Confucius was a great Chinese teacher who lived in the sixth century B.C. The *Analects* presents Confucius' teachings on how people should live to create an orderly and just society.

Primary Source

The Master[1] said: "He who rules by virtue is like the polestar,[2] which remains unmoving in its mansion while all the other stars revolve respectfully around it." (2.1)

The Master said: "To study without thinking is futile.[3] To think without studying is dangerous." (2.15)

Lord Ji Kang asked: "What should I do in order to make the people respectful, loyal, and zealous?"[4] The Master said: "Approach them with dignity and they will be respectful. Be yourself a good son and a kind father, and they will be loyal. Raise the good and train the incompetent, and they will be zealous." (2.20)

The Master said: "Set your heart upon the Way;[5] rely upon moral power; follow goodness; enjoy the arts." (7.6)

The Master said: "A gentleman abides by three principles which I am unable to follow: his humanity knows no anxiety; his wisdom knows no hesitation; his courage knows no fear." Zigong[6] said: "Master, you have just drawn your own portrait." (14.28)

◀ **Confucius** Portrait of the Chinese philosopher Confucius

1. **the Master:** Confucius.
2. **polestar:** the North Star, which appears to remain in the same place in the sky as Earth rotates.
3. **futile:** useless.
4. **zealous:** enthusiastic.
5. **Way:** ideal pattern of behavior.
6. **Zigong:** a student.

DOCUMENT–BASED QUESTIONS

1. What kinds of behavior does Confucius talk about in the *Analects?*

2. What kind of person does Confucius seem to have been?

Chapter Connection For more about Confucius, see Chapter 8, Lesson 2.

from the *Dao De Jing*

By Laozi
Translated by Stephen Mitchell

Background: Laozi was a philosopher who lived in China. The teachings of Laozi are called Daoism. Laozi's *Dao De Jing* ("way of power") was written in the sixth century B.C. The book's main message is that a universal force called the Dao ("way") guides all things. In passage 37 from the *Dao De Jing*, Laozi explains the wisdom of the Dao.

Primary Source

The Dao never does anything,
yet through it all things are done.

If powerful men and women
could center themselves in it,
the whole world would be transformed
by itself, in its natural rhythms.
People would be content
with their simple, everyday lives,
in harmony, and free of desire.

When there is no desire,
all things are at peace.

Laozi Portrait of Laozi, the father of Daoism ▶

DOCUMENT–BASED QUESTIONS

1. What does this passage say prevents people from feeling content and at peace?

2. According to Laozi, how should people overcome the obstacle to peace and contentment?

Chapter Connection For more about Laozi, see Chapter 8, Lesson 2.

Primary Source Handbook

from the *Popol Vuh*

Translated by Dennis Tedlock

Background: The Maya developed a civilization in southern Mexico and Central America around 400 B.C. The *Popol Vuh* is an important Mayan work. The title means "Council Book." The work tells the Mayan story of the creation of the world. The following excerpt tells how the gods ("Bearers, Begetters") created the animals.

Primary Source

Now they planned the animals of the mountains, all the guardians of the forests, creatures of the mountains: the deer, birds, pumas, jaguars, serpents, rattlesnakes, fer-de-lances,[1] guardians of the bushes.

A Bearer, Begetter speaks:

"Why this pointless humming? Why should there merely be rustling beneath the trees and bushes?"

"Indeed—they had better have guardians," the others replied. As soon as they thought it and said it, deer and birds came forth.

And then they gave out homes to the deer and birds:

"You, the deer: sleep along the rivers, in the canyons. Be here in the meadows, in the thickets, in the forests, multiply yourselves. You will stand and walk on all fours," they were told.

So then they established the nests of the birds, small and great:

"You, precious birds: your nests, your houses are in the trees, in the bushes. Multiply there, scatter there, in the branches of trees, the branches of bushes," the deer and birds were told.

When this deed had been done, all of them had received a place to sleep and a place to stay. So it is that the nests of the animals are on the earth, given by the Bearer, Begetter. Now the arrangement of the deer and birds was complete.

▲ **Mayan Vessel** This ceramic vessel shows a dignitary armed with spear and shield sitting on a throne.

1. **fer-de-lances (FEHR•duhl•AN•sihz):** poisonous tropical snakes.

DOCUMENT–BASED QUESTIONS

1. What are some of the creatures that populate the Mayan natural world, and which two are the focus of this story?
2. What is the essential role or task of the animals created by the gods?

Chapter Connection For more about the Maya, see Chapter 9, Lesson 4.

from the **Hebrew Bible: The Creation**

Background: The Book of Genesis is the first book in the Torah, or Hebrew Bible. It tells the history of the Hebrew people. According to Genesis, God created the world in six days. The excerpts below tell what God created on the first and sixth days of creation.

Primary Source

THE FIRST DAY

In the beginning God created the heaven and the earth. And the earth was without form, and void; and darkness was upon the face of the deep. And the Spirit of God moved upon the face of the waters. And God said, "Let there be light": and there was light. And God saw the light, that it was good: and God divided the light from the darkness. And God called the light Day, and the darkness he called Night.

And the evening and the morning were the first day.

THE SIXTH DAY

And God said, "Let the earth bring forth the living creature after his kind, cattle, and creeping thing, and beast of the earth after his kind": and it was so. And God made the beast of the earth after his kind, and cattle after their kind, and every thing that creepeth upon the earth after his kind: and God saw that it was good.

And God said, "Let us make man in our image, after our likeness: and let them have dominion[1] over the fish of the sea, and over the fowl of the air, and over the cattle, and over all the earth, and over every creeping thing that creepeth upon the earth." So God created man in his own image, in the image of God created he him; male and female created he them. And

▲ **Sistine Chapel** **Detail of Michelangelo's Sistine Chapel ceiling, showing the creation of the stars and planets**

God blessed them, and God said unto them, "Be fruitful, and multiply, and replenish[2] the earth, and subdue it: and have dominion over the fish of the sea, and over the fowl of the air, and over every living thing that moveth upon the earth." And God said, "Behold, I have given you every herb bearing seed, which is upon the face of all the earth, and every tree, in the which is the fruit of a tree yielding seed; to you it shall be for meat. And to every beast of the earth, and to every fowl of the air, and to everything that creepeth upon the earth, wherein there is life, I have given every green herb for meat." And it was so. And God saw every thing that he had made, and, behold, it was very good.

And the evening and the morning were the sixth day.

1. **dominion:** authority; control.

2. **replenish:** fill up again.

DOCUMENT–BASED QUESTIONS

1. What does God create on the first day?

2. To whom does God give control over the world's natural resources?

Chapter Connection For more about the ancient Hebrews, see Chapter 10.

from the **Hebrew Bible: Noah and the Flood**

Background: The story of a devastating flood appears among the legends of ancient peoples throughout the world. In the Hebrew Bible, the hero of the story is Noah, who builds an ark to save God's creatures.

Primary Source

And God said to Noah, "I have determined to make an end of all flesh, for the earth is filled with violence because of them. . . . Make yourself an ark of cypress wood. . . . And of every living thing, of all flesh, you shall bring two of every kind into the ark . . . they shall be male and female." . . .

The rain fell on the earth forty days and forty nights. . . . At the end of forty days Noah opened the window of the ark . . . and . . . sent out the dove . . . and the dove came back . . . and there in its beak was a freshly plucked olive leaf; so Noah knew that the waters had subsided from the earth. . . .

Then God said to Noah, "Go out of the ark. . . . Bring out with you every living thing that is with you. . . . I establish my covenant with you, that . . . never again shall there be a flood to destroy the earth."

Noah's Ark Modern painting (1972) showing Noah's Ark ▶

DOCUMENT–BASED QUESTIONS

1. How does Noah know that the waters of the flood have receded?
2. What promise does God make to humankind?

Chapter Connection For more about the ancient Hebrews, see Chapter 10.

from the **Hebrew Bible: Daniel in the Lions' Den**

Background: The Hebrew Bible contains many stories that can be connected to ancient history. One of the most popular of these stories is that of Daniel in the lions' den. This story is set in the court of the Persian king Darius in the sixth century B.C., at a time when the Persians ruled much of Southwest Asia.

Primary Source

It pleased Darius to set over the kingdom a hundred and twenty princes who were to rule the whole kingdom. And over these were three presidents, and of them Daniel was the first. The princes were to give account to them, so that the king would have no troubles.

Daniel was put over the presidents and princes because of his excellent mind. And the king planned to put him over the whole kingdom. Then the presidents and princes tried to find some fault with Daniel concerning the kingdom, but they could find no fault, because he was faithful and loyal, and there was no error or fault to be found in him. And these men said:

"We shall not find any grounds for complaint against Daniel unless it concerns his worship of his God."

So those presidents and princes assembled together before the king and said to him:

"King Darius, live for ever! All the presidents of the kingdom and the governors and the princes, the counselors and the captains, have consulted together about establishing a royal law, by a firm order, that whoever asks anything of any god or man for thirty days, except of you, O king, shall be cast into a den of lions.

"Now, O king, establish this order, and sign the writing, that it may not be changed, according to the law of the Medes and the Persians, which does not change."

Then King Darius signed his name to the writing.

▲ **Mosaic** Daniel in the lions' den as shown in a mosaic in a monastery church in Greece

When Daniel knew that the law was signed and ratified, he went into his house, and his windows being open in his chamber facing Jerusalem, he kneeled down three times a day and prayed and gave thanks to his God just as he had done before.

Then the men came together and found Daniel praying and entreating God. They hurried to the king and reminded him of his order.

"Did you not sign an order that any man asking a favor of any god or man within thirty days, except yourself, O king, shall be thrown into the den of lions?"

(continued)

(continued)

The king answered and said:

"That is true, according to the law of the Medes and the Persians, which does not change."

Then they answered and said to the king: "That Daniel who is one of the children of the captivity of Judah, does not respect you, O king, nor the decree which you have signed, but makes his request three times a day."

When he heard these words, the king was very much displeased with himself, and he set his heart on saving Daniel. He thought until the setting of the sun about how to save Daniel.

Then the men came before the king and said to him: "Remember, O king, that it is the law of the Medes and the Persians that no order or law which the king lays down can be changed."

Then the king commanded them to take Daniel and throw him into the den of lions. And the king said to Daniel: "Your God whom you serve so faithfully, surely he will save you."

Then the king went to his palace and passed the night in fasting. No musical instruments were brought in to him, and he did not sleep at all.

Very early in the morning the king arose and hurried to the den of lions. When he came to the den, he cried out in a sorrowing voice to Daniel and said to him: "O Daniel, servant of the living God, has your God, whom you serve so faithfully, been able to save you from the lions?"

Then Daniel said to the king: "O king, live for ever. My God has sent his angel and has shut the lions' mouths, so that they have not hurt me, because I was innocent in his sight; and I have done no harm to you either, O king."

Then the king was exceedingly glad for him, and commanded that Daniel should be brought up out of the den. So Daniel was brought up out of the den, and no wound of any kind was found on him, because he believed in his God.

Then the king gave commands, and they brought the men who had accused Daniel, and they cast them into the den of lions, and their children and their wives as well. And the lions broke all their bones into pieces.

Then king Darius wrote to all people and nations, and in all the languages of the earth:

"Peace be multiplied to you! I now command that in every part of my kingdom men tremble and fear before the God of Daniel, for he is the living God, unchanging for ever, and his kingdom shall never be destroyed, and his power shall continue to the end. He rescues and saves, and he works signs and wonders in heaven and on earth, he who has saved Daniel from the power of the lions."

So Daniel prospered in the reign of Darius, and in the reign of Cyrus the Persian.

DOCUMENT–BASED QUESTIONS

1. What is the king's attitude toward Daniel?

2. How does the king feel about Daniel's punishment, and what does he do to Daniel's accusers?

Chapter Connection For more about the ancient Hebrews, see Chapter 10.

from the **Hebrew Bible: Proverbs**

Background: A proverb is a short saying that expresses a widely held belief. The Book of Proverbs in the Hebrew Bible provides a rich supply of wisdom. It is traditionally attributed to Solomon. Here is an example from Proverbs 6: 6–11.

Primary Source

Go to the ant, O sluggard,[1]
Observe her ways and be wise,
Which, having no chief,
Officer or ruler,
Prepares her food in the summer,
And gathers her provision in the harvest.
How long will you lie down, O sluggard?
When will you arise from your sleep?
"A little sleep, a little slumber,
A little folding of the hands to rest"—
And your poverty will come in like a vagabond,[2]
And your need like an armed man.

1. **sluggard:** lazy person.
2. **vagabond:** tramp.

▲ **Solomon** King Solomon reading the Torah as shown in a Hebrew biblical text of the 1200s

Primary Source Handbook

DOCUMENT–BASED QUESTIONS

1. What should the sluggard learn by observing the ant?

2. What does the speaker say will happen if the sluggard does not mend his ways?

Chapter Connection For more about the ancient Hebrews, see Chapter 10.

from the **Hebrew Bible: Psalm 100**

Background: The Book of Psalms in the Hebrew Bible served as a hymn book for the temple in Jerusalem. It contains 150 songs on a wide variety of topics. Many have been attributed to King David, who ruled over Israel around 1000 B.C. They remain a part of both Jewish and Christian worship to this day. Psalm 100 is a joyful expression of religious feeling.

Primary Source

Make a joyful noise unto the Lord, all ye lands.
Serve the Lord with gladness;
Come before his presence with singing.
Know ye that the Lord, he is God;
It is he that hath made us,
 and not we ourselves;
We are his people,
 and the sheep of his pasture.
Enter into his gates with thanksgiving,
And into his courts with praise;
Be thankful unto him,
 and bless his name.
For the Lord is good, his mercy is everlasting,
And his truth endureth to all generations.

David David is depicted as a young shepherd playing his pipe in this French manuscript illumination, c. 1250. ▶

DOCUMENT-BASED QUESTIONS

1. How are the faithful told to come into the presence of the Lord?

2. What are some of the qualities of the Lord that are praised in this psalm?

Chapter Connection For more about the ancient Hebrews, see Chapter 10.

from the *Iliad*

By Homer
Translated by Robert Fagles

Background: Homer has long been recognized as one of the world's greatest poets. It is likely that Homer heard singer-poets narrate tales about the Trojan War, a ten-year war waged by Greeks against the wealthy city of Troy, or Ilium, in Asia Minor. In the late 19th century, archaeologists discovered the ruins of ancient Troy. Most scholars now believe that Greek armies probably did attack Troy sometime in the 1200s B.C. Many scholars think that the *Iliad* was created in the 700s B.C. The Greek warrior Achilles enters the battle when his best friend, Patroclus, has been killed by the Trojan hero Hector. Achilles kills every Trojan in his path until he finally meets Hector in single combat outside the city walls.

Primary Source

Athena[1] luring him [Hector] on with all her immortal cunning—
and now, at last, as the two came closing for the kill
it was tall Hector, helmet flashing, who led off:
"No more running from you in fear, Achilles!
Not as before. Three times I fled around
the great city of Priam—I lacked courage then
to stand your onslaught. Now my spirit stirs me
to meet you face-to-face. Now kill or be killed!
Come, we'll swear to the gods, the highest witnesses—
the gods will oversee our binding pacts. I swear
I will never mutilate you—merciless as you are—
if Zeus[2] allows me to last it out and tear your life away.
But once I've stripped your glorious armor, Achilles,
I will give your body back to your loyal comrades.
Swear you'll do the same."

(continued)

1. **Athena (uh•THEE•nuh):** the goddess of wisdom and warfare; protects the Greeks.
2. **Zeus (zoos):** the king of the gods, father of Athena.

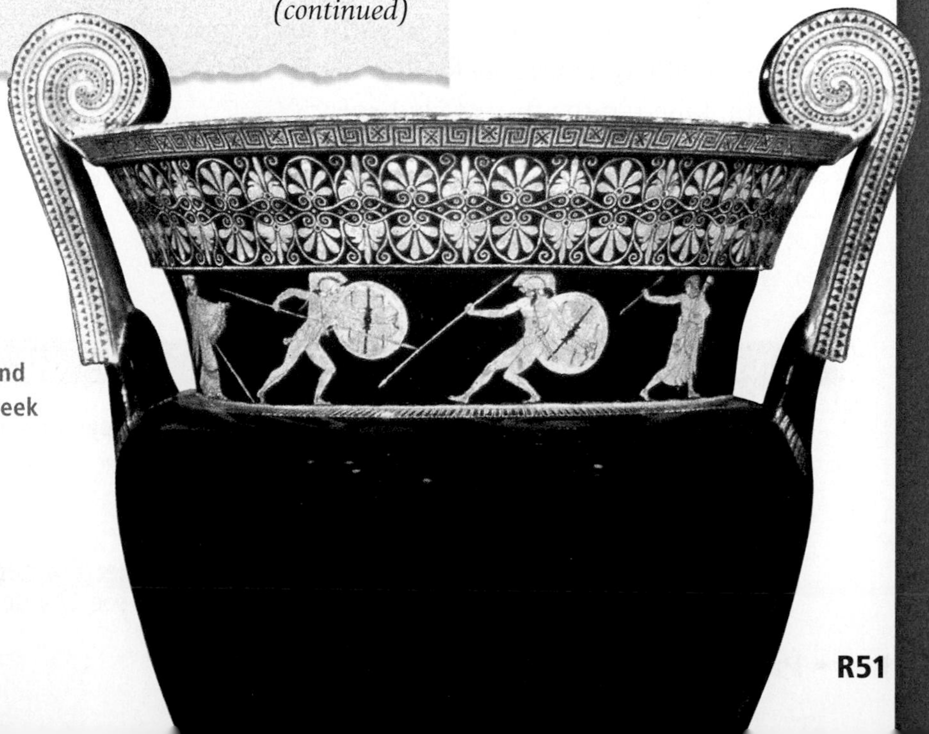

Greek Vase Achilles and Hector duel on this Greek vase, c. 490 B.C. ▶

Primary Source Handbook

▲ **Painting** Achilles in his chariot

(continued)

A swift dark glance
and the headstrong runner[3] answered, "Hector, stop!
You unforgivable, you . . . don't talk to me of pacts.
There are no binding oaths between men and lions—
wolves and lambs can enjoy no meeting of the minds—
they are all bent on hating each other to the death.
So with you and me. No love between us. No truce
till one or the other falls and gluts with blood
Ares[4] who hacks at men behind his rawhide shield.
Come, call up whatever courage you can muster.
Life or death—now prove yourself a spearman,
a daring man of war! No more escape for you—
Athena will kill you with my spear in just a moment.
Now you'll pay at a stroke for all my comrades' grief,
all you killed in the fury of your spear!"

3. **headstrong runner:** Achilles.
4. **Ares (AIR•eez):** the god of war.

DOCUMENT–BASED QUESTIONS

1. What pact does Hector wish to make with Achilles before they fight?
2. Why does Achilles reject the pact?

Chapter Connection For more about Homer and the *Iliad,* see Chapter 11, Lesson 2.

from **Aesop's Fables: The Wolf in Sheep's Clothing**

Background: Aesop (EE•suhp) was a Greek slave who supposedly lived around the sixth century B.C. Aesop's Fables are brief stories that convey lessons about life and conclude with morals that offer useful advice.

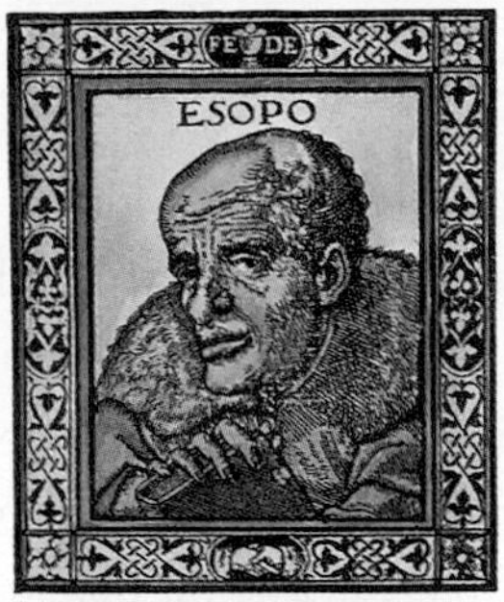

▲ **Aesop** A woodcut of Aesop made in Venice in 1492

Primary Source

A certain wolf could not get enough to eat because of the watchfulness of the shepherds. But one night he found a sheep skin that had been cast aside and forgotten. The next day, dressed in the skin, the wolf strolled into the pasture with the sheep. Soon a little lamb was following him about and was quickly led away to slaughter.

That evening the wolf entered the fold with the flock. But it happened that the shepherd took a fancy for mutton[1] broth that very evening and, picking up a knife, went to the fold. There the first he laid hands on and killed was the wolf.

The evildoer often comes to harm through his own deceit.

1. **mutton:** the meat of a fully grown sheep.

Photograph A humorous illustration of the Aesop fable ▼

DOCUMENT–BASED QUESTIONS

1. What happens to the lamb in this story?

2. What happens to the wolf?

Chapter Connection For more about Aesop, see Chapter 11, Lesson 2.

Primary Source Handbook

Greek Myth: "The Boy Who Flew"

Retold by Anne Rockwell

Background: Many Greek myths focus on individuals who suffer for their prideful or disobedient behavior. Set mainly on the island of Crete in the Aegean Sea, the following story tells the Greek myth of Daedalus (DEHD•uhl•uhs) and Icarus (IHK•uhr•uhs). Daedalus was a brilliant inventor who disobeyed the ruler of Crete; his son, Icarus, disobeyed him. Both suffered for their actions. As this selection opens, Queen Pasiphae (puh•SIHF•uh•EE) of Crete is angry with Daedalus for helping to kill her son, a monster called the Minotaur.

Primary Source

Queen Pasiphae was very angry because, as its mother, she loved the Minotaur, terrible as it had been. Her husband,[1] in order to soothe her, decided to punish Daedalus. He made Daedalus and his son prisoners.

No captain of any ship that sailed to Crete dared take them away because the king had decreed that the inventor and his son could never leave the island. They lived in an isolated tower, where Daedalus had a simple workshop. They had only the seagulls for company. How Daedalus yearned to show Icarus the world beyond their island prison!

One day as Daedalus was watching the gulls wheeling and circling above the surf, he had an inspiration. He shouted down to his son, who was gathering shells on the lonely beach, "Minos may rule the sea, but he does not rule the air!"

▲ **Painting** The fall of Icarus is shown in this painting on the ceiling of the rotunda of Apollo in the Louvre in Paris.

Daedalus had observed how the gulls' wings were shaped, and how they worked. No mortal had ever before figured out how a bird could fly, but Daedalus thought he understood.

He and Icarus began to collect all the gull feathers they could find along the beach. They gathered the large, stiff ones and the tiny, light, downy ones that floated in the breeze. They saved the wax that honeybees made. Then Daedalus made wings of the seagull feathers and the beeswax for himself and Icarus. He worked long and patiently, and Icarus helped him, always doing what his father told him to do.

After they had made two pairs of long, curved wings, Daedalus made two harnesses of leather. He showed Icarus how to place the wings on his shoulders. Then he showed him how to run along the beach until he caught the wind and, like a seagull, flew up into the air.

(continued)

1. **her husband:** King Minos of Crete.

(continued)

Father and son practiced together until, one day, Daedalus decided it was time for them to leave the island. As they rose into the air and headed away from their island prison toward the sea, Daedalus called out to Icarus, "Follow me! Do not fly too low, or you will lose the air and sink into the waves. But do not fly too high, or the heat from the sun will melt the beeswax."

"Yes, Father," shouted Icarus above the sea noises and the wailing of the seagulls who flew beside him.

Higher and higher they flew. At last, Daedalus said, "We will stay at this level all the way. Remember what I told you—follow me!"

As they flew by, fishermen dropped their nets in wonder and farmers stopped at their plows. They thought they were seeing two gods in flight, for surely only gods could fly.

Icarus began to feel more and more sure of himself. He flew upward, then downward. He swooped and soared like a gull, laughing joyously as he did so. He cried out, "Look at me, Father!" and soared upward.

Daedalus beckoned him down, but Icarus thought, He is old and timid while I am young and strong. Surely I can fly a little better than he. Suddenly the boy disappeared into a cloud and flew up and up and up, higher and higher.

Too late, he saw feathers begin to fall from his wings. As the hot sun melted the wax, more and more feathers dropped away. Frantically, the boy flapped his arms in the air, but he could not fly without the wings. Instead, he dropped down and down until he fell into the sea and drowned.

Daedalus flew up in search of his son, calling as he went, "Icarus! Come down to me!"

Then he saw the telltale feathers drifting past him, and he heard the distant splash as Icarus fell into the sea. The old man cried as he continued on his journey, but he flew to freedom. He never made wings for anyone again.

DOCUMENT–BASED QUESTIONS

1. How do Daedalus and Icarus escape from the island?
2. What happens to Icarus?

Chapter Connection For more about Greek myths, see Chapter 11, Lesson 2.

from ***History of the Peloponnesian War***

By Thucydides
Translated by Rex Warner

Background: Thucydides (thoo•SIHD•ih•DEEZ) was a Greek historian who wrote about the bitter 27-year-long war between Athens and Sparta. He was probably in attendance when Pericles, the greatest Athenian statesman of his time, gave a funeral oration for soldiers killed in the first year of the war. In the following excerpt, Pericles speaks of the special qualities of Athens.

Primary Source

"Our love of what is beautiful does not lead to extravagance; our love of the things of the mind does not make us soft. We regard wealth as something to be properly used, rather than as something to boast about. As for poverty, no one need be ashamed to admit it: the real shame is in not taking practical measures to escape from it. Here each individual is interested not only in his own affairs but in the affairs of the state as well: even those who are mostly occupied with their own business are extremely well-informed on general politics—this is a peculiarity of ours: we do not say that a man who takes no interest in politics is a man who minds his own business; we say that he has no business here at all. We Athenians, in our own persons, take our decisions on policy or submit them to proper discussions: for we do not think that there is an incompatibility[1] between words and deeds; the worst thing is to rush into action before the consequences have been properly debated. And this is another point where we differ from other people. We are capable at the same time of taking risks and of estimating them beforehand. Others are brave out of ignorance; and, when they stop to think, they begin to fear. But the man who can most truly be accounted brave is he who best knows the meaning of what is sweet in life and of what is terrible, and then goes out undeterred[2] to meet what is to come."

▲ **Engraving** Portrait of Pericles, the Athenian statesman

1. **incompatibility:** lack of harmony; conflict.
2. **undeterred:** not discouraged.

DOCUMENT–BASED QUESTIONS

1. Why did the Athenians view public discussion as useful before taking action?
2. What was Pericles' definition of courage?

Chapter Connection For more about Pericles' funeral oration, see Chapter 12, Lesson 2, Primary Source.

from *The Life of Caesar*

By Suetonius
Translated by Robert Graves

Background: Julius Caesar was a member of a noble Roman family. He became a great general and sole ruler of Rome. He was assassinated in 44 B.C. More than a century after his death, a Roman historian named Suetonius wrote a biography of this powerful leader.

Primary Source

Caesar was a most skillful swordsman and horseman, and showed surprising powers of endurance. He always led his army, more often on foot than in the saddle, went bareheaded in sun and rain alike, and could travel for long distances at incredible speed in a gig,[1] taking very little luggage. If he reached an unfordable[2] river he would either swim or propel himself across it on an inflated skin; and often arrived at his destination before the messengers whom he had sent ahead to announce his approach. . . .

Sometimes he fought after careful tactical planning, sometimes on the spur of the moment—at the end of a march, often; or in miserable weather, when he would be least expected to make a move. . . . It was his rule never to let enemy troops rally when he had routed them, and always therefore to assault their camp at once. If the fight were a hard-fought one he used to send the chargers[3] away—his own among the first—as a warning that those who feared to stand their ground need not hope to escape on horseback.

1. **gig:** a light two-wheeled carriage drawn by one horse.
2. **unfordable:** uncrossable.
3. **chargers:** horses.

Julius Caesar Bronze statue of Julius Caesar ▼

DOCUMENT–BASED QUESTIONS

1. What were some of the personal qualities of Caesar?
2. What was probably the attitude of Caesar's soldiers toward him?

Chapter Connection For more about Julius Caesar, see Chapter 13, Lesson 3.

from the **New Testament: Parable of the Lost Sheep**

Background: Jesus often taught in parables—stories that teach morals or lessons. In the following parable, Jesus tells

▲ **Brooch** Roman brooch shows the Lamb of God. The halo symbolizes Jesus.

Primary Source

Among the people who gathered to see Jesus were those who were very religious.

"As a teacher of the Law," said one, "I am very concerned to make sure that this wandering preacher is not leading the people astray with what he says."

"As a Pharisee,"[1] added another, "I am worried that he doesn't teach the importance of a pure and holy life." . . .

Jesus waved them over. They stepped forward but then had to wait as a shepherd led his sheep along the path that lay between them, ambling slowly forward so the animals that straggled behind could catch up.

"Just think about shepherds and how they go about their work," said Jesus when they arrived. "Imagine—a shepherd has one hundred sheep. He is leading them along, but when he turns and counts them, he finds that one is missing. What does he do? He leaves the ninety-nine grazing in the pasture and goes looking for the one that is lost.

"And what does he do when at last he finds it? Does he beat it and punish it till it bleats in terror and pain? Of course not! It is his treasure, and he is delighted to find it. So he picks it up and lays it across his shoulders so he can carry it home.

"Then, when it is safely home, he calls to all his friends, 'Today is my happy day. I found my lost sheep. Let us celebrate together!'

"I tell you," said Jesus, "there is more rejoicing in heaven over one sinner who repents of their ways than over ninety-nine respectable people who do not need to repent."

1. **Pharisee:** member of a Jewish sect that emphasized a strict interpretation of the law of Moses.

DOCUMENT–BASED QUESTIONS

1. What does the lost sheep stand for?

2. What sort of message about the fate of sinners does the parable convey?

Chapter Connection For more parables of Jesus, see Chapter 14, Literature Connection.

from the *Annals*

By Tacitus
Translated by Michael Grant

Background: Tacitus was one of the greatest historians of ancient Rome. In the following excerpt, Tacitus tells about a terrible fire that swept Rome in A.D. 64. Many Romans believed that the emperor Nero had ordered the fire set so that he could rebuild Rome according to his own designs.

Primary Source

Of Rome's fourteen districts only four remained intact. Three were leveled to the ground. The other seven were reduced to a few scorched and mangled ruins. To count the mansions, blocks, and temples destroyed would be difficult. They included shrines of remote antiquity, the precious spoils[1] of countless victories, Greek artistic masterpieces, and authentic records of old Roman genius. All the splendor of the rebuilt city did not prevent the older generation from remembering these irreplaceable objects. . . .

But Nero profited by his country's ruin to build a new palace. Its wonders were not so much customary and commonplace luxuries like gold and jewels, but lawns and lakes and faked rusticity[2]—woods here, open spaces and views there. With their cunning, impudent artificialities,[3] Nero's architects and contractors outbid Nature.

1. **spoils:** goods or property seized after a conflict.
2. **rusticity:** resemblance to the countryside.
3. **impudent artificialities:** shameless and unnatural designs.

▲ **Bust** This marble bust portrays the Emperor Nero.

DOCUMENT-BASED QUESTIONS

1. What effect might a public calamity such as a fire have on political stability?
2. How might people at the time have interpreted the event?

Chapter Connection For more about the decline of Rome, see Chapter 15.

A Global View

A religion is an organized system of beliefs and practices, often centered on one or more gods. In this book, you have learned about many different religions and their impact on world history. Religions have guided people's beliefs and actions for thousands of years. They have brought people together. But they have also torn them apart.

Religions are powerful forces today as well. They affect everything from what people wear to how they behave. There are thousands of religions in the world. In the following pages, you will learn about five major religions: Buddhism, Christianity, Hinduism, Islam, and Judaism. You will also learn about Confucianism, an ethical system. Like a religion, an ethical system provides guidance on how to live your life. However, unlike religions, ethical systems do not center on the worship of gods. The chart on the opposite page shows what percentages of the world population practice the five major religions. The map shows where these religions are predominant or where they are practiced by significant numbers.

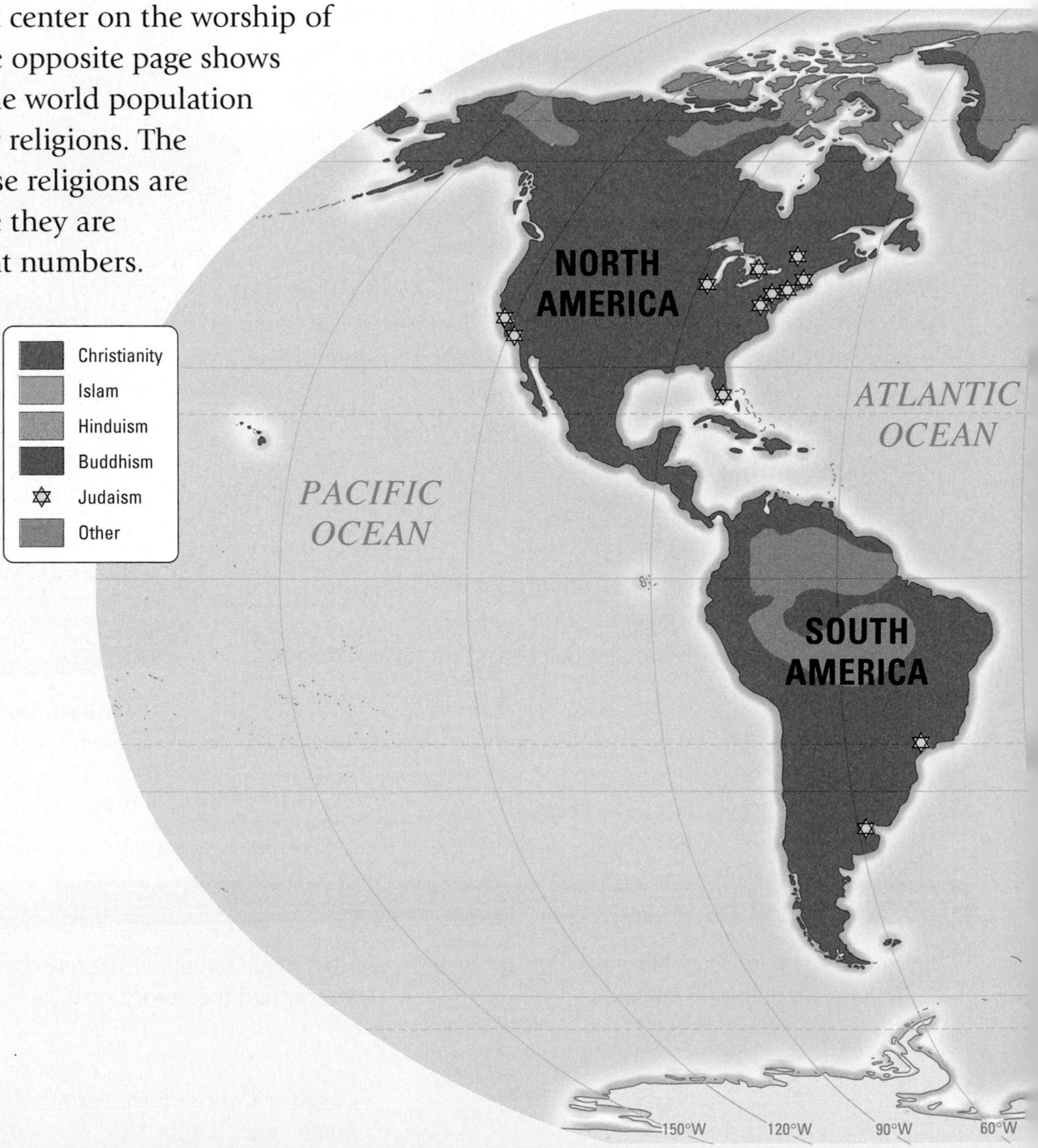

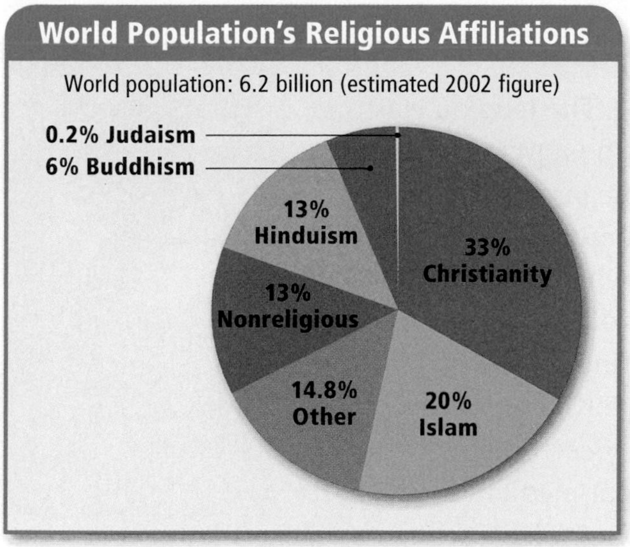

Source: *World Almanac 2003*

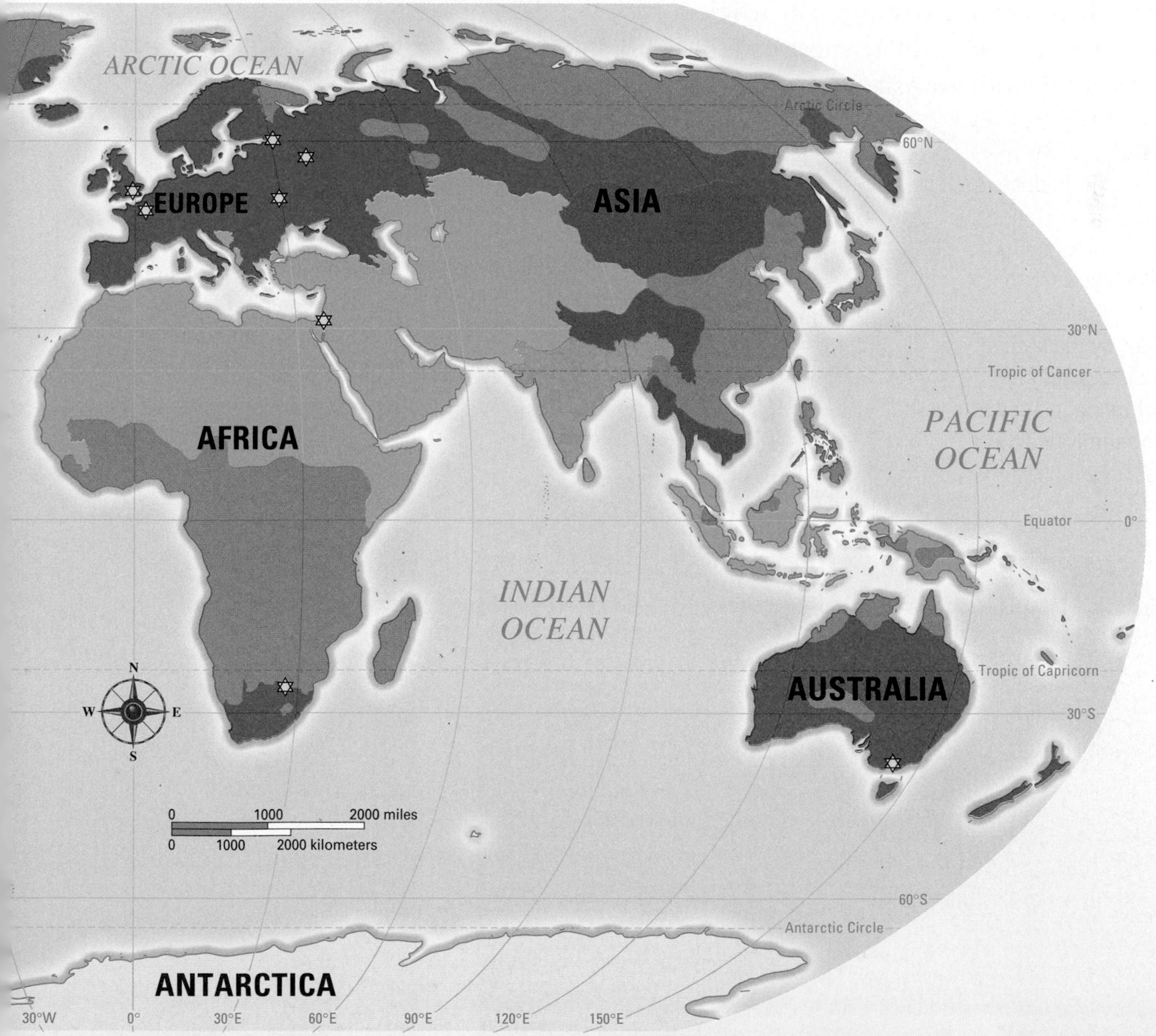

World Religions Handbook

Buddhism

Buddhism began in India in the sixth century B.C. The religion was founded by Siddhartha Gautama (sihd•DAHR•tuh GOW•tuh•muh), who came to be known as the Buddha. *Buddha* means "enlightened one." He was born into a noble family but left home to search for enlightenment, or wisdom. The Buddha is said to have achieved enlightenment after long study. According to Buddhist tradition, he taught his followers that the way to end suffering was by practicing the Noble Eightfold Path. This path involved observing the following: right opinions, right desires, right speech, right action, right job, right effort, right concentration, and right meditation.

After the Buddha's death, Buddhism spread in India, Ceylon, and Central Asia. Missionaries spread the faith. Buddhist ideas also traveled along trade routes. The religion, however, did not survive on Indian soil. Today, most Buddhists live in Sri Lanka (formerly Ceylon), East Asia, Southeast Asia, and Japan.

▼ Buddha
Statues of the Buddha, such as this one in Japan, appear in shrines throughout Asia. Buddhists try to follow the Buddha's teachings by meditating, a way of emptying the mind of thought. They also make offerings at shrines, temples, and monasteries.

▼ Monks
Buddhist monks dedicate their entire life to the teachings of the Buddha. They live together in religious communities called monasteries. There, the monks lead a life of poverty, meditation, and study. In this photograph, Buddhist monks in Myanmar hold their begging bowls.

▲ **Pilgrimage**
For centuries, Buddhists have come to visit places in India and Nepal associated with the Buddha's life. These sites include the Buddha's birthplace and the fig tree where he achieved his enlightenment. Worshipers also visit the site of the Buddha's first sermon, shown here.

Learn More About Buddhism

Symbol The Buddha's teaching, known as the dharma, is often symbolized by a wheel because his teaching was intended to end the cycle of births and deaths. The Buddha is said to have "set in motion the wheel of the dharma" during his first sermon.

Primary Source

The Buddha called his insight into the nature of suffering the Four Noble Truths (see page 234). In the following selection, the Buddha tells his followers how they can end suffering and find enlightenment. The path involves understanding that life on Earth is brief and full of sadness. It also involves giving up selfish desire.

All created things are transitory [short-lived]; those who realize this are freed from suffering. This is the path that leads to pure wisdom.

All created beings are involved in sorrow; those who realize this are freed from suffering. This is the path that leads to pure wisdom.

All states are without self; those who realize this are freed from suffering. This is the path that leads to pure wisdom.

from the Dhammapada
Translated by Eknath Easwaran

Chapter Connection For more about Buddhism, see Chapter 7.

Christianity

Christianity is the largest religion in the world, with about 2 billion followers. It is based on the life and teachings of Jesus, as described in the Bible's New Testament. Jesus, a Jew, taught many ideas from the Jewish tradition. Some biblical prophets had spoken of a day when a promised figure would come to save all of humankind. By the end of the first century A.D., many Jews and non-Jews had come to believe that Jesus was the one who would make this happen. Now called "Christians," they spread their faith throughout the Roman Empire.

Christians regard Jesus as the Son of God. They believe that Jesus entered the world and died to save humanity.

▼ Easter and Palm Sunday

On Easter, Christians celebrate their belief in Jesus' resurrection, or his being raised to heavenly life after he was put to death. The Sunday before Easter, Christians observe Palm Sunday. This day celebrates Jesus' triumphal entry into Jerusalem. Palm branches, like those carried here, were spread before him.

▲ Jesus and the Disciples
Jesus' followers included 12 disciples, or pupils. Jesus passed on his teachings to his disciples. This painting from the 1400s shows Jesus with his disciples.

▼ St. Paul's Cathedral
Paul was one of the apostles who spread Christian beliefs throughout the Roman Empire. Paul started churches almost everywhere he went. Many churches today, such as this great cathedral in London, are named for this apostle.

Learn More About Christianity

Symbol According to the New Testament, Jesus was crucified, or put to death on a cross. As a result, the cross became an important symbol of Christianity. It represents the belief that Jesus died to save humanity.

Primary Source

One of Jesus' most famous sermons is the Sermon on the Mount. In this talk, Jesus provided guidance to his followers. His words were written down in the New Testament, the part of the Bible that describes the teaching of Jesus. In the following verses, Jesus explains that people can be saved by opening their hearts to God and by treating others as they would like to be treated.

"Ask, and it will be given you; seek, and you will find; knock, and it will be opened to you. For every one who asks receives, and he who seeks finds, and to him who knocks it will be opened. Or what man of you, if his son asks him for a loaf, will give him a stone? Or if he asks for a fish, will give him a serpent? If you then, who are evil, know how to give good gifts to your children, how much more will your Father who is in heaven give good things to those who ask him? So whatever you wish that men would do to you, do so to them; for this is the law and the prophets."

Matthew 7:7–12

Chapter Connection For more about Christianity, see Chapter 14.

Hinduism

Hinduism is a way of life guided by religious beliefs and practices that developed over thousands of years. Hindus believe that a supreme being called Brahman is the soul of the universe. The same presence, they believe, can also be found within each person. People can be freed from suffering and desires once they understand the nature of Brahman. The religious practices of Hindus include prayer, meditation, selfless acts, and worship of the various Hindu deities.

Today, Hinduism is the major religion of India and Nepal. It also has followers in Indonesia, Africa, Europe, and the Western Hemisphere.

▼ Festival of Diwali

Diwali, the Festival of Lights, is the most important festival in India. Diwali may have begun as a harvest festival in ancient India. Today, it marks the beginning of the year for many Hindus. They celebrate the festival by lighting candles and lamps, as shown in this photograph.

▲ **Deities**
Brahman often takes the form of three deities in Hinduism. Brahma is the creator of the universe. Vishnu is its protector. Shiva is its destroyer. All three deities are represented in this sculpture.

▼ **Brahmin Priest**
Brahmin priests, like the one shown here, are among Hinduism's religious leaders. These priests take care of the holy images in temples and read from the religion's sacred books.

Learn More About Hinduism

Symbol The syllable *Om* (or *Aum*) is often recited at the beginning of Hindu prayers. *Om* is the most sacred sound in Hinduism because it is believed to contain all other sounds. The syllable is represented by the symbol shown below.

Primary Source

Hinduism has many sacred texts. The Vedas, four collections of prayers, rituals, and other sacred texts, are the oldest Hindu scriptures. They are believed to contain all knowledge, past and future.

The *Bhagavad Gita* is another sacred Hindu text. In this work, Vishnu takes on the personality of a chariot driver named Krishna. Krishna and the warrior Arjuna discuss the meaning of life and religious faith. In this selection, Krishna explains that Brahman cannot be destroyed.

> Weapons do not cut it,
> fire does not burn it,
> waters do not wet it,
> wind does not wither it.
>
> It cannot be cut or burned;
> it cannot be wet or withered;
> it is enduring, all-pervasive,
> fixed, immovable, and timeless.

Bhagavad Gita 2:23–24

Chapter Connection For more about Hinduism, see Chapter 7.

Islam

Islam is a religion based on the teachings of the Qur'an, the religion's holy book. Followers of Islam, known as Muslims, believe that God revealed these teachings to the prophet Muhammad through the angel Gabriel around A.D. 610. Islam teaches that there is only one God—the same God that is worshiped in Christianity and Judaism. In Arabic, God is called Allah. Muslims also believe in the prophets of Judaism and Christianity. In fact, Muslims traditionally refer to Christians and Jews as "people of the book." That is because Christians and Jews have received divine revelations from scriptures in the Bible.

Today, Muslims live in southwestern and central Asia and parts of Africa. Islam also has many followers in Southeast Asia. Muslims show their devotion by performing acts of worship known as the Five Pillars of Islam. These include faith, prayer, charity, fasting, and a pilgrimage to Mecca.

▲ Muslim Prayer
Five times a day—dawn, noon, mid-afternoon, sunset, and evening—Muslims face toward Mecca to pray. Like the people in this photograph, Muslims stop what they are doing when they hear the call to prayer. Everything comes to a halt—even traffic.

▼ The Dome of the Rock
The Dome of the Rock in Jerusalem is one of Islam's holiest sites. The rock on the site is the spot from which Muslims say Muhammad rose to heaven to learn Allah's will. With Allah's blessing, Muhammad returned to Earth to bring God's message to all people.

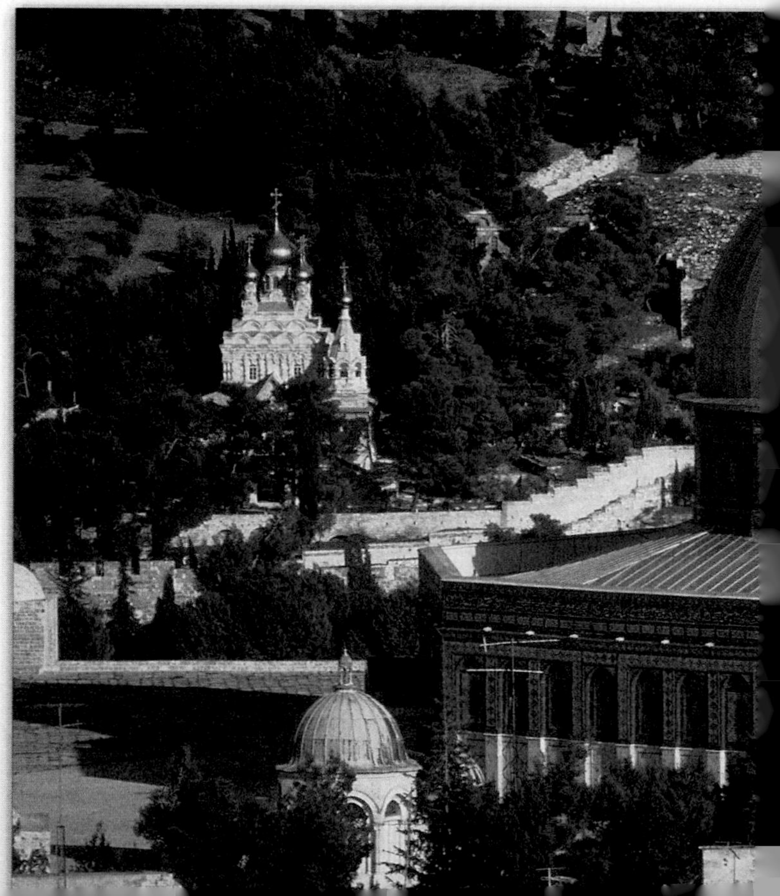

▼ Ramadan

During the holy month of Ramadan, Muslims fast, or do not eat or drink, from dawn to sunset. The family shown here is ending their fast. The most important night of Ramadan is called the Night of Power. This is believed to be the night the angel Gabriel first spoke to Muhammad.

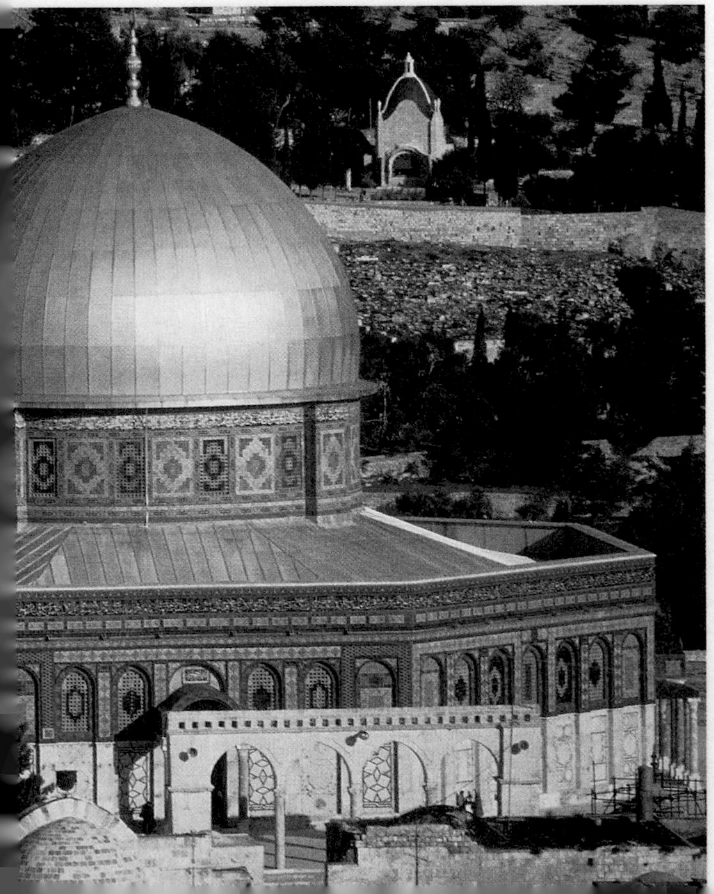

Learn More About Islam

Symbol The crescent moon has become a symbol of Islam. The symbol may be related to the new moon that begins each month in the Islamic lunar calendar.

Primary Source

The Qur'an is the spiritual guide for Muslims. It also contains teachings for Muslim daily life. The following chapter is called the Exordium (introduction). It is also called Al-Fatihah. Muslims recite this short chapter as well as other passages from the Qur'an, when they pray.

In the Name of God, the Compassionate,
the Merciful

Praise be to God, Lord of the Universe,
The Compassionate, the Merciful,
Sovereign of the Day of Judgment!
You alone we worship, and to You alone
we turn for help.
Guide us to the straight path,
The path of those whom You have favored,
Not of those who have incurred Your wrath,
Nor of those who have gone astray.

Qur'an 1:1–6

Judaism

Judaism was the first major monotheistic religion—that is, based on the concept of one God. The basic teachings of Judaism come from the Torah, the first five books of the Hebrew Bible. Judaism teaches that a person serves God by studying the Torah and living by its teachings. The Torah became the basis for the civil and religious laws of Judaism. The followers of Judaism, or Jews, also believe that God set down many moral laws for all of humanity with the Ten Commandments.

Today, there are more than 14 million Jews throughout the world. Many live in Israel, where a Jewish state was created in 1948.

▾ Abraham

According to the Torah, God chose a Hebrew shepherd named Abraham to be the "father" of the Hebrew people. In the 19th century B.C., Abraham led his family to a land that he believed God had promised them. This painting illustrates their journey.

▲ **Rabbi**
Rabbis are the Jewish people's spiritual leaders and teachers. A rabbi often conducts the services in a synagogue, or Jewish house of worship. Like the rabbi shown here, he or she may also conduct the ceremony that marks Jewish children's entrance into the religious community.

▼ **Western Wall**
Many Jews make the pilgrimage to the Western Wall, shown here. The sacred wall formed the western wall of the courtyard of the Second Temple of Jerusalem. The temple was built in the second century B.C. The Romans destroyed it in A.D. 70.

Learn More About Judaism

Symbol The Star of David, also called the Shield of David, is a very important symbol of Judaism. The symbol honors King David, who ruled the kingdom of Israel about 1000–962 B.C.

Primary Source

The Book of Genesis is the first book of the Hebrew Bible and of the Torah. Genesis tells the history of the Hebrew people. It focuses on the individuals with whom God had a special relationship. In the following verses, God speaks to Abraham. His words express a promise of land and a special pledge to the Hebrew people.

Now the Lord said to Abram [Abraham], "Go from your country and your kindred and your father's house to the land that I will show you. And I will make of you a great nation, and I will bless you, and make your name great, so that you will be a blessing. I will bless those who bless you, and him who curses you I will curse; and by you all the families of the earth will bless themselves."

Genesis 12:1–3

Chapter Connection For more about Judaism, see Chapter 10.

World Religions Handbook

Confucianism

Confucianism is an ethical system based on the teachings of the Chinese scholar Confucius. It stresses social and civic responsibility. Confucius was born in 551 B.C., during a time of crisis in China. He hoped his ideas and teachings would restore the order of earlier times to his society. But although Confucius was active in politics, he never had enough political power to put his ideas into practice. After his death, Confucius' students spread his teachings. As a result, his ideas became the foundation of Chinese thought for more than 2,000 years.

Today, Confucianism guides the actions of millions of Chinese people and other peoples of the East. It has also greatly influenced people's spiritual beliefs. While East Asians declare themselves to follow a number of religions, many also claim to be Confucians.

▼ Temple
Although Confucianism has no clergy or gods to worship, temples, like this one in Taiwan, have been built to honor Confucius. In ancient times, the temples provided schools of higher education. Today, many have been turned into museums.

◂ **Confucius**

Confucius believed that society should be organized around five basic relationships. These are the relationships between (1) ruler and subject, (2) father and son, (3) husband and wife, (4) elder brother and junior brother, and (5) friend and friend.

▴ **Confucius' Birthday**

Historians do not know for certain the day when Confucius was born, but people in East Asia celebrate his birthday on September 28. In Taiwan and China, it is an official holiday known as Teachers' Day. The holiday pays tribute to teachers because Confucius himself was a teacher. Here, students in Beijing take part in a ceremony honoring their teachers.

Learn More About Confucianism

Symbol The yin-and-yang symbol represents opposite forces in the world working together. Yin represents all that is cold, dark, soft, and mysterious. Yang represents everything that is warm, bright, hard, and clear. The yin-and-yang symbol represents the harmony that Confucius hoped to restore to society.

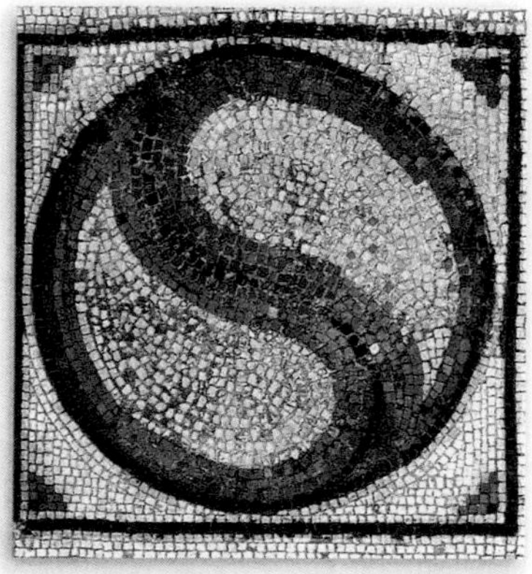

Primary Source

Confucius' teachings were collected by his students in a book called the *Analects*. In the following selections from the *Analects*, Confucius (called the Master) instructs his students about living a moral and thoughtful life.

The Master said: "Even in the midst of eating coarse rice and drinking water and using a bent arm for a pillow happiness is surely to be found; riches and honors acquired by unrighteous means are to me like the floating clouds." (7.16)

The Master said: "When I walk with two others, I always receive instruction from them. I select their good qualities and copy them, and improve on their bad qualities." (7.22)

The Master said: "The people may be made to follow something, but may not be made to understand it." (8.9)

from the ***Analects***
Translated by Raymond Dawson

Chapter Connection For more about Confucianism, see Chapter 8.

Other Important Religions

You have learned about the five major world religions. Now find out about some other important religions: Bahaism, Shinto, Sikhism, and Zoroastrianism. These religions are important both historically and because they have many followers today.

▲ Bahaism

Bahaism (buh•HAH•IHZ•uhm) is a young religion, with more than 7 million followers throughout the world. It was founded in 1863 in Persia (modern-day Iran) by a man known as Bahaullah, which means "splendor of God" in Arabic. Followers believe that, in time, God will make barriers of race, class, and nation break down. When this happens, people will form a single, united society. All of the Baha'i houses of worship have nine sides and a central dome, symbolizing this unity. The Baha'i house of worship shown here is located in Illinois.

▼ Shinto

Shinto, meaning "way of the gods," is Japan's oldest and only native religion. Shintoists worship many gods, called *kami*. They believe that kami are spirits found in mountains, rivers, rocks, trees, and other parts of nature. Shintoists often worship the kami at shrines in their homes. They also celebrate the gods during special festivals, such as the one shown here. Today, there are about 3 million Shintoists, mostly in Japan.

World Religions Handbook

◀ Sikhism

Sikhism was founded in India over 500 years ago by Guru Nanak, a man raised in the Hindu tradition. The religion's 24 million followers, called Sikhs, believe in one God. Like Buddhists and Hindus, Sikhs believe that the soul goes through repeated cycles of life and death. However, Sikhs do not believe that they have to live outside the world to end the cycle. Rather, they can achieve salvation by living a good and simple life. Uncut hair symbolizes this simple life. Many Sikh men cover their long hair with a turban, like the one worn by the man here.

▲ Zoroastrianism

Zoroastrianism (zawr•oh•AS•tree•uh•nihz•uhm) was founded in ancient Persia around 600 b.c. by a prophet named Zoroaster. This prophet taught that Earth is a battleground where a great struggle is fought between the forces of good and the forces of evil. Each person is expected to take part in this struggle. At death, the Zoroastrian god, called Ahura Mazda (ah•HUR•uh MAZ•duh), will judge the person on how well he or she fought. This stone relief shows Ahura Mazda (*right*) giving the crown to a Persian king. Today, there are about 2.5 million Zoroastrians throughout the world.

Comparing World Religions and Ethical Systems

	Buddhism	Christianity	Hinduism	Islam	Judaism	Confucianism
Followers worldwide (estimated 2003 figures)	364 million	2 billion	828 million	1.2 billion	14.5 million	6.3 million
Name of god	no god	God	Brahman	Allah	God	no god
Founder	the Buddha	Jesus	no founder	no founder but spread by Muhammad	Abraham	Confucius
Holy book	many sacred books, including the Dhammapada	Bible, including Old Testament and New Testament	many sacred texts, including the Upanishads	Qur'an	Hebrew Bible, including the Torah	*Analects*
Clergy	Buddhist monks	priests, ministers, monks, and nuns	Brahmin priests, monks, and gurus	no clergy but a scholar class, called the ulama, and imams, who may lead prayers	rabbis	no clergy
Basic beliefs	• Followers can achieve enlightenment by understanding the Four Noble Truths and by following the Noble Eightfold Path of right opinions, right desires, right speech, right action, right jobs, right effort, right concentration, and right meditation.	• There is only one God, who watches over and cares for his people. • Jesus is the Son of God. He died to save humanity. His death and resurrection made eternal life possible for others.	• The soul never dies but is continually reborn until it becomes divinely enlightened. • Persons achieve happiness and divine enlightenment after they free themselves from their earthly desires. • Freedom from earthly desires comes from many lifetimes of worship, knowledge, and virtuous acts.	• Persons achieve salvation by following the Five Pillars of Islam and living a just life. The pillars are faith, prayer, charity, fasting, and pilgrimage to Mecca.	• There is only one God, who watches over and cares for his people. • God loves and protects his people but also holds people accountable for their sins and shortcomings. • Persons serve God by studying the Torah and living by its teachings.	• Social order, harmony, and good government should be based on strong family relationships. • Respect for parents and elders is important to a well-ordered society. • Education is important for the welfare of both the individual and society.

Source: *World Almanac 2004*

Review

MAIN IDEAS

Buddhism (pages R62–R63)

1. How did the Buddha believe that his followers could end their suffering?
2. How did Buddhism spread?

Christianity (pages R64–R65)

3. Why is Jesus important to the Christian religion?
4. What are some Christian beliefs?

Hinduism (pages R66–R67)

5. What is the importance of Brahman in Hinduism?
6. What three deities does Brahman often take the form of?

Islam (pages R68–R69)

7. How do Muslims believe the teachings of the Qur'an were revealed?
8. Why do Muslims traditionally refer to Christians and Jews as "people of the book"?

Judaism (pages R70–R71)

9. What does it mean to say that Judaism is a monotheistic religion?
10. What are the Ten Commandments?

Confucianism (pages R72–R73)

11. What did Confucius hope to restore?
12. What five relationships are important in Confucianism?

Other Important Religions (pages R74–R75)

13. How does Shinto differ from Bahaism, Sikhism, and Zoroastrianism?
14. How is Sikhism similar to Buddhism and Hinduism?

CRITICAL THINKING

15. **COMPARING** What goal do Buddhists and Hindus have in common?
16. **DRAWING CONCLUSIONS** How does Islam affect the everyday lives of its followers?
17. **SUMMARIZING** Which of the religions you have studied are monotheistic?

Standards-Based Assessment

Interpreting a Pie Chart The pie chart below shows what percentages of the population of India practice the major religions. Use the pie chart to answer the following questions.

India's Religious Affiliations

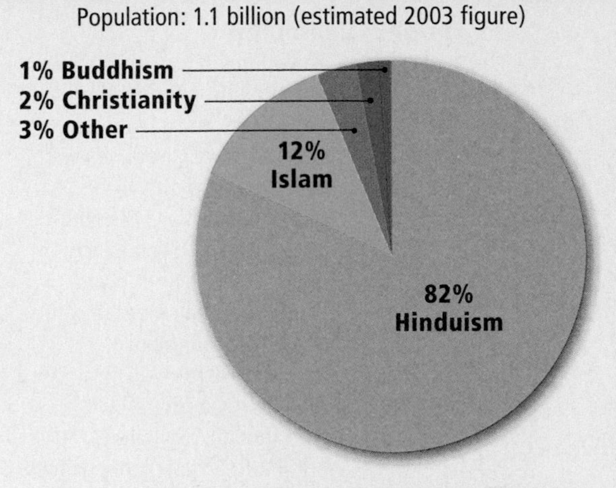

Source: *World Almanac 2004*

1. **What percentage of the people in India practice Hinduism?**
   A. 1 percent
   B. 2 percent
   C. 12 percent
   D. 82 percent

2. **Which religion is practiced by 12 percent of the population?**
   A. Christianity
   B. Hinduism
   C. Buddhism
   D. Islam

Test Practice
ClassZone.com

Additional Test Practice, pp. S1–S33

World Religions Handbook

Glossary

The Glossary is an alphabetical listing of many of the key terms from the chapters, along with their meanings. The definitions listed in the Glossary are the ones that apply to the way the words are used in this textbook. The Glossary gives the part of speech of each word. The following abbreviations are used:

adj. **adjective** ***n.*** **noun** ***v.*** **verb**

Pronunciation Key

Some of the words in this book are followed by respellings that show how the words are pronounced. The following key will help you understand what sounds are represented by the letters used in the respellings.

Symbol	Examples	Symbol	Examples
a	**a**pple [ap•uhl], c**a**tch [kach]	oh	r**oa**d, [rohd], kn**ow** [noh]
ah	b**a**rn [bahrn], p**o**t [paht]	oo	sch**oo**l [skool], gl**ue** [gloo]
air	b**ear** [bair], d**are** [dair]	ow	**ou**t [owt], c**ow** [kow]
aw	b**ough**t [bawt], h**or**se [hawrs]	oy	c**oi**n [koyn], b**oy**s [boyz]
ay	**a**pe [ayp], m**ai**l [mayl]	p	**p**ig [pihg], to**p** [tahp]
b	**b**ell [behl], ta**b**le [TAY•buhl]	r	**r**ose [rohz], sta**r** [stahr]
ch	**ch**ain [chayn], di**tch** [dihch]	s	**s**oap [sohp], i**c**y [EYE•see]
d	**d**og [dawg], rain**ed** [raynd]	sh	**sh**are [shair], na**ti**on [NAY•shuhn]
ee	**e**ven [EE•vuhn], m**ea**l [meel]	t	**t**ired [tyrd], boa**t** [boht]
eh	**e**gg [ehg], t**e**n [tehn]	th	**th**in [thihn], mo**th**er [MUH•thuhr]
eye	**i**ron [EYE•uhrn]	u	p**u**ll [pul], l**oo**k [luk]
f	**f**all [fawl], lau**gh** [laf]	uh	b**u**mp [buhmp], **a**wake [uh•WAYK],
g	**g**old [gohld], bi**g** [bihg]		happ**e**n [HAP•uhn], penc**i**l [PEHN•suhl],
h	**h**ot [haht], ex**h**ale [ehks•HAYL]		pil**o**t [PY•luht]
hw	**wh**ite [hwyt]	ur	**Ear**th [urth], b**ir**d [burd], w**or**m [wurm]
ih	**i**nto [IHN•too], s**i**ck [sihk]	v	**v**ase [vays], lo**v**e [luhv]
j	**j**ar [jahr], ba**dge** [baj]	w	**w**eb [wehb], t**w**in [twihn]
k	**c**at [kat], lu**ck** [luhk]	y	As a consonant: **y**ard [yahrd], m**u**le [myool]
l	**l**oad [lohd], ba**ll** [bawl]		As a vowel: **i**ce [ys], tr**ie**d [tryd], s**igh** [sy]
m	**m**ake [mayk], ge**m** [jehm]	z	**z**one [zohn], rea**s**on [REE•zuhn]
n	**n**ight [nyt], wi**n** [wihn]	zh	trea**s**ure [TREHZH•uhr], gara**ge** [guh•RAHZH]
ng	so**ng** [sawng], a**n**ger [ANG•guhr]		

Syllables that are stressed when the words are spoken appear in CAPITAL LETTERS in the respellings. For example, the respelling of *history* (HIHS•tuh•ree) shows that the first syllable of the word is stressed.

Syllables that appear in SMALL CAPITAL LETTERS are also stressed, but not as strongly as those that appear in capital letters. For example, the respelling of *anthropology* (AN•thruh•PAHL•uh•gee) shows that the third syllable receives the main stress and the first syllable receives a secondary stress.

Glossary

A

Abraham *n.* according to the Bible, a shepherd from the city of Ur in Mesopotamia who became the father of the Hebrews. (p. 325)

absolute ruler *n.* a person who has total power and governs alone. (p. 497)

acropolis (uh•KRAHP•uh•lihs) *n.* a fortified high place in an ancient Greek city, which contained important temples, monuments, and buildings. (p. 396)

Adulis (ah•DOO•lihs) *n.* an ancient city on the Red Sea, which served as the main trading port of the kingdom of Aksum. (p. 198)

Aeneas (ih•NEE•uhs) *n.* a hero of the Trojan War. (p. 431)

afterlife *n.* a life believed to follow death. (p. 159)

agriculture *n.* the cultivation of soil to produce useful crops. (p. 60)

ahimsa (uh•HIHM•SAH) *n.* nonviolence. (p. 233)

Aksum (AHK•SOOM) *n.* an ancient African kingdom on the Red Sea, in what is now Ethiopia and Eritrea. It replaced the kingdom of Kush. (p. 197)

Alexander the Great *n.* a king of Macedonia from 336 to 323 B.C., who conquered parts of Asia and Egypt, spreading Greek culture throughout his empire. (p. 407)

Alexandria *n.* a Hellenistic city in Egypt, on the Mediterranean Sea. Founded by Alexander the Great in 332 B.C., it was noted for its extensive ancient library as well as its lighthouse, one of the Seven Wonders of the World. (p. 408)

alphabet *n.* a set of letters used to represent the individual sounds of a language. (p. 358)

Anatolia *n.* the peninsula between the Mediterranean and Black seas that is now occupied by most of Turkey; also called Asia Minor. (p. 131)

animism *n.* the belief that spirits exist in animals, plants, other natural objects, and natural forces. (p. 205)

aqueduct (AK•wih•DUHKT) *n.* a pipe or channel that carries water from a distant source to a city. (pp. 457, 517)

aquifer *n.* an underground layer of sand, gravel, or spongy rock that contains water. (p. 297)

aristocracy (AR•ih•STAHK•ruh•see) *n.* an upper class or nobility. (p. 373)

artifact *n.* a human-made object. (p. 28)

artisan *n.* a person trained in a particular skill or craft. (p. 67)

Aryan (AIR•ee•uhn) *n.* a member of an Indo-European people who crossed into India around 1500 B.C. (p. 228)

Asoka (uh•SOH•kuh) *n.* the greatest Maurya king, whose reign began in 269 B.C. (p. 236)

Athens *n.* a city-state of ancient Greece, which reached its greatest cultural achievements in the fifth century B.C. It is the capital and largest city of modern Greece. (p. 379)

Augustus (aw•GUHS•tuhs) *n.* the first Roman emperor (originally named Octavian), who became emperor in 27 b.c. (p. 446)

B

Babylonian Captivity *n.* a 50-year period in which the Israelites were held in Babylon, away from their homeland of Judah. During this period, the Israelites became known as Jews. (p. 338)

Bantu *n.* a group of West African peoples that gradually migrated eastward and southward, bringing farming and herding to new regions. (p. 206)

barbarian *n.* a person belonging to a group seen as primitive and uncivilized; especially, a person living outside the ancient Roman Empire. (p. 502)

barracks *n.* a group of buildings used to house soldiers. (p. 380)

bas-relief (BAH•rih•LEEF) *n.* a type of sculpture in which slightly raised figures stand out against a flat background. (p. 516)

bishop *n.* a high-ranking local official in some Christian churches. (p. 485)

Brahmanism (BRAH•muh•NIHZ•uhm) *n.* the early religion of the Aryans in ancient India. (p. 229)

bronze *n.* a metal that is a mixture of copper and tin. (p. 101)

Buddhism *n.* a religion that began in India and is based on the teachings of Siddhartha Gautama. (p. 233)

bureaucracy (byu•RAHK•ruh•see) *n.* a system of organized government departments staffed by appointed officials. (p. 269)

Byzantine (BIHZ•uhn•teen) **Empire** *n.* the Eastern Roman Empire, which was ruled from Constantinople and lasted for about a thousand years after the fall of the Western Roman Empire. (p. 509)

C

Caesar, Julius *n.* a Roman general and politician (100–44 B.C.) who received great support from Rome's commoners and was given the right to rule for life in 44 B.C. He was assassinated the same year. (p. 444)

caste *n.* a social class that a person belongs to by birth. (p. 228)

catapult *n.* an ancient military machine for hurling stones or other objects at enemy troops and fortresses. (p. 405)

cataract (KAT•uh•RAKT) *n.* a steep waterfall. (p. 147)

catholic *adj.* universal. (p. 485)

Chavín (chah•VEEN) *n.* a culture that flourished between 900 and 200 B.C. in the Andes of Peru. (p. 295)

Cicero (SIHS•uh•ROH) *n.* a Roman consul and famous orator who opposed Julius Caesar. (p. 445)

Cincinnatus *n.* a dictator of Rome for one day in 458 B.C. (p. 438)

citizen *n.* a person who is loyal to a particular government and entitled to be protected by that government. (p. 374)

city-state *n.* a political unit that includes a city and its nearby farmlands. (p. 91)

civilization *n.* a human society with an advanced level of development in social and political organization and in the arts and sciences. (p. 89)

civil war *n.* an armed conflict between groups within the same country. (p. 444)

climate *n.* the pattern of weather conditions in a certain location over a long period of time. (p. 12)

code of law *n.* a set of written rules for people to obey. (p. 115)

codex *n.* a book of the type used by early Meso-American civilizations to record important historical events. (p. 310)

Colosseum *n.* a large arena in Rome, where the ancient Romans attended entertainments, such as battles of gladiators. (p. 458)

comedy *n.* a form of drama usually having a happy ending and often making fun of politics, people, and ideas of the times. (p. 412)

Confucianism (kuhn•FYOO•shuh•nihz•uhm) *n.* a philosophy based on the teachings of Confucius (551–479 B.C.), as recorded in the collection called the *Analects*. (p. 260)

consul *n.* one of a pair of elected officials who headed ancient Rome's executive branch and commanded the army. (p. 438)

continent *n.* one of the seven large landmasses of Earth—North America, South America, Europe, Asia, Africa, Australia, and Antarctica. (p. 9)

convert *v.* to convince someone to change his or her religion or beliefs. (p. 477)

creed *n.* a statement of religious beliefs. (p. 486)

crucifixion *n.* an execution by hanging on a cross. (p. 470)

cultural diffusion *n.* the spread of ethnic ideas and customs to other areas of the world. (p. 277)

cuneiform (KYOO•nee•uh•fawrm) *n.* an ancient writing system developed by the Sumerians, made up of wedge-shaped markings. (p. 102)

D

Daoism (DOW•IHZ•uhm) *n.* a belief system said to have begun with the sixth-century-B.C. philosopher Laozi. Daoism emphasizes living in harmony with nature. (p. 262)

David *n.* the king of the Israelites who won control of Jerusalem in 1000 B.C. (p. 336)

Delian League *n.* an alliance of Greek city-states formed at the end of the Persian War to protect Athens and its overseas allies. (p. 395)

delta *n.* the area near a river's mouth where the river deposits large amounts of sand and silt. (p. 147)

democracy *n.* a government in which citizens make political decisions, either directly or through elected representatives. (p. 375)

dharma (DAHR•muh) *n.* the collected teachings of Buddha. (p. 235)

Diaspora (dy•AS•puhr•uh) *n.* the scattering of Jewish people after they were forced out of Judea by the Romans in A.D. 70. (p. 345)

Diocletian (DY•uh•KLEE•shuhn) *n.* a Roman leader who became emperor in A.D. 284 and introduced reforms in Rome's administration, army, and economy. (p. 497)

direct democracy *n.* a form of democracy in which citizens participate directly in running the government. (p. 394)

disciple *n.* one of Jesus' 12 closest followers. (p. 468)

domesticate *v.* to raise and tend (a plant or an animal) to be of use to humans. (p. 59)

drama *n.* a story designed to be performed by actors. (p. 411)

drought (drowt) *n.* a period of little rainfall, in which growing crops becomes difficult. (p. 85)

dynastic cycle *n.* the pattern of the rise and fall of dynasties. (p. 256)

dynasty (DY•nuh•stee) *n.* a line of rulers from the same family. (p. 165)

E

Eastern Orthodox Church *n.* a branch of Christianity that developed in the Byzantine Empire and is not under the authority of the pope. (p. 511)

embalm *v.* to preserve a body after death. (p. 160)

emperor *n.* the ruler of an empire. (p. 113)

empire *n.* a group of territories and peoples brought together under one supreme ruler. (p. 113)

epic poem *n.* a long poem that tells a story of heroes. (pp. 364, 516)

Epistle *n.* one of the letters included in the New Testament, written by Jesus' apostles to early Christian churches to instruct them in Christian beliefs and practices. (p. 480)

exile *n.* forced removal from one's homeland. (p. 120)

Exodus (EHK•suh•duhs) *n.* the migration of the Israelites from Egypt, as told in the Torah. (p. 327)

Ezana (AY•zah•nah) *n.* a strong king of Aksum who came to power in A.D. 325, greatly expanded the kingdom, and made Christianity the official religion. (p. 198)

F

fable *n.* a short story that conveys a moral lesson, often by means of animal characters that possess human characteristics. (p. 364)

fertile *adj.* favorable for the growth of crops and other plants. (p. 147)

Fertile Crescent *n.* an area of rich soil in the Middle East, stretching from the Mediterranean Sea through Mesopotamia to the Persian Gulf. (p. 114)

filial piety *n.* respect for one's parents and ancestors—an important teaching of Confucianism. (p. 261)

floodplain *n.* flat land bordering a river. (p. 84)

fossil *n.* a remain of early life that has been preserved in the ground. (p. 28)

G

Gandhi (GAHN•dee), **Mohandas** (MOH•huhn•DAHS) *n.* a leader who used nonviolence to oppose the British rule of India. (p. 242)

Gentile (JEHN•TYL) *n.* a person who is not Jewish. (p. 478)

geography *n.* the study of Earth and its people. (p. 9)

gladiator (GLAD•ee•AY•tuhr) *n.* in ancient Rome, a trained warrior who engaged in combat to the death to entertain the public. (p. 458)

glyph (glihf) *n.* a symbol, usually carved or engraved, that represents a syllable or a whole word. (p. 310)

Gospel *n.* one of the first four books of the New Testament, describing the life and teachings of Jesus. (p. 468)

government *n.* a system for creating order and providing leadership. (p. 67)

griot (gree•OH) *n.* an official storyteller in an ancient African civilization. (p. 205)

H

Hammurabi (HAM•uh•RAH•bee) *n.* the ruler of the Babylonian Empire from 1792 to 1750 B.C., who expanded the empire. (p. 114)

Han Dynasty *n.* a Chinese dynasty begun in 202 B.C. by Liu Bang, which reunified China. (p. 269)

Hanging Gardens of Babylon *n.* an artificial mountain covered with trees and plants, built by Nebuchadnezzar II for his wife. The gardens are one of the Seven Wonders of the World. (p. 122)

Harappan (huh•RAP•uhn) **civilization** *n.* an ancient Indian culture, dating back to 2500 B.C., that included the people of the entire Indus River region. (p. 221)

Hatshepsut (hat•SHEHP•SOOT) *n.* a female pharaoh of ancient Egypt, who initially ruled with her stepson but declared herself the only ruler in 1472 B.C. (p. 173)

Hellenistic *adj.* relating to the blend of Greek, Persian, Egyptian, and Indian cultures that lasted from the death of Alexander the Great in 323 B.C. until Augustus became emperor in 27 B.C. (p. 408)

helot *n.* an agricultural slave in ancient Sparta. (p. 379)

hemisphere *n.* a half of Earth's surface. (p. 18)

hieroglyph (HY•uhr•uh•GLIHF) *n.* a picture standing for a word or sound. (p. 158)

Himalayas (HIHM•uh•LAY•uhs) *n.* a high mountain range that extends through northern India, southern Tibet, Nepal, and Bhutan. (p. 220)

Hindu-Arabic numerals *n.* the numerals used in the United States and western Europe, which originated in India. (p. 242)

Hinduism *n.* a religion and philosophy developed in ancient India, characterized by a belief in reincarnation and a supreme being who takes many forms. (p. 229)

Hindu Kush (HIHN•doo KUSH) *n.* a mountain range along the northwestern border of India. (p. 220)

hominid (HAHM•uh•nihd) *n.* a human or humanlike creature that walks on two feet. (p. 29)

Horn of Africa *n.* the easternmost projection of the African continent—the region occupied by the present-day countries of Somalia and Ethiopia. (p. 197)

hunter-gatherer *n.* a human being who hunts animals and gathers plants for food, moving to a different location whenever such food becomes scarce. (p. 51)

I

ideal *n.* a thing in its most perfect form. (p. 412)

irrigation *n.* the watering of crops. (p. 61)

isthmus (IHS•muhs) *n.* a narrow strip of land that connects two larger landmasses. (pp. 289, 355)

J

Jesus *n.* a teacher whose life and teachings serve as the basis of the Christian religion. Christians believe Jesus to be the Son of God. (p. 467)

Judaism *n.* the religion of the Hebrews, based on the Hebrew Scriptures and a belief in one God; practiced by Jews today. (p. 326)

justice *n.* fair treatment of people, in keeping with the law. (p. 115)

Justinian *n.* the emperor of the Eastern Roman Empire from A.D. 527 to 565, who ruled with his wife, Theodora, and reconquered lost territories for the empire. (p. 509)

Justinian Code *n.* a revised code of Roman law—including laws dealing with marriage, slavery, property ownership, women's rights, and criminal justice—prepared at the order of the Byzantine emperor Justinian. (p. 510)

K

karma *n.* in Hindu belief, the sum of a person's actions in this life, which determine his or her fate in the next life. (p. 230)

Khufu (KOO•FOO) *n.* the Egyptian pharaoh who, about 2550 B.C., ordered the construction of the largest pyramid ever built. (p. 167)

king *n.* the highest-ranking leader of a group of people. (p. 95)

Kush *n.* an ancient Nubian kingdom that conquered all of upper and lower Egypt in the 700s B.C. (p. 190)

L

landform *n.* a naturally formed feature of Earth's land surface, such as an island, a mountain, or a plateau. (p. 10)

latitude *n.* a measure of distance north or south of the equator. (p. 16)

legalism *n.* the belief that a ruler should use the legal system to force people to obey laws. (p. 259)

legend *n.* a popular story handed down from earlier times, which may be believed to be true but cannot be proved. (p. 431)

linen *n.* a fabric woven from fibers of the flax plant. (p. 149)

longitude *n.* a measure of distance east or west of the prime meridian. (p. 16)

M

maize (mayz) *n.* a type of corn grown by Native American civilizations. (p. 308)

Mandate of Heaven *n.* an ancient Chinese belief that a good ruler had the gods' approval. (p. 256)

Marathon *n.* a plain in ancient Greece, northeast of Athens. (p. 382)

Maya (MAH•yuh) *n.* a civilization of present-day southern Mexico and northern Central America, which reached its height from A.D. 250 to 900. (p. 307)

mercenary *n.* a soldier hired to serve in an army. (p. 496)

Meroë (MEHR•oh•EE) *n.* the capital of the kingdom of Kush from around 590 B.C., located on the Nile and having access to trade routes as well as gold and iron. (p. 192)

Mesoamerica *n.* a region that extends southeastward from central Mexico and includes the countries of Guatemala, El Salvador, and Belize and parts of Honduras and Nicaragua. (p. 292)

Mesolithic (MEHZ•uh•LIHTH•ihk) **Age** *n.* the Middle Stone Age—a period that lasted from about 10,000 to 6000 B.C., during which people began to control fire and develop language. (p. 32)

Mesopotamia (MEHS•uh•puh•TAY•mee•uh) *n.* the area of Southwest Asia between the Tigris and Euphrates rivers—home to many early civilizations. (p. 83)

Messiah (mih•SY•uh) *n.* the savior and king foretold by Jewish prophets. (p. 338)

migration *n.* a movement from one region or country to settle in another. (pp. 52, 206)

missionary *n.* a person who travels to a foreign land to spread his or her religious beliefs. (p. 479)

Moche (MOH•chay) *n.* an ancient culture that inhabited what is now the northern coast of Peru between A.D. 100 and 700. (p. 298)

monotheism (MAHN•uh•thee•IHZ•uhm) *n.* the belief that only one God exists. (p. 326)

monsoon *n.* a seasonal wind that produces a wet or dry period in a region, especially in southern Asia. (p. 220)

mosaic (moh•ZAY•ihk) *n.* a picture created from tiny pieces of colored stone or other material. (p. 515)

Moses *n.* according to the Bible, the prophet who led the Israelites from Egypt and was their lawgiver. (p. 327)

mother culture *n.* a culture that shapes and influences the customs and ideas of later cultures. (p. 303)

mummy *n.* the body of a human or animal that has been preserved and dried out to prevent decay. (p. 160)

myth *n.* a story that explains beliefs, practices, or natural phenomena, often featuring gods and goddesses or other supernatural beings. (p. 362)

N

Nazca (NAHZ•kuh) *n.* an ancient culture that arose near what is now the southern coast of Peru and prospered from 200 B.C. to A.D. 600. (p. 296)

Neolithic (NEE•uh•LIHTH•ihk) **Age** *n.* the New Stone Age—a period that lasted from about 8000 to 3000 B.C. and was marked by the beginning of farming and the development of pottery and weaving. (p. 32)

nirvana (neer•VAH•nuh) *n.* in Buddhism and Hinduism, a state of wisdom which breaks the cycle of reincarnation. (p. 234)

Nok *n.* an ancient African civilization in what is now southeastern Nigeria, noted for its manufacture of iron tools. (p. 205)

nomad *n.* a member of a group of people who have no set home but move from place to place. (pp. 52, 502)

Nubia (NOO•bee•uh) *n.* an ancient region of Africa, which extended from the southern border of Egypt through what is now Sudan. (p. 189)

O

obelisk (AHB•uh•lihsk) *n.* a four-sided shaft with a pyramid-shaped top. (p. 174)

oligarchy (AHL•ih•GAHR•kee) *n.* a government that is controlled by the few, with the basis of power often being wealth. (p. 373)

Olmec (AHL•mehk) *n.* the earliest known Meso-American culture, which flourished from 1200 to 400 B.C. and was centered along the Gulf Coast of what is now southern Mexico. (p. 301)

Olympics *n.* an ancient Greek festival in honor of the god Zeus, which took place every four years and featured competitions in athletics and poetry. (p. 363)

Olympus (uh•LIHM•puhs), **Mount** *n.* the highest mountain in Greece—in Greek mythology, the home of the major gods and goddesses. (p. 361)

oracle bone *n.* an animal bone or turtle shell used by the Shang kings of China to communicate with and influence the gods. (p. 255)

oral history *n.* an unwritten verbal account of an event. (p. 41)

oratory *n.* the art of public speaking. (p. 516)

P

Paleolithic (PAY•lee•uh•LIHTH•ihk) **Age** *n.* the Old Stone Age—a period that lasted from about 2.5 million to 8000 B.C. and was marked by the use of simple stone tools by the earliest humans. (p. 32)

papyrus (puh•PY•ruhs) *n.* a paperlike material made from stems of the papyrus plant and used for writing by the ancient Egyptians. (p. 158)

parable *n.* a simple story that conveys a religious or moral lesson. (p. 468)

Parthenon *n.* a temple of the Greek goddess Athena, built in the fifth century B.C. on the acropolis of Athens. (p. 396)

patrician (puh•TRIHSH•uhn) *n.* one of the wealthy landowners who held the highest positions in government in ancient Rome. (p. 437)

Paul *n.* the most important of the apostles who spread Jesus' teachings. (p. 479)

Pax Romana *n.* a long period of stability and peace in the Roman Empire, beginning in the reign of Augustus, during which the empire grew to its greatest size. (p. 447)

Peloponnesian (PEHL•uh•puh•NEE•zhuhn) **War** *n.* a war between Athens and the Peloponnesian League, led by Sparta, which ended with a Spartan victory in 404 B.C. (p. 400)

Peloponnesus (PEHL•uh•puh•NEE•suhs) *n.* a peninsula forming the southern part of Greece. (p. 355)

peninsula *n.* a body of land that is connected to a larger landmass and surrounded on three sides by water. (pp. 355, 433)

Pericles (PEHR•ih•KLEEZ) *n.* a leader of ancient Athens who set out to strengthen democracy and expand the Athenian empire. (p. 393)

persecute *v.* to oppress or harass. (p. 480)

pharaoh (FAIR•oh) *n.* a king of ancient Egypt. (p. 166)

philosophy *n.* an investigation of basic truths about the universe, based on logical reasoning. (pp. 259, 414)

Phoenician (fih•NIHSH•uhn) *n.* a member of a trading people who lived on the coast of the eastern Mediterranean. (p. 358)

physical map *n.* a map showing landforms and bodies of water. (p. 20)

Piankhi (PYANG•kee) *n.* a king of Kush around 750 B.C., who gained control of almost all of Egypt, becoming pharaoh and uniting the two kingdoms. (p. 190)

pictograph *n.* a picture or drawing that represents a word or an idea in an early system of writing. (pp. 101, 255)

plague (playg) *n.* a disease that spreads very easily and usually causes death, affecting a significant portion of a population. (p. 401)

planned city *n.* a city that is built according to a set design. (p. 221)

plebeian (plih•BEE•uhn) *n.* a member of the common people of ancient Rome, who were allowed to vote but not to hold important government positions. (p. 437)

plunder *v.* to take possessions from by force. (p. 504)

polis (POH•lihs) *n.* a Greek city-state, such as Athens or Sparta. (p. 371)

political map *n.* a map showing features people have created, such as cities, states, provinces, territories, and countries. (p. 19)

polytheism (PAHL•ee•thee•IHZ•uhm) *n.* a belief in many gods or goddesses. (p. 93)

pope *n.* the bishop of Rome and head of the Roman Catholic Church. (p. 485)

primary source *n.* something written or created by a person who witnessed a historical event. (p. 40)

prophet *n.* a spiritual leader who conveys the words and wishes of God or a god. (p. 338)

province *n.* a subdivision of an empire or country. (p. 132)

pyramid (PIHR•uh•mihd) *n.* a structure with four triangular sides that meet at a point. (p. 166)

Q

Qin (chihn) *n.* a state of ancient China. (p. 267)

R

rabbi (RAB•eye) *n.* a religious leader and teacher trained in Jewish law, rituals, and tradition. (p. 346)

Ramses (RAM•SEEZ) **II** *n.* a pharaoh who ruled Egypt for 66 years, greatly expanding the Egyptian empire by conquering surrounding territories. (p. 175)

reincarnation *n.* the rebirth of a soul in another body. (p. 230)

religion *n.* the worship of a god, gods, or spirits. (p. 54)

Remus (REE•muhs) *n.* the twin brother of Romulus. (p. 432)

republic *n.* a form of government in which the people elect leaders and representatives. (p. 432)

resurrection *n.* a return to life after death. (p. 470)

Roman Catholic Church *n.* the branch of Christianity that is under the authority of the pope. (p. 511)

Romulus (RAHM•yuh•luhs) *n.* a legendary hero, descended from Aeneas, who is said to have founded Rome. (p. 431)

Royal Road *n.* a road for government use built by the ancient Persian ruler Darius, which helped unite the empire. (p. 132)

S

satrap (SAY•TRAP) *n.* the governor of a province in the ancient Persian Empire. (p. 132)

scribe *n.* a person who specializes in writing and serves as a record keeper. (pp. 102, 155)

secondary source *n.* an account of a historical event written by someone who did not witness the event. (p. 41)

semiarid (SEHM•ee•AR•ihd) *adj.* having little rainfall and warm temperatures. (p. 84)

senate *n.* a governing body of ancient Rome, made up of 300 members who advised Roman leaders. (p. 438)

Shi Huangdi (shee hwahng•dee) *n.* a Chinese ruler who came to power in 221 B.C. and unified and expanded China by ending internal battles and conquering rival states. (p. 267)

Siddhartha Gautama (sihd•DAHR•tuh GAW•tuh•muh) *n.* an Indian prince who founded Buddhism; also known as the Buddha. (p. 233)

Silk Roads *n.* the overland trade routes along which silk and other Chinese goods passed to Mesopotamia and Europe. (p. 277)

silt *n.* fine, fertile soil deposited by a river. (pp. 84, 147)

slash-and-burn *adj.* relating to a type of agriculture in which patches of land are prepared for planting by cutting down and burning the natural vegetation. (pp. 60, 293)

smelting *n.* the heating and melting of certain rocks to separate the metals they contain. (p. 192)

social class *n.* a group of people with similar customs, backgrounds, training, and income. (p. 67)

Solomon *n.* the third king of Israel, under whom it became a powerful nation. (p. 336)

Sparta *n.* an ancient Greek city-state of the Peloponnesus, noted for its militarism. (p. 379)

specialization *n.* a skill in one type of work. (p. 66)

stele (STEE•lee) *n.* a carved stone slab set upright in the ground, usually commemorating a person or event. (p. 309)

step pyramid *n.* a pyramid whose sides rise in a series of giant steps. (p. 167)

stylus *n.* a sharpened reed used to press markings into clay tablets. (p. 102)

subcontinent *n.* a large landmass that is part of a continent but considered a separate landform. (p. 219)

succession *n.* the order in which members of a royal family inherit a throne or title. (p. 165)

Sumer *n.* an ancient region of southern Mesopotamia, in which civilization arose around 3300 B.C. (p. 89)

surplus *n.* an amount produced in excess of what is needed. (pp. 65, 86)

synagogue (SIHN•uh•gahg) *n.* a building for Jewish prayer and worship and instruction in the Jewish faith. (p. 346)

T

technology *n.* people's application of knowledge, tools, and inventions to meet their needs. (p. 53)

Ten Commandments *n.* the basis of the law of the Israelites, given, according to the Torah, by God to Moses. (p. 327)

terrace *n.* a leveled area on a hillside. (p. 200)

textile *n.* a woven or knitted cloth. (p. 296)

thematic map *n.* a map that presents a particular type of information about a place or region. (p. 21)

toleration *n.* the practice of allowing people to keep their customs and beliefs. (p. 131)

tragedy *n.* a form of serious drama that presents the downfall or ruin of the main character or characters. (p. 412)

trans-Eurasian *adj.* involving the continents of Europe and Asia. (p. 277)

tribute *n.* a payment of money or goods by one ruler to another in order to ensure protection. (p. 120)

Trinity *n.* the union of three persons—Father, Son, and Holy Spirit—in one God. (p. 486)

tropical *adj.* having a warm and rainy climate. (p. 290)

truce *n.* a temporary agreement to stop fighting. (p. 401)

tyrant *n.* a ruler who has taken power illegally and rules without restrictions. (p. 373)

V

vault *n.* an arch that forms a ceiling or roof. (p. 517)

vegetation *n.* the plant life of an area. (p. 12)

Y

Yucatán (yoo•kuh•TAN) **Peninsula** *n.* an area of dense jungle in southeastern Mexico, extending into the Gulf of Mexico and the Caribbean Sea. (p. 292)

Z

Zeus (zoos) *n.* the ruler of the gods in Greek mythology. (p. 361)

ziggurat (ZIHG•uh•RAT) *n.* an ancient Sumerian or Babylonian temple that rose in a series of steplike levels. (p. 92)

Spanish Glossary

A

Abraham *s.* según la Biblia, pastor de la ciudad de Ur en la Mesopotamia, que se convirtió en el patriarca de los hebreos. (pág. 325)

absolute ruler [monarca absoluto] *s.* soberano que tiene poder ilimitado y que gobierna solo. (pág. 497)

acropolis [acrópolis] *s.* cima fortificada de las antiguas ciudades griegas, que contenía templos, monumentos y edificios importantes. (pág. 396)

Adulis *s.* antigua ciudad del Mar Rojo, que servía como el principal puerto mercantil del reino de Aksum. (pág. 198)

Aeneas [Eneas] *s.* héroe de la guerra de Troya. (pág. 431)

afterlife [más allá] s. vida después de la muerte. (pág. 159)

agriculture [agricultura] *s.* cultivo del suelo para producir cosechas útiles. (pág. 60)

ahimsa *s.* no-violencia. (pág. 233)

Aksum *s.* antiguo reino africano del Mar Rojo, en lo que hoy es Etiopía y Eritrea. Reemplazó al reino de Kush. (pág. 197)

Alexander the Great [Alejandro Magno] *s.* rey de Macedonia desde 336 hasta 323 a.C. que conquistó partes de Asia y Egipto y así propagó la cultura griega por todo su imperio. (pág. 407)

Alexandria [Alejandría] *s.* ciudad helenística de Egipto, en el Mediterráneo. Fue fundada por Alejandro Magno en el año 332 a.C. y se caracterizó por su extensa biblioteca antigua además de su faro, una de las siete maravillas del mundo. (pág. 408)

alphabet [alfabeto] *s.* conjunto de letras utilizadas para representar los sonidos individuales de un idioma. (pág. 358)

Anatolia *s.* península entre el Mediterráneo y el mar Negro actualmente ocupada por casi la totalidad de Turquía. También llamada Asia Menor. (pág. 131)

animism [animismo] *s.* creencia de que los animales, plantas, otros objetos naturales y fuerzas naturales tienen espíritu. (pág. 205)

aqueduct [acueducto] *s.* tubería o canal que transporta agua de una fuente distante a una zona poblada. (págs. 457, 517)

aquifer [acuífero] *s.* capa subterránea de arena, grava o rocas esponjosas que contiene agua. (pág. 297)

aristocracy [aristocracia] *s.* clase alta o nobleza. (pág. 373)

artifact [artefacto] *s.* objeto fabricado por el hombre. (pág. 28)

artisan [artesano] *s.* trabajador especializado en un determinado arte u oficio. (pág. 67)

Aryan [ario] *s.* miembro de un pueblo indoeuropeo que emigró a la India hacia 1500 a.C. (pág. 228)

Asoka *s.* el rey más importante de la dinastía mauria, cuyo reinado comenzó en el año 269 a.C. (pág. 236)

Athens [Atenas] *s.* ciudad estado de la antigua Grecia, que alcanzó su máximo esplendor cultural en el siglo V a.C. Es la capital y ciudad más grande de la Grecia moderna. (pág. 379)

Augustus [Augusto] *s.* primer emperador romano (originalmente llamado Octavio), que se convirtió en emperador en el año 27 a.C. (pág. 446)

B

Babylonian Captivity [cautividad babilónica] *s.* período de 50 años durante el cual los israelitas fueron retenidos en Babilonia, lejos de su patria de Judea. Fue durante ese período que los israelitas comenzaron a ser llamados judíos. (pág. 338)

Bantu [Bantúes] *s.* pueblo de África occidental que gradualmente emigró hacia el oriente y hacia el sur, llevando la agricultura y ganadería hacia nuevas regiones. (pág. 206)

Barbarian [bárbaro] *s.* persona perteneciente a un grupo considerado primitivo e incivilizado, especialmente una persona externa al antiguo imperio romano. (pág. 502)

barracks [barraca] *s.* grupo de edificios utilizados para albergar soldados. (pág. 380)

bas-relief [bajorrelieve] *s.* tipo de escultura en la cual las figuras resaltan un poco de un fondo plano. (pág. 516)

bishop [obispo] *s.* autoridad eclesiástica cristiana que supervisa varias iglesias. (pág. 485)

Brahmanism [brahmanismo] *s.* antigua religión de los arios en la antigua India. (pág. 229)

bronze [bronce] *s.* metal resultante de la mezcla de cobre y estaño. (pág. 101)

Buddhism [budismo] *s.* religión que comenzó en la India y se basa en las enseñanzas de Siddhartha Gautama. (pág. 233)

bureaucracy [burocracia] *s.* sistema en el cual el gobierno se divide en departamentos organizados administrados por funcionarios designados. (pág. 269)

Byzantine Empire [imperio bizantino] *s.* Imperio Romano de Oriente, con capital en Constantinopla, que duró aproximadamente cien años hasta la caída del Imperio Romano de Occidente. (pág. 509)

C

Caesar, Julius [César, Julio] *s.* general y político romano (100–44 a.C.) que obtuvo un gran apoyo de los plebeyos de Roma y recibió el derecho de gobernar de por vida en el año 44 a.C. Fue asesinado ese mismo año.. (pág. 444)

caste [casta] *s.* clase social a la cual una persona pertenece desde el nacimiento. (pág. 228)

catapult [catapulta] *s.* antigua máquina militar para arrojar piedras u otros objetos a tropas y fortalezas enemigas. (pág. 405)

cataract [catarata] *s.* cascada grande. (pág. 147)

catholic [católico] *adj.* universal. (pág. 485)

Chavín *s.* cultura que floreció entre los años 900 y 200 a.C. en los Andes peruanos. (pág. 295)

Cicero [Cicerón] *s.* cónsul y famoso orador romano que se opuso a Julio César. (pág. 445)

Cincinnatus [Cincinato] *s.* dictador de Roma por un día en el año 458 a.C. (pág. 438)

citizen [ciudadano] *s.* persona leal a un determinado gobierno y que tiene el derecho de recibir protección por parte de ese gobierno. (pág. 374)

city-state [ciudad estado] *s.* unidad política que comprende una ciudad y sus territorios aledaños. (pág. 91)

civilization [civilización] *s.* sociedad humana con un nivel avanzado de desarrollo en la organización social y política, así como en las artes y ciencias. (pág. 89)

civil war [guerra civil] *s.* conflicto armado entre grupos dentro de un mismo país. (pág. 444)

climate [clima] *s.* conjunto de condiciones atmosféricas en un determinado lugar durante un largo período de tiempo. (pág. 12)

code of law [código de leyes] *s.* conjunto de reglas escritas que los habitantes deben obedecer.(pág. 115)

codex [códice] *s.* libro que utilizaban las primitivas civilizaciones mesoamericanas para registrar acontecimientos históricos importantes. (pág. 310)

Colosseum [Coliseo] *s.* extensa arena de Roma, donde los antiguos romanos presenciaban espectáculos tales como batallas de gladiadores. (pág. 458)

comedy [comedia] *s.* tipo de teatro generalmente con final feliz y que a menudo se burla de la política, las personas y las ideas de la época. (pág. 412)

Confucianism [confucionismo] *s.* filosofía basada en las enseñanzas de Confucio (551–479 a.C.), según se registra en la colección llamada Analects. (pág. 260)

consul [cónsul] *s.* uno de los dos funcionarios electos a cargo del poder ejecutivo de la antigua Roma, que además comandaban el ejército. (pág. 438)

continent [continente] *s.* una de las siete grandes extensiones de tierra del planeta: América del Norte, América del Sur, Europa, Asia, África, Australia y la Antártida. (pág. 9)

convert [convertir] *s.* convencer a alguien de cambiar su religión y sus creencias. (pág. 477)

creed [credo] *s.* declaración de creencias religiosas. (pág. 486)

Crucifixión [crucifixión] *s.* ejecución que consiste en colgar en una cruz. (pág. 470)

cultural diffusion [difusión cultural] *s.* propagación de ideas y costumbres étnicas hacia otras áreas del mundo. (pág. 277)

cuneiform [cuneiforme] *s.* antiguo sistema de escritura desarrollado por los sumerios que consiste en signos con forma de cuña. (pág. 102)

D

Daoism [taoísmo] *s.* sistema de creencias supuestamente iniciado en el siglo VI a.C. por el filósofo Laozi. El taoísmo enfatiza la vida en armonía con la naturaleza. (pág. 262)

David *s.* rey de los israelitas que ganó el control de Jerusalén en el año 1000 a.C. (pág. 336)

Delian League [Liga de Delos] *s.* alianza de ciudades griegas formada al final de la guerra Persa para proteger a Atenas y a sus aliados extranjeros. (pág. 395)

delta *s.* zona cercana a la boca de un río donde el río deposita grandes cantidades de arena y limo. (pág. 147)

democracy [democracia] *s.* gobierno en el cual los ciudadanos toman las decisiones políticas, ya sea en forma directa o mediante representantes elegidos por el pueblo. (pág. 375)

dharma [darma] *s.* enseñanzas del Buda. (pág. 235)

Diaspora [Diáspora] *s.* dispersión del pueblo judío después de ser expulsado de Judea por los romanos en el año70 d.C. (pág. 345)

Diocletian [Diocleciano] *s.* líder romano que se convirtió en emperador en el año 284 d.C. y que introdujo reformas en la administración, el ejército y la economía de Roma. (pág. 497)

direct democracy [democracia directa] *s.* forma de democracia en la cual los ciudadanos gobiernan directamente. (pág. 394)

disciple [discípulo] *s.* uno de los 12 seguidores más cercanos a Jesús. (pág. 468)

domesticate [domesticar] *v.* criar y ocuparse (de una planta o un animal) para que sirva al hombre. (pág. 59)

drama [pieza de teatro] *s.* historia creada para ser representada por actores. (pág. 411)

drought [sequía] *s.* período con poca lluvia, en el cual se hace difícil el cultivo. (pág. 85)

dynastic cycle [ciclo dinástico] *s.* patrón del surgimiento y la caída de las dinastías. (pág. 256)

dynasty [dinastía] *s.* serie de gobernantes de una misma familia. (pág. 165)

E

Eastern Orthodox Church [Iglesia Ortodoxa Oriental] *s.* rama del cristianismo que se desarrolló en el imperio bizantino y no se encuentra bajo la autoridad del papa. (pág. 511)

embalm [embalsamar] *v.* conservar un cuerpo después de la muerte. (pág. 160)

emperor [emperador] *s.* soberano de un imperio. (pág. 113)

empire [imperio] *s.* grupo de territorios y habitantes gobernados por un soberano supremo. (pág. 113)

epic poem [poema épico] *s.* extenso poema que relata una historia de héroes. (págs. 364, 516)

Epistle [Epístola] *s.* una de las cartas incluidas en el Nuevo Testamento, escrita por los apóstoles de Jesús a las primeras iglesias cristianas para transmitirles las creencias y prácticas cristianas. (pág. 480)

exile [exilio] *s.* expulsión forzada de la patria. (pág. 120)

Exodus [Éxodo] *s.* emigración de los israelitas de Egipto, según se relata en el Torah. (pág. 327)

Ezana *s.* poderoso rey de Aksum, que asumió el poder en el año 325 d.C., expandió enormemente el reino y estableció el cristianismo como religión oficial. (pág. 198)

F

fable [fábula] *s.* narración corta que transmite una enseñanza moral, a menudo mediante personajes animales que poseen características humanas. (pág. 364)

fertile [fértil] *adj.* favorable para plantar cultivos y otras plantas. (pág. 147)

Fertile Crescent [Medialuna Fértil] *s.* zona de suelos ricos en el Medio Oriente, que se extiende desde el mar Mediterráneo a través de la Mesopotamia hasta el golfo Pérsico. (pág. 114)

filial piety [amor filial] *s.* respeto de los hijos hacia sus padres y ancestros, enseñanza importante del confucionismo. (pág. 261)

floodplain [llanura de inundación] *s.* superficie de tierra baja adyacente a un río. (pág. 84)

fossil [fósil] *s.* restos de un ser vivo antiguo que se ha preservado en la tierra. (pág. 28)

G

Gandhi, Mohandas [Gandhi, Mahatma] *s.* líder que utilizó la no-violencia para oponerse al gobierno británico en la India. (pág. 242)

Gentile [gentil] *s.* no-judío. (pág. 478)

geography [geografía] *s.* estudio de la Tierra y de sus habitantes. (pág. 9)

gladiator [gladiador] *s.* en la antigua Roma, guerrero entrenado que combatía hasta la muerte para divertir al público. (pág. 458)

glyph [glifo] *s.* símbolo, generalmente esculpido o grabado, que representa una silaba o una palabra entera. (pág. 310)

Gospel [Evangelio] *s.* uno de los cuatro primeros libros del Nuevo Testamento, que describe la vida y enseñanzas de Jesús. (pág. 468)

government [gobierno] *s.* sistema que sirve para crear orden y proporcionar liderazgo. (pág. 67)

griot *s.* narrador oficial en la civilización africana antigua. (pág. 205)

H

Hammurabi *s.* rey del imperio babilónico desde 1792 hasta 1750 a.C., que contribuyó a la expansión de su imperio. (pág. 114)

Han Dynasty [Dinastía Han] *s.* dinastía china comenzada en el año 202 a.C. por Liu Bang, que reunificó la China. (pág. 269)

Hanging Gardens of Babylon [Jardines colgantes de Babilonia] *s.* montaña artificial cubierta por árboles y plantas, construida por Nabucodonosor II para su esposa. Es una de las siete maravillas del mundo. (pág. 122)

Harappan civilization [civilización harappa] *s.* antigua cultura india, que se remonta al año 2500 a.C., y que comprende los pueblos de toda la región del río Indo. (pág. 221)

Hatshepsut *s.* mujer faraón del antiguo Egipto, que al principio reinó junto con su hijastro pero que luego se declaró reina única en el año 1472 a.C. (pág. 173)

Hellenistic [helénico] *adj.* relativo a la mezcla de las culturas griega, persa, egipcia e india que duró desde la muerte de Alejandro Magno en el año 323 a.C. hasta que Augusto se transformó en emperador de Roma, en el año 27 a.C. (pág. 408)

helot [ilota] *s.* esclavo campesino en la antigua Esparta. (pág. 379)

hemisphere [hemisferio] *s.* mitad de la superficie de la Tierra. (pág. 18)

hieroglyph [jeroglífico] *s.* dibujo que representa una palabra o sonido. (pág. 158)

Himalayas [Himalaya] *s.* alta cadena montañosa que se extiende a través del norte de la India, el sur del Tíbet, Nepal y Bhután. (pág. 220)

Hindu-Arabic numerals [números indo-arábigos] *s.* números utilizados en los Estados Unidos y Europa occidental, que tuvieron origen en la India. (pág. 242)

Hinduism [hinduismo] *s.* religión y filosofía desarrollada en la antigua India, caracterizada por una creencia en la reencarnación y en un ser superior que puede tomar distintas formas. (pág. 229)

Hindu Kush *s.* cadena de montañas que se extiende por el límite norte-occidental de la India. (pág. 220)

hominid [homínido] *s.* criatura humana o especie parecida que camina en dos patas. (pág. 29)

Horn of Africa [Cuerno de África] *s.* proyección del extremo oriental del continente africano: región que hoy ocupan los países de Somalia y Etiopía. (pág. 197)

hunter-gatherer [cazador-recolector] *s.* ser humano que caza animales y recolecta platas como alimento, y que cambia de lugar cada vez que su comida escasea. (pág. 51)

I

ideal s. que se encuentra en su forma más perfecta. (pág. 412)

irrigation [irrigación] *s.* riego de los cultivos. (pág. 61)

isthmus [istmo] *s.* angosta lengua de tierra que conecta dos extensiones más grandes de tierra. (págs. 289, 355)

J

Jesus [Jesús] *s.* maestro cuya vida y enseñanzas sirvieron como base de la religión cristiana. Los cristianos creen que Jesús es el hijo de Dios. (pág. 467)

Judaism [judaísmo] s. religión de los hebreos, basada en las escrituras hebreas y en la creencia de un solo Dios, practicada por los judíos hoy en día. (pág. 326)

justice [justicia] *s.* tratamiento equitativo de las personas, en cumplimiento de la ley. (pág. 115)

Justinian [Justiniano] *s.* emperador del Imperio Romano de Oriente de 527 a 565 d.C., quien reinó con su esposa, Teodora, y reconquistó territorios perdidos para el imperio. (pág. 509)

Justinian Code [Código Justiniano] s. código revisado de leyes romanas (incluyendo leyes relativas al matrimonio, esclavitud, posesión de propiedad, derechos de la mujer y justicia criminal) preparado por orden del emperador bizantino Justiniano. (pág. 510)

K

karma *s.* en la creencia hindú, la suma de las acciones de una persona en esta vida, que determina su destino en su próxima vida. (pág. 230)

Khufu *s.* faraón egipcio que, alrededor del año 2550 a.C., ordenó la construcción de la pirámide más grande jamás construida. (pág. 167)

king [rey] *s.* líder de mayor rango de un grupo de personas. (pág. 95)

Kush *s.* antiguo reino nubio que conquistó la totalidad del Alto y el Bajo Egipto en el siglo VIII a.C. (pág. 190)

L

landform [accidente geográfico] *s.* característica natural de la superficie de la tierra, como una isla, montaña o meseta. (pág. 10)

latitude [latitud] *s.* distancia norte-sur con respecto al ecuador. (pág. 16)

legalism [legalismo] *s.* creencia de que un soberano debe utilizar el sistema legal para obligar a las personas a obedecer las leyes. (pág. 259)

legend [leyenda] *s.* narración popular transmitida desde épocas remotas, que puede creerse verdadera pero no puede ser probada. (pág. 431)

linen [lino] *s.* tela tejida con fibras provenientes de la planta de lino. (pág. 149)

longitude [longitud] *s.* distancia este-oeste a partir del primer meridiano. (pág. 16)

M

maize [maíz] *s.* cereal cultivado por las civilizaciones nativas americanas, cuyos granos se encuentran en mazorcas. (pág. 308)

Mandate of Heaven [Mandato del Cielo] *s.* antigua creencia china que postulaba que la autoridad real era producto de la aprobación divina. (pág. 256)

Marathon [Maratón] *s.* llanura en la antigua Grecia, al noreste de Atenas. (pág. 382)

Maya [mayas] *s.* civilización del sur de México y norte de América Central, que alcanzó su máximo esplendor desde el año 250 hasta el año 900 d.C. (pág. 307)

mercenary [mercenario] *s.* soldado contratado para prestar servicio en un ejército. (pág. 496)

Meroë *s.* capital del reino de Kush desde aproximadamente 590 a.C., ubicada en el Nilo y con acceso a las rutas comerciales así como al oro y al hierro. (pág. 192)

Mesoamerica [Mesoamérica] s. región que se extiende hacia el sudeste desde México central y comprende países como Guatemala, El Salvador, Belice y parte de Honduras y Nicaragua. (pág. 292)

Mesolithic Age [Mesolítico] *s.* Edad de Piedra Media: período que duró desde alrededor del año 10.000 hasta el año 6000 a.C., durante el cual el ser humano comenzó a controlar el fuego y a desarrollar el lenguaje. (pág. 32)

Mesopotamia *s.* área del suroeste asiático entre los ríos Tigris y Éufrates, cuna de muchas civilizaciones antiguas. (pág. 83)

Messiah [Mesías] *s.* salvador y rey que predicen los profetas judíos. (pág. 338)

migration [migración] *s.* acción de mudarse de una región o país a otro. (págs. 52, 206)

missionary [misionero] *s.* persona que viaja a otros países para diseminar sus creencias religiosas. (pág. 479)

Moche *s.* antigua cultura que habitó en lo que hoy es la costa norte del Perú entre los años 100 y 700 d.C. (pág. 298)

Monotheism [monoteísmo] s. creencia en la existencia de un solo Dios. (pág. 326)

monsoon [monzón] *s.* viento de estación que produce un período húmedo o seco en una región, especialmente en el sur asiático. (pág. 220)

mosaic [mosaico] *s.* pintura creada a partir de pequeños trozos coloreados de piedra u otro material. (pág. 515)

Moses [Moisés] *s.* según la Biblia, profeta que condujo a los israelitas fuera de Egipto y les entregó las Tablas de la Ley. (pág. 327)

mother culture [cultura madre] *s.* cultura que modela e influye las costumbres e ideas de culturas más recientes. (pág. 303)

mummy [momia] *s.* cuerpo de un humano o animal que ha sido conservado y disecado para evitar que se descomponga. (pág. 160)

myth [mito] *s.* relato que explica creencias, prácticas o fenómenos naturales, con frecuencia protagonizado por dioses y diosas u otros seres sobrenaturales. (pág. 362)

N

Nazca *s.* antigua cultura que surgió cerca de lo que hoy es la costa sur de Perú y prosperó desde el año 200 a.C. hasta el año 600 d.C. (pág. 296)

Neolithic Age [Neolítico] *s.* Nueva Edad de Piedra: Período que duró desde alrededor del año 8000 hasta el año 3000 a.C. y se caracterizó por el comienzo de la agricultura y el desarrollo de la alfarería y el tejido. (pág. 32)

nirvana *s.* en el budismo y el hinduismo, estado de sabiduría que rompe el ciclo de la reencarnación. (pág. 234)

Nok *s.* antigua civilización africana en lo que hoy es el sudeste de Nigeria, caracterizada por la fabricación de herramientas de hierro. (pág. 205)

nomad [nómada] *s.* miembro de un grupo de personas que no tienen hogar fijo y se mudan de un lugar a otro. (págs. 52, 502)

Nubia *s.* antigua región de África, que se extiende desde la frontera sur de Egipto hasta lo que hoy es Sudán. (pág. 189)

O

obelisk [obelisco] *s.* monumento en forma de pilar de cuatro caras que termina en una punta con forma de pirámide. (pág. 174)

oligarchy [oligarquía] *s.* gobierno controlado por una minoría, para el cual la base del poder es a menudo la riqueza. (pág. 373)

Olmec [olmeca] *s.* la cultura mesoamericana más antigua que se conoce, que floreció entre el año 1200 y el año 400 a.C. y se centró en la costa sur del golfo de México. (pág. 301)

Olympics [Olimpíada] *s.* festival de la antigua Grecia en honor del dios Zeus, que se llevaba a cabo cada cuatro años y presentaba competencias atléticas y poéticas. (pág. 363)

Olympus, Mount [Olimpo, Monte] *s.* montaña más alta de Grecia; en la mitología griega, hogar de los dioses y diosas más importantes. (pág. 361)

oracle bone [hueso de oráculo] *s.* hueso de animal o caparazón de tortuga que utilizaban los reyes Shang de China para comunicarse con los dioses e influenciarlos. (pág. 255)

oral history [historia oral] *s.* narración verbal no escrita de un acontecimiento. (pág. 41)

oratory [oratoria] *s.* arte de hablar en público. (pág. 516)

P

Paleolithic Age [Paleolítico] *s.* Antigua Edad de Piedra: período que duró desde el año 2,5 millones hasta el año 8000 a.C. y se caracterizó por el uso de herramientas simples de piedra por parte de los primeros seres humanos. (pág. 32)

papyrus [papiro] *s.* material parecido al papel realizado con hojas de la planta de papiro y que los antiguos egipcios utilizaban para escribir. (pág. 158)

parable [parábola] *s.* narración simple que transmite una enseñanza religiosa o moral. (pág. 468)

Parthenon [Partenón] *s.* templo de la diosa griega Atenea, construido en el siglo V a.C. en la acrópolis de Atenas. (pág. 396)

patrician [patricio] *s.* miembro de una familia adinerada y hacendada que ocupaba los puestos más importantes del gobierno en la antigua Roma. (pág. 437)

Paul [Pablo] *s.* el más importante de los apóstoles que divulgaba las enseñanzas de Jesús. (pág. 479)

Pax Romana *s.* largo período de estabilidad y paz en el Imperio Romano que comenzó con el reinado e Augusto y durante el cual el imperio creció hasta alcanzar su máxima dimensión. (pág. 447)

Peloponnesian War [guerra del Peloponeso] *s.* guerra entre Atenas y la Liga del Peloponeso, liderada por Esparta, que terminó con la victoria de Esparta en el año 404 a.C. (pág. 400)

Peloponnesus [Peloponeso] *s.* península que forma la parte sur de Grecia. (pág. 355)

peninsula [península] *s.* masa de tierra conectada a otra tierra de mayor extensión y rodeada de agua en tres de sus lados. (págs. 355, 433)

Pericles *s.* líder de la antigua Atenas que se propuso reforzar la democracia y expandir el imperio ateniense. (pág. 393)

persecute [perseguir] *v.* oprimir u hostigar. (pág. 480)

pharaoh [faraón] *s.* antiguo rey egipcio. (pág. 166)

philosophy [filosofía] *s.* investigación de las verdades básicas del universo, basada en razonamiento lógico. (págs. 259, 414)

Phoenician [fenicio] *s.* miembro de un pueblo comerciante que vivió en las costas orientales del Mediterráneo. (pág. 358)

physical map [mapa físico] *s.* mapa que muestra relieves y masas de agua. (pág. 20)

Piankhi *s.* rey de Kush alrededor del año 750 a.C., que ganó control de casi todo Egipto, se convirtió en faraón y unificó los dos reinos. (pág. 190)

pictograph [pictografía] *s.* fotografía o dibujo que representa una palabra o una idea en un antiguo sistema de escritura. (págs. 101, 255)

plague [plaga] *s.* enfermedad a menudo mortal que se expande fácilmente y que afecta a una gran parte de la población. (pág. 401)

planned city [ciudad planificada] *s.* ciudad construida según un diseño establecido. (pág. 221)

plebeian [plebeyo] *s.* ciudadano corriente en la antigua Roma, que tenía derecho de voto pero no a ocupar puestos importantes de gobierno. (pág. 437)

plunder [saquear] *v.* tomar posesión de algo por la fuerza. (pág. 504)

polis *s.* ciudad central de una ciudad estado en la antigua Grecia, como por ejemplo Atenas o Esparta. (pág. 371)

political map [mapa político] *s.* mapa que muestra características creadas por el hombre, como ciudades, estados, provincias, territorios y países. (pág. 19)

polytheism [politeísmo] *s.* creencia en muchos dioses o diosas. (pág. 93)

pope [papa] *s.* obispo de Roma y jefe de la Iglesia Católica Romana. (pág. 485)

primary source [fuente primaria] *s.* relato de un acontecimiento histórico narrado por una persona que lo presenció. (pág. 40)

prophet [profeta] *s.* guía espiritual que transmite las palabras y deseos de Dios o de un dios. (pág. 338)

province [provincia] *s.* subdivisión de un imperio o país. (pág. 132)

pyramid [pirámide] *s.* estructura con cuatro lados triangulares que convergen en un punto. (pág. 166)

Q

Qin *s.* estado de la antigua China. (pág. 267)

R

rabbi [rabino] *s.* líder y maestro religioso formado en las leyes, los rituales y las tradiciones judías. (pág. 346)

Ramses II [Ramsés II] *s.* faraón que gobernó Egipto durante 66 años, y que expandió enormemente el imperio egipcio al conquistar territorios vecinos. (pág. 175)

reincarnation [reencarnación] *s.* renacimiento de un alma en otro cuerpo. (pág. 230)

religion [religión] *s.* veneración de un dios, dioses o espíritus. (pág. 54)

Remus [Remo] *s.* hermano gemelo de Rómulo. (pág. 432)

republic [república] *s.* forma de gobierno en la cual los ciudadanos eligen a sus líderes y representantes. (pág. 432)

resurrection [resurrección] *s.* vuelta a la vida después de la muerte. (pág. 470)

Roman Catholic Church [Iglesia Católica Romana] *s.* rama del cristianismo que se encuentra bajo la autoridad del papa. (pág. 511)

Romulus [Rómulo] *s.* héroe legendario, descendiente de Eneas, que fue fundador de Roma. (pág. 431)

Royal Road [Camino Real] *s.* camino para el uso del gobierno construido por el antiguo monarca persa Darío, que ayudó a unificar el imperio. (pág. 132)

S

satrap [sátrapa] *s.* gobernador de una provincia en el antiguo imperio persa. (pág. 132)

scribe [escriba] *s.* persona especializada en escribir y archivar documentos. (págs. 102, 155)

secondary source [fuente secundaria] *s.* relato de un acontecimiento histórico realizado por una persona que no presenció los hechos. (pág. 41)

semiarid [semiárido] *adj.* con poca lluvia y altas temperaturas. (pág. 84)

senate [senado] *s.* cuerpo gubernamental de la antigua Roma, formado por 300 miembros que asesoraban a los líderes romanos. (pág. 438)

Shi Huangdi *s.* soberano chino que asumió el poder en el año 221 a.C. y unificó y expandió la China al acabar con batallas internas y conquistar estados rivales. (pág. 267)

Siddhartha Gautama *s.* príncipe indio fundador del Budismo, también conocido como Buda. (pág. 233)

Silk Roads [Ruta de la seda] *s.* rutas comerciales terrestres por las cuales la seda y otras mercancías chinas pasaban hacia la Mesopotamia y Europa. (pág. 277)

silt [limo] *s.* tierra fina y fértil depositada por un río. (págs. 84, 147)

slash-and-burn [tala y quema] *adj.* tipo de agricultura que consiste en talar y quemar la vegetación natural para obtener parcelas de tierra para el cultivo. (págs. 60, 293)

smelting [fundición] *s.* calentamiento y fundición de ciertas rocas para separar los metales que contienen. (pág. 192)

social class [clase social] *s.* grupo de personas que comparten las mismas costumbres, orígenes, formación y nivel de ingresos. (pág. 67)

Solomon [Salomón] *s.* tercer rey de Israel que transformó su estado en una nación poderosa. (pág. 336)

Sparta [Esparta] s. ciudad estado de la antigua Grecia en el Peloponeso, caracterizada por su militarismo. (pág. 379)

specialization [especialización] *s.* habilidad para un tipo de trabajo. (pág. 66)

stele [estela] *s.* losa esculpida de piedra clavada en el suelo, generalmente en conmemoración de una persona o acontecimiento. (pág. 309)

step pyramid [pirámide escalonada] s. pirámide cuyos lados se elevan en una serie de escalones gigantes. (pág. 167)

stylus [estilo] *s.* punzón afilado utilizado para hacer marcas en lápidas de barro. (pág. 102)

subcontinent [subcontinente] *s.* gran extensión de tierra que forma parte de un continente pero se considera como un accidente geográfico separado. (pág. 219)

succession [sucesión] *s.* orden en el cual los miembros de una familia real heredan un trono o título. (pág. 165)

Sumer [Sumeria] *s.* antigua región del sur de la Mesopotamia, donde surgieron civilizaciones alrededor del año 3300 a.C. (pág. 89)

surplus [excedente] *s.* cantidad producida en exceso de lo que se necesita. (págs. 65, 86)

synagogue [sinagoga] *s.* edificio de culto y oración de los judíos, donde se enseña la fe judía. (pág. 346)

T

technology [tecnología] *s.* aplicación del conocimiento, herramientas e invenciones del ser humano para satisfacer sus necesidades. (pág. 53)

Ten Commandments [Diez Mandamientos] *s.* base de la ley de los israelitas que, según el Torah, Dios entregó a Moisés. (pág. 327)

terrace [terraza] *s.* zona elevada en la ladera de una colina. (pág. 200)

textile [textil] *s.* tela tramada o tejida. (pág. 296)

thematic map [mapa temático] *s.* mapa que representa un tipo específico de información sobre un lugar o región. (pág. 21)

toleration [tolerancia] *s.* práctica de dejar que los demás vivan según sus costumbres y creencias. (pág. 131)

tragedy [tragedia] *s.* forma de teatro serio que representa la caída o la ruina del personaje o personajes principales. (pág. 412)

trans-Eurasian [trans-euroasiático] *adj.* relativo a los continentes de Europa y Asia. (pág. 277)

tribute [tributo] *s.* pago de dinero o mercancías por parte de un monarca a otro a cambio de protección. (pág. 120)

Trinity [Trinidad] *s.* unión de tres personas (el Padre, el Hijo y el Espíritu Santo) en un solo Dios. (pág. 486)

tropical *adj.* con clima cálido y lluvioso. (pág. 290)

truce [tregua] *s.* acuerdo temporal de detener una pelea. (pág. 401)

tyrant [tirano] *s.* soberano que ha tomado el poder en forma ilegal y que gobierna sin restricciones. (pág. 373)

V

vault [bóveda] *s.* arco que forma un cielorraso o techo. (pág. 517)

vegetation [vegetación] *s.* vida vegetal de un área. (pág. 12)

Y

Yucatán Peninsula [península de Yucatán] *s.* zona de selva densa en el sudeste mexicano, que se extiende hacia el golfo de México y el mar Caribe. (pág. 292)

Z

Zeus *s.* dios supremo en la mitología griega. (pág. 361)

ziggurat [zigurat] *s.* antiguo templo sumerio o babilónico construido en una serie de niveles escalonados. (pág. 92)

Index

An *i* preceding an italic page reference indicates that there is an illustration, and usually text information as well, on that page. An *m* or a *c* preceding an italic page reference indicates a map or chart, as well as text information on that page.

A

H

I

N

O

P

Index

Index

Index of Skills

Writing and Speaking

Acknowledgments

This product contains proprietary property of MAPQUEST.COM
Unauthorized use, including copying, of this product, is expressly prohibited.

Text Acknowledgments

LITERATURE CONNECTIONS

Chapter 1, page 34: Excerpt from *A Bone from a Dry Sea* by Peter Dickinson. Copyright © 1993 by Peter Dickinson. Used by permission of Dell Publishing, a division of Random House, Inc.

Chapter 8, page 272: Excerpt from *The Emperor's Silent Army* by Jane O'Connor. Copyright © 2002 by Jane O'Connor. Used by permission of Viking Penguin, a division of Penguin Young Readers Group, a member of Penguin Group (USA) Inc., 345 Hudson Street, New York, NY, 10014. All rights reserved.

Chapter 14, page 473: "The Parable of the Good Samaritan" and "The Prodigal Son," from *Everlasting Stories* by Lois Rock. Copyright © 2004 by Lois Rock. Used with permission of Chronicle Books LLC, San Francisco. Visit ChronicleBooks.com.

PRIMARY SOURCE HANDBOOK

Chapter 2, page R36: Excerpt from *The Man in the Ice* by Konrad Spindler, translated by Ewald Osers. Copyright © 1995 by Ewald Osers. Used by permission of Crown Publishers, a division of Random House, Inc.

Chapter 3, page R37: Excerpt from *The Epic of Gilgamesh*, translated by N. K. Sanders. Copyright © 1960, 1964, 1972 by N. K. Sanders. Used by permission of Penguin books, a division of Penguin Group (USA), Inc.

Chapter 7, page R41: Excerpts from *Bhagavad-Gita*, translated by Barbara Stoler Miller. Copyright © 1986 by Barbara Stoler Miller. Used by permission of Bantam Books, a division of Random House, Inc.

Chapter 8, page R42: Excerpts from *The Analects of Confucius*, translated by Simon Leys. Copyright © 1997 by Pierre Ryckmans. Reprinted by permission of W. W. Norton & Company, Inc.

Chapter 8, page R43: Excerpt from *Tao Te Ching: A New English Version with Foreword and Notes* by Stephen Mitchell. Translation copyright © 1988 by Stephen Mitchell. Used by permission of HarperCollins Publishers Inc.

Chapter 8, page R44: Excerpt from *Popul Vuh* by Dennis Tedlock. Copyright © 1985, 1996 by Dennis Tedlock. Reprinted with the permission of Simon & Schuster Adult Publishing Group.

Chapter 10, page R45: Excerpt from *The Bible Designed to Be Read as Living Literature: The Old and the New Testaments in the King James Version* by Ernest Sutherland Bates. Updated scholarship by Loddwick Allison. Copyright © 1936 by Simon & Schuster, Inc. Copyright renewed © 1964 by Simon & Schuster, Inc. Revised text copyright © 1993 by Loddwick Allison. Reprinted with the permission of Simon & Schuster Adult Publishing Group.

Chapter 11, page R51: "The Death of Hector," from *The Iliad* by Homer, translated by Robert Fagles. Copyright © 1990 by Robert Fagles. Used by permission of Viking Penguin, a division of Penguin Group (USA), Inc.

Chapter 11, page R54: "The Boy Who Flew," from *The Robber Baby: Stories from the Greek Myths* by Anne Rockwell. Copyright © 1994 by Anne Rockwell. Used by permission of HarperCollins Publishers Inc.

Chapter 12, page R56: Excerpt from "Pericles' Funeral Oration," from *History of the Peloponnesian War* by Thucydides, translated by Rex Warner. Copyright © 1934 by Rex Warner. Used by permission of Penguin Group (USA), Inc.

Chapter 13, page R57: Excerpt from *The Twelve Caesars*, translated by Robert Graves. Copyright © 1957 by Robert Graves. Used by permission of Carcanet Press Limited.

Chapter 14, page R58: "The Lost Sheep," from *Everlasting Stories* by Lois Rock. Copyright © 2001 by Lois Rock. Used with permission of Chronicle Books LLC, San Francisco. Visit ChronicleBooks.com.

The editors have made every effort to trace the ownership of all copyrighted material found in this book and to make full acknowledgment for its use. Omissions brought to our attention will be corrected in a subsequent edition.

Art and Photography Credits

COVER, FRONTISPIECE

Background El Castillo. Chichén Itzá, Yucatán, Mexico. Photo © Warren Marr/Panoramic Images/NGSImages.com; *top* Bust of Queen Nefertiti (about 1350 B.C.). From the workshop of Thutmosis. Egypt, 18th dynasty. Painted limestone. H. 50 cm. Inv. 21300. Photo: Margarete Büsing. Photo © Bildarchiv Preussischer Kulturbesitz/Art Resource, New York; *center left* Head of Buddah. © Christie's Images/Corbis; *center right* Giant Olmec head. © Danny Lehman/Corbis *bottom left* Statue of Athena. © Alinari/Bridgeman Art Library; *bottom center* Kuba mask. Private collection. Photo © Aldo Tutino/Art Resource, New York; *bottom right* Augustus coin. © Mimmo Jodice/Corbis.

FRONT MATTER

vi *top* Lucy skeleton. © Science Photo Library; *bottom* Aboriginal rock painting. © Penny Tweedie/Corbis; **vii** *top to bottom* Sitting woman holding a small vase. Louvre, Paris. Photo © Erich Lessing/Art Resource, New York; Detail of the Ishtar Gate. The Granger Collection, New York; Iranian valley. © Alamy Images; **viii** *top to bottom* Double crown illustration. © Wildlife Art Ltd.; Ngady Amwaash. National Museum, Ghana. Photo © Werner Forman/Art Resource, New York; Pyramids at Giza. © Alamy Images **ix** *top to bottom* Shiva sculpture. © Burstein Collection/Corbis; Terracotta soldier on its side. O. Louis Mazzatenta/National Geographic Image Collection; Colossal Olmec head. © Jean-Pierre Courau/Bridgeman Art Library; **x** *top to bottom* Fortress of Masada. © Nathan Benn/Corbis; Zeus on ceramic pot. © Réunion des Musées Nationaux/Art Resource, New York; Equestrian portrait of Alexander the Great in combat. Museo Archeologico Nazionale, Naples. Photo © Alinari/Art Resource, New York; **xi** *top to bottom* Cameo of Augustus Caesar (63 B.C.–A.D. 14). From the Treasury of Boscoreale near Pompeii. Louvre, Paris. Photo © Erich Lessing/Art Resource, New York; Reliquary cross of Justinian (A.D. 500–600). Museum of the Treasury, St. Peter's Basilica, Vatican State. Photo © Scala/Art Resource, New York; Roman aqueduct (1900–1800 B.C.). Pont du Gard, Nimes. Photo © SEF/Art Resource, New York; **xiv** Persian minted coins. © The British Museum; **xxi** Statue of Jupiter. © Araldo de Luca/Corbis; **S32** The cithara-player (A.D. 0–100). Fresco from Stabiae. Museo Archeologico Nazionale, Naples, Italy. Photo © Erich Lessing/Art Resource, New York.

UNIT 1

2–3 Stonehenge. Illustration by Roger Stewart; **3** *top* Paleolithic axe. The Granger Collection, New York; *bottom* Red bull wall painting. © James Mellaart.

Chapter 1

4 *top to bottom* Alfred Wegner. The Granger Collection, New York; Ancient footprint. © John Reader/Science Photo Library/Photo Researchers; Paleolithic hand ax. The Granger Collection, New York; **5** *left to right* Skull. © Science Photo Library/Photo Researchers; Small mask (Neolithic period) from Predionica, Kosovo. Terracotta. Muzej Kosova, Pristina, Serbia and Montenegro. © Erich Lessing/Art Resource, New York; **6** Lasceaux bull. The Granger Collection, New York; **6–7** Lascaux cave. Illustration by Frank Ordaz; **8** Earth from space. © Science VU/NASA/Visuals Unlimited; **10** *top to bottom* San Francisco earthquake aftermath. © Bettmann/Corbis; Transform plates. Illustration by Roberta Polfus; **11** Key West Hurricane. AP/Wide World Photos; **13** Kids making geography poster. Photo by Sharon Hoogstraten; **14** Compass. © Science and Society Picture Library, London; **15** Globe with wooden stand. © Comstock Images/Alamy Images; **22** Historical map of early North America. The Granger Collection, New York; **23** Bust of Ptolemy (geographer, astronomer, mathematician) from the choir stalls of Ulm Cathedral (Alexandria, A.D. 100–200). Cathedral, Ulm, Germany. © Erich Lessing/Art Resource, New York; **24** *left to right* Sextant. © DK Images, Dorling Kindersley Ltd.; Ship by stars. The Granger Collection, New York; **25** *top to bottom* Galileo satellite. © Science Photo Library/Photo Researchers; Car with GPS. © Comstock/Alamy Images; Kid with GPS watch. AP/Wide World Photos; **26** Hominid footprint. © John Reader/Science Photo Library/Photo Researchers; **27** Archeological dig. © Richard T. Nowitz/Corbis; **30** Rift valley. Christophe Ratier/NHPA/Photo Researchers; **31** Lucy skeleton. © Science Photo Library/Photo Researchers; **32** *top to bottom* Anthropomorphic figurine (20,000–18,000 B.C.). Maininsk settlement, Siberia. Photo © The State Hermitage Museum; Neolithic idol (3,000–2,000 B.C.). Usvyaty IV settlement, Pskov region. Photo © The State Hermitage Museum; **33** Australopithecine skull. © Gallo Images/Corbis; **34** *foreground* Magnifying glass. © Getty Images; **34–35** *background* Dusting brush, nail, tape measure. Photo by Sharon Hoogstraten; **35** *right* Trowel. © Dr. Michael B. Collins/Texas Archeological Research Laboratory; **36** Hominid fossils. National Museum of Ethiopia © 1999 Tim D. White/Brill Atlanta; **37** Notebook, note card, shovel handle. Photo by Sharon Hoogstraten; **38** Cave paintings. National Geographic Image Collection; **39** Griot Jeli playing the bolon. Kerouane, Guinea. © David C. Conrad; **40** *left to right* Paleolithic ax. The Granger Collection, New York; Neolithic ax. The Granger Collection, New York; Bronze age ax. The Granger Collection, New York; **41** Rosetta Stone. The Granger Collection, New York; **42** Burial chamber of King Tutankhamen. Tomb of Tutankhamen, Valley of the Kings, Thebes, Egypt. © Scala/Art Resource, New York; **44** Icons. Illustrations by Robert Coleman.

Chapter 2

46 Cavemen during the Ice Age (1800-1899), W. Kranz, after a sketch by Professor Klaatsch. Bibliothèque des Arts Decoratifs, Paris. Photo © Archives Charmet/Bridgeman Art Library; **47** *left to right* Glacier. © Photo Researchers, Inc.; Bronze deer. © ARPL/Topham/The Image Works; Agricultural tool. © The British Museum/Topham–HIP/The Image Works; **48** *inset* Discovery of the Ice Man. © Sygma/Corbis; **48–49** Hunters in the Alps. Illustration by Frank Ordaz; **50** *top to bottom* Man using spear thrower. Illustration by Steve Cowden; Paleolithic spear-thrower with the form of a horse, called "au cheval sautant" (14,000–13,000 B.C.). Carved wood, 28 cm long. MAN 82722. Photo: Jean Schormans. © Réunion des Musées Nationaux/Art Resource, New York; **51** African savanna. © Image Bank/Getty Images; **53** *left to right* Mattock (antler digging tool). © Museum of London/Topham–HIP/The Image Works; Three harpoons used for spearing fish (4,000 B.C.). Bone, early Neolithic. Collections of IDAM. Photo © Erich Lessing/Art Resource, New York; Ax. Museum of London/Topkan–HF/The Image Works; **54** *top to bottom* Native American cave painting. Photo © 2004 Doak Heyser; Australian cave painting. Photo © Pam Gardner/Frank Lane Picture Agency/Corbis; **55** Stag antler headdress. Photo © 2000 The British Museum; **57** Rock painting of animals (produced since the Later Stone Age, probably by the ancestors of Sandawe hunter gatherers still living in the region). The animals predicting may be the favoured game of hunters or hallucinations seen during the shamanistic trance dancing known as simbo. Tanzania National Museum, Dar es Salaam, Tanzania. Photo © Werner Forman/Art Resource, New York; **58** God with a sickle and female idol, both seated on throne-like chairs (4,000–3,000 B.C.). Neolithic sculpture. Tizsa culture, from Szigvar-Tuzkoves and Koekenydomb, Hungary. Koszta Josef Museum, Szentes, Hungary. Photo © Erich Lessing/Art Resource, New York; **59** Sheep grazing landscape in Andes. © Dave Wilhelm/Corbis; **63** Girl growing plants. Photo by Sharon Hoogstraten. **64** Brooch.

Photo © The Museum of London/Topham-HIP/The Image Works; **65** Atlas mountains farming village. © Ben Mangor/SuperStock, Inc.; **66–67** Pottery jar (1850–1550 B.C.), 12.6 cm high, and necklace (1850–1550 B.C.) made of 31 white and brown biconical beads, quartz, 22 cm long, from the Bethlehem area. Canaanite, Bronze Age. Reuben and Edith Hecht Collection, Haifa University, Haifa, Israel. Photo © Erich Lessing/Art Resource, New York; **68** *top to bottom* Seal. Photo © James Mellaart; Dagger. Photo © James Mellaart; **69** Bull wall painting. Photo © James Mellaart; **70–71** Catal Hyuk. Illustrations by Inklink, Florence/Virgil Pomfret; **72** Icons. Illustrations by Robert Coleman; **74** Lasceaux bull. The Granger Collection, New York; Ax. © Museum of London/Topkan-HF/The Image Works, Inc.

UNIT 2

76–77 Ishtar Gate. Illustration by Inklink, Florence/Virgil Pomfret; **77** *top to bottom* Golden helmet from Ur (2450 B.C.). Early dynastic. Iraq Museum, Baghdad, Iraq. Photo © Scala/Art Resource, New York; Orant of Larsa, probably Hammurabi (1792–1750 B.C.), law-giver and sixth king of the Amorite dynasty of Babylon. From Larsa. Bronze, face and hands gold-plated. Louvre, Paris. Photo © Erich Lessing/Art Resource, New York.

Chapter 3

78 *top to bottom* Urn decorated in red (Proto-literate period). Terracotta. From Tell Agrab, Iraq. Iraq Museum, Baghdad, Iraq. Photo © Scala/Art Resource, New York; Sahara desert © Photowood, Inc./Corbis; **79** *top to bottom* Limestone tablet with Sumerian pictographic script. Symbol of the hand indicates the proprietor. End of 4th millenium. Mesopotamia. 5 x 4.2 cm. A) 19936. Louvre, Paris. Photo © Erich Lessing/Art Resource, New York; Mohenjo Daro. © Paul Springett/Alamy Images; **80** *inset* Wheat. © Creatas/PictureQuest; **80-81** Drought. Illustration by Gino D'Achille/Artist Partners; **82** Bull in a Thicket. © The Art Archive/British Museum; **83** Euphrates River. © Alamy Images; **84** Ancient irrigation systems. Illustration by Peter Bull; **85** Reed house. © Jane Sweeney/Lonely Planet Images; **87** Boy making a diagram. Photo by Sharon Hoogstraten; **88** Two gypsum statuettes with folded hands. Male figure, height: 72 cm, Nr. 19752. Female figure, height: 59 cm, Nr. 19751. Eshnunna (Tel Asmar), from the temple carre of the God Abu. Sumerian. Iraq Museum, Baghdad, Iraq. Photo © Erich Lessing/Art Resource, New York; **89** Ruins of Ur. © David Lees/Corbis; **90** Gudea, King of Lagash (2120 B.C.). Sumerian dolerite sculpture. Louvre, Paris. Photo © Scala/Art Resource, New York; **91** *top to bottom* Golden helmet from Ur (2450 B.C.). Early dynastic. Iraq Museum, Baghdad, Iraq. Photo © Scala/Art Resource, New York; Sumerian bronze sword. © 2000 The British Museum; **92–93** Ziggurat. Illustration by Luigi Galante; **95** Sumerian ring (about 3,000 B.C.). Tello-Lagash, Mesopotamia. Louvre, Paris. Photo © Réunion des Musées Nationaux/Art Resource, New York; **97** Cuneiform. © Araldo de Luca/Corbis; **98** Sumerian woman holding a vase. © Erich Lessing/Art Resource, New York; **99** Standard of Ur (2600–2400 B.C.). © The British Museum. **100** Reconstruction of Sumerian wheel. Deutsches Museum, Munich, Germany. Photo © SEF/Art Resource, New York; **101** *top to bottom* Figure of a god on top of a foundation nail (about 2140 B.C.). Male head, perhaps a member of the family of King Gudea of Lagash. Black diorite. Louvre, Paris. Photo © Erich Lessing/Art Resource, New York; Limestone tablet with Sumerian pictographic script. Symbol of the hand indicates the proprietor. End of 4th millenium. Mesopotamia. 5 x 4.2 cm. A) 19936. Louvre, Paris. Photo © Erich Lessing/Art Resource, New York; **102** Cuneiform tablet. © David Lees/Corbis; **103** Assyrian scribe. The Granger Collection, New York; **104** *top to bottom* Sumerian plowing scene. © Ashmolean Museum, Oxford; Farmer plowing field. © Sylvain Saustier/Corbis; **105** *top, left to right* Royal Game of Ur. © 2000 The British Museum; Checkers. Photo by Sharon Hoogstratten; *bottom, top to bottom* Mitannian pottery jar (about 1370–1270 B.C.). Photo © The British Museum/Topham-HIP/The Image Works; Teen using potters wheel. © Tom Stewart/Corbis; 106 Icons. Illustrations by Robert Coleman.

Chapter 4

108 *left to right* Large circular seal with mythical animal from Mohenjo-Daro. Yellow steatite. National Museum of Pakistan, Karachi, Pakistan. Photo © Borromeo/Art Resource, New York; Diorite bust, called the Head of Hammurabi (about 1800 B.C.). Louvre, Paris. Photo © Chuzeville/Réunion des Musées Nationaux/Art Resource, New York (Inv. SB 95); **109** *left to right* Western Zhou dynasty square ding. Bronze. © Asian Art and Archaeology, Inc./Corbis; Ivory head of a woman, thought to be Mona Lisa (720 B.C.). Assyrian. Iraq Museum, Baghdad, Iraq. Photo © Scala/Art Resource, New York; Urn from Monte Alban. Zapotec culture. Museo Nacional de Antropología, Mexico City, D.F., Mexico. Photo © SEF/Art Resource, New York; **110** *inset* Model of a house (2900–2290 B.C.). Early dynastic. Terracotta. Akkadian. National Museum, Aleppo, Syria. Photo © Erich Lessing/Art Resource, New York; **110–111** Collapsed House. Illustration by Roger Stewart; **112** Male head with beard (Sargon), from Niniveh. Bronze or copper. Akkadian. Height, 36 cm. Inv. IM 11331. Iraq Museum, Baghdad, Iraq. Photo © Erich Lessing/Art Resource, New York; **113** Ruins of Uruk © Nik Wheeler/Corbis; **114** Orantes Larsa, probably Hammurabi, law-giver and sixth king of the Amorite dynasty of Babylon. From Larsa. Bronze, face and hands gold-plated. Louvre, Paris. Photo © Erich Lessing/Art Resource, New York; **115** Upper section of the stele of the law code of Hammurabi (about 1792–1750 B.C.). Diorite, from Babylon (found at Susa). First Babylonian dynasty. Louvre, Paris. Photo © Hervé Lewandowki/Réunion des Musées Nationaux/Art Resource, New York; **117** Boy and girl building a monument. Photo by Sharon Hoogstraten; **118** Tree pendant from Nimrud. www.billlyons.com; **119** Capture of Hamanu (stone carving). © Erich Lessing/Art Resource, New York; **121** Palace of Nimrud. © Dagli Orti/The British Museum/The Art Archive; **122** Ishtar Gate (Processional Way) © Ruggero Vanni/Corbis; **123** Dragon detail of Ishtar Gate. The Granger Collection, New York; **126** Hanging gardens of Babylon. © DK Images. Dorling Kindersley, Ltd.; **128** Gold rhyton decorated with winged lion (400–200 B.C.). Achaemenid. Archaeological Museum, Teheran, Iran. Photo © Scala/Art Resource, New York; **129** Iranian valley. © Alamy Images; **131** Surrender of Lachish. © Dagli Orti/The British Museum/The Art Archive; **132** Ruins of ancient Persepolis. Photo © zefa/TH-Foto; **133** Persian coins. © The British Museum; **134–135** Court of Darius. Illustrations by Inklink, Florence/Virgil Pomfret; **136** Icons. Illustrations by Robert Coleman; **138** Male head with beard (Sargon), from Niniveh. Bronze or copper. Akkadian. Height, 36 cm. Inv. IM 11331. Iraq Museum, Baghdad, Iraq. Photo © Erich Lessing/Art Resource, New York.

UNIT 3

140-141 Pyramid builders. Illustration by Angus McBride/Linden Artists, Ltd.; **141** *top to bottom* Sphinx. © Photodisc/Getty Images; Nok head (900 B.C.–A.D. 200). Courtesy Entwistle Gallery, London. Photo © Werner Forman/Art Resource, New York.

Chapter 5

142 *left to right* Harrappan elephant seal. The National Museum, Karachi. Photo © Dagli Orti/The Art Archive; The pyramids at Giza. Old Kingdom. Giza, Egypt. Photo © E. Strouhal and Werner Forman/Art Resource, New York; **143** *top counterclock-wise* The Great Sphinx. © Alamy Images; Step pyramid. © Carl and Ann Purcell/Corbis; Queen Hatshepsut's temple. © Alamy Images; King Ramses II's temple. © Alamy Images; *bottom* Olmec colossal head (1200–900 B.C.). Photo © Gianni Dagli Orti/Corbis; **144** *inset* Ramses stone head. © Michael Melford/Getty Images; **144–145** Death of Ramses II. Illustration by Bill Cigliano; **146** Lotus pendant. © Araldo de Luca/Archivio White Star; **147** The Nile valley. © G.J. Owen, Cambridge; **148** Nile delta. Photo provided by the SeaWiFS project/NASA/Goddard Space Flight Center and ORBIMAGE; **149** Shaduf. © H. Armstrong Roberts; **150–151** Nebamun Hunting Fowl (1425–1400 B.C.). Photo © Archivo Iconografico, S.A./ Corbis; **151** Bracelet from the tomb of Djer (2920–2770 B.C.). Egyptian Museum, Cairo. Photo © Araldo De Luca/Archivio White Star; **152–153** Nile river ship. Illustration by Inklink Firenze; **154** Egyptian mummified cat (Late period, 664–332 B.C.). Stuccoed and painted. Louvre, Paris. Photo © Art Resource, New York; **155** Temple at Luxor. © Tibor Bognar/Corbis; **156** Egyptian social roles. Illustration by Michael Jaroszko; **158** Seated scribe, 3/4 view (Egypt, Fifth Dynasty). Louvre, Paris. Photo © Chuzeville/Réunion des Musées Nationaux/Art Resource, New York; **159** Hieroglyph carving. © Roger Wood/Corbis; **160** Detail of Judgment of the Dead (1400–1300 B.C.). Photo © Historical Picture Archive/Corbis; **161** Head of Anubis (1314–1085 B.C.). Louvre, Paris. Photo © Giraudon/Art Resource, New York; **162** Calendar tomb painting. The Metropolitan Museum of Art, Rogers Fund, 1948. Photo © 1979 The Metropolitan Museum of Art (48.105.52); **163** *clockwise from top left* Egyptian surgical instruments. Photo © Art Resource, New York; Laser surgery. © Corbis Images/ PictureQuest; Stone pyramids. © Philip Coblentz/Brand X Pictures/PictureQuest; Glass pyramid. © Bill Ross/Corbis; **164** Ankh. © Araldo de Luca/Archivio White Star; **165** Pyramids. © Alamy Images; **166** Crown illustrations. © Wildlife Art Ltd.; **167** *top to bottom* Pyramid. © Corbis; Step pyramid. © Corbis; Khufu (Cheops) (Fourth Dynasty). Egyptian Museum, Cairo. Photo © Dagli Orti/The Art Archive; **168** Great pyramid of Khufu. © Alamy Images; **171** Paper pyramid/hand. Photo by Sharon Hoogstraten; **172** Gold mask of King Tutankhamen (Egypt, Eighteenth Dynasty). Egyptian Museum, Cairo, Egypt. © Scala/Art Resource, New York; **173** Queen Hatshepsut's temple. © Art Kowalsky/Alamy Images; **175** Bust of Nefertiti (thought to be an 1800–1900 copy of sculpture in the Egyptian Museum, Berlin). Museo Archeologico, Florence. Photo © Scala/Art Resource, New York; **176** Abu Simbel © Getty Images; **177** Bust of Cleopatra. © Bettmann/Corbis; **178** *inset* The Voyage to Punt: Sailors rowing (New Kingdom, Eighteenth Dynasty). Colored limestone relief, from the temple of Queen Hatshepsut (Maat Ka-Re) (1495–1475 B.C.), in Deir el-Bahri. Aegyptisches Museum, Staatliche Museen zu Berlin, Berlin, Germany. Photo © Erich Lessing/Art Resource, New York; **179** Portraits of Seninefer and Queen Hatshepsut (Eighteenth Dynasty, about 1479–1458 B.C.). Egypt. Painted plaster. Louvre, Paris. Photo © Scala/Art Resource, New York; **178–181** Water and palm trees. © Corbis; **180** Monkeys (1346–1337 B.C.). Wallpainting in the tomb of Pharaoh Tutankhamun (1346–1337 B.C.). Tomb of Tutankhamen, Valley of the Kings, Thebes, Egypt. Photo © Erich Lessing/Art Resource, New York; **181** Two daggers (1600–1000 B.C.). *Left:* crescent-shaped handle, copper, 31 cm long. Middle Kingdom. E 22895. *Right:* bronze, 28.8 cm long, New Kingdom. Louvre, Paris. Photo © Erich Lessing/Art Resource, New York (N 2113 B); **182** Icons. Illustrations by Robert Coleman.

Chapter 6

184 *left to right* Pericles bust. © The British Museum; Nok head, front view (500 B.C.–A.D. 200). Rafin Kura, Nok. Terracotta, 36 cm high. National Museum, Lagos, Nigeria. Photo © Werner Forman/Art Resource, New York; **185** *top to bottom* Sahara desert. © Photowood Inc./Corbis; Rainforest in Gabon. © Gallo Images/Corbis; Savanna with zebras. © Paul Springett/ Alamy Images; Page from an illuminated manuscript, Marici and her followers (Tang Dynasty). Ink on paper, 24 x 22.5 cm. Musée des Arts Asiatiques-Guimet, Paris. Photo © Ravaux/Réunion des Musées Nationaux/Art Resource, New York; **186** *inset* Courtyard and entrance to Ark of the Covenant Temple. Axum, Ethiopia. Photo © Dave Bartruff/Corbis; **186–187** African pilgrimage. Illustration by Frank Ordaz; **188** Kush pottery. Photo © University of Pennsylvania Museum of Archaeology and Anthropology; **189** Cataract on Upper Nile. © Bojan Brecelj/Corbis; **191** The Great Stelae of Piankhi. Photo © Topham/The Image Works; **192–193** Taharqa sphinx. Photo © The British Museum/HIP/The Image Works; **193** Armlet with winged Goddess Mut, from the treasure of Amanishakheto (100–0 B.C.). Meroe, Pyramide N 6. Gold with glass paste inlay, 4.5 cm high. Aegyptisches Museum, Staatliche Museen zu Berlin, Berlin, Germany. © Bildarchiv Preussischer Kulturbesitz/Art Resource, New York (Inv. Mue 2455); **196** The tallest of the still erect stelae at Aksum (A.D. 300–400). Aksumite. Aksum, Ethiopia. Photo © Werner Forman/Art Resource, New York; 197 National Park in Ethiopia. © Robert Preston/Alamy Images; **199** Crown of Aksum. © Sonia Halliday Photographs; **200** Geéz script scroll. Courtesy of BC Galleries, Melbourne; **201** Girl building pillar. Photo by Sharon Hoogstraten; **202** Nok Figure. Terracotta. 12 cm. Private Collection. Courtesy Entwistle, London. Photo Joshua Nefsky, New York. **204** The Sahel and Desertification. Illustration by Stephen R. Wagner; **205** Human bird figure. Nok. Terracotta. 47 x 20 x 22 cm. Photo © Heini Schneebeli/The Bridgeman Art Library; **207** Ngady Amwaash, representing Mweel, sister of the founding ancestor Woot. Kuba culture of Central Zaire. National Museum, Ghana. Photo © Werner Forman/Art Resource, New York; **208** Icons. Illustrations by Robert Coleman; **210** *Nebamun Hunting Fowl* (1400–1425 B.C.). © Archivo Iconografico, S.A./Corbis.

UNIT 4

212–213 The Great Stupa at Sanchi. Illustration by Roger Stewart; **213** *top to bottom* Shiva. © Burstein Collection/Corbis; Vase fanjia (1650–1066 B.C.). From Anyang, China. Bronze, 31 x 14.5 cm. Musée des Arts Asiatiques-Guimet, Paris, France. Inv. MA 6071. Photo © Richard Lambert/Réunion des Musées Nationaux/Art Resource, New York; Mayan pyramid. The Granger Collection, New York.

Chapter 7

214 *left to right* Indus culture necklace. © Archivo Iconografico, S.A./Corbis; Fragment of a statue from the queen's temple at Deir el-Bahari representing Hatshepsut in the form of Osiris (1470–1490). Egyptian Museum, Cairo, Egypt. Photo © Werner Foreman/Art Resource, New York; **215** *left to right* Alexander the Great, so-called Alexander Azara. Copy (200-100 B.C.) of original bust (320 B.C.). Marble, 65 cm high. Louvre, Paris. Photo © Erich Lessing/Art Resource, New York; Horse Sacrifice coin, reign of Samudra Gupta; Lion coin, reign of Kumar Gupta; Chatra and Couchiglia coins, reign of Chandra Gupta (about 500-400 B.C.). National Museum, New Delhi, India. Photo © Borromeo/Art Resource, New York; **216–217** Sarasvati Earthquake. Illustration by Gino D'Achille/Artist Partners; **218** Harappan royal priest. © Jean-Louis Nou/akg-images; **219** Ganges River. © The Image Bank/Getty Images; **220** Summer and winter monsoons. Illustrations by Gary Hincks; **221** Indus valley pictograph seal. The National Museum, Karachi. © Dagli Orti/The Art Archive; **222–223** Mohenjo-Daro ruins. Mohenjo-Daro, Pakistan. Photo © Borromeo/Art Resource, New York; **223** *left to right* Great bath of Mohenjo-Daro. Mohenjo-Daro, Pakistan. Photo © Borromeo/Art Resource, New York; Terracotta pot and lid (1500–1200 B.C.). National Museum, New Delhi, India. © The Bridgeman Art Library; **224** Indus culture bronze tools. © Angelo Hornak/Corbis; **225** Boy making climate graph. Photo by Sharon Hoogstraten; inset Graph paper with bar graph. Photo by Sharon Hoogstraten; 226 Shiva © Burstein Collection/Corbis; **227** Hindu Kush range. © Grant Dixon/Lonely Planet Images; **229** Sweeper with broom (1846). Photo © The British Library/Topham-HIP/The Image Works; **230** Shri Krishna, Indian school. Private collection. Photo © Dinodia Picture Agency, Bombay, India/Bridgeman Art Library; **232** Pillar of Asoka (273–236 B.C.). Maurya Dynasty. Museum, Samath, Uttar Pradesh, India. Photo © Borromeo/Art Resource, New York; **233** Reclining Buddha. © Lindsay Hebberd/Corbis; **234** Siddhartha Gutama. Bodhgaya, Bihar, India. Photo © DPA/SOA/The Image Works; **235** Indian flag. © Royalty Free/Corbis; **236** Vishnu (1750). Photo © Jean-Louis Nou/akg-images; **238** Exterior view of Vishnu temple (500–400 B.C.). Gupta Dynasty. Vishnu temple, Deogarh, Rajasthan, India. Photo © Borromeo/Art Resource, New York; **239** The Iron Pillar and the Quwwat-ul-Islam Masjid. Delhi, India. © The Bridgeman Art Library; **240** Gandhi. © Peter Ruhe/Hulton Archives/Getty Images; **241** Angkor Wat. © The Image Bank/Getty Images; **242** Dance of the Ramayana during a festival in Bangkok. © C. Walker/Topham/The Image Works; **244** *top to bottom* Harappan seal with yoga pose. © Charles and Josette Lenars/Corbis; Modern yoga. © Jose Luis Pelaez, Inc./Corbis; **245** *top, left to right* Ayurvedic herbs and spices. © Botanica; Modern Ayurvedic treatment. © Thinkstock; *bottom, left to right* Sacred bull. © Philadelphia Museum of Art/Corbis; Indian vegetarian food. © Foodpix; **246** Icons. Illustrations by Robert Coleman.

Chapter 8

248 *left to right* Bronze stag figurine. © Royal Ontario Museum/Corbis; Olmec sitting man. © Veintimilla/akg-images; **249** *left to right* Confucious stone engraving. © akg-images; Roman Colloseum. © Royalty Free/Corbis; **250** *inset* Wooden Confucius. © Royalty Free/Corbis; **250–251** Confucius teaching disciples. Illustration by Eric Robson; **252** Vase fanjia (1650–1066 B.C.). Bronze, 31 x 14.5 cm. From Anyang, China. Musée des Arts Asiatiques-Guimet, Paris. Photo © Richard Lambert/Réunion des Musées Nationaux/Art Resource, New York (Inv. MA 6071); **253** Gobi desert. © Keren Su/China Span; **254** Yangtze River. © Alamy Images; **255** Chinese oracle bone (Shang Dynasty, 1766–1122 B.C.). The engraved characters are the earliest known examples of Chinese script. The bones originally used for divination also provide information about rulers battles folk religion and religious rites. British Museum, London. Photo © Werner Forman/Art Resource, New York; **256** Jade dragon. © Royal Ontario Museum/Corbis; **257** Jade pendant in the shape of a dragon (Qing Dynasty, 1644–1911). This pendant, dating to the Quing dynasty was inspired by an example dating to the Zhou dynasty (1050–221 B.C.). British Museum, London. Photo © HIP/Scala/Art Resource, New York; **259** Confucius with his disciples. © Lauros/Giraudon/The Bridgeman Art Library; **260–261** Ceremony honoring Confucius. © Orion Press/Pacific Stock; **261** From *The Analects of Confucius,* edited by Chichung Huang. © 1997 by Chichung Huang. Used by permission of Oxford University Press, Inc.; **262** Drawing of Confucious. © Bettmann/Corbis; **265** *top to bottom* Woodcut of Confucius. © akg-images; Laozi astride a bull, accompanied by a servant (1600–1700). Chinese scroll painting. Bibliotheque Nationale, Paris. Photo © Snark/Art Resource, New York; **266** Jade Funeral Suit. © Alamy Images; **267** Terracotta soldiers. O. Louis Mazzatenta/National Geographic Image Collection; **268** The Great Wall of China. Photo © Hideo Haga/HAGA/The Image Works; **270** Court women (206 B.C.–A.D. 220), François Guénet. Private collection. © François Guénet/akg-images; **271** Flying horse, one leg resting on a swallow (Eastern Han Dynasty). Bronze figure, 34.5 x 45 cm. Excavated 1969 at Wu-Wai, Kansu, China. National Museum, Beijing. Photo © Erich Lessing/Art Resource, New York; **272–273** Terracotta soldier on its side. O. Louis Mazzatenta/National Geographic Image Collection; **274–275** Terracotta army in pit two. O. Louis Mazzatenta/National Geographic Image Collection; **275** Terracotta horses for army. O. Louis Mazzatenta/National Geographic Image Collection; **276** Tang silk tapestry of Buddha. Photo © 2000 The British Museum; **277** Modern silk merchant. © Alamy Images; **278** Silk Road, Afghanistan. © Alamy Images; **281** Girl with notebook and books. Photo by Sharon Hoogstraten; **282** Icons. Illustrations by Robert Coleman.

Chapter 9

284 *top to bottom* Olmec wrestler. © Giraudon/The Bridgeman Art Library; Sphinx with pyramid. © Corbis; **285** Stela depicting a warrior holding a club. Shavin culture, Pre-Columbian. Stone. Cerro Sechin, Peru. Photo © Giraudon/The Bridgeman Art Library. *top to bottom* Mayan rain god. © Robert Harding World Imagery/Alamy Images; Chavin art. © Ken Walsh/The Bridgeman Art Library; Nazca lines. © Roman Soumar/Corbis; Emporer Liu Ban. © The Art Archive/British Library; **286** *inset* The jade burial mask of Pacal (Classic Maya, A.D. 600–700) found in the Temple of the Inscriptions at Palenque.

Museo Nacional de Antropologia, Mexico City, D.F., Mexico. Photo © Werner Forman/Art Resource, New York; **286–287** King Pacal II and his Sons. Illustration by Philip Howe; **288** Quetzal bird. © Michael Maslan Historic Photographs/Corbis; **289** Amazon with people. © Owen Franken/Corbis; **291** *top to bottom* High region of Andes mountains. © The Image Bank/Getty Images; Andes valley region. © Photofrenetic/Alamy Images; **293** Maize. © Macduff Everton/Corbis; **294** Jaguar pendant. Photo © Dumbarton Oaks; **295** Gargoyle at Chavin de Huantar. Photo © Charles and Josette Lenars/Corbis. **297** *top to bottom* Nazca lines hummingbird. © Stockfolio/Alamy Images; Nazca lines parrot. © David Nunuk/Science Photo Library; **298** Moche jug. © Nathan Benn/Corbis; **299** A yellow, blue and red wollen poncho (A.D. 600–700). Nazca/Huari. From the South coast of Peru. Dallas Museum of Art, Dallas, Texas. Photo © Werner Forman/Art Resource, New York; **300** Olmec jade figure. Justin Kerr/The Brooklyn Museum; **302** *inset* Monolithic Olmec head found near La Venta. La Venta, Mexico. Photo © SEF/Art Resource, New York; **302–303** Colossal Olmec head. © Jean-Pierre Courau/The Bridgeman Art Library; **303** Olmec were-jaguar (900–300 B.C.). Photo © Dumbarton Oaks; **305** Girl and boy making time capsule. Photo by Sharon Hoogstraten; **306** Mosaic mask, a funerary gift from tomb 160. It was laid over the face of the dead dignitary to adorn him during his voyage through the Underworld. Jadeite, diopsite, shells, conch-shells, mother of pearl, 34.5 cm high. Inv. 11082, Maya. Tikal, El Peten, Guatemala. Museo Nacional de Arqueologia, Guatemala City, Guatemala. Photo © Erich Lessing/Art Resource, New York; **307** Tikal and surrounding jungle; Temple of the Jaguar (600–900). Guatamala. © Ken Welsh/The Bridgeman Art Library; **309** Stele. © The Granger Collection, New York; **310** *clockwise from top left* Mayan pyramid. © The Granger Collection, New York; Mayan heiroglyphs. © Museo Nacional de Antropologia, Mexico City, Mexico/Giraudon/Bridgeman Art Library; Egyptian heiroglyphs. © Roger Wood/Corbis; Egyptian pyramid. © Giraudon/The Bridgeman Art Library; **311** Maya today. © Danny Lehman/Corbis; **312–313** Illustrations by Inklink, Florence/Virgil Pomfret; **314** Icons. Illustrations by Robert Coleman; **315** Mayan nobleman. © Justin Kerr; **316** *left* Exterior view of Vishnu temple (500–400 B.C.). Gupta Dynasty. Vishnu temple, Deogarh, Rajasthan, India. Photo © Borromeo/Art Resource, New York; *right* Temple of the Jaguar (600–900). Guatamala. © Ken Welsh/The Bridgeman Art Library.

UNIT 5

318-319 Visiting the Temple of Solomon. Illustration by David Bergen; **319** *top to bottom* Hanukkah menorah for the synagogue (1700–1800). Eastern Europe. Brass: cast, cut and engraved. Photo © The Jewish Museum, New York/Art Resource, New York; Apollo of Belvedere, detail of head. Roman copy after Greek original (about 350–320 B.C.). Museo Pio Clementino, Vatican Museums, Vatican State. Photo © Scala/Art Resource, New York; The Parthenon. Photo © Dagli Orti/The Art Archive.

Chapter 10

320 *top to bottom* Russian icon (Abraham and Sarah) (1600–1700). Open Air Museum, Kizhi Island, Russia. Photo © Erich Lessing/Art Resource, New York; Olmec jade head. The Granger Collection, New York; **321** *left to right* Urn from Monte Alban. Zapotec culture. Museo Nacional de Antropologia, Mexico City, D.F. Photo © SEF/Art Resource, New York; Bust of Titus. © Gianni Dagli Orti/Corbis; **322–323** Ruth and Naomi. Illustration by Christian Hook; **324** Torah tik (1919–1925). Iran. The Jewish Museum, New York. Photo © The Jewish Museum, New York/Art Resource, New York; **326** Peregrination of the family of Abraham, Giovanni Benedetto Castiglione. Palazzo Rosso, Genoa, Italy. Photo © Scala/Art Resource, New York; **327** Moses with the Tablets of the Law, Guido Reni. Galleria Borghese, Rome, Italy. Photo © Scala/Art Resource, New York; **328** Deborah. The Granger Collection, New York; **330–331** Moses Parting the Red Sea. Private Collection. Photo © Dagli Orti/The Art Archive; **332** Crossing the Red Sea. The Granger Collection, New York; **333** King in a chariot. Detail from lid of chest of Tutankhamun (Eighteenth dynasty, 1357–1349 B.C.). The king in his chariot hunts desert animals. Stuccoed wood. Egyptian Museum, Cairo, Egypt. © Werner Forman/Art Resource, New York; **334** Mezuzah. © Jewish Museum, London/The Bridgeman Art Library; **335** Sheep in Galilee. © Richard T. Nowitz/Corbis; **336** David (1623-1624), Gian Lorenzo Bernini. Left side, post-restoration. Marble. Galleria Borghese, Rome, Italy. Photo © Scala/Art Resource, New York; **338** Cyrus the Great. The Granger Collection, New York; 339 Pomegranate. Photo © Adar Media/Corbis; **341** King David and King Solomon, detail from "The Resurrection" (1000–1100). Byzantine mosaic. Monastery Church, Hosios Loukas, Greece. Photo © Erich Lessing/Art Resource, New York; **342** Menorah for the synagogue (1700–1800). Brass: cast, cut and engraved. Eastern Europe. The Jewish Museum, New York. Photo © The Jewish Museum, New York/Art Resource, New York; **343** View of ruins (A.D. 150–200). Synagogue, Capernaum, Israel. Photo © Art Resource, New York; **344–345** Masada. © Nathan Benn/Corbis; **346** Boy and rabbi studying the Torah. © Celestial Panoramas/Alamy Images; **347** Girl and boy drawing a fortress. Photo by Sharon Hoogstraten; **348** Icons. Illustrations by Robert Coleman.

Chapter 11

350 *top to bottom* Tiara from Grave III (about 1600–1500 B.C.). Mycenaean. National Archaeological Museum, Athens, Greece. Photo © The Bridgeman Art Library; Olmec sitting man. © Veintimilla/akg-images; **351** *left to right* Gold ring with ornaments (450–400 B.C.). From Ezerovo near Parvomai. Diam. 2.7 cm. Archaeological Museum, Sofia, Bulgaria. Photo © Erich Lessing/Art Resource, New York; Head of a Buddha, from Angkor (Khmer, A.D. 1100–1200). Musée des Arts Asiatiques-Guimet, Paris, France. Photo © Erich Lessing/Art Resource, New York; **352** *inset* Spartan warrior, possibly Leonidas (490–480 B.C.). Archaeological Museum, Sparta, Greece. Photo © Vanni/Art Resource, New York; **352–353** Persian Wars. Illustration by Frank Orday Studio; **354** Fish plate (350–300 B.C.). Red figure vase painting. Louvre, Paris, France. Photo © Réunion des Musées Nationaux/Art Resource, New York; **355** Greek coastline. © Alamy Images; **357** Greek ship. The Granger Collection, New York; **358** Sign language. Seth Perlman/AP/Wide World Photos; **359** Athena/owl coin. The Granger Collection, New York; **360** Heracles leading Alcestris out of the Underworld (about 525–520 B.C.). Black figure amphora, 42.4 cm high. From Vulci. Inv. F 60. Louvre, Paris. Photo © Hervé Lewandowski/Réunion des Musées Nationaux/Art Resource, New York; **361** Mt. Olympus. © Robert Gill; Papilio/Corbis; **362–363** Statue of Zeus (about 500 B.C.). Museo Archeologico Nazionale. Photo © Andrea Baguzzi/akg-images; **363** *clockwise from top* Wheelchair race, Olympic games. AP/Wide World Photos; Apollo of Belvedere, detail of head (about 350–320 B.C.). Roman copy after Greek original. Museo Pio Clementino, Vatican Museums, Vatican State. Photo © Scala/Art Resource, New York; Athena with her owl in flight (about 360 B.C.). *To the right,* Poseidon with the trident. Detail of a a red figure crater. Etruscan vase. Louvre, Paris. Photo © Hervé Lewandowski/Réunion des Musées Nationaux/Art Resource, New York (Inv. CA 7426); Demeter (A.D. 0–100). Carthage, Tunisia. Photo © Jean-Louis Nou/akg-images; **364** "Troy" film still. © Bureau L.A. Collections/Simon Smith-Hutchon/Warner Brothers/Corbis; **365** Cyclops. © Bridgeman Art Library; **366** The Atalanta Lekythos (500–490 B.C.), attributed to Douris. The Cleveland Museum of Art. Leonard C. Hanna, Jr., Fund 1966.114. Photo © The Cleveland Musuem of Art 2004; **367** Artemis. The Granger Collection, New York; **368–369** Acropolis at sunset. © Stone/Getty Images; **368** Statue of Atalanta. © C. M. Dixon. **369** Golden apple. © Creatas/PictureQuest; **370** Water timer. Photo © The American School of Classical Studies at Athens. **371** Ruins of Agora. © Dagli Orti/The Art Archive; **372** Athens aerial. © akg-images; 374 Bust of Solon (630–560 B.C.). Greek. Uffizi, Florence, Italy. Photo © Scala/Art Resource, New York; **375** *counter-clockwise from top* Solid ballot. Photo © The American School of Classical Studies at Athens; Hollow ballot. Photo © The American School of Classical Studies at Athens. Ballot box. Photo © The American School of Classical Studies at Athens; **376** Ostrakon. Greek potsherd. Agora Museum, Athens, Greece. Photo © Scala/Art Resource, New York; **377** Girl and boy making vocabulary cards. Photo by Sharon Hoogstraten. **378** Athena wearing crested helmet and peplos (340 B.C.). Archaeological Museum, Piraeus. Photo © Dagli Orti/Archaeological Museum Piraeus/Art Archive; **379** Attacking warrior (510–500 B.C.). Formerly part of a vessel. Greek bronze, from Dodona, 12.8 cm high. Antikensammlung, Staatlone Museen zu Berlin, Berlin, Germany. Photo © Johannes Laurentius/Bildarchiv Preussischer Kulturbesitz/Art Resource, New York (Inv. Misc 7470); **380** *top to bottom* Barracks. © Anders Ryman/Corbis; Lycurgus Demonstrates the Meaning of Education (1660–1661), Caesar Beotius van Everdingen. Alkmaar. Oil on canvas. Photo © Stedelijk Museum/akg-images; **381** Girls playing knucklebones. The Granger Collection, New York; **384** Fish seller. Illustration by Roger Stewart; **384–385** Life in the Agora. Illustrations by Roger Stewart; **386** Icons. Illustrations by Robert Coleman.

Chapter 12

388 *top to bottom* Oracle at Delphi. © Alamy Images; Parthenon. Todd Gipstein/National Geographic Image Collection; Jerusalem and temple. The Granger Collection, New York; **389** *top to bottom* Lion statues at Delos. © Alamy Images; Portrait statuette of Socrates (about 200 B.C.–A.D. 100). Athenian statesman. Greek. British Museum, London, Great Britian. Photo © HIP/Scala/Art Resource, New York; Olmec artifact. © Veintimilla/akg-images; **390** *inset* Bust of Pericles (about 495–429 B.C.). Museo Pio Clementino, Vatican Museums. Photo © Scala/Art Resource, New York; **390-391** Pericles and others having discussion. Illustration by Ezra Tucker; **392** Caryatids. © Alamy Images; **393** Modern Acropolis aerial. © Digital Vision; **394** Pericles engraving. © akg-images; **396** Parthenon. © Dagli Orti/The Art Archive; **398** Spartan soldier statue. © Alamy Images; **399** Triera, Rafael Monleon y Torres. Watercolor. © Museo Naval Madrid/Dagli Orti/The Art Archive; **400** Pericles, Athens politician (1852), Philipp von Foltz. Photo © akg-images; **403** Boy making a storyboard. Photo by Sharon Hoogstraten; **404** Philip of Macedonia. © Chiaramonti Museum Vatican/Dagli Orti/The Art Archive; **405** Mosaic of the battle between Alexander the Great and Darius III. © Archaeological Museum Naples/Dagli Orti/The Art Archive; inset Alexander the Great mosiac detail. © Archaeological Museum Naples/Dagli Orti/The Art Archive; **406–407** Equestrian portrait of Alexander the Great in combat. Museo Archeologico Nazionale, Naples. © Alinari/Art Resource, New York; **408** Aristotle teaching astronomers (1200–1250). Al-Mubashshir, Mukhtar al-Hikan (The better sentences and most precise dictions). Saljup dynasty. Topkapi Palace Museum, Istanbul, Turkey. Photo © Ms. Ahmet III/Giraudon/Art Resource (3206); **409** Alexandria lighthouse (1800–1899). The Granger Collection, New York; **410** Nike of Samothrace, goddess of victory (about 190 B.C.). Hellenistic. Louvre, Paris. Photo © Erich Lessing/Art Resource, New York; **411** Greek theatre. © Jon Davison/Lonely Planet Images; **412** *top to bottom* Greek comedy mask. © Alfio Garozzo/akg-images; Greek tragedy mask. © akg-images; **413** *clockwise from top* Building in Montpellier, France. Photo © Ric Ergenbright/Corbis; Corinthian column. © Corbis; Doric column. © Alamy Images; Ionic column. © John Hios/akg-images; **414** *left to right* Bust of Plato. Musei Capitolini, Rome. Photo © SEF/Art Resource, New York; Portrait statuette of Socrates (about 200 B.C.–A.D. 100). Athenian statesman. Greek. British Museum, London, Great Britain. Photo © HIP/Scala/Art Resource, New York; **415** *top to bottom* Death of Socrates. © Francis G. Mayer/Corbis; Aristotle. Roman sculpture after Greek original. Galleria Spada, Rome. Photo © Alinari/Art Resource, New York; **417** Archimede's screw. The Granger Collection, New York; **418** *top to bottom* Athlete arriving at Olympic Games (480 B.C.) Classical Greek. Red-figure cup. Goulandris Foundation, Athens. Photo © Dagli Orti/The Art Archive; Cathy Freeman. © Le Segretian Pascal/Corbis; **419** *clockwise from top left* Temple of Hephaestus (600–500 B.C.). Athens, Greece. © Index/Bridgeman Art Library; Lincoln memorial. © Angelo Hornak/Corbis; Greek allotment machine. © Agora Museum, Athens/Dagli Orti/The Art Archive; Jury. © Bob Daemmrich/The Image Works. **420** Icons. Illustrations by Robert Coleman; **422** Bust of Pericles (about 495–429 B.C.). Museo Pio Clementino, Vatican Museums. Photo © Scala/Art Resource, New York.

UNIT 6

424 The Roman Colosseum and the Games. Illustration by Frank Ordaz; **425** Colloseum. Photo © ML Sinbaldi/Corbis; Reliquary cross of Justinian (A.D. 500–600). Byzantine. Museum of the Treasury, St. Peter's Basilica, Vatican State. Photo © Scala/Art Resource, New York; Justinian I with crown and sceptre. Mosaic. S. Apollinare in Classe, Ravenna, Italy. Photo © Erich Lessing/Art Resource, New York.

Chapter 13

426 *top to bottom* She-wolf. © Araldo de Luca/Corbis; Greek temple at twilight. © Getty Images; **427** *left to right* Horse (Han dynasty). Funerary terracotta figurine. Museo d'Arte Orientale, Rome. Photo © Scala/Art Resource, New York; Cameo showing the young Emperor Augustus (63 B.C.–A.D. 14). From the Treasury of Boscoreale near Pompeii. Louvre, Paris. Photo © Erich Lessing/Art Resource, New York; **428** Julius Caesar, Roman statesman. Green slate bust, 41 cm high.

Antikensammlung, Staatliche Museen zu Berlin, Berlin, Germany. Photo © Juergen Liepe/Bildarchiv Preussischer Kulturbesitz/Art Resource, New York (Inv. SK 342); **428–429** The Assassination of Caesar. Illustration by Eric Robson; **430** Detail of Rome with the Tiber and the Anio Fountain, Giovanni Ceccarini. Photo © John Heseltine/Corbis; **431** Palatine Hill. Photo © Scala/Art Resource, New York; **433** Tiber river. © John and Lisa Merrill/Corbis; **434** Farm. © Gary Braasch/Corbis; **436** Lucius Junuis Brutus. © Araldo de Luca/Corbis; **437** Roman Forum. Dave Bartruff/Corbis; **438** Cicero Denouncing Catalina Before the Senate (1800–1899), Cesare Maccari. Wallpainting. Palazzo Madama, Rome, Italy. Photo © Scala/Art Resource, New York; **441** Laurel wreath. © DK Images. Dorling Kindersley Ltd; **442** Imperial eagle figurine from a horse's harness (A.D. 0–100). Ensign bearer. Bronze. Kunsthistorisches Museum, Vienna, Austria. Photo © Erich Lessing/Art Resource, New York; **443** Colosseum today. © ML Sinibaldi/Corbis; **444** Portrait of Caesar. The Granger Collection, New York; **445** Portrait bust of Cicero. Uffizi, Florence, Italy. Photo © Alinari/Art Resource, New York; **446** Roman coins. The Granger Collection, New York; **447** Augustus in a toga. Roman sculpture. Uffizi, Florence, Italy. © Alinari/Art Resource, New York; **449** SPQR sewer grate. Rome, Italy. Photo © Timothy McCarthy/Art Resource, New York; **450–451** Illustrations by Roger Stewart; **452** Cave canem. Pompeiian mosaic. House of the Tragic Poet, Pompeii, Italy. Photo © Scala/Art Resource, New York; **453** View of Hadrian's Villa. Hadrian's Villa, Tivoli, Italy. Photo © Werner Forman/Art Resource, New York; **454** Portrait of a Young Girl (A.D. 0–100). Museo e Gallerie Nazionali di Capodimonte, Naples, Italy. © Lauros/Giraudon/Bridgeman Art Library; **455** Statue of Jupiter. Photo © Araldo de Luca/Corbis; **456–457** Public baths. Illustration by John James; **459** Boy making a mosaic. Photo by Sharon Hoogstraten; **460** Icons. Illustration by Robert Coleman; **461** Relief from Trajan's Column. Column of Trajan, Rome, Italy. Photo © Alinari/Art Resource, New York;

Chapter 14

462 Deer-headed anthropomorphic figure which could represent a shaman undergoing transformation. Peru (north coast), Mochica culture. British Museum, London, Great Britain. Photo © Werner Forman/Art Resource, New York; **463** *left to right* Flying horse, one leg resting on a swallow (Eastern Han Dynasty). Excavated in 1969 at Wu-Wai, Kansu China. Bronze figure, 34.5 x 45 cm. National Museum, Beijing. Photo © Erich Lessing/Art Resource, New York; Colossal bust of Emperor Constantine the Great and other fragments. Palazzo dei Conservatori, Rome, Italy. © Vanni/Art Resource, New York; **464** *inset* Coin of Nero. © Private Collection/The Bridgeman Art Library; **464–465** The burning of Rome. Illustration by Melvyn Grant; **466** Reliquary cross of Justinian (A.D. 500–599). Byzantine. Museum of the Treasury, St. Peter's Basilica, Vatican State. Photo © Scala/Art Resource, New York; **467** Church of the Nativity in Bethlehem. © Celestial Panoramas, Ltd./Alamy Images; **469** The Sermon on the Mount (1295), La Somme Le Roy. Vellum. Bibliotheque Mazarine, Paris, France. © Bridgeman Art Library; **470** Tomb with rolling stone. © Richard Nowitz Photos; **471** Fish with cross, from the Coptic cemetery at Ermant (A.D. 300–399). Limestone relief. Photo © Erich Lessing/Art Resource, New York (Inv. MA 3034); **472–474** Stained glass. From The Story of the Bible in Stained Glass: Christ Church Windows by W. Robert Johnstone and R. Theodore Lutz. Art by Russell Goodman, C.M., and Goodman-Zissoff Studio. Photography by Grant Rushton. Courtesy of Christ Church. The United Church of Canada. Mississauga, Ontario. **476** Communion cup. The Granger Collection, New York; **477** City of Ephesus. © Michael Nicholson/Corbis; **478** *left to right* Nativity (about 1500), Sandro Botticelli. Canvas. The Granger Collection, New York; Mosaic of St. Paul. Photo © Alamy Images; **479** Cruciform page, frontispiece to the Gospel of St. Matthew (A.D. 800–900). Lambeth Palace Library, London. Photo © Bridgeman Art Library; Colossal bust of Constantine the Great and other fragments. Palazzo dei Conservatori, Rome. Photo © Vanni/Art Resource, New York; **480** Portrait of St. Paul, Pompeo Batoni. Basildon Park, Berkshire, Great Britain. Photo © National Trust/Art Resource, New York; **481** A ship, symbol of life, with lowered sails (A.D. 0–50), Naevoleia Tyche. Relief on the mausoleum of C. Munatius Faustus, built by his wife Naevoleia Tyche. From the west side of Via dei sepolcri, Pompeii. Mausoleum of C. Munatius, Rome. Photo © Erich Lessing/Art Resource, New York; **482** Bronze statue of Valentinian I, called The Colossos (A.D. 364–375). Late Roman. Barletta, Italy. Photo © Scala/Art Resource, New York; **483** Rome with St. Peter's dome. © Dennis Degnan/Corbis; **484** Burial niches with fresco "Christ, ruler of the World" (Pantocrator), as followed in Byzantine pattern of the time (800–600 B.C.). Catacomb of S. Callisto, Rome. Photo © Erich Lessing/Art Resource, New York; **485** Constantine mosaic. © The Bridgeman Art Library; **487** Open book. Photo by Sharon Hoogstraten; **487** Student making a pie graph. Photo by Sharon Hoogstraten; **488** Icons. Illustrations by Robert Coleman.

Chapter 15

490 *left to right* Marcus Aurelius relief, Mino da Fiesole. Marble. Bargello, Florence, Italy. © Bridgeman Art Library; Tallest of the still erect stelae at Axum (A.D. 300–499), Axumite. © Werner Forman/Art Resource, New York; **491** Kublai Khan. The Granger Collection, New York; **491** Mayan temple. The Granger Collection, New York; **492** *inset* Roman soldier on horseback attacking a fallen Barbarian. Bronze figurine from a horse's harness, 12 x 9.5 cm. Kunsthistorisches Museum, Vienna, Austria. Photo © Erich Lessing/Art Resource, New York; **492–493** Arrival of the Visigoths. Illustration by Frank Ordaz; **494** Trajan's Column. © Russell Mountford/Lonely Planet Images; **495** Hadrian's Wall. © Sandro Vannini/Corbis; **496** The Tetrarches (A.D. 476–1453). Porpyry. South Marco, Venice, Italy. Photo © Alinari/Art Resource, New York; **497** Colossal head of Constantine the Great. Musei Capitolini, Rome. Photo © Werner Forman/Art Resource, New York; **499** Three students holding a debate. Photo by Sharon Hoogstraten; **500** Ostrogothic jewelery (A.D. 450–550). Photo © The British Museum/Topham-HIP/The Image Works; **501** Istanbul. © Harvey Lloyd/Taxi/Getty Images; **502** Germanic skull. Photo © Archäologisches Landesmuseum der Christian-Albrechts-Universität, Schloss Gottorf, Schleswig, Germany; **504** *left to right* Figurine of Roman Legionnaire. Bronze. Photo © The British Museum; Striding Infantryman (221–206 B.C.), Qin dynasty. Courtesy of the Cultural Relics Bureau, Beijing and The Metropolitan Museum of Art, New York; **507** End of the Roman Empire. The Granger Collection, New York; **508** Justinian I with crown and sceptre. Mosaic. S. Apollinare in Classe, Ravenna, Italy. Photo © Erich Lessing/Art Resource, New York; **509** Hagia Sophia. © H. Spichtinger/zefa; **510** Empress Theodora. © Dagli Orti/The Art Archive; **512** *left to right* Roman cross (1100–1199). Back of walrus ivory cross from Bury St. Edmunds, England. The Granger Collection, New York; Byzantine cross (A.D. 900–1000). Reliquary of the

True cross. Constantinople. Treasury, Cathedral, Limburg an der Lahn, Germany. Photo © Werner Forman/Art Resource, New York; **513** Lion of St. Mark's (A.D. 500–600). Bronze sculpture. S. Marco, Venice, Italy. Photo © Cameraphoto/Art Resource, New York; **514** Praetorian guard bas-relief. © Bridgeman Art Library; **515** Mosaic from Izmir. Getty News Services. (#372147_06); **517** Roman aqueduct. © Miles Ertman/masterfile/zefa; **518** Cross-section of a Roman road. Illustration by Peter Bull; **520** *top to bottom* Pantheon engraving. © Historical Picture Archive/Corbis; U.S. Capitol. © Joseph Sohm/Alamy Images; **521** *clockwise from top left* Roman road photo. © Corbis; Highway interchange aerial. © Kevin Fleming/Corbis; St. Peter catalan (1150). Os de Tremp. Photo © akg-images. Pope John Paul II overlooking St. Peter's square. Photo Arturo Mari/AP/Wide World Photos; **522** Icons. Illustrations by Robert Coleman; **524** Ostrakon. Greek potsherd. Agora Museum, Athens, Greece. Photo © Scala/Art Resource, New York.

PRIMARY SOURCE HANDBOOK

R35 Mary Leaky on site. © Science Photo Library; **R36** Discovery of a mummified body. © Corbis Sygma; **R37** Gilgamesh stone relief. © Musée du Louvre Paris/Dagli Orti/The Art Archive; **R38** Detail of the Stele of Hammurabi. © Gianni Dagli Orti/Corbis; **R39** Detail of *Book of the Dead of Heruben: The Deceased and the Funerary Barge.* Photo © Archivo Iconographico, S.A./Corbis; **R40** Pianki's Monument. © Topham/The Image Works, Inc.; **R41** War chariot. © Dinodia Photo Library; **R42** Confucius. The Granger Collection, New York; **R43** Detail from *Lord of the South Dipper.* Fresco. The Granger Collection, New York; **R44** Mayan vessel. © Museo del Popol Vuh Guatemala/Dagli Orti/The Art Archive; **R45** *Creation of the Stars and Planets,* Michelangelo. Detail of the Sistine ceiling. Sistine Chapel, Vatican Palace, Vatican State. Photo © Scala/Art Resource, New York; **R46** *Noah's Ark* (1972), Monika Cronshagen. Painting. Altonaer Museum, Hamburg, Germany. Photo © akg-images; **R47** *Daniel in the Lions' Den.* Mosaic. Monastery Church, Hosios Loukas, Greece. Photo © Erich Lessing/Art Resource, New York.; **R49** King Solomon reading the Torah (13th century A.D.). British Library, London. Photo © Art Resource, New York; **R50** David, the young shepherd. The Granger Collection, New York; **R51** Achilles and Hector dueling. The Granger Collection, New York; **R52** Achilles dragging the body of Hector around on his chariot, detail from the ceiling of the Sala di Troia (about 1538), Giulio Romano. Fresco. Palazzo Ducale, Mantua, Italy. Photo © The Bridgeman Art Library; **R53** *top* Aesop. The Granger Collection, New York; *bottom* Wolf in sheep's clothes. © Tim Davis/Corbis; **R54** *The Fall of Icarus* (1796), Merry-Joseph Blondel. Fresco. Ceiling of the rotunda of Apollo. Photo © Musée du Louvre Paris/Dagli Orti/The Art Archive; **R56** Pericles. © AKG Images; **R57** Statue of Caesar. © The Art Archive; **R58** Roman brooch with Lamb of God. © The British Museum/Topham-HIP/The Image Works, Inc.; **R59** Bust of Emperor Nero (about A.D. 54–68). Uffizi, Florence. Photo © Scala/Art Resource, New York.

WORLD RELIGIONS HANDBOOK

R62 *bottom* Buddha. © Comstock Images; **R62–R63** *bottom* Young monks with begging bowls. © Dave Bartruff/Corbis; *top* Dhamekha Stupa in the Deer Park. © Lindsay Hebberd/Corbis; **R63** Dharma wheel and deer sculpture on Jokhang Monastery. © David Samuel Robbins/Corbis; **R64** Palm Sunday procession in El Salvador. AP/Wide World Photos; **R64–R65** *top The Tribute Money,* Masaccio. Brancacci Chapel, Santa Maria del Carmine, Florence. Photo © Scala/Art Resource, New York; **R65** *top* © Comstock Images/Getty Images; *bottom* Choir of St. Paul's Cathedral, London. © Angelo Hornak/Corbis; **R66** Indian girl lights a deepawali lamp in Ahmedabad. © Reuters/Corbis; **R67** *bottom* Brahmin priest in Belue, India. © Bennett Dean; Eye Ubiquitous/Corbis; *top left* Heads of Brahma, Vichnu and Shiva (late 800's). Phnom Bok (Siemreap). Musée des Arts Asiatiques-Guimet, Paris. Photo © Erich Lessing/Art Resource, New York; *top right* Ohm symbol © Alamy Images; **R68** Muslim men praying in the street. © Arthur Thévenart/Corbis; **R68-R69** *bottom* Dome of the Rock. © Richard T. Nowitz/Corbis; **R69** *right* Emblem atop Sultan Mosque. © Michael S. Yamashita/Corbis; *left* Family gathers for meal on 13th day of Ramadan. AP/Wide World Photos; **R70** The March of Abraham, Jozsef Molnar. © Archivo Iconografico, S.A./Corbis; **R70–R71** Bar mitzvah. Photograph by Bill Aron; **R71** *bottom Solomon's Wall* Jean-Leon Gerome. © Christie's Images/Corbis; *top* Star of David. Photo © Nathan Benn/Corbis; **R72** *top* Confucius. © SuperStock Inc.; *bottom* Confucius Temple. Taipei. © Yoshio Tomii/SuperStock Inc.; **R73** *right* Shineses ying and yang (200's). Roman. Mosaic. Archaeological Museum, Sousse, Tunisia. Photo © Dagli Orti/Art Archive; *left* Teacher's Day in Beijing. © ImagineChina; **R74** Ba'hai Temple, Wilmette, Illinois. © Royalty-Free/Corbis; **R74–R75** White egret dancers in street festival. © Bob Krist/Corbis; **R75** *right* Ardechir I received his crown from the god Ahura Mazda. © Paul Almasy/Corbis; *left* Portrait of a Nihang. © Chris Lisle/Corbis.

McDougal Littell has made every effort to locate the copyright holders of all copyrighted material in this book and to make full acknowledgment for its use. Omissions brought to our attention will be corrected in a subsequent edition.